AF679709

War: International Law, International Relations, and Just War Theory

War: International Law, International Relations, and Just War Theory – An Interdisciplinary Approach

Antonio F. Perez & Robert J. Delahunty

Published by:

Vandeplas Publishing, LLC – August 2017

801 International Parkway, 5th Floor
Lake Mary, FL. 32746
USA

www.vandeplaspublishing.com

All Rights Reserved
© 2017 by Antonio F. Perez & Robert J. Delahunty

No part of this book may be reproduced, stored in a retrieval system, or transmitted by any means, electronic, mechanical, photocopying, recording, or otherwise, without written permission from the author.

ISBN 978-1-60042-289-8

WAR:
INTERNATIONAL LAW, INTERNATIONAL RELATIONS, AND JUST WAR THEORY
– An Interdisciplinary Approach

ANTONIO F. PEREZ & ROBERT J. DELAHUNTY

Preface

In this volume, we explore the law of war. In our experience as practitioners in the U.S. State Department's Office of the Legal Advisor and the U.S. Department of Justice's Office of Legal Counsel and thereafter as teachers and scholars of international law, however, we have been struck by the dynamic nature of this area and by the ways in which it has been influenced by other disciplines. We believe it is impossible now to discuss the past, present, and future of the law of war without engaging in interdisciplinary dialogue through a focused analysis of concrete cases in which the implications of insights from other disciplines can be revealed and debated.

Accordingly, the book presents what we take to be a distinctive approach to the study of war and its law. It provides a vehicle for students from various disciplines — historical analysis, international relations theory, law and economics, behavioral economics and psychology, science and technology (including the study of the environment), sociology, political philosophy, moral and ethical theory, and comparative religion — to work together in addressing the cutting edge issues presented in the modern law of war. We think practical activity in the law of war - in governments, international governmental and nongovernmental organizations, and elsewhere — now requires an ability to understand the language of practitioners in other disciplines who participate in the formation of new norms and their application in the law of war. And we think practitioners in those other disciplines who participate in the formation and application of the law of war now also need to have an understanding of the distinctive features of international law as a separate discipline. Thus, much as war itself is too important to be left to generals, we think the law of war is too important to be left to international lawyers.

We hope that this book can be used in research seminars in international law at law schools, graduate programs in these various disciplines, and even in advanced courses at the undergraduate level, with the goal of enabling interdisciplinary discussion of the case studies presented in the book. These discussions will enable students to research, analyze and present their own interdisciplinary analyses of current, cutting-edge issues. (We supply examples of possible paper topics below.) We imagine that each case study can be the basis for a single 2-hour discussion per week in a seminar format covering one semester, although the material (depending on the department in which it is used) may warrant additional discussion in a 3- or 4-credit course.

Each case study begins with an essay providing background considerations necessary for a critical reading of the texts that form the basis of each case study. After that introduction, we provide questions that will help focus the student's reading of these texts (sometimes including extensive additional commentary in footnotes helping students relate these texts to the more difficult aspect of their interaction with international law and other disciplines). Finally, after these texts, we supply what we call "theses" concerning the texts (essentially comments and analysis drawing on the interdisciplinary materials we think full discussion of these texts will most fruitfully stimulate).

In this Preface, we describe the structure and logic of the case studies we present and we supply illustrative topics for further research for students under professorial supervision.

Part I of the book presents in two main chapters the major methodological options influencing the study law of war. It begins with traditional international relations theory's realist understanding of the law of war through a focused study of two critical texts — the Melian Dialogue and Mytilenian Debate — in Thucydides' foundational study of the Peloponnesian Wars. (Because of its importance in the development of modern realism, we use the Thomas Hobbes translation of this foundational text in the study of war.) In the second part of the first chapter, we explore the legalist response to traditional realism by focusing on two transformational cases - a domestic Japanese case testing the legality of the U.S. use of nuclear weapons and the more famous Nuremberg Tribunal's prosecution of the Third Reich's war crimes. This chapter provides students with a basic understanding of the sources and methods of international law and its major substantive doctrines.

In the second chapter of Part I, which contains three parts, we move beyond traditional debates between realism and legalism. First, we summarize the underlying international relations theory (including rational choice theory's intersection with the study of strategic behavior), providing reformulation of realist and legalist approaches in terms of modern social science. We then, in a case study concerning North Korea's withdrawal from the Nuclear Non-Proliferation Treaty, explore reformulated realism's use of rational choice theory, law and economics, and science in the study of the international institutions governing international security. Finally, we explore reformulated legalism's use of sociological theories, drawing from critical theory and comparative religion, to offer alternative accounts of West's, primarily U.S.'s, conflict with Iran over Iran's nuclear program. (For purposes of this chapter's exposition of modern methodologies that offer alternatives to rational choice theory, we treat only the initial phase of the U.S.-Iran conflict in the context of the Bush administration's parallel global war on terror. Later developments, including the Obama Administration's negotiations with Iran and the agreement that appears to have emerged from them lie wholly outside the purview of our case study.)

The next two parts of the book provide case studies in the two larger subsets of international law of war - the *jus ad bellum* (Part II), roughly concerning whether or not force may be used; and the *jus in bello* (Part III), roughly concerning the regulation of the means and methods of using force and conducting hostilities. We employ this formal division not only for heuristic purposes to provide structure for our cases studies but also because, as students of international law, we have been trained and write in the Western tradition's synthesis of Christian thought and Greco-Roman classicism, and thus take the Just War Tradition as the point of departure for this synthesis. However, the separation of these two bodies of law in the Just War Tradition, in which violations of each are viewed as independent of violations of the other, is a question to which we return in Part IV, the concluding and synthesizing chapter of this book.

Part II, which was prepared by Professor Perez, explores the *jus ad bellum*. It begins with a didactic chapter dedicated to the evolution of Just War Theory, which served as the historical and moral context for the development of the international *jus ad bellum*. In three cases studies in this part, we examine what appear to be the three main, albeit much debated, rationales that have served as actual or potential justifications for the use of force in international law. The first case study explores the so-called collective security and collective international authorization rationale in the context of the First Gulf War. The second case study explores the so-called humanitarian intervention rationale in the context of the NATO intervention against Serbia to prevent ethnic cleansing in Kosovo. The third case study explores the so-called individual, and perhaps preemptive, self-defense rationale in the context of the U.S. invasion of Iraq in the Second Gulf War.

Part III explores the *jus in bello*. It also begins with a separate chapter dedicated to an explosion of the historical development and framework principles – military necessity, distinction, and proportionality – of the *jus in bello*. The first case study explores these traditional principles in the context of major incidents during NATO's bombing campaign against Serbia during its humanitarian intervention to protect the people of Kosovo; in this connection, it reviews the International Criminal Court for Yugoslavia's Office of the Special Prosecutor's Report (the OTP Report) subsequent evaluation of NATO's action. The next chapter explores more modern extensions of the *jus in bello* to novel areas, focusing on the environmental effects of war and the correlative duties that might arise. This case study concerns the OTP Report's assessment of damage to the environment caused by NATO's actions. Part III concludes with a case study concerning the International Court of Justice's *Advisory Opinion concerning the Legality of the Use of Nuclear Weapons*, which explores the synthesis of the traditional *jus in bello* and other bodies of law that potentially govern the use of force, such as international human rights and environmental law, with principles of moral reasoning grounded in the Just War Tradition. It thus provides a bridge to a concluding chapter in Part IV, which explores the potential linkage of the *jus ad bellum* and *jus in bello* in light of the methodologies utilized in this volume and in light of the traditional Just War Theory which has served as the foundation for the normative critique of war in the Western Tradition.

We think students could use these materials through interdisciplinary methods to explore cutting edge and timely subjects through research papers. Paper topics could include the following subjects:

In the *jus ad bellum*:

- NATO humanitarian intervention in Libya resulting in regime change;
- Russia's intervention in Ukraine and its absorption of Crimea;
- The Western response to the plight of Christians (and other minority religious groups) in the Middle East in the face of the onslaught of the Islamic State;
- The status of the Spratly Island in the South China Sea and the PRC's efforts to change the territorial status quo in the region through, among other things, land reclamation projects;
- The recent efforts of the Japanese Government to reinterpret the Japanese Constitution to permit Japanese military participation in self-defense activities that might include collective self-defense;
- The status of a global commons regime in the Arctic given the foreseeable increase in the military significance of Arctic sea-lanes and the politico-military significance of more accessible strategic resources under the Arctic seabed.

In the *jus in bello*:

- The use of drones by the United States in Pakistan, Yemen, and elsewhere against terrorist targets;
- The intersection of criminal law, the law of armed conflict, and anti-terrorism concerns in the Colombian Civil War;
- The applicability of traditional law of war of discrimination and proportionality to address cyber-warfare attacks (e.g. cyber reprisals) and the risk of an electronic Pearl Harbor;
- The international response to modern, technologically-sophisticated maritime piracy;
- The increasing use and problematic status of private military contractors (the New Hessians?);

- The Ottawa landmines convention and the role of non-governmental organizations in international law-making, taking into account the nation-state's response (e.g. conventional defense and deterrence through landmines on the Korean peninsula).

These topics are only illustrative. We think a professor could fashion a range of paper topics across a single methodology, a single issue-area (such as environmental concerns), or a single doctrinal question (the intersection of human rights law and humanitarian law). But we think a range of paper topics exploring a range of methodologies would best serve the object of this book, which is to promote interdisciplinary fluency and dialogue and achieving ever more sophisticated and respectful disagreement among those holding different views.

We take this opportunity to thank those who have supported us in this project. Professor H. Jefferson Powell kindly read and commented on an early draft of Part One; Professor Robert Miller kindly did the same for a draft of Part IV. We are deeply appreciative of the efforts of our research assistants, Alyssa King (Columbus School of Law, Class of 2015) and Kenneth Knapp (St. Thomas School of Law, Class of 2016). We also thank our respective librarians, Elizabeth Edinger (Head Librarian, Columbus School of Law, The Catholic University of America) and Valerie Aggerbeck (Research Librarian St. Thomas Law School) for their indefatigable assistance. We appreciate the patience and support of our publisher Anton Vandeplas, who has made this project possible. Professor Perez would like to thank his wife and children, Carol, Allie and Nick, for their forbearance while this project cut across many graduations and sports competitions. Professor Delahunty would like to thank the many St. Thomas students he has taught over the years in his International Law course.

Table of Contents

PART I—TABLE OF CONTENTS

PART II—TABLE OF CONTENTS

PART III—TABLE OF CONTENTS

PART IV—TABLE OF CONTENTS

PART I

Chapter 1

Foundational Approaches: Realism and Legalism

Questions of war and peace are foundational to modern international law,[1] philosophy,[2] and international relations theory.[3] This case book is premised on the belief that the study of public international law is best introduced through examining the questions posed by the outbreak of armed conflicts (whether between nations or otherwise), the conduct of such conflicts, the restoration of peace, and the prevention or mitigation of later armed conflicts.

We do not base that belief merely on the fact that the study of such "use of force" questions can provide a convenient starting point for the further study of international law, or that a focus on "use of force" questions can encapsulate or illustrate much of general international law, such as the general law of treaties or the process by which state acts and declarations can give rise to legally binding international norms. Rather, we emphasize the centrality of "use of force" questions to the study of international law because a thorough consideration of the legal issues surrounding the use of force will quickly lead the student into fundamental reflection on the conduct and motivations of states in the international environment, the relationships between international law and strategic state interests, the connections between a state's domestic constitutional order and its behavior in the international arena, the role of human rights and other normative ideals in the formation of a state's foreign policy, and much else besides.

Furthermore, the world of the early twenty-first century is characterized by the unique and dramatic possibilities with respect to war and peace.[4] The decades since the end of the Second

1 See Hugo Grotius, The Laws of War and Peace (1625) (Richard Tuck ed. 2005) (1901 trans., available at *http://oll.libertyfund.org/index.php?option=com_staticxt&staticfile...553).*

2 *See* Immanuel Kant, Perpetual Peace (1795), in Kant: Political Writings (H.S. Reiss ed., 2d ed. 1991); *see generally* Thomas Pangle and Peter Ahrensdorf, Justice Among Nations: On the Moral Basis of Power and Peace (1999).

3 Hans Morgenthau, Politics Among Nations: The Struggle for Power and Peace (1st ed. 1948) (7th ed., *available at www.polsci.buffalo.edu/classes/vesna/PSC644.../).*

4 There is a significant debate over whether current trends will continue. A substantial body of expert opinion holds that war, or at least war between two nuclear-armed Great Powers, is no longer a realistic possibility. But even if so, that would not preclude non-nuclear interstate wars, "proxy" wars fought by state clients of rival Powers, or civil wars. A useful introduction to the debate is Nils Petter Gleditsch, T*he Forum: The Decline of War*, 15 Int'l Stud. Rev. 396 (2013). Bruno Tertrais, *The Demise of Ares: The End of War as We Know It?*, 35 Wash. Q. 7 (2012), also offers a useful summary of the case that inter-state war is on the way out. For major, recent contributions, see Christopher Coker, Can War be Eliminated? (2014); Ian Morris, War! What is it Good For? Conflict and the Progress of Civilization from Primates to Robots (2014); Randall L. Schweller, Maxwell's Demon and the Golden Apples: Global Discord in the New Millennium (2014); Steven Pinker, The Better Angels of Our Nature: Why Violence Has Declined (2011); and John Mueller, The Remnants of War (2004).

For evaluations of the risk of a major interstate war between the U.S. and China, see Thomas J. Christensen, The China Challenge: Shaping the Choices of a Rising Power 37-53 (2015); The Next Great War? The Roots of World War I and the Risk of U.S.-China

World War have been characterized by a relative decline in the occurrence and severity of interstate war (especially in Europe, the scene of two great wars in the twentieth century), though also by the growing incidence of civil wars (especially in Africa), and by the emergence of terrorism on a scale and of a lethality that might match those of interstate wars. The evolution of a zone of peace in Europe and more broadly within the community of liberal democratic states invites the hope of a planetary system that is stable, peaceful, non-violent, prosperous, and free.[5] However, the frequency of civil wars and the threat of mass terrorism raise the fear of a "coming anarchy."[6] Moreover, the ways in which violent conflicts can be fought out have also undergone revolutionary change since the end of the Second World War. On the one hand, nuclear weaponry has created the possibility of mass destruction on a wholly unprecedented scale; on the other, the ready availability of extremely inexpensive weapons such as the AK-47 rifle may have made parts of the world (effectively) unconquerable. Combined, these fundamental changes in the nature of war and the technology by which it is fought seem to carry momentous implications—still imperfectly understood—for the international system of states and the legal régime that governs it.

Finally, because "public international law" at this moment in the emergence of a globalized, multi-civilizational world system is necessarily a highly contested concept, foundational questions, including philosophical and religious questions, are never far from the surface.[7] Extreme positions in both sets of issues hold either that law does *not* matter, or that *only* law matters. The former of these positions we can conveniently label as "realism," the latter as "legalism." A wise Goldilocks, of course, holds otherwise—leaving the hard question of how to mediate between the two extremes. We attempt here to provide materials that will enable and inform those foun-

---

Conflict (Richard N. Rosecranz & Steven D. Miller eds., 2015); Dale C. Copeland, Economic Interdependence and War 436-44 (2015); Christopher Coker, The Improbable War: China, the United States & the Logic of Great Power Conflict (2014); Noah Feldman, Cool War: The Future of Global Competition 129-30, 162-63 (2013) (discussing risks of shooting war, including proxy wars, but also emphasizing likelihood of deepening cooperation); Randall Peerenboom, China Modernizes: Threat to the West or Model for the Rest? 273-81 (2007); and John Mearsheimer, *Can China Rise Peacefully?, in The National Interest* (Oct. 25, 2014) (*available at* http://nationalinterest.org/commentary/can-china-rise-peacefully-10204).

For a study of pre-1914 arguments for "the natural decline of warfare," *see* Paul Crook, *Darwinism, War and History* 98-129 (1994). The idea that humanity is slowly becoming less prone to violence can be traced back in part to the German sociologist, Norbert Elias. See The Civilizing Process (two vols., English trans. 1969 & 1982).

5 For a classic presentation of such ideas from the early post-Cold War period, see Francis Fukuyama, The End of History and the Last Man (1992).

6 *See* Robert D. Kaplan, The Coming Anarchy: Shattering the Dreams of the Post Cold War (2001). There are also those, like the novelist and essayist Umberto Eco, who see a drift towards a "New Middle Ages," decentered from the nation state, but also without the unifying features of a Papacy and Empire. *See* Umberto Eco, *Living in the New Middle Ages, in* Travels in Hyper Reality: Essays 73 (1986). For discussion, *see* John Keane, Reflections on Violence 5–6 (1996); and Pierre Hassner, *Beyond the Three Traditions: The Philosophy of War and Peace in Historical Perspective,* 70 Int'l Aff. 737, 754 (1994).

7 For the thesis that international law emerges from the conditions specific to a particular historical epoch (including the influence of a hegemonic power), *see* Wilhelm G. Grewe, The Epochs of International Law (Michael Byers trans. 2000). Among many studies of the emergence of a post-Western world system, see Parag Khanna, The Second World: Empires and Influence in the New Global Order (2008). On the instability of *any* world system, *see* Andrew Phillips, War, Religion, and Empire: The Tranformation of International Orders (2011). *See generally* Samuel Huntington, The Clash of Civilizations and the Remaking of World Order (1996).

dational discussions, creating a case book that will be usable both for courses in international law and for programs in international relations.

Part I of the book consists of its first two chapters, and can broadly be characterized as a deepening dialogue between two recurring views of the relation between international law and international politics: "realism" and "legalism." In Chapter 1, we outline the competing paradigms of realism and legalism with excerpts from classic texts. Before each excerpt, we provide introductory questions designed to direct and guide the student's reading of that text. After each text, we provide extensive commentary and questions for classroom discussion. Chapter 1.A presents an early realist paradigm through a focused study of key excerpts from Thucydides' celebrated *History of the Peloponnesian Wars.* Chapter 1.B, which presents the alternative legalist paradigm, explicates and scrutinizes the basic premises of contemporary international law through a study of the judgments of the International Military Tribunals at Nuremberg and at Tokyo (the Nuremberg Trial and the Tokyo Trial), as well as a later Japanese court's assessment of the legality of the use of nuclear weapons by the United States at Hiroshima and Nagasaki. The excerpts from these three cases—representing, respectively, the views of judges from the victorious powers in the Second World War, from an Asian colony of one of the victorious Western powers, and from a defeated power—helped to define the post-War system's understanding of both *jus ad bellum* (the legality of going to war) and *jus in bello* (the legality of the means and methods by which warfare is conducted).

In Chapter 2, we carry forward and deepen the dialectic between realism and legalism that governs Chapter 1, examining in depth the relationships between international law and contemporary international relations theory. Chapter 2.A introduces that discussion with an outline of the recent international relations theories grouped under the heading of "realism," concentrating on the so-called "structural realism" (or "neo-realism") of the American scholar Kenneth Waltz.[8] Chapters 2.B and 2.C present in turn the two currently dominant positions in international relations theory: "rational choice" theory, which can be seen as the most sophisticated and nuanced form of "realism," and "constructivism," which has obvious affinities with the "legalist" position studied in Chapter 1.B. We apply and assess each of these approaches by working through two case studies in close detail. Both of those case studies involve nuclear weapons and, more specifically, the Nuclear Non-Proliferation Treaty (the NPT), the "security assurances" given by nuclear-weapon states that relate to the NPT, and the complex regime that now has developed to manage nuclear-related trade. For rational choice theory, our case study is the North Korean nuclear program; for constructivism, the confrontation between the United States and Iran over the latter's nuclear policy.

Part II of the book extends the analytical structures developed in Part I. The distinction marked out in Chapter 1.B between *jus ad bellum* and *jus in bello* provides the structure for

8 *See* Kenneth Waltz, The Theory of International Politics (1979). *See also* Kenneth Waltz, Man, the State and War: A Theoretical Analysis (1954).

Part II of the book. As we have indicated, the law on use of force is ordinarily bifurcated into these two categories—one referring to the legality of initiating armed conflict, the other to the legality of the means and methods by which such a conflict is conducted. In Part II, we focus on three topics in the *jus ad bellum*; in Part III, we turn to three topics in *jus in bello.* The chapters on *jus ad bellum* will consider the use of armed force in three different types of international conflict: as authorized by the United Nations Security Council (focusing on the First Gulf War); for the purpose of humanitarian intervention (the War in Kosovo); and for preemptive and/or preventive purposes (the Second Gulf War). The chapters on *jus in bello* will address three major concerns: combatants and non-combatants (considering the report of the NATO prosecutor on alleged misconduct of allied forces in the War in Kosovo); the extension of the *jus in bello* to nontraditional values, such as environmental harm; and weaponry threatening the international system's existence (focusing on the International Court of Justice's opinion on the legality of nuclear weapons). Finally, the Concluding Thoughts chapter will then examine the question whether a permanently peaceful world order is possible. More particularly, it will consider the alternatives of a unitary planetary government (of some form) versus a continuing "clash of civilizations."

In beginning our study of International Law and International Relations, we start (as foundational studies so often have) with the thought of ancient Greece. We shall examine two lengthy extracts from the enduring classic of the Greek historian Thucydides, entitled *The History of the Peloponnesian War* (hereafter *History*). The two extracts are commonly known (respectively) as the "Mytilenean Debate" and the "Melian Dialogue."

The first extract is Thucydides' account of a debate in the Assembly of the city of Athens in 427 B.C.E. between two speakers, the Athenian politician Cleon and the otherwise unknown Diodotus. The second extract is Thucydides' account of a private dialogue dated to 416 B.C.E. between a delegation sent out by the Athenian generals besieging the city of Melos and the oligarchic leaders of that city. Both colloquies are set in wartime.

In the Mytilenean debate, Cleon, and Diodotus take opposing sides on the question whether the Athenian Assembly should reaffirm its earlier decision to massacre the inhabitants of Mytilene, a city on the Greek island of Lesbos that had been an ally of Athens in its war with Sparta but that had sought to withdraw from that alliance and align itself with the Spartan side. In the debate, Cleon urges the Athenian Assembly to reaffirm its harsh decision, while Diodotus argues that Athens should not destroy the elements of the Mytilenean population that were sympathetic to Athens' cause in the war. In the Melian dialogue, the Athenian ambassadors present an ultimatum to the Melian leaders: either surrender the city peaceably to Athens or face total destruction. The Melians reply by arguing that they have done Athens no wrong, that the gods are on their side, that their honor does not permit them to surrender the city's traditional liberty, and that the Spartans will come to their aid. The Melians choose to resist Athens, do not receive Spartan aid, and are defeated and destroyed.

Very brief sketches of the Peloponnesian War and of Thucydides are in order.[9] As Thucydides' characterizes it, that war was the greatest ever to have been fought in Greece and embraced the whole of the ancient Greek world, from the Greek islands of the coast of modern Turkey to the island of Sicily in what is now Italy. Indeed, the war extended even beyond the boundaries of the Greek world, touching both the North African city of Carthage in the west and the Persian Empire in the east. The chief contenders in the war were the Athenian-led Delian League, consisting of the city of Athens together with its allies and subjects (mostly islands or cities in or near the Ionian Sea), and its chief rival Sparta, the leader of a coalition of Greek cities based mainly in the Peloponnese (the Peloponnesian League). The two main contenders differed in important respects. Athens was a democracy, governed directly by its citizens or *demos* deciding

9 There are many excellent accounts of both the Peloponnesian War and of Thucydides that can be consulted for a richer background. *See, e.g.*, Donald Kagan, The Peloponnesian War (2003) [hereinafter Kagan, Peloponnesian War]; Donald Kagan, Thucydides: The Reinvention of History (2009) [hereinafter Kagan, Reinvention]. For a shorter survey of contrasting accounts, *see* P.J. Rhodes, *Thucydides and the Causes of the Peloponnesian War*, 115 Hermes 154 (1987).

public policy and state strategy at meetings of the Athenian Assembly.[10] Sparta, governed by a complex structure including kings, *ephors* and a popular assembly, was, in effect, an aristocracy that ruled over a conquered slave or *helot* population.[11] Athens was primarily a sea power possessed of a masterful navy, Sparta a land power with what was considered to be Greece's finest army. (Simply put, the Peloponnesian War can be seen as a struggle between a whale (Athens) and an elephant (Sparta)[12]). Athens was dynamic and commercial, Sparta traditionalist and agrarian. Athens was ethnically Ionian, Sparta ethnically Dorian. By and large, those in the Greek world who favored popular rule of democracy sympathized with Athens, while the more aristocratic or oligarchic elements of Greece favored Sparta. Thus the war between Athens and Sparta, though rooted in state rivalry, was overlaid by sharp differences in ideology, ethnicity, and national character. Later readers in the English-speaking world have likened the contest between Athens and Sparta to that between the British Empire and Imperial Germany before the First World War, or to that between the United States and the Soviet Union in the Cold War.

The Peloponnesian War broke out in 431 B.C.E., with a declaration of war by Sparta against Athens. Athens was under the leadership of Pericles, a statesman much admired by Thucydides. Pericles counseled the Athenians to expect a long war with Sparta, to withdraw from most of their land possessions in Attica in mainland Greece, and to wage war against Sparta from the sea. Although Athens seemed at first likely to succeed with the Periclean strategy, it encountered unexpected difficulties once the war began, including a massively lethal and destructive plague in 430 B.C.E. At that point in the war, Athens was weakened, demoralized, and close to bankruptcy. It was then that the Mytileneans, whom Athens considered it had treated well, sought to rebel and join forces with Sparta. Pericles died in 429 B.C.E., leaving Athens to be governed by far less effective successors, the most important of whom were Cleon, Nicias, and (later) Alcibiades. The war went on, with varying fortunes on both sides, until the fragile and inconclusive Peace of Nicias of 429 B.C.E. Five years later, after episodic breaches of the peace on both sides, Athens demanded that the city of Melos, which had hitherto been a neutral, either join its empire or be destroyed. The Melian dialogue dramatizes that encounter between a great imperial power and a small, unaligned one. The destruction of Melos forms, in Thucydides' narrative, the prelude to Athens' decision to invade and conquer the western Greek island of Sicily and its dominant city, Syracuse. That invasion resulted in Athens' resounding defeat. Thereafter,

10 On the importance of oratory in the Athenian politics of the late fifth century, *see* P.J. Rhodes, *Political Activity in Classical Athens,* 106 J. Hell. Stud. 132, 140–41 (1986). For a superb overview of the role of politics in the Greek city state, *see* Paul Rahe, *The Primacy of Politics in Classical Greece,* 89 Am. Hist. Rev. 265 (1984). For a general survey, *see* J.K. Davies, Democracy and Classical Greece (2d ed. 1993).

11 On Sparta, *see* William George Grieve Forrest, A History of Sparta, 950-192 B.C. (1969). The image of Sparta has resonated through Western history. *See* Elizabeth Rawson, The Spartan Tradition in European Thought (1969). Sparta deeply influenced thinkers such as Jean-Jacques Rousseau. *See* Paul Cartledge, *Spartan traditions and receptions,* 181 Hermathena 41 (2006); Judith Shklar, *Rousseau's Two Models: Sparta and the Age of Gold,* 81 Pol. Sci. Q. 25 (1966).

12 For Thucydides' analysis of how the Spartans saw both themselves and their Athenian enemy, *see* Felix M. Wassermann, *The Voice of Sparta in Thucydides,* 59 Classical J. 289 (1964).

in 411 B.C.E., Sparta allied itself with the Persian Empire—an alliance that forced Athens to fight a war on two fronts and that brought about her ultimate defeat. Athens underwent two political revolutions in 411 B.C.E., ending the democracy for a period (it was restored in 410 B.C.E.) and bringing oligarchs to power; later, in 404-03 B.C.E., Athens again succumbed to internal civil strife (*stasis*) and, eventually, to defeat at Sparta's hands.

Thucydides, who was probably born between 460 and 454 B.C.E., lived through the events he describes in the *History,* and indeed for a while played a leading role in them. He was a member of a wealthy Athenian family with significant ties to the north of Greece, was familiar with the brilliant intellectual and artistic currents of fifth century Athens, appears to have been a member of the powerful and cultivated circle around Pericles, and was extraordinarily gifted in his own right. He was elected a general by the Athenian Assembly in 424 B.C.E., but met with military defeat while on campaign in northern Greece at the hands of the Spartan General Brasidas over the city of Amphipolis and was condemned by the Assembly to exile. While in exile, he wrote the *History,* which remained unfinished at his death in 404 B.C.E. He intended the book to be a *ktema es aei*—a possession for all time—and so it has proven to be.

We use the translation of Thucydides' *History* by the great seventeenth century English philosopher Thomas Hobbes (1588-1679). Among many other lasting achievements, Hobbes is widely recognized as a founder of the modern school of international relations theory called "realism." Hobbes' thinking—particularly in his *Leviathan* (1651),[13] which described the state of nature as "a war of all against all"—was deeply influenced by his close reading of, and long engagement with, Thucydides' *History.*[14] Thucydides therefore must be considered essential reading in international relations theory, not only because of the enduring value of his own insights in the *History,* but also because of his place as a precursor of Hobbes' realism, and so of modern realist theory. Furthermore, English-speaking realists for centuries have studied Thucydides in Hobbes' translation. For those approaching the study of international law and international relations, therefore, it is useful to study Thucydides' thought as it is presented in Hobbes' language. Difficult though Hobbes 17th century prose may be, it is no more difficult than Thucydides' original Greek, nor is it appreciably more difficult than more modern English translations. The main texts provided below—the Mytilenean debate and the Melian dialogue—are the two most important passages that international law and international relations scholars have studied in their centuries-old debate on regulation of war.

13 Thomas Hobbes, Leviathan (*available at* http://www.gutenberg.org/files/3207/3207-h/3207-h.htm).

14 An early study of the relationship between Thucydides and Hobbes (including Hobbes' reasons for translating the *History*) is Richard Schlatter, *Thomas Hobbes and Thucydides,* 6 J. Hist. Ideas 350 (1945). Hobbes appears to have become acquainted with Thucydides through his relationship with Francis Bacon, a philosopher, scientist and royal counselor, whose work, *Considerations Touching a War With Spain* (1624), discusses Thucydides. (Hobbes may even have drafted the piece for Bacon.) See Richard Tuck, The Rights of War and Peace: Political Thought and the International Order from Grotius to Kant 127 (1999). For a later discussion of the relationship of Thucydides' thought to Hobbes,' *see, e.g.,* Peter R. Pouncey, The Necessities of War: A Study of Thucydides' Pessimism 151–57 (1980).

1. Study Questions Before Reading the Mytilenean Debate

1) What kind of relationship did Mytilene have with Athens? Was it cooperative? Subordinate? Did it change over time?

2) What motivated the Mytileneans?

3) What motivated the Athenian Assembly initially to order the death of the Mytileneans? Why, and through what process, did the Assembly change its mind?

4) What are Cleon's main arguments? Are they arguments from justice, expediency, or both? What is his criterion for justice? What is his conception of expediency? Is it short-term or long-term?

5) How does Diodotus respond to Cleon?

6) Why does Diodotus apparently appeal solely to expediency and disregard arguments based on humanity?

7) What audiences were Cleon and Diodotus addressing? Each other? The Athenian Assembly? Sparta and its allies? Athens' allies and subjects? Neutral states or Greek public opinion at large? The Gods?

2. The Text of the Mytilenean Debate[15]

Paches, when he came back to Mytilene, took in Pyrrha and Eressus: and having found Salæthus the Lacedæmonian hidden in Mytilene, apprehended him, and sent him, together with those men he had put in custody at Tenedos, and whomsoever else he thought author of the revolt, to Athens. He likewise sent away the greatest part of his army; and with the rest stayed and settled the state of Mytilene and the rest of Lesbos, as he thought convenient. These men, and Salæthus with them, being arrived at Athens, the Athenians slew Salæthus presently [confusing sentence]; though he made them many offers, and amongst other, to get the army of the Peloponnesians to rise from before Platæa; for it was yet besieged. But upon the rest they went to council; and in their passion decreed to put them to death, not only those men there present, but also all the men of Mytilene that were of age; and to make slaves of the women and children: laying to their charge the revolt itself, in that they revolted not being in subjection as others

15 Thucydides, History of the Grecian War 298 –316 (Thomas Hobbes trans., Sir William Molesworth ed., 1843).

were: and withal the Peloponnesian fleet, which durst enter into Ionia to their aid, had not a little aggravated that commotion. For by that it seemed that the revolt was not made without much premeditation. They therefore sent a galley to inform Paches of their decree, with command to put the Mytilenæans presently to death. But the next day they felt a kind of repentance in themselves; and began to consider what a great and cruel decree it was, that not the authors only, but the whole city should be destroyed. Which when the ambassadors of the Mytilenæans that were there present, and such Athenians as favoured them, understood, they wrought with those that bare office, to bring the matter again into debate; wherein they easily prevailed, forasmuch as to them also it was well known, that the most of the city were desirous to have means to consult of the same anew. The assembly being presently met, amongst the opinions of divers others Cleon also, the son of Cleænetus, who in the former assembly had won to have them killed, being of all the citizens most violent and with the people at that time far the most powerful, stood forth and said in this manner:

"I have often on other occasions thought a democracy uncapable of dominion over others; but most of all now for this your repentance concerning the Mytilenæans. For through your own mutual security and openness, you imagine the same also in your confederates; and consider not, that when at their persuasion you commit an error or relent upon compassion, you are softened thus to the danger of the commonwealth, not to the winning of the affections of your confederates: nor do you consider, that your government is a tyranny, and those that be subject to it are against their wills so, and are plotting continually against you; and obey you not for any good turn, which to your own detriment you shall do them, but only for that you exceed them in strength, and for no good will. But the worst mischief of all is this, that nothing we decree shall stand firm, and that we will not know, that a city with the worse laws, if immoveable, is better than one with good laws, when they be not binding; and that a plain wit accompanied with modesty, is more profitable to the state than dexterity with arrogance; and that the more ignorant sort of men do, for the most part, better regulate a commonwealth than they that are wiser. For these love to appear wiser than the laws, and in all public debatings to carry the victory, as the worthiest things wherein to show their wisdom; from whence most commonly proceedeth the ruin of the states they live in. Whereas the other sort, mistrusting their own wits, are content to be esteemed not so wise as the laws, and not able to carp at what is well spoken by another: and so making themselves equal judges rather than contenders for mastery, govern a state for the most part well. We therefore should do the like; and not be carried away with combats of eloquence and wit, to give such counsel to your multitude as in our own judgments we think not good.

"For my own part, I am of the opinion I was before; and I wonder at these men that have brought this matter of the Mytilenæans in question again, and thereby caused delay, which is the advantage only of them that do the injury. For the sufferer by this means comes upon the doer with his anger dulled; whereas revenge, the opposite of injury, is then greatest when it follows presently. I do wonder also, what he is that shall stand up now to contradict me, and shall think to prove that the injuries done us by the Mytilenæans are good for us, or that our calamities are any damage to our confederates. For certainly he must either trust in his eloquence, to make you believe that that which was decreed, was not decreed; or moved with lucre, must with some elaborate speech endeavour to seduce you. Now of such matches [of eloquence] as these, the city giveth the prizes to others; but the danger that hence proceedeth, she herself sustaineth. And of all this you yourselves are the cause, by the evil institution of these matches, in that you use to be spectators of words, and hearers of actions; beholding future actions in the words of them that speak well, as possible to come to pass; and actions already past in the orations of such as make the most of them, and that with such assurance, as if what you saw with your eyes were not more certain than what you hear related. You are excellent men for one to deceive with a speech of a new strain, but backward to follow any tried advice; slaves to strange things, contemners of things usual. You would every one chiefly give the best advice, but if you cannot, then you will contradict those that do. You would not be thought to come after with your opinion; but rather if any thing be acutely spoken, to applaud it first, and to appear ready apprehenders of what is spoken, even before it be out; but slow to preconceive the sequel of the same. You would hear, as one may say, somewhat else than what our life is conversant in; and yet you sufficiently understand not that that is before your eyes. And to speak plainly, overcome with the delight of the ear, you are rather like unto spectators sitting to hear the contentions of sophisters, than to men that deliberate of the state of a commonwealth. To put you out of this humour, I say unto you, that the Mytilenæans have done us more injury than ever did any one city. For those that have revolted through the over-hard pressure of our government, or that have been compelled to it by the enemy, I pardon them. But they that were islanders and had their city walled, so as they needed not fear our enemies but only by sea; in which case also they were armed for them with sufficient provision of galleys; and they that were permitted to have their own laws and whom we principally honoured, and yet have done thus; what have they done but conspired against us, and rather warred upon us than revolted from us, (for a revolt is only of such as suffer violence), and joined with our bitterest enemies to destroy us? This is far worse than if they had warred against us for increasing of their own power. But these men would neither take example by their neighbour's calamity, who are, all that revolted, already subdued by us; nor could their own present felicity make them afraid of changing it into misery: but being bold against future events, and aiming at matters above their strength, though below their desires, have taken arms against us, and preferred force before justice. For no sooner they thought they might get the victory, but immediately, though without injury done them, they rose against us. But with cities that come to great and unexpected prosperity, it is usual to turn insolent: whereas most commonly that prosperity which is attained according to the course of reason, is more firm than that which cometh unhoped for; and such cities, as one may say, do more easily keep off an adverse, than maintain a happy fortune. Indeed we should not formerly have done any honour more to the Mytilenæans than to the rest of our confederates; for then they had never come to this degree of insolence. For it is natural to men to contemn those that observe them, and to have in admiration such as will not give them way. Now therefore let them be punished according to their wicked dealing; and let not the fault be laid upon a few, and the people be absolved. For they have all alike taken arms against us: and the commons, if they had been constrained to it, might have fled hither, and have recovered their city afterwards again. But they, esteeming it the safer adventure to join with the *few,* are alike with them culpable of the revolt. Have also in consideration your confederates: and if you inflict the same punishment on them that revolt upon compulsion of the enemy, that you do on them that revolt of their own accord, who, think you, will not revolt, though on light pretence; seeing that speeding they win their liberty, and failing their case is not incurable? Besides, that against every city we must be at a new hazard, both of our persons and fortunes. Wherein with the best success, we recover but an exhausted city, and lose that wherein our strength lieth, the revenue of it; but miscarrying, we add these enemies to our former, and must spend that time in warring against our own confederates, which we needed to employ against the enemies we have already.

"We must not therefore give our confederates hope of pardon, either impetrable by words or purchaseable by money, as if their errors were but such as are commonly incident to humanity. For these did us not an injury unwillingly, but wittingly conspired against us; whereas it ought to be involuntary whatsoever is pardonable. Therefore both then at first, and now again I maintain, that you ought not to alter your former decree, nor to offend in any of these three most disadvantageous things to empire, *pity, delight in plausible speeches,* and *lenity.* As for pity, it is just to show it on them that are like us, and will have pity again; but not upon such as not only would not have had pity upon us, but must also of necessity have been our enemies for ever hereafter. And for the rhetoricians that delight you with their orations, let them play their prizes in matters of less weight, and not in such wherein the city for a little pleasure must suffer a great damage, but they for their well speaking must well have. Lastly for lenity, it is to be used towards those that will be our friends hereafter, rather than towards such, as being suffered to live, will still be as they are, not a jot the less our enemies. In sum I say only this, that if you follow my advice, you shall do that which is both just in respect of the Mytilenæans, and profitable for yourselves: whereas if you decree otherwise, you do not gratify them, but condemn yourselves. For if these have justly revolted, you must unjustly have had dominion over them. Nay though your dominion be against reason, yet if you resolve to hold it, you must also, as a matter conducing thereunto, against reason punish them; or else you must give your dominion over, that you may be good without danger. But if you consider what was likely they would have done to you, if they had prevailed, you cannot but think them worthy the same punishment; nor be less sensible, you that have escaped, than they that have conspired; especially they having done the injury first. For such as do an injury without precedent cause, persecute most, and even to the death, him they have done it to; as jealous of the danger his remaining enemy may create him: for he that is wronged without cause, and escapeth, will commonly be more cruel than if it were against any enemy on equal quarrel. Let us not therefore betray ourselves, but in contemplation of what you were near suffering, and how you once prized above all things else to have them in your power, requite them now accordingly. Be not softened at the sight of their present estate, nor forget the danger that hung over our own heads so lately. Give not only unto these their deserved punishment, but also unto the rest of our confederates a clear example, that death is their sentence whensoever they shall rebel. Which when they know, you shall the less often have occasion to neglect your enemies, and fight against your own confederates."

To this purpose spake Cleon. After him Diodotus the son of Eucrates, who also in the former assembly opposed most the putting of the Mytilenæans to death, stood forth and spake as followeth.

"I will neither blame those who have propounded the business of the Mytilenæans to be again debated, nor commend those that find fault with often consulting in affairs of great importance. But I am of opinion that nothing is so contrary to good counsel as these two, *haste* and *anger:* whereof the one is ever accompanied with madness, and the other with want of judgment. And whosoever maintaineth that words are not instructors to deeds, either he is not wise, or doth it upon some private interest of his own. Not wise, if he think that future, and not apparent things, may be demonstrated otherwise than by words: interested, if desiring to carry an ill matter, and knowing that a bad cause will not bear a good speech, he go about to deter his opposers and hearers by a good calumniation. But they of all others are most intolerable, that when men give public advice, will accuse them also of bribery. For if they charged a man with no more but ignorance, when he had spoken in vain, he might yet depart with the opinion of a fool. But when they impute corruption also, if his counsel take place he is still suspected; and if it do not take place, he shall be held not only a fool, but also void of honesty. The commonwealth gets no good by such courses: for through fear hereof it will want counsellors. And the state would do their business for the most part well, if this kind of citizens were they that had least ability in speaking; for they should then persuade the city to the fewer errors. For a good statesman should not go about to terrify those that contradict him, but rather to make good his counsel upon liberty of speech. And a wise state ought not either to add unto, or on the other side, to derogate from the honour of him that giveth good advice; nor yet punish, nay nor disgrace the man whose counsel they receive not. And then, neither would he that lighteth on good advice, deliver anything against his own conscience, out of ambition of further honour and to please the auditory; nor he that doth not, covet thereupon, by gratifying the people some way or other, that he also may endear them. But we do here the contrary: and besides, if any man be suspected of corruption, though he give the best counsel that can be given, yet through envy, for this uncertain opinion of his gain, we lose a certain benefit to the commonwealth. And our custom is to hold good counsel, given suddenly, no less suspect then bad: by which means, as he that gives the most dangerous counsel, must get the same received by fraud; so also he that gives the most sound advice, is forced by lying to get himself believed. So that the commonwealth is it alone, which by reason of these suspicious imaginations, no man can possibly benefit by the plain and open way without artifice. For if any man shall do a manifest good unto the commonwealth, he shall presently be suspected of some secret gain unto himself in particular. We therefore, that in the most important affairs and amidst these jealousies do give our advice, have need to foresee further than you, that look not far; and the rather, because we stand accountable for our counsel, and you are to render no account of your hearing it. For if the persuader and the persuaded had equal harm, you would be the more moderate judges. But now, according to the passion that takes you, when at any time your affairs miscarry, you punish the sentence of that one only that gave the counsel, not the many sentences of your own that were in fault as well as his.

"For my own part, I stood not forth with any purpose of contradiction in the business of the Mytilenæans, nor to accuse any man. For we contend not now, if we be wise, about the injury done by them, but about the wisest counsel for ourselves. For how great soever be their fault, yet I would never advise to have them put to death, unless it be for our profit; [nor yet would I pardon them,] though they were pardonable, unless it be good for the commonwealth. And in my opinion, our deliberation now is of the future, rather than of the present. And whereas Cleon contendeth, that it will be profitable for the future, to put them to death, in that it will keep the rest from rebelling: I contending likewise for the future, affirm the contrary. And I desire you not to reject the profit of my advice for the fair pretexts of his; which agreeing more with your present anger against the Mytilenæans, may quickly perhaps win your consent. We plead not judicially with the Mytilenæans so as to need arguments of equity, but we consult of them, which way we may serve ourselves of them to our most advantage hereafter. I say therefore, that death hath been in states ordained for a punishment of many offences, and those not so great, but far less than this. Yet encouraged by hope, men hazard themselves: nor did any man ever yet enter into a practice, which he knew he could not go through with. And a city when it revolteth, supposeth itself to be better furnished, either of themselves or by their confederates, than it is, or else it would never take the enterprise in hand. They have it by nature, both men and cities, to commit offences; nor is there any law that can prevent it. For men have gone over all degrees of punishment, augmenting them still, in hope to be less annoyed by malefactors. And it is likely that gentler punishments were inflicted of old, even upon the most heinous crimes; but that in tract of time, men continuing to transgress, they were extended afterwards to the taking away of life; and yet they still transgress. And therefore either some greater terror than death must be devised, or death will not be enough for coercion. For poverty will always add boldness to necessity; and wealth, covetousness to pride and contempt. And the other [middle] fortunes, they also through human passion, according as they are severally subject to some insuperable one or other, impel men to danger. But hope and desire work this effect in all estates. And this as the leader, that as the companion; this contriving the enterprize, that suggesting the success, are the cause of most crimes that are committed: and being least discerned, are more mischievous than evils seen. Besides these two, fortune also puts men forward as much as anything else. For presenting herself sometimes unlooked for, she provoketh some to adventure, though not provided as they ought for the purpose; and specially cities, because they venture for the greatest matters, as liberty and dominion over others; and amongst a generality, every one, though without reason, somewhat the more magnifies himself in particular. In a word, it is a thing impossible, and of great simplicity to believe, when human nature is earnestly bent to do a thing, that by force of law or any other danger it can be diverted.

"We must not therefore, relying on the security of capital punishment, decree the worst against them, nor make them desperate, as if there were no place to repent, and as soon as they can, to cancel their offence. For observe: if a city revolted should know it could not hold out, it would now compound, whilst it were able both to pay us our charges for the present and our tribute for the time to come. But the way that Cleon prescribeth, what city, think you, would not provide itself better than this did; and endure the siege to the very last, if to compound late and soon be all one? And how can it be but detriment to us, to be at charge of long sieges through their obstinacy, and when we have taken a city, to find it exhausted, and to lose the revenue of it for the future? And this revenue is the only strength we have against our enemies. We are not then to be exact judges in the punition of offenders, but to look rather how by their moderate punishment we may have our confederate cities, such as they may be able to pay us tribute; and not think to keep them in awe by the rigour of laws, but by the providence of our own actions. But we to the contrary, when we recover a city, which having been free and held under our obedience by force hath revolted justly, think now that we ought to inflict some cruel punishment upon them. Whereas we ought rather, not mightily to punish a free city revolted, but mightily to look to it before it revolt, and to prevent the intention of it; but when we have overcome them, to lay the fault upon as few as we can. Consider also, if you follow the advice of Cleon, how much you shall offend likewise in this other point. For in all your cities the commonalty are now your friends, and either revolt not with the few, or if they be compelled to it by force, they presently turn enemies to them that caused the revolt: whereby when you go to war, you have the commons of the adverse city on your side. But if you shall destroy the commonalty of the Mytilenæans, which did neither partake of the revolt, and as soon as they were armed presently delivered the city into your hands: you shall first do unjustly, to kill such as have done you service; and you shall effect a work besides, which the great men do everywhere most desire. For when they have made a city to revolt, they shall have the people presently on their side; you having foreshewn them by the example, that both the guilty and not guilty must undergo the same punishment. Whereas indeed though they were guilty, yet we ought to dissemble it; to the end that the only party now our friend, may not become our enemy. And for the assuring of our dominion, I think it far more profitable voluntarily to put up an injury, than justly to destroy such as we should not. And that same both *justice* and *profit* of revenge, alleged by Cleon, can never possibly be found together in the same thing.

"You therefore, upon knowledge that this is the best course, not upon compassion or lenity, (for neither would I have you won by that), but upon consideration of what hath been advised, be ruled by me, and proceed to judgment at your own leisure against those whom Paches hath sent hither as guilty, and suffer the rest to enjoy their city. For that will be both good for the future, and also of present terror to the enemy. For he that consulteth wisely, is a sorer enemy than he that assaulteth with the strength of action unadvisedly."

Thus spake Diodotus. After these two opinions were delivered, the one most opposite to the other, the Athenians were at contention which they should decree; and at the holding up of hands they were both sides almost equal: but yet the sentence of Diodotus prevailed. Whereupon they presently in haste sent away another galley, lest not arriving before the former they should find the city already destroyed. The first galley set forth before the second a day and a night. But the Mytilenæan ambassadors having furnished this latter with wine and barley cakes, and promised them great rewards if they overtook the other galley, they rowed diligently, at one and the same time both plying their oars, and taking their refection of the said barley cakes steeped in wine and oil; and by turns part of them slept, and the other part rowed. It happened also that there blew no wind against them; and the former galley making no great haste, as going on so sad an errand, whereas the former proceeded in the manner before mentioned, arrived indeed first, but only so much as Paches had read the sentence, and prepared to execute what they had decreed. But presently after came in the other galley, and saved the city from being destroyed. So near were the Mytilenæans to the danger.

But those whom Paches had sent home as most culpable of the revolt, the Athenians, as Cleon had advised, put to death; being in number somewhat above a thousand. They also razed the walls of Mytilene, and took from them all their galleys. After which they imposed on the Lesbians no more tribute, but having divided their land (all but that of the Methymnæans) into three thousand parts, three hundred of those parts [of the choicest land] they consecrated to the gods. And for the rest, they sent men by lot out of their own city to possess it; of whom the Lesbians at the rent of two minæ of silver yearly upon a lot, had the land again to be husbanded by themselves. The Athenians took in all such towns also, as the Mytilenæans were masters of in the continent; which were afterwards made subjects to the people of Athens. Thus ended the business touching Lesbos.

3. Study Questions Before Reading the Melian Dialogue

1) What did the Athenian ambassadors want? What did the Melian representatives want? Why is their return offer of neutrality not adequate for the Athenians?

2) Why did the Melian representatives insist on a private exchange rather than allowing the Athenians to speak to the Melian demos? Are the Melian representatives the leaders of an oligarchic government or of a democratic one?

3) In terms of the substance and frankness of the discussion, does it matter that it is a private conversation between the Athenian ambassadors and the rulers of Melos rather than a public exchange?

4) Does it matter that speakers are nameless rather the named individuals identified in the Mytilenean debate?

5) Does it matter that the speeches here are presented as short, sharp exchanges rather than as extended speeches? Is there a shift in tone from the Mytilenean debate?

6) Are the kinds of arguments made by the Athenians here more like the arguments made by Cleon or more like the arguments made by Diodotus?

7) What, if at all, do the Athenians see as the proper scope of justice? Does it apply in their relations to the Melians, a weaker power? Might it apply in their relations to Sparta, an equal?

8) How do the Athenians see the Melians' interests? How do the Melians disagree? Do they include everything the Melians consider important, such their conception of honor, loyalty, and transcendence?

4. The Text of the Melian Dialogue

The Athenians made war also against the isle of Melos, with thirty galleys of their own, six of Chios, and two of Lesbos. Wherein were of their own, twelve hundredmen of arms, three hundred archers, and twenty archers on horseback: and of their confederates and islanders, about fifteen hundred men of arms. The Melians are a colony of the Lacedæmonians, and therefore refused to be subject, as the rest of the islands were, unto the Athenians; but rested at the first neutral; and afterwards, when the Athenians put them to it by wasting of their land, they entered into open war.

Now the Athenian commanders, Cleomedes the son of Lycomedes, and Tisias the son of Tisimachus, being encamped upon their land with these forces, before they would hurt the same sent ambassadors to deal with them first by way of conference. These ambassadors the Melians refused to bring before the multitude; but commanded them to deliver their message before the magistrates and the few: and they accordingly said as followeth:

Athenians. "Since we may not speak to the multitude, for fear lest when they hear our persuasive and unanswerable arguments all at once in a continued oration, they should chance to be seduced; (for we know that this is the scope of your bringing us to audience before *the few*); make surer yet that point, you that sit here: answer you also to every particular, not in a set speech, but presently interrupting us, whensoever anything shall be said by us which shall seem unto you to be otherwise. And first answer us, whether you like this motion or not?"

Whereunto the council of the Melians answered: "The equity of a leisurely debate is not to be found fault withal; but this preparation of war, not future but already here present, seemeth not to agree with the same. For we see that you are come to be judges of the conference: and that the issue of it, if we be superior in argument and therefore yield not, is likely to bring us war; and if we yield, servitude."

Athenians. "Nay, if you be come together to reckon up suspicions of what may be, or to any other purpose than to take advice upon what is present and before your eyes, how to save your city from destruction, let us give over. But if this be the point, let us speak to it."

Melians. "It is reason, and pardonable for men in our cases, to turn both their words and thoughts upon divers things. Howsoever, this consultation being held only upon the point of our safety, we are content, if you think good, to go on with the course you have propounded."

Athenians. "As we therefore will not, for our parts, with fair pretences; as, that having defeated the Medes, our reign is therefore lawful, or, that we come against you for injury done; make a long discourse without being believed: so would we have you also not expect to prevail by saying, either that you therefore took not our parts because you were a colony of the Lacedæmonians, or that you have done us no injury. But out of those things which we both of us do really think, let us go through with that which is feasible; both you and we knowing, that in human disputation justice is then only agreed on when the necessity is equal; whereas they that have odds of power exact as much as they can, and the weak yield to such conditions as they can get."

Melians. "Well then, (seeing you put the point of profit in the place of justice), we hold it profitable for ourselves, not to overthrow a general profit to all men, which is this: that men in danger, if they plead reason and equity, nay, though somewhat without the strict compass of justice, yet it ought ever to do them good. And the same most of all concerneth you: forasmuch as you shall else give an example unto others of the greatest revenge that can be taken, if you chance to miscarry."

Athenians. "As for us, though our dominion should cease, yet we fear not the sequel. For not they that command, as do the Lacedæmonians, are cruel to those that are vanquished by them; (yet we have nothing to do now with the Lacedæmonians); but such as having been in subjection, have assaulted those that commanded them and gotten the victory. But let the danger of that be to ourselves. In the meantime we tell you this: that we are here now both to enlarge our own dominion, and also to confer about the saving of your city. For we would have dominion over you without oppressing you, and preserve you to the profit of us both."

Melians. "But how can it be profitable for us to serve; though it be so for you to command?"

Athenians. "Because you by obeying, shall save yourselves from extremity; and we not destroying you, shall reap profit by you."

Melians. "But will you not accept, that we remain quiet and be your friends, (whereas before we were your enemies), and take part with neither?"

Athenians. "No. For your enmity doth not so much hurt us, as your friendship will be an argument of our weakness, and your hatred of our power, amongst those we have rule over."

Melians. "Why? Do your subjects measure equity so, as to put those that never had to do with you, and themselves, who for the most part have been your own colonies, and some of them after revolt conquered, into one and the same consideration?"

Athenians. "Why not? For they think they have reason on their side, both the one sort and the other; and that such as are subdued, are subdued by force, and such as are forborne, are so through our fear. So that by subduing you, besides the extending of our dominion over so many more subjects, we shall assure it the more over those we had before; especially being masters of the sea, and you islanders, and weaker (except you can get the victory) than others whom we have subdued already."

Melians. "Do you think then, that there is no assurance in that which we propounded? For here again, (since driving us from the plea of equity you persuade us to submit to your profit), when we have shewed you what is good for us, we must endeavour to draw you to the same, as far forth as it shall be good for you also. As many therefore as now are neutral, what do you but make them your enemies, when, beholding these your proceedings, they look that hereafter you will also turn your arms upon them? And what is this, but to make greater the enemies you have already, and to make others your enemies, each against their wills, that would not else have been so?"

Athenians. "We do not think that they shall be ever the more our enemies, who inhabiting anywhere in the continent, will be long ere they so much as keep guard upon their liberty against us. But islanders unsubdued, as you be, or islanders offended with the necessity of subjection which they are already in: these may indeed, by unadvised courses, put both themselves and us into apparent danger."

Melians. "If you then to retain your command, and your vassals to get loose from you, will undergo the utmost of danger: would it not in us, that be already free, be great baseness and cowardice, if we should not encounter anything whatsoever rather than suffer ourselves to be brought into bondage?"

Athenians. "No; if you advise rightly. For you have not in hand a match of valour upon equal terms, wherein to forfeit your honour; but rather a consultation upon your safety, that you resist not such as be so far your overmatches."

Melians. "But we know that, in matter of war, the event is sometimes otherwise than according to the difference of number in sides: and that if we yield presently, all our hope is lost; whereas if we hold out, we have yet a hope to keep ourselves up."

Athenians. "Hope, the comfort of danger, when such use it as have to spare, though it hurt them, yet it destroys them not. But to such as set their rest upon it, (for it is a thing by nature prodigal), it at once by failing maketh itself known; and known, leaveth no place for future caution. Which let not be your own case, you that are but weak, and have no more but this one stake. Nor be you like unto many men: who though they may presently save themselves by human means, will yet, when upon pressure of the enemy their most apparent hopes fail them, betake themselves to blind ones; as *divination, oracles,* and other such things which with hopes destroy men."

Melians. "We think it, you well know, a hard matter for us to combat your power and fortune, unless we might do it on equal terms. Nevertheless we believe that, for fortune, we shall be nothing inferior; as having the gods on our side, because we stand innocent against men unjust: and for power, what is wanting in us will be supplied by our league with the Lacedæmonians, who are of necessity obliged, if for no other cause, yet for consanguinity's sake and for their own honour, to defend us. So that we are confident, not altogether so much without reason as you think."

Athenians. "As for the favour of the gods, we expect to have it as well as you: for we neither do, nor require anything contrary to what mankind hath decreed, either concerning the worship of the gods, or concerning themselves. For of the gods we think according to the common opinion; and of men, that for certain by necessity of nature they will every where reign over such as they be too strong for. Neither did we make this law, nor are we the first that use it made: but as we found it, and shall leave it to posterity for ever, so also we use it: knowing that you likewise, and others that should have the same power which we have, would do the same. So that forasmuch as toucheth the favour of the gods, we have in reason no fear of being inferior. And as for the opinion you have of the Lacedæmonians, in that you believe they will help you for their own honour: we bless your innocent minds, but affect not your folly. For the Lacedæmonians, though in respect of themselves and the constitutions of their own country they are wont for the most part to be generous; yet in respect of others, though much might be alleged, yet the shortest way one might say it all thus: that most apparently of all men, they hold for *honourable* that which pleaseth, and for *just* that which profiteth. And such an opinion maketh nothing for your now absurd means of safety."

Melians. "Nay, for this same opinion of theirs, we now the rather believe that they will not betray their own colony, the Melians; and thereby become perfidious to such of the Grecians as be their friends, and beneficial to such as be their enemies."

Athenians. "You think not then, that what is profitable must be also safe, and that which is just and honourable must be performed with danger; which commonly the Lacedæmonians are least willing of all men to undergo [for others]."

Melians. "But we suppose that they will undertake danger for us, rather than for any other; and that they think that we will be more assured unto them, than unto any other: because for action, we lie near to Peloponnesus, and for affection, are more faithful than others for our nearness of kin."

Athenians. "The security of such as are at wars, consisteth not in the good will of those that are called to their aid, but in the power of those means they excel in. And this the Lacedæmonians themselves use to consider more than any; and therefore, out of diffidence in their own forces, they take many of their confederates with them, though to an expedition but against their neighbours. Wherefore it is not likely, we being masters of the sea, that they will ever pass over into an island."

Melians. "Yea, but they may have others to send: and the Cretic sea is wide, wherein to take another is harder for him that is master of it, than it is for him that will steal by, to save himself. And if this course fail, they may turn their arms against your own territory, or those of your confederates not invaded by Brasidas. And then you shall have to trouble yourselves, no more about a territory that you have nothing to do withal, but about your own and your confederates."

Athenians. "Let them take which course of these they will, that you also may find by experience, and not be ignorant, that the Athenians never yet gave over siege for fear of any diversion upon others. But we observe that, whereas you said you would consult of your safety, you have not yet in all this discourse said anything, which a man relying on could hope to be preserved by: the strongest arguments you use are but future hopes; and your present power is too short to defend you against the forces already arranged against you. You shall therefore take very absurd counsel, unless excluding us you make amongst yourselves some more discreet conclusion: for [when you are by yourselves], you will no more set your thoughts upon shame; which, when dishonour and danger stand before men's eyes, for the most part undoeth them. For many, when they have foreseen into what dangers they were entering, have nevertheless been so overcome by that forcible word, *dishonour,* that that which is but called dishonour, hath caused them to fall willingly into immedicable calamities; and so to draw upon themselves really, by their own madness, a greater dishonour than could have befallen them by fortune. Which you, if you deliberate wisely, will take heed of; and not think shame to submit to a most potent city, and that upon so reasonable conditions, as of league and of enjoying your own under tribute: and seeing choice is given you of war or safety, do not out of peevishness take the worse. For such do take the best course, who though they give no way to their equals, yet do fairly accommodate to their superiors; and towards their inferiors use moderation. Consider of it therefore, whilst we stand off; and have often in your mind, that you deliberate of your country; which is to be happy or miserable in and by this one consultation."

So the Athenians went aside from the conference; and the Melians, after they had decreed the very same things which before they had spoken, made answer unto them in this manner: "Men of Athens, our resolution is no other than what you have heard before; nor will we, in a small portion of time, overthrow that liberty, in which our city hath remained for the space of seven hundred years since it was first founded. But trusting to the fortune by which the gods have preserved it hitherto, and unto the help of men, that is, of the Lacedæmonians, we will do our best to maintain the same. But this we offer: to be your friends; enemies to neither side; and you to depart out of our land, after agreement such as we shall both think fit."

Thus the Melians answered. To which the Athenians, the conference being already broken off, replied thus: "You are the only men, as it seemeth to us, by this consultation, that think future things more certain than things seen; and behold things doubtful, through desire to have them true, as if they were already come to pass. As you attribute and trust the most unto the Lacedæmonians, and to fortune and hopes, so will you be the most deceived". This said, the Athenian ambassadors departed to their camp. And the commanders, seeing that the Melians stood out, fell presently to the war: and dividing the work among the several cities, encompassed the city of the Melians with a wall. The Athenians afterwards left some forces of their own and of their confederates, for a guard both by sea and land: and with the greatest part of their army went home. The rest that were left, besieged the place. . . .

About the same time the Melians took another part of the wall of the Athenians; they that kept the siege being then not many. But this done, there came afterwards some fresh forces from Athens, under the conduct of Philocrates the son of Demeas. And the town being now strongly besieged, there being also within some that practised to have it given up, they yielded themselves to the discretion of the Athenians: who slew all the men of military age, made slaves of the women and children; and inhabited the place with a colony sent thither afterwards of five hundred men of their own.

5. After Reading the Mytilenean Debate and the Melian Dialogue: Two Theses for Class Discussion

a. Thesis 1—Realism and the Irrelevance of Law and Morality: Thucydides and the "Athenian Thesis"

Many of Thucydides' readers, including both historians and scholars of international relations, have regarded him as a (or the) founder of the "realist" view of international politics.[16] While "realism" comes in several significantly different forms,[17] the core of it can perhaps be stated as follows: The international environment is a realm of "anarchy," in which there is no central government or other authority capable of imposing its will on states (or peoples). States, therefore, cannot look to such a government to resolve disputes that arise between them peaceably

16 The characterization is much disputed and the scholarly writing on the topic voluminous. For studies, *see e.g.*, Richard Ned Lebow, The Tragic Vision of Politics: Ethics, Interests and Orders 14–167 (2003); Thomas L. Pangle & Peter J. Ahrensdorf, Justice Among Nations: On the Moral Basis of Power and Peace 13–32 (1999); Michael W. Doyle, Ways of War and Peace: Realism, Liberalism, and Socialism 49–92 (1997); Peter J. Ahrensdorf, *Thucydides' Realistic Critique of Realism*, 30 Polity 231 (1997); Steven Forde, *International Realism and the Science of Politics: Thucydides, Machiavelli, and Neorealism*, 39 Int'l Stud. Q. 141 (1993); and Steven Forde, *Varieties of Realism: Thucydides and Machiavelli*, 54 J. Pol. 372 (1992). *See also infra* text at notes 25-29. Chapter 2.A offers a fuller treatment of the modern scholarship on realism and its critics.

17 The eighteenth century Swiss philosopher Jean-Jacques Rousseau gave realism an unusually harsh formulation in his Considerations on the Government of Poland (1772) when he wrote: "The most inviolable law of nature is the law of the strongest. No laws, no constitution can be exempted from this law. If you look for the means of guaranteeing yourselves against invasion by a neighbor stronger than you, you are chasing a will-o'-the-wisp." Jean-Jacques Rousseau, Political Writings 236–37 (Frederick Watkins trans. & ed. 1986).

or in accordance with law. Rather, they must rely on their own strength to protect their vital interests or even to ensure their survival. But any other state is at least potentially a threat to the well-being of a state or, ultimately, to its survival, even if that other state does not appear to harbor hostile intentions towards it, but instead appears indifferent or even friendly to it. And, unfortunately, the present or future intentions of one state with regard to another cannot be known with certainty. States, however, strongly desire to protect their interests and, above all, to guarantee their own survival. Accordingly, not knowing the intentions of another state towards it and being aware that that other state might prove to be inimical, each state will take all necessary steps to safeguard its own security. But the best, perhaps the only, way to guarantee a state's security is to enlarge its power (or at least, to prevent other states' power from outdistancing its own). Acting out of rational self-interest (at least as a general rule), each state will therefore strive to acquire sufficient power to overawe any potential enemy state (or combination of them).[18] (This brief description of realism foregrounds the "security dilemma," discussed in detail in Chapter 2.A; other, broader definitions of realism have been put forward.[19])

If the core claims of realism are true, they make the possibility of international law problematic. If, say, a treaty requires a state to act in a manner that would seriously compromise its security or damage its vital interests, then realism predicts that the state will not comply with the treaty. If, on the other hand, treaty compliance would serve the state's security and promote its interests, then realism predicts that the state would act in that way anyway.[20] In the first case, international law is ineffective; in the second, it is superfluous. Either way, international law would make little, if any, difference to a state's conduct.

Thucydides' *History* presents cases that appear to illustrate this logic. The Spartan leader Sthenelaidas persuades the Spartan Assembly to declare war on Athens at least partly on the basis of the fear of further Athenian aggrandizement.[21] Sthenelaidas and the Spartan Assembly consciously ignore the facts—emphasized immediately before in the speech of King Archidamus

18 We examine contemporary realism and its offshoots in detail in Chapter 2. For leading accounts of contemporary realism, see Kenneth Waltz, The Theory of International Politics (1979) and John J. Mearsheimer, The Tragedy of Great Power Politics (2001). Waltz's "defensive" realism stresses states' quest for security; Mearsheimer's "offensive" realism stresses their quest for power. For a collection of essays evaluating realism, *see* The Perils of Anarchy: Contemporary Realism and International Security (Michael E. Brown, Sean M. Lynn-Jones & Steven E. Miller eds., 1995). A brief but highly influential statement of realism is found in E.H. Carr, The Twenty Years Crisis, 1919–1939 (1939).

19 For example, Robert Gilpin, a leading international relations theorist, considers realism to be "a philosophical disposition and set of assumptions about the world." Robert Gilpin, *The Richness of the Tradition of Political Realism,* 39 Int'l Org. 287, 289 (1984). For Gilpin, all forms of realism share three bedrock assumptions: 1) that international affairs are "essentially conflictual . . . Anarchy is the rule; order, justice, and morality are the exceptions;" 2) that "the foundation of political life" lies in "conflict groups," i.e., "in a world of scarce resources, human beings confront one another ultimately as members of groups, and not as isolated individuals"; and 3) that "power and security" take "primacy in all political life." *Id.* at 290.

20 Thucydides illustrates this side of the matter when he ascribes Agamemnon's success in raising a large Greek fleet in the Trojan War, not so much to the oath that Agamemnon's followers had sworn in his support, as to the fact that Agamemnon "exceeded the rest in power." *History*, Book I, ¶ 9.

21 Sthenelaidas' argument rests also, and more importantly, on what he presents as considerations of honor and justice. In Hobbes' translation, Sthenelaidas says: "Wherefore, men of Lacedæmon, decree the war, as becometh the dignity

at the same meeting—that the Treaty of Peace of 446 B.C. between Athens and Sparta required that the parties seek arbitration before going to war, that the Athenians had offered to arbitrate the disputes between themselves and Sparta, and that it would be illegal for Sparta to wage war on Athens in those circumstances.[22] In that instance, international law did not stop Sparta from launching a preventive war out of fear (among other reasons) of the further decline of its power in relation to its main rival. On the other hand, when the Athenian Assembly discusses the Spartan demands, Pericles, Athens' dominant political figure, urges the Assembly to offer legal satisfaction to the Spartans in the manner that the peace treaty provides.[23] Athens would not, however, be appealing to international law for its own sake, but rather to gain a propaganda advantage in the war that both sides are now sure is coming. In this situation, the offer to comply with the treaty is made, not of out a belief in the overriding importance of legal process, but out of Athens' self-interest.[24]

It is questionable whether Thucydides himself was a "realist" in the sense just described.[25] At least some careful students of the *History* argue that however much Thucydides resembles latter-day "realists," he does *not* embrace the view that law and morality are altogether irrelevant to international relations—even if he teaches that "the range of moral choice in international politics" is "radically circumscrib[ed]."[26] Other scholars point to the fact that "Thucydides' history indicates that emotion, in the form of appetite and spirit (honor), was as important [to state behavior] as reason . . . At the deepest levels of interest formation, appetite and spirit rode roughshod over reason."[27] On the other hand, scholars have also found that "[t]here is plenty of

of Sparta; and let not the Athenians grow yet greater, nor let us betray our confederates, but in the name of the Gods proceed against the doers of injustice." *History,* Book I, ¶ 86.

22 As King Archidamus says the Athenians are "content to refer the cause to judgment; and one that offereth himself to judgment, may not lawfully be invaded as a doer of injury." *History,* Book I, ¶ 85. On the Greeks' reliance on arbitration to resolve inter-state disputes and the normative expectations that they would do so, *see* Steve Sheppard, *Laws of War in the Pre-Dawn Light: Institutions and Obligations in Thucydides' Peloponnesian War,* 43 Colum. J. Transnat'l L. 905, 914-19 (2005).

23 *See History,* Book I, ¶ 144 (speech of Pericles urging Athenians to tell the Spartans that "that we will stand to judgment according to the articles [of the peace treaty], and will not begin the war,").

24 Again, it should be noted that Pericles, like King Agis, does not rest his case entirely on considerations of expediency. He also appeals to justice and honor. Compliance with the treaty, he says, "is both just, and for the dignity of the city to answer." *History,* Book I, ¶ 144.

25 *See, e.g.,* Arthur M. Eckstein, *Thucydides, the Outbreak of the Peloponnesian War, and the Foundation of International Systems Theory,* 25 Int'l Hist. Rev. 757, 757, 773 (2003) (arguing that Thucydides shows an "affinity with the fundamental propositions of realism, in particular the impact of a power-transition crisis within a state system," but also finding that unlike later "structural" realists, Thucydides "gives weight to other factors as well as structural process," such as "the specific decisions taken by Athens against Sparta's allies"); and Peter J. Ahrensdorf, *Thucydides' Realistic Critique of Realism,* 30 Polity 231, 233 (1997) (arguing that although "Thucydides does agree with two of the basic tenets of [realism]: namely, the self-interested character of states and the anarchic structure of international politics," nonetheless he "doubts that realism can form the basis of a successful foreign policy because he believes that, although the moral passions and hopes that realism opposes are unreasonable, they are also indelible features of political life").

26 Michael W. Doyle, Ways of War and Peace: Realism, Liberalism, and Socialism 83 (1997). *See also* Clifford Orwin, *The Just and the Advantageous in Thucydides: The Case of the Mytilenean Debate,* 78 Am. Pol. Sci. Rev. 485 (1984).

27 Lebow, *supra* note 16, at 114.

evidence that Thucydides thought that [expediency was] the only way to discuss the relations between states relevant to the actual behaviour of states."[28] Whatever Thucydides himself may have taught, it is certainly arguable that as his *History* presents the Athenians (both leaders and people), *they* were (or took themselves to be) "realists." Accordingly, we may distinguish between the position of Thucydides himself and the "Athenian thesis" of international relations that his speeches, debates and a (single) dialogue impute to the Athenians.[29] Our comments and questions below concern the "Athenian thesis" as dramatized by Thucydides, rather than the views of Thucydides himself.

i. Statements of the Athenian Thesis

a. In Hobbes' translation of the Melian debate, the Athenian ambassadors say: "they that have odds of power exact as much as they can, and the weak yield to such conditions as they can get" (Book V, ¶ 89). In other translations, the statement is rendered more succinctly as: "the strong do what they can and the weak suffer what they must" (Crawley-Lateiner trans. p. 340). Later in the debate, the Athenian ambassadors restate their thesis, saying, "by necessity of nature men will everywhere reign over such as they be too strong for" (Book V, ¶ 105; Hobbes trans.).

In these statements, the Athenian ambassadors appear to be expressing the realist position that states (and individuals) seek to maximize their power. Furthermore, the Athenian ambassadors deny the Melian oligarchs' claim that Sparta, moved by a sense of honor, will go to Melos' assistance (Book V, ¶ 105). Rather, the Athenians say, Sparta will not attempt to protect Melos because it is beyond Sparta's power, and hence not in Sparta's interest, to do so. Sparta will not dare to contend with Athens over the island of Melos, given Athens' indisputable mastery of the sea (Book V, ¶ 109). Although the Spartans use moral language to explain and justify their policies, the Athenians claim that Sparta, no less than Athens, acts only in its own interest (although Sparta may lack Athens' candor, or possibly its self-awareness). See Book V, ¶ 105 (the Spartans "hold for *honorable* that which pleaseth and for *just* that which profiteth").[30] Thus, the Athenians interpret both their own actions and those of Sparta as driven solely by self-interest, and they imply that each of the two states knows that the other acts solely (or at least primarily) from that motive.

---

28 W. Liebeschuetz, *The Structure and Function of the Melian Dialogue,* 88 J. Hell. Stud. 73, 76 (1968).

29 For the distinction between the Athenian thesis and Thucydides' own views, *see* Laurie M. Johnson Bagby, *The Use and Abuse of Thucydides in International Relations,* 48 Int' Org. 131, 136, 141, 143 (1994).

30 The Athenians may be failing to give Sparta her due: the Spartans' reputation for piety—even when religious observances constrained them in wartime—seems generally to have been deserved. As one scholarly study put it, Sparta "was devout, but not to the point of extinction." M.D. Goodman & A.J. Halladay, *Religious Scruples in Ancient Warfare,* 36 Classical Q. 151, 160 (1986).

b. Further evidence of the Athenian thesis appears in the Mytilenean debate, when Diodotus purports to rely exclusively on expediency, i.e., Athens's self-interest, as his argument for clemency. He says (Book III,¶ 44): "We plead not judicially with the Mytileneans as to need arguments of equity but we consult of them which way we may serve ourselves of them to our most advantage hereafter." Plainly, this argument is premised on the rejection of any moral or judicial criterion for decision. The second meeting of the Athenian Assembly, which reversed the decision taken at the first meeting, seems to reveal that the Athenians were eventually moved by a sober and reasoned calculation of their best interests, rather than by the sense of having been wronged or the passionate anger that had motivated their earlier decision. The Assembly's original, vindictive decision to punish Mytilene savagely was a response to what the Athenians saw as act of ingratitude and betrayal, since the Mytilenians had sought and received Spartan support in their efforts to break with the Athenian Empire. Diodotus' argument, which led the Athenians to adopt a humanitarian approach instead of a punitive one, appears to illustrate, in the action of the Athenian Assembly itself, an example of what the Athenian thesis considers to be the true face of international relations. Diodotus offers Athens the image of itself as a calculating, deliberative rational actor, unmoved either by emotions such as anger or pity or by the sense of offended justice; and the Athenian Assembly adapts its conduct to the image of Athens that Diodotus holds up before it.

Even Cleon's defense of the Assembly's original decision seems to provide partial confirmation of the Athenian thesis of the behavior of states (including Athens itself) in international relations. Cleon does indeed appear to argue that, as matter of retributive justice, Mytilene should be punished for its unprovoked betrayal of the Athens.[31] But, like Diodotus, he also appeals to expediency, stating that (Book III, ¶ 40) "if you follow my advice you shall do that which is both just in respect of the Mytileneans *and profitable for yourselves.*" Both speakers in the Mytilenean debate therefore assume that Athens' conduct in international affairs will be governed solely (Diodotus) or partly (Cleon) by an appeal to its self-interest.

c. The Athenians expound their realist view of international relations, not only in their own Assembly or in colloquy with the Melian oligarchs, but also early in the *History* in their debate with the Corinthians before the Assembly of Sparta. In that debate, the Athenians seek to refute the Corinthian charge that Athens has acquired its empire because it is an exceptionally restless, aggressive and, therefore, dangerous power. In their reply, the Athenians contend that they originally acquired their empire from fear and self-interest (though also from honor), and that they have sought to maintain it ever since, because to give it up would be unsafe in view

31 On Cleon's appeal to justice, *see* Orwin, *supra* note 26, at 486–87; Daniel Gerst, *Thucydides and Neorealism,* 33 Int'l Stud. Q. 3, 13–14 (1989).

of Sparta's rivalry.[32] In pursuing that course, the Athenians say, they have behaved no differently from how any other power in their situation would have done. Indeed, the Athenians say, Sparta also arranges affairs in its own region to its best advantage. Generalizing, the Athenians say that it is everywhere the case "for the weaker to be kept under by the stronger" (Book I, ¶¶ 75-76):

> [A]t first we were forced to advance our dominion to what it is, out of the nature of the thing itself; as chiefly for fear, next for honour, and lastly for profit. For when we had the envy of many, and had reconquered some [Greek cities] that had already revolted, and seeing you were no more our friends as you had been, but suspected and quarrelled us, we held it no longer a safe course, laying by our power to put ourselves into your danger. For the revolts from us, would all have been made to you. Now it is no fault for men in danger, to order their affairs to the best. For you also, men of Lacedæmon, have command over the cities of Peloponnesus, and order them to your best advantage. . . . So that, though overcome by three the greatest things, honour, fear, and profit, we have both accepted the dominion delivered us and refuse again to surrender it, we have therein done nothing to be wondered at nor beside the manner of men. Nor have we been the first in this kind, but it hath been ever a thing fixed, for the weaker to be kept under by the stronger. . .

d. The Athenians restate their view after the Melian atrocity during their ill-fated invasion of Sicily. The Athenian ambassador Euphemus ("Good Talker") is seeking to persuade one of the Sicilian states, Camarina, to throw in its lot with the Athenian invaders against the state of Syracuse, the most formidable power on Sicily and Athens' primary target in the campaign. The Syracusan leader Hermocrates has just addressed the Camarenean Assembly, urging it to ally with Syracuse instead. Hermocrates' speech stresses the danger that Athens will pose to the independence of the smaller Sicilian states if it defeats Syracuse, and to the ties of blood and kinship that bind the Camarineans to the (Doric) Syracusans and oppose them to the (Ionian) Athenians. Euphemus seeks to counter Hermocrates by arguing that the regional great power, Syracuse, poses a greater danger to Camarina than Athens does; that for fear of Syracuse, Athens wants Camarina to be strong rather than weak; that Athens bases its policy, not on kinship or blood ties, but only on its own security and interests; and that even if it is tyrannical and exploitative over some of the smaller states it rules, it also treats other subject states leniently—because it is in its interest to do so. So the worst that the Camareneans would have to

32 The statement of the Athenian thesis in this remarkable speech is closely mirrored in Hobbes' Leviathan, Part I, ch. 13, where Hobbes writes:

> So that in the nature of man, we find three principal causes of quarrel. First, competition; secondly, diffidence; thirdly, glory. The first maketh men invade for gain; the second, for safety; and the third, for reputation. The first use violence, to make themselves masters of other men's persons, wives, children, and cattle; the second, to defend them; the third, for trifles, as a word, a smile, a different opinion, and any other sign of undervalue, either direct in their persons or by reflection in their kindred, their friends, their nation, their profession, or their name.

fear from Athens, Euphemus implies, is that Athens would exert a very loose control over them, because anything more oppressive would not serve its interest. Throughout, Euphemus candidly acknowledges that Athens cares for nothing else than its own security and interest—but, somewhat in the manner of Diodotus, he argues that that very concentration on its self-interest will make Athens, in suitable circumstances, a benevolent hegemon. He says (Book VI, ¶ 83):

> Now to a tyrant or city that reigneth, nothing can be thought absurd if profitable; nor any man a friend, that may not be trusted to. Friend or enemy he must be, according to the several occasions. But here it is for our benefit not to weaken our friends, but by our friends' strength to weaken our enemies. This you must needs believe, inasmuch as yonder also [i.e., in the islands of eastern Greece] we so command over our confederates, as every of them may be most useful to us: the Chians and Methymnæans redeem their liberty with providing us some galleys; the most of the rest, with a tribute of money somewhat more pressing. Some again of our confederates are absolutely free, notwithstanding that they be islanders, and easy to be subdued: the reason whereof is this; they are situate in places commodious about Peloponnesus. It is probable therefore, that here also we will so order our affairs as shall be most for our own turn, and most according to our fear, as we told you, of the Syracusians.

e. Elsewhere in the *History*, Thucydides depicts other Greek states as relying on the Athenian thesis that law and morality are irrelevant to international affairs.[33] Of particular interest is one occasion in which the representatives of another Greek state, Corcyra, seek to sway the Athenian Assembly. In Book I, Corcyra's ambassadors are attempting to persuade the Athenian Assembly to come to Corcyra's aid. Corcyra was an "unaligned" state in the remote northwest of Greece, and one of Greece's leading naval powers. Corcyra is faced with a threat from Corinth, the third leading naval power, a commercial rival of Athens, and a potential ally of Sparta against Athens. The Corcyrean ambassadors point out to the Athenians that if Corinth prevails in its conflict with Corcyra, the Corcyrean fleet will be added to that of Corinth, thus creating a naval force that would rival or outstrip that of Athens—and so place Athens in grave jeopardy in the war that is expected to break out soon. The Corcyrean ambassadors note that some Athenians might hesitate to give assistance to Corcyra on the grounds that to do so would violate Athens' legal obligations under the treaty of peace between Athens and Sparta. But the

33 For example, the Syracusan leader Hermocrates, in a speech before the assembled delegates of the Sicilian cities before the Athenian invasion, posits that the several cities of Sicily have acted in their own interests both in going to war with each other and in attempting to compose their differences and make peace. *See History*, Book IV, ¶ 59. To be sure, Hermocrates also urges the delegates to think of Sicily as a unity in whose safety all of their cities have a common interest, distinct from and higher than their several interests. *Id.* at ¶ 60. Realists would, of course, query whether there *could* be such a common interest, and indeed whether Hermocrates, in urging the other Sicilian cities to pursue it, is not disingenuously promoting the interest of his own Syracuse, the dominant power on the island and Athens' primary target, instead.

Corcyreans argue that the Athenians should not hesitate to violate the treaty because it would be in Athens' interest for it to do so. As the Corcyreans say (Book I, ¶ 36):

> If any man now think thus, that what we have spoken is indeed profitable, but fears, if it were admitted, the league [i.e., the peace treaty] were thereby broken: let that man consider, that his fear joined with strength will make his enemies fear, and his confidence, having (if he reject us) so much the less strength, will so much the less be feared.

Thus, both the Corcyreans and the Athenians seem to accept and apply the Athenian thesis, most especially to the actions of the Athenians; and the Athenians apply that view, not only to themselves, but also to the Spartans.

ii. Comments and Questions on the Athenian Thesis

1) Why do the Athenians have to attempt to persuade the Melians to act in accordance with their interests if acting in accordance with one's interests is a necessity of nature? "[I]f all talk of justice and honor is a mere trapping, why are the Athenians so eager to see such talk eliminated?"[34]

2) Isn't the fact that the Athenians had originally decided to destroy Mytilene evidence in itself that sometimes states act on the basis of passions (or of justice) rather than solely on the basis of their interests?

3) Isn't the fact that the Melians chose death rather than subordination to Athens in itself a refutation of the thesis of the Athenian ambassadors? Didn't Melos, or at least a faction of the Melians, choose honor rather than life? (See Bk. V, ¶ 100.)

4) The Melians also rely on the Spartans' conception of their state's honor. (See Book V, ¶ 104.) Did the Melian conception of self-interest therefore encompass the preservation of values, rather than being limited to pure expediency?

5) In light of the disasters that befall Athens after the atrocity at Melos, were the Athenian ambassadors simply "wrong and deluded" about Athens' true interest?[35] If

34 Bagby, *supra* note 29, at 146.

35 *See* Liebeschuetz, *supra* note 28, at 75. Liebeschuetz argues that the Melians were right in warning the Athenians that Athens was going to make many enemies, Sparta would undertake expeditions against the Athenian Empire, and Athens would in time have to fight desperately for self-preservation.

they miscalculated, why did they do so? Or was the Athenians' error deeper than a simple miscalculation of interest?

6) In the Mytilenean debate, Diodotus acknowledges (Book V, ¶ 44) that "either some greater terror than death must be devised or death will not be enough for coercion," thus indicating the belief that expediency or self-interest narrowly construed is not the sole basis of actual human decision-making. Further, in Book I, ¶ 75, Athenian ambassadors to Sparta identify "honor" along with "fear" and "profit" as a motive for establishing the Athenian empire. Did the Athenians always have the narrow, value-neutral conception of self-interest that they seem to embrace in the Melian debate? If they did not, why did they eventually adopt that view?

7) Or is it the case, not that the Athenians have a flawed concept of self-interest, but that the Melians have a mistaken concept of honor? Remember that the Athenian Assembly has already decided on the fate of the Melians, leaving the Athenian ambassadors to Melos no choice but to present the Melians with the choice between surrender or annihilation. Since it is all but certain that the Athenians will prevail in a struggle with the Melians, is it truly dishonorable for the Melians to surrender?[36]

8) Should the Athenians have anticipated that the Melians would not surrender? Some analysts argue that states repeatedly encounter "almost insuperable difficulties" when they attempt to "achieve political means by military ends."[37] (For one thing, states find it hard to think themselves into the enemy's mind, and so cannot reliably predict the enemy's reaction to the use of military force.) Were the Athenians therefore guilty of a failure of imagination more than of anything else?

9) In his famous "Funeral Oration," Pericles had rallied the Athenians to the cause of the war by telling them that the love of honor never grows old, that it matters more than gain, that the Athenian war dead have a lasting glory, and that in the pursuit of freedom, Athens should never decline the dangers of war.[38] In a later speech, Pericles addressed a demoralized and war-weary Athenian Assembly, urging the

36 See A.B. Bosworth, *The Humanitarian Aspect of the Melian Dialogue,* 113 J. Hell. Stud. 30, 41 (1993) ("To confront insuperable odds is not heroic but folly. . . . If one's sense of honour leads one to foreseeable destruction, it is a perverse act of delusion and can bring only dishonour.").

37 *See* David Chuter, *Triumph of the Will? Or, Why Surrender Is Not Always Inevitable,* 23 Rev. Int'l Stud. 381, 394 (1997); *see also* id. at 400.

38 *See History,* Book I, at ¶¶ 43–44.

people to continue the struggle out of love of honor and glory.[39] And before the war had broken out, Pericles had reminded the Assembly that Athens had won glory by opposing the Persian invasion (480 B.C.), even though it had had far fewer resources than Persia and resistance had seemed futile.[40] Don't these Periclean speeches show that, at least early in the war, the Athenians had grasped that honor could motivate state action in international affairs, as well as (or instead of) expediency? Don't they indicate that the Athenian ambassadors at Melos should have understood—if only from their own state's experience in the Persian War—that a state might well resist a much stronger power, even when resistance appeared hopeless?[41] What accounts for the ambassadors' apparent forgetfulness?

10) Diodotus' speech is nearly always read as an appeal to expediency (if an enlarged conception of that) rather than to justice. Is it truer that "[f]rom the depths of Diodotus' argument from interest pipes the still, small voice of justice?"[42]

11) The Melians' arguments draw in part on religious assumptions. In Book V, ¶104, the Melians describe themselves "as having the gods on our side, because we stand innocent against men unjust." Not only do they feel "the gods" will give them strength, but also they seem to feel duty-bound to preserve their traditional liberty, which they regard as "having been a gift from the gods." Thus, the Melians also argue: "trusting to the fortune by which the gods have preserved [our liberty] hitherto ... we will do our best to maintain the same." Don't the actions of the Melians—choosing death rather than submission to Athens—corroborate their view that states may be motivated by more than self-interest narrowly understood, or even by more than an enlarged self-interest understood to include values such as honor?

12) Or are the Melian oligarchs in fact acting out of narrow self-interest in choosing death, whatever they may say about their motivations? Consider that if Melos holds

39 In this speech, Pericles urged the Athenians to fight on for "a present splendour and an immortal glory hereafter." *Id.*, Book II, at ¶ 64.

40 *See id.*, Book I, at ¶ 144 ("For our fathers, when they undertook the Medes, did from less beginnings, nay abandoning the little they had, by wisdom rather than fortune, by courage rather than strength, both repel the barbarian and advance this state to the height it now is at").

41 *See* James V. Morrison, *Historical Lessons in the Melian Episode,* 130 Trans. Amer. Phil. Ass'n 119, 139 n.64 (2000) (noting similarity between Athens' situation in relation to Persia and Melos' situation in relation to Athens). Further, the History has many instances in which small states defy t odds, fight for their liberty against greater powers, and prevail by courage or good luck or both. *See, e.g., History,* Book II, at ¶ 91. Pericles himself stresses to the Athenians—as Melos was later to do—the importance of sheer chance in war. *See id.*, Book I, at ¶ 140.

42 *See* Orwin, *supra* note 26, at 492.

out against Athens, there is at least some chance that it may prevail, even though the odds are great against it. If Melos is not conquered, its oligarchy is likely to survive. On the other hand, if Melos surrenders to Athens, then Athens may not spare its oligarchs (because they may later betray the city to Sparta). Even if Athens does spare them, the opposing faction of Melian democrats who would come to power under Athens' protection would in all likelihood slay them.[43] Do the Melian oligarchs choose to die rather than surrender because they fear that surrender will mean death anyway?

b. Thesis 2—International Politics and Democracy: Thucydides' Account of Democratic Decision-making

One of the central debates of modern international law and international relations theory is the relationship between the internal political structures of a state or system of states and the level of international violence.[44] Drawing on the Kantian claim that "perpetual peace" would arise through the globalization of leagues of republican governments,[45] modern scholars have

43 Note that Melos finally succumbs to Athens because of internal treachery – possibly by the democratic or popular faction. *See History*, Book V, at ¶116. And bear in mind that in Mytilene, the democratic faction, after being given arms, had rebelled against the ruling oligarchs and surrendered the city to the Athenians.

44 Kenneth N. Waltz, Man, The State, and War: A Theoretical Analysis 80–158 (1954) (so-called "second image" analysis).

45 Immanuel Kant, Perpetual Peace *in* Kant: On History 85–154 (Beck ed. 1957). For a representative collection of studies on the "democratic peace" thesis, see Debating Democratic Peace (Michael E. Brown, Sean M. Lynn-Jones & Steven E. Miller eds., 1996); see also David A. Lake, *Powerful Pacifists: Democratic States and War, in* Do Democracies Win Their Wars? 38 (Michael E. Brown, Owen R. Coté, Jr., Sean M. Lynn-Jones & Steven E. Miller eds., 2011). For a review of the issue and the literature surrounding it, see Robert J. Delahunty & John C. Yoo, *Kant, Habermas and the Democratic Peace,* 10 Chi. J. Int'l L. 437 (2010). The thesis does not seem to hold true for democracies in the ancient world. *See* Eric Robinson, *Reading and Misreading the Ancient Evidence for Democratic Peace,* 38 J. of Peace Research 593 (2001). It is also arguable that facets of modern democracies other than their constitutions are causally responsible for "the democratic peace." *See* Azar Gat, *The Democratic Peace Theory Reframed: The Impact of Modernity,* 58 World Politics 73 (2005).

Kant was not the only leading thinker to espouse some form of the democratic peace thesis. Indeed, in the English-speaking world, other figures may have been far more influential in popularizing this hypothesis. Thomas Paine, a leading figure in both the American and French Revolutions, advocated it in his widely read *The Rights of Man* (1791). Paine wrote: "Monarchical sovereignty, the enemy of mankind, and the source of misery, is abolished, and sovereignty is restored to its natural and original place, the nation. . . . Were this the case throughout Europe, the cause of war would be taken away." Thomas Paine, The Rights of Man, in Eric Foner (ed.), 1 Complete Writings, 342 (1995). Likewise, in *Democracy in America* (1835), which also was widely read in the U.S., French thinker Alexis de Tocqueville dedicated a chapter to the topic, "Why Democratic Nations Have A Natural Desire For Peace And Why Democratic Armies Naturally Seek War." De Tocqueville wrote: "The same concerns, fears and passions which distance democratic nations from revolutions also alienate them from war. . . . I think one can accept it as a general and constant rule that, in civilized nations, warlike passions will become less frequent and less intense, as social conditions approach a level of equality." Alexis de Tocqueville, Democracy in America and Two Essays on America 750–51 (1835; Gerald Bevan trans. 2003). Richard Cobden, an early English nineteenth century classical liberal, argued that "The middle and industrious classes of England can have no interest apart from the preservation of peace. The honours, the fame, the emoluments of war belong not to them; the battle-plain is the harvest-field of the aristocracy, watered with the blood of the people." Richard Cobden, 1 Political Works (1835) (*available at* http://oll.libertyfund.org/titles/cobden-the-political-writings-of-richard-cobden-vol-1?q=emoluments+of+war#Cobden_0424-01_330). And in *The Influence of the Aristocracy* (1825), the philosopher John Stuart Mill argued that "[i]t is the interest of the few, to be engaged in continual wars: and this for more reasons than one: 1st, for the glory of the thing, 2ndly for the power it gives them, 3rdly as an excuse for increasing the army and navy, and making more incomes for sons and nephews; and lastly, because in time of war, people think so much of doing harm to others that they have no leisure to think of doing good to themselves: from which cause a period of war is a period of security for political abuses of

advanced the so-called "democratic peace" thesis, arguing that democracies inherently are constituted to promote peace (at least with other democracies).[46] One version of the democratic peace thesis observes that democratic decision-making requires sustained deliberation and enormous effort to reach a consensus on key strategic decisions. It would follow, under this argument, that democracies make reliable international commitments, Thus, this increases predictability in international affairs and reduces misunderstanding, thereby minimizing the chance of war (with other democracies).[47]

In addition to raising the question of realism and the potential irrelevance of international law (Thesis I), Thucydides' account reveals Athens' changing responses to the questions posed by the Mytileneans', Melians', and other smaller states' resistance to her empire. He may be read to argue that, contrary to the democratic peace thesis, democracy itself increases the likelihood of war (whether with other democracies or with non-democracies). He may also be read to argue that the war, exacerbated by plague and other hardships that the war may have caused, induced the further coarsening of Athenian democracy, making it even more reckless, cruel and aggressive.

It should be noted that Thucydides was himself a victim of the Athenian democracy, spending most of the war in exile as punishment rendered by the Athenian Assembly for his defeat at Amphipolis at the hands of the Spartan general Brasidas, thus enabling him to devote his twilight years to writing a history of a war waged by the very democracy that had spurned him.[48] Furthermore, towards the end of the *History* (Book VIII, ¶ 97), Thucydides expresses the view that a "mixed regime" is better than democracy.

i. Democracy Causes Imperialism, War, and Bad War Policy

a. In setting the stage for the debate, Thucydides reports that the Athenian Assembly, in a moment of fury, decided to kill Salaethus, a Spartan prisoner of war whom the Athenian general Paches had captured at Mytilene and shipped back to Athens (Book III, ¶¶ 28, 35-36). The Assembly took this rash and brutal decision even though Salaethus had offered to persuade the

all sorts, sizes, and denominations. As for the many, it is scarcely ever their interest to engage in a war; and never in any that is called a just and necessary one: by which, so far as my observation goes, is always meant, a war that has for its object something either contemptibly silly or detestably wicked: the honours of the flag, the balance of power, or to prevent the establishment of free institutions in foreign countries." John M. Robson (ed.), John Stuart Mill: Collected Works, vol. xxvi – Journals and Debating Speeches Pt. I (1820; 2006) (*available at* http://oll.libertyfund.org/titles/mill-the-collected-works-of-john-stuart-mill-volume-xxvi-journals-and-debating-speeches-part-i?q=balance+of+power#Mill_0223-26_1433).

46 Michael Doyle, *Liberalism and World Politics*, 80 American Political Science Review, 1151–69 (1986).

47 Charles Lipson, Reliable Partners: How Democracies Have Made a Separate Peace (2003).

48 Indeed, according to some ancient biographers, it was Cleon, one of the leading politicians of Athens and perhaps the very same Cleon proposing the punishment of the Mytilene, who brought the charge. *See* Kagan, Reinvention, supra note 9, at 146; *see also* Kagan, Peloponnesian War, *supra* note 9, at 145-6 (suggesting Thucydides' hostility to Cleon in the text makes this claim plausible).

Spartan government to lift its siege of Plataea, an ally of Athens. (Book III, ¶ 36; cp. Book II, ¶ 73 (Plataean alliance with Athens).) The killing of Salaethus and other prisoners of war was a violation of the laws and customs of war that prevailed in Greece.[49] Thucydides may be linking Athenian democracy to a policy of purely self-interested imperialism, and thus to one of extreme and irrational brutality.[50]

b. Cleon's speech in the Mytilenean debate provides evidence that Athens' leaders and people alike understood that they were engaged in a venture of imperial aggression. Cleon argues that, assuming that the Athenian Empire is unjust to its subject peoples, the Athenians must accept the consequences of that injustice—which here would include punishing the Mytileneans unjustly—if they wish to retain their dominion. The price of being "good" or just, Cleon argues, would be the loss of empire the Athenians have already acquired by choice—a price he assumes the Athenians would be unwilling to pay.[51]

True, Cleon seems to question whether the Athenian democracy is capable of executing the means necessary to the ends it has already chosen. He asserts that "I have often on other occasions thought a democracy uncapable of dominion over others; but most of all now for this your repentance concern the Mytilenaeans" (Book III, ¶ 37). But perhaps Cleon is being disingenuous. He knows that the Athenians have shown themselves fully capable of the ruthlessness that he thinks is necessary for successful imperialism, and he is simply trying to shame the Athenians out of any feelings of pity for the Mytileneans by suggesting that democracy may be unequal to the "burdens" of imperial rule.

c. Diodotus' speech succeeds in persuading the Athenian Assembly to reverse its decision of the day before to slaughter the adult males of Mytilene and enslave its women and children. But that success underscores the fickleness of the Athenian people. Popular democracy, Thucydides may be saying, is a badly flawed procedure for making important decisions of state policy. Bear in mind that the Assembly's earlier, brutal decision had also been made after deliberation.[52] However, Thucydides notes the very next day the Athenians "felt a kind of repentance in themselves; and began to consider what a great and cruel decree it was . . . ." (Book III, ¶ 36) And Diodotus, in the very act of persuading the Assembly to reverse itself, alludes to the defects of democracy, asserting his "opinion that nothing is so contrary to good counsel as these two

49 *See* Lebow, *supra* note 16, at 266.

50 On the question whether Athenian democracy (as Thucydides portrays it) inherently tended to imperialism, *see* Steven Forde, *Thucydides on the Causes of Athenian Imperialism*, 80 Amer. Pol. Sci. Rev. 433 (1986); Timothy J. Gilpin, *The Democratic Roots of Athenian Imperialism in the Fifth Century B.C.*, 79 Classical J. 100 (1984).

51 *See History*, Book III, at ¶ 40 ("For if these have justly revolted, you must unjustly have had dominion over them. Nay, though your dominion be against reason, yet if you resolve to hold it, you must also, as a matter conducing thereunto, against reason punish them; or else you must give your dominion over, that you may be good without danger.").

52 *See id.*, Book III, at ¶ 36 ("they went to council").

haste and *anger*: whereof the one is ever accompanied with madness, and the other with want of judgment." (Book III, ¶ 42).

d. Scholars have read the Melian dialogue as a prelude to Athens' disastrous decision to embark on the invasion of Sicily, a large island settled by Western Greeks.[53] The invasion of Sicily was a logical extension of Athens' policy of imperial expansion—an attempt to deny Sparta and its allies of imported Sicilian grain that, if successful, would have brought Sparta and its allies to their knees.[54] Thucydides may be suggesting that the brutality and oppressiveness that the Athenian democracy exhibited at Melos was inextricably linked to the overreaching that finally led Athens to calamity in Sicily.[55]

e. The Syracusan politician Athenagoras identified in Book Six, ¶ 35, as "chief magistrate of the people, and at that time most powerful with the commons," defends decision-making by popular, democratic assemblies as producing results of higher quality than those of oligarchy.[56] But his own speech belies that claim, because he advises the Syracusan assembly that the Athenians will not invade Sicily, and that if they do, Syracuse is well-prepared to meet them—both of which claims are false. Athenagoras is more concerned with discrediting his domestic political opponent Hermocrates (who offers the Syracusans realistic and sober advice, based on keen insight into the nature and ambitions of Athens) than with preparing his countrymen to face the grave danger posed by a foreign enemy. Thucydides may be indicating that democratic decision-making—whether in Athens or elsewhere—is epistemically flawed, leading to over-confidence in a democratic state's own strength, failure to appreciate dangers in the international strategic environment, and an undue focus on domestic political differences.

---

53 *See, e.g.*, Pangle & Ahrensdorf, supra note 2, at 28.

54 Victor Davis Hanson, A War Like No Other: How the Athenians and Spartans Fought the Peloponnesian War 203 (2005).

55 *See* Kagan, Reinvention, supra note 9, at 187; Richard Ned Lebow & Robert Kelly, *Thucydides and Hegemony: Athens and the United States,* 27 Rev. Int'l Stud. 593, 596 (2001) ("The Melian Dialogue . . . represents a crude and dangerous strategy for maintaining hegemony and empire. [Thucydides] clearly contrasts the expanding use of force between early Periclean Athens and the later post-Periclean leadership. Once their empire was based principally on coercion, Athenians had to worry that allies would rebel if they were perceived as weak or irresolute. This fear encouraged an expansionist foreign policy as a means of demonstrating resolve and power, and with it, the kind of risk-taking that threatened serious military losses. The Sicilian expedition, the ultimate expression of this strategy, set in motion the chain of events that led to the collapse of the empire and the defeat of Athens. The Athenians made their fears self-fulfilling."); and Michael G. Seaman, *The Athenian Expedition to Melos in 416 B.C.*, 46 Historia 385, 409 (1997).

56 Athenagoras says: "Some will say, that the democracy is neither a well–governed nor a just state: and that the most wealthy are aptest to make the best government. But I answer first, *democracy* is a name of the whole; *oligarchy*, but of a part. Next, though the rich are indeed fittest to keep the treasure: yet the wise are the best counsellors, and the multitude upon hearing the best judge. Now in a democracy all these, both jointly and severally, participate equal privileges." *History*, Book VI, at ¶ 39.

ii. War Itself Further Debases Democracy, Generating Wider War and Worse War Policy

a. Athens originally saw itself as motivated by noble purposes, not merely by power-seeking, in acquiring its empire. Athenian leaders like Pericles emphasized honor, fame and justice as motives for creating and maintaining the empire. Cleon based his defense of a brutal policy towards Mytilene partly on moral considerations—a demand for retributive justice and a feeling that Athens had been wrongly betrayed. (Book III, ¶ 38) Even Diodotus relied on an enlarged conception of self-interest in advocating a humane policy toward the Mytileneans, and he insisted that the Athenians give weight to other states' values and sense of honor when making their own decisions. (Book III, ¶¶ 46-47).

b. After Pericles' death, Athens seems to become more immoderate, reckless, violent, and degraded. Indeed, one could see the emergence of the three dominant post-Periclean leaders in Athens—Cleon, Alcibiades and Nicias—as Thucydides' way of dramatizing the internal political causes of Athens' fall. Each of Pericles' leading successors is the embodiment of some virtue that Pericles exhibited in governing Athens: Cleon his persuasive skills, Alcibiades his boldness and strategic acumen, Nicias his prudence and caution. Yet while Pericles manages to combine and balance these qualities (to the good of Athens), his three successors, precisely because they do not blend and offset each of them with the others, contributes to Athens' erratic and disastrous course.

c. Cleon in particular launches a devastating attack on Periclean democracy. He charges it with promoting self-deception, "for through your own mutual security and openness, you imagine the same also in your confederates." (Book III, ¶ 37) Then, without mentioning Pericles by name but nonetheless alluding clearly to Pericles' reputation as the wisest of Athenians, he suggests that "the more ignorant sort of men do, for the most part, better regulate a commonwealth than they that are wiser. For these love to appear wiser than the laws, and in all public debating to carry the victory, as the worthiest things wherein to show their wisdom; from whence most commonly proceedeth the ruin of the state they live in." (Book III, ¶ 37). He chastises the demos itself, for "to speak plainly, overcome with the delight of the ear, you are rather like unto spectators sitting to hear the contentions of sophisters, than to men that deliberate of the state of a commmonwealth." (Book III, ¶ 38). Indeed, argues Cleon, the very things most characteristic of debate in the Athenian assembly—"*pity, delight in plausible speeches,* and *lenity*"—are the "three most disadvantageous things to empire." (Book III, ¶ 40.)[57] The process and leadership of Periclean democracy stand accused in Cleon's defense of the decision to destroy Mytilene.

57 Contrast these three alleged vices of democracy in controlling an empire with the three motives that the Athenians have early identified as the causes of their empire: fear, interest and honor. *See id.*, Book I, at ¶ 75. Might it be that Cleon (or

d. Diodotus' defense the Periclean democracy, by contrast, seems more qualified; and it seems to foreshadow the erosion of democracy in the face of the war as Athens suffers one reversal after another. Initially, Diodotus argues for more, not less, speech before the Athenian assembly as the means to achieve "fewer errors." (Book III, ¶ 42.) He fears the practice of imputing corruption to politicians as a means of silencing them, a practice employed against Pericles himself by his enemies[58], for "a good statesman should not go about to terrify those that contradict him, but rather to make good his counsel upon liberty of speech" and "a wise state ought not either to add unto, or on the other side, to derogate from the honor of him that giveth good advice; nor yet punish, nay nor disgrace the man whose counsel they receive not." (Book III, ¶ 42.) However, what the Athenians in fact do, says Diodotus, is "according to the passion that takes you when at any time your affairs miscarry, you punish the sentence of that one only that gave the counsel, not the many sentences of your own that were in fault as well as his." (Book III, ¶ 43.) Thus, Athens' capacity for reasonable deliberation and decision-making is in question for both factions in the Mytilenean debate.

e. Not only the inadequacy of Athens' post-Periclean leadership, but also the continuation of the war itself, seem to incline Athens increasingly towards a narrow and violence-prone conception of its self-interest. By the time of the Melian dialogues, over a decade after the debates over Mytilene, the Athenian Assembly has disappeared from the stage. Thus, we have no account of any deliberations in the Athenian assembly over the fate of the Melians, so perhaps the setting of the Melian dialogue obliquely reveals a transformation in the Athenian Assembly. So, for all that appears, the Assembly may simply have instructed the generals besieging Melos to enslave the city or destroy it. The Assembly may have become more resolute and implacable at a later stage of the war than it had been at the time of the Mytilenean debate. If so, the Athenian commanders would have carried instructions from the Assembly that left them no room for discretion in their dialogue with the Mytileneans. The decision of the Assembly has already been made. An alternative possibility is that purely military decision-making by the generals had displaced political decision-making by the Assembly. As the war went on, the Assembly may have delegated ever greater responsibility over all aspects of the war—political and diplomatic as well as military—to the generals. So the Assembly may simply have authorized the generals to do whatever they thought was necessary to bring the Melians to heel. (That is how Hobbes understood the situation.[59]) Whichever the case, no second ship will come after the Assembly

Thucydides through Cleon) is suggesting that as a democracy rules longer over an empire, its sense of fear yields to lenity, its sense of honor to pity, and its pursuit of interest to pleasure in fine speeches?

58 *See* Michael Grant, The Classical Greeks 67 (1989) (including most notably Pericles' "immoral use of [Athenian] League funds for the construction of magnificent building in Athens").

59 In his preface to the History, Hobbes writes that "if the Athenian people gave in charge to these their captains, to take in the island by all means whatsoever, without power to report back unto them first the equity of the islanders' cause; as is most likely to be true; I see no reason the generals had to enter into disputation with them, whether they should

"repents" to save the Melians from necessity. Democracies at war, Thucydides may be implying, tend to transform themselves into something akin to military dictatorships, and to wage war with indifference to anything but military imperatives.

f. The form of the Melian dialogue reinforces the lack of humanity characteristic of this new, war-consumed Athens. Thus, this depersonalized dialogue, where the Athenian speakers are nameless and may simply be personifications of an abstract "reason of state," is itself an example of speech used as weaponry rather than of speech as reasoned debate or even of speech as elegant and attractive rhetoric. (It is interesting to note that this is the only dialogue, as opposed to debate, in the entire History.[60]) The Athenians rigorously exclude all appeals to morality, justice, or the gods—and even to considerations of prudence regarding the future, or of historical memory regarding the past. They focus on the present alone (though they boast, inconsistently, of Athens' fearlessness in the past, Book V, ¶ 111). Diodotus thus prevails in excising "haste" and "anger." Similarly, Cleon prevails in excising "pity, delight in plausible speeches, and lenity." Conflicting voices are not heard at the price of an impoverished discourse that does not lead to "fewer errors." Has war deprived Athens of the ability to speak and reason even in the ways that had originally seemed characteristic of Athenian democracy? In short, Thucydides' cautionary tale may suggest that even if democracy does not conduce to peace, war itself exacerbates the worst features of democracy, promotes even greater imperial ambition, invites debacles such as the Sicilian expedition, and ultimately destroys the very conditions that make democracy possible.

iii. Questions and Comments on the Thesis

1) The form of democracy that that Thucydides attacks was nothing like that of modern democracy. The democracy he describes made its decisions in a public assembly through procedures simultaneously more and less open than modern liberal, representative democracy.[61] These procedures were more open in the sense that deliberations were open to all and subject to a vote by large, nearly plebiscitary bodies; less open in that fewer kinds of voices could be heard in the Athenian Assembly, given the limitation of political participation rights to a small

---

perform their charge or not, but only whether they should do it by fair or foul means; which is the point treated in this dialogue." Bosworth, *supra* note 36, at 32.

60 *See* Felix Martin Wassermann, *The Melian Dialogue*, 78 Trans. Am. Phil. Ass'n 18, 19 (1947) ("The Melian dialogue is unique in its form. It is the only case in which Thucydides has discarded his device of using speeches to present political conditions and forces").

61 For a classic account of the contrast between the two kinds of democracy, see Benjamin Constant, The Liberty of the Ancients Compared with That of the Moderns (1816) (*available at www.uark.edu/depts/comminfo/cambridge/ancients.html*).

number of men with requisite property, thereby reducing the diversity and quality of information available to moderate decision-making. It is precisely the lack of restraint or reason in democratic deliberation that Thucydides implicitly argues brought Athens to ruin. It is at least arguable that modern democracies are more capable of reasoned decision-making, either in accordance with prudent rational calculation of self-interest or principled, legal-rational behavior in accordance with law and norms. Thus, modern democracies need not be (and are not) as impulsive and irrational as the Athenian democracy on the eve of the Sicilian expedition. Indeed, the habits of internal democratic decision-making may, as liberal international relations theorist posit, make democracies well-suited to translating their rational-legal decision-making process to international decision-making, even on questions of war and peace.[62]

2) The Athenian Democracy may have failed, not because it was too war-like, but because it was not aggressive enough. Arguably, Pericles' moderate policy, seeking a political solution with Sparta, nearly brought Athens to its knees a quarter century before its final collapse at the hands of Spartan-Persian alliance.[63] Rather, it was Pericles' own (undemocratic) domination of the Athenian polis in the early years of the war that prevented the adoption of policies that would have avoided near catastrophe[64]; and it was only the adoption of more aggressive strategies into Spartan territory after Pericles' death that brought Sparta to a temporary peace on terms favorable to Athens.[65] Indeed, the Sicilian expedition failed, so it is argued, because the aristocratic faction in Athens manufactured false charges of impiety against a favorite of the people, Alcibiades, who would have prosecuted the campaign with more vigor. That decision left the command to Nicias, who never believed in the mission and who, like Thucydides, ultimately was repudiated and dishonored by the Athenian people after his death at the hands of the Syracusans and Spartans.[66] If so, Thucydides may be right that democracies can be more war-like, but he may also be wrong that democracies, in being more war-like, are likely to come to ruin. Accordingly, his study may not support his argument that democracy and peace are antithetical.

62 *See* Anne-Marie Slaughter, *International Law in a World of Liberal States,* 6 Eur. J. Int'l Law 503 (1995); Anne Marie Slaughter, A New World Order (2004).

63 For Pericles' overall strategy for the conduct of the war, *see* Kagan, Reinvention, *supra* note 9, at 75-97; Peloponnesian War, *supra* note 9, at 47-54. His fellow Athenians invested Pericles with extraordinary prestige, *see* Kagan, Peloponnesian War, at 69-70. *But see id.* at 80 (rejecting Thucydides' claim that, under Pericles, Athens was a democracy in name only).

64 *Id.* at 69-70.

65 *Id.* at 125–70.

66 *Id.* at 254-55, 321-23.

3) Arguably, the Melian dialogue does *not* reflect the deepening debasement of Athenian democracy. One careful reader of the dialogue has argued that Pericles (as Thucydides portrays him) "would not disapprove of the reasons given by the Athenians for demanding the [annexation] of the strategically located island. [The Athenian ambassadors' voice] is the voice of the inexorable logic of power."[67] The same scholar understands the dialogue, not as "a clash of interests" but as "the struggle of two political ideals and institutions," the conservatism of the small, isolated, tradition-bound, independent-minded Melos and the dynamism and energy of an expanding imperial power.[68]

Transitional Note

Thucydidean thought seems to be premised on a view of what the Greeks called *physis* or "nature," which they understood to be fundamental and unchanging aspects of existence, including human existence. That the essential nature of humanity is to seek power, profit, safety, and distinction seems to be an implicit premise driving much of Thucydides' narrative.[69] The nature of government flows from the nature of humanity, leading ineluctably to disastrous consequences for particular states at both the domestic and the international level. First, human nature makes specific regime types (including democracy) internally unstable, tending always to *stasis* (civil strife), fragmentation and, eventually, dissolution in the pursuit of factional and individual self-interest. Furthermore, since the pursuit of power, profit, security and glory is as essential to the nature of states as it is to that of the individuals who compose them, wars between states appear inevitable. Causality flows in both directions. War unravels the Athenian regime, and that unraveling in turn enables Athenian leaders to display their own thirst for power, interest and distinction ever more nakedly. But the more avid and unapologetic Athens' leaders become in that pursuit, the further Athens is led into self-defeating brutality towards its subjects and ill-considered and over-ambitious foreign adventures. On this interpretation of Thucydides, his History traces out a long arc, in which the drive for power, profit, security and glory results in the creation of a brilliant and dynamic empire, whose very success then generates resistance from a combination of states with similar motivations and capabilities, leading to war, the empire's defeat, *stasis* and eventual dissolution.[70] Pericles (or Thucydides through

67 Wassermann, *supra* note 60, at 24.

68 *Id.* at 25.

69 *See* Pouncey, *supra* note 14, at 20 ("Human nature is the strongest 'binding' concept in Thucydides' work, one with almost an architectonic force. The force lies precisely in this: Whatever the idiosyncrasies of a nation's or an individual's circumstances or temperament, human beings will behave in pretty much the same way in similar circumstances in any age, and under pressure they will behave badly.").

70 *See id.* at 48–53 (analyzing pattern of rise and fall of states that arguably emerges from the *History*).

Pericles) seems to offer us a glimpse of this trajectory when he says, in his final speech to the Assembly, that "all things are made with this law, to decay again" (Book II, ¶ 64).

In such a narrative, what the Greeks called *nomos*—convention, including laws, customs, and perhaps morals—would seem to have little role to play in guiding events, at least in times of war or other great crises. And often, in fact, Thucydides himself seems inclined to that view. For instance, in passing judgment on the atrocities committed by Spartans against the Athenian ally Plataea, a mirror image of the Athenian atrocities at Melos, Thucydides says, in his own voice, that the Spartans acted, not out of a sense of legality or justice, but "altogether for the Thebans' sake, whom they thought useful to them in the war now on foot" (Book III, ¶ 68). If the moralizing, traditionalist Spartans are capable of such atrocities for the sake of self-interest, how can the unapologetically self-interested Athenians—or any other state—realistically be expected to behave otherwise? To be sure, we have seen that Thucydides insists on the significance of other motives, including honor and even respect for justice or legality, in determining the conduct of states and individuals, even in harsh, wartime conditions. But it may nonetheless be fair to say that Thucydides largely discounts the capacity of humans, their governments, and the system of Greek city-states to overcome the necessities of nature by establishing stable "conventions" to govern interpersonal and interstate relations. The drive for power over others and the fear of the dangers that they pose seem, for Thucydides, to be insuperable obstacles to a lasting peace, whether within cities or between them. Thucydides seems to see no escape from what later writers, following Hobbes, have called the "security dilemma."[71]

This "realist" conception of the relationship between *nomos* and *physis*, we have suggested, is opposed what we have called a "legalist" conception. "Legalism" insists on the relevance and efficacy of moral and legal reasoning to human behavior, whether of individuals or of states, and whether in war or in peace. "Legalism," like Athenian (or Thucydidean) "realism," typically incorporates both a certain understanding of "nature" and a certain understanding of "convention." "Legalism" itself characteristically comes in either of two (contrasting) forms. These two forms we may call "naturalist legalism" and "positivist legalism." We shall deal with "naturalist legalism" – or natural law theory -- later in this case book.[72] In the next section, we turn instead to "positivist legalism."[73]

---

71 We discuss the "security dilemma" in Chapter 2.A. For classic formulations of the "security dilemma," *see* John Herz, Political Realism and Political Idealism (1951); Herbert Butterfield, "The Tragic Element in Modern International Conflict," reprinted in Herbert Butterfield, History and Human Relations 9–36 (1952). For discussion, *see* R.J. Delahunty, *Herbert Butterfield, Christianity, and International Law*, 86 U. Detroit Mercy L. Rev. 615 (2009).

72 For now, let it suffice to say that "naturalist legalism" includes components that are both descriptive, akin to the Greek conception of *physis*, and prescriptive, akin to the Greek conception of *nomos*. In opposition to classical Greek realism, it holds that it is in the nature of humanity to seek the good and, further, that humanity *ought* to seek the good. In some versions, Naturalist legalism, both historically and at present, has been related to transcendental conceptions, including religious views, such as those that have been articulated in the debate between "radical Islam" and the "West." For a discussion of that debate, *see infra* Chapter 2.C.

73 The term "positivism" is highly ambiguous. For a brief review of the various meanings that have been given to the term in legal writing, *see* Martii Koskenniemi, From Apology to Utopia: The Structure of International Legal Argument 131 n.

Positivist legalism embraces a certain understanding of how "nature" works—roughly, that provided by the modern scientific world picture[74]—and of the role of "convention." In opposition to naturalist legalism, positivism teaches that law (in a normative sense) is neither of divine origin nor otherwise inscribed in the structure of the universe. Rather, it is wholly man-made law, created by human beings for human needs and purposes. The very term "positive" law derives from the notion that law is "posited" rather than "true."[75] "Positive" law is not true in the sense that nature is true; rather, as in a logical demonstration, it is merely *stipulated* to be true for a defined set of purposes. Thus, positive law is true or valid merely for the purpose of providing a rule for decision, usually in a court that applies the law and declares its consequences. However, positivist legalism differs from realism (and resembles naturalist legalism) in holding that law can be effective in regulating human and state conduct, that individuals and state ought to conform their conduct to the requirements of law, and that failures of compliance are justly sanctionable. The next readings address the concepts and categories through which modern international law, which is usually understood as positive law, has sought to address the hardest questions that arise in the *jus ad bellum*, the problem of aggression, and in the *jus in bello*, the use of nuclear weapons.

In prescribing and enforcing its conventions, positive law speaks, as did Thucydides, to both the domestic and international effects of war. As you consider the premises and mode of reasoning in positivist legalism, also reconsider the Thucydidean questions explored in Chapter 1.A: 1) whether a state's domestic constitutional order relates to the likelihood of its using force; and 2) whether the use of force changes a state's constitutional order over time and, in consequence, changes the state's willingness to use force.

---

258 (Reissued with epilogue 2005).

74 The relationship between scientific understandings of the physical universe and legal or political understandings of the human world can be very close. In the eighteenth century, when the "mechanistic" conception of the universe embodied in Newtonian physics was dominant, the prevailing understanding of the international system was that it reflected a self-equilibrating "balance of power," in which states would frictionally combine together to oppose any power that threatened to dominate the international system. On this form of "balance of power" theory, law had little relevance to the conduct of international affairs, because the liberty of individual states, and the stability and peacefulness of the international system as a whole, would result from the simple computation of relative forces and the desire on the part of weaker states to avoid domination. We discuss the balance of power theory in Chapter 2.A.

75 In a scholarly review of the concept of "positive" law, Roberto Ago identified two characteristic features of nineteenth century legal positivism. First, "[p]ositive law is . . . law which is laid down (*gestez*), and the character of positivity is always conferred on the legal norm by its being derived from some creative act which actually came into being, thus being historically perceptible." Second, "'positive law' . . . now was identified with the idea of law itself. Not only was it stated that law created by formal sources is the only true law, but all those acts which are not direct or indirect manifestations of the will of the state are excluded from the category of 'formal sources' of positive law, for only the state has the power to lay down legal norms." Roberto Ago, *Positive Law and International Law*, 51 Am. J. Int'l L. 691, 697, 698 (1957).

B. LEGALISM: *JUS AD BELLUM* AND *JUS IN BELLO* IN THE POST-SECOND WORLD WAR SETTING

This section addresses the development of the doctrines of *jus ad bellum* (rightful or lawful war) and *jus in bello* (the rightful or lawful conduct of war) in the context of four major judicial opinions from the post-Second World War setting. The first opinion is drawn from the rulings of the International Military Tribunal (IMT), an international military court that was convened by the Allied victors in Europe (the United States, the United Kingdom, the Soviet Union, and France) shortly after the Second World War to hear and decide criminal charges brought by those Allies against major Nazi political, military, and business leaders. These trials before the IMT, together with later trials of lesser defendants before American military tribunals in Nuremberg, Germany, are known and renowned as the "Nuremberg Trials."[76] The second and third opinions are dissents written by two of the judges, Justices B.V.A. Rőling of the Netherlands and Radhabinod Pal of India, in the counterpart trial of major Japanese political and military leaders before the International Military Tribunal for the Far East (IMTFE), convened by the Allied victors over the Japanese Empire—the so-called "Tokyo Trials." The Tokyo Trials were, and remain, less studied than the Nuremberg trials.[77] Finally, the fourth extract is from the opinion of a Japanese national Court in the 1963 *Shimoda Case*, which addressed the legality under international law of the use of the atomic bomb by the United States in 1945 against the Japanese cities of Hiroshima and Nagasaki. Taken together, these four opinions represent a concerted effort to address the horrors of an unprecedentedly violent and destructive war through international law.

76 The IMT was created by the Charter of the International Military Tribunal (also called the London Charter) of August 8, 1945, an international agreement made by the United States, United Kingdom, Soviet Union, and France. The courts that tried the less important defendants were provided for by Control Council Law No. 10, which was promulgated by the International Control Council and signed by American, British, Soviet, and French military commanders on Dec. 20, 1945. In the event, the United States established six such courts, all at Nuremberg (the "United States Military Tribunals"). These military tribunals heard a total of twelve cases between 1946 and 1948, all but one involving multiple defendants. While the IMT was plainly an international court, the lesser tribunals took different and inconsistent stances on the question whether they were American courts that were internationally constituted, or international courts. *See* August von Knieriem, The Nuremberg Trials 96–100 (Elizabeth D. Schmidt trans. 1959).

77 A notable early exception is Richard H. Minear, Victors' Justice: The Tokyo War Crimes Tribunal (1971). For more recent scholarship, *see* Neil Boister & Robert Cryer, The Tokyo International Military Tribunal: A Reappraisal (2008) [hereinafter "A Reappraisal"]. The complete judgments of the IMTFE have been translated into English and published in two volumes. *See* Documents on the Tokyo International Military Tribunal: Charter, Indictment and Judgments (Neil Boister & Robert Cryer eds., 2008)[hereinafter "Document on the Tokyo International Military Tribunal"]. A useful and succinct survey of the Tokyo Trials in found in Roger Clark, Nuremberg and Tokyo in Contemporary Perspective, *in The Law of War Crimes: National and International Approaches* 171, 179–83 (Timothy L.H. McCormack & Gerry J. Simpson eds., 1996). For a review of scholarly writing on the Tokyo Trials, see Gerry Simpson, *Revisiting the Tokyo War Crimes Trials*, 78 Pac. Hist'l Rev. 608 (2009).

1. Legalism: Positivist and Naturalist

The four opinions examined in this section can all be seen as exercises in *legalism.* We introduced the concept of *legalism* briefly in the last section, contrasting it to *realism.* The essential difference between realism and legalism, as we use those terms, is that realism denies, and legalism affirms, that law plays a significant role in determining the conduct of states in international affairs, including war. Realism does not deny that states may profess to be complying with international law, may look for legal justifications for their actions, or may accuse other states of legal violations. But, from the realist viewpoint, such invocations of international law are essentially lip service, at least when the security and vital interests of states are at stake. By contrast, legalism insists that states can, should, and do follow international legal rules, even in situations where they believe that it will damage their security or vital interests to do so.[78] Legalism thus characteristically has an *empirical* component—the claim that states can, and often do, comply with international law, even when they perceive such action as contrary to their self-interest, and a *normative* component—the claim that states should so act.

Further, as we noted in the previous section, legalism has traditionally come in two main forms: positivism and naturalism.[79] In essence, positivism and naturalism differ as to the *sources* of international law.[80] Positivism takes the view that international law consists of rules and standards that arise from the decisions of identifiable law-makers—principally, perhaps only, from states themselves. For a positivist, international law derives from *consent,* as expressed in different ways.[81] Naturalism takes the view that international law derives, at least to a significant

78 Legalism also entails that states are likely to punish serious violations of international law by other states, perhaps particularly so when the violations also threaten the vital national security interests of the responding states. For an historical argument that Britain took Imperial Germany's illegal violation of Belgian neutrality very seriously, so much so, that it helped precipitate Britain's entry into the First World War, *see* Isabel V. Hull, A Scrap of Paper: Breaking and Making International Law during the Great War 16-50 (2014).

79 Legal positivism can take any of several forms. We start from the broad definition given by one of its leading critics, Lon Fuller of the Harvard Law School. Fuller wrote, "By legal positivism I mean that direction of legal thought which insists on drawing a sharp distinction between the law that is and the law that ought to be. Where this distinction is taken it is, of course, for the sake of the law that is, and is intended to purify it by purging it of what [Hans] Kelsen calls 'wish-law.'" Lon L. Fuller, The Law in Quest of Itself 5 (1940). Fuller contrasted legal positivism to natural law, which he characterized as "the view which denies the possibility of a rigid separation of the is and the ought, and which tolerates a confusion of them in legal discussion." *Id.* For classic formulations of "positivism" and "naturalism," *see* H.L.A. Hart, *Positivism and the Separation of Law and Morals,* 71 Harv. L. Rev. 593 (1958) and Lon L. Fuller, *Positivism and Fidelity to Law: a Reply to Professor Hart,* 71 Harv. L. Rev. 630 (1958).

80 It is important to distinguish between legalism and positivism if only because the two are sometimes confused. Legalism is both a theory of the effect of law on the behavior of states and a normative doctrine as to the effect that law should have; positivism is an account of the sources of law. There can therefore be both positivist and non-positivist forms of both legalism and realism. *See* Gerry Simpson, *The Situation on the International Legal Theory Front: The Power of Rules and the Rule of Power,* 11 Eur. J. Int'l L. 439, 451–52 (2000). Contrast Shirley V. Scott, *Is There Room for International Law in Realpolitik? Accounting for the US 'Attitude' Towards International Law,* 30 Rev. Int'l Stud. 71, 80 (2004) ("As a theory internal to international law, legal positivism posits that international law derives from the will of states; legal positivists are aware that states do not always comply with their international law obligations but assume they should do so.").

81 *See, e.g.,* Georg Schwarzenberger, *The Rule of Law and the Disintegration of the International Society,* 33 Am. J. Int'l l. 56, 65 (1939). As one scholar writes, "[i]nternational legal positivism is simply the working out of the private law metaphor

extent, from "nature" rather than from "convention," and may bind states in certain respects whether or not they have not agreed to be so bound, and even if they have deliberately sought to deny such obligations.[82] The readings in this section generally reflect a positivist, rather than naturalist, understanding of international law.

2. The Background Assumptions of Legal Positivism Before 1939

Your critical reading of these materials requires some background knowledge of the professional assumptions that international lawyers and jurists made in the period leading up to the beginning of the Second World War in 1939.[83] Grasping this background is essential for understanding the full significance—indeed, one might fairly say, the revolutionary nature—of these cases, especially those from the IMT and IMTFE.[84]

The architectonic concept for international law in this period was the concept of state *sovereignty*.[85] The definition of sovereignty in its modern form is generally attributed to the sixteenth century French thinker, Jean Bodin.[86] As applied to the international system of states, the

of contract applied to a public legal order."). David Kennedy, *International Law and the Nineteenth Century: History of an illusion*, 17 Quinnipiac L. Rev. 99, 113 (1998).

82 So, for example, Emer de Vattel, a leading eighteenth century theorist, considered an important part of international law (or what he called 'The Law of Nations') to be "necessary, because nations are absolutely bound to observe it. This law contains the precepts prescribed by the law of nature to states, on whom that law is not less obligatory than on individuals." Emer de Vattel, The Law of Nations, or Principles of the Law of Nature, Applied to the Conduct and Affairs of Nations and Sovereigns lxiii (1797). It is noteworthy that naturalist assumptions can be found in Vattel's work, even though modern scholars tend to view him as taking a largely positivist view of the law of nations. *See, e.g.*, Grewe, *supra* note 7, at 374.

83 To be more precise, we should perhaps end this period at 1919, the end of the First World War, not at 1939, the beginning of the Second World War. During the inter-war period, legal ideas began to germinate that came to maturity only after the end of the Second World War. Nonetheless there was sufficient continuity in the international legal system before and after the First World War to mark 1939 as the end of an epoch. For a brief survey of the law of the inter-war period, *see* Robert J. Delahunty & John C. Yoo, *Peace Through Law? The Failure of a Noble Experiment*, 106 Mich. L. Rev. 923 (2008). For a sophisticated critique of periodization, and a alternative narrative of the origins of contemporary international law, *see* Kennedy, *supra* note 81.

84 Even before the Trials began, the eminent German philosopher Karl Jaspers described them as "a herald . . . of the new world order of whose necessity man is now becoming aware." Karl Jaspers, *The Significance of the Nurnberg Trials for Germany and The World*, 22 Notre Dame Law 150, 159 (1946/47).

85 For a highly influential discussion of this concept, see Stephen D. Krasner, Sovereignty: Organized Hypocrisy (1999). For an account of the evolution of the concept of sovereignty in nineteenth century international law, *see* Kennedy, *supra* note 81, at 122–31.

The British international relations theorist Martin Wight interestingly suggested that the dominance of weak, positivist form of international law in period preceding the First World War may have been due to the generally successful and co-operative diplomatic practices of the Great Powers during the nineteenth century, whereas the more robust international law characteristic of the period between and after the major wars of the twentieth century may reflect a diplomacy that is "violent and unscrupulous." Martin Wight, Why Is There No International Theory?, *in* Diplomatic Investigations 29 (Herbert Butterfield & Martin Wight eds., 1966).

86 *See* Jean Bodin, Six Books of the Commonwealth (1576); *see also* Julian H. Franklin, Jean Bodin and the Rise of Absolutist Theory (1973). There are several fine accounts of the pre-history of the modern concept of sovereignty. One recent account locates its origins in the nominalist philosophy of the late medieval period. *See* Jean Bethke Elshtain, Sovereignty:

concept of sovereignty is often said to have emerged in the Peace of Westphalia of 1648, which ended the bitter Thirty Years War in Europe.[87] Some recent scholarship has questioned whether the "Westphalian" moment truly represents a catalyst in the development of the modern international states system.[88] Other scholars contend that Westphalia did indeed mark a constitutional revolution in international affairs—the origin of the modern States system.[89] Whatever the truth may be,[90] the Peace of Westphalian can be regarded, at least symbolically, as marking the birth of that system.[91]

God, State, and Self (2008). Another account emphasizes the significance of the Protestant Reformation in creating the Westphalian system. See Daniel Philpott, Revolutions in Sovereignty: How Ideas Shaped Modern International Relations 97–149 (2001); Daniel Philpott, *The Religious Roots of Modern International Relations,* 52 World Pol. 206 (2000). Still other theories underscore the importance of changes in military technology in fashioning the modern state. *See, e.g.*, Bruce D. Porter, War and the Rise of the State: The Military Foundations of Modern Politics (1994); and Richard Bean, *War and the Birth of the Nation-State,* 33 J. Econ. Hist. 203 (1973). For further accounts of the emergence of the modern state system in Europe (and, with that, the origins of modern "sovereignty"), *see* Perry Anderson, Lineages of the Absolute State (1974); Hendrik Spruyt, The Sovereign State and its Competitors (1994); and Hendrik Spruyt, *The Origins, Development, and Possible Decline of the Modern State,* 5 Ann. Rev. Polit. Sci. 127 (2002). For the (uneasy) relationship between the concept of sovereignty and that of federalism, see Patrick Riley, *Three Seventeenth Century German Theorists of Federalism: Althusius, Hugo and Leibniz,* 6 Publius 7, 16–19 (1976). A sophisticated "constructivist" account of the origin of the early modern state system may be found in John Gerard Ruggie, *Territoriality and Beyond: Problematizing Modernity in International Relations,* 47 Int'l Org. 261, 273–79 (1993); and John Gerard Ruggie, *Continuity and Transformation in the World Polity: Toward a Neorealist Synthesis,* 35 World Pol. 261 (1983). Although Ruggie's explanation of the emergence of the modern idea of sovereignty is (necessarily) complex and many-faceted, we note his emphasis on the importance of the doctrine in Roman law of absolute private property. We discuss constructivism in Chapter 2C.

87 The Westphalian settlement in fact comprehended three treaties: a treaty between Spain and the Netherlands made in Münster on May 15, 1648; a treaty between Sweden and the Holy Roman Empreror, made in Osnabrück on August 6, 1648; and a treaty between France and the Holy Roman Emperor, made on October,24, 1648.

88 *See, e.g.*, Andreas Osiander, *Sovereignty, International Relations, and the Westphalian Myth,* 55 Int'l Org. 251 (2001). For an earlier understanding, *see* Leo Gross, *The Peace of Westphalia, 1648–1948,* 42 Am. J. Int'l L. 20 (1948).

89 *See* Daniel Philpott, Revolutions in Sovereignty: How Ideas Shaped Modern International Relations 82–96 (2001); Daniel Philpott, *The Religious Roots of Modern International Relations,* 52 World Pol. 206, 211 (2000); Daniel Philpott, *The Challenge of September 11 to Secularism in International Relations,* 55 World Pol. 66, 76 (2002)

90 "The positive interpretation of Westphalia regards it as the birth of the modern international order based on sovereign states interacting (formally) as equals within a common secularized legal framework, regardless of size, power or internal configuration. . . . Handbooks of international relations and diplomatic history still commonly take 1648 to frame their discussions, but historians and most political scientists are no longer so confident in asserting the date as a turning point." Peter H. Wilson, The Thirty Years War: Europe's Tragedy 754 (2009).

91 From an *ex post* perspective, Westphalia can be seen as "an important staging post, perhaps the most important, in a long retreat that lasted over several centuries during which time *respublica Christiana* was obliged to surrender more and more authority to the emergent states of Europe. Westphalia is best understood not as a literal moment of change, but rather, as the symbol of a fundamental political transformation of Europe, from a transnational political-theological world, a Catholic Christian theocracy, to a modern secular world based on a system or society of sovereign states." Robert Jackson, Sovereignty 51–52 (2007). In a similar vein, David Armstrong argues that "the Peace of Westphalia may still be regarded as the symbolic origin of the society of states it crystallized." David Armstrong, Revolution and World Order: The Revolutionary State in International Society 33 (1993). Armstrong identifies seven fundamental aspects of the society of states that can be considered "Westphalian": 1) the idea of sovereignty; 2) the equality of states; 3) the balance of power; 4) the idea of international society itself; 5) the right of the society of states to confer legitimacy upon individual states and to lay down a general principle of legitimacy; 6) the conception of international law as a set of voluntarily accepted rules and guidelines appropriate to a society of sovereign states; and 7) the institutionalization of diplomacy. *See id.* at 33–38.

"Sovereignty," in its post-Westphalian conception, had at least two main aspects.[92] First, it meant that states had essentially unfettered discretion to administer their own "internal" affairs.[93] As Judge Max Huber wrote in the 1928 *Island of Palmas Case (U.S. v. Netherlands)*, "[t]he development of the national organisation of States during the last few centuries and, as a corollary, the development of international law, have established this principle of the exclusive competence of the State in regard to its own territory in such a way as to make it the point of departure in settling most questions that concern international relations."[94] *Sovereignty*, in its most basic meaning, was therefore linked inextricably to the powers to control and to protect a *territory*. As the 17th century German philosopher bluntly put it, "Sovereign is he who is master of a territory" and who is "powerful enough to make himself considerable . . . in time of peace and in time of war, by treaties, arms, and alliances."[95] Territorial "sovereignty" is a secular, post-Reformation, Western concept, although it became (and remains) central to a globalized public international law.[96] Thus, in its 1975 *Western Sahara* advisory opinion, the International Court of Justice, despite recognizing the existence of legal, religious, and other ties between the Sherifian State of Morocco and the nomadic tribal peoples of the pre-colonial Western Sahara, concluded nonetheless that Morocco had not been the *territorial sovereign* over the area in question.[97]

---

92 These two aspects of sovereignty, supreme authority inside a country and independence in relation to other states, are interconnected. "Sovereignty is one holistic idea with two conceptual facets: like two sides of a ship's hull, inside and outside. . . . Supremacy and independence cannot exist separately. They can only be distinguished analytically." Jackson, *supra* note 91, at 12.

93 *See, e.g., Nationality Decrees Issued in Tunis and Morocco (French Zone) on November 8th, 1921,* (PCIJ) 1923 WrldCrts E1, [1922] PCIJ 3 (4 Oct. 1922), ¶ 37 ("[E]ach State is sole judge" of "matters which, though they may very closely concern the interests of more than one State, are not, in principle, regulated by international law"). For an analysis of the complications in the idea of sovereignty at issue in this case, *see* Nathaniel Berman, *Imperial Rivalry and the Genealogy of Human Rights: The Nationality Decrees Case,* 94 Am. Soc'y Int'l L. Proc. 53 (2000).

94 *Island of Palmas Case (U.S. v. Netherlands),* 2 Reports of Int'l Arbitral Awards 829, 838 (1928).

95 Gottfried Wilhelm Leibniz, *Entretiens de Philarète et d'Eugène,* quoted in Patrick Riley, *Three 17th Century German Theorists of Federalism: Althusius, Hugo and Leibniz,* 6 Publius 7, 26 (1976). One leading international relations theorist has argued that Leibniz was right in claiming to be "the first to have found the valid definition of sovereignty." John Herz, International Politics in the Atomic Age 53 (1959).

96 Nonetheless, territorially-based claims of sovereignty suffer from (arguably, incurable) indeterminacy. In *Right of Passage Over Indian Territory (Portugal v. India)* (Merits), Judgment of 12 April 1960, ICJ Reports 1960, p. 6, the International Court of Justice adjudicated a dispute between India and Portugal over Portugal's claimed right to move persons and goods, including military personnel and arms, from a Portuguese colony on the Indian coast into another land-locked Portuguese colony in India's interior. Portugal argued that the right of transit was logically implied by its territorial sovereignty over the inland colonies, because without such a right it could not make its sovereign rights and duties effective. India argued on the contrary that as a sovereign "she must have complete, absolute and unrestricted right to regulate the passage of goods, men and traffic." *Id.* at 119 (Chagla, J., dissenting). Discussing this case, Koskenniemi argues that it underscores that "sovereignty" is a purely formal notion with no fixed or determinate content. *See* Koskenniemi, *supra* note 73, at 240–43.

97 *See Western Sahara, Advisory Opinion,* I.C.J. Reports 1975, p. 12, 68 at ¶ 162. The Court specifically acknowledged that "the Sherifian State at the time of the Spanish colonization of Western Sahara was a State of a special character . . . founded on the common religious bond of Islam existing among the peoples and on the allegiance of of various tribes to the Sultan [of Morocco] . . . rather than on the notion of territory." *Id.* at ¶ 95. But the tribes' religious and political ties to the Sultan were, in the Court's judgment, insufficient in themselves to establish Morocco's territorial sovereignty unless the tribes' allegiance to that ruler were "manifested in acts evidencing acceptance of his political authority." *Id.* In his instructive separate opinion, Judge Dillard suggested that the Court had understood "territorial sovereignty" to

As territorial sovereigns, states could make rules that applied throughout their own territories (even to persons not their own nationals who were found within them, such as traders, travelers or missionaries),[98] and to their own subjects or citizens (even if they were found outside their states' territories, *e.g.*, on the "high seas" or international waters). In consequence of this premise, no state had standing to interfere with another state's treatment of the latter's own subjects or nationals, no matter how cruel or unjust it may have been. As the international relations theorist Hedley Bull put it, international law on this point could be seen as "a conspiracy of silence entered into by governments about the rights and duties of their respective citizens."[99] To be sure, states *did* in fact intervene on numerous occasions in the domestic affairs of other states, as Catholic France intervened in the Ottoman Empire to protect persecuted Maronite Christians in Lebanon.[100] But these interventions were often diplomatic "remonstrances" rather than deployments of military force, were widely considered problematic or exceptional, and were sometimes undertaken under the pretense that the state that was subjected to the intervention had "consented" to it.[101] In general, then, sovereignty conferred on states some degree of "impermeability" as against other states, at least with respect to their treatment of their own populations.[102]

Second, sovereignty meant that states were independent, constitutionally separate, and on a plane of equality in "external" affairs. There was no common sovereign above states to which they owed a common allegiance or whom they were duty-bound to obey. As Judge Anzilotti

---

depend on the existence of "a *relationship* in which there is a *sense of obligation* of a special kind . . . [T]he evidence must support the view that the inhabitants of the territory had a sense that the wishes of the Sultan . . . not only 'should' be obeyed out of a feeling of religious affiliation or courtesy, but 'must' be obeyed out of a sense of deferential *obligation*." *Id.* at 125 (Separate Op. of Dillard, J.). Judge Dillard contrasted this understanding of sovereignty from an alternative, Islamic conception that was *not* "patterned on the kind of sense of obligation which now prevails in post-Reformation western oriented societies" and which "permits a dissociation between obligations owed to the State and those owed to religious authority." *Id.* In another separate opinion, Vice-President Ammoun argued, in apparent accord with a more Islamic conception of sovereignty, that the tribes' "allegiance to the Sultan, or sovereign, was equivalent to allegiance to the [Sherifian] State," *id.* at 83 (Separate Op. of Ammoun, V.-P.) and that the Sultan's legal and other relationships to the areas *peoples* constituted, in themselves, a political relationship to *the territory*, *see id.* at 101–02. *See also* Elizabeth Wicks, *State Sovereignty – Towards a Refined Legal Conceptualization*, 29 Anglo-Am. L. Rev. 282, 294 (2000) (commenting on Ammoun opinion); George Joffe, *The International Court of Justice and The Western Sahara Dispute*, at 10–11 (1986) (*available at* www.http://repository.forcedemigration.org/show__metadata.jsp?pid=fmo:59) (Islamic conception of sovereignty based on ruler's relationship to community opposed to Western conception rooted in territoriality); and B.O. Okere, *The Western Sahara Case*, 28 Int'l & Comp. L. Q. 296, 307–08 (1979).

98 As Chief Justice John Marshall said in the early nineteenth century case, *The Schooner Exchange v. M'Fadden*, 11 U.S. 116, 136 (1812):

> The jurisdiction of the nation within its own territory is necessarily exclusive and absolute. It is susceptible of no limitation not imposed by itself. Any restriction upon it deriving validity from an external source would imply a diminution of its sovereignty to the extent of the restriction and an investment of that sovereignty to the same extent in that power which could impose such restriction. All exceptions, therefore, to the full and complete power of a nation within its own territories must be traced up to the consent of the nation itself. They can flow from no other legitimate source.

99 Hedley Bull, The Anarchical Society: A Study of Order in World Politics 80 (1977).

100 *See* Ellery C. Stowell, Intervention in International Law 63–66 (1921).

101 *See* Grewe, *supra* note 7, at 487–96.

102 *See* Herz, *supra* note 95, at 39–108.

wrote in the 1931 *Austro-German Customs Union Case,* "[i]ndependence . . . is really no more than the normal condition of States according to international law; it may also be described as sovereignty (*suprema potestas*) or *external sovereignty,* by which is meant that the State has over it no other authority than that of international law."[103]

The concept of "sovereignty" purported to guarantee the juridical equality of states, large or small, in international law.[104] No state acknowledged any (permanent) higher sovereign or legal superior.[105] As the U.S. Supreme Court Chief Justice John Marshall said with reference to two very (politically and militarily) unequal powers, "Russia and Geneva have equal rights."[106]

"Sovereignty" so understood, as including both internal and external aspects and formal equality with other members of the international community, is by no means the only way to organize international affairs. Indeed, it seems fair to say that it was a legal construct that originated in and reflected the specific historical circumstances of early modern Europe. Other state systems have not been based on the concept of sovereignty in this sense, but on asymmetric relations of dominance and subordination between an imperial "center," like the boundary-less Chinese[107] or Roman Empires, and "peripheries" consisting of client states.[108] Nonetheless, the

---

103 *Customs Régime between Germany and Austria (Protocol of March 19th, 1931),* PCIJ, Ser. A/B, No. 41, 1931 (separate op. of Anzilotti, J.), ¶ 3. Koskenniemi locates the source of the idea of sovereign equality in "skepticism about human capacity to know the good. Values are subjective. In the absence of a universally valid code of values (or at least a method of knowing it), there is no justification to override the values held by some with those held by others. Hence the postulate of sovereign equality." Koskenniemi, *supra* note 73, at 152.

104 This idea embraces what is called "forensic" equality—the idea that "[a]n international tribunal, or a municipal tribunal when giving effect to the international obligations of the State to which it belongs, pays the same attention to the rights of France as it does to the rights of Costa Rica." Arnold McNair, *Equality in International Law,* 26 Mich. L. Rev. 131, 136 (1927). McNair distinguished this type of equality from a) equality of capacity for rights (which not all states had) and b) equality for law-making purposes. For an instance of forensic equality, *see Danzig Legislative Decrees Case,* [1927] PCIJ Rep., Ser. A/B, No. 65 at 39, 66 (separate opinion of Anzilotti, J.).

105 Furthermore, the principle of purely formal or legal sovereign equality imposes limitations on the ability of the great powers to order international affairs as they wish. *See* Michael Byers, Custom, Power and the Power of Rules: International Relations and Customary International Law 75–76 (1999); and Nico Krisch, *International Law in Times of Hegemony: Unequal Power and the Shaping of the International Order,* 16 Eur. J. Int'l L. 369, 396–99 (2005). For example, a robust conception of sovereign equality tends to inhibit coercive intervention by great powers into the affairs of weaker (often, decolonized) states. *See* Benedict Kingsbury, *Sovereignty and Inequality,* 9 Eur. J. Int'l L. 599, 618–20 (1998).

106 *The Antelope,* 23 U.S. 66 (1825).

107 For millennia, China held a hierarchical view of the international order, in which it affirmed pride of place for itself. *See* Christopher Ford, *The Mind of Empire: China's History and Modern Foreign Relations* 4-6 (2015) (discussing China's traditionally "monist" conception of world order). There is an extensive literature on the Chinese "tributary system" or, perhaps better, "Sinosphere." *See, e.g.,* Andrew Phillips, War, Religion and Empire: The Transformation of International Orders 149-260 (2011); Zhang Yongjin & Barry Buzan, *The Tributary System as International Society in Theory and Practice,* 8 Chinese Journal of Int'l Politics 1 (2012); and Zhang Feng, *Rethinking the 'Tribute System': Broadening the Conceptual Horizon of Historical East Asian Politics,* 2 Chinese J. of Int'l Politics 545 (2009). For the suggestion that China may want the restoration of a modernized form of the tributary system, see Martin Jacques, When China Rules the World: The End of the Western World and the Birth of a New Global Order 507-09 (2d ed. 2012). Some contemporary Chinese strategists may even be attempting to create the intellectual framework for such a restoration. *See* William A. Callahan, *Chinese Visions of World Order: Post-hegemonic or a New Hegemony?,* 10 Int'l Stud. Rev. 749 (2008).

108 *See* David Strang, *Anomaly and Commonplace in European Political Expansion: Realist and Institutional Accounts,* 45 Int'l Org. 143, 148 (1991); *see also* Hendrik Spruyt, *The End of Empire and the Extension of the Westphalian System: The Normative Basis of the Modern State Order,* 2 Int'l Stud. Rev. 65, 73–74 (2000). For an analysis of the Roman "client state"

great European expansion from 1500 C.E. onwards gradually forced other non-Western societies into a system organized around "sovereign" states.[109]

a. Sovereignty and the Great Powers

The somewhat simplified depiction of sovereignty given above requires qualification. There were (and are) marked differences in the relative power and standing of states, and these power differentials sometimes translated into legal ones.[110] Throughout nineteenth century Europe, the more powerful states claimed certain *law-making* authorities that the minor states lacked, at least when the great powers acted in concert; and the minor European states usually, if sometimes grudgingly, conceded that claim to authority.[111] For example, the Great Powers occasionally acted in concert to fix disputed international boundaries.[112] And as one eminent legal scholar remarked, "[o]nly the States with navies, perhaps 3 or 4, made most of the law of the sea.

---

system, see Edward N. Luttwak, The Grand Strategy of the Roman Empire: From the First Century A.D. to the Third 20–40 (1976).

109 For studies of the reception of Western international legal concepts in the non-Western world, *see, e.g.*, Immanuel C.Y. Hsu, China's Entrance Into the Family of Nations: The Diplomatic Phase, 1858–1880 (1960); Shogo Suzuki, *China's Perceptions of International Society in the Nineteenth Century: Learning More About Power Politics?*, 28 Asian Perspective 115 (2004); and Jacques deLisle, *China's Approach to International Law: A Historical Perspective*, 94 Am. Soc. Int'l L. Proc. 267 (2000).

110 The international relations scholar Jack Donnelly points out that even though "[s]overeign equality is a foundational principle of the Westphalian order," nonetheless "formal inequalities are standard features of almost all historical international societies," including post-Westphalian ones. Jack Donnelly, *Sovereign Inequalities and Hiercarchy in Anarchy*, 12 Eur. J. Int'l Rel. 139, 144–45 (2006). Donnelly identifies three historically well-established types of formal inequality: 1) that of "outlaw" states; 2) legal inequalities rooted in power differences with no suggestion of normative or legal defect or delict; and 3) the special rights of an "international oligarchy." *Id.* at 145.

111 *See, e.g.*, Gerry Simpson, Great Powers and Outlaw States: Unequal Sovereigns in the International Legal Order (2004); and Krisch, *supra* note 105, at 397–98 (2005). Furthermore, in addition to the differences *within* the prevailing international legal system between the Great Powers in Europe and the minor European powers, there were also legalized differences between so-called "civilized," "semi-civilized" or "barbarous," and "savage" states. *See* James Lorimer, Institutes of International Law: A Treatise of the Jural Relations of Separate Political Communities, vol. I at 93 et seq. (1883); Alexander Orakhelashvili, *The Idea of European International Law*, 17 Eur. J. Int'l L. 315, 318–19 (2006); and Edwin Dewitt Dickinson, The Equality of States in International Law 223–29 (1920). In his 1836 essay *Civilisation*, the nineteenth century British philosopher John Stuart Mill provides a useful contemporary explanation of how these terms were understood. *See* 18 Collected Works of John Stuart Mill 119 (John M. Robson ed. 1977). Later studies include Edward Keene, Beyond the Anarchical Society: Grotius, Colonialism and Order in World Politics (2002); Gerrit W. Gong, The Standard of 'Civilization' in International Society (1984); Antony Anghie, *Finding the Peripheries: Sovereignty and Colonialism in Nineteenth-Century International Law*, 40 Harv. Int'l L. J. 1 (1999); Mark Mazower, *An International Civilization? Empire, Internationalism and the Crisis of the Mid-Twentieth Century*, 82 Int'l Aff. 533 (2006); Schwarzenberg, *supra* note 81, at 63–65; and Gerry Simpson, *Two Liberalisms*, 12 Eur. J. Int'l L. 537 (2001). Some trace of these distinctions may be found in Article 38(1)(c) of the Statute of the International Court of Justice, 59 Stat. 1055, T.S. 993, 3 Bevans 1179, which identifies, as a source of the rules of decision for the International Court of Justice, "the general principles of law recognized by *civilized* nations" (emphasis added).

112 *See* Ann van Wynen Thomas & A.J. Thomas, Jr., *Equality of States in International Law: Fact or Fiction?*, 37 Va. L. Rev. 791, 813–14 (1951). Such "legislative" practices in international affairs are said to have originated at the 1815 Congress of Vienna, at which the assembled Powers made law concerning freedom of passage on Europe's arterial rivers, the slave trade, the rules of diplomatic precedence, and the neutrality of Switzerland. See T.J. Lawrence, The Society of Nations: Its Past, Present, and Possible Future 60–61 (1st ed. 1919). They continued thereafter in the European conference system of the nineteenth century.

Military power, exercised on land and sea, shaped the customary law of war."[113] Indeed, some writers on international law of the period sought to rationalize and justify the formal, legal recognition of these power differentials.[114]

b. "Relative" or "Dependent" Sovereignty

Furthermore, many writers on international law during the period in question explicitly affirmed that sovereignty was divisible or "relative."[115] That affirmation seems inconsistent with the doctrine of sovereign equality, because if sovereign A had the legal authority to direct the conduct of sovereign B even in a single respect, than A and B would seem to be unequal in contemplation of law. Moreover, earlier writers of the stature of Jean Bodin,[116] Thomas Hobbes,[117] Hugo Grotius,[118] Jean-Jacques Rousseau,[119] and Emer de Vattel[120] were understood to have insisted on the indivisibility of sovereignty. Sir William Blackstone forcefully represented this trend when he wrote in his influential Commentaries on the Laws of England (1765-69) that "there is and must be in all [forms of government] a supreme, irresistible, absolute, uncontrolled authority, in which the *jura summi imperii*, or the rights of sovereignty, reside."[121] As late as 1910, the arbi-

113 Byers, *supra* note 105, at 39 (1999) (quoting Oscar Schachter). Nonetheless, even Great Britain, the dominant maritime power of the nineteenth century, frequently found it difficult to impose its views of international sea law on other maritime nations, or to avoid being subjected to their views of it. See Krisch, *supra* note 105, at 388, 391, 394–95.

114 *See, e.g.*, T.J. Lawrence, Essays on Some Disputed Topics in Modern International Law 209, 230–32 (2d ed. 1884) (arguing for candid abandonment of doctrine of sovereign equality and advocating the recognition of the "primacy" of the great powers). We note that even contemporary international law occasionally recognizes—sometimes explicitly, other times implicitly—a privileged legal position for the great powers. Examples of *explicit* recognition include the special privileges accorded to the five Permanent Members of the Security Council under the United Nations Charter and those accorded to the existing nuclear powers under the Nuclear Nonproliferation Treaty. *See* Benedict Kingsbury, *Sovereignty and Inequality,* 9 Eur. J. Int'l L. 599, 600, 610 (1998). Implicitly legalized hierarchy may perhaps be found in the rule for the formation of customary international law that weigh the interests of "specially affected" states more heavily *Id.* at 609 (quoting *Continental Shelf Cases (Denmark v. Germany, Germany v. Netherlands),* [1969] ICJ Rep. 3, 43 at ¶ 73 (Feb. 20)).

115 Thus, Judge Anzilotti referred to "the exceptional and, to some extent, abnormal class of States known as 'dependent States.' These are States subject to the authority of one or more other States. The idea of dependence therefore necessarily implies a relation between a superior State (suzerain, protector, etc.) and an inferior or subject States (vassal, protégé, etc.); the relation between the State which can legally impose its will and the State which is legally compelled to submit to that will." *Customs Régime, supra* note 103, at ¶ 3 (separate op. of Anzilotti, J.).

116 Jean Bodin, On Sovereignty: Four Chapters from the Six Books of the Commonwealth 49 (Julian Franklin ed. & trans. 1992).

117 *See* 3 English Works of Thomas Hobbes, The Leviathan, Pt. II, ch. xviii, ¶ 475; Pt. II, ch. xix, ¶ 482 (Sir William Molesworth ed., 1839). *See* Gregory S. Kavka, *Hobbes's War of All Against All,* 93 Ethics 291, 296–97 (1983) (analysis of Hobbes' argument).

118 *See* Hugo Grotius, The Rights of War and Peace Bk. I, c. III, sec. vii at 62 (A.M. Campbell trans. 1901). But on closer inspection, Grotius proves to have taught that sovereignty was, indeed, divisible. *See* Edward Keene, Beyond the Anarchical Society: Grotius, Colonialism and Order in World Politics 43–44, 48–52 (2002).

119 *See* Jean-Jacques Rousseau, The Social Contract Bk. II, ch. ii (1761; G.D.H. Cole ed. 1923).

120 *See* Emer de Vattel, The Law of Nations Ch. 5, ¶ 227 (1797; Bela Kapossy & Richard Whatmore (eds.) 2010).

121 Sir William Blackstone, Commentaries on the Laws of England, vol. I, pp. 156–57 (1765-69).

tration tribunal in the North Atlantic Coast Fisheries Case ruled that "the modern State, and particularly Great Britain has never admitted partition of sovereignty, owing to the constitution of a modern State requiring essential sovereignty and independence."[122] Nonetheless, candid recognition of the actual practices of international law repeatedly forced both courts[123] and theorists to accept that sovereignty was divisible.[124] For example, the doctrine of the "paramountcy" of Great Britain over the rulers of the princely Native States of India, under which Britain controlled the foreign relations and military affairs of the Native States even while the latter were considered to have retained sovereignty over their "internal" affairs, was a case in which it was generally acknowledged that sovereignty was, in fact, divided.[125] And in a 1937 decision concerning the Philippine Islands, a former U.S. colony, the Supreme Court stated that although the passage of the Philippine Independence Act and the adoption of a Philippine Constitution had "brought about a profound change in the status of the islands and in their relations to the United States, . . . the sovereignty of the United States has not been, and, for a long time, may not be, finally withdrawn. So far as the United States is concerned, the Philippine Islands are not yet foreign territory. By express provision of the Independence Act, we still retain powers with respect to our trade relations with the islands, with certain exceptions set forth particularly in the Act. We retain powers with respect to their financial operations and their currency, and

122 *North Atlantic Coast Fisheries Case (Great Britain v. United States)*, Award of the Tribunal, The Hague, Sept. 7, 1910, at 182 (available at http://www.haguejusticeportal.net/eCache/DEF/5/217.html). The tribunal went on to indicate, however, that the doctrine of incomplete or divided sovereignty was unsuited to States like Great Britain and the United States *"under a system of constitutional government." Id.* (emphasis added). So conceivably the tribunal would have allowed that the doctrine was applicable in other circumstances.

123 *See, e.g., Lighthouses in Crete and Samos (France v. Greece)*, PCIJ Judgment No. 22 (Oct. 8, 1937) at ¶ 38 ("Notwithstanding its autonomy, Crete had not ceased to be a part of the Ottoman Empire. Even though the Sultan had been obliged to accept important restrictions on the exercise of his rights of sovereignty in Crete, that sovereignty had not ceased to belong to him, however it might be qualified from a juridical point of view."). *Compare id.*, Separate Op. of Hudson, J., at ¶ 121 ("It is unnecessary to attempt to place the Crete of this period in a precise legal category. . . . It will suffice to say that after 1899 the Ottoman Government exercised to governmental powers in Crete, and that although the Sultan's flag was ceremoniously flown in Crete until February, 1913, the government of this island was entirely in the hands of the High Commissioner and the Cretans themselves, subject in certain respects to the approval of the four European States. In its external relations, the Cretan Government acted independently of the Ottoman Government, also. . . . If it can be said that a theoretical sovereignty remained in the Sultan after 1899, it was a sovereignty shorn of the last vestige of power. He could neither terminate nor modify the autonomy with which Crete had been endowed against his will and with the sanction of the four European States. A juristic conception must not be stretched to the breaking-point, and a ghost of a hollow sovereignty cannot be permitted to obscure the realities of this situation.").

124 We note the suggestion that those who insisted on the indivisibility of sovereignty confounded a valid definitional point ("divided sovereignty is impossible") with an invalid empirical observation ("a divided configuration of authority structures within a single state is impossible"). *See* Daniel Deudney, Bounding Power: Republican Security Theory from the Polis to the Global Village 53 (2007).

125 See Sir Charles Lewis Tupper, Our Indian Protectorate: An Introduction to the Study of the Relations Between the British Government and its Indian Feudatory 18–19 (1893); Secretary of State for India in Council, The Imperial Gazeteer of India, vol. IV: Administrative 60–61 (1907). A similar case is that of Mongolia, where for a period sovereignty was divided among China, Czarist Russia, and Mongolia itself. By the Kiakhta Agreement of 1915, Russia and Mongolia recognized China's "suzerainty" over Mongolia, with Mongolia however being said to have "autonomy," though without the right to "conclude international treaties with foreign powers respecting political and territorial questions." Questions of Mongolia's foreign relations were to be decided by China, but in consultation with Russia. *See* Ford, *supra* note 107, at 174.

we continue to control their foreign relations. . . Thus, while the power of the United States has been modified, it has not been abolished."[126] Indeed, one scholar has argued that the divided sovereignty was so pervasive outside Europe itself that it provided the foundations on which the "political structures of modern colonial and imperial systems" were built.[127]

Thus, in a series of lectures at Cambridge University in 1887, the English scholar Sir Henry Maine, commenting on the views of John Austin, contended that "this indivisibility of sovereignty, though it belongs to Austin's system, does not belong to International Law. The powers of sovereigns are a bundle or collection of powers, and they may be separated one from another. Thus a ruler may administer civil and criminal justice, may make laws for his subjects and for his territory, may exercise power over life and death, and may levy taxes and dues, but nevertheless he may be debarred from making war and peace, and from having foreign relations with any authority outside his territory."[128] Maine illustrated his point with reference to German, French, and other European nations' relationships with parts of Africa and the Pacific that the Europeans had not annexed, but under which the indigenous peoples were forbidden to engage in foreign relations except as permitted by the "protecting" state. Likewise, the American political scientist Charles Edward Merriam argued in 1900 that "the authorities in international law have been generally inclined to admit the divisibility of sovereignty, and the possibility of a non-sovereign state."[129] Merriam cited treaties between France and Madagascar, which authorized the former to supervise the latter's foreign relations, and between Great Britain and the Transvaal, as cases in point. Another American political scientist, Quincy Wright, analyzed the question in 1923 of who possessed sovereignty over the "mandates territories" that the League of Nations Covenant created out of certain territories and peoples that had belonged to the powers defeated in the First World War.[130] He wrote that "unquestionable instances have existed which can only be described as divided or suspended sovereignty. . . . Confederacies, federations, protectorates, spheres of influence, suzerainties, self-governing dominions, all suggest such a situation."[131]

---

126 *Cincinnati Soap Co. v. United States*, 301 U.S. 308, 319 (1937).

127 Edward Keene, Beyond the Anarchical Society: Grotius, Colonialism and Order in World Politics 93 (2002).

128 Sir Henry Maine, International Law: A Series of Lectures Delivered Before the University of Cambridge, 1887 Lecture III (2d ed. 1915). For Maine's precursors, *see* Keene, *supra* note 127, at 105–07.

129 Charles Edward Merriam, The History of the Theory of Sovereignty since Rousseau 210 (1900).

130 For a study of the "mandate system," see Susan Pedersen, The Guardians: The League of Nations and the Crisis of Empire (2015).

131 Quincy Wright, *Sovereignty of the Mandates*, 17 Am. J. Int'l L. 691, 694 (1923). Wright found that sovereignty over these territories could not be attributed either to the mandatory power, or to the League of Nations, or to the mandated people itself. Nor (he opined) was the sovereignty of the territories placed in suspense. Rather, sovereignty lodged in the mandatory power acting with the League's consent. *Id.* at 697–98. In *The International Status of South-West Africa*, [1950] ICJ Rep. 128 (Advisory Opinion) (July 11), the ICJ dealt with the meaning of "sovereignty" in relation to the former German colony of South West Africa, which under the League of Nations' mandates System had been assigned to the Union of South Africa as "mandatory." The Court ruled that the creation of the mandate "did not involve any cession of territory or transfer of sovereignty to the Union of South Africa." *Id.* at 132. In a separate opinion, Judge McNair took the view that the Mandates system had created "a new relationship between territory and its inhabitants on the one hand and the government which represents them internationally on the other—a new species of international government,

Arthur Berriedale Keith, an international law scholar, began his analysis of the legal relationships within the British Dominions in 1929 by writing that "sovereignty can be divided, and . . . in any country both internal and external sovereignty may be shared by various authorities."[132] These views had become so established that by 1940, the great scholar Hersch Lauterpacht could write that "from the point of view of international law, sovereignty is a delegated bundle of rights . . . and, therefore, divisible, modifiable, and elastic."[133] Although divided or impaired sovereignty in the period before the Second World War was chiefly found in Africa, Asia and Latin America, it also existed in Europe, *e.g.*, under the provisions of the Versailles Treaty that were designed to "demilitarize" Germany and that provided for the continuing military occupation of the German frontier with France and Belgium in the Rhineland,[134] or earlier under the 1815 Treaty of Paris, which had placed the Ionian Islands under a British protectorate.[135]

c. Later Views of Sovereignty

The architectonic role of the concept of sovereignty in international law began to give way after the First World War and still more so after the Second. Proponents of the League of Nations (and, thereafter, of the United Nations) recognized that an international organization of the type they aimed to create, though falling far short of a planetary government, would necessarily possess powers that limited the untrammeled sovereignty of its member states.[136] One such proponent, the eminent British political theorist (Sir) Ernest Barker, in a pamphlet entitled A

---

which does not fit into the old conception of sovereignty and which is alien to it. The doctrine of sovereignty has no application to this new system. Sovereignty over a Mandated Territory is in abeyance." *Id.* at 150 (separate opinion of McNair, J.).

132 Arthur Berriedale Keith, The Sovereignty of the British Dominions 1 (1929).

133 Quoted in David A. Lake, Hierarchy in International Relations 49 (2009) (citing Edward Keene, Beyond the Anarchical Society 108 (2002), who in turn quotes Lauterpacht, Sovereignty and Federation in International Law: The Collected Papers of Hersch Lauterpacht, vol. 3, p. 8 (E. Lauterpacht ed. 1970)). While Keene appears to mean that state sovereignty was delegated by the normative framework of international law, Lauterpacht and Lake appear to view delegated sovereignty more through the prism of the transfer of a portion of the sovereignty held by a state to another state or group of states. For a discussion of the "bundle" of property rights theory of sovereignty, *see* Antonio F. Perez, *Who Killed Sovereignty? Or: Changing Conceptions of Sovereignty in International Law,* 14 Wis. J. Int'l L. 463 (1996).

134 *See* David J. Bederman, *Collective Security, Demilitarization and 'Pariah' States,* 13 Eur. J. Int'l L. 121 (2002). As Bederman notes, decisions concerning military capabilities appear to remain "a protected core of state prerogative that international rules and institutions have yet to effectively penetrate." *Id.* at 137; *see also id.* at 123 (demilitarization regime restricted Germany's "essential sovereignty").

135 *See The Ionian Islands Case* (1855), in John E.P. Wallis (ed.), 8 Reports of State Trials (New Series 1850-1858) at 440 (1898). The opinion holds that although the Ionian Islands were, by treaty, under a British protectorate, Britain's declaration of war against Russia did not automatically place the Islands at war with Russia as well, although Britain could have done so.

136 *See, e.g.,* H.G. Wells, a well-known British historian and novelist of the period, argued on behalf of a League of Nations that "there can be no such thing as a secure and permanent world peace without very considerable qualifications of sovereignty. . . . We must cease to think imperially as we have had to cease thinking parochially; and we must think now in terms of the peace of the world. The League of Nations points straight to a pooling of empires, and it is no good blinking the fact." H.G. Wells, *The League of Free Nations,* in Edith M. Phelps (ed.), Selected articles on a League of Nations 101, 103, 107 ((1919).

Confederation of Nations: Its Powers and Constitution (1918), brought out very clearly that a League would limit sovereignty in at least two main ways: first, as to a sovereign's powers over war and peace; and second, as to a sovereign's powers over its own population.

As to the first limitation, Barker observed that member states would be required both to "surrender their right to make war *proprio motu* [in their own judgment]" and "to accept the duty of making war *motu aliorum* [in the judgment of others], or on the instruction of the League."[137] War, in general, would be supplanted by peaceful methods of dispute resolution—chiefly arbitration (in case of legal differences between states) or conciliation (in cases of policy differences between them); but states that failed to comply with the regulations governing these methods of dispute resolution could themselves become the targets of the collective force marshaled by the League. "If States enter a League on the understanding that they are to try certain alternatives to war, either in lieu of war, or before proceeding to war, they surrender part of that sovereignty which has hitherto entitled them to make war *proprio motu*, according to their own judgment and good pleasure. If States, again, enter a League against any State which refuses to embrace these alternatives to war, they are again, and still more obviously, surrendering their sole and spontaneous sovereignty over war and peace which they have hitherto enjoyed."[138]

As to the second limitation, Barker argued that the League should be empowered to "deal with internal matters inside a State which are of such a nature that, if they are left alone to simmer and ferment, they will gravely affect the relations of that State with other States."[139] Prominent among these internal matters of international concern, Barker wrote, were questions of "national minorities," which he specified as questions arising from "the desires of unredeemed nationalities to join a kindred nation."[140] Beyond that narrow specification of the nationalities problem, Barker also seemed prepared to regard what we would now consider serious human rights violations as also constituting matters of valid international, and therefore League, concern: "Racial massacres, religious pogroms, proscriptions of classes—these are all matters of more than internal consequence."[141] Barker's views here look both forward and backward: forward to the creation of the national minorities regime under the League of Nations[142] and, thereafter, to post-Second World War international human rights law; backward, in that they regard the treat-

---

137 Ernest Barker, A Confederation of the Nations: Its Powers and Constitution 18 (1918).

138 *Id.* at 30.

139 *Id.* at 16.

140 *Id.*

141 *Id.* at 27. As Barker noted, this description of the "minorities problem" would leave the British Empire and Dominions unaffected.

142 *See, e.g., Questions relating to Settlers of German Origin in Poland,* PCIJ Advisory Op. No. 6 (10 Sept. 1923), at ¶¶ 25–33, ¶¶ 39–42, ¶ 90. On the League of Nations' "Minorities Treaties," *see generally* Li-ann Thio, Managing Babel: The International Legal Protection of Minorities in the Twentieth Century 27-98 (2005); and Mark Mazower, *Minorities and the League of Nations in Interwar Europe,* Daedalus (1997) (*available at* http://cf.linnbenton.edu/artcom/social_science/clarkd/upload/MINORITIES%20AND%20THE%20LEAGUE%20OF%20NATIONS%20IN%20INTERWAR%20EUROPE.pdf).

ment of national minorities or other groups subject to persecution as a matter of international concern *only insofar as they affected state-to-state relations.* Thus, even in Barker's progressive vision, the individual had yet to emerge fully as a rights-bearing subject of international law.

d. The "Classic" Conception of Sovereignty Today

As we shall discuss in depth below, the classic conception of sovereignty has by no means emerged unscathed from the experience of the Second World War and, even more, from the human rights revolution that began in the mid-1970s and continues to the present.[143] Many analysts believe that the international order has been (or is being) revolutionized, moving away from the Westphalian system of sovereign states towards a new "constitution." Several phases have been discerned in this putative development: the pre-World War II minority treaties, which institutionalized procedures for international (judicial) intervention on behalf of protected groups in traditionally "internal" state affairs; the intensification of European integration manifested the European Union, which permits the retention of traditional state sovereignty in some areas, but which also provides for supra-national sovereignty in areas specified by European Union law; and the increasing use of the United Nations Charter to sanction international intervention in the "internal" affairs "sovereign" states, including, *e.g.*, Iraq, Serbia, and Libya.[144]

For a variety of reasons, many find the movement away from the Westphalian system to be normatively desirable. At least three kinds of reasons are put forward: economic or social (the national state is wrong-sized to accommodate either the needs of the international economy or the desire for recognition on the part of national minorities); moral (the Westphalian state system encouraged State egoism and helped cause the cataclysms of the First and Second World Wars; the Westphalian system obstructs international protection of minority or at-risk populations); and legal (the Westphalian system impedes the solution of the collective action problems which confront the international community in dealing with, *e.g.*, terrorism or environmental pollution).

Nonetheless, it would be far too soon to declare the Westphalian system dead.[145] Three of the most influential state actors on the international scene—China, India, and Russia—remain deeply committed to it, even if leading Western nations are less so.[146] Further, states that achieved their independence in the post-War period of decolonization are extremely jealous of their prerogatives as sovereigns and hostile to outside (especially Western) interventions (whether military

143 Samuel Moyn, The Last Utopia: Human Rights in History (2010) (discussing origins of contemporary international human rights regime).

144 *See* Daniel Philpott, Revolutions in Sovereignty: How Ideas Shaped Modern International Relations 30–43 (2001).

145 For a critique of the claim that the Westphalian system is, or ought to be, dead, *see* Robert J. Delahunty, *Nationalism, Statism and Cosmopolitanism*, 5 Northwestern Interdisciplinary Law Review 79 (2012).

146 *See, e.g.*, Henry Kissinger, On China (2011).

or other) in their "internal affairs." Votes in the United Nations General Assembly regularly demonstrate that a majority of the world's states are strongly opposed to outside interventions that disregard national sovereignty.[147] Further, sovereignty continues to function "as a progressive, egalitarian principle. . . . The State's permanent sovereignty over national resources is supported by countless UN General Assembly resolutions from 1962 onwards. Use of natural resources is a general sovereignty issue."[148] The concept of state sovereignty thus remains very much with us.

So much, then, by way of outline of the "classic" concept of state sovereignty. The concept unfolded into four key postulates of international law that are especially relevant here. These postulates concern 1) the *sources* of international law; 2) the *subjects* of international law; 3) international *jurisdiction* to prescribe, enforce and adjudicate; and 4) the *immunity* of foreign sovereigns, heads of state and other high-ranking officials. Let us take up each of these postulates in turn.

e. Sources of International Law

The dominant view in the "classical" period was that "all international law [was based] on the consent of States—the 'reciprocity of will,'" so that "only treaty (express consent) and custom (tacit consent) [were to be recognized] as sources of international law."[149] In the stark language of the Permanent Court of International Justice in the 1927 *S.S. Lotus Case*:

> International law governs relations between independent States. The rules of law binding upon States therefore emanate from their own free will as expressed in conventions or by usages generally accepted as expressing principles of law and established in order to regulate the relations between those co-existing independent communities or with a view to the achievement of common aims. Restrictions upon the freedom of States cannot therefore be presumed.[150]

---

147 *See, e.g.*, U.N. General Assembly Resolutions A/Res/58/317 (2004) and A/Res/57/337 (2003), both responding to the U.S. intervention in Iraq. Earlier expressions of the General Assembly's hostility to outside interventions include a series of resolutions condemning the Soviet Union's 1956 invasion of Hungary, *see, e.g.*, Resolution 1131 (XI) (1956); *see also* Quincy Wright, *Intervention, 1956*, 51 Am. J. Int'l L. 257, 274–76 (1957). On the other hand, the General Assembly was concerned with South Africa's (presumably, "internal" or "domestic") racial policies from the late 1940s onward. *See, e.g.*, Resolution 1761 (1962) (finding that apartheid "seriously endangers international peace and security" and referring back to prior General Assembly Resolutions).

148 Koskenniemi, *supra* note 73, at 237.

149 Grewe, *supra* note 7, at 503–04. Thus, Sir Henry Berkeley, the Chief Justice of the Supreme Court of Hong Kong, wrote in 1906 that "the law of nations is that system of rules respecting [nations'] rights established by consent among the civilized and commercial nations of the world, partly written and partly arising out of custom and rendered stable by judicial decisions from time to time." *The Steamship "Prometheus,"* 2 Hong-Kong L. Rpts. 217, (S. Ct. Hong Kong 1906).

150 *The S.S. Lotus Case*, [1927] PCIJ Rep., Ser. A, no 9, at 18. The International Court of Justice has expressed substantially the same idea in the *Nicaragua Case:* "In international law there are no rules, other than such rules as may be accepted by the states concerned." *Military and Paramilitary Activities in and against Nicaragua (Nicar. v. U.S.)*, Merits, [1986] ICJ Rep. 14, 135 at ¶ 269 (June 27). To be sure, this aspect of the *Lotus Case* was and remains controversial. Thus, Judge Bruno Simma, in an ICJ decision on the legality of Kosovo's 2008 declaration of independence, took the Court to task for "upholding the Lotus principle," which he characterized as an "anarchronistic, extremely consensualist vision of

Just as individuals in the "state of nature" could form a political community (i.e., a state) by entering into a "social contract," so in turn states themselves, by express or tacit contract, could form a kind of international society with settled (if somewhat rudimentary) laws of its own.[151] Law in such a system reflects the consent of the law-makers, and consent was expressed in two primary ways: by written treaties[152] or by international custom.[153] "Custom" was understood to mean the general practice of states in their relations with each other, when that practice was guided by *opinio juris,* or a felt sense of obligation.[154] (Custom was, so to say, an informal means of signifying consent, as treaty-making was a formal method of doing so.) Thus while "no one nation can change the law of the sea," the international safety regulations governing the color and placement of lights on vessels traversing the high seas rested "upon the common consent of civilized communities," and were binding upon all nations because they had been "generally accepted as a rule of conduct" and enjoyed "the concurrent sanction of those nations who may be said to constitute the commercial world."[155]

---

international law." *Accordance with international law of the unilateral declaration of independence in respect of Kosovo,* Advisory Opinion of 22 July 2010 at ¶ 2 (Simma, J., dissenting). *See also id.* at ¶ 10 (criticizing the Court's inference from the absence of a prohibition under international law to permissibility as "redolent of a nineteenth-century positivism, with its excessively deferential approach to State consent. "). The vigor of Judge Simma's criticism may attest to the vitality of the *Lotus* principle, however, *see generally* Koskenniemi, *supra* note 73, at 255–60 (analyzing *Lotus* principle as a consequence of the "pure fact" assumption that the power of states is external to and constitutive of international law, as opposed to the "legal" view that state sovereignty is derived from, bounded by and subordinate to conceptually prior international law).

151 Here as elsewhere, "the classical model of international law is a replication at the international level of the liberal theory of the state. The state is implicitly treated as the analogue, on the international level, to the individual within a domestic situation." J.H.H. Weiler, *The Transformation of Europe,* 100 Yale L. J. 2403, 2479 (1991), *reprinted in* J.H.H. Weiler, The Constitution of Europe: "Do the New Clothes Have an Emperor?" and Other Essays on European Integration 10 (1999). Not surprisingly, then, the idea of sovereign equality in international affairs can be traced back to Thomas Hobbes. *See* Thomas & Thomas, *supra* note 112, at 792–94.

152 "[T]he right of entering into international engagements is an attribute of State sovereignty." *Case of the S.S. "Wimbledon,"* PCIJ, Ser. A, No. 1, 1923 at 10 (*available at* http://www.worldcourts.com/pcij/eng/decisions/1923.08.17__wimbledon/).

153 *See* Frederick Pollock, *The Sources of International Law,* 18 L.Q. 418, 419 (1902).

154 The notion of "customary" international law has long perplexed commentators. *See, e.g.,* Koskenniemi, *supra* note 73, at 408–10 (concluding that "modern legal argument lacks a determinate, coherent concept of custom"). If the rules of customary law are based on state consent, how can they (or at least some of them) be said to bind states that have refused to consent to them, or that (like newly independent states) have not had the opportunity to decide whether to consent to them or not? Furthermore, what exactly is the element of *opinio juris*? Is it a state's belief that something is the law, or a state's will that something *be* the law? *See id.* at 417–24. If on the other hand customary legal rules are derived by extrapolation from state practice, then what practices count towards establishing them, given that states may act in a regular or patterned way without considering themselves to be legally bound so to act? How can we distinguish convenience from compliance? *See, e.g., The Asylum Case (Colombia v. Peru),* Judgment of 20 November, [1950] ICJ Reports p. 266, p. 277 (no customary rule emerged from state practice). For a crisp review of some of the issues, *see* David J. Bederman, *Constructivism, Positivism, and Empiricism in International Law,* 89 Geo. L. J. 469, 486–88 (2001). A leading work on the subject is Anthony A. D'Amato, The Concept of Custom in International Law (1971).

155 *The Scotia,* 81 U.S. 170, 187 (1871). As noted above, there was (and is) a tension between the claim that customary law derives from states' consent, and the claim that it binds states regardless of whether they specifically assented to the custom or not. There is judicial support for both views, even in a single opinion. *See, e.g., Continental Shelf Cases (Denmark v. Germany, Germany v. Netherlands),* [1969] ICJ Rep. 3, ¶¶ 37, 39–40, 72 at ¶ 63 (Feb. 20)); *see also Case Concerning Delimitation of the Maritime Boundary in the Gulf of Maine Area (Canada v. U.S.),* Judgment given by the Chambers, ICJ Rep. 1984, p. 246 at ¶ 111 (distinguishing, within the rubric of "customary international law" between a non-consensual "set of norms for ensuring the co-existence and vital co-operation of the members of the international

If there were ever a consensus on these assumptions, it disappeared after the end of the Second World War, if not before. Traditionally, customary law doctrines had drawn objections from revolutionary states[156]; in the post-Second World War period, decolonized and other newly emergent states advanced criticisms of their own. The former group often rejected, and the latter group had had no opportunity to consent to,[157] the rules of customary law. In order to answer such difficulties, "consent" to custom, in some formulations, was conceived to be, not so much a matter of consent to particular rules, as of consent to a process through which particular rules emerged.[158]

The constitutive legal fiction that is at work in the idea of customary law is that states can express their "will" in a legally significant way, allowing them to bind themselves or to decline to be bound. The private law model of a contract was systematically applied to and elaborated within the international legal order. The Nuremberg, Tokyo and Shimoda courts share this premise (though at the Tokyo Trials the prosecution advanced a natural law approach[159]).

f. Subjects of International Law

International lawyers and jurists in this pre-War period also postulated a particular view about the relations between *individuals* and international law. On this view, international law had a "peculiar 'nation-to-nation' character."[160] It "establishes substantive principles for determining

community," and "a set of customary rules whose presence in the *opinio juris* of States can be tested by induction based on the analysis of a sufficiently extensive and convincing practice, and not by deduction from preconceived ideas"). A related problem arises from the doctrine that new states are bound by all rules of customary law which existed at the time they gained their independence, even though they had no role in the development of those rules. *See* Byers, *supra* note 105, at 77, 145 (1999).

156 *See* Armstrong, *supra* note 91, at 15–16, 205. For example, revolutionary France challenged the international legal order of the *ancient regime* by basing legitimacy on national self-determination rather than dynastic rights, by claiming that foreign peoples owed a higher duty to the French Revolution than to their own local rulers, by disregarding arguments based on pre-existing international law in favor of (what was asserted to be) natural law, and by adopting a system of warfare unlimited both in its means and ends. *See id.* at 84–9.

157 *See* Armstrong, *supra* note 91, at 158–98. The attitude of many of these post-1945 states towards international law was neatly summarized by revolutionary Iran's leader, the Ayatollah Khomeini, who once reportedly asked: "What has international law done for the people of Iran?" *Id.* at 167.

158 *See* Byers, *supra* note 105, at 7–8, 142–44, 163 (1999). The American statesman Alexander Hamilton provided a fine example of this kind of reasoning. Arguing that the young United States was no longer a revolutionary state but a member of international society, he wrote that "we have taken our station among nations, have claimed the benefit of the laws which regulated them, and must in our turn be bound by the same laws." Armstrong, *supra* note 91, at 68. Further, the young United States (like other decolonized nations after 1945) eagerly availed itself of the right of a member of the society of states to *reshape* international law, e.g., the rules regarding neutral shipping of contraband. *See id.* at 48.

159 *See* Lawrence Douglas, The Memory of Judgment: Making Law and History in the Trials of the Holocaust 82–83 (2001) (contrasting prosecutorial approaches to natural law at IMT and IMTFE Trials); *see also* Neil Boister & Robert Cryer, A Reappraisal, *supra* note 77, at 291-93.

160 *Banco Naçional de Cuba v. Sabbatino*, 376 U.S. 398, 422 (1964).

whether one country has wronged another."[161] But because *states*, not individuals, were thus the only actors in international law that could inflict or suffer wrongs, *individuals* who believed themselves to have been wronged by a foreign state—*e.g.*, by having their property holdings with in that state's territory confiscated—were expected to "exhaust local remedies [in the foreign state] and then repair to the executive authorities of [their] own state to persuade them to champion [their] claim in diplomacy or before an international tribunal."[162] The mistreatment by one state of the national of another could thus lead the offended state to assert or "espouse" its own right to the "diplomatic protection" of its national's interest as against the offending or "host" state.[163] Significantly, this was regarded as the offended state's assertion of *its* own right.[164] (States had no right to intervene to protect stateless persons, however.[165]) The decision whether to "espouse" the injured individual's cause was, however, discretionary with his state's executive branch, and depended largely on the executive's appreciation of its political relations with the offending state. If the offended state decided to seek redress, the usual channels for dispute resolution were conciliation, mediation, arbitration or some other adjudicative or quasi-adjudicative process. If the offending state did provide a remedy, it was often left to the national's state to decide whether or not to give the proceeds of that remedy to its injured national.

Nonetheless, states *could* confer rights or impose duties directly on individuals or other "private" actors in certain specialized cases. For instance, many "unequal" nineteenth century treaties were made between more powerful Western states and (then) weaker non-Western ones such as Japan, China, or the Ottoman Empire.[166] Under such "unequal treaties," Western nation-

161 *Id.*

162 *Id.* at 422–23.

163 Thus, it was said that the right of territorial sovereignty "has as its corollary a duty: the obligation to protect within the territory the rights of other States, in particular . . . the rights which each State may claim for its nationals in foreign territory." Island of Palmas case (U.S. v. Netherlands), 2 Reports of Int'l Arbitral Awards 829, 839 (1928). Likewise, in *United States v. Arjona*, 120 U.S. 479, 484 (1887), the U.S. Supreme Court said that "[t]he law of nations requires every national government to use 'due diligence' to prevent a wrong being done within its own dominion to another nation with which it is at peace, or to the people thereof."

164 *See The Panevezys-Saldutiskis Railway Case*, P.C.I.J. Judgment no. 29 (Feb. 28, 1939), Series A/B 76, at 16 ("in taking up the case of one of its nationals, by resorting to diplomatic action or international judicial proceedings on his behalf, a state is in reality asserting its own right, the right to ensure in the person of its nationals respect for the rules of international law. This right is necessarily limited to the intervention on behalf of its own nationals because, in the absence of a special agreement, it is the bond of nationality between the state and the individual which alone confers upon the state the right of diplomatic protection, and it is part of the function of diplomatic protection that the right to take up a claim and to ensure respect for the rules of international law must be envisaged.").

165 In the *Dickinson Car Wheel Company Case*, 4 Rep. Int'l Arbitral Awards 669, 678 (1931), the Tribunal wrote that "[a] State . . . does not commit an international delinquency in inflicting an injury upon an individual lacking nationality, and consequently, no State is empowered to intervene or complain on his behalf before or after the injury."

166 *See, e.g.*, Krisch, *supra* note 105, at 396–97; Michael R. Auslin, Negotiating with Imperialism: The Unequal Treaties and the Culture of Japanese Diplomacy (2004) (studying diplomacy of unequal treaties with Japan); Kissinger, *supra* note 146 (unequal treaties and China); Ingrid Detter, *The Problem of Unequal Treaties*, 11 I.C.L.Q. 1069, 1073–75, 1078–80 (1962) (surveying unequal treaties between Western powers and China); Prem Varma, *Unequal Treaties in Modern International Law*, 7 Eastern J. Int'l L. 56, 68–72 (1975) (surveying unequal treaties between Britain and Indian states); and Majid Khadduri, *Islam and the Modern Law of Nations*, 50 Am. J. Int'l L. 358, 365–67 (1956) (surveying unequal treaties between European and Islamic states).

als residing in those countries and accused of crimes under local law were to be tried, not in the courts of the local sovereign, but in their own sovereign's "consular courts" within those territories.[167] One common justification offered for this manifestly unequal practice (which, of course, derogated from the territorial sovereignty of the weaker power) was that they were "essential to the peaceful residence of [Western] Christians within those countries and the successful prosecution of commerce with their people."[168] Later examples of such protections for private individuals or groups in international law are found in the so-called "Minority Treaties" of the period immediately following the First World War.[169] Under these treaties, new nations such as Poland or Czechoslovakia that had emerged after the Versailles Peace Conference of 1919 and older nations such as Hungary, Romania, and Greece undertook not to discriminate against the racial, ethnic, religious, or linguistic minorities within their populations.[170] These treaties were made under the auspices of the League of Nations (the precursor of the United Nations) and were frequently litigated before and enforced by the Permanent Court of International Justice (the precursor of the International Court of Justice). Unlike the treaties creating extra-territorial jurisdiction for (Western) consular courts, the Minority Treaties concerned the protection of individuals *from their own governments*, and, to that extent, represented a remarkable

---

167 For example, Article VI of the Treaty of Amity and Commerce between the United States and Japan, July 29, 1858, declared that "Americans committing offences against Japanese shall be tried in American Consular courts, and, when guilty, shall be punished according to American law. Auslin, *supra* note 166, at 218. *See also* Report of Edward A. Van Dyck, Capitulations of the Ottoman Empire Since the Year 1150 (G.P.O. 1881) (extensive study both of "capitulations" in Ottoman Empire and of Ottoman Empire's place in public international law); Denunciation of the Treaty of November 2nd, 1865, between China and Belgium, PCIJ, Ser. A, No. 8, 1925 (describing rights of Belgians in China under treaty).

168 *In re Ross*, 140 U.S. 453, 463 (1891).

169 On these treaties, *see* Krasner, *supra* note 85, at 90–96 (1999); Mark Mazower, *The Strange Triumph of Human Rights*, 47 Historical J. 379 (2004); Nathaniel Berman, *"But the Alternative is Despair": European Nationalism and the Modernist Revival of International Law*, 106 Harv. L. Rev. 1792 (1993); and Helmer Rosting, *Protection of Minorities by the League of Nations*, 17 Am. J. Int'l L. 641 (1923).

170 A particularly interesting example of the working of these treaties is the 1933 petition to the League of Nations of Franz Bernheim, a German Jew living in Upper Silesia, then a part of Nazi Germany, for relief from the German government's then-recent anti-Semitic legislation. Bernheim relied on the Polish-German Geneva Convention of May 15, 1922, which was part of the general post-War settlement, and which prohibited racial, religious or linguistic discrimination against German nationals and national minorities in Upper Silesia. The German representative to the Council of the League of Nations, apparently seeking to sweep the issue away, conceded at first that "[i]t is obvious that international Conventions concluded by Germany cannot be affected by internal German legislation. Should the provisions of the Geneva Convention have been violated in German Upper Silesia, this can only be due to mistakes on the part of subordinate organs acting under a mistaken interpretation of the laws." Thereafter, however, a League of Nations rapporteur found Germany in violation of the Convention, urged Germany to bring itself into compliance, and asked to be kept informed of the situation. A vigorous discussion in the Council—largely critical of Germany—ensued. Subsequently, a Committee of Jurists designated by the Council issued a report, which the Council, again after prolonged debate, adopted over German and Italian abstentions. *See Bernheim Petition to the League of Nations*, 35 Am. Jewish Y.B. 74 (1933/34). Thereafter Germany complied with its obligations under the Convention and suspended application of the challenged laws to the 10,000 Jews in Upper Silesia until July 15, 1937, i.e., for as long as the relevant parts of the Convention remained in force. *See* Jacob Robinson, And the Crooked Shall be Made Straight: A New Look at the Eichmann Trial 72–73 (1965); *see also* Quincy Wright, *The End of a Period of Transition*, 31 Am. J. Int'l l. 604 (1937) (concerning treaty arrangements for Upper Silesia).

innovation in international law.[171] In either case, however, the creation of such special rights or privileges for individuals under the international law of the pre-War period, including the right to sue or be sued before a national or international court, depended upon special treaty arrangements or customs.

One further, specialized category in which individuals were "subjects" of pre-War international law should be noted. This category formed part of the *jus in bello*, and was conceptualized as a kind of international "common law."[172] The traditional "law of nations . . . prescribe[d], for the conduct of war, the status, rights and duties of . . . enemy individuals."[173] So, for example, it was a rule of the Law of War that "[l]awful combatants are subject to capture and detention as prisoners of war by opposing military forces. Unlawful combatants are likewise subject to capture and detention, but in addition are subject to trial and punishment by military tribunals for acts which render their belligerency unlawful."[174] *Jus in bello* also prescribed rules for the treatment of non-combatant or civilian populations both in wartime and during belligerent occupation.

g. Jurisdiction in International Law

Jurisdiction is an aspect of sovereignty. As Lord Macmillan said, "it is an essential attribute of sovereignty of this realm, as of all sovereign independent States, that it should possess jurisdiction over all persons and things within its territorial limits and in all cases, civil and criminal, arising within these limits."[175]

Basic to pre-War international law conceptions of jurisdiction were the principles of territoriality and of nationality.[176] Under the "territorialist" conception of sovereignty, states were held

---

171 *See* Mark Mazower, *Minorities and the League of Nations in Interwar Europe*, 126 Daedalus 47, 51 (1997) ("The Polish Treaty took international law into uncharted waters. . . . What was new in 1919 was the concern for 'national' rather than exclusively religious rights, for collective rights rather than individual liberties, and the provision for international deliberation."). Some, however, including the French Prime Minister Clemenceau, denied that the minority treaties were novel. *See* Krasner, *supra* note 85, at 92–93.

172 *See Ex parte Vallandigham*, 68 U.S. 243, 249 (1863); In re Yamashita, 327 U.S. 1, 8 (1946); *see also* Alexander N. Sack, *War Criminals and the Defense of Act of State In International Law*, 5 Law. Guild Rev. 288, 295–96 (1945).

173 *Ex parte Quirin*, 317 U.S. 1 (1942).

174 *Id.* at 31. Even so, the law of war crimes was neither internationally codified nor satisfactorily developed at the time of the Nuremberg and Tokyo Trials. *See* J.L. Brierly, *Do We Need an International Criminal Court?*, 8 Brit. Y.B. Int'l L. 81, 84 (1927) ("That there are gaps in the rules is obvious; there is, for instance, no scale of punishments for contraventions whatever, and topics of vital importance . . . are either not regulated by existing rules at all, or regulated by rules which have become anachronisms").

175 Frederick A. Mann, *The Doctrine of Jurisdiction in International Law*, 1964-1 11 Rd C 9, 30 (quoting The Cristina, [1938] A.C. 485, 496–97)).

176 Justice Oliver Wendell Holmes, Jr., provided a succinct restatement of the general pre-War rules of jurisdiction in *American Banana Co. v. United Fruit Co.*, 213 U.S. 347, 355–56 (1909):

> No doubt in regions subject to no sovereign, like the high seas, or to no law that civilized countries would recognize as adequate, such countries may treat some relations between their citizens as governed by their own law, and keep, to some extent, the old notion of personal sovereignty alive. *See The Hamilton*, 207 U. S. 398, 207 U. S. 403; *Hart v. Gumpach*, L.R. 4 P. C.

to be entitled to prescribe rules for the conduct of those on their territory, and to enforce them against violators, including aliens who resided in that territory, or indeed non-nationals who were merely traveling through it.[177] A state's "territory" was deemed to include its "territorial waters"—traditionally, on the seaward side, three miles off its coast.[178] A state's "territory" was also deemed, by legal fiction, to include specific places outside its international boundaries, such as ships that bore the state's flag.[179] States were also assumed to have the power, not merely to enforce rules of conduct for those within their "territory," but also to adjudicate cases arising from events that took place on their territory.[180]

439, 463-464; *British South Africa Co. v. Companhia de Mocambique,* [1893] A.C. 602. They go further at times, and declare that they will punish anyone, subject or not, who shall do certain things, if they can catch him, as in the case of pirates on the high seas. In cases immediately affecting national interests they may go further still and may make, and, if they get the chance, execute, similar threats as to acts done within another recognized jurisdiction. An illustration from our statutes is found with regard to criminal correspondence with foreign governments. Rev.Stat. § 5335. *See further, Commonwealth v. Macloon,* 101 Mass. 1; *Sussex Peerage Case,* 11 Clark & F. 85, 146. And the notion that English statutes bind British subjects everywhere has found expression in modern times and has had some startling applications. *Rex v. Sawyer,* 2 C. & K. 101; *The Zollverein,* Swabey 96, 98. But the general and almost universal rule is that the character of an act as lawful or unlawful must be determined wholly by the law of the country where the act is done. *Slater v. Mexican National R. Co.,* 194 U.S. 120, 194 U.S. 126.

177 Again, as Chief Justice Marshall stated in *The Schooner Exchange,* "[t]h[e] full and absolute territorial jurisdiction [is] alike the attribute of every sovereign and [also renders it] incapable of conferring extraterritorial power." *The Schooner Exchange v. M'Fadden,* 11 U.S. 116, 137 (1812). The U.S. Supreme Court has reaffirmed this principle in the course of denying the habeas petitions of U.S. nationals held in custody by U.S. military forming part of a multinational force in Iraq, who were to be transferred to Iraqi custody for criminal prosecution for violation of local law. "Iraq has a sovereign right to prosecute Omar and Munaf for crimes committed on its soil. As Chief Justice Marshall explained nearly two centuries ago, '[t]he jurisdiction of the nation within its own territory is necessarily exclusive and absolute.' Schooner Exchange v. McFaddon, 7 Cranch 116, 136 (1812)." *Munaf v. Geren,* 553 U.S. 674, 707 (2008).

178 *See Cunard Steamship Co. v. Mellon,* 262 U.S. 100, 122 (1923) ("It now is settled in the United States and recognized elsewhere that the territory subject to its jurisdiction includes the land areas under its dominion and control, the ports, harbors, bays, and other enclosed arms of the sea along its coast, and a marginal belt of the sea extending from the coast line outward a marine league, or three geographic miles"). However, state sovereignty over the territorial sea was limited by the right of "innocent passage" for ships of other states. See J.L. Brierly, The Law of Nations: An Introduction to the International Law of Peace 174 (4th ed. 1949). Furthermore, even when a foreign-flag merchant vessel was inside another sovereign's territorial waters, the latter's general laws were usually considered inapplicable to "matters that involve[d] only the internal order and discipline of the vessel, rather than the peace of the port." *Spector v. Norwegian Cruise Line Ltd.,* 545 U.S. 119, 130 (2005); *see also Wildenhus's Case,* 120 U.S. 1, 12 (1887).

179 *See S.S. Lotus (France v. Turkey),* 1927 PCIJ (ser. A) no. 10. Thus, in *United States v. Flores,* 289 U.S. 137 (1933), the Supreme Court upheld the jurisdiction of the United States to prosecute a murder of an American committed by another American on board a U.S.-flagged vessel in the navigable waters of the Belgian Congo. The Court said:

> [T]he criminal jurisdiction of the United States is in general based on the territorial principle, and criminal statutes of the United States are not by implication given an extraterritorial effect. But that principle has never been thought to be applicable to a merchant vessel which, for purposes of the jurisdiction of the courts of the sovereignty whose flag it flies to punish crimes committed upon it, is deemed to be a part of the territory of that sovereignty, and not to lose that character when in navigable waters within the territorial limits of another sovereignty. . . . Subject to the right of the territorial sovereignty to assert jurisdiction over offenses disturbing the peace of the port, it has been supported by writers on international law, and has been recognized by France, Belgium, and other continental countries, as well as by England and the United States.

Id. at 155–56 (citations omitted).

180 Three distinct types of "jurisdiction" are usually distinguished—"prescriptive" jurisdiction, which goes to the legislative power to extend laws extra-territorially; "adjudicative" jurisdiction, which goes to the courts' power to decide cases; and "enforcement" jurisdiction, which is the executive's power to enforce a law or judgment. *See* Restatement (Third) of the Foreign Relations Law of the United States § 401(1987); *Hartford Fire Ins. Co. v. Calif.,* 509 U.S. 764, 819 (1993) (Scalia, J., dissenting).

Territorialism carried distinct implications for one sovereign's treatment of another sovereign's laws and acts. In general, it was left to each State to decide whether or not to give effect to foreign legislation or foreign court judgments when called upon to do so. The extent to which foreign laws and foreign courts' judgments were recognized and enforced was considered to be a matter of international "comity."[181] The U.S. Supreme Court explained the concept of comity in *Hilton v. Guyot* (1895):

> No law has any effect, of its own force, beyond the limits of the sovereignty from which its authority is derived. The extent to which the law of one nation, as put in force within its territory, whether by executive order, by legislative act, or by judicial decree shall be allowed to operate within the dominion of another nation depends upon what our greatest jurists have been content to call "the comity of nations." Although the phrase has been often criticized, no satisfactory substitute has been suggested.
>
> "Comity," in the legal sense, is neither a matter of absolute obligation, on the one hand, nor of mere courtesy and goodwill, upon the other. But it is the recognition which one nation allows within its territory to the legislative, executive, or judicial acts of another nation, having due regard both to international duty and convenience and to the rights of its own citizens or of other persons was are under the protection of its laws.[182]

Quoting from an earlier Supreme Court decision, the *Hilton* Court added:

> The general practice of civilized countries, the laws of the one will, by the comity of nations, be recognized and executed in another where the rights of individuals are concerned. . . . The comity thus extended to other nations is no impeachment of sovereignty. It is the voluntary act of the nation by which it is offered, and is inadmissible when contrary to its policy, or prejudicial to its interests. But it contributes so largely to promote justice between individuals, and to produce a friendly intercourse between the sovereignties to which they belong, that courts of justice have continually acted upon it as a part of the voluntary law of nation. ...[183]

Further, if a sovereign state's courts might (but were not required to) give effect to the legal acts of a foreign state, they were also expected not to negate the effects of a foreign state's legal acts

181 On the history of the concept of "comity," *see* Joel R. Paul, *The Transformation of International Comity,* 71 Law & Contemp. Probs. 19 (2008). Paul underscores the link between the late nineteenth century's understanding of comity and the idea of sovereign equality. *See id.* at 27. The doctrine of comity retains considerable vitality. *See, e.g., Rep. of Philippines v. Pimentel,* 128 S. Ct. 2180, 2190 (2008) ("There is a comity interest in allowing a foreign state to use its own courts for a dispute if it has a right to do so. The dignity of a foreign state is not enhanced if other nations bypass its courts without right or good cause.").

182 *Hilton v. Guyot,* 159 U.S. 113, 163–64 (1895).

183 *Id.* at 165–66 (quoting *Bank of Augusta v. Earle,* 38 U.S. 519 (1839)).

on the latter's own territory. This was known as the "act of state" doctrine. As explained by the U.S. Supreme Court:

> Every sovereign state is bound to respect the independence of every other sovereign state, and the courts of one country will not sit in judgment on the acts of the government of another done within its own territory. Redress of grievances by reason of such acts must be obtained through the means open to be available of by sovereign powers as between themselves.[184]

Territoriality was not the only traditional basis in international law for the assertion of a state's jurisdiction. A state might also be assumed to be acting lawfully and not in violation of the equal sovereignty of another state when it extended its prescriptive jurisdiction extra-territorially to the conduct of its own nationals when they were abroad.[185] Thus if an American citizen had committed a murder while on holiday in France, he might be tried for murder either in France (on the basis of the territoriality principle)[186] or in the United States (on the basis of the nationality principle).

Territoriality and nationality as jurisdictional bases might collide, however. What was to happen if, for example, a national of state X, a fugitive from justice in his or her own state, were kidnapped by agents of X on the territory of state Y without the latter's knowledge or consent, and then forcibly abducted to X to stand trial there? Did this violation of the territorial sovereignty of state Y operate under international law to nullify the adjudicative jurisdiction of the courts of state X? (To be sure, extradition treaties were intended to prevent any need for such forcible abductions from arising; but such treaties might not exist in some cases, or be disregarded.)[187] In an 1829 English decision, *Ex parte Susannah Scott*, Lord Tenterden ruled that the courts of the state from which the fugitive had fled "cannot inquire" into "the circumstances in which [the fugitive] was brought here," and so were free to assert jurisdiction over

184 *Oetjen v. Central Leather Co.*, 246 U.S. 297, 303 (1918)(citing *Hernandez v. Underhill*, 168 U.S. 250 (1897)).

185 "The competence of the State to prosecute and punish its nationals on the sole basis of their nationality is universally conceded. Such jurisdiction is based upon the allegiance which the person charged with the crime owes to the State of which he is a national." *Research in International Law Under the Auspices of the Faculty of the Harvard Law School: II. Jurisdiction with Respect to Crime*, 29 Am. J. Int'l L. 435, 519 (Supp. 1935).

186 "When an American citizen commits a crime in a foreign country he cannot complain if required to submit to such modes of trial and to such punishment as the laws of that country may prescribe for its own people." *Neely v. Henkel*, 180 U. S. 109, 123 (1901).

187 *See United States v. Rauscher*, 119 U.S. 407, 411–12 (1886) ("It is only in modern times that the nations of the earth have imposed upon themselves the obligation of delivering up these fugitives from justice to the states where their crimes were committed, for trial and punishment. This has been done generally by treaties made by one independent government with another. Prior to these treaties, and apart from them, it may be stated, as the general result of the writers upon international law, that there was no well-defined obligation on one country to deliver up such fugitives to another; and, though such delivery was often made, it was upon the principle of comity, and within the discretion of the government whose action was invoked; and it has never been recognized as among those obligations of one government towards another which rest upon established principles of international law.").

the captive,[188] although current British law has recently evolved.[189] Similarly, in *Ker v. State of Illinois*,[190] an 1886 case involving a U.S. national forcibly seized in and repatriated from Peru, the U.S. Supreme Court cited approvingly to "authorities of the highest respectability which hold that such forcible abduction is no sufficient reason why the party should not answer when brought within the jurisdiction of the court which has the right to try him for such an offense, and presents no valid objection to his trial in such a court."[191]

In addition to territoriality and nationality, other forms of jurisdiction, though less prominent and more contentious, were recognized. In certain cases, international law was understood to permit states to assert jurisdiction with regard to acts *having significant effects within their territory* (the so-called "objective territoriality principle"[192]) or *on their own nationals* (the so-called "passive personality principle"[193]). Further, writers on international law in the early modern period, including the Spaniard Diego Covarruvias and the Dutchman Hugo Grotius,

---

188 *Ex parte Susannah Scott* 9 B. & C. 446, 448 [1829].

189 It appears that Ex parte Scott is no longer good law in the United Kingdom. *See Regina v. Horseferry Road Magistrates' Court, Ex parte Bennett*, [1994] 1 A.C. 42 (UKHL). The different outcomes in Scott and Bennett may perhaps be explained by reference to the jurisprudential shift from regarding irregular abduction as an injury to the territorial sovereign to regarding it as a violation of individual human rights.

190 119 U.S. 436, 444 (1886).

191 For criticism of the prevailing doctrine in light of the Nazi régime's pre-War practice of abducting individuals from foreign states to stand trial in Germany, *see* Lawrence Preuss, *Kidnaping of Fugitives from Justice on Foreign Territory*, 29 Am. J. Int'l L. 502 (1935).

192 *See* Restatement (Third) of the Foreign Relations Law of the United States § 402(3)(1987). The Permanent Court of International Justice's decision in *The S.S. Lotus (France v. Turkey)* stated that "offences, the authors of which at the moment of commission are in the territory of another State, are nevertheless to be regarded as having been committed in the national territory, if one of the constituent elements of the offence, and more especially its effects, have taken place there." *S.S. Lotus (France v. Turkey)*, 1927 PCIJ (ser. A) no. This statement has been cited as support for the principle of objective territoriality. Pre-War United States jurisprudence recognized the jurisdictional principle of objective territoriality to at least some extent. *See United States v. Ford*, 273 U.S. 593, 621–22 (1927) ("Generally the cases show that jurisdiction exists to try one who is a conspirator whenever the conspiracy is in whole or in part carried on in the country whose laws are conspired against."). For a thorough review of the English historical precedents (which also embraced, albeit hesitatingly and only in some cases, objective territoriality jurisdiction), *see Libman v. The Queen*, [1985] 2 S.C.R. 178, ¶¶ 13–27 (Supreme Court of Canada).

193 *Compare* J.L. Brierly, *The 'Lotus' Case*, 44 L. Q. 154, 162 (1928) (viewing both objective territoriality jurisdiction and passive personality jurisdiction as "the juridical by-produce of the aggressive racial nationalism which was launched by the French Revolution and powerfully reinforced by the Italian Risorgimento") and Mann, *supra* note 175, at 92 (doctrine of passive personality "should be treated as an excess of jurisdiction"); *with In re Rohrig, Brunner and Heinze*, Special Court of Cassation (Netherlands 1950) (trans. available in 17 Int'l L. Rpts. 393, 396)(Dutch trial of German officials for war crimes committed in Germany against Dutch nationals; held, Dutch courts had jurisdiction). Traditionally, the United States objected to the "passive personality principle" as a basis for extraterritorial jurisdiction. For example, in the late nineteenth century, the U.S. State Department objected vigorously to Mexico's prosecution of a U.S. national, seized while traveling in Mexico, for having published in a Texas newspaper an article deemed to have criminally libeled a Mexican national. *See Secretary Bayard Firm: No Change in his policy in the Cutting Case. He justifies his action and insists that the United States must maintain its dignity. Comparative quiet at El Paso, in The New York Times* (Aug. 11, 1886). More recently, however, the United States has defended the legitimacy of the passive personality principle as a sufficient jurisdictional basis under international law when applied to the criminal prosecution of terrorism committed against U.S. nationals outside the United States. *See* Lynda M. Clarizio, *United States v. Yunis, 681 F. Supp. 896*, 83 Am. J. Int'l L. 94 (1989); and Restatement (Third) of the Foreign Relations Law of the United States § 402(g)(1987)(approving passive personality for terrorist offenses, other organized attacks on nationals because of their nationality, and attacks on diplomatic representatives).

argued that in the case of certain particularly serious crimes, not only the state on whose territory the offender committed his crimes, but also the state where the offender was to be found, were entitled to prosecute him.[194] Although later developments in international law ran counter to this proposal, even in the eighteenth and nineteenth centuries, it is said, states were permitted to enforce certain laws against certain classes of persons designated as "enemies of mankind"—notably, pirates and slave traders.[195] The enforcement of laws against piracy and slave trading is said to have a matter of *universal* jurisdiction, and *any* state was held to be entitled to capture, try and punish such persons.[196] In part, this was supposedly because the targeted persons either were deemed stateless (like pirates) or operated in the global commons of the sea, outside of any particular state's territorial jurisdiction (pirates again; also slave traders); and in part it was supposedly because of the heinousness of the crimes they were committing.[197] On any account, however, it is clear that very few criminal prosecutions for piracy can be found that depended on universal jurisdiction,[198] while prosecutions for slave trading seem to have been based on "delegated" jurisdiction rather than universal jurisdiction.[199] Universal jurisdiction, both criminal and civil, has, however, become more prominent in the post-Second World War legal environment, especially with regard to certain "international" crimes, *viz.*, genocide, crimes against humanity, and war crimes.[200]

194 *See Case Concerning the Arrest Warrant of 11 April 2000 (Democratic Rep. of Congo v. Belgium)*, 2002 I.C.J. Rep. 3, (separate opinion of President Guillaume).

195 Writing in 1964, Frederick Mann identified "[t]raffic in women and children, trade in narcotics, falsification of currency, piracy and trade in indecent publications" as crimes that, by treaty, had been made the subject of universal jurisdiction. Mann, *supra* note 175, at 95.

196 *See In re Piracy jure gentium*, [1934] A.C. 586, 589 (Privy Council) ("With regard to crimes as defined by international law, that law has no means of trying or punishing them. The recognition of them as constituting crimes, and the trial and punishment of the criminals, are left to the municipal law of each country. But whereas according to international law the criminal jurisdiction of municipal law is ordinarily restricted to crimes committed on its terra firma or territorial waters or its own ships, and to crimes by its own nationals wherever committed, it is also recognized as extending to piracy committed on the high seas by any national on any ship, because a person guilty of such piracy has placed himself beyond the protection of any State. He is no longer a national, but "hostis humani generis" and as such he is justiciable by any State anywhere: Grotius (1583–1645) "De Jure Belli ac Pacis," vol. 2, cap. 20, § 40.").

197 So much, at least, is the conventional view. For a critique, *see* Eugene Kontorovich, *The Piracy Analogy: Modern Universal Jurisdiction's Hollow Foundation*, 45 Harv. Int'l L. J. 183 (2004).

198 *Id.* at 192 (citing Alfred P. Rubin, The Law of Piracy 302, 348 n.50 (2d ed. 1998). For a succinct account of piracy, *see* Max Boot, *Pirates, Then and Now*, 88 For. Aff. 94 (2009)

199 Because sovereignty can be treated as a property right, a portion of the sovereignty's jurisdiction can therefore be transferred to another sovereign or group of sovereigns. For a discussion of "delegated" sovereignty, *see* Keene, *supra* note 133 (citing Lauterpacht). *See also* Rubin, *supra* note 198, at 192–94; Jenny S. Martinez, *Antislavery Courts and the Dawn of International Human Rights Law*, 117 Yale L. J. 550 (2008); The Princeton Principles on Universal Jurisdiction 45 (Stephen Macedo ed., 2001) (*available at* http://lapa.princeton.edu/hosteddocs/unive_jur.pdf).

200 *See, e.g.*, Robert Cryer, Prosecuting International Crimes: Selectivity and the International Criminal Law Regime 84–95 (2003); Donald Francis Donovan & Anthea Roberts, *The Emerging Recognition of Universal Civil Jurisdiction*, 100 Am. J. Int'l L. 142 (2006). For legal justification of this practice in criminal cases, *see. e.g.*, Georg Schwarzenberger, *The Eichmann Judgment: An Essay in Censorial Jurisprudence*, 15 Current Legal Probs. 248, 256 (1962) ("It would . . . be hard to point to evidence of a rule of international law prohibiting the assumption of [national] criminal jurisdiction against an accused actually present in the territory of a sovereign State for crimes he is accused of having committed against foreign

h. Foreign Sovereign Immunity

Fourth and finally, the doctrine of sovereign equality limited the jurisdiction of national courts with respect to foreign sovereigns. "Par in parem non habet imperium"—"An equal has no authority over an equal." Accordingly, it was understood that one sovereign's courts could not assert jurisdiction over another sovereign, at least without the latter sovereign's consent.[201] Thus, in *Compania Naviera Vascongado v. Steamship "Cristina"* [1938] AC 485, 490, Lord Atkin declared it to be "well established" and "beyond dispute" that "the courts of a country will not implead a foreign sovereign, that is, they will not by their process make him against his will a party to legal proceedings whether the proceedings involve process against his person or seek to recover from him specific property or damages." (Foreign sovereigns might, however, be held liable for wrongful acts committed by their authorized agents against other sovereigns, such as wartime sabotage directed against a neutral sovereign.[202])

In its earlier formulation, the immunity of foreign sovereigns to judicial process was often taken to be *absolute*.[203] However, as foreign governments began increasingly to engage in commercial activities (such as operating airlines or transport companies), a *restrictive* view of foreign sovereign immunity took hold. The "restrictive" theory maintained the absolute immunity for foreign sovereigns with regard to their public or governmental acts, but qualified it with respect to "private" activities, including purely commercial ones. In a celebrated letter of May 19, 1952, Jack B. Tate, the Acting Legal Adviser for the U.S. State Department, explained the difference between the earlier and emerging doctrines in this way:

> A study of the law of sovereign immunity reveals the existence of two conflicting concepts of sovereign immunity, each widely held and firmly established. According to the classical or absolute theory of sovereign immunity, a sovereign cannot, without his consent, be made a

---

nationals abroad. . . . In particular, this applies if other States with as close a link, or an even closer link, with the crimes committed, are not able or willing to shoulder the task.").

201 "Intellectually, sovereign immunity is simply a corollary to the principle of the sovereign equality of States; as such, it mandates that no State can claim jurisdiction over another. It is reflected in the principle *par in parem non habet jurisdictionem or par in parem imperium non habet.* From an international relations perspective, immunity exists to promote stable relations between States based on the ability to conduct peaceful diplomacy." Judge Vladen Vereshchetin, *Immunities in International Law in the Jurisprudence of the ICJ,* Press Release 2003/4 (22 Oct. 2003) (*available at* www.icj-cij.org/presscom/index.php?p1=6&p2=1).

202 *See Lehigh Valley Railroad Co. v. Germany (Sabotage Cases),* 8 Repts. of Int'l Arbitral Awards 84 (1930). In that arbitration, Germany agreed to accept liability to damage done to U.S. citizens during the period of American neutrality in the First World War, if the damage could be shown to have resulted from the acts of authorized German agents inside the United States. To like effect is the Zafiro Case. There the United States was held liable for the damage done caused by the improperly supervised crew of a supply ship to Admiral Dewey's fleet in the battle of Manila Bay in 1898. The crew had looted houses and destroyed property belonging to neutral British nationals. See D. Earnshaw et al., *(Great Britain) v. United States (Zafiro Case)* (Philippine War Claim 1925), 6 Rpts. Int'l Arbitral Awards 160.

203 There are historical reasons to doubt that the immunity was universally considered to be absolute. *See* Byers, *supra* note 105, at 110–14.

> respondent in the courts of another sovereign. According to the newer or restrictive theory of sovereign immunity, the immunity of the sovereign is recognized with regard to sovereign or public acts (*jure imperii*) of a state, but not with respect to private acts (*jure gestionis*). There is agreement by proponents of both theories, supported by practice, that sovereign immunity should not be claimed or granted in actions with respect to real property (diplomatic and perhaps consular property excepted) or with respect to the disposition of the property of a deceased person even though a foreign sovereign is the beneficiary.[204]

The doctrine of the immunity of foreign sovereigns was traditionally understood to include immunity for foreign *heads of state.* Heads of state were (and are[205]) taken to be the embodiment of their state's sovereignty: as the U.S. Supreme Court said in 1870, "[t]he reigning sovereign represents the national sovereignty."[206]

Chief Justice John Marshall gave classic expression to the foreign head of state immunity doctrine in *The Schooner Exchange*, when he wrote that "[the] perfect equality and absolute independence of sovereigns, and this common interest impelling them to mutual intercourse, and an interchange of good offices with each other, have given rise to a class of cases in which every sovereign is understood to waive the exercise of a part of that complete exclusive territorial jurisdiction which has been stated to be the attribute of every nation. *One of these is admitted to be the exemption of the person of the sovereign from arrest or detention within a foreign territory.*"[207] Likewise, British cases reflected a similar doctrine. In the 1851 case of *De Haber v. Queen of Portugal*, the Queen's Bench wrote that "an action cannot be maintained in an English court against a foreign potentate, for any thing done, or omitted to be done, in his public capacity as representative of the nation of which he is the head. No English court has jurisdiction to entertain any complaint against him in that capacity. . . . To cite a foreign potentate in a municipal court, for any complaint against him in his public capacity, is contrary to the law of nations, and an insult which he is entitled to resent." [208]

204 App. 2, *Alfred Dunhill of London, Inc. v. Republic of Cuba*, 425 U.S. 682, 711–12 (1976). For contemporaneous commentary, see William W. Bishop, Jr., *New United States Policy Limiting Sovereign Immunity*, 47 Am. J. Int'l L. 93 (1953). Bishop usefully pointed out that the doctrine that a foreign sovereign was not immune from suit for its private activities need not imply that the foreign sovereign no longer enjoyed immunities from execution of an adverse judgment and seizure of its property. Id. at 102. On that issue, *see also* James Crawford, *Execution of Judgments and Foreign Sovereign Immunity*, 75 Am. J. Int'l L. 820 (1981).

205 *See, e.g., Certain Criminal Proceedings in France (Republic of the Congo v. France)*, Order of 17 June 2003, [2003] ICJ 101, 131–32 (dissenting opinion of Judge *ad hoc* de Cara).

206 *The Sapphire*, 78 U.S. 164, 168 (1870).

207 *The Schooner Exchange*, 11 U.S. at 137 (italics added). Further, former heads of state were considered immune for acts done in their sovereign capacity. *See* Quincy Wright, *The Legal Liability of the Kaiser*, 13 Am. Pol. Sc. Rev. 120, 121 (1919). The traditional immunity did not extend, however, to former heads of state for their *private, unofficial* acts. *See Ex-King Farouk of Egypt v. Christian Dior*, 84 Clunet 717, 24 I. L. R. 228, 229 (CA Paris 1957) (Christian Dior "is entitled ... to bring" the ex-King to court "to answer for debts contracted" before his abdication "when, as from the date of his abdication, he is no longer entitled to claim ... immunity" as "Hea[d] of State").

208 *De Haber v. Queen of Portugal*, 17 Q.B. 171, 207 (1851).

Finally, traditional customary international law extended immunity, not only to foreign heads of state, but also to foreign officials of a lower rank, such as prime ministers and foreign ministers. Such immunities came in two forms: immunities which benefited certain state officials *personally* (*ratione personae*) during their tenure of office for their acts or transactions, even private ones; and immunities inuring to covered officials *functionally* (*ratione materiae*), for acts performed in their official capacity.[209]

Perhaps surprisingly, much of the traditional doctrines of head of state (and other officials') immunity remains the law even now, at least in national courts. "National courts and prosecutors have consistently rejected cases against sitting heads of state."[210] The I.C.J. affirmed its continuing vitality in the 2002 *Arrest Warrant Case,* saying, in relation to an incumbent Foreign Minister:

> [T]hroughout the duration of his or her office, he or she when abroad enjoys full immunity from criminal jurisdiction and inviolability. . . In this respect, no distinction can be drawn between acts performed by a Minister for Foreign Affairs in an "official" capacity, and those claimed to have been performed in a "private capacity," or, for that matter, between acts performed before the person concerned assumed office . . . and acts committed during the period of office. [211]

Likewise, the French Cour de Cassation ruled in the 2001 *Ghaddafi Case* that Colonel Mouammar Ghaddafi, then the serving Head of State of Libya, enjoyed immunity against criminal prosecution for his alleged complicity in acts of terrorism that included the murder of French nationals and the destruction of a civilian passenger aircraft.[212]

---

209 On the distinction between personal and functional immunity, *see* Vienna Convention on Diplomatic Relations, Articles 38(1) ("Except insofar as additional privileges and immunities may be granted by the receiving State, a diplomatic agent who is a national of or permanently resident in that State shall enjoy only immunity from jurisdiction, and inviolability, in respect of official acts performed in the exercise of his functions.) and 39(2) ("When the functions of a person enjoying privileges and immunities have come to an end, such privileges and immunities shall normally cease at the moment when he leaves the country, or on expiry of a reasonable period in which to do so, but shall subsist until that time, even in case of armed conflict. However, with respect to acts performed by such a person in the exercise of his functions as a member of the mission, immunity shall continue to subsist."); *Prosecutor v. Blaskic,* Appellate Chamber, International Criminal Tribunal for the Former Yugoslavia, Judgement of 29 October 1997, ¶ 38 ("State officials acting in their official capacity . . . are mere instruments of a State and their official action can only be attributed to the State. They cannot be the subject of sanctions or penalties for conduct that is not private but undertaken on behalf of a State. In other words, State officials cannot suffer the consequences of wrongful acts which are not attributable to them personally but to the State on whose behalf they act: they enjoy so-called "functional immunity. This is a well-established rule of customary international law going back to the eighteenth and nineteenth centuries, restated many times since."); Hazel Fox QC, The Law of State Immunity 665–67 (2d ed. 2008); and Salvatore Zappalà, *Do Heads of State in Office Enjoy Immunity from Jurisdiction in International Crimes? The Ghaddafi Case Before the French Cour de Cassation,* 12 Eur. J. Int'l L. 595, 598–600 (2001).

210 Ingrid Wuerth, *Pinochet's Legacy Reassessed,* 106 Am. J. Int'l L. 731, 741 (2012).

211 *Arrest Warrant Case of 11 April 2000 (Democratic Republic of the Congo v. Belgium),*[2002] I.C.J. Reports 3 at ¶¶ 54-55.

212 *Arrêt relative aux pursuits engagées contre le colonel Kadhaffi,* Cour de Cassation (March 13, 2001), Arrêt no. 1414. For a critique of the Court's reasoning, *see* Salvatore Zappalà, *Do Heads of State in Office Enjoy Immunity from Jurisdiction for International Crimes? The Ghaddafi Case Before the French Cour de Cassation,* 12 Eur. J. Int'l L. 595 (2001).

Recently, on January 14, 2014, a Chamber of the European Court of Human Rights (ECHR) affirmed the general rule of Head of State immunity and applied the rule to a case brought in the U.K. in which private plaintiffs in a civil action sought relief from alleged acts of torture committed by officials of Saudi Arabia acting on behalf of the Saudi government.[213] The ECHR Chamber said that "[t]he weight of authority at international and national level . . . appears to support the proposition that State immunity in principle offers individual employees or officers of a foreign State protection in respect of acts undertaken on behalf of the State under the same cloak as protects the State itself."[214] Moreover, the ECHR Chamber ruled that this immunity was not abrogated because the defendants in the case were alleged to have committed acts of torture, which concededly is an egregious offense under international law:

> [W]hile there is in the Court's view some emerging support in favour of a special rule or exception in public international law in cases concerning civil claims for torture lodged against foreign State officials, the bulk of the authority is . . . to the effect that the State's right to immunity may not be circumvented by suing its servants or agents instead. Taking the applicants' arguments at their strongest, there is evidence of recent debate surrounding the understanding of the definition of torture in the Convention against Torture; the interaction between State immunity and the rules on attribution in the Draft Articles on State Responsibility; and the scope of Article 14 of the Convention against Torture. . . . However, State practice on the question is in a state of flux, with evidence of both the grant and the refusal of immunity ratione materiae in such cases. . . . International opinion on the question may be said to be beginning to evolve, as demonstrated recently by the discussions around the work of the International Law Commission in the criminal sphere. This work is ongoing and further developments can be expected. . . . In these circumstances, the Court is satisfied that the grant of immunity to the State officials in the present case reflected generally recognised rules of public international law.[215]

The ECHR Chamber's decision may be appealed to the Grand Chamber, and the opinion itself makes clear that international opinion on the question of immunity for acts such as torture is "beginning to evolve."[216]

---

213 *Jones v. UK*, European Court of Human Rights, Nos. 34356/06 and 40528/06) (Jan. 14, 2014) (*available at http://hudoc.echr.coe.int/sites/eng/pages/search.aspx#{"appno":["34356/06"],"itemid":["001-140005"]}*).

214 *Id.* at ¶ 204.

215 *Id.* at ¶¶ 213, 215.

216 *Id.*

i. Sovereign Powers as to War and Peace

The "Westphalian" concept of state sovereignty described above also carried extremely broad consequences for international law regarding war and peace—and most especially for the *jus ad bellum,* the law regulating states decisions whether or not to wage war. In its late nineteenth century form, international law had taught that the decision whether or not to wage war was a prerogative whose exercise was within the discretion of every sovereign state.[217] Indeed, this prerogative was considered to be an essential element of sovereignty,[218] if not indeed sovereignty's "ultimate expression and prerogative."[219] In a typical statement of the law for the period, one writer stated that:

> International law, as such . . . does not consider the justice or injustice of a war. From the purely legal standpoint, all wars are equally just or unjust; or, properly speaking, they are neither just nor unjust. International Law merely takes cognizance of the existence of war as a fact, and prescribes certain rules and regulations which affect the rights and duties of neutrals and belligerents during that continuance.[220]

Or again:

---

217 *See* Antonio Cassese, *Realism v. Artificial Theoretical Constructs: Remarks on Anzilotti's Theory of War,* 3 Eur. J. Int'l L. 149, 149–50 (1992) ("It is well known that before 1919 States were at liberty to resort to war either to enforce a legal right or simply to realize their economic or political interests."). *See also* C.A. Pompe, Aggressive War: An International Crime 301–02 (1953) ("[w]ar was a fact, an international phenomenon, and classic [nineteenth century] international law was indifferent towards it . . . A 'legality' of war supposed distinction between just and unjust wars, which may have lingered on in public opinion and may have been defended by some authors, but was not, according to the majority of them, part of international positive law"); Robert H. Jackson, *Nürnberg in Retrospect,* 27 Canadian Bar Rev. 761, 762 (1949) (international law at start of twentieth century had taught that "each state is sovereign, its right absolute, its will unrestrained, and free to resort to war at any time, for any purpose"); F.H. Hinsley, Sovereignty 229–31 (2d ed. 1986); 2 Charles Cheney Hyde, International Law Chiefly as Interpreted and Applied by the United States 189 (1922).

218 *See The S.S. Wimbledon, supra* note 152, dissenting op. of Anzilotti & Huber, JJ., at ¶ 3 ("[t]he right of a state to adopt the course which it considers best suited to the exigencies of its security and to the maintenance of its integrity, is so essential a right that, in case of doubt, treaty stipulations cannot be interpreted as limiting it."). Thus, Robert Jackson, the U.S. Supreme Court Justice who served as the Chief Prosecutor for the U.S. before the IMT, acknowledged in his opening statement at the Trials that "[t]here was a time, in fact I think the time of the First World War, when it could not have been said that war inciting or war making was a crime in law, however reprehensible in morals . . . . The age of imperialistic expansion during the eighteenth and nineteenth centuries added the foul doctrine . . . that all wars are to be regarded as legitimate wars." Robert H. Jackson, The Nürnberg Case 82–83 (1971).

219 Kennedy, *supra* note 81, at 127.

220 Amos S. Hershey, The International Law and Diplomacy of the Russo-Japanese War 67 (1906). Similarly, for the English publicist John Westlake, attempts "to determine in the name of international law the conditions on which a recourse may be had to arms, as that an offer of arbitration shall have been made," merely represent "the counsel of morality," not "rules of law." John Westlake, International Law: Part II – War (1907). And the English legal scholar Arnold McNair described the prevailing view before the First World War as holding that "[w]ar itself was no illegality. Its outbreak might sometimes involve the breach of a treaty or some other international wrong, but it more frequently took rise in circumstances not falling within the sphere regulated by law. It was extra-legal rather than illegal." Arnold D. McNair, *Collective Security,* 17 Brit. Y.B. Int'l L. 150, 152 (1936).

> The voluntary or positive law of nations . . . makes no distinctions . . . between a just and an unjust war. A war in form, or duly commenced, is to be considered, as to its effects, as just on both sides. Whatever is permitted by the laws of war to one of the belligerent powers is equally permitted to the other.[221]

War, in this view, was, like diplomacy, merely a neutral instrument of state policy.[222] It was not, and could not be considered, to be criminal, even if it were unquestionably aggressive. Although the French Revolution had introduced (or rather reintroduced[223]) the idea that wars of aggression and conquest were both legally wrongful and criminally punishable, and although the Versailles settlement at the end of the First World War and the Kellogg-Briand Pact of 1928 represented a tentative and partial recovery of those ideas,[224] it was certainly far from settled, before the Nuremberg and Tokyo Trials, that positive international law encoded such a view.[225]

Pre-WWII *jus in bello* was, however, more developed and less controversial.[226] Articles 228-230 of the Versailles Treaty had stipulated for the trial of individual German defendants for violations of the "laws of war," and in fact there had been several prosecutions of German military officers on such charges before German national courts soon after the First World War. (For example, Captain Emil Mueller was tried, convicted and sentenced to six months' imprisonment for the mistreatment of Allied prisoners of war.[227]) The laws of war in question here were partly

221 Henry Wheaton, Elements of International Law: Text of 1866 with Notes, Carnegie Endowment for International Peace, The Classics of International Law, No. 13 at 313–14 (1936).

222 *See* Carl von Clausewitz, On War, Book VIII, ch. 6.B at 731(Michael Howard & Peter Paret ed. & trans. 1984) ("war is simply a continuation of political intercourse, with the addition of other means").

223 Not unlike the post-World War II period, the European Middle Ages were characterized by a fundamentally legalistic manner of thinking about war. *See* William Stubbs, Seventeen Lectures on the Study of Medieval and Modern History 248 (1887) ("Medieval wars are, as a rule, wars of right; they are seldom wars of unprovoked, never wars of absolutely unjustifiable, aggression; they are not wars of idea, of liberation, or of glory, or of nationality, or of propagandism."). For an argument relating the post-First World War settlement to the medieval scholastic tradition of just war thought, *see* Charles van Völlenhoven, The Three Stages in the Evolution of the Law of Nations (1919). *See also* E.H. Carr, The Twenty Years' Crisis 1919–1939 at 174 (1939) ("Since 1919, natural law has resumed its sway, and theories of international law have become more markedly utopian than at any previous time."). Carr however distinguishes the modern form of naturalism from the traditional one, explaining that the former "connotes no longer something external, fixed and invariable, but men's innate feeling at any given time or place for what 'just law' ought to be." *Id.*

224 *See* Grewe, *supra* note 7, at 422–24. One leading recent historian of the period speaks of "th[e] moralization and politicization of international affairs" that began during and immediately after the First World War. "Conventional morality and domestic notions of law had no place in the world of [pre-War] great power diplomacy and war. By breaching this wall, the architects of the new 'world organization' were quite consciously playing the game of revolutionaries." Adam Tooze, The Deluge: The Great War and the Remaking of Global Order, 1916-1931 at 9 (2014).

225 *See, e.g.*, Cassese, *supra* note 217 (describing evolution of views of prominent Italian jurist and President of the Permanent Court of International Justice, Dionisio Anzilotti, in inter-war period).

226 *See* Hersh Lauterpacht, *The Law of Nations and the Punishment of War Crimes*, 21 Brit. Y.B. Int'l L. 58, 61, 64–65 (1944). For an excellent survey of the roots of *jus in bello*, see Timothy L.H. McCormack, *From Sun Tzu to the Sixth Committee: The Evolution of an International Criminal Law Regime, in* The Law of War Crimes: National and International Approaches 31 (Timothy L.H. McCormack & Gerry J. Simpson eds., 1996).

227 *See* Claude Mullins, The Leipzig Trials: An Account of the War Criminals' Trials and Study of German Mentality (London, 1921); Geo. Gordon Battle, *The Trials before the Leipsic Supreme Court of Germans Accused of War Crimes*, 8 Va.

codified in the great Hague and Geneva Conventions, and partly based on centuries of military customs and practices. Indeed, this body of law, known today also as "international humanitarian law," was widely understood to be based largely on unwritten custom. The so-called "Martens Clause" in the preamble to the 1899 Hague Convention on the Laws and Customs of Land War[228] stated, in language that has regularly been repeated in treaties since then, that:

> Until a more complete code of the laws of war is issued, the High Contracting Parties think it right to declare that in cases not included in the Regulations adopted by them, populations and belligerents remain under the protection and empire of the principles of international law, as they result from the usages established between civilized nations, from the laws of humanity, and the requirements of the public conscience.

The Martens Clause provides a glimpse of the law that was to emerge from the Nuremberg and Tokyo Trials. In particular, by declaring that "populations . . . remain under the protection and empire of the principles of international law," it anticipates the post-Nuremberg view that civilian populations can assert rights directly under international law to protection against extreme abuses at the enemy's hands during wartime.[229] A path goes from the Martens Clause to the *Shimoda* Case.

3. Traditional International Law in the IMT and IMTFE

Much of the interest (and tension) in the IMT and IMTFE opinions reflects the difficulty of fitting the law that was emerging from those decisions into the traditional international legal framework. At the most fundamental level, the Trials posed a powerful challenge to the traditional idea of "sovereignty." Indeed, they can be said to have reconfigured that concept entirely.[230]

L. Rev. 1 (1921); *see generally* Gary Jonathan Bass, Stay the Hand of Vengeance: The Politics of War Crimes Tribunals 58–105 (2000) (overview of legal and political planning for post-First World War trials). These trials are considered a "dismal failure, with only a handful of convictions with light sentences or acquitals [sic] resulting in nine cases, instead of a total of 901 original cases out forward by the Allies." Antonio Cassese, *Reflections on International Criminal Justice,* 61 Mod. L. Rev. 1, 7 (1998).

228 On the meaning and history of the Martens Clause, *see* Antonio Cassese, *The Martens Clause: Half a Loaf or Simply Pie in the Sky?,* 11 Eur. Journal of Int'l Law 197 (2000); Theodore Meron, *The Martens Clause, Principles of Humanity, and Dictates of Public Conscience,* 94 Am. J. Int'l L. 78 (2000); and Chris af Jochnik & Roger Normand, *The Legitimation of Violence: A Critical History of the Laws of War,* 35 Harv. Int'l L. J. 49, 74–76 (1994).

229 *See* Jeremy Sarkin, *The Historical Origins, Convergence and Interrelationship of International Human Rights Law, International Humanitarian Law, International Criminal Law and Public International Law and their Application from at least the Nineteenth Century,* 1 Hum. Rts. & Int'l Leg. Discourse 1 (2007).

230 Nuremberg contributed significantly to the demise of the pre-War doctrine of sovereignty, especially as it related to war. Reflecting the new spirit of international legal scholarship in the immediate aftermath of the Second World War, Philip Jessup observed in 1946 that "[s]overeignty, in its meaning of an absolute, uncontrolled state will, ultimately free to resort to the final arbitrament of war, is the quicksand upon which the foundations of traditional international law are

In order to understand the revolutionary legal implications of the Trials, let us begin by analyzing the charges they involved. Both at Nuremberg and at Tokyo, those charges fell into three main categories. First, they were charged with various offenses relating to the alleged crime of waging a *war of aggression.* (These charges were intended to be the core of the prosecution's case and, if sustained, to become the Trials greatest contribution to the evolution of international law.[231]) Second, they were charged with various *crimes against humanity* occurring in, or related to, the war. (This group of charges in fact became the Trials' most lasting legal legacy.[232]) And third, they were charged with *war crimes*, or offenses against the (more or less traditional) *jus in bello.*

The first category of charges (also called *crimes against peace*) was all but unprecedented. As we have seen, the prevailing view before the Second World War had been that the decision

---

built." Philip Jessup, A Modern Law of Nations: An Introduction 2 (1946); *see also id.* at 157 ("The most dramatic weakness of traditional international law has been its admission that a state may use force to compel compliance with its will."). *See also* Louis Henkin, *That "S" Word: Sovereignty, and Globalization, and Human Rights, Et cetera,* 68 Fordham L. Rev. 1, 3–4 (1999) ("Until 1945, sovereignty, political independence and territorial impermeability meant that how a state treated its own inhabitants was not a subject of international concern. How a state treated its own inhabitants was nobody else's business. That was Hitler. The world stood by, and had nothing to say about it. International law said nothing about it. What went on behind territorial frontiers was cloaked by an iron curtain of sovereignty. The international human rights movement, born during the Second World War, has represented a significant erosion of state sovereignty. And it took Hitler and the Holocaust to achieve that. Since 1945, how a state treats its own citizens, how it behaves even in its own territory, has no longer been its own business; it has become a matter of international concern, of international politics, and of international law.").

231 *See* Bernard D. Meltzer, *Robert H. Jackson: Nuremberg's Architect and Advocate,* 68 Alb. L. Rev. 55, 58 (2004) (former Assistant Trial Counsel for the U.S. Prosecution at the Trials stating that the charge of conspiring to commit crimes against the peace "was viewed as the core of the entire case"); *see also* Edward M. Wise, *The Significance of Nuremberg,* in Belinda Cooper (ed.), War Crimes: The Legacy of Nuremberg 55, 58 (1999) ("At the time . . . the central charges of Nuremberg were supposed to be those of crimes against peace and conspiracy to wage aggressive war. These were characterized by one of the U.S. prosecutors (Sidney Alderman) as 'the heart of the case.' In the very first words of his eloquent opening statement, [U.S. Chief Prosecutor] Justice Jackson referred to 'the privilege of opening the first trial in history for crimes against the peace of the world . . . ' For Jackson and others, the principal legal construct, of the Nuremberg trial was the criminalization of aggressive war. Aggression, said the tribunal's judgment, . . . is 'the supreme international crime.'"); Robert H. Jackson, *Nürnberg in Retrospect,* 27 Canadian Bar Rev. 761, 780 (1949) (summarizing the effects of Nuremberg and stating, "I do think that we have forever laid to rest in the minds of statesmen the vicious assumptions that all war must be regarded as legal and just, and that while the law imposes personal responsibility for starting a street riot, it imposes none for inciting and launching a world war"); and Max Radin, *Justice at Nuremberg,* 24 For. Aff. 369, 376 (1946) (the "greatest prominence" was given to the charge of crimes against the peace, and "it is to these crimes that the largest part of the formal indictment is directed"). In this respect, at least, the Nuremberg Trials may be considered a failure. "No indictment for crimes against peace . . . has followed" the Nuremberg Trials. See Yoram Dinstein, War, Aggression and Self-Defence 110 (3d ed. 2001); *see also* John F. Murphy, Crimes Against Peace at the Nuremberg Trial, *in The Nuremberg Trial and International Law* 141, 153 (George Ginsburgs and V.N. Kudriatsev eds., 1990) ("no prosecutions for crimes against peace have been brought in national courts, and very few countries have made crimes against peace a part of their national criminal codes. In short, from an operational perspective, crimes against peace is a dead letter."). The Statute of the Iraqi Special Tribunal, which tried Saddam Hussein and other ranking Iraqi government defendants, did not give the Tribunal jurisdiction over crimes against the peace, notwithstanding Saddam's invasion of Kuwait. See Coalition Provisional Authority, The Statute of the Iraqi Special Tribunal, Section Three ("Jurisdiction and Crimes") *(available at* http://www.cpa-iraq.org/cgi-bin/prfriendly.cgi?http://www.cpa-iraq.org/human_rights/Stat.).

232 *See* Geoffrey Robertson, Crimes Against Humanity: The Struggle for Global Justice 252 (rev. ed. 2007) ("the great achievement of Nuremberg was count four; the crime against humanity""): *see also* Wise, *supra* note 231, at 58 (the "crowning moral and legal achievement" of the Trials was the prosecution of crimes against humanity); Stephen Breyer, *Crimes Against Humanity, Nuremberg 1946,* 71 N.Y.U. L. Rev. 1161 (1996).

whether to wage war or not was a matter of state sovereignty that could not be judicially reviewed by another other sovereign state or even by the international community at large. Indeed, major powers before the War, including both the United States and Great Britain, had found severe, if not insuperable, difficulties in defining the concept of "aggression."[233] Even to this day, major states, including the United States, have chafed at codifying it in an international criminal code.[234] The second category also represented an innovation, at least insofar as states had previously been thought not to be judicially accountable for the violence—even in the form of mass atrocities—that they practiced against their own citizens or subjects. On that understanding, the Nazi defendants could not be tried for the mass murder and imprisonment of German Jews, German Communists or other German nationals, particularly if those atrocities occurred before the start of the war on September 1, 1939.[235] To meet that legal difficulty, the prosecution at Nuremberg sought to link the Nazis' pre-War atrocities, or at any rate many of them, to the Nazi government's preparations for the War.[236] As discussed above, the third category, unlike the first two, was well established in international law before the start of the

---

233 *See* Denys P. Myers, Origin and Conclusion of the Paris Peace Pact: The Renunciation of War as an Instrument of National Policy 41–42 (1929) (quoting views of British Foreign Minister Sir Austen Chamberlain in the House of Commons, Nov. 24, 1927). U.S. Secretary of State Kellogg, in an address to the Council on Foreign Relations on March 15, 1928, expressly agreed with Chamberlain, noting "the absence of any satisfactory definition of the word 'aggressor' or the phrase 'wars of aggression,'" and finding it "difficult . . . to see how a definition could be agreed upon which would not be open to abuse." Secretary of State Kellogg, *The War Prevention Policy of the United States* (March 15, 1928), reprinted in James Thayer Gerould, Selected Articles on the Pact of Paris, Officially the General Pact for the Renunciation of War 98, 108 (1929). Moreover, in remarks to the American Society of International Law on April 28, 1928, Kellogg emphasized that the right of national self-defense was "inherent," "inalienable" and "implicit in every treaty," and that each state "alone is competent to decide whether circumstances require recourse to war in self-defense." Secretary of State Kellogg, *The French Draft of the Multilateral Treaty for the Renunciation of War, reprinted in id.* at 112, 113. Kellogg's speech "was ultimately made a part of the official record and will stand alongside the treaty as an authoritative commentary." James T. Shotwell, War as an Instrument of National Policy and Its Renunciation in the Pact of Paris 157 (1929).

234 As realists might have predicted, the United States, like other dominant powers of the past, has become reluctant to accept strict international legal restraints on its ability to use force. *See* Krisch, *supra* note 105, at 394; *see also* Shirley V. Scott, *Is There Room for International Law in Realpolitik? Accounting for the US 'Attitude' Towards International Law*, 30 Rev. Int'l Stud. 71, 83–84, 88 (2004).

235 *See* Quincy Wright, World's Destiny and the United States 105 (1941) (Because Germany had not concluded a minority treaty with the League of Nations, "there was no formal ground on which the League of Nations could protest against the beginning of the persecutions in Germany. It was a general principle that a State was free to persecute its own nationals in its own territory as it saw fit.").

236 "[O]ut of concern that they might also be accused of crimes against humanity directed against minority populations within their own territories, or those of their colonies, the four great powers who created the Nuremberg Tribunal limited the scope of the crime [against humanity] to acts committed in association with the waging of an aggressive war. Known to specialists as the 'nexus,' the practical consequence was that no Nazis were convicted at Nuremberg for acts perpetrated prior to the outbreak of the war, on 1 September 1939. . . . The final judgment of the International Military Tribunal confirmed the limited scope of crimes against humanity that had been intended by the four great powers. Although the judgment referred to Nazi atrocities in the 1930s, such as the *Kristallnacht* and the dissemination of the anti-Semitic *Der Sturmer* . . . no convictions were registered for acts committed prior to the formal outbreak of the war." William A. Schabas, Preventing Genocide and Mass Killing: The Challenge for the United Nations 8 (Minority Rights Group International 2006). *See also* Robert Cryer, Prosecuting International Crimes: Selectivity and the International Criminal Regime 206 (2005) (attributing the jurisdictional nexus to war in the crimes against humanity charges to Allied concerns that without it, "not only could colonialism embarrassing for France and the United Kingdom), or the Gulags (still a secret in the USSR) be evaluated with reference to the law, but so could the segregationist policies in the United States").

Second World War. (We return to the question of the prosecution of "aggressive war in Part IV of this volume.)

a. The Nuremberg Trials and the Law of War: Study Questions Before Reading the IMT Opinion

1) How was the International Military Tribunal (IMT) at Nuremberg created? What is the source of its authority? Is it international law? If so, what kind? Is it municipal law, that is to say, the internal law of Germany? Is it both? What about the U.S. Military Tribunals at Nuremberg? Were they U.S. courts or international courts? Were they created under a delegation from the government of occupied Germany? Or had the state of Germany ceased to exist? What are the principles of the law of occupation that bear on these questions? (Hint: *See* Hague Regulations of 1907, art. 42.)

2) What is the meaning of the principle *nullum crimen since lege*? Is it relevant to the IMT's analysis? Is it necessary to the IMT's analysis? Is it a part of international law, domestic law, or both? (Hint: *See* Statute of the Permanent Court of International Justice (the PCIJ), art. 38.)

3) What treaties does the IMT cite for its determinations regarding the legality of aggressive war by states? Do these treaties establish rules of conduct? Do they provide for specific sanctions or remedies? What is the status of these treaties after the commencement of the war? Does the rule bind all states? Why? Why not? (*See generally* Vienna Convention on the Law of Treaties (1970) (the VCLT), arts. 26–32, 34–36, 46, 58, 60–64, and 70–75.) The VCLT, which was adopted in 1970, sets forth rules that are for the most part deemed restatements of the customary international law of treaties. Do you see any exceptions in the VCLT that bear on the foregoing questions?

4) How does the IMT ground its separate conclusion that individuals, and not merely states, can bear legal responsibility for violation of the rule prohibiting aggressive war? What sources does it rely upon? What analogies does it employ? (Hint: *See Shimoda*, below.)

5) How does the IMT describe the basis for, and limits on, any possible superior orders defense to individual criminal responsibility? At the time the IMT rendered its decision, was this doctrine part of international law, domestic law, or both? (*See*

International Law Commission's Articles on State Responsibility, art. 58; *International Law Commission's Principles of International Law Recognized in the Charter of the Nurnberg Tribunal and in the Judgment of the Tribunal,* Yearbook of the United Nations, vol II., p. 374–75 (1950)); *see also* PCIJ Statute, art. 38.)

b. The Text of the IMT Opinion[237]

The jurisdiction of the Tribunal is defined in the Agreement and Charter, and the crimes coming within the jurisdiction of the Tribunal, for which there shall be individual responsibility, are set out in Article 6. The law of the Charter is decisive, and binding upon the Tribunal.

The making of the Charter was the exercise of the sovereign legislative power by the countries to which the German Reich unconditionally surrendered; and the undoubted right of these countries to legislate for the occupied territories has been recognised by the civilised world. The Charter is not an arbitrary exercise of power on the part of the victorious nations, but in the view of the Tribunal, as will be shown, it is the expression of international law existing at the time of its creation; and to that extent is itself a contribution to international law.

The Signatory Powers created this Tribunal, defined the law it was to administer, and made regulations for the proper conduct of the Trial. In doing so, they have done together what any one of them might have done singly; for it is not to be doubted that any nation has the right thus to set up special courts to administer law. With regard to the constitution of the court, all that the defendants are entitled to ask is to receive a fair trial on the facts and law.

The Charter makes the planning or waging of a war of aggression or a war in violation of international treaties a crime, and it is therefore not strictly necessary to consider whether and to what extent aggressive war was a crime before the execution of the London Agreement. But in view of the great importance of the questions of law involved, the Tribunal has heard full argument from the Prosecution and the Defence, and will express its view on the matter.

It was urged on behalf of the defendants that a fundamental principle of all law -international and domestic- is that there can be no punishment of crime without a pre-existing law. "Nullum crimen sine lege, nulla poena sine lege." It was submitted that ex post facto punishment is abhorent to the law of all civilised nations, that no sovereign power had made aggressive war a crime at the time the alleged criminal acts were committed, that no statute had defined aggressive war, that no penalty had been fixed for its commission, and no court had been created to try and punish offenders.

In the first place, it is to be observed that the maxim nullum crimen sine lege is not a limitation of sovereignty, but is in general a principle of justice. To assert that it is unjust to punish those who in defiance of treaties and assurances have attacked neighbouring states without

237 1 Trial of the Major War Criminals before the International Military Tribunal 218–24 (1947) (*available at* http://www.loc.gov/rr/frd/Military_Law/pdf/NT_Vol-I.pdf).

warning is obviously untrue, for in such circumstances the attacker must know that he is doing wrong, and so far from it being unjust to punish him, it would be unjust if his wrong were allowed to go unpunished. Occupying the positions they did in the government of Germany, the defendants, or at least some of them must have known of the treaties signed by Germany, outlawing recourse to war for the settlement of international disputes; they must have known that they were acting in defiance of all international law when in complete deliberation they carried out the designs of invasion and aggression. On this view of the case alone, it would appear that the maxim has no application to the present facts.

This view is strongly reinforced by a consideration of the state of international law in 1939, so far as aggressive war is concerned. The General Treaty for the Renunciation of War of 27th August, 1928, more generally known as the Pact of Paris or the Kellogg-Briand Pact, was binding on sixty-three nations, including Germany, Italy and Japan at the outbreak of war in 1939. In the preamble, the signatories declared that they were:

> "Deeply sensible of their solemn duty to promote the welfare of mankind; persuaded that the time has come when a frank renunciation of war as an instrument of national policy should be made to the end that the peaceful and friendly relations now existing between their peoples should be perpetuated . . . all changes in their relations with one another should be sought only by pacific means . . . thus uniting civilised nations of the world in a common renunciation of war as an instrument of their national policy . . . ."

The first two Articles are as follows:

> "Article I: The High Contracting Parties solemnly declare in the names of their respective peoples that they condemn recourse to war for the solution of international controversies and renounce it as an instrument of national policy in their relations to one another."

> "Article II: The High Contracting Parties agree that the settlement or solution of all disputes or conflicts of whatever nature or of whatever origin they may be, which may arise among them, shall never be sought except by pacific means."

The question is, what was the legal effect of this Pact? The nations who signed the Pact or adhered to it unconditionally condemned recourse to war for the future as an instrument of policy, and expressly renounced it. After the signing of the Pact, any nation resorting to war as an instrument of national policy breaks the Pact. In the opinion of the Tribunal, the solemn renunciation of war as an instrument of national policy necessarily involves the proposition that such a war is illegal in international law; and that those who plan and wage such a war, with its inevitable and terrible consequences, are committing a crime in so doing. War for the solution of international controversies undertaken as an instrument of national policy certainly includes a war of aggression, and such a war is therefore outlawed by the Pact. As Mr. Henry L. Stimson, then Secretary of State of the United States, said in 1932:-

> "War between nations was renounced by the signatories of the Kellogg-Briand Treaty. This means that it has become throughout practically the entire world ... an illegal thing. Hereafter, when nations engage in armed conflict, either one or both of them must be termed violators of this general treaty law.... We denounce them as law breakers."

But it is argued that the Pact does not expressly enact that such wars are crimes, or set up courts to try those who make such wars. To that extent the same is true with regard to the laws of war contained in the Hague Convention. The Hague Convention of 1907 prohibited resort to certain methods of waging war. These included the inhumane treatment of prisoners, the employment of poisoned weapons, the improper use of flags of truce, and similar matters. Many of these prohibitions had been enforced long before the date of the Convention; but since 1907 they have certainly been crimes, punishable as offences against the laws of war; yet the Hague Convention nowhere designates such practices as criminal, nor is any sentence prescribed, nor any mention made of a court to try and punish offenders. For many years past, however, military tribunals have tried and punished individuals guilty of violating the rules of land warfare laid down by this Convention. In the opinion of the Tribunal, those who wage aggressive war are doing that which is equally illegal, and of much greater moment than a breach of one of the rules of the Hague Convention. In interpreting the words of the Pact, it must be remembered that international law is not the product of an international legislature, and that such international agreements as the Pact have to deal with general principles of law, and not with administrative matters of procedure. The law of war is to be found not only in treaties, but in the customs and practices of states which gradually obtained universal recognition, and from the general principles of justice applied by jurists and practiced by military courts. This law is not static, but by continual adaptation follows the needs of a changing world. Indeed, in many cases treaties do no more than express and define for more accurate reference the principles of law already existing.

The view which the Tribunal takes of the true interpretation of the Pact is supported by the international history which preceded it. In the year 1923 the draft of a Treaty of Mutual Assistance was sponsored by the League of Nations. In Article I the Treaty declared "that aggressive war is an international crime," and that the parties would "undertake that no one of them will be guilty of its commission." The draft treaty was submitted to twenty-nine States, about half of whom were in favour of accepting the text. The principal objection appeared to be in the difficulty of defining the acts which would constitute "aggression," rather than any doubt as to the criminality of aggressive war. The preamble to the League of Nations 1924 Protocol for the Pacific Settlement of International Disputes ("Geneva Protocol"), after "recognising the solidarity of the members of the international community," declared that "a war of aggression constitutes a violation of this solidarity and is an international crime." It went on to declare that the contracting parties were "desirous of facilitating the complete application of the system provided in the Covenant of the League of Nations for the pacific settlement of disputes between the states and of ensuring the repression of international crimes." The Protocol was recommended to the members of the League of Nations by a unanimous resolution in the Assembly of the forty-eight members of the League. These members included Italy and Japan, but Germany was not then a member of the League.

Although the Protocol was never ratified, it was signed by the leading statesmen of the world, representing the vast majority of the civilised states and peoples, and may be regarded as strong evidence of the intention to brand aggressive war as an international crime.

At the meeting of the Assembly of the League of Nations on the 24th September, 1927, all the delegations then present (including the German, the Italian and the Japanese), unanimously adopted a declaration concerning wars of aggression. The preamble to the declaration stated:

> "The Assembly:
>
> Recognising the solidity which unites the community of nations;
>
> Being "inspired by a firm desire for the maintenance of general peace;
>
> Being convinced that a war of aggression can never serve as a means of settling international disputes, and is in consequence an international crime...."

The unanimous resolution of the 18th February, 1928, of twenty-one American Republics of the Sixth (Havana) Pan-American Conference, declared that "war of aggression constitutes an international crime against the human species."

All these expressions of opinion, and others that could be cited, so solemnly made, reinforce the construction which, the Tribunal placed upon the Pact of Paris, that resort to a war of aggression is not merely illegal, but is criminal. The prohibition of aggressive war demanded by the conscience of the world, finds its expression in the series of pacts and treaties to which the Tribunal has just referred.

It is also important to remember that Article 227 of the Treaty of Versailles provided for the constitution of a special Tribunal, composed of representatives of five of the Allied and Associated Powers which had been belligerents in the first World War opposed to Germany, to try the former German Emperor "for a supreme offence against international morality and the sanctity of treaties." The purpose of this trial was expressed to be "to vindicate the solemn obligations of international undertakings, and the validity of international morality." In Article 228 of the Treaty, the German Government expressly recognized the right of the Allied Powers "to bring before military tribunals persons accused of having committed acts in violation of the laws and customs of war."

It was submitted that international law is concerned with the action of sovereign States, and provides no punishment for individuals; and further, that where the act in question is an act of state, those who carry it out are not personally responsible, but are protected by the doctrine of the sovereignty of the State. In the opinion of the Tribunal, both these submissions must be rejected. That international law imposes duties and liabilities upon individuals as well as upon States has long been recognised. In the recent case of Ex Parte Quirin (1942 317 US 1), before the Supreme Court of the United States persons were charged during the war with landing in the United States for purposes of spying and sabotage. The late Justice Stone, speaking for the Court, said:

> "From the very beginning of its history this Court has applied the law of war as including that part of the law of nations which prescribes for the conduct of war the status, rights and duties of enemy nations as well as enemy individuals."

He went on to give a list of cases tried by the Courts, where individual offenders were charged with offences against the laws of nations, and particularly, the laws of war. Many other authorities could be quoted, but enough has been said to show that individuals can be punished for violations of international law. Crimes against international law are committed by men, not by abstract entities, and only by punishing individuals who commit such crimes can the provisions of international law be enforced.

The provisions of Article 228 of the Treaty of Versailles already referred to illustrate and enforce this view of individual responsibility.

The principle of international law, which under certain circumstances, protects the representatives of a state, cannot be applied to acts which are condemned as criminal by international law. The authors of these facts cannot shelter themselves behind their official position in order to be freed from punishment in appropriate proceedings. Article 7 of the Chanter expressly declares:

> "The official position of defendants, whether as Heads of State, or responsible officials in government departments, shall not be considered as freeing them from responsibility, or mitigating punishment."

On the other hand the very essence of the Charter is that individuals have international duties which transcend the national obligations of obedience imposed by the individual State. He who violates the laws of war cannot obtain immunity while acting in pursuance of the authority of the State if the State in authorising action moves outside its competence under international law.

It was also submitted on behalf of most of these defendants that in doing what they did they were acting under the orders of Hitler, and therefore cannot be held responsible for the acts committed by them in carrying out these orders. The Charter specially provides in Article 8:

> "The fact that the defendant acted pursuant to order of his Government or of a superior shall not free him from responsibility, but may be considered in mitigation of punishment."

The provisions of this Article are in conformity with the law of all nations. That a soldier was ordered to kill or torture in violation of the international law of war this never been recognised as a defence to such acts of brutality, though, as the Charter here provides, the order may be urged in mitigation of the punishment. The true test, which is found in varying degrees in the criminal law of most nations, is not the existence of the order, but whether moral choice was in fact possible.

c. The Tokyo Trials and the Law of War: Study Questions Before Reading Justice Pal's Dissent

1) What is Justice Pal's view of the basic procedural legitimacy of the International Military Tribunal for the Far East (the IMTFE)? In his view, what conditions would need to be met before the IMTFE, or any similar Tribunal, could be deemed legitimate?

2) What sources does he cite for his views on the views on the legitimacy of the procedure? What do you think he is trying to accomplish rhetorically? Why does Justice Pal participate in a procedure he personally deems illegitimate?

3) How does Justice Pal view the question of individual responsibility for acts of state? To what degree does he accept the idea of individual responsibility for war crimes? How does he relate these views to the jurisdiction of the IMTFE?

4) What is Justice Pal's view of the status of the sources cited by the prosecution for establishing the existence of a crime of aggressive war? Can you identify the criterion he relies on for finding sources that would have legal significance?

d. The Text of Justice Pal's Dissent (Paragraphs 9-15 & 134-145)[238]

According to Dr. Glueck the time has arrived in the life of civilised nations when an international custom should be taken to have developed to hold aggressive war to be an international crime. He insists that an issue of this kind ought not to be disposed of on the basis of blind legalistic conceptualism; it should be dealt with realistically in the light of the practical as well as logical result to which one or the other solution will lead.

Mr. Trainin relies principally on the Moscow Proclamation of October 30, 1943 and emphasises that this marks a new era of development of social life in international community. According to him to facilitate this process of development and to strengthen these new ideas, juridical thought is obliged to forge the right form for these new relations, to work out a new system of international law, and, as an indissoluble part of this system, to direct the conscience of nations to the problems of criminal responsibility for attempts on the foundations of international relations.

In my view, international society has not yet reached the stage where the consequences contemplated by these learned authors would follow.

Even after the formation of the League of Nations we had only a group of coordinated states with their sovereignty intact. The best account of the developments of international society is given by Professor Zimmern in his book entitled "The League of Nations and the Rule of Law." Dr. Schwarzenberger also takes the same view.

> "People learned from the war only 'to substitute the nation of organic association between independent, self-governing and cooperatively minded peoples.' Democracy and centralization do not, it is said belong to the same order of ideas. They are, in essence, as incompatible as freedom and slavery. The League of Nations thus 'while morally a great effort of faith was administratively a great effort of decentralization.'"

It was simply a system of international cooperation.

> "The high contracting parties in order to promote international cooperation and to achieve international peace and security by the acceptance of obligations not to resort to war, by the prescription of open, just and honorable relations between nations, by the firm establishment of the understandings of international law as the actual rule of conduct among governments, and by the maintenance of justice and a scrupulous respect for all treat obligations in the dealings of organised peoples with one another, agreed to this covenant of the League of Nations."

238 Documents on the Tokyo International Military Tribunal: Charter, Indictment, and Judgments, *supra* note 77, at 866–71.

No international community of any higher order came into being. The League showed particularly scrupulous regard for national sovereignty and laid special emphasis on such sovereignty by adopting the principle of unanimous vote. National sovereignty and national interest continued to play the fundamental part in this organisation.

There has no doubt been, since the outbreak of the World War, a feeling on the part of many writers that there should be some restatement of the fundamental principles of international law in terms of international life.

At the same time it must be said that this is yet to happen. The international organisation as it now stands still does not indicate any sign of abrogation of the doctrine of national sovereignty in the near future.

As to the "Widening sense of humanity" prevailing in international life, all that I can say is that at least before the Second World War the powerful nations did not show any such sign. I would only refer to what happened at the meeting of the Committee drafting resolutions for the establishment of the League of Nations when Baron Makino of Japan moved a resolution for the declaration of the equality of nations as a basic principle of the League. Lord Robert Cecil of Great Britain declared this to be a matter of highly controversial character and opposed the resolution on the ground that it "raised extremely serious problems within the British Empire." The resolution was declared lost: President Wilson ruled that in view of the serious objections on the part of some it was not carried.

Coupled with this, if we take the fact that there still continued domination of one nation by another, that servitude of nation still prevailed unreviled and that domination of one nation by another continued to be regarded by the so-called international community only as a domestic question for the master nation, I cannot see how such a community can even pretend that its basis is humanity. In this connection I cannot refrain from referring to what Mr. Justice Jackson asserted in his summing up of the case at Nuremberg. According to him, a preparation by a nation to dominate another nation is the worst of crimes. This may be so now. But I do not see how it could be said that such an attempt or preparation was a crime before the Second World War when there was hardly a big power which was free from that taint. Instead of saying that all the powerful nations were living a criminal life I would prefer to hold that international society did not develop before the Second World War so as to make this taint a crime.

The atom bomb during the Second World War, it is said, has destroyed selfish nationalism and the last defense of isolationism more completely than it razed an enemy city. It is believed that it has ended one age and begun another - the new and unpredictable age of soul.

> "Such blasts as leveled Hiroshima and Nagasaki on August 6 and 9, 1945, never occurred on earth before nor in the sun or stars, which burn from sources that release their energy much more slowly than does Uranium." So said John J. O'Neill, the Science Editor, New York Herald Tribune. "In a fraction of a second the atomic bomb that dropped on Hiroshima altered our traditional

> economic, political, and military values. It caused a revolution in the technique of war that forces immediate reconsideration of our entire national defense problem."

Perhaps these blasts have brought home to mankind "that every human being has a stake in the conduct not only of national affairs but also of world affairs". Perhaps those explosives have awakened within us the sense of unity of mankind, the feeling that:

> "We are a unity of humanity, linked to all our fellow human beings, irrespective of race, creed or color, by bonds which have been fused unbreakably in the diabolical heat of those explosions."

All this might have been the result of these blasts. But certainly these feelings were nonexistent at the time when the bombs were dropped. I, for myself, do not perceive any such feeling of broad humanity in the justifying words of those who were responsible for their use. As a matter of fact, I do not perceive much difference between what the German Emperor is alleged to have announced during the First World War in justification of the atrocious methods directed by him in the conduct of that war and what is being proclaimed after the Second World War in justification of these inhuman blasts.

I am not sure if the atom bombs have really succeeded in blowing away all the pre-war humbugs; we may be just dreaming. It is yet to be seen how far we have been alive to the fact that the world's present problems are not merely the more complex reproductions of those which have plagued us since 1914; that the new problems are not merely old national problems with world implications, but are real world problems and problems of humanity,

There is no doubt that the international society, if any, has been taken ill. Perhaps the situation is that the nations of the international group are living in an age of transition to a planned society.

But that is a matter for the future and perhaps is only a dream.

The dream of all students of world politics is to reduce the complex interplay of forces to a few elementary constants and variables by the use of which all the past is made plain and even the future stands revealed in lucid simplicity. Let us hope it is capable of realization in actual life. I must, however, leave this future to itself with the remark that this future prospect will not in the least be affected even if the existing law be not strained so as to fix any criminal responsibility for state acts on the individual authors thereof in order to make the criminality of states more effective. The future may certainly rely on adequate future provisions in this respect made by the organisers of such future.

During and after the present war, many eminent authors have come forward with contributions containing illuminating views on the subject of "War Criminals-their Prosecution and Punishment". None of these books and none of the prosecutions professed to be prompted by any desire for retaliation. Most of these contributors claim to have undertaken the task because "miscarriage of justice" after World War I shocked them very much, particularly because such failure was ascribable to the instrumentality of jurists who deserved the epithets of being "stiff-necked conceptualists," "strict constructionists," and men "afflicted with an ideological rigor mortis." These Jurists, it is said, by giving the appearance of legality and logic to arguments based on some unrealistic, outworn and basically irrelevant technicality caused the greatest confusion in the minds of ordinary laymen with regard to the problems of war criminals. These, it is claimed, were the chief present-day obstacles to the just solution of the problem and these authors have done their best to remove such obstacles and to supply "not a mere textbook on some remote technically intricate phrase of a branch of law," but "a weapon with which to enforce respect for the tenets of international law with its underlying principles of international justice."

Some of these authors have correctly said that law is not merely a conglomeration of human wisdom in the form of rules to be applied wherever and whenever such rules, like pieces in a jigsaw puzzle, may fit in. "Law is instead a dynamic human force regulating behaviour between man and man and making the existence and continuity of human society possible." Its chief characteristic is that it sterns from man's reasonableness and from his innate sense of justice.

> "Stability and consistency are essential attributes of rules of law, no doubt."

Says such an author:

> "Precedent is the sine qua non of an orderly legal system.
>
> But one must be certain that the precedent has undoubted relevancy and complete applicability to the new station or to the given set of facts. And if applicable precedent is not available, a new precedent must be formed, for at all times law must seek to found itself on common sense and must strive for human justice."

With all respect to these learned authors, there is a very big assumption in all these observations when made in connection with international law. In our quest for international law, are we dealing with an entity like national societies completely brought under the rule of law? Or, are we dealing with an inchoate society in a stage of its formation? It is a society where only that rule has come to occupy the position of law which has been unanimously agreed upon by the parties concerned. Any new precedent made will not be the law safeguarding the peace-loving, law-abiding members of the Family of Nations, but will only be a precedent for the future victor against the future vanquished. Any misapplication of a doubtful legal doctrine here will threaten the very formation of the much coveted Society of Nations, will shake the very foundation of any future international society.

Law is a dynamic human force only when it is the law of an organised society; when it is to be the sum of the conditions of social coexistence with regard to the activity of the community and of the individual. Law stems from a man's reasonableness and from his innate sense of justice. But what is that law? And is international law of that character?

A national society, as I have pointed out above, from the very circumstances of its origin and development, is aware of the bearing of the interests of its own members upon the universal objects of general-humanity, and is thus bound to regard other national societies not only as entitled to rights equal with its own, but as supplementing itself. A national state cannot therefore seek any absolute seclusion, or strive after an absolute self-sufficiency. In this, from the very moment of the origin of national states, international society also came into existence. This also accounts for the circumstance that the period of national states is also marked by the development of the system of international law.

Yet it is difficult to say that this international society is a society under the reign of law. I shall quote extensively from Professor Zimmern, where he very ably and truly characterises international society.

"For anyone", says Professor Zimmern, "trained in the British tradition, the term International Law embodies a conception which is, at its best, confusing and at its worst exasperating. It is never law as we understand it, and it often, as it seems to us, comes dangerously near to being an imposter, a simulacrum of law, an attorney's mantle artfully displayed on the shoulders of arbiter's power.

"A satisfactory political system, in British eyes, is the offspring of a harmonious marriage between law and force. It is the essence of what we call British Constitutionalism. By it is ensured working of two processes, separable in theory for the analysis of the political scientist, but inextricably blended in practice, the observance of the law, or, to use the language of best war controversy, `sanctions' and `peaceful change'. Thus the judge, the legislator and the executive throughout its range, from the Prime Minister to the policeman, form interdependent parts of a single system.

"This constitutional system does not function because it is wound up from outside or impelled from above. Its driving force is supplied from within. It derives its validity from consent; and its energy is constantly renewed and refreshed by contact with public opinion. It is the popular will which the legislature is seeking to embody in appropriate statutes. It is the popular will which the judge is engaged in interpreting and the policeman in enforcing. All these are performing what is felt to be social function. They are adapting the organization of the state, which is the most continuous and potent agency of social service in the community to the permanent and changing needs of society.

> "Seen as a part of this larger whole, law may be defined as social habit formulated into regulations. When these regulations, if any part of them, are felt to be anti-social, no longer in

accordance with the general sentiment of the day, or even repugnant to it, they are changed. Thus the notion of taw and the notion of change, so far from being incompatible, are, in fact, complementary. The law is not a solid construction of dead material, a fixed and permanent monument, it is an integral part of a living and developing society created and transmitted by men.

"Turn now to international law, what do we find? A situation almost exactly the opposite of what has just been described.

"To begin with, where are we to look for the rules and obligations of international law? We shall not find then embodied in the habits of the will, still less in the affections, of a society.

"International law, in fact, is a law without a constitution. And since it is not grounded in a constitution it lacks the possibility of natural growth. Unconnected with a society, it cannot adjust itself to its needs. It cannot gather itself together by imperceptible stages into a system.

"The reason for this is very simple. The rules of international law, as they existed previous to 1914, were, with a few exceptions, not the outcome of the experience of the working of a world society. They were simply the result of the contacts between a number of selfregarding political units-states whose courses, as they moved majestically through a neutral firmament, crossed one another from time to time. The multiplication of these external impacts or collisions rendered it mutually convenient to bring their occasions under review and to frame rules for dealing with them."

In my judgment this is where the international law stands even now and will stand unless and until the political units agree to yield their sovereignty and form themselves into a society. As I have shown elsewhere, the post war United Nations Organization is certainly a material step towards the formation of such a society. I know that as a judge, it is not for me to preach the need for a wider social consciousness or to propound practical solutions for the problems involved in the material interdependence of the modern world. Yet the international relation has reached a stage where even a judge cannot remain silent though the task that is given him is only one of formulation, classification and interpretation. I believe with Professor Lauterpacht that it is high time that international law should recognise the individual as its ultimate subject and maintenance of his rights as its ultimate end. "The individual human being--his welfare and the freedom of his personality in its manifold manifestations -- is the ultimate subject of all law. A law of nations effectively realizing that purpose would acquire a substance and a dignity which would go far toward assuring its ascendancy as an instrument of peace and progress."

This certainly is to be done by a method very different from that of trial of war criminals from amongst the vanquished nations. An international organisation of the kind recommended by Dr. Lauterpacht would not permit a dominating foreign power to claim its dealings with the dominated nation as its "domestic affairs" outside the jurisdiction of the organization.

e. The Tokyo Trials and the Law of War: Study Questions Before Reading Justice Rőlings's Dissent

1) How does Justice Rőling deal with the objection that the charge of crimes against peace is "ex post facto" law? Does he in effect concede that it is? How does he justify his conclusion that the "maxim" prohibiting "ex post facto" law is "not a principle of justice but a rule of policy"? Is his reasoning convincing?

2) Justice Rőling argues that "powers victorious in a 'bellum justum' ... have, according to international law, the right to counteract elements constituting a threat to that newly established order," that they therefore may "retain the custody of the pertinent persons," that they might have chosen "political action" to achieve that end, that the victorious Allies instead chose the "novelty" of "the judicial way" for dealing with the defeated enemy's political and military leadership, and that because the judicial way "affords the vanquished [leadership] more guarantees than mere political action could do," the Tokyo Trials "cannot be regarded as a violation of international law." Is this reasoning sound?

3) Does Justice Rőling provide a coherent principle for distinguishing illegal wars of aggression from other wars? Is his criterion that an illegal war of aggression is a war of conquest? If so, how are wars of conquest to be distinguished from other wars? Or is his view that some, but not all, wars of conquest are illegal aggression? If so, how are legal wars of conquest to be distinguished from illegal ones? Or does his statement that "it is wellnigh impossible to define the concept of initiating or waging a war of aggression both accurately and comprehensively" indicate that no plausible criterion exists for distinguishing between legal and illegal wars?

f. The Text of Justice Rőlings's Dissent[239]

The first occasion on which the punishment of responsible for the war was announced, was on 6 November Stalin's speech commemorating the 26th anniversary of the revolution. In this speech Stalin said:

239 *Id.* at 684-703.

> "In conjunction with our Allies we shall have to...take measures to ensure that all the fascist criminals who are responsible for this war and the suffering peoples have endured shall meet with stern punishment and retribution for all the crimes they have committed no matter in what country they may hide."

On the first of December, 1943, the Cairo Conference Statement was issued, in which Roosevelt, Churchill and Chiang Kai-shek said:

> "The Three Great Allies are fighting this war to restrain and punish the aggression of Japan."

Only the punishment of Japan as a nation is here brought up. One wonders whether such punishment has any bearing upon activity of a tribunal with regard to individual responsibility. Such punishment primarily manifests itself in the destruction of cities, in the loss of territory, and in the humiliation an occupation.

In the Report of Commission I of the London International Assembly, issued in December 1943, it states:

> "It is essential that the categories of crimes in respect of which post-war punishment is required, be stated as precisely as possible. After much discussion the majority of the Commission recommended that a comprehensive view should be taken, including not only the customary violations of the laws of war, but any other serious crime against the local law committed in time of war, the perpetrator of which has not been visited by appropriate punishment. Moreover, in accordance with Stalin's views as expressed on November 6, 1943, the Commission recommended that those responsible for the "crime of war," i.e., unprovoked aggression, should be branded as criminals and adequately punished."

In its "Recommendations," the Commission, having first given the definition its Chairman recommended in October, continued:

> "From this point of view the Commission regards as war crimes especially: (a) the preparation and the waging of an aggressive war and all other acts of aggression (referred to in Marshal Stalin's Declaration of November 6, 1943)..."

Marshal Stalin's idea was further supported in a book by the Soviet-Russian professor A.N. Trainin ("The criminal responsibility of the Hitlerites," Moscow 1944), who, together with Maj. Gen. T.T. Nikitchenko (later the Soviet Member of the I.M.T. at Nuremberg), represented Soviet Russia at the London Conference which resulted in the London Agreement of August 8, 1945.

So far as American policy is concerned, I may quote Sheldon Glueck:

> "Judging from available published data, this idea of including the launching of an aggressive war—a "crime against peace"—among the offenses for which the Axis Powers were to be held liable had its origin, so far as American policy is concerned, in a report to the President made on June 7, 1945, by the American Chief of Counsel for the prosecution of major war criminals."

It was the later Chief of Counsel in Nuremberg, Justice Robert H. Jackson, who in behalf of the U.S. signed the agreements of London of Aug. 8, 1945, concluded between the representatives of the Governments of the U.S., France, U.K., and USSR, "acting in the interests of all the United Nations," in which "crimes against peace" are mentioned as coming within the jurisdiction of the I.M.T.

From the above, it follows that "crimes against peace" were not regarded true crimes before the London Agreement, and were not considered as such before the end of 1943.

* * *

The question has to be faced and answered whether the concept of these crimes was, and could be, created as such by the London Agreement of August 8, 1945, or by the Charter for the IMTFE.

The defense in this case has submitted that this question is of no consequence, in view of the rule invalidating ex post facto law. This argument, however, will not stand examination. If the principle of "nullum crimen sine praevia lege" were a principle of justice, the Tribunal would be bound to exclude for that very reason every crime created in the Charter ex post facto, it being the first duty of the Tribunal to mete out justice. However, this maxim is not a principle of justice but a rule of policy, valid only if expressly adopted, so as to protect citizens against arbitrariness of courts (nullum crimen, nulla poena sine lege), as well as against arbitrariness of legislators (nullum crimen, nulla poena sine praevia lege). Nor does this rule consider the question whether a certain act was criminally wrong at the moment it was committed, but only the question as to whether that act was or was not forbidden under penalty. As such, the prohibition of ex post facto law is an expression of political wisdom, not necessarily applicable in present international relations. This maxim of liberty may, if circumstances necessitate it, be disregarded even by powers victorious in a war fought for freedom. It is, however, neither the task nor within the powers of the Tribunal to judge the wisdom of a certain policy.

As indicated above, aggression was not considered a true crime before and in the beginning of this war, and could not be considered as such for lack of those conditions in international relations on which such a view could be based.

The dreadfulness of World War II may have made us realize the necessity of preventing wars in the future. But we need not discuss here whether the horror of the atomic bomb opened our eyes to the criminality of Japanese aggression.

These horrors of World War II may compel the nations to take the legal steps to achieve the maintenance of peace. This has not been done to date. Consequently, apart from the question as to whether, according to international law, victorious powers, either in a mutual treaty or by order of their Supreme Commander, could bring about a change in the legal situation of aggressive war, the relations of the nations did not change in the sense that even at this moment every illegal war could be qualified as a vile crime.

Positive international law, as existing at this moment, compels us to interpret the "crime against peace," as mentioned in the Charter, in a special way. It may be presupposed that the Allied Nations did not intend to create rules in violation of international law. This indicates that the Charter should be interpreted so that it is in accordance with International Law. There is no doubt that powers victorious in a "bellum justum," and as such responsible for peace and order thereafter, have, according to international law, the right to counteract elements constituting a threat to that newly established order, and are entitled, as a means of preventing the recurrence of gravely offensive conduct, to seek and retain the custody of the pertinent persons. Napoleon's elimination offers a precedent.

The Potsdam Declaration emphasized that duty:

> "There must be eliminated for all time the authority and influence of those who have deceived and misled the people of Japan into embarking on world conquest, for we insist that a new order of peace, security and justice will be impossible until irresponsible militarism is driven from the world."

In his opening statement, the Chief Prosecutor stressed this point of danger:

> "For the accused in the dock are no contrite penitents. If we are to believe their claims as already asserted in this trial, they acknowledge no wrong and imply that if they were set free they would repeat their aggression again and again. So that from the sheer necessity for security they should be forever restrained." (T. 469).

The same thought was expressed by the Russian prosecutor:

> "The accused have not laid down arms. Not only did they plead not guilty, taking advantage of the fact that their criminal actions in the past were thoroughly disguised and the aggressive policy was camouflaged by official lies about Japan's struggle for peace, etc., but they continue actively advocating their criminal aggressive policy which brought innumerable calamities and suffering to millions of people. The conspirators now in the dock are also dangerous because around them rally the most reactionary elements in Japan represented by former generals,

> intelligence agents and diplomats who appearing in this court as witnesses are doing their best to shield their former bosses." (T.p. 39738).

Mere political action, based on the responsibility of power, could have achieved this aim. That the judicial way is chosen to select those who were in fact the planners, instigators and wagers of Japanese aggression is a novelty which cannot be regarded as a violation of international law in that it affords the vanquished more guarantees than mere political action could do.

Again, the chief prosecutor in his opening statement said:

> "This method of constituting an international legal tribunal and permitting such war criminals the privilege of defending themselves and asserting their innocence is but the culmination of the modern and civilized ideals of culture and tolerance which have become crystallized in concrete form." (T. 393).

Crime in international law is applied to concepts with different meanings. Apart from those indicated above, it can also indicate acts comparable to political crimes in domestic law, where the decisive element is the danger rather than the guilt, where the criminal is considered an enemy rather than a villain, and where the punishment emphasizes the political measure rather than the judicial retribution.

In this sense should be understood the "crime against peace," referred to in the Charter. In this sense the crime against peace, as formulated in the Charter, is in accordance with international law. It goes without saying that this conception of the character of the "crime" has certain consequences with regard to the appropriate "punishment."

It appears to me that the Nuremberg Judgment is based upon a somewhat similar conception of the "crimes against peace." Although it qualified the "crime against peace" of initiating a war of aggression as "the supreme international crime, differing only from other war crimes in that it contains within itself the accumulated evil of the whole," yet those defendants found guilty of the crime against peace, who were not, or to a limited degree, found guilty of conventional war crimes, were given only prison sentences (Hess, Doenitz, Raeder, Funk, von Neurath.)

As long as the dominant principle in the crime against peace is the dangerous character of the individual who committed this crime the punishment should only be determined by considerations of security.

In this case, this means that no capital punishment should be given to anyone guilty of the crime against peace only.

At Nuremberg, November 21, 1945 Justice Jackson stated:

> "That four great nations, flushed with victory and stung with injury stay the hand of vengeance and voluntarily submit their captive enemies to the judgment of the law is one of the most significant tributes that Power ever had paid to Reason."

This praise would apply to the Allied Nations in connection with the Pacific War if the crime against peace and the purpose of this trial were understood in the above sense.

In this trial, together with the Nuremberg Trial, the first in which aggression-as-a-crime is at stake, it is not necessary to draw a sharp line between aggression and defense. Here, as the evidence shows, we are dealing with wars which can be called wars of conquest, wars of illegal expansion. These wars of conquest certainly come within the scope of illegal aggression, whatever definition might be given. The question whether the impulses which led to those wars of conquest did, perhaps, originate partly in the defensive sphere, may here be left out of discussion. Insight in the genesis of the crime has but limited importance, as it is not so much retribution for the offense by punishment of the perpetrators which is here being sought, as a measure for protection by elimination of dangerous persons.

It being proved that Japan waged wars of aggression, it is not necessary to inquire in how far treaty provisions, too, were violated. It is clear that "aggression" in the Charter implies and presupposes the illegality of offensive war.

The author of the Charter has been most anxious to cover all the activities, which could be regarded as supporting aggressive war. The indictment has followed this course. It will not be necessary to decide in detail whether someone planned or prepared an aggressive war, or conspired in the accomplishment of the planning, preparation, initiation or waging of such a war. On the other hand, it is hard to find a distinction between initiating and waging, since initiating establishes waging.

More important in this case is the question whether every single member of the government, who votes for war after having entered the government with the purpose of maintaining peace, can be considered to have initiated the war. A similar problem arises in case of someone having entered the government during the war, similarly with the purpose of attempting to achieve peace as soon as possible.

Decision on this point is of great moment for the future. The Judgment must by all means avoid establishing such norms as would tend to create the consequence that individuals supporting peace would be forbidden to hold high office in a government which is inclined to aggressive war, or is in the process of waging an aggressive war.

It may be stated at this point that, unlike other crimes, the crime of aggression is such that the emphasis falls upon the activities in preparation. He who propagates, or plans, or starts the aggression takes upon himself a heavier responsibility than the statesman who cannot but accept the consequences of previous events, or who carries on an established policy.

It is wellnigh impossible to define the concept of initiating or waging a war of aggression both accurately and comprehensively. The simple fact of having been a member of the government which decided for war, or which was in the process of waging a war, is not sufficient. The intention with which one enters such a government is decisive. It should constantly be borne in mind that the question is whether certain activities, mentioned in art, 5a of the Chapter, are such that they can be considered as establishing a crime against peace.

Another problem is whether individuals, other than those forming the Government, can be considered to have waged the war of aggression. As a matter of course, those can be considered so who, without formally belonging to the government, exercise governmental functions. When the Army in a given country assumes a position which makes it the decisive agent in the formulation of the state policy, it can consequently wage war. The Army, if it restricts itself to the proper army function, i.e., to constitute the power which carries out the command of the Government, cannot "wage War." As such, the Army is merely one of the instruments with which war is waged.

Now, the argument could be advanced that at least the military, be they privates or field-marshals assist in the waging, and that those individuals, if conscious of the aggressive character of the war, consequently could be held guilty of criminal participation in the crime.

However, this question need not be answered here, since the Tribunal in any case lacks the jurisdiction to deal with such alleged participation in the crime against peace. Now that the Charter grants jurisdiction only in the case of waging and of some forms of participation in this crime, viz., planning and preparation, other forms are excluded a contrario.

Further on in this opinion, where some individual cases will be treated, there will be opportunity to go into those questions in more detail.

g. The Legality of the Atomic Bomb: Study Questions Before Reading the *Shimoda Case*

1) How does the *Shimoda* court frame the question before it and the Government of Japan's (GOJ) arguments?

2) What is the agreed statement of facts? Why do you think the parties to this case agree on the statement of facts? Are there any missing facts concerning the larger circumstances surrounding, as well as the consequences of, the use of nuclear weapons? What conclusions does the court's statement of facts allow it to draw about the nature of the atomic bomb as a weapon of war?

3) How does the court describe the "premises" for its statement of the applicable law governing nuclear bombing? Are the premises limited to specific legal instruments? Do they include premises about the acceptable mode of legal reasoning to cases

not specifically addressed by those instruments? What does that indicate about the court's views about the nature of international law?

4) What role does the concept of "civilized country" play in the court's analysis? What role does the question of changing technology play in the court's analysis? Are these two concepts in tension? Do they support one another?

5) Does the court focus less on the nature of the weapon and more on the nature of the target and the nature of the use of the weapon in order to assess legality? What does that make of its discussion of the nature of the weapon?

6) What sources does the court invoke to discuss the legality of aerial bombing against particular targets and in particular ways? What is the status of those sources? (Hint: Are "draft" multilateral treaties sources of international law? Cf. VCLT, art. 18 and 31-32.) Is this related to the court's approach or methodology for "finding" the governing principles of law?

7) Which of these possible approaches (nature of weapon, target, and/or use) results in more categorical conclusions? Which approach results in more fact-specific ones? Does the court's reasoning yield a generalized statement about the legality of the use of nuclear weapons or a context-sensitive statement about the legality of a particular use of nuclear weapons?

8) How does the court treat the possibility of a "total war" defense of the indiscriminate use of nuclear weapons? Does the court see the indiscriminate targeting of civilians as a violation of established principles of the law of war?

9) Why does the court think it does not have the authority to issue a remedy on behalf of the victims of the atomic bombings? Do these individuals have rights under international law? When would they? Do they in this case?

10) What is the court's view of individual responsibility for acts in violation of international law? What do you think its view would be of the scope of the "superior orders" defense and whether it could be reconciled with the law of the Nuremberg Trials? What does this tell you about its view of the Nuremberg Trials?

11) Who, in the court's view, has a duty to make reparations under international law? States or persons?

12) What is "diplomatic protection"? As a general matter, does the court think it has domestic legal authority to assert jurisdiction over the U.S. Government to compel it to make reparations for its breach of the law of war? As a general matter, is the principle of sovereign immunity deemed to be a part of Japanese law in this case?

13) Recall that the IMT decided that high ranking German officials acting for the state were not immunized. If the state is immune, and its officials act for the state, can you reconcile the *Nuremberg* and *Shimoda* cases? How does the court distinguish the law governing claims against Germany from the claims Japan may have against the United States? Are there special reasons at work that limit these opinions to the specific contexts of the two wars? Does the court's analysis nevertheless say something about the general implications of the IMT's decision?

14) Does the international strategic environment in which *Shimoda* was decided—including the vital U.S.-Japan security relationship at the height of the Cold War—have anything to do with (1) the court's approach to the question of a blanket prohibition on the use of nuclear weapons, (2) the possibility of a defense of "total war" for particular uses of nuclear weapons that would otherwise violate the law of war, (3) the court's decision with respect its capacity under international law and domestic Japanese law to sanction the Government of the United States, or (4) the court's view of the Nuremberg Trials? Why? Why not?

15) Which parts of the *Shimoda* opinion, if any, fit with a positive conception of international law? Which parts, if any, do not? If it is a positivist conception, is it still a conception of international law rather than international and domestic politics? Why? Why not?

16) What does this tell you about the *Shimoda* court's approach to adjudication? Does the opinion remind you of *Marbury v. Madison* in any way?

17) What significance do you attach to the fact that the opinion was issued on December 7?

18) The *Shimoda* opinion refers to Art. 25 of the Regulations of the 1907 Hague Laws of Land War and to Art. 1 of the 1907 Hague Convention (IX) Concerning Bombardment by Naval Forces. Both provisions prohibit bombardment of "undefended" towns, villages or buildings (although Art. 2 of the latter convention creates an exception for listed military objectives in such localities). Is it reasonable

to extrapolate an analogous rule for aerial bombardment from these rules for land and naval warfare? (Note that Art. 25 prohibits bombardment of undefended towns "by whatever means.")

19) Given that the international community failed to ratify the 1923 draft Hague Rules of Aerial Warfare (also relied upon in *Shimoda*), does that undercut the attempt to infer a prohibition on aerial bombardment akin to those in the Hague Conventions for land and naval warfare?

20) Furthermore, doesn't aerial warfare have distinctive, even revolutionary, characteristics of its own that make it implausible to apply traditional targeting rules for land and naval warfare to it?[240]

21) Does the mere existence of the 1923 draft Rules of Aerial Warfare, even though unratified, support the claim that those rules created, or contributed to creating, customary law?

22) What did the Hague Conventions mean in referring to "undefended" towns? The *Shimoda* opinion maintains that "a defended city is a city resisting any possible occupation attempt by land forces." It seems to infer that all other cities are "undefended," and in particular that cities "far distant from the battlefield" like Hiroshima and Nagasaki are "undefended." Is that inference correct?

23) Might it be that a city that is protected by friendly forces resisting occupation by an encroaching enemy army is a "defended" city, that a city that is laid open to occupation by an encroaching enemy army without resistance is an "undefended" city, and that a city that is in neither situation (because, like Hiroshima and Nagasaki, it is distant from any land battlefield) is *neither* "defended" *nor* "undefended?"[241]

24) Isn't the primary purpose of the Hague rules about "undefended" cities to enable the defender to save them from needless damage and destruction by withdrawing its forces and declaring the cities open to occupation by the enemy army that

240 *See* R.Y. Jennings, *Open Towns,* 22 Brit. Y.B. Int'l L. 258, 260 (1945).

241 For discussion of attempts to interpret and apply the Hague rules during the Second World War, *see* USAF Second Lt. Jerrold F, Elkin, *Application of the "Open City" Concept to Rome 1942–1944,* 22 A,F.L. Rev. 188 (1980/1).

is preparing to attack them?[242] If so, aren't those rules simply irrelevant to the bombardment of hinterland cities like Hiroshima and Nagasaki?[243]

25) Article 59 of the 1997 Additional Protocol 1 to the 1949 Geneva Conventions may be trying to elucidate the Hague Conventions' distinction between defended and undefended cities. That provision reads in part:

a. Art 59. Non-defended localities

1. It is prohibited for the Parties to the conflict to attack, by any means whatsoever, non-defended localities.

2. The appropriate authorities of a Party to the conflict may declare as a non-defended locality any inhabited place near or in a zone where armed forces are in contact which is open for occupation by an adverse Party.

Such a locality shall fulfil the following conditions:

(a) all combatants, as well as mobile weapons and mobile military equipment must have been evacuated;

(b) no hostile use shall be made of fixed military installations or establishments;

(c) no acts of hostility shall be committed by the authorities or by the population; and

(d) no activities in support of military operations shall be undertaken.

26) If Art. 59 is a valid interpretation of the prior Hague rules, were Hiroshima and Nagasaki "non-defended"?

27) The *Shimoda* Court also relies on the prohibition on unnecessary suffering as a general principle of international law. That prohibition is first articulated in the preamble to the St. Petersburg Declaration of 1868 (emphasis added):

a. Considering:

That the progress of civilization should have the effect of alleviating as much as possible the calamities of war;

That the only legitimate object which States should endeavour to accomplish during war is to weaken the military forces of the enemy;

That for this purpose it is sufficient to disable the greatest possible number of men;

That this object would be exceeded by the employment of arms which uselessly aggravate the sufferings of disabled men, or render their death inevitable;

242 *See* Jennings, *supra* note 240, at 260–61.

243 *See* A.P.V. Rogers, *Law on the battlefield* 133 (2d ed. 2004); and Yoram Dinstein, T*he Conduct of Hostilities under the Law of International Armed Conflict* 110 (2d ed. 2010).

That the employment of such arms would, therefore, be contrary to the laws of humanity;

The Contracting Parties engage mutually to renounce, in case of war among themselves, the employment by their military or naval troops of any projectile of a weight below 400 grammes, which is either explosive or charged with fulminating or inflammable substances.

b. Does this language apply to civilians?

28) Does Art. 23(e) of the Regulations to the Hague Laws of Land War, on which *Shimoda* also relies, extend the prohibition on unnecessary suffering to civilians? Examine the other sub-sections of Art. 23 in framing your answer.[244]

29) In a 1996 opinion, *The Legality of the Threat or Use of Nuclear Weapons* (the case study featured in Part III, Chapter 4), the International Court of Justice found that there were two "cardinal principles" of international humanitarian law, of which one "prohibited [causing] unnecessary suffering *to combatants*"(at ¶ 78). In light of that ruling, can it be said that the principle of unnecessary suffering prohibited the attacks on civilians at Hiroshima and Nagasaki?

h. The Text of the *Shimoda* case[245]

Residents of Hiroshima and Nagasaki jointly brought an action against the government of Japan for the damages they and members of their families suffered as a result of the atomic bombings by the United States in August 1945. Among other things, it was alleged that the dropping of the atomic bombs was an unlawful act and that Japan's waiver of claims for damages under domestic and international law against the US gave rise to an obligation for the government of Japan itself to pay damages. The action was dismissed.

The State contended that since neither international customary nor treaty law prohibited the use of atomic bombs at the time, the question of a violation of positive international law did not arise. The Court agreed that the use of nuclear weapons was not expressly prohibited by international law, but it felt that the use a particular weapon was also to be ascertained in light of the principles of international law applicable to the conduct of warfare, in particular the prohibition on indiscriminate bombardment of an undefended city and the prohibition on inflicting unnecessary suffering. Although no generally applicable treaty relative to aerial bombardment was in force at time of the bombing, the Court –on the basis of the Draft Rules of Air Warfare

244 *See* Burrus M. Carnahan, *Unnecessary Suffering, The Red Cross and Tactical Laser Weapons*, 18 Loy. L.A. Int'l & Comp. L.J. 705, 711–12 (1995/6).

245 *Shimoda et al. v. The State*, Tokyo District Court, 7 December 1963 (*available at* https://www.icrc.org/applic/ihl/ihl-nat.nsf/0/aa559087dbcf1af5c1256a1c0029f14d).

(1923) and, by analogy, on the rules applicable to bombardment by land and naval forces– held that the indiscriminate bombing of undefended cities was unlawful under customary law. It further stated that the principle of distinction between military and non-military objectives had not been nullified by the supposed adoption by the belligerents of a doctrine of total war. The bombings of Nagasaki and Hiroshima, as undefended cities, were thus held to have been unlawful acts.

Ruling that individuals did not have rights under international law unless this was specifically recognized in a treaty, the Court took the view that there was no general way open to an individual to claim damages directly under international law. A claim for damages caused by a State to a national of another State could be based on diplomatic protection, but as it is widely recognized in classical international law, any such claim is in fact the State's own claim for damages suffered by its nationals and not the claim of an individual. Thus Japan could waive, and did waive, all its claims –including those deriving from diplomatic protection– against the US under the peace treaty of 1951. It further held that claims by Japanese nationals under domestic law had also been waived.

REASONS:

1. Atomic bombing and its effect.

(1) There is no dispute between the parties about the following facts. Around 8:15 a.m. on August 6, 1945, a B-29 bomber piloted by Colonel Tibbetts, U.S. Army Air Forces, dropped a uranium bomb on Hiroshima under the orders of U.S. President H.S. Truman, and around 11:02 a.m. on the 9th of the same month, a B-29 bomber piloted by Major Sweeney, U.S. Army Air Forces, dropped a plutonium bomb on Nagasaki under the orders of U.S. President Truman. These bombs (hereinafter referred to as "atomic bombs") exploded in the air. A furious bombshell blast with a flash, and both in Hiroshima and in Nagasaki almost all buildings in the cities collapsed. Simultaneously, fire broke out everywhere; and all people who were within a radius of some four kilometers of the epicenter were killed in an instant without distinction of age or sex. A large number of people elsewhere were burned on the skin by the flash, and others, bathed with the radiant rays, suffered from so-called atomic bomb injury. The number of killed and wounded, to say the least, amounted to more than 70,000 and 50,000 respectively, in Hiroshima, and to more than 20,000 and 40,000 respectively, in Nagasaki.

(2) Then, what is the explosion of an atomic bomb? This question is made clear theoretically without any room for doubt, and there are many results of experiment, which are collected into materials by scientists for everyone's use. We will state the principle in brief as follows,

by virtue of the "Effect of Nuclear Weapon" by Samuel Glaston (published by the U.S. Atomic Energy Commission). (Handbook of *Genshiryoku, Bakudan-hen*, in Japanese translation.)

When a free neutron enters into a atomic nucleus of uranium No. 235 or plutonium No. 239, the atomic nucleus is divided in two, and at that moment a large quantity of energy is discharged. Simultaneously, discharged by the reaction of that nuclear fission, more than two neutrons enter into the next atomic nucleus of uranium No. 235 or plutonium No. 239 and cause the reaction of nuclear fission. The neutrons discharged by this second nuclear fission cause the next reaction similarly, and if there is a large quantity of neutrons the reaction of nuclear fission is caused one after another like a chain. In the process, part of the neutrons discharged disperse off, or part are lost by the reaction of atomic nucleus which is not nuclear fission. However, since the loss can be diminished relatively by increasing the quantity of uranium No. 235 or plutonium No. 239, or by reflecting neutrons with reflector placed around, the reaction of nuclear fission is caused one after another like a chain by increasing the quantity of uranium No. 235 or plutonium No. 239 to over the critical quantity; the energy is accumulated and the explosion is caused finally. The time before the explosion is caused is very short, and the energy discharged is tremendous. If a pound of uranium No. 235 or plutonium No. 239 go into full nuclear fission, energy equivalent to the explosion of a 9,000-ton TNT bomb is produced in less than one second. The bombs dropped on Hiroshima and Nagasaki discharge energy equivalent in quantity to 20,000 tons of TNT bombs, but at the present time far stronger weapons which have the energy of megaton class, appear.

(3) Next, we will state in brief the effect caused by the explosion of atomic bombs by virtue of the above-mentioned book.

The first effect comes from the bomb-shell blast. When an atomic bomb explodes in the air, a fire ball composed of gas of very high temperature and very high pressure arises at once and goes up engulfing the surrounding air. From the fire ball, a wave of air (wave from bombardment) of high temperature and high pressure is pushed up at once, and spreads in all directions quickly. When the wave reaches the earth, it destroys buildings and other structures as if an earthquake or typhoon occurred. The range of the effect is very wide. In Nagasaki, houses within 1.4 miles from the epicenter collapsed, those within 1.6 miles suffered rather heavy damage, and even those at the point of 1.7 miles had their roofs and walls damaged.

The second effect comes from the heat rays. When a fire ball is made by the explosion of an atomic bomb in the air, it begins to radiate heat rays composed of heat of high temperature and light. The heat rays include ultraviolate rays as well as visible rays and ultrared rays. The heat rays reach the earth at the same speed as light, set fire to inflammable things on the earth, burn the skin, and cause man's death according to the conditions. In Hiroshima and Nagasaki, 20% to 30% of those killed are presumed killed by burns; and in Nagasaki burns from the heat were recorded as far as 2.5 miles from the epicenter. While the effect of an ordinary high efficient bomb (TNT bomb) is chiefly destruction by bomb-shell blast, the atomic bomb singularly possesses the effect of fire and burn by heat rays, together with destruction by bomb-shell blast.

The third and most peculiar effect comes from the first stage of nuclear radial rays and residual nuclear radioactivity. The radial rays which are radiated within one minute after the explosion of an atomic bomb are composed of neutron, gamma rays, alpha particles and beta particles; and they are called the first stage of nuclear radial rays. Among them, gamma rays and neutron have a flying leg of long range, and, when striking against the human body, they destroy or injure the cells and cause atomic disease (atomic bomb injury) by injury from radial rays. Atomic disease weakens the whole human body, and causes man's death several hours or weeks later; and if he fortunately saves his life a long term is required before his recovery. Also, the radiation of the first stage of nuclear radial rays causes leukaemia, cataract, and abortion of child, has various bad influences on various organs of the human body, and causes hereditarily bad influences.

The radial rays which are radiated chiefly from splinters of the bomb one minute after the explosion, are called the residual nuclear radial rays. These splinters spread wide in the air in the form of corpuscle, cause a radioactive rainfall by sticking to water drops, and flutter down to the earth in the form of the so-called ashes of death. The effect of radial rays on the human body is almost the same as that of the first stage of nuclear radial rays.

(4) Thus, one atomic bomb, even a small-scale bomb like the bombs dropped on Hiroshima and Nagasaki, discharges energy equivalent to a 20,000-ton TNT bomb; and the power of destruction and effect of casualty by the bomb-shell blast are so remarkable that it cannot for a moment be compared with bombs of the past. Moreover, the power of destruction by the bombshell blast is only a part (some 50% of the energy) of the efficiency of atomic bomb; and the effect of incendiary and of casualty by heat rays (some 35% of the energy) has singularity which is not seen in a TNT bomb. We can see the strong power in that 20% to 30% of the deaths in Hiroshima and Nagasaki are presumed to result from burns. However, what strikes us with more terror is the radial rays or radioactivity caused by the atomic bomb; and we have already experienced the terror of atomic disease, leukaemia and various other injuries to the human body, which are caused by radial rays or radioactivity.

Thus, the atomic bomb is far stronger than weapons of the past in power of destruction and casualty. Besides, it has characteristics different from all kinds of weapons of the past in that it inflicts on the human body various kinds of pain and bad influences. We must say that the atomic bomb is really cruel weapon.

2. International law aspects.

(1) There is no doubt that, whether or not an atomic bomb having such a character and effect is a weapon which is permitted in international law as a so-called nuclear weapon, is an important and very difficult question in international law. In this case, however, the point at issue is whether the acts of atomic bombing of Hiroshima and Nagasaki by the United States are regarded as illegal by positive international law at that time. Therefore, it is enough to consider this point only.

(2) As a premise for judging how the above acts of atomic bombing are treated by positive international law, we will begin by considering what international law has existed with regard to war, especially to hostile acts among modern countries since the latter half of 19th Century.

The following are the chronological enumeration of international laws concerning this case:

1868. St. Petersburg Declaration respecting the prohibition of the explosives and incendiaries under 400 grammes.
1899. Convention respecting the Laws and Customs of War on Land (CONVENTION CONCERNANT LES LOIS ET COUTUMES DE LA GUERRE SUR TERRE), concluded at the First Hague Peace Conference; and its annex, Regulations respecting the Laws and Customs of War on Land (REGLEMENT CONCERNANT LES LOIS ET COUTUMES DE LA GUERRE SUR TERRE) (the so-called Regulations respecting War on Land).
1899. Declaration concerning expanding bullets (the so-called Declaration prohibiting dum-dum bullets).
1899. Declaration concerning projectiles launched from balloons in the air (the so-called Declaration prohibiting aerial bombardment).
1899. Declaration concerning projectiles diffusing asphyxiating or deleterious gases (the so-called Declaration prohibiting poison gases).
1907. Convention respecting the Laws and Customs of War on Land (CONVENTION CONCERNANT LES LOIS ET COUTUMES DE LA GUERRE SUR TERRE), which was concluded in the Second Hague Peace Conference (the revision of the Convention of the same name in the First Hague Peace Conference).
1907. Declaration prohibiting aerial bombardment.
1922. Treaty of Five Countries concerning submarines and poisonous gases.
1923. Draft Rules concerning Air Warfare (Draft Rules of Air Warfare).
1925. Protocol prohibiting the use in war of asphyxiating, deleterious or other gases and bacteriological methods of warfare (Protocol respecting the prohibition of poison gases, etc.).
. . .

(3) In the above-mentioned laws and regulations, there is no direct provision with regard to the atomic bomb, a new weapon which appeared during World War II. . . . *However, the prohibition in this case is understood to include not only the case where there is an express provision of direct prohibition but also the case where it is necessarily regarded that the use of a new weapon is prohibited, from the interpretation and analogical application of existing international laws and regulations (international customary laws and treaties). . . .*

(4) There is also an argument that a new weapon is not an object of regulation of international law at all, but such argument has not a sufficient ground as mentioned above. . . .

We cannot deny that in the past, although objections were made by various interests against the appearance of a new weapon because international law was not yet developed, or a hostile feeling was strong against the people of the enemy or pagans, or the advance of general weapons was gradual, new weapons nevertheless came to be regarded as legal with the later advancement of civilization and the development of scientific techniques. This, however, is not always true. This will be clear from the recollection of the existence of the above-mentioned treaties prohibiting the use of dum-dum bullets and poisonous gases. Therefore, *we cannot regard a weapon as legal only because it is a new weapon, and it is still right that a new weapon must be exposed to the examination of positive international law.*

(5) Next, we will examine the international laws and regulations concerned at that time, with regard to the act of atomic bombing. . . . *No general treaty respecting air raids has been concluded. However, according to customary law recognized generally in international law with regard to a hostile act, a defended city and an undefended city are distinguished with regard to bombardment by land forces, and a defended place and an undefended place are distinguished with regard to bombardment by naval forces. Against the defended city and place, indiscriminate bombardment is permitted, while in the case of an undefended city and place, bombardment is permitted only against combatant and military installations (military objectives) and bombardment is not permitted against non-combatant and non-military installations (non-military objectives). Any contrary bombardment is necessarily regarded as an illegal act of hostility. . . .*

(6) With regard to air warfare, there are "Draft Rules of Air Warfare." Article 24 of the Draft Rules . . . prohibit useless aerial bombardment and provide for the principle of military objective first of all. Then, together with that, the Draft Rules distinguish between places in the immediate neighborhood of the operations of land forces and other places, and provide that indiscriminate aerial bombardment against the former is permitted but that against the latter the aerial bombardment of military objectives only is permitted. In these provisions, stricter expressions are used than in the case of bombardment by land and naval forces, but what they mean is understood to be the same as the distinction between the defended city (place) and

undefended city (place). The Draft Rules of Air Warfare cannot directly be called positive law, since they have not yet become effective as a treaty. However, international jurists regard the Draft Rules as authoritative with regard to air warfare. Some countries regard the substance of the Rules as a standard of action by armed forces, and the fundamental provisions of the Draft Rules are consistently in conformity with international laws and regulations, and customs at that time. Therefore, we can safely say that the prohibition of indiscriminate aerial bombardment on an undefended city and the principle of military objective, which are provided for by the Draft Rules, are international customary law, also from the point that they are in common with the principle in land and sea warfare. . . .

(7) Then, what is the distinction between a defended city and an undefended city? Generally speaking, a defended city is a city resisting any possible occupation attempt by land forces. A city which is far distant from the battlefield, and is not in pressing danger of the enemy's occupation, even if there exist defensive installations or armed forces, cannot be said to be a defended city, since there is no military necessity of indiscriminate bombardment; and in this case the bombardment and aerial bombardment only against military objectives is admitted. . . . However, it necessarily follows that in an undefended city, an aerial bombardment directed at a non-military objective, and an aerial bombardment without distinction between military objectives and non-military objectives (the so-called blind aerial bombardment) is not permitted in the light of the above-mentioned principle. . . . *Therefore, the act of atomic bombing on an undefended city, setting aside that on a defended city, should be regarded in the same light as a blind aerial bombardment; and it must be said to be a hostile act contrary to international law of the day.*

(8) It is a well-know fact that Hiroshima and Nagasaki were not cities resisting a possible occupation attempt by land forces at that time. . . . Therefore, *since an aerial bombardment with an atomic bomb brings the same result as a blind aerial bombardment from the tremendous power of destruction, even if the aerial bombardment has only a military objective as the target of its attack, it is proper to understand that an aerial bombardment with an atomic bomb on both cities of Hiroshima and Nagasaki was an illegal act of hostility as the indiscriminate aerial bombardment on undefended cities.*

(9) Against the above conclusion, there is a counter-argument that the war of the day was the so-called total war, in which it was difficult to distinguish between combatant and non-combatant, and between military objective and non-military objective, and that the principle of military objective was not necessarily carried through during World War II.

. . . However, the advocacy of the concept of total war in recent times has the intent of pointing out the fact that the issue of a war is not decided only by armed forces and weapons, but that the other factors, that is to say, chiefly economic factors like source of energy, materials, productive capacity of industry, food, trade, etc., or human factors like population, man-power, etc., have a far-reaching control on the war method and war potential. The concept of total war is not advocated in such a vague meaning as stated above, and there was no actual example of such situation. . . .

(10) During World War II, aerial bombardment was once made on the whole place where military objectives were concentrated, because it was impossible to confirm an individual military objective and attack it where munitions factories and military installations were concentrated in comparatively narrow places, and where defensive installations against air raids were very strong and solid; and there is an opinion regarding this as legal. . . . However, *the legal principle of the aerial bombardment on an objective zone cannot apply to the city of Hiroshima and the city of Nagasaki, since it is clear that both cities could not be said to be places where such military objectives concentrate.*

(11) Besides, the atomic bombing on both cities of Hiroshima and Nagasaki is regarded as contrary to the principle of international law that the means which give unnecessary pain in war and inhumane means are prohibited as means of injuring the enemy. . . . [J]udging from the fact that the St. Petersburg Declaration declares that ". . . considering that the use of a weapon which increases uselessly the pain of people who are already placed out of battle and causes their death necessarily is beyond the scope of this purpose, and considering that the use of such a weapon is thus contrary to humanity. . ." and that article 23(e) of the Hague Regulations respecting war on Land prohibits "the employment of such arms, projectiles, and material as cause unnecessary injury," we can safely see that besides poison, poison-gas, and bacterium the use of the means of injuring the enemy which causes at least the same or more injury is prohibited by international law. The destructive power of the atomic bomb is tremendous, but it is doubtful whether atomic bombing really had an appropriate military effect at that time and whether it was necessary. It is a deeply sorrowful reality that the atomic bombing on both cities of Hiroshima and Nagasaki took the lives of many civilians, and that among the survivors there are people whose lives are still imperilled owing to the radial rays, even today 18 years later. In this sense, *it is not too much to say that the pain brought by the atomic bombs is severer than that from poison and poison-gas, and we can say that the act of dropping such a cruel bomb is contrary to the fundamental principle of the laws of war that unnecessary pain must not be given.*

3. Municipal law aspects.

[T]here is little meaning in the further abstract consideration of the question whether the acts of atomic bombing were contrary to the municipal laws of Japan and the United States. For the existence of the act contrary to municipal law, and the question whether the responsibility for the violation can be placed on some person and before what court the suit can be instituted in order to enforce the responsibility are different questions which must be considered separately. The question in this case is not concretely solved until these points are considered. This point will be commented on later together when the question of responsibility for acts contrary to international law is dealt with.

4. Claims for damages of the sufferers.

. . . President Truman, who ordered the atomic bombing. It is a principle of international law that the State must directly assume responsibility for acts taken by a person as a state organ, and that the person who holds the position as a state organ does not assume responsibility as an individual. . . .

It is still proper to understand that individuals are not the subject of rights in international law, unless it is concretely recognized by treaties as seen in the above example of mixed arbitral tribunals. . . . Indeed, international law permits a state to demand from the other country reparations for damage caused to its nationals, in the name of the state for the sake of its nationals. This is called diplomatic protection, as is generally known. Diplomatic protection is, however, an act based on the state's own right of diplomatic protection and the individual's claim itself is not asserted by this act. The claim for damages is asserted as the state's own claim. Whether the state exercises the right of diplomatic protection is decided by the state in its own judgment, and the state exercises the rights in its name. . . . Accordingly, the possibility left to the individual comes to the question whether he can ask for redress before a domestic court of one or both belligerents. Redress before a Japanese court, however, cannot be asked for. The sufferers must bring an action before a Japanese court against the other country as defendant, in this case, against the United States as defendant, but it is an established principle in international law that a country is not subject to the jurisdiction of the civil courts of other countries; and this principle is also recognized by Japan. . . .

. . .

Everyone has a whole-hearted compassion for those who suffered damages by the dropping of the atomic bombs, which possess the largest-scale and strongest destructive power in human history. It is a common desire of mankind to totally abolish war, or at least to limit it to the minimum and confine damage to the minimum; and for that purpose, we mankind, are persevering in our efforts day and night.

However, if a war unfortunately occurs, it goes without saying that every country is required to minimize damage and to protect its nationals. In this light, the question of State redress on the basis of absolute liability will arise necessarily for war calamity. Actually, there is the "Law respecting Medical Treatment and the Like for Sufferers of the Atomic Bomb" which is related to this case; but it is clear that a law of this scale cannot possibly be sufficient for the relief or rescue of the suffers of the atomic bombs. The defendant State caused many nationals to die, injured them, and drove them to a precarious life by the war which it opened on its own authority and responsibility. Also, the seriousness of the damage cannot compare a moment with that of the general calamity. Needless to say the defendant state should take sufficient relief measures in this light.

That is, however, no longer the duty of the Court, but a duty which the Diet or legislature or the Cabinet or the executive must perform. Moreover, it is by such a procedure that relief measures can be taken not only by the parties to this suit, but also by general sufferers of the atomic bombs: and there lies the raison d'être of the legislature and the administration. It cannot possibly be understood that the above is financially impossible in Japan, which has achieved a high degree of economic growth after the war. We cannot see this suit without regretting the political poverty.

7. Conclusion.

For the above reasons, the plaintiffs' claims in this suit are ruled improper, without considering the other issues; and we can only dismiss the plaintiffs' claims on the merits. Accordingly, applying articles 89 and 93 of the Code of Civil Procedure to the costs of litigation, we decide as in the text of the judgment above.

Civil Affairs Division No. 24, Tokyo District Court.
Presiding Judge T. Koseki (Toshimasa Koseki), Judge Y. Mibuchi (Yoshiko Mibuchi), Judge A. Takakuwa (Akira Takakuwa).

4. After Reading Nuremberg, Tokyo, and Shimoda: Two Theses for Class Discussion

a. Thesis 1—The Limits of Legal Positivism in International Law: While the Opinions Purport to be Grounded on Positivist Premises, They Reveal the Limits of Positivist Legal Reasoning in "Hard" Cases

The Nuremberg and Tokyo Trials are open to serious objections as to both their substantive reasoning and their procedural validity. These objections often measure the Trials against the standards of legal positivism—standards that both the IMT and the IMTFE professed to be following—and find them defective. Even more clearly, the *Shimoda* opinion reveals non-positivist premises in its reasoning. Section 1 below presents arguments that the IMT's judgment with respect to individual criminal responsibility for the crime of aggressive war is substantively flawed when tested by the standards of legal positivism.

Section 2 then addresses the legitimacy of the two Tribunals. In this part, we focus on the IMTFE and Justice Pal's dissent. We also consider the question whether an international tribunal has the capacity to make new positive law in the international legal system.

Section 3 addresses the *Shimoda* court's essentially political technique. Here we discuss the similarity between the *Shimoda* opinion and Chief Justice John Marshall's masterful performance in *Marbury v. Madison*,[246] the 1803 case that established the principle of "judicial review" in American constitutional law. In *Marbury*, the Supreme Court, while ruling that it lacked the power to issue an enforceable remedy, nonetheless took the occasion to articulate a new (and politically opportunistic) set of legal principles—namely, the Court's power of judicial review and thus also to assess the legality of President Thomas Jefferson's conduct. Likewise, the *Shimoda* court, while also denying judicial relief, took the occasion to affirm the illegality of the United States' use of nuclear weapons nearly two decades earlier against Japan.

i. The Legal Reasoning of the IMT conflicts with Positivist Premises

The central positivist objection to the IMT's criminalization of aggressive war was is its *ex post facto* imposition of punishment for conduct that was not criminal at the time it occurred, the so-called principle of legality, non-retroactivity, or *nullum crimen sine lege*.[247] While there are reasons to deny that international law as it stood at the beginning of the Second World War embraced that principle,[248] the prohibition on retroactive criminal laws and punishments was well settled in the domestic legal systems of several Great Powers (including the United

246 *See* Marbury v. Madison, 5 U.S. 137 (1803).

247 For early critiques of this kind, *see* Hans Ehard, *The Nuremberg Trial Against the Major War Criminals and International Law*, 43 Am. J. Int'l L. 223, 236–45 (1948); G. Finch, *The Nuremberg Trial and International Law*, 41 Am. J. Int'l L. 20, 25–37 (1947); Leo Gross, *The Criminality of Aggressive War*, 41 Am. Pol. Sci. Rev. 205 (1947); and Max Radin, *Justice and Nuremberg*, 24 Foreign Affairs 369, 376–82 (April 1946). One early critic of Nuremberg on these grounds later recanted his position. *Compare* Charles E. Wyzanski, Jr., *Nuremberg – A Fair Trial?*, The Atlantic Monthly 66, 67 (April 1946) *with* Charles E. Wyzanski, Jr., *Nuremberg in Retrospect*, The Atlantic Monthly 56 (December 1946).

248 *See* Antonio Cassese, International Criminal Law 139–45 (2003) (arguing that, as of Nuremberg, the principle was not established); *see also* Schwarzenberg, *supra* note 200, at 258 ("If applied in a spirit of common sense and reasonableness, this [Ex post facto] prohibition cannot apply to a statute which, although in form retroactive, actually serves to reassert the standard of civilisation against the kind of relapse into barbarism that had taken place in the Third *Reich*. In particular, this is true if the acts made punishable by a retroactive statute are criminal under the law of any civilized community."); and F.B. Schick, *Crimes against Peace*, 38 Crim. L. & Criminology 445, 459–60 (1947–1948)

States[249]) and had at least some support in the pre-War case law of the PCIJ.[250] Thus, the IMT apparently felt compelled to defend itself against the charge of negating the principle of legality by attempting to construct a positivist legal argument.[251] Nonetheless, the IMT was evasive as to whether a rule of against retroactive criminal sanctions was a part of international law. It stated: "The Charter makes the planning or waging of a war of aggression or a war in violation of international treaties a crime, and it is therefore not strictly necessary to consider whether and to what extent aggressive war was a crime before the execution of the London Agreement [adopting the Tribunal's constitutive instrument, or Charter]."[252] But even if the IMT was correct in stating that as the creature of the London Agreement, it had no power to question the retroactive application of the Charter's law, the distinction would be one without a difference: the question would instead become whether the London Agreement was itself a violation of the principle of legality. And reliance on German law to free the Tribunal from the principle of legality would be equally fruitless, since German law would not supersede international law on the question.[253]

---

249 *See, e.g., Ex parte Garland,* 71 U.S. (4 Wall.) 333 (1866); *Fletcher v. Peck,* 10 U.S. (6 Cr.) 87 (1810); and *Calder v. Bull,* 3 U.S. (3 Dall.) 386 (1798). Indeed, the United States Constitution has two Ex Post Facto Clauses—one for the states (U.S. Const. Art. I, § 10, cl. 1) and another for the United States (U.S. Const. Art. I, § 9, cl. 3). It may be noted, however, that the prohibition on ex post facto penal sanctions formed no part of the law of either Nazi Germany or the Soviet Union. *See* Friedrich Rötter, *The Impact of Nazi Law,* 1945 Wisc. L. Rev. 516, 531 (1945) ("Another means of extending the scope of the penal law was the introduction of the principle of analogy. Acts became punishable where no particular penal law was applicable if the act in question deserved punishment according to the fundamental idea of some penal law, and according to what the Nazis called 'gesundes Volksempfinden,' sound popular feeling. It was left to the judge to decide on the merits of each case whether this provision was to be applied. In that way, the judge was enabled to create law in order to fill gaps in the penal system, and to replace the old rule *nullum crimen sine lege and nulla poena sine lege by the new principle nullum crimen sine poena.*"); F.B. Schick, *War Criminals and the Law of the United Nations,* 7 U. Toronto L.J. 27, 56–57 (1946) [hereinafter Schick, *War Criminals*]; Schick, *supra* note 248, at 460; and Lawrence Preuss, *Punishment by Analogy in National Socialist Penal Law,* 26 J. Crim L. & Criminology 847 (1936).

250 In a 1935 opinion, *Consistency of Certain Danzig Legislative Decrees With the Constitution of the Free City,* the Permanent Court of International Justice explained the principle as follows:

> *Nullum crimen sine lege,* and *Nulla Poena sine lege.* The law alone determines and defines an offence. The law alone decrees the penalty. A penalty cannot be inflicted in a given case if it is not decreed by the law in respect of that case. A penalty decreed by the law for a particular case cannot be inflicted in another case. In other words, criminal laws may not be applied by analogy.

Advisory Opinion of December 4, 1935, Ser. A./B., Fasc. No. 65 at 41, 51. For a discussion of the Court's opinion in the broader context of interwar European nationalism, *see* Nathaniel Berman, *A Perilous Ambivalence: Nationalist Desire, Legal Autonomy, and the Limits of the Interwar Framework,* 33 Harv. J. Int'l L. 353, 372–75 (1992).

251 As discussed below, Justice Röling also attempted to rebut the non-retroactivity charge in the IMTFE case.

252 Trial of the Major War Criminals Before the International Military Tribunal 461 (1948)

253 One might argue that the Tribunal's authority derived not only from international law but also from German law, since all governmental authority in Germany had collapsed at the end of the Second World War and the occupying powers were exercising all the powers of sovereignty over Germany. If so, in exercising those powers of sovereignty, the occupying powers might have been deemed to be executing German law and prosecuting Germans for violations of German law, which in turn might have been deemed to include the crimes specified in the Charter as established prior to the beginning of the war, but without the constraint of prohibition against *ex post facto* punishment, which was not in fact a principle of German law under the Nazi regime. *See Schick, War Criminals, supra* note 249, at 56–57; and Carl Schmitt, The Concept of the Political (George D. Schwab trans., University of Chicago Press, 1996; Expanded edition 2006, with an Introduction by Tracy B. Strong)[1927][2nd ed. 1932] (German legal theoretician whose theory of sovereignty focus on identifying the authority capable of determining the circumstances under which ordinary constitutional rules would not be observed). But this line of argument would attribute to German law internalization of a contradictory set of norms—

The Nuremberg judgment appears to be premised on two claims that are (at least arguably) badly flawed as a matter of positive public international law as it was generally understood at the time the Tribunal was convened. First, established international law prior to Nuremberg made aggressive war an international crime. Second, under established international law, state officers could be held individually responsible for the crime of aggression.

a) The Criminality of Aggressive War: The Kellogg-Briand Treaty or Pact of Paris

In deeming aggressive war to be criminal as of the beginning of the Second World War, the IMT relied principally on the so-called Pact of Paris of 1928 (otherwise known as the Kellogg-Briand Agreement, for the responsible American and French negotiators), to which Allied and Axis powers were parties.[254] The text is worth quoting:

> Article I. The High Contracting Parties solemnly declare in the names of their respective peoples that they condemn recourse to war for the solution of international controversies, and renounce it as an instrument of national policy in their relations with one another.
>
> Article II. The High Contracting Parties agree that the settlement or solution of all disputes or conflicts of whatever nature or of whatever origin they may be, which may arise among them, shall never be sought except by pacific.

Any reliance on this document as the basis for the criminalization of aggressive war fails as an ordinary matter of treaty interpretation. The customary rules of treaty interpretation, now codified in articles 31 and 32 of the VCLT, systematically consider a treaty's a) text, b) context, c) negotiating history and d) the subsequent practice of the parties, in order to determine a treaty's meaning.

a. Text—Even if the Pact of Paris created a norm against aggressive war, its preamble declares that "any signatory Powers which shall hereafter seek to promote its national interests by resort to war should be denied the benefits furnished by this Treaty." Thus, the agreement by

rules against aggressive war, war crimes, and genocide, on one hand; and rules permitting retroactive punishment for aggressive war, war crimes and genocide, on the other. It is unlikely the London Agreement sought to accomplish this result. Rather, it was explicitly imposing an external set of norms, the rules of public international law, on the remnants of the Nazi regime, which had acted through a legal system that the victorious powers believed repeatedly violated accepted rules and principles of international law. And even if the London Agreement were construed to incorporate some portions of German law, for an international tribunal, particularly one discharging the obligations of an occupying power, it is hard to see how domestic German law could trump international law rules, such as the principle of legality. That the IMT defended itself against the charge that its decisions violated the principle of legality seems sufficient to demonstrate that it might well have believed the principle was ordinarily taken to be a part of public international law.

254 *See* 46 Stat. 2343, T. S. No. 796, 2 Bevans 732. For a discussion of the background of the Pact, *see* Jonathan Zasloff, *Law and the Shaping of American Foreign Policy: From the Gilded Age to the New Era,* 78 N.Y.U. L. Rev. 239, 284–86 (2003).

its own terms provides as the sanction for its violation the denial of the right under the treaty to be free from whatever conduct is prohibited under the treaty. It does not even provide for a judicially imposed sanction, much less a criminal sanction.

b. Context—The parties to the treaty knew exactly how to state that war would be a crime, since the League of Nations' Assembly proposal for a draft Treaty of Mutual Assistance on September 29, 1923 expressly provided that "the Contracting Parties solemnly declare that aggressive war is an international crime and severally undertake that no one of them will be guilty of its commission."[255] Thus, if the drafters of the Pact of Paris wanted to criminalize aggressive war, they knew exactly how to do it, and they clearly chose not to do so.

c. Negotiating History—The ratification history reveals precisely why the parties to the Pact of Paris did not wish to criminalize or otherwise sanction aggressive war. They simply could not agree on a definition and wished to reserve for themselves exclusive authority to determine its meaning in individual cases. The United States Senate Foreign Relations Committee reported the treaty "with the understanding that the right of self-defense is in not curtailed or impaired by [its] terms of conditions," and "that [e]ach nation ... is the sole judge of what constitutes the right of self-defense and the necessity and extent of the same," and that "the United States regards the Monroe Doctrine as part of its national security and self-defense."[256] The U.S. Executive Branch shared this view, for Secretary of State Kellogg had placed in the negotiating record a statement that the Pact did not preclude self-defense and that each Power was to be the sole judge of what constituted self-defense.[257] The French Foreign Minister Aristide Briand, in a speech to the assembled dignitaries upon signing the Pact, said: "But, you say, there is no true realism in this Pact. And where are the sanctions? Well, is that realism which exclude from the realm of facts all moral forces, among them that of public opinion?"[258] And the British insisted on a reservation respecting their rights with respect to "regions of the world" that "constituted a special and vital interest" for the British Empire.[259] Certainly as an ordinary matter of the law of treaties, then, Germany would have been entitled in its relations with Allied Powers to the benefit of this restrictive understanding of the effect of the Pact of Paris.

d. Subsequent Practice—Little can be said for a criminal law interpretation of the Pact of Paris on the basis of subsequent practice. Speaking as a private person after he left government service, former U.S. Secretary of State Henry Stimson, in explaining and defending his policy

255 League of Nations, Official Journal. Sp. Supp. No. 13 (1923) at 154, 403.

256 *See* Myers, *supra* note 233, at 68–69.

257 *Id.* at 135–35.

258 James T. Shotwell, War as an Instrument of National Policy and Its Renunciation in the Pact of Paris 185 (1929).

259 Myers, *supra* note 233, at 344, 346–47 (Diplomatic Note of the British Government, May 19, 1928)

of non-recognition of Japanese aggression in Manchuria, described the League's treatment of Japan as "the record of the arraignment, the trial and the condemnation of a great power for the violation of certain new standards of conduct aimed at preventing international aggression."[260] But Stimson's remarks were obviously metaphorical.

Of far greater significance, the parties to the Pact of Paris never asserted that it was violated by German or Japanese aggression during the inter-war period. Indeed, French, German and Russian policy in the days before the Second World War could fairly be characterized as facilitating German aggression against Czechoslovakia, Austria, and Poland.[261] And academic commentary throughout this period held that the Pact of Paris had not established a definite rule of international law criminalizing aggressive war.[262]

b) Individual Criminal Responsibility for Aggressive War: The Versailles Treaty

The IMT's reliance on Article 227 of the Versailles Treaty to make out the claim that individual criminal responsibility for the crime of aggressive war was also established by the beginning of the Second World War is equally unsustainable. Again, the language, its history, and subsequent practice of the parties under the Versailles Treaty do not support the claim made by the Nuremberg Tribunal:

a. Text—This provision would have authorized charging the Kaiser with "a supreme offense against international morality and the sanctity of treaties."[263] The formulation clearly does not refer to any specific rule of international law – let alone any *criminal* rule. The negotiating history (considered below) explains why this is so.

b. Negotiating History—James Brown Scott,[264] a prominent international law scholar, expert on the law of war, and delegate to the Second Hague Peace Conference of 1907, led the United States delegation which rejected the proposal (brought by the Versailles Conference's Commission on the Responsibility of the Authors of the War and the Enforcement of Penalties) to define

260 Henry L. Stimson & McGeorge Bundy, On Active Service in Peace and War 227 (1947); *see generally* Zasloff, *supra* note 254 (for Stimson's interpretation of the Pact in the 1930s).

261 *See generally* Telford Taylor, Munich: The Price of Peace (1979).

262 *See* David Hunter Miller, The Peace Pact of Paris: A Study of the Kellogg-Briand Treaty (1928) (former member of the American Commission to the Versailles Conference); *see also* Edwin Borchard, *The Multilateral Treaty for the Renunciation of War*, 23 Am. J Int'l L. 116, 117–18 (1929) (perhaps the leading American international law scholar of the era).

263 For an exhaustive analysis, see James F. Willis, Prologue to Nuremberg: The Politics and Diplomacy of Punishing War Criminals of the First World War (1982).

264 Scott was a future President of the American Society of International Law and later author of a study of the jurisprudence of leading early modern Catholic naturalist international lawyers Vitoria and Suarez. *See* James Brown Scott, A Catholic Conception of International Law (Georgetown University Press 1934).

Germany's "war of aggression" as "an act directly contrary to positive law, or one which can be successfully brought before a[n] international tribunal."[265] Scott, joined by U.S. Secretary of State Robert Lansing, insisted that the Kaiser should be punished only as "prescribed by the law in force at the time of the commission of the act."[266] Lansing, himself a highly regarded international lawyer while in private practice, later privately wrote to President Woodrow Wilson, describing the proposal as an "international Lynch law."[267] And Scott later suggested the language was changed to the amorphous formulation to acknowledge the reality that there was no positive international law basis for the prosecution.[268]

If so, the negotiating history establishes that the parties understood they were acting on the basis of power, not law—a "Victor's Justice," a "Carthaginian Peace," as Versailles was later described.[269] Certainly for the United States, the Senate's failure to ratify the Treaty of Versailles negated any possible American acquiescence in the proposed trial of the Kaiser.

c. Subsequent Practice—French and British behavior after the entry into force of the Versailles Treaty revealed their own doubts as to the legality of an attempt to prosecute the Kaiser. After the Kaiser sought asylum in neutral Holland, the Allies privately informed the Dutch government that their request was merely *pro forma*.[270] The Dutch Government accordingly responded that it deemed the request political rather than legal.[271] The Kaiser was never extradited for Allied prosecution under Article 227 of the Versailles Treaty; and he was never prosecuted by the Dutch Government, which clearly thus never acquiesced in the view that aggressive war was equivalent to a war crime that it would have had universal jurisdiction to prosecute.[272] The subsequent practice of all parties thus tends to corroborate the view that Article 227 was not understood to establish a norm or rule of positive international law.

---

265 United Nations War Crimes Commission, History of the United Nations War Crimes Commissions and the Development of the Laws of War 237 (HM Stationery Office, London, 1948).

266 *Id.* at 40.

267 Willis, *supra* note 263, at 77 (citations omitted).

268 *See* J.B. Scott, The Trial of the Kaiser, in What Really Happened at Paris 231, 237 (E.M. House & C. Seymour eds., 1921).

269 Etienne Mantoux, A Carthaginian Peace: Or, The Economic Consequences of Mr. Keynes (1946) [1937] (arguing, against John Maynard Keynes, that the Versailles settlement was not nearly harsh enough).

270 *See* Willis, *supra* note 263, at 107.

271 *See id.* at 241.

272 The former Imperial German Chancellor Bethmann-Holweg, who was in office at the time of the War's outbreak, challenged the Allies to try him instead of the Kaiser, on the grounds that he, not the Kaiser, was constitutionally responsible for Germany's decision to go to war. The Allies ignored his offer. *See* Alexander Watson, Ring of Steel: Germany and Austria-Hungary at War 1914-1918 at 558 (2014).

ii. The Procedural Illegitimacy of the International Military Tribunals

The judgments of the Tokyo Tribunal were subject to similar objections, which were exhaustively articulated by Justice Rabhabinod Pal.[273] For present purposes, rather than duplicating those objections, we shall identify and discuss Justice Pal's additional objections as to the procedural legitimacy of the Tokyo Tribunal. The procedural deficiencies of the two Tribunals fall into two categories.

a. Composition of the Tribunal—First, the backgrounds of the Justices who sat on the Tribunals raised questions about the Tribunals' capacity to apply the law neutrally and without bias. All but two of the Justices on the IMTFE were nationals, not of states that had been neutrals in the War, but of states that had either defeated Japan or been badly victimized by it; and only two of the Justices were Asian.[274] Granted, there was no pre-War rule of international law governing the selection of judges on international tribunals to try the crimes prosecuted before the IMT and IMTFE. But the objection might have been expressed as a corollary of the principle of legality, in that a biased tribunal might be strongly inclined to apply (or be perceived as applying) even established international law in an entirely new way. If so, Justice Pal's objections might have been framed in positivist terms. Indeed, Pal cited the leading positivist international legal scholar of the era, University of California law professor Hans Kelsen, to support that argument: "'the victorious states too should be willing to transfer their jurisdiction over their own subjects who have offended the laws of warfare to the same independent and impartial international tribunal.' "[275]

At the same time, Pal also noted that there was "a provision in the Charter itself permitting the judges to decline to take part in the trial if for any reason they consider that they should not do so." He added: "The special difficulty as to the rule of law governing this case, taken with the ordinary uncertainty as to how far our means are sufficient to detect a crime and coupled further with the awkward possibilities of bias created by racial or political factors, makes our position one of very grave responsibility. The accused cannot be found fault with, if, in these circumstances, they entertain any such apprehension, and I, for myself, fully appreciate the basis of their fear."[276]

---

273 *See* Pal, Radhabinod. "Judgment," *in* The Tokyo Judgment: The International Military Tribunal for the Far East (IMTFE) 29 April 1946 – 12 November 1948 (B. V. A. Röling and C. F. Rüter eds., University Press Amsterdam 1977).

274 Justice Pal, an Indian, was a British subject, though India was to achieve its independence from the British Empire soon after. Because of India's unique role in the Second World War, he might plausibly have been regarded as a representative of a "neutral" nation. Justice Delfin Jaramilla of the Philippines was the other Asian justice. However, Jaramilla's freedom from bias might have been questioned, inasmuch as he had been forced by the Japanese Army in the Philippines to take part in the infamous "Bataan death march" of 1942. All twelve of the Justices were appointed by General Douglas MacArthur, the U.S. military commander in charge of the occupation of Japan.

275 Documents on the Tokyo International Military Tribunal, supra note 77, at 816 [12].

276 *Id.* at 817 [14].

In short, Pal seemed to affirm that because of the racial and political backgrounds of the Justices, the IMTFE lacked the neutrality that he viewed as an essential feature of the "administration of justice"; yet, at the same time, he did not himself refuse to serve on the ground that the composition of the Tribunal constituted an "international denial of justice." Pal's argument seems to come down to the essentially subjective assumption that the racial and political background of the Japanese defendants would create an appearance of injustice and a risk of bias on the part of their non-Asian Justices.

b. Authority of the Tribunal—Second, Justice Pal considered the law-making capacity of the tribunals suspect. It is in the context of the IMTFE's perceived, and perhaps inevitable, lack of neutrality that Pal launched a profound attack on the conception of the international legal system that the majority, in his view, relied upon to find as a matter of new, emergent international customary law, authority to punish the crime of aggression.

Pal argued that the global legal order remained, despite aspirations to the contrary, a system of sovereign states. "No international community of any higher order came into being. The League showed particularly scrupulous regard for national sovereignty and laid special emphasis on such sovereignty by adopting the principle of unanimous vote. National sovereignty and national interest continued to play the fundamental part in this organization."[277] While he acknowledged that the "post war United Nations Organization is certainly a material step toward the formation of such a society,"[278] he did not judge that such a community or international society as yet existed.

It was on this ground that he rejected the notion that judges could, analogizing to earlier precedents, bind states to new law to which they have never given their consent. (On this point he continues to stand on reasonably firm ground, as the current International Court of Justice's decisions are binding only as between the parties to the case that have consented to its jurisdiction.[279]) Pal wrote:

> In our quest of international law, are we dealing with an entity like national societies completely brought under the rule of law? Or, are we dealing with an inchoate society in a stage of its formation? It is a society where only that rule has come to occupy the position of law which has been unanimously agreed upon by the parties concerned. Any new precedent made will not be the law safe-guarding the peace-loving, law-abiding members of the Family of Nations, but will only be a precedent for the future victors against the future vanquished. Any misapplication of a doubtful legal doctrine here will threaten the very formation of the much coveted Society of Nations, will shake the very foundations of any future international society. ... Law stems from

277 Documents on the Tokyo International Military Tribunal, supra note 77, at 866 [135].

278 *Id.* at 870 [145].

279 Statute of the International Court of Justice, Art 59, June 26, 1945, 59 Stat. 1055, T.S. 993, 3 Bevans 1179.

man's reasonableness and from his innate sense of justice. But what is that law? And is international law of that character?[280]

For Justice Pal, unlike Justice Jackson,[281] the question answered itself. While domestic law may have natural law foundations, and a domestic judge may exercise a law-making, precedent-establishing capacity, a judge in an international court may not. Thus, because there was no positive law foundation for the crime of aggressive war, and the positive law basis for the international legal system required a strict theory of state consent, the IMTFE was barred from "finding" new rules to govern new circumstances, even for a changing, inchoate international society. Indeed, while acknowledging that the use of atomic weapons may have "destroyed selfish nationalism," he quickly added that this new consciousness was "non-existent at the time the bombs were dropped."[282] Even the use of nuclear weapons was not governed by positive international law on August 6 and 8, 1945.

iii. The Reasoning in the Shimoda Court's Opinion—Legal, Political, or Moral?

Nearly twenty years after Judge Pal's dissent, a civil court in Japan revisited the question of the legality of the use of nuclear weapons, which Judge Pal implicitly deemed lawful under his conception of international law. What is striking about the *Shimoda* court's opinion is that, after all is said and done, it finds that a positive rule of international law, the rule of sovereign immunity, as it was internalized and made applicable to the law governing the dispute as a matter of domestic Japanese law, barred the court from ordering a remedy.

Like the famous *Marbury* decision, much of the opinion is therefore unnecessary to its result, mere dictum, which deflects attention from the court's deeply problematic claim that the nuclear weapons are subject to a prohibition drawn from pre-World War II "Draft Rules of Air Warfare." Those Draft Rules nominally extended the prohibitions of the rules governing land warfare adopted at the Hague Peace Conference of 1907 to air warfare.[283] While the court acknowledged that these rules "cannot directly be called positive law," it went on to say that "international jurists regard the Draft Rules as authoritative," that "[s]ome countries regard the substance of the Draft Rules as a standard of action by armed forces, and the fundamental provisions of the Draft Rules are consistently in conformity with international law and regulations, and customs at that time. Therefore, we can safely say that the prohibition of indiscriminate aerial bombard-

280 *See* Documents on the Tokyo International Military Tribunal, *supra* note 77, at 868 [141–42]

281 "In this connection I cannot refrain from referring to what Justice Jackson answered in his summing up of the case at Nuremberg. According to him, a preparation by a nation to dominate another nation is the worst of crimes. This may be so now. But I do not see how it could be said that such an attempt or preparation was crime before the Second World War when there was hardly a big power which was free from that taint." *Id.* at 867 [137].

282 *Id.* at 867 [138].

283 *See Shimoda, supra* note 245, at 129–31.

ment on an undefended city and the principle of military objective, which are provided for by the Draft Rules, are international customary law."[284] The opinion does not provide the factual basis for these conclusions, so that it is impossible to verify them. More important, it does not discuss the actual practice of states during the war—as it should have in order to address the important question whether, even if rule of customary international law had emerged during the inter-war period prohibiting certain forms of aerial bombing, a superseding rule of customary international had emerged during the Second World War. The failure to discuss evidence and selective discussion of other evidence calls the opinion's legal reasoning into serious question.

Yet the finding of the illegality of the use of nuclear weapons formally justified a powerful statement of facts that must have been deeply embarrassing to Japan's new ally and protector from potential Soviet, Chinese, and North Korean aggression. At the same time, the precise legal theory for the finding of illegality relates to the particular target, an undefended city with no military installations, which allows the court to narrow its dictum so as not to purport to bar the United States from using nuclear weapons in a more discriminate way against military targets when compelled do so under military necessity to defend Japan.

Viewed from this perspective, the opinion operates as a subtle political statement of the highest order (as is underscored by the fact that it was issued on December 7—the anniversary of the Japanese attack on Pearl Harbor). Like the Pal dissent, the *Shimoda* court's opinion makes a rhetorical appeal to the conscience of the powerful, much as the Mytilenes and Melians attempted to do in Thucydides' account. Rather than statements of positive international law, they draw on moral conceptions—conceptions of racial justice and intuitive revulsion against a description of the horrors of weapons of mass destruction—in order to appeal to the conscience of the hegemonic power. *Shimoda* reveals international law as a "weapon of the weak."

b. Thesis 2—The Limits of Legal Positivism in International Law: "Political" Foundations for the Nuremberg and Tokyo Trials

We introduced the concept of *legalism* briefly in the Chapter 1.A, contrasting it to *realism,* and then re-introduced it at the start of this section. Here we give a fuller explanation of what we mean by *legalism.* Our understanding is deeply influenced by Judith N. Shklar's Legalism: Law, Morals, and Political Trials (1964)—a foundational work by an eminent American political scientist that provides an illuminating and original treatment of the Nuremberg and Tokyo Trials.

Shklar defines "legalism" quite narrowly, as "the ethical attitude that holds moral conduct to be a matter of rule following, and moral relationships to consist of duties and rights determined by rules."[285] While that definition is reasonable for purposes of ethical theory, Shklar's work in fact exhibits a different and broader conception of legalism. We therefore prefer to characterize

284 *Id.* at 129.

285 *See* Judith N. Shklar Legalism: Law, Morals, and Political Trials 1 (1964)

"legalism" as a *policy* stance or outlook that displays three main characteristics. First, legalism is *formalist*. That is, it holds that law (especially in the form of criminal justice) is "a self-contained system of norms that is 'there,' identifiable without any reference to the content, aim, and development of the rules that compose it."[286] Insofar as it is formalist, legalism insists that law "must be self-regulating, immune from the unpredictable pressures of politicians and moralists, [and] manned by a judiciary that at least tries to maintain justice's celebrated blindness."[287] Second, legalism requires that law be *efficacious*. That is, that the desire for law-abidingness can, and should be, a sufficient motive in itself for action, causing individuals and states alike to comply with the demands of law for their own sake, regardless of what self-interest or any other motive might seem to dictate. (Indeed, legalism in some forms seems to ignore or deny law's dependence on violence.[288]) Third, legalism requires the *primacy* of law. That is, legalism holds that the satisfaction of the demands of legal justice may and ought to take precedence over any other opposing policy considerations or methods, including those of politics or diplomacy.

The Allied decision to hold criminal trials of the wartime Axis leadership illustrates the legalist mind-set at work. Other policy choices were available, and some indeed were favored, at least for a time, by particular Allied governments.[289] One such option would have been simply to execute the Nazi leaders upon capturing them. Another would have been to try them, but summarily, with a minimum of legal process. A third would have been to leave them judicially unpunished, but forced into exile. Owing chiefly to American pressure, the Allies agreed instead to the large-scale, procedurally demanding criminal trials that were held at Nuremberg and Tokyo. There was, therefore, nothing inevitable about the two great, post-War criminal trials. In

286 *Id.* at 33. *Compare Guido Calabresi, An Introduction to Legal Thought: Four Approaches to Law and to the Allocation of Body Parts,* 55 Stanford L. Rev. 2113, 2114–18 (2003). ("Formalism" is the idea is that law is autonomous, with its own distinctive principles, reasoning processes and modes of establishing facts); Frederick Schauer, *Formalism,* 97 Yale L. J. 509, 510 (1988) (core of formalism is "the concept of decisionmaking according to *rule*").

287 Shklar, *supra* note 285, at 35.

288 *See* Zasloff, *supra* note 254, at 95–101. *See generally* Robert Cover, *Violence and the Word,* 95 Yale L. J. 1601 (1986).

289 On September 15, 1944, President Franklin Roosevelt, meeting with Prime Minister Winston Churchill in Quebec, initialed a proposal that Churchill had brought with him, under which the Nazi leaders would not be tried at all, but would be summarily executed on a political basis upon proof of their identity. Churchill's proposal originated with one of his key legal advisors, Lord Chancellor Sir John Simon. The Quebec decision was also supported by the United States Treasury Department, whose Secretary, Henry Morgenthau, had shortly before, on September 6, 1944, submitted a memorandum to the President that recommended that once the Nazi "arch-criminals" had been apprehended and identified, they "shall be put to death forthwith by firing squads made up of soldiers of the United Nations." *Morgenthau Plan,* App. B. Art. A(1)(b). Roosevelt, largely in response to the pressure of his Secretary of War Henry Stimson, came to regret his approval of the Quebec memorandum (he called it "an egg that I myself laid"), and instead began favoring plans for judicial trials. Even as late as the Yalta Conference in February, 1945, however, both alternatives—summary execution on a political basis, judicial trials on a legal basis—remained open. Indeed, in April 1945, the very month in which the war in Europe ended, the British Cabinet took the position that "for the principal Nazi leaders a full trial under judicial procedure was out of the question." *See generally* Stimson & Bundy, *supra* note 260, at 584–91. The eventual Allied decision in favor of judicial trials instead of summary executions was dictated by the views of Roosevelt's successor, President Harry Truman, to which the British reluctantly yielded.

earlier wars, the leaders of the vanquished states either, like the Kaiser, went into enforced exile (as we have already discussed) or, like Napoleon, were detained indefinitely without trial.[290]

The legalist choice for holding criminal trials posed serious questions for legalism itself, however. As Shklar wrote:

> The main difficulty in pursuing the policy of justice is not that it has nothing to contribute politically. To the extent that it may reinforce legalistic values it is often very constructive, as it was at Nuremberg. That is, however, not the way in which its adherents conceive of their ends. In its exclusiveness, justice as a policy tends to ignore all other political ends and the very social circumstances which condition its effect and even its possibility. Formal justice depends for its social impact upon the total political environment in which judicial actions occur, and its functions cannot be understood in isolation. Yet isolation from politics is its first ideological demand. . . . On the international level of politics a single-minded pursuit of a policy of criminal justice has even graver defects. Since, for justice, law must either be "there" or "not there," it becomes necessary to pretend that a legal system analogous to a well-established domestic order exists. In the case of three of the architects of Nuremberg that meant a system such as prevails in constitutional democracies. That was the first fiction. It led to others, and to a greater concentration on charges which could be squeezed into the mold of municipal law (such as waging aggressive war) than on novel and important charges, like crimes against humanity. . . . History had to be tortured throughout in order to reduce events to proportions similar to those of a model criminal trial within a municipal system. The future was not altogether ignored, but it was seen, characteristically, as the future of law only. The contribution of the Trial was to be made to the future of international criminal law. It was to be an act within a legal system enhancing the strength of that system. To think of either the immediate political needs or the ideological impact of the Trial on Germany would have been to descend to mere politics. Nevertheless, it was these and these alone that justified the Trial.[291]

Legalism, for Shklar, must insist on the irrelevance of "politics" to the outcomes of criminal trials. Only norms and values internal to the trial process itself can be allowed to determine those outcomes. So, for instance, judges must be impartial; defendants must be competently represented by legal counsel of their own choice; the trying court must have jurisdiction over both the subject matter of the charges and the persons charged; reasonable rules of evidence and procedure must be followed; and in short the demands of criminal "due process," as measured by the *domestic* law of a mature liberal legal system, must be met.[292]

---

290 *See* J. Holland Rose, Napoleonic Studies, ch. xii (1904).

291 Shklar, *supra* note 285, at 146–47.

292 *See* Jon Elster, Closing the Books: Transitional Justice in Historical Perspective 88 (2004) (listing elements of due process required for "legal justice").

One obvious merit of legalism's insistence on the irrelevance of politics is that it curbs the tendency of those in power to use the criminal justice system to harass, disgrace or punish their political enemies. Hence, no doubt, the Framers of the U.S. Constitution made it procedurally extremely difficult for the prosecution to prevail on charges of treason.[293] Accordingly, where legalism's precepts are followed, a criminal trial will inevitably pose the risk that *the defendant will not be convicted*—a (legalist) criminal trial is always a kind of *wager.* Further, that risk will be present *even if the defendant's guilt is apparent*—because the conviction must be obtained in accordance with norms internal to the trial process, which are always tilted in favor of the defense.[294] The acquittal of the major Nazi defendants was, therefore, always a genuine possibility once the Allies went forward with the IMT trial, however damaging politically such an outcome might have been; and, in fact, of the 22 Nazi defendants before the IMT, three were acquitted, seven were sentenced to prison, and the remainder received the death penalty.[295]

To secure the just conviction of criminal defendants, however, legalist systems generally demand compliance with the "principle of legality": they require that the defendant be shown to have committed acts *that were criminal under the law as it stood when the act took place. "Nihil crimen sine lege*"—"No crime without a law"—and "*Nihil poena sine crimine*"—"No punishment without a crime"—are, as we have seen, characteristic axioms of legalist systems of justice. Like Justice Pal in the Tokyo Trials, Shklar viewed the retroactivity problem as a fatal defect of the Nuremberg Trials, if they were to be assessed by legalist standards:

> If the principle of legality, the existence of prior law, alone can justify a criminal trial, then the Trial was simply unjust. In order to evade that conclusion some lawyers either invented law on the basis of analogies drawn from their vision of municipal legal systems, or pretended that an international law in the form of custom or accepted usage did exist. The opponents of the Trials had little difficulty in exposing the feebleness of such rationalizations, nor were these necessary except as exercises in legalistic ideology.[296]

Shklar would presumably have disagreed, therefore, with Justice Röling's attempt at the IMTFE Trial to refute the non-retroactivity objection. Röling's argument was, in substance, that the non-retroactivity principle was not a legal rule, but merely "an expression of political wisdom" designed to protect individuals against arbitrariness by legislatures and courts. Röling's claim seems doubtful, however, if only because the non-retroactivity principle is constitutionally entrenched in so many legal systems and thus operates as a general principle of law in the

293 *See* U.S. Const. Art. III, Sec. 3.

294 *See* Elster, *supra* note 292, at 89–90.

295 *Id.* at 22.

296 Shklar, *supra* note 285, at 157.

international legal system as well.[297] Moreover, why did the IMTFE and the Allied powers that convened it *not* act arbitrarily towards the Japanese defendants? Was it because the defendants knew, or ought to have known, before the War that their actions were "crimes against the peace"? To make such a claim was to assume that Japan's pre-War imperialist policies differed in some material ways from those that had been practiced in Asia for decades by Britain, France, Holland, Russia, and the United States—all of whom were sitting in judgment on Japan. That assumption was, to say the least, open to question—as Justice Pal went to extraordinary lengths to show.

As an alternative to Justice Röling's argument, one might look to a theory employed by German courts after the Nuremberg Trials in trying Nazi defendants for acts that had been authorized by the laws of the Third Reich. Those courts sought to meet the retroactivity problem, and thus keep the trials within the ambit of "legalism," by appealing to the "Radbruch formula."[298] (Some post-Cold War courts in a newly unified Germany also invoked the Radbruch formula in criminal trials of former East German border guards who, in compliance with what appeared to be applicable Communist law, had murdered those trying to flee to West Germany.[299]) The formula originally appeared in a celebrated 1946 article, *Statutory Lawlessness and Supra-Statutory Law,* by the German jurisprudential expert and former Minister of Justice, Gustav Radbruch. There Radbruch stated:

> The conflict between justice and legal certainty may well be resolved in this way: The positive law, secured by legislation and power, takes precedence even when its content is unjust and fails

297 Röling's view was anticipated by the Harvard legal scholar Sheldon Glueck, who had argued in a 1944 book, War Criminals: Their Prosecution and Punishment (1944), that there was no ex post facto problem because the trial of the Nazi leadership was justifiable as "a morally legitimate exercise of a political policy on the part of the civilized nations of the world, a policy of expediency enforceable by the will of the victorious United Nations." *Id.* at 126.

298 For accounts of the cases, see David Dyzenhaus, *The Grudge Informer Case Revisited,* 83 N.Y.U. L. Rev. 1000 (2008); Stanley L. Paulson, *Radbruch on Unjust Laws: Competing Earlier and Later Views?,* 15 Oxford J. Leg. Stud. 489, 491 (1995); H.O. Pappe, *On the Validity of Judicial Decisions in the Nazi Era,* 23 Modern L. Rev. 260 (1960); Helen Silving, *In re Eichmann: A Dilemma of Law and Morality,* 55 Am. J. Int'l L. 307, 342–44 (1961); and Paul K. Ryu & Helen Silving, *Error Juris: A Comparative Study,* 24 U. Chi. L. Rev. 421, 465 (1957).

299 The decisions of the German courts in the border guard cases were reviewed and upheld by the European Court of Human Rights in *Case of Streletz, Kessler and Krenz v. Germany,* Applications nos. 34044/96, 35532/97 & 44801/98, Judgment, Strasbourg (22 Mar. 2001). The German Federal Constitutional Court, in reviewing the decision of the German Federal Court of Justice, noted that the latter had found that the "imprecise" criteria of the Radbruch formula had been "supplemented" by later, post-War international human rights law; further, the Federal Constitutional Court expressed the opinion that "[t]o establish punishability there is no need here for recourse to supra-positive legal principles" because it was possible to rely instead on "the values which the [East German legal system] itself took as the basis for its criminal law." *Id.* at 13. The reasoning has led some scholars to argue that instead of constructing an "ideal" East German law, the German courts ought instead to have admitted candidly that they were applying new law to the cases. *See* Elster, *supra* note 292, at 238–39. For further commentary, *see* Rudolf Geiger, *The German Border Guard Cases and International Human Rights,* 9 Eur. J. Int'l L. 540 (1998).

> to benefit the people, *unless the conflict between statute and justice reaches such an intolerable degree that the statute, as "flawed law," must yield to justice.*[300]

Radbruch's formula may have supplied a rationale for later German courts to try, convict, and sentence Nazi and Communist government agents for having committed atrocities that were authorized, or even mandatory, under the laws of their régimes, despite the apparent *ex post facto* problem.[301] In effect, it seemed to provide that laws whose application constituted unbearable acts of injustice and inhumanity were not valid laws at all. Courts punishing such defendants could therefore take the "legalist" position that there was no conflict between the *nullum crimen sine lege* principle and the requirements of material justice.

From Shklar's viewpoint, however, this response to the retroactivity problem would seem to be unpersuasive, insofar as it relies on a non-positivist, natural law-based account of the validity of unjust laws.[302] In her analysis of the Tokyo Trials, Shklar criticized the legal strategy of the chief prosecutor, Joseph Keenan, precisely because "[h]is entire case [was] based on natural law, universal and thoroughly supra-local in its perspectives."[303] Shklar seemed to accept the view that "natural law is capable of too many interpretations in any concrete situation to provide an objective and impersonal basis for international criminal trials."[304] She illustrated that contention by pointing to Justice Bernard's dissent in the Tokyo Trials, which was also based on natural law, but which contradicted the prosecution's version of it. For Justice Bernard, but not for Mr. Keenan, it would have violated the natural law norms of procedural justice to have convicted the defendants on the charge of waging aggressive war. "[T]he charge which Mr. Keenan's natural law supported, Justice Bernard's natural law rejected."[305] For Shklar, then, the

---

300 Gustav Radbruch, *Statutory Lawlessness and Supra-Statutory Law*, 26 Oxford J. of Leg. Stud. 1, 7 (2006) (emphasis added). This is not the only formulation Radbruch gave to his idea, although it was the most influential one. *See* Brian Bix, *Robert Alexy, Radbruch's Formula, and the Nature of Legal Theory*, 37 Rechsttheorie S. 139, 140 (2006). Likewise, Radbruch's formulation is not the only—and may not be the most refined—presentation of the core idea. *See id.* at 139.

301 Article 102, § 2 of the post-Second World War German Constitution or *Grundgestez* emphatically states that an act may be punished only if it is a criminal offense determined by a law in force before the act was committed. *See* Geiger, *supra* note 299, at 547. Furthermore, the Unification Treaty between East and West Germany permitted prosecutions only for acts that were criminal when committed under both nations' legal systems.

302 Scholars disagree over whether Radbruch's post-War writings in fact depended on natural law assumptions or concern legal validity. *See* Stanley L. Paulson, *On the Background and Significance of Gustav Radbruch's Post-War Papers*, 26 Oxford Journal of Legal Studies 17, 35–38 (2006); Thomas Mertens, *Nazism, Legal Positivism and Radbruch's Thesis on Statutory Injustice*, 14 Law & Critique 277 (2003); and Stanley L. Paulson, *Radbruch on Unjust Laws: Competing Earlier and Later Views?*, 15 Oxford J. Leg. Stud. 489, 494–500 (1995). Mertens, for example, argues that Radbruch's main concern was not to justify the apparently retroactive application of criminal law by appeal to natural law or to hold that seemingly valid Nazi-era laws were invalid because contrary to natural law, but instead to argue only that Nazi-era judges were not to be considered criminally liable for having respected then-established criminal law, however horrific it was.

303 Shklar, *supra* note 285, at 181.

304 *Id.* at 185.

305 *Id.*

Radbruch formula might ultimately fail to satisfy the stabilizing requirements of (at least the positivistic form of) "legalism."[306]

Indeed, Shklar went even further than most "legalist" critics of the Nuremberg Trials had done by contending that even the charge of war crimes was untenable:

> The Hague Convention of 1907 did not provide any system of international criminal law to be administered by an international criminal tribunal. The Convention bears not the slightest resemblance to domestic criminal law. The relative antiquity of the conventional war crimes charges does not add anything to their legality. . . . As for the legality of the Hague Convention, it is a chimera. There is no security in relying upon agreements as if they were a part of an operative system of criminal law. An international treaty is simply not analogous to a criminal law. Conventional war crimes are no more, and no less, legal than any other charge made at the Trial.[307]

Nonetheless, Shklar did not condemn the Nuremberg Trials; on the contrary, she saw them as an act of justice, even of legal justice, stating, "[i]ronically, perhaps, a trial without law, in this instance, was still a closer approximation of justice, more in keeping with legalistic values, than any other course of action."[308]

Famously, the German Jewish thinker Hannah Arendt took the diametrically opposite position. Her widely read and controversial book, *Eichmann in Jerusalem* (1963), was based in part on her coverage of the trial of the Nazi bureaucrat Adolf Eichmann as a reporter for *The New Yorker* magazine. Arendt found the Eichmann trial flawed for legalist reasons very similar to those for which Shklar had faulted the Nuremberg and Tokyo Trials. Yet, unlike Shklar, Arendt concluded that a "political" justification for Eichmann's trial was improper:

---

306 We leave open the question whether the rejoinder we are here ascribing to Shklar would be convincing. One might argue that the prohibition on ex post facto criminal laws is an application of the "principle of legality" or "the rule of law," and hence that the prohibition is not consistent even with classical legal positivism. If that claim is correct, then "legalism" could not *both* prohibit retroactive criminal laws and punishments *and* draw the unbridgeable distinction between law and morality Shklar envisions.

307 Shklar, *supra* note 285, at 163.

308 *Id.* at 160. Others scholars agree. *See, e.g.*, Richard Primus, *A Brooding Omnipresence*, 106 Yale L.J. 423, 431 (1996) ("The propriety of Nuremberg rested on the distinctly nonpositivist principle that some things were simply wrong, whether codified or not, and that justice sometimes calls upon courts to act even when they lack formal legal authorization."). In a somewhat similar vein, Gerry Simpson has taken the Nuremberg Trials to represent a "move from history, politics and conscience to crime." Gerry Simpson, *Objective Responsibility: Show Trials and War Crimes Trials*, 4 Int'l Law on Evidence 1, 5 (2006).

> The purpose of a trial is to render justice, and nothing else; even the noblest of ulterior purposes . . . can only detract from the law's main business: to weigh the charges brought against the accused, to render judgment, and to mete out due punishment.[309]

Defending Shklar's approach over Arendt's, Lawrence Douglas has argued that the limits of Arendt's "rule-based vision of legality" have been shown by "narrative jurisprudence."[310] According to Douglas, "for rules-based formalism, questions of narrative are extralegal, while narrative jurisprudence, by insisting that rules fail to exhaust the universe of what counts as law, insists on a more capacious understanding of the legal. . . . Not surprisingly, narrative jurisprudence has treated as its principal object of study the criminal trial. . . . The trial, from this perspective, must be seen not simply as a procedural device whose legitimacy is governed by rules generated within the system of legality itself, but as a complex ritual which produces and suppresses narrative and clarifies and obscures history."[311] On Douglas' view, trials like those of the Axis defendants at Nuremberg and Tokyo or of Eichmann in Jerusalem must, indeed, satisfy some minimum of "legalist" procedural and evidentiary standards (thus, no summary convictions). But they may deviate to some extent from the "rules generated within the system of legality itself" provided that in doing so they serve some higher end—substantive, if not legal—justice, or perhaps even what Friedrich Nietzsche called "great politics" or "politics in the grand style."[312]

Seen in that light, the Nuremberg Trials might be considered as the founding or "constitutional" moment of a new legal order in Europe—and hence as extra-legal rather than "legal." The Yale Law professor Robert Cover argued in a famous law review article that "[e]very legal order must conceive of itself in one way or another as emerging out of that which is itself unlawful. This conception is the mythic or narrative restatement of the positivist's concept of the rule of recognition or *Grundnorm*."[313] As in Aeschylus' *Eumenides,* in which the trial of Orestes served both to mark the end of the cycle of violence in the House of Atreus and to

---

309 Hannah Arendt, Eichmann in Jerusalem: A Report on the Banality of Evil 2–3 (rev'd ed. 2006). For a contrary view, *see* Schwarzenberg, *supra* note 200, at 250 (arguing that even if "the sole legitimate object of a criminal trial is the administration of criminal justice," nonetheless such trials encompass extra-legal ends such as deterrence and correction that "fulfil[] social functions of an essentially educational character. . . . In particular, this is true of sedition and treason trials. In their nature, they are a continuation of politics by other means.").

310 Lawrence Douglas, The Memory of Judgment: Making Law and History in the Trials of the Holocaust 112 (2001).

311 *Id.* at 112–13.

312 *See* Friedrich Nietzsche, Beyond Good and Evil sec. 208 (1886) ("The time for small politics is over: the very next century will bring a struggle for dominion over the earth, the *obligation* for great politics."). *See also* Friedrich Nietzsche, Twilight of the Idols (*"Expeditions of an Untimely Man"*) sec. 11 (1889; R.J. Hollingdale trans. 1993) ("The highest feeling of power and security finds expression in that which possesses *grand style.* Power which is slow to answer; which is conscious of no witness around it; which reposes in *itself,* a law among laws."). On Nietzsche's conception of "grand politics," *see, e.g.*, Tracy B. Strong, Friedrich Nietzsche and the Politics of Transfiguration 210–13 (2000).

313 Robert Cover, *Foreword: Nomos and Narrative,* 97 Harv. L. Rev. 4, 23 (1983).

celebrate the institution of law-governed, democratic Athens,[314] so the Nuremberg Trials were intended to break the cycle of war and revenge that had beset Europe since Germany's triumph over France in the Franco-Prussian War, and to place Germany on law-governed democratic foundations that would consolidate the peace. Nuremberg was an effort in constructing "a normative universe . . . a world of right and wrong, of lawful and unlawful, of valid and void" that combined "law and narrative."[315] "Law" here took the form of the system of positive rules that the Nuremberg courts framed; "narrative" took the form, not only of the harrowing accounts given at the Trials of the Nazis' unprecedented atrocities and lawlessness, but even more of the unforgettable visual imagery both of Nazi concentration camps shown at the Trial and of the Nazi defendants' reactions to watching it.[316] From this perspective, the Nuremberg Trials simply cannot be measured by standards internal to legal positivism. The Trials gave birth to a *Grundnorm* by which positivist legality was subsequently *to be* assessed.[317] Indeed, looking out even further, Nuremberg might yet prove to be the harbinger of a new, non-State-based, post-Westphalian global legal order.[318]

To sum up, the Trials exhibit both the attractions and the perils of legalism. In the self-understanding of the main actors in them, the Trials were an exemplary demonstration of the rule of law at work, uncorrupted by political or other non-legal influences.[319] Yet the convictions

314 On the connections between Aeschylean tragedy and the emergence of Athenian democracy, and on the role of justice as dramatized in *The Oresteia* in supplanting the cycle of vengeance, *see* J. Peter Euben, *Justice and the Oresteia,* 76 Am. Pol. Sci. Rev. 22 (1982).

315 Cover, *supra* note 313, at 4–5. *See also* Theodor Meron, *From Nuremberg to the Hague,* 149 Mil. L. Rev. 107, 109–10 (1995) (describing lawless retaliation and violence that might have occurred in Germany in the absence of the Nuremberg trials).

316 *See* Douglas, *supra* note 310, at 27–37 (discussing effect of film at the IMT Trial).

317 Gerry Simpson suggests that Nuremberg served other "grand" political purposes (different from those we have identified): to vindicate Western progress; to demonstrate that Nazism was an aberration in Western history; and to draw moral demarcations between the Allies and Germany and divert attention from the Allies' own wrongful acts. *See* Gerry Simpson, *Didactic and Dissident Histories in War Crimes Trials,* 60 Alb. L. Rev. 801, 810 (1996–97).

Somewhat similarly, Martii Koskenniemi raises the possibility, in connection with later international criminal trials, that they provide occasions on which "we outsiders admire our own moral sensibilities and capacity for quick compassion, a memory serving our personal and social projects, far removed from the events on trial—perhaps the construction of an 'international community' out of the tragedies of others." Martii Koskenniemi, *Between Impunity and Show Trials,* 6 Max Plannck Y.B. U.N. Law 1, 34 (2002).

318 *See* Frédéric Mégret, *Epilogue to an Endless Debate,* 12 Eur. J. Int'l L. 260, 264 (2001) ("[I]nternational criminal justice threatens to overturn the last pillars of Westphalia. . . . If one is serious about individual criminal responsibility as a concept, therefore, one will sooner or later have to draw all consequences from the fact that it has the ambition of becoming the preferred option for enforcement of what the [international] community increasingly considers as its constitutive norms. As such, it has the potential to replace state responsibility as the ultimate linchpin of the global normative order."). Similarly, Lelia Nadya Sadat has argued that "the repartition of competences between national and international jurisdictions incorporated in the [Rome] Statute as a matter of prescriptive and adjudicative jurisdiction may presage a quasi-federal organization of international legal authority in the future." Lelia Nadya Sadat, *The International Criminal Court and the Transformation of International Law: Justice for the New Millenium* 11 (2002) (quoted in Robert Cryer, *International Criminal Law vs. State Sovereignty: Another Round?,* 16 Eur. J. Int'l L. 979, 993 (2005).

319 This is not to say that the main protagonists did not have other, non-legalist motives. For the argument that the Trials were an early phase of the Cold War struggle, see Francine Hirsch, *The Soviets at Nuremberg: International Law, Propaganda, and the Making of Postwar Order,* 113 Am. Hist. Rev. 701 (2008).

that the Trials produced, at least on the aggressive war charges, were highly problematic under standard legalist premises, as the same actors realized. Moreover, in another irony, the Trials, on legalist premises, could not and should not have had any didactic or "political" function. Yet, at least as Shklar viewed it, the chief justification for the Nuremberg Trials, and its most significant success, lay in creating a radically different political culture in Germany from that of the Nazi period—a political culture in which German élites were reminded of the power and authority of legalism, and in which (West) Germany was reborn as a *Rechtsstaat*—a state in which ordinary criminal trials were conducted fairly, decently and humanely.[320] In a final twist of irony, that welcome political outcome could only have been achieved if the Trials were widely understood as what they in fact were not—as examples of pure legalism at work.[321]

320 *See* Shklar, *supra* note 285, at 169. For an expression of doubt as to whether the Nuremberg Trials achieved that didactic purpose, *see* Koskenniemi, *supra* note 317, at 5–6.

321 *Cf.* Plato, The Republic, Bk II, ¶¶ 414–17 *in* Plato, The Collected Dialogues 658–61 (Hamilton and Cairns eds., 1961) (the so-called "Noble Lie" propagated by the Guardians of the Republic, its overlords, that "all men are brothers," which serves to legitimize the Guardians' rule).

Chapter 2

Modern Reformulations: Neo-Realism, Rational Choice Theory, and Constructivism

In recent years, international law scholars have become increasingly interested in the study of international relations theory,[1] and international relations theorists have reciprocated with a growing interest in international law.[2] This Chapter seeks to explore the applications of international relations theory to deepen the understanding of international law.

In Chapter 1, we explored the dialectic between two continually recurring positions: *realism*, which rejects or minimizes the influence of international law on the conduct of states in

1 A fundamental early study is Kenneth W. Abbott, *Modern International Relations Theory: A Prospectus for International Lawyers,* 14 Yale J. Int'l L. 335 (1989) [hereinafter Abbott, *Modern International Relations Theory].* Abbott's later writings on the interrelationship of the two disciplines include Kenneth W. Abbott, *Toward a Richer Institutionalism for International Law and Policy,* 1 J. Int'l L. & Int'l Rels. 9 (2004/05) [hereinafter "Abbott, *Toward a Richer Institutionalism*"]; Kenneth W. Abbott & Duncan Snidal, *Hard and Soft Law in International Governance,* 54 Int'l Org. 421 (2000); Kenneth W. Abbott, *International Relations Theory, International Law, and the Regime Governing Atrocities in Internal Conflicts,* 93 Am. J. Int'l L. 361 (1999) [hereinafter "Abbott, *Regime Governing Atrocities in Internal Conflicts*"]; Kenneth W. Abbott, *Trust But Verify: The Production of Information in Arms Control Treaties and Other International Agreements,* 26 Cornell Int'l L. J. 1 (1993) [hereinafter "Abbott, *Trust But Verify*"]. Other important articles and book chapters include Anne-Marie Burley, *Law and the Liberal Paradigm in International Relations Theory,* 86 Am. Soc. Int'l L. Proc. 180 (1992); Jack Goldsmith, *Book Review: Sovereignty, International Relations Theory, and International Law,* 52 Stanford L. Rev. 959 (2000); Niels Peterson, *How Rational Is International Law?,* 20 Eur. J. Int'l L. 1247 (2009); Eric Posner & Alan Sykes, *Optimal War and Jus ad Bellum,* 93 Geo. L. J. 993 (2005); Eric Posner, *A Theory of the Laws of War,* 70 U. Chi. L. Rev. 297 (2003); Steven R. Ratner & Anne-Marie Slaughter, *Appraising the Methods of International Law: A Prospectus for Readers,* 93 Am. J. Int'l L. 291 (1999); John K. Setear, *An Iterative Perspective on Treaties: A Synthesis of International Relations Theory and International Law,* 37 Harv. Int'l L. J. 139 (1996); Anne-Marie Slaughter, *International Law and International Relations Theory,* in*The Impact of International Law on International Cooperation: Theoretical Perspectives* (Eyal Benvenisti & Moshe Hirsch eds., 2004); Anne-Marie Slaughter, Andrew S. Tulumello & Stepan Wood, *International Law and International Relations Theory: A New Generation of Interdisciplinary Scholarship,* 92 Am. J. Int'l L. 367 (1998); Anne-Marie Slaughter Burley, *International Law and International Relations Theory: A Dual Agenda,* 87 Am. J. Int'l L. 205 (1993); Richard H. Steinberg & Jonathan M. Zasloff, *Power and International Law,* 100 Am. J. Int'l L. 64 (2006); and Fernando R. Teson, *Realism and Kantianism in International Law,* 96 Am. Soc. Int'l Law. Proc. 113 (1992).

Significant book-length studies include Anthony Clark Arend, Legal Rules and International Society (1999); Michael Byers, Custom, Power and the Power of Rules: International Relations and Customary International Law (1999); Antonia Chayes and Abe Chayes, The New Sovereignty: Compliance with International Regulatory Agreements (1995); Jack Goldsmith & Eric Posner, The Limits of International Law (2005); Andrew T. Guzman, How International Law Works: A Rational Choice Theory (2008); Eric Posner, Perils of Global Legalism (2009); and Joel P. Trachtman, The Economic Structure of International Law (2008). A useful survey of the subject is Michael Byers, *International Law,* inThe Oxford Handbook of International Relations 612 (Christian Reus-Smit & Duncan Snidal eds., 2008) [hereinafter, "Oxford Handbook"].

2 See, e.g., Robert O. Keohane, *Rational Choice Theory and International Law: Insights and Limitations,* 31 J. Leg. Stud. 307 (2002) [hereinafter "Keohane, *Rational Choice Theory and International Law*"]; Robert O. Keohane, *International Relations and International Law: Two Optics,* 38 Harv. Int'l L. J. 487 (1997) [hereinafter "Keohane, *International Relations and International Law*"]; Robert O. Keohane, *International Institutions: Two Approaches,* 32 Int'l Stud. Q. 379 (1988) [hereinafter "Keohane, *International Institutions*"]; Stephen D. Krasner, *Realist Views of International Law,* 96 Am. Soc. Int'l L. 265 (2002); Stephen D. Krasner, *International Law and International Relations: Together, Apart, Together,* 1 Chi. J. Int'l L. 93 (2000).

international affairs, especially those relating to war and national security, and *legalism*, which maintains that international law may, should, and does exert such an influence on states' conduct, even when security is concerned. In Chapter 1.A, we presented realism in terms of its classical roots—realism in the form that Thucydides represented it through the Athenian interlocutors in his *History*. In Chapter1.B, we presented legalism in the form of positivist international law as a response to the threat or use of extreme force by states, such as the Athenian destruction of Melos, the atomic bombing of Hiroshima and Nagasaki, or Hitler's war of aggression and extermination. In this Chapter, we resume studying the conversation between realists and legalists. We do this by examining two dominant schools of contemporary international relations theory: on the one hand, a school called "structural realism" (or "neo-realism") and the developments that have unfolded from it, culminating in what is called "rational choice" theory; and, on the other hand, a schoolcalled "constructivism" that rejects or questions the basic premises of rational choice theory in a way that parallels legalism's idealist response to traditional realism.

Although structural realism remains an important and influential position, a consensus seems to be emerging among international relations scholars that their discipline will be dominated by the debate between rational choice theory and constructivism.[3] At any rate, we shall assume that these are the most plausible international relations theories currently available. Accordingly, we accept that the study of international law will increasingly involve a debate between theories of international law drawn from these two competing viewpoints.

The contrast between the two major trends in international relations thought that will be studied in this Chapter is analogous, in some respects, to the contrast between the kind of realismand legalism that we considered in Chapter 1. The correspondence is by no means exact for at least two reasons.First, both trends offer accounts of international relations, not of international law, althoughthey are the product of a different academic discipline these trends carry significant implications for the study of international law. Second, whereas the contrast between realism and legalism presented in Chapter 1 posed a very stark opposition between two accounts of international law, the two theories highlighted here—rational choice theory and constructivism—suggest far more nuanced and complicated accounts of international law.

We might say that rational choice theory can supply the basis for an account of international law (and specifically of legal positivism) that enables law to play a vital role in constructing international institutions that abate conflict and promote cooperation. Unlike Athenian realism, therefore, contemporary realism, at least as interpreted through rational choice theory, is far from denying that international law can affect the behavior of states. Nonetheless, in their standard formulations, contemporary realism and rational choice theory assume—as Athenian realism did—that states value their survival, security, and even power aggrandizement very highly, and that their behavior is largely driven by those concerns—even when that behavior is unlawful.

3 *See* Peter Katzenstein, Robert Keohane & Stephen Krasner, *International Organization and the Study of World Politics*, 52 Int'l Org. 645, 683 (1998).

We might also say thatjust as legalism envisaged a far more powerful role for international law than Athenian realism did, constructivism also creates the possibility of a greater role for international law than rational choice theory does. In essence, this is because constructivism teaches that states are not locked by the condition of international anarchy into a "security dilemma" that causes them to become so fearful of the threats posed by other states that trust and cooperation between states are problematic. In other words, states are responsive to norms and ideals and can transform themselves in light of them; the desire to be, and to be perceived as, law-abiding can become an important component of a state's self-identity. In constructivist theory, therefore, the norms defined by international law can transform both states and the international system.

Explaining the turn to interdisciplinary work. The turn to this interdisciplinary analysis of international law and international relations had two faces: a descriptive or "positive" side, and a normative side. The positive side sought to describe, predict, and explain what states do—all subjects of undoubted interest to international law. Furthermore, international relations theory offered the prospect of a better understanding of legal phenomena that have a heightened importance in the post-World War II era, including global international institutions such as the United Nations and the World Trade Organization, and the emergence after Nuremberg of an international human rights regime and a set of institutions dedicated to the criminal enforcement of human rights and humanitarian legal norms.

International lawyers sought not only to account for patterns of behavior, but also to use interdisciplinary analysis as a form of advocacy for their preferred world orders: the "normative" side of interdisciplinary research.Thus, some forms of structural realism (including "hegemonic stability" theory[4]) appealed to international lawyers and scholars who preferred reinforcing U.S. sovereignty,[5] while liberal institutionalism appealed to those who favored the subordination of U.S. sovereignty to the interests of the international community, either as an enlightened and self-interested strategyfor the United States or as a just accommodation to the needs of other nations.[6]

The trend also paralleled a broader turn in U.S. domestic legal scholarship to interdisciplinary studies, in which the "law and economics" movement led the way.[7]Like other legal scholars and practitioners, international lawyers were excited about the possible application of economics to their study of a general theory that explored how law and legal institutions might be explained in terms of the basic assumption of rational, self-interested action.

---

4 *See infra* text accompanying notes 178–79.

5 *See* Abbott, *Modern International Relations Theory, supra* note 1.

6 *See* Slaughter and Burley, *supra* note 1.

7 *See* Richard Posner, The Economic Analysis of Law (5th ed. 1998).

Reasons for law students to study international relations theory. Students new to the study of international law (and of international relations) may wonder what profit is to be found in considering a different, and difficult, discipline. So before we begin to outline the various approaches of international relations theory, we offer a brief summary of the reasons why the study of international law can be enriched by some knowledge of international relations theory.[8]

First, international relations theory can equip international lawyers with a theoretical apparatus to diagnose international legal problems andto find regulatory or diplomatic solutions to at least some of them. For instance, concepts of collective good, free-ridership, and market or political failure, or game-theoretic paradigms such as the "prisoner's dilemma," are the stock in trade of international relations theory. International lawyers can avail themselves of these diagnostic and prescriptive tools to explain the origins of legal problems in the relations between states and to develop possible solutions to them. As an international law theorist suggested,

> we can understand arms control agreements as efforts to halt the destructive competition of the Prisoner's Dilemma; ocean dumping treaties as efforts to maintain a collective good against the destructive incentives of the commons; International Civil Aviation Organization rules as devices to coordinate otherwise conflicting and chaotic state behavior; the GATT as an instrument for reducing the transactions costs of detailed trade negotiations; reporting procedures as ways to assure others that one is continuing to comply with agreed obligations; and so on.[9]

To take one example, some international relations theories highlight, as an important factor leading to interstate war, the potential belligerents' imperfect information about the relative distribution of power between them. Not knowing (and perhaps being unable to learn) a prospective opponent's true strength, a potential belligerent may overestimate its own relative strength and may initiate conflict with unsubstantiated confidence.[10] Assuming that this theoretical insight is sound, international lawyers might seek to develop mutual disclosure procedures and regulations under which states could obtain reliable information about other states' actual capabilities in order to restrain the tendency to go to war.

Second, international relations theory can assist international lawyers in explaining international legal rules, norms, practices, and institutions. Unlike the first interest, this concern is less overtly prescriptive and policy-driven; instead, it may seek to analyze what functions international legal rules, norms, practices, and institutions perform and why they have the structure

8 *See* Abbott, *Toward a Richer Institutionalism, supra* note 1, at 10–11 (outlining reasons); Kenneth W. Abbott, *Elements of a Joint Discipline*, 86 Am. Soc. Int'l L. 167 (1992) [hereinafter "Abbott, *Elements of a Joint Discipline*"](same); Slaughter, Tulumello & Wood, *supra* note 1, at 373–78 (same).

9 Abbott, *Elements of a Joint Discipline, supra* note 8, at 170.

10 For a summary of these theories, *see* David Sobek, *The Causes of War* 68–71 (2010). For the classic exposition of the theory, see James D. Fearon, *Rationalist Explanations for War*, 49 Int'l Org. 379 (1995).

they do. For example, one international law scholar has argued that the game-theoretic idea of iterated plays, as applied to international relations, offers the best explanation of the functions performed by the international law of treaties, and of the structure the law assumes.[11]

Third, the study of international relations theory can lead international lawyers to reconceptualize the basis of particular international institutions or even the basis of international law itself. As we have seen in Chapter 1.B, traditional international law placed states at the center of the international legal system. Indeed, individuals and groups were widely understood not to be "subjects" of international law. But "liberal" international relations theory holds that "individuals and groups operating in domestic and transnational society are the primary actors in international relations"—thus pointing the way to "a much broader definition of international law."[12]

Finally, international relations theory can provide international lawyers with a firmer grasp of the possibilities and limits of international law. If, for example, the study of international relations theory convinces readers of the truth of the core claim of "structuralism realism" or "neorealism" that due to the inescapably "anarchic" structure of international affairs, state behavior must be driven by an overriding concern with maximizing security or relative power, then the reader must accept that international law can have little or no influence in guiding the behavior of states, at least where matters of vital national security are at stake.[13] Conversely, if the study of international relations makes it plausible to accept the core claim of "constructivism" that the "structure" of the international system does not dictate that states behave in a power- or security-maximizing way, but that the "process" of state interaction and learning can shape or transform state interests and identities in such a way that "cooperative" security systems based on shared norms can emerge,[14] then the reader will glimpse the possibility of a far more influential role for international law in international affairs.

This Chapter is designed to demonstrate the usefulness of interdisciplinary approaches to the study of international law that draw freely on the insights of competing international relations theories. Drawing on three distinct approaches, it includes three main sections, each of which we present for study as a separate unit or sub-chapter (unlike the materials in chapter 1 of this Part, which we presented in a single chapter as an integrated dialogue between classical realism and positivist legalism).

First, in this sub-chapter, 2.A, we survey some varieties and examine some core theses of modern realism, the long-dominant international relations theory in the United States. In particular, we explain how rational choice theory and constructivism emerged out of, or in reaction

11 *See* Slaughter, Tulumello & Wood,*supra* note 1, at 376 (citing John K. Setear, *Responses to Breach of a Treaty and Rationalist International Relations Theory: The Role of Release and Remediation in the Law of Treaties and the Law of State Responsibility,* 83 Va. L. Rev. 1 (1997)).

12 *See* Slaughter, Tulumello & Wood, *supra* note 1, at 378.

13 *See* Abbott, *Modern International Relations Theory, supra* note 1, at 344 (Kenneth Waltz's international relations theory "implicitly denies the value of international law as a discipline").

14 *See* Alexander Wendt, *Anarchy Is What States Make of It: The Social Construction of Power Politics,* 46 Int'l Org. 391 (1992).

to, the structural realist position. Our narrative proceeds in six phases. First, we will review and outline the main varieties of realist international relations. Second, we will consider realism's historical antecedents in European statecraft in the five centuries since the Renaissance, distilling from that account three major concepts that developed from state practice and reflection on it during that period. Those three concepts, still influential in realist thinking today, are "reason of state," "balance of power" and "balance of trade." Third, we shall then turn to explaining five similarly fundamental concepts that figure in contemporary realist thinking—"anarchy," "rationality," the "security dilemma," "polarity" and "the prisoner's dilemma." This discussion will provide a working account of realism at the point at which it began to spin off alternative, and arguably more refined, forms of international relations theory. Fourth, we shall examine how realism gave rise to "institutionalism"—one of the successor theories that have arguably displaced structural realism—and how institutionalism, in turn, has begotten rational choice theory. Fifth, we shall describe a modification of, or alternative to, both realism and institutionalism that is known as "neoliberalism." Finally, we shall describe and comment on rational choice theory in some detail.

Chapter2.B presents rational choice theory, which draws on the application of economic theory, game theory, and transaction cost economics to the study of international relations. It then examines the law and technical background of a central international security institution of the nuclear era, the Nuclear Nonproliferation Treaty (NPT) and NPT's linkage to the nuclear safeguards regime implemented through the International Atomic Energy Agency (IAEA). The chapter presents as a case study documents relating to the North Korean withdrawal from the NPT after detection of its violations of IAEA safeguards. Finally, we then offer critical commentary on this case study and the rational choice approach to international security law outlined in the section.

Our introduction to different methodological perspectives in Part I of this book closes with Chapter 2.C. We present, under the rubric of constructivism, a case study of Iran's nuclear program, focusing on its rights and obligations under the NPT, specifically, its right to a full "nuclear fuel cycle," which includes such nuclear-weapons sensitive technologies as uranium enrichment and plutonium reprocessing. The case study attempts to explain Iran's behavior in terms of two constructed "identities" of that state—the international community's image of Iran as a "rogue" state, and Iran's image of itself as an "Islamic revolutionary" state at the vanguard of a broad movement throughout the Middle East and world. The case study will consider the constructivist claim that *endogenous* factors—including a state's evolving interpretation of itself—as well as the *exogenous* factor chiefly emphasized by realism—the anarchic structure of the international system—can explain Iran's nuclear policy.

Contemporary international relations theory is marked by a wide variety of approaches.[15] Without question, the most important school of international relations thought in the United States during the Cold War period was "realism,"[16] which was itself divided into different approaches such as "offensive" and "defensive" realism that had different major premises and conclusions about state motivation and behavior.[17] Because of the importance of realism in Cold War (and later) American thought, and also because of its relationship to the "realism" depicted by Thucydides and discussed in Chapter 1.A, we may begin this brief survey of international relations theory by outlining the realist position.

Realism relies on the assumption of "rationalism" – the axiom that states are rational, egoistic actors that seek to promote a certain conception of their own interest without regard to the interests of other states. Realism, so understood, made it difficult to see how or why states should cooperate. Later forms of international relations theory, including "institutionalism" and "rational choice" theory, followed realism in postulating that states acted in a rational, self-interested way; but by augmenting and enriching realism's basic assumptions, these theories provided for the possibility, and explained the actuality, of cooperation between states.

Another leading form of contemporary international relations theory, constructivism, repudiates the realist premise of rationalism, especially insofar as that premise ascribes to states an inherent and unavoidable tendency to pursue a particular form of self-interest to the exclusion of, or in antagonism to, the interests of other states.[18]For constructivism, the interests and identities of states are not unalterable givens, arising out of the anarchic structure of the international system, that is, a system lacking a hierarchical order or structure.Rather, states, like individuals, have a certain pliancy or plasticity in defining their interests and identities, which can be shaped and reshaped within fairly broad margins by their interactions with other states.[19] On this approach, whether states seek to maximize their own power or security or instead prove more willing to cooperate peaceably on the basis of agreed norms and values is not predetermined by the anarchic nature of the interstate system. Rather, what states define as their interests—and therefore what goals they pursue—will be "constructed" from the course of their

15 *See* Jack Snyder, *One World, Rival Theories,* 145 For. Pol'y 52 (2004) (for a wonderful, brief survey of the leading theories).

16 A very useful introduction to this subject is William C. Wohlforth, *Realism, in* Oxford Handbook, *supra* note 1, at 131.

17 *See id.*

18 For introductory accounts, see Ian Hurd, *Constructivism, in*Oxford Handbook, *supra* note 1, at 298; Anthony Clark Arend, Legal Rules and International Society 124-37 (1999); John Gerard Ruggie, *What Makes the World Hang Together? Neo-Utilitarianism and the Social Constructivist Challenge,* 52 Int'l Org. 855, 878–82 (1998); and Keohane, *International Institutions, supra* note 2,389–93.

19 *See* Ted Hopf, *The Promise of Constructivism in International Relations Theory,* 23 Int'l Sec. 171, 175–76 (1998) ("Whereas constructivism treats identity as an empirical question to be theorized within a historical context, neorealism assumes that all units in global politics have only one meaningful identity. That of self-interested states. . . . [N]eorealism further assumes that states have the same a priori interests.").

dealings with other states, the roles they undertake to play in international affairs, and judgments of "appropriateness" associated with those assumed identities. For example, constructivists might point out that states like Canada, Ireland, or even the formerly war-like Sweden have shaped or reshaped their identities to emerge as non-aggressive, peace-promoting actors in international affairs.[20] The interactive processes of international affairs, in other words, may be more important in explaining the behavior of states in the international arena than the nature of the structure in which they act.

1. Structural Realism and Its Roots

Contemporary realism commonly seeks to explain important international events,such as major wars, in terms of the "structure" of interstate relations in conditions of anarchy, hence the name "structural realism," whereas earlier or more "traditional" forms of realism relied not only on the "structural" characteristics of the international system, but even more on the internal features of states acting within that system (for example, whether constitutionally they were democracies or autocracies)and on the particular qualities and interests of the leadership or elites governing those states at any given time. In other words, as the leading American structural realist Kenneth N. Waltz famously put it in his 1954 classic *Man, the State and War*, earlier realists had sought to explain major international events primarily on the basis of the "first image" (the level of individual human actors) or the "second image" (the level of state actors), while he, and those who were to follow him, relied principally on explanations based on the "third image" (the international level).[21] As Waltz later stated when explaining the key difference between his "structuralist" views and the views of earlier realists:

> [Earlier] [r]ealism thinks of causes [of major war and other such international events] as moving in only one direction, from the interactions of individuals and states to the outcomes that their

20 Consider, for example, the Vasa Museum in Stockholm, Sweden. This celebrated site houses the warship *The Vasa*, built at the apex of Sweden's military power, which unfortunately sank on its maiden voyage, was raised to the surface in a fairly well-preserved state in 1961, and thereafter restored and placed in a special museum of its own, together with the human remains and artifacts recovered with it. Rather than representing Sweden's past military prowess, the museum celebrates Sweden's renunciation of the use of force and its current image as a peaceful nation. "Built as a threatening symbol of military power and imperial aggression, it now stands as the peaceful icon of technological creativity and skill. As a popular site of visit among foreign tourists, families, and schoolchildren, it praises the harmless incompetency of Swedish imperialism." Péter Apor, *Museums of civilization, museums of state, museums of identity: national museums in Europe, 1918-2000, in*Peter Aronsson & Gabriella Elgenius, National Museums and Nation-Building in Europe, 1750-2019: Mobilization and Legitimacy, Continuity and Change 33, 53 (2015).

21 *See* Kenneth N. Waltz, Man, the State and War: A Theoretical Analysis12 (1954). For a helpful account of Waltz's criticism of his immediate "realist" predecessors, see Campbell Craig, Glimmer of a New Leviathan: Total War in the Realism of Niebuhr, Morgenthau, and Waltz121–30 (2003). For what appears to be a reformulation of Waltz's categories as "ontological" views of human nature, "mesolevel régime theories" and "macrolevel geopolitical theories," seeJohn Keane, Reflections on Violence 107–11 (1996).

> acts and interactions produce. . . . Students of international politics have typically inferred outcomes from salient attributes of the actors producing them. . . . Governmental forms, economic systems, social institutions, political ideologies—these are but a few examples of where the causes of war have been found. . . . Neorealism [*i.e.,* what we are here calling structural realism] contends that international politics can be understood only if the effects of structure are added to the unit level explanations of traditional realism. By emphasizing how structures affect actions and outcomes, neorealism . . . reconceives the causal link between interacting units and international outcomes. . . . Causes at the level of units interact with those at the level of structure, and because they do, explanation at the unit level alone is bound to be misleading.[22]

The critical (though not the only) structural characteristic of the international system, for Waltz, is anarchy:

> Structural realism presents a systemic portrait of international politics depicting component units according to the manner of their arrangement. For the purpose of developing a theory, states are cast as unitary actors wanting at least to survive, and are taken to be the system's constituent units. The essential structural quality of the system is anarchy—the absence of a central monopoly of legitimate force. Changes of structure and hence of system occur with variations in the number of great powers. The range of expected outcomes is inferred from the assumed motivation of the units and the structure of the system in which they act.[23]

Thus, anarchy is a structure in the sense of being an unalterable (or barely alterable) set of constraints on the behavior of states: it is, effectively, a natural rather than a social phenomenon, comparable, say, to geography.

The "parsimony" of Waltz's structural realism thus consists in this: that while other theories of international relations rely largely on context-specific, unit-level variables (for example, whether a state is capitalist or communist; whether a state's political leadership feels threatened by its domestic political opponents or not) to explain significant international changes (for example,whether major war breaks out or not), structural realism seeks to explain the same outcomes by relying chiefly on the spare assumptions that 1) states are primarily motivated by the desire to survive; 2) states generally act rationally in pursuing the goal of survival;[24] 3) the distribution of power within the system is unequal, that is, states differ, often radically, in power and capabilities; 4) polarity, or the number of states that are dominant powers, is relevant to

22 Kenneth N. Waltz, *The Origins of War in Neorealist Theory, in* Kenneth N. Waltz, *Realism and International Politics* 56, 57–58 (2008) [hereinafter "Waltz, Realism and International Politics"].

23 *Id.* at 58.

24 Waltz is careful to distinguish individual from collective rationality; indeed, his argument is in large part a demonstration that individual rationality may lead to collectively irrational outcomes. *See* Waltz, *supra* note 21, at 191–97.

structural changes within the system (and hence to the likelihood that the events to be explained will occur); and 5) states interact in conditions of international anarchy.

In a nutshell, Waltz finds that wars happen "because there is nothing to prevent them."[25]In a world in which no police force exists to prevent bank robberies, Waltz observes, there will surely be bank robberies. Likewise, he contends, in an anarchic international system where no enforcement authority is able to restrain states from warring, there will surely be wars. The anarchic structure of international relations is "a permissive or underlying cause of war."[26]

Waltz does not, of course, altogether negate the relevance of first- and second-image explanations in accounting for particular wars. Those images furnish the direct, efficient or immediate causes of war. "Structure," on the other hand, explains the inherent tendency of the international state system toward war and preparations for war. Waltz writes:

> [T]he structure of the state system does not directly cause state A to attack state B. Whether or not that attack occurs will depend on a number of special circumstances—location, size, power, interest, type of government, past history and tradition—each of which will influence the actions of both states. If they fight against each other it will be for reasons especially defined for the occasion by each of them. These special reasons become the immediate, or efficient, causes of war. These immediate causes of war are contained in the first and second images. States are motivated to attack each other by the reason and/or the passion of the comparatively few who make policies for states and of the many who influence the few. Some states, by virtue of their internal conditions, are both more proficient in war and more inclined to put their proficiency to the test. Variations in the factors included in the first and second images are important, indeed crucial, in the making and breaking of periods of peace—the immediate causes of every war must be either the acts of individuals or the acts of states.[27]

As Waltz explains structural realism, therefore, the theory seems strikingly different from, even discontinuous with, the realism of the past. One might, therefore, be tempted to conclude that there is little reason to look for the roots of contemporary realism in the work of Waltz's predecessors. And, in fact, the claim of structural realists to a distinguished pedigree for their position, reaching back to Thucydides, through Machiavelli and Hobbes, to the present, is disputable.[28]

---

25 Waltz, *supra* note 21, at 232.

26 *Id.* at 231–32.

27 *Id.* at 232.

28 *See, e.g.*, Brian Schmidt, The Political Discourse of Anarchy: A Disciplinary History of International Relations (1998). Daniel Deudney identifies the German exponents of *realpolitik*—Fichte, Hegel, Weber and others—as the true ancestors of later realism, rather than Thucydides, Machiavelli, Hobbes or Rousseau. *See* Daniel H. Deudney, Bounding Power: Republican Security Theory from the Polis to the Global Village 7, 70–73, 86 (2007). For a contrasting view, *see* Robert G. Gilpin, *The Richness of the Tradition of Political Realism*, 38 Int'l Org. 287, 291 (1984).

First, it might be argued that even if there are some affinities between contemporary realism and those past thinkers, realism as it is now understood is more indebted to microeconomics than it is to any of the great political philosophies of the past.[29] Second, in discounting explanations drawing on first- and second-images, contemporary realism is far more "parsimonious" in its theoretical apparatus than the realism of earlier periods.[30]Third, structural realism arguably differs fundamentally from classical realism in rejecting the latter's pessimistic assumptions about human motivations and their role in explaining international competition.[31]

However,contemporary realism does owe a substantial debt to the past. Waltz's own account of the structural causes of war is largely derived, as he repeatedly acknowledges, from the work of the eighteenth century Swiss philosopher, Jean-Jacques Rousseau. Moreover, the generation of realists that preceded Waltz – including such leading figures as the political theorist Hans Morgenthau,[32] the theologian Reinhold Niebuhr,[33] the historians E.H. Carr[34] and Sir Herbert Butterfield,[35] and the diplomat and historian George Kennan[36]—had, and continue to have, a substantial influence on contemporary realism, even if their explanatory schemes were not methodologically as austere as Waltz's. And those realist thinkers were in turn intimately acquainted with and deeply influenced by the rich Western tradition of thinking about international politics and statecraft that emerged over centuries in the "Westphalian" period. This tradition is embodied in countless state papers and memoranda, manuals of advice for rulers and officials, diplomatic exchanges, mémoires, "political" testaments, occasional writings, legal treatises, works on

29 *See*, e.g., Richard K. Ashley, *The Poverty of Neorealism*, 38 Int'l Org. 225, 240, 279, 283 (1984).

30 Ashley, *supra* note 29, at 270–81. Indeed, Waltz's fundamental distinction between first and second images—man and the state—makes sense only on the assumption that the state possesses legal personality. Thucydides, for whom the city-state is simply a community of human beings, could hardly have accepted Waltz's distinction, see Michael T. Clark, *Realism Ancient and Modern: Thucydides and International Relations*, 26 Pol. Sci. and Pol. 491, 493 (1993).

31 *See* Keith L. Shimko, *Realism, Neorealism, and American Liberalism*, 54 Rev. Pol. 281, 294 (1992) ("In a [structural realist] model which stresses the explanatory power of anarchy, the primary motive for state competition is *fear* of domination by others; in one which emphasizes human nature, the central motive is the *desire* to dominate others. An anarchy model explains the international struggle for power as the tragic result of systemic inadequacies; a human nature model portrays the struggle as the inevitable reflection and extension of man's inadequacies.").

Although Waltz's critique of "first image" explanations aims at classical realism, the latter approach "thought it imperative to explore human nature because our understanding of it necessarily affects our view of realism. The precise character of the compulsions that anarchy exerts on states, the urgency of the threats raised by it, and the prospects for its melioration, are all deeply affected by our view of human nature." Steven Forde, *International Realism and the Science of Politics: Thucydides, Machiavelli, and Neorealism*, 39 Int'l Stud. Q. 141, 145–46 (1995) [hereinafter "Forde, *International Realism*"]. Thus, Thucydides' Athenians posit that their city's behavior is driven, not only by fear for its security in an anarchical international environment, but also by honor and by desire for profit. See id. at 147 (citing *The History of the Peloponnesian War*, Book I, ch. 75); *see also* Steven Forde, *Varieties of Realism: Thucydides and Machiavelli*, 54 J. Pol. 372, 375–76 (1992) [hereinafter "Forde, V*arieties of Realism*"].

32 *See, e.g.*, Hans Morgenthau, Scientific Man vs. Power Politics (1946); Hans Morgenthau et al., Politics Among Nations (1st ed. 1948).

33 *See, e.g.*, Reinhold Niebuhr, Moral Man and Immoral Society (1932); and Reinhold Niebuhr, The Children of Light and the Children of Darkness (1944).

34 *See, e.g.*, E.H. Carr, The Twenty Years' Crisis, 1919-1939: An Introduction to the Study of International Relations (1939).

35 *See, e.g.*, Herbert Butterfield,History & Human Relations (1952).

36 *See, e.g.*, George Kennan, American Diplomacy, 1900-1950 (1951).

statecraft, and elsewhere.[37] Whether or not there is a direct line of ancestry that can be traced from Thucydides through Hobbes and Machiavelli to structural realism, there is some value in examining, at least briefly, the central concepts that were forged in that tradition of thought.

2. Three Key Concepts in Early Modern Realism

In a major study, the English historian Jonathan Haslam has identified three key concepts that emerged from the realist (or proto-realist) tradition in post-medieval Europe. These are: ***reason of state, the balance of power,*** and ***the balance of trade.*** Together these interdependent ideas formed, in Haslam's view, "the core of realist thought in the twentieth century."[38]

a. Reason of State

In very summary form, *reason of state* can be described as the doctrine of the primacy of the state over all competing interests or considerations; it is the teaching that "no value, whether moral or secular, should stand above the security of the state" and so that "the moral rules applicable to the individual were not transferable to the state in its behavior towards citizens or towards other states."[39](In Waltz's formulation, "the conditions of international politics [do not] permit statesmen to think and act in terms of the moral and legal principles that may be both serviceable and acceptable in domestic politics."[40])The doctrine was mainly directed to rulers and those charged with assisting them in governing a state's affairs. It instructed them to pursue the interests of the state (*e.g.*, the interests of the State of France) above the interests of other claimants to their support and loyalty (*e.g.*, the interests of the Papacy), as well as over purely dynastic or personal interests.[41] Moreover, it dictated a policy driven by *rationality,* rather than

---

37 *See* Ashley, *supra* note 29, at 275.

38 Jonathan Haslam, No Virtue Like Necessity: Realist Thought in International Relations Since Machiavelli16 (2002).

39 *Id.* at 15. Important studies of the concept include (Sir) Herbert Butterfield, Raison D'État: The Relations Between Morality and Government: The First Martin Wight Memorial Lecture (1975)[hereinafter "Butterfield, Raison D' État"]; Friedrich Meinecke, Machiavellianism: The Doctrine of Raison D'État and Its Place in Modern History (Douglas Scott trans. 1957). A briefer treatment is found in Daniel Philpott, *The Religious Roots of Modern International Relations,* 52 World Pol. 206, 234–37 (2000). Among primary sources, students should consult The Political Testament of Cardinal Richelieu 71–76 (Henry Bertam Hill trans., 1964).

40 Waltz, *supra* note 21, at 38.

41 For example, under the leadership of the seventeenth century figure Cardinal Richelieu, a high-ranking Catholic prelate and the chief minister of a Catholic state, France intervened decisively against the Imperial-Catholic Hapsburg powers in their contest with the Protestant forces. Richelieu, an adept practitioner of "reason of state," sought to maintain Europe's balance of power and thus prevent the Hapsburgs from achieving universal dominion. Furthermore, although Richelieu considered it necessary to destroy the Huguenot (French Protestant) fortifications in the city of La Rochelle in order to secure the internal unity of France, he was unwilling, unlike his opponent Cardinal de Bérulle, to force conversion to Catholicism upon the defeated Huguenots. For studies of Richelieu's reason of state policy, *see* Butterfield, Raison D' État, *supra* note 39; Donald M. Mackinnon, *Power Politics and Religious Faith: The Fifth Martin Wight Memorial*

(for example) by passion or whim. Although sometimes understood by contemporary realistsas a *description* of how states do or even *must* behave, it is better seen (and in its origins it was seen) as *normative* guidance for how states *should* behave.[42]One normative justification offered for the reason of state doctrine is, therefore, that the rational pursuit of a state's goals in international relations tends towards the limitation of war and the mitigation of its horrors.[43]Another justification was that the doctrine admonished statesmen "to carry out a foreign policy in the interest of the whole nation and not just in the selfish interests of the ruling elite."[44]

In order to understand the doctrine properly, it is essential to bear in mind that it originated in a period when the modern European state was still being formed.[45] Other powerful (and, as we might say, transnational) actors in European affairs, including the Papacy and the Holy Roman Empire, made claims to universal loyalty and obedience over the heads of local rulers, including kings. Likewise, political actors at the sub-state level, such as local lords and magnates, also sought to command the population's allegiance and to extract its resources. The "reason of state" doctrine served to legitimize the priority of the king's claims over the competing claims of the Church, the Empire, and the aristocracy (a development that also contributed to the emergence of the concept of "sovereignty" studied in Chapter I.B). A king's demand for the subject's undivided loyalty was based on the promise that in return for such loyalty he and his forces would provide the population with security within the borders of his realm. The doctrine and practice of "reason of state" enabled the ruler to make good on that promise.

It is also important to see that the doctrine "represented an attempt to order policy to cope with a universal predisposition to conflict."[46] Conflict was understood to arise from passion, which could most effectively be checked by the sober, far-sighted and interest-based calculations of reason.[47] For example, "reason of state" counseled kings to observe the treaties that they had made: the long-term reputational advantages that a policy of treaty-compliance brought were seen generally to outweigh the benefits of breaking a treaty because of another state's momentary weakness, despite the opportunity for making conquests that such vulnerability might

---

Lecture, 6 Brit. J. Int'l Stud. 1 (1980); and R. Harrison Wagner, War and the State: The Theory of International Politics 73–76 (2007).

42 This point is rightly emphasized in Wagner, *supra* note 41, at 63–65.

43 *See* Reinhart Koselleck, Critique and Crisis: Enlightenment and the Pathogenesis of Modern Society 46–48 (1988) ("[I]t was the very primacy of politics that offered an opportunity to meet moral demands as well—by a detour, so to speak, by way of rationalizing both war and the State.").

44 Robert G. Gilpin, *The Richness of the Tradition of Political Realism*, 38 Int'l Org. 287, 303 (1984).

45 For a brief description of that development, *see* Philip Bobbitt, The Garments of Court and Palace: Machiavelli and The World That He Made 21-28 (2013).

46 Haslam, *supra* note 38, at 17.

47 *See* Albert O. Hirschman, The Passions and the Interests (1977).

seem to afford.[48] (Insights from the broad "realist" tradition such as these have been theorized by later rational-choice analysts writing on the significance of "reputation" for state behavior.[49])

Finally, "reason of state" represented an attempt to solve, or at least to mitigate, a problem inherent in the theory and practice of an emerging royal absolutism.If law and custom could no longer check the power of the monarch (as they had in the pre-modern period), how could monarchy be distinguished from tyranny?[50] "Reason of state" doctrine, which purported to identify an objective and rational standard that the monarch could grasp and follow, was one of three overlapping solutions.The other two were "princely virtue," which attempted to instill the habits of self-restraint in the monarch, and "enlightened despotism," which sought to direct absolute power to the pursuit of the common good.[51]

The conception of "reason of state" in early modern realism thus differentiates that body of ideas from later varieties of realism, including structural realism and rational choice theory. Early modern realism is not based on the assumption that states (or individuals) act rationally; on the contrary, it "represents an attempt to improve on what [it] regards as the woefully defective rationality of . . . states."[52]

Although reason of state doctrine has been condemned for centuries as immoral,[53] its most thoughtful defenders see it as a necessary, indeed virtuous, response to a tragic situation.[54]

---

48 Again, we may cite the example of Cardinal Richelieu. Richelieu's conception of statecraft laid considerable emphasis both on what he called "continuous negotiations" and on the sanctity of treaties. *See* Herbert Butterfield, *Diplomacy, in*Studies in Diplomatic History: Essays in Memory of David Bayne Horn357, 365 (Ragnhild Hatton & M.S. Anderson eds., 1970); and Butterfield, Raison D'Etat, *supra* note 39, at 16 ("[O]ne of the most valuable parts" of Richelieu's writing is the emphasis on continuous negotiations[.]"). Richelieu's emphasis on continuous negotiations stemmed from

> his profound belief in the general power of reason and language. "Authority constrains obedience,' he writes in [his] *Testament Politique*, but reason captivates it. It is much more expedient to lead men by means which imperceptibly win their wills than, as is more the practice, by those which coerce them."

G.R. Berridge, *Richelieu,in Diplomatic Theory from Machiavelli to Kissinger* 71, 75 (G.R. Berridge, Maurice Keen-Soper & T.G. Otte eds., 2001). Richelieu also thought that an enlightened self-interest in maintaining "reputation"—which he saw as a key ingredient of a monarch's power—counseled the strict observance of treaties.

> "Kings," he writes, "should be very careful with regard to the treaties they conclude, but having concluded them they should observe them religiously. . . . A great prince should sooner put in jeopardy both his own interests and even those of the state than break his word, which he can never violate without losing his reputation and by consequence the greatest instrument of sovereigns."

Id. at 78.

49 *See, e.g.,*Andrew Guzman, *A Compliance-based Theory of International Law,* 90 Cal. L. Rev. 1823 (2002).

50 On early formulations of the doctrine of royal absolutism in the works of Jean Bodin and his follower, King James I of England, *see* 2 Harold Berman, Law and Revolution: The Impact of the Protestant Reformations on the Western Legal Tradition 234–38 (2003). On the weakening of medieval legal and customary restraints on royal power, *see* Jean Bethke Elshtain, Sovereignty: God, State, and Self 58–64 (2008).

51 *See* Daniel Deudney, Bounding Power: Republican Security Theory from the Polis to the Global Village 69 (2007).

52 *See* Forde, *Varieties of Realism, supra* note 31, *at* 378; *see also* Harvey Mansfield, Jr., *Machiavelli's Political Science,* 75 Am. Pol. Sci. Rev. 293 (1981).

53 Alternatively, reason of state doctrine is criticized for giving no, or only a weak, defense of the values of the societies that it is invoked to defend. *See* Jack Donnelly, *The Ethics of Realism, in* Oxford Handbook, *supra* note 1, at150, 154–55.

54 On the morality of Machiavelli, *see* Bobbitt, *supra* note 45, at 34-45.

Discussing Machiavelli, Kenneth Waltz poses the right question: "Why should the success of the prince in establishing internal order and contriving a defense against external enemies be taken as the criterion by which any act [of statecraft] can be justified? Why define success in terms of princely or state interest instead of, say, in terms of living a moral life?"[55] Machiavelli's answer, says Waltz, appealed to the desperate straits to which Italy had been reduced by her rulers' inability to defend her against foreign invaders. Italy was, Machiavelli said, "a country without dykes or banks of any kind" to be used against foreign foes; had she been "protected by proper measures, like Germany, Spain, and France, this inundation . . . would not have happened at all."[56] In conditions in which a state is unable to defend itself and its people from devastating and repeated foreign invasion, there is no possibility for those within that state of living lives with a measure of independence, decency, and virtue. To secure the state against ruthless foreign enemies of the kind that had made Italy wretched, Machiavelli argued, its rulers must prove to be no less unscrupulous than their opponents. As Waltz puts it, "[i]f by cruelty the dykes and banks are built and kept in good repair, then cruelty is the greatest mercy. If by practicing virtue they are torn down again, then virtue is the greatest vice."[57] And again:

> [T]he leaders of the state may have to choose between behaving *immorally* in international politics in order to preserve the state . . . and . . . abandoning their *moral* obligation to ensure their state's survival in order to follow preferred ways of acting in international politics. The conclusion? Moral behavior is one thing in a system that provides predictable amounts and types of security; another thing where such security is lacking. . . . Those who call 'power politicians' immoral simply because they play the game of power politics have transferred a definition of immorality from one social setting to another, and in the other it is not applicable without serious qualification.[58]

b. The Balance of Power

Realist theories of international relations have also given much prominence to the idea of the "balance of power." Like the reason of state doctrine (to which it was both historically and conceptually linked), balance of power theory emphasized the security of individual states against the encroachments of other states or empires seeking to aggrandize themselves. Additionally, it counseled rationality and long-term calculation in the pursuit of self-interest: the survival of an

55 Waltz, *supra* note 21, 215.

56 *Id.* at 215–16.

57 *Id.* at 216.

58 *Id.* at 207–08; see also R.N. Berki, *Machiavellism: A Philosophical Defense,* 81 Ethics 107, 125–27 (1971).
For a very different view of the statesman's responsibilities, see Michael Loriaux, *The Realists and Saint Augustine: Skepticism, Psychology, and Moral Action in International Relations Thought,* 36 Int'l Stud. Q. 401, 415–17 (1992).

individual state was usually contingent on maintaining the existence of the states system in its entirety against the domination of any single member of the system. Finally, although balance of power thinking accepted the inevitability and, in some circumstances, the desirability, of war (including preventive war), it was considered conducive to maintaining peace, in that it offered a permanent check on individual states' drive to self-aggrandizement.[59]

What exactly is the balance of power theory? As a formal teaching, the balance of power doctrine has developed over the past five centuries.[60]Beginning in the fifteenth century, European statesmen and diplomats thought in terms of a "balance of power," as a means to maintain peace and to prevent one state from dominating others. In 1612, the renowned international lawyer Alberto Gentili argued in his *De Jure Belli Libri Tres* that European states were justified in resisting the claims of universal dominion made both by Spain and the Ottoman Empire. The reflection on and the theorization of the balance of power was brought to new heights in the eighteenth century as observers viewed the policy of maintaining the balance "as something with moral justification of its own, almost independent of any practical value it might have."[61]However, in other eighteenth century formulations, the balance of power was considered more mechanical than moral and voluntaristic; these theorists compared this formulation to gravitational forces in the planetary system or to the "invisible hand" that guides the selfish market choices of individuals into socially beneficent outcomes.[62]As Jean-Jacques Rousseau put it, "[t]he balance existing between the power of these diverse members of the European society is much more a work of nature than of art. It maintains itself without effort, in such a manner that if it sinks on one side, it reestablishes itself very soon on the other."[63]In such formulations, the doctrine posited a (purportedly) natural or mechanical process of alliance diplomacy that

59 Thus, in the account of the eminent nineteenth century German historian Leopold von Ranke, the ascendancy of seventeenth-century France under King Louis XIV had imperiled the independent development of other European states and cultures. "This arrogated supremacy, which was constantly disturbing the peace, threatened to destroy the foundations of European order and development." *See* Leopold von Ranke, *The Great Powers* (1833), *inThe Theory and Practice of History: Leopold von Ranke* 71 (Wilma A. Iggers & Konrad von Moltke trans.)(Georg G. Iggers & Konrad von Moltke, 1973). The solution was found in the balance of power: "The concept of the European balance of power, as it was called, was developed in order that many states might resist the pretensions of the 'exorbitant' court, as it was called." *Id.* at 73.

60 *See* Waltz, *supra* note21, 198–99. Some have placed the origins of this doctrine far earlier than the fifteenth century. Waltz finds the doctrine expounded by Thucydides in the fifth century B.C. and by Polybius in the second century B.C. The eighteenth century philosopher David Hume, in an essay on the balance of power, traced the concept back to ancient Greece. *See* David Hume, *Of the Balance of Power,* in Essays Moral, Political, and Literary (1742) (*available at* http://www.econlib.org/library/LFBooks/Hume/hmMPL30.html).

61 M.S. Anderson, The Rise of Modern Diplomacy 1450-1919at 165 (1993); *see generally id.* at 150–66 (tracing the evolution of the doctrine).

62 *See id.* at 165–68.

63 Randall J. Schweller, *Unanswered Threats: A Neoclassical Realist Theory of Underbalancing,* 29 Int'l Sec. 159, 162 (2004). For an analysis of Rousseau's defense of the balance of power and specifically of his claim that "peace ought to come of itself," *see* Marc Trachtenberg, *The Question of Realism,* 13 Sec. Stud. 156, 174–76 (2003).

would ensure that no single state was able to remain unchecked if it sought to take excessive advantage of its superior position and capabilities.[64]

Thus, the doctrine of the balance of power was thus sometimes taken as prescriptive, sometimes as descriptive, and sometimes as analytical.It went through many mutations and was applied in different, even inconsistent, ways. In an admirable essay, the international relations theorist Martin Wight distinguished no fewer than nine different meanings that the balance of power doctrine had acquired.[65]

Even in its eighteenth century heyday, the balance of power doctrine had severe critics.[66] The great eighteenth-century thinker Immanuel Kant rejected the idea that "a so-called European balance of power" could bring permanent, universal peace. That notion, he said, was "a pure illusion."[67] Kant himself was appalled by the several partitions of Poland by its powerful neighbors—Prussia, Russia, and Austria[68]—that led to the utter annihilation of Poland as a state, the very sort of outcome that the balance of power was supposed to prevent.[69]Studies also suggest that the balance of power system that prevailed in Europe for most of the eighteenth century was in fact far more violent and war-prone than the "concert" system that superseded it after the defeat of Napoleon and the great peace settlement of 1815.[70] As one scholar of the period has written, "[b]alance-of-power politics—the politics of confrontation—generated intolerable international tensions, produced increasingly serious armed conflicts, and inspired progressively

---

64 An alternative, and sounder, understanding of the doctrine would recognize that the efforts to achieve and maintain a balance of power generally encounter considerable friction. The American political theorist Nicolas Spykman affirmed this when he wrote:

> Political equilibrium is neither a gift of the gods nor an inherently stable condition. It results from the active intervention of man, from the operation of political forces. States cannot afford to wait passively for the happy time when a miraculously achieved balance of power will bring peace and security.

Nicholas John Spykman, The United States and the Balance of Power 25 (1943).

65 *See* Martin Wight, Power Politics 173–80 (1978).

66 *See* Michael Sheehan, Balance of Power 103 (1996) (quoting the views of British parliamentarian William Wyndham).

67 *See* Immanuel Kant, *On the Common Saying: 'This May be True in Theory, but it Does Not Apply in Practice,'in*Kant: Political Writings 61, 92 (H.S. Reiss ed., pb. 1977).

68 *See* W.B. Gallie, Philosophers of Peace and War: Kant, Clausewitz, Marx, Engels, Tolstoy 8 (1978).

69 On the other hand, it was generally understood under the balance system that at the end of wars, large states might have to be "compensated" for the loss of territory or population, often at the expense of small states. The Austrian Emperor Joseph II's attempt in 1795 to exchange the Austrian Netherlands for Bavaria is one such case. *See* Paul Schroeder, *Historical Reality vs. Neo-realist Theory,* 19 Int'l Sec. 108, 118 (1994).

70 *See, e.g.,* Paul W. Schroeder, *The 19th Century International System: Changes in the Structure,* 39 World Pol. 1, 2, 10–11 (1986) (arguing that nineteenth century international peace derived mainly from systemic change, reflected in institutional arrangements that differed from the eighteenth century norm); Paul W. Schroeder, *The Nineteenth Century System: Balance of Power or Political Equilibrium?,* 15 Rev. Int'l Pol. 135, 141–42 (1989) (discussing the significance of the balance of power idea in European political and social life); Paul W. Schroeder, *Didthe Vienna Settlement Rest on a Balance of Power?,* 97 Am. Hist. Rev. 683, 684–90, 694, 696, 701–02 (1992) (discussing how the balance of power influenced the Vienna Settlement); Robert Jervis, *From Balance to Concert: A Study of International Security Cooperation,* 38 World Pol. 58 (1985) (discussing the concert system in place from 1815 to 1854); Robert Jervis, *A Political Science Perspective on the Balance of Power and Concert,* 97 Am. Hist. Rev. 716, 718–23 (1992) (analyzing the balance of power idea and its impact on the frequency of war).

extravagant plans of aggression. It neither maintained peace nor preserved the independence of sovereign states; by the time of the French Revolution, the international system had broken down altogether."[71]

What superseded the predatory and unstable eighteenth-century European balance of power system was the so-called "Concert of Europe" system that emerged from the great peace settlement of 1815 at the Congress of Vienna, which reconstituted Europe after several decades of revolution and war.[72] Leading European statesmen affirmed that there was a fundamental difference between the two forms of international order.[73] As the historian Paul Schroeder pungently expressed it, after the Napoleonic wars "European statesmen had learned that eighteenth century poker led to Russian roulette and decided to play contract bridge instead."[74] Scholars disagree over exactly how and why the Concert system differed from the earlier balance of power system.[75]One possible explanation is that the Congress of Vienna consciously sought to create a rough equality of power among the leading states, thus institutionalizing a mechanism that made it easier for blocking coalitions to be formed.[76] This explanation, however, fails to explain why the settlement at Vienna left two of the great powers, Britain and Russia, stronger than any of the other states.[77]

The Concert system brought Europe a "long peace" of almost a century (1815-1914) without a major war involving all the great European powers. Its eventual collapse in the First World

71 Richard B. Elrod, The *Concert of Europe: A Fresh Look at an International System,* 28 World Pol 159, 161–62 (1976); *see also* Robert E. Osgood & Robert W. Tucker, Force, Order, and Justice 102–04 (Johns Hopkins 1967).

72 On the Congress of Vienna, see John G. Ikenberry, After Victory: Institutions, Strategic Restraint, and the Rebuilding of Order After Major Wars(2001) (analyzing Congress from "institutionalist" perspective). A classic study is Henry Kissinger, A World Restored (1957).

73 *See* Carsten Holbrand, The Concert of Europe: A Study in German and British International Theory 1815-1914 17–18 (1970) (quoting views of leading publicist Friedrich Gentz in 1818 on the significant differences between the pre-Revolutionary balance of power and the post-war Congress system); *id.* at 36–37 (discussing the view of Friedrich Ancillon, writer, royal tutor and later Foreign Minister of Prussia, on the merits of Congress system as opposed to pre-Revolutionary balance of power). From its origin in Clause Six of the Quadruple Alliance of the November 20, 1815, it was understood and expected that the Congress system would mark an unprecedented departure in European diplomatic practice. *See* Quadruple Alliance of November 20, 1815, Sir Charles Webster, 2 *The Foreign Policy of Castlereagh 1815-1822* 55–57 (G. Bell and Sons 1963); and Henry Kissinger, A World Restored 215 (1957).

74 Paul W. Schroeder, Austria, Great Britain and the Crimean War: The Destruction of the European Concert 404 (Cornell 1972); *see generally id.* at 401–07 (describing principles that underlay Concert system).

75 For the argument that the master concept of the Congress system was the "Great Power principle," *see* Andreas Osiander, The States System of Europe 1640-1990: Peacemaking and the Conditions of International Stability 232–47 (Oxford 1994). In any event, the Concert's mechanisms were operating, albeit feebly, as late as 1912-1913. *See* Richard Langhorne, The Collapse of the Concert of Europe: International Politics 1890-1914 4 (1981).

76 *See* Edward D. Mansfield, *Concentration, Polarity, and the Distribution of Power,* 37 Int'l Stud. Q. 105, 116–17 (1992). *See also* R. Harrison Wagner, *Peace, War, and the Balance of Power,* 88 Am. Pol. Sci. Rev. 593, 600–01 (1988) (reasoning that in a tri-polar world of equal power distribution among states, if no state wished to diminish the power available to oppose another state's expansion, then, even if every state would prefer to have more resources, no state would want to assist another in expanding, and any state that sought to expand on its own would be opposed by the other two; but arguing also that that reasoning depends on assumptions about the third state's view of the preferences of the potential aggressor state's victim state).

77 *See* Dominic Lieven, Russia Against Napoleon: The True Story of the Campaigns of War and Peace 477, 524 (2008).

War discredited the idea of maintaining peace through the balance of power, particularly so in the mind of the American President, Woodrow Wilson.[78]That rejection of realism's balance of power doctrine served as a catalyst for the creation of new forms of international security. Three major trends, closely linked together under "the famous formula 'Arbitration, Security, and Disarmament,'"[79] dominated international law in the inter-war period.[80] Most importantly, the inter-war period saw the formation of international agreements that called for various kinds of "collective security" measures, including the Covenant of the League of Nations and the Kellogg-Briand Pact, which were designed to prevent or punish offensive war. (The idea of collective security, as we shall see in more detail later, is in some ways the perfect antithesis of the balance of power: a state is assumed to regard aggression directed against *any* member of the states system as equivalent to aggression against itself, instead of evaluating a conflict betweenother states only in terms of its potential effects on its own security.)

The failure of these post-First World War institutions to prevent the recurrence of a major war was one of the principal causes of a renewed and vigorous interest in realism and was signalized by the publication on the eve of the Second World War of a classic work of modern realism, E.H. Carr's *The Twenty Years' Crisis* (1939). Carr's book marked the beginning of the long period, spanning the Cold War and beyond, during which realism dominated international relations thought.[81] In our emerging "multi-polar" world, the balance of power theory remains

---

78 In his celebrated "Peace Without Victory" speech of January 22, 1917, Woodrow Wilson had said:

> The question upon which the whole future peace and policy of the world depends is this: Is the present war a struggle for a just and secure peace, or only for a new balance of power? If it be only a struggle for a new balance of power, who will guarantee, who can guarantee the stable equilibrium of the new arrangement? Only a tranquil Europe can be a stable Europe. There must be, not a balance of power but a community power; not organized rivalries but an organized, common peace.

A League for Peace, Senate Doc. No. 685 (64th Cong., 2d Sess.) Likewise, in his speech presenting the Versailles Treaty to the Senate on July 10, 1919, Wilson identified the balance of power as the cause of the War:

> [The sacrifices of the War] had been exacted because one nation desired dominion and other nations had know no means of defense except armaments and alliances. War had lain at the heart of every arrangement of Europe,—of every arrangement of the world,—that preceded the war. Restive peoples had been told that fleets and armies, which they had toiled to sustain, meant peace; and they now knew that they had been lied to: that fleets and armies had been maintained to promote national ambitions and meant war. They knew that no old policy meant anything else but force, force,—always force. . . . A war in which they had been bled white to beat the terror that lay concealed in every Balance of Power must not end in mere victory of arms and a new balance.

"The Hand of God" in the League of Nations: President Woodrow Wilson Presents the Treaty of Paris to the Senate(available at http://historymatters.gmu.edu/d/4979/). For a searching account of the Wilsonian vision and its aversion to the use of a "balance of power" to maintain peace, *see* Philip Bobbitt, The Shield of Achilles: War, Peace, and the Course of History 359–60 (2002). *See also* Thomas J. Knock, To End All Wars: Woodrow Wilson and the Quest for a New World Order 112–15, 195–96 (1992). For anticipations of Wilson's condemnation of the balance of power and alliance diplomacy in the thought of eighteenth century *philosophes* and the influence of their ideas on early American (and ultimately Wilson's) thought, *see* Felix Gilbert, *The "New Diplomacy" of the Eighteenth Century,* 4 World Pol. 1, 8–9, 13–14, 28, 31–32, 37–38 (1951).

Kellogg-Briand Pact 1928, Aug. 27, 1928, 46 Stat. 2343 (*available at* http://www.yale.edu/lawweb/avalon/imt/kbpact.htm).

79 *See* A.C.F. Beales, The History of Peace: A Short Account of the Organised Movements for International Peace 313 (1931).

80 For an account of these inter-war legal developments, see Robert J. Delahunty & John C. Yoo, *Peace Through Law? The Failure of a Noble Experiment,* 106 Mich. L. Rev. 923, 926–32 (2008).

81 For a perceptive appreciation of Carr, see Jack Goldsmith & Steven D. Krasner, T*he Limits of Idealism,* 132 Daedalus 47 (2003).

attractive to realist-minded scholars and lawyersas a device for ordering international affairs and for maintaining international peace and security.[82]

Proponents of a new balance of power should, however, keep both historical and theoretical issues in mind.[83] First, even assuming that "balancing" in a multi-polar system will occur, there will likely be considerable friction before it can be achieved, and also considerable friction in maintaining it.[84] Balancing is far from being an "automatic equilibrial mechanism": if it were, the outbreak of major wars would be hard to explain, because a potential aggressor would then typically confront an opposing coalition of equal or greater strength and decide to stop its aggression.[85] Rather, building and maintaining a coalition against a common threat presents a kind of collective action problem: the flexibility of alignment that is necessary for successful balancing is arguably likely to occur when *least* needed (*i.e.*, in a world of major states of approximately equal power) and unlikely to occur when *most* needed (in a world in which one power is capable of seeking and achieving hegemony).[86]States may also be unable to align freely with other states that might otherwise be suitable coalition partners because of permanentdifferences between them.The historian Marc Trachtenberg argued that Germany's annexation of the French provinces of Alsace and Lorraine after its victory in the Franco-Prussia War of 1871 foreclosed any possibility of a European coalition that included France and Germany—an outcome detrimental to the interests of *both* powers.[87]Furthermore, prospective members of the coalition may be guided by individual rationality, to the detriment of collective rationality. A potential aggressor usually has several methods by which it can prevent a coalition against it from forming.[88] For example, it can offer side-payments to dissuade another state from joining the hostile coalition (as Hitler in effect did in 1939, by permitting the Soviet Union to seize eastern Poland).[89] Not surprisingly, then, the historical record includes significant cases in which states have failed to balance against an obvious threat. For instance, no durable coalition emerged to counter the

82 For the perspective of an international relations theorist, *see* Christopher Layne, The Peace of Illusions: American Grand Strategy from 1940 to the Present (2006) (advocating that the United States play the role of "offshore balancer"). From a legal perspective, see Robert J. Delahunty & John C. Yoo, *Great Power Security*, 10 Chi. J. Int'l L. 35 (2009).

83 For a review of the literature on balance of power theory, *see* Daniel H. Nexon, *The Balance of Power in the Balance,* 61 World Pol. 330 (2009).

84 *See* Randall L. Schweller, *Bandwagoning for Profit: Bringing the Revisionist State Back In,* 19 Int'l Sec. 72, 93 (1994) ("Balancing is an extremely costly activity that most states would rather not engage in, but sometimes must to survive and protect their values.").

85 *See* Richard Rosecrance & Chih-Cheng Lo, *Balancing, Stability, and War: The Mysterious Case of the Napoleonic International System,* 40 Int'l Stud. Q. 479, 481 (1996).

86 *See* George Liska, *Continuity and Change in International Systems,* 16 World Pol. 118, 122–23 (1963) (arguing against the "myth of flexibility").

87 Marc Trachtenberg, *The Question of Realism,* 13 Sec. Stud. 156, 162–64 (2003).

88 *See* Schweller, *supra* note 84, at 149.

89 *See* Schweller, *supra* note 84, at 94. For other examples, *see id.* at 88–92. "Balancing," therefore, can be conceptualized as a form of the "Stag Hunt" game. *See* Rosecrance & Lo, *supra* note 85, at 480 & n.2; 490. We discuss the Stag Hunt game *infra* notes 172-4.

ambitions of Napoleonic France until 1813, that is, after Napoleon's military weakness had been demonstrated by the failure of his campaign in Russia.[90]

Second, even when a balancing alliance has been formed, it may prove difficult to maintain. Because the interests of a coalition's members are distinct and may even be antagonistic, their partnership in a fluid, multi-polar system is often tenuous. Among other things, coalition members may fear the possibility of "entrapment," being dragged into war over an ally's interest that one does not share, and "abandonment," when an alliance partner switches sides or fails to honor its commitments.[91]

Third, not only do states fail to balance *against* an emerging threat, counter-intuitively perhaps, but also they may align*with*the threat—or at Stephen Walt put it, they may engage in *bandwagoning.*[92] (The Soviet decision to join Hitler in carving up Poland can again serve as an example.) Indeed, the prevailing view is that weak states "tend to bandwagon with a threatening Great Power."[93] Bandwagoning is, in fact, only one of several alternatives that weak states have to balancing (and fighting).Their other options include non-alignment, balancing (but not fighting), allying with other weak states, and fighting alone.[94] The availability of these alternatives helps explain why balancing (and fighting) may fail to occur.

Fourth, an international system that invites balancing may be unusually war-prone rather than peace-making.Where there are several great powers that include a potential emerging "hegemon" like Napoleonic France, Wilhelmine Germany, or (arguably) today's China—a condition that structural realists call "unbalanced multi-polarity"—some evidence indicates that war is especially likely.[95]

---

90 Rosecrance& Lo, *supra* note 85. Several explanations might be given for the failure of the anti-French coalitions that arose between 1792 and 1805, among them the fear of Austria and Prussia that if France were destroyed or even weakened severely, continental Europe would be dominated by Russia instead of France. *See* Frederick W. Kagan, The End of the Old Order: Napoleon and Europe 1801-1805 222 (2006); *see also* Paul W. Schroeder, *The Collapse of the Second Coalition,* 59 J. Mod. Hist. 244 (1987) (analyzing incompatibility within Second Coalition between aims of Austria and those of Britain and Russia).

91 *See* Randall L. Schweller, *Deadly Imbalances: Tripolarity and Hitler's Strategy of World Conquest* 64–65; Jack B. Snyder, *The Security Dilemma in Alliance Politics,* 36 World Pol. 461, 466–68 (1984). Thus, a coalition may itself present a prisoner's dilemma situation, in which defection is the dominant strategy for each coalition member. We discuss the prisoner's dilemma *infra.*

92 *See* Stephen M. Walt, *Alliance Formation and the Balance of World Power,* 9 Int'l Sec. 3, 6–8 (1985).

93 Eric J. Labs, *Do Weak States Bandwagon?,* 1 Sec. Stud. 383, 385 (1992). Labs does not himself accept the general view.

94 *See* Labs, *supra* note 93, at 389–90.

95 *See* Glenn Harold Snyder, *Mearsheimer's World—Offensive Realism and the Struggle for Security: A Review Essay,* 27 Int'l Sec. 149, 167–68 (2002). *See also* Edward D. Mansfield, *Concentration, Polarity, and the Distribution of Power,* 37 Int'l Stud. Q, 105, 117–18 (1992) (noting claims that war is likely when power inequalities exist among leading states); Diego Abente, *The War of the Triple Alliance: Three Explanatory Models,* 22 Latin Amer. Research Rev. 47, 50–51 (1987) (summarizing scholarly arguments that the balance of power tends to result in war, and that periods of known preponderance are periods of peace); Richard N. Rosecrance, *Bipolarity, Multipolarity, and the Future,* 10 J. Conf. Res. 314, 318–20 (1966) (identifying causes of instability in multi-polar systems); *but see* Charles W. Kegley & Gregory A. Raymond, *Must We Fear a Post-Cold War Multipolar System?,* 36 J. Conf. Res. 573 (1992) (arguing that different forms of multipolarity exist, and that some of them may be relatively stable).

Finally, even if the model of the nineteenth century Congress of Europe (rather than that of the unstable eighteenth century balance system) represents the ideal system to be pursued, it may well be that the conditions in which the Congress system flourished were exceptionally benign, and may not be reproducible in our present circumstances.[96]

c. The Balance of Trade

Finally, Jonathan Haslam identifies an economic concept—the *balance of trade*—as a central ingredient of the realist tradition of statecraft.[97] The balance of trade, or what is sometimes called "mercantilism,"[98]complemented both reason of state and the balance of power concepts. In its original form, the balance of trade concept claimedthat national wealth translated into national power, and that national wealth would be most increased if the state could acquire and retain the largest possible share of natural resources, particularly primary commodities. The historical success in the international arena of states such as Great Britain demonstrated the substantial connection between a nation's wealth—more specifically, the depth of its capital markets and the extent of its capacity to borrow in them—and its military and political power.[99] And well before Britain's rise to wealth and power, larger states appeared to have been aware that they could exert political leverage over weaker states by manipulating the terms of their trade with them. Athens' "Megarian Decree" of (perhaps) 433/32 B.C., which Thucydides cites as a pretext for Sparta's declaration of war, is arguably a case in point.[100]

Judged purely as a matter of maximizing global welfare and even national economic welfare, mercantilism has been widely discredited; the "liberal" or "neoclassical" defense of free trade is generally thought to be unanswerable. "Mercantilism," a theory that considers international

96 *See* Stanley Hoffman, *International Systems and International Law,* 14 World Politics 205, 218–19 (1961) (identifying specific features of international environment that made Congress system function successfully); *id.* at 222–23 (specifying conditions that led to the deterioration of the Congress system). Furthermore, as constructivists would be likely to argue, the Congress system may have been able to brake the tendency to major conflict because the great powers conceived of "Europe" as a higher-order, collective entity, with interests and claims of its own that were distinct from and superior to those of individual states—"a European family or a 'higher praetor' which would prevent the warring states from turning inevitable war into inexpiable hate." *Id.* at 222.

97 Haslam, supra note 38, at 16.

98 For a notable study of mercantilism, see Jacob Viner, *Power Versus Plenty as Objectives of Foreign Policy in the Seventeenth and Eighteenth Centuries,* 1 World Pol. 1 (1948); *see also* Charles Wilson, *'Mercantilism': Some vicissitudes of an Idea,* 10 Econ. Hist. Rev. 181 (1957) (reviewing Viner).

99 *See, e.g.,* John Brewer, The Sinews of Power: War, Money and the English State, 1688-1783 (1988).

100 *See* Thucydides, *History of the Peloponnesian War,* Bk. I, paras. 67, 139–40. The Megarian Decree excluded the city of Megara's merchants from the ports of Athens and its Empire, and thus might have functioned as a trade embargo. Robert Gilpin interpreted the Decree as "the political use of economic leverage." Robert G. Gilpin, *The Richness of the Tradition of Political Realism,* 38 Int'l Org. 287, 293 (1984). But others doubt that Athens intended the Decree as a kind of commercial imperialism, and suggest that it may have had religious motives instead. *See* Peter Brunt. T*he Megarian Decree,* 72 Am. J. Philology 269, 276–78 (1951); A. French, *The Megarian Decree,* 25 Zeitschrift für Alte Geschichte 245, 249 (1979) (view that Decree was intended to damage Megara's trade by Empire-wide embargo is "untenable").

trade policy primarily in terms of its effects of national strength,[101] has apparently lost much of its influence (except, arguably, in cases like that of China, which some analysts contend is pursuing a "mercantilist" strategy.[102]) But realists are more interested in maximizing national security and power than in maximizing overall global welfare. That concern can inform realist analyses of, and prescriptions for, international trade policy. Thus, in a work written during the Second World War, the economist Albert O. Hirschman argued that although "the case for free trade, on economic or welfare grounds [is] unanswerable," nonetheless free trade "does not have the additional merit of doing away with the political aspect of international economic relations."[103]In Hirschman's account, the commercial policy of Nazi Germany, especially in relation to south-eastern Europe in the 1930s, was designed to leverage Germany's trade advantages in order to politically control weaker states.[104]

The central idea of Hirschman's analysis was that Germany sought to translate those states' economic dependence on access to German markets into control of their politics and strategy. If Germany with its vast market could largely monopolize the export trade of those smaller economies, they would experience great difficulties, including political unrest, if Germany cut off trade with them. The threat of such a cut-off gave Germany a powerful hold over those states' international behavior.[105] Germany was less likely to suffer from the trade interruption than its smaller partners because a smaller proportion of the German economy would be engaged in international trade.[106] Moreover, Germany did not need to monopolize *all* those states' export trade; it was sufficient to control enough of the trade of vital groups in those

101 Other goals, including aggregate national income, economic growth and political stability, may also enter into "mercantilist" policies. *See* Stephen D. Krasner, *State Power and the Structure of International Trade,* 28 World Politics 317, 319–21 (1976).

102 Thus, some have criticized China's "indigenous innovation" policies, claiming that China is seeking to use its vast market to compel foreign companies to transfer leading-edge technologies and other intellectual property to China. China is considered a "pay-to-play" market for foreign firms because it mandates joint ventures in critical industries and forces technology transfers as requirements for access to its markets. China aims to build "national champion" companies by means that include subsidies and state preferences. *See* James McGregor, *China's Drive for 'Indigenous innovation': A Web of Industrial Policies* (U.S. Chamber of Commerce, July 2010) (*available at* https://www.uschamber.com/sites/default/files/legacy/reports/100728chinareport_0.pdf). The question of China's alleged mercantilism is also analyzed in Eswar Prasad & Shango-Jin Wei, *The Chinese Approach to Capital Inflows: Patterns and Possible Explanations,* National Bureau of Economic Research Working Paper No. 112306 (2005) (*available at* http://www.nber.org/papers/w11306).

103 Albert O. Hirschman, *National Power and the Structure of Free Trade* 76 (1945). For a review and critique of Hirschman's book, which it judges to be "the most highly developed theory of economic dependence and its political uses that we have," *see* R. Harrison Wagner, *Economic Interdependence, Bargaining Power, and Political Influence,* 42 Int'l Org. 461, 462–65 (1988).

104 *See* Hirschman, *supra* note 103 at 34–40. The policy also had the effect of lessening Germany's dependence on overseas markets, from which the effective British blockade of the First World War had cut her off, and from which she would likely be cut off again when, as Hitler planned, war was resumed.

105 Structural Realists have also noted this point. *See* Kenneth N. Waltz, *The Myth of National Interdependence,in* Kenneth N. Waltz, *Realism and International Politics, supra* note 22, at 152, 155.

106 *See* Hirschman, *supra* note 103, at 30.

states to turn them into "a sort of 'commercial fifth column'" working on its behalf.[107] Likewise, Germany could exploit its position as a leading manufacturer of certain specialized finished goods to obtain a predominant or monopolistic position as the supplier of those goods to the states in question. In effect, the smaller states would become like the colonies of older European imperial powers, unable to buy from or sell to any market other than the mother country's. Unlike the colonies, those states presumably would have alternative markets for their exports and alternative sources of supply for their imports, even if the terms of trade with them were less beneficial. But Germany attempted to induce or sustain trade dependency by taking special measures that made it difficult for those states to shift their trade to other partners.[108]For example, Germany demanded "bilateral agreements" that conditioned those states' ability to export to Germany on their receipt of imports from Germany, thus aggravating the difficulties that the small states would experience in attempting to shift either their exports or imports away from Germany.[109]Also, Germany paid above world prices for these countries' exports, prevented the transit of their exports to third countries, blocked payments, and undertook other actions to make these countries dependent on Germany. Further, in order to prevent the development of industry (and the self-dependence in manufactures that would accompany it) within a smaller trading partner, Germany engaged in practices such as predatory dumping. Once trade dependency was achieved, Germany exploited its market power to create both political and economic benefits for itself. On the economic side, it could impose higher tariffs on products in accordance with the level of dependency on the German market, in effect price-discriminating in the sale of access to the German market in the same way that monopolists price discriminate to reap the full advantage of their monopoly power. On the political side, the payoff would come in the form of increased ability to dominate the smaller state's military strategy and foreign policy.

Hirschman believed that economic nationalism of the kind practiced by Nazi Germany was an inherent predisposition of large states, which would always be tempted to use the threat of trade interruption as a tool of power politics. His analysis, therefore, laid the intellectual foundations of the case for the construction of an international trade regime that would limit national autonomy and ensure the (relatively) free movement of goods and services over international borders. In order to prevent price-discrimination or differential market access that flowed from dependency, the post-Second World War General Agreement on Tariffs and Trade (GATT) provided the framework for that regime. The GATT's central ordering principal is the most-favored-nation (MFN) concept, which requires each country to provide tariff treatment no

107 *Id.* at 29.

108 *Id.* at 32.

109 *Id.* at 32–33.

less favorable than that provided to any other country. The MFN clause reduces the risk that differential market access will be leveraged for political or economic power.[110]

3. Contemporary Realism: Five Key Concepts

We have referred occasionally to the concept of "***anarchy***"—one of the lynchpins of any type of realist theory. This concept requires some elaboration here: anarchy enters both into realist explanations of the international system's instability and proneness to conflict and into realist attempts to find ways to avoid conflict and promote cooperation (such as the balance of power theory, considered above). Furthermore, the concept of anarchy is indispensable to realism's diagnosis of international affairs, as seen in the so-called "***security dilemma***," which has been at the center of American international relations studies—including Waltz's form of structural realism[111]—since John Herz introduced it in his vastly influential 1950 essay, *Idealist Internationalism and the Security Dilemma.*[112] But the security dilemma presupposed more than the bare existence of international anarchy.Following the tradition of reason of state, the security dilemma posited that states were ***rational actors,*** and following the traditions of the balance of power and the balance of trade, it asserted that states sought certain substantive goals (*i.e.*, security or, as it may be, power).

The security dilemma was evident in the nuclear arms race between the United States and the Soviet Union. Realists seemed to be unable to propose a solution to the nuclearized form of the security dilemma. Indeed, some realists seem to have concluded that their theory was bankrupt, because the relentless, even if rational, pursuit of security or power entailed the virtual

110 In an important article, Stephen Krasner argued that post-Second World War American "hegemony" favored the creation of a more liberal international trading system. *See* Stephen D. Krasner, *State Power and the Structure of International Trade,* 28 World Politics 317, 319–21 (1976).

111 *See* Andew H. Kydd, *Methodological Individualism and Rational Choice,in*Oxford Handbook, *supra* note 1, at 425, 432 n.5 (2006) (Kenneth Waltz's widely read formulation of structural realism rests essentially on the security dilemma).

112 John Herz, *Idealist Internationalism and the Security Dilemma,* 2 *World Politics* 157 (1950); reprinted in John H. Herz, The Nation-State and the Crisis of World Politics: Essays on International Politics in the Twentieth Century 72–98(1976). Early formulations of the security dilemma can be discerned in Thucydides, History of the Peloponnesian War, Bk. I, para. 23, and in Machiavelli, The Prince Ch. III; *see also* Forde, *International Realism, supra* note 31, at 146–48. For later accounts, applications and criticisms of the security dilemma, *see, e.g.*, Kenneth Booth & Nicholas Wheeler, The Security Dilemma: Fear, Cooperation and Trust in World Politics(2008); John J. Mearsheimer, The Tragedy of Great Power Politics (2001); Charles L. Glaser, *The Security Dilemma Revisited,* 50 *World Politics* 171 (1997); Robert Jervis, *Arms Control, Stability, and Causes of War,* 16 Poli. Sci. Q. 239 (1993); Robert Jervis, *Cooperation Under the Security Dilemma,* 30 World Politics 167, 181 (1978) [hereafter, Cooperation]; Randall L. Schweller, *Neorealism's Status-Quo Bias: What Security Dilemma?,* 5 Sec. Stud. 90 (1991); Barry R. Posen, *The Security Dilemma and Ethnic Conflict,* 35 Survival 27 (1993) (applying concept of security dilemma to intra-state ethnic conflicts in Yugoslavia and elsewhere); Paul Roe, *The Intrastate Security Dilemma: Ethnic Conflict as a 'Tragedy'?,* 36 J. Peace Research 183, 188-92 (1999) (review of literature and critique of Posen); Paul Roe, *Former Yugoslavia: The Security Dilemma That Never Was?,* 6 Eur. J. Int'l Rel. 373 (2000) (arguing that Yugoslav case did not conform to security dilemma paradigm because relevant actors had hostile, rather than non-aggressive, intentions towards each other); Paul Roe, *Which Security Dilemma? Mitigating Ethnic Conflict: The Case of Croatia,* 13 Security Studies 280 (2004) (distinguishing forms of security dilemma and evaluating applicability of each to intra-state ethnic conflict).

certainty of an eventual nuclear holocaust. The indefinite prolongation of nuclear competition between the two major nuclear powers and the increasing availability of nuclear weaponry to other states with less power seemed to guarantee that nuclear weapons would be used. Kenneth Waltz sought to redeem the situation for realism by arguing that the nuclear duopoly of the United States and the Soviet Union tended to make *peace* rather than nuclear war more likely, and argued even more boldly that the acquisition of nuclear weapons by *other* powers would have the same peace-making effects. Waltz's attempted solution to the nuclearized security dilemma drew on the concept of ***polarity,*** which is also foundational to contemporary realism.

Finally, as realism has evolved into rational choice theory, the idea of the "***prisoner's dilemma***"—of which the security dilemma might be seen as one application—has become increasingly prominent. Here too, realism and its offshoots have claimed to find a solution to the security dilemma.

To put the matter simply, if the security dilemma serves as a model for understanding an "anarchic" international environment at the most basic level—so that even when states have no offensive designs on each other, they are nonetheless driven by rational, security-seeking choices to competition, spirals of increasing suspicion and rivalry, arms races, and finally war—and if the security dilemma can itself be understood as a specific form of the prisoner's dilemma, then any solutions that can be found to the prisoner's dilemma might be applicable to international relations, so that cooperation rather than conflict might prevail in at least some types of interstate dealings. Using the core concepts of anarchy, rational action, the security dilemma, and the prisoner's dilemma, theorists of international relations might be able to describe the international environment, to explain the apparently conflict-prone behavior of states, and to devise solutions for preventing or mitigating such conflicts. In this section, we examine each of these five fundamental concepts.

a. Anarchy

Realists invariably take anarchyas the basic condition of the international system. But what is meant by anarchy? In one sense, anarchy can mean "chaos" or "disorder." But realists do not assume that the international system is chaotic—nor should they. As the British international relations theorist Hedley Bull pointed out, "at no stage [in the modern international system] can it be said that the conception of common interests of states, of common rules accepted and common institutions worked by them, has ceased to exert an influence."[113](Bull was a leading figure in the "English school" of international relations theory—an approach that can be seen as a source of constructivism.[114]) Even as between states at war, some common rules are followed

113 Hedley Bull, The Anarchical Society 42 (1977).

114 *See* Tim Dunne, *The English School,in*Oxford Handbook, *supra* note 1, *at* 267 (2008). For a full-scale account, *see* Barry Buzan, From International to World Society: English School Theory and the Social Structure of Globalization (2004).

and some common norms are observed.[115]War can be likened to a primitive, but rule-governed, feud.[116]

What realists mean by anarchy is not the utter absence of rules or conventions but instead "the lack of government."[117] As Kenneth Abbott has explained:

> ["Anarchy"] means instead the power and authority are decentralized, held only by the constituent units, the states. No central institutions are empowered to decide for all. Similarly, authority is not hierarchical: no institution, and no state, can legitimately control the actions of other states by virtue of its position. More powerful states can influence weaker ones, but all are formally equal, a condition reinforced by the "constitutional" rules of classical international law.[118]

The international relations idea of anarchy thus seems to be closely linked to the international law idea of "sovereignty" discussed in ChapterI.B above. The international system seems to be constituted entirely of sovereign states, each of them formally, if not factually,equivalent to each other, and none of them acknowledging the other states'(legal) superiority over its own. If that is what anarchymeans, however, it again does not seem to describe international reality. As we saw in ChapterI.B,the international order has always included semi-sovereign as well as sovereign states: "in some sense, almost all of the states of the world have been semi-sovereigns. Rarely have states enjoyed full autonomy."[119]

However, Abbott's definition of anarchy has another aspect: "No central institutions are empowered to decide for all."[120] Understood in this light, anarchyseems to be a condition in which there is no *global* government. The lack of a *global* government is, of course, compatible with the existence of both sovereign and semi-sovereign states in the international system.

Still, one might argue that this definition merely pushes the question of the meaning of anarchy one stage back. That is, the question becomes: what do we mean by "*government*"?[121] Abbott

---

115 Constructivist scholars in particular stress this point. See Richard E. Price, The Chemical Weapons Taboo 27 (1997) ("[W]ar is a social contest rather than a no-holds-barred drive to extermination. . . . War is a contest of power, and the point of battle is to defeat the opponents' ability to resist according to a legitimated means of adjudicating what counts as power—a means that usually falls short of sheer physical annihilation."); Martha Finnemore, National Interests in International Society69 (1996). *See also* Michael Walzer, Just and Unjust Wars: A Moral Argument With Historical Illustrations24–25 (3d ed. 1977) (criticizing Clausewitz's theory of "absolute" war, and arguing that war is culturally limited).

116 *See* Michael Barkun, Law Without Sanctions: Order in Primitive Societies and the World Community 111 (1968).

117 *See* Helen Milner, *The Assumption of Anarchy in International Relations Theory: A Critique,* 17 Rev. Int'l Stud. 67 (1991), reprinted in David A. Baldwin (ed.), Neorealism and Neoliberalism 145, 147 (1993),

118 Abbott, *Modern International Relations Theory, supra* note 1, at 347.

119 Stephen D. Krasner, *Pervasive not Perverse: Semi-Sovereigns as the Global Norm,* 30 Cornell Int'l L. J. 651, 652 (1997).

120 Likewise, Wohlforth considers anarchy to exist "[w]hen no authority exists that can enforce agreements." Wohlforth, *supra* note 16, at 135.

121 *See* Milner, *supra* note 117, at 148,

speaks of both *power* and *authority*, and both are central attributes of *national* government. In saying that anarchy consists in the lack of global government, then, realists may be saying that there is no single government that has 1) the power, 2) the authority, or 3) both the power and authority to enforce its decisionsagainst all states. It is often unclear which of these criteria realists in fact adopt.One critic of realism contends, for example, that "[l]ack of legitimacy [*i.e.*, authority] seems in the end to be what many international relations scholars have in mind when they talk about anarchy."[122]

b. Rational Action

For realism (as well as the classic international law described in ChapterI.B), states are the only relevant actors in international affairs. Thus, realism takes little or no account in explaining the workings of the international system to non-state actors such as the Roman Catholic Church, the Shell Oil Company, al Qaeda, or the International Committee of the Red Cross. This self-denying ordinance reflects realism's commitment to theoretical parsimony—its desire to explain major international events in terms of the fewest possible factors.

States, of course, differ from each other in significant ways that are often relevant to their interactions with other states. For example, states may differ *constitutionally* (some are democracies; others autocracies; etc.), *ideologically* (some are capitalist; others are communist), *religiously* (some are Islamic; others are secular); *ethnically*; and so on. Further, states differ in material ways that directly affect their security: some states are militarily powerful, others weak; some share borders with historic enemies, others are isolated; some possess vast natural resources, others do not. Finally, states' security strategies are shaped by different kinds of actors.In some states, the military may have a dominant role; in other states, the military is subordinate to elected officials. The popular media may be influential in some states but not others. In some instances, strategy may emerge from competition among the factions of an elite class or from the jockeying of different business interest groups. For contemporary realists, these specific differences do not matter. In Waltz's terms, explanations that rely on such considerations look to the first ("man") or second ("state") images: realism, looking to the third ("structure") image, views states as "unitary"; that is, realism abstracts from a states's "internal" characteristics and differences, important as these might seem in explaining states' interactions with respect to security.[123]

Most importantly of all, for our purposes, realists also ascribe *rationality* to states. In Abbott's terms, realists assume that states "have consistently ordered preferences and choose

122 Milner, *supra* note 117, at 152.

123 For a critique, from a rational choice perspective, of structural realism's postulate of the unitariness of states, *see* Alexander Thompson, *Applying Rational Choice Theory to International Law: The Promise and Pitfalls*, 31 J. Leg. Stud. S285, S291–94 (2002).

among alternative courses of action so as to further those preferences."[124] Note that rationalityfor realists is a *given* characteristic of states, rather than (as it was in the reason of state doctrine) a characteristic that states *ought* to acquire.

Rationality understood in realism's terms leaves two major questions open. First, are a state's "preferences" fixed and unalterable, or may they (as constructivists argue) be altered by a state's interaction with other states and the lessons from these interactions? Second, what is the substantive *content* of a state's preferences? We shall leave the first of these questions for Chapter 2.C. Here we shall briefly addressthe second question.

Realists generally make two main assumptions about the substantive content of states' preferences. First, they posit that states are *self-regarding*: they pursue *their own, individual* interest rather than the interest of another state or of the community of states as a whole. States, in other words, are taken to be, not only rational, but also *egoists*. Second, realists differ over what states take their primary interest or highest-ranked preference to be. For "defensive" realists like Waltz, states aim for their own *security*; for "offensive" realists like John Mearsheimer, states aim for (relative) *power* as against other states. Both defensive and offensive realists appear to agree (in opposition to constructivists) that "material power, whether military or economic or both, is the single most important source of influence and authority in world politics."[125]

c. The Security Dilemma

According to many realist thinkers, the security dilemma arises out of the condition of anarchy. Roughly, the security dilemma affirms that the condition of international anarchy leads to mistrust and hostility, even between states that have fundamentally compatible goals and that harbor no aggressive intentions towards each other. This mistrust and hostility drives these states to engage in destructive arms races and perhaps in war. While some realist thinkers deny that the security dilemma in itself must inevitably lead to war,[126] it does provide a plausible start for identifying the causes of at least *some* wars, including the First World War.[127] We shall introduce the concept of the security dilemma by considering how it might explain the origins of that war.

---

124 Abbott, *Modern International Relations Theory, supra* note 1, at 350. In assuming rationality, structural realism also seems to depart from Thucydides: the Melians' failure to surrender in the face of an overwhelmingly superior Athenian force does not bespeak the rational pursuit of a strategy of survival. *See* Forde, *International Realism, supra* note 31, at145.

125 Ted Hopf, *The Promise of Constructivism in International Relations Theory,* 23 Int'l Sec. 171, 177 (1998). In contrast, constructivism "argues that both material and discursive power are necessary for any understanding of world affairs." *Id.*

126 *See* Fearon, *supra* note 10, at 34–35 ("[T]he fact that under anarchy one state's efforts to make itself more secure can have the undesired but unavoidable effect of making another state less secure" by itself "says nothing about the availability or feasibility of peaceful bargains that would avoid the costs of war. More elaborate arguments are required.").

127 Among recent scholars, Henry Kissinger seems inclined to accept a variant of the "security dilemma" in explaining the origins of the First World War. *See* Henry Kissinger, Diplomacy 170 (1994). For a review and analysis of studies of the causes of the First World War, *see* Samuel R. Williamson, Jr., *The Origins of World War I, in*The Origin and Prevention of Major Wars 225 (Robert I. Rotberg & Theodore K. Rabb eds., 1989).

In 1916, during the First World War, the English writer and historian Goldsworthy Lowes Dickinson had published an insightful, if nowadays neglected, study entitled *The European Anarchy.*[128] In it, Dickinson sought to show that the War had broken out, not because of any intrinsic aggressiveness or militarism on the part of Imperial Germany, but because of the mistrust and suspicion that the Great Powers felt—and could not help but feel—for each other. Dickinson argued that "the defeat of the ideal of a world-order" at the end of Europe's Middle Ages and the ensuing "definite acceptance of international anarchy" had given rise to a "tragic" aftermath on that continent.[129] Emphasizing the importance of the anarchy that attended the decline of the powers of the Pope and Holy Roman Emperor, Dickinson wrote:

> It is as true of an aggregation of States as of an aggregation of individuals that, whatever moral sentiments may prevail, if there is no common law and no common force the best intentions will be defeated by lack of confidence and security. Mutual fear and mutual suspicion, aggression masquerading as defence and defence masquerading as aggression, will be the protagonists in the bloody drama; and there will be, what Hobbes truly asserted to be the essence of such a situation, a chronic state of war, open or veiled. For peace itself will be a latent war; and the more the States arm to prevent a conflict the more certainly will it be provoked, since to one or another it will always seem a better chance to have it now than to have it on worse conditions later. Some one State at any moment may be the immediate offender; but the main and permanent offence is common to all States. It is the anarchy which they are all responsible for perpetuating.[130]

The situation that Dickinson described was diagnosed in more general terms in John Herz's celebrated 1950 article, *Idealist Internationalism and the Security Dilemma.* Herz began his analysis with the concept of an "anarchic" international society, a "social constellation" that he considered to be "fundamental," and that he defined as a condition "where a plurality of otherwise interconnected groups constitute ultimate units of political life, that is, where groups live alongside each other without being organized into a higher unity."[131] In such anarchy, Herz contended,

> there has arisen what may be called the 'security dilemma' of men, or groups, or their leaders. Groups or individuals living in such a constellation must be, and usually are, concerned

128 On Dickinson, *see* the brief sketch in Brian C. Schmidt, The Political Discourse of Anarchy: A Disciplinary History of International Relations160–62 (1998).

129 G. Lowes Dickinson, The European Anarchy 1 (1916 (Dodo ed. (n.d.)).

130 *Id.*

131 John H. Herz, *Idealist Internationalism and the Security Dilemma,* in John H. Herz, The Nation-State and the Crisis of World Politics 72, 72 (1976).

> about their security from being attacked, subjected, dominated, or annihilated by other groups and individuals. Striving to attain security from such attack, they are driven to acquire more and more power in order to escape the impact of the power of others. This, in turn, renders the others more insecure and compels them to prepare for the worst. Since none can ever feel entirely secure in such a world of competing units, power competition ensues, and the vicious circle of security and power accumulation is on.[132]

There is an obvious resemblance between Herz's "security dilemma" and Hobbes' "war of all against all," which similarly seeks to show that even those states who hold no aggressive intentions toward others may nonetheless be compelled to attack them in order to eliminate the potential threats.[133]

Herz's "security dilemma," as applied to international affairs is characterized by certain assumptions and inferences. Let us try to unpack them. First, the security dilemma arises in a condition of anarchy, in which the only relevant actors are states, and in which there is no "higher unity" or central, governing authority. Second, each state is concerned (overridingly, it would seem) with its own security as against threats to its survival posed by (it would seem) the bare existence of other states. (Certainly, Herz offered no further description of a state's specific nature or characteristics; what matters for his analysis is simply that states strongly desire their own security and survival.) Third, states are unaware of, or uncertain about, the intentions of other states towardthem; certainly, they need not *know* that other states are predatory or hostile, or that they have aggressive designs on them. Fourth, states are also unaware of, or uncertain about, the power of other states. Fifth, states' uncertainty about the intentions and capabilities of other states appears to be largely incurable; that is, states appear to have no reliable means of discovering what the true intentionsand capabilities of other states are. Further, even if states had reasonable certainty about other states' *present* intentions, they cannot be certain about their *future* ones. But history shows that states can change rapidly from being unaggressive to being aggressive because of factors like domestic political forces. Sixth, states' desire to preserve their own existence, coupled with their uncertainty regarding the threat posed to their existence by other states, leads them to take precautions against that threat, by acquiring more power, such as by arming themselves.Seventh, other states, perceiving a state taking such defensive measures, becomes more insecure, presumably because they fear that as the first state acquires greater power, it becomes more dangerous, or because they interpret the first

132 *Id.* at 72–73. In 1951, that is, at about the time Herz was writing, the English historian Herbert Butterfield analyzed what he called the "tragic element" in human conflict. *See* Sir Herbert Butterfield, *The Tragic Element in Modern International Conflict,* in (Sir) Herbert Butterfield, *Theory and Human Relations* 9 (1951). Butterfield's conception is strikingly similar to Herz's, and the two are often paired together as co-inventors of the security dilemma. *See* Robert J. Delahunty, *Herbert Butterfield, Christianity, and International Law,* U. Det. Mercy L. Rev. 615 (2009). Kenneth Waltz also propounded a form of the security dilemma not long after Herz and Butterfield had. *See* Waltz, *supra* note 21, at 203–04.

133 *See* Gregory S. Kavka, *Hobbes's War of All Against All,* 93 Ethics 291, 293–95 (1983); *see also id.* at 309 (applying argument to states).

state's armaments program as a signal of aggression. Eighth, feeling more insecure, those other states take counter-measures, which also may include arming themselves. Ninth, the first state, noticing other states acquiring arms or otherwise augmenting their power, feels threatened by the states' counter-measures, and seeks to augment its own power still further—thus triggering an arms race or what Herz calls "a vicious circle of security and power accumulation." Paradoxically, in their efforts to enhance their security, states may unintentionally *decrease* it, and the overall level of security in the states system as a whole. The crux is that "the margin of security for one [country] is the margin of danger for the other."[134]

Herz's security dilemma can be a powerful analytic tool for explaining the state behavior in the international arena. But it is important to see that it rests on assumptions that are challengeable, draws inferences that are problematic, and explains less than it may seem to do. First, as Herz originally laid it out, the security dilemma assumes that states have no reliable way to discover other states' intentions. But that assumption is far too strenuous. It overlooks the possibility of purely voluntary disclosure on the part of one state toward other states, motivated, perhaps, by the belief that such disclosure will be viewed as a gesture of good faith and so will be reciprocated. It also overlooks the fact that a good deal can be inferred from a state's observable behavior in the context in which it acts.[135]Policy making in modern democracies is usually transparent enough to provide a good deal of information about their motivations, and even non-democratic states can, if they choose, send costly signals that their motivations are unaggressive.[136](To be sure, a realist can respond that a significant degree of opacity is likely to remain, as in U.S.-China relations, and that a change of regime can bring about a sudden and drastic change in a state's motivations, as in the collapse of the Weimar government of Germany and the rise of the Nazis.[137]) Furthermore, both diplomacy (and espionage) can provide significant information about a state's intentions and its abilities to execute them.[138] Such information

134 Spykman, *supra* note 64, at 24.

135 *See* Jervis, *Cooperation, supra* note 112, at 199–211.

136 *See* Andrew Kydd, Sheep *in Sheep's Clothing: Why Security Seekers Do Not Fight Each Other,* 7 Sec. Stud. 114, 117, 125–47 (1997).

137 *See* Dale Copeland, *The Constructivist Challenge to Structural Realism: A Review Essay,* 25 Int'l Sec. 187, 199–204 (2000).

138 Historically, diplomacy and espionage have been closely related; both perform important information-gathering functions. Even in classical Greece, where permanent diplomatic missions did not exist, useful intelligence could be derived from or by visiting foreign emissaries: even as a boy, Alexander the Great is said to have interrogated visiting Persian ambassadors about roads and routes in their Empire. *See* J.A. Richmond, *Spies in Ancient Greece,* 45 Greece & Rome 1, 3 (1998). In the early modern period, "[t]he prominence of th[e] information-gathering function meant inevitably that the diplomat was often regarded as little more than a licensed spy." Anderson, *supra* note 60, at 13; *see also* Daniela Frigo, *Introduction,* in Daniela Frigo (ed.), Politics and Diplomacy in Early Modern Italy: The Structure of Diplomatic Practice, 1450-1800 at 10 (2000) ("Behind the pomp that surrounded the Renaissance ambassador on solemn occasions, his function was often and much more realistically viewed as a sort of 'honoured' espionage.'); Edward Vose Gulick, *Europe's Classical Balance of Power: A Case History of the Theory and Practice of One of the Great Concepts of European Statecraft* 55–56 (1955) (in early modern Europe, the function of diplomatic institutions was "watchfulness"). During the Italian Renaissance, "[t]he collecting, processing and packaging of information were the resident's ambassador's main task," and ambassadors were counseled "not [to] behave like a spy." Garrett Mattingly, *Renaissance Diplomacy*

can allay other states' security concerns, at least to some degree. (By contrast, where diplomacy is primitive or non-existent—as it was in the ancient Mediterranean world—the security dilemma is intensified.[139]).

Second, Herz's formulation also seemed to assume it would not matter to states what *kind* of arms—offensive or defensive—that other states acquired. This assumption seems implausible, however: if state A learns that state B is seeking to enhance its security by taking defensive measures that would not lend themselves to offensive uses (such as, perhaps, the defensive French fortifications known as the "Maginot Line"), state B may not feel impelled to take countermeasures designed to bolster its own security.[140]

Third, Herz assumed that states aim at gaining *security*, and so, presumably, would be satisfied if mutual security could be achieved. But that assumption limits the explanatory scope of the model, because states—or at least, *some* states—may in fact harbor aggressive, predatory intentions toward others. Thus, even if the security dilemma can help to solve "a basic puzzle—that even when states have compatible, benign goals, there is competition and conflict"—its explanatory power decreases when some states are greedy.[141]

Finally, we may note that the security dilemma, in Herz's formulation, does not seem able (or even intended) to explain the occurrence of major *war*. There is no reason why an arms race, even if prolonged, should culminate in interstate armed conflict insteadof some states' bankruptcy, exhaustion, or surrender even if, as Dickinson argued, an arms race *did* precede such major conflicts as the First World War. The security dilemma seems more effective as an explanation of *spirals* of mistrust and rivalry rather than, necessarily, of *war*.

d. Polarity

Structural realism, as we have seen, looks to the "structure" or ordering principle of international relations in explaining the interactions of states, especially balancing and major wars. The first, and most important, element of that structure is anarchy. But there are two other elements of structure as well. Second, and less important, is the functional differentiation of states. Because structural realism makes the simplifying assumptions that states are overridingly concerned with survival (or power) and that their internal arrangements do not significantly influence that pursuit, this element plays little role in structural realist theory. The third element

113–14 (1955). Sometimes, of course, ambassadors or their staffs were spies—like the agents of the Spanish Ambassador Eustache Chapuys at the court of King Henry VIII of England. *See id.* at 243–45.

139 *See* Arthur M. Eckstein, Mediterranean Anarchy, Interstate War, and the Rise of Rome 59 (2006).

140 *See* Jervis, *Cooperation, supra* note 112 (discussing whether offense or defense has the advantage, and whether offensive postures can be distinguished from defensive ones, and finding that stability is most likely when defense has the advantage and defensive posture is distinguishable); *see generally* Offense, Defense and War(Michael E. Brown, Owen R. Colé, Jr., Sean M. Lynn-Jones & Steven E. Miller eds., 2004).

141 *See* Glaser, *supra* note 112, at 190–91; *see also* Schweller, *supra* note 112, at 104.

of structure is, however, significant: this is the distribution of power. Because the condition of anarchy as a constant and functional differentiation is disregarded, structural realism could not explain *change* within the international system unless it included a dynamic element. And because the distribution of power across the international system is variable, it can be used to help explain changes in that system.[142]

Structural realists have distinguished three main forms of the distribution of power across the international system. The first is a system characterized by a single preponderant power: *unipolarity* or *hegemony.* The position of the United States after its Cold War victory in 1989 was often taken to exemplify this kind of system. The second kind of system is characterized by the coexistence of two dominant states: *bipolarity.* The paradigm of this kind of system was the post-1945 period, which was dominated by two great powers, the United States and the Soviet Union.[143] The third kind of system features three or more dominant states:*multi-polarity.* The international system as it existed on the eve of the First World War in 1914 was such a multi-polar system: it included the great powers on the continent of Europe—the British, French, Russian, German, Austro-Hungarian, and Italian Empires, together with two rising powers, the United States and the Japanese Empire.[144] The type of "polarity" exhibited by the international system is usually, if crudely, identified by *counting* the number of dominant states —an exercise that appears to require little more than common sense, but that may prove harder than it seems.[145]

In traditional balance of power theory, multi-polarity was generally thought to be more stable (in terms of the frequency, intensity and length of war) than bipolarity.[146] But in a major essay written in 1964, Kenneth Waltz challenged that view, arguing that a "bipolar" world order—such as the world that had existed during the "Long Peace" of the Cold War—was likely to "encourage the limitation of violence in the relations of states."[147] Waltz identified four factors that appeared to explain the nonoccurrence of war after 1945. First, "with only two world powers there are no peripheries."[148] Both the United States and the Soviet Union were vitally concerned with events in widely separated parts of the Earth—Korea, Cuba, Poland, elsewhere. But that concern led to

142 *See* Sobek, *supra* note 10, at 133–34.

143 *See id.*

144 These three forms of power distribution correspond roughly to monopolistic, duopolitistic and oligopolistic market systems. *See* Patrick James & Michael Breecher, *Stability and Polarity: New Paths for Inquiry,* 25 J. Peace Res. 31, 33 (1988); Charles P. Kindleberger, *Review: Scientific International Politics,* 11 World Pol. 83, 86 (1958).

145 *See* Edward D. Mansfield, *Concentration, Polarity, and the Distribution of Power,* 37 Int'l Stud. Q. 105, 108 (1993); Patrick James & Michael Breecher, *Stability and Polarity: New Paths for Inquiry,* 25 J. Peace Res. 31, 32–33 (1988).

146 *See, e.g.,* Morton A. Kaplan, *Balance of Power, Bipolarity and Other Models of International Systems,* 51 Am. Pol. Sci. Rev. 684, 693 (1957) (arguing that a "tight" bipolar system "will not be a highly stable or well integrated system"). *See also* Hans J. Morgenthau, Politics Among Nations: The Struggle for Power and Peace 350–54 (1949).

147 Kenneth N. Waltz, *The Stability of a Bipolar World,inKenneth* N. Waltz, Realism and International Politics, *supra* note 22, at 99, 100.

148 *Id.*

a durable balance: wherever one side threatened to expand, the other resisted, leaving few openings for aggrandizement. Second, "the range of factors included in the competition is extended as the intensity of the competition increases."[149] Thus, the two great protagonists competed diplomatically, militarily, economically, ideologically, and legally; in propaganda, in outer space; and in domestic political arrangements. Hence, the two protagonists attended carefully to even minor shifts in power, tending to keep them in equilibrium. Third, the period was marked by the "nearly constant presence of pressure and the recurrence of crisis."[150] Rather than leading to war, however, brinkmanship tended to moderate conflict: "One's motto may still be, 'push to the limit,' but *limit* must be emphasized as heavily as *push.* Caution, moderation, and the management of crisis come to be of great and obvious importance."[151] Fourth and finally, the power of the United States and the Soviet Union was preponderant as each far outranked the other powers, including Britain, France, China, and Japan. Summarizing, Waltz wrote:

> Taken together, these three factors—the absence of peripheries, the range and intensity of competition, and the persistence of pressure and crisis—are among the most important characteristics of the period since World War II. The first three points combine to produce an intense competition in a wide arena with a great variety of means employed. The constancy of effort of the two major contenders, combined with a fourth factor, their preponderant power, have made for a remarkable ability to comprehend and absorb within the bipolar balance the revolutionary political, military, and economic changes that have occurred.[152]

Waltz's defense of bipolarity was soon challenged,[153] and there is still no consensus among international relations theorists whether bipolarity is more likely to produce international

149 *Id.*

150 Id. at 101.

151 *Id.* at 102.

152 *Id.* at 103. Waltz's argument should be contrasted with the narrower claim that bipolarity *in the specific circumstances that existed after 1945* was exceptionally prone to stability. *See* John Lewis Gaddis, *The Long Peace: Elements of Stability in the Postwar International System,* 10 Int'l Sec. 99, 108–10 (1986).

153 *See, e.g.,* Richard Rosecrance, *Bipolarity, Multipolarity, and the Future,* 10 Conf. Res. 314 (1966).

stability than multi-polarity.[154] Indeed, Harrison Wagner argues powerfully that no consensus is even *possible:* the concept of bipolarity, he contends, simply has no clear meaning.[155]

To the extent that the bipolarity/multi-polarity debate *is* decidable, however, some evidence apparently points in Waltz's favor.If the post-World War II period is the only period in modern history characterized by bipolarity, then no major wars have occurred in a bipolar international system. Further, if the pre-1945 era was multi-polar, then multi-polarity has been accompanied by many wars. But it would be superficial not to subject the evidence to closer analysis. For example, the *concentration* of power in the international system is a variable, distinct from polarity,that appears to be relevant in explaining the occurrence of major wars.[156] Likewise, the number of *decisional centers,* as well as that of *power centers,* may affect stability.[157] Indeed, even the earliest empirical studies of the question found it necessary to bring in distinctions that Waltz's original formulation had not made,[158] and later empirical work, while generally supporting the case for bipolarity, has continued to introduce variations in conceptualization, measurement, and method.[159]

Waltz himself reliedmore on theoretical than empirical arguments in contending that multi-polarity is inherently unstable. In substance, Waltz offered three main theoretical reasons why bipolarity should be more stable than multi-polarity. First, where two blocs are in competition, both will have some interest in maintaining a global balance of power, and the lead nations in each bloc will be capable of achieving that goal. Second, because there are fewer decision-makers,

---

154 For lively examples of the continuing debate, *see* Ted Hopf, *Polarity, The Offense-Defense Balance, and War,* 85 Am. Pol, Sci. Rev. 475 (1991); Manus I. Midlarsky & Ted Hopf, *Polarity and International Stability,* 87 Am. Pol. Sci. Rev. 171 (1993). For examples of formal treatments reaching opposing conclusions, *compare* Alvin M. Saperstein, *The "Long Peace"—Result of a Bipolar Competitive World?,* 35 J. Conf. Res. 68 (1991) (tripolar world in which third party is a significant factor is less stable than a bipolar one) with Karl W. Deutsch & J. David Singer, *Multipolar Power Systems and International Stability,* 16 World Pol. 390 (1964) (frequency and intensity of war expected to diminish as system moves from bipolarity to multi-polarity).

155 *See* R. Harrison Wagner, *What was Bipolarity?,* 47 Int'l Org. 77, 89 (1993). Wagner noted that

> [T]he word bipolarity has at least four distinct meanings in the literature on post-World War II international politics: (1) a condition in which states are polarized into two hostile coalitions; (2) a condition in which there are only two states capable of a strategy of global deterrence; (3) a system of only two states; and (4) a system in which power is distributed in such a way that two states are so powerful that they can each defend themselves against any combination of other states. The first definition . . . is clearly not what recent discussions of the significance of the end of bipolarity have in mind. The second definition is almost universally said to refer to a condition that is independent of bipolarity. . . . The third definition does not apply to any historical international systems. . . . Finally, the fourth definition, far from explaining U.S. and soviet behavior during the cold war, makes their behavior inexplicable [because, for example, of their competition over West Germany]. Thus bipolarity as an explanatory concept is either undefined, irrelevant to post-World War II international politics, or implies behavior that is inconsistent with the behavior it is supposed to explain.

Id.

156 *See* Edward D. Mansfield, *Concentration, Polarity, and the Distribution of Power,* 37 Int'l Stud. Q. 105, 117–19 (1993).

157 Patrick James & Michael Breecher, *Stability and Polarity: New Paths for Inquiry,* 25 J. Peace Res. 31, 33–36 (1988).

158 *See, e.g.,* Michael Hass, *International Subsystems: Stability and Polarity,* 64 Am. Pol. Sci. Rev. 98, 121 (1970) (concluding that "[i]f a state or group of states is willing to accept long wars that are won by aggressor states, bipolarity provides an escape from the more war-prone, character of historical multipolar systems. Multi-polarity entails more violence, more countries at war, and more casualties: bipolarity brings fewer but longer wars").

159 *See* Patrick James, *Structural Realism and the Causes of War,* 39 Mershon Int'l Stud. Rev. 181, 185–91 (1995).

there is less risk of miscalculation of the other side's intentions or its capabilities. Third, while the occurrence of crises would be a recurring aspect of a bipolar situation, the escalation of crises could be more easily prevented than under multi-polarity.

How far should the stability of the Cold War period be attributed to bipolarity, and how much was due to the nuclear stalemate between the two great powers? Some international relations theorists have argued that "the absence of great-power war during the cold war does not demonstrate that bipolarity was instrumental in this outcome. It is just as logical to attribute the long peace to the restraining influence of nuclear weapons."[160] Likewise, the historian John Lewis Gaddis argued near the end of the Cold War that

> the development of nuclear weapons has had, on balance, a stabilizing effect on the postwar international system. They have served to discourage the process of escalation that has, in other eras, too casually led to war. They have had a sobering effect upon a whole range of statesmen of varying degrees of responsibility and capability. They have forced national leaders, every day, to confront the reality of what war is really like, indeed to confront the prospect of their own mortality.[161]

Waltz, however, originally argued that bipolarity rather than the nuclear balance accounted for the stability of the post-1945 international system; at most, second-strike nuclear capabilities "induce[d] an added caution" into the superpowers' dealings with each other.[162] Further, he believed that the world balance would likely be destabilized if other states acquired nuclear capabilities commensurable with those of the two great powers, and argued that "the existence of a number of nuclear states would increase the range of difficult political choices," thus tending to instability.[163]

---

160 Charles W. Kegley, Jr. & Gregory A. Raymond, *Must We Fear a Post-Cold War Multipolar System?,* 36 J. Conf. Res. 573, 579 (1992).

161 Gaddis,*supra* note 152, at 123.

Harrison Wagner has offered yet another account: that the distinctive feature of the Cold War's distribution of power was that one state, the Soviet Union, was near-dominant on the Eurasian continent. This led to the formation of an opposing coalition, led by the United States, which was itself not strong enough to have an incentive to use force to weaken the Soviet Union. *See* R.Harrison Wagner, *What was Bipolarity,* 47 Int'l Org. 77, 79, 94, 102 (1993).

162 Kenneth N. Waltz, *International Structure, National Force, and the Balance of World Power,* in Kenneth N. Waltz, Realism and International Politics 137, 148 (2008).

163 *See* Kenneth N. Waltz, *The Stability of a Bipolar World,in* Kenneth N. Waltz, Realism and International Politics, *supra* note 22, at 99, 102–03. Earlier, John Herz had emphasized the distinction between bipolarity and nuclear armaments, arguing that "the two, in nature and impact, really have nothing to do with each other, and that only by historical accident, as it were, did the conditions that caused each materialize at about the same time." John Herz, International Politics in the Atomic Age33 (1959).

By 1981, however, Waltz had changed his mind dramatically.[164] In *Toward Nuclear Peace,* he argued that "[t]he presence of nuclear weapons makes war less likely," although proliferation "threatens to make wars more intense at the local and not at the global level."[165] He reached this conclusion by finding that nuclear weapons make conquest more difficult, discourage preemptive or preventive war, and dilute the credibility of coercive threats. Nuclear weapons produce these effects chiefly because they reduce the likelihood of miscalculations of the kind that often led to war when only conventional armaments were available:

> Miscalculation causes wars. One side expects victory at an affordable price, whereas the other side hopes to avoid defeat. Here the differences between conventional and nuclear weapons are fundamental. With the former, states are too often tempted to act on advantages that are wishfully discerned and narrowly calculated. In 1914 neither Germany nor France tried very hard to avoid a general war. Both hoped for victory even though they believed their forces to be quite evenly matched. . . . Uncertainty about outcomes does not work decisively against the fighting of wars with conventional weapons. Countries so armed go to war knowing that even in defeat their suffering will be limited. Calculations about nuclear war are made differently, however. A nuclear world calls for a different kind of reasoning. If countries armed with nuclear weapons go to war, their suffering may be unlimited. Of course, it also may not be, but that is not the kind of uncertainty that encourages the use of force. In a conventional world, one is uncertain about winning or losing. In a nuclear world, one is uncertain about survival or annihilation.[166]

The logic of deterrence thus made nuclear armed states cautious and risk-averse in their conflicts with one another. So long as a nuclear state retained sufficient retaliatory capability to mount a second strike that could destroy an attacker's major cities, the attacker would probably be deterred.The cost in suffering a counter-attack would outweigh any gains from a nuclear victory. Waltz accordingly came to conclude in 1990 that nuclear weaponry, not simply bipolarity, had underwritten the Long Peace. He noted that

> [n]ever since the Treaty of Westphalia in 1648, which conventionally marks the beginning of modern history, have great powers enjoyed a longer period of peace than we have known since

164 *See* Kenneth N. Waltz, *The Spread of Nuclear Weapons: More May Better.* Adelphi Papers No. 171 (1981) (*available at* http://www.wiphala.org/waltz25.htm). The consistency of Waltz's changed thinking with the rest of his system is open to question. See Daniel Deudney, Bounding Power: Republic Security Theory from the Polis to the Global Village 78 (2007).

165 Kenneth N. Waltz, *Toward Nuclear Peace,in*Kenneth N. Waltz, Realism and International Politics, *supra* note 22, at 260, 273.

166 *Id.* at 261.

> the Second World War. One can scarcely believe that the presence of nuclear weapons does not greatly explain this happy condition.[167]

Indeed, Waltz claimed that nuclear *proliferation* would be likely to promote peace because it would enable weak but nuclear-armed states to deter attacks by states with much larger military forces.[168] (Readers should keep this point carefully in mind when considering the materials later in this Chapter on the North Korean and Iranian quests for nuclear weaponry.) Some of Waltz's reasons for this (admittedly "unusual") conclusion were specific to the circumstances of the Cold War, like the assumption that "the balance of terror [between the two superpowers] is indestructible."[169] But other reasons may continue to apply: that "nuclear weapons threaten to make the cost of wars immense [and so] make it possible to approach the deterrent ideal"; that "nuclear weapons can be used for defence [sic] as well as for deterrence [and that] [n]o one attacks a defence [sic] believed to be impregnable;" that[n]uclear weapons may make it possible to approach the defensive ideal"; and finally that "[n]ations that have nuclear weapons have strong incentives to use them responsibly. These statements hold for small as for big nuclear powers."[170]

e. The Prisoner's Dilemma

If the security dilemma provides the basic structure of international relations, then it will follow that states, even when their attitudes towards other states are not hostile, will be locked into a spiral of competition that dismayingly makes them increasingly *less* secure. Under the security dilemma, conflict would seem to be all but unavoidable, and cooperation would seem to be all but impossible. The security dilemma might itself be seen as a particular case or specification of an even more general problem—the *prisoner's dilemma*(PD), the paradigm for non-cooperative games.

The PD receives its name from the hypothetical case commonly used to explain its payoff structure. In PD, two prisoners face the choice of whether to maintain their conspiracy (cooperation) or strike a deal with the state for a lesser sentence (defection). Simplified versions of the analysis simply draw ordinal (or merely relative) comparisons among the various outcomes,

---

167 *See* Kenneth N. Waltz, *Nuclear Myths and Political Realities, in*Kenneth N. Waltz, Realism and International Politics, *supra* note 22, at 276, 291–92.

168 *See* Kenneth N. Waltz, *A Reply (to Critics of Sagan and Waltz), in*Kenneth N. Waltz, Realism and International Politics, *supra* note 22, at 294. John Mearsheimer cautiously followed Waltz's lead in arguing that, despite the risk that its example would encourage proliferation, Ukraine should maintain a nuclear deterrent. Mearsheimer conceded that "[n]uclear proliferation does not automatically promote peace and can in some cases even cause war," but he also insisted that "nuclear proliferation sometimes promotes peace." John Mearsheimer, *The Case for a Ukrainian Nuclear Deterrent,* 72 For. Aff. 50, 51 (1993).

169 Waltz, *supra* note 164, at 31.

170 *Id.*

rather than cardinal (or absolute) comparisons of the intensity of each player's payoff for the possible outcomes. Thus, framed in ordinal terms, each player in the PD game is best off if he defects and the other player cooperates, next best off if both cooperate, next worst off if both players defect, and worst off if he cooperates and the other player defects. This last result is known as the "Sucker's Payoff." Plainly, under conditions of uncertainty concerning whether or not the other player will cooperate or defect, the "dominant strategy" for each player in the PD game is to defect: if the other player cooperates, the player is better off by defecting; and, if the other player defects, the player must defect to avoid the Sucker's Payoff. The first incentive is sometimes called an "offensive" incentive to defect; the second, by parity of logic, is called a "defensive" incentive to defect. These incentive structures thus generate the behavioral regularities that realist international relations theorists associate with the perils of anarchy.

To illustrate, suppose both state A and state B confront the choice whether to be armed or unarmed. Assume that the combined payoff for both states would be highest in security terms if both cooperated, that is to say, both remained unarmed. Also suppose that the combined payoff would be lowest if both defected, that is, the states were armed, because neither would achieve security by arming, although arming would entail a cost. Further, suppose that the payoff for each state is highest if it alone armed while the other remained unarmed. Finally, assume also that the states cannot communicate so as to arrange the optimal outcome. Because states, as individual decision-makers facing international anarchy, like individual players in the PD, make decisions solely on the basis of their own preferences with the object of maximizing their own welfare, the PD model explains and predicts the arms race, and other similar outcomes, in the condition of international anarchy. Thus, the PD presents the rational choice theory analogue for the security dilemma.[171]The PD can be described as a cooperation game or non-cooperation game depending on the decisions of the participants.

It is possible, however, that the PD is not the only game in town, so to speak. The international system (or at least some issue-areas or regional situations) may not have a PD payoff structure for cooperation and defection decisions characteristic of the PD. One famous counter-example, the so-called "Stag Hunt" (SH), was suggested by Jean-Jacques Rousseau.[172] In SH, a group of hunters, and only a critical mass of hunters, can capture a stag, which serves for each hunter as his best possible payoff. However, hunters can peel off from the group and individually capture rabbits or other smaller animals. Because unilateral defection produces a lower payoff than cooperation, there is no offensive motive to defect. Only a defensive incentive to defect arises when each hunter judges that the other hunters will defect from the stag hunt.

171 *See generally* Thomas Schelling, The Strategy of Conflict (1960).

172 Jean-Jacques Rousseau, Discourse on the Origins of Inequality Among Men [1754](English translation) (*available at* http://www.constitution.org/jjr/ineq.htm). Some international relations theorists consider the security dilemma an application of the SH, not the PD. *See* Schweller, *supra* note 112.

In short, cooperation becomes a dominant strategy once other players signal their intention to cooperate.[173]

Kenneth Waltz emphasized the significance of Rousseau's parable for contemporary realists, stating that though "[t]he story is simple. . . the implications are tremendous. In cooperative action, even where all agree on the goal and have an equal interest in the project, one cannot rely on others."[174] And certainly, like the PD, the SH demonstrates the intractability of finding a solution to the recurring "collective action" problem that haunts international anarchy.[175] That said, for game theorists, the incentive structure of the SH is far more conducive to cooperation than the PD.

Indeed, leadership by a single player in offering to cooperate, leading the stag hunt, might, like price leadership of a producer in a business cartel, be sufficient to induce cooperation (without additional institutionalization such as a formal agreement to cooperate or other, more extensive forms of integration). Thus, payoff structures that are perceived by the players more to resemble SH than PD are more likely to facilitate cooperation. Indeed, such games are often described as "coordination" games, because cooperation can be assumed once the parties establish a focal point, such as the initial organization of the band of hunters, for cooperation to proceed.

Thus, generally speaking, games fall within two categories: coordination games and cooperation games. In coordination problems, participants to a treaty or practice under customary international law, such as the allocation of a shared resource such as radio spectrum, might have different distributional preferences, but each would coordinate responsibilities and rights once an initial distribution of the resource was established, regardless of whether other parties cooperate or defect. By contrast, in cooperation problems, games may have payoffs that, at the outset, discourage or prevent cooperation. As we shall see below, coordination games suggest the possibility of an escape from the security dilemma.

Before providing a more sophisticated account of an approach to international relations theory grounded on rationalism and game theory, in the following section we provide an account of the emergence of international relations approaches that pay attention to the role of institutions in addressing the collective action problems that are endemic in anarchy. We then supply an account of developments in rational choice theory that draw on ever more sophisticated branches of economics.

---

173 *See* Abbott, *Trust But Verify, supra* note 1, at 21–23. The following text draws extensively on Abbott's seminal article.

174 Waltz, *supra* note 21.

175 *See* Scott Barrett, Why Cooperate? The Incentive to Supply Global Public Goods (2007) (discussing collective action problem).

4. From Structural Realism to Institutionalism and Beyond

Both proponents and critics of structural realism were concerned with the question, "How is it possible that states cooperate—as they do—even when their vital security interests are at stake?" Structural realism seemed to encounter problems in trying to explain the fact of international cooperation and the existence of international institutions that seemed both to reflect and facilitate it. Some structural realists resolutely denied that states could cooperate in ways that would ultimately resolve the security dilemma. They contended that a tendency toward conflict was built into the anarchic structure of international relations, and that short of world government (which would put an end to anarchy) no measures taken by states themselves could ever abate their restless pursuit of security or power. Other structural realists like Robert Gilpin, drawing in part on the later work of Kenneth Waltz,[176] supposed that international institutions could play a limited role in the international system. These realists continued to take anarchy as their point of departure, but saw a partial corrective to anarchy's ills in the idea of *hegemony or hegemonic stability theory.* Finally, some theorists, while carrying over much of realism (including its view of the primacy of states and its rational egoism), developed an *institutionalist* theory, sometimes called *liberal institutionalism.* Robert Keohane pioneered this theoretical perspective. These two lines of thought, while strikingly different, merged in finding a role for international institutions by resolving or attenuating the impediments to international cooperation caused by anarchy. (A variant of liberal institutionalism, known as *neoliberalism,* more recently extends its insights to include the role of sub-state and transnational entities in international institutions.)

We explore the tenets of each of these variants of institutionalist rational-choice theories before providing a detailed account of modern rational-choice institutionalism's theoretical underpinnings in game theory and economic theory, particularly the transaction cost economics of the so-called "new institutional economics."[177]

a. Hegemonic Stability Theory

Some realists suppose that international *institutions* can play a limited role in the international system. A leading neo-realist account of international institutions is the hegemonic

176 Kenneth N. Waltz, Theory of International Politics (1979).

177 *See generally* Oliver Williamson, *The New Institutional Economics: Taking Stock, Looking Ahead,* 38 J. of Econ. Literature 595 (September 2000)[hereinafter "New Institutional Economics"]; The Economic Institutions of Capitalism: Firms, Markets, Relational Contracting (1985)[hereinafter "Economic Institutions of Capitalism"]; and *Transaction Cost Economics: The Governance of Contractual Relations,* 22 J. of Law and Econ. 233 (October 1979)[hereinafter "Transaction Cost Economics"]. The seminal works in this area, however, remain Ronald Coase, *The Nature of the Firm,* 4 Economica 386 (1937) [hereafter, *Nature of the Firm*]; and Ronald Coase, *The Problem of Social Costs,* J. of Law and Econ. 1 (October 1960) (reprinted in Ronald Coase, The Firm, the Market and the Law (1988) [hereinafter, *Problem of Social Cost*]). For Coase's retrospective, *see* Ronald Coase, *The Nature of the Firm: Influence,* 4 J. of Law, Econ. & Org., 33 (1988).

stability theory.[178] This theory supposes that international institutions facilitating cooperation between states can be created by the rational investment of the most powerful state or group of states (the so-called "hegemon") in the creation of such institutions. The theory builds on the U.S.-led creation of international organizations after the conclusion of World War II. These institutions included the United Nations Organization, the International Monetary Fund, the World Bank, and the General Agreement on Tariffs and Trade (what later became the World Trade Organization). This hegemonic stability theory was grounded in the view that the hegemon perceived its self-interest to lie in institutionalizing its position in the international system in exchange for accepting less control of the institutions' day-to-day management. Because of the hegemon's interest in the preservation of the international system that forms the basis for its preferred position, it is willing to bear the initial cost of creating, and a larger than proportionate share of the costs of maintaining, the international institutions that reinforce the status quo. The hegemon is also, however, able to divert or spread some of the direct costs of enforcing its hegemony and to mask its exercise of power, thereby reducing the reputation costs of hegemony. But, in keeping with the core insights of realism, this regime-building process and the regimes thus created are sustainable only so long as the relative power of the hegemon itself subsists.[179]

b. Liberal Institutionalism

A more benign account of this historical process is offered by so-called liberal institutionalist camp, which is most closely associated with the work of Robert Keohane.[180] Keohane's *After Hegemony* first appeared in wake of the apparent collapse of U.S. hegemony after the Vietnam War and the relative decline of U.S. economic power after the oil crises of the 1970s. He argued that international institutions previously explained in terms of the hegemonic stability theory would continue to survive even in the face of decline of the U.S. hegemony. More recently, Keohane has argued that his general theory continues to hold, even if the apparent revival of the U.S. hegemony after the end of the Cold War makes his claim somewhat less testable.[181]

Like structural realism, liberal institutionalism concerns itself with states' interest in creating international institutions. Unlike structural realism, however, liberal institutionalism makes room for potential independence (or "agency") of international institutions as autonomous actors in the international system. In this respect, the agency of international institutions is not

178 *See* Robert Gilpin, U.S. Power and Multinational Corporations (1975); Robert Gilpin, *The Theory of Hegemonic War*, 4 J. Interdisciplinary Hist. 591 (1988).

179 *See* Wohlforth, *supra* note 16, 142.

180 Robert Keohane, After Hegemony: Cooperation and Discord in the World Political Economy (1984).

181 *See* Keohane, Preface to the 2005 edition, After Hegemony: Cooperation and Discord in the World Political Economy, ix–xiii (2005).

tied exclusively to the preferences of hegemonic powers.[182] Rather, institutionalism has focused on the emergence of international "regimes" broadly defined as a set of "principles, norms, rules and decision-making procedures around which actor expectations converge in a given issue-area."[183] This broadened conception of "regimes" is ample enough to accommodate traditional international law in the form of treaties and customs as "norms" or "rules," but it also makes space for "decision-making procedures" in international institutions. Thus, Keohane's theory provides the basis for a wholly new approach to "legalism" in terms more compatible with realism.

Based on what he calls the "realist model of rational egoism,"[184] Keohane employs "rational choice" theory, essentially a game-theoretic model, to explain how states make decisions in international politics.[185] Keohane's central claim is that much international discord results from insufficient information, so that when

> actors have different access to information [asymmetric information, such knowledge held by only one party about its own preferences], obstacles to their collective action and strategic calculations may prevent them from realizing their mutual interest. The mere existence of common interests is not enough: institutions that reduce uncertainty and limit asymmetries in information must also exist.[186]

Keohane then develops a "functional" theory of international regimes or institutions as devices that reduce uncertainty and asymmetric information.[187] In short, because the production of information is costly, states will continue to create international organizations to facilitate international cooperation when those organizations can reduce the costs of obtaining information. His functional theory of international regimes or institutions also draws on economic theory of market structure and competition. Thus, he argues, that like oligopolies in markets, international regimes are "easier to maintain than to construct."[188] This corollary of rational choice theory informs his account of the emergence and continued survival of international institutions even after the hegemonic conditions that may have led to their creation no longer exist.

182 *See* Arthur Stein, *Neoliberal Institutionalism, in*Oxford Handbook, supra note 1, at201.

183 Stephen Krasner, *Structural Causes and Regime Consequences: Regimes as Intervening Variables,* 36 Int'l Org. 185, 185 (1982).

184 Keohane, *supra* note 180, at 67.

185 We provide a more detailed account of game theory below, as background to analyze the strength and weaknesses of efforts to reconstruct international legal theory in terms of rational choice theory. *See infra.*

186 Keohane, *supra* note 180, at 12.

187 *Id.* at 85–109.

188 *Id.* at 102.

For international lawyers, Keohane's systematic application of rational choice theory to account for international organizations opened the door to the possibility of treating international organizations as independent actors and subjects of international law with rights and duties that correspond to the functions they perform.[189]

c. Neoliberalism

Ordinarily, both realism and institutionalism treat states as the units of decision-making. International institutions, if possible at all, are the handiwork of states, designed to perform functions that states believe can be performed at lower cost at higher levels of integration. These models assume what might be called a "black box" or "billiard ball" account of the state, in which the state's preferences are viewed as nothing but the summation of the various sets of preferences of the individuals and groups within the state. Some theorists question the black box model, arguing that international relations theory would provide more powerful (if also more context-specific) explanations if it sought to link a state's behavior to its domestic politics.[190] One approach in this style is called "neoliberalism."[191]

The logic of neoliberalism seems to call for the breakdown of the billiard ball model of states, because domestic non-state actors may be able to interact directly with other states and international organizations created by states, expressing preferences that differ from the states in which they are located. Indeed, sub-state entities may even form cooperative alliances across states, generating international institutions, with their own independent preferences, that differ from those of individual states, groups of states, and international organizations created by states. This approach thus revises the central postulates of liberal institutionalism and the modern international law it purports to describe by broadening the range of subjects of international law to include not only levels of integration above the state but also levels of integration outside of the state and across states. A leading U.S. international legal scholar who became the director of the U.S. State Department's Policy Planning Staff, Anne-Marie Slaughter, has focused on what Keohane and Nye earlier called "transgovernmental relations"[192] as a major element in the new international legal system.[193]

189 *See generally* Dan Sarooshi, *International Organizations and Their Exercise of Sovereign Powers (2005)*; cf. David Bederman, *The Souls of International Organizations: Legal Personality and the Lighthouse at Cape Spartel,* 36 Va. J. Int'l L. 275 (1995-1996).

190 *See* Helen V. Milner, Interests, Institutions and Information: Domestic Politics and International Relations (1997), and Helen V. Milner, *Rationalizing Politics: the Emerging Synthesis of International, American, and Comparative Politics,* 52 Int'l Org. 759 (1998).

191 *See* Andrew Moravcsik, *The New Liberalism, in*Oxford Handbook, *supra* note 1, at 234.

192 *See* Robert O. Keohane and Joseph S. Nye, Jr., *Transgovernmental Relations and International Organizations,* 27 World Pol. 39 (1974).

193 *See* Anne-Marie Slaughter, The New World Order (2004)

Neoliberalism's more inclusive description of the players in the international system may well provide a more accurate appraisal of the determinants in any individual case study, and it may in general provide a mental map that more accurately captures the felt experience of "globalization" in the highly-integrated, post-Internet world. But it fails to provide the theoretical parsimony of the rationalist project. In the language of modern international relations theory, it also signals a move back from "third" image to "second" and "first" image theories of international relations.[194] In other words, neoliberalism requires looking into the internal structure of states and the cultures and individuals within and across those states.

5. Rational Choice Institutionalism's Economic Foundations

As discussed earlier, rational choice institutionalism is grounded not only in **game theory**, but also in what is often called the new institutional economics, which is grounded in Ronald Coase's central insight in his seminal article, *The Nature of the Firm*,explaining the form and level of institutional structure of business organization in terms of **transaction cost economics**, namely, the relative costs of search, bargaining, and policing or enforcing bargains.[195] We take each element in turn and then provide a summary of rational choice theory.

a. Game Theory

Game theory provides an explanatory and predictive model for the behavior regularities observed in various settings or "games" in which the decision on compliance under conditions of uncertainty have varying values or "payoffs." The ordinary model involves a two-player game, in which each player has a decision to make as to whether to comply or not comply, ordinarily labeled "cooperate" or "defect." Modeling becomes even more complex, obviously, as more players are introduced, but these more complex games can sometimes be reduced to two-player games with known incentive structures and more predictable results if the players can be grouped along single parameters, much like alliances.

As we have noted above, "games" can generally be categorized as coordination games or cooperation games. The PD is one kind of cooperation game. In its simplest form as a two-player game in which each player can make only a single move, the PD must produce non-cooperation or mutual defection. If the security dilemma mirrors the structure of the simplest PD game, therefore, states in the security dilemma will never be able to cooperate. Game theory suggests, however, that escape from security dilemma is possible if the conditions of the PD are changed. When games are played iteratively (in the language of game theory, "repeat play"), the

194 *See* Waltz, *supra* note 21.

195 *See* Coase, *The Nature of the Firm*, *supra* note 177.

ability to punish defection in the next iteration coupled with cooperation in the following iteration encourages cooperation in future iterations. The defecting player now perceives a different payoff structure than in a single-play game because opportunistic or offensive defection does not automatically yield a Sucker's Payoff for the victim and opportunistic gains for the defector. In theory, this can result in a relatively stable cycle of cooperation, when the benefits of future cooperation exceed the cost of imposing short-term punishment (whether in forgone benefits or actual self-imposed costs of retaliation borne by the party that reciprocally defects). This is the so-called "tit-for-tat" strategy, which experimental results from tournament play presented by Robert Axelrod also show is rather robust in encouraging cooperation to escape from the PD.[196] Thus, there is some evidence that rational choice theory's prediction of greater cooperation through tit-for-tat strategy in iterated games is borne out by empirical reality.

One of Robert Keohane's central claims concerned the PDsituation, which, like the realists, he assumed to be the most powerful way of modeling international relations. As discussed above, if the PD is a single-play game, it will inevitably produce an outcome of mutual defection that leaves both players with payoffs that are less desirable than those produced by mutual cooperation. Keohane sought to understand how, if the PD was reconceptualized so as to permit iterated plays, the players might instead tend to produce stable outcomes that benefited them both. Translated into the categories of international relations theory, Keohane attempted to prove that the security dilemma could be overcome and patterns of cooperation between states could be established in its place, even in anarchic conditions, and even if states were deemed to be rational actors. Keohane's argument was taken up, extended, and deepened by rational choice theorists.

For rational choice theory, the central paradigm for analyzing anarchy is the game theory model of strategic behavior under conditions of uncertainty.[197] By definition, in conditions of anarchy, there is no mechanism that assures each state that another state will observe its commitments when that other state's interests dictate that it should not fulfill those commitments. States may face a strategic situation, meaning that the effects of their decision depend on the behavior of other states. In other words, uncertainty about the behavior of other states requires states to make decisions about their own compliance based on the risk that other states will not comply.

In short, when states engage in cooperation over time such that they "iteratively" decide whether to cooperate or defect, and benefits of future cooperation exceed the costs of defection, then states might be able to escape the security dilemma. This may entail unpacking or segmenting a set of relationships or performance by both sides in an exchange into multiple performances, in a way that is analogous to repackaging a single contract for the final production of a good or the provision of a service into a series of steps involving the acquisition of inputs,

196 Robert Axelrod, The Evolution of Cooperation (1984).

197 As before, much of our analysis draws here on Abbot's seminal articles.

research, design, production, commercialization, delivery, and ongoing warranties for service, et cetera. By changing the game structure, then, game theory suggests that institutional reforms can transform the relations between states into iterative games, with multiple opportunities for decision-making, and can create the conditions for successful implementation of the tit-for-tat strategy. Rational choice theory in the guise of game theory offers a program for research and policymaking—international regime-building (for international relations theorists) and international law and institution-building (for international lawyers).

For purposes of this introduction, however, the iterative, tit-for-tat strategy is subject to several important caveats that may lessen the likelihood of escaping the security dilemma.[198] First, for tit-for-tat to succeed, players must not be able to foresee that the game will end on a specific move or iteration. Otherwise, through "backward induction" (a condition in which players count backwards from their final move to their current decision to decide whether to cooperate or defect), the payoff structure begins again to approximate a single-play PD situation; in the language of game theory, this causes "unraveling" in the game. In that case, the incentive to avoid the Sucker's Payoff increases in significance.

Second, if a participant has a high discount rate(that is to say, the participant views present gains as more valuable than future gains), then the participant will prefer reaping current gains from defection to future gains from cooperation.[199] One such case may be where the player itself faces so much uncertainty as to its own survival that it is not confident that it will ultimately be able to obtain or internalize the future benefits of cooperation. Unstable or illegitimate players, such as failing states or dictatorships, may therefore be less cooperative than one might expect in an iterative game. Of course, focusing on the nature of the players—that is to say, whether the state is stable because of internal features such as its democratic legitimacy or capacity in economic terms to meet the basic human needs of its population—begins to deviate from rational choice theory's parsimonious disregard of the internal nature of a state.

Third, the rational choice model may pay insufficient attention to distributional issues. A key variable in international relations theory is whether the gains from cooperation are absolute or relative.[200] The distribution of gains raises the question as to whether, at some point in the future, a state that gains more from cooperation can translate those gains into means for denying other states of their initial gains. Under that scenario, even short-term coordination games can be perceived to be collective action problems because the incremental effects of relative

---

198 For an appreciation and penetrating critique of Axelrod's work focusing on its applicability to international relations, *see* Joanna Gowa, *Anarchy, Egoism, and Third Images: The Evolution of Cooperation and International Relations,* 40 Int'l Org. 167 (1986).

199 *See* Axelrod, *supra* note 196; and Guzman, *supra* note 1, at 73–74.

200 *See* Dale C. Copeland, Economic Interdependence and War 35-38 (2015) (applying this distinction to the asymmetrical gains from interstate trade).

gains over time enable a state to achieve a Sucker's Payoff at the final stages of an iterated game.[201]

Fourth, whether viewed as an independent problem or a corollary of the relative gains issue, envy or pride may affect the valuation of the gain from cooperation, such that the disutility from envy or lost pride, perhaps even lost national pride, outweighs the benefits from an absolute gain from cooperation, thus incentivizing defection.

Fifth, and perhaps most important, it may be difficult in repeat-play situations for participants to interpret properly whether the other participant's move represents cooperation or defection. This is because the meaning of the move may depend on private information neither party is willing to reveal. Thus, the risk of misperception may lead to escalatory cycles of defection when cooperation would have been possible if the cooperative nature of the participants' moves could have been verified.[202] (Our case study in Chapter 2.B focuses precisely on the role of the production of information in detecting defection in what might be called an iterative nuclear nonproliferation game.)

The task of rational choice theory, then, is to construct iterative games and design cost-effective methods of providing information that give each party assurance that the other party is cooperating rather than defecting. Either the potential defector must provide the necessary information itself, although this may involve some risk of misrepresentation or other forms of concealment, or the other party must be able to verify independently the potential defector's cooperation or the quantity and quality of its defection, although the access required to allow verification by the other player may create costs for the potential defector, such as the revelation of unrelated information, that would make verification prohibitively costly to the potential defector. As the production of this information is a benefit enabling continued cooperation for all players, an optimal level of contracting is prevented by the cost of concealment and the cost of excessive production of information. Therefore, rational choice theory seeks to reduce these transaction costs in the game.

b. Transaction Costs

In this connection, rational choice theory draws inspiration from the pioneering work of Ronald Coase[203] to account for the emergence of third-party institutions in the same way that lawyer-economists sought to account for the emergence of corporations and other forms of organizations with long-term integration. The so-called "new institutional economics" consid-

---

201 Joseph Grieco, *Anarchy and the Limits of Cooperation: A Realist Critique of the Newest Liberal Institutionalism,* 42 Int'l Org. 485 (1988); Joseph Grieco, Cooperation Among Nations (1990).

202 Robert E. Scott and Paul B. Stephan, The Limits of Leviathan: Contract Theory and the Enforcement of International Law 151–53 (2006) (discussing concept of verifiability by third-party in arms control context).

203 *See* Coase, *The Nature of the Firm, supra* note177; *see also* Williamson, Transaction Cost Economics, *supra* note177.

ers the question of whether firms interact or cooperate through single-shot contracts, repeat play or iterative contracts (sometimes called relational contracts involving long-term supply or production arrangements), or some form of formal integration or shared ownership (such as a joint venture), culminating ultimately in complete integration through acquisition or merger. The central intuition governing this branch of economic analysis is the idea that issues between players are amenable to contractual solutions unless transactions costs impede contract formation.[204] Thus, in multiple player games, the costs of negotiating bilateral contracts may drive players toward multilateral contracts, and the cost of enforcement, including the danger that cooperating players may free ride on the enforcement efforts of other players that are most interested in enforcement, may drive players to delegate much of the enforcement function to joint ventures or other forms of autonomous integration.

From the standpoint of the new institutional economics, then, reducing the transaction costs for the production of information necessary to implement the tit-for-tat solution to the PD necessarily requires a choice concerning the optimal level of integration.This optimal level could range from individualized contract (in the language of international law, a bilateral treaty) to acquisition of the potential defector(annexation), with a range of institutional options such as informal bodies meeting regularly, multilateral treaty organizations without permanent secretariats, organizations with permanent executive bodies, and organizations with quasi-executive, quasi-legislative, and quasi-adjudicatory bodies that approximate the institutional structures of well-organized states.[205]

One possible solution in this rational choice cost-minimization approach is the selection of a third-party to perform assurance and verification functions. The delegation of assurance and verification to a third party can reduce the cost of assurance and verification because, by assumption, the third-party has a smaller incentive than either of the players to conceal or misrepresent the true state of affairs or to acquire unrelated information or reveal non-germane information acquired through its verification activities. Thus, in the search for the proper mixture of the production of information by a potentially-defecting player and the verification of that information by the other player, rational choice theory opens the door to considering institutional solutions to the problem of transaction costs in the production of information necessary to achieve tit-for-tat solutions to PD cooperation problems.

c. Summary of the Rational Choice Approach

To review, in iterative patterns of cooperation and defection, detection of defection will cause reputational losses for the defecting player and authorize the cooperating player to impose the denialof its own cooperation (perhaps also including further retaliation), thereby implementing

204 *See* Ronald Coase, *Problem of Social Cost, supra* note 177.

205 *See generally* Trachtman, *supra* note 1.

tit-for-tat strategy. A rational choice approach to assurance or verification of information about a player's decision will establish regimes that are no more costly than the cooperation benefits they will create. The new institutional economics theory directs attention to questions of institutional design for the production of such information through cost-effective institutions selected along a continuum of possible levels of integration.

We close this discussion with a note of caution. Changes in transaction costs associated with institutional design and revision can make an optimal initial choice suboptimal over time. In theory, in both the initial design and the continued evaluation of a given level of integration for the production of information, the rational choice theory should evaluate the marginal costs and benefits of institution-building. However, if there are substantial fixed costs in the initial phase of institution-building (the development of technical expertise, for example), and these costsor investments dominatethe calculations ofthe costs and benefits of the continued reliance on the institution, then an institution may well continue to survive when alternative levels of integration may have become more cost-effective. Similarly, continuing with the example of development of technical expertise, an institution may have chosen a mode of operation that involved substantial commitment of resources, an initial investment that once undertaken would be perceived as a wasted asset when compared with an alternative mode of operation that would produce the same information or result as lower cost, albeit requiring substantial new fixed costs or investments in institution-building.[206] In these cases, rational choice theory's commitment to welfare maximization in marginal decision-making can lead to the survival of institutions in circumstances under which they no longer minimize transaction costs in the long-run production of information necessary to escape from the Prisoner's Dilemma. States may continue to invest considerable time and money in old, unnecessary institutions.

With this in mind,we turn now to a case study of rational choice institutionalism that raises the question of whether Cold War-era nonproliferation institutions remain optimal in the current political environment.

206 The classic example in the literature is the current QWERTY keyboard, which was optimal in slowing typing rates in an era of typing machines incapable of operating without failure at the speed human dexterity could achieve, but now sub-optimally slows typists in an era of more efficient machinery. *See* Williamson, supra note 177; *see also* Dvorak Simplified Keyboard (***available at*** http://en.wikipedia.org/wiki/Dvorak_Simplified_Keyboard).

B. RATIONAL CHOICE THEORY: THE NUCLEAR NON-PROLIFERATION TREATY AND THE NORTH KOREAN NUCLEAR CRISIS OF 2003

To review Chapter 2.A, from the perspective of an international lawyer, rational choice mediates between the realist and legalist positions by means of modern social science. Specifically, it draws on related disciplines—principally economics but also behavioral psychology—in order to construct international institutions that facilitate verification and assurance of compliance with international obligations. It relies on self-help or collective measures in response to breaches of international obligations—usually taking the form of some kind of retaliation, reciprocal non-compliance, or other harm to the non-complying state that follows from the harm to its reputation as a reliable partner in other joint undertakings.[1] Thus, rational choice theory, drawing from economic analysis, seeks to explain how states can, and very often do, achieve gains in welfare notwithstanding the behavior regularities responding to incentives or payoffs in conditions of anarchy. The cooperative strategies and institutions of cooperation that implement rational choice theory, for an international lawyer, are the constituent doctrines of international law (treaty and custom) and of international organizations as new subjects of international law.

Translated into a theory of international security law, rational choice theory models cooperation in game-theoretic terms. As a theory of international law, it permits one to view international law and institutions as the means through which states can circumvent coordination and cooperation problems that otherwise prevent achievable gains in welfare. Assuming that nuclear non-proliferation is a welfare gain for all concerned states, then the task of a rational choice theory account of international institutions is to determine the optimal level of bilateral, multilateral, and institutional (third-party) measures for the production of information necessary for the implementation of tit-for-tat strategies that reduce the incentives for defection in the prisoner's dilemma (PD) or security dilemma. The move from treaty to international organization is, under this view, much like the move from contract to business organization.[2] This institutionalist reformulation of modern international law moves then to a synthesis of economic theory with classic realist premises of anarchy in the international system. It thus focuses on informal means of enforcement, rather than the typical adjudicatory means of enforcement represented in the IMT and IMTFE.

We now turn to the specific implications of rational choice institutionalism as applied to a particular area of international security law, nuclear nonproliferation. The rational choice theory of international law has obvious implications for nuclear nonproliferation, given the high incentives for non-cooperation or defection, the salience of relative gains, the risk of unraveling given the finality of nuclear Sucker's Payoff, the possibility that states seeking nuclear weapons are the kind of states whose leadership have high discount rates, and the potential

1 *See generally* Andrew T. Guzman, How International Law Works: A Rational Choice Theory (2008).

2 *See generally* Joel P. Trachtman, The Economic Structure of International Law (2008).

for misperception of even cooperative moves given the dual peaceful and military uses of large segments of nuclear material, equipment and technology. In what follows, we explore rational choice theory in the context of a case study of North Korea's (the Democratic People's Republic of Korea's or DPRK's) withdrawal in 2003 from the Nuclear Non-Proliferation Treaty (NPT).

As a preface to the study questions for this case, we provide here, first, the international law of nuclear nonproliferation. In this context, we describe the characteristics of nuclear fuel cycle activities that provide the factual context for the DPRK's withdrawal from the NPT and an overview of the legal structure of the nuclear non-proliferation regime, including the basic structure of the peaceful nuclear cooperation and safeguards. Second, we describe the collective security elements of the regime, which serve as a backdrop to the North Korean withdrawal crisis. (These materials will be of relevance also to our case study of the Iranian crisis and constructivism in Chapter 2.C.) Third, we provide a narrative of the DPRK's attempted withdrawal from the NPT in 1993, the international response, and the DPRK's ultimate withdrawal in 2003.

For readings, we first provide the text of the NPT, which creates an overarching regime governing international possession of nuclear weapons and technologies. Second, we provide the text of the Security Council Resolution approving the so-called "positive" security assurances by the NPT nuclear weapons states designed to induce states to join the NPT and forgo aspirations to nuclear weapons status. Finally, we provide the documents in relation to the DPRK's attempt to break out of the NPT regime and the international response it engendered, resulting in an "Agreed Framework"—nominally, a politically-binding rather than legally-binding set of commitments between the United States and the DPRK—and a multilateral agreement establishing a consortium, the Korean Energy Development Organization (KEDO) to facilitate the implementation of the nuclear supply provisions of the Agreed Framework.[3]

1. The Nuclear Nonproliferation Legal Regime: The Nuclear Fuel Cycle and Atoms for Peace

Early in the nuclear era, it was recognized that there were essentially three pathways for the production of nuclear material necessary to construct a nuclear explosive device based on plutonium, like the bomb used at Hiroshima, or uranium, like the bomb used at Nagasaki: 1) enrichment of uranium in the isotopic form that is fissile or explosive, U235; 2) reprocessing of spent nuclear fuel from light-water reactors using low-enriched uranium; and 3) reprocessing of spent nuclear fuel from heavy-water (the isotope know as deuterium) moderated reactors using naturally-occurring uranium. Enrichment simply refers to the separation of the naturally-occurring fissile or explosive isotopic form of uranium, U235, from uranium ore, which normally contain only .711 percent of U235 and over 99 percent of the fertile form U238, which in a nuclear

3 *See* Korean Peninsula Energy Dev. Org. (Feb. 25, 2015) (*available at* http://www.kedo.org/ap_main.asp).

reactor transmutes through the bombardment of the uranium nucleus with an additional neutron into Pu239, a weapons-usable material. By definition, uranium enriched in excess of 20 percent was deemed highly-enriched uranium (HEU), with lower-grade reactor fuel, usually four to six percent enriched, deemed to be low-enriched uranium (LEU). Various technological methods, ranging from gaseous diffusion, centrifuges, and laser isotope separation have been, and continue to be, developed to achieve uranium isotope separation. Reprocessing is simply the separation from spent nuclear fuel of the fissile, or explosive, plutonium yielded when the predominant naturally-occurring isotope of uranium, U238, is irradiated. The essential or "sensitive nuclear materials" for these pathways to a bomb then are HEU, LEU, and heavy-water. Given the common use of LEU fuel for power reactors, thereby offering the plausible justification for the development of an industrial capacity to enrich uranium, it was widely feared early in the nuclear age that the most likely pathway to nuclear weapons development would be through uranium enrichment.

A paradigm called the "nuclear fuel cycle" thus emerged to describe the range of activities—beginning with the mining of uranium ore; continuing with its transformation into uranium hexafluoride suitable for uranium separation by enrichment techniques; production of uranium fuel for use in power or other reactors; and, ultimately, spent fuel disposal—that enabled states either to produce independently nuclear weapons or sustain nuclear industrial activities. Plausible rationales existed also for the use of plutonium-based fuels, sometimes called mixed-oxide fuels, particular to economize on expensive spent nuclear fuel by developing nuclear fuel cycles that re-used the plutonium contained in spent nuclear fuel, thus in effect producing new reactor fuel in the process of consuming it. As a practical matter, HEU enriched at over 90 percent U235 is said to be bomb-grade.[4]

a. Pre-NPT Atoms for Peace

Thus, from a non-proliferation standpoint, the problem at the beginning of the nuclear age was that nuclear reactors used for entirely peaceful purposes, such as the production of power, can be configured to yield precisely the kind of sensitive nuclear material that create pathways to nuclear weapons. Moreover, the essential equipment, materials, and technology for nuclear reactors are of concern as well, since even natural uranium can be employed through use of a heavy-water reactor and reprocessing to produce a plutonium-based weapon. In this context, in 1954, U.S. President Dwight Eisenhower announced a major shift of U.S. policy in refusing to share nuclear material, equipment, or technology. Fearing that any attempt to maintain a U.S. nuclear monopoly was implausible, given the development of Soviet and British nuclear power,

4 *See generally* Joseph Cirincione, Deadly Arsenals: Tracking Weapons of Mass Destruction 35–42 (2002). The authoritative definitions for the technical terms used above can be found in Article XX of the Statute of the International Atomic Energy Agency. *See* Int'l Atomic Energy Agency [IAEA] Statute, art. 20 (*available at* https://www.iaea.org/about/statute#a1-20).

Eisenhower concluded that only by offering U.S. cooperation, subject to certain safeguards, could the United States discourage states, particularly the defeated Axis Powers Germany and Japan, from developing independent nuclear fuel cycles, which would in turn allow them to develop bomb-manufacturing capabilities. The safeguards initially imposed by the United States as a condition of its willingness to supply nuclear material, equipment, and technology quickly became burdensome and politically embarrassing, leading the United States and other emerging nuclear suppliers to seek to internationalize the system of nuclear safeguards. It was also true that the United States simply faced up to the inevitable reality that it would eventually need to replace its bilateral system of safeguards, as its monopoly in nuclear supply in the initial phase of the Cold War evaporated. It was in this context that the International Atomic Energy Agency (IAEA) was created.[5]

The basic design of the safeguards system is, of course, the central issue in the work of the IAEA. Drawing on the famous Acheson-Lilienthal report and Baruch plan,[6] the original conception was for the IAEA itself to serve as an international repository for nuclear material.[7] Indeed, many provisions of the IAEA Statute make sense only with this vision in mind.[8] However, the IAEA never in practice developed this role and instead its main business became the operation of a safeguards system for the states seeking to achieve the benefits of the peaceful use of the atom.[9] In this sense, the IAEA was always distinct from the specialized agencies of the United Nations, since its statutory purpose from the beginning was not only the development of technical cooperation for human development but also to contribute to international security by applying safeguards.[10]

The initial design for IAEA safeguards grew out of Japan's request in 1958 for the IAEA to arrange the supply of Canadian uranium for a research reactor. Negotiation of a detailed agreement based on the IAEA Statutory provisions proved difficult, and it quickly became apparent that individual negotiations for similar agreements in the future could prove cumbersome and embarrassing to an international organization that would need to justify differential treatment of member states.

Accordingly, over time the IAEA Secretariat developed a concept for a model safeguards agreement, which it ultimately published. The first version appeared in 1961 as GC(V)INF/39, and that was revised in 1963 and published as INFIRC/26. The most complete form of the IAEA

5 *See generally* David Fischer & Paul Szasz, Safeguarding the Atom: A Critical Appraisal 165–69 (1985).

6 For background on these early post-Second World War plans, *see* U.S. Dep't of State, Office of the Historian, *The Acheson-Lilienthal & Baruch Plans, 1946 (available at* https://history.state.gov/milestones/1945-1952/baruch-plans).

7 *See generally* Lawrence Scheinman, The International Atomic Energy Agency and the World Nuclear Order 51 (1987); and Guido Den Dekker, The Law of Arms Control: International Supervision and Enforcement 270–71 (2001).

8 *See* Fischer & Szasz, *supra* note 5, at 142.

9 *Id.* at 169.

10 *Id.* at 165.

pre-NPT safeguards concept appeared in 1965, three years before the conclusion of the NPT, and is known as Information Circular 66—"The Agency's Safeguards System" INFCIRC/66. As amended in INFCIRC/66 rev. 2, this document continues to serve as the basis for non-NPT and non-treaty of Tlatelolco[11] safeguards. Its central premise is that safeguards are applied on plants and largely through the presence and supervision of inspectors, entailing almost continuous supervision of peaceful nuclear activities and an unqualified right of access to safeguarded plants or facilities. That said, creative "contamination" principles extended the scope of INFCIRC/66 safeguards beyond initially agreed facilities. For example, any nuclear material used in a safeguarded facility became subject to safeguards, and insertion of a safeguarded item in an un-safeguarded plant subjected that plant to safeguards as well.[12] While the financial burden was high in this early era in the development of the nuclear industry, the degree of assurance the system provided was commensurate with the burden imposed.

Thus, the trade and development side of the Atoms for Peace grand strategy was always tied to the international security dimension. As the demand for IAEA Safeguards grew with the entry into force of the NPT and Treaty of Tlatelolco, both of which required the imposition of safeguards on peaceful nuclear activities in non-nuclear weapon state (NNWS) parties to those treaties but not on the nuclear weapon state (NWS) parties, IAEA Safeguards were more closely tied to the politico-military structure of the Cold War.

With NPT adherence, which imposed the requirement that NNWS agree to safeguards on all peaceful nuclear activities rather than merely specific material subject to a specific IAEA Safeguards Agreement, it was recognized that the NWS benefited militarily and politically from discrimination not only in their entitlement to possess nuclear weapons, but also economically from their freedom from the duty to subject their peaceful nuclear activities to costly IAEA Safeguards. To remedy this perceived disparity, the NWS gradually accepted the burden of IAEA Safeguards, even though the politico-military rationale for the application of safeguards to a nuclear weapons state was inapplicable.[13] If, for example, a NWS wished to breach its NPT obligation and divert nuclear material to an NNWS, it would not need to use material safeguarded under its IAEA Safeguards Agreement covering material used for peaceful nuclear activities; it could simply divert material, equipment or technology from its un-safeguarded military nuclear activities without risk of IAEA detection.

The more significant impact of the Cold War system on the IAEA safeguards system, however, was not in the number of states which became bound to accept IAEA safeguards but rather on the nature of the safeguards system itself. In the mid-1950s, the European Atomic Energy Community (EURATOM) was formed, together with the European Coal and Steel Community

11 *See* Latin American Nuclear Free Zone Treaty (Treaty of Tlatelolco), Feb. 14, 1967 (*available at* https://www.iaea.org/publications/documents/treaties/treaty-prohibition-nuclear-weapons-latin-america-tlatelolco-treaty).

12 Fischer & Szasz, *supra* note 5, at 92–93.

13 *Id.* at 19–20.

and the European Economic Community—as one of the initial three pillars of the European Community. EURATOM safeguards, which were developed largely for facilitating the development of the nuclear industry in the Federal Republic of Germany as part of its economic reconstruction to counter the Soviet threat, were substantially less intrusive than the emerging IAEA system of safeguards. Germany's higher level of technological capacity made the target of safeguarding plants themselves an expensive and arguably fruitless proposition. Rather, EURATOM safeguards focused on accounting for nuclear material. Adapting IAEA safeguards to EURATOM's requirements proved to be a critical element in securing broader adherence to the NPT.[14] Thus, while the change was not unrelated to the increased cost of imposing safeguards on a large number of states—although the unsurprising truth is that a large number of states have never in fact complied with their NPT obligation to enter into safeguards agreements with the IAEA, for the simple fact that they do not engage in any nuclear activities whatsoever that would require safeguards—the fundamental engine driving the evolution of IAEA Safeguards was the adherence of Germany and Japan to the NPT and the necessity of diluting the safeguards system to secure their adherence as NNWS.

b. The NPT Amendments to Atoms for Peace

After the NPT entered into force on March 5, 1970, and to facilitate compliance with the obligation under Article III.1 of the NPT that NNWS parties enter into a safeguards agreement with the IAEA, the Board of Governors moved to develop a safeguards system that would meet the expectations of the NPT. This process produced INFCIRC/153 in 1971; throughout the Cold War period and beyond, it has served as the model for NPT-compliant safeguards agreements.[15] Strictly speaking, Article III.2 of the NPT provides that each state party only "undertakes not to provide: (a) source or special fissionable material, or (b) equipment or material especially designed or prepared for the processing, use or production of special fissionable material, to any non-nuclear-weapon State for peaceful purposes, unless the source or special fissionable material shall be subject to the safeguards required by this Article."[16]

In principle, then, the NPT called for a safeguards system that was both narrower and broader than the pre-NPT system.[17] On one hand, although the treaty-required safeguards regime for nuclear transfers covers both nuclear material and certain, defined nuclear equip-

14 *See* George Bunn, Arms Control by Committee: Managing Negotiations with the Russians 90 (1992).

15 *See* IAEA, *The Structure and Content of Agreements Between the Agency and States Required in Connection with the Treaty on the Non-Proliferation of Nuclear Weapons*, IAEA Doc. No. INFCIRC/153 (May 1971) [hereinafter INFCIRC/153].

16 *See* Nuclear Nonproliferation Treaty art. 3, ¶ 2, Jul. 1, 1968, 7 I.L.M 809 [hereinafter NPT]. "Special" and "source" nuclear material, as defined in the IAEA Statute, refer to HEU and Pu239 and the materials that can be used to produce such weapons-usable material, such as natural uranium. *See* IAEA Statute, Art. XX, *supra* note 4.

17 *See generally* Mohammed I. Shaker, The Nuclear Non-Proliferation Treaty: Origin and Implementation 649–775 (1980) (providing commonly accepted treaty negotiating history with respect to safeguards, the IAEA and related issues).

ment, the safeguards required by the NPT apply only to the nuclear material itself. In theory, then, a safeguards regime under the NPT could permit the unaccounted-for transfer of sensitive nuclear equipment or technology, or the construction of a nuclear explosive device, up to but not including the point at which source or special nuclear material was introduced, without the application of safeguards.[18] Indeed, as Fischer and Szasz report, the fact that the IAEA had no official information concerning Italy's transfer to Iraq of a so-called "hot cell" (which is a facility that facilitates the development of the skills necessary to operate a full-blown plutonium separation or reprocessing facility) played a role in Israel's decision to bomb the Iraqi facility at Tuwaitha in 1982.[19] On the other hand, safeguards could not be limited to particular facilities; the safeguards required by Article III.1 of the NPT applied to "all source or special fissionable material in all peaceful nuclear activities within the territory of such State, under its jurisdiction, or carried out under its control anywhere,"[20] an obligation that came to be known as the so-called "Fullscope" Safeguards obligations.

However, even if the NPT safeguards obligation was negotiated so as to legitimate EURATOM safeguards, the degree to which the new IAEA Safeguards system would rely less on inspection and more on indirect means to track nuclear material was a matter for interpretation and negotiation. Largely because of the cost involved and the concern of EURATOM countries that the non-proliferation benefits derived from IAEA safeguards would be minimal in relation to the costs involved, the new NPT safeguards system relied less on inspectors continuously supervising peaceful nuclear activities at particular facilities than on following the flow of nuclear material which might be used directly or indirectly for nuclear explosive purposes. Accordingly, the INFCICR 153 drafters designed procedures relating to design, material accountancy, containment and surveillance to assure that no significant quantities of nuclear material could be diverted for non-peaceful use. The concept of "significant quantities" related to an understanding of weapons-design, while design and material accountancy regulation and reporting requirements were intended to ensure that the flow of material could be tracked with a high probability of "timely detection" of evasion. The timeliness of detection was measured in terms of technical understandings of the duration of different pathways to the production of weapons-usable material.

These measures shifted reliance and costs of compliance in the direction of essentially routine planning and reporting phases of the nuclear activities of safeguarded facilities. Thus, the reliance on inspectors was radically reduced, and the right of inspectors to physical access was for the most part limited to so-called "strategic points" in safeguarded facilities,[21] which are the physical locations designated for making measurements relating to accounting of nuclear

18 *See* Fischer & Szasz, *supra* note 5, at 83.

19 *See id.* at 80.

20 *See* NPT, supra note 16, at art. 3, ¶ 1.

21 *See* INFCIRC/153, *supra* note 15, at ¶ 110.

material within or transferred into or out of so-called "material balance areas."[22] In theory, the shift from the safeguarding of facilities under INFCIRC/66 to the safeguarding of material under INFCIRC/153 would be a distinction without a difference when a state's declaration to the IAEA of all the facilities engaging in nuclear activity was accurate. The state's initial declaration under INFCIRC/153 therefore took on special importance, as did the initial so-called "ad hoc" inspections which agency inspectors could undertake before subsidiary arrangements could be concluded identifying the key locations that would serve as the basis for a safeguards regime for the particular state.[23] So-called "routine" inspections required advance coordination with national authorities, and they ordinarily occurred only at critical points of the nuclear fuel cycle. For example, they occurred at the initial and terminal determinations of the "physical inventory" of nuclear material within a so-called "material balance area" for a given timeframe or the actual withdrawal of spent fuel or introduction of nuclear material to a reactor core, usually occurring several months apart. It was recognized that there would be a deviation between the "physical inventory," which was determined by actual measurement, and the so-called "book inventory," which was determined by the physical inventory determined at the initial measurement at any given accounting period and the physical measures of nuclear transfers into and out of a given material balance area. The so-called MUF, or "material unaccounted-for," concept was intended to reflect a recognized and statistically acceptable rate of error or loss in nuclear material accountancy, which would not give rise to concern about diversion of nuclear material.[24] But more important, the ad hoc and routine inspections were clearly limited to the terms of national consent, because advance notice was required, subject to the possibility of no-notice inspections but only in accordance with the principle of "random sampling" rather than as a genuine effort to explore information concerning the possibility of diversion.[25] Thus, one might plausibly argue this scheme left inspectors with little more to do than merely observe the activities of national authorities.[26]

On the other hand, the NPT safeguards system did include new, but untested, "special" or on-demand inspection procedures under paragraphs 73 and 77 of INFCIRC/153. These provisions, which arguably were designed to address the possible gap created by the move to safeguarding of declared nuclear materials of the existence of possible undeclared sensitive nuclear facilities, such as fuel fabrication, nuclear enrichment or reprocessing facilities, were never invoked during the Cold War. (There was, however, one case in 1983 of routine inspection without

22 *See id.* at ¶ 116.

23 *See id.* at ¶ 62 (initial report) and 71(a)(ad hoc inspections); *see also* Dekker, *supra* note 7, at 289.

24 *See* INFCIRC/153, *supra* note 15, at ¶ 102 (book inventory), ¶ 113 (physical inventory), ¶ 111 (material unaccounted-for); and ¶ 30 ("the technical conclusion of the Agency's verification activities shall be a statement, in respect of each *material balance area*, of the amount of material unaccounted for over a specific period, giving the limits of accuracy of the amounts stated") (emphasis in the original).

25 *See id.* at ¶ 83 (notice procedures) and ¶ 84 (no-notice routine inspections based on random sampling).

26 *See generally* Dekker, *supra* note 7, at 290–91.

advance notification, as was ordinarily given for all routine inspections, of a Swedish facility.[27]) The origin of the "special inspections" concept can be traced to the Treaty of Tlatelolco, which, in creating a nuclear weapons free zone in the Americas, also provided for challenge inspections to be carried out by the Organization for the Prohibition of Nuclear Weapons in Latin America (OPANAL) at the expense of the state making the request.[28] It is potentially far more significant a tool in the NPT context, however, which, unlike the Treaty of Tlatelolco, made clear that the creation of even a so-called "peaceful nuclear explosive device" would be a treaty violation.[29] Nonetheless, as will be explained below, both the latent birth defects of the NPT safeguards system—which may have been bargained-for as the price of broad adherence to the NPT during the height of the Cold War—and its immanent possibilities for more aggressive international inspections became the subject of international attention only a generation later during the rise of new threats of proliferation of weapons of mass destruction in the aftermath of the Cold War.

Thus, during the height of the Cold War, the United States' desire not to undermine NATO resulted in a commitment to fashion a system for NNWS safeguards acceptable to EURATOM. But this in turn posed economic competition and sovereign equality concerns in Japan. Indeed, a condition of support in the Japanese legislature for NPT adherence was in effect that Japan receive—to borrow a term from international trade law—"most favored safeguards" treatment from the IAEA; in other words, that safeguards applied to Japan's burgeoning plutonium-based nuclear fuel cycle be no more burdensome than those applied to EURATOM countries. As part of its demand for sovereign equality, Japan demanded and obtained the creation of a special IAEA Committee, the Standing Advisory Group on Safeguards Implementation (or SAGSI), to ensure national representation in technical advice to the IAEA Director General and IAEA Board of Governors.[30] These moves in the direction of equality of treatment and indirect national participation in technical assessments relevant to safeguards implementation could not help but increase the pressure toward dilution of IAEA safeguards, not only in the overall design of the NPT safeguards but also in the rigor of their actual implementation.

---

27 *See* Fischer & Szasz, *supra* note 5, at 31.

28 *See* Treaty of Tlatelolco, Article 16(1)(b)(cited in Fischer & Szasz, *supra* note 5, at 69).

29 *See* Fischer & Szasz, *supra* note 5, at 91; *see generally* Davis R. Robinson, *The Treaty of Tlatelolco and the United State: A Latin American Nuclear Free Zone,* 64 Am. J. Int'l L. 283, 289–90 (1970) (reporting debate over Article 18's provision for peaceful nuclear explosives, under an interpretation of that language advanced by Brazil, Argentina and Nicaragua, and the U.S. view that such an interpretation would undermine the object and purpose of the treaty because it would be impossible to determine whether a nuclear device once constructed would be used only for peaceful purposes rather than as a weapon).

30 *See* Fischer & Szasz, *supra* note 5, at 23–25, 31 n. 3.

2. The NPT Security System: The NPT, Security Council, IAEA, and Supplier Arrangements

In brief, then, the deal permitting German and Japanese NPT accession may have reduced the safeguards burden on NNWS parties to the NPT, but thereby it offered an incentive for adherence to the NPT. Since the safeguards system formed part of a linked set of policies, it would not be fair to say that reducing the quality of IAEA Safeguards had a negative net effect on international peace and security. The benefits from the NPT and Treaty of Tlatelolco were substantial and might well have outweighed whatever losses were suffered. The benefits for states included, of course, those that ensued directly from participation in the new security regime. Such benefits included adoption of UN Security Council Resolution 255, the so-called positive security assurance, under which the Security Council, taking note of declarations by the United States, United Kingdom, and Soviet Union, acknowledged that aggression or the threat of aggression through the use of nuclear weapons against a non-nuclear weapon state would create a qualitatively new situation requiring action by the principal nuclear powers through the Security Council, entailing the exercise of the Security Council's powers under Chapter VII to address the security needs of a NNWS party facing nuclear attack.[31]

However, given the risk of the use of the veto during this period, as well as the probability that any nuclear attack would come from one of the NWS parties to the NPT also serving as Permanent Members of the Security Council,[32] it seems clear that the resolution itself was less a promise of Security Council action than a moral and political commitment by the Great Powers to exercise their own powers on behalf of their allies subject to nuclear attack and a signal to their adversaries that an international norm concerning the use of nuclear force was being forged. Indeed, under Article X of the NPT, which provides that attempts to withdraw from the treaty grounded on "extraordinary events jeopardizing" a state's "supreme national interests" must be notified and explained to the Security Council itself, and given the reporting requirements to the Security Council under the IAEA Statute and Safeguards Agreements for violations of those agreements, it becomes readily apparent that, as a matter of legal design, the Security Council was the appropriate forum for such security assurances. Thus, material breach of a safeguards agreement, withdrawal from the NPT, and the threat or use of nuclear force form a trilogy of "threats to the peace, breaches of the peace, or acts of aggression" well within the continuum of nominal Security Council authority over international peace and security.

Another benefit was the strengthening of the relationship between the NPT, IAEA and U.N. Charter—particularly the Charter's interlocking provisions regarding the threat or use of force under Article 2(4) and its collective security provisions under Chapters VII and VIII—through

31 *See* S.C. Res. 255, U.N. Doc. S/INF/23 (June 19, 1968).

32 *See* Jonathan B. Schwartz, *Controlling Nuclear Proliferation: Legal Strategies of the United States,* 20 L. & Pol'y in Int'l Bus. 1, 9 (1988).

the so-called "negative security assurances." Under a set of political assurances, the United States declared it would not itself use nuclear weapons against a non-nuclear weapon state except in response to attack against itself or one of its allies in association with another nuclear weapon state.[33] This assurance paralleled the geographically more limited assurance provided in the form of an express treaty commitment made under Additional Protocol II to the Treaty of Tlatelolco, under which an adhering party, such as the United States, agreed not to use nuclear weapons against a party to the Treaty of Tlatelolco except in response to an attack by a state party in which it was assisted by a nuclear weapon state.[34] Together, the non-treaty and treaty negative security assurances formed a sturdy set of incentives for states to enter either the NPT or Treaty of Tlatelolco and thereby undertake an obligation to enter into full-scope safeguards agreements with the IAEA under which all source and special nuclear material within a country would be subject to IAEA safeguards.

A final benefit to states provided by the coupling of the NPT, the Treaty of Tlatelolco, and the IAEA safeguards system was a set of export control policies reinforcing the assurance provided by IAEA safeguards. The NPT parties initially implemented their obligation to require IAEA safeguards as a condition of supply not only on the export of nuclear material but also "equipment or material especially designed or prepared for the processing, use or production" of nuclear material by developing in the so-called Zangger Group, named for its chairman, a so-called "Trigger List" of sensitive nuclear equipment, material and technology. NPT parties would deem Trigger List exports subject to NPT safeguards obligations as a condition of supply. This group of NPT parties was later broadened to include suppliers such as France which at that time had not yet joined the NPT, and the items it included was expanded to cover certain technology, equipment, materials, such as heavy water, that were not clearly covered by the NPT requirement of safeguards as a condition of nuclear supply. These new non-treaty commitments, which strictly speaking were not pursuant to the NPT, came to be known as the London Suppliers' Guidelines. A novel development in these non-NPT controls was the pursuit of requirements of "prior consent" on the manner in which nuclear material would be used, such as reprocessing, and on re-exports of transferred items to third-parties.[35] Even more stringent related requirements were unilaterally sought by the United States after the enactment of the Nuclear Nonproliferation Act of 1978, such as reprocessing consent rights and full-scope safeguards as a condition of all nuclear supply.[36] These developments, moving well beyond the terms

33 *See id.* at 9–10 (reporting declaration of President Carter of June 12, 1978).

34 *See* Additional Protocol II to the Treaty of Tlatelolco, Feb. 14, 1967, U.S.T. 754, T.I.A.S. No. 7137, 634 U.N.T.S. 364 (entered into force Dec. 11, 1969; entered into force for U.S. May 12, 1971).

35 *See* Fischer & Szasz, *supra* note 5, at 101–03.

36 *See id.* at 103–04 (noting that the NNPA required merely de facto full-scope safeguards—that is to say, a judgment that safeguards were applied on all nuclear facilities in a country so as to permit the conclusion that the effect of the *de jure* NPT full-scope safeguards requirement was satisfied—rather than the existence of an NPT- or Tlatelolco-compliant safeguards agreement with the IAEA).

of the NPT and INFCIRC/153, reflected decreased confidence in the efficacy of the nonproliferation regime of which the IAEA was only a part. India's detonation of its own "peaceful" nuclear device on May 16, 1974, just as the Zangger Committee produced its Trigger List, together with the emerging reality that important states, such as South Africa, Israel, and Pakistan would remain outside the NPT or the Treaty of Tlatelolco for some time to come, concentrated the minds of nuclear suppliers on the need to move beyond IAEA Safeguards.

Throughout this period, it should be recalled that the NPT was still, so to speak, on probation, since under Article X.2 of the Treaty the parties had determined that a special conference would be held in 1995 to determine whether the Treaty should "continue in force indefinitely" or "be extended for an additional fixed period or periods."[37] Thus, the burden and political insensitivity of IAEA INFCIRC/153 or NPT Full-scope Safeguards would surely become a criterion in the decision of the NPT parties whether or not to extend permanently the NPT. Thus, the mantra of sovereign equality limited substantially the role the IAEA could play in furthering the implementation of the obligation not to assist NNWS in the acquisition of nuclear weapons. Because of the limited role of the IAEA in enforcing the discriminatory distinctions established by the NPT between NWS's and NNWS's, the most the IAEA could do was merely serve as a clearinghouse for the publication and dissemination of the standards agreed to by nuclear fuel cycle suppliers in these other negotiating contexts, such as the Zangger Group and London Supplier Guidelines. In both cases, the IAEA merely published these documents as Information Circulars, neither approving nor disapproving their content.[38]

Additionally, even if the IAEA could have surmounted the perceptual problem of being the instrument of a policy perceived in many circles to discriminate between groups of states, it was even more difficult for states subject to safeguards not to fear that IAEA inspectors were, in some cases at least, agents of foreign powers, especially the NWS, since much of the technical expertise necessary to the formulation and implementation of safeguards of necessity was drawn from experts supplied by the NWS and their allies.[39] To address such potential concerns, the IAEA Statute provided for the independence of the Secretariat and its responsibility to the Board of Governors, and it specifically obligates the Secretariat not to disclose any industrial secrets or other confidential information through performance of its responsibilities.[40] However, nothing in the Statute or safeguards agreements appears to bar the Secretariat from receiving information from interested third parties—whether it be a newspaper account or a foreign intelligence service—so long as the independence and integrity of the Secretariat is not compromised.

---

37 *See* NPT, *supra* note 16, at art. 10, ¶ 2.

38 *See* IAEA, *Communications Received from Members Regarding the Export of Nuclear Material and of Certain Categories of Equipment and Other Material*, IAEA Doc. INFCIRC/209 (Sept. 4, 1974); and IAEA, *Communications Received from Certain Member States Regarding Guidelines for the Export of Nuclear Material, Equipment Or Technology*, IAEA Doc. INFCIRC/254 (Feb. 1978).

39 *See* Fischer & Szasz, *supra* note 5, at 65.

40 *See* IAEA Statute, *supra* note 4, art. 7, ¶ f.

With the forgoing description of nuclear fuel cycle and the legal and non-legal elements of the international nuclear non-proliferation regime in mind, we turn to the DPRK NPT withdrawal crisis.

3. Chronology of the DPRK NPT Withdrawal Crisis

The DPRK relationship with the IAEA dates back to 1977, when INFCIRC/66-type safeguards were applied to Soviet-supplied research reaction located at Yongbyon.[41] The weapons-usable plutonium produced at this research reactor, as well as all other nuclear materials in the DPRK, became subject to full-scope safeguards when the DPRK became a party to the NPT in 1985. But North Korea failed to enter into a safeguards agreement within the 18 month timeframe required under the NPT and insisted, in 1990, that a condition precedent to its doing so would be the withdrawal of all U.S. nuclear weapons from the Korean peninsula, a condition with which President George H.W. Bush finally complied after the end of the Cold War in 1992 as part of a global redeployment of U.S. nuclear forces. In the meantime, however, press reports, presumably based on intelligence information, revealed that in 1989 the DPRK had shut down the plutonium production reactor for a sufficient period, roughly 100 days, to withdraw the spent nuclear fuel and completely refuel the reactor. When the DPRK entered into the NPT-required safeguards agreement in 1992 and made its initial declaration to the IAEA in May 1992, shortly after the revelations that IAEA full-scope safeguards had failed in Iraq to discover an undeclared nuclear weapons program, the DPRK indicated that it had on only one occasion separated extremely small quantities of plutonium, quantities insufficient to build a nuclear explosive device. However, IAEA chemical analysis revealed that the samples made available by the DPRK were drawn from a much larger quantity of separated material derived from several plutonium reprocessing campaigns. In other words, the evidence revealed that North Korea has submitted a materially false initial declaration.[42]

Faced with this challenge, in a scene reminiscent of the UN Security Council session at the height of the Cold War at which photographic intelligence establishing the presence of Soviet nuclear-armed missiles in Cuba was shown to the world, at a Board of Governors meeting in late February 1993, U.S. intelligence photographs revealing Soviet-style nuclear waste storage facilities, as well as the IAEA's own chemical analysis, were presented to the DPRK, thus challenging

41 *See* North Korea Special Collection: IAEA-North Korea: Nuclear Safeguards and Inspections 1977–1989, Monterey Inst. of Int'l Stud. (*available at* http://cns.miis.edu/archive/country_north_korea/nuc/iaea7789.htm).

42 *See generally* Cirincione, *supra* note 4, at 244; *see also* North Korea Special Collection: IAEA-North Korea: Nuclear Safeguards and Inspections 1990, Monterey Inst. of Int'l Stud. (*available at* http://cns.miis.edu/archive/country_north_korea/nuc/iaea90.htm).

the DPRK's initial declaration.[43] On the basis of this evidence, on February 24, 1993, the Board of Governors adopted a resolution demanding within one month IAEA access to the two sites suspected of being part of its nuclear weapons program. The IAEA stated that access to the sites was "essential and urgent."[44] This was the first attempt in the history of the IAEA to demand a "special inspection" for the purpose of ferreting out a possible case of nuclear proliferation.[45] IAEA Director General Hans Blix also sent a copy to the UN Security Council of his telex to the DPRK demanding special inspections of the two suspect locations.[46] Rejecting this demand, on March 12 North Korea announced its withdrawal from the NPT within 90 days as provided for pursuant to Article X of the Treaty, asserting in its notice to the UN Security Council that its "supreme national interests" had been "jeopardized" by U.S. military exercises and the IAEA demand for special inspection of the two suspect sites, but also claiming improper interference by U.S. officials in influencing the IAEA to demand special inspections.[47] Security Council Resolution 825, calling upon the DPRK to retract its notice of intention to withdraw from the NPT, was adopted in this context.[48]

After intense and largely bilateral negotiations between the United States and the DPRK, a day before the notice of withdrawal would have taken effect, North Korea purported to "suspend" its withdrawal from the NPT. But it claimed, because of the circumstances leading to its withdrawal, that it was no longer fully bound by its NPT safeguards agreement, barring the IAEA from even routine inspections needed to assure the "continuity of safeguards," and finally compelling the IAEA Director General in December 1993 to state that IAEA safeguards could no longer provide "meaningful assurances" of non-diversion of nuclear materials.[49] The crisis escalated as the DPRK announced in May 1994 that it would de-fuel its plutonium production reactor, thereby gaining immediate access to fuel that would provide material for several nuclear bombs and would further possibly break the chain of custody that would enable IAEA chemical analysis to determine the precise quantities and composition of the nuclear material that had been produced. Indeed, Director General Blix announced on May 31, 1994, that due to continued North Korean non-compliance with IAEA inspections, North Korea is "no longer [officially] in compliance with IAEA safeguards"; and he made a final appeal to North Korea, asking it

43 *See* North Korea Special Collection: IAEA-North Korea: Nuclear Safeguards and Inspections 1993, Monterey Inst. of Int'l Stud. (*available at* http://cns.miis.edu/archive/country_north_korea/nuc/iaea93.htm) [hereinafter "1993 Special Collection"] (citing David E. Sanger, *West Knew of North Korea Nuclear Development,* N.Y. Times, Mar. 13, 1993 (*available at* http://www.nytimes.com/1993/03/13/world/west-knew-of-north-korea-nuclear-development.html)).

44 *See id.* (citing Don Oberdorfer, The Two Koreas: A Contemporary History 278 (1997).

45 *See* Cirincione, *supra* note 4, at 252 n.21 (citing Leon Sigal, Disarming Strangers: Nuclear Diplomacy with North Korea (1998) (citing and distinguishing special inspection cases in relation to Romania and Sweden)).

46 *See* 1993 Special Collection, *supra* note 43.

47 *See id.*

48 S.C. Res. 825 U.N. Doc. S/RES/825 (May 11, 1993).

49 *See* Cirincione, *supra* note 4, at 245.

to stop withdrawing fuel rods from the 5MW gas-graphite reactor and to allow international inspections to proceed. North Korea's ambassador to the IAEA, Yun Ho-jin, replied that the refueling would continue, stating that a number of fuel rods had already been withdrawn under IAEA camera surveillance and placed in a storage site "pending an inspection agreement."[50] On June 10, the Board of Governors adopted a resolution suspending all technical aid to North Korea, and on June 15 IAEA inspectors left North Korea.[51]

It was in the context of this threat—and in the face of U.S. demands at the UN Security Council for sanctions, as well as the possibility of military action even if the threat of a Chinese veto of threatened sanctions materialized—that former U.S. President Jimmy Carter intervened in a June 16-17 mission to Pyongyang, North Korea, where he helped to arrange a compromise settlement. Even after the July 9 death of North Korean leader Kim Il Sung, this compromise matured into an Agreed Statement on August 12, which in turn yielded on October 21, 1994 a precise set of politically—but not legally—binding commitments, in the so-called "Agreed Framework."[52] The document provided that the DPRK would "freeze" its nuclear program and take a series of steps leading ultimately to full compliance with IAEA safeguards, while the United States and others would form the so-called Korean Energy Development Organization (or KEDO) as a multilateral framework organization to facilitate the construction of a proliferation-resistant light-water nuclear reactors (LWRs) in North Korea and supply heavy fuel oil to replace electrical production that would be lost from shutting down the DPRK's plutonium production reactor.[53] Under Article IV.2 of the Agreed Framework, routine and *ad hoc* inspections would resume only when the commercial supply contract for the LWRs was concluded; and, under Article IV. 3, the DPRK affirmed that it would enter into "full compliance" with IAEA safeguards only after a "significant portion of the LWR project ... is completed, but before delivery of key reactor components...."[54]

The Agreed Framework raised major institutional challenges for the IAEA, both as to its efficacy and the legality of IAEA cooperation in implementing it. The efficacy of the Agreed Framework was always in doubt in many quarters. On one hand, the Agreed Framework in effect deferred special inspections of the undeclared facilities long enough to call into question

50 North Korea Special Collection: IAEA-North Korea: Nuclear Safeguards and Inspections 1994, Monterey Inst. of Int'l Stud. (*available at* http://cns.miis.edu/archive/country_north_korea/nuc/iaea94.htm).

51 *See id.*

52 *See generally* Marian Nash, *Contemporary Practice of the United States Relating to International Law: Peaceful Uses of Nuclear Energy,* 89 Am. J. Int'l L. 96, 119 and 366, 373 (reporting testimony of Secretary of State Warren Christopher Before the Senate Committee on Foreign Relations on January 24, 1995); *see also* Testimony of Ambassador-at-Large Robert Gallucci Before the East Asian and Pacific Sub-Committee of the Senate Committee on Foreign Relations on U.S.-North Korea Nuclear Agreement, *Federal News Service* (Dec. 1, 1994) (affirming that the Agreed Framework was merely a political commitment to which the United States was not bound under international law); *see generally* Antonio F. Perez, *Who Killed Sovereignty?: Or Changing Norms Concerning Sovereignty in International Law,* Wis. J. Int'l L. 463, 479 (1996).

53 *See* Cirincione, *supra* note 4, at 245–46.

54 IAEA, *Agreed Framework of October 21, 1994 Between the United States of America and the Democratic People's Republic of Korea,* IAEA Doc. INFCIRC/457 (Nov. 2, 1994).

whether the truth of North Korea's nuclear program would ever be revealed. Yet, on the other, it was thought that conditioning the provision of key nuclear components essential to the production of any additional plutonium would assure that North Korea could not acquire any additional weapons-usable nuclear material until the IAEA had at least an opportunity to determine the truth about the DPRK's prior nuclear activities.[55] The central premise of this trade-off may have been compromised when it was later revealed that the DPRK also had engaged, like Iraq, in an undeclared uranium enrichment program, establishing an alternative pathway to the production of weapons-usable nuclear material in the form of HEU rather than plutonium.

The U.S. announcement on October 16, 2002, that North Korea had acknowledged to the United States the existence of such a program precipitated a diplomatic crisis yet again. The IAEA offered on October 17 and 18 to send a team to the DPRK or to receive a DPRK team in Vienna, to discuss the issues highlighted by the U.S. announcement, but received no response from Pyongyang. The United States, Japan, South Korea, and KEDO concluded that this action was a violation of the Agreed Framework, the NPT, the DPRK-IAEA Safeguards Agreement, and the North-South Joint Declaration on the Denuclearization of the Korean Peninsula; and the KEDO Board decided to suspend heavy oil deliveries as of the December shipment.[56] Then, on November 29, 2002, the IAEA Board of Governors adopted a resolution recognizing that enriching uranium for nuclear weapons "or any other covert nuclear activities, would constitute a violation of the DPRK´s international commitments, including the DPRK's safeguards agreement with the Agency pursuant to the NPT" and demanding that the DPRK reply and cooperate.[57] The DPRK reply of December 13 to the Director General indicated that, in response to the suspension of oil deliveries, North Korea would lift the freeze on its nuclear activities; on December 22, the DPRK started to cut seals and disable surveillance cameras; on December 27, 2002, it ordered IAEA inspectors to leave North Korea; and on January 10, 2003, it announced that its withdrawal from the NPT would be effective as of January 11, 2003, since all but one day of the notice period had expired in 1993 when it had "suspended" its earlier notice of withdrawal. The official IAEA fact sheet on the situation states:

> The IAEA is not a party to the NPT and hence it is not in the position to determine the status of any State Party's membership of the Non-Proliferation Treaty. NPT States Parties´ comprehensive safeguards agreements with the IAEA provide that such agreements would remain in force as long as the State is party to the Non-Proliferation Treaty.[58]

---

55 *See* Cirincione, *supra* note 4, at 247.

56 News Release, Korean Peninsula Energy Development Organization, Statement of KEDO's Executive Board (Nov. 14, 2002) (*available at* http://kedo.org/news_detail.asp?NewsID=23). The Executive Board includes the European Union, Japan, Republic of Korea, and the United States.

57 IAEA, *Board of Governors Adopts Resolution on Safeguards in DPRK,* IAEA Doc. GOV/2002/33 (Nov. 29, 2002).

58 Fact Sheet on DPRK Nuclear Safeguards, IAEA (*available at* http://www.iaea.org/NewsCenter/Focus/IaeaDprk/fact_sheet_may2003.shtml).

4. Study Questions Before Reading the Nuclear Non-Proliferation Treaty of 1968 and U.N. Security Council Resolution 255 (1970)

1) From the rational choice perspective, is the NPT one bargain or many bargains? Who are the players or groups of players?

2) Can you explain why China did not join for roughly 25 years? Can you explain why North Korea did not join for 25 years? How might these two developments be related?

3) How much of the NPT takes the form of precise legal obligations? Which provisions seem to be specific? Why? How does the NPT contemplate that these obligations will be implemented? Through whom? Under what arrangements?

4) Which provisions seem to give the parties, individually or collectively, the greatest latitude for interpretation? Why?

5) Would you have drafted the NPT with more precision, less precision, or (per Goldilocks) is it just right?

6) Do you see procedures for dispute resolution on the meaning of the treaty or to resolve cases of compliance?

7) What is the relationship between Article X of the NPT and S.C. Res 255? Is the relationship legal or political? Does that matter to the parties?

8) Is there language in Resolution 255 that you would find troubling if you were lawyer or policymaker for a Permanent Member of the Security Council?

9) Is there language in Resolution 255 you would find troubling if you were a state threatened by a potential nuclear adversary?

10) Are the NPT and Resolution 255 worth the paper they are written on? Why? Why not?

a. Treaty on the Non-Proliferation of Nuclear Weapons[59]

Signed at Washington, London, and Moscow July 1, 1968
Entered into force March 5, 1970

The States concluding this Treaty, hereinafter referred to as the "Parties to the Treaty",

Considering the devastation that would be visited upon all mankind by a nuclear war and the consequent need to make every effort to avert the danger of such a war and to take measures to safeguard the security of peoples,

Believing that the proliferation of nuclear weapons would seriously enhance the danger of nuclear war,

In conformity with resolutions of the United Nations General Assembly calling for the conclusion of an agreement on the prevention of wider dissemination of nuclear weapons,

Undertaking to cooperate in facilitating the application of International Atomic Energy Agency safeguards on peaceful nuclear activities,

Expressing their support for research, development and other efforts to further the application, within the framework of the International Atomic Energy Agency safeguards system, of the principle of safeguarding effectively the flow of source and special fissionable materials by use of instruments and other techniques at certain strategic points,

Affirming the principle that the benefits of peaceful applications of nuclear technology, including any technological by-products which may be derived by nuclear-weapon States from the development of nuclear explosive devices, should be available for peaceful purposes to all Parties of the Treaty, whether nuclear-weapon or non-nuclear weapon States,

Convinced that, in furtherance of this principle, all Parties to the Treaty are entitled to participate in the fullest possible exchange of scientific information for, and to contribute alone or in cooperation with other States to, the further development of the applications of atomic energy for peaceful purposes,

---

59 NPT, *supra* note 16. Upon the NPT's indefinite extension in 1995, pursuant to art. 10, ¶ 2, the Security Council reaffirmed Resolution 255. *See* S.C. Res. 984, U.N. Doc. S/RES/984 (Apr. 11, 1995).

Declaring their intention to achieve at the earliest possible date the cessation of the nuclear arms race and to undertake effective measures in the direction of nuclear disarmament,

Urging the cooperation of all States in the attainment of this objective,

Recalling the determination expressed by the Parties to the 1963 Treaty banning nuclear weapon tests in the atmosphere, in outer space and under water in its Preamble to seek to achieve the discontinuance of all test explosions of nuclear weapons for all time and to continue negotiations to this end,

Desiring to further the easing of international tension and the strengthening of trust between States in order to facilitate the cessation of the manufacture of nuclear weapons, the liquidation of all their existing stockpiles, and the elimination from national arsenals of nuclear weapons and the means of their delivery pursuant to a Treaty on general and complete disarmament under strict and effective international control,

Recalling that, in accordance with the Charter of the United Nations, States must refrain in their international relations from the threat or use of force against the territorial integrity or political independence of any State, or in any other manner inconsistent with the Purposes of the United Nations, and that the establishment and maintenance of international peace and security are to be promoted with the least diversion for armaments of the world's human and economic resources,

Have agreed as follows:

Article I

Each nuclear-weapon State Party to the Treaty undertakes not to transfer to any recipient whatsoever nuclear weapons or other nuclear explosive devices or control over such weapons or explosive devices directly, or indirectly; and not in any way to assist, encourage, or induce any non-nuclear weapon State to manufacture or otherwise acquire nuclear weapons or other nuclear explosive devices, or control over such weapons or explosive devices.

Article II

Each non-nuclear-weapon State Party to the Treaty undertakes not to receive the transfer from any transferor whatsoever of nuclear weapons or other nuclear explosive devices or of control over such weapons or explosive devices directly, or indirectly; not to manufacture or otherwise acquire nuclear weapons or other nuclear explosive devices; and not to seek or receive any assistance in the manufacture of nuclear weapons or other nuclear explosive devices.

Article III

1. Each non-nuclear-weapon State Party to the Treaty undertakes to accept safeguards, as set forth in an agreement to be negotiated and concluded with the International Atomic Energy Agency in accordance with the Statute of the International Atomic Energy Agency and the Agency's safeguards system, for the exclusive purpose of verification of the fulfillment of its obligations assumed under this Treaty with a view to preventing diversion of nuclear energy from peaceful uses to nuclear weapons or other nuclear explosive devices. Procedures for the safeguards required by this article shall be followed with respect to source or special fissionable material whether it is being produced, processed or used in any principal nuclear facility or is outside any such facility. The safeguards required by this article shall be applied to all source or special fissionable material in all peaceful nuclear activities within the territory of such State, under its jurisdiction, or carried out under its control anywhere.

2. Each State Party to the Treaty undertakes not to provide: (a) source or special fissionable material, or (b) equipment or material especially designed or prepared for the processing, use or production of special fissionable material, to any non-nuclear-weapon State for peaceful purposes, unless the source or special fissionable material shall be subject to the safeguards required by this article.

3. The safeguards required by this article shall be implemented in a manner designed to comply with article IV of this Treaty, and to avoid hampering the economic or technological development of the Parties or international cooperation in the field of peaceful nuclear activities, including the international exchange of nuclear material and equipment for the processing, use or production of nuclear material for peaceful purposes in accordance with the provisions of this article and the principle of safeguarding set forth in the Preamble of the Treaty.

4. Non-nuclear-weapon States Party to the Treaty shall conclude agreements with the International Atomic Energy Agency to meet the requirements of this article either individually or together with other States in accordance with the Statute of the International Atomic Energy Agency. Negotiation of such agreements shall commence within 180 days from the original entry into force of this Treaty. For

States depositing their instruments of ratification or accession after the 180-day period, negotiation of such agreements shall commence not later than the date of such deposit. Such agreements shall enter into force not later than eighteen months after the date of initiation of negotiations.

Article IV

1. Nothing in this Treaty shall be interpreted as affecting the inalienable right of all the Parties to the Treaty to develop research, production and use of nuclear energy for peaceful purposes without discrimination and in conformity with articles I and II of this Treaty.

2. All the Parties to the Treaty undertake to facilitate, and have the right to participate in, the fullest possible exchange of equipment, materials and scientific and technological information for the peaceful uses of nuclear energy. Parties to the Treaty in a position to do so shall also cooperate in contributing alone or together with other States or international organizations to the further development of the applications of nuclear energy for peaceful purposes, especially in the territories of non-nuclear-weapon States Party to the Treaty, with due consideration for the needs of the developing areas of the world.

Article V

Each party to the Treaty undertakes to take appropriate measures to ensure that, in accordance with this Treaty, under appropriate international observation and through appropriate international procedures, potential benefits from any peaceful applications of nuclear explosions will be made available to non-nuclear-weapon States Party to the Treaty on a nondiscriminatory basis and that the charge to such Parties for the explosive devices used will be as low as possible and exclude any charge for research and development. Non-nuclear-weapon States Party to the Treaty shall be able to obtain such benefits, pursuant to a special international agreement or agreements, through an appropriate international body with adequate representation of non-nuclear-weapon States. Negotiations on this subject shall commence as soon as possible after the Treaty enters into force. Non-nuclear-weapon States Party to the Treaty so desiring may also obtain such benefits pursuant to bilateral agreements.

Article VI

Each of the Parties to the Treaty undertakes to pursue negotiations in good faith on effective measures relating to cessation of the nuclear arms race at an early date and to nuclear disarmament, and on a Treaty on general and complete disarmament under strict and effective international control.

Article VII

Nothing in this Treaty affects the right of any group of States to conclude regional treaties in order to assure the total absence of nuclear weapons in their respective territories.

Article VIII

1. Any Party to the Treaty may propose amendments to this Treaty. The text of any proposed amendment shall be submitted to the Depositary Governments which shall circulate it to all Parties to the Treaty. Thereupon, if requested to do so by one-third or more of the Parties to the Treaty, the Depositary Governments shall convene a conference, to which they shall invite all the Parties to the Treaty, to consider such an amendment.

2. Any amendment to this Treaty must be approved by a majority of the votes of all the Parties to the Treaty, including the votes of all nuclear-weapon States Party to the Treaty and all other Parties which, on the date the amendment is circulated, are members of the Board of Governors of the International Atomic Energy Agency. The amendment shall enter into force for each Party that deposits its instrument of ratification of the amendment upon the deposit of such instruments of ratification by a majority of all the Parties, including the instruments of ratification of all nuclear-weapon States Party to the Treaty and all other Parties which, on the date the amendment is circulated, are members of the Board of Governors of the International Atomic Energy Agency. Thereafter, it shall enter into force for any other Party upon the deposit of its instrument of ratification of the amendment.

3. Five years after the entry into force of this Treaty, a conference of Parties to the Treaty shall be held in Geneva, Switzerland, in order to review the operation of this Treaty with a view to assuring that the purposes of the Preamble and the provisions of the Treaty are being realized. At intervals of five years thereafter, a majority of the Parties to the Treaty may obtain, by submitting a proposal to this effect to

the Depositary Governments, the convening of further conferences with the same objective of reviewing the operation of the Treaty.

Article IX

1. This Treaty shall be open to all States for signature. Any State which does not sign the Treaty before its entry into force in accordance with paragraph 3 of this article may accede to it at any time.

2. This Treaty shall be subject to ratification by signatory States. Instruments of ratification and instruments of accession shall be deposited with the Governments of the United States of America, the United Kingdom of Great Britain and Northern Ireland and the Union of Soviet Socialist Republics, which are hereby designated the Depositary Governments.

3. This Treaty shall enter into force after its ratification by the States, the Governments of which are designated Depositaries of the Treaty, and forty other States signatory to this Treaty and the deposit of their instruments of ratification. For the purposes of this Treaty, a nuclear-weapon State is one which has manufactured and exploded a nuclear weapon or other nuclear explosive device prior to January 1, 1967.

4. For States whose instruments of ratification or accession are deposited subsequent to the entry into force of this Treaty, it shall enter into force on the date of the deposit of their instruments of ratification or accession.

5. The Depositary Governments shall promptly inform all signatory and acceding States of the date of each signature, the date of deposit of each instrument of ratification or of accession, the date of the entry into force of this Treaty, and the date of receipt of any requests for convening a conference or other notices.

6. This Treaty shall be registered by the Depositary Governments pursuant to article 102 of the Charter of the United Nations.

Article X

1. Each Party shall in exercising its national sovereignty have the right to withdraw from the Treaty if it decides that extraordinary events, related to the subject matter of this Treaty, have jeopardized the supreme interests of its country. It shall give

notice of such withdrawal to all other Parties to the Treaty and to the United Nations Security Council three months in advance. Such notice shall include a statement of the extraordinary events it regards as having jeopardized its supreme interests.

2. Twenty-five years after the entry into force of the Treaty, a conference shall be convened to decide whether the Treaty shall continue in force indefinitely, or shall be extended for an additional fixed period or periods. This decision shall be taken by a majority of the Parties to the Treaty.

Article XI

This Treaty, the English, Russian, French, Spanish and Chinese texts of which are equally authentic, shall be deposited in the archives of the Depositary Governments. Duly certified copies of this Treaty shall be transmitted by the Depositary Governments to the Governments of the signatory and acceding States.

IN WITNESS WHEREOF the undersigned, duly authorized, have signed this Treaty.

DONE in triplicate, at the cities of Washington, London and Moscow, this first day of July one thousand nine hundred sixty-eight.

5. Study Questions for DPRK Withdrawal Crisis Documents: S.C. Res. 825 (1993) and the Framework Agreement (1994)

1) Is Security Council Resolution 825 what the Security Council anticipated in Resolution 255 or what the NPT parties anticipated in Article X(1) of the NPT?

2) What threat by North Korea prompted Security Council Resolution 825? What was the basis for North Korea's own decision? What was the role of the IAEA? Does it matter that North Korea did not play a role in the initial development of the NPT or the IAEA? What do you think the DPRK was trying to accomplish by threatening to withdraw from the NPT? What do you think the United States, the other Permanent members of the Security Council, South Korea, and Japan were trying to accomplish? Were their respective strategies legal, political, a combination of the two?

3) Was the Framework Accord the kind of resolution to an attempted withdrawal contemplated by the NPT, Resolution 255, and the IAEA Statute and Safeguards Agreements?

4) From the standpoint of rational choice theory, does the conclusion of the Framework Accord constitute tit-for-tat strategy to reinforce cooperation, a Sucker's payoff for the Security Council, South Korea, and Japan, or something in between?

5) What are the elements of the Framework Accord? How does it differ as a bargain from the NPT itself? If the United States and its allies are deemed the NWS and North Korea is deemed the NNWS for purposes of comparison, are there new commitments by either side? What is the value of those commitments in creating payoffs for both sides? How are transaction cost problems, such as continued assurance and verification, addressed? What new institutions are created to address additional commitments? How are old arrangements revised to address traditional assurance and verification issues? Who will be the participants? Do you see any new participants, either explicitly or implicitly? What will be their level of autonomy? Do you think they could grow to perform functions that range beyond assurance and verification?

a. Security Council Resolution 825 (1993)[60]

Adopted by the Security Council at its 3212th meeting on 11 May 1993

The Security Council,

Having considered with concern the letter from the Minister for Foreign Affairs of the Democratic People's Republic of Korea (DPRK) dated 12 March 1993 addressed to the President of the Council (S/25405) concerning the intention of the Government of the DPRK to withdraw from the Treaty on the Non-Proliferation of Nuclear Weapons (the Treaty) and the report of the Director-General of the International Atomic Energy Agency (IAEA) (S/25556),

60 "The resolution passed with 13 votes, none against and two abstentions from the People's Republic of China and Pakistan, which both called for North Korea to return to the NPT. The Security Council noted with concern the intentions of the DPRK and reaffirmed the "crucial contribution which progress in non-proliferation can make to the maintenance of international peace and security" and called on the North Korean government to be committed and honour its obligations under the Treaty. The resolution also required the Director-General of the IAEA to consult with the DPRK to find a solution and report back in due course. At the insistence of the People's Republic of China, which abstained, the resolution did not make reference to any sanctions if North Korea failed to comply with the Security Council." United Nations Security Council Resolution 825, Wikipedia, http://en.wikipedia.org/wiki/United_Nations_Security_Council_Resolution_825.

Recalling the Security Council Presidential statement of 8 April 1993 (S/25562) in which the members of the Council welcome all efforts aimed at resolving this situation and, in particular, encourage the IAEA to continue its consultations with the DPRK for proper settlement of the nuclear verification issue in the DPRK,

Noting in that context the critical importance of the Treaty, and emphasizing the integral role of IAEA safeguards in the implementation of the Treaty and in ensuring the peaceful uses of nuclear energy, and reaffirming the crucial contribution which progress in non-proliferation can make to the maintenance of international peace and security,

Recalling the Joint Declaration by the DPRK and the Republic of Korea (ROK) on the denuclearization of the Korean Peninsula, which includes establishment of a credible and effective bilateral inspection regime and a pledge not to possess nuclear reprocessing and uranium enrichment facilities,

Noting that the DPRK is party to the Treaty and has concluded a full-scope safeguards agreement as required by that Treaty,

Having also considered with regret the IAEA Board of Governors' findings contained in its resolution of 1 April 1993 that the DPRK is in non-compliance with its obligations under the IAEA-DPRK safeguards agreement (INFCIRC/403), and that the IAEA is not able to verify that there has been no diversion of nuclear materials required to be safeguarded under the terms of the IAEA-DPRK safeguards agreement to nuclear weapons or other nuclear explosive devices,

Noting the letter of reply by the DPRK to the Director-General of the IAEA dated 22 April 1993 which, inter alia, encourages and urges the Director-General to hold consultations with the DPRK on the implementation of the safeguards agreement, noting also that the DPRK has expressed its willingness to seek a negotiated solution to this issue,

Welcoming recent signs of improved cooperation between the DPRK and the IAEA and the prospect of contacts between the DPRK and other Member States,

Calls upon the DPRK to reconsider the announcement contained in the letter of 12 March 1993 and thus to reaffirm its commitment to the Treaty;

Further calls upon the DPRK to honour its non-proliferation obligations under the Treaty and comply with its safeguards agreement with the IAEA as specified by the IAEA Board of Governors' resolution of 25 February 1993;

Requests the Director-General of the IAEA to continue to consult with the DPRK with a view to resolving the issues which are the subject of the Board of Governors' findings and to report to the Security Council on his efforts in due time;

Urges all Member States to encourage the DPRK to respond positively to this resolution, and encourages them to facilitate a solution;

Decides to remain seized of the matter and to consider further Security Council action if necessary.

b. Agreed Framework Between The United States of America And The Democratic People's Republic of Korea[61]

Geneva, October 21, 1994

Delegations of the governments of the United States of America (U.S.) and the Democratic People's Republic of Korea (DPRK) held talks in Geneva from September 23 to October 21, 1994, to negotiate an overall resolution of the nuclear issue on the Korean Peninsula.

Both sides reaffirmed the importance of attaining the objectives contained in the August 12, 1994 Agreed Statement between the U.S. and the DPRK and upholding the principles of the June 11, 1993 Joint Statement of the U.S. and the DPRK to achieve peace and security on a nuclear-free Korean peninsula. The U.S. and the DPRK decided to take the following actions for the resolution of the nuclear issue:

I. Both sides will cooperate to replace the DPRK's graphite-moderated reactors and related facilities with light-water reactor (LWR) power plants.

1) In accordance with the October 20, 1994 letter of assurance from the U.S. President, the U.S. will undertake to make arrangements for the provision to the DPRK of a LWR project with a total generating capacity of approximately 2,000 MW(e) by a target date of 2003.
   The U.S. will organize under its leadership an international consortium to finance and supply the LWR project to be provided to the DPRK. The U.S., representing the international consortium, will serve as the principal point of contact with the DPRK for the LWR project.
   The U.S., representing the consortium, will make best efforts to secure the conclusion of a supply contract with the DPRK within six months of the date of this Document for the provision of the LWR project. Contract talks will begin as soon as possible after the date of this Document.
   As necessary, the U.S. and the DPRK will conclude a bilateral agreement for cooperation in the field of peaceful uses of nuclear energy.

2) In accordance with the October 20, 1994 letter of assurance from the U.S. President, the U.S., representing the consortium, will make arrangements to offset the energy foregone due to the freeze of the DPRK's graphite-moderated reactors and related facilities, pending completion of the first LWR unit.
   Alternative energy will be provided in the form of heavy oil for heating and

61 *See* Agreed Framework, U.S.-N. Kor., Oct. 21, 1994 (*available at* http://www.armscontrol.org/print/2475).

electricity production.
Deliveries of heavy oil will begin within three months of the date of this Document and will reach a rate of 500,000 tons annually, in accordance with an agreed schedule of deliveries.

3) Upon receipt of U.S. assurances for the provision of LWR's and for arrangements for interim energy alternatives, the DPRK will freeze its graphite-moderated reactors and related facilities and will eventually dismantle these reactors and related facilities.
The freeze on the DPRK's graphite-moderated reactors and related facilities will be fully implemented within one month of the date of this Document. During this one-month period, and throughout the freeze, the International Atomic Energy Agency (IAEA) will be allowed to monitor this freeze, and the DPRK will provide full cooperation to the IAEA for this purpose.
Dismantlement of the DPRK's graphite-moderated reactors and related facilities will be completed when the LWR project is completed.
The U.S. and the DPRK will cooperate in finding a method to store safely the spent fuel from the 5 MW(e) experimental reactor during the construction of the LWR project, and to dispose of the fuel in a safe manner that does not involve reprocessing in the DPRK.

4) As soon as possible after the date of this document U.S. and DPRK experts will hold two sets of experts talks.
At one set of talks, experts will discuss issues related to alternative energy and the replacement of the graphite-moderated reactor program with the LWR project.
At the other set of talks, experts will discuss specific arrangements for spent fuel storage and ultimate disposition.

II. The two sides will move toward full normalization of political and economic relations.

1) Within three months of the date of this Document, both sides will reduce barriers to trade and investment, including restrictions on telecommunications services and financial transactions.

2) Each side will open a liaison office in the other's capital following resolution of consular and other technical issues through expert level discussions.

3) As progress is made on issues of concern to each side, the U.S. and the DPRK will upgrade bilateral relations to the Ambassadorial level.

III. Both sides will work together for peace and security on a nuclear-free Korean peninsula.

1) The U.S. will provide formal assurances to the DPRK, against the threat or use of nuclear weapons by the U.S.

2) The DPRK will consistently take steps to implement the North-South Joint Declaration on the Denuclearization of the Korean Peninsula.

3) The DPRK will engage in North-South dialogue, as this Agreed Framework will help create an atmosphere that promotes such dialogue.

IV. Both sides will work together to strengthen the international nuclear non proliferation regime.

1) The DPRK will remain a party to the Treaty on the Non-Proliferation of Nuclear Weapons (NPT) and will allow implementation of its safeguards agreement under the Treaty.

2) Upon conclusion of the supply contract for the provision of the LWR project, ad hoc and routine inspections will resume under the DPRK's safeguards agreement with the IAEA with respect to the facilities not subject to the freeze. Pending conclusion of the supply contract, inspections required by the IAEA for the continuity of safeguards will continue at the facilities not subject to the freeze.

3) When a significant portion of the LWR project is completed, but before delivery of key nuclear components, the DPRK will come into full compliance with its safeguards agreement with the IAEA (INFCIRC/403), including taking all steps that may be deemed necessary by the IAEA, following consultations with the Agency with regard to verifying the accuracy and completeness of the DPRK's initial report on all nuclear material in the DPRK.

Source: Department of State

Robert L. Gallucci	Kang Sok Ju
Head of Delegation of the United States of America, Ambassador at Large of the United States of America	Head of the Delegation of the Democratic People's Republic of Korea, First Vice-Minister of Foreign Affairs of the Democratic People's Republic of Korea

6. Thesis I—Rational Choice Theory, International Law, and the North Korean NPT Withdrawal Crisis

In general terms, our focus has been on the role that the design of international institutions, drawing on rational choice theory, can play in "enforcing" compliance with international obligations. "Enforcement" in the sense we intend need not involve "legal" sanctions imposed by a court after adjudication; nor does "non-compliance" here necessarily amount to a treaty violation that non-judicial sanctions might be used to deter or punish. As we discuss further below, "enforcement" can also work through such "informal" ways as the loss of reputation for behavior that is not, in itself, forbidden by a treaty or other "legal" rule.

Furthermore, the regimes or institutions described in this section do not generally involve high degrees of transfer of sovereign authority to international institutions.[62] While the NPT system is linked, as we will show, to the UN Charter's collective security system, the NPT itself and the institutions specifically constructed to "enforce" it include both formal, "legal" elements, like the UN Charter, and informal or "non-legal" elements. That is to say, the NPT system is partly formed without specific multilateral or bilateral treaty commitments. Both legal and non-legal arrangements involve a high degree of institutionalization, even if sanctions for non-compliance do not take the form found in adjudicatory settings. We explore how these complex institutions, both legal and non-legal, implement a basic set of policies—that the international community should seek to halt the growth of the number of nuclear weapons states, seek ultimately complete abolition of nuclear weapons, and in the interim, increase the confidence of all states that nuclear materials and technologies used for peaceful purposes will not be diverted to nuclear weapons use.

We consider first whether and how the international regime built around the NPT fits a rational choice model. We then explore how the rational choice theory, as illustrated by the NPT, suggests a novel understanding of international "law." Finally, we address whether the rational choice model provides a meaningful or adequate account of the North Korea withdrawal crisis.

62 In Part II, Chapter 2, we will consider a regime, specifically the UN Charter's collective security system, that seeks to transfer substantially greater sovereign authority.

a. A Rational Choice Explanation of the NPT/IAEA Regime

The central premise of the NPT is that joint gains can be achieved for all states through non-possession of nuclear weapons. Indeed, Article VI of the NPT nominally includes a legally-binding promise to "pursue negotiations in good faith on effective measures relating to cessation of the nuclear arms race at an early date and to nuclear disarmament," and to pursue a "treaty on general and complete disarmament under strict and effective international control."

From the rational choice perspective, nuclear proliferation might be seen as a PD game: each state will seek nuclear weapons to avoid the nuclear Sucker's Payoff—destruction at the hands of, or else submission to, the state with nuclear weapons. But that is to envisage nuclear proliferation as modeling the one-shot, two-player game—and it does not. Nuclear proliferation is a multi-shot, multi-player game, or at least an array of multi-shot, two-player games. Those games fell into three categories. First, proliferation could be seen primarily as a PD game between the two leading nuclear powers of the Cold War: the United States and the Soviet Union. While each would benefit from making nuclear weapons available to its own allies while the other did not, both would avoid the Sucker's Payoff if *neither* side's allies had such weapons. Alternatively, proliferation could be seen primarily as a PD game between the "club" of Nuclear Weapons States (NWS) as a whole and its "opponent," the world of Non-Nuclear Weapon States (NNWS). In a third category, proliferation subsumed a set of PD games between pairs (or triads, etc.) of *regional* powers, neither (or none) of which were nuclear-armed, but each of which might, by gaining regional hegemony, forcing one into the Sucker's Payoff if it acquired nuclear weapons while the other did not. India and Pakistan, or Brazil and Argentina, are examples of such PD couples. (Further complicating the simple, two-player, one-shot PD model, nuclear proliferation was an iterated or multi-shot game—though also one that seemed unlikely to last indefinitely, for the simple reason that if nuclear proliferation was practiced sufficiently widely for sufficiently long, the use of nuclear weapons appeared inevitable. When Waltz learned to stop worrying and love the bomb,[63] he called into question the basic security architecture of the modern era.)

The games in each of these three categories represented security dilemmas; each presented opportunities for nuclear cooperation, whether taking the form of a reduced arms race or avoiding the race altogether. Plainly, the key to transforming this many-faceted PD game into one that facilitates cooperation is producing information that allows each party to the NPT to be reasonably confident of the continued cooperation of the other parties. Yet the multiplicity of players, negotiating numerous purely bilateral agreements proved to be prohibitively costly.[64]

63 *See* Dr. Strangelove or: How I Learned to Stop Worrying and Love the Bomb (1964) (summary *available at* http://www.imdb.com/title/tt0057012/plotsummary). For Waltz's views, *see* Kenneth N. Waltz, The Spread of Nuclear Weapons: More May Be Better, Adelphi Paper No. 171 (1981) (*available at* http://polsci.colorado.edu/sites/default/files/10B_Waltz.pdf).

64 Early pre-NPT efforts by the United States to provide assurance and verification regimes through bilateral nuclear safeguards agreements, therefore, we quickly set aside in favor of an IAEA-centered assurance and verification system

The IAEA was, however, considered capable of performing the assurance and verification functions needed to produce "timely warning" of threatened defection from NPT commitments. The IAEA's capability formed the basis of a bargain under which the NNWS accepted full-scope IAEA safeguards in exchange for the NWS' acceptance of obligations to supply the NNWS with nuclear materials.[65] Thus, the IAEA became the institutional vehicle for the resolution of the nuclear security dilemma through its ability to produce information of a party's intent to defect, and to produce it early enough for other parties to avoid the Sucker's Payoff.

The parties' commitments in part took the form of relatively precise legal obligations, with compliance or performance representing cooperation and breach constituting defection. But cooperation and defection also took somewhat less "legalized" forms. Because of ongoing debate concerning the risk associated with the transfer of varying kinds of nuclear material, equipment, and technology to certain states, a more informal arrangement emerged to implement supplier obligations, first through the Zangger Committee and then through the NSG. These informal exporters' cartels enabled nuclear supplier states (a much smaller group than all the parties to the NPT or IAEA) to coordinate joint supply policies without the large delegation costs of transferring that function to an independent body (such as the IAEA). These supplier cartels might not have been able to agree on precise criteria for implementing the cartel, and so they avoided reducing their informal agreement to a formal treaty.

Furthermore, the expansive right to withdraw under Article X of the NPT when a party "decides that extraordinary events, related to the subject matter of this Treaty, have jeopardized the supreme interests of its country," enabled states to join the NPT at relatively low initial cost, provided timely warning of a threatening party's defection became available. And the so-called "positive security assurances" provided by the NWS, which were adopted by the Security Council both at the adoption of the NPT and its subsequent indefinite extension, provided some additional insurance against the risk of the Sucker's Payoff for states that might be especially at risk in the event of defection by another party.

Thus, the overall NPT/IAEA regime fitted squarely within the paradigm of rational choice theory and the methods that it prescribes for escaping from the security dilemma. But is this regime a "legal" construct; and, if so, in what sense?

b. Is the NPT Regime a Creature of International "Law"?

Significantly, the NPT régime involved varying degrees of legalization, at least within the terms of traditional international legal doctrine of the sources of international law. For international lawyers, the regime created a puzzle that could only be explained by a revised conception

for the peaceful use of nuclear material and technology.

65 The safeguards entailed a complex schedule of obligations, with performance measured by technical experts over time and reports to political organs (including the IAEA Board of Governors and, eventually, the UN Security Council).

of international "law" that treated even informal elements of cooperation as a type of law. Rational choice theory provided the conceptual resources for this enlarged understanding of "law."

For rational choice theory, all or nearly all states have an important interest in being able to make bargains with other states. But in international anarchy, bargains may be difficult or impossible to enforce, inasmuch as there are no courts or police and injured parties must rely primarily on self-help. To overcome the difficulty in making credible commitments, therefore, states have an interest in acquiring and maintaining a *reputation* as promise-keepers. They may do this by sedulously keeping their bargained-for commitments to other states, even when short-term advantage would seem to dictate reneging on their promises.

Breaching a promise thus typically carries a cost for the breaching state, in that it diminishes its reputation and credibility and so makes it harder for it to enter into future bargains with other states.[66] "Breach of a promise" (unlike "reputation") is a legal term, not a category of international relations. For rational choice theorists, then, what lawyers would call the "breach" of a treaty or other international obligation matters only because it signals to other parties that the breaching party is less reliable than other parties had previously supposed. Lawyers influenced by rational choice theory may conclude that behavior by a party that diminishes its reputation for compliance should be taken to *constitute* a breach or violation of international law. Much as Justice Oliver Wendell Holmes, Jr.'s "bad man" theory of the law collapsed the existence of a legal obligation into a prediction about what courts would do,[67] so here international lawyers might collapse the breach of an international obligation into a prediction about reputational losses.

Under this approach, failure of a member of the NSG, for example, to honor an informal commitment not to supply a potential proliferator with nuclear technology or equipment might harm the supplier's reputation every bit as much as a technical breach of an IAEA safeguards agreement—and thus count as an NPT "breach." Further, a knowing and concealed breach of an informal, "non-legal" obligation may harm a state's reputation for cooperation more than a public but merely technical breach of a formal, "legal" obligation expressed in a treaty—so that the former constituted a "breach, but the latter might not. And a perfectly "lawful" withdrawal from the NPT (perhaps as in the case of North Korea's withdrawal) might harm a state's reputation for cooperation even more than breach of a "non-legally-binding" commitment or a "legally-binding" commitment. Thus, under a rational choice theory of international law, deviation from any of the recognized modes of cooperation would have the same deleterious effects on a state's reputation—and could therefore be treated as a violation of international law.

A "rational choice" theory of international law along these lines would arguably have to repudiate the traditional requirement of "state practice" as a condition for the emergence of a

66 The significance of "reputation" is central to the rational choice account of international law. *See* Guzman, *supra* note 1.

67 *See* Oliver Wendell Holmes, Jr., *The Path of the Law*, 10 Harv. L. Rev. 457 (1897).

rule of customary international law—a topic we discussed in Chapter 1.B *supra*. The reputational effects of not complying with a norm follow when the non-complying party is acting in a way that is not accepted by the other members of the international community, and acceptance of a norm may be established without state conduct in accordance with the norm; rather, acceptance may occur or be expressed through public statements alone. Thus, a rational choice theory of international law grounded on reputational effects might reduce customary law to *opinio juris* alone, as manifested in such non-treaty statements as U.N. General Assembly Resolutions, which are technically merely "recommendations" to states. Possible examples of this so-called "instant custom" are the U.N. Universal Declaration on Human Rights,[68] the so-called Friendly Relations Declaration,[69] and more recently, the claim by some states, mainly those that do not themselves engage in substantial military operations, that "unprivileged combatants" are entitled to Prisoner-of-War status and treatment, notwithstanding the substantial state practice to the contrary by states that do engage in military operations.[70] Of course, when public statements alone can serve as law, it leaves the discipline of international law open to the criticism that most of what passes today for international law is not truly law but merely international politics or rhetoric by another name. Interestingly enough, this criticism is most closely associated with writers who *espouse* a rational choice approach to international law.[71]

c. The North Korean Withdrawal Crisis

One view of the North Korean (DPRK) withdrawal crisis is that it is entirely explicable in terms of rational choice theory and an international law theory grounded on it. The central premise of this account is that the DPRK was not subject to international law in any significant way *because it had no reputation for compliance to protect through continued cooperation.* The very isolation of the North Korean regime—both from its nominal allies (Russia and China) as well as from its likely adversaries (South Korea, Japan, and the United States)—reduced its incentives to cooperate over time. In short, North Korea may have rationally judged that no level of cooperation could achieve a significant change in its perceived reputation, thus causing it to cooperate or defect based solely on the short-term payoff structure of a non-iterated PD game.

A second reason for which North Korea's defection may have been predicted may have been that the iterated game of nuclear nonproliferation under the NPT required reliance on a set of institutions, such as the IAEA and NSG, in which North Korea placed little confidence. The DPRK was not involved in the creation of these institutions; rather, as a late entrant in

68 U.N. GAOR, 3d Sess., 183d plen. mtg., U.N. Doc. A/RES/3/217/A (Dec. 10, 1948).

69 U.N. GAOR, 25th Sess., Supp. No. 28, at 121, U.N. Doc. A/8028 (Oct. 24, 1970).

70 *See infra* Part III, Chapter 1.

71 *Cf.* Eric Posner, The Perils of Global Legalism (2009); and Jack L. Goldsmith and Eric A. Posner, The Limits of International Law (2005).

the nuclear non-proliferation game, it might reasonably have viewed these entities as skewed toward South Korea and Japan, together with its allies in the West. (By parity of reasoning, China's late entrance into the NPT, coupled with China's potential adversary relationship with North Korea, may have reduced China's own capacity to reassure the DPRK as to the IAEA's reliability.) Thus, North Korea might have seen the IAEA as a potential means of intelligence collection on matters unrelated to the IAEA's narrow verification functions, thereby reducing the degree to which North Korea would cooperate towards the IAEA in a way that would provide other states assurance as to its peaceful intentions and facilitate the IAEA's verification activities.

Finally, it may be that North Korea's behavior was plainly rational in the sense that the nuclear nonproliferation game, for North Korea, is not a game in which gains from nonproliferation can be achieved by both sides, but is rather a true zero-sum game in which the very fate of the DPRK is at issue. Under this view, facing an existential threat emanating from an alliance between its near neighbors, Japan and South Korea, and the United States, North Korea rightly viewed its task as dividing the United States from its allies; it thus insisted on a separate dialogue that would undermine South Korean and Japanese confidence in the United States. Additionally, under this view, the rational North Korean strategy was to use the nuclear dialogue with the United States and its allies as a vehicle for a much broader political dialogue on the terms for the continued survival of the DPRK. North Korea's payoffs or goals were to extract benefits that would materially support the regime internally and increase its status and legitimacy both internally and externally in other venues.[72] Viewed from this perspective, the West cooperated while the DPRK defected; the West then received the Sucker's Payoff—in the form of a new commitment to provide North Korea with a new fuel cycle based on light-water, proliferation-resistant nuclear reactors, equal to the level of technology available in South Korea and mediated by public/private consortium in which North Korea would be treated as an equal; substantial, free oil supplies, reducing the risk of economic collapse in North Korea; and an enhanced, direct dialogue with the world's remaining superpower, the United States. In return, the DPRK agreed to inspections under IAEA auspices that were less intrusive than the inspection rights to which the IAEA was entitled under the applicable Safeguards Agreement, IAEA Statute, and NPT.

In this non-iterative game, the United States, South Korea, and Japan may have feared irrational behavior by the DPRK—the possibility that the regime would use nuclear weapons in a final, desperate act of self-immolation; or regime collapse that would impose the burden of reconstruction mainly on South Korea but, to a lesser degree, on Japan and the United States. This fear perhaps induced them to accept the Sucker's Payoff when rational choice theory itself

72 On possible motives for North Korea's nuclear program, *see* Jonathan D. Pollack, *North Korea's Nuclear Weapons Program to 2015: Three Scenarios, in* Combating Weapons of Mass Destruction 263, 265–70 (Nathan E. Busch & Daniel H. Joyner eds., 2009).

might have predicted a strategy of noncooperation, leaving the DPRK to its own fate. Perhaps perversely, it is the risk that the DPRK would commit suicide—a risk not contemplated by the assumptions of rational choice theory's rational egoism—that may best explain the North Korean nuclear withdrawal crisis.[73]

7. Thesis 2—Does the North Korean Crisis Suggest that Rational Choice Theory Needs to be Revised or Supplemented in Order to Provide a Better Account of an International Legal Solution to the Perils of Anarchy?

We now ask whether international lawyers and the policy makers whom they advise can rely on rational choice theory alone in framing legal solutions for problems like that posed by the North Korean withdrawal crisis. The case study raises at least two important possibilities.

First, one might argue that rational choice does indeed explain the crisis satisfactorily and, even further, that it explains why states may be moving away from the IAEA-based regime to resolve the information problems associated with nuclear cooperation as well as by supplementing deterrence with more direct forms of coercion, albeit at higher cost.

Second, one might argue that rational choice theory as currently constituted does not fully explain the crisis. Rather, suggested by the Framework Accord, and the creation of the nuclear supply consortium KEDO to provide a public-private institutional vehicle for cooperation on the Korean Peninsula, liberal institutionalism's thicker characterization of the shape of international law and international society may supplement, complicate, and perhaps ultimately even replace a rational choice theory built on the "billiard ball" model of the state.

We now consider these possibilities in turn:

a. An Apologist Narrative: The Argument from the International Economics Branch of Rational Choice Theory

One hypothesis, fully within the terms of rational choice theory, is that existing international institutions, the IAEA and the Security Council, are not optimal in stemming nuclear proliferation, and others are needed to supplement or augment them. On this supposition, the Proliferation Security Initiative (PSI)—advanced by the United States for the interdiction

73 Not to be overlooked is the possibility that North Korea's leaders were also seeking to leverage their bargaining position with China. China's continued support is indispensable for the survival of the North Korean regime, yet it would be foolish for North Korea's leaders to assume that that support will always be available. Certainly contemporary China no longer has the ideological affinity with China that it once felt. A North Korean nuclear capability might serve to warn China that if it failed to ensure the survival of the North Korean government, China could be drawn down along with it. As a former Chinese student of one of us pointed out, Beijing is nearer to North Korean missile sites than Tokyo is.

of international maritime transfers of weapons of mass destruction, materials, and precursor agents—might provide an even more effective solution to the problem of proliferation.[74]

The increasing salience of the PSI and other such informal practices or institutions (such as so-called "coalitions of the willing") may serve to confirm a prediction made by the new "institutional economics" branch of rational choice theory.[75] That form of rational choice theory argues that the optimal international organization for the performance of the functions necessary to resolve the nuclear security dilemma may entail lesser levels of integration with less fixed investment in the creation of free-standing, autonomous institutions.[76] As a consequence, the cooperative action to produce the information needed to escape the security dilemma would be undertaken through entities that lacked formal independent status or legal personality, such as that held by the IAEA or even the United Nations.[77]

b. A Revisionist Narrative: The Argument from the Theory of Two-Level Games

The second hypothesis calls into question the premises of rational choice analysis (and, by extension, the usefulness of international institutions based on that theory). In effect, the Framework Accord contemplated a whole new era of nuclear cooperation between North and South Korean stakeholders in nuclear power development. The cooperative efforts needed to build a common nuclear fuel cycle on the Korean Peninsula might have led to deepening peninsular unification—first, economic and, ultimately, political. And it could have provided assurances to neighboring powers, such as Japan, China, Taiwan, and the United States, that a combined peninsular nuclear capability would not turn a unified Korea into a security threat for its neighbors, destabilizing Japan's, and perhaps also Taiwan's, status as an NNWS. Can rational choice theory explain why North Korea rejected such an enticing offer?

The answer may be yes, but only if rational choice theory is substantially modified. The problem here seems to be whether the "black box" model of international relations—which serves

---

74 For a close study of the PSI as an international practice or institution, and an analysis of its legal aspects, *see* James R. Holmes & Andrew C. Winner, *The Proliferation Security Initiative, in* Combating Weapons of Mass Destruction 139, 140–48 (Nathan E. Busch & Daniel H. Joyner eds., 2009). *See also* John C. Yoo & Glenn M. Sulmasy, *The Proliferation Security Initiative: A Model for International Cooperation,* 35 Hofstra L. Rev. 405 (2006).

75 *See* Oliver Williamson, *The New Institutional Economics: Taking Stock, Looking Ahead,* 38 J. of Econ. Literature 595 (Sept. 2000)

76 This might be analogized to a move from a joint venture to a long-term relational contract. In other words, the IAEA could be viewed as a sharing of sovereign authority, or ownership, in respect of the function of verification of non-proliferation, while the PSI could be viewed as a long-term contract between an among supplier states in which their good faith, albeit *ad hoc,* efforts to interdict proliferation-sensitive transfers of nuclear equipment, materials and technology require no further institutionalization or investment or precise terms for cooperation or burden-sharing. *See* Chapter 2.A, *supra* text accompanying notes 203-04 (discussing the transaction cost economics approach in relation to institutional design).

77 *See Advisory Opinion on Reparations For Injuries Suffered in the Service of the United Nations,* I.C.J Rep. 174 [1949] (establishing the legal capacity of the United Nations to bring claims based on injury suffered to its agents in violation of international law as if that international organization were a state),

as a starting-point for many accounts of rational choice theory (such as Andrew Guzman's) —is sufficient to explain the international behavior of states. The North Korean withdrawal crisis may suggest the black box needs to be opened and its contents examined.

Arguably, North Korea's withdrawal from the NPT and its nuclear bluster were not motivated by purposes a rational egoist state would have. As we have seen, it was precisely North Korea's reputation for *noncompliance* with international law that induced the United States and its allies to continue to negotiate with it, at each step in the process providing it with additional benefits. Why did North Korea then not accept the offer of the even greater benefits that would flow from peninsular unification? An answer might be found in a form of rational choice theory that is enriched by the logic of "two-level games." In such games, states' international behavior is considered to be the output, not only of its systemic interactions with other states, but also of the interactions of the state's domestic interest groups, factions and constituencies. Payoffs for cooperation and defection at one level of a game need to be balanced against payoffs for cooperation and defection at another level of the game.[78]

Such a two-level game analysis could allow the rational choice theorist to take account of the North Korean leadership's desire to survive and maintain itself in power, and in general to behave in a manner contrary to the interests of the North Korean state as such. (As we saw in discussing reason of state doctrine, what is rational for a state may not be rational for its rulers, and vice-versa.) On this account, the danger of regime collapse and correlative need for external conflict to sustain internal legitimacy may provide an (enriched) rational choice explanation for North Korea's behavior. But the rational choice theorist could only attempt this kind of explanation at the price of forgoing a measure of parsimony—it would be necessary to peer into the internal dynamics of the North Korean regime.

Two- (or multi-) level game theory may carry implications for international law. For example, one might treat the South Korean nuclear power industry as a "player" who interacts with the South Korean Government on the domestic (or second level) and thus constrains that government's interaction with North Korea. But the *South* Korean nuclear power industry through its role in KEDO may also "play" a game with *North* Korea that further constrains the interaction between the South and North Korean Governments. To the extent that this three-player game includes not only two states but also a third, non-state actor interacting with both, it generates new subjects of international law. This revised version of rational choice theory could support neoliberalism's claim that non-state actors also have rights and duties under international law.[79]

78 Robert D. Putnam, *Diplomacy and Domestic Politics: The Logic of Two-Level Games*, 42 Int'l Org. 427 (1988).

79 *See supra* Chapter 2.A Parts 4 & 5.

Postscript and Bridge to Chapter 2.C: Back to a Thucydidean Future?

One might argue that rational choice's usual premises do not account for a large range of state behavior, so that rational choice theory needs to be augmented in certain ways (for example, by introducing second-level games). A more radical view might reject even more of the structural realist tradition and its rational choice successors, returning in the process to realism's classical roots.

As Richard Ned Lebow argued, the Greek philosophical tradition identified "four generic explanations for compliance: fear, interest, honor, and habit."[80] What behavioral economists call irrationalities that impede welfare-maximizing behavior by individuals or groups in collective action problems,[81] classical political realists called "universal drives (appetite and spirit), a powerful emotion (fear) and routine practices (habit)," although "[t]heir relative importance varies within and across societies and epochs."[82] For Lebow, one causal chain for a set of preferences yielding what rationalists would call "defection" relies primarily on "appetite" and "spirit." Thus:

> Spirit- and appetite-based societies are delicately balanced even when well-functioning. Both motives are advanced through competition, and spirit-driven competition for standing is particularly intense because of its relational nature. When not held in check by reason, competition for either honor and standing (spirit) and wealth (appetite) can transgress the accepted constraints and lead to a rapid unraveling of order. Imbalance in the direction of spirit can intensify intra-elite competition to the point where a critical mass of elite actors comes to fear that they will be denied standing or even forfeit their lives. This fear becomes paramount when one actor or faction (or state or alliance) appears to be on the verge of capturing the mechanisms of state (or abusing its power to establish unwanted authority over others) in pursuit of its parochial goals. In these circumstances, violence or welfare may break out, brought about through a bid for domination by one side or preemption by the other. Imbalance in the direction of appetite on the part of an elite is likely to lead to both emulation and resentment by other actors. It risks unraveling the social order through the widespread violation of *nomos* and increasing class tensions that ultimately lead to the same kind of fear and responses to it associated with an excess of spirit.[83]

Under Lebow's theory, we cycle back to Thucydides' account of the Peloponnesian War, or at least to the cultural assumptions that shaped Thucydides' narrative. Lebow accordingly describes Homer, with whom Thucydides is in dialogue, as "the first theorist of honor, and his

80 *See* Richard Ned Lebow, A Cultural Theory of International Relations 4 (2008).

81 *See supra* Chapter 2.A Part 5.

82 Lebow, *supra* note 80, at 5.

83 *Id.* at 27.

account in the *Iliad*" as "unrivaled in its understanding of this motive and its consequences, beneficial and destructive, for societies that make it a central value."[84]

Lebow's analysis suggests a return to a "thick" description of states' behavior that introduces first- and second-, as well as third-level, images. Moreover, it suggests that individuals and groups within a state, and perhaps the state itself, are *agents* in creating and changing a state's preferences and interests. Most importantly of all, it suggests that that competition over "*standing*" and "*honor*," no less than competition over security and power, may determine the international conduct of states. Constructivism, the topic of the next section, advances all three of these claims.

From this angle, one could view the problem of nuclear nonproliferation as an exercise in norm creation.[85] Are states that are motivated primarily by motives other than rational egoism "uncivilized"? Under such a view, the attempted de-legitimization of so-called "rogue" states seeking nuclear weapons parallels (and might be derived from) nineteenth-century international law's hierarchical distinction between "civilized" and "uncivilized" states, which limited "sovereign equality," excluded some states from international society, and served to justify outside intervention. We return, therefore, to a focus on regime type as the source of threats to international peace and security, a theme explored in Chapter 1.A, Thesis 2, in our analysis of the so-called "democratic peace" hypothesis.

In the next section, Chapter 2.C, we turn to a fuller discussion of constructivism as an alternative theoretical approach mediating between realism and legalism. Our case study in that section focuses on Iran's attempt to acquire what it claims are peaceful nuclear fuel cycle capabilities that it is permitted to create under the NPT. Iran's opponents, led by the United States, argue that it is a "rogue" or "pariah" state that should be condemned by the international community for breaching basic NPT norms. Part of Iran's counter-argument is that its leadership role as a "revolutionary Islamic" state would justify it in departing from those norms—though it also denies that it has done so. Even from this brief description, it should be apparent that states' images of themselves or of other states—the United States' self-image as the leader of the free world, its image of Iran as a "rogue" state, Iran's image of the United States as the "great Satan," and Iran's self-image as a "revolutionary" and "Islamic" state—could well structure the interactions between the two sides. And at the core of constructivism is the claim that such state identities decisively influence their relations with each other.

84 *Id.* at 5.

85 *See* Ethan Nadelmann, *Global Prohibition Regimes: The Evolution of Norms in International Society*, 44 Int'l Org. 479, 484–86 (1990) (laying out stages in evolution of international norms); *id.* at 493–97 (discussing rise of anti-slavery norm).

C. CONSTRUCTIVISM, OR WHEN WORLDS COLLIDE: THE IRANIAN NUCLEAR CRISIS—THE CONFLICT BETWEEN "CIVILIZED" AND "ROGUE" STATES

We turn now to constructivism, a theory of international law that is foreshadowed in Hedley Bull's foundational work, *The Anarchical Society*, on the idea of "international society,"[1] and in the work of Bull's colleagues and followers in the English School.[2] The constructivist trend in international relations theory comes to fruition in the seminal work of Alexander Wendt,[3] considered at length later in this section.

The section is divided into four main parts. The first part discusses constructivism in some depth, looking especially to its power to explain how states frame their political, legal, and ideological debates with each other, thereby explaining their conduct in international affairs. Here we begin by considering the historical and theoretical origins of constructivism. Next, we provide an overview or summary of its teachings. Then we consider constructivism's account of international society. We then outline the main differences between constructivism and realism. Finally, we discuss Alexander Wendt's constructivist theory of the inevitability of a world state.

In the second part of this section, as our case study, we provide an overview of the religious and ideological foundations of the Iranian government and an account of that nation's nuclear program.

In the third and fourth parts of this section, we provide documents presenting the views of leaders of the United States and Iran that frame the political and ideological context for the U.S.-Iran legal dispute. We then build on Chapter 2.B's discussion of the nuclear non-proliferation regime by presenting, through the relevant International Atomic Energy Agency (IAEA) and U.N. Security Council documents, the elements of the legal dispute concerning Iran's compliance with its NPT and IAEA obligations. Thereafter, in our two concluding theses, we examine the merits of constructivism as an approach to understanding the dispute over Iran's nuclear program.

We think it is illuminating to examine constructivism in the context of the Iranian nuclear program (and Western challenges to it) for the following reason.

Constructivism, as we have already said, regards states as thoroughly socialized actors whose identities, roles, and reputations are central to their conduct on the international stage. So it would accord with constructivism to try to understand the conflict between the United States and Iran in terms of the identities they ascribe to each other. Mirroring the categories of "classic" nineteenth century law, which distinguished between the supposedly "civilized" states that were recognized as full members of the "family" or "community" of nations and the supposedly "semi-civilized" or "barbaric" states or societies that were, at best, kept in the international

1 Hedley Bull, The Anarchical Society: A Study of Order in World Politics (1977).

2 As noted above, *see* text at Part I.3, the English School's approach has helped to form constructivism.

3 Alexander Wendt, Social Theory of International Politics (1999).

community's waiting room,[4] the United States and much of the international community seem prepared to regard Iran as (variously) a "rogue," "outlaw," or "pariah" state.[5]

Although it may at first seem implausible that those nineteenth century legal constructs are still with us (even in a modernized and deracialized form[6]), it takes no great ingenuity to see how the categories of "civilized," "semi-civilized," and "barbarous" societies could map on to the Cold War distinctions between "first," "second" and "third" or "underdeveloped" worlds. Likewise, the more current distinction between "democracies" and "autocracies"[7] surely echoes the distinction between the "civilized" and "semi-civilized" states.

The fact is that the contemporary international system uneasily combines a professed regard for the principle of sovereign equality,[8] and its corollary that the "essentially domestic" affairs of states are not matters of international concern, with a commitment to protect people from human rights violations at the hands of their own governments[9] and the corollary of *that* principle that international (usually, Western) intervention in the internal affairs of states may be

---

4 *See* Chapter 1.B.

5 At this stage, we will not pause to consider whether the category of "rogue" (etc.) states evidences an attempted revision of the *jus ad bellum, see infra* Part II, Chapters 1–4, or whether it is related to the concept of unlawful combatant in the *jus in bello, see infra* Part III, Chapters 1–4.

6 International law's "civilized/uncivilized" categorization was, at its inception, unembarrassedly Euro-centric and racial. Its deracialization began with the admission of non-Western states such as Ottoman Turkey and, later, Japan into international society. The war against Nazi Germany, which had inscribed racism into its essence, and which was also unquestionably "European," changed all that. The Nazis regarded other Europeans (among others, the Slavs) much as the European colonizers had regarded their colonial populations, sought to apply to them the methods that those colonizers had used in ruling over their subject peoples, and considered their program of territorial conquest as, in substance, one of raising the level of "civilization" in eastern and south-eastern Europe. *See* Mark Mazower, Hitler's Empire (2008). On the other side, the United States and its allies fought the war largely in the name of "civilization." The Allies' victory over Nazi Germany made it impossible for them thereafter to regard states as presumptively "civilized" merely because they were European or because their populations were predominantly white, or to regard non-white, non-European states as presumptively "uncivilized."

7 *See* Robert Kagan, The Return of History and the End of Dreams (2008).

8 *See* U.N. Charter, art. 2.

9 *See* World Summit Outcomes Resolution, UNGA Resolution 60/1 (A/RES/60/1) (September 16, 2005). The key statements of an international consensus are found in ¶¶ 138 and 139 of this General Assembly Resolution:

> Paragraph 138 states: "Each individual State has the responsibility to protect its populations from genocide, war crimes, ethnic cleansing and crimes against humanity. This responsibility entails the prevention of such crimes, including their incitement, through appropriate and necessary means. We accept that responsibility and will act in accordance with it. The international community should, as appropriate, encourage and help States to exercise this responsibility and support the United Nations in establishing an early warning capability."

Paragraph 139 states: "The international community, through the United Nations, also has the responsibility to use appropriate diplomatic, humanitarian and other peaceful means, in accordance with Chapters VI and VIII of the Charter, to help protect populations from genocide, war crimes, ethnic cleansing and crimes against humanity. In this context, we are prepared to take collective action, in a timely and decisive manner, through the Security Council, in accordance with the Charter, including Chapter VII, on a case-by-case basis and in cooperation with relevant regional organizations as appropriate, should peaceful means be inadequate and national authorities manifestly fail to protect their populations from genocide, war crimes, ethnic cleansing and crimes against humanity. We stress the need for the General Assembly to continue consideration of the responsibility to protect populations from genocide, war crimes, ethnic cleansing and crimes against humanity and its implications, bearing in mind the principles of the Charter and international law. We also intend to commit ourselves, as necessary and appropriate, to helping States build capacity to protect their populations from genocide, war crimes, ethnic cleansing and crimes against humanity and to assisting those which are under stress before crises and conflicts break out."

permissible, and perhaps even mandatory.[10] As one perceptive analyst of international law has observed, the current international legal system seems to be attempting to combine two governing, but perhaps inconsistent, norms: a norm of *toleration* and a norm of *civilization*.[11] The former principle derives from the standard that classic nineteenth century law prescribed for the interactions between European or other "civilized" states; the latter derives from the law's prescriptions for civilized states' dealings with their non-Western colonies, the "uncivilized" societies.

1. Constructivism

As noted, constructivism must be understood in light of the historical and political context in which it arose. Indeed, understanding its specific teachings, as well as its theory of international society, its relationship to realism and rational choice theory, and its implications for the future of international society, must begin with constructivism's place in the history of ideas.

a. The Sources of Constructivism

Why has constructivism taken hold as an influential school of international relations theory, rivaling and even threatening to displace all forms of realism? We think that constructivism can be seen as the outgrowth of two distinct but converging developments, one historical, the other theoretical.

Just as contemporary realism took shape under the pressure of major international events—the collapse of the Versailles Treaty regime and the destruction of the international institutions had it created, the rise of the Axis powers, the Second World War, and the ensuing Cold War—so, viewed *historically*, constructivism is a product of the post-Cold War international environment. It reflects the confluence of six major changes in the international system that took place at about that time: 1) the international human rights regime that grew out of Nuremberg and, later, the 1975 Helsinki Accords,[12] and the challenge to the traditional state-centered conception of international relations that the human rights movement posed;[13] 2) the increasing

10 *See Legality of the Use of Force Case (Provisional Measures (Yugoslavia v. Belgium),* ICJ 1999 (pleadings of Belgium, 10 May 1999, CR 99/15) (arguing that armed humanitarian intervention is compatible with article 2(4) of the UN Charter) (discussed in Simon Chesterman, Just War or Just Peace? 46 (2001)).

11 Edward Keene, Beyond the Anarchical Society: Grotius, Colonialism and World Politics 2–6 (2002).

12 Final Act of the Conference on Security and Cooperation in Europe, Aug. 1, 1975, 14 I.L.M. 1292 (1975) (the Helsinki Final Act).

13 As discussed in the Postscript to Chapter 1, the post-Nuremberg transformation of international law made the nature of the state and its conduct towards its citizens a matter of international concern. Part of that change involved the creation of new international human rights institutions, which in turn gave the international human rights movement a new dynamic. But this regime-building exercise in international human rights law and institutions gave rise to a new division among that states, distinguishing states that respected basic human rights from states that do not. This post-Nuremberg

visibility and importance of non-state actors in the international arena, including non-governmental organizations;[14] 3) the success of new forms of international governance, epitomized by the European Union, that had substantially abridged the traditional prerogatives of state sovereignty;[15] 4) the transformation in the posture of the Soviet bloc under Mikhail Gorbachev from one of hostility toward the West to one of a willingness to reduce its armaments even without reciprocation and otherwise to cooperate with the West (all actions seemingly hard for realists to explain); 5) the ensuing victory of the liberal, capitalist democracies over the Soviets, together with the spread of democracy to places where it had not flourished before, including much of Eastern Europe, the Iberian peninsula, and Latin America[16], and the apparent promise of a durably peaceful world order that the West's victory brought; and 6) the expansion of the North Atlantic Treaty Alliance into much of the former Soviet bloc and the apparently indisputable hegemony of the United States as the "sole remaining super-power" in a "unipolar" world.[17] To put the matter simply: if realism was suited to an international environment in which disorder and war seemed to be the normal condition, constructivism is better suited to an international environment in which order, peace, and progress seemed to be normal.[18]

Viewed as a matter of *theory*, constructivism grew out of widespread perceptions of the inadequacies of structural realism (and of the institutionalism that followed it). The criticisms were of three different kinds. The first kind of criticism came from within international relations theory itself because structural realism failed to theorize the actual workings of the international system correctly. The second kind of criticism came from historians, who found that state practice did not match structural realism's predictions. The third criticisms were normative, stating that despite adopting the pose of scientific neutrality, structural realism in fact concealed strong normative commitments, foreclosing ways of viewing international relations that might challenge hierarchy and domination. Let us approach each of these three lines of criticism in turn.

---

development accelerated with the end of the Cold War—the final settlement of the Second World War through German unification, the UN Security Council's Agenda for Peace, and the Charter of Paris.

14 *See supra* Chapter 2.B (discussing institutionalist rational choice theory).

15 *See* J.H.H. Weiler, *The Transformation of Europe,* 100 Yale L.J. 2403 (1991); and J.H.H. Weiler, The Constitution of Europe: 'Do the New Clothes Have an Emperor?' and Other Essays on European Integration (1999).

16 *See* Francis Fukuyama, The End of History and the Last Man (1992); *but see* Samuel P. Huntington, The Clash of Civilizations and the Remaking of World Order (1997).

17 *See* Charles Krauthammer, *The Unipolar Moment,* Foreign Affairs, Vol. 70, No. 1, America and the World 1990/91 23–33 (1990/1991); *but see* John J. Mearsheimer, *Back to the Future: Instability in Europe After the Cold War,* in The Perils of Anarchy: Contemporary Realism and International Security 78 (Michael E. Brown, Sean M. Lynn-Jones & Steven E. Miller eds., 1995) (predicting the return of multipolarity).

18 Wendt himself draws support for constructivism from the observations that in the post-Cold War world, "most states follow international law most of the time, . . . war and security dilemmas are the exception rather than the rule, Great Powers no longer tend to conquer smaller ones, and free trade is expanding rather than contracting." Alexander Wendt, *Constructing International Politics,* 20 Int'l Sec. 71, 76 (1995).

Richard Ashley's lengthy and important 1984 paper *The Poverty of Neorealism* exemplifies the first kind of criticism.[19] Ashley argued that structural realism harbored a deep, internal inconsistency: on the one hand, it regarded the structure of international politics as constituted entirely by states, leaving structure no independent explanatory value; on the other hand, as a form of structuralism, realism should suppose that structure constitutes states and, accordingly, has explanatory power. According to Ashley, structural realism regards states as the only actors in international affairs, leaving the structure of international politics to emerge entirely from the states' interactions. International relations flow from the distribution of power among states, their hierarchy, and their interests. But in that case, the structure of international politics cannot explain the conduct of states. It is merely "an emergent property produced by the joining of units having a prior existence."[20] On the other hand, to be considered a form of *structuralism*, the theory *should* ascribe a substantial explanatory role to the framework in which states act.[21] Ashley contends that states are constituted by such structures, rather than constituting them, and said "neorealism is statist before it is structuralist."[22] Thus, the post-Westphalian structure of "sovereignty" was the matrix of an international political order in which the actors were *states*;[23] the pre-Westphalian structure constituted a different international order consisting largely of *non-state* actors. Ashley's diagnosis of realism's error here parallels the more general criticism of the "contractarian tradition" (including Hobbes and Rousseau) advanced by the nineteenth century German philosopher G.W.F. Hegel, a powerful influence on constructivism. Hegel argued that far from it being true that the state can be reduced to the sum of associated individuals, "it is only as a member [of a state] that the individual gains concrete objectivity, genuine individuality, and ethical life."[24]

Ashley also strenuously attacked structural realism for its "individualist and rationalist premises," which he argued it shares with what he called "utilitarianism."[25] Ashley explained that

> [u]tilitarian theories of *action* hold that actors behave rationally, in the narrow instrumentalist sense. Actors strive to serve their intrinsic . . . desires or ends in the most efficient means

19 Richard K. Ashley, *The Poverty of Neorealism,* 38 Int'l Org. 225 (1984).

20 *Id.* at 240.

21 *See id.* at 254–56.

22 *Id.* at 241.

23 To grasp what Ashley seems to mean here, consider that without the institution of slavery, there would be no slaves. In that sense, the practice or institution of slavery precedes or "constitutes" the units within it. Sovereignty is a kind of practice or institution that creates states, if to be a "state" is to have certain roles in relation to other states, to enjoy certain rights with respect to them (*e.g.*, diplomatic immunity or a right against external intervention) and to be bound by certain duties towards them (*e.g.*, reciprocation).

24 Fred Dallmayr, *The Discourse of Modernity: Hegel and Habermas,* 84 J. Phil. 682, 691–92 (1987). *See also* Richard B. Pippin, *What is the Question for Which Hegel's Theory of Recognition is the Answer?*, 8 Eur. J. Phil. 155, 162–63 167 (2000).

25 Ashley, *supra* note 19, at 243.

possible. Social *interaction* is . . . instrumental coactions or exchange among individual actors, each party regarded as an external object or instrument in the eyes of the rationally acting other. Utilitarian theories also hold that, at base, *social order* . . . derives entirely from equilibria . . . in the instrumental relations and mutual expectations among rational egoistic individuals.[26]

Because structural realism "approaches the international system from a utilitarian point of view" (though substituting states for individuals),[27] it cannot satisfactorily explain the concept of "social power behind or constitutive of states and their interests,"[28] nor give an account of the "rules, norms, mutual expectations, or principles of practice prior to or independent of [states], their essential ends, and their capabilities."[29]

If Ashley's early paper was an influential statement of objections to structural realism by international relations theorists, a 1994 paper by Paul Schroeder, *Historical Reality vs. Neo-realist Theory,*[30] marshaled many of the objections raised by the historical profession. Schroeder tested Waltz's theory of how the international system worked against the record of European state practices in the Westphalian era from 1648 to 1945, and concluded that Waltz's predictions as to how states would behave in anarchy were largely unfounded. For instance, Schroeder determined that states did not generally resort either to self-help or to counter-hegemonic balancing when faced with security threats. Perhaps even more helpful to constructivists, Schroeder concluded that throughout the Westphalian period, both great and small states sought survival (among other ways) through "specializing" in "certain important international functions or fill[ing] particular vital roles within the system that no other unit could do or do as well."[31] Specialization led individual states to expect other powers to recognize their functions, to support these other states in the performance of these functions, and even to accept the other states' primacy in some areas on functional grounds.

Even structural realists and those sympathetic to them acknowledged explanatory deficits in the theory.[32] Steven Walt, for instance, argued that Waltz was mistaken in supposing that states allied to balance against *power*; instead, Walt argued that states allied to balance against *threats.*[33] Britain, France, and Germany did not balance against the United States after the Second

26 *Id.*

27 *Id.* at 244.

28 *Id.* at 244.

29 *Id.* at 245.

30 Paul Schroeder, *Historical Reality vs. Neo-realist Theory,* 19 Int'l Sec. 108, 115–20 (1994). Waltz responded to Schroeder's findings in Kenneth N. Waltz, *Evaluating Theories,* 91 Am. Pol. Sci. Rev. 913 (1997).

31 Schroeder, *supra* note 30, at 125.

32 *See, e.g.,* Robert O. Keohane, *International Institutions: Two Approaches,* 32 Int'l Stud. Q. 379, 388 (1988) (pointing out that formal game-theoretic models needed to be situated in institutional contexts in order to explain state interactions, and that realism's assumption of "unitariness" of state required modification in light of the problem of agency costs).

33 *See* Steven M. Walt, The Origins of Alliances 5 (1987).

World War, although it was the greatest single *power.* Instead, they joined the United States in balancing against the Soviet Union, which they saw as the greatest *threat.* But what is a "threat"? Understanding the Soviet Union and not the United States as a "threat" seemed to depend on the European states' understanding of their own identities and interests and of the Soviets' intentions with regard to them. But "a theory of threat perception" is "precisely what a constructivist account of identity offers."[34]

Finally, critics of structural realism advanced *normative* objections to it. Ashley was one of the most vehement of these critics, arguing that structural realism was less a science than an ideology, carrying a concealed totalitarian impulse within itself. As Ashley said, it

> treats the given order as the natural order, limits rather than expands political discourse, negates or trivializes the significance of variety across time and place, subordinates all practice to an interest in control, bows to the ideal of a social power beyond responsibility, and thereby deprives political interaction of those practical capabilities which make social learning and creative change possible. What emerges is an ideology that anticipates, legitimizes, and orients a totalitarian project of global proportions: the rationalization of global politics.[35]

It was an impressive catalogue of vices.

History and theory thus set the stage for the emergence of constructivism in the late 1980s as a force in international relations theory. But what, exactly, is constructivism? We take that question up next, focusing on the work of perhaps the most notable constructivist, Alexander Wendt.

b. The Teachings of Constructivism

At the core of constructivism, as Wendt explained in 1992, are the teachings that 1) "the fundamental structures of international politics are social rather than strictly material" and 2) that "these structures shape actors' identities and interests, rather than just their behavior."[36] Wendt did *not* deny that the third-image "structures" of international society explain the behavior of states, and to that extent he agreed with the realists. But unlike them, he maintained that the structures are socially "constructed." He offered a structuralism that is "sociological rather than micro-economic."[37]

For Wendt, the structures of the international order "are defined, in part, by shared understandings, expectations, or knowledge . . . A *security dilemma,* for example, is a social structure composed of intersubjective understandings in which states are so distrustful that they make

34 Ted Hopf, *The Promise of Constructivism in International Relations Theory,* 23 Int'l Sec. 171, 187 (1998).

35 Ashley, *supra* note 19, at 228.

36 Wendt, *supra* note 18, at 71–72.

37 *Id.* at 73.

worst-case assumptions about each others' intentions, and as a result define their interests in self-help terms."[38] The security dilemma is not, therefore, a condition imposed on states because of the brute fact of anarchy; rather, it results from state *agency*—from what states *make* of anarchy. States could transform anarchy into a *security community* marked by trust and cooperation instead of a security dilemma marked by mistrust and competition.[39] "Ideas," in short, determine "interests" or "preferences," rather than being determined by them.

Consider an example that Wendt offered to illustrate the importance of "ideas" or "meanings" in defining and structuring interstate relations. Wendt wrote that "500 British nuclear weapons are less threatening to the United States than 5 North Korean nuclear weapons."[40] Why is this? The obvious answer is that the United States perceives Britain as a friend and ally and North Korea as a foe. The example provides Wendt with an opportunity to explain that material resources such as a nuclear arsenal "only acquire meaning for [state] action through a structure of shared knowledge in which they are embedded. . . . Material capabilities as such explain nothing; their effects presuppose structures of shared knowledge, which vary and which are not reducible to capabilities."[41]

Wendt's opposition to materialism does not mean that he denied the importance of "material" factors or "hard" power.[42] Seeking to distinguish his views from neoliberalism, Wendt explained that his claim "is not that ideas are more important than power and interest, or that they are autonomous from power and interest. Power and interest are just as important and determining as before. The claim is rather that power and interest have the effects they do in virtue of the ideas that make them up."[43]

In addition to arising from shared meanings and including material resources, the structures of international society, for Wendt, are capable —through state agency—of being altered, perhaps radically. He noted that "[t]he Cold War was a structure of shared knowledge that governed great power relations for over forty years, but once they stopped acting on this basis,

---

38 *Id.*

39 The concept of a "security community" was developed by the political scientist Karl W. Deutsch. *See, e.g.*, Karl W. Deutsch et al., Political Community and the North Atlantic Area: International Organization in the Light of Historical Experience (1957). According to Deutsch, "[a] security community is a group of people which has become integrated. Integration is defined as the attainment of a sense of community and of institutions and practices strong enough and widespread enough to ensure for a 'long' time, dependable expectations of 'peaceful change' among its population." *Id.* at 5. "Security communities" include a variety of types. In the international area, "security communities" in which member states retain their sovereignty include such "zones of peace" as the European Union or the U.S.-Canada dyad. The concept of a security community has proven to be of considerable interest to constructivist scholars. For a review of Deutsch's (and later) work on the topic and the relation of Deutsch's thinking to Waltz's realism, *see* Wolf-Dieter Eberwein, *The Future of International Warfare: Toward a Global Security Community?*, 16 Int'l Poli. Sci. Rev. 341, 346–48 (1995).

40 Wendt, *supra* note 18, at 73.

41 *Id.*

42 *See* Joseph S. Nye, Jr., Soft Power: The Means to Success in World Politics (2005).

43 Wendt, *supra* note 3, at 135.

it was 'over.'"[44] In emphasizing the malleability of state interests and the structures they form, Wendt wrote:

> [T]o the extent that interests are constructed by beliefs we can have more hope of changing them than we could if they simply reflected human nature (short of genetic engineering). It may be difficult for an actor to change its interests if the beliefs that constitute it are part of a culture that simultaneously constitutes the interest of other actors. This helps explain why culture tend to reproduce themselves once created. But the fact remains that if interests are made of ideas, the discursive processes of deliberation, learning, and negotiation are potential vehicles of foreign policy and even structural change that would be neglected by a materialist approach.[45]

Realists assume (uncritically, as constructivists see it) that an anarchic international environment will necessarily be one in which states are antagonistic. Constructivists deny that either hostility or rivalry is a necessary outcome of international anarchy any more than friendship and cooperation are. What becomes of anarchy is what the agency of states, guided by the meanings they attribute to their relations with other states, makes of it. Thus, Wendt invited his readers to consider how states would respond if they discovered that an extra-terrestrial power was seeking to communicate and interact with them (a modernized, science fiction version of the Hobbesian "state of nature"). Wendt argued that states would not necessarily regard the alien forces as threatening or hostile. Instead, they would try to interpret its efforts at communication to see what sense should be made of them: were the aliens trying to signal an interest in peaceable relations, trade, and the pursuit of common objectives, or were they signaling a desire for exploitation and conquest?[46] There is nothing inevitable about regarding the aliens as "foes" rather than "friends" or "neutrals."

Even at the level of individuals rather than states, constructivists argue, extreme conditions that approximate to anarchy do not necessarily tend to result in competition and violence. Consider a case in which an ocean liner has begun to sink. Who will occupy the lifeboats? Is there necessarily a struggle for survival of all against all? Or do women and children go first, and the crew last? Do the young and strong seat themselves, or do they help the elderly and infirm? "Determining the outcome will require knowing more about the situation than about the distribution of material power or the structure of authority. One will need to know about the culture, norms, institutions, procedures, rules, and social practices that constitute the actors and the structure alike."[47] In short, even in an extreme situation in which real life approximates the state of nature, anarchy is what social construction makes of it.

44 Wendt, *supra* note 18, at 74.

45 Wendt, *supra* note 3, at 135.

46 *Id.*

47 Ted Hopf, *supra* note 34, at 173.

At a minimum, Wendt's work has called attention to aspects of international society that other international relations theories have ignored or left unexplained. Just as realism found intuitive support in the observable phenomena of state interaction—their mistrust of each other, the persistent "collective action" problems they find in trying to cooperate, their frequent rivalry or aggression—so too does constructivism. Cooperation no less than conflict is easily observed in international relations. The pursuit of common ideals is as marked a feature as the competitive quest for more powerful weapons or for greater natural resources. Changes in consciousness influence state conduct just as changes in material power do. Even in wartime, belligerent states comply with common rules, follow common customs, and honor common norms.[48] The history of international relations demonstrates that states can and do subordinate their self-interest to an overriding concern for the welfare of a broader community of states. The nineteenth-century Concert of Europe, discussed in Chapter 2.A, is arguably a case in point. History also appears to show that the role or function of a state within the international system, or the identity that is ascribed to it, can explain its international behavior no less than (or even more than) its power position alone.[49] Likewise, history demonstrates that the dominant self-images of states can undergo fundamental change, and that this transformation can have vast consequences for their behavior on the international stage. Germany's post-War transformation from an aggressive dictatorship to the peaceable *Rechtsstaat* it is today illustrates the point.[50] States do care (though how much may be disputed) about the well-being of the international communities and organizations to which they belong, about their reputation among other states, about the legitimacy and law-abidingness of their interactions with other states, and about the image they project to the international community, including not only to other states but also to their own and other states' people.[51] Norms are not invariably "epiphenomenal" in accounting for the behavior of states.[52]

48 *See* Martha Finnemore, National Interests in International Society 69 (1996).

49 For cases including the Habsburg monarchy, *see* Schroeder, *supra* note 30, at 127–29.

50 On the other hand, the possibility that states will radically reorient their foreign policies gives realism an opening for criticizing constructivism. As our discussion of the security dilemma showed, *see* Chapter 2.A, Part 3.c, states will fear other states—even *status quo* powers—because of their uncertainty regarding those other states' motives, intentions and capabilities. Thus, realists argue, even in a world of wholly unaggressive, non-revisionist powers, there will be a built-in tendency to war. A large part of the uncertainty in the security dilemma concerns other states *future* motives and intentions: if state A fails to forecast the rise of aggressiveness on the part of state B, state A may lose the lead-time it needs to maintain its relative power as to B. But on constructivist principles, because a state can fundamentally reorient its foreign policy, it can become *more* instead of *less* aggressive; and other states ignore that possibility at their peril. Thus, even though Germany pursued mildly revisionist policies under the Weimar government of the 1920s, it became dramatically more aggressive and threatening after the Nazis came to power. Ironically, then, the "mutability of human ideational structures at the domestic level"—which constructivism emphasizes—"reinforces [other states'] great uncertainty about future intentions at the interstate level." Dale C. Copeland, *The Constructivist Challenge to Structural Realism: A Review Essay*, 25 Int'l Sec. 187, 212 (2000).

51 For an extended argument for states' concern with "legitimacy," *see* Ian Hurd, After Anarchy: Legitimacy and Power in the United Nations (2007).

52 *See, e.g.*, Hendrik Spruyt, *The End of Empire and the Extension of the Westphalian System: The Normative Basis of the Modern State Order*, 2 Int'l Stud. Rev. 65, 81 (2000) (analyzing influence of Western ideals and norms, especially among

This is not to say that the "constructed" identities of states must, in the near-term at least, always lead in the direction of greater international peace and cooperation. Some historical cases suggest the opposite. For example, one scholar has argued that as European practices and public law entered more deeply into the consciousness of nineteenth-century Japan, Japan's traditional view of its relation to China—that of a "younger brother" to an "older brother" in the "family" of East Asian states—began to change, so that Japan increasingly began to view China through a European prism, that is, as a "semi-civilized" state that was ripe for colonization and exploitation.[53] Another scholar argued that in the course of its nineteenth century encounters with the West and Japan, classical China's conception of world order was transformed from one that was "based more on culture than on politics" and that had rested "legitimacy . . . more on proclaimed moral virtue than compelling military power" to one that posited a "Hobbesian world of structural anarchy . . . buttressed by might rather than right. The traditional view of China as the center of a global Confucian order became obsolescent, and was replaced by a gradual but inexorable turn to the ideas of classical realism."[54] Still, for constructivists, it is important to recognize both that the meaning these two Asian states found in their relationship to each other governed their military and political policies, and that their self-understandings underwent significant change because of their interactions with and learning from other, European states.

c. Constructivism and the Society of States

Recall the view of Hedley Bull and the English School that states form an international society, not merely an aggregate. Recall too Richard Ashley's claim that structural realism was "statist before it is structuralist." Constructivism adopts both these positions: states form a society, and that society creates a structure from which states emerge.[55]

What does it mean to say that states both form a society and emerge from it? Part of what it means is that states are not, and never have been, in a state of nature. They have always belonged to a socialized world.[56] Further, the world in which they act is not anarchic, if that means an environment utterly without norms, rules, conventions, and laws. Like anything that

local elites in colonial societies, in bringing about decolonization).

53 *See* Shogo Suzuki, *China's Perceptions of International Society in the Nineteenth Century: Learning More About Power Politics?*, 28 Asian Perspective 115 (2004).

54 Steve Chan, *Chinese Perspectives on World Order, in International Order and the Future of World Politics* 197, 199–201 (T.V. Paul & John A. Hall eds., 1999).

55 Constructivism also owes a major debt to Hegel in these respects: Hegel taught that states were *constituted* by their relations to other states, and more specifically by their *recognition* by other states—including recognition through war. *See* Hans-Martin Jaeger, *Hegel's Reluctant Realism and the Transnationalization of Civil Society*, 28 Rev. Int'l Stud. 497, 500–01, 507–09 (2002).

56 Wendt was careful to insist, however, that states have an identity that is not dependent on their interactions with other states, and indeed that they have certain essential needs, including security. *See* Copeland, *supra* note 50, at 192 (2000).

can reasonably be called a society, the society of states has certain ground-rules that apply to all who claim membership within it. As Bull argued, "[o]rder in the great society of all mankind has been attained . . . through general acceptance of the principle that men and territory are divided into states, each with its own proper sphere of authority, but linked together by a common set of rules."[57] Bull's position obviously entails the denial of the Hobbesian (and realist) claim that "international politics is an arena in which there are no rules restricting states in their relations with one another."[58]

To be a "state," accordingly, is not merely to be able to exercise power over a certain population within a certain territory; it is to claim *legitimacy* or *right* when doing so. Moreover, to be a "state" is to claim and to concede certain rights and obligations in relation to other states. In the case of international society in the nineteenth century, these ground-rules were largely matters of reciprocity: as sovereigns, states claimed and conceded jurisdiction over particular populations and territories, insisted on formal equality in their dealings with other states, accorded and expected certain immunities from each others' jurisdictions, held themselves and other states to the enforcement of any treaties they had made, and reserved to themselves the right to enforce their rightful claims against each other, by violence if necessary. In the twenty-first century, these ground-rules probably also include respect for certain basic human rights (although that norm, unlike the nineteenth century ones, is not a matter of reciprocity). These ground-rules *constitute* the international society of states and must be accepted by any entity that claims membership in it. They are also the basic framework of international law.

In addition to these constitutive rules, international society creates what have been called regulative rules.[59] Most of the substance of international law consists of regulative rules. Take, for example, the rule that the territorial sea of a coastal state extends three miles (now, generally, twelve miles) out from its shore. That is a regulative rule of international law, reflecting a reasonable accommodation of the interests of coastal states, chiefly in protecting the security of their land from invasion or incursion, and the interests of seafaring states in having the greatest expanse possible open to their maritime traffic.

Constructivism follows Bull and the English School in emphasizing that international society is rule- and norm-governed, that states may appeal to common rules and norms in their relations with other states, and that those appeals will be likely to affect the actions both of the states to whom they are directed and of other members of the international community. Constructivism also follows the English School in recognizing that international society evinces a strong tendency toward cooperation between states, and that the patterns of interaction between states tend to stabilize and even become normative over time.

57 Keene, *supra* note 11, at 134–35.

58 *Id.* at 135.

59 For the distinction between constitutive and regulative rules, *see* John Gerard Ruggie, *What Makes the World Hang Together? Neo-Utilitarianism and the Social Constructivist Challenge,* 52 Int'l Org. 855, 871 (1998).

Realists will insist that achieving security against perceived threats remains a vital, even overriding, concern of states. But even here, constructivism claims to yield insights that are less readily grasped from a realist perspective. In a severe contest over security, states will be deeply concerned with the international community's perceptions of themselves and their adversaries. Bringing an adversary into general disrepute, causing it shame, discrediting it in the minds of its own people, or isolating it from other states are all weapons of strategic value to states in their contests with each other. In their concentration on the material bases of state power, realists have tended to discount these "ideational" factors. Moreover, constructivists have shed light on how "weak" states can use these ideational weapons against the "strong" (just as, of course, the "strong" can turn them against the "weak," or each other). Although South Africa under the apartheid regime had powerful friends and backers in the Western community of states, it was gravely weakened by the campaign of third world states in the U.N. General Assembly to have it characterized and demeaned as a "pariah" state.

Language, discourse, and narrative are among the great instruments of international power politics. The power to name is of inestimable strategic value. For instance, that is why so much hinges, simply in terms of power politics, on whether the United States succeeds in branding Iran as a "rogue" state and in persuading the Security Council that Iran must be sanctioned for breaching its legal obligations under the NPT.[60] In emphasizing the importance of shame, honor, and standing in international politics, constructivism makes contact with rational choice theory's account of reputation on the one hand, and with Thucydides' notions of fame on the other.

How does constructivism differ from realism? We can identify at least five major differences:

i. Rational Egoism

Wendt argued that "[r]ealists of all stripes believe that states do what they do because it is in their national interest, and that the national interest is self-regarding with respect to security."[61] Wendt noted that this "rationalist model of man" has "received its most systematic use in economics . . . and is now seen as the core of the 'economic' approach to human behavior, from where it has been colonizing other social sciences."[62] In his view, realism insists that states see each other as existential enemies. Wendt replied that interests "should not be seen as an exclusively 'realist' variable."[63] It follows that that international anarchy implies a security dilemma only under rational egoist premises.

Wendt described three distinct "cultures of anarchy"—Hobbesian, Lockean, and Kantian. (These are offered as ideal types rather than as faithful accounts of the thought of these

60 *See* infra text accompanying note 199.

61 Wendt, *supra* note 3, at 113.

62 *Id.* at 116–17 (citation omitted).

63 *Id.* at 114.

theorists.[64]) Rational choice theory also distinguished between different views of international society, but in terms of payoff structures given by a specific set of capabilities. For example, game theory distinguishes between a Hobbesian Prisoner's Dilemma and a Rousseauean Stag Hunt, in which different incentive structures from different payoffs for cooperation or defection yield different dominant strategies.[65] Wendt's non-materialist account emphasized the sociological and relational aspects of these competing visions.

Thus, the Hobbesian culture is characterized as a state of "enmity," in which "[e]nemies are constituted by representations of the Other as an actor who (1) does not recognize the right of the Self to exist as an autonomous being, and therefore (2) will not willingly limit its violence toward the Self."[66] It is a culture in which enemies treat each other as objects, rather than subjects with entitlements. This "objectification" of other states was, for Wendt, the central, but unjustified, premise of realism in general and rational choice theory in particular.

Lockean culture, by contrast, is characterized by "rivalry." Wendt contrasted it with Hobbesian culture in the following terms:

> unlike enemies, rivals expect each other to act as if they recognize their sovereignty, their 'life and liberty', as a *right*, and therefore not to try to conquer or dominate them. Since state sovereignty is territorial, in turn, this implies recognition of a right to some 'property' as well. Unlike friends, however, the recognition among rivals does not extend to the right to be free from violence in disputes.[67]

Thus, in this culture, territorial sovereignty serves as a kind of buffer state between the culture of enmity and the culture of friendship, leading to an intermediate state of rivalry.

Finally, the Kantian culture of anarchy is "based on the role structure of friendship."[68] While Wendt conceded that the literature and empirical basis for this culture is thin, he defined it as "a role structure in within which states expect each other to observe two simples rules: (1) disputes will be settled without war or the threat of war (the rule of nonviolence) and (2) they will fight as a team if the security of any one is threatened by a third party (the rule of mutual aid)."[69] In his more recent work, Wendt elaborated on his view of Kantian anarchy, drawing on what he called "thin recognition," in which one is "seen by others as a legitimate locus of needs

64 *Id.* at 246–312.

65 *See supra* Chapter 2.A.

66 Wendt, *supra* note 3, at 260.

67 *Id.* at 279.

68 *Id.* at 298.

69 *Id.* at 298–99.

and agency—as a 'subject' rather than an 'object.'"[70] Wendt coupled this with what he called "Hegel's teleological view that the end of the state is not just to protect its members' physical security, but to make their subjectivity possible, which cannot be realized until all are recognized as subjects."[71] Viewed this way, the Kantian culture of anarchy seems to be the negation of the Hobbesian model.

In each of these cultures, in Wendt's view, values are internalized by states (respectively, as narcissism, individualism, and solidarism),[72] thus giving rise to interests grounded on these shared beliefs. It is these beliefs, not a given distribution of capabilities, which in turn give rise to behaviors that culturally reinforce those values. Yet, as noted above, those values can change in response to human agency, thus permitting progressive moves from Hobbesian to Lockean to Kantian culture. To be sure, constructivism seems to permit regression as well as progress. A demilitarized Japan enjoying peaceful relations with its neighbors may internalize the role of an expansionist, power-seeking colonizer, and regional hegemon, modeling itself on the behavior of the great European powers. But in Wendt's later thought, constructivism rules out regression, except as a temporary and reversible phenomenon. The international order moves, however haltingly, from a Hobbesian culture to a Kantian one. (We shall shortly discuss this view.)

ii. Preferences

Realism—including rational choice theory—typically posits that states have a very limited number of goals. In the realist view, the contents of states' preferences are narrowly defined, and those preferences are necessarily weighted and ranked in a particular order.[73] Constructivism, as already noted, disputes both assumptions. First, it maintains that states seek a wide array of goals—fame, glory, good repute among other states, et cetera—in addition to the realist goals of security and material power. Second and no less important, constructivism affirms that the order in which these preferences are ranked and the weight that states give to them are highly variable. In other words, states that formerly sought material power with little regard for other goals may rank that goal below a reputation for being peaceable, or while still ranking it higher may give it much less weight.

---

70 Alexander Wendt, *Why a World State is Inevitable: Teleology and the Logic of Anarchy*, 9 *European Journal of International Relations* 491 (December 2003).

71 *See id.*

72 *Id.* at 266–78 (Hobbesian psychoanalytic infantile regression); *id.* at 285–98 (Lockean possessive individualism), and *id.* at 302–07 (Kantian solidarity).

73 *See* Robert O. Keohane, *International Institutions: Two Approaches*, 32 Int'l Stud. Q. 379, 381 (1988) (arguing that structural realist conception of rationality "generates hypothesis about actual human behavior only when it is combined with auxiliary assumptions about the structure of utility functions and the formation of expectations").

iii. Pluralism

Constructivism postulates a plurality of international actors as the unit level, unlike realism, which parsimoniously posits only states. Moreover, even where Wendt focused on a constructivist account of the "state system" alone, he also argued against the view that "world politics and the state system are equivalent, or even that states are more important than other international actors, whatever that might mean. Lots of things come under the heading of '[international relations].' The state system is just one."[74] Thus, theorists should look across states and outside of states; and they must also look inside the "black box" that realists make of the state in order to understand the state's international behavior.

iv. Endogeny vs. Exogeny

Structural realism seeks explanations for state action at Waltz's "third image" level—that is, in terms of the "anarchic" structure in which states find themselves. Wendt did not deny the existence of such a structure, nor its explanatory importance. As we have noted, however, he insisted that "structure" is itself thoroughly socialized—a construct made by states. Moreover, Wendt believed (in realism's terms) that "second images" are indispensable in the study of international relations: realism is too parsimonious. He distinguished between independent or "exogenous" elements (which are treated as "givens" or "constants" in a theory of international relations) and dependent or "endogenous" elements (which are explained and treated as variables) in a theory of international relations. Contrasting constructivism with realism, Wendt argued that, for the most part, "material" elements should not be treated as exogenous (as they are in realism), but rather should be "endogenized." Furthermore, endogenous, state-specific explanations are needed to supplement exogenous, structure-dependent explanations. What states do can only be explained by reference to what they take themselves to be and what they want to become.

v. Teleology and Agency

Realists typically assume that the division of the international systems into states is unalterable. Although realists can acknowledge the possibility of a world state that would put an end to anarchy, they doubt that such a possibility will be realized. The closest approximation to a true world state, in realist terms, was perhaps the U.S.-U.S.S.R. condominium or power duopoly that dominated global affairs during the Cold War. Not even post-Cold War globalization, Waltz argued, can disturb the primacy of the state in international affairs. The state is resilient because

74 Wendt, *supra* note 70, at 194.

it is still necessary.[75] And Mearsheimer has contended that in due course, the post-Cold War international environment will be marked by multi-polarity and the resumption of great power rivalry.[76]

In his later work, Wendt boldly challenged this realist assumption. If "anarchy is what states make of it," then human beings—through states—can change the international system for the better (or worse). If international structures are the products of human agency, it is at least conceivable that international anarchy might be ended through the institution of a world state. Wendt's argument ventures far beyond that conclusion, however, holding that a unitary world state is not merely conceivable, but inevitable. That startling thesis—which, if true, would spell the end of the Westphalian state and, with it, realism—deserves consideration under the general rubric of constructivism.

2. Wendt's Argument for the Inevitability of a World State

While much of Wendt's thesis appears to appropriate vocabulary having classical origins, such as teleology and honor, Wendt's thesis actually is grounded in a specific modern philosophical tradition, is based on a highly nuanced and modern conception of teleology that purports to reject classical premises, and is reliant on an equally modern conception of honor that also purports to deviate from classical premises. He synthesized these argument with his descriptive account of various cultures of anarchy to provide what he claimed to be a necessary historical progression through these various stages of anarchy on the road to a "world state." We take each element in turn and then close with some final thoughts on the meaning and limits of Wendt's project.

a. The German Philosophical Tradition

Wendt's view that a unitary world state is inevitable draws heavily on the ideas of two great German "idealist" philosophers—Immanuel Kant and G.W.F Hegel. This is so in at least four important ways. First, both Kant and Hegel believed in the possibility, indeed necessity, of teleogical explanations. Teleological explanations (roughly, explanations in terms either of end states or of purposes[77]) are to be contrasted with explanations in terms of mechanical or efficient causes, which are typical of physics and other natural sciences. Further, teleological explana-

75 *See* Kenneth N. Waltz, *Globalization and Governance,* 32 Pol. Sci. and Pol. 693 (1999). *See also* Stephen D. Krasner, *Abiding Sovereignty,* 22 Int'l Pol. Sci. Rev. 229, 241–48 (2001) (identifying reasons for "resilience" of sovereignty).

76 *See* Mearsheimer, *supra* note 17. *Contrast* John Gerard Ruggie, *Territoriality and Beyond: Problematizing Modernity in International Relations,* 47 Int'l Org. 139, 142–44 (1993).

77 Teleological explanations may refer either to end states or to purposes, both of which are embraced in the concept of "design." *See* Wendt, *supra* note 70, at 8. A teleological explanation of the growth and maturation of a puppy in terms

tions must be applied to the *totality* of natural phenomena.[78] Thus, Kant argued that the human intellect is irresistibly inclined to conceive of nature as an intelligible structure whose varied facets fit together to make it a unified and coordinated whole.[79] Kant maintained that there is an "interest of reason" in searching for such a systemic unity. In Kant's view:

> The speculative interest of reason makes it necessary to regard all order in the world as if had originated in the purpose of a supreme reason. Such a principle opens out to our reason, as applied to the field of experience, altogether new views as to how the things of the world may be connected according to teleological laws, and so enables it to arrive at their greatest systematic unity.[80]

Second, not only natural phenomena, but human history must also be seen as a totality tending towards a final goal.[81] Third, as a political matter, the end of human history is the formation of some kind of global federation or, conceivably, supra-national union.[82] Fourth, Wendt's account

---

of end states would point to its final form as an adult dog. A teleological explanation of a hammer would point to the human purposes it is intended to serve. The latter type of explanation is goal-seeking; the former is end-directed.

78 Wendt expressed no views relevant to this Kantian claim.

79 That is not to say that Kant taught that nature *is* purposively designed, still less that he would disparage the search for mechanical causality. Kant believed that we cannot know whether nature is purposive or not, and he emphasized the centrality of mechanical causality for a scientific understanding of the world. But Kant also "[saw] an inherent thought process built into the very modus operandi of the human mind" that leads us to teleological explanations, "because reason's inherent commitment to intelligibility enmeshes us in the idea of the world as a great purposive whole—unified into a grand system under the aegis of purposive principles." Nicholas Rescher, *Kant's Teleological Theology, in* Nicholas Rescher, Kant and the Reach of Reason: Studies in Kant's Theory of Rational Systematization 99, 104–05 (2000). *See also* Yirmiyahu Yovel, Kant and the Philosophy of History 160 (1980); and Michael C. Williams, *Reason and* Realpolitik: *Kant's "Critique of International Politics,"* 25 Can. J. Pol. Sci. 99, 114–17 (1992).

80 Burleigh Taylor Wilkins, *Teleology in Kant's Philosophy of History,* 5 Hist. & Theory 172, 179 (1966).

81 *See* Yovel, *supra* note 79, at 135–42; *see also* Sharon Anderson-Gold, *Kant's Ethical Anthropology and the Critical Foundations of the Philosophy of History,* 11 Hist. Phil. Q. 405, 409–10 (1994). Teleological explanations of discrete historical phenomena may be attractive and in some cases plausible. Thus, one might see the Napoleonic Wars, not as the outgrowth of a random lust for power, but as expressive of a widespread desire for a peaceful unified European order or federation that rejected the continuous power struggles of the *ancient regime*—an order that was approximated by the century of peace ushered in by the Concert of Europe system. *See* Wilkins, *supra* note 80, at 183. Kant's view goes beyond such discrete instances by positing a teleological explanation for *universal* history.

82 Here Wendt went beyond either Kant or Hegel. Although Kant did in places suggest that human history should end in a unitary world state, his more considered view appears to be that the best attainable outcome would be a world league or federation of republics. *See* R.J. Delahunty & John C. Yoo, *Kant, Habermas and Democratic Peace,* 10 Chi. J. Int'l L. 437, 443–45, 449–52 (2010). For an alternative interpretation weighting the "cosmopolitan" aspects of Kant's thought more heavily, *see* Andrew Hurrell, *Kant and the Kantian Paradigm in International Relations,* 16 Rev. Int'l Pol. 183 (1990). Wendt himself believed that Kant saw the culmination of world history as consisting of "a world of republican states" that "remain egoists who retain sovereignty." Wendt, *supra* note 70, at 3.

Hegel is usually considered to be a kind of realist who denies the possibility and desirability of a world state. *See, e.g.,* Charles Taylor, Hegel 447–49 (1977). However, some scholars note that although Hegel did not explicitly envisage that history would culminate in a world state, he allowed for the possibility of some higher form of sovereignty than the nation state. *See, e.g.,* Andrew Vincent, *The Hegelian State and International Politics,* 9 Rev. Int'l Stud. 191, 202 (1983) ("[I]f one looks carefully at the structure of Hegel's system, it is quite obvious that the state is transcended by the true Hegelian method. Hegel argues that the state, with regard to the development of Spirit, is still but a stage characterized by imperfection, finiteness, incompleteness and contingency."). Other scholars suggest that although Hegel denied that a world state would emerge, it is in fact the necessary

of the successive phases through which history works in order to attain a world state resembles Hegel's "dialectical" method as *he* traced out the course of world history.

Wendt identified different stages through which "cultures of anarchy" pass in the evolution of the world state. He treated each phase as, in effect, an attempted "solution" to the problem of international instability and violence—a solution that breaks down for internal reasons, causing it to be superseded by the next phase, which, by changing the "boundary conditions" of its predecessor, achieves a more satisfactory (but still unstable) outcome. His procedure resembles Hegelian dialectics, which "deal with the contradiction between certain historical forms and the basic purposes sought in them."[83] And just as Hegel saw world history as driven by the "cunning of reason," through which individuals, even while acting on their personal interests or passions, served as the "unconscious tools and organs" of the world spirit,[84] so too Wendt saw human action as unintentionally leading to a world state. Likewise, Wendt's reliance on man's disposition to violence and war resembles Kant's notion that the "cunning of nature" leads paradoxically to the realization of a rational political system.[85]

Wendt departed from both Kant and Hegel, however, by emphasizing the dramatic technological changes that have greatly increased the costs of war and the scale on which it is possible to organize states.[86] For Wendt, the end of history can therefore be nothing short of a *world state*—by which he means, following the German sociologist Max Weber, an organization that, at a minimum, possesses a monopoly on the legitimate use of organized force within a global society.[87]

Wendt saw a world state as inevitably emerging from the interaction of a process and a structure. What makes it inevitable, he argued, is the interaction between a self-organizing, "bottom-up" process and a structural, "top-down one": struggles for "recognition" mediated by technological change at the micro-level, conditioned by the logic of anarchy at the macro-level.[88]

outcome of his thought. *See* Thomas L. Pangle & Peter J. Ahrensdorf, Justice Among Nations: On the Moral Basis of Power and Peace 214 (1999). *See generally* Hans-Martin Jaeger, *Hegel's Reluctant Realism and the Transnationalization of Civil Society,* 28 Rev. Int'l Stud. 497, 503–04 (2002) (evaluating evidence for and against ascribing to Hegel the view that human history trends toward a world state); Thom Brooks, *Hegel's Theory of International Politics: A Reply to Jaeger,* 30 Rev. Int'l Stud. 149 (2004) (making the case for considering Hegel a realist).

83 Taylor, *supra* note 82, at 132.

84 *See* G.H.R. Parkinson, *Hegel, Marx and the Cunning of Reason,* 64 Phil. 287, 291 (1989) (quoting Hegel's *Philosophy of Right* para. 344 (1821)).

85 *See* Yovel, *supra* note 79, at 8–9. 140–41, 146–48. For Wendt, as for Kant, the "cunning of nature" is by no means the only, or dominant, factor driving this development. *See* Wendt, *supra* note 70, at 493-94, 508-10.

86 *Id.* at 508-09.

87 *Id.* at 526-28. Wendt's world state will incorporate more than these minimal "Weberian" features, however.

88 *Id.* at 529.

b. Teleological Explanation

In characterizing this process as "teleological," Wendt carefully marked two distinctions. The first distinction is that between intentional and non-intentional teleological processes; the second between evolutionary and developmental forms of teleological explanation. A teleological process is intentional when it is goal-seeking, as for example, when a wolf forages for rabbits. It is *non-intentional* when it is directed toward an end because of non-conscious "boundary conditions," as when a puppy grows into an adult dog. The process leading to a world state is, for Wendt, chiefly a non-intentional one. Second, teleological explanations are "evolutionary" when they address a question about origins. Thus, we might explain a zebra's stripes in an evolutionary way by showing how stripes were functional for the survival of zebras in natural selection. A teleological explanation is "developmental" when it addresses the question of how things work or what purposes they serve in some larger system, not how they originate. It is forward-looking rather than backward-looking. Wendt's argument about world state formation is developmental, not evolutionary.

As we have noted, Wendt's teleological explanation also draws on the interaction of a "bottom-up" process and a "top-down" structure. Neither the process nor the structure by itself is teleological: teleology emerges from their interaction.[89] The bottom up process is a form of "self-organization," that is, a process that creates a systemic order through the interactions of its elements following local rules. Wendt illustrated self-organization by reference to the emergence of a balance of power among states, as explained by Robert Jervis. On this view, by virtue of individual states' responses to local threats, an ordered, systemic pattern of balancing arises and persists over time, without any central coordination. The top-down structure stems from macro-level organizing principles or boundary conditions, which separate a system from its environment and impose a degree of "closure" on its internal processes.[90] Wendt invited readers to think about top down explanations in terms of a "program."[91] He illustrated his meaning by a different account of the emergence of a balance of power—Kenneth Waltz's. Whereas Jervis' process-based theory looked to the micro-level at how individual states perceived and reacted to threats, Waltz by contrast looked to the macro-level at how the anarchic structure of the international system "selects" for balancing: over time states that fail to balance are simply eliminated by a kind of natural selection, leaving only balancers.[92]

Wendt's teleological scheme also drew on the idea of "final causation." Top-down causation by itself does not explain change; bottom-up explanation introduces change but does not explain its direction. Finality, which refers to the role of end-states in channeling system dynamics

89 *Id.* at 496-501.

90 *Id.* at 517-20 (transition from Hobbesian to Lockean order).

91 *Id.* at 500.

92 *Id.* at 500-01.

towards certain outcomes, is therefore also necessary in a fully teleological account.[93] To round out the scheme, therefore, Wendt introduced the idea of end-states as "attractors." There are several kinds of "attractors," among them that of a "fixed-point" (corresponding to the idea of equilibrium in economics). Once a system has locked into such an end state, it will sustain itself in that pattern, absent outside disruption. Thus, in Waltz's theory, anarchy creates the boundary conditions for a system whose "attractor" is the fixed-point, end-state of "balancing."

Wendt's teleological account of world state formation combines the various causal elements contained in this scheme: bottom-up causation; top-down causation; and an "attractor" end-state. (These correspond to the traditional "mechanical," "formal" and "final" types of causation.[94]) For the most part, Wendt downplayed the "material" factors tending to cause a world state—notably, the nuclear dimension, which makes a world state the only means through which nuclear holocaust can be avoided.[95] Characteristically, Wendt focused instead on the "ideational" side of the causal story.[96]

---

93 *Id.* at 501-02.

94 The classification of causes into four kinds—mechanical or efficient; formal; final and material—goes back to Aristotle. The standard illustration is a house, which can be said to be caused by its builder (mechanical or efficient causality), its design (formal causality), its purpose of providing human habitation (final causality) or the materials from which it is made (material causality). *See* Aristotle, Physics, Bk. II, Ch. 3.

95 Wendt, *supra* note 70, at 507-10.

96 Wendt refers briefly to the "material" argument presented by Daniel Deudney for the emergence of a planetary "nuclear republican union." Daniel Deudney, *Nuclear Weapons and the Waning of the Real-State,* 124 Daedalus 209, 227 (1995). Deudney's argument is a powerful one that differs from Wendt's in several crucial ways.

Deudney contends that the invention and spread of nuclear weaponry "has reversed the security problem as it presented itself throughout almost all of human history. Two fundamental features of the world—the velocity and the volume of violence—shape the appropriate type of security-providing institution [which Deudney calls the '*real*-state']. In the past both were low. . . . In a nuclear world, the old problems that the *real*-state needed to solve largely have been solved, while new problems have emerged for which the *real*-state is ill-suited. . . . In a world dominated by nuclear explosives, ballistic missiles, and planet-spanning information systems, the volume of violence has reached the absolute, and the velocity of violence nears the instantaneous." *Id.* at 218–19. These technological or "material" changes in the nature of war, Deudney argued, entail the collapse of the *real*-state:

> Nuclear weapons fundamentally challenge the *real*-state because they deny the possibility that a political order of less than universal scope can monopolize violence capability within its territory. Prior to the advent of nuclear explosives, the scale requirements of military viability dictated that an entity be of approximately continental scale, as the two world wars demonstrated. With the advent of nuclear explosives, an entity must encompass the entire globe, or else monopolize all nuclear capability (in which case one state would be secure, and all the rest insecure). Nuclear weapons are to the *real*-state what gunpowder was to the medieval fief: a technology that renders it militarily enviable.

Id. at 214.

Deudney differed from Wendt in thinking that the best and most likely solution to this problem is "[n]either a world state nor the simple multistate system" but "an institution that contains and paralyzes nuclear capability but does not aggregate all territory into one state. . . . Instead of a world state, it is more appropriate to expect the territorial state system to be augmented by an institution for the comprehensive containment of nuclear capability." *Id.* at 219–20.

Deudney's work builds on (but is more sophisticated than) the work of earlier theorists who considered some form of world government to be the only possible escape from nuclear catastrophe. These thinkers included, surprisingly if also intermittently, the realist Hans Morgenthau. *See, e.g.*, Hans Morgenthau, The Purpose of American Politics 308 (1960); *see also* Hans Morgenthau, *The Four Paradoxes of Nuclear Strategy,* 58 Am. Pol, Sci. Rev. 23 (1964); James P. Speer II, *Hans Morgenthau and the World State,* 20 World Pol. 207 (1968). For criticisms of these earlier arguments for world government, *see* Gregory S. Kavka, Moral Paradoxes of Nuclear Deterrence 127–46 (1987).

c. Struggles for Recognition

The bottom-up (or micro-level) aspect of Wendt's explanation is what he called "the struggle for recognition." The top down (or macro-level) aspect is what he called the "culture of anarchy."[97] Because the concept of "recognition" plays a crucial role in Wendt's overall explanation of world state formation,[98] we must consider it with care.

The concept of "recognition" is imported from Hegel's system.[99] For Hegel, "[t]he desire for recognition is . . . the quintessentially human desire. . . . The desire to be recognized is not just another desire that we happen to have; it is the core human desire, central to our sense of well-being, our sense of who and what we are."[100] Human beings wish to appear to be worthy in the eyes of others, to be treated with consideration, decency, and respect, even to be admired or loved. They do not, however, wish to accord such consideration generally to other human beings. Recognition may not be reciprocal. Hence, "struggles for recognition" arise in which one person or group demands the recognition that another person or group refuses to grant. So imperative is the desire for recognition that struggles for recognition often turn into matters of life and death. Individuals and groups may well value recognition more than security or survival.[101]

Wendt distinguished two kinds of "recognition," which he called "thin" and "thick."[102] "Thin" recognition is, essentially, a juridical notion. It means, in substance, equal citizenship and equal rights under the law.[103] "Thick" recognition, Wendt explained, means being respected or esteemed by significant "Others." "Thick" recognition is afforded to an individual when he or she, for example, is seen as smart, virtuous, part of the in-crowd, and so on. It does not involve

97 Wendt, *supra* note 70.

98 *Id.* at 51-16.

99 Wendt's understanding of Hegel may well be informed by the extremely influential and widely read work of Hegel's commentator, Alexandre Kojève. *See* Michael S. Roth, *A Problem of Recognition: Alexandre Kojève and the End of History*, 24 Hist. & Theory 293, 296–99 (1985).

100 Steven D. Smith, Hegel's Critique of Liberalism 116–17 (1989).

101 Hegel's celebrated dialectic of the "master-slave relationship" in his *Phenomenology of the Spirit* (1807) explains both how compelling the need for recognition can be and how futile the attempt to wrest it from another must be. *See* Taylor, *supra* note 82, at 153–57. That humans risk death for the sake of winning recognition from others proves how overridingly important achieving recognition can be. Some combatants, however, when facing death, realize their attachment to life and will chose it, even at the cost of enslavement. The victor may spare the vanquished in order to make him his slave, thus apparently achieving two aims: first, that of confirming his sense of his own worth (he has valued himself as more than a mere life) and, second, that of securing another to recognize that worth. However, recognition is worth nothing unless it comes from someone the master recognizes as fully human—and in the master's eyes, the slave is not fully human. Hence the futility of the master's demand: he seeks to exact from the slave what he also makes it impossible for the slave to give.

102 Wendt, *supra* note 70, at 511.

103 *Id.*

rights, and is not legally enforceable.[104] By contrast, a "Hegelian" state, Wendt said, is a state that accords thin recognition to all its members. In other words, a "Hegelian" state is a "Weberian" state, a bureaucratic regime that also guarantees equal citizenship and respect to all. According to Wendt, in such a state the desire of all actors for recognition is satisfied, and one can therefore expect it to be highly stable.[105]

We cannot expect such stability, however, in a state that affords unequal recognition to its members—for example, a slave state like Athens, Sparta, the American Confederacy, or to a lesser degree in a state like the Ottoman Empire, which subordinated its Christian and Jewish subjects legally and in other ways to its Muslim subjects.[106] Wendt contended that eventually, the desire for recognition undermines systems that do not satisfy them.[107]

Wendt saw the struggle for recognition as a pervasive feature of international relations, and as the, or at least a, major cause of conflict. Thus, Wendt appeared to regard nationalism as an aspect of the demand for recognition, reflecting the "embeddedness" of individuals within national groups.[108] Moreover, since groups as well as individuals seek recognition, groups may seek to change international boundaries in order to create the conditions in which their collective identities can be recognized. Wendt thought it appropriate to regard states as the primary units representing groups in their cross-boundary struggles for recognition with other groups.[109] Even this summary account should make it plain how much explanatory weight the concept of "recognition" carries in Wendt's scheme.[110]

---

104 Other accounts combine features of both "thin" and "thick" recognition in a single concept. *See* Robert B. Pippin, *What is the Question for Which Hegel's Theory of Recognition is the Answer?*, 8 Eur. J. Phil. 155, 167 (2000).

105 Wendt, *supra* note 70, at 512, 524-25.

106 On the legal and social condition of the Christian and Jewish *dhimmi* in the Ottoman Empire, *see* Mark Movsesian, *Elusive Equality: The Armenian Genocide and the Failure of Ottoman Legal Reform*, 4 U. St. Thomas J. L. & Pub. Pol'y 1, 7–10 (2010).

107 Wendt, *supra* note 70, at 513.

108 *Id.* at 515-16.

109 *Id.*

110 Struggles for group recognition serve for him as the, or a, leading cause of the conflicts endemic to the international system and, therefore, of its chronic instability; and that instability in term, conjoined with the anarchic structure of international affairs, drives the system to seek the stability that only a world state can provide. One can agree with Wendt both that unequal recognition is an important cause of instability and that the desire for recognition fuels much interstate conflict without, however, accepting that international conflicts can generally be resolved by according equal recognition—in Wendt's "thin" sense—to the aggrieved contestant. Groups may simply prefer to live within the shelter of their own states, even if offered full civic equality within the ambit of a larger state. For any number of reasons, groups may prefer to occupy a distinctive political space of their own, rather than sharing a larger space, even on equal terms, with another group.

Thus, the "Velvet Divorce" of Slovakia from the unitary Czechoslovakian state in 1992 was not due to the legal or civic subordination of the Slovak population in post-Communist Czechoslovakia, but to other causes. The American slaveholders of the Confederacy did not secede because they were denied equal recognition as citizens, or threatened with such denial. The desire of the Muslim rebels in Kashmir to secede from India and join the Islamic state of Pakistan is also not attributable to India's refusal to accord them equal recognition with its other citizens. France's promise to extend equal citizenship to Algerian Muslims did little to allay the Algerian demand for national independence. The conflict between Israelis and Palestinians undoubtedly stems in part from the demand of the Palestinians for greater recognition; but in large part it also seems to be a contest over the possession and control of a particular land. *See* Lea Brilmayer, *Secession and Self-Determination: A Territorial Interpretation*, 16

d. Cultures of Anarchy

Coupled with the bottom-up demand for recognition are the top-down boundary conditions established by anarchy. Wendt wrote: "What drives the system forward is the logic of anarchy, which through downward causation conditions struggles for recognition in two ways: by making it possible for them to be pursued through organized violence, and by generating military technology that makes the costs of such violence less and less tolerable."[111] Wendt identified five successive "cultures," culminating in a world state, that progressively limit struggles for recognition in ways that keep their costs manageable. Despite being a "local attractor" that provides some measure of relief from struggles for recognition, however, each of the cultures short of a world state proves to be unstable. The inadequacies of each culture, therefore, are only provisionally cured by creating new boundary conditions, which in turn leads to the formation of a new culture. Only when boundary conditions are created by the world state can the system achieve self-sustaining stability.

Briefly, the successive "cultures" (conceived of as an analytical rather than historical progression) are: (1) the "system of states," or the Hobbesian culture of complete non-recognition or enmity;[112] (2) the "society of states," or the Lockean culture in which states recognize each other (as rivals), but do not recognize the rights of each others' citizens;[113] (3) "world" or "cosmopolitan" society, or a universal security community that extends recognition to individuals as well as to states (which proves unstable because it provides for no collective protection against aggression on the part of "rogue" states); (4) the Kantian culture of collective security or "friendship" (which improves on the universal security community by establishing a duty of mutual aid, but which at bottom remains anarchic because states retain their sovereignty, and which permits secession); and finally (5) the world state, which abolishes any remaining state sovereignty in local actors by creating a planetary Weberian state that holds a global monopoly over the legitimate use of violence. Throughout the unfolding of this sequence, the international system is driven by the quest for greater stability in the face of the mounting cost of (now, chiefly nuclear) violence.[114]

Yale J. Int'l L. 177 (1991). Thus, to the extent that international conflict derives from struggles for recognition, therefore, some of it would seem to be due to demands for "thicker" forms of recognition than mere legal equality. Indeed, some conflicts over recognition seem to be due simply to the desire to *exclude* or *dominate* other groups: stability may be too costly if it comes at the price of equality. Taken in itself, then, the demand for recognition cannot make a world state inevitable.

111 Wendt, *supra* note 3, at 259-79.

112 For a non-constructivist account of the instability of a Hobbesian world in which rulership is based entirely on fear, *see* Gregory S. Kavka, *Rule by Fear,* 17 Nous 601, 614–16 (1983).

113 Wendt, *supra* note 3, at 279-97

114 Not everyone would agree with Wendt that the international system attaches so much weight to the avoidance of nuclear conflict. Writing in 1964, Waltz observed that "[w]here weapons of horrible destructive power exist, stability necessarily appears as an important end. It will not, however, be everyone's highest end. . . . The unity and self-dependence of Europe may, for example, rank higher as goals than international stability." Kenneth N. Waltz, The Stability of a Bipolar World, in Realism and International Politics 99, 116–17 (2008).

Wendt devoted some attention to the question why the transformation of the Kantian culture of collective security into a world state is necessary and inevitable. A "crucial" part of his answer looped back to the concept of recognition. Wendt wrote:

> Recognition that is not enforceable by a common power is in the end not really recognition at all, since it depends on the goodwill and choice of the recognizer. Genuine recognition means that the recognized has a right to recognition, and the Self therefore has a *duty* to the Other. Genuine recognition is about obligation, not charity. Only when acting on behalf of the Other has become an enforceable obligation is recognition secure.[115]

Wendt also considered the question why a world state should be stable—a fixed point attractor—rather than, for example, a "periodic attractor" that collapses into cycles of anarchy? (Although no world state has ever existed, the closest historical precedents are discouraging. Even empires ostensibly based on the ideal of civic equality, like Napoleon's in Italy, have proven highly vulnerable to collapse.[116]) Part of Wendt's answer is that, while war would become insurgency and terrorism would become crime, a world state would have the capability to prevent secession, giving it a stronger "homeostatic logic" than any culture of anarchy.[117] The case of the Union victory over the secessionist Confederacy in the American Civil War reinforces Wendt's point.[118]

Wendt did not, however, rely primarily on the coercive power of a world state to ensure its stability (that would, after all, defeat the claim that its stability stems mainly from its provision

---

115 Wendt, *supra* note 70, at 524.

116 *See* Timothy Parsons, The Rule of Empires: Those Who Built Them, Those Who Endured Them, and Why They Always Fail 231–88 (2010); *see also* David A, Bell, The First Total War: Napoleon's Europe and the Birth of Warfare as We Know It 265–74 (2007).

117 Wendt, *supra* note 70, at 525.

118 On the other hand, even if secession were more difficult in a world state than in an anarchic culture (and that seems an open question), it would not be impossible: what is to prevent part of the world state's armed forces from taking up arms against the government, or local élites from organizing violent resistance to it? Furthermore, rebellion can come from below as well as from above: what has been called the "Kalashnakov Revolution"—the wide diffusion of small arms, above all the AK-47—has placed an extraordinary capability for violence in the hands of small, weak groups, making the territories they control effectively unconquerable by great powers (including those with nuclear arms), as the experiences of the Soviet Union in Afghanistan and the United States in Iraq have shown. *See* Daniel Deudney, Bounding Power: Republican Security Theory from the Polis to the Global Village 255 (2007). Why should a world state be any more successful at suppressing such low-technology forces of resistance? Finally, it is not at all obvious why the coercive powers of a world state would be more likely to eliminate the risk of a nuclear attack on civilians than the existing international system is: if non-state actors such as al-Qaeda can threaten to acquire and use weapons of mass destruction in the current international system, what is to stop similar groups from posing such threats under a world state?

The "Kalashnikov Revolution" is named for the Soviet assault rifle, the Avtomat Kalashnikova 1947 or AK-47, of which some 300 million are in circulation. The AK 47 is responsible for a quarter of a million deaths annually, is the weapon of choice for fighting forces from Africa, the Middle East and Central America to Los Angeles, and is sold in many countries for less than the price of a chicken. *See* Larry Kahaner, *Weapon of Mass Destruction,* in *The Wash. Post* (Nov. 26, 2006) (*available at* http://www.washingtonpost.com/wp-dyn/content/article/2006/11/24/AR2006112400788_pf).

of full recognition to all). Instead, Wendt argued that the world state could be organized so as to cope effectively with what he identified as the three main threats to its stability: the likelihood of a democratic deficit in its political institutions, the influence of nationalism, and the absence of an external Other to "recognize" the world state.[119] Oddly, Wendt did not identify religion—including a religion like Islam, which advances its own claims to form a world state—as a potential threat to the durability of his world state, or at least a recurring source of instability and violence within it.

e. Comments on Wendt's Argument for a World State

Wendt's account of the "inevitable" formation of a world state is complex and multi-faceted. Even our lengthy summary of it does not do justice to all the questions it poses. Here we will offer only a brief reflection on his argument.

The world state, in Wendt's telling, will be materially feasible because of the emerging technology of surveillance and coercion, and practically feasible because even great powers will prefer to give up their sovereignty rather than face the risk or nuclear war with "rogue" nations, yet not so despotic that it will unravel, as communications technology will facilitate representation at larger scales of geographic political organization and practices such as subsidiarity and delegation of power will mitigate concerns over a democratic deficit.[120] Wendt wrote: "My guess is that a world state will emerge within 100 years, which makes the process potentially relevant to policymakers and scholars today . . . ."[121] He thus fused a teleological claim about the world-state with a claim about human agency. Like Marxist-Leninist theory, where the "withering away of the state" is coupled with a call to revolutionary activity, particularly on the part of the intelligentsia, [122] Wendt's constructivism calls for human action and intentionality in bringing an end to anarchy, while also supposing that the end of anarchy is historically foreordained. In doing so, however, Wendt's constructivism, again like Marxism-Leninism, veers towards self-contradiction: how can the theory combine its belief in historical inevitability with its belief in creative human action, its determinism with its voluntarism?

Wendt's teleological account of the emergence of a world state is, perhaps, more specifically Western and even Christian than he acknowledged. His indebtedness to German idealist thought of the late eighteenth and early nineteenth century is apparent. Through those influences (Kant and Hegel were both Lutheran, if unorthodox, thinkers), Wendt is the legatee of

119 Wendt, *supra* note 70, at 525-28.

120 *Id.* at 526.

121 *Id.* at 491-92.

122 *See* Karl Marx, The Communist Manifesto (1848) (English translation) (*available at* https://www.marxists.org/archive/marx/works/1848/communist-manifesto/); and V.I. Lenin, What is to be Done? (1902)(English translation) (*available at* https://www.marxists.org/archive/lenin/works/1901/witbd/).

a Christian vision of history.[123] Even the conflict in Wendt's system between determinism and voluntarism mirrors the traditional difficulty in Christian thought of reconciling the freedom of human action with predestination and divine foreknowledge.[124]

Armed with this account of constructivism, let us test how far it illuminates international law and politics. Our case study, as mentioned above, is the confrontation between the Unites States and Iran over the Iran's nuclear program.

3. The U.S.-Iranian Nuclear Confrontation—Background to the Iranian Crisis

We approach the study of the conflict over Iran's nuclear policy in three stages. First, we will outline the sources and teachings of "radical Islamism." At least under the rule of the Ayatollah Ruholla Khomeini, the leader of the 1979 Iranian Revolution and the founder of the modern Islamic Republic of Iran, Iran was the most energetic proponent of Radical Islam. Second, we will attempt to overview Iran's grand strategy under Khomeini and his recent successors. Finally, we shall examine the conflict over Iran's nuclear policy up to the point in time at which the terms of the confrontation crystallized, roughly 2006.

a. Radical Islam

Classically, Islamic thought distinguished between two "worlds"—the *dar al-islam* and the *dar al-harb.* As Patricia Crone, an eminent British scholar of classical Islam, explained, the *dar al-islam* world is conceived of as "the abode of Islam, or what one might more idiomatically call the Muslim world. This was the world in which Islamic law held sway and in which there were rights and duties, human warmth, peace, and brotherhood."[125] The *dar al-harb* world (also known as the *dar al-kufr* or "abode of unbelief") was "the abode of war, or what we might more fashionably call the realm of 'The Other.' This was the world in which there was no legal (as opposed to de facto) order."[126] For much of Islamic history, the *dar al-harb* was, to a great extent, Christendom, or the civilization shaped by the Christian religion.[127] While an antagonistic relation existed between the two "abodes" or "worlds," the relationship could be, and often was,

123 To be more accurate, Wendt's (like Hegel's) is a kind of "gnostic" Christianity, making salvation available to a cognitive elite that can penetrate into the hidden plan of world history. For a classic account of Gnosticism, *see* Hans Jonas, The Gnostic Religion: The Message of the Alien God and the Beginnings of Christianity (1958).

124 *See, e.g.*, Martin Luther, On the Bondage of the Will (1525)(English translation) (*available at* http://www.archive.org/stream/martinlutheronth00luthuoft/martinlutheronth00luthuoft_djvu.txt).

125 Patricia Crone, God's Rule: Government and Islam: Six Centuries of Medieval Islamic Political Thought 359 (2004).

126 *Id.*

127 For medieval Christian understandings of Islam, *see, e.g.*, R.W. Southern, Western Views of Islam in the Middle Ages (1962).

softened in many ways (e.g., if non-Muslim states entered into long-term tributary relationships with Muslim ones), the *dar al-harb* was, in the final analysis, illegitimate. As explained by Crone:

> [The *dar al-harb* world] had no right to exist, like states denied diplomatic recognition in modern times. Though truces could temporarily suspend hostilities between it and the abode of Islam, the relationship between them could never be one of real peace. Muslims were legally obliged to wage holy war against *dar al-harb* until it ceased to exist or the world came to an end, whichever would be sooner.[128]

> "Holy war" or *jihad* thus took the form of "missionary warfare. It is directed against infidels [*i.e.,* non-Muslims], who may not be guilty of any act of hostility against Muslims (their very existence is a cause of war), and its aim is to incorporate the infidels in the abode of Islam, preferably as converts, but alternatively as *dhimmis* [*i.e.,* protected minority religious communities within a Muslim polity], until the whole world has been subdued.[129]

To say that medieval Islamic thought held such a conception of international (or rather, civilizational) relations is not, of course, to say that the same conception remains dominant in the Muslim world or among leading Muslim thinkers. Contemporary Muslim legal scholars, drawing on Koranic sources, have rejected the traditional view that the relations between the "abode of Islam" and the "abode of war" must be marked by war, arguing instead that "peace is the normal organizing principle which should govern foreign relations in Islam, while fight[ing] is an exception."[130] Nonetheless, there is a body of contemporary Islamic thought that continues to subscribe to the traditional position, or at least to something that resembles it.

This trend can be called "Islamism" or "radical Islamism." What we call "radical Islamism" should be distinguished both from the attempt to fuse Islam with nationalism within the context of a particular State, and from "pan Islam," the movement to unify the entire Muslim world into a single state.[131] Radical Islamism, as we define it, is the view that the entire world, whether Muslim or not, should be under Islamic rule.

---

128 *Id.* at 362.

129 *Id.* at 365.

130 Mohammed Abo-Kazleh, *Rethinking International Relations Theory in Islam: Toward a More Adequate Approach,* 5 Alternatives: Turkish J. Int'l Rels. 41, 51 (2006); *see also* Sheik Wahbeh al-Zuhiki, *Islam and International Law,* 87 IRRC 269, 278–79 (2005). Furthermore, as several leading experts have emphasized, the classical concept of *jihad* in Islam has undergone a significant mutation (or distortion) at the hands of contemporary jihadists such as Osama bin Laden. *See, e.g.,* Fawaz A. Gerges, The Far Enemy: Why Jihad Went Global 3–9 (2005).

131 Other authors use the term "Islamism" to refer to a trend of thought that fuses religion with nationalism. In this understanding, "Islamism is a political philosophy that seeks to establish an Islamic state . . . built upon a distinctly Islamic moral framework." Reza Aslan, Beyond Fundamentalism: Confronting Religious Extremism in the Age of Globalization 23 (2010). What we are calling "Islamism" rejects the idea of the nation state as anathema to Islam and advocates its transcendence in a global political structure. "Islamism" as we use the term is therefore closer to what Aslan calls "jihadism," *id.* at 23, or "religious transnationalism," *id.* at 32.

One of the most influential early thinkers in the radical Islam movement was the twentieth century Indian Muslim writer, Abul Ala Mawdudi.[132] Mawdudi taught that:

> [T]he power to rule over the earth has been promised to the whole community of [Muslim] believers. . . . A state of this sort cannot evidently restrict the scope of its activities. Its approach is universal and all-embracing. Its sphere of activity is coexistent with the whole of human life. . . . [It would] destroy those regimes opposed to the precepts of Islam and replace them with a government based on Islamic principles. . . . not merely in one specific region. . . . but [as part] of a comprehensive Islamic transformation throughout the entire world.[133]

Another remarkable radical Islamist thinker was the Egyptian Sayyid Qutb.[134] Qutb also believed in a bipolar world of conflict between the *dar al-Islam* and the *dar al-jahilliyah* (the abode of ignorance or pagandom[135]); so long as the *dar al-jahilliyah* continues, a state of war would exist, and Muslims would be required to engage in a globalized *jihad.* Such *jihad* would continue until it resulted in the establishment of God's sovereignty throughout the world and the "extermination" of "all the Satanic forces and their ways of life."[136] Qutb's "vision of peace is one in which Islam is 'established in its entirety in the world' and all people bow in submission before God rather than human beings.'"[137]

Likewise, what we are calling "Islamism" must be distinguished from "pan-Islamism." Unlike the view we are considering here—that a unitary *world* political community should be formed on the religious principles of Islam—"pan-Islamism" holds that the *Muslim* world should form a separate and unitary state. *See* Hans Küng, Islam: Past, Present & Future 456–57 (John Bowden trans. 2007). For brief studies of Sayyid Jamaluddin al-Afghani, who is often credited with the revival of pan-Islamism, *see* Roxanne L. Euben, Enemy in the Mirror: Islamic Fundamentalism and the Limits of Modern Rationalism 96–105 (1999); Nikki R. Keddie, *The Pan-Islamic Appeal: Afghani and Abdulhamid II,* 3 Middle Eastern Stud. 46 (1966). For a comprehensive treatment, *see* Jacob M. Gerdau, The Politics of Pan-Islam: Ideology and Organization (1990). Hopes for (and fears of) a pan-Islamic empire flourished after the attack of September 11, 2001—though in the view of one author, it represented only "an unrealistic phantasy" comparable to "a union of, say, the English-speaking world." Ali A. Allawi, The Crisis of Islamic Civilization 139, 154 (2009).

132 For a useful study of Mawdudi's life and ideas, *see* Ayesha Jalal, Partisans of Allah: Jihad in South Asia 242–65 (2008). Mawdudi was "the first Muslim thinker to arrive at a sweeping condemnation of modernity and its incompatibility with Islam, and to formulate a definition of the danger it constituted." Emmanuel Sivan, Radical Islam: Medieval Theology and Modern Politics 22 (enlarged edn. 1990). Like other radical Islamic thinkers such as Sayyid Qutb, Mawdudi has exercised an important influence on later radical Islamist movements, including al Qaeda.

133 Efraim Karsh, Islamic Imperialism: A History 207–08 2006. Elsewhere, Mawdudi seems to anticipate Samuel Huntington's theory of a "clash of civilizations." *See* Abul Ala Maududi, A Short History of the Revivalist Movement in Islam 22–24 (Al-Ashari trans. 1963).

134 A useful introduction to Sayyid Qutb's ideas is his *Milestones* (1988) (English translation) (*available at* http://majalla.org/books/2005/qutb-nilestone.pdf). For studies of Qutb, *see* Paul Berman, Terror and Liberalism 60–106 (2004); Natana J. Delong-Bas, Wahhabi Islam: From Revival and Reform to Global Jihad 256–66 (2004); Roxanne L. Euben, Enemy in the Mirror: Islamic Fundamentalism and the Limits of Modern Rationalism 49–92 (1999).

135 The term *jahilliya* refers in the historical sense to the condition of Arab society before the revelation announced by the prophet Mohammed. In Qutb's usage, it also refers to the pervasive, contemporary condition of both Muslim and non-Muslim societies in rejecting true Islam. In that sense, the term might even be translated as "modernity."

136 Quoted in DeLong-Bas, *supra* note 134, at 264.

137 Delong-Bas, *supra* note 134, at 265 (quoting *Milestones, supra* note 135, at 122).

Proponents of an Islamic world state have not all been, like Mawdudi and Qutb, simply thinkers and activists without state power at their disposal. The Iranian revolutionary leader Ayatollah Ruhollah Khomeini did have the power of the state of Iran at his disposal. Khomeini "viewed Western imperialism as the latest manifestation of the millenarian struggle between the House of Islam and the House of War," and envisaged an "Islamic world order [that] would see the territorial state transcended by the broader entity of the umma [*i.e.,* the community of Muslim believers.]"[138] When in power, Khomeini pursued a policy directed largely against Western ideas and influences including Soviet Communism. He said:

> We [Iran] have repeatedly shown in our foreign and international policy that we have been and are intent on expanding the influence of Iran in the world and lessening the domination of the world devourers. Now, if the servants of the United States cite this policy as being expansionist and motivated to establish a great empire, we will not fear it but welcome it. . . . We are intent on tearing out the roots of corrupting Zionism, Capitalism, and Communism in the world. We have decided to rely on God Almighty to destroy the regimes which are based on these three pillars, in order to spread the regime of the messenger of God [Mohammed].[139]

Khomeini also called for the export of the Islamist revolution in Iran to other countries. He said:

> [T]he Iranian revolution is not exclusively that of Iran, because Islam does not belong to any particular people. . . . We will export our revolution throughout the world because it is an Islamic revolution. The struggle will continue until the calls 'there is no god but Allah and Muhammed is the messenger of Allah' are echoed all over the world.[140]

b. The Legacy of the Iranian Revolution

Iran's grand strategy in international relations bears Khomeini's lasting imprint. Although Khomeini died in 1989, Iran remains (according to the respected expert and Obama Administration adviser Ray Takeyh) "a society whose essential political identity is still conditioned by [Khomeini's] legacy. . . . As the Islamic Republic charts its course, Khomeini remains the central actor in Iran's melodrama."[141] Under the leadership of the Grand Ayatollah Ali Hoseyni Khameini, appointed Khomeini's successor as Supreme Leader (*Velāyat-e faqih*) after Khomeini's death in 1989, and Iran's former President Mahmoud Ahmadinejad, Iran arguably pursued a foreign policy defined by "great power pretentions more than ideology," as realists

138 Karsh, *supra* note 133, at 216–17,

139 Quoted in John Kelsay, Islam and War: A Study in Comparative Ethics 39 (1993).

140 Quoted in Karsh, *supra* note 133, at 217.

141 Ray Takeyh, Hidden Iran: Paradox and Power in the Islamic Republic 9–10 (2006) [hereinafter "Takeyh, Hidden Iran"].

would predict.[142] And, unquestionably, Iran's international behavior has changed significantly since the revolutionary, war-torn Khomeini-period. Nonetheless, Takeyh counseled that it would be mistaken to conclude "that Islamism no longer drives the policies of Iran's rulers."[143]

Ahmadinejad himself, as well as other members of Iran's recent leadership, were active participants in the 1979 revolution against the Shah, whom they considered to be the United States' puppet. These leaders were forged in the 1980-88 Iran-Iraq War, in which the United States tilted toward Iraq and, sporadically, engaged in conflict with Iran.[144] These heirs of Khomeini regard the Iranian Revolution as "a remarkable historical achievement that the United States could neither accept nor accommodate," and they believe that "[t]he only means by which Iran could secure its independence and achieve its national objectives was through confrontation with the West."[145] Thus:

> [c]o-existence with the 'Great Satan' is viewed as tantamount to an appeasement of evil. Ahmadinejad has plainly declared that 'Our nation is on the path of progress, and on this path has significant no need for the United States.' Not since Khomeini has there been an Iranian [ruling] faction so fundamentally averse to dialogue and compromise with the United States.[146]

Other scholars saw Ahmadinejad as challenging the United States on the fundamental ground of "legitimacy." Like Khomeini, he was said to be "campaigning for Iran to assume leadership, first in the world of Islam and then in the international community. . . [I]f Iran does lead, it will do so under the banner of Islam."[147] Therefore, a constructivist approach centered on Iran's embattled self-image, no less than a realist approach emphasizing Iran's security needs, may be essential to understanding Iran's past, and even current, strategy.

On the plane of international relations, Khomeini's revolution fused together a religiously-inspired vision of the existing world order, which it held to be dominated by powers implacably hostile both to Islam and to the nation of Iran; a belief in radical Islamism, together with the corollary that its own revolution had to be exported; a readiness or even a desire for a continuous state of war, both with other Muslim states and with the United States; disdain for public international law, both because it was seen as a tool for Western domination and because the West itself cynically disregarded it; and an equal disdain for diplomacy or engagement with

142 *See* Ray Takeyh, Guardians of the Revolution: Iran and the World in the Age of the Ayatollahs 260 (2011) [hereinafter Takeyh, "Guardians of the Revolution"].

143 *Id.*

144 *See The Oil Platforms Case (Islamic Republic of Iran v. United States)*, Judgment, 2003 ICJ Reports 161 (2003) (adjudicated Iran's claims against the United States arising out of several such instances).

145 Takeyh, Guardians of the Revolution, *supra* note 142, at 225.

146 *Id.* at 240 (sic; translation as quoted).

147 John Kelsay, Arguing the Just War in Islam 209–10 (2007).

Iran's perceived opponents, coupled with a willingness to endure, or even welcome, international isolation.

Khomeini's revolution was rooted in Shi'ism, a form of Muslim belief that has long prevailed in Iran, but that is distinctly a minority position in the Muslim world as a whole.[148] Shi'ism has been characterized as "a religion of protest" because from the time of its origin in the seventh century, "protesting power and leading revolutionary outbursts against the status quo has been second nature to Shi'ism."[149] This consideration may help to explain much of revolutionary Iran's international behavior under Khomeini. As the voice of protest on behalf of the oppressed against oppressive and predatory rulers, Shi'ism is not easily deployed as a justification for or ideology of state power. Consequently, if only to protect the legitimacy of his own Shi'ite regime, Khomeini had to keep Shi'ism "always in a combative mode and revolutionary posture, forever, for as long as he lived."[150]

Khomeini laid claim to the political and spiritual leadership, not only of Iran, but also of the Shi'ite world beyond Iran, and indeed of the Muslim world as a whole. Khomeini and his followers sought to persuade the Iranian people that their revolution was a "new Karbala"—thus equating its significance to that of the seventh century battle in which Ali, whom Shi'ites view as the rightful successor to the prophet Mohammed, was slain, and which is the most sacred event in Shi'ism. Khomeini also had himself designated as an "Imam," a title that, in Shi'ite discourse, suggested that he was the Supreme Leader of global Shi'ism.[151] But even more, as we have seen, Khomeini sought to characterize the Iranian Revolution:

> not as a Shia one but an Islamic one. . . . He posed as a champion of Islamic revival, and presented the Iranian revolution as the Islamic revolution that the Sunni thinkers of the Muslim Brotherhood and Jamaat-e Islami had been claiming was necessary if Islam's fortunes were to be restored. Iran, the bastion of Shiism, was also the vanguard of the global Islamic revolution.[152]

---

148 The overwhelming majority of the world's Muslims are Sunni, another branch of Islam that has historically been highly antagonistic towards Shi'ism. Shi'ism is also a minority position throughout the Arab parts of the Muslim world, with the exception of Iraq, where Shi'ites form a clear majority. There is also a large Shi'ite population in Lebanon, leading some Sunni leaders to speak of an emerging "Shi'ite crescent" that extends from Iran to the Mediterranean coast. *See* Vali Nasr, The Shia Revival: How Conflicts within Islam Will Shape the Future (2006); Yitzak Nakash, Reaching for Power: The Shi'a in the Modern Arab World (2006). For an account of the origins and early history of Shi'ism, *see* Jonathan P. Berkey, The Formation of Islam: Religion and Society in the Near East 600-1800 130–36 (2003). Hamid Dabashi gives a compelling account of this form of Islamic belief in his Shi'ism: A Religion of Protest (2011).

149 Hamid Dabashi, Iran: A People Interrupted 179 (2007).

150 *Id.* at 217.

151 *See* Ervand Abrahamian, *Empire Strikes Back: Iran in U.S. Sights,* in Bruce Cummings, Ervand Abrahamian & Moshe Ma'oz, Inventing the Axis of Evil 116 (2004) ("[I]n the past, shi'is had reserved this title, with its notion of sacred infallibility, for the lawful descendants of the Holy Prophet whom they termed the Twelve Imams.").

152 Nasr, *supra* note 148, at 137.

It followed from these claims that Iran had a right and duty to export its revolution to other parts of the Islamic world, overturning their existing regimes if need be. As noted by Takeyh:

> [t]he essence of Khomeini's message was that the vitality of his Islamist mission was contingent on its relentless export. Moreover, because God's vision was not to be confined to a single nation, Iran's foreign policy would be an extension of its domestic revolutionary turmoil . . . . For the grand ayatollah, the global order was divided between states whose priorities were defined by Western conventions and Iran, whose ostensible purpose was to redeem a divine mandate. All local regimes had a choice—they could sustain their allegiance to the West or conform to the new Islamic epoch launched by Iran.[153]

Indeed, Article 11 of the Iranian Constitution prescribes that the nation "must constantly strive to bring about the political, economic, and cultural unity of the Islamic world."[154]

Prominent among the local regimes targeted by Iran was Saudi Arabia, a "Wahhabist" Sunni kingdom whose foundations were as theological as those of Iran.[155] For much of the 1980s, therefore, Iran was locked in a contest with the Saudis.[156] The battle was fought out on two planes, one geopolitical and the other theological. Iranians and Saudis vied for strategic dominance in the Persian Gulf. Both nations claimed to possess the truest and most faithful type of Muslim régime.

The Saudi-Iranian contest lay behind the Iran-Iraq War (1980-88). The war began with Iraq's opportunistic invasion in 1980 of what it saw as a weakened and vulnerable Iran, and ended eight years later in what was tantamount to an Iraqi defeat. Seeing secular but Sunni Iraq as its main line of defense against Iran, the Saudis, and other Sunni Arab states in the region gave Iraq their support. (As we shall see in Part II, Chapter 2, Iraq's perception that the support of its Sunni allies was radically insufficient was a direct cause of its invasion of Kuwait in 1990 and of the war in the Gulf that ensued.)

Additionally, revolutionary Iran's foreign policies throughout the Khomeini period repeatedly intersected and conflicted with those of the United States. The Iranian Revolution was itself directed against the Shah of Iran, who had long enjoyed American support, was seen as

---

153 Takeyh, Guardians of the Revolution, *supra* note 142, at 18.

154 Iranian Government Constitution (English transalation) (*available at* http://www.iranonline.com/iran/iran-info/goverment/constitution-1.html).

155 On the theological foundations of the Saudi state, *see* John L. Esposito, Islam: The Straight Path 189–90 (1991). On the origins and doctrines of Wahhabism, *see* Delong-Bas, *supra* note 134.

156 Epitomizing the struggle was the confrontation between Saudi security forces and Iranian pilgrims during the annual pilgrimage of Muslims to Mecca in 1987. The clash resulted in over 400 deaths. The Saudis claimed that the Iranians had engaged in a premeditated riot in which many of them were crushed to death; the Iranians charged that the Saudis had provoked and massacred the pilgrims. The episode took place, not only on a religiously highly charged occasion and near Islam's most sacred places, but also at a time of acute political tension in which the U.S. had introduced its naval forces into the Gulf to protect the flow of oil from being disrupted by the Iran-Iraq War. After the incident, Saudi and Iranian leaders exchanged bitter insults and accusations and intensified their competition for predominance in Islam. *See* Martin Kramer, Arab Awakening and Islamic Revival 161 (1996).

a faithful American ally, and had in fact been installed in power in 1953 in a coup orchestrated by the U.S. Central Intelligence Agency that brought down Iran's democratically-elected government.[157] (That intervention has left a lasting, and seemingly incurable, scar in the Iranian memory.) Further, the early stages of the Iranian Revolution were marked by the takeover of the U.S. Embassy in Tehran, ostensibly by revolutionary students acting independently of Khomeini's government. (There is reason to believe that Khomeini was aware of the students' plans and had approved them beforehand.[158] In any event, his government refused to remove the students, endorsed their actions, and exploited the hostage crisis to its own advantage.) The occupation of the Tehran Embassy was traumatic for the United States, gravely wounded President Jimmy Carter's re-election campaign, and left a lasting memory in the American mind — as lasting as the Iranians' memory of the 1953 coup. Further contributing to the deterioration of relations between the United States and Iran were the U.S. policy of support for Iraq during its war with Iran;[159] the bombing of a U.S. Marine base in Lebanon on October 23,1983 by the Iranian-sponsored Hezbollah organization, which resulted in the deaths of 241 Americans; the collapse of an attempted *rapprochement* between the two sides in the "Iran-Contra" scandal of 1986-87; and the destruction in 1988 of an Iranian civil aircraft, Iran Flight 655, by the U.S. Navy vessel *Vincennes.*

Iran under and after Khomeini's rule has disparaged international law, viewing it as fashioned to serve the interests of the West.[160] Khomeini's own public career began with his attacks in the early 1960s on the so-called "capitulation laws" that would have given U.S. forces stationed in Iran the equivalent of diplomatic immunity from local law.[161] Iranian nationalists perceived these laws as latter-day counterparts of the "unequal treaties" discussed above in Chapter I.B; they were taken to rest on the assumption that the West was "civilized" and the non-West not. Khomeini denounced the laws on precisely that basis. He argued that in enacting the law, the Iranian Assembly:

> has acknowledged that Iran is a colony; it has given America a document attesting that the nation of Muslims is barbarous; it has struck out all our Islamic and national glories with a black line. . . . If the Shah should run over an American dog, he would be called to account but if an American cook should run over the Shah, no one has any claims against him.[162]

157 *See* Takeyh, Hidden Iran, *supra* note 141, at 85–95; Ali M. Ansari, Confronting Iran: The Failure of American Foreign Policy and the Next Great Conflict in the Middle East 27 (2006).

158 *See* Takeyh, Guardians of the Revolution, *supra* note 142, at 39–41.

159 *See id.* at 98–99.

160 *See* Ansari, *supra* note 157, at 203 (referring to "historical distrust Iranians had for Western legalism").

161 Takeyh, Guardians of the Revolution, *supra* note 142, at 14.

162 Roy Mottahedeh, The Mantle of the Prophet: Religion and Politics in Iran 245–46 (1985).

During Khomeini's rule, Iran conspicuously violated international law (specifically, the inviolability of diplomatic premises) by its conduct during the takeover of the U.S. Embassy in Tehran.[163]

The Iranians also observed that the West remained silent during the Iran-Iraq War when Saddam Hussein deployed chemical weapons against Iran—a gross violation of the laws of war that Iran, perhaps for reasons of religious law,[164] appeared not (at least initially) to have reciprocated.[165] The Iraqi use of forbidden chemical weapons was no secret to the West. In a hearing before the U.S. House of Representatives Armed Services Committee, Tariq Aziz, Iraq's Foreign Minister, stated: "Yes, of course we use chemical weapons. They are savages and we need to defend ourselves. We would use nuclear weapons if we had them."[166] In pointed remarks to the U.N. General Assembly in 2005, Iranian President Ahmadinejad criticized the West for its silence in the 1980s over Iraq's use of chemical weapons: "Who, in fact, armed Saddam with those weapons? What was the reaction of those who claim to fight against WMDs regarding the use of chemical weapons then?"[167]

Finally, in the post-Khomeini period, Iranian leaders appear to have concluded that the United States' invasion of Iraq in 2003 without prior authorization from the U.N. Security Council confirmed that the United States regarded international law merely instrumentally, to be followed when serviceable and disregarded when not.[168]

Iran's hostility toward the West during the Khomeini period, its attempts to revolutionize its near neighbors, its brutalization of its own people (including the minority religious community of the Bahai), its terrifying tactics during the war with Iraq (which included using teenage Iranians as the means to detonate landmines), its involvement in acts of terrorism, and its rejection of international law all contributed to Iran's isolation from the world community. Far from regretting that outcome, Khomeini welcomed it. "We must become isolated in order to become independent," he declared.[169] Iran's willingness to accept isolation made it easier, of course, for

163 *See Case Concerning United States Diplomatic and Consular Staff in Tehran (U.S. v. Iran)*, Judgment, 1980 I.C.J. Reports 3 (1980).

164 *See* Karl Vick, *Iran's Gray Area on Nuclear Arms*, The Wash Post (June 21, 2006) (*available at* http://www.washingtonpost.com/wp-dyn/content/article/2006/06/20/). AR2006062001584. One may also note, however, that Iran had significantly less chemical weaponry capability than Iraq. See Edward M. Spiers, A History of Chemical and Biological Weapons 106–07 (2010).

165 *See* John Kelsey, Islam and War: A Study in Comparative Ethics 50 (1993); *but see* Spiers, *supra* note 166, at 106–07 (occasional Iranian use later in war).

166 Takeyh, Guardians of the Revolution, *supra* note 142, at 98.

167 Takeyh, Hidden Iran, *supra* note 141, at 148.

168 *See* Ansari, *supra* note 157, at 204.

169 Takeyh, Guardians of the Revolution, *supra* note 142, at 58.

Western states to characterize Iran as a "rogue," "outlaw," or "pariah" state. Ahmadinejad also seemed unconcerned about such matters.[170]

Khomeini's grand strategy was successful in protecting Iran from defeat at the hands of Iraq and in safeguarding the Iranian Revolution from subversion by the United States. Those were considerable achievements. However, in part because the historic enmity between Shi'ite and Sunni Muslims created a firewall against the spread of Shi'ite ideas, Khomeini's strategy failed to export revolution throughout the Islamic world. Iran's support for Hezbollah won it a valuable ally in Lebanon, but at the cost of earning it a reputation for supporting terrorism. In hindsight, Khomeini's Islamic Republic had little attraction as a model for the outside world, and indeed little attraction for the people of Iran. For example, it is said that Iranian taxi drivers will not stop to pick up clerics as passengers because of the disagreement of the Iranian people with their leadership.[171]

Nonetheless, Khomeini's successors admired his revolutionary model and, as we have argued, were in many ways deeply influenced by it.[172] Moreover, owing largely to the United States' interventions in two nations bordering Iran—Afghanistan in 2001 and Iraq in 2003—Khomeini's successors have had a much greater opportunity to achieve regional hegemony than he did. Both Afghanistan under the Taliban and Iraq under Saddam Hussein were deeply hostile to Iran. The United States' success in removing Saddam and the Taliban from governing power benefitted Iran. Moreover, the emergence of a Shi'ite-dominated state in Iraq not only eliminated a formidable foe, but also gave Iran a sympathetic neighbor open to Iranian influences. In any event, Iran's star is seen in the region to be rising, and that of the United States to be fading.

In that strategic environment, the question of Iran's nuclear program (which, incidentally, originated under the Shah in 1972) becomes vital.[173] At one end of the spectrum of defensive to offensive motives, Iran's experience during its war with Iraq may have taught it that it could never be secure if it faced an opponent armed with weapons of mass destruction while it was without them itself.[174] Was the nuclear program designed simply to give Iran bargaining chips,

---

170 Ansari, *supra* note 157, at 231.

171 *See* Nikki R. Keddie, *Secularism & Its Discontents,* Daedalus 14, 26 (Summer 2003).

172 For instance, Iran provides support for the Sunni-dominated organization Hamas, which seeks to fuse Islam with Palestinian nationalism. Iran's strident opposition to Israel also seems designed to attract non-Shi'ite Muslims.

173 For accounts of Iran's nuclear program from a variety of perspectives, *see,* for example, Ansari, *supra* note 157, at 197–206, 221–25; Dabashi, *supra* note 150, at 237–40; Sharon Squassoni, *The Iranian Nuclear Program, in Combating Weapons of Mass Destruction: The Future of International Nonproliferation Policy* 281 (Nathan E. Busch & Daniel H. Joyner eds., 2009); Takeyh, Hidden Iran, *supra* note 141, at 140-60; and Takeyh, Guardians of the Revolution, *supra* note 142, at 242–50.

174 *See* Ervand Abrahamian, *Empire Strikes Back: Iran in U.S. Sights,* in Bruce Cummings, Ervand Abrahamian & Moshe Ma'oz, Inventing the Axis of Evil 138 (2004). Former Iranian President Rafsanjani made this argument bluntly when he said:

> With regard to chemical, bacteriological, and radiological weapons it was made very clear during the [Iran-Iraq] war that these weapons are very decisive. It was also made clear that the moral teachings of the world are not very effective when war reaches a serious state and the world does not respect its own resolutions and closes its eyes to the violations and all the

which it could exchange in due course for benefits from the West—such as membership in the World Trade Organization, long-overdue capital investment in its oil fields, or release of Iranian assets frozen in the West?[175] Was Iran's nuclear program even designed for creating weaponry, rather than merely reducing its growing energy needs and thereby reducing its long-term dependency on foreign oil refineries?[176] Yet, perhaps Iran was seeking, not its own security, but rather the extension of its power, pursuing even regional hegemony? Could Iran have been seeking membership in the exclusive "club" of nuclear powers, with intermediate- or even long-range delivery capability, as befits its status as *the* dominant regional power? Finally, at the other extreme, was Iran driven by apocalyptic fantasies of destruction of its adversaries, risking even its own annihilation, as former President Ahmadinejad's crude threats of destroying Israel might have suggested?[177] Whatever the motive or set of motives (and they may have shifted over time), the Iranian government framed its nuclear program as a core element of national identity, printing the symbol of the atom on 50,000 rial bills.[178]

Furthermore, it is important to remember that Iran is a specifically *Islamic* state. But Iran's religious and political leaders have reportedly said on several occasions that Islamic law forbids nuclear weapons: they are *haram* or forbidden.[179] It has even been reported that the Ayatollah Khomeini issued a *fatwa* or religious ruling forbidding the production of nuclear weapons.[180] But other ranking Iranian religious leaders appear to disagree. For example, the Ayatollah Jalalodine Taheri said in 2006 that stockpiling nuclear weapons, using them for deterrence or

---

> aggressions which are committed in the battlefield. We should fully equip ourselves both in the offensive and defensive use of chemical, bacteriological and radiological weapons.

Takeyh, Guardians of the Revolution, *supra* note 142, at 245.

175 *See* Mohsen Milani, *Iran's U.S. Policy,* 88 For Aff. 46, 51 (2009).

176 *See* Mohammed Sahimi, Pirouz Majtahed-Zadeh & Kaveh L. Afrasiabi. *Energy: Iran Needs Nuclear Power,* The New York Times (Oct. 14, 2003) (*available at* http:/www.nytimes.com/2003/10/14/opinion/). Analysts have found that, despite Iran's vast reserves of hydrocarbons, its dependence on revenue generated by the export of oil can be taken to suggest that its "claim to need nuclear power might be genuine, an indicator of distress from anticipated revenue shortfalls." Roger Stern, *The Iranian Petroleum Crisis and United States National Security,* 104 Proc. Nat'l Acad. Sci. 377, 377 (2007). The Israeli analyst Paul Rivlin had earlier concluded that public information did not permit a judgment as to whether Iran's plan to meet its demand for electricity from nuclear power plans made sense economically. *See* Paul Rivlin, *Iran's Energy Vulnerability,* 10 Middle East Rev. Int'l Aff. 103 (2006).

177 Timeline: Israel and Iran statements, Reuters, March 29, 2010 (*available at* http://www.reuters.com/article/idUSTRE62S1E520100329).

178 *Id.*

179 Supreme Leader Ayatollah Ali Khameini has said on more than one occasion that "Islam is opposed to nuclear weapons." *See* Edward Yeranian, *Iran's Supreme Leader Khameini Says Islam Opposes Nuclear Weapons,* VANews.com (Feb. 19, 2010); *see also Use of Nuclear Arms 'Haram', Says Khameini,* The Times of India (Apr. 16, 2010). Another Iranian Ayatollah, Hussein-Ali Montazeri issued a ruling that "[i]n light of the scope of death and destruction they bring, and in light of the fact that such weapons cannot be used solely against an army of aggression but will invariably sacrifice the lives of innocent people, even if those innocent lives are those of future generations nuclear weapons are not permitted according to reason or Sharia." Abbas Milani, *Exclusive: A Green Ayatollah's Fatwa Against Nukes,* The New Republic (Oct. 20, 2009) (Milani trans.) (*available at* http://www.tnr.com/blog/the-plank/exclusive-green-ayatolah).

180 *See* Karl Vick, *Iran's Gray Area on Nuclear Arms,* The Wash. Post (June 21, 2006).

even deploying them in self-defense, might be permissible.[181] U.S. intelligence sources have also suggested that statements by the Iranian leadership that nuclear weapons are forbidden might be considered deceptions of an enemy that are legitimate under the doctrine of *taqiyya.*[182] What sense, then, is to be made of these reported rulings?

With those questions in mind, we turn to an examination of the Iranian nuclear program in the light of international law and international relations theory.

c. Iran's Dispute with the IAEA and the Security Council

The ongoing dispute between the IAEA and the Security Council, on one hand, and Iran, on the other, has had a checkered history.[183] But most chronologies begin with President George Bush's State of the Union Address in 2002, given shortly after the attacks of 9/11, in which he described Iraq, Iran, and North Korea as an "axis of evil" and warned of the proliferation of long-range missiles being developed in these countries.[184] In September 2002, Russian technicians begin construction of Iran's first nuclear reactor at Bushehr. On September 12, 2003, the IAEA Board adopted a resolution on nuclear safeguards in Iran, calling on Iran to accelerate cooperation with the IAEA and provide the full transparency needed for the Agency to complete its verification job.[185] Iran then indicated it was suspending its uranium enrichment program and would allow tougher UN inspections of its nuclear facilities, including a commitment to sign the so-called Additional Protocol and accept its expanded special inspections regime.[186] However, in August-September 2005, Tehran confirmed that it has resumed uranium conversion at its Isfahan plant and insisted that its program was for peaceful purposes and offered a legal defense

181 *Id.*

182 *See* Reza Kahlili, *An Ex-CIA Spy Explains Itan's Quest for Nuclear Weapons,* The Christian Science Monitor (Mar. 24, 2010), On the doctrine of *taqiyya, see* Raymond Ibrahim, *How Taqiyya Alters Islam's Rules of War,* 17 Middle East Q. 3 (Winter 2010).

183 For a detailed chronology, *see* Iran Profile-Timeline, BBC News, 14 July 2015 (*available at* http://news.bbc.co.uk/2/hi/middle_east/806268.stm).

184 *See id.*

185 *See* Board of Governors Resolutions: Implementation of the NPT Safeguards Agreement in the Islamic Republic of Iran, GOV/2003/69 (September 12, 2003) (*available at* http://www.iaea.org/Publications/Documents/Board/2003/gov2003-69.pdf).

186 See Board of Governors Resolution: Implementation of the NPT Safeguards

Agreement in the Islamic Republic of Iran, GOV/2003/81 (26 November 2003) (*available at* http://www.iaea.org/Publications/Documents/Board/2003/gov2003-81.pdf).

for its right to do so.[187] While the IAEA found Iran in violation of its safeguards obligations,[188] it did not report Iran's noncompliance to the UN Security Council. In January 2006, Iran broke the IAEA seals at its nuclear research facility in Natanz and announced its intention to cease what it called its "voluntary suspension" of nuclear research activities—presumably the code for its weapons-related enrichment and reprocessing activities.[189] Only thereafter, on February 4, 2006, did the IAEA respond by reporting Iran to the UN Security Council.[190] On August 31, 2006, the UN Security Council deadline for Iran to halt its work on nuclear fuel passed.[191] On December 26, 2006, the UN Security Council imposed sanctions on Iran's trade in sensitive nuclear materials and technology.[192]

The saga continues up to the present with various twists and turns: the Obama Administration and American allies are currently engaged in delicate negotiations with the Iranian government on nuclear and other issues. Our case study, however, is not intended to cover and analyze that unfolding story: it is neither possible nor, for our purposes, necessary to do so. Rather, our intention is to explain by means of the case study the differences between realist/rational choice and legalist/constructivist accounts of the emergence of legal and political conflict. Since the contours of the conflict, and the precise legal positions taken by the parties, crystallized by 2006, we deem that terminus an appropriate point at which to take stock. However, the later phases of the negotiations may form the basis for additional research using the methods developed in this volume.

187 Communication dated 1 August 2005 received from the Permanent Mission of the Islamic Republic of Iran to the Agency, INFCIRC/648 (August 1, 2005)(providing general statement of Iranian position, including defense of its legal right to undertake sensitive nuclear activities) (*available at* http://www.iaea.org/Publications/Documents/Infcircs/2005/infcirc648.pdf).

188 *See* Board of Governors Resolution: Implementation of the NPT Safeguards Agreement in the Islamic Republic of Iran, GOV/2005/77 (September 24, 2005) (*available at* http://www.iaea.org/Publications/Documents/Board/2005/gov2005-77.pdf).

189 Iran To Resume Suspended Nuclear Research and Development, IAEA Press Release 2006/01 (January 3, 2006) (*available at* http://www.iaea.org/NewsCenter/PressReleases/2006/prn200601.html); and Iran Begins Removal of IAEA Seals at Enrichment-related Locations, IAEA Press Release 2006/02 (January 10, 2006) (*available at* http://www.iaea.org/NewsCenter/PressReleases/2006/prn200602.html).

190 *See* Board of Governors Resolution: Implementation of the NPT Safeguards Agreement in the Islamic Republic of Iran, GOV/2006/14 (February 4, 2006) (*available at* http://www.iaea.org/Publications/Documents/Board/2006/gov2006-14.pdf).

191 S.C. Res. 1696, adopted July 31, 2006 (*available at* un.org).

192 S.C. Res. Resolution 1737, adopted December 23, 2006) (*available at* http://www.iaea.org/NewsCenter/Focus/IaeaIran/unsc_res1737-2006.pdf).

4. Study Questions and Documents on the U.S.-Iran Confrontation

a. Study Questions for Documents on the Political-Ideological Dispute between the United States and Iran

1) In Wendt's framework for "cultures of anarchy," how would you describe the values reflected in President Bush's "Axis of Evil" speech? In Iranian Ayatollah Khamene'i's response, his "Axis of Unity" Speech?

2) Relying on these speeches, if you were a legal advisor for the U.S. State Department, how would you write your memorandum to the IAEA arguing that Iran was in breach of its IAEA and NPT obligations? How would you balance the need for technical precision, given the legal and factual complexity involved, against rhetorical considerations?

3) If you were a legal advisor to the Iranian Ministry of Foreign Affairs, how would you write your brief defending Iran from such allegations? Would you strike the balance between legal precision and rhetorical effect in the same way that the U.S. Legal Advisor might?

4) If you were a legal and political advisor to the U.S. State Department, without reading the documents in Part B of this section, how would you frame your argument that Iran should be subject to sanctions?

5) If you were a legal and political advisor to the Iranian Ministry of Foreign Affairs, without reading the documents that are in Part B of this section, how would you write your argument that Iran should not be subject to sanctions? To whom would you address the argument? (Hint: As we will discuss in Part II of this book, a single negative vote by a Permanent Member of the Security Council—the United States, United Kingdom, France, Russia, or People's Republic of China, which are also the five NPT NWSs—blocks a Security Council Resolution.)

b. President George W. Bush's "Axis of Evil" Speech[193]

Our nation will continue to be steadfast, and patient and persistent in the pursuit of two great objectives. First, we will shut down terrorist camps, disrupt terrorist plans and bring

193 President George W. Bush, State of the Union Address, January 29, 2002 (*available at* http://archives.cnn.com/2002/ALLPOLITICS/01/29/bush.speech.txt/).

terrorists to justice. And second, we must prevent the terrorists and regimes who seek chemical, biological, or nuclear weapons from threatening the United States and the world.

Our military has put the terror training camps of Afghanistan out of business, yet camps still exist in at least a dozen countries. A terrorist underworld—including groups like Hamas, Hezbollah, Islamic Jihad and Jaish-i-Mohammed—operates in remote jungles and deserts, and hides in the centers of large cities. While the most visible military action is in Afghanistan, America is acting elsewhere. We now have troops in the Philippines helping to train that country's armed forces to go after terrorist cells that have executed an American and still hold hostages. Our soldiers, working with the Bosnian government, seized terrorists who were plotting to bomb our embassy. Our Navy is patrolling the coast of Africa to block the shipment of weapons and the establishment of terrorist camps in Somalia.

My hope is that all nations will heed our call and eliminate the terrorist parasites who threaten their countries and our own. Many nations are acting forcefully. Pakistan is now cracking down on terror, and I admire the strong leadership of President Musharraf. But some governments will be timid in the face of terror. And make no mistake about it: If they do not act, America will.

Our second goal is to prevent regimes that sponsor terror from threatening America or our friends and allies with weapons of mass destruction. Some of these regimes have been pretty quiet since September 11, but we know their true nature. North Korea is a regime arming with missiles and weapons of mass destruction, while starving its citizens. Iran aggressively pursues these weapons and exports terror, while an unelected few repress the Iranian people's hope for freedom.

Iraq continues to flaunt its hostility toward America and to support terror. The Iraqi regime has plotted to develop anthrax and nerve gas and nuclear weapons for over a decade. This is a regime that has already used poison gas to murder thousands of its own citizens, leaving the bodies of mothers huddled over their dead children. This is a regime that agreed to international inspections, then kicked out the inspectors. This is a regime that has something to hide from the civilized world.

States like these, and their terrorist allies, constitute an axis of evil, arming to threaten the peace of the world. By seeking weapons of mass destruction, these regimes pose a grave and growing danger. They could provide these arms to terrorists, giving them the means to match their hatred. They could attack our allies or attempt to blackmail the United States. In any of these cases, the price of indifference would be catastrophic.

We will work closely with our coalition to deny terrorists and their state sponsors the materials, technology, and expertise to make and deliver weapons of mass destruction. We will develop and deploy effective missile defenses to protect America and our allies from sudden attack. And all nations should know: America will do what is necessary to ensure our nation's security. We'll be deliberate, yet time is not on our side. I will not wait on events while dangers gather. I will not stand by as peril draws closer and closer. The United States of America will not permit the world's most dangerous regimes to threaten us with the world's most destructive weapons.

c. Ayatollah Khamene'i's "Axis of Unity" Speech[194]

In the name of God, the Merciful, the Compassionate . . . .

The anniversary of the demise of His Eminence the Imam [Khomeini]— may he be admitted to God's paradise - is, on the one hand, an opportunity for the nation to convey its affection and respect for its noble Imam. On the other hand, it is an opportunity for those whose hearts are infatuated with the Imam, his ideals and strategic ideas and principles, to reiterate their loyalty and commitment once again. Therefore, 14th Khordad of every year [4th June] has a special importance for political analysts the world over. Today, in all parts of the country, the people are showing the kind of affection and love for their noble Imam that has now become customary . . . .

The Islamic revolution, as a new and unique phenomenon, was able to revive the rays of hope in the hearts of people in Muslim societies. Everyone in the Islamic world and even outside it realized that our revolution was not emulating the slogans uttered by the untrustworthy tongues of the Eastern and Western regimes. They realized our revolution was a new phenomenon that had a new vitality and momentum. As a result, with the establishment of our Islamic Republic, all over the Islamic world, Muslim nations achieved a new momentum and a new sense of hope . . . .

Islamic revolution is not weak.

The reason why the dominant arrogant powers led by America work so hard against the Islamic revolution is that they want to destroy this focal point and this origin here. They know as long as this spring is boiling and as long as the focal point of this new thinking is alive here, they cannot discourage the nations of the world in their quest for justice. Therefore, they try to do one of these two things: Either they try to destroy this origin here totally, or as they know that this is not possible with the awakening of the nation and its being lively; they try to destroy the content of the Islamic Republic although its facade may be still there.

They try to change the directions and orientations. They try to distort the principal and clear concepts of Islamic revolution and Islamic Republic. Of course, they keep propagating all over the world that the Islamic Republic is declining and is becoming weak. This is part of the everyday propaganda of the enemies of this revolution and this system. Some simple-minded people may believe this. It may depress some of our friends across the world and make our enemies happy. But this is not an historical or scientific forecast. This a propaganda trick.

194 Speech of Imam Khamene'i at Imam Khomene'i's mausoleum in Teheran, June 4, 2002 (*available at* http://www.islam-pure.de/imam/speeches/speech2002.htm31012002).

If the Islamic revolution is weak and old and incapable, why they spend billions of dollars to oppose the Islamic revolution? If the Islamic revolution is breathless, why America comes to face this revolution with all of its military and propaganda equipment and makes its tone increasingly violent everyday? No. This revolution is alive, dynamic and progressing. The movement and the basic trends of the revolution are still alive . . . .

Unfortunately, the enemies of the state ascribe all weaknesses - even if they concern only one institution, to the state itself. The state has firm foundations. It has clear contours. The mode of reasoning and the rationale behind the main contours of the state are immutable.

Need for vigilance in the face of foreign threats

The officials and executives of the Islamic state, be they in the legislature or the executive or the judiciary, or the armed forces or anyone who is working anywhere, must overcome their weaknesses. The way to ensure prosperity for this nation is to implement the very principles that our magnanimous Imam defined and which were incorporated into the constitution. The nation has expressed its loyalty to them a number of times.

It became clear that the enemy opposed those very principles. The enemy opposes everything that may prevent its infiltration. The enemy intends to infiltrate through different channels. The Iranian nation, particularly our officials, must be vigilant. Praise be to God, they have already demonstrated their vigilance. During all these years, our dear nation has demonstrated that it is aware of those things. What the enemy must know is that it will not be able to force the nation to surrender by addressing it in a peremptory manner or by using the language of force and bullying.

What is clear to our nation is that any foreign domination in this country would threaten their religious and material happiness and would impose inferiority and humiliation on them. Today America talks to the world—not only to us—with the literature of arrogance. America speaks of war in order to expand its domination and influence in the world. This is arrogance. Any nation and any government that is intimidated with this literature and this way of treatment and surrenders to it, is digging its own grave and acting against itself.

The regime of America, sees it as its right to treat the nations with force and talk to governments with the language of force. You see that America humiliates Arab governments and exerts pressure on Arab nations. It takes as many advantages as it can. It wholeheartedly supports the usurper regime of Israel against the world of Islam and the Arab world. It is planning to expand its influence. And this causes hatred around the world.

Therefore, America is becoming more and more hated in the world everyday. You saw this demonstration of tens of thousands of people in European cities against the American president in his recent trip. This is unique in the world. It is unprecedented. What does this mean?

In the world of Islam the regime of America is the most hated regime. This is according to the polls they have taken themselves. Now it has been clear that it is not merely in the world of

Islam. In Russia, in various European countries, this public hatred against the regime of America and its leaders is on the rise day by day. What they are going to do with this public hatred?

Our nation is a nation of dignity. It attaches importance to its independence and dignity. It does not accept and tolerate insults by anyone. No government and no regime in the world is entitled to insult the Iranian nation for their independent stances.

Unity is the only thing that can stop America's impudence.

. . . .

These principles in which the people believe, which are trusted by the people, loved by the people—these principles are the axis of unity. People should not look elsewhere for the axis of unity. Everyone should show their loyalty to these principles again and again, with their words and pens, in their speeches, with their behavior, whether officials or other people involved in politics.

This becomes the axis of unity. This is what national unity means. We are not saying that the different preferences that exist among the people and the political groups must be removed from the country's political arena. No, this is neither possible nor beneficial.

Differences of opinion should not lead to conflict.

However, such differences of opinion must not lead to conflict or create rifts. That is the main point. Everyone must observe this unity and preserve it. That is the way to defend this country and that is a barrier to the enemy's audacious onslaught. They are constantly threatening us and they are talking about it and repeating it all the time.

At the same time, our officials have a gargantuan task as well. Officials of our country must serve the people and they must be indefatigable in their efforts. They will have to work hard and around the clock. It does not make any difference whether they are in the executive branch in the government, or in the legislature as Majlis deputies or in the Judiciary and judicial institutions throughout the country.

They must be serious and they must try to implement the principles of the revolution and the Imam and they must follow this course of action. In fact, that means putting the constitution into practice. They must work regardless of any special considerations and they must make efforts like that. They must not permit their time to be spent on doing other things. Everyone is duty-bound to do so.

5. Study Questions and Documents for the Actions of the IAEA and the Security Council

1) Why does the IAEA approve two separate resolutions—one finding Iran not in compliance with its safeguards obligations; the other reporting that non-compliance to the Security Council? Is this a legal decision? A political decision?

2) Similarly, why does the Security Council adopt two separate resolutions—one threatening sanctions; the other imposing sanctions? Is this a legal decision? A political decision?

3) What are the specific factual findings that permit the IAEA and the Security Council to make the decisions required in each resolution? .

4) What procedures are employed in each case? Do they seem fair to you? Would additional procedures have changed the decisions of the IAEA or the Security Council?

5) Viewed from the standpoint of third-parties, do these resolutions indicate the nuclear non-proliferation regime has teeth after the detection of a violation, that its norms are in jeopardy, or is the situation somewhere in between?

a. Iran's Legal —IAEA Information Circular 648[195]

IAEA
International Atomic Energy Agency

Information Circular

INFCIRC/648
Date: 1 August 2005

General Distribution
Original: English

Communication dated 1 August 2005 received from the Permanent Mission of the Islamic Republic of Iran to the Agency

The Secretariat of the Agency received on 1 August 2005 a Note Verbale dated 1 August 2005 from the Permanent Mission of the Islamic Republic of Iran (Iran). In accordance with the request contained in the Note Verbale, the text is attached herewith for the information of all Member States.

In the Note Verbale, Iran informed the Agency, inter alia, that Iran had "decided to resume the uranium conversion activities at UCF [Uranium Conversion Facility] in Esfahan on 1 August 2005." Iran requested the Agency "to be prepared for the implementation of the Safeguards related activities in a timely manner prior to the resumption of the UCF activities."

In response to the Note Verbale, the Agency, in a letter dated 1 August 2005, informed Iran that, in order to implement effective safeguards at UCF, the Agency would need to install additional surveillance equipment at the input and output stages of certain process lines prior to any resumption of any such activities and that, prior to the planned movement of U_3O_8, the Agency would need to verify the nuclear material in question. The Agency further informed Iran that, to that end, the Agency was in the process of preparing the necessary equipment for UCF, and would expect to be in a position to install the equipment some time next week. The Agency also informed Iran that, "to ensure continuity of knowledge, it is essential that Iran refrain from removing the Agency's seals and from moving any nuclear material at UCF until such time as the surveillance equipment is installed and the Agency has verified the material."

In its resolution adopted on 29 November 2004 (GOV/2004/90), the Board, inter alia, welcomed Iran's decision to continue and extend its suspension of all enrichment related and reprocessing activities, and underlined that the full and sustained implementation of the suspension, which was a voluntary, non-legally-binding, confidence building measure, to be verified by the Agency, was essential to addressing outstanding issues. The Board also requested the Director General to continue verifying that the suspension remained in place and to inform Board Members, inter alia, should the suspension not be fully sustained. By means of this Information Circular, the Director General is informing the Members of the Board of Governors, as well as all Member States, accordingly.

195 *Communication Dated 1 August 2005 Received from the Permanent Mission of the Islamic Republic of Iran to the Agency*, IAEA INFCIRC/648 Aug. 1, 2005 (*available at* https://www.iaea.org/sites/default/files/publications/documents/infcircs/2005/infcirc648.pdf).

Permanent Mission of the
Islamic Republic of Iran
to the United Nations and other
International Organizations in Vienna

جمهوری اسلامی ایران
نمایندگی دائم نزد دفتر ملل متحد و سازمانهای بین‌المللی
وین

URGENT

Verbal Note No.: 350-1-17/928

The Permanent Mission of the Islamic Republic of Iran to the United Nations and other International Organizations in Vienna presents its compliments to the Secretariat of the IAEA and has the honour to state the following:

Since early 1980s, Iran's peaceful nuclear program and its inalienable right to nuclear technology have been the subject of the most extensive and intensive campaign of denial, obstruction, intervention and misinformation.

- Valid and binding contracts to build nuclear power plants were unilaterally abrogated;
- Nuclear material rightfully purchased and owned by Iran were illegally withheld;
- exercise of Iran's shareholder's right in several national and multinational nuclear power corporations were obstructed;
- Unjustified and coercive interventions were routinely made in order to undermine, impede and delay the implementation of Iran's nuclear agreements with third parties; and
- Unfounded accusations against Iran's exclusively peaceful nuclear program were systematically publicized.

While Iran's rights under the NPT have continued to be grossly and systematically violated, and while major state parties to the Treaty have persisted in their non-compliance with many of their obligations under Articles I, IV and VI of the Treaty in general, and under paragraph 2 of Article IV vis-a-vis Iran in particular, Iran nevertheless continued diligently to comply with all its obligations under the Treaty. At the same time and merely in order to prevent further illegal and illegitimate restrictions on the exercise of its rights, Iran was forced to be discrete in its legal activities, avoiding to disclose the details of programs, which, in nearly all cases, it was not any way obliged to disclose in accordance with its obligations under its safeguards agreement with the IAEA.

In October 2003, Iran entered into an agreement with France, Germany and the United Kingdom with the explicit expectation to open a new chapter of full transparency, cooperation and access to nuclear and other advanced technologies. Iran agreed to a number of important transparency and voluntary confidence building measures and immediately and fully implemented them.

- It signed and immediately began full implementation of the Additional Protocol;
- It opened its doors to one of the most expansive and intrusive IAEA inspections;

1

LEONARD BERNSTEIN-STRASSE 8 STG 2 TOP 22.5, 1220 VIENNA, AUSTRIA Tel: (00431) 26 99 660, Fax: (00431) 26 99 791, e-mail: pm.iran@aon.at

- It provided a detailed account of its peaceful nuclear activities, all of which had been carried out in full conformity with its rights and obligations under the NPT;
- It began and has continuously maintained for the past 20 months a voluntarily suspension of its rightful enrichment of Uranium as a confidence building measure;
- It further expanded in February and November 2004, following agreements with E3/EU in Brussels and Paris respectively, its voluntary suspension to incorporate activities which go well beyond the original Agency's definition of "enrichment" and even "enrichment-related" activities.

Iran has worked closely with the Agency, during the course of the last two years, to deal with the issues and questions raised about its peaceful nuclear program. All significant issues, particularly those related to the sources of HEU, have now been resolved. Indeed, except for few questions, mostly speculative, nothing more remains to close this Chapter.

The Agency's thorough inspections of Iran repeatedly confirmed Iran's statement that any amount of inspection and scrutiny will never show the slightest diversion into military activity. The Director-General confirmed in Paragraph 52 of his November 2003 report that "to date, there is no evidence that the previously undeclared nuclear material and activities referred to above were related to a nuclear weapons programme." After one more year and over a thousand person-days of the most rigorous inspections, the Director-General again confirmed in Paragraph 112 of his November 2004 report that "all the declared nuclear material in Iran has been accounted for, and therefore such material is not diverted to prohibited activities."

Regrettably, Iran received very little, if anything, in return and instead has repeatedly expanded its voluntary confidence building measures only to be reciprocated by broken promises and expanded requests. The October 2003 promises of the E3 on nuclear cooperation and regional security and non-proliferation have yet to be even addressed. The February 2004 commitment by the E3 to "work actively to gain recognition at the June 2004 Board of the efforts made by Iran, so that the Board works thereafter on the basis of Director-General reporting if and when he deems it necessary, in accordance with the normal practice pertaining to the implementation of Safeguards Agreements and the Additional Protocol", in response to Iran's expansion of its suspension to include assembly and component manufacturing was not fulfilled, until Iran agreed in November 2004 to the expansion of voluntary suspension to include the Uranium Conversion Facility which had been originally defined by the Secretariat of the IAEA as outside the scope of any definition of "enrichment-related activities". And the E3/EU has yet to honor its recognition, in the Paris Agreement of November 2004, of "Iran's rights under the NPT exercised in conformity with its obligations under the Treaty, without discrimination."

After over three months of negotiations following the Paris Agreement, it became evident the E3/EU simply wanted prolonged and fruitless negotiations, thereby prejudicing the exercise of Iran's inalienable right to resume its legal enrichment activities, and did not have the intention or the ability to present its proposals on objective guarantees on peaceful nature of Iran's nuclear program, as well as firm guarantees on economic, technological and nuclear cooperation and firm commitments on security issues.

In a further testament to Iran's desire to ensure the success of the negotiations, so that Iran's rightful nuclear program could also enjoy the support and confidence of the West, Iran suggested to the E3/EU to ask the IAEA to develop technical, legal and monitoring modalities for Iran's enrichment program as objective guarantees to ensure that Iran's nuclear program will remain exclusively for peaceful purposes. While one member of E3/EU accepted the suggestion, lack of consensus among the E3 prevented resort to the IAEA as an authoritative and impartial framework for solving the impasse.

Finally, on March 23, 2005, Iran offered a collection of solutions for objective guarantees suggested by various independent scientist and observers from the United States and Europe. The package included:

1. Strong and mutually beneficial relations between Iran and the EU/E3, which would provide the best guarantee for respect for the concerns of each side;

2. Confinement of Iran's enrichment program, in order to preclude through objective technical guarantees any proliferation concern:
    a. Open fuel cycle, to remove any concern about reprocessing and production of plutonium;
    b. Ceiling of enrichment at LEU level;
    c. Limitation of the extent of the enrichment program to solely meet the contingency fuel requirements of Iran's power reactors;
    d. Immediate conversion of all enriched Uranium to fuel rods to preclude even the technical possibility of further enrichment;
    e. Incremental and phased approach to implementation in order to begin with the least sensitive aspects of the enrichment program and to gradually move to enrichment as confidence in the program would be enhanced;

3. Legislative and regulatory measures
    a. Additional Protocol;
    b. Permanent ban on the development, stockpiling and use of nuclear weapons through binding national legislation;
    c. Enhancement of Iran's export control regulations;

4. Enhanced monitoring
    a. Continued implementation of the Additional Protocol; and
    b. Continuous on-site presence of IAEA inspectors at the conversion and enrichment facilities to provide unprecedented added guarantees.

Extraneous pressures prevented timely and serious consideration by E3/EU of this proposal which has the potential of providing a framework in which concerns of all sides are reasonably allayed. Even Iran's further effort to salvage the process by suggesting the negotiated commencement of implementation of phase 1 of that proposal on limited resumption of the work of the UCF - which had never had any past alleged failures, and is virtually proliferation free — with additional confidence building and surveillance and monitoring measures was misconstrued by the E3/EU as an ultimatum.

In order to correct any wrong perception about an ultimatum and to ensure that no opportunity was spared for an agreed settlement, Iran agreed to extend the period of full suspension for another two months, in response to a commitment made by the E3/EU ministers in Geneva to finally present their comprehensive package for the implementation of the Paris Agreement by the end of July or early August 2005, that is nearly nine months after the Agreement.

Iran made it clear in Geneva that any proposal by the E3/EU must incorporate E3/EU's perception of objective guarantees for the gradual resumption of the Iranian enrichment program, and that any attempt to turn objective guarantees into cessation or long-term suspension were incompatible with the letter and spirit of the Paris Agreement and therefore unacceptable to Iran.

Eager to salvage the negotiations, in a message to the Ministers, Iran offered the most flexible solution to the E3/EU as they were finalizing their package:

- Commencement of the work of Esfahan plant (UCF) at low capacity and under full scope monitoring, while arrangements for import of the feed material and export of the product are worked out with you and other potential partners; (Negotiations on these arrangements have already started and preliminary agreement has been reached.)
- Further negotiations on a mutually acceptable arrangement for an initial limited operation at Natanz or allowing the Agency to develop an optimized arrangement on numbers, monitoring mechanism and other specifics for such an initial limited operation at Natanz;
- Negotiations for full scale operation of Natanz would continue on the premise that it would be synchronized with the fuel requirements of light water reactors.

Against all its sincere efforts and maximum flexibility, Iran has not received a proposal as of today, and all public and diplomatic information, particularly the letter of 29 July 2005 of the E3 Ministers, indicate that the content of the eventual proposal will be totally unacceptable. We have been informed that the proposal not only fails to address Iran's rights for peaceful development of nuclear technology, but even falls far short of correcting the illegal and unjustified restrictions placed on Iran's economic and technological development, let alone providing firm guarantees for economic, technological and nuclear cooperation and firm commitments on security issues. While we had made it crystal clear that no incentive would be sufficient to compromise Iran's inalienable right to all aspects of peaceful nuclear technology, such offers of incentives are in and of themselves demeaning and totally incommensurate with Iran and its vast capabilities, potentials and requirements.

It is now self-evident that negotiations are not proceeding as called for in the Paris Agreement, due to E3/EU policy to protract the negotiations without the slightest attempt to move forward in fulfilling their commitments under the Tehran or Paris Agreements. This protracted continuation is solely geared to serve the purpose of keeping the suspension in place for as long as it takes to make the cessation a *fait accompli.* This is contrary to the letter and spirit of the Paris Agreement and is not in line with principles of good faith negotiations.

After such long period of negotiations and so much that Iran has done to restore confidence and the flexibility that it has shown, there is no pretext for any further delay in the implementation of the first phase of Iran's proposal, by limited resumption of UCF at Esfahan, which is free from any past alleged failures, and is virtually proliferation free. With additional proposed arrangements, it should leave no excuse for anyone.

It must be underlined that all States party to the NPT, without discrimination, have an inalienable right to produce nuclear energy for peaceful purposes. As this right is "inalienable", it cannot be undermined or curtailed under any pretext. Any attempt to do so, would be an attempt to undermine a pillar of the Treaty and indeed the Treaty itself.

Iran, like any other Non-Nuclear-Weapon State, has no obligation to negotiate and seek agreement for the exercise of its "inalienable" right, nor can it be obligated to suspend it. Suspension of Uranium enrichment, or any derivative of such suspension, is a voluntary and temporary confidence-building measure, effectuated by Iran in order to enhance cooperation and close the chapter of denials of access to technology imposed by the west on Iran. It is not an end in itself, nor can be it construed or turned into a permanent abandonment of a perfectly lawful activity, thereby perpetuating, rather than easing, the pattern of denial of access to technology.

The suspension has been in place for nearly 20 months, with all its economic and social ramifications affecting thousands of families. The E3/EU has failed to remove any of its multifaceted restrictions on Iran's access to advanced and nuclear technology. In a twist of logic, it has attempted to prolong the suspension, thereby trying to effectively widen its restrictions instead of fulfilling its commitments of October 2003 and November 2004 to remove them.

As the IAEA Board of Governors has underlined, suspension "is a voluntary, non-legal binding confidence building measure". When the Board itself explicitly recognizes that suspension is "not a legally-binding obligation", no wording by the Board can turn this voluntary measure into an essential element for anything. In fact the Board of Governors has no factual or legal ground, nor any statutory power, to make or enforce such a demand, or impose ramifications as a consequence of it.

In light of the above, Iran has decided to resume the uranium conversion activities at the UCF in Esfahan on 1 August 2005.

The Agency is hereby requested to be prepared for the implementation of the Safeguards related activities in a timely manner prior to the resumption of the UCF activities.

The Islamic Republic of Iran wants to ensure that no effort is spared in order to reach a negotiated resumption of its enrichment activities. It is therefore, prepared to continue in good faith and in an expeditious and result-oriented manner, its negotiations with E3/EU. Meanwhile, Iran will continue to maintain its voluntary suspension of all enrichment-related activities. It is to be noted that the UCF was not originally considered by the Agency to be included in such category.

Iran is committed to non-proliferation and elimination of nuclear weapons, and considers nuclear weapons and capability to produce or acquire them as detrimental to its security. Iran will continue to abide by its obligations under the NPT and will continue to work actively for the establishment of a zone free from weapons of mass destruction in the Middle East.

The Permanent Mission of the Islamic Republic of Iran to the United Nations and other International Organizations in Vienna requests the Secretariat this Note to be officially circulated as INFCIRC document and avails itself of this opportunity to renew to the Secretariat of the IAEA the assurances of its highest consideration.

Vienna, 1 August 2005

To the
IAEA Secretariat

Attn.: Dr. Mohamed ElBaradei
Director-General of the IAEA

b. IAEA Resolution Finding Iran in Noncompliance with its Safeguards Obligations[196]

IAEA Board of Governors GOV/2005/77 (adopted on 24 September 2005)
Implementation of the NPT Safeguards
Agreement in the Islamic Republic of Iran

Resolution The Board of Governors,

(a) Recalling the resolutions adopted by the Board on 11 August 2005 (GOV/2005/64), 29 November 2004 (GOV/2004/90), 18 September 2004 (GOV/2004/79), 18 June 2004 (GOV/2004/49, 13 March 2004 (GOV/2004/21), 26 November 2003 (GOV/2003/81) and on 12 September 2003 (GOV/2003/69), the statement of the Board of 19 June 2003 (GOV/OR.1072) and the Chairman of the Board's conclusions of March 2005 (GOV/OR.1122) and of June 2005 (GOV/OR.1130),

(b) Recalling that Article IV of the Treaty on the Non Proliferation of Nuclear Weapons stipulates that nothing in the Treaty shall be interpreted as affecting the inalienable rights of all the Parties to the Treaty to develop research, production and use of nuclear energy for peaceful purposes without discrimination and in conformity with Articles I and II of the Treaty,

(c) Commending the Director General and the Secretariat for their professional and impartial efforts to implement the Safeguards Agreement in Iran, to resolve outstanding safeguards issues in Iran and to verify the implementation by Iran of the suspension,

(d) Recalling Iran's failures in a number of instances over an extended period of time to meet its obligations under its NPT Safeguards Agreement (INFCIRC 214) with respect to the reporting of nuclear material, its processing and its use, as well as the declaration of facilities where such material had been processed and stored, as reported by the Director General in his report GOV/2003/75 dated 10 November 2003 and confirmed in GOV/2005/67, dated 2 September 2005,

(e) Recalling also that, as deplored by the Board in its resolution GOV/2003/81, Iran's policy of concealment has resulted in many breaches of its obligation to comply with its Safeguards

196 *Implementation of the NPT Safeguards Agreement in the Islamic Republic of Iran*, IAEA Board of Governors Resolution GOV/2005/77, Sept. 24, 2005 (*available at* https://www.iaea.org/sites/default/files/gov2005-77.pdf).

Agreement,

(f) Recalling that the Director General in his report to the Board on 2 September 2005 noted that good progress has been made in Iran's correction of the breaches and in the Agency's ability to confirm certain aspects of Iran's current declarations,

(g) Noting that, as reported by the Director General, the Agency is not yet in a position to clarify some important outstanding issues after two and a half years of intensive inspections and investigation and that Iran's full transparency is indispensable and overdue,

(h) Uncertain of Iran's motives in failing to make important declarations over an extended period of time and in pursuing a policy of concealment up to October 2003,

(i) Concerned by continuing gaps in the Agency's understanding of proliferation sensitive aspects of Iran's nuclear programme,

(j) Recalling the emphasis placed in past resolutions on the importance of confidence building measures and that past resolutions have reaffirmed that the full and sustained implementation of the suspension notified to the Director General on 14 November 2004, as a voluntary, non-legally binding confidence building measure, to be verified by the Agency, is essential to addressing outstanding issues,

(k) Deploring the fact that Iran has to date failed to heed the call by the Board in its resolution of 11 August 2005 to re-establish full suspension of all enrichment related activities including the production of feed material, including through tests or production at the Uranium Conversion Facility,

(l) Also concerned that Iran has to date failed to heed repeated calls to ratify the Additional Protocol and to reconsider its decision to construct a research reactor moderated by heavy water, as these measures would have helped build confidence in the exclusively peaceful nature of Iran's nuclear programme,

(m) Noting that the Director General reported that the Agency "continues to follow up on information pertaining to Iran's nuclear programme and activities that could be relevant to that programme" and that "the Agency's legal authority to pursue the verification of possible nuclear weapons related activity is limited" (GOV/2005/67),

(n) Endorsing the Director General's description of this as a special verification case, and

(o) Noting that the Agency is still not in a position to conclude that there are no undeclared nuclear materials or activities in Iran,

1. Finds that Iran's many failures and breaches of its obligations to comply with its NPT Safeguards Agreement, as detailed in GOV/2003/75, constitute non compliance in the context of Article XII.C of the Agency's Statute;

2. Finds also that the history of concealment of Iran's nuclear activities referred to in the Director General's report, the nature of these activities, issues brought to light in the course of the Agency's verification of declarations made by Iran since September 2002 and the resulting absence of confidence that Iran's nuclear programme is exclusively for peaceful purposes have given rise to questions that are within the competence of the Security Council, as the organ bearing the main responsibility for the maintenance of international peace and security; GOV/2005/77

3. Requests the Director General to continue his efforts to implement this and previous Resolutions and to report again, including any further developments on the issues raised in his report of 2 September 2005 (GOV/2005/67) to the Board. The Board will address the timing and content of the report required under Article XII.C and the notification required under Article III.B.4;

4. In order to help the Director General to resolve outstanding questions and provide the necessary assurances, urges Iran:
   (i) To implement transparency measures, as requested by the Director General in his report, which extend beyond the formal requirements of the Safeguards Agreement and Additional Protocol, and include access to individuals, documentation relating to procurement, dual use equipment, certain military owned workshops and research and development locations;
   (ii) To re-establish full and sustained suspension of all enrichment-related activity, as in GOV/2005/64, and reprocessing activity;
   (iii) To reconsider the construction of a research reactor moderated by heavy water;
   (iv) Promptly to ratify and implement in full the Additional Protocol;

(v) Pending completion of the ratification of the Additional Protocol to continue to act in accordance with the provisions of the Additional Protocol, which Iran signed on 18 December 2003;

5. Calls on Iran to observe fully its commitments and to return to the negotiating process that has made good progress in the last two years;

6. Requests the Director General to continue his efforts to implement the Agency's Safeguards Agreement with Iran, to implement provisionally the Additional Protocol to that Agreement, and to pursue additional transparency measures required for the Agency to be able to reconstruct the history and nature of all aspects of Iran's past nuclear activities, and to compensate for the confidence deficit created; and

7. Decides to remain seized of the matter.

c. IAEA Resolution Referring Iran to the UNSC[197]

IAEA Board of Governors GOV/2006/14
(adopted 4 February 2006)

Implementation of the NPT Safeguards
Agreement in the Islamic Republic of Iran

The Board of Governors,

(a) Recalling all the resolutions adopted by the Board on Iran's nuclear programme,

(b) Recalling also the Director General's reports,

(c) Recalling that Article IV of the Treaty on the Non Proliferation of Nuclear Weapons stipulates that nothing in the Treaty shall be interpreted as affecting the inalienable rights of all the Parties to the Treaty to develop research, production and use of nuclear energy for peaceful purposes without discrimination and in conformity with Articles I and II of the Treaty,

197 *Implementation of the NPT Safeguards Agreement in the Islamic Republic of Iran,* IAEA Board of Governors Resolution GOV/2006/14, Feb. 4, 2006 (*available at* https://www.iaea.org/sites/default/files/gov2006-14.pdf).

(d) Commending the Director General and the Secretariat for their professional and impartial efforts to implement the Safeguards Agreement in Iran, to resolve outstanding safeguards issues in Iran and to verify the implementation by Iran of the suspension,

(e) Recalling the Director General's description of this as a special verification case,

(f) Recalling that in reports referred to above, the Director General noted that after nearly three years of intensive verification activity, the Agency is not yet in a position to clarify some important issues relating to Iran's nuclear programme or to conclude that there are no undeclared nuclear materials or activities in Iran,

(g) Recalling Iran's many failures and breaches of its obligations to comply with its NPT Safeguards Agreement and the absence of confidence that Iran's nuclear programme is exclusively for peaceful purposes resulting from the history of concealment of Iran's nuclear activities, the nature of those activities and other issues arising from the Agency's verification of declarations made by Iran since September 2002,

(h) Recalling that the Director General has stated that Iran's full transparency is indispensable and overdue for the Agency to be able to clarify outstanding issues (GOV/2005/67),

(i) Recalling the requests of the Agency for Iran's cooperation in following up on reports relating to equipment, materials and activities which have applications in the conventional military area and in the civilian sphere as well as in the nuclear military area (as indicated by the Director General in GOV/2005/67),

(j) Recalling that in November 2005 the Director General reported (GOV/2005/87) that Iran possesses a document related to the procedural requirements for the reduction of UF6 to metal in small quantities, and on the casting and machining of enriched, natural and depleted uranium metal into hemispherical forms,

(k) Expressing serious concerns about Iran's nuclear programme, and agreeing that an extensive period of confidence-building is required from Iran,

(l) Reaffirming the Board's resolve to continue to work for a diplomatic solution to the Iranian nuclear issue, and

(m) Recognising that a solution to the Iranian issue would contribute to global nonproliferation efforts and to realising the objective of a Middle East free of weapons of mass destruction, including their means of delivery,

1. Underlines that outstanding questions can best be resolved and confidence built in the exclusively peaceful nature of Iran's programme by Iran responding positively to the calls for confidence building measures which the Board has made on Iran, and in this context deems it necessary for Iran to:
    - re-establish full and sustained suspension of all enrichment-related and reprocessing activities, including research and development, to be verified by the Agency;
    - reconsider the construction of a research reactor moderated by heavy water;
    - ratify promptly and implement in full the Additional Protocol;
    - pending ratification, continue to act in accordance with the provisions of the Additional Protocol which Iran signed on 18 December 2003;
    - implement transparency measures, as requested by the Director General, including in GOV/2005/67, which extend beyond the formal requirements of the Safeguards Agreement and Additional Protocol, and include such access to individuals, documentation relating to procurement, dual use equipment, certain military-owned workshops and research and development as the Agency may request in support of its ongoing investigations;

2. Requests the Director General to report to the Security Council of the United Nations that these steps are required of Iran by the Board and to report to the Security Council all IAEA reports and resolutions, as adopted, relating to this issue;

3. Expresses serious concern that the Agency is not yet in a position to clarify some important issues relating to Iran's nuclear programme, including the fact that Iran has in its possession a document on the production of uranium metal hemispheres, since, as reported by the Secretariat, this process is related to the fabrication of nuclear weapon components; and, noting that the decision to put this document under Agency seal is a positive step, requests Iran to maintain this document under Agency seal and to provide a full copy to the Agency;

4. Deeply regrets that, despite repeated calls from the Board for the maintaining of the suspension of all enrichment related and reprocessing activities which the Board has declared essential to addressing outstanding issues, Iran resumed

uranium conversion activities at its Isfahan facility on 8 August 2005 and took steps to resume enrichment activities on 10 January 2006; GOV/2006/14

5. Calls on Iran to understand that there is a lack of confidence in Iran's intentions in seeking to develop a fissile material production capability against the background of Iran's record on safeguards as recorded in previous Resolutions, and outstanding issues; and to reconsider its position in relation to confidence-building measures, which are voluntary, and non legally binding, and to adopt a constructive approach in relation to negotiations that can result in increased confidence;

6. Requests Iran to extend full and prompt cooperation to the Agency, which the Director General deems indispensable and overdue, and in particular to help the Agency clarify possible activities which could have a military nuclear dimension;

7. Underlines that the Agency's work on verifying Iran's declarations is ongoing and requests the Director General to continue with his efforts to implement the Agency's Safeguards Agreement with Iran, to implement the Additional Protocol to that Agreement pending its entry into force, with a view to providing credible assurances regarding the absence of undeclared nuclear material and activities in Iran, and to pursue additional transparency measures required for the Agency to be able to resolve outstanding issues and reconstruct the history and nature of all aspects of Iran's past nuclear activities;

8. Requests the Director General to report on the implementation of this and previous resolutions to the next regular session of the Board, for its consideration, and immediately thereafter to convey, together with any Resolution from the March Board, that report to the Security Council; and

9. Decides to remain seized of the matter.

d. Security Council Ultimatum Resolution and Debate[198]

"*The Security Council,*

"*Recalling* the Statement of its President, S/PRST/2006/15, of 29 March 2006,

198 S.C. Res. 1696, SC/8792 (July 31, 2006) (available at http://www.un.org/News/Press/docs//2006/sc8792.doc.htm).

"*Reaffirming* its commitment to the Treaty on the Non-proliferation of Nuclear Weapons, and recalling the right of States Party, in conformity with Articles I and II of that Treaty, to develop research, production and use of nuclear energy for peaceful purposes without discrimination,

"*Noting* with serious concern the many reports of the IAEA Director General and resolutions of the IAEA Board of Governors related to Iran's nuclear programme, reported to it by the IAEA Director General, including IAEA Board Resolution GOV/2006/14,

"*Noting* with serious concern that the IAEA Director General's report of 27 February 2006 (GOV/2006/15) lists a number of outstanding issues and concerns on Iran's nuclear programme, including topics which could have a military nuclear dimension, and that the IAEA is unable to conclude that there are no undeclared nuclear materials or activities in Iran,

"*Noting* with serious concern the IAEA Director General's report of 28 April 2006 (GOV/2006/27) and its findings, including that, after more than three years of Agency efforts to seek clarity about all aspects of Iran's nuclear programme, the existing gaps in knowledge continue to be a matter of concern, and that the IAEA is unable to make progress in its efforts to provide assurances about the absence of undeclared nuclear material and activities in Iran,

"*Noting* with serious concern that, as confirmed by the IAEA Director General's report of 8 June 2006 (GOV/2006/38) Iran has not taken the steps required of it by the IAEA Board of Governors, reiterated by the Council in its statement of 29 March and which are essential to build confidence, and in particular Iran's decision to resume enrichment-related activities, including research and development, its recent expansion of and announcements about such activities, and its continued suspension of co-operation with the IAEA under the Additional Protocol,

"*Emphasizing* the importance of political and diplomatic efforts to find a negotiated solution guaranteeing that Iran's nuclear programme is exclusively for peaceful purposes, and *noting* that such a solution would benefit nuclear non-proliferation elsewhere,

"*Welcoming* the statement by the Foreign Minister of France, Philippe Douste-Blazy, on behalf of the Foreign Ministers of China, France, Germany, the Russian Federation, the United Kingdom, the United States and the High Representative of the European Union, in Paris on 12 July 2006 (S/2006/573),

"*Concerned* by the proliferation risks presented by the Iranian nuclear programme, *mindful* of its primary responsibility under the Charter of the United Nations for the maintenance of international peace and security, and *being determined* to prevent an aggravation of the situation,

"*Acting* under Article 40 of Chapter VII of the Charter of the United Nations in order to make mandatory the suspension required by the IAEA,

"1. *Calls upon* Iran without further delay to take the steps required by the IAEA Board of Governors in its resolution GOV/2006/14, which are essential to build confidence in the exclusively peaceful purpose of its nuclear programme and to resolve outstanding questions,

"2. *Demands*, in this context, that Iran shall suspend all enrichment-related and reprocessing activities, including research and development, to be verified by the IAEA,

"3. *Expresses* the conviction that such suspension as well as full, verified Iranian compliance with the requirements set out by the IAEA Board of Governors, would contribute to a diplomatic, negotiated solution that guarantees Iran's nuclear programme is for exclusively peaceful purposes, *underlines* the willingness of the international community to work positively for such a solution, *encourages* Iran, in conforming to the above provisions, to re-engage with the international community and with the IAEA, and *stresses* that such engagement will be beneficial to Iran,

"4. *Endorses*, in this regard, the proposals of China, France, Germany, theRussian Federation, the United Kingdom and the United States, with the support of the European Union's High Representative, for a long-term comprehensive arrangement which would allow for the development of relations and cooperation with Iran based on mutual respect and the establishment of international confidence in the exclusively peaceful nature of Iran's nuclear programme (S/2006/521),

"5. *Calls upon* all States, in accordance with their national legal authorities and legislation and consistent with international law, to exercise vigilance and prevent the transfer of any items, materials, goods and technology that could contribute to Iran's enrichment-related and reprocessing activities and ballistic missile programmes,

"6. *Expresses* its determination to reinforce the authority of the IAEA process, strongly supports the role of the IAEA Board of Governors, *commends and encourages* the Director General of the IAEA and its Secretariat for their ongoing professional and impartial efforts to resolve all remaining outstanding issues in Iran within the framework of the Agency, *underlines* the necessity of the IAEA continuing its work to clarify all outstanding issues relating to Iran's nuclear programme, and *calls upon* Iran to act in accordance with the provisions of the Additional Protocol and to implement without delay all transparency measures as the IAEA may request in support of its ongoing investigations,

"7. *Requests* by 31 August a report from the Director General of the IAEA primarily on whether Iran has established full and sustained suspension of all activities mentioned in this resolution, as well as on the process of Iranian compliance with all the steps required by the IAEA Board and with the above provisions of this resolution, to the IAEA Board of Governors and in parallel to the Security Council for its consideration,

"8. *Expresses* its intention, in the event that Iran has not by that date complied with this resolution, then to adopt appropriate measures under Article 41 of Chapter VII of the Charter of the United Nations to persuade Iran to comply with this resolution and the requirements of the IAEA, and *underlines* that further decisions will be required should such additional measures be necessary,

"9. *Confirms* that such additional measures will not be necessary in the event that Iran complies with this resolution,

"10. *Decides* to remain seized of the matter."

Action on Text

The Council adopted the text as resolution 1696 (2006), by a vote of 14 in favour to 1 against (Qatar).

Statements

…

JOHN BOLTON (United States) said four months had passed since the Council had called on Iran to suspend its nuclear programme. Two months had passed since the EU-3 (France, Germany, United Kingdom) + 3(China, Russian Federation, United States) had made its generous offer. That diplomatic effort had been preceded by more than three years of Iranian non-compliance with Non-Proliferation Treaty and its International Atomic Energy Agency (IAEA) safeguards agreement. Sadly, Iran had defied the international community by continuing its pursuit of nuclear weapons, and the continued defiance of its leadership demanded a strong response from the Council. He was pleased that the Council had taken clear and firm action in passing the resolution. The pursuit of nuclear weapons constituted a direct threat to international peace and security, and demanded a clear statement by the Council in the form of a tough resolution. It sent an unambiguous message to Iran, namely to take the steps set out by the IAEA Board of Governors, including full and sustained suspension of all enrichment-related and reprocessing activities, and suspend construction of its heavy-water reactor.

Iran should understand that the United States and others would ensure that financial transactions associated with proliferation activities would be impeded, he said. He expected Iran — and all other Member States — to immediately act in accordance with the resolution. It was the first Security Council resolution on Iran in response to its nuclear programme, reflecting the gravity of the situation and the Council's determination. He hoped the resolution would demonstrate to Iran that the best way to end its international isolation was to give up its pursuit of nuclear weapons. He hoped Iran would make the strategic decision that pursuit of weapons of mass destruction made it less, and not more, secure. Members needed to be prepared, however, that Iran might chose a different path. That was why the United States expressed its intention to adopt measures under Article 41 of the Charter, if Iran did not comply with the resolution.

EMYR JONES PARRY (United Kingdom) said that Iran's nuclear activities and its history of concealment had raised pressing questions about whether that country's programme was as it claimed – solely for peaceful purposes. He was deeply concerned over Iran's failure to cooperate fully with IAEA. After more than three years, the Agency was still unable to conclude that there was no undeclared nuclear material or related activities in Iran, including activities with a possible nuclear military dimension; that remained unanswered. The international community had shown great patience and given Iran many opportunities to show that it had no intentions to create nuclear weapons, but, unfortunately, Iran had not taken the necessary steps to build confidence.

Nevertheless, he said, his country remained committed to working towards a negotiated solution. On 6 June, Javier Solana had presented Iran with a new set of far-reaching and imaginative proposals for a comprehensive agreement, offering a way forward, one that would give Iran everything it needed to achieve its stated ambition of developing a modern civil nuclear-power industry. That included, among other things, support for building light-water power reactors, as well as legally binding assurances relating to the supply of nuclear power material, for which it would not have to depend on a single foreign supplier. The proposals would also offer Iran, among other benefits, significant trade benefits, including with the European Union. When Mr. Solana had presented the proposal, he had made it clear that it was essential for Iran to take the steps required by the IAEA Board of Governors, namely, full suspension of all uranium enrichment and reprocessing activities, including research and development, to be verified by the Agency.

If Iran suspended enrichment, the United Kingdom would be prepared to suspend further activity in the Security Council, he said. Continuation of enrichment-related and reprocessing activities, including research and development, would allow Iran to develop know-how to produce fissile material, which could be used for the production of nuclear weapons. The proposal had suggested a procedure to review the moratorium once confidence in Iran's intention had been restored. He was deeply disappointed that Iran had given no indication that it was ready to seriously engage in that proposal or take the necessary steps signalling its readiness to begin. A full suspension was required to help build confidence and create the atmosphere of trust necessary for negotiations. Those talks could not succeed if Iran continued the activities, which were a main source of international concern.

A Security Council resolution, which made mandatory the IAEA required suspension, was significant. Should Iran refuse to comply, he would work towards the adoption of measures under the Charter's Article 41. Should it implement the decision of the IAEA and the Council, and enter into negotiations, he would be ready to hold back from further action in the Council. He reaffirmed that the proposal conveyed to Iran by the six countries on 6 June remained valid. The choice was now Iran's. He urged and encouraged it to implement the steps required by the IAEA Board and the Security Council.

VITALY CHURKIN (Russian Federation) said the resolution expressed the need for Iran to establish full cooperation with IAEA, to clarify outstanding questions and for restoring confidence in its nuclear programme. The main purpose of the text was to support IAEA's efforts to resolve Iran's nuclear problem. The Agency should continue to play a central role in resolving non-proliferation issues in the context of Iran's nuclear programme. He hoped that, with the Council's support, it would be easier for IAEA to do that job. By acting under Article 40 of the Charter, the Council had rendered mandatory suspension of all uranium-enrichment activities. If Iran did not comply, members had expressed the intention to take appropriate action under Article 41. It was crucial to note that, it followed from the resolution, any additional measures that could be required to implement the resolution ruled out the use of military force.

He said the resolution should help to clarify outstanding issues and restore trust in its nuclear programme. This measure should be viewed as an interim measure, for the period necessary for resolving the issue. If Iran complied with the resolution, members would be prepared to refrain from any further action. If negotiations yielded a positive solution to the problem, no additional steps against Iran would be taken in the Council. The resolution also established a provision for Tehran's broad cooperation to meet Iran's energy requirements. It also reaffirmed the proposals transmitted to Iran on 6 June. His delegation hoped that Tehran would seriously view the contents of the resolution and would take the necessary steps to redress the situation.

ZIU ZHENMIN (China) said, since the beginning of the year, the issue of Iran's nuclear programme had attracted more and more attention. IAEA had conveyed to the Council a number of reports and resolutions related to the issue. China had all along indicated that the purpose for the Council's review of the issue was to safeguard the international nuclear non-proliferation mechanism, strengthen IAEA's authority and role, reinforce the endeavour of the Agency's Director General to clarify outstanding issues relating to Iran's nuclear programme, promote diplomatic efforts and commit to finding an appropriate solution to the issue through political and diplomatic means.

For the same purpose, the Council had issued a presidential statement on 29 March and had just adopted a resolution, he said. Regrettably, the Iranian side had yet to respond positively to the requests of the IAEA Board of Governors and the Council's calls. The resolution explicitly demanded that Iran suspend all enrichment-related and reprocessing activities. It expressed the intention, in the event that Iran failed to comply with the resolution, that the Council shall adopt appropriate measures under Article 41 of the Charter to persuade Iran to comply with the resolution and IAEA's requirements. On the other hand, in the event that Iran fulfils the above obligations and return to the negotiating table, it would not be necessary for the Council to adopt additional measures.

He said the resolution had stressed in many paragraphs the importance of finding a negotiated solution through political and diplomatic efforts. It had underlined the irreplaceable key role of IAEA in handling the issue. It had endorsed the "package proposals" put forward by China, France, Germany, Russia, the United Kingdom and the United States in early June, and emphasized that the proposals were important efforts for a comprehensive arrangement, which would allow for the development of bilateral relations and cooperation based on mutual respect and the establishment of international confidence in the exclusively peaceful nature of Iran's nuclear programme.

A belated appropriate solution to the Iran's nuclear issue was due to lack of trust among the main parties involved, he said. Whether now or in the future, the Council could not handle the issue single-handedly. Dialogue and negotiations were the only way out. IAEA should always be the main mechanism for dealing with the issue. Any measures adopted by the Council should serve the purpose of diplomatic efforts. According to Article 25 of the Charter, all Member States were obliged to carry out Security Council resolutions. Under the current circumstances, China urged Iran to practice restraint, earnestly implement the requirements of the resolution and make an early response to the "package proposals", so as to create conditions for increasing trust and promoting dialogue and negotiation.

He called upon all the other parties to adopt a highly responsible attitude towards world peace, security and stability and the international nuclear non-proliferation mechanism; remain confident and calm; practice restraint; explore new ways of thinking; and continue to creatively carry out diplomatic efforts for the settlement of Iran's nuclear issue. He welcomed any ideas conductive to conducting talks, breaking the stalemate and reaching compromises. During the current sensitive period, it was essential for Iran and for all practices concerned not to take any steps that would harm diplomatic efforts and might lead to complications or even loss of control. He called upon all parties to resume, as soon as possible, dialogue and negotiations for the proper solution of Iran's nuclear issue. China would continue its efforts to maintain world and regional peace and stability, safeguard and strengthen international non-proliferation mechanisms, and enhance political and diplomatic efforts for the solution of Iran's nuclear issue.

...

Speaking in his national capacity, JEAN-MARC DE LA SABLIÈRE (France), whose delegation holds the Council's presidency for July, said that the resolution had been made necessary by the fact that Iran, despite the three meetings with Mr. Solana, had not been willing to seriously address the substance of the proposals of 6 June on behalf of the six countries. Thus, there had been no alternative other than to resume the activity placed on hold in the Council. He was glad that the 15-member body, through today's vote, had supported the efforts of those six countries. France, together with Germany, would underline the following elements: the text had made the suspension requested by the IAEA mandatory, but that did not mean end to negotiations, and he had reaffirmed the proposals made on 6 June to Iran; if Iran refused to comply, the Council would work under Article 41 of Chapter VI of the Charter; and if Iran did comply and resumed negotiations, the Council could abstain from such action. He appealed to Iran to comply with the substantive proposals submitted to it last month.

JAVAD ZARIF (Iran) said his delegation had requested to be given an opportunity to speak before the Council took action, so that it would be appraised of the views of the concerned party before it adopted a decision. His previous request to speak before the Council when it adopted a presidential statement on 29 March had also been denied. It was indicative of the degree of transparency and fairness that the Security Council had adopted a presidential statement and a draft resolution, without allowing the views of the concerned party to be heard. For the record, he would make the statement intended for presentation before action. He expressed profound appreciation to Qatar for the negative vote based on their principles, as well as their legitimate concern for the regime.

He said it was not the first time that Iran's endeavours to stand on its own feet and make technological advances had faced the stiff resistance and concerted pressure of some powers permanently represented in the Council. Iran's struggle to nationalize its oil industry had been touted in a draft resolution submitted in October 1951 by the United Kingdom and supported by the United States and France as a threat to international peace and security. That draft had preceded a coup d'état, organized by the United States and United Kingdom, in a less veiled attempt to restore their short-sighted interests. More recently, Saddam Hussein's massive invasion of Iran in 1980 had not troubled the same permanent members to consider it a threat to international peace and security.

Over the past several weeks, the Council had been prevented from moving to stop the massive aggression against the Palestinian and Lebanese people and the resulting terrible humanitarian crises, he said. The Council would not have the slightest chance of addressing the oppressor's nuclear arsenal. Likewise, the Council had been prevented from reacting to the daily threats of resort to force against Iran uttered at the highest levels by the United States, the United Kingdom and the lawless Israeli regime, in violation of the Charter. On the other hand, in the past few years, a few big Powers had spared no efforts in turning the Security Council into a tool for attempting to prevent Iran from exercising its inalienable right to nuclear technology for peaceful purposes, recognized explicitly under the NPT.

The people and Government of Iran were determined to exercise their inalienable right to nuclear technology for peaceful purposes and build on their own scientific advances in developing various peaceful aspects of that technology, he continued. At the same time, as the only victims of the use of weapons of mass destruction in recent history, they rejected the development and use of all those inhumane weapons on ideological, as well as strategic, grounds. Iran's leader had issued a public and categorical religious decree against the development, production, stockpiling and use of nuclear weapons. Iran had also clearly stressed that nuclear weapons had no place in its military doctrine.

He noted that, in order to dispel any doubt about its peaceful nuclear programme, Iran had enabled IAEA to carry out a series of inspections, which had amounted to the most robust inspection of any IAEA Member State, including more than 2,000 inspector days of scrutiny in the past three years; the signing of the Additional Protocol on 18 December 2003 and implementing it immediately, until 6 February 2006; the submission of more than 1,000 pages of declarations in accordance with the Additional Protocol; and permitting inspectors to investigate baseless allegations, by taking the unprecedented step of providing repeated access to military sites.

Consequently, he said, all IAEA reports since November 2003 had been indicative of the peaceful nature of the Iranian nuclear programme. In November of that year and in the wake of sensational media reports on the so-called 18 years of concealment by war, IAEA had confirmed that "to date, there is no evidence that the previously undeclared nuclear material and activities ...were related to a nuclear weapons programme". The same can be found in other IAEA reports, as recent as February 2006.

Much had been made, included in today's resolution, of a statement by IAEA that it was not yet in a position to conclude that there were no undeclared nuclear materials or activities in Iran, he said. The sponsors had ignored, however, the repeated acknowledgement by the IAEA Director General that the process of drawing such a conclusion was a time-consuming process. They had also ignored the addendum to the *2005 IAEA Safeguards Implementation Report*, released in June 2006, which indicated that 45 other countries were in the same category as Iran, including 14 European and several members of the Council.

Iran's peaceful nuclear programme posed no threat to international peace and security, he said. Dealing with the issue in the Council was, therefore, unwarranted and void of any legal basis or practical utility. Far from reflecting the international community's concerns, the approach of the sponsors flouted the stated position of the overwhelming majority of the international community, clearly reflected in the most recent statements by foreign ministers of the Non-Aligned Movement and the Organization of the Islamic Conference, and partly reflected in the June 2006 IAEA Board Chairman's Conclusion.

Claiming to represent the international community, the EU-3, in their so-called package of incentives of last August, had asked Iran to "make a binding commitment not to pursue fuel cycle activities". A cursory look at the chronology of events since last August indicated that Iran's rejection of that illegal and unwarranted demand had, and continued to be, the sole reason for the imposition of resolutions and statements on the IAEA Board and the Council.

Today's action by the Council — which was the culmination of those efforts aimed at making the suspension of uranium enrichment mandatory — violated the fundamental principles of international law, the NPT and IAEA resolutions. It also ran counter to the views of the majority of United Nations Member States, which the Council was obliged to represent. The sole reason for pushing the Council to take action was that Iran had decided, after over two years of negotiations, to resume the exercise of its inalienable right to nuclear technology for peaceful purposes, by partially reopening its fully safeguarded facilities and ending a voluntary suspension. Iran's right to enrich uranium was recognized under the NPT. And, upholding the right of States parties to international regimes was as essential as ensuring respect for their obligations. Those regimes, including the NPT, were sustained by a balance between rights and obligations. Threats would not sustain the NPT or other international regimes. Ensuring that members could draw rightful benefits from membership, and non-members were not rewarded for their intransigence, did.

"Yet, exactly the opposite is the trend today", he said. Today, the world was witness to a dangerous trend. While members of the NPT were denied their rights and punished, those who defied the NPT, particularly the perpetrators of current carnage in Lebanon and Palestine, were rewarded by generous nuclear cooperation agreements. "This is one awkward way to safeguard the NPT or ensure its universality", he said.

The trend, he added, had reached a horrendous, and indeed ridiculous, state with the Israeli regime. That regime, a non-member of the NPT, whose nuclear arsenal was coupled with its expansionist, repressive and state-terror policies, was repeatedly recognized as the most serious threat to regional and international peace and security. Yet, it had the audacity to cry wolf about Iran's peaceful nuclear programme and lead a global campaign of threats, lies, deception, pressure, blackmail and outright extortion. In spite of the massive political and propaganda machine, no one in today's world could accept the convoluted logic that it was okay for some to have nuclear weapons, while others were prevented from developing nuclear energy.

Another destructive trend was the imposition of arbitrary thresholds, which were often a function of bilateral considerations, rather than objective or technical criteria, he said. The new threshold regarding enrichment was as arbitrary as the previous ones, and was simply another excuse to begin a trend to prevent the realization of the rights of the NPT members to peaceful use, while, according to the United States Ambassador, non-members could "legitimately" continue producing nuclear bombs.

He said it had been argued that the Council's intervention was needed to ensure cooperation by Iran with IAEA, and to bring Iran back to the negotiating table. He suggested that, in order to achieve that goal, Security Council involvement was not needed. In fact, the Council's involvement hindered, rather than helped the ongoing process, because it was designed as an instrument of pressure. Iran's cooperation with the Agency was far more extensive and comprehensive before action was imposed on the Board to engage the Council. As for coming back to the negotiating table, Iran had always been ready for negotiations. For almost three years, Iran had tried to sustain or even resuscitate negotiations with the EU-3. Iran had offered far-reaching proposals to usher in a new era of cooperation, in August 2004, in January, March, April, July and September 2005, and in January, February and March 2006.

Throughout that period, Iran had adopted extensive and extremely costly confidence-building measures, including suspension of its rightful enrichment activities for two years, to ensure the success of negotiations, he said. All along, it had been the persistence of some to draw arbitrary red lines and deadlines that had closed the door to any compromise. That tendency had single-handedly blocked success and, in most cases, killed proposals in their infancy. That had been Washington's persistent strategy ever since Iran and the EU-3 had started their negotiations in October 2003. "Only the tactics have changed", he said.

"All along, the threats by some to bring this issue before the Council and take it out of its proper technical and negotiated structure has loomed large over the negotiations and has impeded progress, derailed discussions and prevented focus on a mutually acceptable resolution," he said. The manner in which negotiations over the recently proposed package had been conducted was a further indication of the same propensity to resort to threats and the lack of a genuine will to reach a mutually acceptable resolution. Iran had publicly, and in a show of good faith, reacted positively to that initiative and had indicated its readiness to engage in fair, non-discriminatory and result-oriented negotiations about the package, within a mutually agreed time frame and without preconditions. Yet, an arbitrary deadline had been set, ex post facto, without any justification, and only to serve the totally ulterior objective of "maximizing pressure".

Indeed, it had taken the EU-3 nearly five months, from March to August 2005, to consider a very serious proposal by Iran last year and, even then, the EU-3 had come up with a response that did not address any elements of that proposal, he noted. And yet, while Iran had clearly stated that it required three more weeks to conclude its evaluation of the proposed package and come up with a substantive reaction, it was astonishing to see that the EU-3 and the United States were in such a rush to prematurely hamper the path of negotiations by imposing a destructive and totally unwarranted Council resolution. Compare that rush to the fact that some of the very same Powers had for the last three weeks prevented any action, not even a 72-hour truce, by the Council on the urgent situation in Lebanon. "You be the judge of how much credibility this leaves for the Security Council. Millions of people around the world have already passed their judgement."

Concluding, he said it was pertinent to ask what the motive was behind the long-standing urge of some permanent members to bring Iran before the Council. Was it anything but pressure and coercion? That approach would not lead to any productive outcome and, in fact, it could only exacerbate the situation. The people and Government of Iran were not seeking any confrontation and had always shown their readiness to engage in serious and result-oriented negotiation, based on mutual respect and equal footing. They had also showed, time and again, their resilience in the face of pressure, threat, injustice and imposition.

e. Security Council Resolution Imposing Sanctions[199]

Resolution 1737 (2006)
Adopted by the Security Council at its 5612th meeting, on
23 December 2006

The Security Council,
Recalling the Statement of its President, S/PRST/2006/15, of 29 March 2006, and its resolution 1696 (2006) of 31 July 2006,

Reaffirming its commitment to the Treaty on the Non-Proliferation of Nuclear Weapons, and recalling the right of States Party, in conformity with Articles I and II of that Treaty, to develop research, production and use of nuclear energy for peaceful purposes without discrimination,

Reiterating its serious concern over the many reports of the IAEA Director General and resolutions of the IAEA Board of Governors related to Iran's nuclear programme, reported to it by the IAEA Director General, including IAEA Board resolution GOV/2006/14,

Reiterating its serious concern that the IAEA Director General's report of 27 February 2006 (GOV/2006/15) lists a number of outstanding issues and concerns on Iran's nuclear programme, including topics which could have a military nuclear dimension, and that the IAEA is unable to conclude that there are no undeclared nuclear materials or activities in Iran,

Reiterating its serious concern over the IAEA Director General's report of 28 April 2006 (GOV/2006/27) and its findings, including that, after more than three years of Agency efforts to seek clarity about all aspects of Iran's nuclear programme, the existing gaps in knowledge continue to be a matter of concern, and that the IAEA is unable to make progress in its efforts to provide assurances about the absence of undeclared nuclear material and activities in Iran,

Noting with serious concern that, as confirmed by the IAEA Director General's reports of 8 June 2006 (GOV/2006/38), 31 August 2006 (GOV/2006/53) and 14 November 2006 (GOV/2006/64), Iran has not established full and sustained suspension of all enrichment-related and reprocessing activities as set out in resolution 1696 (2006), nor resumed its cooperation with the IAEA under the

Additional Protocol, nor taken the other steps required of it by the IAEA Board of Governors, nor complied with the provisions of Security Council resolution 1696 (2006) and which are essential to build confidence, and

Deploring Iran's refusal to take these steps,

199 S.C. Res. 1737 (Dec. 23, 2006) (*available at* http://www.un.org/ga/search/view_doc.asp?symbol=S/RES/1737(2006)).

Emphasizing the importance of political and diplomatic efforts to find a negotiated solution guaranteeing that Iran's nuclear programme is exclusively forpeaceful purposes, and *noting* that such a solution would benefit nuclear nonproliferation elsewhere, and *welcoming* the continuing commitment of China, France, Germany, the Russian Federation, the United Kingdom and the United States, with the support of the European Union's High Representative to seek a negotiated solution,

Determined to give effect to its decisions by adopting appropriate measures to persuade Iran to comply with resolution 1696 (2006) and with the requirements of the IAEA, and also to constrain Iran's development of sensitive technologies in support of its nuclear and missile programmes, until such time as the Security Council determines that the objectives of this resolution have been met,

Concerned by the proliferation risks presented by the Iranian nuclear programme and, in this context, by Iran's continuing failure to meet the requirements of the IAEA Board of Governors and to comply with the provisions of Security Council resolution 1696 (2006), *mindful* of its primary responsibility under the Charter of the United Nations for the maintenance of international peace and security,

Acting under Article 41 of Chapter VII of the Charter of the United Nations,

1. *Affirms* that Iran shall without further delay take the steps required by the IAEA Board of Governors in its resolution GOV/2006/14, which are essential to build confidence in the exclusively peaceful purpose of its nuclear programme and to resolve outstanding questions;

2. *Decides*, in this context, that Iran shall without further delay suspend the following proliferation sensitive nuclear activities:

   (a) all enrichment-related and reprocessing activities, including research and development, to be verified by the IAEA; and

   (b) work on all heavy water-related projects, including the construction of a research reactor moderated by heavy water, also to be verified by the IAEA;

3. *Decides* that all States shall take the necessary measures to prevent the supply, sale or transfer directly or indirectly from their territories, or by their nationals or using their flag vessels or aircraft to, or for the use in or benefit of, Iran, and whether or not originating in their territories, of all items, materials, equipment, goods and technology which could contribute to Iran's enrichment-related, reprocessing or

heavy water-related activities, or to the development of nuclear weapon delivery systems, namely:

(a) those set out in sections B.2, B.3, B.4, B.5, B.6 and B.7 of INFCIRC/254/Rev.8/Part 1 in document S/2006/814;

(b) those set out in sections A.1 and B.1 of INFCIRC/254/Rev.8/Part 1 in document S/2006/814, except the supply, sale or transfer of:
   (i) equipment covered by B.1 when such equipment is for light water reactors;
   (ii) low-enriched uranium covered by A.1.2 when it is incorporated in assembled nuclear fuel elements for such reactors;

(c) those set out in document S/2006/815, except the supply, sale or transfer of items covered by 19.A.3 of Category II;

(d) any additional items, materials, equipment, goods and technology, determined as necessary by the Security Council or the Committee established by paragraph 18 below (herein "the Committee"), which could contribute to enrichment-related, or reprocessing, or heavy water-related activities, or to the development of nuclear weapon delivery systems;

4. *Decides* that all States shall take the necessary measures to prevent the supply, sale or transfer directly or indirectly from their territories, or by their nationals or using their flag vessels or aircraft to, or for the use in or benefit of, Iran, and whether or not originating in their territories, of the following items, materials, equipment, goods and technology:

(a) those set out in INFCIRC/254/Rev.7/Part2 of document S/2006/814 if the State determines that they would contribute to enrichment-related, reprocessing or heavy water-related activities;

(b) any other items not listed in documents S/2006/814 or S/2006/815 if the State determines that they would contribute to enrichment-related, reprocessing or heavy water-related activities, or to the development of nuclear weapon delivery systems;

(c) any further items if the State determines that they would contribute to the pursuit of activities related to other topics about which the IAEA has expressed concerns or identified as outstanding;

5. *Decides* that, for the supply, sale or transfer of all items, materials, equipment, goods and technology covered by documents S/2006/814 and S/2006/815 the export of which to Iran is not prohibited by subparagraphs 3 (b), 3 (c) or 4 (a) above, States shall ensure that:

(a) the requirements, as appropriate, of the Guidelines as set out in documents S/2006/814 and S/2006/985 have been met; and

(b) they have obtained and are in a position to exercise effectively a right to verify the end-use and end-use location of any supplied item; and

(c) they notify the Committee within ten days of the supply, sale or transfer; and

(d) in the case of items, materials, equipment, goods and technology contained in document S/2006/814, they also notify the IAEA within ten days of the supply, sale or transfer;

6. *Decides* that all States shall also take the necessary measures to prevent the provision to Iran of any technical assistance or training, financial assistance, investment, brokering or other services, and the transfer of financial resources or services, related to the supply, sale, transfer, manufacture or use of the prohibited items, materials, equipment, goods and technology specified in paragraphs 3 and 4 above;

7. *Decides* that Iran shall not export any of the items in documents S/2006/814 and S/2006/815 and that all Member States shall prohibit the procurement of such items from Iran by their nationals, or using their flag vessels or aircraft, and whether or not originating in the territory of Iran;

8. *Decides* that Iran shall provide such access and cooperation as the IAEA requests to be able to verify the suspension outlined in paragraph 2 and to resolve all outstanding issues, as identified in IAEA reports, and *calls upon* Iran to ratify promptly the Additional Protocol;

9. *Decides* that the measures imposed by paragraphs 3, 4 and 6 above shall not apply where the Committee determines in advance and on a case-by-case basis that such supply, sale, transfer or provision of such items or assistance would clearly not contribute to the development of Iran's technologies in support of its proliferation sensitive nuclear activities and of development of nuclear weapon delivery systems, including where such items or assistance are for food, agricultural, medical or other humanitarian purposes, provided that:

(a) contracts for delivery of such items or assistance include appropriate end-user guarantees; and

(b) Iran has committed not to use such items in proliferation sensitive nuclear activities or for development of nuclear weapon delivery systems;

10. *Calls upon* all States to exercise vigilance regarding the entry into or transit through their territories of individuals who are engaged in, directly associated with or providing support for Iran's proliferation sensitive nuclear activities or for the development of nuclear weapon delivery systems, and *decides* in this regard that all States shall notify the Committee of the entry into or transit through their territories of the persons designated in the Annex to this resolution (herein "the Annex"), as well as of additional persons designated by the Security Council or the Committee as being engaged in, directly associated with or providing support for Iran's proliferation sensitive nuclear activities and for the development of nuclear weapon delivery systems, including through the involvement in procurement of the prohibited items, goods, equipment, materials and technology specified by and under the measures in paragraphs 3 and 4 above, except where such travel is for activities directly related to the items in subparagraphs 3 (b) (i) and (ii) above;

11. *Underlines* that nothing in the above paragraph requires a State to refuse its own nationals entry into its territory, and that all States shall, in the implementation of the above paragraph, take into account humanitarian considerations as well as the necessity to meet the objectives of this resolution, including where Article XV of the IAEA Statute is engaged;

12. *Decides* that all States shall freeze the funds, other financial assets and economic resources which are on their territories at the date of adoption of this resolution or at any time thereafter, that are owned or controlled by the persons or entities designated in the Annex, as well as those of additional persons or entities

designated by the Security Council or by the Committee as being engaged in, directly associated with or providing support for Iran's proliferation sensitive nuclear activities or the development of nuclear weapon delivery systems, or by persons or entities acting on their behalf or at their direction, or by entities owned or controlled by them, including through illicit means, and that the measures in this paragraph shall cease to apply in respect of such persons or entities if, and at such time as, the Security Council or the Committee removes them from the Annex, and *decides further* that all States shall ensure that any funds, financial assets or economic resources are prevented from being made available by their nationals or by any persons or entities within their territories, to or for the benefit of these persons and entities;

13. *Decides* that the measures imposed by paragraph 12 above do not apply to funds, other financial assets or economic resources that have been determined by relevant States:

(a) to be necessary for basic expenses, including payment for foodstuffs, rent or mortgage, medicines and medical treatment, taxes, insurance premiums, and public utility charges or exclusively for payment of reasonable professional fees and reimbursement of incurred expenses associated with the provision of legal services, or fees or service charges, in accordance with national laws, for routine holding or maintenance of frozen funds, other financial assets and economic resources, after notification by the relevant States to the Committee of the intention to authorize, where appropriate, access to such funds, other financial assets or economic resources and in the absence of a negative decision by the Committee within five working days of such notification;

(b) to be necessary for extraordinary expenses, provided that such determination has been notified by the relevant States to the Committee and has been approved by the Committee;

(c) to be the subject of a judicial, administrative or arbitral lien or judgement, in which case the funds, other financial assets and economic resourcesmay be used to satisfy that lien or judgement provided that the lien or judgement was entered into prior to the date of the present resolution, is not for the benefit of a person or entity designated pursuant to paragraphs 10 and 12 above, and has been notified by the relevant States to the Committee;

(d) to be necessary for activities directly related to the items specified in subparagraphs 3 (b) (i) and (ii) and have been notified by the relevant States to the Committee;

14. *Decides* that States may permit the addition to the accounts frozen pursuant to the provisions of paragraph 12 above of interests or other earnings due on those accounts or payments due under contracts, agreements or obligations that arose prior to the date on which those accounts became subject to the provisions of this resolution, provided that any such interest, other earnings and payments continue to be subject to these provisions and are frozen;

15. *Decides* that the measures in paragraph 12 above shall not prevent a designated person or entity from making payment due under a contract entered into prior to the listing of such a person or entity, provided that the relevant States have determined that:

(a) the contract is not related to any of the prohibited items, materials, equipment, goods, technologies, assistance, training, financial assistance, investment, brokering or services referred to in paragraphs 3, 4 and 6 above;

(b) the payment is not directly or indirectly received by a person or entity designated pursuant to paragraph 12 above; and after notification by the relevant States to the Committee of the intention to make or receive such payments or to authorize, where appropriate, the unfreezing of funds, other financial assets or economic resources for this purpose, ten working days prior to such authorization;

16. *Decides* that technical cooperation provided to Iran by the IAEA or under its auspices shall only be for food, agricultural, medical, safety or other humanitarian purposes, or where it is necessary for projects directly related to the items specified in subparagraphs 3 (b) (i) and (ii) above, but that no such technical cooperation shall be provided that relates to the proliferation sensitive nuclear activities set out in paragraph 2 above;

17. *Calls upon* all States to exercise vigilance and prevent specialized teaching or training of Iranian nationals, within their territories or by their nationals, of disciplines which would contribute to Iran's proliferation sensitive nuclear activities and development of nuclear weapon delivery systems;

18. *Decides* to establish, in accordance with rule 28 of its provisional rules of procedure, a Committee of the Security Council consisting of all the members of the Council, to undertake the following tasks:

(a) to seek from all States, in particular those in the region and those producing the items, materials, equipment, goods and technology referred to in paragraphs 3 and 4 above, information regarding the actions taken by them to implement effectively the measures imposed by paragraphs 3, 4, 5, 6, 7, 8, 10 and 12 of this resolution and whatever further information it may consider useful in this regard;

(b) to seek from the secretariat of the IAEA information regarding the actions taken by the IAEA to implement effectively the measures imposed by paragraph 16 of this resolution and whatever further information it may consider useful in this regard;

(c) to examine and take appropriate action on information regarding alleged violations of measures imposed by paragraphs 3, 4, 5, 6, 7, 8, 10 and 12 of this resolution;

(d) to consider and decide upon requests for exemptions set out in paragraphs 9, 13 and 15 above;

(e) to determine as may be necessary additional items, materials, equipment, goods and technology to be specified for the purpose of paragraph 3 above;

(f) to designate as may be necessary additional individuals and entities subject to the measures imposed by paragraphs 10 and 12 above;

(g) to promulgate guidelines as may be necessary to facilitate the implementation of the measures imposed by this resolution and include in such guidelines a requirement on States to provide information where possible as to why any individuals and/or entities meet the criteria set out in paragraphs 10 and 12 and any relevant identifying information;

(h) to report at least every 90 days to the Security Council on its work and on the implementation of this resolution, with its observations and recommendations, in particular on ways to strengthen the effectiveness of the measures imposed by paragraphs 3, 4, 5, 6, 7, 8, 10 and 12 above;

19. *Decides* that all States shall report to the Committee within 60 days of the adoption of this resolution on the steps they have taken with a view to implementing effectively paragraphs 3, 4, 5, 6, 7, 8, 10, 12 and 17 above;

20. *Expresses* the conviction that the suspension set out in paragraph 2 above as well as full, verified Iranian compliance with the requirements set out by the IAEA Board of Governors, would contribute to a diplomatic, negotiated solution that guarantees Iran's nuclear programme is for exclusively peaceful purposes, *underlines* the willingness of the international community to work positively for such a solution, *encourages* Iran, in conforming to the above provisions, to re-engage with the international community and with the IAEA, and *stresses* that such engagement will be beneficial to Iran;

21. *Welcomes* the commitment of China, France, Germany, the Russian Federation, the United Kingdom and the United States, with the support of the European Union's High Representative, to a negotiated solution to this issue and encourages Iran to engage with their June 2006 proposals (S/2006/521), which were endorsed by the Security Council in resolution 1696 (2006), for a long-term comprehensive agreement which would allow for the development of relations and cooperation with Iran based on mutual respect and the establishment of international confidence in the exclusively peaceful nature of Iran's nuclear programme;

22. *Reiterates* its determination to reinforce the authority of the IAEA, strongly supports the role of the IAEA Board of Governors, *commends* and *encourages* the Director General of the IAEA and its secretariat for their ongoing professional and impartial efforts to resolve all remaining outstanding issues in Iran within the framework of the IAEA, *underlines* the necessity of the IAEA continuing its work to clarify all outstanding issues relating to Iran's nuclear programme;

23. *Requests* within 60 days a report from the Director General of the IAEA on whether Iran has established full and sustained suspension of all activities mentioned in this resolution, as well as on the process of Iranian compliance with all the steps required by the IAEA Board and with the other provisions of this resolution, to the IAEA Board of Governors and in parallel to the Security Council for its consideration;

24. *Affirms* that it shall review Iran's actions in the light of the report referred to in paragraph 23 above, to be submitted within 60 days, and:

(a) that it shall suspend the implementation of measures if and for so long as Iran suspends all enrichment-related and reprocessing activities, including research and development, as verified by the IAEA, to allow for negotiations;

(b) that it shall terminate the measures specified in paragraphs 3, 4, 5, 6, 7, 10 and 12 of this resolution as soon as it determines that Iran has fully complied with its obligations under the relevant resolutions of the Security Council and met the requirements of the IAEA Board of Governors, as confirmed by the IAEA Board;

(c) that it shall, in the event that the report in paragraph 23 above shows that Iran has not complied with this resolution, adopt further appropriate measures under Article 41 of Chapter VII of the Charter of the United Nations to persuade Iran to comply with this resolution and the requirements of the IAEA, and underlines that further decisions will be required should such additional measures be necessary;

25. *Decides* to remain seized of the matter.

S/RES/1737 (2006)
Annex

A. Entities involved in the nuclear programme

1. Atomic Energy Organisation of Iran
2. Mesbah Energy Company (provider for A40 research reactor – Arak)
3. Kala-Electric (aka Kalaye Electric) (provider for PFEP – Natanz)
4. Pars Trash Company (involved in centrifuge programme, identified in IAEA reports)
5. Farayand Technique (involved in centrifuge programme, identified in IAEA reports)
6. Defence Industries Organisation (overarching MODAFL-controlled entity, some of whose subordinates have been involved in the centrifuge programme making components, and in the missile programme)
7. 7th of Tir (subordinate of DIO, widely recognized as being directly involved in the nuclear programme)

B. Entities involved in the ballistic missile programme

1. Shahid Hemmat Industrial Group (SHIG) (subordinate entity of AIO)
2. Shahid Bagheri Industrial Group (SBIG) (subordinate entity of AIO)
3. Fajr Industrial Group (formerly Instrumentation Factory Plant, subordinate entity of AIO)

C. Persons involved in the nuclear programme

1. Mohammad Qannadi, AEOI Vice President for Research & Development
2. Behman Asgarpour, Operational Manager (Arak)
3. Dawood Agha-Jani, Head of the PFEP (Natanz)
4. Ehsan Monajemi, Construction Project Manager, Natanz
5. Jafar Mohammadi, Technical Adviser to the AEOI (in charge of managing the production of valves for centrifuges)
6. Ali Hajinia Leilabadi, Director General of Mesbah Energy Company
7. Lt Gen Mohammad Mehdi Nejad Nouri, Rector of Malek Ashtar University of Defence Technology (chemistry dept, affiliated to MODALF, has conducted experiments on beryllium)

D. Persons involved in the ballistic missile programme

1. Gen Hosein Salimi, Commander of the Air Force, IRGC (Pasdaran)
2. Ahmad Vahid Dastjerdi, Head of the AIO

6. Thesis 1—Does Iran's Conduct Comply with the NPT or Is It the Behavior of a "Rogue" State?

Is a constructivist explanation of the U.S. – Iran dispute necessary? Can a rational choice explanation supply an adequate account? If a rational choice explanation is not adequate, does constructivism supply a better account? We take each question in turn.

a. A Rational Choice Account of the Crisis

A rational choice account of the crisis is founded on the premise that the NPT regime addresses, here as in all other cases, the security dilemma. Both the United States (and its allies) and Iran are viewed as rational egoists. Under this view, the U.S. invasion of Afghanistan and

Iraq, together with U.S. rhetoric about Iranian policies, may have suggested to Iran that it faces a much greater risk of a Sucker's Payoff—a U.S. invasion undeterred by an independent Iranian nuclear weapons capability. That change may have de-stabilized the basis for the earlier cooperation between the United States and Iran within the NPT regime.

On this analysis, the United States and its allies responded to Iranian defection from a previously stable game by beginning to employ a tit-for-tat strategy through the political organs of the IAEA and the UN. Iran is presented with a series of escalating consequences for its own defection, in the hope of inducing it at some step in the process to walk back. Thus, Iran's first move is to engage in preliminary steps toward the creation of a full nuclear fuel cycle, including the weapons-sensitive activities of full-scale enrichment (in an energy security context, given Iran's massive oil reserves, that belies Iran's purported peaceful intentions). The IAEA responds with a finding of non-compliance, seeking to induce Iranian cooperation. Continued non-cooperation by Iran induces the IAEA to take the next incremental step of referring the matter to the U.N. Security Council. Continued Iranian noncompliance induces the U.N. to threaten sanctions. Finally, Iran's failure to respond induces the Security Council to impose discriminate sanctions, continuing to leave open the possibility of further tit-for-tat responses designed to induce Iranian cooperation at some optimal point in which the benefits of future cooperation and costs of further defection persuade Iran to change course. Plainly, on this view, the United States and its allies are playing a prisoners dilemma game, signaling their intention and hoping through a process of incremental defection to persuade Iran that it has misperceived U.S. intentions, which present no real risk to it of a Sucker's Payoff.

The formal structure of the legal debate maps onto this rational choice account. Legal claims concerning Iranian violations focus on Iran's technical breach of safeguards obligations, but are also framed as an Iranian attempt to breach its core NPT obligations. In this context, the formal legal argument against Iran reaches Iran's right to full nuclear fuel cycle capabilities, as a countermeasure under the law of state responsibility for a material breach under the law of treaties. The procedural rules for communication between the IAEA and U.N. Security Council transfer the legal debate, now settled, to an international political process for action by a nominally neutral third party, the U.N. Security Council. The institutionalized nonproliferation regimes thus set a boundary between law and policy that is crossed once the Security Council's discretionary authority to impose sanctions is engaged. Rational choice theory thus provides a recognizable theory of international law, creating a boundary between law and policy that legitimizes international law and, arguably, restores the normative claim that all NPT parties are governed by a set of rules that help them escape from the security dilemma.

b. A Constructivist Theory of the U.S.-Iran Crisis?

Constructivism would describe the legal and political conflict between the United States and Iran as, ultimately, a conflict over competing ideas, norms, and identities rather than a contest over security, power or material resources. A constructivist analysis would therefore attempt to describe and understand the conflict primarily in terms of its ideational origins. If constructivism is to be a viable alternative to realism and rational choice, it must provide a richer account of the competing "interests" at stake in the conflict, how they came to be formed, and whether they might be reconciled. Consider, then, how Wendt's constructivism might be applied to characterize each side's view of the current international order.[200]

For the United States, international anarchy presents, in substance, what Wendt called a Lockean culture (though one in which not all states are equally sovereign). In Iran's vision, international anarchy combines characteristics from each of Wendt's two other cultures. Iran views the Western world through a Hobbesian lens, and the Muslim world through a Kantian one. Iran's Hobbesian image of the Western world is congruent with the traditional Islamic vision of the *dar al-harb*, its Kantian picture of the Muslim world with the traditional *dar al-Islam.*

i. The Lockean Culture of Anarchy in the "Axis of Evil" Speech

The U.S. view of Iran's place in the international order focused on two crucial ideas—first, Iran's status as a rogue state; second, Iran's breach or threatened breach of the "nuclear taboo."[201]

As we have previously explained,[202] the Lockean culture of anarchy is grounded in the principle of territorial sovereignty, coupled with the assumption of international rivalry. However, Lockean culture operates within a range between the purely hierarchical Hobbesian culture and the non-hierarchical Kantian culture. It is thus possible for a Lockean conception of the world order to regard sovereignty as divisible. States may hold different degrees of sovereignty and individual rights may be opposable to sovereign rights. Degrees of sovereignty and protection of individual rights permit a distinction to be drawn between the "civilized," which are full members in good standing of the society of states, and the "uncivilized," states or societies that are

200 We should not be taken to be suggesting that only one constructivist description of the conflict is available. Indeed, as we shall soon argue, the inability of constructivism to supply a fully determinate description of the U.S.-Iran conflict is a *failing* in the theory.

201 The "nuclear taboo" can be defined as the "powerful *de facto* prohibition against the first use of nuclear weapons. The taboo is not the behavior (of non-use) but rather *the normative belief about the behavior.*" Nina Tannenwald, The Nuclear Taboo: The United States and the Non-Use of Nuclear Weapons Since 1945 10 (2007). When the term is used in this sense, it reflects the "forbidden" quality of a taboo and has its origins in Freudian analysis of primitive forms of social organization, which on this account coalesce through ritual and sacrifice involving holy, or "totemic," objects and unholy, or "taboo," objects. *See* Sigmund Freud, Totem and Taboo (Strachey trans. 1950).

202 *See supra* note 67 and accompanying text.

unable or unwilling to exercise the rights and fulfill duties of full members.[203] Thus, in a Lockean culture, Iran's sovereignty may be conditioned on its regard for "civilized" international norms, including both the nuclear taboo and human rights. Though a Lockean culture acknowledges the pervasive phenomenon of international rivalry, it may insist that rivalry be bounded by a set of rules that check its drift into Hobbesian enmity.

On this interpretation, the U.S. characterization of Iran as a "rogue" state drew on its Lockean conception of the international order. Rogue states are conceptualized as having two inter-linked aspects: a tendency toward violence against their own population (or some part of it) and a tendency toward aggression against other states. As a rogue state, Iran's human rights violations against its own people (including what is seen as massive electoral fraud) undercut the conditions of its limited sovereignty. A sovereign may forfeit its right against external intervention if it commits serious human rights abuses against its own people or does not truly "represent" them. Further, the characterization of Iran as a rogue state was supported by its repeated attacks on the legitimacy, sovereignty, and existence of other states, predominantly Israel. Iran was considered a "rogue" state because of its alignment with other "rejectionist" Middle Eastern states, such as Syria, that challenged the regional status quo, its assistance to groups that are considered to be terrorist, like Hamas and Hezbollah, and its threatened breach of the nuclear taboo.

Iran's human rights violations against its own people were also taken to signal Iran's readiness to threaten the sovereignty, territory, and population of other states. Lockean states accordingly perceived Iran as viewing them as Hobbesian "enemies" rather than Lockean "rivals," and so as posing an "existential" threat to them. Calling Iran part of "an axis of evil," as President George W. Bush did, evoked the image of Nazi Germany—the paradigmatic "uncivilized" state in post-colonial terms. Iran was thought, like Germany after its defeat in 1945, to have lost its entitlement to equal treatment as a fully sovereign state.

The characterization of Iran as a rogue state is a matter of international politics rather than international law; but it is likely to carry legal consequences. If Iran is a rogue state, then Lockean states can legitimately seek to have it sanctioned under international law. They can press the Security Council to deny Iran the full measure of its rights as a party to the NPT legal regime—namely, those relating to weapons-sensitive nuclear technology. Both in law and in policy, the United States and its allies sought to "reproduce" the anarchical culture of limited, Lockean sovereignty in relation to Iran.

ii. Hobbesian and Kantian Cultures of Anarchy—the "Axis of Unity" Speech

The Iranian view of the world order drew on two different categorical schemes—one secular and contemporary, the other Islamic and traditional. First, Iran used the same (secular)

203 *See* Keene, *supra* note 11.

categories of international law and international politics as the United States does to describe the relations between the two countries, but it systematically reversed the application of those categories, projecting them back against the United States and the West. Second, especially in relation to the rest of the Islamic world, Iran employed a discourse of unity and conflict that was drawn from the classical Islamic theory of international relations.

When using contemporary, secular categories, Iran laid claim under general international law to equal sovereignty with United States, and so to equality of rights as a party to the NPT. Iran advanced a legal theory of the NPT that is predicated on Iran's sovereign equality and that entitled it to enjoy the same NPT rights to reprocessing and enrichment technology as the United States does. The legal debate was carried on in accordance with the standard rules of engagement of general international law.

Further, when using the discourse of contemporary international politics, Iran beamed back against the United States and its allies the very categories that they sought to apply to Iran and other Muslims. Thus, for Iran, the United States was a "rogue" state that threatens the stability of the international order by its hegemonic drives; Iran was not. And the Western world, not Islam, is a "failed civilization" that "has taken a wrong turn."[204] What Western liberal optimists saw as the "end of history" and the triumph of the Western model, Iran saw as the end of *Western* history. Thus, in a letter to President George W. Bush, President Ahmadinejad wrote: "Liberalism and Western style democracy have not been able to help realize the ideals of humanity. Today these two concepts have failed. Those with insight can already hear the sounds of the shattering and fall of the ideology and thoughts of the Liberal democratic systems."[205] Language of this kind is the common idiom of international politics, and so is fully intelligible to Western and secular audiences (though they may deny its applicability).

Second, Iran also conceived itself to have a special mission to further the unification of the people of Islam in the face of Western imperialism and secularism. If the United States projected itself as the leader of the "free world," Iran counter-claimed the leadership of the Muslim world. Iran accused the United States and its Western allies of waging a religious and civilizational war on Islam and, indeed, of posing an "existential" threat to it. By urging Muslims to form an "axis of unity," the Ayatollah Khamenei conceptualized this clash as a phase of the millennial contest between the *dar al harb* and the *dar al-Islam.* In calling for an "axis of unity," Iran was not addressing the United States so much as the Islamic world, particularly the Middle East and U.S. allies in the Persian Gulf. Turning its face to the Islamic world, Iran invoked the language of "friendship," drawing on the logic of the Kantian culture of anarchy,[206] which forms the basis for Iran's appeal for solidarity among the Islamic peoples. Unity for some members of the com-

---

204 Kelsay, *supra* note 147, at 211.

205 *Text of Iranian President Ahmadinejad's letter to President George W. Bush* (released by Iranian Republic News Agency, updated May 6, 2006) (*available at* http://ww.thefinalcall.com/).

206 *See supra* notes 68–71 and accompanying text.

munity of states, under this Kantian logic, necessarily excluded the non-Islamic world. Turning instead toward the United States, Iran used the rhetoric of "enemy," characteristic of the logic of a Hobbesian culture.[207]

7. Thesis 2—Constructivism and its Discontents

If constructivism is to hold its own against realism and rational choice modeling as a theory of international relations, a constructivist theory should be able to generate descriptions of "structures" such as the U.S.-Iran conflict that permit the interactions of the states within such structures to be explained and that offer testable predictions about their future interactions.[208] Much as rational choice theory seeks to anchor its explanations of state behavior in the concept of "reputation," constructivism often seeks to do the same with the concept of "identity." As one leading constructivist has said:

> Identities are a congealed reputation, that is, the closest one can get in social life to being able to confidently expect the same actions from another actor time after time. Identities subsume reputation; being a particular identity is sufficient to provide necessary diagnostic information about a state's likely actions with respect to other states in particular domains.[209]

Explanation by reference to state identities seems most like to enable diagnosis and prediction when state identities are stable, as they often are. No doubt Switzerland's identity as a "neutral" and China's identity as a "great power" are secure. As we have just seen, however, state identities are often contested and unsettled. What diagnosis should constructivists make of the situation in which the United States sought to have Iran identified as a rogue state, and Iran threw that claim back against the United States? When the United States characterized the Soviet Union as an "Empire of Evil," or when some third world states sought to identify Israel's Zionism as "racism"?

State identities may be indeterminate for at least two reasons: first, a state itself may be unsure what identity it holds, perhaps because influential domestic political actors are propounding

207 For some U.S. allies Iran uses the rhetoric of "rivalry," strategically differentiating them from the United States.

208 This is true even if constructivism is an "approach" rather than a "theory," because constructivist approaches will generate "theories." It is also true even if a constructivist theoretical explanation will look different from a realist or rational choice explanation because, for example, it employs a different kind of causality or because it introduces many more variables. If constructivism cannot be measured against other international relations theories on explanatory and predictive grounds, it is no more an alternative to them than the study of history is.

209 Ted Hopf, *supra* note 34, at 190.

different views of what that identity should be;[210] and second, different members of the international community may contest a state's claim to a particular identity and seek to impose a different identity on it. The indeterminacy of state identities and the frequency with which they are contested make it problematic to frame a plausible constructivist theory of state interaction, at least when such a theory is intended to be anchored in state identities.

Consider the difficulty that the indeterminacy of state identities seems to pose for a constructivist theory of the U.S.-Iran conflict. We have assumed thus far that the United States envisages the international order as a Lockean culture, pervaded by rivalry rather than by either stark enmity or friendship. But what if the United States in fact envisages the international order essentially as Iran claims that it does? What, in other words, if the United States *saw itself* as a "crusader" state, locked in a civilizational conflict with the Muslim world and posing an existential threat to it? What if the United States considered it to be its mission to "civilize" and "modernize" the Muslim world through a program of imposing (forcibly, if need be) political democratization, market economics, and the ratification of specific human rights norms including Western conceptions of religious liberty and gender relationships? Many have argued that the self-image of the United States under the second Bush Administration gave rise to precisely that program; some (including, of course, the Iranians) would argue that the U.S. "crusader" identity is far deeper and more enduring. Unless a constructivist theory can specify which U.S. identity is the true one, it would seem to have limited explanatory and predictive power. In particular, without more determinacy, a constructivist theory would not do much to illuminate the U.S.-Iran conflict.

Or consider the problem from the opposite direction. Suppose that instead of viewing international politics as a Lockean or Hobbesian culture, the United States currently views it as a Kantian one? More specifically, suppose, as Water Russell Mead has done, that the fundamental policy objective of the Obama Administration is to promote world governance and, ideally, a form of global union that, once it came to fruition, would bring "realist" or "Hobbesian" anarchy to an end.[211] Assuming that the United States now takes such a "Kantian" perspective, the United States might well conclude that Iran's pursuit of nuclear weapons, if not checked, would result in widespread nuclear proliferation, a clear demonstration of the ineffectiveness of international law and the defeat of the project of global unity. Because Iran is unlikely to be dissuaded from its course by peaceful, diplomatic means, the United States would therefore be driven to attack Iran's nuclear facilities. On this account of U.S. foreign policy goals, a war between the United States and Iran is more likely to happen than if the United States was preoccupied with "realist" issues like the regional balance of power in the Persian Gulf.

---

210 Indeed, in emphasizing the importance of human agency in fashioning identities, constructivists should surely grant this point.

211 *See* Walter Russell Mead, *Nuking Westphalia: Obama's Deep Convictions Point to War With Iran* (posted on July 16, 2010) (*available at* http://blogs.the-american-interest.com/wrm/2010/07/16/nuking-westphalia).

Here again, the problem of the indeterminacy of identity arises. Without a specification of the "true" identity of the United States, a constructivist theory would be helpless in explaining the U.S.-Iran conflict and in predicting how it is likely to unfold.

Postscript: Revisiting Athens and Nuremberg?

Our inquiry in this chapter has taken us through modern international relations theory, offering sophisticated and inter-disciplinary reformulations of the basic realist-legalist divide that formed the subject of our study of Thucydides' Melian dialogue and Mytilenean debate, on one hand, and the war crimes tribunals and Shimoda Court's opinions on aggression and nuclear war, on the other. In our somewhat dialectical presentation, an interpretation of Athenian realism that gives primacy to the facts of human nature in causing war is challenged by a post-Nuremberg interpretation of legalism that proposes to govern human nature with a system of legal commands made effective through adjudication. In response, a nominally scientific approach to the study of human nature—international relations theory—provides pragmatic solutions war-creating tendencies of human nature, as it is hypothesized in rational choice theory; and these solutions gives rise to institutional solutions or various forms. Finally, constructivism challenges modern international relations theory's narrow conception of human nature as egoistic and acquisitive and argues that institutional structures, such as states and perhaps international organizations, reflect values that are chosen and can reflect norms and commitments, much as legalism holds that human nature can be regulated and subordinated.

Thus, what is striking is that what we have called Athenian realism —with its attention to a broad range of human motivations, including "honor"—re-emerges through constructivism's attention to personal "recognition." But that theoretical complexity is challenged by a demand for theoretical parsimony, which in turn is deemed too parsimonious, leaving out important considerations. To provide an example, transcendental values reflected in the Mytilenean leadership's invocation of the will and favor of the gods are resurrected in the religious ideologies that play central roles in the constructivist account of the U.S.-Iran conflict.

In our account of legalism, we alluded briefly to the two possible forms of legalism—naturalist legalism and positivist legalism—and deferred discussion of naturalist legalism. We now turn to naturalist legalism, because it plays a central role in the intellectual history of the *jus ad bellum*, which is the subject of Part II.

For now, we note that, like positivist legalism and constructivism, naturalist legalism makes normative demands, and failure to meet those demands may incur opprobrium on political, legal, or moral grounds. Furthermore, like Athenian realism and rational choice theory, naturalist legalism purports to describe what is true. What, if anything, makes naturalist legalism true, however, is an objective moral and legal order inscribed into the heart of things.

Part II

Chapter 1

Introduction to *the Jus ad Bellum*: The Just War Tradition in Western Thought

In Part I of this volume we considered extreme positions in traditional and modern debates concerning the relation between international politics and law on the question of war. The traditional debate is between realism, which treats law as a nullity, and legalism, which treats law as controlling. We suggest that the modern debate between neorealist theories (such as rational choice and related, institutionalist conceptions of international politics) and constructivist theories recapitulates the basic realist-legalist divide. Our case studies have demonstrated the application and limits of each of these theoretical perspectives on the study of war, and its relation to international politics and law, in concrete circumstances involving the common question of mass destruction or use and potential use of weapons of mass destruction—a realist account of the Melian dialogue and Mytilenian debate; a legalist account of responsibility for the bombings of Hiroshima and Nagasaki; a neorealist or rationalist account of the North Korean withdrawal from the Nuclear Non-Proliferation Treaty; and a constructivist account of the conflict between Iran and the West, particularly the United States, over Iran's right to nuclear-weapons related nuclear technology. We have not systematically explored the relation between war and moral theories that may or may not underlay theories of international politics, law, and war.

Part II of this book turns to the moral question. While we have alluded to the so-called Just War Theory (JWT) as a quasi-legal construct earlier in this volume, particularly in connection to providing a background to the rise of modern legalist approaches, we initially treated 19th and 20th century European legalism as a complete and consistent system. By this we mean that it addressed all questions in the legal order concerning war, including the question of mass destruction, and depended on no postulates or axioms outside of the legal order itself for its legitimacy or justification. We depart from this approach now to explicate fully both the intellectual origins of international legalism and provide an independent account of the relation between international politics and international law. Under this approach, one might suggest that an independent set of normative commitments have a gravitational attraction for the ongoing development of systems of international politics and international law, even in relation to such ultimate questions as the threat or use of nuclear weapons. Again, under this view, one even could see the effect of moral imperatives underlying JWT in neo-realist and constructivist reformulations of realism and legalism; for, as neorealism's foray into institutionalism takes into account learned cooperation, constructivism's dynamic account of the logical, system-driven move to Kantian ethics in international law and politics makes a necessity of virtue.

In Part II of this part of the book, we will explore the central thesis that moral concerns play an unavoidable role even in questions of war in the context of the threshold legal issues arising in the *jus ad bellum*—that is to say, whether force may be used. In Chapter 2, we explore the politics, law and morality of collective security through the prism of first Gulf War as a case study. In Chapter 3 we address collective humanitarian intervention by NATO against Serbia to protect the people of Kosovo. In Chapter 4, we focus on the question self-defense and preemptive self-defense in the context of the Second Gulf War. These cases may merge into each other. For example, one could see the Second Gulf War, as many lawyers did, as the lawful resumption of the collective security framework that richly described and justified the First Gulf War; and one could equally, as many moralists did, see it as justified collective humanitarian to protect the Iraqi people through the overthrow of a tyrant, Saddam Hussein. Accordingly, one could view chapter 3's discussion of Kosovo as a bridge between chapters 2 and 4. We will explain in these chapters how each debate concerning the legality and legitimacy of the use of force ultimately can be reduced to a debate held in terms of the JWT. And, in Part III of this book, we explore the thesis of the centrality of JWT in relation to the so-called *jus in bello*—that is to say, how force is to be used—in additional cases studies.

Any discussion of the influence of the Just War Tradition on modern international law debates on the use of force, thus, is well served to begin with the classical and Biblical sources of the modern Just War Tradition. In this introductory section, as a prelude for our case studies on modern international law and the three distinct grounds available for formally lawful and morally legitimate uses of force—self-defense, defense of others, and humanitarian intervention—we explore the roots of the Just War Tradition through an exposition of the thought of its chief advocates, as though they were engaged in a conversation that has spanned the centuries, albeit with some attention to the historical circumstances in which they wrote and to some extent conditioned their thought. We begin with the classical Greco-Roman tradition, turn then to religiously-based moral conceptions, and conclude with Just War Theory's modern reformulations (both in religiously-inspired and in non-theological but morality-based theories) in the context of a post-Westphalian system of international law and politics. There may be other non-classical and non-Biblical approaches that describe the moral basis for evolution of modern thought, or provide a standpoint for moral criticism of international politics and international law. We do not study these important questions. Rather, in explaining the modern international legal system's competing views on the use of force, we observe that in the tradition in which we write, Classical and Christian thought have formed the central paradigm for discussing the morality of war over the centuries.

The tension between the realist and legalist perspectives on war finds expression in the earliest Western thinker on the subject, Cicero. As one of the last great statesmen of the Roman Republic, he gave the first significant thought to the question of Just War. Cicero, an advocate of order and a philosopher who reformulated Stoic thought and made it the groundwork for a theory of the law of nations, is widely thought to be the founder of systematic analysis of Just War.[1]

That said, Cicero's complex thought is not inattentive to the insights of realism. Cicero has been cited repeatedly for his statement in *Pro Milone* that "in times of war, the laws fall silent" ("silent enim leges inter arma"),[2] thus suggesting a disdain for legalist strictures on the use of force. This speech defended Milo, who stood accused of the murder of Publius Clodius Pulcher in a battle on the Appian Way outside the city of Rome. The trial occurred in the waning days of the Roman Republic, when Clodius and Milo were the heads of contending gangs in the city and served as henchmen for the Caesarian and Pompeian factions, and thus foreshadowing the outbreak of full-scale civil war shortly after the trial. In a sense, civil order had already broken down in Rome. Thus, description of the battle as occurring in "a time of war" was not too far from the truth. Milo was killed in the course of a true battle between armed gangs, suggesting that a state of civil war existed, subjecting neither faction to lawful authority. This interpretation of Cicero's remark put him squarely in the realist camp.

However, the context for his remark locates it in larger set of views that are grounded in Cicero's commitment to Just War reasoning concerning war. Cicero essentially argued that Milo engaged in legitimate self-defense. Admittedly, this was not the ordinary case of self-defense in a typical case of murder. Yet, Cicero's essential claim was that Milo was under attack from Clodius and his forces, had no room for retreat, and used necessary and proportionate force to defend himself. Cicero went on to argue that Milo's conduct was ruled by the "inborn law" (or "*nata lex*") that "we are not taught through instruction, but through natural intuition" *(or "non instituti, sed imbuti suus").*[3] Killing Clodius under such circumstances, argued Cicero, should not result in Milo's conviction for murder and, as was ultimately the case, his ostracism or banishment from Rome.[4] Thus, Cicero's arguments in this trial under civil law drew from a larger set of views concerning pre-social, unlearned, and thus "natural" inclinations. What are the roots of this insight, and how does it relate to his theory of the Just War?

1 *See generally* Thomas Pangle & Peter Ahrensdorf, Justice Among Nations: On the Moral Basis of Power and Peace 51–72 (1999).

2 Cicero, Pro Tito Annio Milone ad iudicem oratio, section 11 (English trans.) (*available at* http://www.perseus.tufts.edu/hopper/text?doc=Perseus%3Atext%3A1999.02.0020%3Atext%3DMil.%3Asection%3D11) [hereinafter after Pro Milone].

3 *Id.* at 10

4 *Id.* at 10.

The roots of Ciceronian thought lie in the Stoic normative worldview,[5] rather than a positive conception of international law. The Greek Stoic tradition, as Cicero inherited it, focused on the question of moral counsel for the wise, the philosopher, who alone is capable of reaching "true" virtue through the life of contemplation. Viewed this way, the life of the wise person was a commitment to virtue in itself, a set of "perfect" virtues that constitute obedience to a rational ordering or natural law commanded by the gods. These virtues transcend immediate personal gain and, thus, the parochial advantages of particular groups; accordingly, the Stoic views only a cosmopolitan perspective as consistent with individual ethics. Revealed sometimes in dreams through divine intervention to the best of the wise, the true virtues form the basic postulates for all moral reasoning for traditional Greek stoicism.[6] The traditional Stoic perspective is sometimes thought to represent a kind of extreme form of Platonism, privileging the "wise" or "guardians" as in Plato's Republic.[7]

Cicero's general theory of international law and his specific Just War Theory must be viewed in this Stoic context, particularly in Greek stoicism's cosmopolitan standpoint. But Cicero's reformulation of Stoicism made it usable as a system of practical ethics for a political class engaging in transnational politics, such as the leadership of the late Roman Republic. Unlike traditional stoicism, Cicero's stoicism pays attention to the so-called "median" or "imperfect" duties—such as self-preservation, independence, one's own material wealth in moderation, one's own health, those goods for one's family—within the reach of the average person, the people who populate a political order and whose consent and support are necessary for its survival. In this respect, Cicero hews more closely to Aristotle than Plato, making philosophy an eminently practical art directed to relating individual virtue to the conditions for a sustainable political order.[8] The "law of nature" first revealed in Stoic cosmopolitanism as revised by Cicero is thus made accessible to most human beings across societies, not merely for the contemplative life of the few. It also forms the basis of what Cicero, for the first time, called the *ius gentium—the "law of nations" or, as more precisely translated, the "law of peoples."*[9] According to Cicero's Gaius Laelius, "Nor will there be one law for Rome, a different law for Athens, or different laws at one time and then another; but for all nations and for all time one sempiternal and immutable law, and one common as it were magistrate and ruler over all."[10]

This transnational law and ethic forms the basis for Cicero's Just War Theory. Cicero recognizes that Stoic cosmopolitanism is a means to an end, the ultimate goal of true virtue. But in

5 Pangle & Ahrensdorf, *supra* note 1, at 54.

6 *Id.* at 52–54.

7 *See generally* Plato, The Republic (Benjamin Jowett ed. 1941)

8 *See generally* Aristotle, Nicomachean Ethics (Robert C. Bartlett & Susan D. Collins trans. 2012)

9 *See* Ethical Writings of Cicero: De Offciis; De Sentecute; De Amicitia, and Scipio's Dream bk. III, para. 23 (Andrew P. Peabody trans., 1887) [hereinafter Ethical Writings]; *see also* Pangle & Ahrensdorf, supra note 1, at 54, 275–76 n.9.

10 *Id.* at bk. III, para. 35.

the interim, practical life demands an intermediate and temporary view of the virtue that can be achieved through a law of nations. This law consists in recognition that "the human race" is united in a "society" comparable to the parts of the body. This "organic analogy," foreshadowing medieval thought, demands that the welfare of each part be pursued by seeking the welfare of the whole.[11] This ordering principle is enforced by the law of nations or nature, yet also is recognized in positive law of all particular communities.[12] In one of Cicero's most famous passages concerning duties to strangers, he proclaims:

> [T]he general lesson is clear enough. [L]et whatever can be given away without detriment be bestowed, even on a stranger. From which we derive those common principles: do not check flowing water, allow the lighting of his fire at your fire, if someone asks, given him trustworthy counsel in his deliberations; give whatever is useful to those who receive but not hurtful to the giver. These principles should be followed, and we should always be contributing something to the common utility.[13]

And, as Cicero continues much later in this treatise, "they do wrong who keep strangers from the use of their cities and exclude them; [for] to prohibit strangers fro the use of one's city is inhuman."[14]

In terms of the specific Just War Theory, Cicero, through his character the statesman Gaius Laelius in Cicero's *Republic*, goes on to proclaim: "No war is ever undertaken by the best city except for honor or safety; ... those wars are unjust, that are undertaken without cause. Now no war can be justly waged except for the cause of punishing or repelling enemies... Our people, however, now holds sway over the whole earth through defending its allies.... Do we not observe that dominion has been given, by nature herself, to what is best—with the greatest consequent benefit to those who are weaker?"[15]

Cicero's altruism may have a transcendental, theological component. Cicero writes that the law of nation's recognition of the reasonableness of generosity and altruism thus implies that it is "more according to nature to undergo the greatest labors and troubles in order to help and save all nations, if possible, in the manner of the heroic Hercules, whom human fame has assigned the for the memory of his beneficial actions a place in the council of heaven, than it is to live in solitude not only free from troubles but reveling in the greatest pleasures and abounding in riches and excelling in beauty and strength."[16] He adds:

11 *Id.* at bk. III, para 21–22.

12 *Id.* at bk. III, para. 23.

13 *Id.* at bk. I, paras. 51–52.

14 *Id.* at bk. III, para. 47.

15 Ethical Writings, *supra* note 9, at bk. III, paras. 34–35.

16 *Id.* at bk. III, para. 25.

> if nature has prescribed this, that a human being should want to take care of another human being, however he may be, simply for the reason that he is a human being, then according tot the same nature it is necessary that the interest of each is a common interest. If this is so, we are all embraced by one and the same law of nature; and if this is so, we are certainly prohibited by the law of nature from doing wrong to another....Moreover, those who say that citizens must be respected, but not outsider, sunder the common association of the human race; once this is gone, kindness, generosity, goodness, and justice are utterly destroyed; and those who destroy this must be judged impious even toward the immortal gods.[17]

Thus, even if the law of nation's cosmopolitan ethics is not warranted by reason itself, it would be independently justified by serving the will of the gods.

Setting aside this theological issue until we consider the Christian reformulation of the Just War Theory, the rational sufficiency of the law of nature makes it possible for Cicero to articulate a set a views on the justice of war he considers compelling to anyone committed to the Stoic premises, the pursuit of the "happy life" and "greatness of soul."[18] These premises, and the general stance they prescribe for a theory of international justice, lead directly to the specific features of Cicero's conception of the just war. Thus, Cicero rejects retribution as a just cause for war, favoring instead rehabilitation and deterrence. Arguing that war is only a last resort to maintain the peace by punishing and thereby deterring injury caused by a guilty state against an innocent state, he writes: "There are, moreover, certain duties to be observed toward those by whom you have been done an injustice. In fact there is a proper way to exact retribution and to punish; I know that is suffices if that party, who has committed wrong, should repent the wrongdoing, in order that he should not do it again and others be deterred from injustice."[19] And the preference for peace followed from a view of war as necessary only when there is a deviation from cosmopolitan justice; for, "as there are two ways of deciding an issue, one through discussion, the other through force, the former appropriate for human beings, the later for beasts, if one is not permitted to use the superior methods recourse must be had to the inferior. Wherefore wars must be undertaken for this cause: that life may go on in peace without injustice."[20]

In its particulars, Cicero's Just War Theory often appears inconsistent with a pure ethic of altruism. For Cicero, promises need not always be kept, when to do so would be of "no utility to the person to whom one promised; nor, if the keeping does greater harm to you than it does good to the one to whom you promised, is it against duty to prefer the greater good to the lesser."[21] Moreover, when two powers both believe that each is challenging the other's deserved rule or

17 *Id.* at bk. III, paras. 27–28.

18 *Id.* at bk. III, paras. 47, 18–19, 22.

19 *Id.* at bk. I, paras. 33, 88–89.

20 *Id.* at bk. I, paras. 34–35.

21 *Id.* at bk. I, paras. 31–32.

reputation, Cicero seems to believe that such wars between them would serve the common good and the community of nations because such war, if fought with restraint, represents the natural expression of the ambition to rule—the natural need for glory and honor. And expansion seemed to be an essential feature of Roman republicanism, as Cicero advises: "Those who would guard the republic should ... by whatever means they can, either in war or at home, augment the republic by empire, farmlands, and revenues. These are the things that belong to great men, these are the things that were performed over and over again in our forefather's time, and those who pursue these kids of duties will attain, along with the supreme advantage of the republic, both gratitude and great glory."[22]

Thus, Cicero appears to see no real tension between self-interest and the common good, given his view of the essential justice of Roman republicanism. Indeed, even such Roman wars of expansion must be understood to be subordinated to the larger conception that "natural" pursuit of glory and honor and, thus, have built into them principles of restraint which serve the common good. As Cicero makes clear: "When it is truly the case that war is fought for supremacy, and glory is what is sought, the causes must in every way conform to ... the just causes of war. But these wars, in which the glory of rule is the end, must be waged with less bitterness – just as even with fellow citizen we contend in one way if he is an enemy, in another if he is a rival (with the one we contend for honor and dignity, with the other for our heads and reputations)."[23] Yet, in making this distinction, Cicero also seems to recognize that rational altruism has its limits, for altruism is found in "the degree to which persons are conjoined, in the same proportion they should be shown kindness."[24] Thus, as its spokesman Gaius Laelius suggests, Cicero's theory reflects a synthesis with, but perhaps also a rationalization of, the then prevailing view of the Roman Republic's elite that Roman expansion played a central, positive role in history.

As one relaxes the assumption of the essential rightness of Roman republicanism, however, Cicero's Just War Theory also serves as the basis for a critical perspective, one that foreshadows early modern Just War Theory's use to condemn imperial corruption at the end of the Roman Empire and imperial expansion by Spain at the end of the feudal era. In short, Cicero's Just War Theory provides a framework for explaining the decline of the Roman Republic by the medium of his account of Scipio Africanus the Younger's dream—which, although Scipio does not hold to be of divine origin, provides the basis for his thought in an implicit reference to the Greek Stoic tradition. The dream sequence appears in Cicero's *Republic.*[25] The spokesman is significant, for his father, Scipio Africanus, played central role in Roman history, which is critical to the proper interpretation of the dream; for Scipio's victories to end the Second Carthaginian or

22 *Id.* at bk. I, para. 38; *id.* at bk. II, para. 85.

23 *Id.* at bk. I, para. 38; *id.* at bk. II, para. 85.

24 *Id.* at bk. I, para. 50.

25 Cicero, On the Republic bk. I, para. 10 (Jonathon Powell ed., 2009); *see also* Pangle & Ahrensdorf, *supra* note 1, at 56–57.

Punic War and to establish Roman military supremacy in Asia Minor marked the rise of Rome as a world power.[26] Rome's victory in the Second Punic War, after years of the Carthaginian General Hannibal's operations in Italy, was viewed by Romans as the vindication of the Roman system, for Hannibal was never able to garner the support of Rome's Italian allies. From the Roman perspective, Scipio's wise leadership reflected the virtues of the Roman system, which in turn warranted Roman expansion through the natural expansion throughout the Mediterranean world of Rome's system of Italian alliances, thus forging a transnational political order.[27] When Scipio, through Cicero, explains that even Romulus, the founder of Rome, perpetrated injustices, he signals Cicero's view that Roman power was not unambiguously moral. Through Scipio, Cicero offers a vision of "the true beauty of nature and the true satisfaction of contemplation, in the light of which transpolitical vision he has become convinced of the pettiness of Rome and indeed of all political action."[28] Scipio's dream's subversive quality is to see evil at the root and inception of Roman power.

For Cicero, whose generation witnessed a war against Rome by its Italian allies and the breakdown of the consensual rules or political association within the Roman ruling class itself, the central question was how to explain the decline of the Roman system from the international solidarity and internal consensus of the period of Rome's rise to power under Scipio and his successors. Through the teachings of the dream, Cicero appropriates Scipio's authority to question the continued legitimacy of Roman power, which in his generation had been employed externally for personal gain. This is demonstrated most notably in Caesar's conquest of Gaul, which was viewed by many as a war of aggression and a paradigmatically unjust war, bringing Caesar spoils and power that in turn was, at the time of Cicero's composition of Scipio's Dream, bringing Rome to the verge of civil war.[29] As Rome ceased to operate externally on the basis of Stoic cosmopolitan principles underlying Cicero's Just War Theory, the natural consequence of violation of natural law was the decline of Rome's system of consensual external rule, thus the war of the allies, followed shortly by the civil wars between Sulla and Marius and then ultimately a generation later between Pompey and Caesar.

Thus, Cicero during the last year of his life writes an epitaph for the Roman Republic:

> The truth is that as long as the empire of the Roman people was maintained through acts of beneficence rather than injustice, wars were waged either on behalf of allies or for the empire, wars were terminated with clemency or only the necessary harshness, our senate was a refuge for kings, populaces, and nations, our magistrates and rulers strove to win glory only from the equitable and faithful defense of provinces and allies; and thus our rule could more truly

26 *See* Michael Grant, History of Rome, 122–27, 137–38 (1978).

27 *Id.* at 147–48.

28 Pangle & Ahrensdorf, *supra* note 1, at 56.

29 *See* Christian Meier, Caesar: A Biography 235–37, 346–348 (1982).

> be called a paternal protectorate of the empire earth rather than an empire. This policy and disciplined declined gradually, and in truth after Sulla's victory we abandoned it.... By Justice, then, are we punished. If we had not allowed the crimes of many to go unpunished, such license would never have come to center on one man... And thus while the house of walls of the city stand and remain—through even they how fear the worst crimes—the true republic we have completely lost.[30]

Thus, Cicero's account of the relation between Just War Theory and cosmopolitan ethics provides a paradigm for the use of Just War Theory for a critical account of current political developments. It thus serves as the immediate backdrop to Christian view of war, which takes an initially critical and subversively pacifist form but then reformulates Classical Stoicism's Just War Theory in Christian terms.

30 *See* Ethical Writings, *supra* note 9, at bk. II, paras. 26–29.

Despite the legacy from Classical Stoicism, late antiquity and medieval Just War Theory's development as a continuous tradition of thought and dialogue, is widely believed to be more deeply rooted in the early and medieval Christian conceptions of political order.31 We turn first to the early Christian pacifist tradition, and its qualifications, as the backdrop to Christian Just War Tradition. Then we turn to Augustine's response, formulating a theory for the legitimate use of force. Next we consider the medieval synthesis of classical and Christian thought in the writings of Thomas Aquinas. We then consider, in the context of the European discovery of the Americas and the rise of the modern system of states, the late medieval scholastic extension of Aquinas's Just War Theory and the Protestant Christian response.

1. Christian Pacifism

In the last half century, discussion of the early Christian perspective on the use of force must begin British-born, American-Protestant Roland Bainton, who argued that early Christianity took an absolutist position of pacifism, but later became a qualified acceptance of use of force through Just War Theory, and finally was transmogrified into active support for use of force in a Crusader mentality.[32] The implicit, if not explicit, argument underlying his pacifist position, under which all war is unjust and Christians may never use force, is Bainton's understanding of original Christianity. Under this view, it is only through the transformation of Christianity from a subversive sect into a state religion of a state fighting defensive war against barbarian invader that Christianity formulates a provisional and partial justification for use of force in Just War Theory.33 The story continues with Christianity serving as the ideological basis for offensive Crusader War against Islam and to suppress heresy at home.[34]

However, Bainton's historical claim concerning the pacifist position of the early Christian Church has recently come under attack. J. Daryl Charles argues that Bainton and his followers have misread the early Christian fathers.[35] Bainton and his followers, argues Charles, correctly claim that the leading early Church fathers Tertullian and Origen, writing in the second century

31 *See generally* Howard M. Hensel, Christian Belief & Western Just War Thought, 29–86 in Asian and Western Perspectives on the Legitimate Use of Military Force (2010).

32 *See* Roland H. Bainton, Christian Attitudes toward War and Peace: A Historical Survey and Critical Re-evaluation (1960). For Bainton's pacifist roots, *see* Wikipedia: Roland Bainton (*available at* https://en.wikipedia.org/wiki/Roland_Bainton.) (reporting Bainton's ordination as a Congregationalist Minister, marriage to a Quaker, and father's pacifism).

33 *Id.* at 85–100.

34 *Id.* at 109–116.

35 *See* J. Daryl Charles, *Pacifists, Patriots, or Both?: Second Thoughts on Pre-Constantinian Early-Christian Attitudes toward Soldiering and War,* 13 Logos 17 (2010).

of Christianity, vigorously opposed Christian participation in the military, but that their writing also suggests that it was only after 170 A.D. or so that Christian participation in the military became an issue warranting commentary and correction. This description of Christian practice suggests the possible normative position that the first century of Christian thought on the matter treated pacifism as a compelled inference from Christian moral teaching.[36] But, claims Charles, a close reading of Tertullian and Origen, among other early Church fathers, makes clear that Christians may well have participated in the military earlier than Bainton and his follows suppose.[37] More important, he argues that both Tertullian and Origen held no categorical view against use of force by the state. Rather, in the case of Tertullian, Charles shows that Tertullian's objection to Christian participation in the military was instrumental. It was because soldiers engaged in practices that smacked of idolatry — such as devotion to the Roman military standards, the legion's "eagle," and because the military was generally populated also with devotees of Mithraism, a sect in fierce competition with Christianity — that Tertullian vigorously opposed Christian enlistment.[38] As for Origen, Charles argues that his argument against Christian participation did not reflect a principled objection to the goals of the state in using force but rather the belief that Christians could better serve the Empire and its legitimate military objectives through prayer.[39] In short, neither early Christian practice nor early Christian teaching unambiguously compels pacifism. Indeed, Charles goes so far to suggest that Bainton's own theological commitments have colored his view of the history and textual sources in favor of finding an early Christian pacifist consensus when the evidence is at least ambiguous.[40]

That is not to say that early Christian pacifism does not find strong roots in early Christian teaching. Indeed, as we show below, Augustine's formulation of Christian Just War Theory makes no sense except in a context in which serious disagreement is possible within the sources available to Christian theologians and philosophers. The textual sources of Christian pacifism are clear, most notably the command of Jesus' Sermon on the Mount — "Resist not evil, turn the other check…."[41] Moreover, the pacifist position accords with the early Christian view that otherworldly values should take priority to seeking relative justice on earth, given that the imminence of Christ's Second Coming in the *parousia*, or end of time, is what all Christians should look as their primary test for moral guidance.[42] Similarly, the otherworldly quality of early Christian thought was influenced by Platonist categories of thought that framed not only Christian theology through the theory of transubstantiation, distinguishing between the true

36 *Id.* at 17–22.

37 *Compare* Bainton, *supra* note 32, at 71–74 *with* Charles, *supra* note 35, at 51 n.48.

38 *See* Charles, *supra* note at 25–29.

39 *See* Charles, *supra* note at 29–33.

40 *Id.* at 23, 49 n.17.

41 *Matthew 5 & Luke* 6.

42 *See* Bainton, *supra* note 32, at 75–76.

ideal "Form" of a thing and its mere appearance, but also Christian ethics. As Plato wrote, Socrates held it "worse to do than to suffer wrong."[43] Neoplatonism thus played a central part in pacifist thought generally and in Christian pacifism in particular.[44] Thus, like the older Greek Stoic view's Platonic tendencies, emphasizing "perfect" virtue and cosmopolitan idealism, pacifist Christian neo-Platonic thought gave less attention than Cicero's Stoic reformulation to the practical tension between justice and peace in this world.

That said, if Charles's critique of Bainton is correct, the historical evidence is at least ambiguous as to the practice of pacifism. Moreover, early Christians had good reason to struggle over the relation between their ideal and practical commitments, given Paul's authoritative injunction in his *Letter to the Romans* concerning the role and authority of the state:

> Let every person be subject to the governing authorities. For there is no authority except from God, and those that exist have been instituted by God. Therefore whoever resists the authorities resists what God has appointed, and those who resist will incur judgment. For rulers are not a terror to good conduct, but to bad. Would you have no fear of the one who is in authority? Then do what is good, and you will receive his approval, for he is God's servant for your good. But if you do wrong, be afraid, for he does not bear the sword in vain. For he is the servant of God, an avenger who carries out God's wrath on the wrongdoer.[45]

Thus, pacifism was at least a permissible position to early Christians in the circumstances of the first two centuries of the Christian era, during a time of relative peace and security. It did not mean it was the only possible position or indeed the position most consistent with the best understanding of the faith as historical circumstances changed.

Indeed, Augustine's Just War Theory, like Cicero's Just War Theory, may be viewed as responses, within the open space permitted by the textual sources and traditions available to Christians, to changing circumstances — for classical Stoics, such as Cicero, the imminent fall of the republic; or for Christians, such as Augustine, the impending fall of the empire.

2. Augustine

Christian-Platonism's pacifist tendencies did present a problem once Christians began to participate in governance and the Roman state's very existence was at risk in the late 4th and early 5th centuries of the Christian era. With the destruction of the Roman army by Goth invaders

43 Plato, The Gorgias, para. 474(b).

44 *See* Bainton, *supra* note 32, at 29 and 95.

45 *Romans* 13: 1–4.

at the battle of Adrianople in 378 A.D.,[46] and the sack of Rome by Visigoth forces under Alaric in 410 A.D.,[47] the central question for Augustine of Hippo in his *City of God* was to provide an explanation for the Roman Empire's apparent, imminent collapse. More practically, Augustine's writings served to guide Christians as to the rightfulness of their undertaking any measures, including participation in the military, required to stem that collapse or deal with the consequences of ongoing barbarian invasions.[48] As its title suggests, Augustine's central objective, drawing on the Christian Neoplatonic and eschatological traditions, was to console Christians suffering in the "city of man" by focusing their attention on the life of the world to come, the "City of God." That said, Augustine's specific guidance as to Christian participation in war reflects a series of premises concerning the Christian view of the state, its purposes, the responsibility of political leadership, and the practical duties of participation of citizens or subjects that underlay his formulation of the Just War Theory. Explicating those initial assumptions is thus essential to achieving an understanding of the specific features for Just War Theory and their evolution within the tradition of Christian thought over the centuries as the Christian view of the state, the responsibilities of political leadership, and the practical duties of citizens or subjects also evolved.

a. Foundational Assumptions

Although Augustine's presentation is not systematic, his overall theological commitments are well-organized. First, he argues from the ideal conception of the "Heavenly City," which is "a perfectly ordered and perfectly harmonious fellowship in the enjoyment of God, and a mutual fellowship in God; the peace of the whole universe is the tranquillity of order—and order is the arrangement of things equal and unequal in a pattern which assigns to each its proper position."[49] This phrase, the *"tranquillitas ordinis"* or "tranquility of order," has served as a central organizing principle for much subsequent Just War Theory, and it therefore warrants some explication. Augustine makes clear that what he has in mind is the good imbued in nature by God, for "not even the nature of the Devil himself is evil, in so far as the Devil has a nature; it is perversion that makes it evil. And so the Devil did not stand firm in the truth, and yet he did not escape the judgment of the truth. He did not continue in the tranquillity of order...."[50]

Second, this nature is imbued by God for the good of God's human creation and, accordingly, requires man to "observe two rules: first, to do no harm to anyone, and, secondly, to help everyone whenever possible." Thus, "in the household of the just man who 'lives on the basis of

46 *See* Noel Emmanuel Lenski, Failure of Empire: Valens and the Roman State in the Fourth Century A.D. (2002).

47 *See* Michael Kulikowski, Rome's Gothic Wars: From the Third Century to Alaric (2007).

48 *See* St. Augustine, Concerning the City of God Against the Pagan (Bettenson trans. 1972) [Hereinafter COG].

49 *Id.* at bk. XIX, ch.13.

50 *Id.*

faith' and who is still on pilgrimage [in the city of man] far from that Heavenly City, even those who give orders are the servants of those whom they appear to command. For they do not give orders because of a lust for domination but from a dutiful concern of the interests of others, not with pride in taking precedence over others, but with compassion in taking care of others."[51]

Third, it follows that "peace," properly understood, is the realization of the Christian duty to "take care" of others in accordance with a substantive conception of what is good for humans, namely:

> [In] establishing the mortal race of mankind as the greatest ornament of earthy things, [God] has given to mankind certain good things suitable to this life. These are: temporal peace, in proportion to the short span of a mortal life – the peace that consists in bodily health and soundness, and in fellowship with one's kind; and everything necessary to safeguard or recover this peace – those things, for example, which are appropriate and accessible to our senses: light, speech, air to breathe, water to drink, and whatever is suitable for the feeding and clothing of the body, for the care of the body and the adornment of the person. And all this is granted under the most equitable condition: that every mortal who uses aright such goods, goods designed to serve the peace of mortal men, shall receive goods greater in degree and superior in kind, namely, the peace of immortality, and the glory and honour appropriate to it in a life which is eternal for the enjoyment of God and of one's neighbor in God, whereas he who wrongly uses those mortal goods shall lose them, and shall not receive the blessings of eternal life.[52]

Thus, the specific conception of "peace" entails a conception of distributive justice; if "taking care" of others means pursuing "peace," it means seeking the realization of the substantive conception of justice embodied in "true peace."

In pursuing this peace, Augustine also descends to the pragmatic question of a theory of the state. To begin with, Augustine makes clear that the fact that a state has power does not legitimize it. In a deservedly famous passage, he writes:

> Remove justice, and what are kingdoms but gangs of criminals on a large scale? What are criminal gangs but petty kingdoms? A gang is a group of men under the command of a leader, bound by a compact of association, in which the plunder is divided according to an agreed convention. ... For it was a witty and truthful rejoinder which was given by a captured pirate to Alexander the Great. The king asked the fellow, "What is your idea, in infesting the sea?" And the pirate answered, with uninhibited insolence, "The same as yours, in infesting the earth! But because

51 *Id.* at bk. XV, ch.14.

52 *Id.* at bk. XIX, ch.13.

I do it with a tiny craft, I'm called a pirate: because you have a mighty navy, you're called an emperor."[53]

But the state is capable of seeking justice, for "it would be incorrect to say that the good which [the earthly city] desires are not goods, since even that city is better, in its own human way, by their possession. For example, that city desires an earthly peace, for the sake of the lowest goods; and it is that peace which it longs to attain by making war.... Now when the victory goes to those who were fighting for the juster cause, can anyone doubt that the victory is a matter for rejoicing and the resulting peace is something to be desired?"[54] At the same time, holds Augustine, the justice and peace pursued by the state through war are always imperfect and incomplete, when compared the perfect and complete justice and peace of the "city of God," for "if the higher goods are neglected," in the pursuit of justice and peace in the "city of man," or the goods of the city of man "are loved more than the goods which are believed to be higher, the inevitable consequence is fresh misery, and an increase of the wretchedness" in the city of man.[55] In sum, just wars are imperfectly and incompletely just and may never be viewed as more than imperfect means to imperfect ends. Christians can do no better, though they can easily be tempted to follow the Ciceronian path and do worse, given man's fall from grace. The state and its wars must be viewed with suspicion.

b. Specific Just War Criteria

This overall theology thus generates a theory of justice and ethics that has enormous implications for Christianity's attitude toward both Cicernian Just War Theory and early Christian pacifism. To begin with, Augustine rejected important elements of the Roman Ciceronian heritage, condemning it for treating virtue as a means to the end of fame rather than an end in itself, for "Cicero himself could not disguise this fact; in his treatise ..., speaking of the appointment of a chief of state, he lays it down that he must be 'nourished by glory', and goes on to recall that it was the greed for glory that inspired his ancestors to many famous and admirable achievements.... And even in his philosophical writings Cicero dies not disguise this pernicious doctrine...."[56] Thus, Augustine squarely rejects the realist leanings of Cicero's reformulated Stoic approach to Just War Theory.

Confronting the pacifist challenge, Augustine first attempts to seize the moral high ground, arguing that "peace is the desired end of war."[57] But this is not mere peace as the absence of war;

---

53 *Id.* at bk. IV, ch. 4.

54 *Id.* at bk. XV, ch. 6.

55 *Id.* at bk. V, ch. 4.

56 *Id.* at bk. V, ch.14.

57 *Id.* at bk. XIX, ch.12.

it is rather the peace that reflects justice, "for a man who has learnt to prefer right to wrong and the rightly ordered to the perverted, sees that the peace of the unjust, compared with the peace of the just, is not worthy even of the name of peace."[58]

Second, it follows for Augustine that it is "the injustice of the opposing side that lays on the wise man the duty of waging wars…."[59] Rather, in order to pursue true peace, peace with justice, Christians must use force in discharging their duty to "love" others, rectifying injustice done to them and protecting them from injustice. Augustine makes clear that the state, both internally and externally, may kill without violating the Biblical injunction against murder. Thus, specific reasons or "causes" giving rise to the duty of waging war include the state's "self-defense" of its own people, defense of other states, seeking recovery or reparation from those who initiate war, and punishing a state that itself fails to correct or punish a wrong for which it is responsible.[60] He makes clear that "the commandment against killing was not broken by those who have waged wars on the authority of God, or those who have imposed the death penalty on criminals when representing the authority of the State in accordance with the laws of the state, the [most just] and most reasonable source of power."[61] Even some of Rome's wars were just by this standard, for when "they were subjected to unprovoked attacks by their enemies, they were forced to resist not by lust for glory in men's eyes but by the necessity to defend their life and their liberty."[62]

Third, Augustine adds that, in discharging this duty, the just warrior is the reluctant warrior, for the "wise man … will rather lament the fact that he is faced with the necessity of waging just wars; for if they were not just, he would not have to engage in them, and consequently there would be no wars for a wise man."[63]

In sum, much of what later becomes the core of the Just War Tradition—the object of war is peace; war is warranted only by just cause; and war must be pursued with right intention, thus only as a last resort when truly necessary—flows from Augustine's theological commitments and the theory of the state which these theological commitments imply.

Throughout, Augustine gave priority to the "will," rather than "reason," which in turn is driven by "love," associating virtue with the "right order of our love" — that is say, towards love's proper objects: God and, as commanded by Jesus' teaching in the Sermon on the Mount, other

58 *Id.* at bk. XIX, ch.12.

59 *Id.* at bk. XIX, ch.7.

60 *See* Pangle & Ahrensdorf, *supra* note 1, at 77.

61 COG, *supra* note 49, at bk. I, ch. 21.

62 *Id.* at bk. III, ch.10.

63 *Id.* at bk. XIX, ch.7.

persons.[64] Thomas of Aquinas, by contrast, gave greater prominence to "right reason" in the identification of humanity's objective good and the means to achieving that good.[65]

3. Aquinas's Synthesis

The basic formula Aquinas promulgates is that war must be declared a legitimate authority, for a just cause, and with right intention.[66] This formal test, like Augustine's approach, is grounded on an overarching theory of morality and politics that supplies the criteria for implementing each component part of the test. We explicate that theory and then explain how it supplies the criteria for applying the formal elements of the test in the specific institutional context of the era in which Thomas theorized.

Like Augustine, the Thomas's argument for why a war can be just begins with *New Testament* exegesis, albeit treating the text as the target for a *contrario* reasoning. (The medieval scholastic tradition exemplified in Thomas's writings proved a thesis by articulating and then refuting the objections to that thesis.) Thomas's first "objections" to the possibility of just war are Jesus's commands in *Matthew* 26:52 that "all who take the sword shall perish by the sword" and *Matthew* 5:39 "not to resist evil" and Paul's admonition to Christians in *Romans* 12:19 against "revenging yourselves."[67] In refuting the pacifist inferences that could be drawn from these texts, Thomas proceeds by premises grounded in the Christian virtue of charity or love of others. Here, the central move that reconciles Jesus's commands and Paul's admonition is the emphasis Thomas gives to Augustine's criterion of legitimate authority, "for it is not the business of a private individual to declare war, because he can pursue his right (*ius sum prosequi*) before the judgment of his superior. Moreover, it is not the business of a private person to summon together the people, which has to be done in wartime. And as the care of the common weal is committed to those who are in authority, it is their business to watch over the common weal of the city, kingdom, or province subject to them."[68] Drawing on Paul's statement in Romans 13:4 exculpating from sin those who use force as God's agents — "He beareth not the sword in vain: for he is God's minister, an avenger to execute wrath upon him that doth evil" — Thomas argues "just as it is licit for them to have recourse to the material sword in defending the common weal against internal dis-

64 *See* Pangle & Ahrensdorf, *supra* note 1, at 74 (interpreting Augustine to lack faith in human reason since, while humans were created as rational creatures, that "blessed situation has been lost forever on earth because of original man's wanton disobedience").

65 *See id.* at 83 (interpreting Thomas to argue that "the moral law ... is known prior to and without any necessary dependence on faith").

66 Thomas Aquinas, Summa Theologica II-II, *reprinted in* The Ethics of War: Classic and Contemporary Readings 176 (Reichberg, Syse and Begby eds., 2006) [hereinafter Summa Theologica].

67 *Id.*

68 *Id.* at 177.

turbances, as when they punish malefactors, ... so too, it is their business to have recourse to the sword of war in protection the common weal against external enemies."[69] Following Augustine, Thomas maintains that "a just cause is required, namely that those who are attacked, should be attacked because they deserve it on account of some fault (*culpa*)."[70] Now, when "legitimate authority" is promoted by a "just cause" to execute the "wrath" of God, this superficially vengeful state of mind takes on a special meaning when implemented, so that "it is necessary that those waging war should have a rightful intention, so that they intend the advancement of good, or the avoidance of evil .... For it may happen that the war is declared by the legitimate authority, and for a just cause, and yet be rendered illicit through a vile intention."[71] Those who execute the "wrath" of God must, consistent with Scripture, do so with a spirit of charity.

Aquinas's "commitment to the idea that earthly political life can and should be animated by moral virtue seems to make him even more certain than was St. Augustine that there exists a legal order governing the relations among nations, an order that must be adhered to and enforced" yields increased attention to "right intention."[72] It may also be, however, that this increased attention to "right intention" and the capacity of persons to achieve virtue in the city of man reflects Aristotle's influence and diverges from Augustine's more pessimistic view of human nature. Indeed, Aristotle's understanding of "virtue" or, more precisely, a set of virtues as the means through which the "rational soul" pursues happiness, the supreme good in earthly life,[73] deeply influenced Aquinas, who wrote an extensive commentary on Aristotle's *Nicomachean Ethics*.[74] In this text, Aristotle held that a properly political order could encourage virtue[75] and that "the law in ordaining what is good is not burdensome."[76] On this view, rationality, not faith alone, could provide the source for virtue, and right intention's increased salience in Aquinas's Just War Theory could well reflect the possibility for a secular, natural law basis for authoritative criteria for engaging in war.

In sum, the notion appears to be that those who act for others, by assumption members of the state exercising public authority and discharging their Christian duty of care for others, must do what private citizens may not do on their own behalf. Viewed from this perspective, the

69 *Id.*

70 *Id.*

71 *Id.*

72 Pangle & Ahrensdorf, *supra* note 1, at 87.

73 *See* Aristotle, *supra* note 8, at books I–IV.

74 *See* St. Thomas Aquinas, Commentary on Aristotle's Nicomachean Ethics (1964).

75 *See* Aristotle, *supra* note 8, at bk. X, ch. 9

76 *Id.* at bk. X, ch. 9, para. 1180, lines 23–24.

precise elements of Thomas's argument implement the central motivating ideal that Christians should be imbued with a spirit of Christian charity or love of others.[77]

Implementing a Just War Theory based on charity in terms of Augustine's tests of legitimate authority, just cause, and right intention yield specific insights about institutional questions Thomas faced in the radically different political context in which he wrote when compared to the Church-State unity of Augustine's late Roman Empire. Thomas theorized in an era of divided authority: Papal power was in competition with secular authority; the Pope legitimized the Crusades and competed effectively with monarchy in the struggle for wealth and power in Europe; yet the Church's legitimacy was called into question because of these excesses; and, finally, with the invasion of Aristotelian and other secular influences, the Papacy was on the verge of being held in "captivity" in Avignon under control of the French Kings.[78] Thus, Thomas distinction between privately- and publicly-authorized violence placed the state at the center of decision-making as to the use of force, a notable assertion in a medieval world in which state authority continued to depend, in theory at least, on Papal recognition. In further support of the state, Thomas reasoned from the premise that "those who are in authority" may suppress "internal disturbances" through force on the same basis as "war," which by assumption is not an "internal" disturbance.[79] And these two forms of disturbances, corresponded to internal and external threats to the supremacy or sovereignty of the state, foreshadowing European political theory's "discovery" of sovereignty with two faces, one internal and other external. In these formulations, Thomas appears to reinforce monarchical claims of authority against Papal supervision.

At the same time, Thomas suggested by implication that there may be institutional and pragmatic limits on state sovereignty in decisions concerning war. In justifying the exclusion of private persons from war-making decisions, he noted that it is "not the business of a private individual to declare war, because he can pursue his right... before the judgment of his superior" and "not the business of a private person to summon together the people, which has to be done in wartime." The first criterion may suggest an institutional concern that alternative dispute resolution must be pursued where possible, perhaps implying a kind of "last resort" requirement akin to suggestions in Augustine's formulas. The second criterion may also suggest

77 In Thomas's language, there is some ambiguity as to the addressees of the "just cause" and "right intention" criteria, since Thomas seems to suggest that it is only as to those "waging war" who must have "right intention." *See* St. Thomas, Summa Theologica, *supra* note 66, at 177. The concept of intention for public authority is analogous to the intention of agents of public authority when public authority is a single human agent such as a prince, but collective intentions, as in the case of oligarchies or democracies or other multiple-entity decision-makers, are not immediately commensurable with individual intentions. This complex question in implementing JWT we reserve for later discussion. For purposes of this discussion, it seems reasonable to assume that the "just cause" that provides a basis for legitimate authority to act includes not only an objective ground that suffices as a cause but a subjective intention to act on the basis of that ground. Cluttering our exposition of Thomist thought at this stage adds little to the progression of Just War Theory.

78 *See generally* Thomas Bokenkotter, A Concise History of the Catholic Church 168–192 (1979).

79 *See* St. Thomas, Summa Theologica, supra note 66, at 177 ("just as it is licit for them to have recourse to the material sword in defending the common weal against internal disturbances ...").

another practical institutional requirement, under which only those with sufficient authority to organize a force capable of showing a "probability of success" have the right under Just War theory to declare or commence war, since a pointless war could not, by assumption, be carried out for a just cause with right intention. It might be inferred that these institutional constraints on private war where applicable should equally constrain public war. If so, Thomas's notion of "superior authority" and the need to "summon the people" may serve as vehicles for transferring the locus of legitimate authority to third parties; for example, they could take a subsidiary, special meaning when conflicts arise between Christian princes that could be adjudicated by the Papacy as that "superior authority" or when the war in question is between the "people" of all of Christendom and the powers of Islam. Indeed, as international organization supplants national authority, Aquinas might be read as favoring federal, con-federal or supranational organization as actual or potential "legitimate authority." If so, it would be possible to construct criteria that would be viewed as authoritative from the viewpoint of several actors, a multilateral rather than unilateral approach to Just War Theory.

Finally, for Aquinas, the precise ground for just cause—*culpa* or fault—also skirts the divide between secular and religious authority. Technically, in Aquinas's lexicon, it may correspond to theological sin,[80] thus suggesting that non-secular decision-makers alone would exercise competence in the precise determinations as to whether a cause was just. On the other hand, *culpa* also served as a criterion for what became tort liability in private law legal systems in the West as well,[81] thus facilitating a secular interpretation of Aquinas's just cause requirement.

In sum, the nuances in Thomas's formulations open the door to accommodating institutional preferences for competing claims of Papal and secular authority and competing visions of moral and legal authority.

4. Catholic Neo-scholasticism in Victoria and Suarez

The possible secular and multilateral elements of Aquinas's Just War Theory seem to come to fruition in the teaching of the so-called Spanish neo-scholastics, Vitoria and Suarez. Like Augustine, but unlike Thomas Aquinas, Vitoria and Suarez faced a special historical problem that frames any discussion of their Just War Theory. For Augustine, the sack of Rome, the decline of Roman power, and the evident need for Christians to rise up to defend the community invited sustained reflection on the reconciliation of Biblical charity with the use of force. For Vitoria and Suarez, Spanish power's offensive extension to the West Indies and, in particular,

80 *See* Janet E. Smith, Moral Terminology and Proportionalism, http://www.aodonline.org/aodonline-sqlimages/shms/faculty/SmithJanet/Publications/MoralPhilosophy/MoralTerminology.pdf.

81 *See* Richard Epstein, Cases and Materials on the Law of Torts 30 (2009) (fault forms the ordinary basis for liability in tort).

the destruction of the Peruvian Inca Empire, formed the challenge to Christian thought.[82] Spain, in this era, nominally asserted special rights through the Spanish King's concurrent authority as Holy Roman Emperor, making a special claim of inheriting the temporal authority of the Roman Empire perpetuated by successive Papal investitures, "in theory coterminous with Latin Christendom itself, and endowed with a special mission of preserving and extending the Christian faith."[83] These Spanish thinkers, building on traditional discourse of Thomas Aquinas and the other late-medieval scholastics, confronted the Spanish King's theoretical claim. They needed therefore to formulate criteria to establish the limits of Spanish power in a manner consistent with Just War Tradition inherited from Augustine and Aquinas.

At the same time, the Spanish neo-scholastics wrote in the practical context of an emerging multi-polar European system of states. Vitoria wrote at the beginning of the Reformation while Suarez wrote a half-century later, after Protestant powers had become clearly established as permanent players in the European system of states. Thus, it was becoming increasingly important to address the Just War question in terms that were persuasive not only to the Spanish Kings but also other members, Catholic and Protestant, of the emerging European system of states. In doing so, however, the Spanish neo-scholastics provided the central apparatus for what became the Grotian conception that formed the basis for eviscerating, in effect, traditional Just War Theory in the aftermath of the 16th and 17th century Wars of Religion. Marking the end of those war, the Peace of Westphalia effectively delegitimized theologically-grounded unifying principles; thus, efforts to limit war were channeled from the *jus ad bellum* into the *jus in bello*.[84]

a. Vitoria's Subversive Defense of Spanish Power

Vitoria's Just War Theory reasoning begins with Aquinas, but his engagement with the problem of the Spanish conquest of the Amerindians takes him in an even more secular and multilateral direction than is foreseeable even in Aquinas's thought. Like Augustine and Aquinas, Vitoria supposes that war may be justified in terms of the tranquility of order, for this "proof

---

82 *See* Pangle & Ahrensdorf, supra note 1, at 88–89.

83 *See generally* R.R. Palmer & Joe Colton, A History of the Modern World 32 (1978).

84 *See* Tyler Rauert, Early Modern Perspectives on Western Just War Thought, *in* The Prism of War: Asian and Western Perspectives on the Use of Military 88 (Howard M. Hensel ed., 2010) ("each sovereign had the right and the authority to decide when just cause for war existed, and the search for a definition of justice by an overarching ideology was in effect abandoned within international law" but "one may not set aside the rules of war on behalf of a just cause").

Previously, Catholic Just War Theory had not sharply distinguished between *jus ad bellum* and *jus in bello*. According to John Finnis, "The distinction between *jus ad bellum* and *jus in bello* is scarcely part of the Catholic natural law tradition." John Finnis, The Ethics of War and Peace in the Catholic Natural Law Tradition, in The Ethics of War and Peace: Religious and Secular Perspectives 25 (Terry Nardin ed., 1996). According to Pangle & Ahrensdorf, "The sharp distinction between just cause of war and just prosecution of war arises on the basis of a specifically modern attempt, with roots in Grotius, but diverging from the spirit of the Scholastic Just War doctrine, to deny the possibility of distinguishing between wars whose cause is just and war whose cause is unjust—and then to erect a new sort of just conduct-of-war doctrine, in which the moral limits are not derived from policing authority of the just combatants." Pangle & Ahrensdorf, *supra* note 1, at 103. We reconsider the relationship between the *jus ad bellum* and the *jus in bello* in Part IV of this volume.

is based on the purpose and good of the whole world. Surely it would be impossible for the world to be happy -- indeed, it would be the worst of all possible worlds -- if tyrants and thieves and robbers were able to injure and oppress the good and the innocent without punishment, whereas the innocent were not allowed to teach the guilty a lesson in return."[85] Like Aquinas, he relies on a domestic analogy for the grounding of the right to war on the pursuit of vengeance upon a wrongdoer, for "there can be no vengeance where there has not first been a culpable offense....Likewise, a prince cannot have greater authority over foreigners than he has over his own subjects; but he may not draw the sword against his own subjects unless they have done some wrong; therefore he cannot do so against foreigners except in the same circumstances."[86] Thus, it is "lawful to avenge the injury done by the enemy, and to teach the enemy a lesson by punishing them for the damage they have done."[87]

Indeed, for the prince, rightful vengeance may be the only justification for war. Vitoria distinguishes between "offensive" and "defensive" war, but suggests that, ultimately, the same criteria control both kinds of war. With a caveat, he maintains that "there can be no doubt about the rights of defensive war...." While Vitoria acknowledges that "a private person... has the right to defend himself and his property," he adds the qualification that a private person "does not have the right to avenge injury, nor even, indeed, to seize back property which has been taken from him in the past. Self-defence must be a response to immediate damage, made in the heat of the moment."[88] But "the same proof holds true for offensive war; that is to say, not only war in which property is defended or reclaimed, but also war in which vengeance for an injury is sought..."; for, "even defensive war could not conveniently be waged unless there were also vengeance inflicted on the enemy for the injury they have done, or tried to do. Otherwise, without the fear of punishment to deter them from injustice, the enemy could simply grow more bold about invading a second time."[89] Thus, the practical requirements for vengeance in defensive war imply the legitimacy of vengeance even when unnecessary to provide restitution to the victim of injustice and deter further injustice.

The logic of these arguments seems to be based on a conception of global governance. Drawing on the notion that "the law of the Gospels does not prohibit anything which is permitted by natural law,"[90] Vitoria grounds this right to war, not in the execution of God's justice, but rather in a particular conception of natural law as grounded on practical requirements for order;

85 *See* Francisco de Vitoria, Political Writings, On the Law of War (Pagden & Lawrence eds., 1991), *reprinted in* The Ethics of War: Classic and Contemporary Readings 310 (Reichberg, Syse and Begby eds., 2006) [hereinafter "Law of War"].

86 *Id.* at 314.

87 *Id.* at 316.

88 *Id.* at 311. To the extent, thus, that Vitoria articulates a self-defense test that requires "imminence," it is linked to the question of competence or legitimate authority rather than whether there is a just cause for war.

89 *Id.* at 310.

90 Id. at 309.

for, "the world could not exist unless some men had the power and authority to deter the wicked by force from doing harm to the good and the innocent. Yet those things which are necessary for the governance and the conservation of the world belong to natural law." Thus, "this is his right by the law of nations and the authority of the whole world."[91] This "authority of the whole world" is the seed of a secular, yet universal conception of Just War Theory. Significantly, it is grounded on Vitoria's intuition concerning the practical requirements for maintaining order on the international level.

The significance of this approach is made clear in Vitoria's specific critique of Spain's claim of a right to use force against the Amerindians. Vitoria plainly rejects paternalist grounds for use of force, for "no Christian emperor, with the benefit of the advice of the most holy and wise popes, has ever declared war on unbelievers simply because they refused to accept the Christian religion."[92] Moreover, relying on Aquinas, Vitoria argues: "it is foolhardy and imprudent of anyone to believe a thing without being sure it comes from a trustworthy source, especially in matters to do with salvation. But the barbarians could not be sure of this, since they did not know who or what kind of people they were who preached the new religion to them." Thus, "the faithful man would not believe them unless he could see that they were credible, either by palpable signs or by some other means," so that "where there are no such signs nor any other persuasive factor, the barbarians are not obliged to believe." In sum, "those who are not Christians cannot accept the judgment of the pope, since the pope cannot condemn or punish them by a right other than that he is the vicar of Christ";[93] and "Christian princes, even on the authority of the pope, may not compel the barbarians to give up their sins against the law of nature, nor punish them for such sins."[94] It follows, for Vitoria, that "the Spaniards cannot use this pretext to attack them or conduct a just war against them."[95]

That said, Vitoria presents an artful compromise grounded in natural law through which Spanish objectives might be achieved through more peaceful and internationally palatable means. He hypothesizes the "just titles" by which Amerindians might have come under Spanish rules, the chief of which is predicated on the sociability of man and communities under "the law of nations (*ius gentium*), which either is or derives from natural law."[96] This reference to the *ius gentium*, a Roman concept, suggests a return to the non-theological foundations of Ciceronian Just War Theory, albeit without, in Vitoria's hands, its expansionist orientation. Rather, Vitoria

91 *Id.* at 316.

92 *See* Francisco de Vitoria, Political Writings, On the American Indians, *reprinted in* The Ethics of War: Classic and Contemporary Readings 296 (Reichberg, Syse and Begby eds., 2006)[hereinafter "American Indians"]. This account is consistent with the traditional view of the Crusades as being grounded on the protection of Christian rights in the Holy Land rather than some *mission civilisatrice.*

93 *Id.* at 298.

94 *Id.* at 297.

95 *Id.* at 295–96.

96 *Id.* at 300.

supposes, based on the natural law right to trade and to impart and receive information, that the Spaniards would be justified to use force both to vindicate their own rights and to protect the right of the Indians themselves. He writes:

> if the barbarians, either in the person of the masters or as a multitude, obstruct the Spaniards, after reasoning with them to remove any cause of provocation, may preach and work for the conversion of the people even against their will, and may if necessary take up arms and declare war on them, insofar as this provides the safety and opportunity needed to preach the Gospel. And the same holds true if they permit the Spaniards to preach, but do not allow conversions, either by killing or punishing the converts to Christ, or by deterring them by threats or other means. This is obvious, because such actions would constitute a wrong committed by the barbarians against the Spaniards, as I have explained, and the latter therefore have just cause for war. Second, it would be against the interests of the barbarians themselves, which their own prince may not justly harm; so the Spaniards could wage war on behalf of their subjects for the oppression and wrong which they were suffering, especially in such important matters.[97]

The requirement of "reasoning with" the barbarians is, moreover, central to the equal respect to which the "barbarians" are entitled, for:

> if the barbarians attempt to deny the Spaniards in these matters which I have described as belonging not the law of nations (ius gentium), that is to say from trading and the rest, the Spaniards ought first to remove any cause of provocation by reasoning and persuasion, and demonstrate with every argument at their disposal that they have not come to do harm, but wish to dwell in peace and travel without any inconvenience to the barbarians. Andy they should demonstrate this not merely in words, but with proof.... But if reasoning fails to win the acquiescence of the barbarians, and they insist on replying with violence, the Spaniards may defend themselves, and do everything needful for their own safety. It is lawful to meet force with force. And only in this eventuality, but also if there is no other means of remaining safe, they may build forts and defences, and if they have suffered an offence, they may on the authority of their prince, seek redress for it in war, and exercise the other rights of war.[98]

For Vitoria, it seems to follow that restraint in war is a corollary of the duty to reason with the enemy, as a procedural condition precedent to the ripening of a right to use force. But it may also follow from Vitoria's own doubts about the substantive capacity of reason itself to provide universally-acceptable answers.

---

97 *Id.* at 305.

98 *Id.* at 302.

Vitoria's theological commitments may well explain his diminished faith in reason. In adjudicating questions of sin, the concept of "invincible" or unavoidable ignorance had widespread medieval scholastic acceptance as an excuse. Vitoria's central innovation is to extend it equally to Christian and non-Christian Amerindians, giving each equal moral respect. Not only does Vitoria hold that in matters of salvation, the "barbarians" may be entitled, initially at least, to adopt a questioning attitude, but for the first time in Just War Theory, he advances the notion that war can be just on both sides.[99] By this he means that each side in a war may be entitled to take the position that it has just cause. He holds that "where there is provable ignorance either of fact or of law, the war may be just in itself for the side which has true justice on its side, and also just for the other side, because they wage war in good faith and are hence excused from sin. Invincible error is a valid excuse in every case."[100] He writes: "the barbarians may still be understandably fearful of men whose customs seem so strange, and who they can see are armed and much stronger than themselves. If this fear moves them to mount an attack to drive the Spaniards away or kill them, it would indeed be lawful for the Spaniards to defend themselves, within the bounds of blameless self-defence."[101] Yet,

> it is not incompatible with reason, indeed, when there is right on one side and ignorance on the other, that a war may be just on both. For instance, the French hold Burgundy on the mistaken but colourable belief that it belongs to them. Now our emperor Charles V has a certain right to that province and may seek to recover it by war, but the French may defend it. The same may be true of the barbarians. This is a consideration which must be given great weight. The laws of war against really harmful and offensive enemies are quite different from those against innocent or ignorant ones.[102]

Thus, as Vitoria raises the Amerindians to the moral status of the French, he so qualifies Just War Theory that it does not effectively discipline the use of force, including erroneous use of force by Amerindians, whenever "colorable" claims of right can be asserted by contending parties.

But the moral equality of the Amerindians did also open the door to limited uses of force against them to prevent injustice -- in other words, in an early formulation of modern humanitarian intervention, to save them from themselves. Discussing the Amerindian practice of human sacrifice, Vitoria writes that, as "barbarians are all our neighbors, ... princes, may defend them from ... tyranny and oppression ... not only to the actual moment when they are being

99 *See* Pangle & Ahrensdorf, *supra* note 1, at 93 (where Vitoria "introduces an innovation" but "it would appear that Vitoria understands himself to be simply uncovering the implications of Thomistic doctrine").

100 Vitoria, Law of War, *supra* note 85, at 322.

101 Vitoria, American Indians, *supra* note 92, at 303.

102 *Id.*

dragged to death; [but] they may also force the barbarians to give up such rites altogether."[103] For Vitoria, Just War Theory would not warrant use of force to subject the Amerindians to Spanish rule, if it was not necessary to prevent human sacrifice and protect the Amerindians themselves from the specific wrong of human sacrifice. Thus, rather than emphasize Spain's legitimate authority, Vitoria's interpretation of Just War Theory highlighted Spain's just cause and right intention. In so doing, for critics of Spanish power, he opened the door to it inquiry into whether the means chosen truly reflected the reasons for which the Spanish subjected the Amerindians to centuries of colonial rule.

b. Suarez's Subversive Defense of Just War Theory

Suarez, unlike Vitoria, gives real teeth to the distinction between "offensive" and defensive" wars—applying to cases of "offensive" war even greater limitations, given the importance of the need for "certitude."[104] On the other hand, Suarez builds on Vitoria's work on humanitarian intervention to protect the Amerindians from the consequences of tyranny, such as human sacrifice. Thus, it is from the duty to protect others from unjust rule, rather than a generalized right to execute universal justice, that Suarez fashions a robust theory of humanitarian intervention that is coupled with a right to revolution against tyranny, arguably linking democracy, domestic justice, and international intervention.

Restating traditional doctrine, Suarez begins with the premise that "a Christian prince may not declare war save either by reason of some injury inflicted or for the defense of the innocent."[105] In other words, war is always motivated by the pursuit of justice. Thus, Suarez distinguishes between "offensive" and "defensive" war solely in terms of whether the prior injustice that gives rise to war "has already occurred." But he defines as "defensive" war one's efforts "without notable delay ... to protect himself and to reinstate himself in possession."[106] This extended right of self-defense is plenary, since it accords with natural law, and is sometimes even "prescribed" by "the order of charity."[107] Suarez thus offers a formula for "defensive" war that appears to open the door to a robust approach toward the defense of others, including, as we shall see, the innocent victims of unjust regimes.

On the other hand, for Suarez, offensive war is subject to more rigid scrutiny along the lines of the traditional Just War criteria. Because it relates to the duty of the state -- and here Suarez

103 *Id.* at 306.

104 Francisco Suarez, Selections from Three Works of Francisco Suarez, The Classics of International Law, 828 (Williams et. al trans., 1944) *reprinted in* The Ethics of War: Classic and Contemporary Readings 357 (Reichberg, Syse and Begby eds., 2006)]hereinafter "Selections"].

105 *Id.* at 355.

106 *Id.* at 342.

107 *Id.* at 341.

uses the term "commonwealth" to make clear that his approach is not limited to "princely" rule -- to perform what Suarez calls "vindicative justice." Drawing on Vitoria's hierarchical approach, Suarez observes the "supreme prince may punish his own subjects when they harm others, so may he avenge himself on another prince or commonwealth . . . because the prince of whom we are speaking has no superior in temporal affairs; therefore, if the offender is not prepared to give satisfaction, he may be compelled to do so by war."[108] Indeed, "an incomplete commonwealth, or whosoever in temporal affairs is under a superior, cannot justly declare war without the authorization of that superior."[109]

And, in addition to sharpening the criteria of legitimate authority, Suarez tightens restraints that flow from just cause and right intention. He argues that public authority may not have recourse to war without "diligent examination," for "reason demands that in any matter whatsoever, deliberation and diligence should be applied, commensurate with it importance."[110] Moreover, for Suarez, the statesman must take the attitude of the "just judge,"[111] and, "if he is acting in good faith, should assess what is right [by seeking the counsel] of prudent and learned men"; indeed, "he may follow their judgment, if by [this consultation] his right is made clear to him."[112] As to the case of mistaken just cause, here Suarez seems to reverse the pro-war inference that might be drawn from Vitoria's insight that war can be "just on both sides" because of the "invincible ignorance" of one or both parties; for, analogizing to domestic legal disputes, Suarez maintains that "if the rights of the parties in question are at all times entirely equal, there is no reason which would allow [the judge] to allot the whole property to either party; and therefore the judge is bound to divide the property. Or, if this cannot be advantageously done, it will be necessary to satisfy both sides, in some fashion. Hence, in a question involving war, the princes shall be bound to this same attitude."[113]

In short, Suarez's refinements to Just War Theory could be interpreted to reinvigorate the Thomist commitment to reason, albeit not for the rational fulfillment of absolute ends, but rather as a reasonable basis for self-restraint. Suarez writes:

> it is impossible that the Author of nature should have left human affairs, governed as they are by conjecture more frequently than by any sure reason, in such a critical condition that all controversies between supreme princes and commonwealths would be settled only by war, for such a condition would contrary to wisdom and the common good of the human race; and therefore it would be contrary to justice. Furthermore, if this condition prevailed, those persons would as

108 *Id.* at 343.

109 *Id.* at 344.

110 *Id.* at 357.

111 *Id.*

112 *Id.* at 359.

113 *Id.* at 358.

> a rule possess the greater right who were the more powerful, and [this right] would have to be measured by arms, which is manifestly a barbarous and absurd supposition.[114]

Yet, it may be that Suarez's strict criteria and critical self-doubt in favor peace, both as a matter of natural law and as a consequence of the theological view of human society as amenable to reason, apply fully only where conflicts of property between states are involved, where a state's apparent self-interest is engaged, and where the defects of reason must be attenuated by the examination of conscience.

The force of these limitations appears to diminish, however, when Suarez turns to the vindication of the rights of others. Vitoria's position only indirectly provided authority to convert the Amerindians; while he rejected a right to convert those invincibly ignorant of Christian truth, he authorized the use of force to enable the Amerindians to have access to Christian truth, apparently only as a corollary of the natural rights to trade and, thus, to seek and impart information. Beginning with Vitoria's libertarian, free trade insight but transforming it into a substantive conception of the good, Suarez notes:

> if any nation should worship the one God and observe the laws of nature, while another nation practiced idolatry and lived contrary to natural reason, then the former state would have the right to send missionaries to instruct [the citizens of the latter state], and to free them from their errors. And if the nation were forcibly prevented, then war could justly follow. This holds first, because such a right is entirely keeping with nature; secondly, because the defense of the innocent would be involved in that procedure, since it is only reasonable to think that, there would not fail to be some who wished to be taught the natural truths necessary for an upright and virtuous life, and who would be wickedly impeded in the attainment of this wish.[115]

Suarez makes clear that it is the superiority of Christian "truth," rather than the right of the Amerindians to choose, that forms the core of his reasoning when, after affirming the right to defend the "innocent," he asserts that "if a commonwealth subject to an infidel princes wishes to accept the law of Christ and the unbelieving king prohibits that acceptance, then Christian princes have the right to defend that innocent people. But if the same commonwealth wishes to submit to the law of unbelievers -- for example, to the Mohammedan [law] -- and its prince is oppressed to this submission, then an infidel Turkish prince would not have a similar right of war against that other prince. The reason for this distinction is that to prevent the acceptance of the law of Christ does indeed involve grievous injustice and harm, whereas there is no injury at all in prohibiting the acceptance of another law."[116] In short, unlike Vitoria who

114 *Id.*

115 *Id.* at 355–56.

116 *Id.* at 355–56.

relied on neutral criteria concerning the right to trade in information as the basis for use of force in the conversion of the Amerindians, because of the harm done to the Indians from the sub-standard or repressive ideas governing them in pre-Spanish America, Suarez grounded the force of force on the substantive superiority of Christian ideas. In sum, the right to defend the innocent includes the right to protect them from the injustice of suffering impediments to the right of any person not to be "wickedly impeded" in the "attainment" of the "virtuous life" of the Christian.

The substantive underpinnings of Suarez's views on humanitarian intervention in the defense of others may well be connected to his view concerning the limits on state power, which in turn is grounded in a theory of limited government and popular sovereignty. In other words, governments become aggressors when they deprive their citizens of their rights, and the people themselves may have a right to do what others may do in their defense on humanitarian grounds. Suarez's thus argues that whole people, not only the Amerindians subject to tyranny, may also use force against an unjust or tyrannical prince. His "reason supporting these statements is that the tyrant in question is the attacker, and is iniquitously waging war against the commonwealth and its separate parts. By consequence, all those parts have the right of defense."[117] In other words, this right of self-defense is a natural right that can be exercised by private persons.[118] In this connection, Suarez provides an additional justification for the overthrow of "tyrants" that opens the door to a democratic element in his theory of government, one that places at least some responsibility on the people as a whole for the use of force by the state. He argues "the commonwealth, as a whole, is superior to the prince, for the commonwealth, when it granted him his power, is held to have granted it upon these conditions: that he should govern politically, and not tyrannically; and that, if he did not govern thus, he might be deposed."[119] Yet, perhaps because tyrannicide is not a pure case of self-defense, even Suarez recognizes that it cannot be an absolute right and is subject, instead, to the same criteria of doubt and restraint Suarez insists upon for offensive war. He argues that "[in order that such an uprising may justly occur] the situation must be one in which it is observed that the king does really and manifestly behave in a tyrannical manner; and the others conditions laid down for a just war must concurrently be present...."[120]

In sum, subject to his consistent theme of reasonable self-doubt and restraint, Suarez clearly opens the door to a right to revolution, presumably on pro-democratic principles, to enforce limits or "conditions" on delegated power. Moreover, the logic of his position seems to intimately connection to his authorization for humanitarian intervention to defend or vindicate the

117 *Id.* at 369.

118 *Id.*

119 *Id.*

120 *Id.* at 370.

rights of an innocent people, as in the Amerindian case, as against a tyrant exceeding his powers and thereby committing aggression against them and depriving them of their rights.

5. A New Legal Order Without Just War Theory: Protestant Voluntarism and Rebellion Against Reason

With the Renaissance turn toward secular humanism, which revived classical natural law thought, and Protestant Reformation, which buttressed the emerging multilateral and pluralist European state system, Spanish neo-scholastic and imperialist Just War Theory faced theoretical and practical challenges. Theoretically, Protestantism theology's commitment to individual will, rather than deference to hierarchy, and its skeptical treatment of human reason as a basis for valid moral judgments, had the effect for many of reducing confidence in community judgments concerning the dictates of reason. This in turn called into question scholasticism's confidence in the hierarchically-structured community of reasoned judgment reflected in Catholic moral teaching. In addition, the revival of secular thought rendered purely religious justifications less generally persuasive. Practically, the emergence of Protestant political powers, particularly in England and the Netherlands, contesting Spanish imperial claims based on the unity of Christian political universe under the Holy Roman Empire, increased the demand for theories that would compete with Spanish neo-scholasticism. In the Italian Protestant Alberico Gentili's, writing in exile from Oxford, political realism drew on the subversive elements in Spanish thought, taking them to their logical conclusions and on behalf of English power essentially negating Just War Theory. In Dutchman Hugo de Groot's (Grotius) attempt to synthesize traditional Christian Just War Theory with classical natural law theory, in the context of a pluralist international order, the pursuit of completeness may have sacrificed coherence -- leaving modern international law, which he is said to have fathered, bereft of any real limits on the use of force.

a. Gentili's Religious and Political Realism

It is unsurprising that Gentili's Protestantism posed a fundamental challenge to traditional Just War Theory, both in his premises and his specific conclusions. Emphasizing individual free will, in contrast to the medieval Catholic synthesis of individual reason in light of the guidance of a hierarchical community, Gentili insisted that "mind and whatever belongs to our mind are not affected by any external power or potentate, and the soul has no master save God only, who alone can destroy the soul." Thus, "religion ought to be free."[121] While the dissident Vitoria may have shared this conclusion, Gentili blankedly asserted "the Spanish were not just in giving...

121 Alberico Gentili, On the Law of War, Bk. I, Ch. 9, The Classics of International Law (John C. Rolfe trans. 1933) *reprinted in* The Ethics of War: Classic and Contemporary Readings 375 (Reichberg, Syse and Begby eds., 2006) [hereinafter Gentili].

the pretext of religion as the reason for their war with the Indians."[122] Again, using a formula that appears consistent with the Catholic's Vitoria reliance on the medieval theological construct "invincible ignorance," Gentili questioned the capacity of Just War Theory to provide reliable judgments in particular cases, where there is what he called "justifiable ignorance." He added that "our jurists are not in the habit of admitting ignorance as a defense," but Gentili was "driven to this distinction by the weakness of our human nature, because of which we see everything dimly, and are not cognizant of the purest and truest form of justice, which cannot conceive of both parties to a dispute being in the right." Moreover, he added, "it is doubtful on which side justice is, and if each side aims at justice, neither can be called unjust."[123] Finally, while preserving the theoretical possibility of relying on Just War Theory to determine that some wars are unjust uses of force, he made the practical point that "although it may sometimes happen . . . it will not occur very often ... that injustice is clearly evidenced on one of the two sides...."[124] Thus, for Gentili, drawing on a central Protestant premise in opposition to the Roman Church's claim of universal truths binding on all believers, it was the defects of human nature and reason that compelled the conclusion that war can be just on both sides, or at least not unjust. In short, Gentili creates a presumption against the invalidity, perhaps even a presumption in favor of the validity, of claims states make to use force.

This presumption also suggests an overall theory of state sovereign equality, one under which judgment concerning the use of force by states is not only theoretically difficult but also practically impossible, as experience indicated that most cases were incapable of resolution according to the "clearly evident" standard Gentili articulated. Gentili asserted that "reason shows that war has its origin in necessity; and this necessity arises because there cannot be judicial processes between supreme princes or free peoples unless they themselves consent, since they acknowledge no judge or superior."[125] While consistent with traditional Just War Theory concerning "legitimate authority," in a Protestant context where no credit is given either to the Papacy or the Holy Roman Emperor as potential "superior authorities," Gentili's theoretical move represented a radical break with traditional thought. If there were any doubt, Gentili's political realism becomes clear in his receptivity even to preventive war under a subjective interpretation of the criterion of "necessity," for a state "ought not to delay, or wait to avenge at one's peril an injury which one has received, if one may at once strike at the root of the growing plant and check the attempts of the adversary who is meditating evil."[126]

Perhaps more important, Gentili broke with the domestic analogy that seemed to inform traditional Just War Theory. He noted the argument that, in the case of an individual defense, a

122 *Id.* at 376.

123 *Id.* at 374.

124 *Id.* at 375.

125 *Id.* at 373.

126 *Id.* at 376.

"just cause for fear is demanded; suspicion is not enough. Now a just fear is defined as the fear of a greater evil, a fear which might properly be felt even by a man of great courage."[127] Yet, perhaps following the great divorce between private and public morality effected in his fellow Italian Machiavelli's thought, Gentili claimed: "in the case of great empires I cannot in reality accept that definition, which applies to private affairs. For if a private citizen commit some offense against a fellow citizen, reparation may be secured through the authority of a magistrate. But what a prince has done to a prince, no one will make good." This implied that justice has nothing to do with the relations between states and that law, whether grounded in some theory of right or simply as a description or state practice, also seems far removed. Instead, although Gentili insisted that he does not believe that a state may go to war merely "as soon as someone becomes too powerful," he held that "no general rule can be laid down with regard to the matter...."[128] In sum, preventive war seemed to come as a corollary of the separation of private and public morality, or perhaps the removal of morality from the relations between states; thus, Just War Theory became practically, if not theoretically, irrelevant.

b. The Grotian Synthesis

It is a matter of conventional wisdom that Hugo Grotius' synthesis of traditional Just War Theory with the increasingly secular rationality and multilateral political system of post-Westphalia Europe make his writings the starting point for the study of modern international law. But close inspection of his system reveals that it is closer to a wholesale uprooting of the premises of the Just War tradition than pragmatic adjustment; it may signal, rather, a return to the classical tradition of Just War, albeit with a Stoic orientation. His theory offered a nuanced philosophical analysis of the meaning of law, its relation to the objects of an international community governed by law, a conception of individual rights of states as subjects of that community in respect of the use of force for their own ends and to serve others, and a theory of the psychology of states and statesmen exercising those individual rights.

Grotius, when translated into English, appeared to use the term "*ius*" or "law" in at least three distinct senses, which in his original Latin retains its distinct meanings. First, law is "that which is just in relation to the rational beings who together form human society"; second, it is an "objective rule of conduct"; and, third, it is "a right vesting in a person" or subject, meaning a theory of subjective rights.129 In other words, Grotius's theory of international law encompassed a set of jurisprudential commitments concerning the nature of international society and, therefore, the law that governs it; a body of specific rules giving rise to rights, with a doctrine of

127 *Id.* at 377.

128 Gentili, *supra* note 121, at 377.

129 Hugo Grotius, On the Law of War and Peace, Prolegomena, para. 6, *reprinted in* The Ethics of War: Classic and Contemporary Readings 392 (Reichberg, Syse and Begby eds., 2006) [hereinafter Grotius].

sources for determining the specific content of those rules that is consistent with his theory of international society; and a concept of a system of rights and duties based on accepted rules that may be asserted as normative claims, whether or not subject to a system of dispute resolution.

Concerning "law" in the first sense of rational order, Grotius articulated a theory of the international community. Of course, Gentili wholly rejected the Just War Tradition's domestic analogy in his discussion of preventive war.[130] But Grotius premised his discussion of international society with the recognition of the human desire felt for society, for "among the traits characteristic of man is an impelling desire for society, that is, for community, not of any and every sort, but peaceful, and organized according to the measure of his intelligence, with those who are of his own kind, which the Stoics called *oikeiosis*."[131] Grotius then rejected the notion Gentili's divorce of international society from domestic society, rejecting the claim that "the standard of justice ... in the case of individuals within the state is inapplicable to a nation or the ruler of a nation."[132] Rather, he observed, "there is no state so powerful that it may not in some time need the help of others outside itself, either for purposes of trade, or even toward of the force of many foreign nations united against it."[133] Notably, this practical assessment forms the basis for inferring a need for states to cooperate, both to achieve their defensive objectives of avoiding losses and to achieve the affirmative objectives of improving their positions.

However, the needs of states, unlike Victoria's more ambitious conception of the purposes of international order as pursuing "happiness,"[134] are limited to a more modest objective. For Grotius, rationality commands that "no community can be maintained without law." And he made clear that he had in mind only the minimum requirements of community life, noting that this is what "Aristotle proved by the memorable example of brigands," so that "surely also that community which bands together the human race, or a number of nations, has need of law..."[135] Thus, it is the minimum requirements of cooperation of states as a "community of brigands," rather than a community pursuing "happiness," or any other conception of the good, that forms the basis for Grotius's theory of the international community of states. Built into this practical conception appears to be the rejection of any theologically-grounded claim that international society of necessity pursues or serves a common purpose. As Grotius famously wrote: "What we have been saying would have a degree of validity even if we should concede that which cannot be conceded without the utmost wickedness -- that there is no God or that the affairs of men are of no concern to Him."[136]

130 Gentili, *supra* note 121, at 377.

131 Grotius, *supra* note 129, at 388.

132 *Id.* at 390.

133 *Id.*

134 *See* Vitoria, *supra* note 86, at 311.

135 Grotius, *supra* note 129, at 390.

136 *Id.* at 389.

Grotius's conception of the nature of international society also had practical implications for his theory of how the precise rules of international law arise. It is a theory that is predicated on the honor of thieves, built on their own judgments of their own needs, for "just as the laws of each state (*civitatis*) have in view the advantage of that state, so certain laws could, and obviously did, originate between all or most states (*inter civitatis*) by mutual consent, aiming at the advantage, not of individual nations, but of this great global community (*universitatis*). And this is what is called the law of nations (*ius gentium*), whenever we distinguish that term from the law of nature (*iure naturalis*)."[137] The criterion of "mutual consent" accords with his view of the minimum requirements of international society as the source of international law, for the felt needs of states should be sufficient to bring them by agreement to those rules truly necessary for the "maintenance" of the international community in whose maintenance states have a common interest. It the will of states, rather than the will of God, that gives rise to order and law in international society.

Together with his minimalist conception of international society, Grotius's voluntarist conception of the doctrine of sources for finding international rules carries implications for his Just War Theory. First, he postulated that "right reason and the nature of society ... do not prohibit all use of force, but only that use of force which is repugnant to society, that is, which infringes upon another's right."[138] The apparent import of this formulation, when extended to international law -- that states have a right to use force unless there is a prohibitory rule based on state practice -- created a right against the use of force. On the other hand, he restated the traditional Just War formula of "just cause" to resort to war "to prevent imminent harm" and when "injury either is to be repaired or punished."[139] These apparently conflicting presumptions -- one permitting war unless it is forbidden; the other authorizing war only when it comports with some authorizing rule can be invoked -- are reconciled only in Grotius's theory of the psychology of states and the circumstances under which either test might be met. In theory, states are given broad latitude; in practice principles of circumspection and prudence generally call for restraint.

Grotius's formula appears to include defense or restitution of property taken wrongfully, self-defense, and some notion of just punishment on behalf of community interests. It is clear enough that Grotius frames his discussion on what constitutes a "wrong" against property in terms of his thin conception of international society. Rather than invoke a conception of distributive justice, under which a state may be affirmatively entitled to change the status quo to accord with a more just distribution of entitlements, he relied on the concept of "commutative" justice, which plainly authorizes use of force in self-help only to repair a prior wrongful taking.[140]

137 *Id.*

138 *Id.* at 394.

139 *Id.* at 401.

140 *Id.* at 404.

His discussion of the use of force in self-defense suggested even greater limitations than the procedural condition suggested by the commutative justice criterion with respect to the property of states. Ruling out preventive war in nominal self-defense, he affirmed that "Human life exists under such conditions that complete security is never guaranteed to us."[141] Foreshadowing what later came to be known as the *Caroline test, he argued for strict conditions on preemptive self-defense, for "the danger must be immediate."*[142] While acknowledging room for disagreement since some "theologians and jurists who would extend their indulgence somewhat further," he maintained the aggressor "cannot rightly *(iure) be killed, either if the danger can in any other way be avoided, or if it is not altogether certain that the danger cannot be otherwise avoided."*[143] Yet, he advanced a doctrine of mistakes, which gave a state with a reasonable basis in good faith for anticipating an imminent, certain attack some latitude for action, for "even if the assailant be blameless ... the right to protect oneself *(ius se tuendi) is not thereby taken away."*[144] But the absence of good faith did not seem to play much of a role in Grotius's calculus, since "in making war a wrong may arise from the intent of a party who engages in hostilities," but, "while these things do indeed convict of wrong the party that makes war, yet when a justifiable cause is not lacking they do not render the war itself properly unjust."[145] In short, rightful intention did not seem to play the role of a strict requirement in Grotius's *jus ad bellum.*

One might observe that Grotius advanced apparently conflicting insights -- skepticism toward preventive and preemptive war; deference to reasonable mistakes; but diminished reliance on good faith or right intention. However, a common psychological premise regarding the behavior of states and statesmen explains these apparent conflicts -- that is, skepticism concerning the capacity of human agents to avoid acting on the basis of their self-interest when they putatively act for the sake of others. The premise seems also rooted in Hugo Grotius's Dutch Protestant formation, which, like Gentili's realism, recognized the fallibility of human reason and the danger of any projects predicated on the capacity of reason to discover and realize universally binding truth. It also accords with Grotius's minimalist conception of order in international society, one that rejects international altruism, whether based on theological or non-theological imperatives. Thus, preventive or preemptive wars are questionable because human fear is likely to be inordinate; reasonable mistakes are inevitable in light of defective reason; and proving subjective right intention becomes an insuperable obstacle to objectively just uses of force given the prevalence of self-interest and bad faith. If there were any doubt about the role this psychological premise in Grotius's Just War Theory concerning self-defense and defense of

141 *Id.* at 405.

142 *Id. See also infra* Part II, Chapter 4, notes 16–33 and accompanying text.

143 *Id.*

144 *Id.* at 402.

145 Grotius, *supra* note 129, at 412.

state property, those doubts are resolved in Grotius's skepticism towards a third possible ground for the use of force, vindicating the interests of justice through humanitarian intervention.

While Grotius accepts in theory the possibility of use of force to vindicate justice by protecting other states or communities, the practical limits he imposes on such uses of force make it doubtful that he would ever approve such measures. In considering whether "peoples may rightly wage war on account of things done contrary to the law of nature, although not against them or their subjects," he acknowledged that "it is more honorable to avenge wrongs done to others than done to oneself, since in the case of wrongs done to oneself it s more to be feared though a sense of personal suffering one may exceed the proper limit or at least prejudice one's mind."[146] But, quoting Plutarch, he noted also that to "'impose civilization upon barbarous peoples is a pretext which may serve to conceal greed for what is another's.'"[147] In view of this danger, he held that "with regard to the laws of nature it is right to pardon those who are hampered by weakness of their powers of reasoning or deficient education."[148] Indeed, "wars undertaken to inflict punishment are under suspicion of being unjust, unless the crimes are very atrocious and most evident, or there is some other coincident reason."[149] Moreover, to defend even a limited right to humanitarian intervention and to reject the argument that only its proper jurisdiction or an injury to the state itself gives rise to a right to use force, he relied not only on reason and opinion but also noted that the right is "confirmed also by the usage of all nations."[150] Thus, in limiting humanitarian intervention, Grotius seemed to rely on the need for evidence of mutual consent reflected in state practice. In so doing, he coupled a presumption against humanitarian intervention with an affirmative burden of proof of its acceptance by states. For Grotius, it is proof of established custom that validates claims that, if based on natural law and reason alone, would be deemed spurious.

To review, coupled with the people's right, which is grounded in self-defense, to overthrow unjust government -- presumably including unjust Amerindian and even Protestant governments that impede the attainment of virtuous Christian life -- Suarez's defensive conception of Just War Theory provided a playbook for Spanish imperialism during the Wars of Religion. Promoting that Spanish conception of Christian civilization becames, on this view, justified as the defense of the innocent. And, if war is a means through which justice is vindicated, defined as restitution for the innocent and punishment for the wrongdoer, Vitoria's notion that both sides may not be in violation of the requirements of Just War Theory undermined the justice-seeking capacities of Just War Theory. It also undermined the capacity of third parties to choose sides and to come to the defense of the innocent in a manner free from moral doubt. With the

146 *Id.* at 407.

147 *Id.* at 408.

148 *Id.* at 409.

149 *Id.*

150 *Id.*

collapse of Just War Theory, each state became free -- morally and, if as Vitoria supposed the *ius gentium* was coterminous with the natural law, legally -- to use force; and every third-party state was also compelled not to use force, since it had no moral or legal basis to act other than its own self-interest, to assist an "innocent" against a "wrongdoer." Without a basis for choosing sides, states were free to use force at their will,[151] and a law of neutrality emerged to restrain third-party use of force.[152] Accordingly, Vitoria's conceptual apparatus, coupled with increasing practical doubt in case analysis, gave rise to a radically different approach to the law of war than imagined by Just War Theory during the millennium between Augustine and the Renaissance and Reformation recovery of secular thought and emergence of multi-polar system of states.

War became a question of might, discussed in the language or *realpolitik* or balance of power, rather than right. Gentili explicitly adopted this approach. Grotius attempted in practice to steer between the Scylla of rationalist, universalist and idealist traditional Just War Theory and the Charybdis of a voluntarist, pluralist, and realist balance of power theory. However, his skepticism concerning rationally-derived universal truths, his minimalist conception of international order, and his insistence on state practice as the source of international law uprooted the premises of traditional Just War Theory as well. Thus, a Protestant backlash against the Spanish imperial ambitions during the Wars of Religion marked the interment of the Just War tradition during the centuries following the Peace of Westphalia, until the tradition was resurrected in the aftermath of Nagasaki and Nuremberg.

C. Post-Westphalian Just War Theory

Falling into desuetude, Just War Theory in the centuries following Westphalia was explicitly or implicitly rejected. Hobbes's realist, social contract theory was premised on the state of nature's being a state of war. He observed that "in all times, Kings, and Persons of Soveraigne authority, because of their Independency, are in continual jealousies, and in the state and posture of Gladiators...," so that in "this war of every man against every man this also is consequent; that nothing can be Unjust."[153] Kant's legalist proposal for a federation of republican states as a practical means for achieving world peace explicitly rejected the premises of traditional Just War Theory under which the punishment to enforce justice and intervention to protect the innocent within a state might serve as just causes for use of force. Instead, Kant advanced "Six Preliminary Articles of a Perpetual Peace between Nations," the 5th of which famously states: "No state shall forcibly interfere in the constitution and government of another state," for to

151 *See generally* Wilhelm Grewe, The Epochs of International Law 279–342 (Michael Byers trans. 2000) (describing the "balance of power" era) [hereinafter Epochs].

152 *See id.* at 371–93; *see also* Stephen C. Neff, The Rights and Duties of Neutrals: A General History 192–96 (2000) (discussing the challenge the post-World War II revival of Just War thinking posed for the law of neutrality).

153 Thomas Hobbes, Leviathan 90 *reprinted in* The Ethics of War: Classic and Contemporary Readings 446 (Reichberg, Syse and Begby eds., 2006).

do so "would make the autonomy of all other states insecure."[154] He thus supposed in that each state is entitled to "autonomy" as though it were an individual agent with free will. It followed that punishment was never a just cause, since "war is only a regrettable expedient for asserting one's rights by force within as state of nature, where no court of justice is available to judge with legal authority. In such cases, neither party can be declared an unjust enemy, for this would already presuppose a judge's decision; only the outcome of the conflict, as in the case of a so-called 'judgment of God', can decide who is in the right. A war of punishment (*bellum punitivum*) between states is inconceivable, since there can be no relationship of superior to inferior among them."[155] Kant's "judgment of God" here had no theological content, but rather drews on the liberal, Lockean tradition that was premised on individual rights and limited government, in which the "appeal to heaven" is not a claim of practical authority in the here and now, but rather, where "there is no judge on earth," one must answer for one's decision only later, "at the great day to the Supreme Judge of all men."[156]

Thus, non-intervention, coupled with the idea of state autonomy in the form of the principle of "self-determination," played a central role in the drafting of the Charter of League of Nations.[157] The degree to which, in current international law, it finds expression in Article 2(7) of the United Nations Charter is a matter of enormous debate. For present purposes, it is sufficient to note that Article 2(7) provides, as follows: "Nothing contained in the present Charter shall authorize the United Nations to intervene in matters which are essentially within the domestic jurisdiction of any state...."[158] Chapter VII of the Charter, of course, authorizes the U.N. Security Council to adopt "enforcement measures" through its "decisions" as to "maintain or restore international peace and security" when the Council "determine[s] the existence of any threat to the peace, breach of the peace, or act of aggression."[159] At the same time, in "discharging" its "duty" with respect to the maintenance of international peace and security, Article 24(2) of the Charter requires the Council "to act in accordance with the ... Principles of the Organization,"[160] thus including the non-intervention principle. Yet, Article 2(7) provides that "this principle shall not prejudice the application of enforcement measures under Chapter VII,"[161] which appears to give the Council at least some authority to supersede the non-intervention principle of the

---

154 Immanuel Kant, Perpetual Peace, *reprinted in* The Ethics of War: Classic and Contemporary Readings 520–21 (Reichberg, Syse and Begby eds., 2006).

155 *Id.* at 522.

156 John Locke, Two Treatises on Civil Government, Second Treatise 127, *reprinted in* The Ethics of War: Classic and Contemporary Readings 466 (Reichberg, Syse and Begby eds., 2006).

157 League of Nations, Covenant of the League of Nations, (Apr. 28, 1919) (*available at* http://www.refworld.org/docid/3dd8b9854.htm); *see generally,* Margaret MacMillan, Paris 1919: Six Months that changed the World (2001).

158 U.N. Charter art. 2, para. 7.

159 U.N. Charter arts. 39–42.

160 U.N. Charter art. 24, para. 2.

161 U.N. Charter art. 2, para. 7.

legalist international order. At least initially, as we will discuss, the superpower conflict between the U.S. and Soviet Union rendered the interventionist interpretation of the U.N. Charter moot, thereby suppressing the question of collectively-authorized intervention for reasons of justice, either to punish a wrongdoer or protect the innocent, as contemplated by traditional Just War Theory. Instead, the law on use of force seemed to evidence a divorce of international politics and law from the Just War Tradition.

The specific debates that give rise to the modern recovery of Just War Theory in the West begin with two major moral challenges, which arguably more properly ought to be discussed in terms of *jus in bello* reasoning but were framed in a way that invoked, and arguably distorted, the traditional *jus ad bellum.* The first debate focused on the American use of nuclear weapons during the Second World War against Japan in order to secure Japan's unconditional surrender (as well as, for that matter, the destruction of German cities through non-nuclear aerial bombardment to secure Germany's unconditional surrender). The second debate considered the U.S. retaliatory threat to use nuclear weapons in order to deter nuclear attacks by the Soviet Union and the possible NATO first-use of tactical weapons in Europe to defeat conventional military invasion of Western Europe by the Warsaw Pact. The two debates invited religiously-inspired moralists to consider the meaning of the Just War tradition in the entirely new context of weapons of mass destructions in a world without an established international authority yet with the form of a potential supranational judge, namely the U.N. Security Council.

We now consider how it is possible to view these contemporary, religiously-inspired debates through the prism of the earlier debate between Augustinian and Thomist approaches -- one emphasizing the defects of human reason; the other placing greater reliance on reason's capacity to understand and pursue the common good through collective action. These debates in time prompted a formal response from the Catholic Church, both the U.S. Conference of Catholic Bishops and the Vatican itself, prompting in turn critical commentary by Catholics and other Christians purporting to recover the original Just War Tradition. Finally, secular commentary attempted to reframe much of Just War Theory in terms of competing strands of liberal and communitarian political theory. We take each development in turn.

1. The Augustinian Revival

Paul Ramsey, writing from the Augustinian tradition of Protestant theologians, attempted to convince Christian pacifists that nuclear weapons were not intrinsically evil in the struggle against the Soviet Union but that the use or threat of use of such weapons required moral justification. Situating himself in this intermediate position, Ramsey began with the central question whether "reliance on nuclear weapons for deterrence hypothetically commit us, here and now, to murder, there and then?"[162] To resolve the basic *jus ad bellum* question concerning whether such war could ever be justified, Ramsey resorted to what appeared to be a version of the traditional medieval doctrine of "double effect." The critical distinction, for Ramsey, was between nuclear deterrent strategies that targeted enemy forces, so-called "counterforce" strategies, and strategies that that target enemy civilians, sometimes called "city-busting." According to Ramsey, "collateral civilian damages that would result from counter-force warfare in its maximum form may itself be quite sufficient to deter either side from going so high and to preserve the rules and tacit agreements limiting conflict in a nuclear age. In that case, deterrence during the war and collateral civilian damage are both 'indirect' effects' of a plan and action of war which would be licit or permitted by the traditional rules of civilized conduct in war. To say that counter-force strikes over an enemy's own territory are licit or permitted is to say that one can morally intend and be 'conditionally willing' to engage in such a war. ... The deterrent effect, of which we are now speaking, is then, as it were, an indirect effect of the foreseeable indirect effects of legitimate military conduct."[163] It is argued by some that Ramsey's willingness to extend Just War principles to nuclear deterrence reflected his Augustinian worldview[164] -- recognition of the prevalence of evil in human affairs, particularly as reflected in the ambitions and practices of the Soviet Union; indeed, on another view, Ramsey was "a Protestant soldier" who "would have Americans gird themselves for a long continuous struggle with the forces of evil."[165]

2. A Thomist Response

In reviving the Just War Tradition to address the most difficult moral issue in the nuclear age, it seemed to many, however, that Ramsey had reduced the "right intention" element of traditional Just War Theory to absurdity. Writing from the standpoint of Thomas Aquinas's Catholic synthesis of classical Aristotelian virtue ethics and Christian charity, G.E.M. Anscombe deemed the Allied war policy during the Second World War to fail the "right intention" element of traditional Just War Theory. She held that if "a government's intentions cannot be known to be unjust because they are vague, that vagueness itself vitiates them. But the case is even clearer than this. For the truth is that government's professed intentions are not merely vague, but unlimited. ...What does this mean but that our intentions are so unlimited that there is no point at which we or the Germans could say to our government: 'Stop fighting; for your conditions are

162 Paul Ramsey, The Limits of Nuclear War, *reprinted in* The Ethics of War: Classic and Contemporary Readings 620 (Reichberg, Syse and Begby eds., 2006).

163 *Id.*

164 *See* Reichberg, Introductory Note to Paul Ramsey, supra note 163, at 615 (evidencing "little interest in the historical dimensions of just war theory, apart from St. Augustine, whom he often quoted").

165 Michael Walzer, Just and Unjust Wars: A Moral Argument with Historical Illustrations 279 (1977)

satisfied.'" In short, her view was that Britain's policy was "incomprehensible, except as a policy, of opposing German injustice, but of trying to preserve the status quo and that an unjust one."[166]

In the same essay, written well-before the Allied fire-bombing of German cities and American use of nuclear weapons in Japan to secure -- immorally, as Anscombe had already argued -- German and Japanese "unconditional surrender," Anscombe further insisted that the principle of "double effect" did not justify indiscriminate use of force so as to cause disproportionate harm to the innocent. There was an important distinction, she asserted, between "making one group of persons a target, to kill others by accident, and to make a group of persons a target, in order -- by attacking them all -- to attack some members of the group who are persons who may legitimately be attacked."[167] Here she saw a connection with what she also saw as a settled Just War principle: "No action can be excused whose consequences involve a greater evil than the good of the action itself, whether these consequences are accident or not. Double effect therefore only excused a grave incidental consequence where the balance of the total effects of an action is on the side of the good."[168]

Extending these insights to nuclear deterrence, Anscombe rejected Ramsey's use of the doctrine of double effect -- in an Orwellian reference, calling it "double-think about double-effect."[169] Anscombe acknowledged the "distinction between the intended, and the merely foreseen, effects of a voluntary action is indeed absolutely essential to Christian ethics. For Christianity forbids a number of things as being bad in themselves. But if I am answerable for the foreseen consequences of an action or refusal, as much as for the action itself, then these prohibitions break down. If someone innocent will die unless I do a wicked thing, then on this view I am his murderer in refusing, so that all that is left for me is to weigh the evils."[170] Yet, for Asncombe, a line must be drawn, for "it may be impossible to take the thing (or people) you want to destroy as your target; it may be possible to attack it only by taking as the object of your attack what includes large numbers of innocent people. Then you cannot very well say they died by accident. Here your action is murder."[171] In short, a principle of proportionality, or what later became known as "comparative justice," seemed to inform Anscombe's critique of Ramsey's defense of the application of the principle of double effect to the question of nuclear deterrence.

---

166 G.E.M Anscombe, The Justice of the Present War Examined, 74-75 (1981), *reprinted in* The Ethics of War: Classic and Contemporary Readings 632 (Reichberg, Syse and Begby eds., 2006) [hereinafter Present War].

167 *Id.* at 631.

168 *Id.* at 630.

169 G.E.M. Anscombe, War and Murder (1961), *reprinted in* The Ethics of War: Classic and Contemporary Readings 628–29 (Reichberg, Syse and Begby eds., 2006) [hereinafter War and Murder].

170 *Id.* at 629.

171 G.E.M Anscombe, Mr. Truman's Degree (1981), *reprinted in* The Ethics of War: Classic and Contemporary Readings 630 (Reichberg, Syse and Begby eds., 2006) [hereinafter Truman's Degree]

3. The Catholic Bishops—A New Catholic Synthesis and its Critics

In light of criticism of his use of the principle of "double effect," Ramsey acknowledged that he should have described the deterrent effect as a "direct and wanted effect of the unwanted, indirect, collateral consequence of even a just use of nuclear weapons."[172] The debate among the philosophers attempting to revive the Just War Tradition informed the attempt of the U.S. Conference of Catholic Bishops to reformulate traditional Just War Theory to address the danger of nuclear war during the 1980s, the last decade of the Cold War.

In its pastoral letter *The Challenge of Peace*,[173] the Catholic Bishops of the United States attempted to summarize the legacy of the Just War Tradition and offer guidance to Roman Catholics and others concerning its implications for the morality of the possession and threat or use of nuclear weapons on the terms articulated as the official policy of the United States, which purported to exclude the direct targeting of civilians.[174] The central conclusions of the Bishops' reading of the Just War Tradition are that "Catholic teaching begins in every case with a presumption against war"; that "[o]ffensive war of any kind is not morally justifiable"; and that, with respect to nuclear weapons, "[e]ven defensive response to unjust attack can cause destruction which violates the principle of proportionality, going far beyond the limits of legitimate self-defense."[175] Indeed, the Bishops concluded that, "[i]f nuclear deterrence exists only to prevent the use of nuclear weapons by others, the proposal to go beyond this to planning for prolonged periods of repeated nuclear strikes and counter-strikes, or 'prevailing' in nuclear war, are not acceptable. They encourage notions that nuclear war can be engaged in with tolerable human and moral consequences.... Nuclear deterrence should be used as a step on the way toward progressive disarmament."[176]

In the course of making these arguments, the Bishops attempted to systematize the Just War Tradition into a doctrine, with specific criteria to be applied as a form of rules:

---

172 Ramsey, *supra* note 162, at 620 n.14.

173 The Challenge of Peace: God's Promise and Our Response, A Pastoral Letter on War and Peace (May 3, 1983), *reprinted in* The Ethics of War: Classic and Contemporary Readings 680 (Reichberg, Syse and Begby eds., 2006) [hereinafter Challenge of Peace].

174 The Challenge of Peace reports that its analysis relied upon "the letter of January 15, 1983, of Mr. William Clark, national security adviser, to Cardinal Bernardin. Mr. Clark states: 'For moral and political reasons, the United States does not target the Soviet civilian population as such. There is no deliberately opaque meaning conveyed in the last two words. We do not threaten the existence of Soviet civilization, by threatening Soviet cities. Rather, we hold at risk the war-making capability of the Soviet Union—its armed forces, and the industrial capacity to sustain war. It would be irresponsible for us to issue policy statements which might suggest to the Soviets that it would be to their advantage to establish privileged sanctuaries within heavily populated areas, thus inducing them to locate much off their war fighting capability within those urban sanctuaries." *Id.* at 679.

175 *Id.* at 670–61.

176 *Id.* at 680.

a. Just Cause – "only to confront 'a real and certain danger,' i.e., to protect innocent life, to preserve conditions necessary for decent existence, and to secure basic human rights."[177]

b. Competent Authority – because "the right to use force has always been joined to the common good," war must be "declared by those with responsibility for public order," a requirement which "is particularly important in a democratic society."[178]

c. Comparative Justice – in answering the question whether "the values at stake are critical enough to override the presumption against war.... [I]n a world of sovereign states recognizing neither a common moral authority nor a central political authority, comparative justice stresses that no state should act on the basis that is has 'absolute justice' on its side...."[179]

d. Right Intention – "war can be legitimately intended only for the reasons set forth above as a just cause" and means "pursuit of peace and reconciliation, including avoiding unnecessarily destructive acts or imposing unreasonable conditions (e.g., unconditional surrender)."[180]

e. Last Resort – requiring that "all peaceful alternatives must have been exhausted" and, in this connection, while recognizing that "[n]o international organization currently in existence has exercised sufficient internationally recognized authority to be able either to mediate effectively in most cases or to prevent conflict," the Bishops "regret the apparent unwillingness of some to see in the United Nations organization the potential for world order which exists and to encourage its development."[181]

f. Probability of Success – rejecting "irrational resort to force or hopeless resistance when the outcome of either will clearly be disproportionate or futile."[182]

g. Proportionality – that "the damage to be inflicted and the costs incurred by war must be proportionate to the good expected by taking up arms," taking into account

177 *Id.* at 671.

178 *Id.*

179 *Id.* at 672.

180 *Id.*

181 *Id.* at 673.

182 *Id.*

> that "in today's interdependent world even a local conflict can affect people everywhere; this is particularly the case when the nuclear powers are involved."[183]

Like Anscombe, the Bishops' synthesis stands in direct opposition to Ramsey's acceptance of nuclear deterrence. In its new *Catechism of the Catholic Church* issued a decade later,[184] the Vatican seemed to take a more nuanced position, stating: "The prohibition of murder does not abrogate the right to render an unjust aggressor unable to inflict harm. Legitimate defense is a grave duty for whoever is responsible for the lives of others or the common good."[185] It seemed to frame the use of force only in terms of a right and duty of public officials, competent authority, to use force in self-defense. This reading is further suggested by the Vatican's reference to self-defense as the only enumerated exception stated in the Vatican II document *Gaudium et Spes* from the duty of "all citizens and all governments" to "work for the avoidance of war."[186] Thus, the Vatican's formulation seems to share the U.S. Bishops' objection to "offensive war," leaving open however the question whether self-defense for the Vatican includes the U.S. Bishops' approval of the right and duty to "to protect innocent life, to preserve conditions necessary for decent existence, and to secure basic human rights."[187] Yet, the Vatican seemed to follow the U.S. Bishops in demanding that "[t]he strict conditions for legitimate defense by military force require rigorous consideration"; specifically, that "the damage inflicted by the aggressor on the nation or community of nations must be lasting, grave, and certain"; that "all other means of putting an end to it must have been sown to be impractical or ineffective"; that "there must be serious prospect of success"; and that "the use of arms must not produce evils and disorder graver than the evil to be eliminated," noting further that the "power of modern means of destruction weighs very heavily in evaluating this condition."[188] In short, describing these elements as the "traditional elements enumerated in what is called the 'just war' doctrine," the Vatican, like the U.S. Bishops, appears to insistent on last resort, probability of success, and proportionality of harm. At the same time, the Vatican does not appear to have explicitly adopted a commitment to comparative justice or asserted a right to make prudential judgments as to the morality of deterrence, since the *Catechism* clearly states that the "evaluation of these conditions for moral legitimacy belongs to the prudential judgment of whose who have responsibility for the common good."[189] The negative implication of this formula is that

---

183 *Id.*

184 *See* Catechism of the Catholic Church: With Modifications from Editio Typica (U.S. Conference of Catholic Bishops trans. 1995) [hereinafter Catechism].

185 *Id.* at 618, para. 2321.

186 *Id.* at 615, para. 2308.

187 Challenge of Peace, *supra* note 173, at para. 86.

188 Catechism, *supra* note 184, at 615, para. 2309.

189 *Id.*

the precise factual judgments required in casuistry -- the discussion of concrete cases -- is the province of neither the Bishops nor the Vatican.

Indeed, to many others, the Bishops' approach, even as reformulated after the end of the Cold War,[190] seemed wholly inconsistent with the core Just War Tradition. For these critics, even some Catholic critics such as George Weigel,[191] the Bishops reformulated the requirements of Just War Theory in ways that departed from the central Just War idea that it is the responsibility of public authority to make the prudential judgments that further the *tranquillitas ordinis* or "common good," which was first articulated by Augustine as the central postulate of Just War thought. But the most systematic response to the Bishops has come from Ramsey's former student, James Turner Johnson, who continued to insist that "[c]lassically[,] the use of force in response to a threat to values was justified in four ways: to protect the innocent, to recover something wrongfully taken, to punish evil, and to defend against a wrongful attack in progress."[192] In re-calling the vindicative justice dimension of traditional Just War Theory, Weigel and Johnson sought to reinvigorate the capacity of Western states to view the question of use of force through the prism of their responsibility to exercise power, not just in their own interest, but also in the interest of the international community as a whole. About the U.S. Bishops, wrote Johnson, "once one has begun by describing war as something negative, it is conceptually impossible to describe it as a way to peace."193 Rather than focus on what states may not do, argued Johnson, the Just War Tradition has focused on what states can do to promote true peace, defined to include justice, and thus serve the common good.

Johnson also took issue with the Bishops' precise formulation of the specific Just War criteria. Rather than treat each of the seven criteria as essential requirements of the tradition, Johnson argued that only four specific requirements served as true duties, or what he called "deontological (primary) criteria," in the Just War Tradition:

a. Sovereign Authority – a "duly authorized representative of a sovereign political entity"; in traditional terms, "persons or communities with no political superior."

190 For an extension and modest reformulation of the Bishops' position, *see* The Harvest of Justice is Sown in Peace, National Conference of Catholic Bishops (1993), *reprinted in* The Ethics of War: Classic and Contemporary Readings 681 (Reichberg, Syse and Begby eds., 2006).

191 *See* George Weigel, Tranquillitas Ordinis: The Present Failure and Future Promise of American Catholic Thourght on War and Peace (1989).

192 James Turner Johnson, Does Defense of Values by Force Remain a Moral Possibility?, *reprinted in* The Ethics of War: Classic and Contemporary Readings 662 (Reichberg, Syse and Begby eds., 2006).

193 *See* James Turner Johnson, The War to Oust Saddam Hussein: Just War and the New Face of Conflict 29 (2005) [hereinafter "War to Oust Saddam Hussein"].

b. Just Cause – "the protection and preservation of value in the face of injustice"; in traditional terms, "retaking persons, property or other values wrongly taken" and "punishment of evil";

c. Right Intention – an "intent" that is "in accord with just cause and not territorial aggrandizement, intimidation, or coercion"; in traditional terms, negatively stated, avoiding "hatred of the enemy" and "implacable animosity," or, positively stated, "the aim of producing peace"; and

d. The Aim of Peace – "establishing domestic and international stability, security and peaceful interaction"; in traditional terms, the "positive aspect of the criterion of right intention."[194]

In Johnson's review of the history, "last resort," "reasonable hope of success," and "proportionality of ends" -- what the Bishops described as duties (see e, f, and g above); and the Vatican included in its revised *Catechism* -- serve only as "prudential (supportive) criteria," meaning that they inform the application of the deontological criteria.[195] This does not necessarily mean that Johnson's reformulation conflicts with the Bishops' specific views. For example, the Bishops' acceptance of deterrence only on the condition of its use as a means toward eventual abolition might be formulated in terms of the deontological criteria of "right intention" or "aim of peace" criteria, such that deterrence truly serve the goals of peace rather than the extension of U.S. power. To illustrate, the Bishops could be deemed to hold that no use of nuclear weapons could reflect "right intention," since the goal of peace and pursuing the common good could never be realized by using force in a way that causes more harm than good. On the other hand, since their specific arguments relate to what Johnson called "prudential" criteria, if the Bishops were to follow the Vatican's apparent view that application of prudential elements is not the province of the Bishops, it may be difficult to reformulate the Bishops' precise guidance as to the morality of possession, use or threat of use of nuclear weapons in terms as demanding as the Bishops employed in *The Challenge of Peace.* What clearly disappears from Johnson's reconstruction of Just War Theory is the Bishops' commitment to "comparative justice." But it seems self-evident that Johnson's approach demands that Just War Theory not include a "presumption against war" that the Bishops had deemed so central to their project.[196]

---

194 *Id.* at 38.

195 *Id.*

196 *See* Challenge of Peace, *supra* note 173, at 672.

4. Secular and Non-Christian Approaches of the Just War Tradition

In the aftermath of the Vietnam War, American moral philosopher and political scientist Michael Walzer sought to provide a non-realist, non-legalist approach to questions of justice in war. Walzer rooted his approach only in part on the specific teachings of previous theoreticians. Rather, he sought to expound what he viewed as a kind of "shared" or "common" morality, "shared not because we arrive at the same conclusions as to whose fight unjust and whose unjust, but because we acknowledge the same difficulties on the way to our conclusion, face the same problems, talk the same language."[197] But because "proper method of practical morality is casuistic in character," he believed it was only through a discussion of cases and examples that he could establish his general claim that there was such a "common" morality in questions of use of force.[198] Yet, although he did not claim is was necessary or even possible to defend the foundations for such a morality -- with a precise account of his theory of "personality, action and intention" -- he suggested that the "morality I shall expound is in its philosophical form a doctrine of human rights."[199] Central to this discussion, then, is the role of state sovereignty as the means to protecting those rights, for the "theory of ends in war is shaped by the same rights that justify fighting in the first place -- most importantly, by the right of nations, even of enemy nations, to continued national existence and, except in extreme circumstances, to the political prerogatives of nationality."[200] By parity of reasoning, he argued, "when a government turns savagely upon its own people, we must doubt the very existence of the political community to which the idea of self-determination might apply."[201] In his discussion, then, Walzer rejected realism's absolute commitment to state sovereignty, but he also rejected legalism's often formalistic justifications for ignoring state sovereignty.

Walzer thus challenged, in a sustained argument, what he described as the modern "legalist" position that force may be used only in self-defense to repel and to punish aggression.[202] To take one example, in the context of a discussion of humanitarian intervention, he argued that the law simply runs out, in many cases, requiring independent justification for the morality of any given use of force. Thus, the absence of legal authority does not preclude moral legitimacy. Walzer notes: "many lawyers prefer to stick to the paradigm. That doesn't require them, on their view, to deny the (occasional) need for intervention. They merely deny legal recognition

197 Walzer, *supra* note 165, at xiv–xv.

198 *Id.* at xvi. While Johnson approves what appears to be Walzer's refusal to adopt the Bishops' position that there is a "presumption against war" in Just War reasoning, he sharply disagrees with Walzer's emphasis on casuistry, arguing that Walzer's reasoning "needs to be accompanied by the disciplined criteria found in classic just war tradition." War to Oust Saddam Hussein, *supra* note 193, at 33.

199 Walzer, *supra* note 165, at xvi.

200 *Id.* at 123.

201 *Id.* at 101.

202 *Id.* at 58–63.

to that need."[203] Similarly, the existence of formal legal authority does not guarantee morality. Discussing humanitarian intervention by India in 1971 to protect and liberate East Pakistanis in what is now known as Bangladesh, notwithstanding the absence of Security Council authorization, Walzer writes:

> Nor is it clear to me that action undertaken by the UN, or by a coalition of powers, would necessarily have a moral quality superior to that of the Indian attack. What one looks for in numbers is detachment from particularist views and consensus on moral rules. And for that, there is at present no institutional appeal; one appeals to humanity as a whole. States don't lose their particularist character merely by acting together. If governments have mixed motives, so do coalitions of governments. Some goals, perhaps, are cancelled out by the political bargaining that constituencies the coalition, but others are super-added; and the resulting mix is as accidental with reference to the moral issue as are the political interests and ideologies of a single state.[204]

Thus, "any state capable of stopping the slaughter has the right, at least, to try to do so."[205] And Walzer even leaves open the possibility of regime-change as the "outer limit," only "in cases where the criminality of the aggressor state threatens those deep values that political independence and territorial integrity merely stand for in the international order, and when the threat is in no sense accidental or transitory but is inherent in the very nature of the regime."[206] Where humanitarian intervention is authorized to "stop the slaughter," one would imagine that regime-change would be justified as the "outer limit" in appropriates cases as well.

In this respect, Walzer appears to track the more recent thinking of John Rawls on questions of global justice. Rawls' *Theory of Justice* had offered a philosophical defense, based on a conception of what he called "justice as fairness," of the modern, liberal welfare-state on social contract and Neo-Kantian grounds. However, it gave rise to sustained criticism from communitarians -- such as Michel Sandel[207] and Walzer himself[208] -- and was extended to supply a theory of international justice only others,[209] not by Rawls himself. When he finally turned to the question of international justice in an essay based on lectures he delivered at Oxford after the end of the Cold War, *The Law of Peoples*,[210] he rejected the idea that international society could be, like domestic societies, based exclusively on a common "comprehensive" theory of the good, such as

203 *Id.* at 106.

204 *Id.* at 107.

205 *Id.* at 108.

206 *Id.* at 113.

207 *See generally* Michael Sandel, The Limits of Liberalism (1982).

208 *See generally* Michael Walzer, Spheres of Justice: A Defense of Pluralism and Equality (1983).

209 *See, e.g.*, Charles R. Beitz, Political Theory and International Relations (1979).

210 *See* John Rawls, Collected Papers 529–564 (Samuel Freeman ed., 1999).

his own theory of "justice as fairness." He viewed international society as a pluralist system in which each state is entitled to advance within its jurisdiction its own competing conception of the common good.[211] Because "justice as fairness" could not be extended to what he called "hierarchical" societies, then the "law of peoples" could not be based on a comprehensive conception of the good, such as "justice as fairness."

However, Rawls, like Walzer, also distinguished between international legalism and international morality, arguing that "international law" is "an existing, or positive, legal order, however incomplete it may be in some ways, lacking, for example, an effective scheme of sanctions such as normally characterizes domestic law," while "the law of peoples" is "a family of political concepts with principles of right, justice, and the common good, that specify the content of a liberal conception of justice worked up to extend to and to apply to international law. It provides concepts and principles by which the law is to be judged."[212] Moreover, given the Kantian roots of Rawls' *Theory of Justice*, specifically Rawls' commitment to individual liberty as a principle of justice having priority even over communitarian claims (as well as over distributive justice), it should not then have come as a surprise to Rawls' students that Rawls would then adopt the Kantian position that nominally insists on nonintervention as a bedrock principle of international society. In short, for Rawls, it is the autonomy of the "people" that constitutes any given state.[213]

Drawing on these premises, Rawls identified the minimum content of the "law of peoples," primarily the universality of basic human rights. On this basis, Rawls argued that there is a moral basis to intervene to protect basic human rights, for "[h]uman rights are a special class of rights designed to play a special law in a reasonable law of peoples for the present age."[214] Thus, human rights are "a necessary condition for a state's legitimacy," when they are in place "sufficient to exclude justified and forceful intervention by other peoples, say by economic sanctions, or in grave cases, by military force," and "set a limit of pluralism among peoples."[215] Like Walzer, then, Rawls held that "human rights" form the foundational principle for a theory of humanitarian intervention, although he insisted this foundation was not located within explicitly a "comprehensive" view of the "common good" in international society as a whole. Thus, for both Walzer and Rawls, justified use of force must be defended exclusively in terms that are not grounded on a foundational comprehensive set of commitments, such as the religions premises upon which traditional Just War Theory was grounded.

Yet, Walzer's most recent contribution to the question of humanitarian intervention may move beyond the exclusively secular justifications advanced in his earlier work, albeit from the

---

211 *See id.* at 544–51.

212 *Id.* at 536.

213 *See id.* at 539–49; compare Kant, *supra* note 154, at 520.

214 *See* Rawls, *supra* note 210, at 539–49.

215 *Id.* at 554–55.

communitarian perspective that is more inclined to promote humanitarian intervention than the liberal and Kantian tradition in which Rawls theorized. For Walzer, the right to intervene should no longer be separated from the duty to intervene.[216] He offered two plausible accounts -- one nominally secular and Marxist; the other theological and Jewish. Drawing on Marx's dictum -- "from each according to his abilities, to each according to his needs" -- Walzer argued that "obligatory giving" is part of our common morality.[217] But he did not begin his analysis there, for the medieval Jewish philosopher Maimonides maintained, "following Talmudic precedents, that insofar as Jewish communities in the Diapora had coercive power, they could legitimately force their members to give *tzedekah,*"[218] which, Walzer noted, "is commonly translated as 'charity,' but which comes from the same root as the word for 'justice'."[219] Thus, for Walzer:

> the negative act of not contributing is a positive theft. And since theft is unjust, you are acting not only uncharitably but also unjustly by not giving, which is why coerced *tzedekah* is legitimate. I called this a theological argument, but it is possible even for nonbelievers to accept that, in some sense, it is true and right. Or nonbelievers can translate the argument into secular language: some part of everyone's wealth belongs to the political community which makes economic activity and peaceful accumulation possible -- and it can and should be used to promote the well-being of all the members of the community.[220]

But extending this idea to humanitarian intervention may be problematic, perhaps even for Walzer. The Jewish tradition seems to be predicated on the coercive power of the community. Walzer held there is "no higher authority to which people can appeal for help. The United Nations sometimes clams to be such an authority, but its repeated failures to rescue those in need of rescuing give the lie to the claim."[221] Moreover, he acknowledged that it is at least "sometimes" true that "military interventions will inevitably be the work of rich and powerful states acting imperially" and will "end in domination."[222] But he nevertheless insisted that "[c]harity and justice together require that rich and powerful states contribute disproportionately to the common good or, better that they contribute in proportion to their disproportionate wealth."[223] Like the object of *tzedekah,* however, the goal of humanitarian intervention must be to enable the recipient of charity/justice to "help themselves," to avoid "enduring eco-

216 *See* Michael Walzer, *On Humanitarianism: Is Helping Others Charity, or Duty, or Both?,* 90 Foreign Affairs 69–80, (2011).

217 *Id.* at 72.

218 *Id.* at 71.

219 *Id.* at 70.

220 *Id.* at 71.

221 *Id.* at 75.

222 *Id.* at 77.

223 *Id.*

nomic or political dependency -- the creation of pauper populations or of satellite states and puppet governments."[224] Thus, in this connection, Walzer insisted that attempts to engage in "regime change," as "when the U.S. Army tried to bring democracy to Iraq in 2003," constitute "ideological, not humanitarian, projects. They aimed at repair but not at relief, whereas humanitarianism aims a repair only after, and in order to sustain, relief."[225] Finally, for Walzer, the duty of humanitarian intervention continues to be a principle of international justice, rather than a judicially-enforceable norm of international law.[226] What is striking about this proposal is that it enables us to end our preliminary discussion of the Just War tradition's teaching on the *jus ad bellum* precisely where the Christian roots of the tradition began, with the obligation of charity.[227]

With this admittedly superficial and incomplete discussion of the Stoic, medieval Christian, and various modern understandings of the Just War Tradition as a species of moral reasoning, we now turn to a discussion of the modern legal regime on the use of force. In the next three chapters in the context of our three case studies -- on collective security in response to aggression by Iraq against Kuwait; on humanitarian intervention by NATO to protect innocent Kosovars from Serbia; and on preemptive self-defense by the U.S. and its allies, coupled with rationales based on the protection of the innocent and the punishment of evil, to justify the overthrow of the regime of Saddam Hussein in Iraq -- we shall consider the enduring relevance of the Just War Tradition as possible center of gravity for the evolution of international law.

224 *Id.* at 79.

225 *Id.* at 80.

226 *Id.* at 79

227 One might also search the Islamic tradition for parallels. *See, e.g.*, James Turner Johnson, The Holy War Idea in Western and Islamic Traditions (1997).

Chapter 2

The First Gulf War: Collective Security and the Defense of Others

In the next two chapters, we consider humanitarian intervention and preemptive self-defense against a tyrant, which in Just War terms could be described as the protection of the innocent and the vindication of justice by punishing evil. Here, we consider the classical Just War causes of defense of another against an aggressor, a wrongdoer, combined with the return of property. The wrongdoer, in this case, was Saddam Hussein's Iraq; the victim was Kuwait, whose state and state property were to be returned. The charity was performed by the coalition of states, primarily the United States, which went to war to defend Kuwait from aggression and to seek the restoration of what Kuwait has lost. This oversimplified explanation of the First Gulf War ignores the niceties of the positive international law regime through which these events are more commonly described. We turn to these events now, including a description of the positive international law regime governing collective security, the precise facts of the case, together with preliminary questions on the central documents; and we return in our commentary on the case to the relationship between these two descriptions. In our commentary, we also consider the realist, legalist, rational choice, and constructivist understandings of the problem of war developed in Part I of this volume.

We begin, however, with the historical background of the international legal regime in effect during the First Gulf War—the U.N. Charter and its predecessor, the League of Nations.

1. The League of Nations

The failure of the League of Nations[1] to secure the peace in Europe in the aftermath of the First World War forms the necessary context for the United Nations Charter.[2] The League's creation was one of President Wilson's famous Fourteen Points,[3] his proposal for the basis for a settlement to the war.[4] Notwithstanding British influence, the proposal represented uniquely American aspirations to replace the 19th century Concert of European monarchies, balance the power of international politics, and replace the pre-war system of alliances, which Wilson and many other Americans believed had given rise to unprecedented destruction.[5] The Wilsonian program envisaged, instead, that self-determination of peoples, democracy, and collective security would serve as the foundations for a new, peaceful, and just world order.[6] The head of the French delegation at the Versailles peace conference, George Clemenceau, observed: "God himself was content with Ten Commandments."[7] Our focus here is on the collective security aspect of the Wilsonian program—its nature, premises, design features, and the reasons for its failure—as a precursor to the United Nations.

The collective security system Wilson had in mind must be understood in terms of its opposition to the traditional alliance system. As Henry Kissinger points out, the term "collective security" has been extended to include alliance systems such as NATO.[8] That is plainly not what Wilson had in mind. Rather, the alliance system that triggered the First World War, as described

1 League of Nations Covenant (June 28, 1919) (*available at* http://avalon.law.yale.edu/20th_century/leagcov.asp).

2 United Nations Charter (June 26, 1945) (*available at* http://www.un.org/en/documents/charter/).

3 Point XIV provides: "A general association of nation must be formed under specific covenants for the purpose of affording mutual guarantees of political independence and territorial integrity to great and small states alike." Margaret MacMillan, Paris 1919: Six Months that Changed the World 496 (2001).

4 The seeds of the proposal came to Wilson in a note from British Foreign Minister Grey even before the United States entered the war. Grey wrote: "Would the President propose that there should be a League of Nations binding themselves to side against any Power which broke a treaty or which refused, in case of dispute, to adopt some other method of settlement than that of war?" Letter from Sir Edward Grey to Colonel Edward M. House (Sept. 22, 1915) (quoted in Henry Kissinger, Diplomacy 223 (1994)).

5 *See generally* A.J.P. Taylor, The Struggle for Mastery in Europe 1848–1918 (1954).

6 Kissinger, *supra* note 4, at 221–22.

7 MacMillan, *supra* note 3, at 33 (citations omitted).

8 Kissinger, *supra* note 4, at 247.

by Barbara Tuchman a half century ago,[9] "[was] directed against specific threats and defined precise obligations for specific groups of countries linked by shared national interests or mutual security concerns."[10] This series of conditional alliances addressed specific contingencies in contractual form. If country A attacked country B, would country C come to the defense of country A? If country C did come to the defense of country A, would country D come to the defense of country B? Wilson's proposed a collective security scheme that, in Kissinger's words, "is theoretically designed to resist any threat to the peace, by whoever might pose it and against whomever it might be directed."[11] Collective security thus protects all states from any attack, defending "international law in the abstract, which it seeks to sustain in much the same way that a judicial system upholds a domestic criminal code."[12] In an effort to persuade the French to accept the League, Wilson and his British counterpart David Lloyd George included a proposed "guarantee" that would have converted the basic structure of the Versailles settlement into something more like the traditional alliance system of the past. However, the United States never joined the League, the British withdrew this commitment in light of the American withdrawal, and the alliance aspect of the settlement never entered into force, thereby leaving the League in the form of the collective security arrangement as originally conceived.[13]

Thus, it is worth exploring Wilson's premises in advancing collective security as the solution to the problems that gave rise to the war. For Wilson, it was the alliance system itself—which reinforced an unjust territorial status quo in Europe suppressing the self-determination of peoples with repressive monarchies—that caused the war. He viewed his own role as a mediator and insisted on calling the United States an "associated" power, rather than an ally of the French, British, and Italians.[14] His vision was, in Margaret MacMillan's view, "a liberal and a Christian vision."[15] It was liberal, according to E.H. Carr, as it consisted of an attempt to translate to the international sphere "rationalism" and its "belief in the infallibility of public opinion."[16] If it was "Christian," it was because Wilson deemed international harmony to be a natural condition.[17] For Carr, the League represented the institutional manifestation of the 19th century utopian belief liberals called the "harmony of interests,"[18] an idea closely connected to free trade ideol-

9 *See* Barbara Tuchman, The Guns of August (1962).

10 Kissinger, *supra* note 4, at 247.

11 *Id.*

12 *Id.*

13 *See id.* at 237–38.

14 *See id.* at 226;

15 MacMillan, *supra* note 3, at 13.

16 Edward Hallet Carr, The Twenty Years' Crisis, 1919-1939: An Introduction to the Study of International Relations 26 (1946); *see also* Kissinger, *supra* note 4, at 232.

17 *See* Kissinger, *supra* note 4, at 232.

18 *See* Carr, *supra* note 16, at 41–62.

ogy that also formed part of Wilson's Fourteen Points.[19] Thus, according to MacMillan, the final rejection of the League in the United States reflected the fundamentally opposing views of Wilson and his opponent in the U.S. Senate, Henry Cabot Lodge: "Wilson put his trust in the League and collective security as a way to end war. Lodge, a pessimist with little faith in the perfectibility of human nature, preferred to trust power."[20] For Wilson, apparent conflict required merely the prodding of public discussion and public opinion to assert itself. Thus, if the Versailles conference got wrong the particulars, such as specific border arrangements, the League would serve much like a government, not unlike the U.S. Federal Government,[21] to correct its errors.[22] Indeed, Lord Cecil, the leading advocate for the League before Parliament and its principal British drafter, proved to have the zeal of a convert to Wilson's position when he averred, we "rely upon is public opinion... and if we are wrong about it, then the whole thing is wrong."[23]

The formal structure of the League reflects precisely these two features—an attempt to construct a collective security system and the absence of any credible enforcement mechanism other than the possibility of further action. Under Article I, the parties agreed to "condemn recourse to war for the solution of international controversies, and renounce it as an instrument of national policy in their relations with one another."[24] But this provision never defined "war,"[25] which left open the possibility that it excluded uses of force short of war, such as limited, but necessary and proportionate, acts of self-defense,[26] or reprisals seeking the redress of wrongs committed in violation of international law.[27] Setting even that ambiguity aside, it was clear that the League's collective security provisions necessarily related only to a subset of war, specifically only "aggressive war"; for Article 10 provides that: "The members of the League under-

---

19 Wilson Third Point called for "The removal, so far is possible, of all economic barriers and the establishment of an equality of trade conditions among all the nations consenting to the peace and associating themselves for its maintenance." MacMillan, *supra* note 3, at 495.

20 *Id.* at 152.

21 *See* Kissinger, *supra* note 4, at 223.

22 *See id.* at 230.

23 Carr, *supra* note 16, at 35 (quoting Lord Cecil's argument).

24 League of Nations Covenant art. 1.

25 We have discussed this terminological gap earlier in the context of our assessment of the effect of the subsequent Kellog-Briand Pact on the legality of the Nuremberg and Tokyo prosecutions of German and Japanese leadership for the "crime of aggression." As we shall soon see, the precise scope of the term "war" also left important ambiguities unresolved in relation to the scope of the "inherent" or pre-Charter right of self-defense preserved for states under the law of the UN Charter. *See infra* Part II, Chapter 4.

26 *See* Charles Cheney Hyde, International Law 239 (1945) (reporting the Caroline incident and U.S. Secretary of State Webster's assertion that British use of force in 1837 against a private U.S. ship supporting Canadian insurgents required a showing of necessity and proportionality).

27 *See* Green Hackworth, Digest of International Law 154–55 (reporting the Naulilaa incident, in which German reprisal against Portuguese forces for the alleged murder of Germans in Angola was neither necessary to remedy nor proportionate to any wrong that may have been committed).

take to respect and preserve as against external aggression the territorial integrity and existing political independence of all Members of the League. In case of any such aggression or in case of any threat or danger of such aggression the Council shall advise upon the means by which this obligation shall be fulfilled." Articles 12, 13, and 15 created obligations for states not to "resort to war" unless members had first exhausted the political and legal dispute resolution processes available to them, submission to the League Council or international arbitration. In this context, Article 14 of the League Covenant called for the creation of a Permanent Court of International Justice.[28] The architecture of these provisions thus suggested that arbitration under Articles 12 and 13, impliedly through the mechanism of Article 14, would transform disputes that could give rise to war into questions of law to be decided by the Permanent Court of International Justice. Accordingly, under Article 16, it was only when a member had resorted to war "in disregard of" these procedural requirements stated "in Articles 12, 13, or 15" that it would "ipso facto be deemed to have committed an act of war against all other Members of the League, which hereby undertake immediate to subject it" to economic sanctions. Article 16 then provides: "It shall be the duty of the Council in such case to recommend to the several Governments concerned what effective military, naval, or air force the Members of the League shall severally contribute to the armed forces to be used to protect the covenants of the League. The Members of the League agree further that they will support ... the Members of the League who are cooperating to protect the covenants of the League."[29] Finally, "Any Member of the League which has violated any covenant of the League may be declared to be a no longer a Member of the League by a vote of the Council concurred in by the Representatives of all the other Members of the League represented therein."[30]

In sum, the collective security commitment of the members of the League was structured to enforce a process, rather than a set of substantive entitlements, as there were no agreed definitions of "war" or "aggression." Thus, the commitment each state made has been described as a "tautology"; for Article 10's language, that "the Council shall advise upon the means by which [the territorial integrity and existing political independence of all Members would be protected against external aggression] shall be fulfilled," meant that "the League of Nations would agree to that on which it could agree. This was, of course, what the nations of the world would typically have done even if there had been no Covenant; and this was precisely the circumstances which traditional alliances sought to remedy by invoking the formal obligation of mutual assistance for specifically defined circumstances."[31]

Even Article 16's measures were to be effected only through "recommendations" and ill-defined obligations of "mutual support," and conditioned upon the conclusion that a member

28 League of Nations Covenant arts. 10, 12, 13, 14 and 15.

29 *Id.* at art. 16.

30 *Id.*

31 Kissinger, *supra* note 4, at 237.

had "resorted to war in disregard" of the procedural requirements. Yet, nothing in the document provided procedures or criteria for determining whether or not a member had in fact done so. Thus, as British scholar Derek Bowett noted, "it was left to each member to decide whether a breach had occurred or an act of war had been committed, so that even the obligation to apply economic sanctions ... was dependent on the member's own view of the situation."[32] Indeed, only the expulsion provision of Article 16 provided a specific mechanism and sanction for a determination by the League Council that a member had violated its obligations under the League. As it turned out, the expulsion of the Soviet Union after its invasion of Finland in 1939 signaled the final demise of the League.[33]

The League Covenant was, in substance, what lawyers call a mere "agreement to agree," even if it created institutions, procedures, and expectations. Yet, that Germany would have a motive and the ability to overturn the Versailles settlement could have been, and indeed was, foreseen by its authors. England's Lloyd George understood fully that Germany would be able to rely on the self-determination principle to overturn the territorial settlements. In his March 25, 1919 memorandum to Wilson, he wrote: "I can not conceive any greater cause of future war than that the German people, who have certainly proved themselves one of the most vigorous and powerful races in the world should be surrounded by a number of small states, many of them consisting of people who have never previously set up a stable government for themselves, but each of them containing large masses of Germans clamouring for reunion with their native land?"[34] Indeed, England's Lord Balfour had even earlier foreseen the specific case that would give rise to the Second War, namely Germany's dissatisfaction with the existence of a Polish state separating it from its historic nucleus of Prussia; for, if "Poland were made an independent kingdom, becoming a buffer state between Russia and Germany, France would be at the mercy of Germany in the next war, for this reason, that Russia could not come to her aid without violating the neutrality of Poland."[35] The Versailles settlement did include provision for reparations, but ultimately Germany paid little because of its economic collapse following the war; and Versailles provided for plebiscites in the Saar, bordering France, and Upper Silesia, bordering Poland—in part, because of the strategic coal deposits these territories possessed; in part, because of the substantial German populations they shared—but they, too, eventually were reincorporated into Germany.[36] And, even though France failed in its effort to reverse Bismarck's achievement of German unification by creating a separate buffer state in the Rhineland, the demilitariza-

32 D.W. Bowett, The Law of International Institutions 18 (1982).

33 *See* Resolution Adopted by the Council of the League of Nations, League of Nations, Official Journal 506 (Dec. 14, 1939); Assembly Resolution League of Nations' Expulsion of the U.S.S.R., Office Journal 540 (Dec. 14, 1939) (*available at* http://www.ibiblio.org/pha/policy/1939/391214a.html).

34 Kissinger, *supra* note 4, at 241 (citations omitted).

35 *Id.* at 243 (citations omitted).

36 *See generally* Raymond J. Sontag, A Broken World, 1919-39 (1971); MacMillan, *supra* note 3, 166–203.

tion provisions, especially the demilitarization of the Rhineland, appeared initially to diminish Germany's capabilities. However, the French and British military commands recognized very quickly that German rearmament was inevitable and could come as early as within a decade.[37] It remains widely debated whether Germany's pre-World War II expansionist policies were simply a continuation of her pre-World War I imperial ambitions or, instead, reflected the design failures of the Versailles settlement and the geopolitical vacuum it created. But the fact remains that, in due course, Adolf Hitler's *revanchist* and *irredentist* Germany launched aggressive war.[38] This received history lesson thus formed the backdrop to proposals to create a successor to the League of Nations.[39] Most important, in the eyes of some observers, was the breakdown of the Franco-English-American "alliance," as the means of balancing German power.[40]

2. The United Nations

Reflecting an effort not to repeat the mistakes of the past, the Charter's provisions evidence a substantial departure from the pure collective security regime of the League Covenant, its absence of enforcement powers, and its limited view of the threat to the peace as arising from only "war" and "aggression." We consider the original Charter design, what we call "the alliance element; next describe the limited realization of the Charter's ambitions during the Cold War; finally, we turn to how seeds planted during the Cold War grew a dramatic expansion of the Security Council's enforcement powers into matters that, for most of the Cold War, were regarded as falling within the sovereignty of states.

a. The Alliance Element

Recognizing the failure to take account of the need to preserve alliance solidarity that makes any system of collective security work, President Roosevelt's proposal for a post-war

37 *See* Kissinger, *supra* note 4, at 250–51.

38 *Compare* A.J.P. Taylor, The Origins of the Second World War (1961) (treating war as avoidable and viewing German policies as limited essentially to revision of Versailles), *with* Telford Taylor, Munich: The Price of Peace (1979) (treating war as unavoidable response to German aggression and viewing German policies as an attempt to achieve expansionist goals leading to domination of Eastern Europe). Taylor's overall view no doubt was influenced by his experience as a member of the American prosecutorial team in the aftermath of the Second World War. See Telford Taylor, The Anatomy of the Nuremberg Trials: A Personal Memoir (1992). But there is substantial evidence to support his understanding of Germany's overall project in the 20th century. See Fritz Fischer, Germany's Aims in the First World War (C.A. Macartney trans. 1967) (showing through analysis of documentary record that Germany's pre-war policies and war aims in the First World War constituted an attempt to establish German domination of the so-called "Mitteleuropa," meaning what was then called Central Europe and is now called Eastern Europe).

39 *See generally* Carr, *supra* note 16.

40 *See* Kissinger, *supra* note 4, at 229 (distinguishing the case from the success of the Holy Alliance in preserving, at least for a time, the Concert of Europe after the Congress of Vienna in 1815).

international organization began with the notion that the United States, Britain, Soviet Union, and China would serve as four "policemen" who would "work together to preserve the peace."[41] Roosevelt wanted some form of "collective security but he knew from the experience of the 1920s that collective security required enforcers and this was to be the role of the Four Policemen."[42] The veto power of the Permanent Members of the Security Council, now including France, ensured that future decisions of the body on substantive matters retained the basic characteristic of alliance diplomacy. Indeed, the preservation of this alliance seemed to be the *sine qua non* for agreement, for Stalin's acquiescence in the final accord was conditioned on his understanding that the Security Council would not have the authority to expel a member without its consent, as the League had expelled the Soviet Union in 1939.[43] Similarly, the alliance component was reflected in the otherwise unfathomable provision in the Charter concerning Japan and Germany. This provision, validating "action, in relation to any state which during the Second World War has been an enemy of any signatory of the present Charter, taken or authorized as a result of that war by the Governments having responsibility for that action," in effect recognized the de facto partition of Germany following the war and the continuing authority of the four powers occupying Germany (the U.S., U.S.S.R, Britain, and France in respect of Berlin) and Japan.[44] It was only with the end of the Cold War when the Security Council alliance was partially reconstituted that German reunification was possible and the Second World War legally came to an end.[45]

One view, thus, is that the full exercise of Security Council powers is conditioned on the legality of the veto, which in turn would appear to compel the Permanent Five to act in concert if they are to act at all. But another possible inference is that, if the Permanent Five cannot act in concert, the matter is outside the scope of the "law" governed by the UN Charter.

b. The Possibility of Enforcement Authority

The Charter's initial design clearly contemplated that the Security Council, would act as it deemed appropriate through "recommendations" and "decisions." "Decisions" would, under

41 *Id.* at 396 (citations omitted).

42 *Id.* at 397.

43 Stephan C. Schlesinger, Act of Creation: The Founding of the United Nations 64 (2003).

44 U.N. Charter art. 107.

45 *Compare* John Lewis Gaddis, The Cold War: A New History 248–52 (2005) (providing a conventional politico-military explanation of the end of the Cold War through German unification), *with* Philip Bobbitt, The Shield of Achilles: War, Peace, and the Course of History 631–36 (2002) (arguing that the legal end of the Cold War amounted to a revision of the settlement concluded to end the Second World War in the UN Charter, effectively treating these arrangements as amendments to the UN Charter).

Articles 25,[46] 48,[47] and 103,[48] be deemed "binding" on all members. These decisions could take two forms. First, under Article 41, the Council could decide on economic or other non-military sanctions, which it defined as "measures not involving the use of armed force," and the Council could then "call upon the Members of the United Nations to apply such measures."[49] Second, "[s]hould the Security Council consider that measured provide for in Article 41 would be inadequate, it may take such action by air, sea, or land forces as may be necessary to maintain or restore international peace and security."[50] To implement military measures through UN action, UN forces would be required. Thus, article 43 provided that "All Members of the United Nations, in order to contribute to the maintenance of international peace and security, undertake to make available to the Security Council, on its call and in accordance with a special agreements, armed forces, assistance and facilities, including rights of passage, necessary for the purpose of maintaining international peace and security."[51]

At the same time, the Charter's design does not preclude the legality of other alliance systems as the means for implementing the decisions of the Security Council. Whereas Winston Churchill had sought a regional security system—preserving the "spheres of influence" reflected in the British Empire, Soviet Union, and U.S. supremacy in the Western hemisphere[52]—nothing like this formally survives in Chapter VIII of the Charter, which reflected the triumph of the U.S. position favoring globalism over the U.K.'s insistence on regionalism as the basic structure for managing international peace and security under the new order.[53] Article 53(1) of the Charter provides that: "The Security Council shall, where appropriate, utilize such regional arrangements or agencies for enforcement action under its authority. But no enforcement action shall be taken under regional arrangements or by regional agencies without the authorization of the Security Council ...."[54]

---

46 Article 25 provides: "The Members of the United Nations agree to accept and carry out the decisions of the Security Council in accordance with the present Charter."

47 Article 48(1) provides: "The action required to be carry out the decisions of the Security Council for the maintenance of international peace and security shall be taken...as the Security Council shall determine." Article 48(2) further provides that such "decisions shall be carried out by the Members of the United Nations directly and through their action in the appropriate international agencies of which they are members."

48 Article 103 provides: "In the event of a conflict between the obligations of the Members of the United Nations under the present Charter and their obligations under any other international agreement, their obligations under the present Charter shall prevail."

49 U.N. Charter art. 41.

50 U.N. Charter art. 42 (emphasis added).

51 UN Charter art. 43, para. 1.

52 *See* Kissinger, *supra* note 4, at 406–14; Schlesinger, *supra* note 43, at 58–59.

53 *Id.*

54 *See* U.N. Charter art. 53, para. 1 (adding an exception relative to enforcement measures separately authorized under Article 107 against the former "enemy" states).

As it would happen, with the rise of the Cold War, the agreements contemplated in Chapter VII never came into effect. Indeed, the only case of so-called UN forces implementing Chapter VII "decisions" involved United States and allied forces deployed in Korea. These forces operated nominally under a U.N.-flag pursuant to Security Council Resolution 84,[55] which was adopted only in the absence of the Soviet representative who was protesting the Security Council's failure to seat the representatives of the People's Republic of China after the victory of the Communist forces over the Nationalist forces in the Chinese civil war. That said, in the Korean conflict, the Security Council never made a "decision" binding on states pursuant to Articles 25, 48 and 103 of the Charter.[56] Later, when the United States claimed that its quarantine of Cuba was authorized by the Organization of the American States (the OAS) as an "enforcement" measure pursuant to Chapter VIII of the Charter,[57] it appeared to disregard the clear language of Article 53(1). Throughout the Cold War, one can safely say, the Security Council failed to function in the manner contemplated by its authors.

But with the collapse of Permanent Five Cooperation, two significant developments appeared to fill the gap of Security Council enforcement in practical and legal terms—so-called "Blue Helmets," meaning the rise of UN peacekeeping operations as efforts in preventative diplomacy and confidence-building measures; and the progressive development of the international law regarding the use of force.

First, as a result of the impasse that followed the Korean War, the General Assembly adopted the Uniting for Peace Resolution, declaring its power under Article 10 of the Charter to make "recommendations to Members for collective measures, including in the case of the breach of the peace or act of aggression the use of armed force when necessary...."[58] Legal authority was found in the General Assembly's power to make "recommendations" under Article 10, albeit not when "the Security Council is exercising in respect of any dispute or situation the functions assigned to it ... unless the Security Council so requests."[59] The question of how to determine when the Security Council is "exercising ... the functions assigned to it" raised critical interpretive questions. It soon followed that the UN itself began to engage in preventative diplomacy through the deployment of so-called "Blue Helmets," peacekeeping forces provided by members states with the consent of member states, and thus without raising the issue of whether a Security Council decision under Chapter VII was required to bind states to cooperate in enforcement actions. Legal authority was found also in the Security Council's authority in Chapter VII of the Charter

55 *See* S.C. Res. 84, U.N. Doc. S/RES/1588 (Jul. 7, 1950).

56 *See* Lori Damrosch, Louis Henkin, Sean Murphy, & Hans Smit, International Law: Cases and Materials 1227–28 (5th ed. 2009).

57 *See* M. Whiteman 4 Digest of International Law 523–24 (1965).

58 Uniting for Peace Resolution, G.A. Res. 377, U.N. Doc. A/1775 (Nov. 3, 1950).

59 U.N. Charter arts. 10 & 12.

to make "recommendations" to member states for the "peaceful settlement" of their disputes.[60] Initially, these peacekeeping forces were funded out of the general budget of the organization, but a constitutional crisis ensued when France and the Soviet Union objected to expenditures in respect of the UN force in the Congo, when the UN's participation in the Congolese civil war conflicted with French and Soviet interests. Although the International Court of Justice in its 1962 *Certain Expenses of the United Nations Advisory Opinion* supported the constitutional authority of the Security Council and General Assembly,[61] the practical resolution was to shift funding for U.N. peacekeeping operations to voluntary contributions outside the scope of the General Assembly's budget authority under the Charter.

Second, the General Assembly began to focus on clarifying the meaning of the Charter's prohibition under Article 2(4) against "the threat or use of force against the territorial integrity or political independence of any state, or in any other manner inconsistent with the Purposes of the United Nations,"[62] language which appeared to go beyond the scope of the League's prohibition against "recourse to war" and "external aggression." Thus, the General Assembly engaged in what appeared to be law-making projects to define the precise scope of unpermitted uses of force under the Charter and customary international law. In its 1970 Declaration on Friendly Relations,[63] the General Assembly purported to interpret the UN Charter provisions relating to the use of force,[64] and these interpretations of the law of the Charter and customary

60 *See* U.N. Charter arts. 33-38.

61 *See* Certain Expenses of the United Nations, Advisory Opinion, 1962 I.C.J. 151 (Jul. 20).

62 U.N. Charter art. 2, para. 4.

63 *See* Declaration on Principles of International Law Concerning Friendly Relations and Cooperation among States in Accordance with the Charter of the United Nations, G.A. Res. 2625 (Oct. 24, 1970).

64 The pertinent provisions, which become of enormous significance in the jurisprudence of the International Court of Justice, are as follows:

> "Every State has the duty to refrain in its international relations from the threat or use of force against the territorial integrity or political independence of any State, or in any other manner inconsistent with the purposes of the United Nations. Such a threat or use of force constitutes a violation of international law and the Charter of the United Nations and shall never be employed as a means of settling international issues.

A war of aggression constitutes a crime against the peace, for which there is responsibility under international law.

In accordance with the purposes and principles of the United Nations, States have the duty to refrain from propaganda for wars of aggression.

Every State has the duty to refrain from the threat or use of force to violate the existing international boundaries of another State or as a means of solving international disputes, including territorial disputes and problems concerning frontiers of States. Every State likewise has the duty to refrain from the threat or use of force to violate international lines of demarcation, such as armistice lines, established by or pursuant to an international agreement to which it is a party or which it is otherwise bound to respect. Nothing in the foregoing shall be construed as prejudicing the positions of the parties concerned with regard to the status and effects of such lines under their special regimes or as affecting their temporary character.

States have a duty to refrain from acts of reprisal involving the use of force.

Every State has the duty to refrain from any forcible action which deprives peoples referred to in the elaboration of the principle of equal rights and self-determination of their right to self-determination and freedom and independence.

Every State has the duty to refrain from organizing or encouraging the organization of irregular forces or armed bands including mercenaries, for incursion into the territory of another State.

international law ultimately proved highly influential to the International Court of Justice.[65] Perhaps recognizing the need for consensus on the meaning of the concept of "aggression," the General Assembly then adopted a Resolution on the Definition of Aggression,[66] although the difficulty of the negotiation and plethora of interpretive statements made by states upon its adoption revealed that the apparent consensus was illusory.[67]

In sum, while in practice collective security arrangements failed during the Cold War, the Security Council and General Assembly's interpretation of their own powers, to engage in peacekeeping and progressive development of international law, became significant in assessing the powers of states to engage in "individual or collective self-defense."[68] In addition, as we

---

Every State has the duty to refrain from organizing, instigating, assisting or participating in acts of civil strife or terrorist acts in another State or acquiescing in organized activities within its territory directed towards the commission of such acts, when the acts referred to in the present paragraph involve a threat or use of force.

The territory of a State shall not be the object of military occupation resulting from the use of force in contravention of the provisions of the Charter. The territory of a State shall not be the object of acquisition by another State resulting from the threat or use of force. No territorial acquisition resulting from the threat or use of force shall be recognized as legal. Nothing in the foregoing shall be construed as affecting:

(a) Provisions of the Charter or any international agreement prior to the Charter regime and valid under international law; or

(b) The powers of the Security Council under the Charter.

65 *See* Military and Paramilitary Activities in and Against Nicaragua (Nicar. v. U.S.), 1986 I.C.J. 4 (June 27) (treating the content of the Friendly Relations Declaration, which had been adopted unanimously, as evidence of customary international law concerning the "use of force," which is regarded as identical to the law of the Charter).

66 *See* Definition of Aggression, G.A. Res. 3314 (XXIX) (Dec. 14, 1974). Article 3 provides: "Any of the following acts, regardless of a declaration of war, shall, subject to and in accordance with the provisions of article 2, qualify as an act of aggression:

(a) The invasion or attack by the armed forces of a State of the territory of another State, or any military occupation, however temporary, resulting from such invasion or attack, or any annexation by the use of force of the territory of another State or part thereof,

(b) Bombardment by the armed forces of a State against the territory of another State or the use of any weapons by a State against the territory of another State;

(c) The blockade of the ports or coasts of a State by the armed forces of another State;

(d) An attack by the armed forces of a State on the land, sea or air forces, or marine and air fleets of another State;

(e) The use of armed forces of one State which are within the territory of another State with the agreement of the receiving State, in contravention of the conditions provided for in the agreement or any extension of their presence in such territory beyond the termination of the agreement;

(f) The action of a State in allowing its territory, which it has placed at the disposal of another State, to be used by that other State for perpetrating an act of aggression against a third State;

(g) The sending by or on behalf of a State of armed bands, groups, irregulars or mercenaries, which carry out acts of armed force against another State of such gravity as to amount to the acts listed above, or its substantial involvement therein.

67 The United States, for example, does not consider the resolution to be an authoritative interpretation of the Charter or to codify customary international law. *See* Sean D. Murphy, *Contemporary Practice of the United States Relating to International Law*, 95 Am. J. Int'l L. 387, 400–01 (2001) (reporting U.S. position at the negotiations on the International Criminal Court); *but see* Elizabeth Wilmhurst, Audiovisual Library of International Law, Definition of Aggression (*available at* http://untreaty.un.org/cod/avl/ha/da/da.html) (stating "Difficult compromises were necessary to reach consensus on the text. Interpretative statements to express particular interpretations of the Definition were made by Government delegations on adoption of the Definition both in the special committee and in the General Assembly."). Wilmburst, who seems to believe consensus was adopted, resigned from her position as deputy legal adviser in the U.K.'s Foreign Office in opposition to the Second Gulf War. *See* Ewen MacAskill, *Adviser Quits Foreign Office Over Legality of War*, The Guardian, (Mar. 23, 2003).

68 Article 51 of the Charter provides: "Nothing in the present Charter shall impair the inherent right of individual or collective self-defense if an armed attack occurs against a Member of the United Nations, until the Security Council has

have already discussed in the context of our assessment of the Nuremburg and Tokyo Trials, the attention was given to the question of aggression as an "international crime" for which leaders may bear personal criminal responsibility in international and domestic courts links the *jus ad bellum* to the *jus in bello*. We will discuss the "law" of "aggression" as an international crime in greater detail in Part III of this volume. For now, it is sufficient to note that the jurisprudence developed in international courts created by the Security Council under its Chapter VII powers seems to have served as a powerful impetus for the creation of a permanent International Criminal Tribunal (the ICC) in the 1998 Rome Statute.[69] This in turn has generated yet another process to define "aggression," now for purposes of individual criminal responsibility. To a degree, the General Assembly and ICC processes now seem to suggest the "legalist" interpretation of the Wilsonian vision reflected in the League Covenant and Permanent Court of International Justice—projecting liberal domestic premises onto the international sphere treating aggression as a species of crime and deterring it through the imposition of criminal punishment, rather than through political and economic sanctions or forcible countermeasures permitted under Chapter VII. Yet, as we will discuss in Part III, the precise relationship between the Security Council's "enforcement" powers and the ICC's responsibilities raised difficult legal and political issues, given the potential conflict between their respective decisions in particular cases. Suffice it to say for now that the rise of the ICC is not unrelated to the Security Council's own changing understanding after the end of the Cold War of the scope of its enforcement powers, to which we now turn.

c. The Constitutional Dimension of Chapter VII—Multidimensional Threats

Despite the tensions in managing the peace during the Cold War, the text of the Charter also suggests that the powers of the Security Council are not limited to the question of "war" or "external aggression" alone, as was the focus of the League Covenant.[70] Rather, Article 39 of the Charter plainly authorizes the Security Council to "determine the existence of any threat to the peace, breach of the peace, or act of aggression and ... decide what measures shall be taken ... to maintain or restore international peace and security."[71] Thus, the plain text seems to contemplate that "threats to the peace" form a category different from "war" or "acts of aggression," which had been the limit of Article 10 of the Covenant of the League of Nations. Admittedly,

taken measures necessary to maintain international peace and security. Measures taken by Members in the exercise of this right of self-defense shall be immediately reported to the Security Council and shall not in any way affect the authority and responsibility of the Security Council under the present Charter to take at any time such action as it deems necessary in order to maintain or restore international peace and security." U.N. Charter art. 51.

69 *See* Rome Statue of the International Criminal Court, July 17, 1998, 2187 U.N.T.S. 3 (entered into force Jul. 1, 2002).

70 *See supra* text accompanying note 26 (discussing The Caroline and Naulilaa incidents as evidence of uses of force short of war regulated by international law notwithstanding the right of states to engage in war).

71 U.N. Charter art. 39.

Article 2(7) provides, as follows: "Nothing contained in the present Charter shall authorize the United Nations to intervene in matters which are essentially within the domestic jurisdiction of any state...."[72] While non-intervention in the internal affairs of states, in furtherance of the principle "self-determination," had played a central role in the drafting of the Charter of League of Nations,[73] the Charter's writ would run further. Chapter VII, moreover, authorizes the U.N. Security Council to adopt "enforcement measures" through its "decisions" as to "measures" to "maintain or restore international peace and security" when the Council "determine[s] the existence of any threat to the peace, breach of the peace, or act of aggression."[74] At the same time, in "discharging" its "duty" with respect to the maintenance of international peace and security, Article 24(2) of the Charter requires the Council "to act in accordance with the ... Purposes and Principles of the Organization,"[75] thus including the non-intervention principle. Yet, Article 2(7) specifically provides that "this principle shall not prejudice the application of enforcement measures under Chapter VII,"[76] which appears to give the Security Council at least some authority to supersede the non-intervention principle that had served as a core postulate of the League Covenant.

If the Charter's text does not foreclose an interpretation that authorizes the Security Council to find "threats to the peace" in matters that had previously been thought to reside within the domestic jurisdiction of states, it remained unclear to many whether the Security Council was authorized to do so. In 1946, at the very beginning, grave doubts were raised when the Council rejected Poland's request for sanctions against Fascist Spain, tabling the question after a Security Council subcommittee drew the conclusion that Spain's domestic human rights violations did not constitute a threat to neighboring states.[77] Indeed, for much of the history of the United Nations until the end of the Cold War, U.N intervention in the internal affairs of states was seen as deeply problematic, initially meeting resistance even in the most egregious cases of Rhodesia and South Africa's racial practices.[78]

But, very tentatively, in the Rhodesia and South Africa cases, the Security Council was able to link the internal practices of those states to "threats to the peace" justifying Chapter VII "decisions" imposing economic sanctions. In the case of Rhodesia (now Zimbabwe), it found a threat to the British Commonwealth through Rhodesia's nominally provocative and unlawful,

---

72 U.N. Charter art. 2, para 7.

73 *See generally* MacMillan, *supra* note 3.

74 U.N. Charter arts. 39–42.

75 U.N. Charter art. 24, para. 2.

76 U.N. Charter art. 2, para 7.

77 *See* David Johnson, *Sanctions and South Africa*, 19 Harv. Int'l L. J. 887, 892 (1978) (discussing and distinguishing Spanish precedent).

78 *See generally* Louis B. Sohn, Rights in Conflict: The United Nations and South Africa (1994) (discussing resistance to intervention against racial policies in Rhodesia (now Zimbabwe) and South Africa (including then South-West Africa, now Namibia, ignoring, in Sohn's view, the human rights provisions of the Charter)).

"unilateral" declaration of independence,[79] although here the Commonwealth reaction may have been the threat to the peace. Later, imposing sanctions on South Africa, it cited cross-border attacks against so-called Front Line states supporting internal resistance to South Africa's apartheid policies in its unlawful occupation of South-West Africa (now Namibia) and South Africa proper, although the *sui generis* nature of South Africa's occupation of Namibia following the termination of the League of Nations mandate reduced the case's value as a precedent.[80]

Nonetheless, on the broadest possible view of these precedents, Article 24(2)'s requirement that the Security Council act "in accordance with the Purposes and Principles" of the United Nations may also suggest that Security Council decisions to address "threats to the peace" must take into account a broader conception of the "peace" as more than merely the absence of "war" or the absence of "aggression." That conception of peace could be found in all of the "Purposes" and "Principles" of the United Nations, which include, most plainly in Article 1, "collective measures ... in conformity with the principles of justice and international law."[81] In this connection, it may be worth noting that the Charter begins with the majestic words "We the Peoples of the United Nations," which seem to go beyond the right of states and suggest instead that the rights of peoples may be of equal weight in its interpretation.[82] Finally, Article 103 of the Charter operates as a kind of Supremacy Clause, elevating the UN Charter's status in relation to all other treaties, arguably giving it a kind of quasi-constitutional status. In short, the text, coupled with a broad reading of the Rhodesia and South Africa precedents, opened the door to myriad possibilities that would go well beyond the scope of the practice of the United Nations and, especially, the Security Council, in the first thirty-five years of its operation.

Turning to the First Gulf War, we note that our discussions of the Coalition's efforts to protect Iraqi Kurds and Shi'ites in the aftermath of the First Gulf War will lay the groundwork for our discussion of the question of humanitarian intervention in the following chapter. This goes directly to the question of the potential expansion and transformation of the Security Council's authorities under the U.N Charter. For now, we turn to the events leading to the First Gulf War as a necessary background to an analysis of whether it represents the realization of the U.N's original design as a mixed collective security-alliance regime, a traditional exercise of balance of power politics, or something else still.

79 *See* S.C. Res. 221, U.N. Doc. S/RES/221 (Apr. 9, 1966) (authorizing U.K. to "use force if necessary" to enforce Commonwealth oil embargo against Rhodesia); S.C. Res. 232, U.N. Doc. S/RES/232 (Dec. 16, 1966) (imposing sanctions, including an arms embargo).

80 *See* S.C. Res. 418, U.N. Doc. S/RES/418 (Nov. 4, 1977) (imposing arms embargo); *cf.* S.C. Res. 276, U.N. Doc. S/RES/276 (Jan. 30, 1970) (declaring the illegality of South Africa's continued presence in South-West Africa given its violation of the terms of the mandate and declaring duty of states not to recognize the validity of South African acts pursuant to its continuing occupation); *and* Legal Consequences for States of the Continued Presence of South Africa in Namibia (South West Africa) Notwithstanding Security Council Resolution 276 (1970), 1971 I.C.J. 3, 16 (1971) Advisory Opinion (confirming the legal effect of S.C. Res. 276 and G.A. Res. 2145 (XXI) (Oct. 27, 1966), which had purported to terminate the mandate).

81 U.N. Charter art. 1, para. 1.

82 U.N. Charter Preamble.

B. THE FIRST GULF WAR—THE INTERNATIONAL RESPONSE

When the United States mobilized an international coalition to reverse Saddam Hussein's conquest of Kuwait, in the views of some, the U.S. reaction to Iraq's invasion may have been as surprising to Saddam Hussein as was the U.S. reaction to North Korea's invasion of South Korea in June 1950. There, North Korean and Soviet leaders had "taken at face value the pronouncements of leading Americans that had placed Korea outside the American defense perimeter."[83] The U.S. had supported Iraq during the bloody Iran-Iraq War of the 1980s,[84] which had imposed great burdens on the Iraqi economy, and perhaps Iraq believed the U.S. owed it a debt of gratitude for this proxy war, in line with traditional Cold War premises. Iraq complained that Kuwait's oil price strategy, together with its alleged "slant" drilling into Iraqi fields, reduced Iraq's fair share of the proceeds from the exploitation of Iraqi oil, and in turn reduced Iraq's ability to recover from the effects of the war.[85] Iraq's grievances concerning the demarcation of the Iraq-Kuwait boundary were longstanding.[86] Ironically, the unsettled borders of the Middle East had grown out of the tenuous territorial settlements emerging out of the Versailles conference, when the principle of self-determination ran into the buzz saw of the Sykes-Picot agreement under which Britain and France carved up the carcass of the Ottoman Empire.[87] In this context, Hussein's discussions with the American ambassador may have led him to believe the U.S. considered the Iraq-Kuwait border was not inviolable.[88]

However, when Iraq invaded Kuwait in August 1990, the Security Council reacted in the context of an international system that had experienced a radical break from the Cold War. Soviet President Gorbachev's reforms has initiated a process that resulted in the fall of the Berlin Wall, the collapse of the Soviet-allied regimes in Eastern Europe, the re-unification of Germany in the so-called "4+2" negotiations (the four occupying powers, the U.S., U.K., Soviet Union and France, as well as East and West Germany), and ultimately the unraveling of the Soviet Union.[89] At the same time, internal turmoil followed in China after the Tiananmen Square Protests of 1989.[90]

83 Kissinger, *supra* note 4, at 250.

84 *See* Alan Friedman, Spider's Web: The Secret History of How the White House Illegally Armed Iraq (1993).

85 *See* Joe Stork and Ann M. Lesch, *Background to the Crises: Why War?*, 167 Middle East Report 11–18 (1990).

86 *See generally* Keesing's Border and Territorial Disputes 245–47 (Alan J. Day ed., 2nd. ed. 1987).

87 *See generally* MacMillan, *supra* note 3, at 380–409.

88 *See* John Mearsheimer & Stephen Walt, *An Unnecessary War*, 134 For. Pol. 54 (2003). They argue that Saddam Hussein had approached the U.S. to find out how it would react to an invasion into Kuwait. U.S. Ambassador April Glaspie, consistent with U.S. policy not to intervene in this territorial dispute, commented that "[W]e have no opinion on the Arab–Arab conflicts, like your border disagreement with Kuwait." They add: "The U.S. State Department had earlier told Saddam that Washington had 'no special defense or security commitments to Kuwait.'" On the basis of this, Mearsheimer and Walt conclude "The United States may not have intended to give Iraq a green light, but that is effectively what it did."

89 *See generally* George H.W. Bush & Brent Scowcroft, A World Transformed (1998)(the President and his National Security Council Advisor's account of the U.S. role in these epochal events).

90 *See* Keesing's, Record of World Events, vol. 35 at 36587 (1989).

Both of these U.S. rivals, therefore, had diminished their willingness to challenge the United States.[91] Thus, perhaps for the first time in its history, the Security Council seemed united, albeit under leadership structure that some called a "Unipolar Moment."[92] The ensuing Security Council Resolutions and Coalition strategy for implementing them represented, for their chief strategists President George Bush and his National Security Adviser Brent Scowcroft, a self-conscious attempt to create what Bush would call a "New World Order." Employing rhetoric that recalled President Wilson's performance on the way to Versailles, Bush proclaimed:

> We stand today at a unique and extraordinary moment. The crisis in the Persian Gulf, as grave as it is, also offers a rare opportunity to move toward an historic period of cooperation. Out of these troubled times ... a new world order ...can emerge: a new era—freer from the threat of terror, stronger in the pursuit of justice, and more secure in the quest for peace. An era in which the nations of the world, East and West, North and South, can prosper and live in harmony. A hundred generations have searched for this elusive path to peace, while a thousand wars raged across the span of human endeavor. Today that new world is struggling to be born, a world quite different from the one we've known. A world where the rule of law supplants the rule of the jungle. A world in which nations recognize the shared responsibility for freedom and justice. A world where the strong respect the rights of the weak.[93]

Thus, the Gulf War was to be the "precedent" for the creation of this "new world order."[94] Initially, it would appear to be a precedent protecting the "territorial integrity" of existing states from forcible revision, but in time it would stand for much, much more.

Immediately after Iraq invaded Kuwait, the Security Council adopted Resolution 660, "acting under Articles 39 and 40" of the UN Charter, demanding "that Iraq withdraw immediately and unconditionally all its forces to the positions in which they were located on 1 August 1990."[95] When Iraq refused to comply, days later the Security Council adopted Resolution 661, in which—"affirming the inherent right of individual or collective self-defence, in response to the armed attack by Iraq against Kuwait, in accordance with Article 51 of the Charter"—it imposed a series of economic sanctions. These included, except for medical or humanitarian aid, a ban on imports, as well as the promotion or transfer of funds in support of imports from Iraq or

---

91 *See* Kissinger, *supra* note 4 at 250 ("domestic upheavals in the Soviet Union and China gave the permanent members of the UN Security Council an incentive to maintain America's goodwill").

92 Charles Krauthammer, *America and the World 1990/91: The Unipolar Moment,* 70 For. Aff. 23 (1990).

93 George H.W. Bush, Toward a New World Order (Sept. 11, 1990) (address to a joint session of Congress and the nation concerning Persian Gulf).

94 *See* Derek Chollet & James Goldgeier, America Between the Wars: The Misunderstood Years Between the Fall of the Berlin Wall and the Start of the War on Terror 8–19 (2008) (discussing the "Iraq precedent").

95 S.C. Res. 660, U.N. Doc. S/RES/660 (Aug. 2, 1990).

Kuwait; a ban on arms exports to Iraq or Kuwait; and financial sanctions.[96] In Resolution 662 a few days later, the Security Council stated that it "decided" that Iraq's annexation of Kuwait was invalid and it "called upon states not to recognize the purported annexation.[97] A week later, in Resolution 664, again acting under Chapter VII, the Council, perhaps fearing the taking of hostages, directed Iraq to respect the consular rights of third-party nationals.[98] Enforcement appeared doubtful, however, until the Security Council adopted Resolution 665, which, without specifically citing any of the provisions of Chapter VII, called upon states to take "such measures commensurate to the specific circumstances" that would be "necessary" to enforce the Council's economic sanctions against Iraq.[99] Clearly, the Council hoped that depriving Iraq of the fruits of its acquisition of Kuwait through strict enforcement of the embargo of Iraqi and Kuwaiti oil exports might compel Iraqi compliance.[100] Later resolutions continued to call attention to Iraq's failure to observe the requirements of the previous resolutions, such as Iraq's imprisonment of certain foreign nationals, in effect as hostages.[101] Meanwhile, U.S. forces and other Coalition forces, including from Egypt, Saudi Arabia, Britain, France, Argentina, and Canada, were engaging in a dramatic military build-up in the Persian Gulf.[102] Finally, in the face of continued Iraqi noncompliance and after the United States made the strategic decision to increase its deployment of forces in the region, the Council adopted Resolution 678 in late November 1990. This gave Iraq "one final opportunity, as a pause of goodwill," to comply with the Council's demands. And, unless Iraq complied on or before January 15, 1991, it authorized the United Nations to "use all necessary means to uphold and implement resolution 660 (1990) and all subsequent relevant resolutions and to restore international peace and security in the area...."[103] Iraq did not comply and was forcibly ejected from Kuwait in a ground war that lasted less than a week.[104]

96 S.C. Res. 661, U.N. Doc. S/RES/661 (Aug. 6, 1990).

97 S.C. Res. 662, U.N. Doc. S/RES/662 (Aug. 9, 1990) (providing that the Council "Decides that annexation of Kuwait by Iraq under any form and whatever pretext has no legal validity, and is considered null and void; and that it "Calls upon all States, international organizations and specialized agencies not to recognize that annexation, and to refrain from any action or dealing that might be interpreted as an indirect recognition of the annexation").

98 *See* S.C. Res. 664, U.N. Doc. S/RES/664 (Aug. 18, 1990) ("Demands that Iraq permit and facilitate the immediate departure from Kuwait and Iraq of the nationals of third countries and grant immediate and continuing access of consular officials to such nationals"; and "Further demands that Iraq take no action to jeopardize the safety, security or health of such nationals").

99 S.C. Res. 665, U.N. Doc. S/RES/665 (Aug. 25, 1990) ("Calls upon those Member States co-operating with the Government of Kuwait which are deploying maritime forces to the area to use such measures commensurate to the specific circumstances as may be necessary under the authority of the Security Council to halt all inward and outward maritime shipping in order to inspect and verify their cargoes and destinations and to ensure strict implementation").

100 The preamble to Resolution 665 noted the Council's concerns, "in particular at the conduct of the Government of Iraq in using Iraqi flag vessels to export oil ..." *Id.* at para. 5.

101 *See, e.g.*, S.C. Res. 667, U.N. Doc. S/RES/667 (Sept. 16, 1990) (demanding "the immediate release of those foreign nationals," in effect taken hostage).

102 *See* Damrosch et al., *supra* note 56, at 1230.

103 S.C. Res. 678, U.N. Doc. S/RES/678 (Nov. 29, 1990).

104 *See* Damrosch et al., supra note 56, at 1231.

Recognizing the existence of a new situation with the cessation of hostilities effective March 2, 1991,[105] the Security Council set the terms for a comprehensive settlement adopted in Security Council Resolution 687.[106]

This, of course, was not the end of the story, as the Security Council continued to adopt a series of resolutions to deal with the aftermath of the war. One important effort, which we will discuss in greater detail in our next chapter concerning use of force for the purpose of humanitarian intervention, was Security Council Resolution 688.[107] Kurdish populations in northern Iraq, and the Shi'ites in southern Iraq, had launched uprisings against the weakened Iraqi regime, with the hope of securing autonomy or perhaps even independence. The central government responded with brutal attacks on these civilian populations, and the Security Council demanded that Iraq, "as a contribution to remove the threat to international peace and security in the region, immediately end this repression."[108] This formulation appears to have been part of the basis for the legal rationale advanced by U.S. and U.K. when they imposed "no-fly zones," which ensured that Iraqi Government air forces could not systematically slaughter Kurds and Shi'ites in those zones. In short, the Coalition gave enough assistance to prevent continued mass murder but not enough to allow the Kurds or southern Shi'ites to achieve the political goal of partitioning Iraq.

But most of the Security Council's energy was devoted to addressing concerns about Iraq's nuclear weapons program, when it was discovered by the inspections authorized under Resolution 687 that Iraq had come perilously close to developing nuclear weapons. When we take up the question of self-defense, and particularly the question of pre-emptive self-defense, we will discuss the Security Council's efforts to seek Iraqi compliance with the disarmament provisions of Resolution 687. For now, suffice it to say that with time the Permanent Five coalition at the Security Council began to erode and, in due course, the enforcement of Resolution 687's disarmament provision became problematic.

105 *See* S.C. Res. 686, U.N. Doc. S/RES 686 (Mar. 2, 1991) ("Taking note of the suspension of offensive combat operations by the forces of Kuwait and the Member States cooperating with Kuwait pursuant to resolution 678 ...").

106 *See* S.C. Res. 687, U.N. Doc. S/RES/687 (Apr. 3, 1991).

107 *See* S.C. Res. 688, U.N. Doc. S/RES/688 (April 5, 1991).

108 *Id.* at para. 2.

1. Reading Questions

1) What is the precise legal basis for Coalition use of force in Iraq under Resolution 678? Is it Article 42, Article 51, or something else? Does Resolution 687 look like a proposal for a treaty with Iraq? If so, who are the parties? Does it resemble a statute enacted by a legislature? Something else? (Please review Chapter 1B.)

2) How are the politico-military circumstances surrounding the First Gulf War like or unlike those surrounding the First World War and the Versailles settlement? How are they like or unlike those surrounding the Second World War? Do the answers to these questions affect your answers to question 1? Was partition of the defeated power more or less likely because of politico-military considerations? Was partition of the defeated power more or less likely because of legal considerations? Which sets of factors were more important in each case and why? (Please review Chapter 1A.)

3) In which of these cases—Versailles, the terms of the peace following the Second World War, and the terms settling the First Gulf War—were the costs and benefits of collective action greater? Are there any differences in pre-existing institutional structures that affect your answer to these questions? What similarities and distinctions would a rational choice analyst find in these cases to explain how the wars arose and the terms of their settlements? (Please review Chapter 2C.)

4) To the extent that human agency affected the outcomes in these cases, what values or visions were involved, and how were they alike or different? What is the relation, if any, between your answers to the preceding questions and this question? Please review Chapter 2B.)

5) Is it artificial to view any of these cases as isolated incidents or must the First Gulf War, its aftermath and effects on Iraq's internal sovereignty (with respects to its treatment of its minorities) and external sovereignty (with respect to its force posture), and the Second Gulf Wars be considered part of one continuous process with multiple dimensions, legal and otherwise? Is this also a better way of viewing the progression from League Covenant, to the UN Charter, to the final

re-unification of Germany at the end of the Cold War? If so, is the Iraqi situation better understood in terms of a debate between two views: one in which Iraq is a wrongdoer disturbing the *tanquillitas ordinis*, and states acting through the Security Council, vindicated the claims of justice; the other in which the members of the Coalition, making pre-textual claims of just cause, appropriated the forms of legality of the international community to pursue an imperialist agenda to control the flow of oil from the Middle East? Are your answers to questions 1-4 affected by your views as to the relevance of this question? (Please review Part II, Introductory Chapter.) Please reconsider these questions as you read our next chapters on humanitarian intervention and self-defense.

2. **Documents**

a. United Nations Security Council Resolution 660 (1990)[109]

The Security Council,

Alarmed by the invasion of Kuwait on 2 August 1990 by the military forces of Iraq,

Determining that there exists a breach of international peace and security as regards the Iraqi invasion of Kuwait,

Acting under Articles 39 and 40 of the Charter of the United Nations,

1. *Condemns* the Iraqi invasion of Kuwait;

2. *Demands* that Iraq withdraw immediately and unconditionally all its forces to the positions in which they were located on 1 August 1990;

3. *Calls upon* Iraq and Kuwait to begin immediately intensive negotiations for the resolution of their differences and supports all efforts in this regard, and especially those of the League of Arab States;

4. *Decides* to meet again as necessary to consider further steps with to ensure compliance with the present resolution.

---

109 S.C. Res. 660, para. 19, 45 U.N. SCOR, U.N. Doc. S/RES/660 (Aug. 2, 1990).

b. United Nations Security Council Resolution 678 (1990)[110]

The Security Council,

Recalling, and reaffirming its resolutions 660 (1990) of 2 August (1990), 661 (1990) of 6 August 1990, 662 (1990) of 9 August 1990, 664 (1990) of 18 August 1990, 665 (1990) of 25 August 1990, 666 (1990) of 13 September 1990, 667 (1990) of 16 September 1990, 669 (1990) of 24 September 1990, 670 (1990) of 25 September 1990, 674 (1990) of of 29 October 1990 and 677 (1990) of 28 November 1990.

Noting that, despite all efforts by the United Nations, Iraq refuses to comply with its obligation to implement resolution 660 (1990) and the above-mentioned subsequent relevant resolutions, in flagrant contempt of the Security Council,

Mindful of its duties and responsibilities under the Charter of the United Nations for the maintenance and preservation of international peace and security,

Determined to secure full compliance with its decisions,

Acting under Chapter VII of the Charter,

1. *Demands* that Iraq comply fully with resolution 660 (1990) and all subsequent relevant resolutions, and decides, while maintaining all its decisions, to allow Iraq one final opportunity, as a pause of goodwill, to do so;

2. *Authorizes* Member States co-operating with the Government of Kuwait, unless Iraq on or before 15 January 1991 fully implements, as set forth in paragraph 1 above, the foregoing resolutions, to use all necessary means to uphold and implement resolution 660 (1990) and all subsequent relevant resolutions and to restore international peace and security in the area;

3. *Requests* all States to provide appropriate support for the actions undertaken in pursuance of paragraph 2 of the present resolution;

4. *Requests* the States concerned to keep the Security Council regularly informed on the progress of actions undertaken pursuant to paragraphs 2 and 3 of the present resolution;

5. *Decides* to remain seized of the matter.

110 S.C. Res. 678, 45 U.N. SCOR, U.N. Doc. S/RES/678, at 27 (Nov. 29, 1991).

c. Security Council Resolution 687 (1991)[111]

The Security Council,

Recalling its resolutions 660 (1990) of 2 August 1990, 661 (1990) of 6 August 1990, 662 (1990) of 9 August 1990, 664 (1990) of 18 August 1990, 665 (1990) of 25 August 1990, 666 (1990) of 13 September 1990, 667 (1990) of 16 September 1990, 669 (1990) of 24 September 1990, 670 (1990) of 25 September 1990, 674 (1990) of 29 October 1990, 677 (1990) of 28 November 1990, 678 (1990) of 29 November 1990 and 686 (1991) of 2 March 1991,

Welcoming the restoration to Kuwait of its sovereignty, independence and territorial integrity and the return of its legitimate Government,

Affirming the commitment of all Member States to the sovereignty, territorial integrity and political independence of Kuwait and Iraq, and noting the intention expressed by the Member States cooperating with Kuwait under paragraph 2 of resolution 678 (1990) to bring their military presence in Iraq to an end as soon as possible consistent with paragraph 8 of resolution 686 (1991),

Reaffirming the need to be assured of Iraq's peaceful intentions in the light of its unlawful invasion and occupation of Kuwait,

Taking note of the letter sent by the Minister for Foreign Affairs of Iraq on 27 February 1991 and those sent pursuant to resolution 686 (1991),

Noting that Iraq and Kuwait, as independent sovereign States, signed at Baghdad on 4 October 1963 "Agreed Minutes Between the State of Kuwait and the Republic of Iraq Regarding the Restoration of Friendly Relations, Recognition and Related Matters", thereby recognizing formally the boundary between Iraq and Kuwait and the allocation of islands, which were registered with the United Nations in accordance with Article 102 of the Charter of the United Nations and in which Iraq recognized the independence and complete sovereignty of the State of Kuwait within its borders as specified and accepted in the letter of the Prime Minister of Iraq dated 21 July 1932, and as accepted by the Ruler of Kuwait in his letter dated 10 August 1932,

Conscious of the need for demarcation of the said boundary,

Conscious also of the statements by Iraq threatening to use weapons in violation of its obligations under the Geneva Protocol for the Prohibition of the Use in War of Asphyxiating, Poisonous or Other Gases, and of Bacteriological Methods of Warfare, signed at Geneva on 17 June 1925, and of its prior use of chemical weapons and affirming that grave consequences would follow any further use by Iraq of such weapons,

Recalling that Iraq has subscribed to the Declaration adopted by all States participating in the Conference of States Parties to the 1925 Geneva Protocol and Other Interested States, held

111 S.C. Res. 687, 45 U.N. SCOR, U.N. Doc. S/RES/687 (Apr. 3, 1991).

in Paris from 7 to 11 January 1989, establishing the objective of universal elimination of chemical and biological weapons,

Recalling also that Iraq has signed the Convention on the Prohibition of the Development, Production and Stockpiling of Bacteriological (Biological) and Toxin Weapons and on Their Destruction, of 10 April 1972,

Noting the importance of Iraq ratifying this Convention,

Noting moreover the importance of all States adhering to this Convention and encouraging its forthcoming Review Conference to reinforce the authority, efficiency and universal scope of the convention,

Stressing the importance of an early conclusion by the Conference on Disarmament of its work on a Convention on the Universal Prohibition of Chemical Weapons and of universal adherence thereto,

Aware of the use by Iraq of ballistic missiles in unprovoked attacks and therefore of the need to take specific measures in regard to such missiles located in Iraq,

Concerned by the reports in the hands of Member States that Iraq has attempted to acquire materials for a nuclear-weapons programme contrary to its obligations under the Treaty on the Non-Proliferation of Nuclear Weapons of 1 July 1968,

Recalling the objective of the establishment of a nuclear-weapons-free zone in the region of the Middle East,

Conscious of the threat that all weapons of mass destruction pose to peace and security in the area and of the need to work towards the establishment in the Middle East of a zone free of such weapons,

Conscious also of the objective of achieving balanced and comprehensive control of armaments in the region,

Conscious further of the importance of achieving the objectives noted above using all available means, including a dialogue among the States of the region,

Noting that resolution 686 (1991) marked the lifting of the measures imposed by resolution 661 (1990) in so far as they applied to Kuwait,

Noting that despite the progress being made in fulfilling the obligations of resolution 686 (1991), many Kuwaiti and third country nationals are still not accounted for and property remains unreturned,

Recalling the International Convention against the Taking of Hostages, opened for signature at New York on 18 December 1979, which categorizes all acts of taking hostages as manifestations of international terrorism,

Deploring threats made by Iraq during the recent conflict to make use of terrorism against targets outside Iraq and the taking of hostages by Iraq,

Taking note with grave concern of the reports of the Secretary-General of 20 March 1991 and 28 March 1991, and conscious of the necessity to meet urgently the humanitarian needs in Kuwait and Iraq,

Bearing in mind its objective of restoring international peace and security in the area as set out in recent resolutions of the Security Council,

Conscious of the need to take the following measures acting under Chapter VII of the Charter,

1. Affirms all thirteen resolutions noted above, except as expressly changed below to achieve the goals of this resolution, including a formal cease-fire;

A

2. Demands that Iraq and Kuwait respect the inviolability of the international boundary and the allocation of islands set out in the "Agreed Minutes Between the State of Kuwait and the Republic of Iraq Regarding the Restoration of Friendly Relations, Recognition and Related Matters", signed by them in the exercise of their sovereignty at Baghdad on 4 October 1963 and registered with the United Nations and published by the United Nations in document 7063, United Nations, Treaty Series, 1964;

3. Calls upon the Secretary-General to lend his assistance to make arrangements with Iraq and Kuwait to demarcate the boundary between Iraq and Kuwait, drawing on appropriate material, including the map transmitted by Security Council document S/22412 and to report back to the Security Council within one month;

4. Decides to guarantee the inviolability of the above-mentioned international boundary and to take as appropriate all necessary measures to that end in accordance with the Charter of the United Nations;

B

5. Requests the Secretary-General, after consulting with Iraq and Kuwait, to submit within three days to the Security Council for its approval a plan for the immediate deployment of a United Nations observer unit to monitor the Khor Abdullah and a demilitarized zone, which is hereby established, extending ten kilometres into Iraq and five kilometres into Kuwait from the boundary referred to in the "Agreed Minutes Between the State of Kuwait and the Republic of Iraq Regarding the Restoration of Friendly Relations, Recognition and Related Matters" of 4 October

1963; to deter violations of the boundary through its presence in and surveillance of the demilitarized zone; to observe any hostile or potentially hostile action mounted from the territory of one State to the other; and for the Secretary-General to report regularly to the Security Council on the operations of the unit, and immediately if there are serious violations of the zone or potential threats to peace;

6. Notes that as soon as the Secretary-General notifies the Security Council of the completion of the deployment of the United Nations observer unit, the conditions will be established for the Member States cooperating with Kuwait in accordance with resolution 678 (1990) to bring their military presence in Iraq to an end consistent with resolution 686 (1991);

C

7. Invites Iraq to reaffirm unconditionally its obligations under the Geneva Protocol for the Prohibition of the Use in War of Asphyxiating, Poisonous or Other Gases, and of Bacteriological Methods of Warfare, signed at Geneva on 17 June 1925, and to ratify the Convention on the Prohibition of the Development, Production and Stockpiling of Bacteriological (Biological) and Toxin Weapons and on Their Destruction, of 10 April 1972;

8. Decides that Iraq shall unconditionally accept the destruction, removal, or rendering harmless, under international supervision, of:

   (a) All chemical and biological weapons and all stocks of agents and all related subsystems and components and all research, development, support and manufacturing facilities;

   (b) All ballistic missiles with a range greater than 150 kilometres and related major parts, and repair and production facilities;

9. Decides, for the implementation of paragraph 8 above, the following:

   (a) Iraq shall submit to the Secretary-General, within fifteen days of the adoption of the present resolution, a declaration of the locations, amounts and types of all items specified in paragraph 8 and agree to urgent, on-site inspection as specified below;

(b) The Secretary-General, in consultation with the appropriate Governments and, where appropriate, with the Director-General of the World Health Organization, within forty-five days of the passage of the present resolution, shall develop, and submit to the Council for approval, a plan calling for the completion of the following acts within forty-five days of such approval:

(i) The forming of a Special Commission, which shall carry out immediate on-site inspection of Iraq's biological, chemical and missile capabilities, based on Iraq's declarations and the designation of any additional locations by the Special Commission itself;

(ii) The yielding by Iraq of possession to the Special Commission for destruction, removal or rendering harmless, taking into account the requirements of public safety, of all items specified under paragraph 8 (a) above, including items at the additional locations designated by the Special Commission under paragraph 9 (b) (i) above and the destruction by Iraq, under the supervision of the Special Commission, of all its missile capabilities, including launchers, as specified under paragraph 8 (b) above;

(iii) The provision by the Special Commission of the assistance and cooperation to the Director-General of the International Atomic Energy Agency required in paragraphs 12 and 13 below;

10. Decides that Iraq shall unconditionally undertake not to use, develop, construct or acquire any of the items specified in paragraphs 8 and 9 above and requests the Secretary-General, in consultation with the Special Commission, to develop a plan for the future ongoing monitoring and verification of Iraq's compliance with this paragraph, to be submitted to the Security Council for approval within one hundred and twenty days of the passage of this resolution;

11. Invites Iraq to reaffirm unconditionally its obligations under the Treaty on the Non-Proliferation of Nuclear Weapons of 1 July 1968;

12. Decides that Iraq shall unconditionally agree not to acquire or develop nuclear weapons or nuclear-weapons-usable material or any subsystems or components or any research, development, support or manufacturing facilities related to the above; to submit to the Secretary-General and the Director-General of the International Atomic Energy Agency within fifteen days of the adoption of the present resolution a declaration of the locations, amounts, and types of all items specified above; to place all of its nuclear-weapons-usable materials under the exclusive control, for custody and removal, of the International Atomic Energy Agency, with the

assistance and cooperation of the Special Commission as provided for in the plan of the Secretary-General discussed in paragraph 9 (b) above; to accept, in accordance with the arrangements provided for in paragraph 13 below, urgent on-site inspection and the destruction, removal or rendering harmless as appropriate of all items specified above; and to accept the plan discussed in paragraph 13 below for the future ongoing monitoring and verification of its compliance with these undertakings;

13. Requests the Director-General of the International Atomic Energy Agency, through the Secretary-General, with the assistance and cooperation of the Special Commission as provided for in the plan of the Secretary-General in paragraph 9 (b) above, to carry out immediate on-site inspection of Iraq's nuclear capabilities based on Iraq's declarations and the designation of any additional locations by the Special Commission; to develop a plan for submission to the Security Council within forty-five days calling for the destruction, removal, or rendering harmless as appropriate of all items listed in paragraph 12 above; to carry out the plan within forty-five days following approval by the Security Council; and to develop a plan, taking into account the rights and obligations of Iraq under the Treaty on the Non-Proliferation of Nuclear Weapons of 1 July 1968, for the future ongoing monitoring and verification of Iraq's compliance with paragraph 12 above, including an inventory of all nuclear material in Iraq subject to the Agency's verification and inspections to confirm that Agency safeguards cover all relevant nuclear activities in Iraq, to be submitted to the Security Council for approval within one hundred and twenty days of the passage of the present resolution;

14. Takes note that the actions to be taken by Iraq in paragraphs 8, 9, 10, 11, 12 and 13 of the present resolution represent steps towards the goal of establishing in the Middle East a zone free from weapons of mass destruction and all missiles for their delivery and the objective of a global ban on chemical weapons;

D

15. Requests the Secretary-General to report to the Security Council on the steps taken to facilitate the return of all Kuwaiti property seized by Iraq, including a list of any property that Kuwait claims has not been returned or which has not been returned intact;

E

16. Reaffirms that Iraq, without prejudice to the debts and obligations of Iraq arising prior to 2 August 1990, which will be addressed through the normal mechanisms, is liable under international law for any direct loss, damage, including environmental damage and the depletion of natural resources, or injury to foreign Governments, nationals and corporations, as a result of Iraq's unlawful invasion and occupation of Kuwait;

17. Decides that all Iraqi statements made since 2 August 1990 repudiating its foreign debt are null and void, and demands that Iraq adhere scrupulously to all of its obligations concerning servicing and repayment of its foreign debt;

18. Decides also to create a fund to pay compensation for claims that fall within paragraph 16 above and to establish a Commission that will administer the fund;

19. Directs the Secretary-General to develop and present to the Security Council for decision, no later than thirty days following the adoption of the present resolution, recommendations for the fund to meet the requirement for the payment of claims established in accordance with paragraph 18 above and for a programme to implement the decisions in paragraphs 16, 17 and 18 above, including: administration of the fund; mechanisms for determining the appropriate level of Iraq's contribution to the fund based on a percentage of the value of the exports of petroleum and petroleum products from Iraq not to exceed a figure to be suggested to the Council by the Secretary-General, taking into account the requirements of the people of Iraq, Iraq's payment capacity as assessed in conjunction with the international financial institutions taking into consideration external debt service, and the needs of the Iraqi economy; arrangements for ensuring that payments are made to the fund; the process by which funds will be allocated and claims paid; appropriate procedures for evaluating losses, listing claims and verifying their validity and resolving disputed claims in respect of Iraq's liability as specified in paragraph 16 above; and the composition of the Commission designated above;

F

20. Decides, effective immediately, that the prohibitions against the sale or supply to Iraq of commodities or products, other than medicine and health supplies, and prohibitions against financial transactions related thereto contained in resolution

661 (1990) shall not apply to foodstuffs notified to the Security Council Committee established by resolution 661 (1990) concerning the situation between Iraq and Kuwait or, with the approval of that Committee, under the simplified and accelerated "no-objection" procedure, to materials and supplies for essential civilian needs as identified in the report of the Secretary-General dated 20 March 1991, and in any further findings of humanitarian need by the Committee;

21. Decides that the Security Council shall review the provisions of paragraph 20 above every sixty days in the light of the policies and practices of the Government of Iraq, including the implementation of all relevant resolutions of the Security Council, for the purpose of determining whether to reduce or lift the prohibitions referred to therein;

22. Decides that upon the approval by the Security Council of the programme called for in paragraph 19 above and upon Council agreement that Iraq has completed all actions contemplated in paragraphs 8, 9, 10, 11, 12 and 13 above, the prohibitions against the import of commodities and products originating in Iraq and the prohibitions against financial transactions related thereto contained in resolution 661 (1990) shall have no further force or effect;

23. Decides that, pending action by the Security Council under paragraph 22 above, the Security Council Committee established by resolution 661 (1990) shall be empowered to approve, when required to assure adequate financial resources on the part of Iraq to carry out the activities under paragraph 20 above, exceptions to the prohibition against the import of commodities and products originating in Iraq;

24. Decides that, in accordance with resolution 661 (1990) and subsequent related resolutions and until a further decision is taken by the Security Council, all States shall continue to prevent the sale or supply, or the promotion or facilitation of such sale or supply, to Iraq by their nationals, or from their territories or using their flag vessels or aircraft, of:

    (a) Arms and related materiel of all types, specifically including the sale or transfer through other means of all forms of conventional military equipment, including for paramilitary forces, and spare parts and components and their means of production, for such equipment;

(b) Items specified and defined in paragraphs 8 and 12 above not otherwise covered above;

(c) Technology under licensing or other transfer arrangements used in the production, utilization or stockpiling of items specified in subparagraphs (a) and (b) above;

(d) Personnel or materials for training or technical support services relating to the design, development, manufacture, use, maintenance or support of items specified in subparagraphs (a) and (b) above;

25. Calls upon all States and international organizations to act strictly in accordance with paragraph 24 above, notwithstanding the existence of any contracts, agreements, licences or any other arrangements;

26. Requests the Secretary-General, in consultation with appropriate Governments, to develop within sixty days, for the approval of the Security Council, guidelines to facilitate full international implementation of paragraphs 24 and 25 above and paragraph 27 below, and to make them available to all States and to establish a procedure for updating these guidelines periodically;

27. Calls upon all States to maintain such national controls and procedures and to take such other actions consistent with the guidelines to be established by the Security Council under paragraph 26 above as may be necessary to ensure compliance with the terms of paragraph 24 above, and calls upon international organizations to take all appropriate steps to assist in ensuring such full compliance;

28. Agrees to review its decisions in paragraphs 22, 23, 24 and 25 above, except for the items specified and defined in paragraphs 8 and 12 above, on a regular basis and in any case one hundred and twenty days following passage of the present resolution, taking into account Iraq's compliance with the resolution and general progress towards the control of armaments in the region;

29. Decides that all States, including Iraq, shall take the necessary measures to ensure that no claim shall lie at the instance of the Government of Iraq, or of any person or body in Iraq, or of any person claiming through or for the benefit of any such person or body, in connection with any contract or other transaction where its

performance was affected by reason of the measures taken by the Security Council in resolution 661 (1990) and related resolutions;

G

30. Decides that, in furtherance of its commitment to facilitate the repatriation of all Kuwaiti and third country nationals, Iraq shall extend all necessary cooperation to the International Committee of the Red Cross, providing lists of such persons, facilitating the access of the International Committee of the Red Cross to all such persons wherever located or detained and facilitating the search by the International Committee of the Red Cross for those Kuwaiti and third country nationals still unaccounted for;

31. Invites the International Committee of the Red Cross to keep the Secretary-General apprised as appropriate of all activities undertaken in connection with facilitating the repatriation or return of all Kuwaiti and third country nationals or their remains present in Iraq on or after 2 August 1990;

H

32. Requires Iraq to inform the Security Council that it will not commit or support any act of international terrorism or allow any organization directed towards commission of such acts to operate within its territory and to condemn unequivocally and renounce all acts, methods and practices of terrorism;

33. Declares that, upon official notification by Iraq to the Secretary-General and to the Security Council of its acceptance of the provisions above, a formal cease-fire is effective between Iraq and Kuwait and the Member States cooperating with Kuwait in accordance with resolution 678 (1990);

34. Decides to remain seized of the matter and to take such further steps as may be required for the implementation of the present resolution and to secure peace and security in the area.

1. Thesis 1—How Does Each of our Models Shed Light on the International Response to Iraq's Invasion of Kuwait?

a. The Legalist Account

The literature on the Security Council's resolutions in connection with Iraq's invasion of Kuwait is vast, and much of it grapples with the central question of whether the Security Council's decisions implemented the original design of the Charter. Some hold that the Council worked "as it was supposed to work according to the design of its framers";[112] others hold that the Council legitimately was moving outside the scope of its original powers;[113] others question the legitimacy of the Council's legal innovations;[114] and still others find the Council's actions irregular under its original design but justified by implicit amendments to the Charter's formal rules, given the end of the Cold War and the adoption of important new legal instruments affording the basis for the legitimacy of the Council's exercise of new powers.[115] Why does the "legalist" debate give rise to so many conflicting perspectives?

The original Charter design envisioned "enforcement" action by the Security Council itself under forces that would be deployed under U.N. command and control pursuant to Article 43.[116]

112 *See, e.g.*, Abram Chayes, The Use of Force in the Persian Gulf, *in* Law and Force in the New International Order 3–7 (Damrosch & Scheffer eds., 1991) (State Department Legal Adviser during the Cuban Missile Crisis).

113 *See, e.g.*, Jose E. Alvarez, *The Once and Future Security Council*, Wash. Q., 5, 6 (Spring 1995) (noting that the Charter never worked as intended and that, contrary to popular wisdom, it is not working now as it was originally intended).

114 For important critiques of the legitimacy of Security Council action, *see* Burns H. Weston, *Security Council Resolution 678 and the Persian Gulf Decision Making: Precarious Legitimacy*, 85 Am. J. Int'l L. 516 (1991) (questioning the initial authorization of enforcement action by the U.S. with respect to Iraq); David D. Caron, *The Legitimacy of the Collective Authority of the Security Council*, 87 Am. J. Int'l L. 552 (1993) (critiquing the so-called "reverse veto," under which once the Security Council authorization is given for enforcement action, such as with respect to Iraq, the veto by one Permanent Members, such as the United States, prevents the international community from disenabling the Permanent Member exercising its veto from lawfully undertaking further enforcement action).

115 *See, e.g.*, Philip Bobbitt, The Shield of Achilles: War, Peace, and the Course of History 636–39 (2002) (arguing that the Charter of Paris in 1990 constituted a treaty of peace closing the epochal war between parliamentary democracy and its fascist and communist competitors, in which the internal constitutional principles of what Bobbitt calls "market states" were confirmed as the new constitutional principles of the international system); and Antonio F. Perez, *On the Way to the Forum: The Reconstruction of Article 2(7) and the Rise of Federalism Under the United Nations Charter*, 31 Tex. Int'l L. J. 353, 402-04 (1996) (suggesting that the UN Security Council Declaration approving the Secretary-General's "Agenda for Peace"—describing self-determination and democracy as emerging central principles in the post-Cold War international legal system—operated as the proposal for a newly amended Charter).

116 Article 43 specifically contemplated the establishment of U.N. forces pursuant to agreement with Member States, which would turn over command and control to the U.N. See U.N. Charter art. 43, para. 1 ("All Members of the United Nations, in order to contribute to the maintenance of international peace and security, undertake to make available to the Security Council, on its call and in accordance with a special agreement or agreements, armed forces, assistance, and facilities, including rights of passage, necessary for the purpose of maintaining international peace and security."). These

Because the Council merely purported to "authorize" the use of force by a state or group of Member States to address putative threat to the peace, it has not been clear whether these actions constituted "enforcement" measures within the meaning of Article 42, an authorization by the Security Council of individual or collective self-defense under Article 51, or yet some third source of inter-textual power of the Security Council.[117] (The Rhodesia "authorization" to the U.K. arguably provided the only, albeit distinguishable, precedent for "enforcement" action undertaken by states rather than the UN itself.) It was observed, therefore, that if collective intervention is authorized other than as an enforcement measure pursuant to Article 42, the question arises whether the exception for "enforcement measures under Chapter of the Charter" from the "domestic jurisdiction" principle of Article 2(7) is applicable.[118] Indeed, contemporaneously, the U.N. Under-Secretary-General for Legal Affairs and a future member of the International Court of Justice, Carl-August Fleischhauer, took the view that U.N. Resolution 678 authorizing use of force against Iraq to repel it from Kuwait was not "adopted under Article 42," and thus did "not provide for a collective enforcement action by the United Nations," but was instead simply "the exercise of power of the Council under Chapter VII."[119] If so, many of the Council's decisions in Resolution 687 were arguably problematic if imposed directly on Iraq without its consent. Thus, if Resolution 687's terms received Iraq's consent, as though it were a treaty, any legal concerns relating to the UN's duty of non-intervention would have been resolved. The precise wording of Resolution 687 takes these concerns into account and demands Iraq's consent. Yet, the Secretary-General, Boutros Boutros-Ghali, a respected international law scholar, took a different view from that of his Legal Adviser, specifically referring to Resolution 678 as "enforcement action."[120] But Oscar Schachter, perhaps the most respected authority on the law of the United Nations, held that the Coalition action in the First Gulf War could be characterized either as one

---

were the "air, sea, or land forces" Article 42 contemplated would be used by the United Nations to "maintain or restore international peace and security." *Id.* art. 42.

117 *See* Oscar Schachter, *United Nations Law in the Gulf Conflict,* 85 Am. J. Int'l L. 452, 459 (1991) (concluding that such authorizations may well be consistent with both Articles 42 and 51); *see also* Sean D. Murphy, *The Security Council, Legitimacy, and the Concept of Collective Security After the Cold War,* 32 Colum. J. Transnat'l L. 201, 226 (1994) (claiming that so-called "major power functions" legitimately flow from the collective security conception of the Charter) (noting that it is no doubt possible to argue that the specific provisions of Chapter VII do not exhaust the power of the Security Council under the Charter, since, as Article 24(2) suggests in enumerating the provisions identifying the "specific powers" of the Council, the Council may well have "general" powers as well to maintain international peace and security in accordance with the Charter's "Purposes and Principles").

118 *See* Murphy, *supra* note 117, at 227.

119 Carl-August Fleischhauer, *Remarks on Compliance and Enforcement in the United Nations System,* 85 Am. Soc'y Int'l L. Proc. 429, 431 (1991).

120 *See* United Nations, General Assembly, Supplement to an Agenda for Peace: Position Paper of the Secretary-General on the Occasion of the Fiftieth Anniversary of the United Nations, P 78, U.N. Doc. A/50/60 (1995) (characterizing the Council's authorization to use force in the Korean, Iraq-Kuwait, Somalia, Rwanda, and Haiti cases as "enforcement action") [Supplement to Agenda for Peace].

of Security Council-authorized collective self-defense under Article 51 or as enforcement action whose implementation was delegated to the Coalition to be undertaken under article 42.[121]

b. The Realist Response

Yet these legalist metaphysics seem far removed for the political reality of the situation. It can be argued that this Council-authorized collective action against interstate aggression occurred only during the brief interlude between the end of the two superpowers' Cold War struggle and the more recent emergence of challenges to American global hegemony.[122] Only in those unusual and likely unrepeatable circumstances was the United States able to gather sufficient votes within the Security Council to obtain authorization to use force to address what it and its coalition allies considered to be a serious breach of the peace in the Middle East. Moreover, like the Korean intervention, the First Gulf War was the handiwork of U.S. diplomatic resourcefulness and military strength, rather than a genuine example of "collective security." Although the presence in the U.S.-led coalition of military forces from thirty-three countries contributed significantly to the political success of the endeavor, "militarily all aspects of this war were dominated by U.S. forces."[123] Rather than considering the First Gulf War as evidence that the Charter's collective security system can work, it is more realistic to view the episode as a hegemon's intervention attempt to stabilize a troubled region, a view that seems to be shared by constructivist critics,[124] and classical realist advocates,[125] of U.S. power. On this theory, if it was true that the Iraqi invasion of Kuwait presented an extraordinary opportunity to revitalize the Charter's collective security arrangements, then why was the opportunity not taken in the early

121 *See* Schachter, supra note 117, at 452–63. Because of this potential overlap, Schachter considered the question, which is of central significance to our study of self-defense in Chapter 4, whether a Chapter VII resolution could oust a state of its "inherent" rights. Schachter opined: "A Council decision that calls on an invader to withdraw and to cease hostilities is certainly a necessary measure, but it could not in be intended to deprive the victim state of its right to defend itself when the invader has not complied with the Council's order. A reasonable construction of the provision in Article 51 would recognize that the Council as the authority to adopt a measure that would require armed action to cease even if that action was undertaken in self-defense. However, this would not mean that *any* measure would preempt self-defense. The intent of the Council as expressed in its decision would determine whether the right to use force in self-defense has been suspended by the Council." *Id.* at 458 (emphasis in the original). A similar debate arose in connection with the asserted right of Bosnia-Herzegovina to "self-defense" from Serbia when the Security Council imposed an arms embargo during the Balkan Wars of the early 1990s that had the effect later on of favoring Serbian forces in the region after Bosnia-Herzegovina had secured its de facto independence. *See* S.C. Res, 713, U.N. Doc. S/RES 713 (Sept. 25, 1991) (acting under "Chapter VII" to impose an arms embargo on then "Yugoslavia").

122 It was during this brief interlude that President George H.W. Bush delivered an address to Congress, ironically on September 11, 1990, in which he first envisaged "'a new world order."' *See Adam Roberts, A New Age in International Relations?,* 67 Int'l Aff. 509, 519 (1991) (citation omitted).

123 Trevor N. Dupuy, *How the War Was Won*, National Rev., 29 (Apr. 1, 1991).

124 *See* Martti Koskenniemi, *The Place of Law in Collective Security*, 17 Mich. J. Int'l L. 455, 460–61 (1996) (noting arguments that the Council's action "has not reflected the collective interests of United Nations members as a whole, but only the special interests and factual predominance of the United States and its Western allies within the Council").

125 *See* Kissinger, *supra* note 4, at 350 ("In the Gulf War, collective security was invoked as a justification of American leadership, not as a substitute for it.").

1990s to conclude special agreements under Article 43 to provide national military contingents as standby forces for the Council's future use?[126] Indeed, perhaps the most revealing argument that emerged from the public debate in the United States regarding whether or not to spill American blood to liberate Kuwait was Secretary of State James Baker's famous explanation that the war was about "jobs, jobs, jobs"; yet, like Schachter's assessment that a legalist description is equally amenable to collective self-defense and collective security accounts, it may be that both idealist and realist rationales were in the minds of the relevant decision-makers, since aggression by Iraq to acquire control of a dominant share of the world's oil could be viewed not only as wrongful but also as a threat to the world economy.[127]

c. Rational Choice Perspectives

Rational choice theory draws attention to the difficulties involved in constructing and sustaining any alliance mechanism, much less collective security regimes that are defined, as we have, to protect the status quo from any forcible reversal. The League of Nations limited its goals by defining "defection" from cooperation as "war" or "aggression." The Charter's more ambitious definition under Article 2(4) and Chapter VII defined defection as "any use of force against the territorial integrity or political independence" of states and any "threats to the peace, breaches of the peace, or acts of aggression." One could view the General Assembly's Uniting for Peace Resolution and its attempt to define aggression, when lack of cooperation between the members of the Security Council paralyzed that body, as an effort to reduce the scope of the definition of defection to "aggression," and thereby to restore the less ambiguous approach of the League collective security regime. On the other hand, one could view the General Assembly's efforts as attempts to raise the reputational costs of defection for the hegemonic powers through more precise articulation of the applicable norms. With the end of the Cold War, the costs of cooperation through the adoption of a Security Council Chapter VII resolution diminished transaction costs for the United States, as the United States no longer had to bargain with the Soviet Union or China for votes at the Security Council. At the same time, the benefits of cooperation through

126 *See* Koskenniemi, *supra* note 124, at 461.

127 The Gulf War, Part A, Frontline (Jan. 28, 1997) (transcript *available at* http://www.pbs.org/wgbh/pages/frontline/gulf/script_a.html). As major participants recalled years later:

> Bernard Trainor: George Bush rose up in righteous anger and called this aggression a la the Nazi era.
>
> Pres. George Bush: The fight is about naked aggression!
>
> Bernard Trainor: The American people didn't quite understand that. Then the next argument was that the war was about oil. We had to protect oil.
>
> Pres. George Bush: If control of the world's great oil reserves fell into the hands of that one man, Saddam Hussein.
>
> Bernard Trainor: The banners came out in Harvard Square, "Hell, no. We won't go. We won't die for Texaco." That really didn't - didn't resonate. And then, if you recall, Jim Baker got up there and said it's about "jobs, jobs, jobs."
>
> James Baker: If you want to sum it up in one word, it's jobs.
>
> Bernard Trainor: The American people said, "Huh? What's this all about?"

the Security Council may have increased for the United States, since the potential long-term effects of Security Council-approved use of force created a perceived cost for potential future regional aggressors in the less stable and more uncertain environment following the Cold War, particularly in light of the emerging risk of proliferation of weapons of mass destruction. If so, as the costs of working through the Security Council declined and the benefits of obtaining resolutions that would legally-bind their targets (or, in the language of rational choice theorists, at least impose increased reputational costs for noncompliance) increased, the U.S. incentive to invest in norm-creation through making the effort required to produce and act through Security Council Chapter VII resolutions finally reached a tipping point.

However, a rational choice explanation of these events is clearly sensitive to fleeting calculations of the relevant costs and benefits involved. And it makes the sustainability of these decisions and the likelihood of continued cooperation among the members of the Coalition that defeated Iraq, even under continuing U.S. hegemony, problematic, given the costs of sustaining any cooperative behavior. Moreover, any collective security system, as even defenders of the concept have admitted, is intrinsically liable to fall prey to the common problems of collective action, including free-ridership.[128] Thus, in exposing the inherent design flaws in collective security theory, John Mearsheimer noted: "even if states agree to act automatically and collectively to meet aggression, there would surely be difficulty determining how to distribute the burden. States will have strong incentives to pass the buck and get other states to pay the heavy price of confronting an aggressor."[129] More generally, states will have incentives to enjoy their share of the public global goods—peace and order—produced by a collective security system, while avoiding the costs of providing those goods. Since enforcement costs can be high, while the national interests of particular great powers in addressing a particular threat to the peace may be marginal, the incentives to be a free rider may be irresistible. Moreover, if a hegemonic power like the United States were willing to assume most of the burden of providing the relevant public global goods (as, one might argue, it sought to do in the Second Gulf War), its challengers might have incentives to exploit their positions within the system in order to weaken the hegemon's power (as, one might also argue, France and Russia did in the Security Council debates preceding the Second Gulf War). And, as apparent U.S. hegemony through the 1990's declined, the hegemon's ability to reward cooperation and punish defection would decline even further, thereby further increasing free-riding incentives.[130]

Indeed, from a rational choice perspective, the lessons to be drawn from the fate of the Versailles settlement and frustration of the original purposes of the UN Charter during the Cold

128 *See* Eric A. Posner & Alan O. Sykes, *Optimal War and the Jus Ad Bellum*, 93 Geo. L.J. 993, 1001–12, 1019 (2005).

129 John J. Mearsheimer, The False Promise of International Institutions, in Theories of War and Peace 329, 361 (Michael E. Brown et al. eds., 1998)

130 *See generally* Chollet & Goldgeier, *supra* note 94 (discussing the breakdown of weapons inspections in Iraq and the negotiations for Resolution 1441).

War similarly foreshadow the erosion of the legitimacy of the legal and political settlement reflected in Security Council Resolutions 678 and 687. The Versailles settlement failed as predicted; indeed, many observers now view the First and Second World Wars as one continuous struggle,[131] and the tenuous peace in Europe observed since the end of the Second World War can be explained more readily by reference to other factors. Thus, some scholars argue that the bipolar system of the Cold War was an important force in maintaining the peace, finding such a system to be intrinsically more stable than a multi-polar or uni-polar, system.[132] The threat that a conventional war in Europe might also lead to a nuclear exchange may also have deterred recourse to armed force.[133] Since war is often caused by imperfect information regarding rivals' capabilities and intentions, the incentives to go to war may well have been reduced by the development of photo-reconnaissance and other technologies, or by the arms inspections regimes fostered by disarmament treaties, that made the superpowers more transparent to each other.[134] Other analysts see the U.S.-Soviet conflict, which pitted a large land power against a commercial maritime republic, as "an elephant-whale" confrontation in which the specific power-projection capabilities of the antagonists made full-scale conflict unlikely.[135] The greater political stability of European states,[136] the persisting memories of the devastation of the two great twentieth century wars fought largely on the European continent, and the power of the two Cold War hegemons to maintain the peace within their European spheres of influence[137] were also likely to have been important contributory factors.[138] In short, a rationalist might see the First Gulf War as an unstable cost-benefit calculus unlikely to repeat itself in the near future.

---

131 *See supra* text accompanying note 38 (discussing Fischer).

132 *See* John Lewis Gaddis, The Long Peace: Inquires into the History of the Cold War 221–23 (1987); Mearsheimer, *supra* note 129, at 3, 24–25; *see also* Eyal Benvenisti, The US and the Use of Force: Double-edged Hegemony and the Management of Global Emergencies, 15 Eur. J. Int'l L. 677, 687 (2004); *but see* Daniel S. Geller & J. David Singer, Nations at War: A Scientific Study of International Conflict 115–17 (1998) (surveying empirical studies of relationships between "polarity" and warfare, and reporting that some findings show "high numbers of crises during bipolar periods" but also "lower war magnitudes than with multipolar systems," and that other findings indicate "the lack of a substantive linear relationship between the number of great powers and warfare").

133 *See* Gaddis, *supra* note 132, at 230–31; and Mearsheimer, *supra* note 129, at 25–26; *see also* Evan Luard, The Blunted Sword: The Erosion of Military Power in Modern World Politics 31–32 (1988); Kenneth Waltz, *The Spread of Nuclear Weapons: More May Better,* Int'l Inst. for Strategic Studies, Adelphi Papers No. 171, (1981) (available at http://www.mtholyoke.edu/acad/intrel/waltz1.htm.).

134 *See* Gaddis, *supra* note 132, at 232–33; and Stephen Van Evera, Causes of War 24–33, 137–42 (1999).

135 *See* William R. Thompson, *Principal Rivalries,* 39 J. Conflict Resol. 195, 209–10 (1995).

136 *See* Evan Luard, War in International Society 68 (1986).

137 The NATO alliance might be viewed, not only as a means of deterring attack by Soviet forces, but also as a device by which American hegemony over Western Europe was subtly enforced. *See* Christopher Layne, *America as European Hegemon,* Nat'l Int., 17, 19 (2003).

138 For other factors coloring recent Western attitudes to war, including cultural changes, *see* Jeremy Black, Why Wars Happen 222–26, 229–32 (1998); *see also* Michael Howard, The Invention of Peace 98–113 (2000).

d. A Constructivist Epilogue

In view of legalist indeterminacy and realist-rationalist despair, a constructivist would see the attempt to construct "A New World Order" as quixotic or, more likely, raw propaganda for domestic consumption. Thus, the objective conditions of this period in international relations render the Kantian logic of "The New Order" inappropriate in the Hobbesian or Lockean logic of the current world environment.

2. Thesis 2—The Just War Prism's Gravitational Pull

Yet, the central appeal of the First Gulf War is that, to some degree, President Bush's articulation of U.S. war aims may have hewed more closely to the central tenets of the Just War tradition. The war meets the classic criteria of the Just War Theory—even if the U.S. motives were mixed, but there was a Just Cause: for plainly innocent Kuwaitis and the Kuwaiti state were the objects of a brutal attack; and there was wrongful taking of the property of the Kuwaiti state and its people (what a leading commentator on Middle Eastern affairs, Fouad Adjami, called one of the greatest "heists" in human history).[139] United States and the Security Council did not, explicitly at least, advance goals other than the reversal of the invasion, the return of this property, and just compensation. This demonstrated a "right intention" to re-establish the status quo ante. In fact, prospectively, the UN and Coalition rhetoric did no more than aspire to advance international order and, in the words of Resolution 678, "restore international peace and security in the area," although this perhaps left open whether "peace and security in the area" would be defined expansively to include a modicum of justice, the *tranquillitas ordinis.* The proportionality of the means used by the Coalition was further evidenced by its limited objectives, namely, its willingness to bring about a cessation of hostilities immediately after the Coalition completed the liberation of Kuwait. Regime change, which was never an explicit part of the mandate of Resolution 678, never became an explicit Coalition military objective (whether or not it might have become militarily feasible, a matter of great debate years later).[140]

Thus, one might agree that positive international law raised serious questions about the validity of the Council's "authorization"; that realist accounts called into question the motive and effects of the projection of U.S. military power into the Middle East; that rational choice analysis viewed the Coalition as unstable and the norms is was attempting to enforce and generate as doubtful; and that constructivist insights suggest that, like Versailles, where Wilson and his interlocutors never had a true meeting of the minds, the Security Council's temporary coalition masked deeper disagreements about the premises of world order. Granting all that, it seems

139 *See* Fouad Adjami, *The Summer of Arab Discontent,* 69 Foreign Affairs 1 (1990–91) (discussing the annexation of Kuwait).

140 *See generally* Bush and Scowcroft, *supra* note 89.

clear that the First Gulf War—through its appeal to moral principles that can be framed in terms of the Just War Tradition—legitimized change in the UN law of collective security.

We consider in the next chapter the First Gulf War's impetus, in particular the effect of Resolution 688, for legal change on the question of collective humanitarian intervention; and, in the following chapter, we consider the impact of the international community's experience in implementing the arms control provisions of Resolution 678 for the right of individual and collective right of self-defense against rogue states possessing, or threatening to possess, weapons of mass destructions.

Chapter 3

The Kosovo Crisis: Collective Humanitarian Intervention

In this chapter we consider the question of humanitarian intervention. We focus in particular on the case of the 1999 NATO bombing of Serbia in order to protect the people of Kosovo without an explicit Chapter VII authorizing resolution. We will also consider the subsequent legal and political debates surrounding this intervention. But to locate properly this study in its full context, we first explore the general and specific historical background. First, we discuss the pre-Versailles background for the protection of populations from genocide and other forms of oppression. This begins with interventions for the Greeks, Bulgarians, and Cubans, and the failure to intervene to save the Armenian people during the Armenian Genocide during the First World War. Second, we consider the lessons drawn from the origins of Second World War for the U.N. Charter, which appeared to delegitimize the practice of humanitarian intervention for the better part of the Cold War. Third, we consider the cases of collective humanitarian intervention in the aftermath of the end of the Cold War—cases in which the Security Council authorized intervention, in Iraq, Somalia and Haiti—and cases in which the UN failed to act, such as Rwanda and Bosnia-Herzegovina. Next, we explore in detail the background to the Kosovo affair as a prelude to your review of the key documents concerning the legal debate on the legality of the NATO intervention. This review includes excerpts from the defense offered before the International Court of Justice by NATO representatives during the bombing. It also includes the text of Security Council Resolution 1244, which was adopted following the bombing, not only to oversee an international process designed to reach an agreed Serb-Kosovar settlement on the status of Kosovo but also, in the interim, protect the people of Kosovo. These two documents provide the main sources for ex ante justification and ex post ratification of the NATO action. Finally, we comment on these and subsequent developments from realist, rational choice, legalist, constructivist, and Just War Theory perspectives.

With increased attention of the international media, the question of humanitarian intervention has recently become increasingly pressing (the so-called CNN effect). It is an idea with a long pedigree. We first explore its roots in the period leading to the Versailles Peace Conference, turn to the inter-war period and the reaction to the inter-war period in the U.N. Charter, and finally explore tentative steps of the international community to reclaim the practice of the 19th century.

1. The 19th Century Pre-History of Humanitarian Intervention

Humanitarian intervention as a political policy, and perhaps as an international legal concept, is a child of the 19th century. At the Congress of Vienna, which settled the Napoleonic Wars, Great Britain insisted on including abolishing the slave trade within French jurisdiction.[1] Following the Congress, the so-called "Concert of Europe" of the victorious powers—Britain, Russia, Prussia, and Austria (what later became the Austro-Hungarian Empire)—and defeated France sought to maintain the peace. But soon, liberal Britain and the conservative, monarchical powers of Russia, Prussia, and Austria (which came to be known as the Holy Alliance), became divided over the question of internal reform and fear of another French revolution, thus raising the question of intervention in the internal affairs of states.[2] When the Holy Alliance intervened to suppress anti-monarchical uprisings in the first half of the 19th century, liberals advocating for pro-democratic reform throughout Europe came to support non-intervention as a vehicle for ensuring that nascent democratic movements throughout Europe would not be suppressed by Russian, Prussian, or Austrian troops.[3]

In the aftermath of Russian intervention to defend Austrian power from Hungarian nationalist uprising after the "revolutions" of 1848,[4] English liberal John Stuart Mill argued that the doctrine of non-intervention could work only if "despots" and "free states" both played by the same rules. Accordingly, he argued that "liberal states" should engage in counter-intervention if despotic states intervened, in order to balance the scales of power.[5] But Mill seemed to feel the need to justify the policy not only on pragmatic grounds but also normatively, arguing "it seems now to be an admitted doctrine" that "outside powers are warranted in demanding that the context shall cease, and a reconciliation take place on equitable terms of compromise. Intervention of

1 *See* Gary Bass, Freedom's Battle: The Origins of Humanitarian Intervention 18 (2008).

2 *See* Henry Kissinger, A World Restored: Metternich, Castlereagh, and the Problems of Peace, 1812–22 (1973).

3 *See* Bass, *supra* note 1, at 353.

4 *See id.*

5 *See id.* at 355 (citing John Stuart Mill, A Few Words on Nonintervention, *in* Dissertations and Discussions: Political, Philosophical and Historical, vol. 3, 256–62 (1882)).

this description has been repeatedly practiced during the present generation, with such general approval, that its legitimacy may be considered to have passed into a maxim of what is called international law."[6] Nonetheless, Mill's views notwithstanding, even if counter-intervention were good policy, its legality continued to be under question.

Despite these doubts, support for intervention in the 19th century increased as it coalesced with concern over the atrocities committed by the Ottoman Empire in maintaining its control over its subject Christian peoples. Reports of the Turkish massacre of the rebellious Greek population on the island of Scio prompted the formation of the London Greek Committee to lobby for British intervention.[7] The question of humanitarian intervention in Greece deeply divided the Concert of Europe, with Austrian and Prussia opposed to intervention.[8] Indeed, the Ottoman Empire could reasonably ask why British attention focused on human rights violations in the Ottoman Empire rather than those committed by the Emperors of the Holy Alliance. When British officials objected to the sale into slavery of refugees from Scio, an Ottoman official replied: "Why do not the Christian Sovereigns interfere to prevent the Emperor of Russia from sending his subjects into Siberia? Because there is one law of humanity for Turkey and another for Russia!"[9] Notwithstanding the suggestion that British intervention reflected imperialism rather than humanitarianism, in time a coalition of French and Russian forces joined the British to defeat the Ottoman fleet at the battle of Navarino in 1827. This established European military supremacy, shattered Ottoman power in Greece, and served as the midwife to Greek independence.[10] The Greek situation served as a paradigm for humanitarian intervention for European liberals. And, as Mill suggested, it could be extended to other cases as the improvement of communications made the knowledge of repeated Ottoman atrocities more widely available. Indeed, for the next quarter-century, the great "Eastern Question"—meaning the inevitable dissolution of Ottoman power in Eastern Europe through regular national uprisings coupled with repressive measures shocking the conscience of the West—became the central issue in European Great Power politics.[11]

England was caught on the horns of a dilemma, however. While an ally to Russia on the question of Greece, England's geopolitical interests in limiting Russian expansion complicated Britain's policy as Ottoman atrocities continued; for Russian intervention to protect peoples under Ottoman rule threatened to bring Russian power in proximity with territories under British control. Similarly, to ensure France would not substantially undermine Ottoman power, England insisted that French intervention in Syria to protect Lebanese Christians ("Maronites") be limited

---

6 Mill, *supra* note 5, at 257 (quoted in Bass, *supra* note 1, at 41–42).

7 *See* Bass, *supra* note 1, at 67–79.

8 *See id.* at 363–64.

9 *Id.* at 358 (citations omitted).

10 *See id.* at 137–51.

11 *See generally* A.J.P. Taylor, The Struggle for Mastery in Europe 1848–1918 (1954).

in time and space.[12] The most important manifestation of this dilemma was Conservative British Prime Minister Disraeli's opposition in 1877 to Russian intervention to protect Bulgarians, even after massacres committed by Ottoman forces, because it would expand Russian and Austrian power, resulting in territorial gains for both (including Bosnia, occupied by Austria in 1878 and annexed finally in 1908, as payoff for supporting Russia).[13] Disraeli also held Russia partially responsible for the massacres since its Pan-Slav propaganda and policies had, in Disraeli's view, stimulated the Bulgarian uprising and thus brought upon the Bulgarians the wrath of the Ottoman Empire.[14] The question of intervention and its conflict with British Imperial policy became a central issue for former Prime Minister Gladstone during his famous campaign wresting power from Disraeli—the so-called "Midlothian" campaign of 1878-80, named for the seat for which Gladstone himself campaigned.[15] Thus, humanitarian intervention galvanized the British public into rejecting the calculations of *realpolitik* and doubts about international legality.

Humanitarian impulses played a similar role in U.S. foreign policy during this era, beginning with the Spanish-American War and leading up to President Wilson's proposed Fourteen Points. Beginning in 1896 Spanish General Valeriano Weyler initiated a policy of forcing Cuban peasants to "concentrate"—in what became known as the first "concentration camps"—in order to separate them from Cuban rebel forces seeking independence.[16] In 1894, the Ottoman Empire embarked on a policy of repressing Armenians in a manner so grotesque that the Hearst newspapers, which agitated for war against Spain, reported that "Cuba is our Armenia" and that the "American people will not tolerate in the Western Hemisphere the methods of the Turkish savages in Armenia, no matter what the cost of putting an end to them might be."[17] As it turned out, the war with Spain resulted ultimately in Cuban independence but also the annexation by the U.S. of Spanish-controlled Puerto Rico, Guam, and the Philippines, in the course of which U.S. forces fought a nearly decade-long counterinsurgency campaign to suppress independence forces in the Philippines.[18] Years later, Felix Frankfurter, a future U.S. Supreme Court Justice, was so concerned about the effect of the war on the reputation of the United States that he suggested that any future U.S. interventions in the Western Hemisphere receive multilateral authorization through a Pan-American international organization.[19]

---

12 *See generally* Bass, *supra* note 1, at 163–232.

13 *See id.* at 299–304.

14 *See id.* at 346.

15 *See id.* at 305–12.

16 *Id.* at 317.

17 Quoted in Bass, supra note 1, at 317 (citations omitted).

18 *See id.* at 317–18.

19 *See id.* at 363.

Yet, a decade later, despite this ambiguous legacy, for President Wilson the liberation of Cuba was "precursor to a wider U.S. defense of liberty in Poland, Bohemia, and Yugoslavia."[20] For Wilson, domestic repression was a factor causing the First World War and self-determination was the logical solution to the source of the problem. Thus, although the war began in the Balkans with the murder of the Archduke Francis Ferdinand by a Serbian fanatic objecting to Austrian control, Wilson extended his program outside Europe. The Twelfth of the famous Fourteen Points stated: "The Turkish possessions of the present Ottoman Empire should be assured a secure sovereignty, but the other nationalities which are now under Turkish rule should be assured an undoubted security of life and an absolutely unmolested opportunity of autonomous development ..."[21] Whatever Wilson's true intentions, at Versailles he faced the political problem of the pre-existing Sykes-Picot agreement of 1916, in which Britain and France had already made plans to carve up the Ottoman Empire in the Middle East.[22] And, with respect to Armenia in particular—even after the "Young Turks" orchestrated the murder of at least several hundred thousand and perhaps more than a million Armenians during 1915-1916 (in what later came to be called "Genocide")[23]—neither Wilson nor the French or British were prepared to accept responsibility for Armenia as a mandate under the new League of Nations system.[24] At the same time, the rhetoric of Versailles, together with rules and institutions developed during the inter-war period to protect minority rights,[25] seemed to legitimize the aspirations that had given rise to humanitarian intervention by the major powers of Europe and the United States. Some even viewed the Versailles Treaty and the creation of the League of Nations as a return to the core Just War Theory idea that the whole international community had a right and duty to protect the innocent.[26] In the United States, a leading international law scholar and member of the U.S. delegation at the Versailles Conference, James Brown Scott, upon returning to the U.S. began work to recover the Just War Tradition, ultimately leading to the publication of his study of the work of the Spanish neo-scholastics, Vitoria and Suarez.[27] All this was to come crashing down as German troops marched into Prague in 1938.

---

20 *Id.* at 318.

21 Quoted in Margaret MacMillan, Paris 1919: Six Days That Changed the World 496 (2003).

22 *See* Bass, *supra* note 1, at 334–35.

23 *See generally* Samantha Power, A Problem form Hell: America and the Age of Genocide (2003).

24 *See* Bass, *supra* note 1, at 319–40.

25 *See generally* Nathaniel Berman, *But the Alternative is Despair: European Nationalism and the Modernist Renewal of International Law*, 106 Harv. L. Rev. 1792 (1993) (detailing provisions of Versailles and subsequent inter-war practice providing for the protection of minorities in the states after Versailles).

26 *See* Stephen C. Neff, War and the Law of Nations 292–93 (2005) (commenting on the reaction of Pope Pius XI on the 600th anniversary of the canonization of Thomas Aquinas, the principal author of medieval Catholic Just War Theory).

27 *See* James Brown Scott, The Catholic Conception of International Law (1934).

2. The Lessons of the Second World War and the U.N. Charter

In a sense, the road to the post-World War II period's delegitimizing of humanitarian intervention runs through the Sudetenland. President Wilson never expected the Versailles Conference to make definitive territorial settlements under the principle of self-determination. Rather, he expected the League of Nations to discharge a continuing responsibility for correcting whatever mistakes the peacemakers had made and adjusting the settlement to take into account changing circumstances.[28] One of those possible mistakes was the inclusion of the Sudetenland ("south-land") Germans[29] in the new state of Czechoslovakia. While Sudetenland Germans comprised a substantial percentage of the population of Bohemia, they had been under Austro-Hungarian, not German, control for centuries. Thus, German representatives at the Versailles conference made little effort to campaign for the Sudetenland's inclusion in Germany, preferring instead to focus on other territorial objectives.[30] It would, in any event, have been a lost cause, since the Sudetenland's inclusion in Czechoslovakia was essential to the survival of that state for two reasons. First, Czechoslovakia could "not survive economically without the Sudetenland's sugar refineries, glassworks, textile mills, smelters and breweries." Second, the "Czechs needed the old frontiers, which ran along mountains and hills, to defend themselves."[31] But Czechoslovakia was a "Slav state." And the principals at Versailles, particularly U.S. Secretary of State Robert Lansing, feared that the principle of self-determination was being unduly compromised. To accommodate these concerns, the Czechs gave to their minorities, including the Sudetenland Germans, several "guarantees: their own schools, freedom of religion, even proportional representation, so that they could have their own representatives. Czechoslovakia was going to be the Switzerland of central Europe."[32]

This Czechoslovakia, the dream palace of the Versailles Conference, came crashing down in late 1938, in what was later seen as the turning point in Hitler's war of aggression.[33] It appeared at first to be the logical continuation of the politics of the Versailles settlement. In 1935 the promised plebiscite in the Saar, supervised by the League of Nations as promised by the Versailles Treaty, resulted in the reunification of the primarily German-speaking Saar with Germany. Nominally, Germany and German-speaking Austria were unified in the so-called *Anschluss*.[34]

28 *See* Sean Murphy, Humanitarian Intervention: The United Nations in an Evolving World Order 59 (1996) (suggesting that internal violations of human rights could constitute "disputes" for purposes of submission to international dispute resolution within the meaning of the League of Nations Covenant).

29 *See* MacMillan, *supra* note 21, at 235.

30 *See id.* at 237.

31 *Id.* at 236.

32 *Id.* at 237–38.

33 *See generally* Telford Taylor, Munich: The Price of Peace (1980); *See* Chapter 3, *supra; see also* Niall Ferguson, The War of the World: Twentieth-Century Conflict and the Descent of the West, 345–68 (2006).

34 *See* R.R. Palmer and Joel Colton, A History of the Modern World 794 (1978).

This set the stage for a German politico-military and psychological campaign, culminating at the Munich Conference in September 1938 in Western acquiescence in Germany's acquisition of the Sudetenland, with enormous consequences for the European balance of power.[35] Germany sought to delegitimize public resistance through a sustained propaganda campaign targeting British elites.[36] Returning from Munich, British Prime Minister Neville Chamberlain famously minimized his concession to German power, calling it a "quarrel in a faraway country between people of whom we know nothing."[37] Chamberlain hoped that "appeasing" aggrieved Germany would bring a final settlement—what Chamberlain called "peace with honor" and "peace in our time"—but his conclusions were premised on a fundamental misunderstanding of German objectives. Indeed, when England's foreign policy "accepted the legitimacy of 'self-determination' for the Sudeten Germans, it implicitly accepted the legitimacy of Hitler's goal of a Greater Germany"—in Poland, Lithuania, and throughout Central and Eastern Europe.[38] Germany claimed to be acting not only to fulfill the dream of Versailles, but also to protect Germans living under non-German governments from persecution, for Hitler complained to Chamberlain that the Czechs were "using force against my countrymen in the Sudetenland"; and, as German troops marched into the Sudetenland, he proclaimed "wild excesses have taken place in many villages to which again numerous Germans have fallen victims. From hour to hour the appeals for help from victims and persecuted are increasing."[39] Thus, the claim of humanitarian intervention, alloyed with the right of self-determination, served Nazi politico-military purposes against Czechoslovakia and the rest of Europe. Thus, the argument for humanitarian intervention became so tied to German imperialism that, in the collective memory of the following generation, the 19th century legacy of humanitarian intervention was forgotten or rejected.

In the aftermath of the Second World War, the United Nations in Article 2(4) of the Charter appeared to adopt a rule preventing the threat or use of force "against the territorial integrity or political independence of any state, or in any other matter inconsistent with the Purposes of the United Nations."[40] It may be possible to parse this language and its negotiating history to construct arguments supporting humanitarian intervention as not "against the territorial integrity or political independence of a state" and, indeed, actually consistent rather "inconsistent with

35 According to Niall Ferguson, "Hitler gained immediately after Munich. With Czechoslovakia emasculated, Germany's eastern frontier was significantly less vulnerable. Moreover, in occupying the Sudetenland, the Germans acquired at a stroke 1.5 million rifles, 750 aircraft, 600 tanks, and 2,000 field guns, all of which were to prove useful in the months to come. Indeed, more than one in ten of the tanks used by the Germans in their Western offensive of 1940 were Czech-built. The industrial resources of Western Bohemia further strengthened Germany's war machine, just as the *Anschluss* has significantly added to Germany's supplies of labour, hard current and steel." Ferguson, *supra* note 33, at 367–68.

36 *See* Bass, *supra* note 1, at 39.

37 *Id.* at 19 (citations omitted); and Ferguson, *supra* note 33, at 345 (citations omitted).

38 *See id.* at 346–48.

39 Bass, *supra* note 1, at 39 (citations omitted).

40 U.N. Charter, art. 2, para. 4.

the Purposes of the United Nations" (which include "self-determination" and "promoting and encouraging respect for human rights").[41] But the consensus at the end of the Cold War was that these views did not reflect the dominant interpretation of the Charter or the practice of states.[42] Perhaps no other conclusion was possible in light of the experience of German aggression and the Munich Conference.

Commenting on arguments for an exception, Professor Oscar Schachter's summary of the state of the law concerning humanitarian intervention at the end of the Cold War remains canonical:

> These arguments, appealing as they seem to be have failed to win the explicit support of the international community of States or of any significant segment of that community. No United Nations resolution has supported the right of a State to intervene on humanitarian grounds with armed troops in a State that has not consented to such intervention. Nor is there evidence of State practice and related *opinion juris* on a scale sufficient to support a humanitarian exception to the general prohibition against non-defensive use of force.... It is true that, in a few cases, the action of an intervening army outside of its borders was seen as serving a humanitarian end because it saved innocent lives from death or injury. Whether these cases can be considered as precedents accepted as law is dubious, especially as no intervening state claimed a legal right based on that ground. Thus, when Indian troops acted to protect Bengalis in East Pakistan in 1971 from Pakistani troops, India asserted the action was necessary to protect its borders.... Despite much sympathy for the East Pakistani Bengalis, the great majority of States were clearly unwilling to legitimize India's armed action as a permissible exception to Article 2(4).... A second case that some lawyers have viewed as humanitarian intervention occurred when Tanzanian troops moved into Uganda following a Ugandan frontier incursion repulsed by Tanzania. Actually, Tanzania claimed self-defense rather than a right of humanitarian intervention ... A claim of humanitarian intent was used by Vietnam to support armed action in Cambodia in 1978 against the Pol Pot forces.... The majority of States in the United Nations have rejected the Vietnamese contentions and called for the withdrawal of its troops.... Our sympathy for victims of atrocities should not obscure the lessons of past invasions claimed to be humanitarian. Past armed interventions, going back to the 19th century incursions by imperial powers, have shown that intervening States have invariably had their own political agenda. They imposed conditions that were not freely chosen by the people of the country in question. They often obtained special advantages and exacerbated internal conflicts. It is hardly surprising that governments have refrained

41 U.N. Charter, art. 1 paras. 2, 3. Indeed, many authors have done so. *See, e.g.*, Simon Chesterman, Just War or Just Peace?: Humanitarian Intervention in International Law 48–53 (2001).

42 *See* Chesterman, *supra* note 41, at 50 n.29 (acknowledging consensus contrary to his revisionist views).

from adopting a general rule for humanitarian intervention. Indeed, I believe no government has actually declared itself as favoring so broad an exception to the rule against force.[43]

With the end of the Cold War and the activation of the Security Council, however, the practice of states appeared to revive the 19th century tradition of multilateral humanitarian intervention, albeit initially only with explicit Security Council authorization under Chapter VII of the Charter.

3. The Post-Cold War Emerging Practice of Collective Humanitarian Intervention under Chapter VII Authorization

It is difficult to understand the political and legal context of humanitarian intervention by NATO without considering the legal and practical difficulties the United Nations experiences in Somalia and Haiti, as well as the cases of non- or misfeasance by the Security Council and the rest of the international community in Rwanda and Bosnia-Herzegovina. But these cases in turn cannot be understood without an assessment of the paradigm established in the aftermath of the First Gulf War to save Iraqi Kurds from extermination by the defeated regime of Saddam Hussein.

a. The "Precedent" of the First Gulf War—Security Council Resolution 688

After the liberation of Kuwait from Iraqi occupation in early 1991, the Security Council's adopted Resolution 688, "condemn[ing] the repression of the Iraqi civilian population in many parts of Iraq, including most recently in Kurdish populated areas, the consequences of which threaten international peace and security in the region." It also demanded that "Iraq, as a contribution to remove the threat to international peace and security in the region, immediately end this repression." [44] To many, this seemed to signal a new view about the legitimacy and legality of humanitarian intervention. On the other hand, others viewed it as potentially illegitimate

43 Schachter, International Law in Theory and Practice 123–25 (1991); *but see, e.g.,* Anthony D'Amato, International Law: Process and Prospect 57–73 (1987); Fernando R. Tesón, Humanitarian Intervention: An Inquiry into Law and Morality (1997)(interpreting the positive law to accord with non-positivist norms).

44 S.C. Res. 688, op. paras. 1-2, U.N. Doc. S/RES/688 (April 5, 1991) [hereinafter S.C. Res. 688]. This highly debated Resolution provides, as follows:

The Security Council,

Mindful of its duties and its responsibilities under the Charter of the United Nations for the maintenance of international peace and security,

Recalling of Article 2, paragraph 7, of the Charter of the United Nations,

Gravely concerned by the repression of the Iraqi civilian population in many parts of Iraq, including most recently in Kurdish populated areas, which led to a massive flow of refugees towards and across international frontiers and to cross-border incursions, which threaten international peace and security in the region,

Deeply disturbed by the magnitude of the human suffering involved,

Taking note of the letters sent by the representatives of Turkey and France to the United Nations dated 2 April 1991 and 4 April 1991, respectively (S/22435 and S/22442),

projection of U.S., British and French power into the Middle East, facilitated by the earlier U.S. call for an uprising by the Iraqi people to overthrow Saddam Hussein,[45] echoing Disraeli's suggestion that Russia had incited Bulgarian uprisings against Ottoman rule. The truth may lie somewhere in between.

The immediate context for the adoption of Resolution 688 was reports of a developing humanitarian catastrophe in Iraq, especially northern Iraq where remaining Iraq military units were slaughtering Kurds who had taken advantage of the defeat of Iraqi forces in Kuwait to attempt to secede. Previous such Kurdish uprisings had been suppressed by Saddam Hussein through the use of chemical weapons. In this situation, the measures employed by the Iraqi military attacking Kurdish villages resulted in an estimated two million civilian refugees, including perhaps one million Kurds attempting to cross the border into primarily Kurdish territories in Turkey. In the face of this potential catastrophe, France proposed and, after extensive negotiations, the Security Council on April 5 adopted Resolution 688.[46] On April 7, concerned no doubt in part by the risk of the possible effects in fomenting Kurdish separatism in Turkey, the Turkish President called for the creation of internationally-supervised "safe havens" in Iraq for the Kurdish people. The next day British Prime Minister called for the creation of UN-protected Kurdish enclaves in northern Iraq, believing that 'the rubric exists within [resolution] 688 to avoid the need for a separate resolution." On April 10, the United States announced that it would enforce a prohibition against any Iraqi fixed- or rotary-wing aircraft flying north of the 36th parallel," the so-called northern "no-fly zone," which left strategic Iraqi oil reserves near the city of largely Kurdish Kirkuk outside Coalition protection, thereby reducing the incentive for Kurdish

---

Taking note also of the letters sent by the Permanent Representative of the Islamic Republic of Iran to the United Nations dated 3 and 4 April 1991, respectively (S/22436 and S/22447),

Reaffirming the commitment of all Member States to the sovereignty, territorial integrity and political independence of Iraq and of all States in the area,

Bearing in mind the Secretary-General's report of 20 March 1991(S/22366),

1. Condemns the repression of the Iraqi civilian population in many parts of Iraq, including most recently in Kurdish populated areas, the consequences of which threaten international peace and security in the region;
2. Demands that Iraq, as a contribution to remove the threat to international peace and security in the region, immediately end this repression and express the hope in the same context that an open dialogue will take place to ensure that the human and political rights of all Iraqi citizens are respected;
3. Insists that Iraq allow immediate access by international humanitarian organizations to all those in need of assistance in all parts of Iraq and to make available all necessary facilities for their operations;
4. Requests the Secretary-General to pursue his humanitarian efforts in Iraq and to report forthwith, if appropriate on the basis of a further mission to the region, on the plight of the Iraqi civilian population, and in particular the Kurdish population, suffering from the repression in all its forms inflicted by the Iraqi authorities;
5. Requests further the Secretary-General to use all the resources at his disposal, including those of the relevant United Nations agencies, to address urgently the critical needs of the refugees and displaced Iraqi population;
6. Appeals to all Member States and to all humanitarian organizations to contribute to these humanitarian relief efforts;
7. Demands that Iraq cooperate with the Secretary-General to these ends;
8. Decides to remain seized of the matter.

45 *See* Chesterman, *supra* note 41, at 196–206.

46 *Id.* at 130–31 (citations omitted).

secession. At the same time, the United States warned Iraq to cease attacks on the Kurdish population and, when Iraq failed to comply, on April 16 announced that "consistent with resolution 688," U.S. troops would enter Iraq north of the 36th parallel to establish safe-havens for the Kurdish population, the so-called "Provide Comfort" operation. During August 1992, to protect the southern Iraqi Shi'ites from similar threats from the central authorities in Baghdad, the United States and its allies established a second "no-fly zone" below the 32nd parallel.[47]

While the United States and United Kingdom relied on Resolution 688, they did not initially explain the basis for their legal theory. In January 1993 Coalition forces relied again on Resolution 688 to attack Iraqi missile launchers threatening to challenge the southern no-fly zone, as well as to respond to other violations by Iraq of its obligations under Resolution 687.[48] In defending the legality of those operations, the Secretary-General of the U.N., Boutros Boutros-Ghali, asserted: "the forces that have carried out the raid have received a mandate from the Security Council, according to Resolution 678, and the cause of the raid was a violation by Iraq of Resolution 687 concerning the ceasefire. So, as Secretary-General of the United Nations, I can say that this action was taken and conforms to the resolutions of the Security Council and conforms to the Charter of the United Nations."[49] In relying on Resolution 678 and 687, the Secretary General made no explicit reference to Resolution 688, although Coalition authorities relied on Resolution 688 for both no-fly zones. Resolution 678 authorized the Coalition "to use all necessary means to uphold and implement Resolution 660 (1990) [calling for the withdrawal of Iraqi forces from Kuwait] and all subsequent relevant resolutions and to restore international peace and security in the area."[50] Thus, insofar as Resolution 688 determined that the Iraq's repressive measures "threatened international peace and security in the region,"[51] it might have been read to authorize the Coalition to take "all necessary means," including operation Provide Comfort and the establishment of no-fly zones, to "restore international peace security in the area." Indeed, no nation objected to Operation Provide Comfort.[52]

But, for reasons we will discuss further in our case study concerning the Second Gulf War, the claim that Resolution 678 provided the Coalition members with continuing legal authority to use force to implement any and all Security Council resolutions concerning Iraq has proved contentious.[53] Indeed, by late 1992, the British explicitly relied only on customary international law rather

---

47 *See id.* at 197–99 (citations omitted).

48 *See generally* Part II, Chapter 2, *supra,* at nn. 105-106.

49 Quoted in Chesterman, *supra* note 41, at 201 (citations omitted).

50 S.C. Res. 678, 45 U.N. SCOR at 27, U.N. Doc. S/RES/678 (November 29, 1990).

51 *See* S.C. Res. 688, *supra* note 44, at para. 2.

52 *See* Chesterman, *supra* note 41, at 200 (citing Nigel Rodley, Collective Intervention to Protect Human Rights and Civilian Populations: The Legal Framework, *in* To Loose the Bands of Wickedness: International Intervention in Defense of Human Rights 235, 233 (Rodley ed. 1992)).

53 *See* Chesterman, *supra* note 41, at 201–03.

than Security Council authorization to defend their participation in humanitarian intervention in Iraq to protect the Kurds and Shi'ites.[54] Thus, the British were not inclined to interpret Resolution 678, at least on this point, to give the Coalition broad and continuing authority.

Moreover, even if the authority to use force under Resolution 678 survived the adoption of Resolution 687, the negotiating history and context of Resolution 688 calls into question whether it should have been interpreted to give rise to enforcement authority for humanitarian violations in Iraq, much less suggesting that such occasions in general are within the scope of the Security Council's authority under Chapter VII. Because Resolution was 688 was adopted in the special context of a series of Security Council resolutions treating the overall situation in Iraq, including the destabilizing, indirect effects of the Security Council authorized use of force, one could easily view it as an aberration and a unique situation. Second, on its own terms it may have actually reinforced the principle of nonintervention. It was the first of the Iraq Security Council Resolutions following Iraq's invasion of Kuwait not to state explicitly that the Council was acting under Chapter VII; it referred instead to Article 2(7), in a crucial amendment necessary to secure the requisite votes for its adoption, particularly the support the USSR and acquiescence of the PRC as Permanent members of the Council who could veto its adoption.[55] Moreover, in its preambular language the resolution referred to "the repression ...in Kurdish populated areas, which led to a massive flow of refugees towards and across international frontiers and to cross-border incursions, which threaten international peace and security in the region."[56] Thus, it was arguably only the trans-boundary effects of domestic repression that justified the Council's judgment of fact that the internal situation was within its jurisdiction under Chapter VII.[57] Indeed, a study of the legislative history of the Resolution reveals that only France (albeit the resolution's drafter whose views might be entitled to significant weight) asserted that the "[v]iolations of human rights such as those now being observed become a matter of international interest when they take on such proportions that they assume the dimension of a crime against humanity."[58] States could thus reasonably hold the view that Resolution 688 at most evidenced Security Council Chapter VII authority to intervene to stop domestic atrocities only when those atrocities have substantial international effects.

In sum, if Resolution 688 was a precedent for UN-authorized humanitarian intervention, it was a transitional precedent, since its ambiguous language and context could safely allow states

54 In a written response to a question from Parliament to the Foreign and Commonwealth Office of Legal Counsel, Anthony Aust replied: "Resolution 688, which applies not only to northern Iraq but to the whole of Iraq, was not made under Chapter VII. Resolution 688 recognized that there was a severe human rights and humanitarian situation in Iraq and, in particular, northern Iraq; but the intervention in northern Iraq, "Provide Comfort" was in fact, not specifically mandated by the United Nations, but the state taking action in northern Iraq did so in exercise of the customary international law principle of humanitarian intervention." Quoted in Chesterman, *supra* note 41, at 204.

55 *Id.* at 132 (citations omitted).

56 S.C. Res. 688, *supra* note 44, at preamble para. 3.

57 *See* Chesterman, *supra* note 41, at 132.

58 Quoted in Chesterman, *supra*, at 132–33 (citation omitted).

and scholars to rely on the narrowest possible interpretation of the Security Council's authority in respect of atrocities committed within states. On the other hand, even under the narrow theory of Resolution 688 under which the authority to intervene is predicated on refugee flows, it would be hard to imagine any substantial program of domestic repression that would not result in a flow of refugees. In practice, it might prove hard to confine the precedent. The logic of this argument seems to have been fully corroborated by subsequent Security Council practice.

b. Subsequent Practice of UN-authorized Humanitarian Intervention

After the First Gulf War, the Permanent Five of the Security Council were able to reach consensus on a number of other humanitarian missions, most notably in Somalia and Haiti. These seemed initially to be legitimate and expand humanitarian intervention, albeit bordering on pro-democratic intervention. But in time, mission creep, selectivity, and operational ineffectiveness called into doubt the U.N.'s capacity to authorize or implement humanitarian intervention legitimately and effectively.

With the collapse of the regime of Siad Barre in January 1991 as a result of the decline of Soviet influence, a power vacuum ensued in Somalia, sparking a clan-based civil war in which access to food was used as a weapon. By late January 1992, the office of the U.N. High Commissioner for Refugees (UNHCR) was reporting that 140,000 Somali refugees had reached Kenya with more coming every day. The Security Council, "Gravely alarmed at the rapid deterioration of the situation in Somalia and the heavy loss of human life and widespread material damage resulting from the conflict in the country and aware of its consequences on the stability and peace in the region," imposed an arms embargo.[59] Then, after the Secretary General reported to the Council that relief operations could continue only through an enforcement operation authorized by the Security Council,[60] the Council intervened to prevent a humanitarian catastrophe. It "[e]xpress[ed] grave alarm at continuing reports of widespread violations of international humanitarian law occurring in Somalia, including reports of violence and threats of violence against personnel participating lawfully in impartial humanitarian relief activities; deliberate attacks on non-combatants, relief consignments and vehicles, and medical and relief facilities; and impeding the delivery of food and medical supplies essential for the survival of the civilian population," and on this basis authorized "the Secretary-General and Member States cooperating in the offer [of the United States] to use all necessary means to establish ... a secure environment for humanitarian relief operation in Somalia...."[61] The Somalia intervention thus advanced the case for the legality of UN-authorized humanitarian intervention under Chapter VII of the

59 *See* S.C. Res. 733, U.N. Doc. S/RES/733 (Jan. 23, 1992) (imposing an arms embargo on Somalia based on the conclusion that the humanitarian crisis in Somalia posed "a threat to international peace and security").

60 *See* Chesterman, *supra* note 41, at 141.

61 S.C. Res. 794, para. 8, U.N. Doc. S/RES/794; 47 U.N. SCOR at 63, U.N. Doc. S/INF/48 (1992) (Dec. 3, 1992).

Charter beyond Resolution 688, with the Secretary General calling it the first time in the history of the UN that it had intervened "militarily for strictly humanitarian purposes."[62] Like the Iraqi-Kurdish situation, refugee flows from Somalia were deemed to give rise to a threat to international peace and security. But, unlike the Iraqi-Kurdish situation, the conflict, although giving rise to a similar humanitarian catastrophe, was of entirely domestic origin.

But the Somalia humanitarian intervention did not come without political costs. By late 1993, U.S. forces deployed in support of the U.N. relief operation became embroiled in the Somali civil war, with American corpses dragged through the streets of Mogadishu, images that were flashed before the American viewing public. In the United States at least, this "mission creep" delegitimized the use of U.S. ground forces for "nation building" and humanitarian intervention.[63] This "Somalia syndrome" that followed may have played a role in discouraging the Security Council from taking action against the Rwandan Genocide of April 1994 when, according to the Secretary General, somewhere between 250,000 and 500,000 Rwandan Tutsis were massacred by Rwandan Hutus nearly and perhaps another 1.5 million were displaced.[64] Much of the human cost occurred well after the scale of the Hutu campaign was known, as the commander of pre-existing U.N. mission of peacekeepers (U.N. Mission in Rwanda or UNAMIR), made clear that UNAMIR lacked the resources and mandate to take action to prevent further massacres. The initial rejection of a French offer to intervene with Security Council authorization was rejected, because of France's close relationship with the genocidal Hutu regime).[65] Thus, it was only after months of delay that the United Nations finally adopted a Chapter VII resolution accepting France's offer to deploy force using "all necessary means" to "(a) [c]ontribute to the security and protection of displaced persons, refugees and civilians at risk in Rwanda, including through the establishment and maintenance, where feasible, of secure humanitarian areas; and (b) [p]rovide security and support for the distribution of relief supplies and humanitarian relief operation."[66] But by then, it was too late. While French forces did play a marginal role beginning in late June, it was the Tutsi rebels based in the borderland with Uganda (the Rwandan Patriotic Front) under the leadership of Paul Kagame that overthrew the Rwandan Hutu-dominated government and brought the genocide to a halt.[67] The effect of Western reluctance, however, was to call into question the Security Council's impartiality in deciding whether to intervene to stop a humanitarian catastrophe.

The perception that the Security Council was engaging in selective humanitarian intervention was exacerbated by the Council's eventual response to the situation in Haiti. In that case,

62 Chesterman, *supra* note 41, at 142 (citation omitted).

63 *See* Derek Chollet & James Goldgeier, America Between the Wars 72–83 (2008); Chesterman, *supra* note 41, at 143.

64 *See* Chesterman, *supra* note 41, at 144–45 (citations omitted).

65 *See id.* at 145–47.

66 S.C. Res. 929, para. 3, U.N. Doc. S/RES/929 (June 22, 1994) (referencing the humanitarian objectives set forth in paras. 4(a) and (b) of Resolution 925); S.C. Res. 925, U.N. Doc. S/RES/925 (June 8, 1994).

67 *See* Power, *supra* note 23, at 380–81.

the September 30, 1991 overthrow of the democratically-elected President of Haiti Jean-Bertrand Aristide caused internal strife, which in turn caused refugee flows. Yet, these refugee flows were firmly suppressed through U.S. interdiction activities on the high seas. Accordingly, while the Organization of American States adopted economic sanctions against Haiti, no Security Council Resolution followed because of resistance from China and the vast majority of states. That said, as conditions within Haiti worsened, the Security Council finally acted in June 1993 under Chapter VII against the de facto Haitian authorities.[68] Resolution 841 imposed an arms embargo and economic sanctions, in light of, among other things, "the incidence of humanitarian crises, including mass displacements of population, becoming or aggravating threats to international peace and security," because "the persistence of this situation contributes to a climate of fear of persecution and economic dislocation which could increase the number of Haitians seeking refuge in neighbouring Member States and [because the Council was] convinced that a reversal of this situation is needed to prevent its negative repercussions on the region."[69] Finally, after these measures failed to force the de facto authorities to withdraw, on July 31, 1994, the Security Council in Resolution 940 authorized the use of multilateral force through "all necessary means," along the lines of Resolution 678 with respect to the Iraq-Kuwait conflict, to "facilitate the departure of the military authorities ... and return of the legitimately elected President" of Haiti.[70] With former U.S. President Jimmy Carter brokering an agreement, Aristide was returned to power without the use of force. If there were reservations about the Security Council-mediated coup, it was because of the dominance of the U.S. role in its own neighborhood, resurrecting fears of regional hegemony along the lines of earlier U.S. interventions in the region, most recently during the Cold War.[71]

In what may be the low point in the history of the United Nations, the murder of thousands of Bosnian Muslims in July 1995 may have crystallized doubts about the U.N's capacity and willingness to prevent humanitarian catastrophe, thereby resurrecting the 19th century criticism that there was "one law of humanity" for Christians, and another for non-Christians. The U.N. role began when the process of dissolution of the Socialist Federal Republic of Yugoslavia (SFRY) careened out of control through the early 1990s. The former province of Slovenia, after only brief fighting, achieved its independence with the Brioni agreement of July 7, 1991. Croatian independence took longer, as Croatian forces battled the Yugoslav National Army (JNA) and Croatian Serb militias until a ceasefire was achieved on January 2, 1992.[72] When the fighting was at its height, the Security Council adopted under Chapter VII a mandatory embargo of arms "to

68 *See generally* Chesterman, *supra* note 41, at 152–55.

69 S.C. Res. 841, preambular paras. 9, 11, and operative paras. 5–6, U.N. Doc. S/RES/841 (June 16, 1993).

70 S.C. Res. 941, U.N. Doc. S/RES/941 (July 31, 1994).

71 *See* Chesterman, *supra* note 41, at 155 (citations omitted).

72 *See* U.N. Secretary-General, Pursuant to General Assembly Resolution 53/15 The Fall of Srebrenica, para. 11, U.N. Doc. A.54/549 (Nov. 15, 1995) [hereinafter "Report on The Fall of Srebrenica"].

Yugloslavia."[73] The effect of the embargo, however, was to complicate the U.N. role in the Balkans, for it denied arms not only to the JNA and Serb militias but also to forces in the remaining disaffected members of the Yugoslav federation attempting to defend themselves from Serb forces.

As Bosnian Muslins became victims of what came to me known as "ethnic cleansing," the United Nations did step into action. The UN Protection Force (UNPROFOR) had been established in February 1992 to interpose only between Serbian and Croat forces.[74] In April 1992, however, Bosnia-Herzegovina joined Slovenia and Croatia in being recognized as independent states by both the United States and the European Community.[75] UNPROFOR's mandate, together with the obligation of all parties not to impair UNPROFOR's freedom of movement, was now expanded to extend to Sarajevo and its airport in Bosnia-Herzegovina.[76] After continued conflict, the Security Council, in an unprecedented decision, "demand[ed] that all parties and others concerned treat Srebrenica and its surroundings as a safe area which should be free from any armed attack or any other hostile act" and to cooperate in UNPROFOR's enforcement of this "safe area."[77] The Security Council, acting under Chapter VII, then authorized NATO air strikes to enforce UNFROFOR's mandate.[78] Yet, as detailed in the Secretary-General's 1999 report on the "Fall of Srebrenica," on July 11, 1995 Bosnian Serb paramilitaries overran Srebrenica and killed over 8000 Bosnian Muslims. UNPROFOR's Dutch units did nothing because the Minister of Defense of the Netherlands, fearing that Serb forces would take action against the Dutch units, intervened to terminate NATO air action directed at the Serb forces attacking Srebrenica.[79]

As the truth became more widely known, Western public opinion turned in favor of a more active role NATO.[80] This resulted in an intense campaign of NATO air strikes, nominally to enforce the prior UN Security Council Chapter VII resolutions, and an agreement settling Bosnia-Herzegovina's status was brokered by the United States at Dayton and formally signed

---

73 S.C. Res. 713, para. 6, U.N. Doc. S/RES/713 (Sept. 25, 1991).

74 *See* S.C. Res. 743, U.N. Doc. S/RES/743 (Feb. 21, 1992).

75 *See* Lori Damrosch, Louis Henkin, Sean Murphy, & Hans Smit, International Law: Cases and Materials 318–20 (5th ed. 2009); See U.S. Recognition of Former Yugoslav Republics, 3 Dep't of State Dispatch 287 (April 13, 1992).

76 *See* S.C. Res. 757, U.N. Doc. S/RES/757 (May 30, 1991) (with para. 10 stating the Council's decision: "States, parties and others concerned shall cooperate fully with UNPROFOR, the Conference on Yugoslavia and the European Community Monitor Mission and respect fully their freedom of movement and the safety of their personnel," and para. 17 stating the Council's demand that "all parties and others concerned create immediately the necessary conditions for unimpeded delivery of humanitarian supplies to Sarajevo and other destinations in Bosnia and Herzegovina, including the establishment of a security zone encompassing Sarajevo and its airport and respecting the agreements signed in Geneva on 22 May 1992"); *see also* S.C. Res. 758, op. para. 2, 8, U.N. Doc. S/RES/758 (June 8, 1992).

77 S.C. Res. 819, para. 1, U.N. Doc. S/RES/819 (Apr. 16, 1993).

78 *See* S.C. Res. 836, U.N. Doc. S/RES/836 (June 4, 1993).

79 *See* Report on The Fall of Srebrenica, *supra* note 72, at para. 306; *See also* Damrosch, *supra* note 75, at 1261–62 and 1329; and Chesterman, *supra* note 41, at 173.

80 *See generally* Power, *supra* note 23, at 411–441.

at Paris on December 14, 1995.[81] The settlement was then approved by the Security Council acting under Chapter VII, under which a new Stabilization Force (SFOR) replaced UNFROFOR,[82] which in turn remained in Bosnia-Herzegovina until 2004 when it was replaced by forces from the European Union.[83]

In sum, while the legitimacy of collective humanitarian intervention under Chapter VII authorization may have received substantial support, the Council's decision and the implementation of its decisions left much to be desired. In Somalia and Haiti, it is arguable that the United Nations did too much. While resolutions were formally grounded on the humanitarian crisis and the threat of refugee flows as a threat to international peace and security, the core of the Security Council's complaint in Somalia was an ongoing civil war and in Haiti the overthrow of a democratically-elected government. Questions that were historically at the core of the non-intervention doctrine, especially in Haiti, were now the ultimate source of the evil; preventing a threat to the peace required preventing repression and refugee flows, which in turn required a change in government.

But in Rwanda and Bosnia, it appeared that the United Nations did too little, too late. Whatever their true cause, these experiences delegitimized the perceived consensus that specific UN-authorization was a condition precedent to collective humanitarian intervention when the Council as a whole refused to act. Assignment of blame for the U.N.'s failure to prevent the massacre at Srebrenica—whether in the design of the governing Security Council resolutions, their implementation by UN peacekeepers, or the support provided by the Member States comprising NATO—has spawned enormous controversy. Secretary General Koffi Annan --writing after the NATO in 1999 intervention without U.N. authorization to save the Kosovars from Yugoslavia – rationalized that "the Security Council, although acting under Chapter VII of the Charter, had provided no resources or mandate for UNPROFOR to impose its demands on the parties."[84] Yet, whatever the true cause, decision-makers in NATO countries could reasonably be expected to make determined efforts to avoid further Srebrenicas.

This background forms part of the legal and political context in which NATO acted in 1999 to defend the Kosovars from Serbia, in the absence of specific U.N. authorization under a Chapter VII resolution. A full understanding of the NATO decision, however, also requires an understanding of the historical context of the dispute between the Serbs and the Kosovars, which came to a climax in 1999.

---

81 *See* General Framework Agreement for Peace in Bosnia and Herzegovina, U.N. Doc. S/1995/999 (Nov. 30, 1995), 35 I.L.M. 75 (1996).

82 *See* S.C. Res. 1031, U.N. Doc. S/RES/1031 (Dec. 15, 1995).

83 *See* Damrosch, *supra* note 75, at 1262.

84 Report on the Fall of Srebrenica, *supra* note 72, at para. 56.

Until its declaration of independence in February 2008, Kosovo (or, in Albanian, "Kosova") was formally a province of about 4,200 square miles (somewhat smaller than the state of Connecticut) located in southern Serbia.[85] In 1999, Kosovo was the scene of the last of the four "Yugoslav wars"—Slovenia (1991), Croatia (1991-1992), Bosnia (1992-1995), and Kosovo (1999)—that attended the breakup of the former Socialist Federated Republic of Yugoslavia (SFRY or the former Yugoslavia).[86] In addition to the four violent secessions from the former Yugoslavia, a fifth secession occurred when the then-union of Serbia and Montenegro in the Federal Republic of Yugoslavia (FRY) ended with the peaceful secession of the latter on June 3, 2006.[87] Montenegro was admitted into the United Nations on June 28, 2006.[88] Prior to 1999 and for many decades before that, the population of Kosovo was overwhelmingly Albanian in ethnicity and Moslem in faith.[89] Historically, however, Kosovo was an important part of the religious and cultural inheritance of the Serbs, a Slavic and Orthodox Christian people, and was known to them as "Old Serbia."[90]

The former Yugoslavia became an independent state in December 1918, almost immediately after the end of the First World War.[91] From the beginning it was an ethnically and religiously divided state, predominantly populated by Slavic peoples, of which the two largest groups were the Serbs and the Croats.[92] The state was formed by the unification of the two southern states of Serbia and Montenegro with the former Austro-Hungarian territories of Croatia, Dalmatia, and Bosnia-Herzegovina.[93] (Serbia had previously seized Kosovo from the decaying Ottoman Empire during the First Balkan War (1912) and had thereafter annexed it.[94]) Relations between the major ethnic groups in the Yugoslav state from 1918 onward were difficult: the Croats feared and resented what they considered to be Serb domination of the state, while the Serbs had joined

85 *See generally* Noel Malcolm, Kosovo: A Short History (1998) (detailing the history of the Yugoslav state).

86 *See* Philip Bobbitt, The Shield of Achilles: War, Peace, and the Course of History 432 (2002).

87 *See* Yehuda Z. Blum, *Was Yugoslavia a Member of the United Nations in the Years 1992–2000?*, 101 Am. J. Int'l L. 800, 800 n. 2 (2007).

88 *See* G.A. Res. 60/264, U.N. Doc. A/RES/60/264 (June 28, 2006).

89 *See* Piotr Eberhardt, Ethnic Groups and Population Changes in Twentieth-Century Central-Eastern Europe 385–94 (Jan Owsinski trans., 2003).

90 *See* Peter Popham, Serbia Endorses Bomb Attack on Kosovo Border, The Independent, Feb. 20, 2008, at 18 (noting the view of Serbs "who are bitterly resentful of the fact that the province known as the historic heartland of 'Old Serbia' should have broken free").

91 *See* David Fromkin, Kosovo Crossing 128–30 (1999) (describing the events leading to the recognition of Yugoslavia as a nation); MacMillan, *supra* note 21, at 109–24 (detailing the circumstances of Yugoslavia's origin).

92 For a magisterial account of the peoples of the former Yugoslavia, their origins, and their ideologies before unification, *see generally* Ivo Banac, The National Question in Yugoslavia: Origins, History, and Politics 21–115 (1984).

93 *See id.* at 115–40 (detailing the establishment of the Yugoslav state).

94 *See id.* at 296 (describing the Serbian occupation and annexation of Kosovo in 1912–13).

the state precisely because they had intended to build it around themselves.[95] Nonetheless, geopolitical realities, including fear of encroachments by Italy, Hungary, or Bulgaria, tended to hold the union together.[96] With the invasion of Yugoslavia by Nazi Germany in the spring of 1941, however, inter-ethnic conflict broke out.[97] Joining in the German victory "was the Croatian Ustase leader Ante Pavelic, who became Croatia's wartime leader" and eventually oversaw the killing of nearly half a million ethnic Serbs.[98] Resistance to the German occupation was divided between forces loyal to the pre-war monarchy and Communist partisans led by Josip Broz, himself an ethnic Croat who was better known by his *nom de guerre* "Tito."[99]

The Communist movement took power at the conclusion of the Second World War and proclaimed the Federal People's Republic of Yugoslavia in November 1945.[100] This Yugoslav state was constituted on the principle of what might be called ethno-federalism. This federal structure was sacrosanct, it being seen as one of the pillars of the communist Yugoslavia that emerged as a result of the Partisan struggle during World War II. Thus it appeared as a cardinal figure of all of communist Yugoslavia's constitutional documents (from 1946 to 1974). However, due to political control exercised by the highly centralized Communist Party of Yugoslavia, in reality the Yugoslav state in the immediate post-World War II years was a highly centralized state.[101] In this respect the leadership role of Tito was crucial. The state's "federal" structure consisted of six constituent "republics"—Serbia (including the provinces of Kosovo and Vojvodina), Croatia, Slovenia, Macedonia, Bosnia-Herzegovina, and Montenegro, whose boundaries were defined, with the notable exceptions of the Albanian majority in Kosovo and the Hungarian majority in Vojvodina, largely in terms of population distribution by ethnicity. As one scholar reports: The boundaries of the constituent republics corresponded more or less to the territorial distribution of particular ethnic groups, so that each ethnic group inhabited a particular constituent republic. However, some ethnic groups, such as the Serbs, formed significant minorities within constituent republics other than their own. There were also ethnic groups that did not have their own constituent republic, such as the Albanians and the Hungarians, who were concentrated respectively in the autonomous provinces of Kosovo and Vojvodina, within Serbia. According to the 1991 census, the last before the Yugoslav wars began, "five of the six republics were

95 *See* MacMillan, *supra* note 21, at 110 (describing the "separate nationalisms" growing in the region).

96 *See* Fromkin, *supra* note 91, at 141–43 (noting the perceived external threats to the Yugoslav state which allowed "the new borders to harden in the public mind").

97 *See* Malcolm, *supra* note 85, at 290 (detailing the circumstances of the German invasion and Yugoslavia's unconditional surrender).

98 Fromkin, *supra* note 91, at 145.

99 *See id.* at 146 (noting that Broz became better known as "Tito"); Malcolm, *supra* note 85, at 297–302 (describing the two resistance movements that emerged during the German invasion).

100 *See* Richard C. Frucht, Eastern Europe 431 (2005) (noting that the Communist-controlled Constituent Assembly established the Federal People's Republic of Yugoslavia on November 29, 1945).

101 *See* Peter Radan, The Break-up of Yugoslavia and International Law 147 (2002).

substantially mono-ethnic"; Bosnia was the exception.[102] Slovenia was 88% Slovene; Croatia 78% Croat; Serbia 66% Serb; Macedonia 65% Macedonian; Montenegro 62% Montenegrin. Because Albanian Kosovars boycotted the 1991 census, their exact numbers are unknown, but they are believed to have been 85% of the population of Kosovo.[103] However, substantial ethnic Serb minority populations existed outside Serbia, particularly in the Republics of Croatia and Bosnia-Herzegovina. Serbia's acceptance of the post-1945 system of internal borders was therefore conditional upon the Yugoslav federation's remaining centralized.[104]

Persisting ethnic tensions within the former Yugoslavia, though in general successfully suppressed by the Tito régime, led to constitutional changes in 1963 and again in 1974.[105] Under the 1974 constitution, which remained in force until the SFRY's breakup, a Presidential Council directed the government's affairs at the federal level. The Council consisted of the heads of the six republics together with the heads of the autonomous provinces Kosovo and Vojvodina. The chair of the Council rotated among its members.[106] The 1974 constitutional arrangements "gave the autonomous provinces of Kosovo and Vojvodina a status equivalent in most ways to that of the six republics themselves," including the right to issue their own constitutions, and confirmed rights earlier granted to the autonomous provinces to a role in federal economic decision making and even foreign policy.[107] Malcolm suggests that the 1974 constitution did not take the further step of making Kosovo a "republic" largely for fear that it might secede and join with Albania.[108] Indeed, some analysts contend that Yugoslavia's Communist régime had deliberately "'gerrymandered' the Constitution 'as a means of weakening the state's largest ethnic element,' the Serbs.""[109] As a result, the 1974 constitution was extremely unsatisfactory to many Serbs, who preferred a more centralized state, despite ethnic Serbian predominance in the federal Yugoslav Army and the federal governmental apparatus.[110] A well-known memorandum written in 1986 by sixteen members of the Serb Academy of Arts and Sciences set forth the causes of Serb dissatisfaction with the existing Yugoslav state. In particular, the authors of the memorandum claimed that Kosovo was experiencing the "physical, political, legal and cultural" genocide of the province's Serb population, owing to the intimidation and discrimination they allegedly encountered

102 Michael Mann, The Dark Side of Democracy 363 (2005).

103 *See* Thomas D. Musgrave, Self-Determination and National Minorities 114 (1997).

104 *See* Radan, *supra* note 101, at 152.

105 *See* Fromkin, *supra* note 91, at 146 (noting the manner in which ethnic unrest contributed to changes to the constitution).

106 *See* Heike Krieger, The Kosovo Conflict and International Law 1 (2001) (describing this presidential council as a "federal presidency" composed of "two representatives of each republic and one from each autonomous province").

107 *See* Malcolm, *supra* note 85, at 327.

108 *See id.* at 328.

109 Mann, *supra* note 102, at 365.

110 *See id.* at 364–65 (describing Serbian frustrations with the 1974 constitutional changes).

at the hands of the Kosovar Albanian provincial authorities.[111] The complaints expressed by these Serbian intellectuals, while controversial, were by no means groundless. As one scholar points out, there is "a strong argument" that the failure of the Kosovar Albanian majority after the grant of provincial autonomy in 1974 to reassure the Kosovar Serb minority that its rights and interests would be respected lay behind much of the trouble that was to ensue in the 1980s.[112]

During the Cold War, Yugoslavia, as a "non-aligned" (if also Communist) state, occupied a special place in NATO strategy that gave it continuing access to Western credit and Western markets. The conclusion of the Cold War, however, coupled with the foreign debt crisis of the late 1980s, cost Yugoslavia its niche position in the global economy and exposed it to competition from newly independent Central European states. The resulting strains destabilized Yugoslavia, encouraged its most "Westernized" components (Slovenia and Croatia) to seek independence, and fed the rise of nationalist and secessionist movements throughout the federation.[113]

In the late 1980s, Slobodan Milosevic, a former Communist opportunistically drawing on Serbian nationalism, began to emerge as Serbia's leading political figure.[114] Milosevic first gained prominence in April 1987 in the small town of Kosovo Field, next to the site of the famous battle of June 28, 1389, in which the forces of the Serb medieval empire under Prince Lazar Hrebeljanovic were defeated by the army of the Ottoman Sultan Murad I.[115] Visiting the town as a Communist Party deputy leader, Milosevic witnessed Kosovar Albanian police beating Serbs—an event he may have prearranged—and was televised exclaiming: "[N]ever again will you be beaten."[116]

Milosevic became President of Serbia in May 1989[117] and, in breach of the 1974 constitution, soon thereafter revoked Kosovo's and Vojvodina's status as autonomous provinces.[118] Serbia's leadership had sought on various occasions to change Kosovo's de facto status as a republic under the federation's 1974 constitution but had been unsuccessful because of the objections of the other republics.[119] However, continued pressure by the Kosovar Albanians for formal republican status for Kosovo throughout the 1980s provoked Serbia to take unilateral action to

---

111 *See* Memorandum of the Serbian Academy of Arts and Sciences (1986), http://www.trepca.net/english/2006/serbian_memorandum_1986/serbia_memorandum_1986.html .).

112 *See* Michael McGwire, *Why Did We Bomb Belgrade?*, 76 Int'l Aff. 1, 4 (2000).

113 *See id.* at 2.

114 *See* Mann, *supra* note 102, at 369–76 (detailing the rise of Milosevic beginning in the late 1980s).

115 Some scholars question whether the Serb forces even suffered defeat at Kosovo Field. In any case, Serbia's loss of independence was not complete until 88 years later, with the fall of Smederevo. *See* Branimir Anzulovic, Heavenly Serbia: From Myth to Genocide 38–39 (1999).

116 Mann, *supra* note 102, at 370.

117 *See* Krieger, *supra* note 106, at 524.

118 *See* Mann, *supra* note 102, at 370.

119 *See* Radan, *supra* note 101, at 197.

change its constitution in 1989 and again in 1990 to curtail Kosovo's autonomy.[120] The two key events were a 1989 amendment to the Serbian constitution, followed by a new constitution for Serbia in 1990. Some scholars date the current crisis in Kosovo to these 1989-1990 constitutional changes, which were accompanied by other Milosevic-inspired measures against the Albanian Kosovars.[121] Thereafter Milosevic instituted a program of discrimination against the Kosovar ethnic Albanian majority, leading to their exclusion from employment, education, and health care benefits.[122] The Albanian Kosovars fought back and, in a referendum organized by para-governmental institutions, voted for independence.[123] Likewise, an underground parliament and government, led by Ibrahim Rugova as President, were created in 1992.[124]

Kosovo was not itself the site of major armed conflict during the second (Croatian) and third (Bosnian) Yugoslav wars, but it was keenly interested in the 1995 Dayton Accords, under which the international community imposed a settlement to the war in Bosnia.[125] The Albanian Kosovars had expected that the Dayton Accords would grant them some future status, but instead they found themselves ignored.[126] Their frustration led to the formation of the Kosovo Liberation Army (KLA), which began an insurgency targeting Serb security forces.[127] The Serbian authorities retaliated with a program of systematic reprisals and village clearances against the Albanian Kosovars.[128] These measures intensified throughout 1998.[129] On September 23, 1998, the U.N.

120 *See id.*

121 *See* Miranda Vickers, Between Serb and Albanian: A History of Kosovo 234–35 (1998); Richard Caplan, *International Diplomacy and the Crisis in Kosovo*, 74 Int'l Aff. 745, 748, 751 (1998).

122 *See id.* at 751 (describing Albanian expulsion from employment and education); Human Rights Watch/Helsinki, Open Wounds: Human Rights Abuses in Kosovo 126 (1993) (explaining that in July and August 1990 the health care system in Kosovo was placed under "emergency management" by the Serbians leading to massive layoffs of Kosovar Albanian healthcare workers).

123 *See* Assembly of the Republic of Kosova, Results of the Referendum (Oct. 19, 1991), *reprinted in* Former Yugoslavia Through Documents: From Its Dissolution to the Peace Settlement 765–66 (Snezana Trifunovska ed. 1999) (stating that of the 1,051,357 eligible voters of Kosova, 87.01% participated in the referendum, and of those 87.01%, 99.87% voted in favor of independence).

124 For a detailed account of political developments in Kosovo between 1989 and 1992, *see* Radan, *supra* note 101, at 198–200.

125 *See* Paul C. Szasz, Introductory Note, General Frame Work Agreement for Peace in Bosnia and Herzegovina, *supra* note 81, (1996) (explaining the implementation of the General Framework Agreement and the role of the international community in concluding the treaty).

126 *See* Mark S. Ellis, *The Consequences of the Kosovo Conflict on Southeastern Europe*, 34 Int'l L. 1193, 1194 (2000) (explaining that Dayton created expectations among Kosovar Albanians for "some degree of independence" but that Kosovo was left off the agenda at Dayton and this signaled to Kosovo's leaders that their efforts to gain international support would be fruitless).

127 *See* Malcolm, *supra* note 85, at 353–55 (explaining that after Kosovo was ignored at Dayton, some Kosovar Albanians began taking more "direct action" including shootings and bombings targeted at Serb officials and that by the summer of 1997 a group calling itself the "Kosovo Liberation Army" was claiming responsibility for the attacks).

128 *See* Mann, *supra* note 102, at 387 (explaining how Serb police attempted to wipe out the KLA in 1998); *see also* Eleanor Lumsden, *An Uneasy Peace: Multilateral Military Intervention in Civil Wars*, 75 N.Y.U. J. Int'l L. & Pol. 795, 828–29 (2003) (noting that Serbian forces began to carry out reprisals on both the rebel forces and Albanian villagers and civilians).

129 *See generally id.* at 829 (noting that in 1998 Milosevic began a program of ethnic cleansing of Kosovar Albanians).

Security Council adopted Resolution 1199, which expressed "[g]rave concern[]" over "excessive and indiscriminate use of force" by the Serb security forces and military that had "resulted in numerous civilian casualties and ... the displacement of over 230,000 persons from their homes." The Resolution further expressed alarm over an "impending humanitarian catastrophe" and reaffirmed the Council's commitment to "a peaceful resolution of the Kosovo problem which would include an enhanced status for Kosovo, a substantially greater autonomy, and meaningful self-administration."[130] Nonetheless the inter-ethnic conflict grew worse, culminating in a massacre in the village of Raçak in January 1999 that left forty-five Albanian Kosovars dead.[131]

In February 1999, the so-called Contact Group—France, Germany, Italy, Russia, the United Kingdom, and the United States[132]—summoned Serb and Albanian Kosovar negotiators to a conference in Rambouillet, France, in order to secure their agreement to an interim settlement.[133] The talks failed. The Kosovar Albanian delegation, which (unlike Bosnia-Herezegovina at the time of the NATO air strikes leading to the adoption of the Dayton Plan)[134] had not been recognized by the NATO countries as representing an independent state, was persuaded only with extreme difficulty to accept the Rambouillet plan; the Serbs refused to sign at all.[135] Soon after, the Serbs renewed their offensive against Kosovo.[136] At that point, without a Security Council resolution explicitly authorizing the use of "all necessary means" to protect the Kosovars, Western military forces in the North Atlantic Treaty Organization (NATO) intervened with air strikes against Serbia and its forces in Kosovo.[137] The NATO air war began on March 24, 1999, and continued until June 9, 1999.[138] On March 26, Russia introduced a Security Council resolution to condemn that NATO action, which was defeated by a vote of 12 to 3 (with Russia, China and Namibia voting in favor).[139] Following the commencement of NATO's air attacks, Serb forces in Kosovo massively intensified their efforts at ethnic cleansing, driving over 800,000 Albanian Kosovars

---

130 S.C. Res. 1199, preamble, U.N. Doc. S/RES/1199 (Sept. 23, 1998).

131 *See* Timothy W. Crawford, *Pivotal Deterrence and the Kosovo War: Why the Holbrooke Agreement Failed,* 116 Pol. Sci. Q. 499, 519 (2001).

132 *See* Marc Weller, *The Rambouillet Conference on Kosovo,* 75 Int'l Aff. 211, 212 (1999).

133 Ivo H. Daalder & Michael E. O'Hanlon, Winning Ugly: NATO's War to Save Kosovo 76–77 (2000).

134 *See supra* text accompanying notes 125-126.

135 For analysis of the Rambouillet Conference, *see* McGwire, *supra* note 112, at 7–10, 13–15. McGwire argues that the Western powers in the Contact Group set up the Conference to fail, thus positioning themselves to make war on Serbia. *Id.* at 13.

136 *See* John Janzekovic, The Use of Force in Humanitarian Intervention: Morality and Practicalities 179 (2006) (describing how the "Serbian military and police forces immediately stepped up the intensity of their operations against the ethnic Albanians in Kosovo" once the Serb delegation walked out of the Rambouillet conference).

137 *See id.* at 180 (noting that the U.S. and NATO began Operation Allied Force after the Serbs refused to comply with the Rambouillet peace proposal).

138 *See* NATO's Role in Relation to the Conflict in Kosovo, NATO (July 15, 1999), http:// www.nato.int/kosovo/history.htm [hereinafter NATO's Role].

139 *See* U.N. Doc. S/PV.3989 at 6 (Mar. 26, 1999); *see also* Damrosch, *supra* note 75, at 1207.

out of Kosovo.[140] Also, during the NATO campaign, Yugloslavia applied to the International Court of Justice, seeking provisional measures ordering NATO to stop the bombing. Although the arguments advanced by both sides joined issue on the legality of humanitarian intervention without Security Council authorization, the ICJ did not reach the question. On June 2, 1999, the ICJ on jurisdictional grounds refused to grant provisional measures.[141]

Then, on June 10, 1999, without remedy at the Security Council or the ICJ, Milosevic agreed to withdraw Serb forces from Kosovo, opening the way to an international settlement.[142] This settlement was embodied in SCR 1244 (1999).[143] Broadly speaking, SCR 1244 authorized the establishment of a United Nations civil administrative mission in Kosovo ("UNMIK"), and the deployment of a NATO-led security force (KFOR) into that province.[144] Kosovo was thus placed under a transitional U.N. administration pending the outcome of a negotiation process intended to resolve its final political status.[145]

1. Postscript

Kosovo's Albanians differ from their Serb neighbors ethnically, religiously, and linguistically.[146] The pre-1998 history of Serb-Albanian relations was unquestionably marked by severe conflict, including mass ethnic cleansing.[147] Yet, the closely entwined histories of Kosovo and Serbia also included periods of coexistence and symbiosis. From a long-term perspective, "Kosovo was essentially a pluralistic society, where various ethnic groups coexisted, many languages were spoken and all major religions of the Balkans were represented."[148] Kosovo today, however, is

140 For accounts of the 1999 war and its background, *see* Daalder & O'Hanlon, *supra* note 133; and Power, *supra* note 23, at 441–73.

141 *See* Legality of Use of Force (Yugoslavia v. Belg., Fr., Ger., Neth., Port., Spain, U.K. and U.S.A.), 1999 I.C.J. 124 (June 2) (judgment); See Yugoslavia v. U.K., CR 99/23, Verbatim Records, 1999 I.C.J. (*available at* http://www.ess.uwe.ac.uk/Kosovo/Kosovo-International_Law9.htm) (arguments of Yugoslavia and United Kingdom).

142 *See* NATO's Role, *supra* note 138 (describing the NATO withdrawal from Kosovo on June 10 after verifying the withdrawal of Yugoslav forces following the conclusion of the Military-Technical Agreement on June 9, 1999).

143 *See* S.C. Res. 1244, U.N. Doc. S/RES/1244 (June 10, 1999).

144 *Id.* at para. 5; see also United Nations Interim Administration in Kosovo, UNMIK Fact Sheet (July 2008) (*available at* http:// www.unmikonline.org/intro.htm) (discussing the establishment of UNMIK).

145 *See* Enrico Milano, *Security Council Action in the Balkans: Reviewing the Legality of Kosovo's Territorial Status,* 14 Eur. J. Int'l L. 999, 1003 (2003) (describing the UN transitional administration); *see also* S.C. Res. 1244, supra note 143, para. 11(a) ("promoting the establishment, pending a final settlement, of substantial autonomy and self-government in Kosovo").

146 *See* Jonathan I. Charney, *Self-Determination: Chechnya, Kosovo and East Timor,* 24 Vand. J. Transnat'l L. 455, 460 n. 18 (2001) (noting that the Albanians in Kosovo are distinct from the "majority population in terms of language, ethnicity, religion, culture, and social organization"); *see also* Malcolm, *supra* note 85, at 10–40 (discussing the development of the culture, language and religion of the Albanians).

147 *See, e.g., id.* at 335 (describing the deaths of Kosovar Albanians in the 1980s).

148 Ger Duijzings, Religion and the Politics of Identity in Kosovo 9 (2000).

effectively a "cleansed," mono-ethnic zone. Since NATO's intervention in 1999, about two-thirds of the ethnic Serb population of Kosovo, or some 200,000 people, have been forced out.[149]

The costs of the United Nations' activities in administering Kosovo have been substantial. Since 1999, the U.N. has spent approximately US $53 billion in Kosovo, or roughly US $2,800 per capita per year, over a hundred times its per capita aid for the rest of the world. Nonetheless, Kosovo remains impoverished, with close to half its residents living on less than US $4.80 a day and with youth unemployment at around 75%, and it is reported to be riddled with corruption and dominated by organized crime figures. Allegations of corruption and criminality have also been leveled against UNMIK administrators.[150] Moreover, despite the presence of KFOR, ethnic violence, now largely directed against Serbs, has persisted in Kosovo.[151] The political process failed to resolve the question of Kosovo's final status in a manner acceptable to all the parties. In the view of the Western powers, it appeared that any agreement between the Serbian authorities and the Kosovar Albanians was simply out of reach.

On February 17, 2008, Kosovo declared its independence from Serbia.[152] On February 18, the EU Foreign Ministers agreed to provide a wide range of political, military, diplomatic, and financial support to the new state of Kosovo.[153] Several major Western governments, including the United States, United Kingdom, France, Germany, and Italy, swiftly recognized Kosovo as a sovereign, independent state, although Serbia, supported by Russia, has vigorously contested the legality both of Kosovo's secession and of the Western powers' support for it.[154] On October 8, 2008, United Nations General Assembly adopted a resolution requesting an Advisory Opinion from the ICJ on whether the unilateral declaration of independence of Kosovo was in accordance with international law.[155] On July 22, 2010 the ICJ advised that Kosovo's declaration of independence was not in violation of international law.[156] Yet the narrowness of the ICJ's reasoning left many questions unanswered concerning the existence and scope of the Kosovar people's

---

149 *See* Mann, *supra* note 102, at 356 (noting that during 1999, Kosovar Albanians pressured almost 200,000 Serbs, amounting to two-thirds of the population, to leave Kosovo).

150 *See* Walter Mayr, The Slow Birth of a Nation, Spiegel Online Int'l, Apr, 24, 2008, http://www.spiegel.de/international/world/0,1518,549441,00.html.).

151 *See* Independent International Commission on Kosovo, The Follow-Up of the Kosovo Report: Why Conditional Independence? 19 (2001) (*available at* http://www.alb-net.com/pipermail/albsa-info/2001-November/002393.html (finding KFOR's inability to restrain violence against Kosovo's Serb minority "the greatest single failure since the NATO intervention" and "a moral disgrace").

152 *See* Dan Bilefsky, Kosovo Declares Independence, Int'l Herald Trib, Feb. 18, 2008, at 1.

153 *See* Press Release, Council of the European Union, 2851st Council Meeting, General Affairs and External Relations 2 (Feb. 18, 2008) (*available at* http://www.consilium.europa.eu/ueDocs/cms_ Data/docs/pressData/en/gena/98818.pdf).

154 *See* Nicholas Kulish & C.J. Chivers, Kosovo Independence Gets Mixed Reaction Worldwide, San Diego Union-Trib., Feb. 19, 2008, at A11 (reporting that the Serbian President described Kosovo as a "false state" and that Russia believed the declaration to be "null and void").

155 *See* G.A. Res. 63/3, U.N. GAOR, A/RES/63/3 (Oct. 8, 2008).

156 *See* Advisory Opinion on the Accordance with International of the Unilateral Declaration of Independence in Respect of Kosovo, 2010 I.C.J., General List No. 141 (July 22) (*available at* http://www.icj-cij.org/docket/files/141/15987.pdf).

right to self-determination and to statehood, as well as the interaction of any such rights with Resolution 1244 or with the rights of Serbs within Kosovo.[157]

In any event, what followed in Kosovo was clearly the fruit of the NATO humanitarian intervention in 1999. We now turn to the possible legal justifications for that action. We supply text that form the basis for these arguments: first, the international law argument for humanitarian intervention supplied contemporaneously before the ICJ; second, the possible ratification of the NATO action through the adoption by the Security Council of Resolution 1244. We then critique these arguments on our commentary.

157 For a discussion of these and other issue related to Kosovo's declaration of independence, *see* Robert J. Delahunty & Antonio F. Perez, *The Kosovo Crisis: A Dostoievskian Dialogue on International Law, Statecraft, and Soulcraft,* 42 Vand. J. Transnat'l L. 15 (2009).

C. QUESTIONS AND DOCUMENTS

Before reading the following documents, as well as afterwards, it might be helpful for you to consider the following questions.

1. Reading Questions

1) To what extent was NATO intervention motivated by an imperialistic agenda? To what extent was humanitarianism a pretext for self-interested, but defensive, motives? From the standpoint of neighboring NATO countries, can you distinguish clearly between defensive and offensive motives? Can you imagine or role-play a strategy session at a meeting of NATO military and diplomatic leadership considering whether to use force in 1999 in light of the decade-long EU, US, and NATO role in the Balkans? Perform a similar exercise in developing a draft proposal for what became Resolution 1244.

2) Based on U.N. practice and precedents, how would you make a lawyerly case that a Security Council resolution under Chapter VII to authorize NATO bombing was within the authority granted to the Security Council under Chapter VII? How would you draft arguments to the contrary? Compare you arguments to the kinds of arguments that were actually made by lawyers for Yugoslavia and the United Kingdom.

3) Can you see any reasons why forming coalitions to adopt or implement a UN mission in Kosovo would be difficult? What are the relative politico-military and diplomatic advantages and disadvantages of the apparent NATO strategy of acting militarily first, without even seeking a vote on an authorizing resolution at the Security Council, and diplomatically second by obtaining a subsequent Security Council Resolution providing a roadmap for a long-term political settlement? As a general matter, when important national interests are stake, do these national interests include humanitarian concerns? If so, how? Is the Security Council capable of acting quickly enough actually to prevent an imminent humanitarian catastrophe? How would a rational choice theory of international law consider these questions? How do these questions relate to whether S.C. Res. 1244 should be deemed to have ratified the NATO intervention?

4) What factors play a role in developing an international consensus favoring humanitarian intervention? What factors impede the formation of such a consensus? What is the relation of humanitarian intervention to the broader question of the legitimacy of forms of government and dominant ideologies, such as religious conceptions, or the role of national identity? How would a constructivist view of international law consider these issues? How would you argue that these issues playing a controlling role in the Serbian-Kosovar conflict? Does it follow that they played an equally important role in the decisions of the states favoring and opposing intervention? How do your answers to these questions relate to whether S.C. Res. 1244 should be deemed to have ratified the NATO intervention?

5) Would replacing a discussion in terms of realism, legalism, rational choice theory and constructivism with a focus on Just War criteria provide a better basis for consensus and effectiveness in humanitarian intervention? Would they more accurately describe and predict the circumstances under which states act? Or are the criteria sufficiently vague that the same realist, legalist, rational choice and constructivist concerns, reframed in terms of competing views of the Just War tradition, would prevent consensus? Under a Just War Theory, does it matter that Kosovo was merely a province of Yugoslavia and not an independent state? Would it have been possible for the U.S. and EU to recognize Kosovo as an independent state and then provide Kosovo assistance under Article 51 of the Charter right to collective self-defense? If so, would that be bending the forms of international law to accommodate it to requirements of the Just War Tradition?

2. Documents

a. United Kingdom's Argument[158]

12. Mr. President, we must not let our careful and lawyerly analysis of these jurisdictional factors obscure our view of the real situation in Kosovo, of the human misery and suffering caused by the planned and deliberate actions and policies of the Government whom our opponents come here to represent, of the massive and shocking oppression of an entire ethnic population and the dire effects of this on neighbouring States. Let me simply give you a description containing some facts and figures – some of which you have had already – which I will do as dispassionately as I

158 Legality of Use of Force (Yugoslavia v. U.K.), CR/99/34, May 11, 1999 (*available at* http://www.ess.uwe.ac.uk/Kosovo/Kosovo-International_Law9.htm) [hereinafter Argument of the U.K.] (excerpts from the argument of the United Kingdom (Attorney-General, the Rt. Hon. Mr. John Morris).

can despite the great indignation and outrage they have caused amongst ordinary people in my country. I do so, Mr. President, not in my words or the words of the British Government, but in those of the United Nations High Commissioner for Refugees, briefing in person the members of the Security Council on 5 May of this year – a week after these proceedings were started.

13. "The situation of women, men and children fleeing the Province of Kosovo and Metohija, in the Federal Republic of Yugoslavia, is increasingly desperate. Kosovo is being emptied – brutally and methodically – of its ethnic Albanian population. In the last three days alone [she said], about 37,000 new refugees and internally displaced people have arrived in Albania, the former Yugoslav Republic of Macedonia, and the Republic of Montenegro. More trains with thousands of refugees have arrived last night at the Yugoslav/Macedonian border. Ethnic cleansing and mass forced expulsions are yielding their tragic results faster than we can respond . . . Fragile and unprepared countries are bearing the brunt of one of the largest refugee flows Europe has seen in the twentieth century. Seven hundred thousand people have already been forced to leave their homes."

14. Mrs. Ogata went on to say, in a passage which is very important to put the allegations you heard from counsel for the Federal Republic of Yugoslavia in their right perspective:

"This refugee crisis is not new. Last year, more than a quarter of all asylum requests in Europe were by people from Kosovo. Up to 23 March, when UNHCR had to reluctantly leave the province following a decision of the United Nations Security Coordinator, it was providing assistance to 400,000 people displaced or otherwise affected by fighting inside the province, and to 90,000 refugees and displaced people outside Kosovo."

15. So, Mr. President, the Applicant has brought before you claims that 1,200 of its civilians have been killed in a seven-week military campaign – all civilian deaths are a source of sadness – but expects you to ignore that over 700,000 Kosovars have been driven from their homes: 700,000, nearly three-quarters of a million, over one-third of the entire population of Kosovo. How could anyone remain unmoved by that description, by those figures? They are of course confirmed by reports we get from our own diplomatic missions in neighbouring countries. Isn't it strange that there is not one word about them in the Application and request filed with the Court? Mrs. Ogata is in no doubt that the root cause is (and I quote again) "the systematic and intolerable violence being waged against an entire population, and the failure to prevent it." Nor could anyone who simply watches the television screen and reads the newspapers. Doesn't that make one pause and think about the true motive and purpose behind the attempt of the Federal Republic of Yugoslavia to move this Court to action in its favour?

16. This Court is of course familiar, Mr. President, with cases in which one litigating party says that a dispute is about such-and-such and the other party complains that so-and-so has also to be brought within it or taken into account. Those cases have to be judged each on its own merits. This case is however one that can *only* be understood against the background of why my country (together with others) is waging the military action complained of, and that is precisely (in Mrs. Ogata's words again) to prevent the systematic and intolerable violence being waged against an entire population. Everyone knows that, as does the applicant State itself. I will allow myself one final quotation - this time from a British source - to show that what we are doing is not *against* any people or population, but *for* the rescue of the Kosovar Albanians from their desperate plight.

17. Speaking, Mr. President, in the Security Council on 24 March, the day the military action began, the United Kingdom's Permanent Representative described it as "an exceptional measure to prevent an overwhelming humanitarian catastrophe."

"Under present circumstances in Kosovo [he went on] there is convincing evidence that such a catastrophe is imminent. Renewed acts of repression by the authorities of the Federal Republic of Yugoslavia would cause further loss of civilian life and would lead to displacement of the civilian population on a large scale and in hostile conditions. Every means short of force has been tried to avert this situation. . . . The force now proposed is directed exclusively to averting a humanitarian catastrophe, and is the minimum judged necessary for that purpose."

18. Contrary to what was suggested by counsel for the Applicant yesterday, those have always been the terms in which the British Government have presented their position in Parliament. My learned friend, Professor Brownlie, referred to a statement by the Prime Minister in the House of Commons on 23 March of this year. He suggested that this statement revealed an ambivalence on the part of my Government about the motives and legal basis for our action. Mr. President, it does nothing of the kind. What the Prime Minister said was that we would act "primarily to avert what would otherwise be a humanitarian disaster in Kosovo." Later in his statement he said:

"We must act to save thousands of innocent men, women and children from humanitarian catastrophe – from death, barbarism and ethnic cleansing by a brutal dictatorship . . ."

The motives for our action could not have been more clearly stated. They give the lie to counsel's suggestion yesterday that, in acting to halt humanitarian catastrophe in one Province of the Federal Republic of Yugoslavia, the British Government should have been seeking to bring humanitarian catastrophe to the civilian population in any other part of their country, still less intending to destroy any population group as such.

19. Mr. President, I will not deal in detail with the jurisdiction element. Professor Greenwood will cover that. I only want respectfully to remind you that, even if the Applicant's optional clause declaration was a valid acceptance of the Court's jurisdiction, its application against the United Kingdom is plainly excluded by the 12-month clause in our acceptance. But to the Applicant that crucial fact seems to be of no account. In fact, judging from what we have been hearing in Court over the last two days, the Applicant seems to have launched claims in pretty well identical terms against a whole series of different respondents without any regard to the terms on which each respondent may be within the jurisdiction of the Court – in fact without regard to whether some respondents are within the jurisdiction at all. That is hardly a sign of respect towards the judicial process of the Court.

20. Apart from the optional clause, which is clearly not applicable, the only other basis invoked is Article IX of the Genocide Convention. But, Mr. President, the same cavalier attitude permeates the Applicant's submissions on this point too. They give us virtually no indication of what conduct is actually alleged against the United Kingdom or of how that conduct might fall within the scope of the Genocide Convention. Nothing in the Applicant's written or oral submissions comes even near to a plausible allegation that the United Kingdom has breached its obligations under the Convention or threatens to do so. The factual allegations recited, even if all were proved true and even if we were responsible for them, are not genocide. Nor is there the slightest shred of evidence of genocidal intent. So where is there in any meaningful sense a dispute between us over the interpretation, application or fulfillment of the Genocide Convention?

21. I have explained, Mr. President, that what we are doing is designed to save one ethnic group, not – *not* – to destroy another. But what we do know with absolute certainty is that the authorities of the Federal Republic of Yugoslavia have been systematically engaged in what has acquired the eerie name of "ethnic cleansing." I gave you the shocking figures earlier. There is ample evidence that the ultimate aim is the forced removal of the entire ethnic Albanian population from the geographical area.

22. Mr. President, distinguished Members of the Court, the Applicant would have you believe that the situation in Kosovo is simple, a case of unwarranted external intervention. Counsel told you yesterday that if once the external intervention was stopped, the situation inside Kosovo would resolve itself into a model of ethnic harmony. You will know that such a depiction is wholly incredible. It is a travesty of the facts. It tries to banish from view the desperate humanitarian circumstances which led to our actions and the relief of which is our sole purpose. Not only that, but it tries to blind you to what happened since, as a result of the calculated policies of the Federal Republic of Yugoslavia. What the world requires – what in our submission

international law requires – is that the inhabitants of Kosovo are able to return to their homes, are able to live there in peace and to rebuild their shattered lives. It is obvious that that requires far more than just the application of some simplistic nostrum: "stop the bombing." It means that the people of Kosovo must be protected against new atrocities. That is the reason why the G-8 Foreign Ministers adopted on 6 May seven principles designed to ensure the safe and free return of all refugees and displaced persons and conditions for a peaceful and normal life for all inhabitants in Kosovo.

23. So the Court, with respect, must ask itself what the effect would be of granting the provisional measures which the Federal Republic of Yugoslavia is urging upon it. The Court, with respect, is bound to consider that. But the Court may readily reach the conclusion that what the Federal Republic of Yugoslavia wants to achieve is to use the Court's processes to secure for itself a free hand to complete its planned campaign of "ethnic cleansing." At present the military action, directed specifically at the means of pursuing the oppression of the Kosovar Albanians, is the only thing holding the oppressors back. Imagine, imagine what the situation would be in the refugees' tented camps next winter if that restraint were lifted. Imagine the public reaction if a judicial proceeding in this Court were to lead to that result.

24. I come therefore, Mr. President, to my final point. This is whether the Court ought to be entertaining this request from the Federal Republic of Yugoslavia at all. I have already described it, in its careless disregard of the legal requirements, as an abuse of the process of the Court. It deserves to be dismissed on that ground alone. There is, however, Mr. President, a deeper point. In my own legal system a remedy like "provisional measures" would lie at the discretion of the Court. In considering whether or not to exercise that discretion, the Court would weigh up all the equities. In weighing up all the equities, the Court would pay particular attention as to whether the party seeking its assistance came with clean hands. The Court would not, however, allow its process to be used as an engine to assist turpitude. I can see no reason why exactly the same principles should not be applied by this honourable Court. They are deeply rooted in the essential nature of the judicial function. They should be regarded as "general principles of law" within the meaning of Article 38 of the Statute.

25. For this reason, as much as for any other, the Court should summarily dismiss the request.

b. United Nations Security Council Resolution 1244 (1999)[159]

The Security Council,

159 S.C. Res. 1244, U.N. SCOR, U.N. Doc. S/RES/1244 (June 10, 1999).

Bearing in mind the purposes and principles of the Charter of the United Nations, and the primary responsibility of the Security Council for the maintenance of international peace and security,

Recalling its resolutions 1160 (1998) of 31 March 1998, 1199 (1998) of 23 September 1998, 1203 (1998) of 24 October 1998 and 1239 (1999) of 14 May 1999,

Regretting that there has not been full compliance with the requirements of these resolutions,

Determined to resolve the grave humanitarian situation in Kosovo, Federal Republic of Yugoslavia, and to provide for the safe and free return of all refugees and displaced persons to their homes,

Condemning all acts of violence against the Kosovo population as well as all terrorist acts by any party,

Recalling the statement made by the Secretary-General on 9 April 1999, expressing concern at the humanitarian tragedy taking place in Kosovo,

Reaffirming the right of all refugees and displaced persons to return to their homes in safety,

Recalling the jurisdiction and the mandate of the International Tribunal for the Former Yugoslavia,

Welcoming the general principles on a political solution to the Kosovo crisis adopted on 6 May 1999 (S/1999/516, annex 1 to this resolution) and welcoming also the acceptance by the Federal Republic of Yugoslavia of the principles set forth in points 1 to 9 of the paper presented in Belgrade on 2 June 1999 (S/1999/649, annex 2 to this resolution), and the Federal Republic of Yugoslavia's agreement to that paper,

Reaffirming the commitment of all Member States to the sovereignty and territorial integrity of the Federal Republic of Yugoslavia and the other States of the region, as set out in the Helsinki Final Act and annex 2,

Reaffirming the call in previous resolutions for substantial autonomy and meaningful self-administration for Kosovo,

Determining that the situation in the region continues to constitute a threat to international peace and security,

Determined to ensure the safety and security of international personnel and the implementation by all concerned of their responsibilities under the present resolution, and acting for these purposes under Chapter VII of the Charter of the United Nations,

1. Decides that a political solution to the Kosovo crisis shall be based on the general principles in annex 1 and as further elaborated in the principles and other required elements in annex 2;

2. Welcomes the acceptance by the Federal Republic of Yugoslavia of the principles and other required elements referred to in paragraph 1 above, and demands the full cooperation of the Federal Republic of Yugoslavia in their rapid implementation;

3. Demands in particular that the Federal Republic of Yugoslavia put an immediate and verifiable end to violence and repression in Kosovo, and begin and complete verifiable phased withdrawal from Kosovo of all military, police and paramilitary forces according to a rapid timetable, with which the deployment of the international security presence in Kosovo will be synchronized;

4. Confirms that after the withdrawal an agreed number of Yugoslav and Serb military and police personnel will be permitted to return to Kosovo to perform the functions in accordance with annex 2;

5. Decides on the deployment in Kosovo, under United Nations auspices, of international civil and security presences, with appropriate equipment and personnel as required, and welcomes the agreement of the Federal Republic of Yugoslavia to such presences;

6. Requests the Secretary-General to appoint, in consultation with the Security Council, a Special Representative to control the implementation of the international civil presence, and further requests the Secretary-General to instruct his Special Representative to coordinate closely with the international security presence to ensure that both presences operate towards the same goals and in a mutually supportive manner;

7. Authorizes Member States and relevant international organizations to establish the international security presence in Kosovo as set out in point 4 of annex 2 with all necessary means to fulfil its responsibilities under paragraph 9 below;

8. Affirms the need for the rapid early deployment of effective international civil and security presences to Kosovo, and demands that the parties cooperate fully in their deployment;

9. Decides that the responsibilities of the international security presence to be deployed and acting in Kosovo will include:

   (a) Deterring renewed hostilities, maintaining and where necessary enforcing a ceasefire, and ensuring the withdrawal and preventing the return into Kosovo of Federal and Republic military, police and paramilitary forces, except as provided in point 6 of annex 2;

(b) Demilitarizing the Kosovo Liberation Army (KLA) and other armed Kosovo Albanian groups as required in paragraph 15 below;

(c) Establishing a secure environment in which refugees and displaced persons can return home in safety, the international civil presence can operate, a transitional administration can be established, and humanitarian aid can be delivered;

(d) Ensuring public safety and order until the international civil presence can take responsibility for this task;

(e) Supervising demining until the international civil presence can, as appropriate, take over responsibility for this task;

(f) Supporting, as appropriate, and coordinating closely with the work of the international civil presence;

(g) Conducting border monitoring duties as required;

(h) Ensuring the protection and freedom of movement of itself, the international civil presence, and other international organizations;

10. Authorizes the Secretary-General, with the assistance of relevant international organizations, to establish an international civil presence in Kosovo in order to provide an interim administration for Kosovo under which the people of Kosovo can enjoy substantial autonomy within the Federal Republic of Yugoslavia, and which will provide transitional administration while establishing and overseeing the development of provisional democratic self-governing institutions to ensure conditions for a peaceful and normal life for all inhabitants of Kosovo;

11. Decides that the main responsibilities of the international civil presence will include:

(a) Promoting the establishment, pending a final settlement, of substantial autonomy and self-government in Kosovo, taking full account of annex 2 and of the Rambouillet accords (S/1999/648);

(b) Performing basic civilian administrative functions where and as long as required;

(c) Organizing and overseeing the development of provisional institutions for democratic and autonomous self-government pending a political settlement, including the holding of elections;

(d) Transferring, as these institutions are established, its administrative responsibilities while overseeing and supporting the consolidation of Kosovo's local provisional institutions and other peace-building activities;

(e) Facilitating a political process designed to determine Kosovo's future status, taking into account the Rambouillet accords (S/1999/648);

(f) In a final stage, overseeing the transfer of authority from Kosovo's provisional institutions to institutions established under a political settlement;

(g) Supporting the reconstruction of key infrastructure and other economic reconstruction;

(h) Supporting, in coordination with international humanitarian organizations, humanitarian and disaster relief aid;

(i) Maintaining civil law and order, including establishing local police forces and meanwhile through the deployment of international police personnel to serve in Kosovo;

(j) Protecting and promoting human rights;

(k) Assuring the safe and unimpeded return of all refugees and displaced persons to their homes in Kosovo;

12. Emphasizes the need for coordinated humanitarian relief operations, and for the Federal Republic of Yugoslavia to allow unimpeded access to Kosovo by humanitarian aid organizations and to cooperate with such organizations so as to ensure the fast and effective delivery of international aid;

12. Encourages all Member States and international organizations to contribute to economic and social reconstruction as well as to the safe return of refugees and displaced persons, and emphasizes in this context the importance of convening an

international donors' conference, particularly for the purposes set out in paragraph 11 (g) above, at the earliest possible date;

14. Demands full cooperation by all concerned, including the international security presence, with the International Tribunal for the Former Yugoslavia;

15. Demands that the KLA and other armed Kosovo Albanian groups end immediately all offensive actions and comply with the requirements for demilitarization as laid down by the head of the international security presence in consultation with the Special Representative of the Secretary-General;

16. Decides that the prohibitions imposed by paragraph 8 of resolution 1160 (1998) shall not apply to arms and related matériel for the use of the international civil and security presences;

17. Welcomes the work in hand in the European Union and other international organizations to develop a comprehensive approach to the economic development and stabilization of the region affected by the Kosovo crisis, including the implementation of a Stability Pact for South Eastern Europe with broad international participation in order to further the promotion of democracy, economic prosperity, stability and regional cooperation;

18. Demands that all States in the region cooperate fully in the implementation of all aspects of this resolution;

19. Decides that the international civil and security presences are established for an initial period of 12 months, to continue thereafter unless the Security Council decides otherwise;

20. Requests the Secretary-General to report to the Council at regular intervals on the implementation of this resolution, including reports from the leaderships of the international civil and security presences, the first reports to be submitted within 30 days of the adoption of this resolution;

21. Decides to remain actively seized of the matter.

Annex 1—Statement by the Chairman on the conclusion of the meeting of the G-8 Foreign Ministers held at the Petersberg Centre on 6 May 1999

The G-8 Foreign Ministers adopted the following general principles on the political solution to the Kosovo crisis:

- Immediate and verifiable end of violence and repression in Kosovo;
- Withdrawal from Kosovo of military, police and paramilitary forces;
- Deployment in Kosovo of effective international civil and security presences, endorsed and adopted by the United Nations, capable of guaranteeing the achievement of the common objectives;
- Establishment of an interim administration for Kosovo to be decided by the Security Council of the United Nations to ensure conditions for a peaceful and normal life for all inhabitants in Kosovo;
- The safe and free return of all refugees and displaced persons and unimpeded access to Kosovo by humanitarian aid organizations;
- A political process towards the establishment of an interim political framework agreement providing for a substantial self-government for Kosovo, taking full account of the Rambouillet accords and the principles of sovereignty and territorial integrity of the Federal Republic of Yugoslavia and the other countries of the region, and the demilitarization of the KLA;
- Comprehensive approach to the economic development and stabilization of the crisis region.

Annex 2—Agreement should be reached on the following principles to move towards a resolution of the Kosovo crisis:

1. An immediate and verifiable end of violence and repression in Kosovo.

2. Verifiable withdrawal from Kosovo of all military, police and paramilitary forces according to a rapid timetable.

3. Deployment in Kosovo under United Nations auspices of effective international civil and security presences, acting as may be decided under Chapter VII of the Charter, capable of guaranteeing the achievement of common objectives.

4. The international security presence with substantial North Atlantic Treaty Organization participation must be deployed under unified command and control and authorized to establish a safe environment for all people in Kosovo and to facilitate the safe return to their homes of all displaced persons and refugees.

5. Establishment of an interim administration for Kosovo as a part of the international civil presence under which the people of Kosovo can enjoy substantial autonomy within the Federal Republic of Yugoslavia, to be decided by the Security Council of the United Nations. The interim administration to provide transitional administration while establishing and overseeing the development of provisional democratic self-governing institutions to ensure conditions for a peaceful and normal life for all inhabitants in Kosovo.

6. After withdrawal, an agreed number of Yugoslav and Serbian personnel will be permitted to return to perform the following functions:
   - Liaison with the international civil mission and the international security presence;
   - Marking/clearing minefields;
   - Maintaining a presence at Serb patrimonial sites;
   - Maintaining a presence at key border crossings.

7. Safe and free return of all refugees and displaced persons under the supervision of the Office of the United Nations High Commissioner for Refugees and unimpeded access to Kosovo by humanitarian aid organizations.

8. A political process towards the establishment of an interim political framework agreement providing for substantial self-government for Kosovo, taking full account of the Rambouillet accords and the principles of sovereignty and territorial integrity of the Federal Republic of Yugoslavia and the other countries of the region, and the demilitarization of UCK. Negotiations between the parties for a settlement should not delay or disrupt the establishment of democratic self-governing institutions.

9. A comprehensive approach to the economic development and stabilization of the crisis region. This will include the implementation of a stability pact for South-Eastern Europe with broad international participation inrder to further promotion of democracy, economic prosperity, stability and regional cooperation.

1. Thesis 1—How Does Each of Our Models Shed Light on the International Response to NATO Intervention to Save the Kosovars from Serbian Ethnic Cleansing?

a. The Realist Account

When South African Nelson Mandela judged that "Africans and Asians had to envy the willingness of the world to save Kosovo,"[160] he echoed the 19th century Ottoman objection that states engaging in humanitarian intervention acted as though "there was one law of humanity" for preferred groups and another for disfavored groups.[161] This criticism sounds in the more recent concern that the International Criminal Court has focused primarily on prosecuting Africans, as crimes against humanity and war crimes have been committed in Africa alone since the ICC Statute has come into force.[162] Authors from widely-varying political perspectives now apparently share the view that humanitarian intervention is inevitably an exercise in hegemonic power.[163] But others hold that imperialism, if it is necessary to save lives, is a global good; and the problem is that states capable of engaging in humanitarian intervention simply lack the courage of their convictions to rid the world of radical evil. Indeed, under such views, the self-defense rationale we will later explore in relation to the Second Gulf War and the final overthrow of Saddam Hussein was unnecessary, and limitations on humanitarian intervention in such cases should simply be ignored.[164]

Yet, a realist response to the question might also consider the unintended effects of humanitarian intervention. For example, in Kosovo, the United States and European Union could not intervene militarily through NATO and then diplomatically through the deployment of UNMIK without changing the situation on the ground—in particular, the expectations of the Kosovars who, like the Bulgarians protected by Russia in the 19th century and the Kurds protected by the U.S. and U.K. in late 20th century, came to believe that they too could have their own state.[165]

160 Quoted in Bass, *supra* note 1, at 23 (citations omitted).

161 *See id.*

162 *See id.*

163 *See* Bass, *supra* note 1, at 480 n.6; Andrew Bacevich, American Empire: The Realities and Consequences of U.S. Diplomacy (2002); Chalmers Johnson, The Sorrows of Empire: Militarism, Secrecy, and the End of the Republic (2004); and Patrick J. Buchanan, A Republic, Not an Empire: Reclaiming America's Destiny (1999)).

164 *See* Bass, *supra* note 1, at 480 n.7 (citing Niall Ferguson, In Praise of Failed Diplomacy, N.Y. Times, Mar. 23, 2003 (discussing Second Gulf War as successful humanitarian intervention to overthrow a tyrant, Saddam Hussein); Timothy Garton Ash, Gambling on America, Guardian, Oct. 3, 2002.

165 *See* Bass, *supra* note 1, at 366.

In short, under this strand of realism, responsibility for consequences comes with power, and power inevitably corrupts those who exercise it,[166] thus requiring humility and restraint in the exercise of power as a necessary corrective, what modern realists call the moral virtue of prudence.[167] (This strand of the realist critique may well overlap with constructivist and Just War Theory.) Perhaps, then, a realist might have questioned the Kosovo intervention, asking whether NATO was prudent in the manner it used force when the benefits of action, both to the Kosovars and the members of NATO were not clear, and the potential effects in NATO-Russia relations and on future international legal cooperation were hard to define.

Whether understood as a description of international politics as the pursuit of power or a sophisticated account of international politics based on a deep understanding of human nature, the realist contribution to the debate on humanitarian intervention seemingly treats law as irrelevant. The rationalist analysis makes that point explicit, treating law only as a factor, to the extent it reflects potential reputational costs.

b. The Rational Choice Critique

We sketch out here a series of questions that would need to be answered to address the problem of humanitarian intervention from a rational choice perspective we explored in Chapter 2A. The rationalist perspective reformulates the realist perspective in light of a sophisticated use of the new institutional economics and game theory to model effective decisions and institution-building to reach optimal levels of humanitarian intervention.

A rational choice approach to the question of humanitarian intervention would, at least as a first-approximation, view it simply through a consequentialist analysis that balances the benefits and costs of intervention solely in terms of the lives and value of the lives lost by action or inaction. Under this view, one would focus on the costs of non-intervention in Kosovo, including the death of Kosovars and potential loss of their culture and third-party effects, such as the risk of refugee flows toward Albania; together these effects would not appear to generate substantial concerns for the Balkans generally and even less so for the European Union. Like the situation in Haiti, it would appear that problem could be contained. Perhaps hindsight bias should be avoided. However, from the rational choice standpoint, it seems reasonable to argue that NATO intervention ultimately did more harm than good for Kosovars, since it triggered perhaps more extreme measures by the Serb authorities in attempting to wipe out the Kosovar population rather than merely drive it into exile. On the other, the problem on that score might not have been the choice to intervene but rather the decision not to deploy ground troops. And

166 *See* Reinhold Niebuhr, Moral Man and Immoral Society: A Study in Ethics and Politics (1960); John Patrick Diggins, Why Niebuhr Now? (2011) (drawing on Niebuhr's warnings about the need for caution in the exercise of power to criticize recent U.S. foreign policy decisions).

167 *See* Bass, *supra* note 1, at 359 ("Kissinger rightly praises Castlereagh and Metternich for almost a century of peace. These leaders had a morality of prudence.").

the negative long-term effects on Kosovo might have been due to the implementation of S.C. Res. 1244 and continued Russian resistance rather than the initial steps taken by NATO.[168] In short, the cost-benefit implications of a decision may depend on whether the decision is framed in terms of incremental decisions or the overall pattern of decisions implied by the initial choice to act.

But even if under this analysis NATO should have intervened, on second approximation, the analysis would quickly become more complex and problematic. Coalition building for humanitarian intervention is not a costless activity. Humanitarian interveners will face the cost of building coalitions for humanitarian intervention and the opportunity costs of deploying the political resources necessary to build those coalitions on a particular humanitarian intervention rather than other humanitarian interventions or even other important global public goods. In addition, because deployment of forces by a state engaging in humanitarian intervention may have ancillary benefits in projecting power, the intervening state's motives could be either offensive (namely, to project power) or defensive or altruistic (perhaps preventing costly refugee flows or avoiding the psychological costs of seeing harm done to a populations with whom the intervening state shares some trait, such as religion or ethnicity), or some mixed-motive combination. Other states will view the game as a Prisoner's Dilemma or some version of a cooperative game depending on their perception of the payoffs involved, whether the game is amenable to repeat play, and whether effective signaling is possible. Thus, even if offensive motives do not dominate, misperception may create the need for expensive, indeed wasteful, confidence-building measures.[169]

In the case of NATO's bombing campaign, this may have been the last move in the longstanding game played by the U.S., EU, and Russia in the Balkans. Tit-for-tat based cooperation may have been difficult to achieve since most of the potential value in the game had been distributed in the preceding ten years. In other words, the "shadow of the future" was not likely to facilitate cooperation, incentivizing both Russia and NATO to pursue unilateral strategies of offensive defection as the game drew to a close. Moreover, even if these incentives for defection could have been overcome, the perception in Russia that NATO was further projecting its power into an area that had previously been under Russian influence suggests that the costs of achieving consensus at the Security Council would have been prohibitive—much as securing authorization for U.S. intervention in Haiti took a full two years after OAS sanctions were secured through U.S. diplomacy. Thus, Russia no doubt viewed the game as one in which it was liable to the Sucker's payoff, since the EU, if not also the U.S., through humiliation of a Russian ally would gain substantial political benefits.

---

168 *See supra* text accompanying notes 144–151 (discussing the political and economic effects of UNMIK's deployment).

169 *See* John Gerard Ruggie, *Multilateralism: The Anatomy of an Institution, in* Multilateralism Matters: The Theory and Praxis of an Institutional Form (1993).

Finally, a third approximation of rational choice analysis would view the case through the optic of the relevant rules that should have been applied, in the context of building a rule-utilitarian approach to norm building for future cases. From this perspective, it is useful to begin the analysis with the premise that governments will always struggle with imperfect information. Thus, when rules or policies on humanitarian intervention dictate a general level of intervention, particular decisions on humanitarian intervention will be erroneous from the standpoint of maximizing global welfare. Some rules may be over-inclusive, yielding too much intervention (perhaps Haiti) or too intrusive an intervention (perhaps Somalia), and sometimes the result will be under-inclusive, with states intervening not often enough (perhaps Rwanda) or not intrusively enough (perhaps Srebrenica in Bosnia-Herzegovina).

Judgments about the likelihood of error and their likely types ex post should be factored into the development of rules or policies on humanitarian intervention ex ante, in order to maximize accuracy in overall decision-making on humanitarian intervention. From a global welfare standpoint, intervention can be excessive when the intervening state perceives the gains from intervention to exceed the true gains and the costs of intervention to be less than the true costs. For example, an intervening state might intervene to achieve gains unrelated to the humanitarian purpose; also, an intervening state might underestimate the true costs, perhaps through unanticipated failures in implementation or an unanticipated level of political resistance from other actors in the international system, which might perceive the intervening state as acting imperialistically rather than to further the global public good. From a global welfare standpoint, humanitarian intervention can be insufficient when the intervening state perceives the costs of intervention as greater than the true costs or perceives the benefits of intervention as less than the true benefits.

Thus, in general, rules ex ante should take into account the relative likelihood of these kinds of errors. For example, when the risk of imperialistic or pre-textual use of legal authority to intervene is high, rules against humanitarian intervention should be strong. When the risk of imperialistic or pre-textual use is low, prohibitory rules should be relaxed. Thus, if one thinks the rules against humanitarian intervention are based on the probability of errors that come from external biases toward the acquisition of power, it could be conjectured that the rules against humanitarian intervention should be relaxed. Other kinds of error could also be considered in the process of rule formation. For example, different factual situations give rise to different degrees of domestic support for humanitarian intervention. Thus, parallel compensatory strategies, to take account of these domestic biases, should also be part of international rule formation. The sources of error, and need for correction, are manifold.

In the current contexts, if one thinks the sources of error are primarily external, until recently, the decline of Cold War competition between the United States and Russia has reduced the likelihood that either the United States or Russia will engage in imperialistically motivated humanitarian intervention. Also, the demand or need for humanitarian intervention throughout the world has increased since the end of the Cold War, as failed states have become more common (in view, among other things, of the declining support failing states receive from the U.S. or Russia after the decline of Cold War competition) and therefore the incidence of repression by fragile governments may have increased.

But if one thinks the rules against humanitarian intervention are based on the probability of errors from internal sources of bias toward intervention, it may be that those rules should be retained. With the increase of mass communication, the payoff for humanitarian politics in western countries may have increased. In the words of one commentator, the emergence of "saintly logrolls" can make intervention politically-beneficial.[170] It might be noted that the political costs of non-intervention were greater in Greece and Yugoslavia (given the duration of the violence and therefore the likelihood of sustained press attention) than in Bulgaria and Rwanda, where the massacres occurred within a shorter timeframe and received, because of their relative lack of access to international media, somewhat less attention.[171] A domestic-politics explanation of the political costs and benefits of humanitarian intervention thus complicates the analysis of whether some states are more prone than others to make errors of excessive humanitarian intervention, not only because of the likelihood that a state's demographic diversity will engage the interests of its population in some atrocity somewhere in the world or because of the openness of its press or the responsiveness of its political system to public outrage.

In short, with increasingly complex factors to evaluate the quality of decision-making in individual cases and the quality of the rules that govern this area, what is a rationalist to do? The imponderables required in a rational choice analysis do seem, however, to suggest that costs of NATO's intervention may have exceeded its benefits, and the legal instability perceived by the legalist perspective suggests that the international legal system as a whole was left in tatters. Indeed, NATO's intervention may have played an unintended role in encouraging the breakdown of the Charter regime for collective security, as suggested by the Legalist and Constructivist responses below and our analysis of the law of self-defense in the following chapter.

c. The Legalist Response

In the particular case of the NATO intervention, respected authority argues that S.C. Res. 1244 retroactively validated the operation.[172] However, a close reading of the text of the resolution and its negotiating history does not indicate any intent to ratify NATO's action among all the states whose consent would have been required to adopt an authorizing resolution ex ante.

170 Bass, *supra* note 1, at 478–79 (citations omitted).

171 *See id.* at 375.

172 *See* Louis Henkin, *Kosovo and the Law of Humanitarian Intervention,* 93 Am J. Int'l L. 824 (1999) (noted human rights scholar and former president of the American Society of International Law).

One might argue that Russia acquiesced in the results of NATO's intervention, thereby approving it.[173] But this says nothing about the views of China or Namibia, both of which supported the proposed Russian resolution condemning the NATO action.[174] Rather, the resolution "reaffirm[s] the commitment of all Member States to the sovereignty and territorial integrity of the Federal Republic of Yugoslavia and the other States of the region."[175] Moreover, at least two international bodies of experts writing shortly afterwards implicitly rejected the ratification argument.[176] Thus, one might argue that, even if a formal argument to that effect has some surface plausibility, whether ratification is possible in a doubtful case of legality is a completely different question from whether ratification should be inferred in a case of clear illegality.

As to ex ante justification, while some U.S. scholars suggest that authorization was implied by prior Security Council resolutions imposing an arms embargo and deploying a UN Verification Mission,[177] the U.S. issued no formal legal opinion defending the substantive legality of NATO conduct on this or any other grounds.[178] And it seems clear that neither the U.S. nor the U.K. before the ICJ was prepared to argue that there was advance Security Council authorization for the NATO bombing campaign.[179] It is worth noting that before the ICJ, Yugoslavia was represented by one of the world's leading authorities on international law and use of force, Britain's Ian Brownlie, who in his May 11 argument before the ICJ was able to rely upon virtually every respected authority in the international legal community to argue that state practice and international legal doctrine rejected the legality of humanitarian intervention without UN

173 *See* Damrosch, *supra* note 75, at 1209 (because Russia was willing to participate in KFOR).

174 *See supra* text accompanying note 139.

175 S.C. Res. 1244, preamble, U.N. Doc. S/RES/1244 (June 10, 1999).

176 The so-called R2P Report states: "Interventions by ad hoc coalitions (or, even more, individual states) acting without the approval of the Security Council, or the General Assembly, or a regional or sub-regional grouping of which the target state is a member, do not – it would be an understatement to say – find wide favour. Even those countries involved in the Kosovo intervention, and prepared to passionately defend its legitimacy by reference to all the threshold and precautionary criteria we have identified in this report, for the most part acknowledge its highly exceptional character, and express the view that it would have been much preferable to have secured the Security Council's – or failing that the General Assembly's – endorsement. One view that has some currency is that an *ex post facto* authorization, of the kind that has occurred for the African regional instances mentioned above, might conceivably have been obtained in the Kosovo and Rwanda cases, and may offer a way out of the dilemma should any such case occur again in the future." *See* The Responsibility to Protect: Report of the International Commission on Intervention and State Sovereignty, para. 6.36 (Dec. 2001) [hereinafter R2P Report] (*available at* http://www.iciss.ca/report-en.asp). The Report thus appears to suggest that no subsequent ratifying resolution was adopted by the Security Council; *see also* Independent International Commission, Kosovo Report, Chapter 6 (2000).

177 *See* Sean D. Murphy, *Contemporary Practice of the United States Relating to International Law*, 93 Am. J. Int'l L. 628, 631–32 (1999); Ruth Wedgwood, *NATO's Campaign in Kosovo*, 93 Am. J. Int'l L. 835–37 (1999) (relying on Security Council Resolutions 1160 1199, and 1203). Damrosch, however, notes that the language of those resolutions evidences recognition that Russia and China would have used their veto to prevent a Chapter VII authorizing resolution. See Damrosch, *supra* note 75, at 1264.

178 *See id.* at 1208.

179 *See* Arguments of the U.K., *supra* note 158.

authorization under Chapter VII of the Charter.[180] The U.K., by contrast, focused on the facts, as though the facts alone provided justification, although it suggested as a legal argument that Yugoslavia though its conduct lacked the "clean hands" necessary to entitle it to a remedy from the Court. The first argument suggests that the legal order is irrelevant to the Court's decision, since the morality of the U.K.'s conduct supplies the justification for its action. In short, the question has moved beyond the limits of the positivist legal order. The second argument is akin to the treatment of Yugoslavia as a "rogue" state outside the international legal order.[181] Construed this way, however, both arguments identify limits to the scope of the legal order. Noted commentators also viewed the case as ungovernable by the traditional law. Some viewed NATO's conduct as "illegal but justifiable," and, by analogy, not punishable as if under a domestic law rule of mitigation or excuse of criminal responsibility.[182] Others viewed it as evidencing the fundamental rupture and collapse of a UN Charter-based legal order.[183]

Yet, outside the chambers of the ICJ, NATO's intervention engendered a legalist debate. The Secretary-General posed the central questions in his speech that fall before the General Assembly:

> To those for whom the greatest threat to the future of international order is the use of force in the absence of a Security Council mandate, one might ask—not in the context of Kosovo—but in the context of Rwanda: If, in those dark days and hours leading up to the genocide, a coalition of States had been prepared to act in defense of the Tutsi population, but did not receive prompt Council authorization, should such a coalition have stood aside and allowed the horror to unfold?
>
> To those for whom the Kosovo action heralded a new era when States and groups of States can take military action outside the established mechanisms for enforcing international law, one might ask: Is there not a danger of such interventions undermining the imperfect, yet resilient security system created after the Second World War, and of setting dangerous precedents for future interventions without a clear criterion to decide who might invoke these precedents, and in what circumstances?[184]

The General Assembly, on the occasion of the UN's 50th anniversary, gave its answer in the so-called "World Summit Outcome."[185] The compromise struck a balance between state sover-

180 *See* Legality of Use of Force (Yugoslavia v. U.K.), CR/99/24, May 11, 1999 (citing Simma, Schachter, Akehurst, Dinstein, and Randezhofer).

181 *See* Part I, Chapter 2C (discussing the problem of "rogue" states from a constructivist perspective).

182 *See* Thomas Franck, Recourse to Force: State Action Against Threats and Armed Attacks 180–84 (2002).

183 *See generally* Michael J. Glennon, Limits of Law, Prerogatives of Power (2001).

184 Report of the Secretary-General, U.N. Doc. A/54/PV.4 (Sept. 20, 1999).

185 *See* G.A. Res. 60/1, U.N. GAOR, U.N. Doc. A/60.L.1 (Sept. 16, 2005) [hereinafter World Summit Outcome].

eignty with Charter law. On one hand, states recognized that "[e]ach individual State has a responsibility to protect its populations from genocide, war crimes, ethnic cleansing and crimes against humanity. This responsibility entails the prevention of such crimes, including their incitement, through appropriate and necessary means.... The international community should, as appropriate, encourage and help States to exercise this responsibility and support the United Nations in establishing an early warning capability."[186] In short, the General Assembly recognized that state sovereignty, under Article 2(7), was limited and that a state's treatment of its own "populations" was a matter of international concern.

That said, the General Assembly appeared to close the door to unilateral or collective intervention by states absent a Security Council authorization under Chapter VII. It declared:

> The international community, through the United Nations, also has the responsibility to use appropriate, diplomatic, humanitarian and other peaceful means, in accordance with Chapters VI and VII of the Charter, to help to protect populations from genocide, war crimes, ethnic cleansing and crimes against humanity. In this context, we are prepared to take *collective action, in a timely and decisive manner, through the Security Council, in accordance with the Charter, including Chapter VII*, on a case-by-case basis and in cooperation with relevant regional organizations as appropriate, should peaceful means be inadequate and national authorities are manifestly failing to protect their populations from genocide, war crimes, ethnic cleansing and crimes against humanity. We stress for the General Assembly to continue consideration of the responsibility to protect populations from genocide, war crimes, ethnic cleansing and crimes against humanity and its implications, bearing in mind the principles of the Charter and international law. We also intend to commit ourselves, as necessary and appropriate, to helping States build capacity to protect their populations from genocide, war crimes, ethnic cleaning and crimes against humanity and to assisting those which are under stress before crises and conflicts break out.[187]

In so doing, the General Assembly appeared to approve the Post-Cold War practice of Security Council-authorized humanitarian intervention, even in cases without demonstrable third-party international effects. Failures to discharge the "responsibility to protect" alone would seem to justify the Security Council's determination that, within the meaning of Chapter VII of the Charter, there was a "threat to the peace." Thus, the document could be read to suggest that only Security Council action can authorize forcible humanitarian intervention in the prescribed cases, since it contemplated "timely and decisive" Security Council action in such cases. On the other hand, the language does not explicitly address the question of whether even Security Council-authorized intervention is consistent with the Charter when a humanitarian

186 *Id.* at para. 138.

187 *Id.* at para. 139 (emphasis added).

emergency arises in a circumstance that does not fall within the categories specified in the resolution; nor does it explicitly address the question whether states retain any residual right to undertake humanitarian intervention when Security Council action is not "timely and decisive." In short, the language replicated the legal impasse at the Security Council during the Cold War.

Thus, continued legal uncertainty characterized the legalist response reflected in the World Summit Outcome, precisely because it remained within the terms of traditional Charter law, but as amended by the sustained practice of the Security Council during the 1990s. Traditional legal scholars, including the legal advisors to leading governments, have not perceived a rupture in the legal order, but rather a slight change of trajectory to normalize Security Council practice.[188]

Nonetheless, the resolution noted the "responsibility," rather than the "duty" of States, to "protect" their "populations," rather than their "population."[189] Thus, the General Assembly's resolution does not use the language of rights and duties, suggesting that no legal enforcement was contemplated. Yet, in using the term "populations,"[190] the resolution seems to contemplate that a state is composed of multiple groups, each receiving separate and distinct kinds and levels of protection. One could argue that these concepts reflect constructivist debates about the nature of international law on the issue of humanitarian intervention. A constructivist reading of the World Summit Outcome Resolution would look beneath the legalist surface of the General Assembly's response to notice shifting foundations of international law in response to the dialogue provoked by the NATO humanitarian intervention to save Kosovars and create Kosovo as an independent state.

d. A Constructivist Perspective

The rationalist and legalist perspectives seem to share the premise that states are the units of action in humanitarian intervention. While the rationalist perspective views the question as a "simple" exercise in welfare maximization, the legalist perspective views the question in terms of the formulation and application of norms embodied in the rules of the international legal system. For the most part, for the rationalist the effective units of decision-making are the states that are responsible for humanitarian crises and the states that are capable of intervening with the requisite military or political assets. For the legalist, rights and duties are held by subjects of

188 *See generally* Michael Wood, *International Law and the Use of Force: What Happens in Practice?*, 53 Indian Journal of International Law 345, 363 (2013)(British Member of the U.N.'s International Law Commission opining that "for the present, and absent further practice, claims [of humanitarian intervention in Iraq in 1991 and Kosovo in 1999] may have to rely on some exceptional defence or justification of necessity, such as is found in domestic legal systems, rather than on positive law"); *see also* Michael Matheson, Council Unbound: The Growth of UN Decision Making on Conflict and Postconflict Issues after the Cold War 139 (2006)(U.S. member of the International Law Commission and U.S. and former Acting Legal Advisor of U.S. State Department noting that "the U.S. has never asserted the doctrine [and] there is a much stronger legal and political basis for forcible humanitarian intervention under Chapters VII and VIII.").

189 World Summit Outcome, *supra* note 185, at para. 138.

190 *Id.*

international law; thus, the right to intervene is held by states, and the right against intervention is held by states. The UN Charter, in Articles 2(4) and 51, as discussed above, provide the framework for a legalist response to the question. But what if states are no longer the effective or the exclusive holders of rights and duties in the international community?

Constructivism thus draws attention to the transformational implications of the transnational debate prompted by the Kosovo intervention. In September 2000 the Canadian government launched an "International Commission on Intervention and States Sovereignty" (ICSS), which in December 2001 presented a report to the General Assembly entitled "The Responsibility to Protect," coining the phrase "R2P."[191] In its reply to the Secretary General's question,[192] the ICSS advised:

> 2.25 The emerging principle in question is that intervention for human protection purposes, including military intervention in extreme cases, is supportable when major harm to civilians is occurring or imminently apprehended, and the state in question is unable or unwilling to end the harm, or is itself the perpetrator. The Security Council itself has been increasingly prepared in recent years to act on this basis, most obviously in Somalia, defining what was essentially an internal situation as constituting a threat to international peace and security such as to justify enforcement action under Chapter VII of the UN Charter. This is also the basis on which the interventions by the Economic Community of West African States (ECOWAS) in Liberia and Sierra Leone were essentially justified by the interveners, as was the intervention mounted without Security Council authorization by NATO allies in Kosovo.
>
> 2.26 The notion that there is an emerging guiding principle in favour of military intervention for human protection purposes is also supported by a wide variety of legal sources - including sources that exist independently of any duties, responsibilities or authority that may be derived from Chapter VII of the UN Charter. These legal foundations include fundamental natural law principles; the human rights provisions of the UN Charter; the Universal Declaration of Human Rights together with the Genocide Convention; the Geneva Conventions and Additional Protocols on international humanitarian law; the statute of the International Criminal Court; and a number of other international human rights and human protection agreements and covenants.

---

191 R2P Report, *supra* note 176.

192 *See id.* at Foreword ("NATO's intervention in Kosovo in 1999 brought the controversy to its most intense head. Security Council members were divided; the legal justification for military action without new Security Council authority was asserted but largely unargued; the moral or humanitarian justification for the action, which on the face of it was much stronger, was clouded by allegations that the intervention generated more carnage than it averted; and there were many criticisms of the way in which the NATO allies conducted the operation. At the United Nations General Assembly in 1999, and again in 2000, Secretary-General Kofi Annan made compelling pleas to the international community to try to find, once and for all, a new consensus on how to approach these issues, to 'forge unity' around the basic questions of principle and process involved.").

Some of the ramifications and consequences of these developments will be addressed again in Chapter 6 of this report as part of the examination of the question of authority.

2.27 Based on our reading of state practice, Security Council precedent, established norms, emerging guiding principles, and evolving customary international law, the Commission believes that the Charter's strong bias against military intervention is not to be regarded as absolute when decisive action is required on human protection grounds. The degree of legitimacy accorded to intervention will usually turn on the answers to such questions as the purpose, the means, the exhaustion of other avenues of redress against grievances, the proportionality of the riposte to the initiating provocation, and the agency of authorization. These are all questions that will recur: for present purposes the point is simply that there is a large and accumulating body of law and practice which supports the notion that, whatever form the exercise of that responsibility may properly take, members of the broad community of states do have a responsibility to protect both their own citizens and those of other states as well.[193]

The R2P Report's central claim, then, is that not only Security Council but also the "members of the broad community of states" have a "responsibility to protect not only "their own citizens"—a concept accepted expressly by the World Summit Outcome resolution of the General Assembly—but also "those of other states as well." Moreover, in an obvious reference to the use of force along the lines of that taken by NATO with respect to Kosovo, the R2P suggests that "decisive action" may be taken by states for humanitarian intervention without Security Council authorization. Although sponsored by the Government of Canada, the R2P Report did not speak for states; rather, chaired by Gareth Evans, a former Canadian Cabinet Minister, and Mohammed Sahnoun, an Algerian then serving as a Special Advisor to the UN Secretary-General, the ICSS and its Advisory Group represented a broad range of inter-governmental, international non-governmental, and private organizations, yet all speaking in their individual capacities.[194] And, although it received support from the Canadian government, it drew its funding largely from private sources.[195] In short, for a constructivist, the R2P Report spoke for transnational civil society.

Perhaps this is why, in relation to Kosovo at least, the R2P Report focused less on the forms of sovereignty, the rights of states, and rigid adherence to Charter law than on the rights of peoples, the capacities of regional organizations, and the duties of international actors. The

193 *Id.* at paras. 2.25–27.

194 *See id.* at Annex A (Members); Annex B (Advisory Board).

195 *See id.* at Annex B (Funding) ("ICISS was funded by the Canadian Government, together with major international foundations including the Carnegie Corporation of New York, the William and Flora Hewlett Foundation, the John D. and Catherine T. MacArthur Foundation, the Rockefeller Foundation, and the Simons Foundation. ICISS is also indebted to the Governments of Switzerland and the United Kingdom for their generous financial and in-kind support to the work of the Commission.").

R2P Report contemplated viewing Yugoslavia's sovereignty as suspended,[196] treating action by regional organizations acting within their sphere of competence as a substitute for advance Security Council authorization,[197] and resolutions adopted by the General Assembly under the Uniting for Peace resolution as vehicles for legitimizing collective intervention when the Security Council had not acted.[198]

But, more important, from a constructivist standpoint, are the implicit premises for international law as a whole. One implication focuses on the process through which the R2P Report was produced, reflecting the growing authority of transnational civil society; the other, the substantive implications of the report, as well as the General Assembly's World Summit Outcome resolution, for international law doctrine. A constructivist response to the question of humanitarian intervention, then, could thus take two forms: one that focuses on higher units, meaning international organizations and norms; and another that focuses lower units, meaning the "peoples" exercising rights to existence and protection even from their own governments. From a constructivist perspective, the R2P Report thus reflects a move from the Lockean premises of the current international system to Kantian or world-state perspectives we explored in Chapter 2C.

Indeed, a constructivist approach, viewing the question of humanitarian intervention from the top level of transnational civil society, suggests that "a crucial shift" has occurred between the 19th century and the present, such that support for humanitarian intervention now reflects a social consensus based on "legal understandings and the rules or norms of international organizations" and "a dense web of international legal obligations to protect human rights."[199] From this standpoint, the R2P Report reflects the beginning of process internalizing the implications of the growing importance of international organizations and the culture and legalization of human rights. Moreover, while the practitioners of international organization politics and human rights advocacy, not generally states, were the motive forces behind the R2P Report, the ICSS also was in dialogue with Member States of the United Nations. Some of the conclusions

196 *See id.* at para. 5.26 ("Yugoslavia could be said to have temporarily had its sovereignty over Kosovo suspended, though it has not lost it *de jure*. The objective overall is not to change constitutional arrangements, but to protect them.").

197 *See id.* at para. 6.34 ("It is much more controversial when a regional organization acts, not against a member or within its area of membership, but against a non-member. This was a large factor in the criticism of NATO's action in Kosovo since it was outside NATO's area. NATO argues, nevertheless, that the conflict in Kosovo had the potential to spill over NATO borders and cause severe disruption, and was thus a matter of direct concern to it. Other regional and sub-regional organizations which have mounted military operations have acted strictly within their geographical boundaries against member states.").

198 *See id.* at para. 6.30 ("Although the General Assembly lacks the power to direct that action be taken, a decision by the General Assembly in favour of action, if supported by an overwhelming majority of member states, would provide a high degree of legitimacy for an intervention which subsequently took place, and encourage the Security Council to rethink its position. The practical difficulty in all of this is to contemplate the unlikelihood, in any but very exceptional case, of a two-thirds majority, as required under the Uniting for Peace procedure, being able to be put together in a political environment in which there has been either no majority on the Security Council, or a veto imposed or threatened by one or more permanent members - although Kosovo and Rwanda might just conceivably have been such cases. The Commission believes, nonetheless, that the mere possibility that this action might be taken will be an important additional form of leverage on the Security Council to encourage it to act decisively and appropriately.").

199 Martha Finnemore, The Purposes of Intervention: Changing Beliefs about the Use of Force 21 (2003).

of the R2P Report plainly influenced the UNGA's World Summit Outcome resolutions, such as acceptance of the legality of Chapter VII authority in wholly domestic violations of fundamental human rights; others, such collective intervention without Security Council authorization have not yet been accepted, but neither have they been completely rules out.

Indeed, a constructivist might find in the UNGA's World Summit Outcomes resolution evidence for an emerging conception of international law that would authorize intervention to protect "populations" within states, even if primary responsibility for their protection rests with their own states.[200] It has been suggested that Article 51 of the Charter provides a legal basis for humanitarian intervention.[201] Under this view, drawing on Rawls' later writings on international society, the existence of states from a moral standpoint is justified only as the ordering principle that the true actors in international society, the "peoples" that constitute states, would choose under reasonable conditions and assumptions as the basic institutions of international society.[202] It is "peoples"—and one sets aside for purposes of exposition the difficult question of how to define a "people"—that have rights, in fact what might be deemed "natural rights." And here the constructivist argument takes note of the equally authoritative French translation of Article 51 of the U.N. Charter, which refers to the "*inherent right* of individual or collective self-defense if an armed attack occurs against a member of the United Nations" as a "*droit naturel*," or natural right.[203] Thus, the natural right of peoples is built into the text of Article 51, and nothing in Article 51 precludes interpreting that right to extend to an "armed attack" or use of force against the right-holder, a "people" within a "Member State," coming from the government of that "Member state." Under this theory, the NATO intervention is an exercise of the right of "collective self-defense" under Article 51 of the Charter.[204] And to be more precise, the theory treats the notion of "collective self-defense" as two-fold: one that includes regional collective security function served by a pre-existing set of legal obligations, such as the NATO's mutual defense commitments; and more fundamental right that encompasses voluntary "defense of others," which in turn amounts to a right to rescue along the lines of the emerging R2P.[205] Thus, even the First Gulf War was not an exercise in "collective security" at all, at least in the established understanding of "collective self-defense," under which the United States and other Coalition members viewed the

200 *See* World Summit Outcome, *supra* note 185, at para. 138.

201 *See* George P. Fletcher & Jens David Ohlin, Defending Humanity: When Force is Justified and Why 129–154 (2008).

202 *Id.* at 146–47 (citing John Rawls, The Law of Peoples (1999)).

203 Fletcher & Ohlin, *supra* note 200, at 145 9 (citation omitted).

204 *See id.* at 151–52. Fletcher and Ohlin find the theory questionable as applied to Somalia because of doubt as to whether an attack occurred on a "people"; and they reject it for the Second Gulf War, since individual pre-emptive self-defense, rather than collective self-defense on humanitarian grounds, was the true rationale for the use of force. *See id.* at 152–54.

205 *See id.* at 68–78 (relying on the original French text of the Charter text, better translated into English as "legitimate defense," to view a strand of "collective" self-defense as encompassing the "defense of others," which under French law and the law of other civil law jurisdictions, but not under the common law, contemplates a duty to defend or rescue others).

matter primarily through the optic of their own interest, albeit shared with the Government of Kuwait, to repel aggression, because of the risk that aggression posed for them.[206] Instead, under the revised theory, it was a case of altruistic, humanitarian intervention, a case of international rescue, evidencing the emerging R2P.[207] Constructivism, by reconfiguring foundational premises, thus would re-interpret the legalist order so as to internalize changing values.[208]

Arguably, such a constructivist approach works out the implications of the rhetoric of self-determination that influenced the Versailles Conference and, to a lesser degree, the UN Charter.[209] It is a move from the "law of states" to a "law of peoples."[210]

2. Thesis 2—The Just War Theory's Gravitational Pull

An alternative, however, is to consider the moral basis for action, on the theory that natural law provides an independent basis for principled legal decision-making. Under this view, where the law of the UN Charter does not conform to the natural legal order, it is no longer governing law. Under the traditional Just War Theory, moreover, the focus is less on the "rights" of the victims and the parallel "rights" of Member States of the United Nations to defend victims than on the proper purposes of those with authority to act on behalf of the community. One might view the U.K.'s primary argument from the facts in defending NATO's intervention as a Just War Theory argument, for it did not seem to rely on international law at all. At the same time, the British argument made no systematic case on moral grounds in terms of the disciplined criteria of the Just War Tradition,[211] giving rise to criticism that in effect NATO treated its intervention as a form

206 This appears to be the common understanding of the right of collective self-defense under which the state providing assistance does so because of some interest it has in the defense of the targeted state. *See* Derek Bowett, Self-Defenses in International Law 201–02 (1958). The reference to "collective" self-defense, as well Chapter VIII's provisions relating to "regional security" organizations, as is widely-known, were included at least in part to satisfy the desire of Latin American Governments to avoid invalidating their own regional security regime under the recently-adopted Act of Chapultepec, the so-called Rio Treaty. *See* Ruth B. Russell, A History of the United Nations Charter 698 (1958). This self-interested rationale for collective self-defense is precisely the rationale that forms the target for constructivist revisionism. *See* Fletcher & Ohlin, *supra* note 200, at 80–83.

207 Fletcher & Ohlin, Defending Humanity, *supra* note 200, at 70–72.

208 The ICJ's current understanding of international law, as Fletcher and Ohlin know, takes a much narrower view of the "inherent" right of collective self-defense preserved by the Charter. *Id.* at 136–37 (citing the ICJ's rejection of the converse argument for self-defense asserted by a state, Israel, against attack by a non-state entity, elements of the Palestinian "people,"; *see* Advisory Opinion on the Legal Consequences of the Construction of a Wall in the Occupied Palestinian Territory, 2004 I.C.J. Rep.)).

209 *See* Fletcher & Ohlin, *supra* note 200, at 138–40 (for discussion of this emerging legal right, citing Antonio Cassese, Self-Determination of Peoples 67–99 (1995); Heather Wilson, International Law and the Use of Force by National Liberation Movements 55–88 (1988)).

210 *See generally* John Rawls, The Law of Peoples (1999) (arguing that protection of human rights from large-scale violations constitutes a necessary exception to the rule of non-intervention necessary in an international legal order constituted by liberal and hierarchical states); *See supra* Part II Introduction.

211 *See* Argument of the U.K., *supra* note 158.

of "civil disobedience" that offers no principled justification and, from the legalist perspective, fundamentally challenges the legal order via *ipse dixit*.[212]

Without clear justification in traditional legal forms, commentators have turned to explicitly moral analysis. Gareth Evans, who chaired the ICSS responsible for the R2P Report, has in fact suggested that something like Just War criteria be followed in decisions concerning humanitarian intervention—enumerating: the seriousness of the harm (which seems to track "Just Cause"), a proper purpose (which seems to equate with "Right Intention'), last resort, proportional means, and a balance of consequences.[213] And in a discussion of the NATO humanitarian intervention in Libya in 2011, recounting the long international debate on humanitarian intervention during the last decade, even a realist suggested that "we could have simply stayed with the concept of just war, which remains as valid today as it did in the time of Thomas Aquinas."[214] Moreover, by 2013, when considering whether to intervene in Syria to protect rebels and others from the use of chemical weapons by the Assad regime, the British Government framed its legal rationale in terms that recalled several of the elements of the Just War Tradition, thus providing a much more systematic account that it did before the ICJ in the case of Kosovo.[215]

It is unclear, however, whether Evans' formula, or the British approach to Syria, is rooted in the teleological system that shaped the Thomist and Spanish neo-scholastic understanding of Just War criteria. Under that formula, the pursuit of the common good and the achievement of true peace with justice, the so-called *transquillitas ordinis*. Clarity on this question would be essential in understanding how to apply Evans' criteria; for, perhaps, the ongoing duty to pursue the *tranquillitas ordinis* would create a presumption for humanitarian action, while a rights-based approach would, practically speaking, impose a burden of persuasion on the "innocent"

212 *See* Fletcher & Ohlin, *supra* note 200, at 135–36 (criticizing a defense of humanitarian intervention that eschews legal forms of justification).

213 *See* Gareth Evans, The Responsibility to Protect: from an Idea to an International Norm 15, 23–24, *in* Responsibility to Protect: The Global Moral Compact for the 21st Century (Cooper & Kohler eds., 2009). Leading scholars on the questions have adopted similar approaches. *See, e.g.*, Chesterman, *supra* note 41, at 228–229.

214 David Rieff, Saints Go Marching In, The National Interest, 6, 15 (July/Aug. 2011) ("[W]e could have simply stayed with the concept of just war, which remains as valid today as it did in the time of Thomas Aquinas.").

215 *See* Policy paper: Chemical weapon use by Syrian regime: UK government legal position, August, 29, 2013)(Office of the Prime Minister)(*available at* https://www.gov.uk/government/publications/chemical-weapon-use-by-syrian-regime-uk-government-legal-position/chemical-weapon-use-by-syrian-regime-uk-government-legal-position-html-version).

The paper provides conditions for British intervention, perhaps even unilateral intervention, provided:

(i) there is convincing evidence, generally accepted by the international community as a whole, of extreme humanitarian distress on a large scale, requiring immediate and urgent relief;

(ii) it must be objectively clear that there is no practicable alternative to the use of force if lives are to be saved; and

(iii) the proposed use of force must be necessary and proportionate to the aim of relief of humanitarian need and must be strictly limited in time and scope to this aim (i.e. the minimum necessary to achieve that end and for no other purpose).

Arguably, condition (i) identifies a Just Cause; (ii) embodies the last resort doctrine, and (iii) includes both the right intention criterion, that there be no other purpose, and a related requirement of proportionality of harms.

victims of atrocities. The most recent debate in the Just War Tradition has focused precisely on this question, namely, whether there is a "presumption against war."[216]

Indeed, in a close moral case such as Kosovo, the burden of moral persuasion would seem to dictate the result of one's analysis, as it would under a legal analysis. One might argue that evaluation of the so-called prudential criteria of the Just War Tradition,[217] namely the balance of harms question under a presumption against war—in light of all the factual uncertainties and the admittedly *post hoc* judgment that NATO intervention actually had the effect of accelerating and worsening the humanitarian catastrophe suffered by the Kosovars—would argue against intervention. At the same time, however, moralists reviewing the application of these prudential criteria would give enormous deference to NATO's factual judgments. Yet, in applying the absolutely binding, or so-called deontological criteria,[218] one could argue the Kosovars own partial culpability and NATO's own interest—particularly the EU's interest in projecting its power into the Balkans to avoid refugee flows and the consequent costs, and to extend the European political system ultimately into the Balkans—called into question the morality of NATO's conduct under the Just Cause and Right Intention criteria. One could question whether NATO's possibly imperial and selfish intentions falsified its nominally humanitarian just cause of saving Kosovars, who in turn were not wholly innocent through their violation of the human rights of Serbians in Kosovo.[219] The NATO intervention, under this view, would revive concerns about reliance on Just War Theory to impose Western culture on unassimilated populations (treating Slavic, in this case Serbian, eastern European culture in the same way the Spanish Conquistadors had treated aboriginal culture in the Americas, which has spawned the Spanish neo-scholastic revival of the Just War Tradition to discipline the Spanish Empire's expansionist tendencies).[220] But if the presumption against war does not control, it would be hard to find fault with NATO's decisions.

Thus, in the humility required by the Just War tradition, one wonders whether casuistry under JWT would advance the cause of moral clarity—filling the gap left by the realist and legalist acceptance of the status quo, and the indeterminacy of the rationalist and constructivist visions of the future—to make sense of Kosovo.

---

216 *See supra* Part II Introduction, text accompanying notes 175–93 (discussing debate between traditional understanding of James Turner Johnson and "presumption against war" articulated by the American Catholic Bishops and defended by Gregory Reichberg).

217 *See* James Turner Johnson, Part II Introduction, text accompanying notes 194–96.

218 *See id.*

219 *See* Delahunty & Perez, *supra* note 157, at 116-142 (discussing EU recognition of an independent Kosovo, debate between Grand Inquisitor and Fr. Zossima with respect to the EU's overall policy objectives in the Balkans).

220 *See supra* Part II Introduction, text accompanying notes 82–120.

What is clear is that the Kosovo case requires students, scholars, activists, and governments alike to meditate on the relationship between power, welfare, law, and morality. It tests the Charter system on the use of force, the meaning and consequences of the right to self-determination of peoples in international law, and the intersection of these two concepts in the collective right of self-defense. We now turn to another way in which the traditional *jus ad bellum* debate has fractured international opinion in the aftermath of the end of the Cold War: the question of the use of force preemptively to address the threat of terrorist use of weapons of mass destruction. If the Kosovo case raised the question of the outer limits of the right of collective self-defense (or to intervene in the domestic affairs of states to save the innocent), the Second Gulf War raises the question of the outer limits of the right of self-defense. But under a Just War Theory, the right of self-defense by those in authority in a state can always be reduced to the duty to defend the members of the political community for whom those in authority are responsible. Both rights, under the Just War Tradition, are in fact duties of charity that must be viewed as a species of the same obligation, even if they are subjectively understood as a matter of international law.

Chapter 4

The Second Gulf War: Preemptive Self-Defense

In the aftermath of the September 11, 2001 attacks by Al Qaeda against the United States, the Bush administration articulated what has come to be known as the Bush Doctrine, which on its own terms describes a strategy of "preemptive" use of force to address the threat of use of weapons of mass destruction (WMD) by "rogue states and terrorists."[1] It seems quite clear that the Bush Doctrine supplied the context for the policy decision leading to the war and provided at least part of the domestic political rationale through which the administration persuaded the U.S. Congress to provide domestic legal authorization for the use of force. [2] Admittedly, in its formal statement of the international legal theory it used to persuade the U.S. Congress to grant

1 *See* The National Security Strategy of the United States (Sept. 17, 2002), http://georgewbush-whitehouse.archives.gov/nsc/nss/2002/index.html.). It states:

> For centuries, international law recognized that nations need not suffer an attack before they can lawfully take action to defend themselves against forces that present an imminent danger of attack. Legal scholars and international jurists often conditioned the legitimacy of preemption on the existence of an imminent threat—most often a visible mobilization of armies, navies, and air forces preparing to attack.
>
> We must adapt the concept of imminent threat to the capabilities and objectives of today's adversaries. Rogue states and terrorists do not seek to attack us using conventional means. They know such attacks would fail. Instead, they rely on acts of terror and, potentially, the use of weapons of mass destruction—weapons that can be easily concealed, delivered covertly, and used without warning.
>
> The targets of these attacks are our military forces and our civilian population, in direct violation of one of the principal norms of the law of warfare. As was demonstrated by the losses on September 11, 2001, mass civilian casualties is the specific objective of terrorists and these losses would be exponentially more severe if terrorists acquired and used weapons of mass destruction.
>
> The United States has long maintained the option of preemptive actions to counter a sufficient threat to our national security. The greater the threat, the greater is the risk of inaction— and the more compelling the case for taking anticipatory action to defend ourselves, even if uncertainty remains as to the time and place of the enemy's attack. To forestall or prevent such hostile acts by our adversaries, the United States will, if necessary, act preemptively.
>
> The United States will not use force in all cases to preempt emerging threats, nor should nations use preemption as a pretext for aggression. Yet in an age where the enemies of civilization openly and actively seek the world's most destructive technologies, the United States cannot remain idle while dangers gather. We will always proceed deliberately, weighing the consequences of our actions.

2 *See* Congressional Joint Resolution Authoring Use of Force against Iraq, Pub. L. No. 107-243, 116 Stat. 1499 (2002) [hereinafter Iraq Resolution], providing, in pertinent part, as follows:

> Whereas after the liberation of Kuwait in 1991, Iraq entered into a United Nations sponsored cease-fire agreement pursuant to which Iraq unequivocally agreed, among other things, to eliminate its nuclear, biological, and chemical weapons programs and the means to deliver and develop them, and to end its support for international terrorism;
>
> Whereas the efforts of international weapons inspectors, United States intelligence agencies, and Iraqi defectors led to the discovery that Iraq had large stockpiles of chemical weapons and a large scale biological weapons program, and that Iraq had an advanced nuclear weapons development program that was much closer to producing a nuclear weapon than intelligence reporting had previously indicated;
>
> Whereas Iraq, in direct and flagrant violation of the cease-fire, attempted to thwart the efforts of weapons inspectors to identify and destroy Iraq's weapons of mass destruction stockpiles and development capabilities, which finally resulted in the withdrawal of inspectors from Iraq on October 31, 1998;

domestic legal authorization,[3] and in its explanation to the United Nations Security Council,[4] the Bush Administration relied on prior Security Council authorization rather than the Bush Doctrine's theory of preemptive self-defense. Yet, it is the Bush Doctrine that has received the greatest attention, giving rise to enormous criticism as an unlawful and immoral policy of "preventive" war, rather than a theory of legitimate, anticipatory self-defense. The Bush Doctrine's theory of preemptive self-defense remains important largely because of its potential use in

---

> Whereas Iraq both poses a continuing threat to the national security of the United States and international peace and security in the Persian Gulf region and remains in material and unacceptable breach of its international obligations by, among other things, continuing to possess and develop a significant chemical and biological weapons capability, actively seeking a nuclear weapons capability, and supporting and harboring terrorist organizations;...
>
> Whereas the current Iraqi regime has demonstrated its capability and willingness to use weapons of mass destruction against other nations and its own people;
>
> Whereas the current Iraqi regime has demonstrated its continuing hostility toward, and willingness to attack, the United States, including by attempting in 1993 to assassinate former President Bush and by firing on many thousands of occasions on United States and Coalition Armed Forces engaged in enforcing the resolutions of the United Nations Security Council;
>
> Whereas members of al Qaida, an organization bearing responsibility for attacks on the United States, its citizens, and interests, including the attacks that occurred on September 11, 2001, are known to be in Iraq;
>
> Whereas Iraq continues to aid and harbor other international terrorist organizations, including organizations that threaten the lives and safety of United States citizens;
>
> Whereas the attacks on the United States of September 11, 2001, underscored the gravity of the threat posed by the acquisition of weapons of mass destruction by international terrorist organizations;
>
> Whereas Iraq's demonstrated capability and willingness to use weapons of mass destruction, the risk that the current Iraqi regime will either employ those weapons to launch a surprise attack against the United States or its Armed Forces or provide them to international terrorists who would do so, and the extreme magnitude of harm that would result to the United States and its citizens from such an attack, combine to justify action by the United States to defend itself ...

3 *Id.*, which provides, in pertinent part, as follows:

> Whereas after the liberation of Kuwait in 1991, Iraq entered into a United Nations sponsored cease-fire agreement pursuant to which Iraq unequivocally agreed, among other things, to eliminate its nuclear, biological, and chemical weapons programs and the means to deliver and develop them, and to end its support for international terrorism;
>
> Whereas in 1990 in response to Iraq's war of aggression against and illegal occupation of Kuwait, the United States forged a coalition of nations to liberate Kuwait and its people in order to defend the national security of the United States and enforce United Nations Security Council resolutions relating to Iraq;...
>
> Whereas United Nations Security Council Resolution 678 (1990) authorizes the use of all necessary means to enforce United Nations Security Council Resolution 660 (1990) and subsequent relevant resolutions and to compel Iraq to cease certain activities that threaten international peace and security, including the development of weapons of mass destruction and refusal or obstruction of United Nations weapons inspections in violation of United Nations Security Council Resolution 687 (1991), repression of its civilian population in violation of United Nations Security Council Resolution 688 (1991), and threatening its neighbors or United Nations operations in Iraq in violation of United Nations Security Council Resolution 949 (1994);
>
> Whereas in the Authorization for Use of Military Force Against Iraq Resolution (Public Law 102-1), Congress has authorized the President to use United States Armed Forces pursuant to United Nations Security Council Resolution 678 (1990) in order to achieve implementation of Security Council Resolution 660, 661, 662, 664, 665, 666, 667, 669, 670, 674, and 677";
>
> Whereas in December 1991, Congress expressed its sense that it "supports the use of all necessary means to achieve the goals of United Nations Security Council Resolution 687 as being consistent with the Authorization of Use of Military Force Against Iraq Resolution (Public Law 102-1)," that Iraq's repression of its civilian population violates United Nations Security Council Resolution 688 and "constitutes a continuing threat to the peace, security, and stability of the Persian Gulf region," and that Congress, "supports the use of all necessary means to achieve the goals of United Nations Security Council Resolution 688";
>
> Whereas the Iraq Liberation Act of 1998 (Public Law 105-338) expressed the sense of Congress that it should be the policy of the United States to support efforts to remove from power the current Iraqi regime and promote the emergence of a democratic government to replace that regime ....

4 *See* William H. Taft & Todd F. Buchwald, *Preemption, Iraq, and International Law*, 97 Am. J. Int'l L. 563, 563 (2003) (exposition by the sitting U.S. State Department Legal Advisor and his deputy of the official position of the U.S. Government).

other situations not governed by the thicket of Security Council resolutions directed towards Iraq, such as the potential acquisition and/or use of WMD by other so-called rogue states. It also is relevant, both as a matter of background customary international law and as a matter of legal-policy concerning the development of international law, to future U.S. interpretations of Security Council resolutions relating to the potential use of WMD by terrorists and rogue states. Thus, in this chapter we focus on the so-called right of "preemptive self-defense," the Second Gulf War, and the general problem of self-defense against potential use of WMD by terrorists or so-called rogue states.

To examine the debate on the Bush Doctrine and its relevance to the legal and political debates surrounding the Second Gulf War, first we consider the traditional background law of self-defense, exploring the traditional customary law and the law of the U.N. Charter, as it was debated by multiple actors in the international system, including but not limited to the International Court of Justice. Then, we explore the circumstances giving rise to the Second Gulf War. With this background, we supply a set of questions, exploring the meaning and effects of Security Council Resolution 1441, [5] which gave Saddam Hussein one last chance to comply with prior Security Council resolutions; the formal legal justifications advanced by the U.S. and U.K. for the Coalition use of force in their letters to the UN Security Council; and Security Council Resolution 1483,[6] which provided the terms for international recognition of the Coalition occupation of Iraq after the overthrow of the Hussein regime. These two resolutions provide bases for alternative viewpoints of the legal issues: one focusing on ex ante authorization under customary international law or the law of the UN Charter; the other, comparable to Resolution 1244 in respect of NATO's humanitarian intervention to save Kosovars,[7] suggesting a theory of ex post ratification or, less favorably, the excuse of an otherwise unlawful aggressive war. Finally, in our commentary on these issues, we explore legalist, realist, rationalist, constructivist, and Just War Theory interpretations of these issues and events.

5 *See* S.C. Res. 1441, U.N. SCOR, 57th year, U.N. Doc. S/RES/1441 (2002).

6 S.C. Res. 1483, U.N. SCOR, 58th year, U.N. Doc. S/RES/1483 (2003).

7 *See* Part II, Chapter 3, *supra*.

A. THE LAW OF SELF-DEFENSE

Most discussion of the law of self-defense begins with the UN Charter and Article 2(4),[8] which provides:

> All Members shall refrain in their international relations from the threat or use of force against the territorial integrity or political independence of any state, or in any other manner inconsistent with the Purposes of the United Nations....

and Article 51,[9] which provides:

> Nothing in the present Charter shall impair the inherent right of individual or collective self-defense if an armed attack occurs against a Member of the Untied Nations, until the Security Council has taken measures necessary to maintain international peace and security. Measures taken by Members in exercise of this right of self-defense shall be immediately reported to the Security Council and shall not in any way affect the authority and responsibility of the Security Council under the present Charter to take at any time such action as it deems necessary in order to maintain or restore international peace and security.

Thus, the text of Article 51 implicitly references not only article 2(4), which prohibits use of force, but also Chapters VII and VIII. Chapters VII, as we have already discussed,[10] authorizes UN "enforcement action" and now, under the law of the First Gulf War, UN authorization for states or groupings of states to use force. Chapter VIII similarly permits the Security Council to "utilize ... regional arrangements or agencies for enforcement action under its authority," but further provides that "no enforcement action shall be taken under regional arrangements or by regional agencies without the authorization of the Security Council...."[11] Thus, the scope for unilateral use of force by states, at least as provided under a naïve reading of the Charter, turns on four questions: first, whether force is prohibited under Article 2(4); second, it is authorized by the Security Council under Chapters VII or VIII; third, if it is prohibited by Article 2(4) and not authorized under Chapters VII or VIII, whether it is permitted under Article 51; and fourth, whether, even if it is permitted under Article 51, it is nonetheless prohibited under the Security Council's authority under Article 51 to exercise it powers under Chapter VII and VIII?

8 U.N. Charter art. 2, para. 4.

9 U.N. Charter art. 51.

10 *See* Part II, Chapter 2, *supra.*

11 U.N. Charter art. 53, para.1 (albeit subject to an exception against the "enemy states"). *See* Chapter 3, *supra* (discussing "enemy states" clause of the Charter and similar war settling and alliance features of the U.N. Charter).

Some initially argued that the Charter's language could be read narrowly. Article 2(4)'s prohibition on use of forces might apply only to force against "the territorial integrity or political independence" of states or otherwise in a "manner inconsistent with the Purposes" of the United Nations. But initial post-Charter understanding of the potential abuse of claims of humanitarian intervention, even when not intended to subordinate a state but rather intended to further human rights, which is a "Purpose" of the UN, militated in favor of a broad interpretation of Article 2(4).[12] Moreover, the negotiating history of the Charter in the view of most observers reflects an intent, not to limit the scope of prohibition, but rather to emphasize or expand it.[13] Of course, as the collective security regime envisaged by the Charter's drafters collapsed with the onset of the Cold War, it became more plausible to argue that the Charter's prohibition might operate more narrowly than initially understood[14] or, indeed, even to claim that the Charter, at least as a treaty, may no longer reflect binding law because there has been a "fundamental change of circumstances" giving states the right to treat its provisions as inoperative.[15] If, however, the Charter's prohibition remains in force, as a matter of treaty or as evidence of customary international law, an assumption that seems to be widely shared, the critical question -- setting aside for a moment the potential effects of Chapters VII and VIII, which is of crucial relevance for the legal debate on the Second Gulf War -- becomes the scope of a state's "inherent right of individual and collective self-defense" when facing "an armed attack" under Article 51 of the Charter and customary international law.

1. The Pre-Charter Customary International Law Background

The customary international background to the Charter is, for the most part, opaque, since pre-Charter law, as we have discussed, had not clearly laid out the contours of a prohibition on the use of force or correlative rights of self-defense. However, in the immediate aftermath of the Second World War, the so-called *Caroline* standard seems to have risen to prominence. Strictly speaking, the standard, as articulated in the 19th century by U.S. Secretary of State Daniel Webster, provides that use of force in self-defense is limited to cases in which the "necessity of the self-defense is instant, overwhelming, and leaving no choice of means, and no moment of

12 *See* Part II, Chapter 3, *supra.*

13 *See* Yoram Dinstein, War and Aggression 87 n. 26 (2005) (citing A. Randelzhofer, Article 2(4), The Charter of the United Nations: A Commentary, Vol. I, 112, 123 (B. Simma ed., 2002)).

14 *See, e.g.*, Julius Stone, Aggression and World Order: A Critique of United Nations Theories of Aggression (1958); and Thomas Franck, *Who Killed Article 2(4)? Or: Changing Norms Governing the Use of Force by States,* 64 Am. J. Int'l L. 809 (1970).

15 *See* Robert J. Delahunty, *Paper Charter: Self-Defense and the Failure of the United Nations Collective Security System,* 56 Cath. U. L. Rev. 871 (2007).

deliberation."[16] The standard was cited in response to claims of self-defense at the Nuremberg and Tokyo Tribunals[17] -- at the Nuremberg Tribunal to reject the German claim of preemptive self-defense against Great Britain when Germany attacked Norway in 1940;[18] and at the Tokyo Tribunal to justify the Netherlands' declaration of war against Japan as an immediate response to Japanese attacks against the United States and Great Britain.[19] While one could debate whether either case reflects a correct application of the *Caroline* standard,[20] what seems to matter is that the *Caroline* standard was invoked by the powers responsible for the Charter as their understanding of the scope of the "inherent" or pre-Charter right of self-defense, and that the *Caroline* standard has been invoked as evidence for why the Bush Doctrine violates both the Charter and customary international law.[21] A close review of the facts and context for the incident that gave rise to the standard, therefore, seems appropriate.

The *Caroline* incident occurred in 1837 during the Canadian rebellion against the U.K.[22] Some U.S. nationals along the border sympathized with the Canadian rebels and sought to assist them. The United States government attempted to suppress these activities by its own nationals, but was unsuccessful.[23] In December 1837, a group of armed men, many of them U.S. nationals, seized Navy Island on the Canadian side of the Niagara River, and used it as a base for attacking the Canadian mainland. The *Caroline*, a steamer bearing the U.S. flag, was used to make trips between New York and Navy Island and convoy men and material to the Canadian rebels.[24] The British commander, observing this activity, resolved to destroy the *Caroline* while it was in Canadian territory at Navy Island.[25] As it happened, however, the *Caroline* had returned to U.S. territory, carrying twenty-three U.S. nationals on board, when the British fell upon it and destroyed it.[26] U.S.

16 The Caroline, 2 Moore, Digest of International Law 412 (1906); Charles Cheney Hyde, International Law 239 (1945), *reprinted in* Lori Damrosch, Louis Henkin, Sean Murphy, International Law, Cases and Materials, 1134–35 (5th ed. 2009).

17 For a discussion of the Tribunals, *see* Chapter 1B.

18 *See* Judgment of the International Military Tribunal for the Trial of German Major War Criminals, Cmd. 6964, at 28–29 (1946).

19 *See* The Tokyo Judgment: The International Military Tribunal for the Far East, April 29, 1946– November 12, 1948 382 (B.V.A. Roling and C. F. Ruter, eds., 1977).

20 *See* Delahunty, *supra* note 15, at 911–13.

21 For the common post-Charter reading, *see* Michael Bothe, *Terrorism and the Legality of Pre-emptive Force*, 14 Eur. J. Int'l L. 227, 231 (2003).

22 *See generally* R.Y. Jennings, *The Caroline and McLeod Cases*, 32 Am. J. Int'l L. 82 (1938) (providing the standard account of the factual background of the Caroline incident); *see also* Letter from Daniel Webster, U.S. Sec'y of State, to Lord Ashburton, British Special Minister (July 27, 1842) (*available at* http://www.yale.edu/lawweb/avalon/diplomacy/britain/br-1842d.htm) [hereinafter "Webster Letter"] (providing this letter and other important primary materials of the Caroline case).

23 *See* Jennings, *supra* note 22, at 82.

24 *See id.* at 83.

25 *Id.* at 83–84.

26 *Id.* at 84.

diplomatic protests, made originally in 1838, were renewed in 1841 by Secretary of State Daniel Webster.[27] Webster's letter of July 27, 1842 to the British Special Minister Lord Ashburton is the now-classic statement of the *Caroline* doctrine. In that letter, Webster maintained that under the circumstances, "[i]t will be for [the British g]overnment to show a necessity of self-defence, instant, overwhelming, leaving no choice of means, and no moment for deliberation."[28]

Recent scholarship has re-examined the development of the *Caroline* doctrine and shown that it was reformulated and misstated by many legal writers in the post-Charter period.[29] This scholarship reveals that the prevailing pre-Charter understanding limited the doctrine's restrictions on self-defense only "to extra-territorial uses of force by a state in peacetime against another state that was unable or unwilling to prevent its territory from being used as a base of operations for hostile activities against the state taking action."[30] The doctrine was originally not conceived to impose requirements applying to every occasion of lawful self-defense. For example, a state could properly use armed force to defend its own sparsely inhabited territory from forcible incursions by another state's military, even if the need for such counter-force was "neither 'instant' nor 'overwhelming.'"[31] The common post-Charter view "that the narrow restrictions of the *Caroline* doctrine apply to all uses of force by a state in self-defense under customary international law" is, therefore, mistaken.[32] Indeed, if the Nuremberg Tribunal and IMTFE citations to the *Caroline* went beyond the narrow proposition for which the incident stood, the question arises whether these citations evidenced, not the established customary international law on the use of force, but rather a forward-looking revision in accordance with new principles, including but not limited to those found in the Charter's broader prohibition on uses of force.[33]

2. The Charter Text and Customary International Law

To the extent, however, that the *Caroline* standard is part of the context for interpreting the Charter, it has been understood by many to relax to some extent the Charter's textual requirement for an actual "armed attack." A right to preemption, therefore, is viewed by some as an exception to the clear language of the Charter, which should be construed narrowly, thus reinforcing a broad reading of the Charter's prohibition on the use of force. [34] Under this reading,

27 *Id.* at 85

28 Webster Letter, *supra* note 22.

29 *See* Timothy Kearley, *Raising the Caroline*, 17 Wis. Int'l L. J. 325 (1999).

30 *Id.* at 325, 336–38.

31 *See id.* at 326.

32 *Id.* at 330.

33 *See* Chapter 1B, *supra.*

34 *See generally* Ian Brownlie, International Law and the Use of Force by States (1963).

the "inherent right of self-defense" survives only when an actual "armed attack" has commenced or in order to preempt such an armed attack, but only when the *Caroline* standard is satisfied.

3. Post-Charter Practice and Interpretations

Interpretation of the Charter does not stop, however, with its text and customary international law background. The practice of UN organs and of states under the Charter is an indispensable source, especially early practice following the adoption of the Charter. Significantly, as early as 1949, the ICJ advanced a narrow view of the right of self-defense in the *Corfu Channel Case*,[35] when British naval forces -- exercising the right of innocent passage through an international waterway and after having suffered damage from mines laid in Albania's territorial sea -- took forcible measures to clear the waterway of mines. The ICJ rejected Britain's claim. The Court conceded that Albania was internationally responsible for laying the mines and not warning the U.K. about the mines. Nonetheless, it rejected the U.K. argument that it was entitled to take "possession of the evidence" and to engage in "self-help," which was an argument of self-defense by another name. Implicitly, however, the laying of mines in this international waterway did not constitute an "armed attack" on the U.K., and the U.K. therefore did not have the right to use force. Recognizing the onset of the Cold War and the lack of consensus at the Security Council, the ICJ nonetheless noted that it could "only regard the alleged right of intervention as the manifestation of a policy of force, such as has, in the past, given rise to more serious abuses and such as cannot, whatever be the present defects in international organization, find a place in international law." It added that, "to ensure respect for international law, of which it is the organ, the Court must declare that the action of the British Navy constituted a violation of international law."[36] Thus, the ICJ advanced a vision of itself as "the organ" of international law within the international legal system with competence to pronounce upon legal questions relating to the use of force, even by Permanent Members of the Security Council such as the U.K.

On the other hand, some intervening state practice seemed to offer contrary evidence, suggesting that the term "armed attack" could be construed more broadly to include measures short of an actual armed attack. Instigating what became known as the Cuban Missile Crisis in October 1962, the Soviet Union, notwithstanding private pledges to President Kennedy to the contrary, earlier that year deployed nuclear missiles in Cuba.[37] President Kennedy, shortly after discovering the deployment through U.S. U-2 spy-plane over-flights of Cuba, on October 22, 1962 publicly demanded the withdrawal of those weapons, declaring that this "urgent transformation of Cuba into an important strategic base -- by presence of ... large, long-range, and clearly

35 *See* The Corfu Channel Case [U.K. v. Albania], 1949 I.C.J. Rep. 4 (Jul. 9, 1949).

36 *Id.* at 34–35.

37 *See* Don Munton & David A. Welch, The Cuban Missile Crisis: A Concise History 53 (2007).

offensive weapons of sudden mass destruction -- constitutes an explicit threat to the peace and security of all the Americas, in flagrant and deliberate defiance of the Rio Pact of 1947, the traditions of this nation and hemisphere... and my own pubic warning to the Soviet..." On October 23 the Permanent Council of Organization of American States, meeting as the Provisional Organ of Consultation under the Rio Treaty meet and voted "to take all measures, individually and collectively, including the use of armed force, which they may deem necessary to ensure that the Government of Cuba cannot continue to receive supplies which may threaten the peace and security of the Continent and to prevent the missiles in Cuba with offensive capability from ever becoming an active threat to the peace and security of the Continent."[38] The same day, the President ordered what he termed a "quarantine" of Cuba -- a term coined by the Deputy Legal Adviser to the Department of State, to avoid using the term 'blockade" and thereby avoid the appearance of asserting belligerent rights that the U.S. would assert under the law of war.[39] At the same time, the U.S. prepared contingency plans to take military action against Soviet forces in Cuba; but these plans were never implemented when the U.S. and Soviet Union came to an understanding under which, among other things, the missiles were withdrawn.[40] It is widely believed, however, that war may have been inevitable without the withdrawal of the missiles.[41]

The legality of the U.S. conduct was widely questioned at the time. Former Secretary of State Dean Acheson, also a renowned international lawyer, famously said:

> The power, position and prestige of the United States had been challenged by another state; and law simply does not deal with such questions of ultimate power -- power that comes close to the sources of sovereignty. I cannot believe that there are principles of law that say we must accept destruction of our way of life. One would be surprised if practical men, trained in legal history and thought, had devised and brought into a state of general acceptance a principle condemnatory of an action so essential to the continuation of pre-eminent power as that taken by the United States....[42]

Moreover, to the extent the law mattered, there appeared to be a disconnect between the theory of law publicly articulated by U.S. officials and the theory of law that guided private deliberations.

38 Whiteman, *The Cuban Missile Crisis*, 1962, 4 Dig. of U.S. Prac. of Int'l L. 523–24 (1965).

39 *See* Quincy Wright, *The Cuban Quarantine*, 57 Am. J. Int'l L. 546 (1963) (rejecting the view that the U.S. action was authorized as a pacific blockage not amounting to an act of war, that it was authorized under Article 51 of the Charter, or that it was authorized under the Charter of the OAS and the Rio Treaty).

40 For a discussion of the settlement, involving implicit and explicit commitments concerning future U.S. action towards Cuba and the withdrawal of comparable U.S. missiles deployed in Turkey, *see* John Lewis Gaddis, We Now Know 268–74 (2007).

41 *See* Scott Silverstone, Preventive War and American Democracy 123 (2007) (viewing war as inevitable if the Soviets had not withdrawn the missiles).

42 The Cuban Quarantine, Remarks by the Honorable Dean Acheson, 57 A.S.I. L. Proc. 13, 14 (1963).

The public legal theory of the U.S. was that it was authorized to act by the OAS, which was a Chapter VIII regional organization. Publicly, moreover, the U.S. took no position as to whether it also was entitled to exercise the right of self-defense. Indeed, the Deputy Legal Advisor for the U.S. Department of State Leonard Meeker specifically stated that the "quarantine" was "considered not to contravene Article 4, paragraph 2, because it was a measure adopted by a regional organization in conformity with the provisions of Chapter VIII of the Charter." He added, "The purposes of the [OAS] were considered to be consistent with the purposes and principles of the United Nations as provided in Article 52. This being the case, the quarantine would no more violate Article 2, paragraph 4, than measures voted by the Council under Chapter VII, by the General Assembly under Articles 10 and 11, or taken by the Unite Nations Members in conformity with Article 51."[43]

Yet, the U.S. argument seemed frivolous. Article 52 provides only that "[n]othing in the present Charter precludes the existence of regional arrangements or agencies for dealing with such matters relating to the maintenance of international peace and security as are appropriate for regional action, provided that such arrangements or agencies and their activities are consistent with the Purposes and Principles of the Untied Nations."[44] Meanwhile, Article 53(1) also clearly provided that "no enforcement action shall be taken under regional arrangement or by regional agencies without the authorization of the Security Council..."[45] And, since the quarantine would have constituted "enforcement action" if undertaken pursuant to UN authorization, as Meeker seemed to concede, the absence of specific Security Council authorization, which was impossible due to the threat of Soviet veto, the U.S. quarantine could not have been justified under Article 53 as "enforcement action" by a "regional arrangement."[46] It appears significant that Meeker did not refer at all to Article 53, but suggested that the U.S. action was no less justified than state action under Article 51. Because it is no more possible to suggest that the Soviet Union engaged in an "armed attack" against the United States by deploying WMD in Cuba than to suggest that U.S. had engaged in an "armed attack" against the Soviet Union by deployed WMD on the Soviet periphery, if justified in terms of self-defense, the U.S. action would have to be regarded as preemptive self-defense. Alternatively, if both sides had engaged in "armed attacks" for purposes of Article 51, both sides would have been entitled to exercise the right of self-defense in an ongoing belligerency.

In fact, it is now clear that in their internal deliberations senior U.S. government officials believed, and were so advised by their Department of Justice lawyers, that the U.S. was entitled to rely on a theory of individual self-defense.[47] It has been suggested that the U.S. advanced as a

43 Leonard Meeker, *Defensive Quarantine and the Law*, 57 Am. J. Int'l L. 523, 524 (1963).

44 U.N. Charter art. 52, para. 1.

45 U.N. Charter art. 53, para. 1.

46 *See* Wright, *supra* note 39.

47 *See* The Kennedy Tapes: Inside the White House during the Cuban Missile Crisis (Ernest R. May & Philip D. Zelikow, eds., 1997).

public legal justification the OAS theory knowing it to be inconsistent with the plain text of the Charter but believing it to do less damage to U.S. interests by expanding the U.S. public theory of the scope of Article 51 in a way that could be relied upon by the Soviet Union in the future to the detriment of U.S. interests.[48] Thus, given the gap between public pronouncements and private views, as suggested by Secretary Acheson's statement, the precise relation between law and politics in the Cuban Missile Crisis has never been clear.

Indeed, the debate over the legacy of the Cuban Missile Crisis may ultimately require a debate about sources and methods in international law, in turn reflecting conflicting theories of jurisprudence. Under traditional positivist theories, the public articulation of the legal theory for state conduct constitutes the *opinio juris* that is necessary to establish evidence of legal obligation as a matter of customary international law and is also relevant to establishing subsequent practice as evidence of the meaning of a treaty.[49] Alternatively, a legal realist approach focuses on the degree to which the action taken reflects a state's actual understanding of the law as a guide to its likely future conduct, as well as the actual legitimating effect of conduct regardless of the reasons given for its validity.[50] Under the former view, because the U.S. never asserted a right of self-defense, nothing in the Cuban Missile Crisis reveals anything about the right of self-defense. Under the latter view, U.S. practice in the Cuban Missile Crisis evidenced an understanding of the "inherent" right of self-defense under Article 51 of the Charter as not limited to cases involving actual armed attacks -- indeed, as not being limited even to threats that would satisfy the strict standards of the *Caroline* test, since there was no evidence whatsoever of an "immediate" risk of a Soviet first-strike from Cuba against the United States. But international acceptance of U.S. conduct, where the U.S. never had to veto a resolution of condemnation, reveals something about international acceptance of the operational theory under which the U.S. acted. Because, however, the U.S. never publicly articulated its theory, describing the operational U.S. theory of the law of self-defense that would explain U.S. conduct in the Cuban Missile Crisis would require an imaginative reconstruction. It might focus on the U.S. understanding that the likelihood and gravity of the threat had risen in a way (i.e., by means of surprise, thus signaling aggressive intent) and to a level (i.e., constituting a new nuclear first-strike capability for the Soviet Union and thus substantially shifting the balance of power) that was not acceptable and thus warranted defensive measures.[51] But these would be tentative and provisional

48 *See* Abram Chayes, The Cuban Missile Crisis: International Crises and the Role of Law (1974) (former U.S. Legal Adviser during the Cuban Missile Crisis defending the relevance of international law to decision-making in the crisis).

49 *See generally* Schachter, International Law in Theory and Practice (1991).

50 *See generally* Michael Reisman and Andrew Willard, International Incidents: The Law that Counts in World Politics (1988).

51 For commentators describing the Cuban Missile Crisis as a case of preemptive self-defense, *see, e.g.*, Ruth Wedgewood, *The Fall of Saddam Hussein: Security Council Mandates and Preemptive Self-Defense*, 97 Am. J. Int'l L. 576 (2003); and John C. Yoo, *Using Force*, 71 U. Chi. L. Rev. 729 (2004). For commentary attempting to defend the U.S. action under a theory of Just War incorporating elements of likely harm even without an armed attack, see Michael Doyle, Striking First: Preemption and Prevention in International Conflict 70–78 (2008).

hypotheses that would need to be reconciled with other precedents. In short, the status of the Cuban Missile Crisis as a legal precedent is fraught with questions.

Nearly a quarter century later, however, the issue returned to the ICJ in the *Nicaragua Case*.[52] There, the ICJ took what to some seemed a view of the right of individual and collective self-defense consistent with the theory it had articulated in the *Corfu Channel Case*. Nicaragua had persuaded the Court to accept jurisdiction under the so-called optional clause of the ICJ Statute and the U.S.-Nicaragua Treaty for Friendship, Commerce and Navigation (FCN).[53] But in substance Nicaragua asserted a violation of the use of force provisions of the UN Charter when the U.S., among other things, provided military and other assistance to paramilitary forces based in Honduras engaging in armed attacks in Nicaragua, and itself laid mines in Nicaragua's territorial and internal waters and engaged in covert attacks against Nicaragua ports, oil installations, and a naval base.[54] Although the United States had withdrawn from the proceedings, the ICJ considered the U.S. legal defense that its actions under the right of individual and collective self-defense were lawful countermeasures to Nicaragua's intervention to support an insurgency in El Salvador and to de-stabilize Honduras.[55]

Although the Court gave effect to the so-called multilateral treaty reservation of the United States, under which the United Nations Charter could not be applied in a dispute between the U.S. and Nicaragua unless all other parties to the Charter were also before the Court,[56] thus making the Charter itself technically inapplicable, the ICJ nonetheless found the law of the Charter concerning use of force to reflect customary international law and relied on, among other things, the General Assembly's Resolution Defining Aggression and the so-called Friendly Relations Declaration to define customary international law's precise terms.[57] In so doing, it specifically relied on the General Assembly Resolution on the Definition of Aggression to conclude that neither the U.S. nor Nicaragua by the mere provision of assistance had engaged in an "armed attack" by the mere provision of assistance,[58] because it saw:

> no reason to deny that, in customary law, the prohibition of armed attacks may apply to the sending by a State of armed bands to the territory of another State, if such an operation, *because of its scale and effects, would have been classified as an armed attack rather than as a mere frontier*

52 *See* Military and Paramilitary Activities in and Against Nicaragua (Nicar. v. U.S.), 1986 I.C.J. Rep. 14, 14 (June 27).

53 *See id.* at 392 (rejecting, among other defenses going to jurisdiction and admissibility, the U.S. argument that the ICJ was not competent to address questions of international peace and security, which, in the U.S. view, were properly the province of only the Security Council).

54 *See id.* at paras. 75–86.

55 *See id.* at para. 11 (noting the U.S. failure to appear and defend in the merits phase).

56 *See id.* at paras. 173–74.

57 *See id.* at paras. 175–95.

58 *See id.* at para. 195; see also Resolution on the Definition of Aggression, supra Part II, Chapter 2, note 66.

incident had it been carried out by regular armed forces. But the Court does not believe that the concept of "armed attack" includes not only acts by armed bands where such acts occur on a significant scale but also assistance to rebels in the form of the provision of weapons or logistical or other support.[59]

The ICJ then distinguished between the conduct of Nicaragua and that of the United States, stating: "while the concept of an armed attack includes the dispatch by one State of armed bands into the territory of another State, the supply of arms and other support to such bands cannot be equated with armed attack." [60] Accordingly, it found that the United States -- which had "dispatched" the Nicaraguan *Contras,* or counter-revolutionary forces, from bases in Honduras -- had violated the customary international law analogue to Article 2(4).[61] Because it judged that as a matter of customary international law, the right of self-defense was predicated on a prior

59 *Id.* at para. 195 (emphasis added). No doubt the United States may have viewed as illegitimate the ICJ's reliance on the General Assembly's resolutions. *See generally* Part II, Chapter 2, *supra* note 6 (noting U.S. qualification concerning the extent to which the General Assembly's definition of "aggression" reflected customary international law). Yet, assuming the insurgencies in Honduras and El Salvador has risen to the level of belligerency, thus triggering international obligations of neutrality, the distinction the ICJ drew between mere "provision of weapons or logistical or other support" and the "the sending by a State of armed bands to the territory of another State" was a distinction that may have found support in the pre-Charter U.S. practice in the application of rules concerning the rights and duties of neutrals, under which the U.S. took the view that it was barred only from making territory it controlled "a base" of support for a belligerent. *See* Stephen C. Neff, The Rights and Duties of Neutrals 188–90 (2000) (discussing the so-called "Destroyers-for-Bases" Agreement, in which the United States viewed the provision of excess military ships to the United Kingdom not to violate its duties of neutrality but judged that the building of new ships in the United States, for the purpose of providing those ships to the United Kingdom, would convert the United States into a "base" of support for the United Kingdom in violation of U.S. duties of neutrality). *See* Great Britain—U.S. Transfer of U.S. Destroyers, 203 UNTS 201 (Sept. 2, 1940); Robert H. Jackson, *Opinion on Exchange of Over-Age Destroyers for Naval and Air Bases,* 34 Am. J. Int'l L. 728 (1940) (legal opinion of the Attorney General of the United States); *but see* Friedman, The Changing Structure of International Law 265–66 (1964) (describing the traditional pre-Charter law of neutrality, as least as it was understood in the context of the 1936-39 Spanish Civil War, as forbidding neutral governments from providing any military assistance). Even more recently, the United States had taken the position that Americans landing at the Bay of Pigs, who had been organized and trained for a military expedition to overthrow the Castro government in Cuba, were not subject to U.S. prosecution under the Neutrality Act, which is intended to implement U.S. neutrality obligations under international law, because the expedition was launched from Guatemala (and not, in the words of the statute, "carried on from thence," meaning sent from the United States). *See* Whiteman, *supra* note 38, at 275–76.

60 *Id.* at para. 247.

61 The ICJ stated:

> As to the claim that United States activities in relation to the contras constitute a breach of the customary international law principle of the non-use of force, the Court finds that, subject to the question whether the action of the United States might be justified as an exercise of the right of self-defence, the United States has committed a prima facie violation of that principle by its assistance to the contras in Nicaragua, by "organizing or encouraging the organization of irregular forces or armed bands . . . or incursion into the territory of another State", and "participating in acts of civil strife ... in another State", in the terms of General Assembly resolution 2625 (XXV). According to that resolution, participation of this kind is contrary to the principle of the prohibition of the use of force when the acts of civil strife referred to "involve a threat or use of force". In the view of the Court, while the arming and training of the contras can certainly be said to involve the threat or use of force against Nicaragua, this is not necessarily so in respect of all the assistance given by the United States Government. In particular, the Court considers that the mere supply of funds to the contras, while undoubtedly an act of intervention in the internal affairs of Nicaragua, as will be explained below, does not in itself amount to a use of force.

Id. at para. 228; *see also id.* at para. 238.

armed attack,[62] the U.S. violation of the customary norm reflecting the Charter prohibition could not be justified as an exercise of the customary law right of individual or collective self-defense.

Moreover, according to the ICJ's understanding of the facts, it was not clear that the procedural requirements relating to the assertion of the right of "collective" self-defense were satisfied. The Court acknowledged that El Salvador considered itself under armed attack by Nicaragua and requested the United States to provide it assistance.[63] The ICJ also found that Honduras had asserted before the Security Council in 1984 that Nicaragua had engaged in aggression against it and had requested U.S. assistance.[64] However, none of the countries putatively exercising rights under Article 51 ever made the notification to the Security Council required by Article 51.[65] Appearing to apply a principle of *estoppel*, the ICJ also noted circumstances in which the United States had maintained that failure to observe this requirement undercut a state's claim to be acting under Article 51.[66] While not essential to the ICJ's reasoning and conclusions, this line of analysis suggested that states, as a matter of customary international law, would be required to make public requests for assistance from other states, if they were to seek to rely on the customary law equivalent of their Article 51 right to collective self-defense.

The effect of Court's reasoning was substantially to narrow the right of self-defense, both individual and collective. The narrow definition of "armed attack" limited responsive options and incentivized support, below certain thresholds, for insurgents or terrorists. Moreover, as to the right of collective self-defense, ICJ seemed to insist on contemporaneous and public requests for assistance. If so, it is possible that, still imprisoned by the prism of the Cold War, the ICJ was concerned that subsequently manufactured requests, under pressure from the United States or some other Great Power, would transform the right of collective self-defense into a sword for aggression rather than a shield from armed attack.[67] But, in doing, so it certainly gave the advantage to aggressors against states that feared public confrontation, and perhaps it also exacerbated threats that might follow the victim's revelation that it was turning to its adversary's adversary for assistance.

At the same time, Israel, not having a veto at the Security Council, was condemned on several occasions during the Cold War for what could be characterized as preemptive and, in some cases, preventive uses of force. First, during the Six Day War of 1967, Israel's "preemptive" strike against Egyptian forces did not receive unambiguous support, even when Egyptian forces were mobilized and poised to launch an attack against Israel after Egypt had already imposed a blockade against Israel in the Gulf of Aqaba.[68]

---

62 *See id.* at paras. 211, 232.

63 *See id.* at para. 48.

64 *See id.* at paras. 231, 234.

65 *See id.* at paras. 234–35.

66 *See id.* at para. 235.

67 *See* Delahunty, *supra* note 15 (criticizing this aspect of the opinion).

68 *See* Michael Walzer, Just and Unjust Wars 82–85 (2006) (calling Israel's action a case of legitimate anticipation). Some argue, however, that Israel never specifically claimed the right to use force preemptively, relying rather on alleged prior

Second, after Israel's 1981 attack on an Iraqi nuclear facility ("Osirak"), the Security Council adopted Resolution 487 condemning Israel's use of force.[69] Like the legal theory it advanced at the time of the Six Day War, which then also was seen as problematic, Israel maintained that it was justified to use force since it was in a continuing state of war with Iraq.[70] More important, Israel could argue that Iraq's clearly articulated intention was to destroy Israel, if necessary through the use of nuclear weapons, and that the Iraqi plutonium production capability that Israel destroyed by all accounts had no other reasonable purpose but to enable Iraq to develop plutonium-based nuclear weapons.[71] Yet the attack was deemed by the Security Council not to satisfy the *Caroline* standard.[72] Perhaps most important to the Council's reasoning in condemning Israel's preemptive use of force, however, was that Iraq was a member of the NPT and IAEA in good standing and, under the terms of the NPT and IAEA, the Council "recognize[d] the inalienable sovereign right of Iraq, and all other States, especially the developing countries, to establish programmes of technological and nuclear development to develop their economy and industry for peaceful purposes in accordance with their present and future needs and consistent with the internationally accepted objectives of preventing nuclear-weapons proliferation."[73] By contrast, Israel appeared to be the outlaw nation, since it was not a party to the NPT and had a nuclear weapons program outside of IAEA safeguards.[74] Thus, the Council also called upon Israel "urgently to place its nuclear facilities under IAEA safeguards."[75] Yet, Israel's a characterization of Iraq as an emerging international outlaw seems more persuasive today in hindsight than it was at the time it was

attacks by Egyptian forces, claims that were not generally accepted. *See* Christine Gray, International Law and the Use of Force 130–131 (2004). Others argue, however, that Israeli authorities knew that Nasser's Egypt had mobilized his forces merely as a "bluff" and that he had no intention of attacking. *See* Richard K. Betts, Striking First: A History of Thankfully Lost Opportunities, 17 Ethics and Int'l Aff. 17–24 (2003); *see also* Gray, *supra* note 13, at 131 n. 152 (citing Dinstein). But others hold that, even if Egypt did not intend to strike, its strategic mobilization which in turn compelled Israel to mobilize its civilian military, left Israel with no practical alternative but to strike, satisfying the *Caroline* standard's requirements. *See* Doyle, *supra* note 51, at 16–17, 53–54.

69 *See* S.C. Res. 487, para. 1, U.N. Doc. S/RES/487 (June 19, 1981) (describing Israel's attack as a violation of the Charter, having cited article 2(4), and thus by negative inference not an exercise of the right of self-defense under Article 51).

70 *See* Dinstein, *supra* note 13, at 186 (conceding the illegality of Israel's conduct but for the continuing state of war theory); *see also* Anthony D'Amato, *Israel's Air Strike Upon the Iraq Nuclear Reactor,* 77 Am. J. Int'l L. 584, 588 (1983) (discussing a possible nuclear weapons exception to Charter law).

71 For recent, qualified defense of Israel's action, in light of the full historical record, *see* Doyle, *supra* note 51, at 78–84 (citing, id. at 78–79 n.53, sources debating the question based on contemporaneously available public records).

72 *See* U.N. SCOR 36th Sess. U.N. Doc. at S/PV.2285-88 (June 16–19, 1981) (verbatim transcript of Security Council discussion, in which several delegations cite the *Caroline* as the controlling formulation of the right of anticipatory or preemptive self-defense and judge that the standard was not satisfied in this case). For further discussion, *see* Oscar Schachter, *The Right of States to Use Armed Force,* 82 Mich. L. Rev. 1620, 1633–35 (1984) (referring to reliance on the *Caroline* standard on this case, albeit acknowledging that it may not have reflected customary international law prior to the adoption of the Charter).

73 S.C. Res. 487, para. 4, *supra* note 69.

74 *See* U.N. Doc. S/PV.2285-88, *supra* note 72; *see also* Chapter 2B, *supra* (discussing nuclear non-proliferation regime and Israel's refusal to adhere).

75 S.C. Res. 487, para. 5, *supra* note 69.

made, in light of the discoveries made by Coalition forces in the aftermath of the First Gulf War (although, in some ways, the episode may have forced the diversification and acceleration of the Iraqi nuclear weapons program and thereby increased the danger).[76]

Third, the Security Council again condemned Israel, albeit this time with the U.S. abstaining,[77] for its October 1, 1985 attack on the PLO Headquarter in the suburbs of Tunis, Tunisia, in order punish and thereby deter the PLO from future terrorist attacks against Israeli citizens. Resolution 573, however, framed Israel's attack as an "act of armed aggression perpetrated by Israel against Tunisian territory in flagrant violation of the Charter of the United Nations, international law and norms of conduct."[78] Implicitly drawing on the principles of attribution articulated by the ICJ in the *Nicaragua Case*, the Security Council refused to attribute the PLO's conduct to Tunisia; thus, in a use of force against Tunisia, the question of self-defense from "armed attacks" by non-state entities attributable to a state did not even arise. The Council rejected, therefore, Israel's claim that in order to deter future attacks it could respond in self-defense to prior terrorist attacks by a non-state entity being harbored by a state.[79]

Yet, notwithstanding international censure of Israel's use of force, very shortly thereafter, the U.S. also seemed to claim the right to preempt future attacks. On April 14, 1986 it launched an aerial attack on "the headquarters, terrorist facilities, and military assets that support[ed]" Libyan dictator Muammar Qadhafi's "subversive facilities," including his personal compound. [80] The U.S. conceded the attack was in response to a Libyan-sponsored attack on U.S. soldiers stationed in Berlin,[81] in which case it could have been viewed as "defensive armed reprisal" that, during a belligerency or war, is conditionally lawful, if conducted in accordance with rules of necessity and proportionality,[82] but is now thought to be unlawful under Charter law.[83] However, the United States then argued that the attack was a "mission fully consistent with Article 51 of the UN Charter." The U.S. explained: "We believe that this preemptive action against terrorist installations will not only diminish Colonel Qadhafi's capacity to export terror, it will provide

76 *See* Dan Reiter, *Preventive Attacks against Nuclear Programs and the 'Success' at Osirak*, 12 Nonproliferation Rev. 355–71 (2005). The episode thus raises important questions concerning the potential gap between publicly-available sources of information and the kind of sensitive information which states may not wish to reveal, for fear of compromising sources and methods of collecting intelligence, yet may need to rely upon in their decisions to use force.

77 *See* Marian Nash Leich, *Resort to War and Armed Force*, 80 Am. J. Int'l L. 165 (1986).

78 S.C. Res. 573, para. 1, U.N. Doc. S/RES/571 (Oct. 4, 1985).

79 *See* Gray, *supra* note 68, at 160–61 (citing O'Brien, *Reprisals, Deterrence and Self-Defense in Counterterror Operations*, 30 Va. J. Int'l Law. 421 (1990) (defending U.S. and Israeli theories).

80 Presidential Statement of April 14, 1986, U.S. Dept. of State, Selected Documents No. 24 (quoted in Damrosch, *supra* note 16, at 1179) [hereinafter Presidential Statement].

81 *See* Damrosch, *supra* note 16, at 1179.

82 *See* The Naulilaa, Part II, Chapter 2, *supra* note 27.

83 *See* Dinstein, *supra* note 13, at 228–29 (reporting common understanding of scholarship that Charter law now prohibits forcible reprisals but state practice, including the 1986 U.S. attack, that appears to falsify this scholarly consensus).

him with incentives and reasons to alter his criminal behavior."[84] Thus, even though the attack could have been viewed as a forcible reprisal or punishment against Libyan wrongdoers, the U.S. described it as "preemption," the use of force prospectively to deter future attacks. Thus, in some ways, the U.S. justification was reasoned in terms very similar to the grounds Israel had provided as its basis for its attack on the PLO Headquarters in Tunis, Tunisia, albeit directed towards a state's own responsibility for terrorist conduct rather than, at least in the terms understood by Israel, at a non-state entity, the PLO, given sanctuary within a state, Tunisia.

In sum, except where a state, such as the United States, could exercise its veto, Security Council practice evidenced little support for preemptive defense claims against states, much less preemptive self-defense claims against non-state entities whose conduct could not, under the demanding test articulated by the ICJ in the *Nicaragua Case*, be attributed to another state.

4. Post-Cold War Practice

It was not until the rise of Al Qaeda that Security Council practice evidenced support for the proposition that an "armed attack," for purposes of Article 51, might be attributed to non-state entities, with the United States now explicitly advancing the theory that would have justified Israel's 1986 attack on the PLO Headquarters in Tunis. In August 7, 1998, when terrorist bombs devastated U.S. Embassy buildings in Nairobi, Kenya and Dar-es-Salaam, Tanzania, U.S. intelligence attributed these attacks to Al Queda. While condemning the attack in Security Council Resolution 1189, and stating that "every Member State has the duty to refrain from organizing, instigating, assisting or participating in terrorist acts in another State or acquiescing in organized activities within its territory directed towards the commission of such acts," the Council did not make reference to Chapter VII or otherwise suggest that the United States had been a victim of an "armed attack" under Article 51.[85] Two weeks later, however, after U.S. intelligence connected the attacks to Al Queda, the U.S., relying on Article 51, launched cruise missile strikes at what it claimed were Al Qaeda associated facilities: a pharmaceutical plant in Sudan alleged to be making chemical weapons for use by Al Qaeda; and training camps in Afghanistan.[86] A year later, after the U.S. had indicted Osama bin Laden on criminal charges relating to the Embassy attacks, and after the Taliban authorities in Afghanistan had refused to extradite bin Laden to the United States, as previously demanded by the Security Council, the Council in Resolution 1267 did invoke its Chapter VII powers, imposing economic sanctions on Afghanistan

84 Presidential Statement, *supra* note 80, at 1179.

85 S.C. Res. 1189, U.N. Doc. S/RES/1189 (Aug. 13, 1998).

86 *See* Sean D. Murphy, *Contemporary Practice of the United States Relating to International Law*, 93 Am. J. Int'l. L. 161–67 (1999).

for its failure to comply.[87] The resolution did not specifically describe the Embassy bombings as "armed attacks," for purposes of Article 51.[88] Rather, consistent with the ICJ's understanding in the *Nicaragua Case* of the law on use of force, it "deplored" that the "Taliban continues to provide safe haven to Usama bin Laden and to allow him and others associated with him to operate a network of terrorist training camps from Taliban-controlled territory and to use Afghanistan as a base from which to sponsor international terrorist operations."[89] Thus, neither Resolution 1189 nor Resolution 1267 indicated that the United States had suffered an armed attack, triggering its right to self-defense under the Charter against Al Queda itself; however, by attributing state responsibility under the *Nicaragua Case* test to Afghanistan, albeit not to Sudan, it seemed to legitimize the U.S. use of force in self-defense against Afghanistan.

But with the Al Qaeda attacks of September 11, 2001, the legal situation arguably changed dramatically. In Resolution 1368, the Council recognized "the inherent right of individual or collective self-defence in accordance with the Charter" and viewed those attacks, "like any act of international terrorism, as a threat to international peace and security."[90] Simultaneously, the NATO Council met to consider action in light of Article 5 of the NATO Treaty, which provided an "armed attack against one or more" members of NATO "shall be considered an attack against them all," under which they would exercise "the right of individual and collective self-defense recognized by Article 5" of the UN Charter; the Council then issued a statement that, "if it is determined that the attack was directed from abroad against the United States, it shall be regarded as a n action covered by Article 5."[91] Shortly thereafter, in Resolution 1373, the Security Council again found the attacks, "like any act of international terrorism, constitute a threat to international peace and security"; reiterated the "inherent right of individual or collective self-defence as recognized by the Charter of the United Nations"; and, finally, reaffirmed the "need to combat by all means, in accordance with the Charter of the United Nations, threats to international peace and security caused by terrorist acts."[92] The language of these resolutions thus suggested the recognition that the right of self-defense in the context of terrorism could be exercised through a series of measures over time, akin to a theory of belligerent reprisals governed by the law of war. Moreover, by invoking its Chapter VII powers, the Security Council imposed measures designed to prevent financial support for any form of terrorism, directing those measures not only at support from states harboring terrorism but also, regardless of whether the conduct was attributable to state support, to any private support for terrorist organizations themselves.[93]

---

87 *See* S.C. Res. 1267, U.N. Doc. S/RES/1267 (Oct. 15, 1999).

88 *Id.*

89 *Id.* at preamble.

90 S.C. Res. 1368, preamble, para. 1, U.N. Doc. S/RES/1368 (Sept. 12, 2001).

91 North Atlantic Treaty, Apr. 4, 1949, 63 Stat. 2241, 34 U.N.T.S. 243. *See* Damrosch, *supra* note 16, at 1190–91.

92 S.C. Res. 1373, preamble, U.N. Doc. S/RES/1373 (Sept. 28, 2001.)

93 *See id.*

If so, although nothing in the resolutions explicitly defined the Al Qaeda attacks as "armed attacks" for purposes of Article 51, they clearly could be read to signal increasing international recognition that Chapter VII collective enforcement measures could be directed at sub-state organizations as such and, by parity of reasoning, that unilateral exercise of the right of self-defense could be directed at a sub-state organization as well. They could also be read to view the "inherent right of self-defense" as authorizing measures to deter future acts of terrorism, along the lines of the U.S. theory justifying its 1986 bombing of Libya and, perhaps, Israel's 1985 bombing of the PLO Headquarters in Tunisia.

Skirting this ambiguity, however, on October 2, the NATO Secretary-General announced that it had "clearly been determined that the individuals who carried out the attacks belonged to the worldwide terrorist network of Al-Qaida, headed by Osama bin Laden and protected by the Taliban regime in Afghanistan."[94] The NATO statement thus seemed to be framed so as to open the door to a right to self-defense against sub-state entities yet also to make out the connection required by the *Nicaragua Case* between the state harboring, or acting as a "base" for, a terrorist organization and the terrorist organization itself, which the ICJ had deemed necessary to trigger a right to self-defense in response to an armed attack under customary international law and Article 51.

5. Dissonance in the Views of the Security Council, the ICJ, and States

In retrospect, these resolutions may have signaled an emerging difference of view between the ICJ, a majority of the Security Council, and some Member States on the scope of the right of self-defense. Of course, the resolutions could be viewed as consistent with the ICJ's rules for attributing the conduct of a non-state actor to a state under in the *Nicaragua Case*, since the Taliban's support for Al Qaeda seemed by far to exceed the support provided, as the facts were understood by the ICJ, by the Government of Nicaragua to rebels in El Salvador or by the Government of Tunisia to the PLO. However, insofar as the resolutions suggested that an ongoing struggle gave the target state the right to respond to prior acts of terrorism with armed attacks to deter future such acts, they began to edge towards the U.S. position in the 1986 Libyan attack and Israel's position in the 1985 attack on the PLO Headquarters in Tunis. On the other hand, nothing in these resolutions or NATO practice could be analogized to the Cuban Missile Crisis. That said, the Cold War itself, when viewed as an ongoing struggle, could be analogized to Israeli's conflict with the PLO, the U.S.'s struggle with Libyan sponsored terrorism, and thus the U.S.'s ongoing "war" with Al Qaeda. If so, the use of force by states against Al Qaeda would, if they satisfied the ordinary *jus in bello* criteria of necessity and proportionality for "defensive armed reprisals," have been lawful under the customary law of war and, because of the Taliban's responsibility for Al Qaeda's conduct, could have been directed against Afghanistan as well.

94 Quoted in Damrosch, *supra* note 16, at 1190–91.

Clearly, this view of the scope of the "inherent right of self-defense" under Article 51 was the legal theory buttressing U.S. attacks against Sudan and Afghanistan in 1998, in response to Al Qaeda's bombing of the U.S. Embassies in Tanzania and Kenya.[95] Thus, by 1998 the U.S. had taken the view that significant cooperation with terrorist organizations, thus threatening future cooperation in attacks against U.S. life and property, justified the use of armed force in self-defense against the cooperating state.

If so, then one way of viewing the question before the international community in the debate on the Second Gulf War was whether the Gulf War, too, was an ongoing struggle. Would the Charter's prohibition of even defensive armed reprisals continue to control the relations between Iraq and the Coalition? Would the traditional law of belligerency permit the resumption of hostilities? Issues of law and fact would need to be resolved to answer these questions.

In the same way that Israel took the view that the ongoing right of defensive armed reprisal survived the Charter's adoption, so that the continuing state of war between Israel and its adversaries justified Israel's use of force in the Six Day War, the attack on the Iraqi nuclear facility, and Israel's targeting of the PLO's Headquarters, the U.S. and its Coalition allies could argue that their continuing rights of self-defense survived the temporary armistice concluding the First Gulf War. Thus, if the law of defensive armed reprisal survived, and if the U.S. was engaged in a continuing struggle with Iraq, then the Second Gulf War was not a case of preemptive use of force but rather a case of defensive armed reprisal or the simple continuation of hostilities. On one other hand, the adoption of a series of Security Council resolutions arguably superseded the defensive rights of states.

Also, the legal conclusion would turn on one's view of the facts: with conflicting sides framing the facts either as a discontinuous set of conflicts or a continuous struggle. Under the first view, at each stage, the identity of the first user of force (i.e., the party responsible for an "armed attack" that in turn gave rise to a right of self-defense) would be in issue and outcome determinative of the question of legality; under the second, there was a continuous struggle in which each party always could respond lawfully to force with force, subject only to the requirement of necessity and proportionality under the *jus in bello*.

With this description of the legal and rhetorical differences of opinion as of March 2003 among the Security Council, the ICJ, and some Member States, we turn to a statement of the critical facts giving rise to the Second Gulf War. For, under one view of the law and facts, the Coalition of forces lead by the U.S. launched aggressive war in violation of Article 2(4); while, under the alternative view, the U.S. and its allies were engaging in a continuing exercise of the collective right of self-defense, either with the approval of the Security Council under Security Council Resolution 678 or at least without being barred from further lawful acts of self-defense by Security Council Resolutions 687 and 1441.

95 *See* Murphy, *supra* note 86, at 161–67 (1999).

B. THE SECOND GULF WAR

In the aftermath of the First Gulf War, the Security Council adopted what appeared to be final terms governing Iraq's re-integration in the international community. Paragraph 33 of Resolution 687 states that the Security Council: "Declares that, upon official notification by Iraq to the Secretary-General and to the Security Council of its acceptance of the provisions above, a formal cease-fire is effective between Iraq and Kuwait and the Member States cooperating with Kuwait in accordance with resolution 678 (1990)..."[96] The most important substantive provisions of Resolution 687, however, after discovery of the scope of the unsafeguarded Iraq nuclear weapons program in clear violation of the NPT and IAEA Statute, were those relating to international supervision and control of Iraq's activities relating to all weapons of mass destruction, whether nuclear, chemical or biological. Through the creation of a special organ of the Security Council, the UN Special Commission (UNSCOM), coupled with delegation of Security Council authority to the IAEA, then headed by Secretary General Hans Blix, the Security Council established a unique arms control regime for Iraq, denying it freedom not to join the NPT and imposing inspection obligations on it greater than those undertaken by any other state.[97] In short, like the Versailles demilitarization arrangements imposed on Germany, Resolution 687 treated Iraq as an international pariah. Within months, however, Iraqi's initial noncompliance and questions of interpretation of Iraq's obligations under these arms control provision of Resolution 687 prompted the Security Council to adopt Resolution 707, which condemned Iraqi noncompliance and, among other things, clarified UNSCOM's inspection rights and determined that Iraq retained "no ownership interest in items to be destroyed, removed or rendered harmless pursuant to" resolution 687.[98] Yet, Iraqi continued to test the resolve of the UN and the Coalition to enforce the provisions of Resolution 687.

In January of 1993, apparently without specific UN authorization through a new Security Council resolution, Coalition forces (including U.S., U.K. and French warplanes) launched air strikes in response to what they described as "cease-fire violations," which included unauthorized Iraqi incursions into Kuwaiti territory, Iraq's refusal to comply with its obligations to cooperate in UNSCOM and IAEA inspections, and measures threatening Coalition enforcement of

---

96 S.C. Res. 687, U.N. Doc. S/RES/687. The precise legal status of this unprecedented clause was unclear, remains unclear. If viewed as an Armistice Agreement, there is some authority that violation by Iraq only of the cease-fire provisions of the agreement would give the other parties to the Armistice Agreement the right to resume hostilities. The Secretary General of the U.N. has stated that "The very logic of armistice agreements shows that infringements of other articles cannot serve as a justification for an infringement of the cease-fire article." *See* Report of the Secretary-General, UN. Doc. S/3596, at 7 (1956) (report concerning armistice agreements between Israel and various Arab states); *accord* International Law Commission Comment on the Separability of Treaty Provisions, II Yb. I.L.C. 237–39 (1966) (commentary on drafts of what later became the Vienna Convention on the Law of Treaties).

97 *See* S.C. Res. 687, *supra* note 96, at paras. 7-14. These provisions for inspection rights went well beyond any previous inspection regimes effected through the IAEA. *See* Part I, Chapter 2B, *supra* (discussing the evolution of international arms control inspections).

98 *See* S.C. Res. 707, para. 4, U.N. Doc. S/RES/707 (Aug. 15, 1991).

the no-fly zones.[99] The Secretary General also issued a statement supporting the Coalition's action: "the forces that have carried out the raid have received a mandate from the Security Council, according to resolution 678, and the cause of the raid was a violation by Iraq of resolution 687 concerning the ceasefire. So, as Secretary-General of the United Nations, I can say that this action was taken and conforms to the resolutions of the Security Council and conforms to the Charter of the United Nations."[100] At this point, therefore, setting aside the longstanding debate whether the Coalition was undertaking enforcement action under Chapter VII as the Security Council's delegee or exercising its own right of collective self-defense under Article 51,[101] there seemed to be general consensus that in principle Coalition forces were free, without an additional authorizing resolution, to use force against Iraq to compel its compliance with Security Council resolutions concerning WMD. The debate, if any, focused on whether Coalition action was within the scope of whatever mandate existed.

Iraqi's compliance with the exceptionally intrusive verification procedures required was always problematic but again reached a crisis point in 1998, with the withdrawal of UNSCOM inspectors from Iraq because of Iraqi obstruction of UNSCOM's implementation of its mandate[102] coupled with Iraq's refusal to permit UNSCOM inspectors or a successor team of inspectors

---

99 *See* Damrosch, *supra* note 16, at 1236; *see also* R.W. Apple, *U.S. and Allied Planes Hit Iraq: Bombing Missiles in South in Reply to Hussein's Defiance,* N.Y. Times, Jan. 14, 1993, at A1 (describing French participation). France, however, publicly disassociated itself partially from the Coalition action, arguing that the United States had exceeded its mandate in attacking the Iraqi nuclear weapons facility at Zafaraniyah. *See* Simon Chesterman, Just War or Just Peace: Humanitarian Intervention 201–02 (2001). And questions remained concerning whether Coalition authority to enforce the WMD provisions of Resolution 687 extended to enforcement of the no-fly zones established by U.S. and U.K. in northern and southern Iraq pursuant to their understanding of their authority under Resolutions 678, 687 and 688 (relating to the Iraq's suppression of Kurds and Shi-ites). *See* Part II, Chapter 3, *supra* (discussing debate concerning whether the no-fly zones were authorized by the Security Council).

100 Transcript of Press Conference by Secretary-General Boutros Boutros-Ghali, Following Diplomatic Press Club Luncheon in Paris, U.N. Doc. SG/FM/4902 Rev. 1, at 1 (Jan. 14, 1993) (discussed in Chesterman, Humanitarian Intervention, *supra* note 99, at 201; *see also* Christine Gray, *After the Ceasefire: Iraq, the Security Council, and the Use of Force,* 65 Brit. Yb. Int'l L. 135, 167 n. 264)).

101 *See generally* Part II, Chapter 2, *supra.*

102 *See generally* Richard Butler, The Greatest Threat: Iraq, Weapons of Mass Destruction, and the Crisis of Global Security (2000) (account of UNSCOM Chairman). Yet Butler's role in allegedly spying for the U.S. and submitting reports that exaggerated Iraq's non-compliance, in the view of his French deputy, gave rise to claims that the Coalition attacks were unwarranted. *See* Siddarth Varadarajan, Frontier Rugs: Review of The Carpet Wars by Christopher Kremmer, Wash. Post, (Sept. 30, 2002) (*available at* http://svaradarajan.blogspot.com/2002/09/frontier-rugs-review-of-carpet-wars-by.html). According to Vraradrajan: "Buried within Kremmer's Iraq narrative is the fascinating, and hitherto unpublished, testimony of Eric Fournier, a senior French diplomat posted to India after spending a year as political advisor to Richard Butler, chief of the UN Special Commission on Iraq (UNSCOM). Tasked with inspecting and destroying Iraqi stocks of proscribed weapons, UNSCOM had become a tool for US policy, and Butler -- a mediocre but ambitious Australian diplomat -- was a more than willing accomplice. Simply put, Butler used UNSCOM repeatedly to trigger a crisis with Iraq so the US would have an excuse to continue attacking it. So provocative was UNSCOM in their dealings with the Iraqis that UN humanitarian officials posted in Baghdad told me they used to refer to the weapons inspectors as 'unscum.'" With the US preparing once again to bomb Iraq, Fournier's account is strikingly relevant: "Why did the bombings occur in December 1998? Well, because Richard Butler reported that the Iraqis had not cooperated with inspections, even though more than three hundred had taken place in a few weeks and only a handful had been a problem. Three out of three hundred did not go perfectly smoothly...the report, drafted like that, was a good excuse for some members of the Security Council to take action."

to resume inspections.[103] In response to Iraqi noncompliance, U.S. and U.K. forces launched a series of air strikes in December 1998, continuing with air attacks and additional bombing for the following eight months.[104] The U.S. and U.K. relied, among other things, on Security Council Resolution 1205, which had condemned Iraq's decision to cease cooperation with UNSCOM, calling it a "flagrant violation" of Resolution 687.[105] Deeming this to confirm that Iraq had materially breached its obligations, the United States and United Kingdom took the position that the Security Council finding also gave them the right to enforce the terms of the ceasefire, including the arms control obligations, although Russia explicitly objected.[106] Whatever consensus existed in 1993 supporting the legal theory for Coalition enforcement action appeared to have fractured.

Thus, the Security Council, in an olive branch to Iraq, proposed the resumption of inspections by a new entity, the United Nations Monitoring, Verification and Inspection Commission (UNMOVIC), which was created by Security Council Resolution 1284 as a successor to UNSCOM.[107] The Secretary-General of the United Nations appointed Dr. Hans Blix of Sweden to be the Commission's Executive Chairman. He served from March 1, 2000 to June 30, 2003. To resolve concerns about the impartiality of UNSCOM inspectors, many of whom were seconded to the UN from service in national governments, UNMOVIC inspectors were employees of the United Nations.[108] But Iraq refused to accept further inspections even under this proposal.

After the Al Qaeda attacks on September 11, 2001, the Bush Administration viewed the risk of Iraqi support for Al Qaeda terrorism, in view of with Iraq's continued, unsafeguarded programs for the development of WMD, to raise unacceptable risks of further terrorism through the use of WMD.[109] After the U.S. military operations during 2001-02 broke the Taliban's stranglehold on Afghanistan and eliminated Al Qaeda training camps there,[110] the Bush Administration turned to the threat posed by Iraq. On Sept. 12, 2002, speaking to the U.N. General Assembly, President Bush asserted that the use of force against Iraq might be necessary to enforce existing Security Council resolutions and eliminate the grave threat Iraq posed to international

103 *See* Damrosch, *supra* note 16, at 1236.

104 *See* Sean Murphy, *Contemporary Practice of the United States relating to International Law: Continuation of Air Attacks and Sanctions against Iraq,* 94 Am. J. Int'l L. 102–04 (2000); Murphy, *Contemporary Practice,* 93 Am. J. Int'l L. 471 (1999).

105 *See* Damrosch, *supra* note 16, at 1236.

106 *See* Gray, *supra* note 68, at 266–67 (reporting Russian objections and noting that other states also disputed the U.S./U.K. position).

107 *See* S.C. Res. 1284, U.N. Doc. S/RES/1284 (Dec. 17, 1999).

108 *See* UNMOVIC: Basic Facts (*available at* http://www.unmovic.org/) ("Unlike its predecessor, UNSCOM, the staff of UNMOVIC were employees of the United Nations.").

109 *See generally* Bob Woodward, Plan of Attack (2004) (detailing the decision-making process over a two-year period in which the Bush administration decided to launch the Second Gulf War).

110 *See generally* Bob Woodward, Bush at War (2002) (discussing legal basis for these operations under international law).

peace and security.[111] The White House also released the National Security Strategy document in which it announced what appeared to be a grand strategy of preemption to respond to emerging threats coupling rogue states with support for terrorist use of WMD.[112] Under this increased pressure, on September 16, 2002 Iraq finally announced its acceptance of the deployment of UNMOVIC and IAEA inspectors.[113] President Bush had asked for, and on October 16 finally received, domestic legal authorization from Congress to use force against Iraq to enforce Security Council Resolutions.[114] Then, on November 8 the Security Council adopted Resolution 1441, giving Iraq "one final opportunity to comply" and providing for additional elements for the inspections regime, which Iraq by letter dated Nov. 16 also accepted.[115] Resolution 1441 required Iraq to submit by December 8 a "currently accurate, full, and complete declaration" on "all aspects of its programmes to develop chemical, biological, and nuclear weapons, ballistic missiles, and other delivery systems."[116] After studying this declaration and beginning inspections, UNMOVIC Director General Hans Blix was not able to report to the Security Council that Iraq had complied fully with its obligations under Resolution 1441.[117] U.S. Secretary of State Colin Powell also reported to the Security Council U.S. allegations of noncompliance by Iraq, which were discussed and debated by the Security Council.[118] Nevertheless, both the facts relating to the existence of the Iraqi WMD capability, and the legal question whether Resolution 1441 barred or permitted further action (as well as whether the Coalition had legal authority to use force irrespective of Resolution 1441) were hotly contested, with a group of countries led by France, Germany and Russia opposing action.

Unable either to reach consensus at the Security Council on an additional resolution or to compel the Iraqi regime to leave power, the U.S., U.K. and their Allies commenced combat operations in Iraq on March 19-20, 2003, bringing to a climax the contentious debate on the legality of the Coalition action and further dividing the Security Council and much of the world. The U.S.'s strategic objectives in defeating and occupying Iraq, in addition to eliminating Iraq's WMD capabilities, was to overthrow the regime of Saddam Hussein (in effect the so-called policy of "regime change") and, thereafter, transform Iraq into a pluralist democracy that would

111 *See* George W. Bush, U.N. General Assembly in New York Address (Sept. 12, 2002), 38 Weekly Comp. Pres. Doc. 1529 (Sept. 16, 2002).

112 *See* The National Security Strategy of the United States, *supra* text accompanying note 1.

113 Letter from the Secretary-General addressed to the President of the Security Council, S/2002/1034 (Sept. 16, 2002).

114 *See* Resolution Authorizing Use of Force Against Iraq, *supra* note 2.

115 *See* S/2002/1242 (annex), (Nov. 13, 2002).

116 *See* S.C. Res. 1441, para. 3, U.N. Doc. S/RES/1441.

117 *See* Note of the Secretary General Transmitting UMOVIC Report pursuant to Paragraph 12 of Resolution 1284 (Dec. 17, 1999), S/2003/32 (Annex, paras. 71–73) (Twelfth Quarterly UNOVIC Report) (*available at* http://www.un.org/Depts/unmovic/new/documents/quarterly_reports/s-2003-232.pdf); *see also* U.N. Doc. S/PV.4692, at 3; U.N. Doc. S/PV/4714, at 5 (2003).

118 *See* S/PV.4701 (2003), S/PV.4714 (2003).

no longer violate the human rights of its people, including Kurds and Shi'ites, and which would serve as an example for the promotion of democracy throughout the Middle East.[119] On May 8 by letter from their Permanent Representatives to the UN, the U.S. and U.K., speaking for Coalition forces and their governments, recognized their legal responsibilities as "occupying powers" under the laws of war.[120] Then, on May 22, the Security Council adopted Resolution 1483,[121] which addressed the legal consequences of the situation in Iraq, including the application of limits on the discretion of occupying powers under the laws of war, giving rise to still further debate concerning whether, and to what extent, the Security Council had ratified Coalition conduct. While evidence of WMD-related activities were discovered by occupying forces, no actual WMD were ever found in Iraq, despite the general consensus of Western intelligence agencies before the war that Hussein had a significant WMD program; nor were any significant connections between Iraqi intelligence and Al Qaeda established.[122]

With this review of the contested law and facts as of the Coalition intervention, we now turn to the key resolutions concerning the legality of the Coalition invasion and occupation of Iraq. We then provide commentary, again in terms of realist, legalist, rationalist, constructivist, and Just War perspectives.

---

119 *See* Woodward, *supra* note 109.

120 Letter from the Permanent Representatives of the U.K. and the U.S. to the U.N. addressed to the President of the Security Council, S/2003/538 (May 8, 2003).

121 S.C. Res. 1483, U.N. Doc. S/RES/1483 (May 22, 2003).

122 *See generally* Bob Woodward, State of Denial (2006) (discussing the findings of the Iraq Survey Group, headed first by David Kay and later by Charles Duelfer, that no WMD were found in post-war Iraq).

C. CASE STUDY—SECURITY COUNCIL RESOLUTIONS ON THE SECOND GULF WAR

1. Reading Questions

1) The drafting of Resolution 1441 appears to have been intentionally ambiguous, as are many negotiated documents, hoping to avoid a conflict:

   a. Imagine that you are a U.S. or U.K. lawyer-diplomat seeking to ensure that Resolution 1441 could be interpreted to allow the Coalition to argue persuasively that it would have legal authority to use force, either as a matter of enforcing Security Council Resolutions or exercising the Coalition's right of self-defense. How would you improve the drafting of Resolution 1441 in order to strengthen your case?

   b. Imagine you are a French, German or Russian lawyer-diplomat seeking to ensure that Resolution 1441 could be interpreted to require yet another UN authorizing resolution to allow the Coalition to argue persuasively that it would have legal authority to use force, either as a matter of enforcing Security Council Resolutions or exercising the Coalition's right of self-defense. How would you improve the drafting of Resolution 1441 in order to strengthen your case?

   c. Which set of lawyers would need to make more changes to construct a better argument? Is Resolution 1441 closer to the preferred U.S.-U.K. position or the French-German-Russian position?

   d. Resolution 1483 might be reviewed from the same perspective. Consider the same sets of questions in relation to whether (i) the Coalition's action is ratified and (ii) whether the Coalition is denied legal authority to engage in regime change in accordance with its view of the preferred political, economic, social and religious order in Iraq. In this connection, what do you make of the similarity of this debate with the debate concerning the legal effect of Resolution 1244 concerning Kosovo with respect to the legality of NATO's humanitarian intervention in 1999?

2) If you were an ICJ judge, would you need to look to the negotiating history, or *travaux préparatoires*, of the Resolution to resolve the debate? If so, do the rules

that govern treaty interpretation govern the interpretation of Security Council resolutions? Are you convinced the statements by the parties to the dispute advancing their preferred interpretation are reliable? Would such statements, if made prior to or contemporaneous with the adoption of the resolution, at least bar the other side to the dispute, by some principle of *estoppel*, from relying on the Resolution to establish its preferred position? Does the rise of the International Criminal Tribunal change the stakes for countries and their officials when they launch aggressive war? Even if under international criminal law leaders launching aggressive war could not be justified, might they be excused from criminal liability on grounds of necessity or reasonable mistake of fact?

3) Even if the Coalition were entitled to exercise self-defense right, did it satisfy the *Caroline* criteria? What was the threat? How would it have been viewed under the *Nicaragua* test? Is the *Nicaragua* test workable for WMD threats? Even if necessary, was the use of force proportionate? How would a realist view the necessity and proportionality criteria? How would a realist theorist view the authority of the Security Council? How would a rational choice theorist view the problem of reasonable mistakes about the existence of WMD?

4) How, if at all, does it matter that Iraq had become a unique player in the international legal system, as a consequence of Resolution 687 and the subsequent Security Council resolutions? How does it mater, if at all, that in effect the Coalition and Iraq had been engaging in armed struggle for over a decade? How does it matter, if at all, that the Security Council in a range of other matters during the 1990s had dramatically expanded its exercise of its Chapter VII power? How would a constructivist view the problem of reasonable mistakes about the existence of WMD?

5) How does it matter, if at all, that consensus on the exercise of Chapter VII powers appeared to have fractured in NATO's humanitarian intervention to protect Kosovo in 1999 and the intervenors had chosen to defend themselves before the ICJ on moral, rather than legal, grounds? How would you make a case for the overthrow of the Hussein dictatorship on humanitarian grounds? Was the case still sound in 2003 after inspectors were again in Iraq? Should the Coalition have waited for another humanitarian crisis? Were the members of the Coalition the right states to undertake a humanitarian overthrow of the tyranny in Iraq? How would a Just War Theorist view the conduct of the U.S. and its Coalition partners, as well as the positions of the French, Germans and Russians? Systematically consider the

following questions: Was there legitimate authority? Whose authority? Just cause? Which cause? Right intention? Whose intention and which intention? How would a Just War Theorist view the problem of reasonable mistakes about the existence of WMD when the information underlying the mistake cannot be made public for fear of compromising intelligence sources and methods?

2. Documents

a. Please review U.N. Security Council Resolutions 678 and 687 in Chapter 2—The First Gulf War: Collective Security and the Defense of Others

b. UN Security Council Resolution 1441 (2002)[123]

The Security Council,

Recalling all its previous relevant resolutions, in particular its resolutions 661 (1990) of 6 August 1990, 678 (1990) of 29 November 1990, 686 (1991) of 2 March 1991, 687 (1991) of 3 April 1991, 688 (1991) of 5 April 1991, 707 (1991) of 15 August 1991, 715 (1991) of 11 October 1991, 986 (1995) of 14 April 1995, and 1284 (1999) of 17 December 1999, and all the relevant statements of its President, Recalling also its resolution 1382 (2001) of 29 November 2001 and its intention to implement it fully,

Recognizing the threat Iraq's non-compliance with Council resolutions and proliferation of weapons of mass destruction and long-range missiles poses to international peace and security,

Recalling that its resolution 678 (1990) authorized Member States to use all necessary means to uphold and implement its resolution 660 (1990) of 2 August 1990 and all relevant resolutions subsequent to resolution 660 (1990) and to restore international peace and security in the area,

Further recalling that its resolution 687 (1991) imposed obligations on Iraq as a necessary step for achievement of its stated objective of restoring international peace and security in the area,

Deploring the fact that Iraq has not provided an accurate, full, final, and complete disclosure, as required by resolution 687 (1991), of all aspects of its programmes to develop weapons of mass destruction and ballistic missiles with a range greater than one hundred and fifty kilometres, and of all holdings of such weapons, their components and production facilities and locations, as well as all other nuclear programmes, including any which it claims are for purposes not related to nuclear-weapons-usable material,

Deploring further that Iraq repeatedly obstructed immediate, unconditional, and unrestricted access to sites designated by the United Nations Special Commission (UNSCOM) and

123 S.C. Res. 1441, U.N. Doc. S/RES/1441 (Nov. 8, 2002).

the International Atomic Energy Agency (IAEA), failed to cooperate fully and unconditionally with UNSCOM and IAEA weapons inspectors, as required by resolution 687 (1991), and ultimately ceased all cooperation with UNSCOM and the IAEA in 1998,

Deploring the absence, since December 1998, in Iraq of international monitoring, inspection, and verification, as required by relevant resolutions, of weapons of mass destruction and ballistic missiles, in spite of the Council's repeated demands that Iraq provide immediate, unconditional, and unrestricted access to the United Nations Monitoring, Verification and Inspection Commission (UNMOVIC), established in resolution 1284 (1999) as the successor organization to UNSCOM, and the IAEA, and regretting the consequent prolonging of the crisis in the region and the suffering of the Iraqi people,

Deploring also that the Government of Iraq has failed to comply with its commitments pursuant to resolution 687 (1991) with regard to terrorism, pursuant to resolution 688 (1991) to end repression of its civilian population and to provide access by international humanitarian organizations to all those in need of assistance in Iraq, and pursuant to resolutions 686 (1991), 687 (1991), and 1284 (1999) to return or cooperate in accounting for Kuwaiti and third country nationals wrongfully detained by Iraq, or to return Kuwaiti property wrongfully seized by Iraq,

Recalling that in its resolution 687 (1991) the Council declared that a ceasefire would be based on acceptance by Iraq of the provisions of that resolution, including the obligations on Iraq contained therein,

Determined to ensure full and immediate compliance by Iraq without conditions or restrictions with its obligations under resolution 687 (1991) and other relevant resolutions and recalling that the resolutions of the Council constitute the governing standard of Iraqi compliance,

Recalling that the effective operation of UNMOVIC, as the successor organization to the Special Commission, and the IAEA is essential for the implementation of resolution 687 (1991) and other relevant resolutions, Noting that the letter dated 16 September 2002 from the Minister for Foreign Affairs of Iraq addressed to the Secretary-General is a necessary first step toward rectifying Iraq's continued failure to comply with relevant Council resolutions, Noting further the letter dated 8 October 2002 from the Executive Chairman of UNMOVIC and the Director-General of the IAEA to General Al-Saadi of the Government of Iraq laying out the practical arrangements, as a follow-up to their meeting in Vienna, that are prerequisites for the resumption of inspections in Iraq by UNMOVIC and the IAEA, and expressing the gravest concern at the continued failure by the Government of Iraq to provide confirmation of the arrangements as laid out in that letter,

Reaffirming the commitment of all Member States to the sovereignty and territorial integrity of Iraq, Kuwait, and the neighbouring States,

Commending the Secretary-General and members of the League of Arab States and its Secretary-General for their efforts in this regard,

Determined to secure full compliance with its decisions, Acting under Chapter VII of the Charter of the United Nations,

1. Decides that Iraq has been and remains in material breach of its obligations under relevant resolutions, including resolution 687 (1991), in particular through Iraq's failure to cooperate with United Nations inspectors and the IAEA, and to complete the actions required under paragraphs 8 to 13 of resolution 687 (1991);

2. Decides, while acknowledging paragraph 1 above, to afford Iraq, by this resolution, a final opportunity to comply with its disarmament obligations under relevant resolutions of the Council; and accordingly decides to set up an enhanced inspection regime with the aim of bringing to full and verified completion the disarmament process established by resolution 687 (1991) and subsequent resolutions of the Council;

3. Decides that, in order to begin to comply with its disarmament obligations, in addition to submitting the required biannual declarations, the Government of Iraq shall provide to UNMOVIC, the IAEA, and the Council, not later than 30 days from the date of this resolution, a currently accurate, full, and complete declaration of all aspects of its programmes to develop chemical, biological, and nuclear weapons, ballistic missiles, and other delivery systems such as unmanned aerial vehicles and dispersal systems designed for use on aircraft, including any holdings and precise locations of such weapons, components, subcomponents, stocks of agents, and related material and equipment, the locations and work of its research, development and production facilities, as well as all other chemical, biological, and nuclear programmes, including any which it claims are for purposes not related to weapon production or material;

4. Decides that false statements or omissions in the declarations submitted by Iraq pursuant to this resolution and failure by Iraq at any time to comply with, and cooperate fully in the implementation of, this resolution shall constitute a further material breach of Iraq's obligations and will be reported to the Council for assessment in accordance with paragraphs 11 and 12 below;

5. Decides that Iraq shall provide UNMOVIC and the IAEA immediate, unimpeded, unconditional, and unrestricted access to any and all, including underground, areas, facilities, buildings, equipment, records, and means of transport which they wish to inspect, as well as immediate, unimpeded, unrestricted, and private access to

all officials and other persons whom UNMOVIC or the IAEA wish to interview in the mode or location of UNMOVIC's or the IAEA's choice pursuant to any aspect of their mandates; further decides that UNMOVIC and the IAEA may at their discretion conduct interviews inside or outside of Iraq, may facilitate the travel of those interviewed and family members outside of Iraq, and that, at the sole discretion of UNMOVIC and the IAEA, such interviews may occur without the presence of observers from the Iraqi Government; and instructs UNMOVIC and requests the IAEA to resume inspections no later than 45 days following adoption of this resolution and to update the Council 60 days thereafter;

6. Endorses the 8 October 2002 letter from the Executive Chairman of UNMOVIC and the Director-General of the IAEA to General Al-Saadi of the Government of Iraq, which is annexed hereto, and decides that the contents of the letter shall be binding upon Iraq;

7. Decides further that, in view of the prolonged interruption by Iraq of the presence of UNMOVIC and the IAEA and in order for them to accomplish the tasks set forth in this resolution and all previous relevant resolutions and notwithstanding prior understandings, the Council hereby establishes the following revised or additional authorities, which shall be binding upon Iraq, to facilitate their work in Iraq:
   – UNMOVIC and the IAEA shall determine the composition of their inspection teams and ensure that these teams are composed of the most qualified and experienced experts available;
   – All UNMOVIC and IAEA personnel shall enjoy the privileges and immunities, corresponding to those of experts on mission, provided in the Convention on Privileges and Immunities of the United Nations and the Agreement on the Privileges and Immunities of the IAEA;
   – UNMOVIC and the IAEA shall have unrestricted rights of entry into and out of Iraq, the right to free, unrestricted, and immediate movement to and from inspection sites, and the right to inspect any sites and buildings, including immediate, unimpeded, unconditional, and unrestricted access to Presidential Sites equal to that at other sites, notwithstanding the provisions of resolution 1154 (1998) of 2 March 1998;
   – UNMOVIC and the IAEA shall have the right to be provided by Iraq the names of all personnel currently and formerly associated with Iraq's chemical, biological, nuclear, and ballistic missile programmes and the associated research, development, and production facilities;
   – Security of UNMOVIC and IAEA facilities shall be ensured by sufficient United Nations security guards;
   – UNMOVIC and the IAEA shall have the right to declare, for the purposes of freezing a site to be inspected, exclusion zones, including surrounding areas and transit corridors, in which Iraq

will suspend ground and aerial movement so that nothing is changed in or taken out of a site being inspected;

- UNMOVIC and the IAEA shall have the free and unrestricted use and landing of fixed- and rotary-winged aircraft, including manned and unmanned reconnaissance vehicles;
- UNMOVIC and the IAEA shall have the right at their sole discretion verifiably to remove, destroy, or render harmless all prohibited weapons, subsystems, components, records, materials, and other related items, and the right to impound or close any facilities or equipment for the production thereof; and
- UNMOVIC and the IAEA shall have the right to free import and use of equipment or materials for inspections and to seize and export any equipment, materials, or documents taken during inspections, without search of UNMOVIC or IAEA personnel or official or personal baggage;

8. Decides further that Iraq shall not take or threaten hostile acts directed against any representative or personnel of the United Nations or the IAEA or of any Member State taking action to uphold any Council resolution;

9. Requests the Secretary-General immediately to notify Iraq of this resolution, which is binding on Iraq; demands that Iraq confirm within seven days of that notification its intention to comply fully with this resolution; and demands further that Iraq cooperate immediately, unconditionally, and actively with UNMOVIC and the IAEA;

10. Requests all Member States to give full support to UNMOVIC and the IAEA in the discharge of their mandates, including by providing any information related to prohibited programmes or other aspects of their mandates, including on Iraqi attempts since 1998 to acquire prohibited items, and by recommending sites to be inspected, persons to be interviewed, conditions of such interviews, and data to be collected, the results of which shall be reported to the Council by UNMOVIC and the IAEA;

11. Directs the Executive Chairman of UNMOVIC and the Director-General of the IAEA to report immediately to the Council any interference by Iraq with inspection activities, as well as any failure by Iraq to comply with its disarmament obligations, including its obligations regarding inspections under this resolution;

12. Decides to convene immediately upon receipt of a report in accordance with paragraphs 4 or 11 above, in order to consider the situation and the need for

full compliance with all of the relevant Council resolutions in order to secure international peace and security;

13. Recalls, in that context, that the Council has repeatedly warned Iraq that it will face serious consequences as a result of its continued violations of its obligations;

14. Decides to remain seized of the matter.

Annex—Text of Blix/El-Baradei letter
United Nations Monitoring, Verification and Inspection Commission
The Executive Chairman
International Atomic Energy Agency
The Director General
8 October 2002

Dear General Al-Saadi,

During our recent meeting in Vienna, we discussed practical arrangements that are prerequisites for the resumption of inspections in Iraq by UNMOVIC and the IAEA. As you recall, at the end of our meeting in Vienna we agreed on a statement which listed some of the principal results achieved, particularly Iraq's acceptance of all the rights of inspection provided for in all of the relevant Security Council resolutions. This acceptance was stated to be without any conditions attached.

During our 3 October 2002 briefing to the Security Council, members of the Council suggested that we prepare a written document on all of the conclusions we reached in Vienna. This letter lists those conclusions and seeks your confirmation thereof. We shall report accordingly to the Security Council.

In the statement at the end of the meeting, it was clarified that UNMOVIC and the IAEA will be granted immediate, unconditional and unrestricted access to sites, including what was termed "sensitive sites" in the past.

As we noted, however, eight presidential sites have been the subject of special procedures under a Memorandum of Understanding of 1998. Should these sites be subject, as all other sites, to immediate, unconditional and unrestricted access, UNMOVIC and the IAEA would conduct inspections there with the same professionalism.

H.E. General Amir H. Al-Saadi Advisor Presidential Office Baghdad Iraq

We confirm our understanding that UNMOVIC and the IAEA have the right to determine the number of inspectors required for access to any particular site. This determination will be made on the basis of the size and complexity of the site being inspected. We also confirm that Iraq will be informed of the designation of additional sites, i.e. sites not declared by Iraq or previously inspected by either UNSCOM or the IAEA, through a Notification of Inspection (NIS) provided upon arrival of the inspectors at such sites.

Iraq will ensure that no proscribed material, equipment, records or other relevant items will be destroyed except in the presence of UNMOVIC and/or IAEA inspectors, as appropriate, and at their request.

UNMOVIC and the IAEA may conduct interviews with any person in Iraq whom they believe may have information relevant to their mandate. Iraq will facilitate such interviews. It is for UNMOVIC and the IAEA to choose the mode and location for interviews.

The National Monitoring Directorate (NMD) will, as in the past, serve as the Iraqi counterpart for the inspectors. The Baghdad Ongoing Monitoring and Verification Centre (BOMVIC) will be maintained on the same premises and under the same conditions as was the former Baghdad Monitoring and Verification Centre. The NMD will make available services as before, cost free, for the refurbishment of the premises.

The NMD will provide free of cost: (a) escorts to facilitate access to sites to be inspected and communication with personnel to be interviewed; (b) a hotline for BOMVIC which will be staffed by an English speaking person on a 24 hour a day/seven days a week basis; (c) support in terms of personnel and ground transportation within the country, as requested; and (d) assistance in the movement of materials and equipment at inspectors' request (construction, excavation equipment, etc.). NMD will also ensure that escorts are available in the event of inspections outside normal working hours, including at night and on holidays.

Regional UNMOVIC/IAEA offices may be established, for example, in Basra and Mosul, for the use of their inspectors. For this purpose, Iraq will provide, without cost, adequate office buildings, staff accommodation, and appropriate escort personnel.

UNMOVIC and the IAEA may use any type of voice or data transmission, including satellite and/or inland networks, with or without encryption capability. UNMOVIC and the IAEA may also install equipment in the field with the capability for transmission of data directly to the BOMVIC, New York and Vienna (e.g. sensors, surveillance cameras). This will be facilitated by Iraq and there will be no interference by Iraq with UNMOVIC or IAEA communications.

Iraq will provide, without cost, physical protection of all surveillance equipment, and construct antennae for remote transmission of data, at the request of UNMOVIC and the IAEA. Upon request by UNMOVIC through the NMD, Iraq will allocate frequencies for communications equipment.

Iraq will provide security for all UNMOVIC and IAEA personnel. Secure and suitable accommodations will be designated at normal rates by Iraq for these personnel. For their part, UNMOVIC and the IAEA will require that their staff not stay at any accommodation other than those identified in consultation with Iraq.

On the use of fixed-wing aircraft for transport of personnel and equipment and for inspection purposes, it was clarified that aircraft used by UNMOVIC and IAEA staff arriving in Baghdad may land at Saddam International Airport. The points of departure of incoming aircraft will be decided by UNMOVIC. The Rasheed airbase will continue to be used for UNMOVIC and IAEA helicopter operations. UNMOVIC and Iraq will establish air liaison offices at the airbase. At both Saddam International Airport and Rasheed airbase, Iraq will provide the necessary support premises and facilities. Aircraft fuel will be provided by Iraq, as before, free of charge.

On the wider issue of air operations in Iraq, both fixed-wing and rotary, Iraq will guarantee the safety of air operations in its air space outside the no-fly zones. With regard to air operations in the no-fly zones, Iraq will take all steps within its control to ensure the safety of such operations.

Helicopter flights may be used, as needed, during inspections and for technical activities, such as gamma detection, without limitation in all parts of Iraq and without any area excluded. Helicopters may also be used for medical evacuation. On the question of aerial imagery, UNMOVIC may wish to resume the use of U-2 or Mirage overflights. The relevant practical arrangements would be similar to those implemented in the past.

As before, visas for all arriving staff will be issued at the point of entry on the basis of the UN Laissez- Passer or UN Certificate; no other entry or exit formalities will be required. The aircraft passenger manifest will be provided one hour in advance of the arrival of the aircraft in Baghdad. There will be no searching of UNMOVIC or IAEA personnel or of official or personal baggage. UNMOVIC and the IAEA will ensure that their personnel respect the laws of Iraq restricting the export of certain items, for example, those related to Iraq's national cultural heritage. UNMOVIC and the IAEA may bring into, and remove from, Iraq all of the items and materials they require, including satellite phones and other equipment. With respect to samples, UNMOVIC and IAEA will, where feasible, split samples so that Iraq may receive a portion while another portion is kept for reference purposes. Where appropriate, the organizations will send the samples to more than one laboratory for analysis.

We would appreciate your confirmation of the above as a correct reflection of our talks in Vienna.

Naturally, we may need other practical arrangements when proceeding with inspections. We would expect in such matters, as with the above, Iraq's co-operation in all respect.

Yours sincerely,

(Signed)

Hans Blix Mohamed ElBaradei

Executive Chairman Director General United Nations Monitoring, International Atomic Energy Agency

Verification and Inspection Commission

c. Letter dated 20 March 2003 from the Permanent Representative of the United Kingdom of Great Britain and Northern Ireland to the United Nations addressed to the President of the Security Council[124]

I have the honour to inform you on behalf of my Government that the Armed Forces of the United Kingdom – in association with those of the United States and Australia – engaged in military action in Iraq on 20 March 2003. The action is continuing.

The action follows a long history of non-cooperation by Iraq with the United Nations Special Commission (UNSCOM), the United Nations Monitoring, Verification and Inspection Commission (UNMOVIC) and the International Atomic Energy Agency (IAEA) and numerous findings by the Security Council that Iraq has failed to comply with the disarmament obligations imposed on it by the Council, including in resolutions 678 (1990), 687 (1991) and 1441 (2002). In its resolution 1441 (2002), the Council reiterated that Iraq's possession of weapons of mass destruction constitutes a threat to international peace and security; that Iraq has failed, in clear violation of its obligations, to disarm; and that in consequence Iraq is in material breach of the conditions for the ceasefire at the end of hostilities in 1991 laid down by the Council in its resolution 687 (1991). Military action was undertaken only when it became apparent that there was no other way of achieving compliance by Iraq.

The objective of the action is to secure compliance by Iraq with its disarmament obligations as laid down by the Council. All military action will be limited to the minimum measures necessary to secure this objective. Operations will be conducted in accordance with the international laws of armed conflict. Targets have been carefully chosen to avoid civilian casualties.

I would be grateful if you could circulate the text of the present letter as a document of the Security Council.

(*Signed*) Jeremy Greenstock

d. Letter dated 20 March 2003 from the Permanent Representative of the United States of America to the United Nations addressed to the President of the Security Council[125]

Coalition forces have commenced military operations in Iraq. These operations are necessary in view of Iraq's continued material breaches of its disarmament obligations under relevant Security Council resolutions, including resolution 1441 (2002). The operations are substantial

124 Letter from the Permanent Representative of the U.K. to the U.N. addressed to the President of the Security Council, S/2003/350 (Mar. 21, 2003).

125 Letter from the Permanent Representative of the United States of America to the United Nations addressed to the President of the Security Council, S/2003/351 (Mar. 20, 2003).

and will secure compliance with those obligations. In carrying out these operations, our forces will take all reasonable precautions to avoid civilian casualties.

The actions being taken are authorized under existing Council resolutions, including its resolutions 678 (1990) and 687 (1991). Resolution 687 (1991) imposed a series of obligations on Iraq, including, most importantly, extensive disarmament obligations, that were conditions of the ceasefire established under it. It has been long recognized and understood that a material breach of these obligations removes the basis of the ceasefire and revives the authority to use force under resolution 678 (1990). This has been the basis for coalition use of force in the past and has been accepted by the Council, as evidenced, for example, by the Secretary-General's public announcement in January 1993 following Iraq's material breach of resolution 687 (1991) that coalition forces had received a mandate from the Council to use force according to resolution 678 (1990).

Iraq continues to be in material breach of its disarmament obligations under resolution 687 (1991), as the Council affirmed in its resolution 1441 (2002). Acting under the authority of Chapter VII of the Charter of the United Nations, the Council unanimously decided that Iraq has been and remained in material breach of its obligations and recalled its repeated warnings to Iraq that it will face serious consequences as a result of its continued violations of its obligations. The resolution then provided Iraq a "final opportunity" to comply, but stated specifically that violations by Iraq of its obligations under resolution 1441 (2002) to present a currently accurate, full and complete declaration of all aspects of its weapons of mass destruction programmes and to comply with and cooperate fully in the implementation of the resolution would constitute a further material breach.

The Government of Iraq decided not to avail itself of its final opportunity under resolution 1441 (2002) and has clearly committed additional violations. In view of Iraq's material breaches, the basis for the ceasefire has been removed and use of force is authorized under resolution 678 (1990).

Iraq repeatedly has refused, over a protracted period of time, to respond to diplomatic overtures, economic sanctions and other peaceful means, designed to help bring about Iraqi compliance with its obligations to disarm and to permit full inspection of its weapons of mass destruction and related programmes. The actions that coalition forces are undertaking are an appropriate response. They are necessary steps to defend the United States and the international community from the threat posed by Iraq and to restore international peace and security in the area. Further delay would simply allow Iraq to continue its unlawful and threatening conduct. It is the Government of Iraq that bears full responsibility for the serious consequences of its defiance of the Council's decisions. I would be grateful if you could circulate the text of the present letter as a document of the Security Council.

(*Signed*) John D. Negroponte

e. Security Council Resolution 1483 (2003)[126]

The Security Council,

Recalling all its previous relevant resolutions,

Reaffirming the sovereignty and territorial integrity of Iraq,

Reaffirming also the importance of the disarmament of Iraqi weapons of mass destruction and of eventual confirmation of the disarmament of Iraq,

Stressing the right of the Iraqi people freely to determine their own political future and control their own natural resources, welcoming the commitment of all parties concerned to support the creation of an environment in which they may do so as soon as possible, and expressing resolve that the day when Iraqis govern themselves must come quickly,

Encouraging efforts by the people of Iraq to form a representative government based on the rule of law that affords equal rights and justice to all Iraqi citizens without regard to ethnicity, religion, or gender, and, in this connection, recalls resolution 1325 (2000) of 31 October 2000,

Welcoming the first steps of the Iraqi people in this regard, and noting in this connection the 15 April 2003 Nasiriyah statement and the 28 April 2003 Baghdad statement,

Resolved that the United Nations should play a vital role in humanitarian relief, the reconstruction of Iraq, and the restoration and establishment of national and local institutions for representative governance,

Noting the statement of 12 April 2003 by the Ministers of Finance and Central Bank Governors of the Group of Seven Industrialized Nations in which the members recognized the need for a multilateral effort to help rebuild and develop Iraq and for the need for assistance from the International Monetary Fund and the World Bank in these efforts,

Welcoming also the resumption of humanitarian assistance and the continuing efforts of the Secretary-General and the specialized agencies to provide food and medicine to the people of Iraq,

Welcoming the appointment by the Secretary-General of his Special Adviser on Iraq,

Affirming the need for accountability for crimes and atrocities committed by the previous Iraqi regime,

Stressing the need for respect for the archaeological, historical, cultural, and religious heritage of Iraq, and for the continued protection of archaeological, historical, cultural, and religious sites, museums, libraries, and monuments,

Noting the letter of 8 May 2003 from the Permanent Representatives of the United States of America and the United Kingdom of Great Britain and Northern Ireland to the President of the Security Council (S/2003/538) and recognizing the specific authorities, responsibilities, and obligations under applicable international law of these states as occupying powers under unified command (the "Authority"),

126 S.C. Res. 1483, U.N. SCOR, U.N. Doc. S/RES/1483 (May 22, 2003).

Noting further that other States that are not occupying powers are working now or in the future may work under the Authority,

Welcoming further the willingness of Member States to contribute to stability and security in Iraq by contributing personnel, equipment, and other resources under the Authority,

Concerned that many Kuwaitis and Third-State Nationals still are not accounted for since 2 August 1990,

Determining that the situation in Iraq, although improved, continues to constitute a threat to international peace and security,

Acting under Chapter VII of the Charter of the United Nations,

1. Appeals to Member States and concerned organizations to assist the people of Iraq in their efforts to reform their institutions and rebuild their country, and to contribute to conditions of stability and security in Iraq in accordance with this resolution;

2. Calls upon all Member States in a position to do so to respond immediately to the humanitarian appeals of the United Nations and other international organizations for Iraq and to help meet the humanitarian and other needs of the Iraqi people by providing food, medical supplies, and resources necessary for reconstruction and rehabilitation of Iraq's economic infrastructure;

3. Appeals to Member States to deny safe haven to those members of the previous Iraqi regime who are alleged to be responsible for crimes and atrocities and to support actions to bring them to justice;

4. Calls upon the Authority, consistent with the Charter of the United Nations and other relevant international law, to promote the welfare of the Iraqi people through the effective administration of the territory, including in particular working towards the restoration of conditions of security and stability and the creation of conditions in which the Iraqi people can freely determine their own political future;

5. Calls upon all concerned to comply fully with their obligations under international law including in particular the Geneva Conventions of 1949 and the Hague Regulations of 1907;

6. Calls upon the Authority and relevant organizations and individuals to continue efforts to locate, identify, and repatriate all Kuwaiti and Third-State Nationals or the remains of those present in Iraq on or after 2 August 1990, as well as the

Kuwaiti archives, that the previous Iraqi regime failed to undertake, and, in this regard, directs the High-Level Coordinator, in consultation with the International Committee of the Red Cross and the Tripartite Commission and with the appropriate support of the people of Iraq and in coordination with the Authority, to take steps to fulfill his mandate with respect to the fate of Kuwaiti and Third-State National missing persons and property;

7. Decides that all Member States shall take appropriate steps to facilitate the safe return to Iraqi institutions, of Iraqi cultural property and other items of archaeological, historical, cultural, rare scientific, and religious importance illegally removed from the Iraq National Museum, the National Library, and other locations in Iraq since the adoption of resolution 661 (1990) of 2 August 1990, including by establishing a prohibition on trade in or transfer of such items and items with respect to which reasonable suspicion exists that they have been illegally removed, and calls upon the United Nations Educational, Scientific, and Cultural Organization, Interpol, and other international organizations, as appropriate, to assist in the implementation of this paragraph;

8. Requests the Secretary-General to appoint a Special Representative for Iraq whose independent responsibilities shall involve reporting regularly to the Council on his activities under this resolution, coordinating activities of the United Nations in post-conflict processes in Iraq, coordinating among United Nations and international agencies engaged in humanitarian assistance and reconstruction activities in Iraq, and, in coordination with the Authority, assisting the people of Iraq through:

   (a) coordinating humanitarian and reconstruction assistance by United Nations agencies and between United Nations agencies and non-governmental organizations;

   (b) promoting the safe, orderly, and voluntary return of refugees and displaced persons;

   (c) working intensively with the Authority, the people of Iraq, and others concerned to advance efforts to restore and establish national and local institutions for representative governance, including by working together to facilitate a process leading to an internationally recognized, representative government of Iraq;

(d) facilitating the reconstruction of key infrastructure, in cooperation with other international organizations;

(e) promoting economic reconstruction and the conditions for sustainable development, including through coordination with national and regional organizations, as appropriate, civil society, donors and the international financial institutions;

(f) encouraging international efforts to contribute to basic civilian administration functions;

(g) promoting the protection of human rights;

(h) encouraging international efforts to rebuild the capacity of the Iraqi civilian police force; and

(i) encouraging international efforts to promote legal and judicial reform;

9. Supports the formation, by the people of Iraq with the help of the Authority and working with the Special Representative, of an Iraqi interim administration as a transitional administration run by Iraqis, until an internationally recognized, representative government is established by the people of Iraq and assumes the responsibilities of the Authority;

10. Decides that, with the exception of prohibitions related to the sale or supply to Iraq of arms and related materiel other than those arms and related materiel required by the Authority to serve the purposes of this and other related resolutions, all prohibitions related to trade with Iraq and the provision of financial or economic resources to Iraq established by resolution 661 (1990) and subsequent relevant resolutions, including resolution 778 (1992) of 2 October 1992, shall no longer apply;

11. Reaffirms that Iraq must meet its disarmament obligations, encourages the United Kingdom of Great Britain and Northern Ireland and the United States of America to keep the Council informed of their activities in this regard, and underlines the intention of the Council to revisit the mandates of the United Nations Monitoring and Verification Commission and the International Atomic Energy Agency as set forth in resolutions 687 (1991) of 3 April 1991, 1284 (1999) of 17 December 1999, and 1441 (2002) of 8 November 2002;

12. Notes the establishment of a Development Fund for Iraq to be held by the Central Bank of Iraq and to be audited by independent public accountants approved by the International Advisory and Monitoring Board of the Development Fund for Iraq and looks forward to the early meeting of that International Advisory and Monitoring Board, whose members shall include duly qualified representatives of the Secretary-General, of the Managing Director of the International Monetary Fund, of the Director-General of the Arab Fund for Social and Economic Development, and of the President of the World Bank;

13. Notes further that the funds in the Development Fund for Iraq shall be disbursed at the direction of the Authority, in consultation with the Iraqi interim administration, for the purposes set out in paragraph 14 below;

14. Underlines that the Development Fund for Iraq shall be used in a transparent manner to meet the humanitarian needs of the Iraqi people, for the economic reconstruction and repair of Iraq's infrastructure, for the continued disarmament of Iraq, and for the costs of Iraqi civilian administration, and for other purposes benefiting the people of Iraq;

15. Calls upon the international financial institutions to assist the people of Iraq in the reconstruction and development of their economy and to facilitate assistance by the broader donor community, and welcomes the readiness of creditors, including those of the Paris Club, to seek a solution to Iraq's sovereign debt problems;

16. Requests also that the Secretary-General, in coordination with the Authority, continue the exercise of his responsibilities under Security Council resolution 1472 (2003) of 28 March 2003 and 1476 (2003) of 24 April 2003, for a period of six months following the adoption of this resolution, and terminate within this time period, in the most cost effective manner, the ongoing operations of the "Oil-for-Food" Programme (the "Programme"), both at headquarters level and in the field, transferring responsibility for the administration of any remaining activity under the Programme to the Authority, including by taking the following necessary measures:

    (a) to facilitate as soon as possible the shipment and authenticated delivery of priority civilian goods as identified by the Secretary-General and representatives designated by him, in coordination with the Authority and the Iraqi interim administration, under approved and funded contracts previously concluded by the previous Government of Iraq, for the humanitarian relief of the people of Iraq, including, as necessary, negotiating adjustments in the terms or conditions of these contracts and respective letters of credit as set forth in paragraph 4 (d) of resolution 1472 (2003);

(b) to review, in light of changed circumstances, in coordination with the Authority and the Iraqi interim administration, the relative utility of each approved and funded contract with a view to determining whether such contracts contain items required to meet the needs of the people of Iraq both now and during reconstruction, and to postpone action on those contracts determined to be of questionable utility and the respective letters of credit until an internationally recognized, representative government of Iraq is in a position to make its own determination as to whether such contracts shall be fulfilled;

(c) to provide the Security Council within 21 days following the adoption of this resolution, for the Security Council's review and consideration, an estimated operating budget based on funds already set aside in the account established pursuant to paragraph 8 (d) of resolution 986 (1995) of 14 April 1995, identifying:
   (i) all known and projected costs to the United Nations required to ensure the continued functioning of the activities associated with implementation of the present resolution, including operating and administrative expenses associated with the relevant United Nations agencies and programmes responsible for the implementation of the Programme both at Headquarters and in the field;
   (ii) all known and projected costs associated with termination of the Programme;
   (iii) all known and projected costs associated with restoring Government of Iraq funds that were provided by Member States to the Secretary-General as requested in paragraph 1 of resolution 778 (1992) of 2 October 1992; and
   (iv) all known and projected costs associated with the Special Representative and the qualified representative of the Secretary-General identified to serve on the International Advisory and Monitoring Board, for the six month time period defined above, following which these costs shall be borne by the United Nations;

(d) to consolidate into a single fund the accounts established pursuant to paragraphs 8 (a) and 8 (b) of resolution 986 (1995);

(e) to fulfil all remaining obligations related to the termination of the Programme, including negotiating, in the most cost effective manner, any necessary settlement payments, which shall be made from the escrow accounts established pursuant to paragraphs 8 (a) and 8 (b) of resolution 986 (1995), with those parties that previously have entered into contractual obligations with the Secretary-General under the Programme, and to determine, in coordination with the Authority and the Iraqi interim administration, the future status of contracts undertaken by the United Nations and related United Nations agencies under the accounts established pursuant to paragraphs 8 (b) and 8 (d) of resolution 986 (1995);

(f) to provide the Security Council, 30 days prior to the termination of the Programme, with a comprehensive strategy developed in close coordination with the Authority and the Iraqi interim administration that would lead to the delivery of all relevant documentation and the transfer of all operational responsibility of the Programme to the Authority;

17. Requests further that the Secretary-General transfer as soon as possible to the Development Fund for Iraq 1 billion United States dollars from unencumbered funds in the accounts established pursuant to paragraphs 8 (a) and 8 (b) of resolution 986 (1995), restore Government of Iraq funds that were provided by Member States to the Secretary-General as requested in paragraph 1 of resolution 778 (1992), and decides that, after deducting all relevant United Nations expenses associated with the shipment of authorized contracts and costs to the Programme outlined in paragraph 16 (c) above, including residual obligations, all surplus funds in the escrow accounts established pursuant to paragraphs 8 (a), 8 (b), 8 (d), and 8 (f) of resolution 986 (1995) shall be transferred at the earliest possible time to the Development Fund for Iraq;

18. Decides to terminate effective on the adoption of this resolution the functions related to the observation and monitoring activities undertaken by the Secretary-General under the Programme, including the monitoring of the export of petroleum and petroleum products from Iraq;

19. Decides to terminate the Committee established pursuant to paragraph 6 of resolution 661 (1990) at the conclusion of the six months period called for in paragraph 16 above and further decides that the Committee shall identify individuals and entities referred to in paragraph 23 below;

20. Decides that all export sales of petroleum, petroleum products, and natural gas from Iraq following the date of the adoption of this resolution shall be made consistent with prevailing international market best practices, to be audited by independent public accountants reporting to the International Advisory and Monitoring Board referred to in paragraph 12 above in order to ensure transparency, and decides further that, except as provided in paragraph 21 below, all proceeds from such sales shall be deposited into the Development Fund for Iraq, until such time as an internationally recognized, representative government of Iraq is properly constituted;

21. Decides further that 5 percent of the proceeds referred to in paragraph 20 above shall be deposited into the Compensation Fund established in accordance with resolution 687 (1991) of 3 April 1991 and subsequent relevant resolutions and that, unless an internationally recognized, representative government of Iraq and the Governing Council of the United Nations Compensation Commission, in the exercise of its authority over methods of ensuring that payments are made into the Compensation Fund, decide otherwise, this requirement shall be binding on a properly constituted, internationally recognized, representative government of Iraq and any successor thereto;

22. Noting the relevance of the establishment of an internationally recognized, representative government of Iraq and the desirability of prompt completion of the restructuring of Iraq's debt as referred to in paragraph 15 above, further decides that, until December 31, 2007, unless the Council decides otherwise, petroleum, petroleum products, and natural gas originating in Iraq shall be immune, until title passes to the initial purchaser, from legal proceedings against them and not be subject to any form of attachment, garnishment, or execution, and that all States shall take any steps that may be necessary under their respective domestic legal systems to assure this protection, and that proceeds and obligations arising from sales thereof, as well as the Development Fund for Iraq, shall enjoy privileges and immunities equivalent to those enjoyed by the United Nations except that the above-mentioned privileges and immunities will not apply with respect to any legal proceeding in which recourse to such proceeds or obligations is necessary to satisfy liability for damages assessed in connection with an ecological accident, including an oil spill, that occurs after the date of adoption of this resolution;

23. Decides that all Member States in which there are:

(a) funds or other financial assets or economic resources of the previous Government of Iraq or its state bodies, corporations, or agencies, located outside Iraq as of the date of this resolution, or

(b) funds or other financial assets or economic resources that have been removed from Iraq, or acquired, by Saddam Hussein or other senior officials of the former Iraqi regime and their immediate family members, including entities owned or controlled, directly or indirectly, by them or by persons acting on their behalf or at their direction, shall freeze without delay those funds or other financial assets or economic resources and, unless these funds or other financial assets or economic resources are themselves the subject of a prior judicial, administrative, or arbitral lien or judgement, immediately shall cause their transfer to the Development Fund for Iraq, it being understood that, unless otherwise addressed, claims made by private individuals or non-government entities on those transferred funds or other financial assets may be presented to the internationally recognized, representative government of Iraq; and decides further that all such funds or other financial assets or economic resources shall enjoy the same privileges, immunities, and protections as provided under paragraph 22;

24. Requests the Secretary-General to report to the Council at regular intervals on the work of the Special Representative with respect to the implementation of this resolution and on the work of the International Advisory and Monitoring Board and encourages the United Kingdom of Great Britain and Northern Ireland and the United States of America to inform the Council at regular intervals of their efforts under this resolution;

25. Decides to review the implementation of this resolution within twelve months of adoption and to consider further steps that might be necessary;

26. Calls upon Member States and international and regional organizations to contribute to the implementation of this resolution;

27. Decides to remain seized of this matter.

1. The Bush Doctrine for the Second Gulf War -- the Realist Critique?

Realists are divided about whether the Second Gulf War reflected realist political thought. Indeed, the debate about what the Bush Administration was trying to achieve in the Second Gulf War continues and is mired in controversy. A senior Defense Department official was quoted, shortly after the U.S. occupation began but before it became clear that stocks of WMD would not be found, that the WMD rationale was not the true reason for the war, but rather a "bureaucratic compromise," giving rise to international criticism that the Bush Administration had deceived the world as to its *casus belli*.[127] Yet the Pentagon quickly corrected the record, pointing out that the transcript of the interview actually stated that multiple reasons persuaded the Bush Administration to act, with WMD as "the core reason" but with the Hussein regime's support for terror and mistreatment of its own people, as well as the relation between WMD and terror, also playing roles.[128] But even to the extent "regime change" was the rationale for the Administration's strategy, the term conceals an important ambiguity: was the "regime" to be changed simply and merely the leadership of Saddam Hussein, who had shown an intention and capability to use WMD during the Iran-Iraq War in the 1980s, circumvent international arms control inspectors both before and after the First Gulf War, and to support terrorism; or was the "regime" to be changed the overall political system in Iraq, which would be replaced with a pluralist democracy for the purpose of promoting regime-change throughout the region?

Under the broader understanding of regime change, the WMD issue and Iraq's links to Al-Qaeda were simply added as public justifications for a strategy of regional transformation.[129] Thus, critics have viewed the Bush Administration's policy of promoting democracy in the Middle East through preemptive use of force and unilateralism (here understood as to be without Security Council authorization) as rooted in what some call "American exceptionalism"[130]

127 *See Wolfowitz Comments Revive Doubts over Iraq's WMD,* USA Today, (May 30, 2003) (*available at* http://www.usatoday.com/news/world/iraq/2003-05-30-wolfowitz-iraq_x.htm).

128 According to a tape recording made by the Pentagon, the actual quote is, "The truth is that for reasons that have a lot to do with the U.S. government bureaucracy we settled on the one issue that everyone could agree on, which was weapons of mass destruction, as the core reason." After reciting this language, a report on the Pentagon's account continues: "After a brief pause to take another phone call, Wolfowitz continues, 'There have always been three fundamental concerns. One is weapons of mass destruction, the second is support for terrorism, the third is the criminal treatment of the Iraqi people. Actually, I guess you could say there's a fourth overriding one, which is the connection between the first two.'" Jamie McIntyre, *Pentagon challenges Vanity Fair Report,* CNN (May 30, 2003) (*available at* http://www.cnn.com/2003/US/05/30/wolfowitz.vanity.fair/).

129 *See* Mark Danner, *The Secret Way to War,* 52 The New York Rev. of Books (June 9, 2005) (*available at* http//www.nybooks.com/articles/18034).

130 *See* Harold Koh, *On American Exceptionalism,* 55 Stan. L. Rev. 1479, 1515–26 (2003).

and others call the consistent U.S. grand strategy of expanding, in Thomas Jefferson's words, the "empire of liberty."[131] Under this view, the invasion of Iraq in 2003 was the logical extension of the Clinton administration's policy of "democratic enlargement"; this is because "democratic enlargement" was grounded on the neo-Wilsonian theory that democracies do not go to war against each other[132] coupled with the judgment that liberal democracy had in fact triumphed at the end of the Cold War, thus serving as the wave of the future in a new era for humanity[133] in which international law had begun to recognize an emerging "democratic entitlement" as a human right of all peoples.[134] The extension by the Bush Administration, which was criticized by some of the original proponents of democratic enlargement,[135] was only that the Clinton Administration's policy now required a willingness to move the triumph of liberal democracy along through forcible intervention, since Iraqi cooperation with Al Qaeda presented a short-term threat that required accelerating history; viewed this way, the Bush doctrine was the logical successor of Clinton administration policy and an offshoot of Wilson's liberal internationalism.[136]

131 *See* John Lewis Gaddis, Surprise, Security and the American Experience (2004) (arguing that a neo-Wilsonian, neo-federalist foreign policy better serves U.S. interests today). For Jefferson's use of the phrase, *see generally* Robert W. Tucker and David C. Hendrickson, Empire of Liberty: The Statecraft of Thomas Jefferson (1992).

132 *See* White House, A National Security Strategy of Engagement and Enlargement 2 (Feb. 1995). The overarching geopolitical strategy of "democratic enlargement," as articulated by the President's National Security Adviser Anthony Lake, focused on democracy both in international and internal governance. It claims that the national interest requires that "democracy be at once the foundation and the purpose of the international structures [the United States builds] through this constructive diplomacy: the foundation, because the institutions will be a reflection of their shared values and norms; the purpose, because if [the United States'] economic institutions are secure, democracy will flourish." Thus, it set forth as an objective the establishment of "[a] framework of democratic enlargement that increases our security by protecting, consolidating and enlarging the community of free market democracies." *Id.* at 7. Much of this geopolitics was based on the theory that, because democratic states are not inclined to go to war, the enlargement of the area of democracy by democratization, perhaps even the forced democratization, of currently undemocratic states, is likely to lead to a so-called liberal peace. For a useful exchange on this issue, *compare* Christopher Lane, *Kant or Cant: The Myth of the Democratic Peace,* 19 Int'l Sec. 5, 7–10, 45–49 (1994) (arguing that a pro-interventionist foreign policy by the United States would lead to more war rather than peace), and David E. Spiro, The Insignificance of the Liberal Peace, 19 Int'l. Sec. 50, 51–52 (challenging the statistical significance of the empirical support offered for the Democratic Peace hypothesis) *with* Bruce Russett, *Correspondence: And Yet It Moves,* 20 Int'l Sec. 164 (1995) (Russett, the high priest of Democratic Peace theory, responds to these criticisms). For an argument that, even if the premise that democratic states are peaceful is right, it may be that internal processes of transformation to democracy makes a state more, not less, aggressive during the transitional period, *see* Edward D. Mansfield & Jack Snyder, *Democratization and War,* For. Aff. 79 (May/June 1995).

133 *See* Frances Fukuyama, The End of History and the Last Man (1992) (neo-Hegelian account of the triumph of liberal democracy).

134 *See* Thomas M. Franck, *The Emerging Right of Democratic Governance,* 86 Am. J. Int'l L. 46 (1992) ("Increasingly, governments recognize that their legitimacy depends on meeting a normative expectation of the community of states.").

135 For a criticism of the Bush Administration's neoconservative foreign policy in Iraq by an author most responsible for the view that liberal democracy had triumphed with its victory in the Cold War, *see* Frances Fukuyama, America at the Crossroads: Democracy Power and the Neoconservative Legacy (2006) (claiming his earlier work had been misinterpreted and misapplied by the neocons); *see also* James Mann, Rise of the Vulcans: The History of Bush's War Cabinet (2004) (discussing neo-conservative vision of, among other, senior Defense Department official Paul Wolfowitz and State Department official John Bolton); and Jacob Heilbrunn, They Knew They Were Right: The Rise of the Neocons (2008) (analyzing philosophical foundations of neoconservative foreign policy).

136 Tony Smith, Wilsonianism After Iraq: The End of Liberal Internationalism?, *in* The Crisis of American Foreign Policy: Wilsonianism in the Twenty-First Century 51 (essays by G. John Ikenberry, Thomas J. Knock, Anne-Marie Slaughter, and Tony Smith (2009) [hereinafter "The Crisis of American Foreign Policy"].

Liberal-internationalists have rejected this account of the Bush doctrine, claiming that the essence of Wilsonian theory was multilateralism, not democratic enlargement as such.[137] The debate about the Wilsonian legacy takes several turns, with liberal internationalists taking the view that Wilson's intervention in the Mexican civil war in 1914 manifested a policy of forcible, pro-democratic regime change, while others hold that by Versailles Wilson had abandoned coercion as a means of democratic enlargement.[138] Still, as Thucydides might have said, Wilson's strategy could be described as "unilateral democratic enlargement when you can, multilateral democratic enlargement when you must."[139] For realists, however, regardless of whether it was pursued unilaterally or multilaterally, the policy of democratic enlargement fails "by overstating threats from nonliberal states and underestimating the difficulty of transforming the world in our image."[140]

On the other hand, to the extent the U.S. rationale was simply the connection between WMD capabilities and Saddam Hussein's support for terrorism against the U.S., it fell squarely within the realist tradition. Alberico Gentili, one of the first international lawyers to begin to break with the Just War Tradition, endorsed "preventive war" simply on the ground of fear alone, since no superior authority can with certainty defend a state.[141] Indeed, Hobbes, the modern father of realist political theory, placed fear at the center of his thought, noting, in relation to his premature birth when his mother heard of the coming Spanish Armada in 1588, that "my mother gave birth to twins: myself and fear."[142] For realists, the Hobbesian tradition, which is though to be part of early modern international law in the thought of Grotius, the "law of nature" implies a "right of nature," which allows a state to take measures to defend itself yet never to inflict unnecessary harm.[143] Under this view, war to prevent a future war under less favorable conditions is morally justified. War for other reasons, such as the imposition of democracy or the protection of human rights in another state, is not.

Political realism then, in a Hobbesian international system, morally and prudentially justified preventive war against Iraq only when that war was limited to the objective of eliminating

137 *See* Anne-Marie Slaughter, The Crisis of American Foreign Policy, *supra* note 136, at 89.

138 *See* Michal Desch, Woodrow Wilson's War, Jan/Feb Nat. Int. 87, 89 (2009) (discussing this debate).

139 *Cf.* Chapter 1A, *supra* (Thucydides famous dictum that "states do what they can and accept what they must").

140 Desch, *supra* note 138, at 89.

141 Gentili writes: "A just cause for fear is demanded: suspicion is not enough. Now a just fear is defined as the fear of a greater evil, a fear which might properly be felt even by a man of great courage. Yet in the case of great empires I cannot readily accept that definition, which applies to private affairs. For if a private citizen commit some offence against a fellow citizen, reparation may be secured through the authority of a magistrate. But what a prince has done to another prince, no one will make good." Reichberg, The Ethics of War, at 377 (excerpting Gentili, Bbk. I, Chap. XIV of De Belli Libre Tres, Three Books on the Law of War).

142 Encyclopedia of World Biography: Thomas Hobbes (*available at* http://www.notablebiographies.com/He-Ho/Hobbes-Thomas.html).

143 *See generally* Richard Tuck, Rights of War and Peace (1999)(interpreting both Grotius and Hobbes to defend universal morality, albeit on minimalist terms that are consistent with political realism).

Iraq's WMD capabilities and overthrowing a government that had an interest in sharing those capabilities with terrorists who had themselves demonstrated a capability and interest in using WMD against the United States. Thus, from a realist perspective, the decision to go to war was simply a question of whether the President believed at the time the decision was made that "Saddam Hussein posed a threat to the United States that was far greater than the likely cost of removing him from power."[144] Indeed, for some realists, that the United States found no actual stocks of WMD but did find evidence of Iraqi research and development activities was sufficient evidence of danger so as to justify, from a realist perspective, the decision to invade.[145] Defending the administration, they claim that the broader "regime change" rationale, defining the "regime" to be not just the Hussein leadership group but also the overall political system in Iraq, was never the true justification for the war; it was instead a rationalization constructed after the fact when WMD stockpiles were never found.[146] Alternatively, the Bush Administration's error, if any, was to diverge from a realist approach, necessarily entailing cooperation with the UN in order to obtain multilateral approval of the occupation through Resolution 1483. Thus, for realists, the mistake, always worse than a crime,[147] was succumbing after-the-fact to the liberal internationalist ambition to seek to occupy Iraq to transform its regime into a liberal democracy that would respect the rights of the Iraqi people and promote democracy through the region.[148]

From the realist perspective, Security Council authorization could never serve as a legal *sine qua non*, since the Charter regime of collective security had fallen into desuetude, as least as early as the Korean War when the Soviets began to exercise their veto, certainly during the Cuban Missile Crisis, and most recently when the Russians and Chinese had blocked authorization for NATO's humanitarian intervention in Kosovo.[149] Furthermore, the substantive moral legitimacy of Security Council decisions has always been in question given the character of some of the governments that serve as Permanent Members.[150] Finally, the Security Council's resistance in

144 Richard Pearl, Ambushed on the Potomac, Jan/Feb Nat. Int. 38 (2009).

145 *See id.* at 40 ("the salient issue was not whether Saddam had stockpiles of WMD but whether he could produce them and place them in the hands of terrorists").

146 *See generally* Douglas Feith, War and Decision: Inside the Pentagon at the Dawn of the War on Terror (2008) (former Undersecretary of Defense for Policy during the Second Gulf War detailing shift in the administration's public rhetoric towards democracy promotion in the region as no evidence of WMD stocks was uncovered); *see also* Pearl, *supra* note 144, at 42–44 (citing Feith). Feith's account has been praised by noted U.S. foreign policy realists, including Henry Kissinger, James Schlesinger, and Fred Ikle, as the best account of the decision to go to war yet available.

147 *See* Encyclopedia of World Biography: Charles Maurice de Talleyrand (2004) (in a comment attributed to him on the kidnapping and execution of the Duc d'Enghien at Napoleon's command: "It was worse than a crime, it was a mistake.") (*available at* http://www.encyclopedia.com/topic/Charles_Maurice _de_Talleyrand.aspx).

148 *See* Pearl, *supra* note 144, at 41.

149 *See* Delahunty, *supra* note 15, at 871.

150 *See generally* Lea Brilmayer, American Hegemony: Political Morality in a One-Superpower World (1994) (questioning not only the moral authority of the repressive governments that have served on the Security Council but also the moral validity of decision by the Council that, as of the time of writing, represented the extraordinary power the U.S. wielded at the end of the Cold War).

Resolutions 1441 and 1483 to approve fully Coalition use of force and full U.S. discretion as occupying power evidenced the resistance of Russia, France, and Germany, not the wisdom of the international community; indeed, resistance to the U.S. agenda reflected longstanding geopolitical objectives of each of these powers to strengthen their access to commerce and other advantages that flowed from a close relationship with Saddam Hussein and to undermine U.S. hegemony.[151] Because of political realism's recognition that fear, pride, and the pursuit of power and honor motivate humanity, including the U.S., it has little use for self-interested Security Council debates; realists would call, instead, for a debate closer to home, with the U.S. Congress rather than the Security Council deciding,[152] or even a successor League of Democracies, as was proposed in the aftermath of the war and occupation by an alliance of liberal internationalists and neoconservatives.[153] Under traditional realist theory, the Hobbesian "right of nature" to defend oneself should be exercised by those who are to be defended or at least those closest to them, not by blundering altruists.

In sum, for political realists, Gentili's endorsement of preventive war follows necessarily from a realist understanding of the state of international society. It is not then objectionable for preemptive war under the Bush Doctrine to operate in practice as a form of preventive war. It follows, under a realist theory of international law, that the core of the Bush doctrine was its appropriately expansive claims about the law of self-defense: namely, first, its insistence that increased risk could justify earlier, anticipatory action than would otherwise be permissible;[154] and, second, its claim that those who "harbored" terrorists would be held responsible by the United States.[155] In short, under this view, the essence of the Bush doctrine was a justified challenge to the jurisprudence of the ICJ, under which the U.S. right of self-defense was limited by the *Caroline* test's "imminence" requirement and the *Nicaragua Case*'s restrictive rules on the attribution of state responsibility for harboring terrorists. A realist's objection to the Second Gulf War is only that the Bush Administration was insufficiently "realist."

151 *See* Delahunty, *supra* note 15, at 938.

152 *See* Richard Tuck, Comment *in* Michael W. Doyle, Striking First: Preemption and Prevention in International Conflict 119, 127 (Stephen Macedo ed., 2008)[hereinafter "Striking First"].

153 *See* G. John Ikenberry and Anne-Marie Slaughter, Forging a World of Liberty Under Law: U.S. National Security in the 21st Century (The Woodrow Wilson School for Public and Int'l Aff., 2007); *see also* Final Report of The Princeton Project on National Security (2006) (*available at* http://www.princeton.edu/~ppns/report/FinalReport.pdf) (liberal internationalist proposal); and Robert Kagan, *The Case for a League of Democracies*, Financial Times, May 13, 2008) (neoconservative endorsement).

154 *See* The National Security Strategy of the United States, *supra* note 1.

155 *See* Pearl, *supra* note 144, at 38–39.

2. Did the Second Gulf War Violate International Law? -- A Legalist Reply

For the realist, international law seems to work from the bottom-up, starting with the law of self-defense. For the Charter legalist, international law seems to work seamlessly from the top-down. Yet, even for legalists, the debate (on whether the Coalition was authorized to use force and whether, if not, the Security Council subsequently ratified its action) has been endless.[156] Most simply put, the gist of this debate concerns the interpretation of paragraph 12 and 14 of Security Council Resolution 1441. This exquisitely-negotiated document provided that, if the Council's designated agents, led by Hans Blix, determined that Iraq was not in compliance with its disarmament obligations under SCR 687, then the Council would meet to "consider the situation," and it concluded by stating that the Council remained "seized" of the matter.[157] The U.S. position was that Resolution 1441 did not require further action by the Security Council for the Coalition to act on Iraq's "material breach" and, therefore, nothing in the resolution barred the Coalition from acting based on its consistent interpretation of Security Council resolutions in earlier circumstances, especially 1993 and 1998-99.[158]

The negotiating history tells a more complex story, however, at least to the interpretation of Resolution 1441.[159] Russia made clear her view that a fresh resolution would be necessary to determine the consequences that would flow should Mr. Blix's team find persisting Iraqi violations. The Russian Ambassador stated that "in the event of any kind of disagreement about disarmament matters -- it is the heads of UNMOVIC and IAEA who will report that to the Security Council, and it is the Council that will consider the situation that has developed."[160] This understanding seemed to be affirmed in the French statement at the adoption of Resolution 1441, asserting that, upon a report by Mr. Blix that Iraq had violated its obligations, "the Council would meet immediately to evaluate the seriousness of the violations and draw the appropriate conclusions." Furthermore, the French ambassador made reference to a joint statement to be issued later that day by France, Russia, and China, "stressing the scope of the text of the resolution just adopted," under which "all elements of automaticity have disappeared from the

156 *See Debate: Adjudicating Operation Iraqi Freedom*, 100 ASIL Proc. 179–202 (2006); *see also* Lori Fisler Damrosch & Bernard Oxman, *Agora: The Future Implications of the Iraq Conflicts*, 97 Am. J. Int'l L. 553–57 (2003), *reprinted in* The American Society of Int'l Law, Selections from the American Journal of Int'l Law: Future Implications of the Iraq Conflict (2004) (describing the range of views that exists, with excerpts from relevant Security Council Resolutions and from Contemporary Practice of the United States Relating to International Law); and Taft & Buchwald, *supra* note 4, at 557–63 (presenting the U.S. State Department Legal Advisor's statement and defense of U.S. legal position).

157 S.C. Res. 1441, paras. 12 and 14, *supra* note 5.

158 *See* Taft & Buchwald, *supra* note 156.

159 *See* Michael C. Wood, *The Interpretation of Security Council Resolutions*, 2 Max Planck, Y.B. U.N.L. 73, 89–95 (1998) (senior U.K. legal adviser stating that interpretation of Security Council resolutions, like the interpretation of treaties under the Vienna Convention on the Law of Treaties and the customary international law of treaty interpretation, should take into consideration their "plain meaning," their "object of its object and purpose," and their "travaux préparatoires" or negotiating history).

160 U.N. Doc. S/PV.4644, at 8 (Nov. 8, 2002).

resolution."[161] Thus, in their joint statement, the three veto-wielding members of the Security Council, who later refused to join in the Coalition invasion Iraq, made clear their understanding that they had not authorized the other two permanent members of the Council to invade Iraq. Rather, Russia, France, and China declared: "Resolution 1441 (2002) adopted today by the Security Council excludes any automaticity in the use of force. In this regard, we register with satisfaction the declarations of the representatives of the United States and the United Kingdom confirming this understanding in their explanations of vote, and assuring that the goal of the resolution is the full implementation of the existing Security Council resolutions on Iraq's weapons of mass destruction disarmament. All Security Council members share this goal."[162] Finally, the Press Release of the Security Council itself reported the views of the Council's members, particularly its permanent members, that the Council itself would be the final decision-maker in determining the significance and consequences of any violations by Iraq; that Council members said that their views had been taken into account in the final version of the draft, which was co-sponsored by the United States and the United Kingdom; that the representative of France welcomed the two-stage approach required by the resolution, saying that the concept of "automaticity" for the use of force had been eliminated; and that the representatives of China and the Russian Federation stressed that only UNMOVIC and the IAEA had the authority to report violations by Iraq of the resolution's requirements.[163]

Subsequent practice and general principles of treaty interpretation also do not undercut the French, Russian and German position. Russia and France (joined by Germany, which shortly thereafter took a seat as a non-permanent member of the Security Council) maintained that view throughout the occupation of Iraq, even when acquiescing in the adoption of subsequent Security Council Resolutions intended to deal with the consequences of the invasion. Thus, Security Council 1483 arguably did not ratify this invasion; for Russia, Germany, and France made clear in supporting that Resolution that it was their intent to ensure respect for international humanitarian law by the occupying powers and to rebuild the framework for collective decision making.[164] At a minimum, these statements by France, Russia and Germany placed the U.S. and U.K on notice of their interpretations of the effect of the adoption of Resolution 1483, *estopping* them from arguing that France, Germany and Russia had acquiesced in the U.S. and U.K. interpretation of Resolution 1441.[165]

---

161 *Id.* at 5 (statement by French Ambassador Levitte).

162 Press Release, Joint Statement from the Popular Republic of China, the Federation of Russia, and France (Nov. 8, 2002) (*available at* http://www.un.int/france/documents_anglais/021108_cs_france_irak_2.htm).

163 *See* Press Release, Security Council, Security Council Holds Iraq in "Multilateral Breach" of Disarmament Obligations, Offers Final Chance to Comply, Unanimously Adopting Resolution 144, U.N. Doc. SC/7564 (Nov. 11, 2002).

164 *See* UN Doc. S/PV.4761, at 3–7 (May 22, 2003) (an ambassador from each country describing its intent in supporting the Resolution).

165 *See* Temple Preah Vihear (Cambodia v. Thailand), 1962 I.C.J. 6, 39–51 (June 15) (treating estoppel as a general principle of international law); *id.* at 143–44 (Spender, J., dissenting) (stating elements of estoppel concept); Vienna Convention on

But even if it did not ratify the prior Coalition use of force, as to the legal consequences of the Coalition invasion, Resolution 1483 is remains amenable to at least two interpretations. Under one theory, the resolution is "relevant" to the question of international acceptance of the U.S. invasion that Resolution 1483 granted the U.S. and U.K. "effective legal control over Iraq's economy and political process until an internationally recognized government takes power."[166] Accordingly, it deemed the invasion neither illicit nor sanctionable. On the other, it reflects a less trusting view of the occupation because, in part, of the transformation of the law of occupation since the Second World War. That transformation substantially reduced the freedom of the occupying power to reform completely the economy and society of the occupied state, in effect depriving the U.S. of the absolute discretion it had enjoyed in Germany and Japan following the Second World War.[167] It is true the U.S. seemed to argue that, properly construed, Resolution 1483 gave it at least some room for discretion in economic and political reform in Iraq beyond what would have been permitted under the law of war, although the more moderate British view found authority only for economic reform measures that would merely supplement occupation law.[168] Yet, if the basic premise for the U.S. invasion of Iraq in March 2003 was an occupation that would do for Iraq what U.S. occupation had done for Nazi Germany and Imperial Japan, then the imposition of occupation law through the operation of Security Council Resolution 1483 evidenced some degree of disapproval of the U.S. strategic objectives for the war, if not also the legal theory that sustained those strategic objectives.[169] In sum, one might view the ambivalent

---

the Law of Treaties, art. 31, para. 3(c), May 23, 1969 [hereinafter "VCLT]" (instructing courts to consider as a general rule of interpretation "[a]ny relevant rules of international law applicable in the relations between the parties"); and Martti Koskenniemi, From Apology to Utopia: The Structure of International Legal Argument 357–58 (2005) (describing bases of estoppel doctrine and noting difficulty of distinguishing it from "acquiescence"). *See generally* Hersch Lauterpacht, Private Law Sources and Analogies of International Law with Special Reference to International Arbitration (1970) [1926] (discussing use of general principles of private law, such as estoppel, to fill in the gaps of public international law).

166 John Norton Moore, Toward Incentive Theory 74 (2004).

167 *See* David Scheffer, *Beyond Occupation Law*, 97 Am. J. Int'l L. 842, 848 (2003) (viewing U.S. discretion as occupying power as limited by the "law of war").

168 *See* Remarks of John B. Bellinger, II, Legal Adviser, U.S. Dep't of State, U.N. Security Council Resolutions and the Application of Int'l Humanitarian Law, International Conference, (Sept. 9, 2005) (*available at* http://www.state.gov./s/l/c8183.htm); *see also* J.L. Dorosin, *Jus in Bello: Occupation Law and the War in Iraq*, 98 ASIL Proceedings 117, 119 (2004) (State Department attorney-adviser stating: "Resolution 1483 provided authorities that supervene any inconsistent limitations that may be contained in other bodies of international law, including occupation law"). The British view of the legal effect of Resolution 1483 was characteristically more nuanced. As the British Secretary of State for Foreign and Commonwealth Affairs wrote: "Occupation law does indeed constrain the capacity of the Occupying Power to carry out economic reform... That position is supplemented by Security Council Resolution 1483, and in particular paragraph 8(e) which envisages assistance to the people of Iraq for the promotion of economic reconstruction." Second Report from the Foreign Affairs Committee, Foreign Policy Aspects of the War Against Terrorism, Session, 2003–04, Response of the Secretary of State for Foreign and Commonwealth Affairs, Mar. 2004, Cm. 6162, at 8. Contrary to the U.S. view, the United Kingdom's view thus appears to limit Resolution 1483 to authorize only economic reform and only to supplement, but not to supersede or contradict, otherwise applicable occupation law. *But see* Stefan Talmon, Security Council Treaty Action, 62 Revue Hellenique de Droit International 65 (2009) (treating statements of U.S. and U.K. as consistent).

169 For a criticism of the U.S. legal strategy in terms of its failure to establish in advance the legal conditions that would enable the U.S. to achieve is strategic objectives, *see* Antonio F. Perez, *Legal Frameworks for Economic Transition in Iraq—Occupation Under the La of War vs. Global Governance under the Law of Peace*, 18 The Transnational Lawyer 53 (2004).

reaction of the Security Council to the Coalition's use of force here, like the Security Council's ambivalent reaction in Resolution 1244 to NATO's humanitarian intervention to save Kosovo,[170] as suggesting a mixed response: a pattern of accommodation to noncompliance coupled with limited sanctions, signaling something less than approval and something less than punishment.

Yet, even assuming nothing in Resolution 1441 barred U.S. action, the U.S. legal position was also necessarily premised on the revival of its rights under Resolution 678. On this score, the U.S. view necessarily held that ordinary principles of law in the performance and breach of multilateral treaties could be extended to the interpretation Security Council resolutions; in other words, Security Council Resolution 687 was not a bilateral treaty between the U.N. and Iraq but rather a multilateral treaty between the Member States of the UN and Iraq. Further, it held under those principles that Iraq's material breach of a series of Security Council resolutions, including Resolution 687, gave the United States and other states, as parties to that treaty, the right to suspend the effect of resolution 687: either because of the nature of Iraq's obligation and the effect of its breach on all parties; or because of the special effect of its breach on the U.S. and its other Coalition partners involved in the first Gulf War.[171] Thus, suspension of that treaty revived U.S. rights to use force under resolution 678.[172]

Clearly, the frame of reference explaining the Coalition's use of force in the First Gulf War would matter. For, if one took the view that the Coalition engaged in "enforcement action" under Chapter VII as the agent of the Security Council and UN, then it would be easier to view Resolution 678 as a bilateral treaty between the UN and Iraq, giving the Coalition members no rights. However, if the Coalition's use of force in the First Gulf War were viewed as an exercise of collective self-defense rights under Article 51, with the approval of the Security Council under Chapter VII, then it would be easier to view Resolution 687 as a multilateral arrangement between the parties in conflict, with the UN serving as guarantor of the ceasefire's terms.[173]

Finally, the debate seemed to raise foundational questions about the basic role of the UN Charter, UN Security Council, and their relation to the rights and duties of Member States, in

---

170 *See* Part II, Chapter 3, *supra* (discussing the extent to which, if at all, Resolution 1244 ratified NATO's use of force).

171 *See* VCLT, art. 60(2)(b) ("providing that a "material breach of a multilateral treaty" entitles "a party specially affected by the breach to invoke it as a ground for suspending the operation of the treaty in whole or in part in the relations between itself and the defaulting State") and 60(2)(c) (providing that a "material breach of a multilateral treaty" entitles "any party other than the defaulting State to invoke the breach as a ground for suspending the operation of the treaty in whole or in part with respect to itself if the treaty is of such a character that a material breach of its provisions by one party radically changes the position of every other party with respect to the further performance of its obligations under the treaty"); *see also* Moore, *supra* note 166, at 137 n.21 (discussing VCLT Article 60(2)(c) and asserting that arms control agreements, such as the WMD provisions of Resolution 687, are believed to fall within this category). One could also argue that the U.S., as well as the other Coalition states which had used forced against Iraq in the First Gulf War, were "specially affected" for purposes of VCLT Article 60(2)(b) and, therefore, were entitled to suspend the ceasefire provisions of Resolution 687 even without showing that Iraq's material breach "radically change[d] the position of every other party with respect to the further performance of its obligations under the treaty," as required by Article 60(2)(c).

172 *See* Taft & Buchwald, *supra* note 156.

173 *See* Part II, Chapter 2, *supra* note 117 (discussing whether Resolution 678 constituted enforcement action, approval of collective self-defense or perhaps, as according to Oscar Schachter, it could be viewed as either).

which the "constitutional" status of the UN Charter may be debated. Under one view, the Charter is something like a constitution for international society,[174] a partial (albeit functionally amendable) constitution with limited powers in specified areas,[175] a fractured or failed constitution,[176] or part of a set of legal instruments that together form an overall constitutional structure;[177] alternatively, the Charter resolution would be viewed merely a treaty subordinate to the dispositive treaties between the Great Powers settling major wars.[178] Another way to put the question is whether the decisions of the Security Council are more like treaties or more like the statutes of a legislative organ?[179] Did that change between the First Gulf War, when the Council was acting generally in unison, and the Second Gulf War, after the NATO humanitarian intervention may have irretrievably divided the Council and restored the Cold War pattern of paralysis and acrimony?[180] Without answers to these prior questions, there seems to be no authoritative basis within available precedent for resolving whether Resolutions 678 and 687 are more like treaties or contracts between states or laws promulgated by the Security Council that bind states.

Finally, the U.S. legal position was arguably premised on the belief that, in invading Iraq and overthrowing Saddam Hussein, it satisfied the standards for the exercise of the right to

174 *See* Bardo Fassbender, *United Nations Charter as Constitution of the International Community*, 36 Colum. J. Transnational L. 529 (1998).

175 See Antonio F. Perez, *On the Way to the Forum: The Reconstruction of Article 2(7) and the Rise of Federalism Under the United Nations Charter*, 31 Tex. Int'l L. J. 353, 402–04 (1996) (suggesting that the Charter's meaning was understood to have changed with the U.N. Security Council Declaration approving the Secretary-General's "Agenda for Peace," which described self-determination and democracy as emerging central principles in the post-Cold War international legal system, thus operated as the proposal for a de facto amended Charter, and following Security Council approval authorized Chapter VII action not only in ordinary cases of armed conflict across borders but also wholly domestic genocide and military coups).

176 Simpson raises the question of whether NATO's 1999 intervention in Kosovo was the "foundational moment" of a project of international "regime building" in which the West sought to overthrow the UN Charter as the "constitution" of the world legal order and to install a régime of regional hegemony instead. *See* Gerry Simpson, Great Powers and Outlaw States 194 (2004). Simpson sees the great European peace settlement at the Congress of Vienna in 1815 as establishing a kind of international constitution akin to the UN Charter of 1945. *Id.* at 177. He then compares NATO to the Holy Alliance of the early nineteenth century, led by Russia and joined by Prussia and Austria. *Id.* at 199–222. The Holy Alliance was committed to a policy of armed intervention (in Spain, for instance) to protect monarchist institutions from revolution. The Alliance's policy seemed to Britain and the United States to threaten the foundation of the Congress of Vienna's international legal order, which rested on the idea of the equality of sovereign states and their freedom from outside interference. *Id.* at 91–131. NATO's intervention in Kosovo in 1999 likewise represented a revolution against the constitutional principles of the UN Charter, especially the requirement that non-self-defensive uses of force be approved by the Security Council. *Id.* at 199–222. Simpson even compares the "mystical" Prime Minister Tony Blair to the Russian Czar Alexander I, the founder of the Holy Alliance (and President Bill Clinton to Austria's Count Metternich, who joined the Holy Alliance for opportunistic reasons). *Id.* at 202–03.

177 *See* Andreas Paulus, The International Legal System as a Constitution, *in* Ruling the World?: Constitutionalism, International Law and Global Governance 69 (Jeffrey Dunoff & Joel Trachtman eds., 2009).

178 *See* Philip Bobbitt, The Shield of Achilles: War, Peace, and the Course of History 636–39 (2002) (arguing that the Charter of Paris in 1990 constituted a treaty of peace closing the epochal war between parliamentary democracy and its fascist and communist competitors, in which the internal constitutional principles of "market states" were confirmed as the new constitutional principles of the international system).

179 A number of views have been advanced on the role the Security Council might play, if any, as a legislature body. *See, e.g.*, Stefan Talmon, *The Security Council as World Legislature*, 99 Am. J. Int'l L. 175 (2005).

180 *See* Simpson, *supra* note 176.

self-defense. Here, the U.S. seems to have viewed this particular "preemptive use of force" as "certainly lawful where, as here, it represents an episode in an ongoing broader conflict initiated—without question—by the [Iraq]."[181] Yet, despite the efforts made by U.S. State Department lawyers to narrow the scope of the U.S. legal theory to a question of the *jus in bello*, the U.S. legal theory engaged not only a specific debate concerning the rights of states in the face of Security Council indecision but also a more general debate over the circumstances under which self-defense rights may be exercised against sub-state entities, such as terrorist organizations. It thus called into question the U.S. interpretation of Security Council Resolutions 1368 and 1373.[182] The U.S. theory also took a broad view of the circumstances under which the conduct of those entities can be attributed to states. It thus called into question the *Nicaragua* test.[183] Finally, the U.S. had argued that it was the risk of Iraqi support for Al Qaeda, given Iraq's assumed possession of WMD, that give rise to the "necessity" for self-defense. In other words, the U.S. also argued that the new conditions of WMD use by sub-state entities (who were as threatening as states but, unlike states, could not be deterred by the threat of retaliation) also gave rise to the need for "preemptive" action, thus re-interpreting the *Caroline* test to meet modern circumstances.[184]

This debate concerning the necessity and proportionality of self-defense shortly thereafter reached in the jurisprudence of the ICJ and the reports of international bodies created by the UN to study these underlying issues. In a series of decisions following the war, the ICJ called each of the major propositions of the U.S. legal theory into question. As to the right to respond against an armed attack against sub-state entity, in its advisory opinion on the *Legal Consequences of Construction of a Wall in the Occupied Palestinian Territory*, the ICJ asserted: "Article 51 of the Charter thus recognizes the existence of an inherent right of self-defence in the case of armed attack by one State against another State."[185] This language seemed to rule out the possibility of relying on Article 51 to respond to an attack by a sub-state entity that was not attributable, under the rules of the ICJ, to another state. On the other hand, the ICJ did recognize the validity of Security Council Resolutions 1368 and 1373. It stated: "The Court notes that Israel exercises control in the Occupied Palestinian Territory and that, as Israel itself states, the threat which it regards as justifying the construction of the wall originates within, and not outside, of that territory. The situation is thus different from that contemplated by Security Council resolutions 1368 (2001) and 1373 (2001), and therefore Israel could not in any event invoke those resolutions

181 Taft & Buchwald, *supra* note 4, at 11.

182 *See supra* text accompanying notes 90–92 (that Resolutions 1368 and 1373, together with the NATO determination of an armed attack by Al Qaeda with Taliban support for purposes of the NATO Treaty, triggered the U.S. right to self-defense).

183 *See supra* text accompanying notes 52–67 (discussing the ICJ's attribution rules).

184 *See supra* text accompanying note 1 (The National Security Strategy of the United States).

185 Legal Consequences of Construction of a Wall in the Occupied Palestinian Territory, 2004 I.C.J. 136, 194 at para. 139 (July 9) [hereinafter "Construction of a Wall"].

in support of its claim to be exercising the right of self-defence."[186] Thus, the ICJ's implicit interpretation of Resolutions 1368 and 1373 is that they are predicated on the attribution of responsibility for Al Qaeda's attack on the United States to Afghanistan, making the attack an "armed attack" by a "State" for purposes of Article 51. U.S. anti-terrorism policies targeting terrorist groups operating in states test would continue, therefore, to be legally problematic if they did not satisfy the ICJ's test for attribution.

If so, this made crucial the rules of attribution the Court articulated in the *Nicaragua Case.* In the interim, one other international juridical organ had considered the question of attribution, albeit in the separate context of determining whether the conduct of the Republika Srpska (Serb Republic) forces in Bosnia-Herezegovina during the Bosnian civil war could be attributed to the Federal Republic of Yugoslavia (the FRY) so as to trigger the application of the laws and customs of war governing international armed conflict. If the conduct was not attributable, its followed that the conduct of the Serb Republic within the Bosnian confederation that included the Serb Republic would be governed by the less rigorous standards of international humanitarian law governing non-international armed conflict. The International Criminal Tribunal for Yugoslavia, which had been created by Chapter VII resolution as a creature of the United Nations (the ICTY),[187] determined that the "effective control" test utilized by the ICJ in the *Nicaragua Case* was too stringent and did not comport with international law principles of state responsibility. Rather, it believed that only a "lower degree of control" (i.e., "overall control" of the FRY) was sufficient.[188] In *Application of the Convention on the Prevention and Punishment of the Crime of Genocide (Bosnia & Herzegovina v. Serbia & Montenegro),*[189] the ICJ nonetheless reaffirmed its reasoning in the *Nicaragua Case* and disagreed with the ICTY that the conduct of the Serb Republic could be attributed to the FRY.[190] The ICJ effectively rejected the "overall control" test, noting that, if:

> [it were] employed to determine whether or not an armed conflict is international, which was the sole question which the Appeals Chamber [of the ICTY] was called upon to decide, it may well be that the test is applicable and suitable; the Court does not however think it is appropriate to take a position on the point in the present case, as there is no need to resolve it in the present proceeding. On the other hand, the ICTY presented the "overall control" test as equally application under the law of State responsibility for the purpose of determining -- as the Court is required to do in the present case -- when a State is responsible for acts committed

---

186 *Id.*

187 *See* S.C. Res. 827, U.N. Doc. S/RES/827 (May 25, 1993).

188 *See* Prosecutor v. Tadic, I.C.T.Y. Case No. IT-94-1-AR72, paras. 102–45 and 162 (1999) (Judgment of Appeals Chamber).

189 *See* Application of the Convention on the Prevention and Punishment of the Crime of Genocide (Bosn. & Herz. v. Serb. & Montenegro), 2007 I.C.J. 191 (Feb. 26) [hereinafter The Genocide Case].

190 *Id.* at para. 394.

> by paramilitary units, armed forces which are not among its official organs. In this context, the argument in favor of that test is unpersuasive.[191]

In sum, whatever purchase the more expansive ITCY test for attribution may have had in determining which law of armed conflict governed a situation, and even on this issue the ICJ's concession was qualified, the *Nicaragua Case* test would continue to control generally for purposes of attribution of the conduct of "armed bands" to sovereignty states.[192] In short, the ICJ reiterated its skepticism on attribution, and thereby weakened any case the U.S. could have made that that terrorist conduct, including that of Al Qaeda, would have been attributable to Iraq.

Finally, the ICJ imposed a very heavy burden of proof that a state would need to show to establish the necessity and proportionality of its exercise of the right of self-defense from an "armed attack" by an "armed band" subject to the "effective control" of a state. In the *Oil Platforms Case*,[193] the ICJ found that U.S. use of force against Iran was neither necessary nor proportionate. During the Iran-Iraq conflict in the 1980s, Iran retaliated against Iraq, then an ally of the United States, with attacks on neutral-flag ships coming from or destined for ports in Kuwait and Saudi Arabia. To protect neutral commerce, the United States re-flagged the neutral ships so as to fly under the U.S. flag, but these ships continued to be attacked by Iranian forces. In addition, Iran laid mines in international waters, resulting in damage to a U.S. naval vessel. In response, the U.S. attacked and destroyed two Iranian offshore oil production installations, oil platforms, which the U.S. claimed were used as a staging facilities for attacks by Iranian forces against shipping in the Gulf.

Although the basis for jurisdiction was the U.S.-Iran Treaty of Amity, as in the *Nicaragua Case* the Court found the customary international law of self-defense, which governed the use of force under the treaty, to be coterminous with the law of the Charter. First, the ICJ asserted that the U.S. carried the burden of proof that its vessels "were of such a nature as to be qualified as 'armed attacks' within the meaning of that expression in Article 51 of the United Nations Charter, and as understood in customary law on the use of force," thereby apparently insisting on an actual "armed attack" rather than a threat of an armed attack as a necessary condition for the exercise of the right of self-defense.[194] Second, and perhaps more important, the Court did not find the evidence sufficient to show that Iranian responsibility for the missile attack the U.S.

---

191 *Id.* at para. 404.

192 Indeed, the ICJ made this clear on facts comparable to those of the *Nicaragua Case*, if anything further limiting the right of self-defense. In *Armed Activities on the Territory of the Congo*, the ICJ rejected Uganda's argument that it was properly exercising its right of self-defense when it was "actively extending" support to irregular forces in the Congo opposing the Congolese government, even though it was responding to the Congolese government's provision of support to anti-Ugandan insurgents who were engaging in cross-border attacks from Congo into Uganda. *See* Armed Activities on the Territory of the Congo (Dem. Rep. Congo v. Uganda), 2005 I.C.J. 168, para. 147 (Dec. 19).

193 *See* Oil Platforms Case (Iran v. U.S.), 2003 I.C.J. 161, paras. 72–78 (Nov. 14).

194 *Id.* at para. 51.

alleged had been directed at U.S.-flagged ship. After carefully reviewing the evidence submitted by the United States, much of it of a highly technical nature, including satellite imagery and other intelligence information,[195] the Court concluded that the U.S. bore "the burden of proof of the existence of an armed attack by Iran against the United states," which "had not been discharged." Finally, it considered the proportionality of the U.S. response. It noted that, if the U.S. response to the Iranian missile attack on a U.S. re-flagged Kuwaiti tanker was necessary, then the response might have been proportionate. But it did not think that retaliatory measures against the oil platforms was a proportionate response to the Iranian laying of mines in international waters that caused damage to a U.S. naval vessel.[196]

Also, in its advisory opinion on the *Legal Consequences of Construction of a Wall in the Occupied Palestinian Territory*,[197] the ICJ said it was "not convinced" that wall was "the only means" to safeguard Israel from terrorist attacks originating in the Palestinian-controlled territory, which Israel thought was the "necessity" justifying the wall's construction. This stringent test, if applied literally, would limit state discretion beyond even what the ICJ must have intended; for, if several possible means are available, no single means could serve as the "only means" available for exercising the right of self-defense, rendering each means improper. Could this possibly be what the ICJ intended?

Whatever its precise intent, the ICJ's advisory opinion on the *Legal Consequences of Construction of a Wall in the Occupied Palestinian Territory*, coupled with its judgment in the *Oil Platforms Case*, may well signal ICJ resistance to approving virtually any use of force by the U.S. or Israel. At a minimum, none of these determinations, all in the immediate aftermath of the Second Gulf War, could be viewed as favorable to any case the U.S. might wish to make in the future, based on intelligence information, for the exercise of its right of self-defense to deter future attacks by a state, much less groups supported by states such as Iran. The Court's jurisprudence, therefore, represents at some level a response to the legal theories advanced by the U.S. in the Second Gulf War, as well as Israel in its earlier attack on the PLO Headquarters in Tunisia. As the United States and its allies sought to adapt or amend the legal postulates the ICJ had thought were established, the ICJ reasserted the supremacy of views it has asserted at the beginning of the Charter legal order in the *Corfu Channel Case*, when it declared itself "the organ" of "international law."[198]

In September 2003, during the aftermath of the Second Gulf War, the Secretary General of the UN constituted a special commission of eminent persons, including among others former

195 *Id.* at paras. 50–51.

196 *Id.* at para. 77.

197 *See* Construction of a Wall, *supra* note 185, at 195 para. 40.

198 The Corfu Channel Case, *supra* note 35, at 34–35.

U.S. National Security Advisor Brent Scowcroft, who had opposed the Second Gulf War,[199] to study and evaluate existence institutions and policies on collective security.[200] On December 1, 2004, after the ICJ issued its judgments in the *Oil Platforms Case* and its advisory opinion *Concerning the Construction of a Wall in the Occupied Territories*, the eminent persons group submitted its findings, the Report of the Secretary-General's High-Level Panel on Threats, Challenges and Change, A More Secure World: Our Shared Responsibility (HLP Report).[201] The HLP Report recognized that in the case of "non-imminent or non-proximate" threats, "good arguments for preventive military action, with good evidence to support," could be "put to the Security Council," with the implication that Security Council authorization might lawfully be forthcoming.[202] However, it explicitly opposed "unilateral preventive action" and "the rewriting or reinterpretation of Article 51."[203] A year later, the Secretary General issued his own report to the United Nations, In Larger Freedom: Towards Development, Security and Human Rights for All (In Larger Freedom).[204] There, he reaffirmed his own opposition to preemptive use of force where the threat was not "imminent" but rather "latent."[205] But he took the position that crimes against humanity could also, like latent threats, constitute threats to international peace and security within the competence of the Security Council, which therefore also could be the subject of collective action based on Security Council authorization under Chapter VII.[206] Finally, he called for a Security Council resolution articulating the principles the Council would consider when deciding whether to authorize use of force in circumstances of emerging threats when state action was not permitted under existing law.[207] He thus supported the conclusions of the High-Level Panel Report on the preemptive use of force; the R2P Report with respect to humanitarian intervention;[208] and, albeit without citing its decisions and advisory opinions, the

199 *See* Steven Mufson, *Scowcroft Urges Restraint on Iraq*, Wash. Post, Aug. 5, 2002, at A4 ("Scowcroft, who advised Bush's father during the Persian Gulf War," on CBS's 'Face the Nation' "warned that a U.S. invasion of Iraq "could turn the whole region into a cauldron and, thus, destroy the war on terrorism.").

200 *See* Note by the Secretary General, Follow-up to the Outcome to the Millennium Summit, paras. 1–3, A/59/565 (Dec. 2, 2004) (transmitting Report of High-Level Panel on Threats, Challenges and Change).

201 *See* Report of the Secretary-General's High-Level Panel on Threats, Challenges and Change, A More Secure World: Our Shared Responsibility (Dec. 1, 2003), paras. 189–90, Annex to Note by the Secretary General, Follow-up to the Outcome to the Millennium Summit, A/59/565 [hereinafter "Report of the High-Level Panel"].

202 *Id.* at paras. 189–190.

203 *Id.* at paras. 191-192.

204 *See* Report of the Secretary-General, In Larger Freedom: Towards Development, Security and Human Rights for All, (Mar. 21, 2005), A/59/2005, Follow-up to the Outcome of the Millennium Summit [hereinafter In Larger Freedom].

205 *See id.* at paras. 124–25 (suggesting that the line reflected the consensus position of international lawyers; thus, implicitly endorsing the *Caroline* test).

206 *Id.* at para. 125

207 *Id.* at para. 126.

208 *See generally* Part II, Chapter 3, *supra.*

reasoning of the ICJ in the jurisprudence in which the ICJ had implicitly criticized the proposed expansion of the right of self-defense.

In short, a legalist counter-attack from the ICJ, the Secretary General, and a group of international experts representing transnational civil society, sought to delegitimize the U.S.'s challenge during the Second Gulf War to the existing conception of positive international law. These actors also rejected the extension of the reasoning underlying the NATO action on Kosovo without Security Council authorization to the Gulf War, which for many would have served as the best rationale for the overthrow of Saddam Hussein. In short, these voices reaffirmed the "legalist paradigm," as it has been called by moral philosopher Michael Walzer,[209] and rejected the proposed Bush doctrine's attempt to substitute legalism with a focus on the costs of nonintervention in the face of WMD threats and humanitarian catastrophes and the foregone benefits of installing democratic regimes.

3. A Rationalist Response

If Legalism and Realism are speaking at cross-purposes, rational choice theory or rationalist-institutionalism, which we have described as rooted in neo-realism, attempts to respond to the insights of realism in terms the allow it to engage in a dialogue with with legalism's theory of multilaterally-managed, democratic enlargement. The rationalist critique of the Bush Doctrine focuses on its approach to assessing the nature of the threat posed by WMD and their possible use by terrorists, but pays attention to developing an optimal set of rules.

Rationalism differs substantially from legalism, however, in its approach to the basis for international law and the authority of international institutions. Instead of focusing on right process and compliance with formalities, such as decision-making by the Security Council, it is grounded on a compliance theory of international law that is not exhausted by the decisions of international tribunals.[210] The legitimacy of a legal rule turns, not only on whether it is in "accordance with right process," but also on its effectiveness in pulling "those to whom it is

209 *See* Walzer, *supra* note 68, at 75 (viewing the paradigm as authorizing response on;y to actual and imminent attacks).

210 *See* W. Michael Reisman, International Incidents: Introduction to a New Genre in the Study of International Law, *in* International Incidents: The Law that Counts in World Politics 3, 15 (W. Michael Reisman & Andrew R. Willard eds., 1988) ("If law is to be found in significant part in the application of norms to particular cases and controversies, it is plain that such applications in international politics must be sought in a much wider range of arenas than the highly formalized and structured judicial fora of domestic systems."). As Sean Murphy further explains, "[i]n the context of international law relating to the use of military force, law is best seen as a means of predicting global reactions to a proposed use of such force." That is, "when a lawyer says that a proposed course of action would be unlawful, the lawyer is really saying that in the past, international society has decided that such an action is wrongful and, in similar circumstances, will likely do so again." Sean D. Murphy, *The Doctrine of Preemptive Self-defense*, 50 Vill. L. Rev. 600, 704 (2005) (describing realist approach); cf. Abram Chayes & Antonia Handler Chayes, The New Sovereignty: Compliance with International Regulatory Agreements 118, 127 (1995).

addressed toward consensual compliance."[211] But, even legalists might be viewed as incorporating rationalist thought in their theory of international law; for, when they emphasize the *opinio iuris* component of customary international law formation (i.e., holding that conduct can be "discursively" legitimated through the reasons given), they mean that acceptance of those reasons in turn can affect the actual costs other states impose on the state using force. Thus, even in the Cuban Missile Crisis, according to a former State Department's Legal Advisor, "the requirement of justification suffuses the basic process of choice. There is a continuous feedback between the knowledge that the government will be called upon to justify its action and the kind of action that can be chosen."[212]

For realists who turn to rationalist thought, the reasons given are clearly subordinate to the calculation of interest that explains ultimately the decision to use force and the reactions of other states, including the states on the Security Council. As we shall see, constructivist proponents of "discursive" justification would view the Security Council through the lens of a thought-experiment requiring "ideal speech" conditions.[213] Realists, by contrast, would view decision-making at the Security Council substantively, as wholly subordinating to the national interest;[214] and procedurally they would view Security Council decision-making as standardless and secretive.[215] Thus, rationalists reject the liberal-internationalist suggestion that the Security Council serves as a kind of "global jury."[216] Rather, what matters is what states do and why they do it, which is explained primarily by calculations of interest, rather than statements of justification. Thus, increasingly, rationalist theory takes into account behavioral contexts to assess more accurately probable behaviors, taking into account actual subjective perceptions, especially in ways that diverge from the model of rational behavior that underlies traditional economic analysis.[217]

---

211 Thomas M. Franck, *Legitimacy in the International Legal System*, 82 Am. J. Int'l L. 705, 711 (1988); *see also* Chayes & Chayes, *supra* note 200, at 118, 127; and Thomas M. Franck, *The Power of Legitimacy and the Legitimacy of Power*, 100 Am. J. Int'l L. 88, 103 (2006).

212 Abram Chayes, The Cuban Missile Crisis: International Crises and the Role of Law 103 (1974).

213 *See* Jurgen Habermass, The Theory of Communicative Action (Thomas McCarthy trans., 1984) (suggesting that fair procedure becomes the justification for a fair outcome).

214 *See* Ruth Wedgewood, *Unilateral Action in the UN System*, 11 Eur. J. Int'l L. 349, 351 (2000).

215 *See* Ian Johnstone, *Security Council Deliberations: The Power of the Better Argument*, 14 Eur. J. Int'l L. 437, 438, 452–53 (2003) (pointing out deficiencies in Security Council procedures).

216 As Hans Blix, former Secretary General of the IAEA and head of UNMOVIC, wrote after the Second Gulf War, "We would properly react if a judge on a court allowed his vote for the death penalty in one case to be influenced by another judge's offer of support in a different case. Is this any different from one state urging another to vote for an authorization of the use of armed force which will inevitably lead to death and destruction?" Hans Blix, Disarming Iraq 218 (2004); *see also* Thomas M. Franck, Fairness in International Law and Institutions (1995) (suggesting viewing the Security Council as a "global jury").

217 *See, e.g.*, Christine Jolls, Cass Sunstein, & Richard Thaler, *A Behavioral Approach to Law and Economics*, 50 Stan. L. Rev. 1471 (1998).

From the rationalist perspective, then, the ICJ *Oil Platforms* decision's nominally objective, *ex post* review of U.S. decision-making is deeply flawed, because it failed to account for the subjective experience of decision-makers under exigent circumstances. According to one former State Department lawyer, "The concept of discretion contains within it the premise of decision-maker judgment, but third-party assessment of such judgment would require an examination of perceptions and the reasonableness of decisions based on them. Yet objective responsibility, a dominant theory of state responsibility, holds that [i]n the absence of any specific requirement of a mental element . . . it is only the act of a State that matters, independently of any intention."[218] Moreover, under this view, any attempt to describe patterns of expectations in terms of rigid legal rules fails to capture the substantial indeterminacy in legal doctrine.[219] This is perhaps more true in international law than perhaps any other body of law, where the possibility of a gap in the law, the so-called *non liquet*, is often debated.[220] For a rationalist, then, recognition of fact- and law-indeterminacy are necessary to model accurately the behavior of states and, therefore, to determine how best to develop institutions that encourage welfare-maximizing behavior.

For a rationalist, conflict is avoidable if both sides to the conflict have perfect information about their respective capacities and capabilities. This knowledge would enable the parties to reach a settlement that is a welfare-maximizing solution reflecting the real distribution of power

218 David Kaye, *Adjudicating Self-Defense: Discretion, Perception, and the Resort to Force in International Law*, 44 Colum J. Int'l L. 149–50 (2005) (citing Articles on Responsibility of States for Intentionally Wrongful Acts, in Report of the International Law Commission on the Work of Its Fifty-third Session, U.N. GAOR, 56th Sess., Supp. No. 10, at 73, U.N. Doc. A/56/10 (2001), *reprinted in* James Crawford, The International Law Commission's Articles on State Responsibility: Introduction, Text and Commentaries 84 (2002)). Kaye adds: "It looks only to whether a particular act is in conformity with a specified rule of international law applicable to the acting state." *Id.* at 150 (citing André Nollkaemper, *Concurrence Between Individual Responsibility and State Responsibility in International Law*, 52 Int'l & Comp. L. Q. 615, 617 (2003) ("The conduct of the state as a legal person is assessed against an objective standard.")). And as Kaye notes, "[t]his is essentially what was done in *Oil Platforms*, where the ICJ refused to look at the intent behind U.S. actions impugned by Iran and examined only the outcomes—specific responses to specific attacks on U.S. shipping. It is largely a principle that works against discretion in the adjudication of international legal rules." Kaye, *supra*, at 150.

219 *See* Kaye, *supra* note 218, at 146 (citing Russell B. Korobkin, *Behavior Analyss and Legal Form: Rules vs. Standards Revisited*, 79 Or. L. Rev. 23, 26 (2000) ("In real world situations, however, the distinction between rules and standards is often less extreme, and the two types of legal forms are better understood, as a descriptive matter, as endpoints of a spectrum than as dichotomous categories.")).

220 *Compare* Anthony D'Amato, *Legal Uncertainty*, 71 Cal. L. Rev. 1 (1983) (treating law as a binary system, in which there are no gaps because either the plaintiff wins or the defendant wins); *with* W. M. Reisman, *International Non-Liquet: Recrudescence and Transformation*, 3 Int'l Law. 770, 773 (1969) (arguing, not theoretical gaps in the law, but institutional and pragmatic considerations explain and justify the decisions that in effect are non-liquets even if the Court does not describe them as such); *see also* Julius Stone, *Non-Liquet and the Function of Law in the International Community*, 35 Brit. Y.B. Int'l L. 124 (1959) (critiquing Siorat and Lauterpacht, infra, and concluding that there is no rule prohibiting non-liquet); L. Siorat, Le Probleme des Lacunes en Droit International: Contribution a L' Etude des Sources du Droit et De La Fonction Judiciaire (1958) (arguing that State practice suggests that international law in some cases actually requires a non-liquet); and H. Lauterpacht, The Function of Law in the International Community 127–38 (1966); Hersch Lauterpacht, Some Observations on the Prohibition of "Non-Liquet' and the Completeness of the Legal Order, in Symbolae Verzijl 196, 199 n.2 (Martinus Nijhoff ed., 1958) (arguing that a non-liquet in a contentious case is forbidden as a matter of law but recognizing that "the problem assumes a different complexion" in advisory opinions).

and preferences.[221] WMD programs in secretive societies are inherently hard to defect, however, as the U.S. experience with Iraq revealed after the intelligence failure to discover Iraq's unsafeguarded nuclear weapons program before the First Gulf War. But this failure was coupled with the U.S. intelligence and law enforcement community's failure to anticipate Al Qaeda's September 11, 2001 attacks on the Pentagon and World Trade Center,[222] which no doubt played a role in making the intelligence community risk-averse in the period before the Second Gulf War.[223] The catastrophic harm that WMD may cause also skews judgments of risk, despite low probability, in the direction of extreme risk-aversion, much like Pascal's famous wager under which one ought to be willing to believe in God when weighing the infinite gain of eternal bliss against suffering the infinite loss of eternal damnation, even if the probability of their actually being a God were infinitesimally small.[224] This kind of thinking has given rise to the so-called "precautionary principle" in international environmental law[225]-- which for the Bush Administration in the terrorism context became known as "the one percent doctrine," meaning that a one percent chance of a WMD attack was unacceptable and required preemptive use of force.[226] Leading students of law and economics have voiced concerns about the degree to which democracies are prone to exaggerate the risk of extreme outcomes.[227]

Perhaps more important, the transmission and receipt of information about intentions is particularly problematic in the relations between democracies and rogue regimes and terrorist organizations. Because, for the rational choice theorist, risk of misperception is a key cause of war,[228] effective signaling of intentions and capabilities reduces the risk of war. Thus, while the effectiveness of signaling between democracies explains democratic peace theory's promise

221 *See* Jide Nzelibe and John Yoo, *Rational War and Constitutional Design,* Yale L.J. 2512, 2527–28 (2006) (citing James D. Fearon, *Signaling Foreign Policy Interests: Tying Hands Versus Sinking Costs,* 41 J. Conflict Resol. 68, 69 (1997), and *Domestic Political Audiences and the Escalation of International Disputes,* 88 Am. Pol. Sci. Rev. 577, 578 (1994)).

222 *See generally* Lawrence Wright, The Looming Tower: Al-Qaeda and the Road to 9/11 (2006); Report of the National Commission on Terrorist Attacks Upon the United States (2004).

223 See Bob Woodward, *supra* note 109, at 422 (CIA Director reportedly stating that the presence of WMD in Iraq was a "slam dunk"); *see also* The Commission on the Intelligence Capabilities of the United States Regarding Weapons of Mass Destruction, Report to the President of the United States (2005) (*available at* http://govinfo.library.unt.edu/wmd/report/wmd_report.pdf).

224 *See* Blaise Pascal, *Pensées,* Part III, sec. 233 (*available at* http://www.gutenberg.org); *see generally* Wikipedia: Pascal's Wager (*available at* http://en.wikipedia.org/wiki/Pascal%27s_Wager).

225 *See, e.g.,* Rio Declaration on Environment and Development, The United Nations Conference on Environment and Development, Report of the United Nations Conference on the Human Environment, Stockholm, 5–16 (*available at* http://www.unep.org/Documents.multilingual/Default.asp?DocumentID=78&ArticleID=1163) (Principle 15 states: states should adopt a "precautionary approach," under which "[w]here there are threats of serious or irreversible damage, lack of full scientific certainty shall not be used as a reason for postponing cost-effective measures to prevent environmental degradation.").

226 *See* Ron Suskind, The One Percent Doctrine: Deep Inside America's Pursuit of its Enemies since 9/11 62 (2006).

227 *See* Cass R. Sunstein, Laws of Fear: Beyond the Precautionary Principle 83, 89, 104 (2005) (noting various ways in which the Bush administration exaggerating the consequences of 9/11); Richard A. Posner, Catastrophe: Risk and Response 148–49 (2004) (taking issue with Pascal's famous wager and arguing for a more moderate precautionary principle).

228 *See generally* Robert Jervis, Perception and Misperception in International Politics (1976).

that democracies do not go to war with each other, it is the impediments to effective signaling between democracies and rogue states or terrorist organizations that explains why the risk of conflict is so much greater.[229] For a rational choice theorist, the traditional *Caroline* imminence test made sense misperception and error. For "[r]equiring that a specific attack be about to occur helps ensure that a defender exhaust other, non-forcible means and it reduces the likelihood of mistakes, insofar as waiting until that point is more likely to expose an adversary's true intentions, perhaps through visible preparations."[230] It also ensures that states not use force in circumstances that might unnecessarily provoke escalation of conflict, which is the rational choice explanation some liberal-intenationalists have given for endorsing unilateral humanitarian intervention but not unilateral preemptive use of force against states with potential WMD capabilities.[231]

But circumstances may have changed, making the *Caroline* test arguably irrational. To the extent the international community does express its assessment of relevant risks through the Security Council, the Council has made clear, after the Second Gulf War in Resolution 1540 which implicit acknowledges the concerns that gave rise to U.S. preemption, that the "proliferation of nuclear, chemical and biological weapons, as well as their means of delivery, constitutes a threat to international peace and security."[232] Moreover, because of uncertainties as to the perceived risks of harm from rogue states and terrorist organizations and the perceived incapacity of all parties effectively to signal intentions, WMD possession by rogue states and terrorist organizations is likely to lead to excessive precaution and, therefore, excessive preemptive self-defense.

A rationalist reply to this conundrum is perhaps to address the problem by trying to produce more information. Thus, a rationalist strategy might require states to articulate and defend their grounds of preemptive use of force in response to WMD threats by reference to "factors that a reasonable state would consider in evaluating a potential threat under capability uncertainty."[233] This would, like tort law, judge the decision-maker in light of the facts and circumstances known to the decision-maker at the time of the decision, incentivizing conduct toward a welfare-maximizing result, much like economic interpretations of the "reasonable person" standard in the law of torts.[234] Because states would be measured in terms of objective factors, democracies sufficiently concerned to consider preemption would try to produce the maximum

229 *See* Nzelibe and Yoo, Rational War Design, *supra* note 221, at 2526–30 and 2532–36.

230 Matthew C. Waxman, *The Use of Force Against States that Might Have Weapons of Mass Destruction*, 31 Mich. J. Int'l L. 1, 7–8 (2009) (citing Eric A. Posner & Alan O. Sykes, *Optimal War and Jus Ad Bellum*, 93 Geo. L.J. 993, 1000 (2005).

231 *See* Harold Koh, *in* Striking First, *supra* note 152, at 99, 106 (arguing there was no real risk of retaliation or escalation as a result of NATO's humanitarian intervention to save Kosovo).

232 S.C. Res. 1540, preamble, U.N Doc. S/RES/1540 (Apr. 28, 2004).

233 Waxman, *supra* note 230, at 47.

234 *See generally* Richard Posner, Economic Analysis of Law 167–68 (1992) (under which the reasonable person is a cost-minimizer or, alternatively, a welfare-maximizer).

possible objectively verifiable information to support their risk-assessments; and target states would be incentivized toward greater transparency (such as, for Iraq, greater cooperation with UNMOVIC), with the possible effect of strengthening institutional patterns of cooperation through the Security Council or other international institutional frameworks.[235] To a rational choice theorist, increased institutional cooperation would help to resolve the incentives of the so-called the Prisoners' Dilemma between democracies and rogue state, increasing the possibility for tit-for-tat strategy to build patterns of cooperation and compliance. This forward-looking perspective would be less concerned with whether or not the U.S. violated international law in the Second Gulf War than in seeking how to modify the relevant security "game" between the "players," including not only the processes but also the rules governing decision-making, to achieve welfare gains in the future.

Yet, the search for objective factors to evaluate what is essentially a subjective judgment also has turned in other, arguably constructivist, directions. One view, advanced by a former State Department Legal Advisor, would focus also on whether or not the past behavior of the target state suggests an intention to use WMD or share WMD with a terrorist organization.[236] But to the extent this view is predicated on framing the target as an "outlaw" state, it seems to divide the international community into law-abiding and rogue states, thereby transforming an international order nominally premised on "sovereign equality."[237] Another view, which borrows from the domestic law of self-defense, suggests relying on arguments based on the principle of reciprocity, as well as publicly available facts, to excuse from responsibility for aggression states that engage in preemptive use of force.[238] But this view replaces a system of sovereign states with Kantian principles akin to those that would govern a cosmopolitan world government. Finally, although we defer discussion to Part IV, one could reject entirely any focus on objective standards for the *jus ad bellum*, ultimately collapsing it into the *jus in bello*, which has always focused on the subjective intention of the wrongdoer,[239] thus viewing what appears to be preemption as actually occurring in the context of an ongoing struggle; this, in fact, was what the U.S. State Department argued was the best understanding of the facts leading up to the Second Gulf War.[240]

---

235 *See* Waxman, *supra* note 230, at 54–57 and 62–70 (discussing the kinds of objective evidence as to capabilities and intentions that would satisfy an "objective standards" approach to preemptive use of force).

236 *See* Abraham D. Sofaer, *On the Necessity of Pre-emption*, 14 Eur. J. Int'l L. 209 (2003).

237 As Emmerich de Vattel's foundational 18th century treatise averred: "A dwarf is as much of man as a giant; a small republic is no less a sovereign state than the most powerful kingdom. By the necessary consequence of equality, whatever is lawful for one nation, is equally lawful for any other; and whatever is unjustifiable in the one, is equally so in the other." Preliminaries, The Law of Nations 18–19 (1967).

238 *See* George P. Fetcher & Jean David Ohlin, Defending Humanity 155–176 (2008).

239 As one State Department lawyer observed, "when it ratified Additional Protocol I to the 1949 Geneva Conventions, the United Kingdom conveyed its understanding that military decision-makers' actions must be assessed on the basis of "information from all sources which is reasonably available to them at the relevant time." Kaye, *supra* note 218, at 161.

240 *See* Taft & Buchwald, *supra* note 4, at 563.

We turn now to a discussion of these two transformative, constructivist strategies for managing preemptive self-defense against WMD threats, and then turn in the following section to the third approach, focusing on subjective intention and wrongfulness, revisiting the so-called Just War Tradition's interpretation of anticipatory use of force.

4. Constructivism's Critique

One could view the legal debate concerning the preemption doctrine as a set of conflicting attempts to reconstruct a fundamentally Lockean international legal order: one in the direction of Hobbesian unilateralism, under which dominant powers seek to eradicate revolutionary threats; the other in which globalist forces seek to move the international system in a Kantian direction of world government.[241]

On one side, as applied to the international system, Hobbes central insight was that the state of nature implies a right of nature for any state to do whatever is necessary for it to survive; and, in the state of nature, any man can kill another other man, thus giving rise to a basic state of fear.[242] Thus, even according to a former U.S. State Department Legal Advisor—who moderately suggests only a modification of the *Caroline* test—the argument about the threat posed Iraq's potential capabilities needed to be understood in view of the revolutionary nature of its foreign policy. Under his view, "Iraq also poses a continuing threat to use conventional forces or weapons of mass destruction in light of its prior conduct and avowed motives. It has twice attacked states in the Gulf area in pursuit of its avowed aim of 'reestablishing' an 'Arab Nation' with its capital in Baghdad. If allowed to continue to develop weapons of mass destruction, including nuclear arms, Iraq could use or threaten to use those arms to disrupt or disrail international efforts to prevent Iraq from achieving its geopolitical objectives."[243] Indeed, his argument focused on the fact that, "in recent statements, Saddam acknowledges that he cannot win a war with the US, but he asserts that Iraq must nonetheless resist being forced to submit to US or UN pressure. He equates his situation to that of a Muslim hero, being tested along with the Iraqi people by God to demonstrate their willingness to confront evil."[244] Accordingly, the root prem-

241 *See generally* Part I, Chapter 2C (discussing Alexander Wendt's constructivist models—Hobbesian, Lockean, and Kantian—of the international system).

242 *See generally* Part I, Chapters 1A and 2C (discussing Hobbesian view of international system).

243 Sofaer, *supra* note 236, at 221.

244 *Id.* at 222. Sofaer cites Ambassador Joseph Wilson, former US diplomat who had extensive contact with Saddam Hussein and Iraq, who reported that he "learned firsthand ... what the CIA psychiatrists have said for years: Saddam is an egomaniacal sociopath whose penchant for high-risk gambles is exceeded only by a propensity for miscalculation." *Id.* at 222 (citing How Saddam Thinks, San Jose Mercury News, Oct. 13, 2002, Sec. P. at 1.). The citation here to Wilson's estimate of Hussein's psychology and likely behavior, of course, is a variance with Wilson's own focus on Iraq's true capabilities, which grew out of his involvement in the controversy concerning a very specific aspect of Iraq's capabilities. In an investigative mission for the U.S. before the war, Wilson was unable to verify reports that Iraq attempted to obtain

ise for a relaxation of the *Caroline* test is thus an objective assessment from the standpoint of a reasonable observer of the behavior and intentions of the state possessing WMD, rather than an objective assessment of the state's capabilities.

But this view necessarily requires an assessment of whether or not the regime in question is satisfied with the status quo or seeks to revise it. Viewed from that perspective, it hearkens back to the approach of the victorious powers at the Congress of Vienna, the Versailles Conference, and the UN Charter to suppress revolutionary forces that had given rise to war or could give rise to renewed war.[245] Indeed, the dominant image of Iraq the Bush Administration employed to justify the coming war to the American people was as part, like Iran and North Korea, of "an Axis of Evil."[246]

Viewed from a constructivist perspective, in essence, the proposed reinterpretation of the *Caroline* test—in terms to accommodate objective review of an assessment of an incommensurable threat requiring preemptive action—turns on a subjective assessment; it is predicated on an overall view of the target state as a revolutionary power, a rogue state that no longer is willing to play by the accepted rules of the international system and seeks instead to overturn that system. Under this view, preemptive use of force responds to a revolutionary state through revolutionary change in the domestic order of the target state. Thus, preemption as the means enables regime change as an end, so that occupying forces can eliminate the revolutionary tendencies that drive the target state towards revolutionary objectives, thus avoiding a challenge to the hegemonic status quo. Under this view, the Second Gulf War's policy of "regime change" to spread democracy in the Middle East, flowed logically out of the legal theory of preemption, which was grounded in the changing Iraqi regime's psychology and intentions, which were rooted in the Iraqi government's appeal to a Baathist secularized version of Islamic revolutionary thought; in other words, preemption was the necessary means for achieving that regime change.

---

from Niger yellowcake uranium, a precursor material for the production of nuclear weapons. *See* Joseph Wilson, What I Didn't Find in Africa, N.Y. Times, July 6, 2003.

245 *See generally* Kissinger, A World Restored: Metternich, Castlereagh and the Problems of Peace 1812–1822 (1954) (describing efforts to prevent the revival of revolution in Europe, especially in France); and Margaret MacMillan, Paris 1919: Six Months that changed the World 63–74 (2001) (excluding revolutionary Russia from the discussions at Paris); U.N. Charter, art. 107 (the enemy states clause, seeking to facilitate continued suppression of revolutionary forces in Italy, Japan and Germany.

246 According to President Bush, "Iraq continues to flaunt its hostility toward America and to support terror. The Iraqi regime has plotted to develop anthrax, and nerve gas, and nuclear weapons for over a decade. This is a regime that has already used poison gas to murder thousands of its own citizens—leaving the bodies of mothers huddled over their dead children. This is a regime that agreed to international inspections—then kicked out the inspectors. This is a regime that has something to hide from the civilized world. States like these, and their terrorist allies, constitute an axis of evil, arming to threaten the peace of the world. By seeking weapons of mass destruction, these regimes pose a grave and growing danger. They could provide these arms to terrorists, giving them the means to match their hatred. They could attack our allies or attempt to blackmail the United States. In any of these cases, the price of indifference would be catastrophic." *See* George W. Bush, State of the Union Address, Office of the Press Secretary, Jan. 29, 2002, http://georgewbush-whitehouse.archives.gov/news/releases/2002/01/print/20020129-11.html).

Together, however, preemption and broad regime change challenged the sub-rules of the international system of sovereign equality, seeking to expand the *Caroline* test and requiring a degree of discretion to effect regime change during occupation that international law would not normally sanction. The legalist reaction to these reconstructive projects was negative. Through the *ICJ Oil Platforms Case* and other decisions, the Report of the High-Level Panel, and the Secretary-General Report In Larger Freedom, legalism reaffirmed the *Caroline* test, except as approved by the security Council; and, in Security Council Resolution 1483, legalism insisted on compliance with principles of occupation law that required the occupying power to respect the sovereign equality and rights of self-determination of the Iraqi people, in theory leaving the door open to their choosing to incorporate revolutionary Islamic principles in their new government.

Another view of the controversy, this one Kantian, analogizes to the principles of domestic criminal law, as though states were subject to the authority, both moral and practical, of a world government. Whereas as Hobbesian constructivism's interpretation of the Second Gulf War takes into account the post-Cold War emergence of proliferation of WMD, the Kantian perspective takes as its point of departure the post-Cold War growth of international criminal law. The Kaiser, it will be recalled, was never actually tried, even thought the Versailles Treaty had made provision under an amorphous legal standard.[247] Additionally, while the victorious powers had no difficulty prosecuting the Germans and Japanese for war crimes and related crimes against humanity, their prosecution for aggression, "crimes against the peace," was controversial, to say the least.[248] But the Nuremberg Tribunal's citation to the *Caroline* test formally suggested that a use of force in self-defense that failed the test could be considered an act of aggression, entailing international criminal responsibility.[249]

That thought lay dormant for more than half a century, until the end of the Cold War, when the creation of international courts to apply international criminal law exploded onto the scene. Initially, post-Cold War international criminal tribunals reflected the expansion of the concept of "threat to the peace" under the Chapter VII authorities of the Security Council,[250] which had come to believe that war crimes and crimes against humanity exacerbated war and that their prosecution would further international peace. So, acting under Chapter VII of the Charter, the Council created the International Criminal Tribunal for the Former Yugoslavia (the ICTY), as a special international criminal tribunal with competence limited to addressing the war crimes and crimes against humanity committed during the non-international, and then international,

247 *See generally* Part I, Chapter 1B, *supra.*

248 *Id.*

249 *See supra* note 18 (citing Judgment of the International Military Tribunal for the Trial of German Major War Criminals, Cmd. 6964, at 28–29 (1946)).

250 *See supra* Part II, Chapter 3 (discussing the expansion of this concept to authorize UN intervention in Iraq after the Second Gulf War to protect the Kurds, in Somalia to prevent refugee flows caused by famine, and in Haiti to restore elected government following a coup d'etat).

armed conflict that followed the dissolution of Yugoslavia.[251] Commensurate with its expanding understanding of its own powers under Chapter VII, following the Rwandan genocide, [252] the Council then extended the ICTY precedent to establish the International Criminal Tribunal for Rwanda (the ICTR), which prosecuted genocide, crimes against humanity and other offenses under international humanitarian law governing non-international armed conflict.[253] The Security Council, have determined that the establishment of such tribunals could further "international peace and security," did so on a number of occasions.[254]

But as these international criminal tribunals proliferated, political pressure rose for a "truly" international criminal tribunal outside of Security Council control. After the preparatory work of the International Law Commission and more than a year of meetings of preparatory committees under the auspices of the General Assembly, a conference of plenipotentiary representatives of states met in Rome in 1998 and adopted a Statute for an International Criminal Court (the ICC), under which cases could be referred for investigation and prosecution not only by the Security Council but also any state, as well as even the ICC's own chief prosecutor acting independently.[255] The Rome Statue entered into force with the requisite 60 ratifications in 2002, and now has been ratified by well over one hundred states, although without the participation of the U.S., China, Russia, India, and Israel.[256] Initially, the ICC was competent to prosecute the crime of genocide, crimes against humanity and war crimes.[257] While the "crime of aggression" was listed as a possible basis for jurisdiction, the Rome Statute made clear that the ICC would not prosecutes such offenses until the parties, in a subsequent review conference, in accordance with article 121 and 123 [of the Statute] defined the crime and set out the conditions under which the Court would exercise jurisdiction."[258]

The criminalization of aggression, once a the post-World War II fantasy, may now be on the verge of becoming an international reality; and, if so, it poses a serious threat to the preemptive theory advance by the Bush Administration in the Second Gulf War. A review conference did meet in Kampala, Uganda from May 31-June 11, 2010, which adopted a proposed amendment to the Rome Statute that would define the crime of aggression as an act which by its "character,

251 *See* S.C. Res. 827, U.N. Doc. S/RES/827 (May 25, 1993). *See generally* Damrosch, *supra* note 16, at 1327–31 (discussing ever expanding activities of ICTY to include subsequent war crimes committed by Yugoslav authorities against Kosovo, leading to the first indictment ever by an international criminal tribunal of a sitting Head of State, Slobodan Milosevic).

252 *See* Part II, Chapter 3, *supra.*

253 *See* S.C. Res. 955, U.N. Doc. S/RES/955 (Nov. 8, 1994). *See generally* Damrosch, *supra* note 16, at 1341–44 (discussing operations of the Rwanda Tribunal).

254 *See* Damrosch, *supra* note 16, at 1344–40 (excerpting discussion of Security Council practice in Murphy, Principles of International Law 430–36 (2006).

255 *See* Rome Statute of the International Criminal Court, July 17, 1998, 2187 U.N.T.S. 3. [hereinafter "Rome Statute"].

256 *See* Damrosch, *supra* note 16, at 1350.

257 *See* Rome Statute, *supra* note 255, at art. 5(1)(a), (b), and (c).

258 *Id.* at art. 5(2).

gravity, and scale constitute a manifest violation of the Charter of the United Nations." It also defines an "act of aggression" in terms of the UN General Assembly Resolution Defining Aggression,[259] which in turn had been central to the jurisprudence of the ICJ in the *Nicaragua Case*.[260] Thus, by relying on the General Assembly's resolution Defining Aggression, the proposed amendment to the Rome Statute implicitly endorses the *Nicaragua Case*'s understanding of the level of support required to constitute an armed attack, and thereby undercuts the Bush Doctrine's understanding of the need for preemptive use of force when support even at lower levels pose the danger of WMD use by terrorist organizations. Although there remain grave doubts as to whether this proposed amendment will ever enter into force,[261] the Rome Statute, as amended, might then criminalize actions like the Second Gulf War, subjecting U.S. leaders engaging in similar conduct in the future to international criminal responsibility.[262]

This criminalization of aggression might be understood to reflect an attempt to impose the moral values of the international community and to subordinate the nominal global hegemon, the United States, with veto power at the Security Council,[263] to the discipline of the interna-

---

259 *See* Assembly of the Parties, Article 8, Crime of Aggression, Resolution RC/Res. 6 (Annex) (*available at* http://www.icc-cpi.int/iccdocs/asp_docs/Resolutions/RC-Res.6-ENG.pdf). The text provides as follows:

> 1. For the purpose of this Statute, "crime of aggression" means the planning, preparation, initiation or execution, by a person in a position effectively to exercise control over or to direct the political or military action of a State, of an act of aggression which, by its character, gravity and scale, constitutes a manifest violation of the Charter of the United Nations.
>
> 2. For the purpose of paragraph 1, "act of aggression" means the use of armed force by a State against the sovereignty, territorial integrity or political independence of another State, or in any other manner inconsistent with the Charter of the United Nations. Any of the following acts, regardless of a declaration of war, shall, in accordance with United Nations General Assembly resolution 3314 (XXIX) of 14 December 1974, qualify as an act of aggression:
>
> (a) The invasion or attack by the armed forces of a State of the territory of another State, or any military occupation, however temporary, resulting from such invasion or attack, or any annexation by the use of force of the territory of another State or part thereof;
>
> (b) Bombardment by the armed forces of a State against the territory of another State or the use of any weapons by a State against the territory of another State;
>
> (c) The blockade of the ports or coasts of a State by the armed forces of another State
>
> (d) An attack by the armed forces of a State on the land, sea or air forces, or marine and air fleets of another State;
>
> (e) The use of armed forces of one State which are within the territory of another State with the agreement of the receiving State, in contravention of the conditions provided for in the agreement or any extension of their presence in such territory beyond the termination of the agreement;
>
> (f) The action of a State in allowing its territory, which it has placed at the disposal of another State, to be used by that other State for perpetrating an act of aggression against a third State;
>
> (g) The sending by or on behalf of a State of armed bands, groups, irregulars or mercenaries, which carry out acts of armed force against another State of such gravity as to amount to the acts listed above, or its substantial involvement therein.

260 *See supra* text accompanying notes 52–66 (discussing the *Nicaragua Case* and its reliance on UNGA Res. 3314).

261 *See* Beth Van Schaack, *Negotiating at the Interface of Power & Law: The Crime of Aggression* (*available at* http://ssrn.com/abstract_16668661) (discussing issues placing in doubt future entry into force). Strictly speaking, however, advocates for the amendments point out that once 30 states adopt the proposed amendments, a conference of the parties could agree by two-thirds vote after January 1, 2017 to activate the amendments and permit the Court to exercise jurisdiction in such cases. See Coalition for the International Criminal Court (*available at* http://www.iccnow.org/?mod=aggression).

262 For a debate on the ICC's proposed criminalizing of aggression, *see Symposium: The Codification of the Crime of Aggression,* 20 Eur. J. Int'l L. 1099–1156 (2009).

263 *See* Jose Alvarez, International Organizations as Law-makers 199–216 (2005) (discussing "hegemonic" influence of the United States at the U.N. Security Council).

tional community through an organ not subject to that veto. Under this view, the U.S. would be the rogue state. Accordingly, this constructivist project would view the criminalization of aggression as the logical extension of the ordinary criminal law processes of domestic law to the international plane, finding its intellectual roots the retributivist aspects of Kantian thought.[264] Perversely, this may bring the *Caroline* test for anticipatory self-defense back to the domestic law origins from which it arose, for some commentary suggests the test was formulated to deal, not with the question of international responsibility, but rather the question of the individual responsibility of the British officers in question being prosecuted in the domestic courts of the United States for an ordinary criminal offense.[265]

In the case of the Second Gulf War, following such a criminal law model, assuming preemptive use of force was *prima facie* a "manifest violation" of the Charter of the UN, the question then becomes whether that criminal responsibility can be defended on the basis of a mistake of fact as to the presence of WMD in Saddam Hussein's Iraq. Article 32(1) of the Rome Statute provides that "A mistake of fact shall be a ground for excluding criminal responsibility only if it negates the mental element required by the crime."[266] Thus, the Rome Statute does provide for a "mistake of fact" defense, although it does not define the precise contours of such a defense. One approach for filling this gap would be to insist that only "reasonable" mistakes of fact would "negate" the requisite intent; indeed, if one were to analogize to domestic criminal law, a defender may use force only when the "defender reasonably believes 'such force is immediately necessary for the purpose of protecting himself against he use of unlawful force by such other person on the present occasion.'"[267] The emphasis now placed on "immediate necessity" for "the present occasion" bears some similarity to the *Caroline* test. Accordingly, commentators employing this schema "would be hard put to apply [it] to the prolonged ten-year period in which the United Nations imposed sanctions on Iraq and conducted inspections to control its supply of weapons. Nothing in particular had happened to support the decision to invade on March 20, 2003—or indeed, in 2003 rather than 2004."[268] On this view, the U.S. could not change its mind when no material facts had changed.

Moreover, other procedural features of Kantian logic would undermine U.S. arguments. First, the Kantian principle of reciprocity rejects grounding an argument of "imminence for the

---

264 *See* Fletcher & Ohlin, supra note 238, at 156–57 (noting that while, "Kant, surprisingly, argued in favor of preemptive war ... much has changed since Kant's time.").

265 As Greig observes, the British government's argument may have been merely that the British subject, who was being prosecuted in New York for the murder of two United States citizens killed in the destruction of the *Caroline*, should be released on grounds of self-defense. If so, then Webster's formulation in reply would have addressed a question of domestic, not international, law. *See* D. W. Greig, International Law 883–86 (1976); *see also* D.W. Greig, *Reciprocity, Proportionality, and the Law of Nations*, 34 Va. J. Int'l L. 295, 322 n. 91 (1994).

266 Rome Statute, *supra* note 255.

267 Fletcher & Ohlin, *supra* note 238, at 163 (citing the U.S. Model Penal Code and noting that other countries have adapted their penal codes in recent years to approximate this formulation).

268 *Id.* at 166.

present occasion" on the nature of the Hussein regime, for the Kantian categorical imperative requires the imposition of criminal punishment only on the basis of "a reciprocal rule that all states can live by," rather than the status of the potential attacker as a "rogue" state.[269] Second, under this view, the legal defense of "reasonable mistake" as to the "imminence for the present occasion" could be grounded on secret information to be judged only by those who claim the defense, which would "turn the doctrine of preventive war into a farce." Rather, the "only solution is to require that the evidence be, in some manner, publicly available to the international community (say, through the General Assembly or the Security Council) and not relegated to the president's hip pocket."[270] These reciprocity and publicity criteria would ensure that moral judgment of the community, for the issue is "not just whether the United States believed that Hussein had weapons of mass destruction; the issue is whether it was objectively reasonable for any country to believe, with the information available, that he posed a danger with these weapons."[271]

Finally, under the best understanding of modern criminal law, even if the U.S. met this objective test for reasonable mistake, it might have been "excused," albeit not "justified." A "justified" use of force by the U.S. would have been predicated on the wrongfulness of Iraq's conduct and would have deprived Iraq of the moral and legal right to use force, thereby making it criminally responsible for its use of force. By contrast, a reasonable mistake of fact by the United States as to whether use of force against Iraq was "immediate necessity" for "the present occasion," merely excusing the U.S. and its leaders from international criminal responsibility, would not deprive Iraq of its right to resist.[272]

In sum, the criminal law model challenges the basically utilitarian approach of rational choice theory for managing the question of preemptive self-defense. The rational choice analysis of the question of reasonable mistakes seeks only to maximize social welfare by taking into account ex ante decision-making with imperfect information under conditions of uncertainty. An optimal rational choice theory would, however, require states also to some degree to internalize the costs of their avoidable errors. Accordingly, the international community might seek to impose of civil sanctions, such as a scheme for reparations paid by the mistaken attacker to those harmed by its mistake.[273] This approach might also be analogized to a so-called "condi-

---

269 *Id.* at 168–9.

270 *Id.* at 171 (presumably, if the Security Council veto is used, resorting to the General Assembly for a recommendation under the Uniting for Peace Resolution).

271 *Id.* at 174.

272 According to Fletcher and Ohlin, "If a preventive invasion is justified, then the conduct is lawful and not a case of aggression. Iraq therefore has no right to resist, and its use of defensive force is illegal. This follows the model of domestic self-defense. If you are justified in using legitimate defense against our attacker, your attacker cannot legally use force to fend off counter counterattack." *Id.* at 172 (distinguished "justified" from merely "excused" uses of force in self-defense).

273 *See, e.g.*, Alan Buchanan & Robert O. Keohane, Preventive Use of Force: A Cosmopolitan Institutional Proposal, Ethics and International Affairs 1–22 (2004).

tional" privilege of necessity in the common law of torts, under which to save one's property one may use force against another's property but must pay for the damage done to that property (unlike the so-called absolute version of the privilege, in which no payment is required when one acts to save the property of the community as a whole).[274] Even under the public necessity rationale, however, although the common law seems to take the view that no compensation is owed to the innocent victim of force used under a reasonable mistake of fact, those relying on the Roman civil law tradition might take a different view and require compensation for any harm to a wholly innocent third-party.[275] If so, to the extent that civil sanctions are imposed on mistaken defender or mistaken uses of forces for the defense of others or as a matter of public necessity, the moral sense of the international community might begin to internalize new norms along Kantian lines, opening the door to the transformation of tort into crime.

Walking through that door, explicit criminalization of aggression, by contrast, would pursue a different agenda—one in which a global legal community enforces its norms against an imperial power. The criminal law model, thus, might serve objectives comparable to those served by Just War Theory, in which the good of the community as a whole is always the sole criterion for the exercise of power. And a reconstruction of the international law of aggressive war in terms of modern domestic criminal law would, like the Just War Theory of Thomas Aquinas, justify the use of force only on one side, depriving the other side of its right of self-defense. Only when, under a theory of excuse, one acknowledges the limited capacities of human beings acting under conditions of necessity (like the Spanish neo-scholastic theory of invincible ignorance) can war be just on both sides.[276] Thus, an attempt to reconstruct the international law of use of force into a form of domestic criminal law,[277] like traditional Just War Theory, seems to presume that war must serve the needs of the whole community.

---

274 *See generally* John L. Diamond, et. al, Understanding Torts (2000); and Richard Epstein & Catherine Sharkey, Cases and Materials on Tort 34 (10th ed. 2012) (describing self-defense as a universally-recognized affirmative defense to civil liability).

275 *See* Justinian's Digest 9.2.45.4 ("Persons who do damage because they cannot otherwise defend themselves are innocent; for all statutes and legal systems allow one to repel force by force. But if in order to defend myself I throw a stone at my adversary, but hit, not him but a passer-by, I shall be liable under the Lex Aquilia [the general tort statute]; for one is allowed to strike only the person who uses force, and then only when it is done for the purpose of protection and not revenge as well.") (quoted in Epstein, *supra* note 274, at 34).

276 *See* Part II, Chapter 1, *supra* text accompanying notes 82–120 (discussing Spanish Neo-Scholastic shift in Just War Theory on the question of invincible ignorance).

277 *See* Part I, Chapter 2C, *supra* (discussing Wendt's cosmopolitan theory transforming international law of use of force into a form of criminal law).

5. The Gravitation Pull of Just War Theory (JWT)

These realist, legalist, rationalist and constructivist debates have also elicited a reaction from Just War Tradition. While the scholarly response is impressive,[278] perhaps the most influential contribution comes from the High-Level Panel Report to the Secretary-General of the United Nations, which explicitly referred to a version of Just War criteria as the grounds for Security Council authorization of use of force for defense against non-imminent threats and humanitarian intervention.[279] These criteria—seriousness of threat, proper purpose, last resort, proportional means, and balance of consequences—plainly draw on the Just War Tradition. However, the HLP Report's understanding of Just War Theory seems to oscillate between traditional and modern understandings; as such may or may not be consistent with elements of the Bush doctrine (depending on how that doctrine in interpreted); contains important ambiguities that complicate how its implementation would vary from implementation of alternative approaches, such as the Bush doctrine; and, finally, in its failure to justify its assumptions, raises foundational questions about the legitimacy of the international order it claims exists.

The HLP Report, in its overall approach, does clearly vary from traditional, and even recent, formulations of Just War Theory. It does not distinguish the traditional doctrine's mandatory criteria from what commentators have called the non-deontological criteria relating to "balance of harms" and "proportionate means." Instead, the HLP Report appears to give all the criteria equal weight.[280] It does not explicitly impose a "presumption against war," thus appearing to

278 *See e.g.*, Buchanan & Keohane, *supra* note 273, 1–22 (2004) (treating the Security Council as the superior authority competent to apply a modern version of Just War criteria); William C. Bradford, *The Duty to Defend Them: A Natural Law Justification for the Bush Doctrine of Preventive War,* 79 Notre Dame L. Rev. 1365, 1395 n.102 (2004) (characterizing the necessity standard as a defense justifying otherwise illegal conduct without regard to Security Council authorization); and Doyle, *supra* note 51 (purporting to write in the Just War Tradition and favoring a rule requiring initial, but nonbinding, resort to the Security Council); *but see* Fetcher & Ohlin, *supra* note 238, at 169 (insisting on reciprocity and publicity to avoid "righteous goals" that would serve as "the modern secular analogue to the just wars of the Christian tradition").

279 *See* High-Level Panel Report, *supra* note 201, at para. 207. It states:

> In considering whether to authorize use of force, the Security Council should always address—whatever other considerations it may take into account—at least the following five basic criteria of legitimacy:
>
> (a) *Seriousness of threat.* Is the threatened harm to state or human security of a kind, and sufficiently clear and serious, to justify prima facie the use of military force? In the case of internal threats, does it involve genocide and other large-scale killing, ethnic cleaning or other serious violations of humanitarian law, actual or imminently apprehended?
>
> (b) *Proper purpose.* Is it clear that the primary purpose of the proposed military action is to halt or avert the threat in question, whatever other purposes or motives may be involved?
>
> (c) *Last resort.* Has every non-military option for meeting the threat in question been explored, with reasonable grounds for believing that that other measures will not succeed?
>
> (d) *Proportional means.* Are the scale, duration and intensity of the proposed military action the minimum necessary to meet the threat in question?
>
> (e) *Balance of Consequences.* Is there a reasonable chance of the military action being successful in meeting the threat in questions, with the consequences of action not likely to be worse than the consequences of inaction?

280 *See* Part II, Chapter 1, *supra* text accompanying notes 193–97 (discussing synthesis presented in the scholarship of James Turner Johnson).

separate itself from the recent turn in American Catholic formulations of Just War Theory,[281] although neither does its focus on harms that must be threatened before force may be used endorse a teleological conception in which forces may be used, in the traditional sense, of furthering the common good – seeking, in order words, the *tranquillitas ordinis*, of peace and justice.[282] Premised only on the possibility of Security Council authorization even when the "imminence" requirement set forth in the *Caroline* test is not met for self-defense, moreover, it suggests it does not treat the *Caroline* test as the only just cause permitted by Just War Theory. Indeed, its support for acts of charity under the rubric of humanitarian intervention is plainly consistent with late antiquity and medieval Just War Theory.

However, given the absence of a presumption against recourse to force or casuistry (via hypotheticals or actual cases) explaining how the HLP Report would be applied, it is difficult to determine the HLP Report's understanding of the relationship of the Bush doctrine (both in its narrow form of preemptive self-defense and its broad form of regime change) to Just War Theory. This lack of specificity is troubling, since modern students of the Just War Tradition, reviewing the medieval and early modern sources, have concluded that the Just War Tradition may be inconsistent with both the *Caroline* test and the Bush doctrine, if the Bush doctrine is interpreted narrowly to address only the risk of harm imposed by a state's capabilities and behavior without regard to the wrongfulness of the state's conduct.[283] If the Bush doctrine is interpreted more broadly to address the wrongful of the target regime, then the HLP Report may on this view undercut the Just War Tradition's implementation through the Bush doctrine.

281 *See* Part II, Chapter 1, *supra* text accompanying notes 174–90 (discussing American Catholic Bishops Pastoral letter, The Challenge of Peace).

282 *See* Part II, Chapter 1, *supra* text accompanying note 192.

283 *See, e.g.*, Gregory M. Reichberg, *Preventive War in Classical Just War Theory,* 9 J. Hist. Int'l Law 5–34 (2007). According to Reichberg the better view seems to be that the traditional Just War Theory would reject the Caroline test. He notes that Thomas Aquinas warns that "due care" ought to be taken to judge fairly, thus avoiding "when a man, from slight indications, esteems another man's wickedness as certain." *Id.* at 11 (quoting Saint Thomas I-II, q. 60). But he notes that within the same passage Aquinas observes that "when we have to apply a remedy to some evil, whether our own or another's, in order for the remedy to be applied with greater certainty of a cure, it is expedient to take the worst for granted, since if the remedy be efficacious against a sores evil, much more is it efficacious against a lesser evil." *Id.* at 11–12 (quoting Saint Thomas I-II q. 60, art. 4). Reichberg further notes that Grotius believed that "public authority may be justified in undertaking long-term preemptive action only when the target of such action (which may be the leadership of another state) has been found guilty of conspiracy to commit future aggression. In other words, a discernible wrong must have been committed if such preemption is to have a ground in sound moral and legal principle." *Id.* at 22 (citing Grotius, The Laws of War and Peace, Bk. II, I, V, paras. 1–2). From this and other sources, Reichberg reasons that, so long as it is a response to wrongdoing by legitimate authority, which under Just War Theory is entitled to vindicate justice, preemption is a prudential question upon which reasonable minds can differ. In other words, the "immediacy" and "necessity" requirements of the *Caroline* test apply only when the actor is not a public authority and therefore must ordinarily turn to "superior authority" before resorting to the use of force. *Id.* at 7–10, 31–33. Thus, even if the Bush Administration is not subject to "superior authority," if its argument for preemptive use of force is based solely on the quantum of probable effects of another state's behavior, rather than some prior wrongfulness, the Bush doctrine it is not consistent with the core Just War teaching that force may be used only to address a wrong causing harm – such as harm to self, harm to one's property, or harm to others. *Id.* at 31–33. If, however, in the particular cases that the Bush doctrine is applied, it is applied to address a threat caused by some prior wrong—such as the Hussein government's unlawful possession of WMD, future aggression such as another campaign against Kuwait, or the gross violation of the human rights of the Iraq people—the wrongfulness of Iraq's conduct might permit preemptive use of force.

The HLP Report's variation from the Just War Tradition might also be noticed in its details, depending of course on their precise interpretation. It replaces "just cause" with "seriousness of threat," but defines the threat "to state or human security" so as to include "internal" threats. Thus, unlike the traditional Just War Theory, it does not focus on a prior wrong, although it might be possible to construe the test to assume the existence of some prior wrong since external threats might be deemed to be unlawful and internal threats must rise to the level of violation of "humanitarian law." The HLP Report also replaces "right intention" with "proper purpose," a formulation that seems to replace the subjective inquiry into human intention with an objective inquiry into the attributed "purpose" of collective bodies, such as states and their legislatures or even the Security Council itself. On the other hand, apparently relying on the traditional Augustinian sensibility that first gave rise to the Christian Just War Theory, which recognizes human evil even in cases of ostensibly charitable acts of humanitarian intervention, the HLP Report demands only that the "primary purpose" seek to address the threat. It thus recognizes that there will be unavoidably uncharitable secondary purposes. Finally, and perhaps most important, it does not refer to the "legitimate authority" requirement of the traditional Thomist test. Thus, the HLP Report may well be assuming that Security Council authorization prima facie satisfies that requirement. Here, the HLP Report assumes without demonstrating that the Security Council operates as a legitimate "superior authority" for purposes of Just War Theory; in short is substitutes a procedural criterion for a substantive analysis.

Thus, the HLP Report raises the most important question for a Just War theorist. Does the exercise of "legitimate authority" require Security Council authorization generally, given the defects in its capacity to exercise power and impose its will independently from the individual or collective resources of states? Is Security Council authorization required when doubts are raised concerning whether the Security Council can serve as the "superior authority," because of its bias in particular cases either in imposing the will of the veto-bearing powers or when one or more veto-bearing powers blocks action? In short, is the Security Council the "superior authority" required by Just War Theory for the approval necessary for recourse to war—a body that could rebut the inference that the use of force serves private, rather than public purposes, or does not serve the common good.[284] The debate concerns in what sense, if at all, the UN Charter serves as a supranational constitution, and whether the Security Council is an executive or legislative organ of the government under that constitution.[285]

One extreme position, of course, is that Security Council authorization is an absolute condition for use of force by states for the moral legitimacy of use of force, regardless of its legality. This to be the view expressed not only in the High-Level Panel Report, but also the Secretary-General's

284 *See supra* Part II, Chapter 1 and text accompanying notes 192 (discussing George Weigel's study of the *tranquillitas ordinis* in the thought of Augustine and Aquinas).

285 *See supra* text accompanying notes 174–178 (noting range of views on this question, ranging from Fassbender to Bobbitt).

Kofi Annan's own view stated in his report, In Larger Freedom.[286] Drawing on the realist and neo-realist rational-choice traditions, however, it is difficult at present to view the Security Council as the equivalent of a transnational government. Thus, the other extreme position is that the Security Council's authorization, given the Council's composition and procedures, has no special impact on moral questions.[287] An intermediate position, however, is that states should seek Security Council authorization, where possible, but that the failure of the Security Council to act does not operate as an absolute bar to use of force.[288] This position, which acknowledges that neither the purely Hobbesian nor the purely Kantian views of international society are adequate descriptions, or perhaps even normatively attractive, mediates between two competing views about the future of the world order—one in which a Coalition of liberal-democratic states seeks to order international society so as to marginalize and transform so-called "rogue" states; another in which the sovereign equality of states and their sovereignty is subordinated to an emerging cosmopolitan ideal of global governance, chiefly through the Security Council's monopoly on the means of legitimation.[289] And, under the intermediate view, the Security Council's action and inaction would not be the final word.[290] It would be at least possible to argue that the "legitimate authority" criterion of the Just War tradition might have been satisfied by the U.S., U.K. and its allies when they sought, but failed, to receive in Resolution 1441 the explicit support of the members of the Security Council and then took action—knowing that, because of the expected veto of at least France and Russia, explicit authorization would not be forthcoming.

If, however, under this view, the Security Council is not that "superior authority" whose authorization is necessary to conduct a just war, then Just War Theory must grapple anew with the question of "superior authority." In an era when, for democracies at least, the "people" are the superior authority and authorize war—in some polities, through their elected representatives after a public process of debate and decision—the determination of "legitimate authority" and "right intention" have become problematic. Thus, a Just War Theory for modern democracies would certainly prefer seeking "legitimate authority" in national governments rather than international organizations.[291] Yet, if the people in varying constitutional processes determine whether

286 *See supra* text accompanying notes 156–209 (discussing the legalist position); *compare* Buchanan & Keohane, *supra* note 273 (requiring Security Council authorization).

287 *See supra* text accompanying notes 127–55 (discussing the realist and neo-realist positions); *compare* Bradford, *supra* note 278 (not requiring Security Council authorization).

288 *See* Doyle, *supra* note 51, at 61–62 (former assistant to UN Secretary General).

289 *See supra* text accompanying notes 241–76 (outlining two possible versions of constructivist thought).

290 As Doyle argues, "[r]ather than enjoying a monopoly, the council will now know that its actions are subject to the 'market 'of alternative judgment." Doyle, *supra* note 51, at 62.

291 *See* Antonio F. Perez, *The Modern Relevance of Legitimate Authority and Right Intention in the Just War Tradition*, 51 Cath. U. L. Rev.15 (2001) (arguing that the Second Gulf War should be fought by the United States, if it was to be fought at all, with authorization from the U.S. Congress prior to seeking authorization from the U.N. Security Council, in contrast to the procedure preceding the First Gulf War in which Security Council authorization was obtained prior to congressional authorization).

to use force with just cause, how does Just War theory determine whether the "people" or their representatives have "right intention"? Does it depend on the specific national constitution and whether the executive is free to use force without advance parliamentary authorization. Even more difficult—particularly in cases such as the Second Gulf War in which the information upon which the people makes their judgments through their representatives is not, or cannot, be publicly disclosed–is determining the level of diligence that is required in forming "right intention."

Traditional Just War theorists, such as Suarez, suggested that before acting the "prince" should call upon the "counsel of learned and prudent men."[292] Perhaps legislatures providing advance authorization for the use of force today could function as the equivalent of the "counsel of learned and prudent men." Alternatively, as one theorist suggests, independent national commissions could review ex post the judgments of political authorities (including, in democracies, not only the people but also their elected representatives who respond to people).[293] Without adopting a criminal law model,[294] or a civil law damages model,[295] such measures might be serviceable to determine whether "reasonable mistakes of fact" absolve decision-makers from moral responsibility for their invincible ignorance under the "right intention" prong of Just Cause Theory.

And even if Suarez's suggestion for independent review could be transformed into a modern regime for independent institutional review, the procedures of such a body—including their access to information—and their substantive standards for decision-making would need to be appropriate. For example, in the complex case of the Second Gulf War, how would an independent commission review the degree of deference that U.S. intelligence analysts and decision-makers should have been given in relying on the apparent judgments of other intelligence agencies around the world that Saddam Hussein's Iraq possessed WMD? And, perhaps more important, would "intention" be viewed in the context of baseline of peace between U.S. and Iraq or taking into account the decade-long conflict, just as the legal question of preemption under the *Caroline* test can be avoided by focusing on the duration of the conflict between Iraq and the U.S., in which each side had made earlier uses of force? In other words, should the morality of the use of force in Iraq truly been analyzed on the basis of criteria developed for questions of *jus ad bellum* or should it have been considered under the moral criteria that govern the *jus in bello.*

We now turn to the *jus in bello.* It may be that a full understanding of the legality and legitimacy of the Second Gulf War requires consideration of both perspectives if, as the Bush Administration asserted, the Second Gulf War was only a theater of operations in the larger Global War against Terror.

---

292 *See supra* Part II, Chapter 1, text accompanying note 112 (discussing Suarez's teachings).

293 *See* Doyle, *supra* note 51, at 62.

294 *See* Fletcher & Ohlin, Defending Humanity, *supra* note 238 (conditioning "reasonable mistakes" excuse on satisfaction of publicity criterion).

295 *See* Buchanan & Keohane, *supra* note 273 (suggesting ex post review to determine whether damages should paid to justified claimants by state using force).

PART III

Chapter 1

Introduction to the *Jus in Bello*

We now turn to the *jus in bello*, its origins, its sources and underlying principles, and threshold jurisdictional questions in the definition of armed conflict required to apply the law and its principles. In light of these jurisdictional requirements, we offer some concluding thoughts on the possible application of these norms to asymmetric warfare by sub-state terrorist organizations and individuals.

A. ORIGINS OF THE *JUS IN BELLO*

Over the centuries, in many civilizations and cultures, a body of law developed that reflects moral judgments, imposes the judgments on military commanders and their subordinates, and holds them liable, usually criminally, for violations of these moral judgments. This body of law is now often called "international humanitarian law" or the "humanitarian law of war." In its usual name, it is called the *jus in bello.*[1] The *jus in bello* forms part of that larger body of thought and practice that the philosopher Michael Walzer called the "war convention"—the "set of articulated norms, customs, professional codes, legal precepts, religious and philosophical principles, and reciprocal arrangements that shape our judgments of military conduct."[2]

In the International Court of Justice's 1996 case, *The Legality of the Threat or Use of Nuclear Weapons* (which we shall study in detail in Chapter 4), Judge Weeramantry wrote powerfully about the origins and history of the *jus in bello*:

> Humanitarian law and custom have a very ancient lineage. They reach back thousands of years. They were worked out in many civilizations—Chinese, Indian, Greek, Roman, Japanese, Islamic, modern European, among others. . . . It is today a substantial body of law, consisting of general principles flexible enough to accommodate unprecedented developments in weaponry, and firm enough to command the allegiance of all members of the community of nations. This body of general principles exists in addition to over 600 special provisions in the Geneva Conventions and their Additional Protocols, apart from numerous other conventions on special matters such as chemical and bacteriological weapons. It is thus an important body of law in its own right.[3]

---

1 The term "*jus in bello*" is itself comparatively recent, *see* Robert Kolb, *Origin of the Twin Terms Jus ad Bellum/Jus in Bello,* 320 IRRC 554 (1997). But, the existence of norms, conventions, and legal rules regulating and restraining combat or protecting victims of war is not. See Carsten Stahn,"'*Jus ad Bellum,*' '*Jus in Bello*' . . . '*Jus Post Bellum*'?—*Rethinking the Conception of the Law of Armed Force,* 17 Eur. J. Int'l L. 921, 925 (2007).

2 Michael Walzer, Just and Unjust Wars: A Moral Argument With Historical Illustrations 44 (3d ed. 2000) [hereinafter Walzer, Just and Unjust Wars]. Walzer specifically took issue with Carl von Clausewitz's view that war is intrinsically limitless. *See infra* note 26. Walzer maintained (much as constructivists would) that "war is a social creation. At particular points in time, it takes shape in particular ways, and sometimes at least that resist the 'utmost exertion of forces." *Id.* at 24. And elsewhere, more bluntly, Walzer said: "it is wrong to cut the throats of [the enemy's] wounded or to shoot them down when they are trying to surrender. These judgments are clear enough . . . and they suggest that war is still, somehow, a rule-governed activity, a world of permissions and prohibitions—a moral world, therefore, in the midst of hell." *Id.* at 36.

3 *Legality of the Threat or Use of Nuclear Weapons, Advisory Opinion,* 1996 ICJ Rep. 226, 429, 443–44 Weeramantry, J., dissenting).

As Judge Weeramantry pointed out, *jus in bello* is a centuries-old body of law,[4] evidence of which can be identified in the ancient world,[5] including the societies of Israel,[6] Greece,[7] Rome,[8] China,[9]

4 *See generally* Christopher Greenwood, *Historical Development and Legal Basis, in* The Handbook of Humanitarian Law in Armed Conflicts 1, 12–23 (Dieter Fleck ed. 1995) (summary of history of *jus in bello*); Martin van Creveld, The Culture of War 129–49 (2008) (surveying rules of war in different periods and societies).

5 For a survey of the law of war in the ancient Mediterranean civilizations of Israel, Greece, and Rome, *see* David J. Bederman, International Law in Antiquity 242–49 (2001). A more skeptical approach is found in Arthur Eckstein, Mediterranean Anarchy, Interstate War and the Rise of Rome 37–42, 79–80 (2009).

6 *See Deuteronomy* 20:19–20; 2 *Kings* 6:22–23. In the ancient world, the Jewish historian Josephus detailed, in his book *Against Apion*, a summary of the Jewish rules of war, saying that Moses had required the Jews to be "considerate even to those who have been adjudged enemies. He does not allow us to burn up their country or to cut down their fruit trees, and forbids even the spoiling of fallen combatants; he has taken measures to prevent outrage to prisoners of war, especially women. . . . [He] bade us even in an enemy's country to spare and not to kill the beasts employed in labour. Thus, in every particular, he had an eye to mercy." Quoted in Martin Goodman, Rome and Jerusalem: The Clash of Ancient Civilizations 326 (2007). The great Jewish medieval thinker Moses Maimonides dealt with the *jus in bello* in his The Laws of Kings and Their Wars. *See* Rambam, *Mishne Torah, Yad Hachzakah* (Rabbi Avraham Yaakov Finkel ed. & trans. 2001). *See also* George Horowitz, The Spirit of Jewish Law 149–52 (1953) (Biblical *jus in bello* as rabbinically elaborated); Rabbi Michael Broyde, *Battlefield Ethics in the Jewish Tradition*, 95 Proc. Am. Soc. Int'l L. 92 (2002); Guy Roberts, *Judaic Sources of and Views on the Laws of War*, 37 Naval L. Rev. 221, 230–33 (1988); Norman Solomon, *Judaism and the Ethics of War*, 87 Int'l Rev. Red Cross 295 (2005). *See generally* 2 Walther Eichrodt, Theology of the Old Testament 336 (J.A. Baker trans. 1967) (Israelite laws of war mark "a weakening of the tendency to ascribe autonomous validity to the political sphere"). For the modern Ethical Code of Israeli Defense Forces, *see* Israel Defense Forces:

Ruach Tzahal - Code of Ethics, Jewish Virtual Library (*available at* http://www.jewishvirtuallibrary.org/jsource/Society_&_Culture/IDF_ethics.html).

7 Thucydides referred to these conventions as "the common institutions of Greece." Thucydides, *History of the Peloponnesian War* 3.69.1 (Hobbes translation). Josiah Ober listed twelve rules of war that the Greek city states considered binding in wars against each other during the period of hoplite dominance (from about 700 BC to about 450 BC). Josiah Ober, *Classical Greek Times, in* Michael Howard, George J. Andreapoulos & Mark R. Shulman, The Laws of War: Constraints on Warfare in the Western World 12, 13 (1994) [hereinafter Howard et al., The Laws of War]. Ober argued that these conventions began to disappear under the pressure of Athens' radical and innovative strategy for fighting the Peloponnesian War. *See also* Adriaan Lanni, *The Laws of War in Ancient Greece*, 26 Law and History Review 469 (2008). Richard Ned Lebow, The Tragic Vision of Politics: Ethics, Interests and Orders 164 (2003) (summarizing Thucydides' account of common Greek customs of war); J.E. Lendon, Soldiers & Ghosts: A History of Battle in Classical Antiquity 41–57 (2005) (analyzing the conventions of hoplite warfare). Also, in The Republic, Plato's Socrates, when addressing the question "How shall our soldiers treat their enemies?", lays down certain laws of war applicable to conflicts between Greek city-states: that Greeks not enslave each others' cities or citizens; that they not despoil enemy dead, except of armor; that spoils not be offered at temples; and that enemy territory and houses not be devastated. *See* The Republic of Plato 165–68 (Benjamin Jowett trans., 3d ed. 1888). Socrates made clear that these rules apply to conflict between Greeks and Greeks, which he considered a kind of "civil war," but not (at least in full force) to war with "barbarians," which he took to be "war" in the proper sense. In warring against non-Greeks, Socrates said, Greeks may treat their enemies as they treat other Greeks in actual practice.

8 *See* Alan Watson, International Law in Archaic Rome: War and Religion 50–52 (1993) (noting that different legal rules were applied to the treatment of a conquered people or city depending on whether it surrendered "in trust" ["in fidem"] or "into the dominion" ["in dicionem"]). The great Roman orator and politician Cicero expounded certain rules of war in his *De Officiis (Of Moral Duties)*. *See generally* Thomas L. Pangle & Peter J. Ahrensdorf, Justice Among Nations: On the Moral Basis of Power and Peace 66–70 (1999).

9 *See* Johan Huizinga, Homo Ludens: A Study of the Play Element in Culture 97 (1950).

and India,[10] as well as in classical Islam,[11] in the medieval societies of Japan[12] and of Europe,[13] and in traditional Africa.[14]

What now constitutes the corpus of international *jus in bello* began to take shape in early modern Europe between about AD 1550 and AD 1700[15]—a period which also, not coincidentally,[16] saw the rise of the modern state and the decline (though not the complete disappearance[17]) of the traditional doctrine of *jus ad bellum.*[18] A new normative framework for the emerging states system was necessary, not only to "fill[] the void created by the collapse of the unity and authority provided by the Church of Rome," but also to accommodate the growing centralization of

---

10 *See* Nagendra Singh, *Armed Conflicts and Humanitarian Laws of Ancient India,* in Studies and Essays on International Humanitarian Law and Red Cross Principles in Honor of Jean Pictet 53 (Christophe Swinarski ed., 1984); *see also* John Ferguson, War and Peace in the World's Religions 30–31 (1977); V.S. Mani, *International Humanitarian Law: An Indo-Asian Perspective,* 83 Int'l Rev. Red Cross 59 (2001); Lakshmikanth R. Penna, *Written and Customary Provisions Relating to the Conduct of Hostilities and Treatment of Victims of Armed Conflicts in Ancient India,* 271 Int'l Rev. Red Cross 333 (1989); Manoj Kumar Sinha, *Hinduism and International Humanitarian Law,* 87 Int'l Rev. Red Cross 285, 291–94 (2005); K.N. Upadhyaya, *The Bhagavad Gitā on War and Peace,* 19 Phil. E. & W. 159 (1969).

11 *See United States Diplomatic and Consular Staff in Tehran (U.S. v. Iran),* 1980 I.C.J. 2 (May 24) (Tarazi, J., dissenting); Sohail H. Hashmi, *Interpreting the Islamic Ethics of War and Peace, in* Islamic Political Ethics: Civil Society, Pluralism and Conflict 194 (Sohail H. Hashmi ed., 2002); James Turner Johnson, The Holy War Idea in Western and Islamic Traditions 115–27 (1997); John Kelsay, Islam and War: A Study in Comparative Ethics 57–76 (1993); Majid Khadduri, War and Peace in the Law of Islam 102 (1955) (quoting the instructions of Abu Bakr on the first Syrian expedition); Rudolph Peters, Jihad in Classical and Modern Islam 9–17 (1996) (collecting *ahádith* [sayings of the prophet Muhammad]); M.K. Ereksoussi, *The Koran and the Humanitarian Conventions,* 14 Int'l Rev. Red Cross 273 (1962); Ella Landau-Tasseron, *"Non-Combatants" in Muslim Legal Thought,* Research Monographs on the Muslim World, Series No. 1, Paper No. 3 (Hudson Institute Dec. 2006) (*available at* http://www.hudson.org); Sheik Wahbeh al-Zuhili, *Islam and International Law,* 87 Int'l Rev. Red Cross 269, 282–83 (2005).

12 *See* Karl F. Friday, Samurai, Warfare and the State in Early Medieval Japan 135–63 (2004).

13 *See* Philippe Contamine, War in the Middle Ages 260–302 (Michael Jones trans. 1984); Leslie C. Green, The Contemporary Law of Armed Conflict 23–25 (2d ed. 2000); Johnson, *supra* note 11, at 102–12; Richard W. Kaeuper, Chivalry and Violence in Medieval Europe 169–85 (1999) (discussing the differing implications of ideals of chivalry for knights and for non-combatants); Richard Ned Lebow, A Cultural Theory of International Relations 257 (2008); Theodore Meron, *Medieval and Renaissance Ordinances of War: Codifying Discipline and Humanity, in* War Crimes Law Comes of Age 1, 1–10 (1998); Pangle & Ahrensdorf, *supra* note 8, at 73–88; Robert C. Stacey, *The Age of Chivalry,* in Howard et al., The Laws of War, *supra* note 7, at 27; Louis J. Swift, *Augustine on War and Killing: Another View,* 66 Harv. Theol. Rev. 369, 380–83 (1973).

14 *See* Yolanda Diallo, *Humanitarian Law and Traditional African Law,* 179 Int'l Rev. Red Cross 57 (1976).

15 *See* Geoffrey Parker, *Early Modern Europe,* in Howard et al., The Laws of War, *supra* note 7, 40, 41. Arguably, the prevalence of *jus ad bellum* theory in Europe before the seventeenth century had *inhibited* the growth of *jus in bello.* See Lynn H. Miller, *The Contemporary Significance of the Doctrine of Just War,* 16 World Pol. 254, 258 (1964); *see also* Inis L. Claude, Jr., Just Wars: *Doctrines and Institutions,* 95 Pol. Sci. Q. 83, 91 (1980).

16 *See* Carl Schmitt, The *Nomos of the Earth in the International Jus Publicum Europaeum* 152–53 (G.L. Ulmen trans. 2006).

17 On the beginning of the severance of *jus in bello from jus ad bellum, see e.g.,* Serena K. Sharma, *Reconsidering the Jus Ad Bellum/Jus In Bello Distinctions, in* Jus Post Bellum: *Towards a Law of Transition From Conflict to* Peace 9, 14–15 (Carsten Stahn & Jann K. Kleffner eds., 2008). On the persistence of just war theory, *see* Joachim von Elbe, *The Evolution of the Concept of Just War in International Law,* 33 Am. J. Int'l L. 665 (1939); Hans Kelsen, *Quincy Wright's A Study of War and the Bellum Justum Theory,* 53 Ethics 208, 209–10 (1943).

18 On the transformation and secularization of *jus ad bellum* doctrine in the early modern period, the increasingly anachronistic character of the doctrine, and the origin of the conditions for modern *jus in bello, see* Stephen C. Neff, War and the Law of Nations: A General History 95–102 (2005); *see also* Robert D. Sloane, *The Cost of Conflation: Preserving the Dualism of Jus ad Bellum and Jus in Bello in the Contemporary Law of War,* 34 Yale J. Int'l L.47, 60–64 (2009); Robert J. Delahunty & John C. Yoo, *Making War,* 93 Cornell L. Rev. 123, 140–49 (2007).

military power and domestic legitimacy in territorially-based states.[19] The search for new rules to govern the conduct of hostilities, evident in the work of the seventeenth century Dutch thinker Hugo Grotius, reflects the interests of such states both in limiting the pervasiveness of "private" violence and in applying standards of instrumental rationality to their violence against each other.[20]

Nonetheless, the modern European tradition of *jus in bello* was firmly rooted in the past. The military historian Geoffrey Parker argued that "the laws in war in Europe have rested since the Middle Ages upon the same five foundations,"[21] which he identified as 1) prescriptive texts, including the Bible, Roman law, canon law, and the writings of figures such as St. Augustine and St. Thomas Aquinas; 2) the teachings promulgated from the eleventh century onward by the Peace of God and the Truce of God;[22] 3) various military manuals and articles of war that were issued by national armed forces;[23] 4) customs arising from the practice of war; and 5) combatants' growing appreciation of the advantages of restraint in warfare, including honoring truces and surrenders and sparing captives and the wounded.[24]

---

19 A. Claire Cutler, *The 'Grotian Tradition' in International Relations*, 17 Rev. Int'l Stud. 41, 44 (1991).

20 *See* Ian Clark, Waging War: A Philosophical Introduction 40 (1988).

21 Parker, *Early Modern Europe, supra* note 15, at 41.

22 For accounts of the "peace movements" leading to these developments, *see* H.E.J. Cowdrey, *The Peace of God and the Truce of God in the Eleventh Century*, 46 Past & Present 42 (1970); Loren C. Mackinney, *The People and Public Opinion in the Eleventh-Century Peace Movement,* 5 Speculum 181 (1930). The Peace of God sought to protect certain classes of persons and their goods at all times from war's harms; the Truce of God was an attempt to stop all warfare at certain times. Both can be said to be the outcomes of "peace movements." The canons of the Council of Narbonne (1054) illustrate eleventh century legislation in the area.

23 For discussion of the articles of war promulgated by both royalist and parliamentary forces in English Civil War of the seventeenth century, *see* Barbara Donagan, *Codes and Conduct in the English Civil War,* 118 Past & Present 65, 83–87 (1988) [hereinafter Donagan, *Codes and Conduct*]: *see also* Barbara Donagan, *Atrocity, War Crime, and Treason in the English Civil War,* 99 Am. Hist. Rev. 1137, 1142 (1994) [hereinafter Donagan, *Atrocity, War Crime, and Treason*].

24 Another major historian, John Nef, sensed "the presence of a new chivalry—adjusted to novel and horrible weapons, hitherto unused," in Diego Velásquez's great painting from (perhaps) 1634 to 1635, *The Surrender at Breda (Las Lances),* which portrayed the surrender in 1625 of the defeated Dutch forces under Justin of Nassau to the Italian aristocrat and Spanish commander, the Marquis of Spinola. See John U. Nef, War and Human Progress: An Essay on the Rise of Industrial Civilization 139 (1950) [hereinafter Nef, War and Human Progress]. Spinola's siege of Breda had been a spectacular display of engineering and skill that had attracted distinguished visitors from all over Europe. The siege had been an exhausting one for both sides. Nonetheless, General Spinola's terms for the garrison's surrender were magnanimous—reflecting, perhaps, seventeenth century Spanish ideals for the treatment of defeated enemies. For accounts of the cultural background and significance of Velázquez' painting, *see* Robin Wagner-Pacifici, The Art of Surrender: Decomposing Sovereignty at Conflict's End 29–36 (2005); Jonathan Brown & John H. Elliott, A Palace for A King: The Buen Retiro and the Court of Philip IV 185–93 (rev'd ed. 1980). "In spite of the religious wars [of the seventeenth century]," Nef wrote, "Europeans had at their disposal remnants of the medieval conception of universal Christian community. They also had remnants of the old chivalry and the pageantry that accompanied it." Nef, War and Human Progress, at 139.

Others have also thought that the "gentling" of intra-European warfare owed much to Christianity. The eighteenth century Scottish Enlightenment philosopher and economist Adam Smith argued in his Lectures on Justice, Police, Revenue, and Arms (1763) that "[t]his superior degree of humanity was introduced during the time of Popery. We never find it among the Greeks and Romans, notwithstanding all their attainments. The Pope was considered as the common father of Christendom, the clergy were under his subjection, and he had intercourse by his legates with all the courts of Europe. By this they were more nearly connected, and he obliged them to treat one another with more humanity. The Holy War too, which at that time was undertaken by most of the princes in Europe, made them turn their arms against all those of a different religion, who they thought deserved

Von Clausewitz, too, thought that the seventeenth century saw the beginning of a new rationality and humaneness in warfare—though he attributed this less to the persisting influence of medieval Christianity than to "intelligence."[25] As von Clausewitz noted:

> It had ceased to be in harmony with the spirit of the times to plunder and lay waste the enemy's land, which had played such an important role in antiquity, in Tartar days and indeed in medieval times. It was rightly held to be unnecessarily barbarous, an invitation to reprisals, and a practice that hurt the enemy's subjects rather than their government—one therefore that was ineffective and only served permanently to impede the advance of general civilization. Not only in its means, therefore, but also in its aims, war increasingly became limited to the fighting force itself. Armies, with their fortresses and prepared positions, came to form a state within a state, in which violence gradually faded away.[26]

Thus, beginning about the middle of the nineteenth century, modern humanitarian practice and law began to assume a more definite form. On business travel in Italy on June 24, 1859, the young Swiss banker Henri Dunant happened upon large numbers of wounded soldiers in a church in the village of Castiglione. The soldiers were casualties from the battle of Solferino, which had been fought on that day between the armies of France and Sardinia on the one side and Austria on the other. The battle of Solferino was the most appalling that Europe had seen since that at Waterloo. Within ten hours, more than 6,000 soldiers were killed and more than 30,000 were wounded. Franco-Sardinian medical services were overwhelmed. Moved by the suffering and distress of the wounded men, Dunant, who was without any medical training, did what he could to help them. But the memory of what he had seen haunted him. In 1862, he published, at his own expense and at no cost to anyone who would take a copy, a book entitled

---

to be treated in the most cruel manner, but when they came to be engaged in a war among themselves, as they had all been on one side in that common cause, and as they thought that Christians should not be treated in the same manner with infidels, a greater degree of humanity was introduced." *Id. (available at* http://oll.libertyfund.org/titles/smith-lectures-on-justice-police-revenue-and-arms-1763?q=degree+of+humanity#Smith_1647_541).

25 Carl von Clausewitz, On War 85 (Michael Howard & Peter Paret (trans.) 1991) ("If, then, civilized nations do not put their prisoners to death or devastate cities and countries, it is because intelligence plays a larger part in their methods of warfare and has taught them more effective ways of using force than the crude expression of instinct.").

26 *Id.* at 714. Von Clausewitz, of course, referred here only to wars *within* Europe, not to wars by Europeans against non-European states and peoples, or against the natives of remote parts of Europe such as the highland Scots and the Irish. On the former, see Jeremy Black, Culloden and the '45 187–88 (1990); on the latter, *see* Donagan, *Codes and Conduct, supra* note 23, at 70–71, 93–95; Donagan, *Atrocity, War Crime, and Treason, supra* note 23, at 1148. Wars waged by "Western" European powers such as Sweden against "Eastern" European powers such as Russia also displayed a savagery not found elsewhere, which included the use of bayonets, a weapon not often employed elsewhere. Such practices have been explained in part by "the traditional European's view of the Slav as less entitled than his own people to civilized treatment." Nef, War and Human Progress, *supra* note 24, at 253. Moreover, von Clausewitz was very well aware that, even if eighteenth century intra-European war was "limited" in the ways he described, the advent of the wars of the French Revolution and of Napoléon changed all that. *See* Gunther Rothenberg, *The Age of Napoleon*, in Howard et al., The Laws of War, *supra* note 7, 86, 86–87 (criticism of von Clausewitz); *see also* David A. Bell, The First Total War: Napoleon's Europe and the Birth of War as We Know It (2007); *and* J.F.C. Fuller, The Conduct of War 1789-1961 at 26–58 (1992 ed.).

Un Souvenir de Solferino (*A Memory of Solferino*), which described the horrors that he saw and which concluded by asking: "Would it not be possible, in time of peace and quiet, to form relief societies for the purpose of having care given to the wounded in wartime by zealous, devoted and thoroughly qualified volunteers?" Dunant's call was heeded and led to the foundation of the International Committee of the Red Cross (ICRC), which is widely considered to be the leading international non-governmental organization dedicated to promoting humanitarian law.[27]

At very nearly the same time, the *jus in bello* began to be codified in multilateral treaties among states.[28] Thus appeared such landmark instruments as the 1863 Lieber Code—used by the Union Army in the American Civil War,[29] which is regarded as the origin of "Hague Law"; the 1864 Geneva Convention for the Amelioration of the Condition of the Wounded in Armies in the Field,[30] from which "Geneva Law" is derived; and the 1868 Declaration of St. Petersburg,[31] which introduced restrictions on the use of certain types of weaponry in war. The Hague Conferences of 1899 and 1907 issued important conventions that regulate the conduct of warfare and the use of weaponry, including the 1907 Convention (IV) with Respect to the Laws and Customs of War on Land.[32] The Nuremberg and Tokyo Trials made notable additions to the *jus in bello*, in such spheres as the liability of commanding officers and their subordinates. The four

27 *See* François Bugnion, *From Solferino to the Birth of Contemporary International Humanitarian Law* (ICRC April 22, 2009) (*available at* http://www.icrc.org/eng/resources/documents/article/other/solferino-article-bugniomn-240409.htm); *see also* Jean Pictet, *The First Geneva Convention*, 271 IRRC 277 (1989). Although Dunant was unquestionably a pioneer, there were of course precedents for his work. "Two hundred ninety-one bipartite treaties regulating the treatment of the wounded and sick were concluded in Europe from 1581 to 1864." Fritz Grob, The Relativity of War and Peace: A Study in Law, History, and Politics 162 (1949).

28 Adam Roberts, *Land Warfare: From Hague to Nuremberg, in* Howard et al., The Laws of War, *supra* note 7, 116, 119 ("Up to the mid-nineteenth century the laws of war did exist, but in a form very different from today: in custom, in broad principles, in national laws and military manuals, and in religious teaching. The second half of the nineteenth century was . . . an era of belief in progress in controlling war. Indeed, that characteristic modern encapsulation of the laws of war—the multilateral treaty setting out principles in this field for states to follow—was only invented in the second half of the nineteenth century.").

29 *See* Int'l. Comm. of the Red Cross, Instructions for the Government of Armies of the United States in the Field (Lieber Code) (n.p. 1863) (at http://www.icrc.org/ihl.nsf/FULL/110?OpenDocument). For a brilliant analysis of the origins, application and lasting effects of the Lieber Code, see John Fabian Witt, Lincoln's Code: The Laws of War in American History (2013). *See also* Burrus M. Carnahan, *Lincoln, Lieber and the Laws of War: The Origins and Limits of the Principle of Military Necessity*, 92 Am. J. Int'l L. 213 (1998).

30 *See* Convention for the Amelioration of the Condition of the Wounded in Armies in the Field, 22 August 1864 (*available at* https://www.icrc.org/ihl/INTRO/120?OpenDocument). This convention marks the point at which the rules of *jus in bello* began to become multilateral.

31 *See* Declaration Renouncing the Use, in Time of War, of Explosive Projectiles Under 400 Grammes Weight, Dec. 11, 1868, 138 Consol. T.S. 297(*available at* http://www.icrc.org/ihl.nsf/FULL/130?OpenDocument).

32 Convention (IV) Respecting the Laws and Customs of War on Land and in Its Annex: Regulations Concerning the Laws and Customs of War on Land, Oct. 18, 1907, 36 Stat. 2277 (*available at* http://www.icrc.org/ihl.nsf/385ec082b509e76c41256739003e636d/1d1726425f6955aec125641e0038bfd6).

Geneva Conventions of 1949,[33] replacing the two Geneva Conventions of 1929,[34] introduced new and more extensive protections for the victims of armed conflicts, including especially non-combatants in enemy or occupied territory. Owing largely to the demands of Third World and Communist bloc nations,[35] the 1949 Conventions were significantly modified by two "Additional Protocols" in 1977 (hereafter Protocol I and Protocol II).[36]

The *jus in bello* continues to undergo dynamic change—in treaty law, case law and evolving custom. For example, various courts—the International Court of Justice; special international courts, especially the International Criminal Tribunal for the Former Yugoslavia (the ICTY);[37] and national courts, such as the Supreme Court of Israel—have contributed significantly in recent decades to the definition and development of customary *jus in bello* rules. The role of these courts will be discussed further in later chapters.

---

33 *See* Geneva Convention for the Amelioration of the Condition of the Wounded and Sick in Armed Forces in the Field, Aug. 12, 1949, 6 U.S.T. 3114, 75 U.N.T.S. 31 [hereinafter Geneva I]; Geneva Convention for the Amelioration of the Condition of Wounded, Sick and Shipwrecked Members of Armed Forces at Sea, Aug. 12, 1949, 6 U.S.T. 3217, 75 U.N.T.S. 85 [hereinafter Geneva II]; Geneva Convention Relative to the Treatment of Prisoners of War, Aug. 12, 1949, 6 U.S.T. 3316, 75 U.N.T.S. 135 [hereinafter Geneva III]; Geneva Convention Relative to the Protection of Civilian Persons in Time of War, Aug. 12, 1949, 6 U.S.T. 3516, 75 U.N.T.S. 287 [hereinafter Geneva IV].

34 *See* Geneva Convention Relative to the Treatment of Prisoners of War, July 27, 1929, 47 Stat. 2021, 118 L.N.T.S. 343; Geneva Convention for the Amelioration of the Condition of the Wounded and Sick in Armies in the Field, July 27, 1929, 47 Stat. 2074, 118 L.N.T.S. 303.

35 *See* Antonio Cassese, *Wars of National Liberation and Humanitarian Law,* in Studies and Essays on International Humanitarian Law and Red Cross Principles in Honor of Jean Pictet (Christophe Swinarski, ed.), *supra* note 10, at 313; Richard Baxter, *Human Rights in War,* 31 Bull. Am. Acad. Arts and Sciences 4, 8–9 (1977).

36 Additional Protocol I; Protocol Additional to the Geneva Conventions Relating to the Protection of Victims of Non-International Armed Conflicts, June 8, 1977, 1125 U.N.T.S. 609 [hereinafter Additional Protocol II].

37 For a measured assessment of the contribution of the ICTY's jurisprudence to contemporary *jus in bello, see* Michael N. Schmitt, *Military Necessity in International Humanitarian Law: Preserving the Delicate Balance,* 50 Va. J. Int'l L. 795, 817–22 (2010). *See also* Christopher Greenwood, *International Humanitarian Law and the Tadić Case, in* Essays on War in International Law 457, 472–74 (2006).

B. "HAGUE LAW" AND "GENEVA LAW"

Many scholars speak of "Hague Law" and "Geneva Law," and it is true that the two bodies of law exhibit certain characteristic differences of coverage and emphasis. As the International Court of Justice explained in its decision in *The Legality of the Threat or Use of Nuclear Weapons,*[38] '"Hague Law and, more particularly, the Regulations Respecting the Laws and Customs of War on Land, fixed the rights and duties of belligerents in their conduct of operations and limited the choice of methods and means of injuring the enemy in an international armed conflict," while '"Geneva Law' . . . protects the victims of war and aims to provide safeguards for disabled armed forces personnel and persons not taking part in hostilities."[39] Nonetheless, as the Court went on to say, "[t]hese two branches of the law applicable in armed conflict have become so closely interrelated that they are considered to have gradually formed one single complex system, known today as international humanitarian law."[40]

Although it seems fair to say that "Hague Law" regulates the conduct of hostilities and the means and methods of warfare while "Geneva Law" concerns the protection of persons, the distinction is not as clear-cut as it may appear, if only because the protection of the civilian population (a primary aim of "Geneva Law") can only be accomplished if the means of combat are regulated. In addition, "Hague Law" has to a great extent been absorbed into "Geneva Law" in Part III of Protocol I to the Geneva Conventions, which regulates the means of combat.[41]

38 *Legality of the Treat or Use of Nuclear Weapons,* Advisory Opinion, July 8, 1996, 1996 ICJ Rep. 226.

39 *Id.* at ¶ 75.

40 *Id.* at ¶ 75.

41 These points have been noted by the Constitutional Court of the Republic of Colombia. *See* How Does Law Protect in War? 1357, 1357–58 (International Committee of the Red Cross, Marco Sassòli & Antoine A. Bouvier eds., 1999).

C. THREE FUNDAMENTAL PRINCIPLES IN CONTEMPORARY *JUS IN BELLO*: MILITARY NECESSITY, DISTINCTION, AND PROPORTIONALITY

Although the *jus in bello* consists, for the most part, of specific and detailed rules, it is founded upon a small number of bedrock principles. Three of these principles are: 1) military necessity, 2) distinction and 3) proportionality.[42] (The principle of proportionality might itself be derived from the more basic principles of necessity and distinction.[43]) In some places, the *jus in bello* may make explicit reference to one or more of these principles; in other places, a reference may be implicit. The interpretation and application of the *jus in bello* is, however, guided and informed throughout by these principles. In what follows, we shall give a brief and introductory outline of each of the principles.

1. The Principle of Military Necessity

The principle of military necessity is at once fundamental to the *jus in bello* and yet highly elusive.[44] It seems possible to distinguish several different forms that the idea of "military necessity" has taken. Of these, the first (factual or material military necessity) is non-legal and the second (reason of war) is inadmissible in current law. "Military necessity" does figure in current *jus in bello* in other analytically distinct, yet sometimes conflicting and sometimes overlapping, forms (as a constraint, as an exception, as an excuse, and as a pervasive element in the law of war).

a. Material Military Necessity

Let us begin with the celebrated definition of "military necessity" set out in Article 14 of the Lieber Code:

---

42 Some writers identify further (or fewer) principles. For example, writers identify the principle of unnecessary suffering. *See, e.g.*, Gary Solis, The Law of International Armed Conflict: International Humanitarian Law in War 250–51 (2010); Françoise Hampson, *Winning by the Rules: Law and Warfare in the 1980s*, 11 Third World Q. 31, 47 (1989). They also identify the principle of humanity. *See, e.g.*, A.P.V. Rogers, Law on the Battlefield 7 (2d ed. 2004). Finally, writers identify the principle of chivalry. *See* Lt. Col. William J. Fenrick, *The Rule of Proportionality and Protocol I in Conventional Warfare*, 98 Mil. L. Rev. 91, 93–94 (1982) [hereinafter Fenrick, *The Rule of Proportionality*] (finding "continued, though somewhat limited, vitality" in this principle).

43 *See* Rogers, Law on the Battlefield, *supra* note 42, at 7 (military necessity as element in proportionality); Fenrick, *The Rule of Proportionality, supra* note 42, at 92 (Protocol I "accommodates the needs of humanity with the practical inevitabilities of warfare" by requiring proportionality).

44 *See* Michael N. Schmitt, *Military Necessity and Humanity in International Humanitarian Law: Preserving the Delicate Balance*, 50 Va. J. Int'l L. 795, 796 (2010) [hereinafter Schmitt, *Military Necessity and Humanity*] ("No principle is more central . . . nor more misunderstood."); Nobuo Hayashi, *Requirement of Military Necessity in International Humanitarian Law and International Criminal Law*, 28 Boston U. Int'l L. J. 39, 41 (2010) ("[F]ew concepts are so fundamental to warfare . . . are more elusive.").

> Military necessity, as understood by modern civilized nations, consists in the necessity of those measures which are indispensable for securing the ends of the war, and which are lawful according to the modern law and usages of war.

Lieber's definition has two parts. Military necessity consists in the necessity of measures that are both a) indispensable and b) lawful. The first of these two elements can be taken as a fair account of "military necessity" in its widest sense. That is, measures that are "necessary" (if not always "indispensable") to achieve or further either specific aims in combat or, more widely, the overall military objectives of the war. Understood in this sense, "military necessity is essentially a matter of identifying the range of realistic courses of action of generating the desired outcome, and selecting and pursuing one that is superior to the others on the strength of its chances and resource efficiency."[45] Military necessity here has a factual or "material" rather than a legal meaning.

b. "Kriegsräson" or Reason of War

The term "*kriegsräson*" or "reason of war" refers to a doctrine expoused by the German Army since the nineteenth century. As Michael Walzer explained it, "[t]he doctrine justifies not only whatever is necessary to win the war, but also whatever is necessary to reduce the risks of losing, or simply to reduce losses or the likelihood of losses in the course of the war."[46] *Kriegsräson* so understood could serve as a kind of legal trump card, justifying violations of the requirements of the *jus in bello* whenever they collided with the pursuit of military objectives. Such a doctrine would obviously strip the *jus in bello* of any restraining effects, and it was emphatically rejected at Nuremberg. The American Military Tribunal in *The Hostage Case* rejected the reason of war doctrine when it said: "We do not concur in the view that the rules of warfare are anything less than they purport to be. Military necessity or expediency do not justify a violation of positive rules. International law is prohibitive law."[47]

---

45 Hayashi, *supra* note 44, at 44–45.

46 Walzer, Just and Unjust Wars, *supra* note 2, at 144. There were in fact several different formulations of the doctrine. In one version, the doctrine allowed that the normal rules of war were binding on a belligerent under ordinary circumstances, but ceased to be so in exceptional cases of urgent necessity. *See* Jesse S. Reeves, *The Neutralization of Belgium and the Doctrine of* Kriegsraison, 13 Mich. L. Rev. 179, 180 (1915). Further, the doctrine appears to have permitted exceptions only to customary law, not to treaty law. *Id.* at 181. In another and broader version, the one to which Walzer refers, the doctrine of *kriegsräson* meant "that the ordinary laws of war cease to be binding upon a belligerent whenever their observance would defeat the attainment of the object of the war." James Wilford Garner, 2 International Law and the World War 196 (1920).

47 *United States v. List (The Hostage Case)*, Case No. 7 (Feb. 19, 1948), *reprinted in* 11 Trials of War Criminals Before the Nuremberg Military Tribunals Under Control Council Law No. 10 (hereafter TWC), at 1256 (1950). For a survey of Nuremberg case law on the subject, *see* Myres S. McDougal & Florentino P. Feliciano, Transnational Law of War and World Public Order 676–78 (1994).

Yet, the American rejection of German doctrine in this case added little to the law of war, for in the Lieber Code's definition, military necessity also does not appear as a legal constraint. Rather, two steps are needed before "military necessity" can be invoked as a legal defense of a measure. First, the measure has to be shown to be a "necessity" in the factual or material sense. Second, the measure has to be shown to be compliant with the rules of war—in other words, that it is legally *permissible.* It appears in the guise of the first step in *The Hostage Case,* when the Tribunal stated that "[m]ilitary necessity . . . does not permit the killing of innocent inhabitants for purposes of revenge or for the satisfaction of a lust to kill."[48] Killing of innocent inhabitants "*for purposes of revenge*" is killing them without a specifically *military* reason, as is killing them "for the satisfaction of *the lust to kill.*" It was only because measures taken for those reasons lack any *military* rationale that the Tribunal treated them as violations of a limit imposed by "military necessity." This is a limited inquiry indeed.

c. Military Necessity as a Legal Constraint

"Military necessity" has, however, emerged as a genuine as a constraint in the *jus in bello.* The French legal scholar Henri Meyrowitz pointed to a draft submitted by the Russian delegation to the 1874 diplomatic conference in Brussels that led to the (unratified) *Project of an International Declaration Concerning the Laws and Customs of War.* The Russian proposal stated in part: "To achieve the object of war, every means and method conforming to the laws and customs of war and justified by the necessities of war are allowed." In Meyrowitz's view, this sentence "[was] the best formulation of the notion—or rather the principle—of necessity in the law of war" because it "highlight[ed] the normative role of the notion or principle of 'military necessity.'"[49] As Meyrowitz explicated it, the Russian formulation "state[d] that for means and actions to be lawful, it is not enough for them to be in accordance with the rules of the law of war; their choice and the use made of them must also be justified by military necessity."[50] Meyrowitz contrasted the 1874 Russian statement with Article 14 of the Lieber Code, quoted above. Under the Lieber Code, a measure is permissible if, first, without regard to any question of legality, it is militarily necessary and, second, it is not legally forbidden. Under the Russian draft, a measure is forbidden unless, first, it is not otherwise legally forbidden and, second, is justified by military necessity.

Meyrowitz pointed to Article 52(2) of Additional Protocol I as a contemporary example of how "military necessity" can function as a legal constraint.[51] Article 52(2) states:

---

48 *The Hostage Case, supra* note 47, 11 TWC 1254.

49 Henri Meyrowitz, *The Principle of Superfluous Injury or Unnecessary Suffering From the Declaration of St. Petersburg to Additional Protocol I of* 1977, 299 IRRC 98, 106–07 (1994).

50 *Id.* at 107.

51 *Id.* at 113 (finding Article 52(2) to be "the most remarkable application . . . of the principle of necessity").

> Attacks shall be limited strictly to military objectives. In so far as objects are concerned, military objectives are limited to those objects which by their nature, location, purpose or use make an effective contribution to military action and whose total or partial destruction, capture or neutralization, in the circumstances ruling at the time, offers a definite military advantage.

Thus, in Meyrowitz' analysis, Article 52(2) imposes two tests, both of which must be satisfied for an "attack" to be lawful. First, attacks must be limited to "military objectives." This is a categorical rule of law (in effect, the principle of distinction). Second, an attack must also be justified as a military necessity. When the "objective" is an "object," it must be "mak[ing] an effective contribution to military action" and its total or partial destruction must "in the circumstances ruling at the time, offer[] a definite military advantage." As Meyrowitz noted, this two-part test seems to mirror the tests proposed by the 1874 Russian draft. Further, by referring to "the circumstances ruling at the time," Article 52(2) reflects the fluid and situational nature of "military necessity."

However, understanding how "military necessity" functions as a legal constraint also helps explain the view expressed by some scholars that the current *jus in bello* is insufficiently protective of (some) combatants. In considering whether the Allied Coalition's conduct during the First Gulf War satisfied the requirements of *jus in bello,* Françoise Hampson raised the question of the Coalition's attacks on retreating Iraqi forces. She noted, correctly, that

> [t]he destruction of the opposing armed forces . . . does not appear to require the justification of military necessity. . . . The Iraqi forces had not surrendered, nor had they abandoned their weapons so as to evince an intention either to surrender or at least no longer to continue fighting. Nor, at that time, had the Iraqi political leadership entered into cease-fire negotiations. While the Iraqi forces may have looked like a disorganized and defeated rabble, they could also have been engaged in a tactical retreat prior to regrouping. The coalition forces, legally speaking, need not prove the necessity of the attacks. The attacks were lawful.[52]

Article 52(2) confirms Hampson's analysis. It declares that only "military objectives" may be attacked. Then it requires a further showing of military necessity before "objects" within that class may be targeted. But military objectives include military personnel as well as "objects." Thus, by implication, Article 52(2) permits attacks on military personnel even if those attacks are not justified by military necessity.

52 Françoise Hampson, *Proportionality and Necessity in the Gulf Conflict,* 86 Proc. Am. Soc. Int'l L. 45, 53–54 (1992); *see also* Stephen L. Carter, The Violence of Peace: America's Wars in the Age of Obama 59 (2011); William J. Fenrick, *International Law and Combat Casualties,* 21 Eur. J. Pop. Revue Europeénne de Démographie 167, 172 (2005) ("Combatants . . . may . . . be attacked at any time, sleeping, eating, marching to the rear, unless they have surrendered or are injured and have ceased to take part in hostilities.").

Hampson expressed understandable discomfort with that conclusion. The retreating Iraqi forces did not merely look like, but were, a "disorganized and defeated rabble." There were reports that "the coalition forces showed some reluctance to go on attacking an unresisting enemy."[53] In other words, Allied soldiers and pilots felt revulsion at the needless killing of the retreating Iraqi soldiers. Hampson also observed that "[e]ven if conduct is not unlawful, a military commander must consider whether it is wise,"[54] implying that it would not have been wise to gun down these Iraqi forces. And finally she pointed out that "the lawfulness of attacks against a clearly defeated enemy could be made a matter of legal regulation by providing that an attack against enemy forces is unlawful unless it can be proved to be necessary."[55]

d. Military Necessity as an Exception

At various places, the Hague and Geneva Conventions mark out express exceptions from an otherwise applicable rule for cases of military necessity. Again, the *Hostage Case* provides a useful statement of this form of military necessity:

> The destruction of property to be lawful must be imperatively demanded by the necessities of war. Destruction as an end in itself is a violation of international law. There must be some reasonable connection between the destruction of property and the overcoming of the enemy forces. . . . Private homes and churches may even be destroyed if necessary for military operations.[56]

The Tribunal is apparently referring here to Article 23(g) of the Annex to the 1907 Hague Convention IV Respecting the Laws and Customs of War on Land. That provision prohibits the destruction or seizure of enemy property unless "imperatively demanded by the necessities of war." Other treaties detailing *jus in bello* rules have exceptional clauses of a similar kind. For example, Article 53 of the 1949 Fourth Geneva Convention prohibits a belligerent occupying force from destroying protected property "except where such destruction is rendered absolutely necessary by military operations."[57] Article 49 of the same Convention prohibits a belligerent

53 Hampson, *supra* note 52, at 54.

54 *Id.*

55 *Id.* Under an earlier, eighteenth century version of the "war convention," just such a rule was apparently applied. *See* James Q. Whitman, The Verdict of Battle: The Law of Victory and the Making of Modern War (2012).

56 *The Hostage Case, supra* note 47, 11 TWC 1254.

57 *See Beit Sourik Village Council v. Gov't of Israel,* HCJ 2056/04 at ¶ 32 (Sup. Ct. of Israel 2004) ("[T]he military commander is authorized—by the international law applicable to an area under belligerent occupation—to take possession of land, if this is necessary for the needs of the army. See articles 23(g) and 52 of the Hague Conventions; article 53 of the Fourth Geneva Convention. . . . To the extent the construction of the fence [*i.e.,* the wall or security perimeter erected by Israel in the occupied territories of the West Bank] is a military necessity, it is permitted, therefore, by international law.").

occupier, regardless of motive, to engage in "[i]ndividual or mass forcible transfers, as well as deportations of protected persons from occupied territory" to any other country, but further states that "[n]evertheless, the Occupying Power may undertake total or partial evacuation of a given area if the security of the population or *imperative military reasons* so demand" (emphasis added). Article 4 of the 1954 Hague Cultural Property Convention allows the waiver of some protection for covered property "in cases where military necessity imperatively requires such a waiver." Exceptional clauses for military necessity are found in Arts. 54(5), 62(1), 67(4) and 71(3) of Additional Protocol I. Other clauses of Additional Protocol I, *e.g.*, Article 54 (3), might be construed as exceptions created to reflect military necessity.

The Nuremberg case law occasionally dealt with the scope of such exceptions for (alleged) military necessity. Here we may illustrate the decisional law by briefly considering part of an opinion by an ICTY Trial Chamber in its 2005 judgment in the *Strugar* case.[58] The question posed in this case was whether the defendant should be held liable for the war crime of "devastation without military necessity" for his role in the shelling of the Old Town of Dubrovnic. The Trial Chamber took the position that "military necessity may usefully be defined for present purposes with reference to the widely acknowledged definition of military objectives in Article 52 of Additional Protocol I."[59] One commentator argued that this may be an error, contending that Article 52 goes to the legality of targeting a property while military necessity goes to the legality of the property's "destruction."[60] On this interpretation, if an "attack" on a property is forbidden by Article 52 (because the property is not a "military objective"), there can then be no question of justifying its destruction by reference to "military necessity"; and, if an "attack" on a property is legal (because it is a "military objective"), there is no further need to justify its destruction by reference to "military necessity."

e. Military Necessity as Permissive or Exculpatory

A more controversial way of understanding military necessity is to see it as permissive or exculpatory. *The Hostage Case* once more suggests such a conceptualization:

> Military necessity permits a belligerent, subject to the laws of war, to apply any amount and kind of force to compel the complete submission of the enemy with the least possible expenditure of time, life and money. In general, it sanctions measures by an occupant necessary to protect the safety of his forces and to facilitate the success of his operations. It permits

58 *Prosecutor v. Strugar,* Case No. IT-01-42-T, Trial Judgment (Jan. 31, 2005).

59 *Id.* at ¶ 295.

60 Hayashi, *supra* note 44, at 112–13.

> the destruction of life of armed enemies and other persons whose destruction is incidentally unavoidable by the armed conflicts of the war.[61]

What must be noted, however, is that the Tribunal was careful to speak here of military necessity as "permitting" or "sanctioning" measures only "subject to the laws of war." If a measure is forbidden by the laws of war, "military necessity" cannot authorize, justify, or excuse it. Far from being the equivalent of *kriegsräson,* this form of military necessity is its opposite.

This understanding of "military necessity" has the support of the overwhelming majority of the scholarly commentators. Thus Nobuo Hayashi wrote:

> To most commentators, military necessity has no place in international humanitarian law outside the confines of specific exceptional clauses. Permitting military necessity pleas *de novo* for deviations from unqualified rules would risk making the law unduly volatile and subservient to the exigencies of war. The relevant judicial decisions to date are also in support of this view.[62]

The justification most commonly tendered for this view is that the needs of military forces in armed conflict have already been taken into consideration when the relevant rules of *jus in bello* were framed.[63] Hence, it would overweight military values (and underweight humanitarian ones) if deviation from those rules were permitted, even in exceptionally urgent cases. Again, Hayashi stated the rationale well:

> Having taken military necessity into consideration, the law simply does not permit any deviation from the prescription of its norms on account of military necessity, save where such a possibility is expressly envisaged beforehand by way of exceptional clauses. The very existence of express military necessity exceptions in certain places indicates, *a contrario,* that no implicit military necessity exception, justification or excuse is intended elsewhere. That is so because, had the framers of unqualified rules intended to allow deviations on account of military necessity at all, they would have appended exceptional clauses to that effect. Accordingly, where a rule is unqualified, military necessity does not except, justify or excuse contrary behavior.[64]

---

61 *The Hostage Case, supra* note 47, 11 TWC 1254.

62 Hayashi, *supra* note 44, at 55 (footnotes and citations omitted); *accord* Schmitt, *Military Necessity and Humanity, supra* note 44, at 796, 805.

63 *See, e.g.,* William J. Fenrick, *supra* note 52, at 169.

64 Hayashi, *supra* note 44, at 56. The practical effect of these arguments can be illustrated by a situation depicted in the film *Saving Private Ryan.* A group of soldiers is sent on a mission behind enemy lines. They encounter an enemy combatant and capture him. They cannot carry out their mission, however, if they bring him along. If they release him, he will alert his comrades to their presence. The solution seems to be to kill him; but that is forbidden by the *jus in bello* (even though they might have killed him before taking him captive). *See* Protocol I, Art. 49. They must therefore abort their mission, after releasing the prisoner, returning with him, or otherwise ensuring his safety. *See Schmitt, Military Necessity and Humanity, supra* note 44, at 805.

Is it in fact correct to say that deviations from unqualified *jus in bello* rules in the name of military necessity are never permissible?

We offer four observations on that question. First, the reasoning in support of the view that deviations from unqualified rules are always impermissible seems to be strongest in the case of treaty rules, which ordinarily are carefully negotiated, with the participation of the armed forces of the states involved, and thus reflect the careful weighing of military and humanitarian interests.

Second, *jus in bello* includes exceptional clauses for the sake of humanitarian interests as well as for military ones. So, if deviations from unqualified rules are impermissible in the name of military necessity, then they should also be impermissible in the name of humanitarianism: *both* types of interests have been balanced together in unqualified rules.[65] Yet that conclusion seems uncertain, because deviation from unqualified rules for humanitarian reasons, in proper cases, should be permissible.[66] If such deviations from unqualified treaty rules are allowable for humanitarian reasons, why should they not be allowable in equally compelling cases of military necessity?

Third, even when considerations of "military necessity" are reflected in an unqualified rule, different interpretations of that rule may legitimately give greater (or lesser) weight to those interests.[67] In such cases, when interpreting what appears to be an "unqualified" rule, military practice may (reasonably) calibrate the balance between military necessity and humanitarian concerns in a way that gives greater weight to the former.

Fourth and most controversially, it is arguable that deviations from unqualified *jus in bello* rules in the name of military necessity might be permissible in certain unusually compelling circumstances, especially when the humanitarian purposes of the *jus in bello* would also be promoted by such deviations.

---

65 As noted in Hayashi, *supra* note 44, at 56–57.

66 For example, during the 1982 Falklands Islands War, the British held a large number of Argentine prisoners of war on military vessels pending their repatriation, in contravention of the unqualified rule in Article 22 of the Third Geneva Convention forbidding such practices. In relevant part, Article 22 states that "Prisoners of war may be interned only in premises located on land." This was done for humanitarian reasons: the conditions of detention were more humane than any realistic alternative, and repatriation would be possible sooner. Hayashi, *supra* note 44, at 56–57.

67 Consider, Article 18(1) of the Second Geneva Convention, which states that "[a]fter each engagement, Parties to the conflict shall, without delay, take all possible measures to search for and collect the shipwrecked, wounded and sick, to protect them against pillage and ill-treatment, to ensure their adequate care, and to search for the dead and prevent their being despoiled." The reference here to "all possible" rescue measures indicates that military necessity has been factored into the rule to some extent; but how broadly should the duty to rescue be understood? If one weights humanitarian interests more heavily, the efforts required could entail substantial risks for rescuers. But one might reasonably give the military interests greater weight. Accordingly, a leading U.S. legal expert on the law of submarine warfare wrote:

> The Second Geneva Convention requires all ships, including submarines, to "take all possible measures" to search for and collect survivors after each engagement. However, the practice of states during World War II suggests the rule more likely to be followed in war at sea, is more limited and applies *only to the extent that military exigencies permit.* If such humanitarian efforts would subject the submarine to undue additional hazard or prevent it from accomplishing its military mission, U.S. Navy guidance calls for the location of possible survivors to be passed at the first opportunity to a surface ship, aircraft, or shore facility capable of rendering assistance.

J. Ashley Roach, *Legal Aspects of Modern Submarine Warfare*, 6 Max Planck Y.B. of U.N. Law 367, 378–79 (2002) (emphasis added).

To be sure, "military necessity" has been abused too often when cited to defend departures from the rules and customs of war. Once that defense is admitted, it can be argued, the way to atrocities lies open. Indeed, surely it accords better with our initial moral intuitions to reject "military necessity" categorically as a defense for violating unqualified rules rather than to consider engaging in torturing prisoners or murdering innocent civilians.[68]

Yet, historical examples can be identified for both sides of the argument—some opponents citing French atrocities during the Algerian war for national liberation; [69] some proponents citing the U.S. use of nuclear weapons to end the war against Japan, thus avoiding an invasion that might have been more destructive that nuclear warfare even to the Japanese.[70] Thus, these questions should instill some doubt about the prevailing view that military necessity can never serve as a defense of the breach of an unqualified *jus in bello* rule. The central problem is that even assuming that the rules of *jus in bello* generally accommodate both military and humanitarian interests well, in some important applications they can disserve both. As Eric Posner has pointed out, the fact that "limiting the destructiveness of weapons and tactics does not necessarily minimize the loss of life and destruction of property" is deeply problematic for any view that assumes that *jus in bello* rules must serve humanitarian purposes.[71] "The contrary view, which

68 *See* Thomas Nagle, *War and Massacre*, 1 Phil. & Pub. Aff. 123, 126 (1972) ("[I]t is particularly important not to lose confidence in our absolutist intuitions, for they are often the only barrier before the abyss of utilitarian apologetics for large-scale murder."); *id.* at 128 (moral absolutism "requires us to forgo certain potentially useful military measures, such as the slaughter of hostages and prisoners. . . . It means that we cannot deliberate on whether such measures are justified by the fact that they will avert still greater evils, for as intentional measures they cannot be justified in terms of any consequences whatever."). For a more recent argument for maintaining an absolute ban on torture based on the singularity of each person, *see* Ahimud Gilead, Torture and Singularity, 19 Pub. Aff. Q. 26 (2005).

69 There, the French General Jacques Massu "justified the widespread use of torture and related practices by his para[troopers] during the Battle of Algiers as the only credible response ('an eye for an eye, a tooth for a tooth') to the [Algerian insurgents'] challenge for the control of the city of Algiers." Paul Kennedy & George J. Andreopoulos, *The Laws of War: Some Concluding Reflections* 214, 218, in Howard et al., The Laws of War, *supra* note 7.

70 Let us assume, for the sake of the argument, that the United States flagrantly violated the *jus in bello*, as was concluded in *Shimoda*. But what if the U.S. decision was intended to, and did, save many more lives than were lost in the attacks? Assume further that the lives saved included not only those of U.S. soldiers, airmen, and sailors (an interest subsumable under "military necessity"), but also those of Japanese civilians (who might otherwise have been starved to death through a prolonged Allied submarine blockade), Japanese military personnel (who would have died if the conflict with the United States and its Allies had dragged on), Russian combatants (Russia had just entered the war against Japan) and Chinese civilians and combatants (who would have died if Japan's campaigns in China had gone on longer). On those assumptions, the U.S. decision to use atomic weapons served humanitarian purposes, as well as the military interest in reducing the number of combatant deaths on our side. In light of all these circumstances, should the U.S. actions be considered permissible, or not?

For a carefully reasoned analysis of whether this was in fact the case, *see* Michael Bess, Choices Under Fire: Moral Dimensions of World War II 198–253 (2006); *see also* Fenrick, *The Rule of Proportionality*, *supra* note 42, at 121–22 ("If the proportionality equation is to be drawn between the innocent civilian casualties at Hiroshima and Nagasaki and the enormous casualties, many of them civilian, which would be caused by attempting to end the war in other ways, it is less clear that the losses were disproportionate."). For a passionate critique of any reasoning of this kind, *see* Eyal Weizman, The Least of All Possible Evils: Humanitarian Violence from Arendt to Gaza 8-10 (2011).

71 Eric Posner, *A Theory of the Laws of War*, 70 U. Chi. L. Rev. 297 (2003). Such was the vision of war of the Union Army General William Tecumseh Sherman during the American Civil War. In Sherman's view, showing humaneness to Southern civilians merely prolonged the war and aggravated the ensuing suffering. Sherman's outlook is epitomized in his September 12, 1864 letter to the City Council of Atlanta, Georgia (*available at* http://history.ncsu.edu/projects/

has been asserted time and again, is that short-term ruthlessness reduces long-term suffering. Massive destruction promises to end a war earlier rather than later, and to deter future wars. Nuclear weapons, it is often argued, kept the peace during the Cold War."[72] If compliance with the rules of *jus in bello* in some circumstances both inhibits the pursuit of military aims and causes more loss and suffering, then why, in those cases, should one comply with them?

f. Military Necessity as a Pervasive Element of the *Jus in Bello*

The final form that "military necessity" has taken is that of a pervasive element in forming the *jus in bello.* In that form, "military necessity" is said to be balanced against the "principle of humanity" in forming the *jus in bello.* Michael Schmitt has explained this form of military necessity as follows:

> Although the catalogue of direct references to military necessity in [*jus in bello*] is slim, the principle pervades the entire body of law by undergirding individual rules. In this central role, military necessity exists in equipoise with the principle of humanity, which seeks to limit the suffering and destruction incident to warfare. . . . [*Jus in bello*] represents a carefully thought out balance between the principles of military necessity and humanity.[73]

Schmitt's view of military necessity is accepted by many other scholars. For example, Major-General Rogers found an important role for military necessity as "an element of the rule of proportionality . . . in trying to achieve a balance between the, sometimes conflicting, aims of military success and humanitarian protection."[74]

This understanding of military necessity appears to account, not only for discrete rules of the *jus in bello,* but also for its most basic features. Take, for instance, the decision of the drafters of Protocol I to relax the previously stringent requirements for entitlement to the privileges and immunities of being a lawful "combatant." Before Protocol I, it had generally been assumed that the protections accorded to combatants by the Hague and Geneva Conventions generally required them to be members of a state's regular armed forces, or at any rate to wear some fixed distinctive emblem or sign that distinguished them from civilians and to carry their arms openly.[75] The chief rationale behind these requirements was that if combatants were readily

---

cwnc/items/show/23). On Sherman, *see generally* John Bennett Walters, General William T. Sherman and Total War, 14 J. Southern Hist. 447 (1948).

72 Posner, *supra* n. 71. For a discussion and critique of this common position, *see* Richard M. Price, The Chemical Weapons Taboo 38–43 (1997).

73 Schmitt, *Military Necessity and Humanity, supra* note 44, at 796, 798.

74 Rogers, Law on the Battlefield, *supra* note 42, at 7.

75 Certain categories of exceptions were permitted, as for example, the *levée en masse* (or "people in arms"). For the general rule, *see Osmin bin Haji Mohamed Ali et al. v. Public Prosecutor,* Privy Council (U.K.), July 29, 1968, [1969] 1 A.C. 430

identifiable to each other, the risk that they would mistakenly fire on noncombatants would be significantly reduced. By modifying these requirements in response to the claims made on behalf of guerrilla fighters in national liberation wars, Protocol I rebalanced the Geneva Conventions' relative weighting of necessity and humanity in favor of the claim of necessity and against the humanitarian interest in heightened protection for civilians.

2. The Principle of Distinction

The principle of distinction, like that of military necessity, lies at the core of *jus in bello.* At a first approximation, the principle of distinction authorizes the intentional use of force against combatants, but prohibits its intentional use against non-combatants. Otherwise put, combatants are both legally "privileged" to use force, but also legally "liable" to have force directed against them.[76] Non-combatants or "civilians" enjoy a legal "immunity" against uses of force directed against them.

There can be no question that the principle of distinction—and more especially the allied principle of civilian immunity—is foundational in contemporary *jus in bello.* As the Supreme Court of Israel explained in its 2005 decision, *Public Committee against Torture in Israel v. Gov't of Israel*:

> Customary international law regarding armed conflicts distinguishes between combatants and military targets, and non-combatants, in other words, civilians and civilian objectives. . . . According to the basic principle of distinction, the balancing point between the State's military need and the other side's combatants and military objectives is not the same as the balancing point between the state's military need and the other side's civilians and civilian objectives. In general, combatants and military objectives are legitimate targets for military attack. Their lives and bodies are endangered by the combat. They can be killed and wounded. . . . Opposite the combatants and military objectives stand the civilians and civilian objectives. Military attack directed at them is forbidden.[77]

(persons claiming to be members of Indonesian Armed Forces, who had committed acts of sabotage in Singapore during what was assumed to be an international armed conflict in which the Geneva Conventions applied, and who were arrested while in civilian clothes, were held not entitled to prisoner of war status). On the *levée en masse, see, e.g.,* R. Ernest Dupuy, *The Nature of Guerrilla Warfare,* 12 Pacific Aff. 138, 141, 144–45 (1939).

76 *See Prosecutor v. Galić,* Case No. IT-98-29-T at ¶ 48 n.88 (Dec. 5, 2003) ("Combatant status implies not only being considered a legitimate military objective, but also being able to kill or wound other combatants or individuals participating in hostilities, and being entitled to special protections when hors-de-combat, *i.e.,* when surrendered, captured or wounded.").

77 *Public Committee against Torture in Israel v. Gov't of Israel,* HCJ 769/02 at ¶ 23 (Sup. Ct. Israel 2005) (*available at* http://www.haguejusticeportal.net/Docs/NLP/Israel/Targetted_Killings_Supreme_Court_13-12-2006.pdf). We shall defer until later chapters such questions as how to define "combatants" and "civilians," whether there are both "privileged"

After the Second World War, Sir Hersch Lauterpacht wrote:

> [I]t is in [the] prohibition, which is a clear rule of law, of intentional terrorization—or destruction—of the civilian population as an avowed or obvious object of attack that lies the last vestige of the claim that war can be legally regulated at all. Without that irreducible principle of restraint there is no limit to the licence and depravity of force.[78]

Moreover, in contemporary *jus in bello,* the principle of distinction is firmly established in both treaty and customary law.[79]

Indeed, the principle, especially insofar as it confirms the immunity of civilians, is considered "sacrosanct."[80] Civilian immunity is not to be balanced against military interests or necessities. It is, in that sense, an absolute. Thus, the ICTY Trial Chambers in the 2003 *Galić* case was correct to reject formulations in earlier opinions that had characterized deliberate attacks against civilians as unlawful only if they were "not justified by military necessity."[81] Rather, the Court pointed out, the applicable rule (Article 51(2) of Protocol I) "states in clear language that civilians and the civilian population as such should not be the object of attack. It does not mention any exceptions. In particular, it does not contemplate derogating from this rule by invoking military necessity."[82] Similarly, on several recent occasions, the United Nations Security Council stressed the overriding importance of protecting civilians during armed conflict. For example, in reauthorizing the International Security Assistance Force (ISAF) in Afghanistan in 2008, the Council recognized:

> the efforts taken by ISAF and other international forces to minimize the risk of civilian casualties, and *call[ed] on* them to take additional robust efforts in this regard, notably by the continuous review of tactics and procedures and the conduct of after-action reviews and investigations in cooperation with the Afghan Government in cases where civilian casualties have occurred and when the Afghan Government finds these joint investigations appropriate.[83]

---

and "unprivileged" combatants, what constitutes "direct participation in hostilities," and so on. Here, we are chiefly concerned with exploring the development and bases of the principle of distinction.

78 Sir Hersch Lauterpacht, *The Problem of the Revision of the Law of War,* 29 Brit. Y.B. Int'l L. 360, 368 (1952).

79 *See Public Committee against Torture in Israel v. Gov't of Israel, supra* note 77, at ¶ 29 (Article 51(2) of Additional Protocol I "constitutes customary international law").

80 *Galić, supra* note 76, at ¶ 57 n.102 (Dec. 5, 2003). For a more critical view, see Jeremy Rabkin & John C. Yoo, *A Return to Coercion: International Law and New Weapons Technologies,* 42 Hofstra L. Rev. 1187 (2014).

81 *Galić, supra* note 76, at ¶ 42.

82 *Id.* at ¶ 44.

83 S.C. Res. 1833 (2008).

Likewise, in authorizing Member States to intervene in Libya in 2011, the Council permitted them "to take all necessary measures . . . to protect civilians and civilian populated areas under threat of attack in the Libyan Arab Jamahiriya, including Benghazi, while excluding a foreign occupation force of any form on any part of Libyan territory."[84] In effect, outside intervention was authorized, but only for the specific purpose of protecting endangered civilians. Indeed, press accounts reported that NATO sought to avoid killing, not merely disproportionately many, but *any,* civilians.[85]

Yet despite its signal importance in current international law, the actual codification of the principle of distinction came late. It was not explicitly mentioned in treaty law until 1977, when it appeared as Article 48 of Protocol I:

> In order to ensure respect for and protection of the civilian population and civilian objects, the Parties to the conflict shall at all times distinguish between the civilian population and combatants and between civilian objects and military objectives and accordingly shall direct their operations only against military objectives.[86]

To be sure, the principle of distinction was adumbrated well before 1977. We now consider the historical development of the principle of distinction and critique the varying rationales that have been offered to defend it. We then offer some concluding thoughts on the principle of distinction.

a. Development of the Principle of Distinction

Medieval Latin Christianity accorded immunity to various categories of non-combatants. Pope Gregory IX identified eight such classes, including monks, friars, pilgrims, travelers, merchants, peasant cultivators, women, and children.[87] Medieval writers like Christine de Pizan, a French noblewoman, argued on the basis of chivalric values for the immunity of the poor and

84 S.C. Res. 1973 (2011).

85 *See* Con Coughlin, *Libya: On a Wing and a Prayer,* The Telegraph (May 29, 2001) (*available at* http://www.telegraph.co.uk/comment/columnists/concoughlin/8545476/Libya-On-a-wing). Critics of NATO's performance argued that by refusing to tolerate even lawful levels of civilian casualties, NATO was prolonging the Libyan conflict and ultimately causing more civilian deaths. *See* Anthony H. Cordesman, *Libya: Will the Farce Stay With US (And France and Britain)?,* Center for Strategic & International Studies (Apr. 20, 2011) (*available at* http://csis.org/publication/libya-will-farce-stay-us-and-france-and-britain).

86 *See* Protocol Additional to the Geneva Conventions or 12 August 1949, and Relating to the Protocol of Victims of International Armed Conflicts (Protocol I), 16 ILM 1391 (1978) (entered into force 1985).

87 *See* Hugo Slim, *Why Protect Civilians? Innocence, Immunity and Enmity in War,* 79 Int'l Aff. (Royal Institute of Int'l Aff.) 481, 493 (2003) [hereinafter Slim, *Why Protect Civilians?*]; James T. Johnson, *The Meaning of Non-Combatant Immunity in the Just War/Limited War Tradition,* 39 J. Am. Acad. Rel. 151, 154–55 (1971). For general accounts of the emergence of the doctrine of non-combatant immunity, *see* Helen M. Kinsella, The Image Before the Weapon: A Critical History of the Distinction between Combatant and Civilian (2011); Gunnar Lind, *Genesis of the Civilian in the Western World, 1500-2000,* in Gunner Lind (ed.), Civilians at War from the Fifteenth Century to the Present 44 (2013). We would note, however, that

innocent.[88] Both secular and religious jurists in the late Middle Ages, including the fourteenth century writer Lucas de Penna and the fifteenth century theologian Antonino of Florence, also affirmed the immunity of various categories of non-combatants.[89] In the early modern period, legal scholars like the Spanish Dominican Francesco de Vitoria maintained that it was always wrong, even in a just war, intentionally to kill the "innocent."[90] Hugo Grotius wrote that even though "[f]rom the moment we are at war, all those who belong to the hostile state become our enemies," nonetheless "our right to wound and kill being founded on self-defence, or on the resistance opposed to us, we can with justice wound or take the life on none except those who take an active part in the war."[91]

Nineteenth century codifications, while characteristically emphasizing the protection of combatants rather than civilians, did shelter civilians as well, at least indirectly. Thus, the preamble to the 1868 Declaration of St. Petersburg affirms that "the only legitimate object which States should endeavour to accomplish during war is to weaken the military forces of the enemy" and that "for this purpose it is sufficient to disable the greatest possible number of men." Attacks on civilians or civilian property would seem not, except incidentally, to "weaken the military forces of the enemy," nor to "disable the greatest possible number of [fighting] men." Here we can discern, at least in part, the contemporary legal principle of non-combatant immunity. A more explicit nineteenth century statement of the principle of discrimination (though here qualified by military necessity) can be found in the Lieber Code.[92] Reflecting these humanitarian nineteenth century views, the English legal scholar J.M. Spaight wrote in 1911 that "[t]he separation of armies and peaceful inhabitants into two distinct classes is perhaps the greatest triumph of International Law."[93]

Thus, during the first part of the twentieth century, the principle of distinction, though largely uncodified, could arguably be said to have emerged as a part of customary international law. In the aftermath of the First World War, which provided a glimpse of the terrifying potential of air

---

the clergy, pilgrims, the poor, women, and even children played an active part, including combat, in Church-sponsored crusades. *See* Walter Porges, *The Clergy, the Poor, and the Non-Combatants on the First Crusade,* 21 Speculum 1 (1946).

88 *See* Susan J. Dudash, *Christine de Pizan and the "Menu People,"* 78 Speculum 788, 798–99 (2003); Johnson, *supra* note 87, at 156.

89 *See* Richard Shelly Hartigan, *Noncombatant Immunity: Reflections on Its Origins and Present Status,* 29 Rev. Pol. 204, 214–15 (1967).

90 Vitoria included specific classes of persons, among them women and children, among the "innocent," and extended the principle of immunity to wars with non-Christians. *See* Richard Shelly Hartigan, *Francesco de Vitoria and Civilian Immunity,* 1 Pol. Theory 79, 84 (1973).

91 Robert Wayne Gehring, *Protection of Civilian Infrastructure,* 42 Law & Contemp. Probs. 86, 87 (1978).

92 Article 22 of that Code states: "As civilization has advanced during the last centuries, so has likewise steadily advanced, especially in war on land, the distinction between the private individual belonging to a hostile country and the hostile country itself, with its men in arms. The principle has been more and more acknowledged that the unarmed citizen is to be spared in person, property and honor as much as the exigencies of war will admit."

93 James Spaight, War Rights on Land (1911).

warfare,[94] states attempted to erect legal barriers to the intentional or indiscriminate bombardment of their cities and civilian populations from the air. The 1923 Hague Draft Rules of Aerial Warfare (which were never ratified) would have provided that "[a]erial bombardment for the purpose of terrorizing the civilian population, of destroying or damaging private property not of a military character, or of injuring non-combatants is prohibited" (Article 22) and that "[a]erial bombardment is legitimate only when directed at a military objective" (Article 24(1)). In 1932, the General Commission of the League of Nations Disarmament Conference adopted a resolution providing that "air attack against the civilian population shall be absolutely prohibited."[95] A unanimous resolution of the League of Nations Assembly, adopted on September 30, 1938, declared that "[t]he intentional bombing of civilian populations is illegal" and that "[o]bjectives aimed at from the air must be legitimate military objectives and must be identifiable." Also in 1938, British Prime Minister Neville Chamberlain told the House of Commons that belligerents were "prohibited to launch attacks against civilian populations as such . . . [and] distinction must be made at all times between persons taking part in the hostilities and members of the civilian population to the effect that the latter be spared as much as possible."[96]

Of course, none of these pronouncements was of the least avail in preventing the enormous losses of civilian life and property that occurred as a direct and intended result of aerial bombardments during the Second World War. Nor, despite the fact that British and American leaders had condemned the bombardment of civilians before the War, did the Allied governments observe such restraints.[97] The atomic attacks on the civilian populations of Hiroshima and Nagasaki were merely the culmination of the practice of area bombardment that the United States and Great Britain had engaged in for years against their German and Japanese adversaries, a practice that itself grew out of the pre-War military doctrines of both states.[98] British and American bombing objectives were set out in the "Casablanca directive," which resulted from the January 1943 meeting in Casablanca, Morocco between President Franklin D. Roosevelt and Prime Minister Winston Churchill. Issued to British and American Bomber Commands on February 4, 1943, the directive declared that the primary objectives of the Allies' bombing

---

94 The German "Gotha raids" against London and southern England of 1917–18, though causing few casualties, caused consternation in Britain. The "Smuts memorandum" of 1917 warned of the presciently of the potential scope and power of air war. *See* Ward Thomas, The Ethics of Destruction: Norms and Force in International Relations, 104, 106 (2001).

95 Lester Nurick, *The Distinction between Combatant and Noncombatant in the Law of War*, 39 Am. J. Int'l L. 680, 691 (1945).

96 R. George Wright, *Noncombatant Immunity: A Case Study in the Relation Between International Law and Morality*, 67 Notre Dame L. Rev. 335, 337 (1991/2).

97 *See, e.g.*, Slim, *Why Protect Civilians?*, *supra* note 87, at 489–91.

98 For U.S. and British pre-War military doctrines of air war and their common emphasis on the punishment of civilians, *see* Thomas, *supra* note 94, at 110–25; Robert A. Pape, *Bombing to Win: Air Power and Coercion in War* 58–66 (1996). For an account of how the legal and moral thinking of the period was woven together with U.S. doctrines of air power, *see* Lt. Col. Peter R. Faber, *The Development of US Strategic Bombing Doctrine in the Interwar Years: Moral and Legal?*, 7 U.S. A.F. Acad. J. Legal Stud. 111 (1996/97).

campaign included "the undermining of the morale of the German people to the point where their capacity for armed resistance is fatally weakened."[99]

The *jus in bello,* as the Allies interpreted it, fully sanctioned those practices. Telford Taylor, the Chief Counsel at the war crimes trials at Nuremberg (and later a professor at the Columbia School of Law), stated in his final report on the trials that "[m]any of the provisions of the 1907 Hague Convention . . . were antiquarian. . . . [T]he ruins of German and Japanese cities. . . bore witness that aerial bombardment of cities and factories has become a recognized part of modern warfare as carried on by all nations."[100]

The outcomes of the Nuremberg and Tokyo Trials supported Taylor's conclusion. "Destructive methods of warfare by all sides, involving the massacre of civilians, were not condemned or even legally challenged. By leaving morale bombing and other attacks on civilians unchallenged, the Tribunal conferred legal legitimacy on such practices."[101] In the *Einsatzgruppen Case,* a Nuremberg Trials decision handed down by a U.S. military tribunal, the court condoned attacks on civilian populations when designed to induce surrender, including attacks with atomic weapons.[102] With exquisite irony, another U.S. military tribunal sitting in Yokohama convicted a Japanese military commission for having tried and punished two captured American flyers for having carpet-bombed Kobe and Osaka, sentencing the Japanese Judicial Officer on the commission to hang.[103]

U.S. Army Captain in the Judge Advocate General's Department very reasonably concluded in 1945 that the principle of distinction "has been so whittled down by the demands of military necessity that it has become more apparent than real."[104] Another legal scholar writing in 1945 considered "the inviolability or immunity of civilians from the effects of military operations" to be an "irrational and sentimental popular opinion. . . . [I]t has become logical to bring pressure to bear on the civilian population in order that they may induce the government to yield."[105] One

99 The Casablanca directive is reproduced in Winston S. Churchill, The Second World War (Vol. 5): Closing the Ring 458 (1951, 1985).

100 Quoted in Tami Davis Biddle, *Air Power,* in Howard et al. The Laws of War, *supra* note 7, at 146, 155.

101 Chris af Jochnick & Roger Normand, *The Legitimation of Violence: A Critical History of the Laws of War,* 35 Harv. Int'l L. J. 49, 91 (1994).

102 "[T]here . . . is no parallelism between an act of legitimate warfare, namely the bombing of a city, with concomitant loss of civilian life, and the premeditated killing of all members of certain categories of the civilian population in occupied territory. . . . [A]s grave a military action as is an air bombardment, *whether with the usual bombs or by atomic bomb,* the . . . only purpose of the bombing is to effect the surrender of the bombed nation." *U.S. v. Otto Ohlendorf et al.,* (Case # 9), 4 War Crimes Comm'n, U.N., Trials of War Criminals Before the Nuremberg Tribunals Under Control Council Law No. 10 at 1, 467 (1948) (emphasis added).

103 *See* Robert W. Miller, *War Crimes Trials at Yokohama,* 15 Brook. L. Rev. 191, 207–08 (1948/9).

104 Nurick, *supra* note 95, at 680.

105 Ellery Stowell, *The Laws of War and the Atomic Bomb,* 39 Am. J. Int'l L. 784, 785 (1945).

scholarly commentator has written that the weather "had a greater impact than the laws of war or theories of morality" on the Anglo-American bombing campaigns.[106]

Yet, today, the principle of distinction, perhaps now more than ever before, is entrenched, not merely in the *jus in bello,* but in the practices of Western militaries and the consciousness of Western publics.[107] Rather than being discarded after the Second World War as impracticable and obsolete, the principle came over the course of the Cold War to be more widely honored, leading to its codification in 1977. Indeed, Western governments are deeply embarrassed even by lawful air strikes that cause civilian casualties.[108] During the early stages of the First Gulf War, when two U.S. stealth fighters unintentionally killed over 200 Iraqi civilians (including women and children) in the Al Firdos bunker (which had been identified as an Iraqi command-and-control center), the Chairman of the U.S. Joint Chiefs of Staff, Gen. Colin Powell, and the U.S. theater commander, Gen. Norman Schwarzkopf, both recognized that the strike had caused major political and media problems for the Allied Coalition, and all but ended the strategic air war campaign against objectives in Baghdad (including the Iraqi leadership).[109] In other words, Western governments and publics seem so committed to the principle of distinction that even compliance with the legal restraints that codify the principle seems insufficient.[110] Does the principle deserve its central place in the *jus in bello*? In the following section, we explore the question of the justifications for the principle of distinction.

---

106 Tami Davis Biddle, *Bombing by the Square Yard: Sir Arthur Harris at War, 1942-1945,* 21 Int'l Hist. R. 626, 662 (1999).

107 This change may be due in part to the reputed "CNN effect," which "postulates that public opinion can be so moved by images of suffering that it demands action, even where inappropriate." Lawrence Freedman, *Victims and Victors: Reflections on the Kosovo War,* 26 Rev. Int'l Stud. 335, 338 (2000). Whether the "CNN effect" is genuine or not is debated. *See, e.g.,* Piers Robinson, *The CNN Effect: Can the News Media Drive Foreign Policy?,* 25 Rev. Int'l Stud. 301, 308 (1999) (finding it open whether the media have triggered humanitarian interventions, but suggesting a theoretical model that "predicts media influence on government policy only when there exist[] policy that is uncertain and media coverage that is framed to advocate a particular course of action"); Peter Viggo Jakobsen, *Focus on the CNN Effect Misses the Point: The Real Media Impact on Conflict Management Is Invisible and Indirect,* 37 J. Peace Res. 131, 138 (2000) (claiming that "the impact of media coverage on Western conflict management is less direct than the CNN effect argument suggests. Its direct impact in the pre- and post-violence phases is negligible since they receive very little coverage. Direct impact is greater in the violence phase but limited, nevertheless. The CNN effect is only relevant in a handful of cases, and even though media generated pressure may make a difference to policy by putting military intervention on the agenda in situations where governments are reluctant to use force, interventions are unlikely to follow unless they can be conducted quickly with low risk of casualties.").

108 This was true of the U.S. government during the War in Vietnam. Restraints on the aerial bombardment of targets in North Vietnam were imposed, not only for legal reasons, but also because of the effects that even lawful attacks were expected to have on domestic and world public opinion. The North Vietnamese government was, however, largely successful in its efforts to portray the U.S. attacks as systematically unlawful. *See* Robert A. Pape, Bombing to Win: Air Power and Coercion in War 195–210 (1996); W. Hays Parks, *Rolling Thunder and the Law of War,* 22 Air U. Rev. 2 (1982); W. Hays Parks, *Linebacker and the Law of War,* 34 Air U. L. Rev. 2 (1983).

109 *See* Thomas, *supra* note 94, at 87–88.

110 Restrictions on targeting due to political rather than legal constraints also narrowed the U.S. bombing campaign in the 1960s during the Vietnam War—to the point, one writer argues, of condemning it to ineffectiveness. *See* W. Hays Parks, *Rolling Thunder and the Law of War,* 22 Air U. Rev. 2 (1982); *see also* W. Hays Parks, *Linebacker an d the Law of War,* 34 Air U. L. Rev. 2 (1983).

b. Rationales for the Principle of Distinction

The principle of distinction has two aspects: one is the immunity of non-combatants from intentional or indiscriminate violence; the other is the liability of combatants to such violence. Can one justify this unequal treatment? "[W]hich is the greater evil—the humane killing of non-combatants or the burning of combatants to death by flame-throwers?"[111]

The most persuasive arguments have turned on the distinction between war as a conflict between states rather than peoples; on the distinction between the "innocence" of non-combatants and the "guilt" of combatants; and, finally, on the distinction between dangerousness of combatants and the non-dangerousness of non-combatants. We consider each set of arguments in turn.

i. War as a Conflict between States

A classic defense of the principle of distinction is to be found in the writings of Jean-Jacques Rousseau. Rousseau argued that war is a relation between *states,* not between individuals. Thus when war exists, one state has a right to seek another state's defeat or even destruction. The destruction of an enemy state does not require the destruction of its *people,* but only of those who defend that state by arms, and who therefore, in a sense, are that state. Rousseau wrote:

> [w]ar is not . . . a relationship between one man and another, but a relationship between one State and another, in which individuals are enemies only by accident, not as men, nor even as citizens, but as soldiers. . . . Since the aim of war is the destruction of the enemy State, one has the right to kill its defenders as long as they bear arms; but as soon as they lay down their arms and surrender they cease to be enemies or the enemy's instruments, and become simply men once more, and one no longer has a right over their life. It is sometimes possible to kill the State without killing a single one of its members; and war confers no right that is not necessary to its end.[112]

Yet, Rousseau's argument suffers from at least two major weaknesses, both of which became visible in the twentieth century. One weakness concerned total war, the other with non-international war.[113]

111 Clark, *supra* note 20, at 93.

112 Jean-Jacques Rousseau, The Social Contract and other Later Political Writings 46-7 (Victor Gourevitch ed. 1997).

113 Indeed, both total war and guerrilla war came to the fore not long after Rousseau, during the French Revolutionary and Napoleonic Wars. *See* David A. Bell, *The First Total War: Napoleon's Europe and the Birth of Warfare as We Know It* (2007).

In total wars (such as the First and Second World Wars[114]), it is plausible to say that one "people" is at war with another "people." The majority of a belligerent's civilian population is likely to be engaged, directly or indirectly, in sustaining the state's war effort. Demoralizing the civilian population's support for the government and its will to resist are considered to be essential to victory. Methods aimed at causing civilian suffering or death are held to be legitimate (like the British blockade of Germany in the First World War). Even the extermination or enslavement of the enemy's population may be a major war aim, as was the case with Germany's attack on Russia in the Second World War. Rousseau's distinction between combatants and non-combatants became harder to justify in theory and vastly more difficult to observe in practice.

The problem was even worse with non-international war, such as wars of national independence, guerrilla wars, and civil wars. In these wars, one of the parties to the conflict is not a state. In short, whatever its merits in cases in which war is a relation between state and state, Rousseau's argument has less force when war is a contest between one people and another, or between a state and a people or popular movement.

ii. "Innocence" and "Guilt"

Forms of the principle of distinction have also traditionally been defended in terms of the "innocence" of non-combatants and the "guilt" of combatants. Because combatants choose to engage in conflict with other combatants, it is argued, they may properly attack and kill one another. Those who consent to combat must bear its risks. But non-combatants have not chosen to subject themselves to these risks; and combatants have no right to use violence against them.

Whether or not such reasoning is persuasive when applied to armed combat between knightly castes or other élite groups of military professionals, it has little application to wars between conscript armies. Moreover, for many non-conscripts, there may be little choice whether or not to enlist: military careers have often been the only realistic choice of occupation for the poor and uneducated.[115] And even when alternative occupations are open to them, recruits may enlist because they have poor information about their governments' policies or war aims: government propaganda and dominant opinion may convey false or misleading accounts of the objectives for which recruits will find themselves fighting.

---

114 The influential Italian inter-war theorist of air power, Giulio Douhet, wrote in 1921: "The prevailing forms of social organization have given war a character of national totality – that is, the entire population and all the resources of a nation are sucked into the maw of war. And, since society is now definitely evolving along this line, it is within the power of human foresight to see now that future wars will be total in character and scope." Giulio Douhet, *The Command of the Air* 5-6 (Dino Ferrari trans. 1942).

115 A recent study has found that the poor and uneducated have been disproportionately many among U.S. military casualties in the wars in Korea, Vietnam, and Iraq. *See* Douglas L. Kriner & Francis X. Shen, The Casualty Gap: Causes and Consequences of American Wartime Inequalities (2010).

More sophisticated and plausible defenses of the principle of distinction in terms of "innocence" and "guilt" have, however, been advanced. In the formulation given by Robert Fullinwider, the argument draws on an analogy from the criminal law.[116] Consider the case in which Attacker (A) opens fire on a street against Target (T). Posit that A might have any one of several different motives for the attack: that A has been urged on by his wife; that he is in debt to mobsters for a sum he cannot pay, and has accepted their offer to cancel the debt if he kills T, a crusading district attorney; or whatever. The criminal law permits T to defend himself from A by using lethal force himself: self-defense allows T, in those circumstances, to kill A. But even if T knows the motive for A's attack, he may not turn violence on A's wife (although she may be urging A on) or on the mobsters (although they may be watching from a nearby parked car). Fullinwider argued that the same criminal law principles should govern the analysis of armed conflict. A state no less than an individual may kill in self-defense. Thus, it may use lethal force against those who attack it, placing it in direct and immediate jeopardy. These are, Fullinwider says, the armed forces of the attacking state. But just as A may not attack T's wife or the mobsters watching nearby, so a state may not attack an enemy state's noncombatants, whatever their role in causing the attack. Justifiable self-defense does not extend that far, either in the case of an individual or the state.

However, appealing as Fullinder's argument may be, it is ultimately unsatisfactory. First, T undoubtedly has a legal right under the criminal law to defend himself from A. But if T counter-attacks, does A have a legal right to defend himself from T? The answer is that A does not; he merely compounds his original wrong in attacking T if he responds to T's counter-attack with continuing lethal force, except where the victim has a duty to retreat.[117] Under the *jus in bello,* however, even the armed forces of an aggressor are normally considered to have the right to defend themselves against the armed forces of the victim state. In other words, the wrongness of an attack under the *jus ad bellum* does not deprive an aggressor's forces of their right to defend themselves in battle. So while Fullinder's account might justify civilian immunity, it does not (fully) explain combatants' liability.

Second, under the criminal law, T is only entitled to engage in reasonably necessary self-defense.[118] So if T can disable A by wounding rather than killing A, he may not kill A, and in some common law jurisdictions if T can avoid being killed by fleeing from A, he has a duty to retreat. But in armed conflict, it is generally held, an enemy's armed forces are liable to be killed;

116 Robert K. Fullinwider, *War and Innocence,* 5 Phil. & Pub. Aff. 90 (1975). Thomas Nagel made a similar argument, although it is based on a moral principle—respect for other persons—rather than on criminal law. As Nagel articulated it, this is the principle that "whatever one does to another person intentionally must be aimed at him as a subject, with the intention that he receive it as a subject. It should manifest an attitude to *him* rather than just to the situation, and he should be able to recognize it and identify himself as its object." Thomas Nagel, *War and Massacre,* 1 Phil. & Pub. Aff. 123, 136 (1972).

117 *See* Diamond, Levine & Bernstein, Understanding Torts 36–37 (5th ed. 2013) (indicating that the "duty to retreat" is a minority view among U.S. jurisdictions).

118 Similar principles govern tort law. *Cf. id.* at 35–39.

there is no general duty to incapacitate rather than kill the enemy. Moreover, a defending force has no legal duty to avoid combat or retreat, if that can be done safely. Once combat is offered, it may be joined.

Third, unless under a doctrine of reasonable mistake, although T may not fire on A's wife or the mobsters (unless, by participating in A's attack, they make themselves "attackers" as well), the state, acting through the criminal law, subjects them to punishment for their roles in bringing about A's crime.[119] Thus, even if their "guilt" does not justify T in attacking them, it will be nonetheless be punished under the domestic law of a well-functioning criminal justice system. But what about "guilty" civilians who have incited, paid for, and supported a war of aggression? Absent a functioning system of international criminal justice, who will punish them, if not the armed forces of the victim state? Perhaps they should go unpunished, as the principle of discrimination would imply. But then the defense of that principle, to be complete, would need to show why such punishment should be withheld.

Accordingly, we think that the combatant/noncombatant distinction cannot fully be explained and justified in terms of the guilt/innocence distinction made by criminal law and the doctrine of self-defense.

iii. Dangerousness/Non-dangerousness

Both of the previous accounts hint at another possible justification for the principle of distinction: that combatants may always be attacked because of their dangerousness, while noncombatants may never be attacked because they are non-dangerous. Rather than relying on an analogy from the criminal law, this argument would invoke a comparison to the civil law's treatment of dangerous persons and objects. Thus, rather than comparing enemy armed forces to assailants using deadly force in violation of the criminal law, one might compare them, for example, to the violently insane, who may be civilly confined, not as punishment for crime, but as an administrative measure for the protection of others.[120]

Ordinarily, of course, the civil law does not permit the use of deadly force against human persons who are deemed dangerous. Less violent measures, such as confinement and treatment, are usually employed. But the destruction of dangers is commonly authorized by the civil law with respect to animals or material objects. It may be permissible, such as to destroy a stand

---

119 *Cf. id.* at 36 ("The belief need not be correct, however.").

120 Thomas Nagel's defense of the principle of distinction has some resemblance to the argument here. Although Nagel based his defense on the idea of the "innocence" of noncombatants, he was not referring to "moral innocence." Rather, "innocent" in his argument "means 'currently harmless,' and it is opposed not to 'guilty' but to 'doing harm.'" Nagel, *War and Massacre, supra* note 116, at 139. Thus, he distinguished combatants from noncombatants "on the basis of their immediate threat or harmfulness." *Id.* at 140. Combatants may legitimately be attacked because "they are armed and are using their arms in pursuit of certain objectives." *Id.* at 140. Attacks on non-combatants are illegitimate because such attacks are directed to what is "peripheral" rather than to "the cause of danger." *Id.*

of red cedar trees infected with a rust plant disease that, if not controlled, would spread to a neighboring apple orchard.[121] Can the principle of distinction be defended on a similar basis?

Again, the suggested analogy is imperfect, at least in a range of cases. Not all enemy combatants are dangerous, even if they are armed. Yet, under the usual understanding of the *jus in bello*, all may properly be targeted. Nor are all non-combatants "innocent," even in the sense of posing no threat of harm. Consider a U.S. soldier, who is on duty at a military base in Singkiang, far from the European theater, in early 1945, in a kitchen on the base peeling potatoes for dinner. The soldier may lawfully be killed by a stray German combatant, even though he poses only a highly attenuated danger to Germany. Conversely, civilians may pose significant dangers. A physicist working in 1944 at a university laboratory or research institute on the design of an atomic bomb is a far graver threat to Germany than the soldier in Singkiang; a Nazi radio propagandist inciting troops on the Eastern Front to murder Jews and Bolsheviks may be more dangerous than a German corporal drinking coffee in a café in occupied Denmark.

Furthermore, this argument, like the one that preceded it, does not explain why we should be legally justified in killing enemy combatants when it may be possible merely to incapacitate them, if incapacitation is sufficient to contain their dangerousness. No such duty to mitigate lethal force exists under the *jus in bello.*

c. Concluding Thoughts on the Principle of Distinction

The principle of distinction has deep roots in human nature. We are appalled at gratuitous cruelty to the helpless or those unable to defend themselves. Our sense of justice rebels at rude violence to the innocent. We feel an aching pity at the sight of children burned by incendiary weapons or left mutilated by cluster bombs. The distraught woman who carries a dead child in her arms is indelibly etched in our imaginations. The victims of war remind us of our common humanity.

We are likely to be far less outraged when violence is inflicted on those who bring it with them and who can defend themselves against it. Force can legitimately be used to answer those who are guilty of using force. We do not pity those who would shatter the political communities to which we belong, steal our resources, or impose on us a hated way of life. Even when we do not consider an armed enemy to be a criminal, we may consider him to be a deadly threat, and we think it justified to do what is necessary to meet that threat.

One modern defender, in the aftermath of the rampant violation of the principle during the wars of the last century, supports the distinction (or at least the idea of civilian immunity) in the following way:

---

121 *See Miller v. Schoene,* 276 U.S. 272 (1928).

> At root, there seem to be three quite obvious reasons why civilians should be protected in war. These spring respectively from arguments of morality, prudence and self-interest. First, because all life is precious, it is morally right to limit violence as much as possible. Second, prudential arguments suggest that it is wise not to kill and wreck more widely than necessary, because this will mean you leave less to conquer and the extremity of your violence may raise new enemies and make peace more difficult to make. Finally, because the conduct of war can often be reciprocal, it is in your interest not to do certain things to your enemy lest he do them to you in return.[122]

Yet, these arguments may be subject to the following objections. First, if "all life is precious," then the lives of military combatants are precious too, and, if it is "morally right to limit violence as much as possible," then it is right to limit violence against combatants.[123] Second, prudence indeed instructs us that "it is wise not to kill and wreck more widely than necessary."[124] But that recognition cannot justify the principle of non-combatant immunity, if only because military commanders have often argued (sometimes with good reason) that military necessity requires them to target and attack civilians. Third, reciprocity can indeed induce states at won not to attack their adversaries' civilians, for fear that those adversaries might respond in kind. But the principle of distinction is supposed to be binding even as against an adversary that does not observe it.

Thus, while the experience of the twentieth century suggests a range of these considerations that bear on, and support, the principle of distinction, none of them fully and satisfyingly justifies it. Perhaps, as Michael Walzer suggested, explicating what he called the "war convention," its justification is "conventional," not "natural," to be found in experience, practice, and tradition, not in abstract reasoning or deductive logic.[125]

3. The Principle of Proportionality

Proportionality "is recognized today as a general principle of international law" and "plays a central role in the law regarding armed conflict."[126] Thomas Franck has identified three different settings in which the principle of proportionality is relevant to the law of armed conflict:

122 Slim, *Why Protect Civilians?, supra* note 87, at 482.

123 *Id.*

124 *Id.*

125 *See* Walzer, Just and Unjust Wars, *supra* note 2.

126 *Beit Sourik Village Council v. Gov't of Israel, supra* note 57, at ¶ 37. For an investigation of the origins of the concept of proportionality in the *jus in bello, see* Jeremy Rabkin, *Proportionality in Perspective: Historical Light on the Law of Armed Conflict,* 16 San Diego Int'l L. J. 263 (2015).

1) Disputes regarding a state's use of force in light of the Article 2(4) and 51 of the U.N. Charter;

2) Disputes regarding a state's choice of weapons and tactics in light of the constraints of Hague/Geneva law;

3) War crimes trials in which the measures a defendant has taken in armed conflict are assessed in relation to the objectives of the conflict. [127]

Proportionality applies to uses of force other than armed combat between one belligerent and another. The principle regulates the use of force by a belligerent against a neutral state or in its territory when the belligerent has been attacked from forces operating within the neutral state or the neutral has violated its duties to that belligerent.[128] But here we are concerned with proportionality in the *jus in bello*, that is, its applications to the means and methods of war and to the assessment of individual criminal liability.

In a rough and ready sense, the basic idea of "proportionality" seems clear enough. Armed combat cannot be carried on without causing unwanted or unintended harm to non-combatants. But *some* restraints on even unintended harm to civilians must be observed. It is beyond all reason to destroy a city in order to kill a sniper. More demandingly, even small combat units on patrol should be expected to realize that no attack should be carried out "when no reasonable person could doubt the strictly limited military significance of the chosen target as compared with the severe damage the attack may clearly be expected to cause among the civilian

127 Thomas M. Franck, *On Proportionality of Countermeasures in International Law*, 102 Am. J. Int'l L. 715, 719 (2008).

128 *See* Enzo Cannizaro, *The Rule of Proportionality in the Law of International Countermeasures*, 12 Eur. J. Int'l L. 889, 911 n.65 (2001); Note, *International Law and Military Operations against Insurgents in Neutral Territory*, 68 Colum. L. Rev. 1127, 1137, 146–47 (1968). It also constrains the use of force as a countermeasure against the unlawful interference by a coastal state with another state's armed vessels' right of innocent passage. *See The Corfu Channel Case*, [1949] ICJ 4 (Apr. 19). In authorizing member states to use force to ensure compliance with its ban on military flights over Bosnia airspace, the Security Council specified that they were permitted to use all necessary measures "proportionate to the specific circumstances and the nature of the flights." S.C. Res. 816 at ¶ 4 (1993); *see also* S.C. Res. 787 at ¶ 12 (1992) (authorizing member states "to use such measures commensurate with the specific circumstances as may be necessary" to enforce Bosnian War arms embargo); *but see* Judith G. Gardam, *Legal Restraints on Security Council Military Enforcement Action*, 17 Mich. J. Int'l L. 285, 317 (1995/6) ("It is by no means 'uncontested' that the rules of customary international law apply to the forces acting in pursuance of Chapter VII Security Council powers."). Proportionality figures in the law of weaponry, as when states balance the military uses and value of blinding lasers against the suffering they cause or even their long-term impact on society. *See* Burrus M. Carnahan & Marjorie Robertson, *The Protocol on "Blinding Laser Weapons": A New Direction for International Humanitarian Law*, 90 Am. J. Int'l L. 484, 485 (1996). Proportionality is relevant to the law of belligerent occupation. Thus, the Supreme Court of Israel has held that the principle of proportionality under both international law and Israeli domestic regulates the activities of a military commander governing an occupied territory in balancing security needs against harm to humanitarian values (the interests of local inhabitants affected by the measure). *Beit Sourik Village Council v. Gov't of Israel*, *supra* note 57, at ¶¶ 36- 39. Proportionality is also relevant to armed conflict (though perhaps not to the law of armed conflict) in other ways, as for example, when the question arises whether wartime derogations from individual human rights law are disproportionate.

population."[129] The principle of proportionality is thus designed to be a rule of reason, accommodating the pursuit of military victory to the protection of non-combatant life and property. Proportionality, therefore, has been seen as a derivative principle that emerges from the balancing of "military necessity" against "humanity."[130]

Although they do not speak expressly in terms of "proportionality," Articles 51and 57 of Protocol I include the most authoritative statement of the principle of proportionality in contemporary *jus in bello.* Article 51(4) prohibits all "indiscriminate attacks," and Article 51(5) provides a non-exhaustive list of prohibited attacks, including, *inter alia* "(b) an attack which may be expected to cause incidental loss of civilian life, injury to civilians, damage to civilian objects, or a combination thereof, which would be excessive in relation to the concrete and direct military advantage anticipated." Article 57(2)(a)(iii) further provides, in pertinent part, that "[w]ith respect to attacks, . . . those who plan or decide upon an attack shall . . . refrain from deciding to launch any attack which may be expected to cause incidental loss of civilian life, injury to civilians, damage to civilian objects, or a combination thereof, which would be excessive in relation to the concrete and direct military advantage anticipated. Article 57(2)(b) provides that "an attack shall be cancelled or suspended if it becomes apparent that the objective is not a military one or is subject to special protection or that the attack may be expected to cause incidental loss of civilian life, injury to civilians, damage to civilian objects, or a combination thereof, which would be excessive in relation to the concrete and direct military advantage anticipated . . . ."[131]

Of particular note is the language in these articles prohibiting any "attack which may be expected to cause incidental loss of civilian life, injury to civilians, damage to civilian objects, or a combination thereof, which would be excessive in relation to the concrete and direct military advantage anticipated."[132] Three characteristics of this compact formula stand out. First, the requirement of proportionality expressed here applies over and above the principle of

129 Frits Kalshoven & Liesbeth Zegveld, Constraints on the Waging of War: An Introduction to International Humanitarian Law 109 (ICRC 2001).

130 *See, e.g.*, Bengt Anderberg, Ove E. Bring & Myron L. Wolbarsht, *Blinding Laser Weapons and International Humanitarian Law,* 29 J. Peace Res. 287, 288 (1992).

131 *See* Protocol Additional to the Geneva Conventions or 12 August 1949, and Relating to the Protocol of Victims of International Armed Conflicts (Protocol I), 16 ILM 1391 (1978) (entered into force 1985).

132 Note that "attack," as used here, is a "technical term relating to a specific military operation limited in time and place, and covers attacks carried out both in offence and in defence. The jurisprudence of [the ICTY] has defined 'attack' as a course of conduct involving commission of acts of violence." *Galić, supra* note 76, at ¶ 52.

Despite that welcome clarification, the meaning of the term "attack" as used in Protocol I is problematic. Article 49(1) states that "'Attacks' means acts of violence against the adversary, whether in offence or defence." But that definition "is broad enough to designate the act of a single soldier shooting a rifle as an attack." Fenrick, The *Rule of Proportionality, supra* note 42, at 101–02. It seems necessary, therefore, to consider the surrounding context of an occurrence of the term in Protocol I in order to ascertain its meaning. Thus, because an "attack" in Article 51 and 57 envisages a preceding planning process and the possibility of targeting several military objectives, those provisions may not relate to "an operation below divisional . . . level." Fenrick, *Rule of Proportionality, supra* note 42, at 102, 107 ("[T]he negotiating record . . . indicates that responsibility [under Article 57(2)(a)] is to be placed at a relatively high level of the command structure"); *id.* at 107–08, 112 (further evidence from negotiating record).

distinction.[133] That is, even if a commander had focused an attack solely on a military objective and had carefully avoided targeting any civilian objectives, the attack would still be unlawful unless the proportionality requirement was met. Second, the harm that an attack "may be expected" to cause to civilian or civilian objects must not be "excessive in relation to the concrete and direct military advantage anticipated."[134] Difficult to interpret though this language undoubtedly is,[135] it is clear that "[t]he standard is 'excessive' (a comparative concept), not 'extensive' (an absolute concept)."[136] Thus, if an attack causes a very high number of civilian casualties and other losses (500 deaths, let us say), it may still be proportionate, if those harms are not excessive when balanced against the "concrete and direct military advantage anticipated." On the other hand, even very small civilian damage may be disproportionate if it is "excessive" to the anticipated "military advantage."[137] Third, the formula, like other definitions of "proportionality," encapsulates a two-part test: a "proportionality of effectiveness" (expressing the idea of military necessity or advantage) and a "proportionality of value" (expressing the idea that military advantage should not be outweighed by its destructiveness).[138]

The formulas raise serious interpretive issues,[139] which are still being hammered out in judicial opinions, military manuals, reports by non-governmental organizations, and scholarly publications. For our purposes, the opinion of the ICTY Trial Chamber in the 2003 *Galić* case provides a useful and concise analysis of how Protocol I's distinction and proportionality requirements are intended to work together:

> The practical application of the principle of distinction requires those who plan or launch an attack take all feasible precautions to verify that the objectives attacked are neither civilians nor civilian objects, so as to spare civilians as much as possible. Once the military character of a target has been ascertained, commanders must consider whether striking this target is "expected

133 *See* Michael N. Schmitt, *Precision Attack and International Humanitarian Law,* 87 IRRC 445, 456–57 (2005) [hereinafter Schmitt, *Precision Attack*].

134 Protocol Additional to the Geneva Conventions or 12 August 1949, and Relating to the Protocol of Victims of International Armed Conflicts (Protocol I), Article 51(5)(b), 16 ILM 1391 (1978) (entered into force 1985).

135 According to an eminent U.S. military lawyer and scholar, the standard of "excessiveness" had historically "enjoyed a high threshold – condemning only collateral civilian casualties so excessive as to be tantamount to the intentional attack of the civilian population or to a total disregard for the safety of the civilian population." W. Hays Parks, *Linebacker and the Law of War,* 34 Air U. Rev. 2, n. 47 (1983) (*available at* http://www.airpower.maxwell.af.mil/airchronicles/aureview/1983/jan-feb/parks.html).

136 Schmitt, *Precision Attack, supra* note 133, at 457.

137 On the negotiating history of the term "excessive" in Arts. 51 and 57, *see* Fenrick, The *Rule of Proportionality, supra* note 42, at 102–06.

138 *See* David R. Mapel, *Prudence and the Plurality of Value in International Ethics,* 52 J. Pol. 433, 436 (1990).

139 Michael Schmitt raises some of these difficulties: "How certain must one be of the resulting collateral damage and incidental injury before it is 'expected'? What does the phrase 'concrete and direct' mean in practice? How 'military' must the advantage be to count? Most importantly, how does one compare dissimilar values (civilian harm and military gain) at all, let alone over time in different combat situations and across cultures?" Schmitt, *Precision Attack, supra* note 133, at 457.

> to cause incidental loss of life, injury to civilians, damage to civilian objectives or a combination thereof, which would be excessive in relation to the concrete and direct military advantage anticipated." If such casualties are expected to result, the attack should not be pursued. The basic obligation to spare civilians and civilian objects as much as possible must guide the attacking party when considering the proportionality of an attack. In determining whether an attack was proportionate it is necessary to examine whether a reasonably well-informed person in the circumstances of the actual perpetrator, making reasonable use of the information available to him or her, could have expected excessive civilian casualties to result from the attack.[140]

The *Galić* Court added several explanatory notes to this discussion. First, the requirement in Article 57(2)(a) that precautions must be "feasible" means that they must be "practicable or practically possible."[141] Second, the negotiating history of the expression "concrete and direct" shows that "the advantage must be 'substantial and relatively close,' and that 'advantages which are hardly perceptible and those which would only appear in the long term should be disregarded.'"[142] Further, the Court cited with apparent approval to the International Committee of the Red Cross's [ICRC] view that "a military advantage can only consist in ground gained or in annihilating or in weakening the enemy armed forces."[143] The ICRC's view, however, has been criticized as unduly restrictive by preventing enemy military personnel from reaching and slaughtering members of a minority ethnic group that an intervening force is attempting to protect.[144] Third, "the rule of proportionality [in Protocol I] does not refer to the actual damage caused nor to the military advantage achieved by an attack, but instead uses the words 'expected' and 'anticipated.'"[145] Thus the review of the decision-maker's choice has to be made on the basis of the information (reasonably) available to him at the time, not on the basis of

140 Galić, *supra* note 76, at ¶ 58.

141 *Id.* at n.105. For further discussion, *see* Fenrick, *The Rule of Proportionality, supra* note 42, at 108–09.

142 *Id.* at n.106.

143 *Id.* (internal citation omitted).

144 It would appear to follow, for example, that harm to civilians cannot be balanced against such gains to the attacker as demoralizing the enemy's people or causing popular dissatisfaction with the enemy government, interrupting the flow of the enemy's wartime propaganda, or perhaps even reducing the chances that the attacker's own military forces, weaponry or material will be destroyed. These and other questions are pressed in Major Jeanne M. Meyer, *Tearing Down the Façade: A Critical Look at the Current Law on Targeting the Will of the Enemy and Air Force Doctrine,* 51 A.F. L. Rev. 143 (2001). Meyer contended that such restrictive understandings of military "objectives" and "advantages" do not correspond to state practice, which has long regarded it as a legitimate use of air power to achieve political, diplomatic and psychological advantages over an enemy. *See id.* at 166–71. For example, NATO's use of air power in Kosovo was intended to influence the political decisions of the Serb leadership and to undermine popular support for the Milosevic government. Meyer claimed that a restrictive interpretation of Protocol I would call the legality of such uses of air power into question. *But see* Yoram Dinstein, The Conduct of Hostilities under the Law of International Armed Conflict 93 (2d ed. 2010) (Forcing a change in negotiating attitudes "cannot be deemed a proper military advantage"). For a brief summary of the negotiating record regarding the standard for determining the meaning of "concrete and direct military advantage" in Arts. 51 and 57, *see* Fenrick, *The Rule of Proportionality, supra* note 42, at 106–07.

145 *Galić, supra* note 76, at n.109.

hindsight. Finally, although the Court itself did not emphasize this, we may note that it framed the applicable standard of review in terms of what "a reasonably well-informed person" in the attacker's position, rather than what a "reasonable commander" in that situation, would have expected.

In short, the principle of proportionality, like the principles of military necessity and distinction, which, as our discussion reveals, the principle of proportionality in turn modifies, raises as many questions as it answers. In the eyes of some critics, the principle is so indeterminate as to be useless, or even harmful. Thus, Eyal Weizman writes:

> Although violence is in constant need of measurement, the principle of proportionality provides no scale, no formulas and no numerical thresholds. Instead, it demands assessment on a case-by-case basis, within parameters that are always relative, situational and immanent. It demands the estimation of aims, impacts and side effects, intended and unintended consequences – which is also to say, the measurement of lesser and greater evils, their exchange and sometimes even transfer – in an economy of a real or imaginary 'worst-case scenario' and in an attempt to keep the overall level of violence to the minimum necessary . . . . Military lawyers and experts in international humanitarian law are the first to accept the fact that the predictions required for proportionality analysis are always contingent, immanent and prone to subjective interpretations. Contemporary debates about IHL concern precisely the impossibility of bringing together in practice the legal demand that violence be measured, and the impossibility of doing so.[146]

146 Weizman, *supra* n. 70, at 12. Assessments of proportionality are arguably impossible to make as a conceptual matter even if the calculus is stripped down to a mere body count. Even assuming that in the wake of an attack it was possible to identify all the casualties *(i.e.,* no bodies destroyed or unidentifiable) and to distinguish between the civilians and combatants among them (which assumes an agreed-upon definition of those categories), the "exchange rate" of these deaths would be uncertain. Should the death of a civilian child count for more, less or the same as the death of an eighty year old civilian or the death of a civilian of military age? And should the death of a "high value" terrorist be measured against that of one, two or more civilians? In 2002, the former head of the International Law Division in the Israeli military, Daniel Reisner, challenged a group of experts on law and military ethics to determine what ratio of "collateral" civilian deaths they would consider legitimate in the context of an attack on and killing of a single armed militant. The average of the answers given was 3.14 (or, roughly, π). *See* Weizman, *supra* note 70, at 13. Should militaries work with that "exchange rate," or is it arbitrary?

To take a real world case, consider the report of an independent commission of scholars and experts to the United Nations Human Rights Council on the conduct of Israeli and Palestinian forces in Gaza since mid-summer 2014. *See* Report of the independent commission of inquiry established pursuant to Human Rights Council resolution S-21/1, A?HRC/29/52 (June 24, 2015) (*available at* http://www.ohchr.org/EN/HRBodies/HRC/CoIGazaConflict/Pages/ReportCoIGaza.aspx). In the context of Israeli strikes by precision-guided weapons (*i.e.,* drones) on residential building in Gaza, the commission found a total of 216 Palestinian fatalities in some 15 cases of strikes, including 115 children and 50 women (*id.* at ¶ 36). As against this, the commission "found indications of possible military objectives in . . . nine [of the fifteen] cases" (*id.* at ¶ 38). In those cases, the commission considered that the attacks were targeted at individuals "on account of their alleged links to the police, Hamas or an armed group" *(id.* at ¶ 39). Evaluation of whether the casualties in those attacks included combatants was not possible in part because Israel, in large part for security reasons, declined to provide relevant information about its intended targets (*id.* at ¶ 75).

Is the death of some 216 persons, of whom the great majority were presumably civilians and 115 of whom were children, to be considered disproportionate to the killing of (let us suppose) nine or so (suspected) terrorist operatives? Surely it would seem so (but what if the slain terrorists were of extraordinarily "high value"?). The independent commission itself did not affirm that the attacks (taken as a whole) were disproportionate. It did, however, assign to Israel the burden of *demonstrating* the legality of the attacks *(id.* at ¶ 40):

Yet, even before reaching these difficult questions of necessity, distinction and proportionality, legal policy makers and on-the-ground decision-makers, including combatants and their commanders, authors of rules of engagement, and those engaged in various stages of legal review, including ultimately municipal and international courts, must face the additional complex jurisdictional, or threshold, questions concerning whether the law of war is even applicable and, if so, which set of rules, those governing international or non-international armed conflict, apply.

Given the absence of information suggesting that the anticipated military advantage at the time of the attack was such that the expected civilian casualties and damage to the targeted and surrounding buildings were not excessive, there are strong indications that these attacks could be disproportionate, and therefore amount to a war crime.

The United States' drone strike programs in Pakistan, Afghanistan and Yemen, like that of Israel in Gaza and the West Bank, has drawn substantial legal and humanitarian criticism. For a well informed and sharply critical review of the U.S. program, *see* Grégoire Chamayou, A Theory of the Drone (Janet Lloyd trans. 2015).

D. JURISDICTIONAL QUESTIONS—EXISTENCE OF ARMED CONFLICT HUMANITARIAN VS. HUMAN RIGHTS LAW; AND INTERNATIONAL OR NON-INTERNATIONAL ARMED CONFLICT

Before the *jus in bello* can be applied to any situation, two main "jurisdictional" questions need to be addressed. The first question is whether the situation is one of "armed conflict." If it is not, *jus in bello* will not be applicable, although other kinds of law (such as criminal law or human rights law) are likely to apply. If, however, the situation is an "armed conflict," then a second further question arises as to the correct categorization of that conflict. Is it an inter-state or international conflict? Are there forms of violence that constitute "armed conflict" yet fall outside the definitions of the two types of armed conflict—international and "non-international"—contemplated by the Geneva Conventions? Depending on the categorization selected, different *jus in bello* regimes will control. And those regimes may assign very different rights and obligations to the parties to the conflict.

1. The Existence of an "Armed Conflict"

It may often be uncertain, and contentious, whether an "armed conflict," a term of only recent origin,[147] to which the *jus in bello* would apply has arisen. In its 1995 *Tadic* decision, the Appeals Chamber of the ICTY propounded the following tests for the existence of an "armed conflict":

> An armed conflict exists whenever there is a resort to armed force between States or protracted armed violence between governmental authorities and organized armed groups or between such groups within a State. International humanitarian law applies from the initiation of such armed conflicts and extends beyond the cessation of hostilities until a general conclusion of peace is reached; or, in the case of internal conflicts, a peaceful settlement is achieved.[148]

147 For the rewriting of legal doctrine in terms of "armed conflict" rather than the more traditional "war," *see* Nathaniel Berman, *Privileging Combat? Contemporary Conflict and the Legal Construction of War*, 43 Colum. J. Transnat'l L. 1, 15–16 (2004). During the 1930s, that is, before the term "armed conflict" came into general use in international instruments, aggressor states had often denied that they were engaged in legal "war," describing their actions instead as "intervention[s] of a sort of police character. Prominent examples are the Japanese invasion of China, the German dismemberment of Czechoslovakia, the occupation of Bessarabia." W. Friedmann, *International Law and the Present War*, 26 Trans. Grotius Soc. 211, 216 (1940).

148 *Prosecutor v. Tadic*, ICTY Appellate Chamber, Oct. 2, 1995, at ¶ 70 (*available at* http://www.icty.org/x/cases/tadic/acdec/en/51002.htm). For commentary, *see, e.g.*, Christopher Greenwood, *International Humanitarian Law and the* Tadic *Case*, 7 Euro. J. Int'l L. 265 (1996).

The *Tadic* tests have been widely accepted.[149] Yet, there will inevitably be many problems in applying them.

One set of questions relates to the status of the participants. Is it even *possible* for an "armed conflict" subject to the *jus in bello* to arise if one of the parties to the conflict is not a State?[150] Does *any* kind of "armed force" between states and organized armed groups rise to the level of "armed conflict" for purposes of the *jus in bello*?[151] What about large-scale armed violence between police or military forces of a state and narco-militias?[152] Is there an "armed conflict" if the Indian Navy attacks and destroys Somali pirates preying on merchant shipping?[153] How should we view the November 2008 attack by the Laskar-e-Taiba group on the city of Mumbai, India, which killed 172 people, overwhelmed local police contingents, and required the Indian government to deploy army and marine units into combat? What about the United States' counter-terrorist

149 *See, e.g., Case Concerning Armed Activities on the Territory of the Congo (Congo v. Uganda),* 2005 ICJ 169, ¶ 25 (Separate Op. of Simma, J.); *Prosecutor v. Lubanga,* Case No. ICC_01/04-01/06, *Decision on the Confirmation of the Charges* ¶ 233 (Jan. 29, 2007); *Prosecutor v. Norman, Fofana & Kondewa: Decision on Appeal Against "Decision on Prosecution's Motion for Judicial Notice and Admission of Evidence,* Case No. SCSL-2004-14-AR73at ¶ 32 (Separate Op. of Ayoola, J.) (Special Court for Sierra Leone, May 16, 2005); *Prosecutor v. Rutaganda,* Case No. ICTR-96-3-T, Trial Chambers, Judgment, ¶ 92 (ICTR Dec. 6, 1999), 39 I.L.M. 557, 574-75 (May 2000); *How is the Term "Armed Conflict" Defined in International Humanitarian Law?,* International Committee of the Red Cross (ICRC) Opinion Paper 2 (March 2008).

150 *See Public Committee against Torture in Israel v. Gov't of Israel, supra* note 77, at ¶ 11 ("[T]here is no longer any doubt that an armed conflict can exist between a state and groups and organizations which are not states. That is due, *inter alia,* to the military ability and means which such organizations have, as well as their willingness to use them."); *id.* at ¶ 21 ("Our starting point is that the law that applies to Israel and the terrorist organizations in the [Occupied Territories] is the international law dealing with armed conflicts.").

151 Protocol II, though applicable to internal armed conflicts, states in terms that it "shall not apply to situations of internal disturbances and tensions, such as riots, isolated and sporadic acts of violence and other acts of a similar nature, as not being armed conflicts." Art. 1(2).

152 There is a highly-charged debate within Colombia over the question whether that State is engaged in an "armed conflict" with the Fuerzas Armadas Revoluçionarias de Colombia ("FARC"). Colombian President Manuel Santos has publicly supported legislation that would describe Colombia's ongoing struggle with the FARC as an "armed conflict." *See 'Hace Rato Hay Conflict Armado', Dice J.M. Santos (available at* http://www.eltiempo.com/justicia/ARTICULO-WEB-NEW__NOTA__INTERIOR). Santos' predecessor, former President Alvaro Uribe, immediately and emphatically disagreed, arguing that the State was engaged in a struggle with a criminal terrorist organization. According to Uribe, categorizing the struggle as an "armed conflict" would confer a political status, and thus a measure of legitimacy, on the FARC. *See Uribe Pide a Santos Que No Reconozca la Existencia de un Conflict Armado en Colombia (available at* http://www.google.com/hostednews/afp/article/ALeqM5gmDa8NTNUyOSOO60bCWaIU).

The FARC itself, beginning as a Marxist-Leninist movement, has over time become a kind of "alternative State" within Colombia, profiting from its ties to the drug trade, with weak ideological commitments. *See* Román D. Ortiz, *Insurgent Strategies in the Post-Cold War: The Case of the Revolutionary Armed Forces of Colombia,* 25 Stud. in Conflict & Terrorism 127, 137 (2002) ("[T]he rebels have taken on the role of a parallel state authority in areas where narcotics are produced. In fact, they have provided the peasants and dealers involved in the business basic services such as justice, maintenance of public order, and defense against the operations of the army and the police."). The FARC has rejected the notion that the *jus in bello* applies to its conflict with the Colombian State. *See* Gabriel Marcella, *The United States and Colombia: The Journey from Ambiguity to Strategic Clarity* 20 (May 2003) (*available at* http://www.strategicstudiesinstitute.army.mil/pdffiles/PUB10.pdf).

153 *See, e.g.,* Douglas Guilfoyle, *The Laws of War and the Fight Against Somali Piracy: Combatants or Criminals?,* 11 Melbourne J. Int'l L. 1 (2010) (not an armed conflict); *c.f.* Ruth Wedgwood, *What Do You Do with a Captured Pirate?, in Defining Ideas: A Hoover Institution Journal* (Mar. 1, 2009) (*available at* http://www.hoover.org/publications/defining-ideas/article/5558) (arguing that "the only trouble is that the West is still tangled in the postmodern confusion of the law of armed conflict, human rights law, solipsistic views of national jurisdiction, and a lack of common sense").

actions since 9/11 against al Qaeda?[154] Is the German Army (*Bundeswehr*) engaged in armed conflict in Afghanistan when its soldiers open fire on Afghans attempting to drive a car at high speed and despite warning shots through a *Bundeswehr* road-block?[155] Was Israel engaged in "armed conflict" when it invaded Lebanon during "Operation Peace in Galilee" in 1982 to combat the Palestinian Liberation Organization, even though the operation was not directed against the State of Lebanon?[156] If a United Nations peacekeeping force, backed by French helicopters, fires rockets into the compound where a claimant to the Presidency of the Côte d'Ivoire resides and destroys the heavy weapons surrounding that compound, acting pursuant to a Security Council Resolution authorizing it "while impartially implementing its mandate, to use all necessary means to carry out its mandate to protect civilians under imminent threat of physical violence,"[157] is the peacekeeping force engaged in an "armed conflict"?

Another set of questions relates to the conduct of the participants. How "protracted" does the violence in question need to be? May a state of armed conflict last only three days?[158] Is an attack on a military facility by forty civilians lasting only thirty hours sufficiently prolonged to count as an armed conflict?[159] What if the violence is sporadic and discontinuous, but nonetheless occurs over a prolonged period of time?[160] Is "intensity" a better criterion than duration, or at least necessary in addition to it?[161] What factors or circumstances count in determining

154 Former U.S. State Department Legal Adviser Harold Koh has stated that the United States is engaged in an "armed conflict with al-Qaeda, the Taliban and associated forces." Harold Hongju Koh, *The Obama Administration and International Law* (Mar. 25, 2010) (*available at* http://www.state.gov/s/l/releases/remarks/139119.htm).

155 The original answer given by German authorities was No: Germany was engaged in a "stabilization mission," not "armed conflict," in Afghanistan. See Constantin von der Groeben, *Criminal Responsibility of German Soldiers in Afghanistan: The Case of Colonel Klein*, 11 German L. J. 469, 470 (2010). Subsequently, however, the German government declared that the situation in Afghanistan was an "armed conflict." *See id.* at 475.

156 Yes, according to the Supreme Court of Israel. *See Al Nawar v. Minister of Defence*, H.C. (High Court) 574/82, 16 Isr. Y.B. Hum. Rts. 321, 323; and How Does Law Protect in War? 819, 820 (Marco Sassoli & Antoine Bouvier eds., 1999).

157 *See* S.C. Res. 1975 (2011); *see also* UN Secretary-General Ban Ki-Moon, *Statement on the Situation in Côte d'Ivoire* (Apr. 10, 2011) (*available at* http://www.un.org/apps/news/infocus/sgspeeches/); *and* David Smith, *Gbagbo Comes Under Attack from Ground Assault* (Apr. 11, 2011) (*available at* http://www.guardian.co.uk/world/2011/apr/11/gbagbo-attack-ground-assault/). French military assistance was authorized in a series of Security Council Resolutions. *See. e.g.*, S.C. Res. 1962 (2010).

158 Yes, according to the ICTY. See Prosecutor v. Boskoski et al., IT-04-82-PT, Aug. 22, 2005; *Prosecutor v. Limaj et al.*, IT-03-66-T, Nov. 30, 2005.

159 Yes, according to the Inter-American Commission on Human Rights. *See Juan Carlos Abella v. Argentina*, Case 11.137, Inter-Amer. C.H.R. Report No. 55/97/OEA/Ser.L/V/II.95 Doc. 7 rev (1997).

160 Berman, *supra* note 147, at 25–27, 32–33 (noting that discontinuity is a common characteristic of contemporary warfare and poses a difficulty in applying *Tadic* formula).

161 *See Prosecutor v. Haradinaj* (Judgment), ICTY Trial Chamber I, Case No. IT-04-84-T, at ¶ 49 (Apr. 3, 2008):

> The criterion of protracted armed violence has therefore been interpreted in practice, including by the *Tadić* Trial Chamber itself, as referring more to the intensity of the armed violence than to its duration. Trial Chambers have relied on indicative factors relevant for assessing the "intensity" criterion, none of which are, in themselves, essential to establish that the criterion is satisfied. These indicative factors include the number, duration and intensity of individual confrontations; the type of weapons and other military equipment used; the number and calibre of munitions fired; the number of persons and type of forces partaking in the fighting; the number of casualties; the extent of material destruction; and the number of civilians fleeing combat zones. The involvement of the UN Security Council may also be a reflection of the intensity of a conflict.

"intensity"?[162] When does recourse to armed force in the interactions between states reach the level of armed conflict? In the 1982 Falklands/Malvinas War between Great Britain and Argentina, neither state officially recognized a state of war. Is such recognition necessary for inter-state armed conflict?[163] Was "Operation Eagle Claw," the abortive U.S. military operation in April 1980 to rescue the hostages held in the U.S. Embassy in Tehran an "international armed conflict"?[164] Does the answer change when non-state actors are involved? Was Israel engaged in "armed conflict" with Hamas on May 31, 2010, when the Israeli Defense Force boarded the *Mavi Marmara*, a Comoros-flagged vessel on the high seas bound for Gaza with the announced intent of breaching Israel's naval blockade of Gaza, or was Israel's engagement with Hamas insufficiently "protracted" or "intense" to meet the tests for armed conflict?[165] Should there be a sliding scale analysis requiring greater intensity or duration when non-state actors are involved?

A third set of questions clearly relates both to status and conduct. The "organization" criterion for non-state actors is problematic.[166] What kind and degree of "organization" is necessary?[167] Did the Kosovo Liberation Army (the KLA) achieve a sufficient level of "organiza-

---

162 In *Prosecutor v. Boskoski & Tarculovski*, Case No. IT-04-82-T, Judgment at ¶¶ 177- 78 (July 10, 2008), the ICTY Trial Chamber summarized earlier rulings on this question as follows:

> Various indicative factors have been taken into account by Trial Chambers to assess the "intensity" of the conflict. These include the seriousness of attacks and whether there has been an increase in armed clashes, the spread of clashes over territory and over a period of time, any increase in the number of government forces and mobilisation and the distribution of weapons among both parties to the conflict, as well as whether the conflict has attracted the attention of the United Nations Security Council, and whether any resolutions on the matter have been passed. Trial Chambers have also taken into account in this respect the number of civilians forced to flee from the combat zones; the type of weapons used, in particular the use of heavy weapons, and other military equipment, such as tanks and other heavy vehicles; the blocking or besieging of towns and the heavy shelling of these towns; the extent of destruction and the number of casualties caused by shelling or fighting; the quantity of troops and units deployed; existence and change of front lines between the parties; the occupation of territory, and towns and villages; the deployment of government forces to the crisis area; the closure of roads; cease fire orders and agreements, and the attempt of representatives from international organisations to broker and enforce cease fire agreements. At a more systemic level, an indicative factor of internal armed conflict is the way that organs of the State, such as the police and military, use force against armed groups. In such cases, it may be instructive to analyse the use of force by governmental authorities, in particular, how certain human rights are interpreted, such as the right to life and the right to be free from arbitrary detention, in order to appreciate if the situation is one of armed conflict.

163 No. *See* Françoise Hampson, *Winning by the Rules: Law and Warfare in the 1980s*, 11 Third World Q. 31, 42 (1989); Michael A. Meyer, *Liability of Prisoners of War for Offenses Committed Prior to Capture: The Astiz Affair*, 32 Int'l & Comp. L. Q. 948, 957–58 (1983).

164 Yes, according to one commentator. *See* Fenrick, *The Rule of Proportionality*, *supra* note 42, at 98.

165 According to the Supreme Court of Israel, "a continuous situation of armed conflict has existed [between Israel and Hamas] since the first intifada [of 1987-92]." *Public Committee against Torture in Israel v. Gov't of Israel*, *supra* note 77, at ¶ 16; *see also* The Turkel Commission, *The Public Commission to Examine the Maritime Incident of 31 May 2010, Report, Part one* at ¶¶ 37–46 (Jan. 2010). But this assumption is questioned in Douglas Guilfoyle, *The Mavi Marmara Incident and Blockade in Armed Conflict*, Brit. Y.B. Int'l L. (2011) (*available at* www.bybil.oxfordjournals.org).

166 *See* William V. O'Brien, *The Rule of Law in Small Wars*, 541 Ann. Amer. Acad. Pol. & Soc. Sci. 36, 43 (1995) ("At what point does a small, relatively ineffective resistance movement reach the magnitude and demonstrate the capabilities that would warrant granting them belligerent status involving rights and duties under the international law of war? Conventional law on this subject is confused.").

167 According to the ICTY Trial Chamber in *Prosecutor v. Haradinaj*, *supra* note 161, at ¶ 60:

> an armed conflict can exist only between parties that are sufficiently organized to confront each other with military means. State governmental authorities have been presumed to dispose of armed forces that satisfy this criterion. As for armed groups, Trial Chambers have relied on several indicative factors, none of which are, in themselves, essential to establish whether the

tion" for its activities in relation to Serbian forces in and after mid-1998 to count as an "armed conflict"?[168] How should we view conflicts involving non-state actors within a territory in which the state structures have disintegrated?[169] What if a conflict between two organized armed bands is fought out beyond the boundaries of any state (*e.g.*, a conflict in international waters between competing groups of pirates, the traditional "enemies of mankind," *hostes humanis generis*)? Do the new "enemies of mankind," a terrorist network such as al Qaeda, display the requisite "organization"?[170] What about its affiliates or "franchisees"?

"organization" criterion is fulfilled. Such indicative factors include the existence of a command structure and disciplinary rules and mechanisms within the group; the existence of a headquarters; the fact that the group controls a certain territory; the ability of the group to gain access to weapons, other military equipment, recruits and military training; its ability to plan, coordinate and carry out military operations, including troop movements and logistics; its ability to define a unified military strategy and use military tactics; and its ability to speak with one voice and negotiate and conclude agreements such as cease-fire or peace accords.

168 Yes, according to the Trial Chamber of the ICTY. *See Prosecutor v. Limaj,* Case No. IT-03-66-T, Judgment, ¶¶ 171-3 (Nov. 30, 2005):

> The Chamber is satisfied that before the end of May1998 an armed conflict existed in Kosovo between the Serbian forces and the KLA. By that time the KLA had a General Staff, which appointed zone commanders, gave directions to the various units formed or in the process of being formed, and issued public statements on behalf of the organisation. Unit commanders gave combat orders and subordinate units and soldiers generally acted in accordance with these orders. Steps have been established to introduce disciplinary rules and military police, as well as to recruit, train and equip new members. Although generally inferior to the VJ and MUP's equipment, the KLA soldiers had weapons, which included artillery mortars and rocket launchers. By July 1998 the KLA had gained acceptance as a necessary and valid participant in negotiations with international governments and bodies to determine a solution for the Kosovo's crisis, and to lay down conditions in these negotiations for refraining from military action. ... The ability of the KLA to engage in ... varied operations is a further indicator of its level of organisation. . . . In view of the above the Chamber is persuaded and finds that an internal armed conflict existed in Kosovo before the end of May 1998. This continued until long after 26 July 1998.

169 A 1998 ICRC document notes this point.

> Where structures have disintegrated, there is no clear distinction between persons directly engaged in an armed conflict and civilians and no chain of command; and there is confusion about the international humanitarian war applicable among the parties to the conflict. . . . Situations where State structures have disintegrated in the course of an armed conflict are usually characterized by a lack of effective leadership capable of ensuring respect for international humanitarian law. . . . The distinction between persons directly participating in an armed conflict and civilians tends to blur, as members of local militias rarely wear distinctive signs and mingle with civilians.

Chairman's Report, First Periodical Meeting on International Humanitarian Law, Geneva, Jan. 19-23, 1998, *reprinted in* How Does Law Protect in War? 507, 508, 509 (International Committee of the Red Cross, Marco Sassòli & Antoine A. Bouvier eds., 1999).

170 No, according to Sylvain Vité, *Typology of Armed Conflicts in International Humanitarian Law: Legal Concepts and Actual Situations,* 91 IRRC 69, 93 (2009) (Al Qaeda appears to be "a loosely connected, clandestine network of cells" that does not meet "the organization criterion"). By contrast, Michael Scheuer found that al Qaeda is more like "an insurgent organization" than a "terrorist group." For Scheuer, terrorist groups "are small; obsessively secretive; aim at publicity, not victory; constitute a lethal nuisance, not a national security threat to the nation-state; and are subject to defeat by decapitation or attrition. Insurgent groups, on the other hand, are much larger; balance the need for secretiveness with the need for propaganda; aim at victory and define what constitutes victory; pose genuine security threats to nation-states; and put so much effort into succession-planning that neither decapitation nor attrition is likely." Michael Scheuer, Osama Bin Laden 73 (2011).

2. Categorizing "Armed Conflicts"

War has traditionally (if also somewhat misleadingly) been described as a "game for sovereigns."[171] Non-sovereigns have repeatedly engaged in armed conflicts or "wars," and those conflicts were often regulated, at least to some extent, by *jus in bello.* [172] Historically, non-state actors, mercenaries, for example, often served as combatants on behalf of, or as authorized by, state sovereigns. [173] Moreover, a sovereign might find itself "at war" with non-state actors, such as a violent armed band that had broken away from an Indian tribe. Rebels, insurgents, guerrillas, saboteurs, mercenaries, and pirates are among the kinds of armed combatants of whom the *jus in bello* has treated.[174]

Nonetheless, the paradigmatic case of armed conflict to which the *jus in bello* applies has been and remains that of international or state-to-state warfare. These are sometimes referred to as "common Article 2" conflicts because they fall under a provision, Article 2, which is common to all four of the 1949 Geneva Conventions.[175] In relevant part, that provision states that "the present Convention shall apply to all cases of declared war or of any other armed conflict which may arise between two or more of the High Contracting Parties, even if the state of war is not recognized by one of them" (emphasis added). Since only states are (or could be) "contracting parties" to the Geneva Conventions, the armed conflicts regulated by the Conventions are, centrally at any rate, conflicts between states.[176]

171 *See* Frédéric Mégret, *Jus in Bello and Jus ad Bellum,* 100 Proc. Am. Soc. Int'l L. 121, 121 (2006) ("What makes war war (rather than a brawl, or a feud), according to the *jus in bello* has traditionally been that it is conducted by the sovereign . . . .").

172 Transborder violence by non-state actors at the behest of states was common in the early modern period. For an explanation of the decline of that practice, *see* Janice E. Thomson, Mercenaries, Pirates, & Sovereigns (1994).

173 The U.S. Constitution contemplates such state-sanctioned authorization of what otherwise would be private war-making in the "Letters of Marque and Reprisal" Clause. *See* U.S. Const. Art. I, sec. 8, cl. 11.

174 The U.S. Supreme Court recognized these categories in its 1901 decision in *Montoya v. United States,* 180 U.S. 261 (1901). In that case, the question was whether the depredations committed by "an organized company of men constituting a band in itself, acting independently of any other band or tribe, and carrying on hostilities against the United States," amounted to "a war," so as to relieve the government of statutory liability to compensate settlers for those depredations. *Id.* at 265. The Court observed that "the fact that Indians are engaged in acts of general hostility to settlers, especially if the government has deemed it necessary to dispatch a military force for their subjugation, is sufficient to constitute a state of war." *Id.* at 267

175 *See* Solis, *supra* note 42, at 150.

176 For that reason, states engaged in armed conflict with non-state actors, including national liberation movements, traditionally concluded that captured enemy combatants were not entitled to legal protection of prisoners of war under the Third Geneva Convention. Thus, the French government during the Algerian War (1954–62) faced the issues whether the Algerian rebellion was an "armed conflict" subject to the laws of war and, more particularly, whether Algerian rebels captured in combat were entitled to prisoner of war status. The Cour de Cassation (France's highest court) ruled that an Algerian rebel captured while fighting with an "armed band" was not entitled to prisoner of war status—although it implied that he would have been, had he been fighting with a regular Algerian military unit. *See Jean Touscoz, Etude de la Jurisprudence Intern Française Sur les Aspects Internationaux de l'Affaire d'Algérie,* 9 Annuaire Français de Droit International 953, 960 & n.24 (1963). During the Vietnam War, the United States denied prisoner of war status under the Third Geneva Convention to captured Vietcong combatants, although it "accord[ed] them treatment roughly equivalent to that required for bona fide POWs." *See* William V. O'Brien & Anthony C. Arend, *Just War Doctrine and*

However, contemporary armed conflict is by no means limited to international conflicts. Indeed, such conflicts appear to be happening less frequently than in the past.[177] Contemporary *jus in bello* has accordingly been updated to reach both the armed struggles of the post-Second World War period against the European colonial powers in Africa and Asia—wars of "national liberation"—and civil or "internal" wars.[178] Broadly, Additional Protocol I was intended to adapt the 1949 Geneva Conventions to suit the conditions of wars of national liberation;[179]Additional Protocol II was addressed (effectively) to civil or other "internal" armed conflicts.[180] The specific requirements established by these different legal regimes (Geneva, Protocol I, Protocol II) are intended to reflect the characteristics of the different forms of armed conflict to which they apply.

It is often difficult to determine whether an armed conflict is or is not "international" in the sense of "common" Article 2 of the Geneva Conventions.[181] The categorization of a conflict may, however, entail substantive legal consequences, because the treaty regime established by the Geneva Conventions, and extended by Additional Protocol I, is far more robust than that established by Additional Protocol II. Furthermore, the liability of a foreign state for actions committed by the forces it is assisting in an "internal" conflict may be implicated if its assistance "internationalizes" the conflict.[182] A decision by the ICTY Appeals Chamber in the *Tadic* case

---

the International Law of War, 1 Military Medical Ethics 221, 236 (2003) (*available at* http://www.bordeninstitute.army.mil/published_volumes/ethicsVol1/ethicsVol1.html). Likewise, Israel had to deal with the question whether Palestinian Liberation Organization participants in the ongoing conflicts in the Middle East were entitled to the legal status of prisoners of war, and concluded that they were not. *See id.; see also* Fritz Kalshoven, *Problems of the Law of Armed Conflict in Lebanon*, 77 Proc. Am. Soc. Int'l L. 214, 239 (1983).

177 There are, of course, recent examples of interstate armed conflict, such as the 1982 Falklands War between the United Kingdom and Argentina or the 2003 Gulf War between the U.S-led Coalition and Iraq.

178 In the post-1945 world, civil wars have been the most deadly form of armed conflict. One study has estimated the 1945–1999 direct death toll for 127 civil wars at 16.2 million, or about five times the count for the 3.3 million battle deaths in 25 international armed conflicts of that period. *See* James Fearon & David Laitin, *Ethnicity, Insurgency and Civil War*, 97 Am. Poli. Sci. Rev. 75, 75 (2003). Another study has found that of the 111 armed conflicts recorded for the period 1989–2000, only 7 were international. *See* Peter Wallensteen & Margareta Sollenberg, *Armed Conflict, 1990–2000*, 38 J. Peace Res. 629, 632 tbl.II (2001).

179 Under Article 1(4) of Protocol I, the Geneva Conventions are extended to "armed conflicts in which peoples are fighting against colonial domination and alien occupation and against racist regimes."

180 The scope of Protocol II is restricted to conflicts in the territory of a State party between its armed forces and "dissident armed forces or other organized armed groups which, under responsible command, exercise such control *over a part of its territory* as to enable them to carry out sustained and concerted military operations and to implement this Protocol." *Id.* Art. I(1) (emphasis added). It is well-understood that the coverage of Protocol II does not extend to all internal armed conflicts. *See* R.R. Baxter, *Modernizing the Law of War*, 78 Mil. L. Rev. 165, 169 (1977); and Daniel Smith, *New Protections for Victims of International Armed Conflicts: The Proposed Ratification of Protocol II by the United States*, 120 Mil. L. Rev. 59, 66–69 (1988).

181 *See, e.g.*, Geneva Convention For the Amelioration of the Condition of the Wounded and the Sick in the Armed Forces in the Field, Art. 2, Aug. 12, 1949, 6 U.S.T. 3114, T.I.A.S. No. 3362, 75 U.N.T.S. 31 (entered into force Oct. 21, 1950) ("[T]he present Convention shall apply to all cases of declared war or any other armed conflict which may arise between two or more High Contracting Parties, even if the state of war is not recognized by one of them."). For an analysis of common Article 2 in the context of the Israeli naval blockade of Gaza, *see* Guilfoyle, *supra* note 165 (concluding that the conflict between Israel and Hamas is at most a non-international armed conflict).

182 *Prosecutor v. Tadic, supra* note 148, at ¶ 97 ("[T]he legal consequences of the characterization of [an armed] conflict as either internal or international are extremely important. Should the conflict eventually be classified as international,

provides useful guidance. The question before the Chamber was whether, in the circumstances prevailing in late 1992, the Army of the Federal Republic of Yugoslavia (the FRY), a recognized state, exercised sufficient control over the Army of the so-called "Serbian Republic of Bosnia and Herzegovina" (the VRS), which was not recognized as a state, in the VRS' internal conflict with the state of Bosnia-Herzegovina as to make that conflict "international" for purposes of the Geneva Conventions?[183] The question arose because the FRY Army had formally withdrawn from Bosnia-Herzegovina after May 12, 1999, yet continued to support the VRS in various ways in its continuing conflict with the Bosnia government. From the prosecution's perspective, the relationships between the FRY and the VRS were sufficiently close that the actions of the latter could be imputed to the former. From the defense perspective, the FRY and the VRS were merely "allies." Whether or not the actions of the VRS for which its members were being prosecuted constituted "grave breaches" of the Geneva Convention depended on whether or not the conflict was "international."[184] For the Appeals Chamber, this depended on whether the VRS "could be considered *de iure* or *de facto* organs of a foreign power, namely the FRY.[185] Recognizing that the VRS was not a *de jure* organ of the FRY, the Appeals Chamber articulated "an overall control" test to decide whether the VRS was the *de facto* organ of the FRY. Thus, the

> control required by international law may be deemed to exist when the State (or, in the context of an armed conflict, the Party to the conflict) *has a role in organizing, coordinating or planning the military actions* of the military group, in addition to financing, training and equipping or providing operational support to that group. Acts performed by the group or members thereof may be regarded as acts of *de facto* State organs regardless of any specific instruction by the controlling State concerning the commission of those acts.[186]

Concluding that "the link between the [FRY] and VRS clearly went far beyond mere coordination or cooperation between allies and, in effect, the renamed Bosnian Serb army still comprised one army under the command of the General Staff of the [FRY Army]," the Appeals Chamber found that the VRS was indeed the de facto organ of the FRY,[187] thus triggering the application of the more demanding grave breach provisions of the *jus in bello* governing international armed conflict.

---

it would *inter alia* follow that a foreign State may in certain circumstances be held responsible for violations of international law perpetuated by the armed groups acting on its behalf.")

183 *See id.* at ¶¶ 68 et seq.

184 The relevant war crimes charged against the *Tadic* defendants were made subject to prosecution under Article 2 of the ICTY Statute. To fall within the scope of that provision, the armed conflict had to be "international" and the victims had to be "protected" under the Geneva Conventions. *See Tadic, supra* note 148, at ¶ 80; *Tadic,* Appeals Chamber, Decision of Oct. 2, 1995, Separate Op. of Shidwa, J., at ¶¶ 110–12.

185 *Tadic, supra* note 148, at ¶¶ 84, 87.

186 *Id.* at ¶¶ 131, 137.

187 *Id.* at ¶¶151–52.

E. THE *JUS IN BELLO* IN THE WAR ON TERROR—THE DEBATE OVER COMMON ARTICLE 3

We now consider the applicability of modern *jus in bello* to U.S. and allied action in Afghanistan and elsewhere in response to the attacks of September 11, 2001. The United States was plainly at war with the Taliban government of Afghanistan, suggesting that that conflict, at least, was "international" (because the parties to that conflict were both considered to be states). But the United States was also at war with a non-state terrorist organization, al Qaeda, which was closely aligned with Taliban-governed Afghanistan. Should that conflict also have been considered "international" because of the close ties between al Qaeda and Taliban? Or should it not have been so considered because the United States was also at war with al Qaeda elsewhere outside the territorial limits of Afghanistan, and/or because al Qaeda was not a state actor? The Taliban government was itself also entangled in a civil war with the Northern Alliance. That conflict in itself was clearly not "international." But did it become "internationalized" once the United States attacked Afghanistan and began cooperating with the Northern Alliance? Was the civil war in Afghanistan merged (so to say) into the inter-state U.S.-Taliban conflict, or did it remain a separate conflict subject to different treaty norms?

Article 3, which is found in all four of the Geneva Conventions of 1949, creates a kind of "mini"-regime for regulating certain forms of armed conflict, providing that in "the case of armed conflict not of an international character occurring in the territory of one of the High Contracting Parties, each Party to the conflict shall be bound to apply, as a minimum," certain provisions, including humane treatment, avoiding violence to life and person, not taking hostages, avoiding outrages to personal dignity, passing sentences or carrying out executions only on the basis of judgments by previously constituted courts, and care of the wounded and the sick in respect of certain, defined persons.[188] When the United States was attacked by al Qaeda

188 *See, e.g.*, Geneva Convention For the Amelioration of the Condition of the Wounded and the Sick in the Armed Forces in the Field, Art. 3, Aug. 12, 1949, 6 U.S.T. 3114, T.I.A.S. No. 3362, 75 U.N.T.S. 31 (entered into force Oct. 21, 1950). The text provides, as follows:

(1) Persons taking no active part in the hostilities, including members of armed forces who have laid down their arms and those placed hors de combat by sickness, wounds, detention, or any other cause, shall in all circumstances be treated humanely, without any adverse distinction founded on race, colour, religion or faith, sex, birth or wealth, or any other similar criteria. To this end the following acts are and shall remain prohibited at any time and in any place whatsoever with respect to the above-mentioned persons:

(a) violence to life and person, in particular murder of all kinds, mutilation, cruel treatment and torture;

(b) taking of hostages;

(c) outrages upon personal dignity, in particular, humiliating and degrading treatment;

(d) the passing of sentences and the carrying out of executions without previous judgment pronounced by a regularly constituted court affording all the judicial guarantees which are recognized as indispensable by civilized peoples.

(2) The wounded and sick shall be collected and cared for.

An impartial humanitarian body, such as the International Committee of the Red Cross, may offer its services to the Parties to the conflict.

The Parties to the conflict should further endeavour to bring into force, by means of special agreements, all or part of the other provisions of the present Convention.

forces on September 11, 2001, however, questions arose whether the United States was engaged in an "armed conflict" and, if so, which form of *jus in bello*, if any, applied to that conflict: the Geneva Conventions; Protocol I; Protocol II; or common Article 3? These were, and remain, vigorously disputed questions. We now explicate the debate.

The dominant view was that the United States was indeed, for purposes of the *jus in bello*, engaged in an "armed conflict."[189] Recognizing that the United States had a right to respond as a matter of self-defense under Article 51 of the U.N. Charter, the Security Council's Resolution 1368 of September 12, 2001 appeared to sanction the view that the attacks constituted an armed conflict to which some form of *jus in bello* would apply. Moreover, the Council indicated that the attacks posed a "threat to international peace and security," enabling it to take military action under Chapter VII.[190] The decisions taken at the time by NATO and by the U.S. Congress confirmed that understanding.[191]

Yet, granting that the situation on 9/11 was an "armed conflict," what form of the *jus in bello*, if any, was applicable? Legal scholars have long puzzled over the meaning of "not of an international character."[192] The U.S. Executive Branch, in initially drawing the conclusion the conflict with al Qaeda was not governed by common Article 3, took the view that that article applied to civil wars.[193] There are at least three textual reasons for thinking so. First, civil wars are, by and

---

The application of the preceding provisions shall not affect the legal status of the Parties to the conflict.

189 For a robust defense of this conclusion, *see* Mark Osiel, The End of Reciprocity: Terror, Torture, and the Law of War 114–17 (2009). That the United States is "at war" is denied by other writers, who maintain that criminal law and human rights law rather than the *jus in bello* govern the U.S. conflict with al Qaeda. *See, e.g.*, Marco Sassòli, *Jus ad Bellum and Jus in Bello—The Separation Between the Legality of the Use of Force and Humanitarian Rules to be Respected in Warfare: Crucial or Outdated?, in* International Law and Armed Conflict: Exploring the Faultlines—Essays in Honour of Yoram Dinstein 241, 261 (Michael N. Schmitt & Jelena Pejic eds., 2007) (stating that "the typical law enforcement situation" is "the appropriate legal framework for all parts of the 'war on terror' not taking place within an international armed conflict (such as the conflict between the US and Afghanistan in 2001/2002) or amounting to a non-international armed conflict")). For a survey of the debate, *see* Monica Hakimi, *International Standards for Detaining Terrorism Suspects: Moving Beyond the Armed Conflict-Criminal Divide,* 33 Yale J. Int'l L. 369, 376–79 (2008).

190 *See* S.C. Res. 1368 (2001); *see also* Christopher Greenwood, *International Law and the Pre-Emptive Use of Force,* 4 San Diego Int'l L. J. 7, 17 (2003).

191 For NATO, *see* Press Release, Statement by the North Atlantic Council on Collective Defense (Sept. 12, 2001); for Congress, *see* Authorization for the Use of Military Force, Pub. L. No. 107-40, 115 Stat. 224.

192 *See, e.g.*, James G. Stewart, *Towards a Single Definition of Armed Conflict in International Humanitarian Law: A Critique of Internationalized Armed Conflict,* 85 IRRC 313, 318 (2003) ("[O]ne of the most assured things that might be said about the words 'not of an international character' is that no one can say with assurance precisely what they were intended to convey.") (quoting Tom Farer, *Humanitarian Law and Armed Conflicts: Towards the Definition of "International Armed Conflict",* 71 Colum. L. Rev. 37, 43 (1971)); *see also* W. Michael Reisman & James Silk, *Which Law Applies to the Afghan Conflict?,* 82 Am. J. Int'l L. 459, 463 n.17 (1988) (collecting authorities who have complained of the uncertain meaning and application of Article 3). Reisman and Silk themselves understood Article 3 "apparently [to] apply to all other [non-Article 2] conflicts in which one party to the Conventions is engaged."

193 *See* Robert J. Delahunty, *Is the Geneva POW Convention 'Quaint'?,* 33 Wm. Mitchell L. Rev. 1635, 1639–41 (2007). Although the language of common Article 3 might well be argued to apply to wars of national liberation or decolonization as well, the practice of major state parties to the Geneva Conventions did not accord with that interpretation, and Protocol I was designed in part to cure the resulting uncertainty. *See id.* at 1639 n.16. Thus, both Britain and France had denied the applicability of Article 3 to wars of decolonization in (respectively) Kenya and Algeria. *See* Fabian Klose, *The Colonial Testing Ground: The International Committee of the Red Cross and the Violent End of Empire,* Humanity 107 (Spring 2011)

large, "not of an international character," in that the parties to them are usually an established national government on the one side and a rebel force on the other.[194] Although the rebel forces would normally be seeking either to overthrow the national government or to secede from its authority, they would generally not have acquired international recognition as a government. So the conflict would not be "international," in that the parties to it were not both sovereign states. Second, for the same reason, the rebel forces would not normally be considered to be a "Party" to the Geneva Conventions. Non-state actors are, in general, not even legally competent to enter into treaties.[195] The rebel forces would, however, be a "Party to the conflict," and the fact Article 3 uses that language would again indicate that the provision is directed to civil wars. Third, the language of the final clause, which provides that application of the Article's substantive provisions "shall not affect the legal status of the Parties to the conflict," seems designed to allay fears on the part of national governments that by applying Article 3 to their dealings with rebel or insurgent forces, they would be taken to be overtly or implicitly "recognizing" them, either as a "belligerent" under international law[196] or even as another sovereign. The final clause

(*available at* http://muse.jhu.edu). However, the question was vigorously disputed at the time. About mid-way through the Algerian War, France appeared to accept that the Article applied to that conflict. *See* Eldon Van Cleef Greenberg, *Law and the Conduct of the Algerian Revolution,* 11 Harv. Int'l L. J. 37, 47–50 (1970); and Touscoz, *supra* note 176, at 957.

194 Civil wars could indeed *become* "internationalized" by the intervention of outside states, as the Spanish Civil War of 1936–39 was by the interventions of Germany, Italy, and the Soviet Union, and it was understood that "the Spanish Civil War has obscured the distinction between civil and international law." Friedmann, *supra* note 147, at 216–17. But an internationalized civil war like that in Spain was not the standard case; nor did the Spanish War erase the traditional distinction between international and internal or civil wars. The distinction between international and civil wars is deeply entrenched in the Western legal consciousness, though civil conflict was traditionally deemed not to be "true" war to which ordinary *jus in bello* applied. "Not until 1949 . . . were rules on the waging of civil strife embodied in international conventions, and even then only in a very rudimentary fashion." Stephen C. Neff, War and the Law of Nations 367 (2005).

195 *See* Robert J. Delahunty & John C. Yoo, *Statehood and the Third Geneva Convention,* 46 Va. J. Int'l L. 131, 140–41 (2005). Non-state forces may, however, make "special agreements" with states, as Article 3 itself provides.

196 Not all "rebel" or "insurgent" forces were accorded the status of "belligerents." *See* Elbert Jay Benton, International Law and Diplomacy of the Spanish-American War 13 (2010 reprint of 1908 ed.) (distinguishing recognition of "insurgency" from recognition of "belligerency" for purposes of law of neutrality). Toward the outset of the U.S. Civil War, the Union government was anxious not to concede in any way the Confederate government's claim to be a sovereign state. It, therefore, was unwilling to apply the international law of war to the hostilities with the Confederacy. Instead, the Union would have preferred to apply federal criminal law to the Confederates in arms, treating the rebellion as a large-scale criminal conspiracy somewhat akin to the 1794 Whiskey Rebellion that President George Washington had called out federal troops to suppress. However, President Lincoln gradually, if reluctantly, began to recognize the Confederacy as a "belligerent." *See* Burrus M. Carnahan, Act of Justice: Lincoln's Emancipation Proclamation and the Law of War 38–39, 43–50, 61–70 (2007). Recognition of an insurgent organization in a civil war as a "belligerent" entails that the organization has rights and duties under international law. *See The Three Friends,* 166 U.S. 1, 57 (1896) ("[T]he recognition of belligerency, while not conferring all the rights of an independent state, concedes to the government recognized the rights, and imposes upon it the obligations, of an independent state in matters relating to the war being waged."). Yet, recognition of belligerency by neutral third parties, which may be forced upon them, may be highly objectionable to an established government engaged in a civil war. *See The Three Friends,* 166 U.S. at 52. Thus, when Britain, France, and other European sovereigns formally recognized the Confederacy as a "belligerent," the Union objected strenuously. *See* Joseph H. Beale, Jr., *The Recognition of Cuban Belligerency,* 9 Harv. L. Rev. 406, 412–17 (1896). Furthermore, recognition of belligerency places some legal limits on how the established government may treat the rebels or insurgents, especially under its domestic criminal law. For example, "regular" enemy combatants may be held to be legally "privileged" to use lethal force against the established government's soldiers and citizens, and hence not subject (if captured) to prosecution under the detaining state's criminal law for having committed such acts of violence.

of Article 3 seems to be intended to remove that obstacle to achieving humanitarian objectives in civil wars.[197]

As a structural matter, this reading of the relationship between Article 3 and the rest of the Geneva Convention makes clear sense. The great bulk of the Geneva Conventions applies to international armed conflicts (Article 2 conflicts); a special (and rudimentary) legal regime applies to internal armed conflicts (effectively, civil wars). Furthermore, the relationship of the Geneva Conventions to the later Protocols also makes good sense: Protocol I carried the 1949 Conventions forward by assimilating wars of national liberation (between states and proto-states) to traditional "international" conflicts; Protocol II carried the Conventions forward by developing common Article 3's rudimentary regime for internal or civil conflicts into a more detailed set of requirements. Furthermore, Article 3 presupposes that rebels or insurgents will be no less bound by its requirements than the States that are parties to the Geneva Conventions. But how can such reciprocity be explained, given that rebels or insurgents are not signatories to those treaties and indeed are not competent to become parties to them? Several theories have been offered as solutions to this problem. Thus, "Article 3 might be considered as devolving upon all citizens of an original signatory State ... or as binding on rebel groups pretending to exercise state authority, because the state itself is so bound."[198] But those explanations assume that Article 3 applies to a conflict between a signatory State and its own nationals, or between such a State and a movement of its own nationals claiming to be a government. In other words, Article 3 is legally binding on both sides only in a case of civil war.

There is also substantial evidence that the drafters of the 1949 Geneva Conventions had intended Article 3 to apply to civil wars.[199] Those drafters had plainly not anticipated and provided for the wars between states and national liberation movements that had made the adoption of Protocol I necessary. Still less had they anticipated and provided for war between states and international terrorist organizations. In the jurisprudential universe of the late 1940s, "armed conflict" was either "international" (i.e., between states) or "non-international" (i.e., within states), and the latter type of conflict was regulated by international law only in a rudimentary way.[200] Furthermore, before the 9/11 attacks, what little judicial opinion there was took Article 3 to apply to "internal or civil wars of a purely domestic nature."[201]

197 This was, indeed, the ICRC's view. *See* Delahunty, *supra* note 193, at 1641 & n.23.

198 Greenberg, *supra* note 193, at 52.

199 *See* Farer, *supra* note 192, at 50–51(noting that some of the negotiators distinguished between types of civil conflict, of which at least some, and perhaps all, fell under Article 3, though allowing that some civil wars might also have been intended to fall under the Convention as a whole).

200 *See Prosecutor v. Tadic, supra* note 148, at ¶¶ 96–97. The Spanish Civil War of the 1930s—to which some third-party states insisted that a measure of international *jus in bello* applied—was a precedent in the mind of the drafters of the Geneva Conventions for a (very modest) degree of international legal regulation of similar intra-state conflict. *See id.* at ¶¶ 100–01. *See* Antonio Cassese, *The Geneva Protocols of 1977 on the Humanitarian Law of Armed Conflict and Customary International Law,* 3 U.C.L.A. Pac. Basin L.J. 55, 104–05(1984).

201 *United States v. Noriega,* 746 F. Supp. 1506, 1534 (S.D. Fla. 1990).

Legal scholars before 9/11 had also widely understood common Article 3 in that sense.[202] For example, a leading Italian scholar (and later ICTY Judge) Antonio Cassese wrote that "Article 3 of the Geneva Conventions is meant to protect only victims *of civil wars* who '[take] no active part in the hostilities.' . . . State practice developed after 1949 shows that Article 3 [has made it] legally impossible for any State to deny the applicability of those fundamental safeguards *in cases of civil strife*" (emphases added).[203] The ICRC experts in the 1960s understood Article 3 only to limit State Parties' actions "as regards their own nationals in a case of internal conflicts."[204] Asked to consider the question, "In which cases is article 3 legally applicable?," the ICRC's Commission of Experts responded in terms that limited the scope of the provision to "internal" conflicts between "a legal government" and "rebel groups."[205] Indeed, immediately after 9/11, at least some outside the U.S. Executive Branch, applying what appeared to be the traditional tests for international and non-international armed conflict, thought the conflict with al Qaeda could fall outside of both of these categories.[206]

Despite this evidence, the U.S. Supreme Court rejected the Executive Branch's interpretation in its decision in *Hamdan v. Rumsfeld*.[207] There, interpreting U.S. law in a manner it deemed con-

---

202 For collections of the scholarly authorities, see Robert J. Delahunty & John C. Yoo, *What is the Role of Human Rights Law in the War on Terror?*, 59 DePaul L. Rev. 803, 807 n.20 (2010); and Delahunty, *supra* note 193, at 1641 & nn.22, 23, 24, 25. Other relevant authorities are cited in Curtis A. Bradley, *The Military Commissions Act, Habeas Corpus, and the Geneva Convention*, 101 Am. J. Int'l L. 322, 326 n.28 (2007); *see also* Osiel, *supra* note 189, at 52–53 (discussing pre-*Hamdan* scholarship).

One somewhat variant approach was suggested in 1989 by Françoise Hampson. She advanced the possibility that Protocol II had amended common Article 3 by adding "organizational requirements, territorial control and a minimum threshold of disruption to the criteria of applicability of common Article 3." Alternatively, she suggested, those criteria might be considered "implicit" in Article 3. Françoise Hampson, *Winning by the Rules: Law and Warfare in the 1980s*, 11 Third World Q. 31, 44 (1989). In either case, it would be manifest that common Article 3 did not apply to the conflict with al Qaeda.

203 Cassese, *supra* note 200, at 107–08.

204 *Humanitarian Aid to the Victims of Internal Conflicts: Meeting of a Commission of Experts in Geneva*, 23 IRRC 79, 79 (1963).

205 The Commission said:

> Article 3 . . . tends to guarantee respect for the essential principles of these [four Geneva] Conventions in the case of conflicts which, by reason of their internal character, do not entail the putting into effect of all the Conventions. It must be a question of an internal "armed" conflict which gives rise to "hostilities." . . . In the Commission's opinion, the existence of an armed conflict, within the meaning of article 3, cannot be denied if the hostile action, directed against a legal government, is of a collective character and consists of a minimum amount of organization. In this respect . . . one should take into account . . . the number and framework of the rebel groups, their installation or action on a part of the territory, . . . the methods employed by the legal government to re-establish order, etc.

Id. at 82–83. The Commission went on to speak of the terms of the settlement of a conflict to which Article 3 applies in terms that can refer only to a war between a government and its own nationals or subjects. *See id.* at 83.

206 Nathaniel Berman emphasized the difficulty of the question:

> The attacks did not meet the test for "international armed conflict" because they were not inter-state attacks. Nor would Al-Qaeda meet the traditional test for "belligerency status," since it had not established a government over a relatively stable territory. Yet neither did the attacks seem to fit within the rubric of "non-international armed conflicts." It would be quite a stretch to say that they fell within the Geneva Conventions' Article 3 category of conflicts "not of an international character occurring within the territory of one of the High Contracting Parties," let alone the stricter definition in definition in Protocol II. The attacks seemed too trans-border in nature (and not even proto-inter-state) to be international in the traditional sense.

Berman, *supra* note 147, at 32.

207 548 U.S. 557, 562 (2006).

sistent with background treaty law, the Court determined that, for purposes of U.S. law, common Article 3 would be deemed applicable to all "armed conflicts" other than international armed conflicts, and not only civil wars.[208] Accordingly, unless and until the U.S. Congress enacts superseding legislation or the Executive Branch, with Senatorial advice and consent or perhaps even by congressional-executive agreement, ratifies a superseding treaty modification, the U.S. armed conflict with al Qaeda must now be considered an "Article 3 conflict"; and this also implies, since the two categories are mutually inconsistent, that it cannot be considered an Article 2 conflict.[209]

---

208 Justice Stevens explained:

> the phrase "not of an international character" bears its literal meaning. . . . Although the official commentaries accompanying Common Article 3 indicate that an important purpose of the provision was to furnish minimal protection to rebels involved in one kind of "conflict not of an international character," *i.e.,* a civil war, the commentaries also make clear "that the scope of the Article must be as wide as possible." In fact, limiting language that would have rendered Common Article 3 applicable "especially [to] cases of civil war, colonial conflicts, or wars of religion," was omitted from the final version of the Article, which coupled broader scope of application with a narrower range of rights than did earlier proposed iteration.

Id. at 562 (citations omitted).

209 Because the conflict is governed by Article 3, it cannot as such be an Article 2 conflict. Article 3 expressly contemplates that unless the other provisions of the Geneva Conventions are adopted by "special agreement" between the parties to the conflict, they do not apply. *See Prosecutor v. Tadic,* Appeals Chamber, *supra* note 148, at ¶¶ 103–04 ("Common Article 3 contains . . . a procedural mechanism inviting parties to internal conflicts to agree to abide by the rest of the Geneva Conventions. As in the current conflicts in the former Yugoslavia, parties to a number of internal armed conflicts have availed themselves of this procedure to bring the law of international armed conflicts into force with respect to their internal hostilities. . . . Agreements made pursuant to common Article 3 are . . . [a] vehicle through which international humanitarian law has been brought to bear on internal armed conflicts."); *see* Solis, *supra* note 42.

We conclude our introductory survey of the *jus in bello* with a brief consideration of its emerging relationship to International Human Rights Law (IHRL). Traditionally, *jus in bello* was thought to apply to international armed conflict and, in an extenuated way, to non-international armed conflict, while IHRL was conceived to regulate the peacetime dealings between a state and its citizens (or others subject to its territorial jurisdiction). In recent years, however, IHRL has begun to penetrate areas previously thought to be subject only to the "special" law of armed conflict. This extension of IHRL, which is becoming increasingly accepted, has been largely been driven by judges (particularly those on the European Court of Human Rights) and United Nations commissions. It has usually taken the form of finding that a state's "jurisdiction" attaches to certain of its extra-territorial acts, as *e.g.*, when it is in (formal or functional) occupation of a foreign territory or when it is holding detainees from a foreign conflict outside its own territory. "Jurisdiction" is sometimes said to arise in such cases because the state, though acting extra-territorially, is considered to be exercising "effective control" over the relevant situation. Because many states' rights obligations usually attach wherever it exercises "jurisdiction," IHRL has been held to apply even in such conditions.[210] Whether or not this trend in the law is misguided,[211] it is by now sufficiently well established to require discussion.

We have already discussed he extraordinary difficulty of distinguishing "armed conflict" from "peace" in many contemporary circumstances. But that fact alone does not explain the increasing penetration of IHRL into situations of armed conflict. International and regional courts have also emphasized that IHRL has at least some application to what are undoubtedly situations of international armed conflict, such as the Second Gulf War. Thus, the International Court of Justice ("ICJ") has said that "[i]n principle, the right not arbitrarily to be deprived of one's life applies also in hostilities."[212] Other international courts and juridical bodies have generally followed the lead of the ICJ. In a September 2014 decision arising out of the Second Gulf War, the Grand Chamber of the European Court of Human Rights ("ECtHR") relied upon the ICJ's jurisprudence, "which has held that international human rights law and international humanitarian law may apply concurrently."[213] Accordingly, in *Hassan v. United Kingdom*, the

210 For a survey of the main steps in the relevant case law, *see* Oliver De Schutter, International Human Rights Law 149-87 (2d ed. 2014).

211 For review and criticism of the earlier case law, *see* Robert J. Delahunty & John C. Yoo, *International Human Rights Law and the War on Terror*, in Thomas Cushman (ed.), Routledge International Handbook of Human Rights 610 (2011).

212 *Legality of the Threat or Use of Nuclear Weapons* (ICJ Advisory op. July 8, 1996) at ¶ 25 (*available at* http://www.icj-cij.org/docket/files/95/7495.pdf) [hereinafter *Nuclear Weapons Case*].

213 *Case of Hassan v. UK*, Judgment (Grand Chamber, ECtHR September 10, 2014) at ¶77 (*available at* http://hudoc.echr.coe.int/sites/eng/pages/search.aspx?i=001-146501#{"itemid":["001-146501"]}). The ECtHR documented the relevant ICJ rulings at *id.* at ¶¶ 35-37.

ECtHR applied provisions of the European Convention on Human Rights[214] to the detention of an Iraqi civilian who had been arrested and held by the British military on suspicion of being an enemy combatant during the phase of active hostilities in an international armed conflict.

Administrative bureaucracies have ploughed the same furrow. Thus, in March 2014, the United Nations Human Rights Council adopted a resolution that (emphasis added):

> Urges all States to ensure that any measures employed to counter terrorism, including the use of remotely piloted aircraft or armed drones, comply with their obligations under international law, including the Charter of the United Nations, *international human rights law* and international humanitarian law, in particular the principles of precaution, distinction and proportionality. . . .[215]

The consequences of this novel understanding of IHRL are significant for IHL, or the law of armed conflict. First, IHRL demarcates the boundaries of IHL: where the latter does not apply, the former, by default, does apply. Second, even when IHL rules govern, IHRL norms may be invoked in interpreting and applying IHL. Thus, even in situations of armed conflict, "among the military means [employed], one must choose the means whose harm to the human rights of the harmed person is smallest."[216]

Assuming that human rights obligations do attach in at least some situations of armed conflict, it would of course follow that the right *to life* would be protected in that context. All of the most important international human rights documents concur in affirming the right to life. For example, Article 3 of the 1948 Universal Declaration of Human Rights states that "[e]veryone has the right to life, liberty and security of person."[217] Likewise, Article 6(1) of the 1976 International Covenant on Civil and Political Rights states that "[e]very human being has the inherent right to life. This right shall be protected by law. No one shall be arbitrarily deprived of his life."[218] As these and other international instruments insist, any deprivation of human life must be non-arbitrary. In particular, the consensus view is that any use of lethal force "must be *necessary* and *proportionate* and intentional force can be used only where strictly necessary to

214 *See* European Convention on Human Rights (*available at* http://www.hrcr.org/docs/Eur_Convention/euroconv.html).

215 *See* United Nations Human Rights Council, *Ensuring use of remotely piloted aircraft or armed drones in counter-terrorism and military operations in accordance with international law, including international human rights and humanitarian law,* Resolution A/HRC/ 25, L.32 (March 24, 2014) (*available at* http://www.un.org/ga/search/view_doc.asp?symbol=A/HRC/25/L.32).

216 *Public Committee against Torture in Israel v. Gov't of Israel, supra* note 77, at ¶ 40.

217 Universal Declaration of Human Rights Declaration, United Nations General Assembly in Paris on 10 December 1948, General Assembly Resolution 217 A (III) (*available at* http://daccess-dds-ny.un.org/doc/RESOLUTION/GEN/NR0/043/88/IMG/NR004388.pdf?OpenElement).

218 International Covenant on Civil and Political Rights, adopted and opened for signature, ratification and accession by General Assembly resolution 2200A (XXI) of 16 December 1966 entry into force 23 March 1976 (*available at* http://www.ohchr.org/en/professionalinterest/pages/ccpr.aspx).

protect against an imminent threat to life."[219] In the context of IHRL, these terms carry different meanings from those they bear in IHL. '"Necessary' means that there are no less serious alternatives available to achieve the aim, for example using baton rounds instead of live ammunition to disperse a crowd. 'Proportionate' requires that the means used, e.g. lethal force, is not out of proportion to the aim pursued, for example shooting to arrest an unarmed man who has committed a petty theft."[220] Thus, the use of lethal force might be permissible if it were strictly necessary to protect a human life in some hostage situations. On the other hand, a suspect's involvement in planning past terrorist operations, even if taken to be indicative of dangerousness, would not, in itself, be a lawful ground for intentionally killing him or her.

In the leading case of *McCann v. U.K.*,[221] the Grand Chamber of the ECtHR elucidated the meaning of the right to life as affirmed in Article 2 of the European Convention on Human Rights. In that case, British Special Forces in Gibraltar shot and killed three terrorists from Northern Ireland who were members of the Irish Republican Army. Although the Grand Chamber agreed that the soldiers believed for good reasons that the three men were about to launch an attack, it ruled that the killings were disproportionate because British planning had not taken necessary precautionary measures beforehand:

> [T]he use of lethal force would be rendered disproportionate if the authorities failed, whether deliberately or through lack of proper care, to take steps which would have avoided the deprivation of life of the suspects without putting the lives of others at risk.[222]

Thus, under this view, use of drones to attack and kill suspected terrorists would violate IHRL, even if the suspects were reasonably thought to pose an imminent danger, unless the State had considered alternative, less violent means of forestalling the danger beforehand and had found that no alternative to lethal force was available. If the suspects could have been arrested and interrogated without undue danger to others (including law enforcement officials), then IHRL would have mandated the use of those less violent procedures.

Furthermore, this legal obligation would hold even if (as is usually the case) the drone attacks occurred outside the territory of the State that had authorized them. The ECtHR's 2014 *Hassan* case illustrates such reasoning: there, the British armed forces in Iraq who had detained the petitioner's brother had effective control over him in their detention center, thus causing the U.K.'s obligations under the European Convention to attach.

---

219 Christof Heyns, *Report of the Special Rapporteur on extrajudicial, summary or arbitrary executions*, U.N. General Assembly A/68/382 (Sept. 13, 2013) at ¶ 33 (emphasis added).

220 Ilias Bantekas & Lutz Odette, *International Human Rights: Law and Practice* 316 (2013).

221 21 E.H.R.R. 97 (1995) (*available at* http://hudoc.echr.coe.int/sites/eng/pages/search.aspx?i=001-57943#{"itemid":["001-57943"]}).

222 *Id.* at ¶ 35.

The extra-territorial use of drones to kill suspected terrorists does, however, pose certain problems even under this approach. Drones enable a State to kill without exercising effective control over a foreign territory and without taking the targeted suspect into custody. Accordingly, it can be argued that even after *Hassan,* the jurisdictional requirement for the application of IHRL to drone killings does not exist.

The case law on this subject is sparse and inconclusive. In a 2001 decision, *Banković et al. v. Belgium,*[223] the Grand Chamber of the ECtHR held that persons who had been killed by NATO air attacks on a Serbian radio station during the Kosovo War did not fall within the "jurisdiction" of any of those NATO States for the purposes of applying the European Convention's prohibition on arbitrary deprivation of life. Although later ECtHR decisions (including *Hassan*) seem to have narrowed the scope of *Banković,* it remains a precedent for an exception from IHRL for extra-territorial drone warfare.

Nevertheless, it seems unlikely that courts and human rights bodies would recognize such an exception. For one thing, it seems incongruous that IHRL should permit a State to act extra-territorially through an aerial platform positioned above a foreign country in a way in which it would be unlawful for it to act were that platform located above its own territory. Further, the initiation of the drone strike would normally occur within the attacking State, and the lapse of time between the decision to strike and the death of the target would be negligible. In that situation, the IHRL violation might be deemed to have occurred *on the attacking State's territory,* and so within its "jurisdiction."[224]

With these thoughts, we conclude our introduction to the *jus in bello.* We turn next to three lengthy case studies in the *jus in bello*—one dealing with conventional warfare; a second dealing with the extension of the law of war to nontraditional interests, namely, environmental harms; and a third dealing with non-conventional warfare, namely the threat or use of nuclear weapons.

223 *See* Banković et al. v. Belgium (*available at* http://hudoc.echr.coe.int/sites/eng/pages/search.aspx?i=001-22099#{"itemid":["001-22099"]}).

224 The question whether State A had jurisdiction over a death in State B where the missile or other agent that caused the death had been released in A was disputed in Anglo-American common law. Some courts concluded that State A had jurisdiction over the murder, others denied that proposition. Compare *People v. Botkin,* 98 P. 861 (Cal. 1908) (State may punish a crime even if only portions of it are committed within that State) with *State v. Hall,* 114 N.C. 909 (1894) (Court refused to exercise jurisdiction over a person who fired a shot from North Carolina that killed a victim in Tennessee). For an extensive review of the common law cases, *see People v. Duffield,* 387 Mich. 300, 307-28 (1972). The Court in *Duffield* concluded that "as between counties the common-law rule is that jurisdiction to prosecute for . . . homicide lies at the place where the blow was given. There appears no common law case on the question of where jurisdiction lies when a blow would be given in England and death would occur outside of England, for example, in France. Although it is conceivable that this situation might conduct [sic] to a different result, we are of the opinion that the logic of the situation would rest jurisdiction where the blow was given regardless of where the victim died." Id. at 328.

Chapter 2

Jus in Bello: The ICTY Office of the Prosecutor's Report on NATO's Aerial Campaign in the War in Kosovo—Necessity, Distinction, and Proportionality in Practice

The primary focus of this chapter will be on the application of *jus in bello* rules, particularly as articulated in the 1977 Additional Protocol I to the Geneva Conventions, to an armed conflict in the Balkans. This conflict was "traditional" in one way: it was a war between states. Yet it was also "non-traditional" in at least two other ways: it overlapped with a war between a state, Serbia,[1] and a non-state actor, the Kosovo Liberation Army (the KLA)[2]; and one of the parties to the inter-state conflict, NATO, was or claimed to be motivated by humanitarian purposes to protect the Serbia's Albanian Kosovar minority, rather than national interests as usually defined. Yet, no doubt to NATO's surprise and dismay, the legality of its conduct also came under review by the International Criminal Tribunal for the Former Yugoslavia (the ICTY), or more exactly, by the prosecutor and the Office of the Prosecutor (the OTP) of the ICTY.

The review of NATO's conduct undertaken by the ICTY prosecutor and the OTP was prompted by evidence and allegations of war crimes made against NATO by leading non-governmental organizations (NGOs) and by Serbia. Although the review did not result in a decision to investigate and prosecute NATO before the ICTY on charges of war crimes, OTP's report to the prosecutor on its review, which the prosecutor eventually adopted, is a document of extraordinary interest to students of contemporary *jus in bello.* The Report illustrates how the basic principles of the *jus in bello*—necessity, distinction and proportionality—are or may be applied in a range of situations that are likely to be common on the contemporary battlefield. More specifically, the Report chiefly addresses the application of those principles to the use of *air power* in contemporary armed conflict.[3] However, the Report reveals the extent of the difficulties of

1 We shall designate the same entity as "Serbia," "the Federal Republic of Yugoslavia," the "FRY," or occasionally "Yugoslavia." Strictly, "Serbia" refers to the dominant part of the FRY or "Yugoslavia," which then also included Montenegro.

2 NATO seemed to have provided the KLA with covert support, including training, aid and equipment, and to have tailored its air campaign to help prevent a KLA defeat at Serbian hands. *See* Anthony H. Cordesman, *The Lessons and Non-Lessons of the Air and Missile Campaign in Kosovo* 230–34 (rev'd August 2000) (*available at* http://csis.org); *see also* Tom Walker and Aidan Laverty, *CIA Aided Kosovo Guerrilla Army,* THE SUNDAY TIMES, London, UK (March 12, 2000).

3 Because of the United States' dominance as an air power, legal questions relating to its use are particularly important to U.S. policymakers and the U.S. public. "The speed and agility of air power, combined with its ability to deliver firepower precisely and with relatively low risk to U.S. personnel across the spectrum of conflict, often make it the military instrument of choice for policymakers. However, the heightened risk of collateral damage when operating in urban environments partially offsets U.S. technological superiority and provides adversaries with expanded opportunities

applying, not simply those basic principles, but the formulations they are given in Protocol I, to those battlefield situations. Our case study is thus designed to enable students to reach a more informed judgment of the merits and flaws of Protocol I—undoubtedly the leading statement of contemporary *jus in bello,* yet a treaty that the United States has declined to ratify, and that continues to draw serious criticism. In this context, it places in sharp relief issues concerning prosecutorial discretion in international criminal law, much like the Nuremburg cases and the Tokyo Trials.

First, we briefly describe NATO's air campaign in the War in Kosovo; and then we examine the ICTY, its origins, establishment, legality, and jurisdiction. Second, we provide an overview of the basic facts of the disputed NATO attacks and the law of war issues raised by NATO's targeting decisions. Third, we then provide study questions and relevant excepts from the Final Report to the Prosecutor. Finally, we provide analytical commentary on the issues raised by the Final Report and conclude with a Thesis that compares "legalist" and "realist" views of the Report.[4]

to exploit U.S. adherence to certain norms." Matthew C. Waxman, International Law and the Politics of Urban Air Operations 1–2 (2000) (*available at* http://www.rand.org/publications/mr/mr1175/.).

4 The Final Report also sheds light on the complex questions in the institutionalization of international law, particularly the interactions between governments and international judicial bodies like the ICTY. The presence of these relatively novel judicial actors on the scene of armed conflict, and their activities in seeking to regulate it, are increasingly important factors in contemporary state practice with respect to armed conflict. They also invite analysis from the rational choice and constructivist perspectives developed earlier in this volume. But we limit this initial chapter on the *jus in bello* to an exploration of the realist and legalist critiques of the performance of the ICTY.

1. NATO's Air Campaign

The NATO air campaign against Serbia began on March 24, 1999. President William J. Clinton articulated its goal as forcing Serbian leaders to "understand the imperative of reversing course" in their "offensive against innocent civilians in Kosovo"; yet the President specifically ruled out the possibility of a ground war, announcing that he "did not intend to put our troops in Kosovo to fight a war."[5] Other NATO leaders shared that position.[6] NATO expected that after a few days of air strikes (chiefly on Serbian air defenses and radar sites), an intimidated Serbian government would return to the bargaining table. That assumption was a spectacular mistake. Instead of being cowed by NATO's air strikes, Serbia ramped up its brutal ethnic cleansing in Kosovo. By March 27, it was clear that NATO's opening salvo had failed. On March 27, NATO authorized attacks on a broader array of targets in Serbia and on Serbian forces operating in Kosovo, seeking mainly to interdict lines of communication and to strike Serbian military choke points, storage and marshaling areas, and tank concentrations.[7] Partly because of bad weather and partly because of Serbian elusiveness, NATO again met little success. During the second week of the campaign, NATO escalated its attacks still further, striking "infrastructure targets in Serbia" including bridges and the main water supply to Novi Sad and, on April 6, the main telecommunications building in Pristina.[8] Again, the campaign appeared to be stalled. "By the end of the first month, as many as 80 percent of the strikes conducted had been revisits to fixed targets that had been attacked at least once previously."[9] Attacks on state radio and television stations in Belgrade first took place on April 21. In the same attack, U.S. cruise missiles struck at the offices of Milosevic's political party. NATO had begun targeting what it saw as "the four

5 Ivo H. Daalder & Michael E. O'Hanlon, Winning Ugly: NATO's War to Save Kosovo 97 (2000).

6 *Id.* at 96–97. Later in the campaign, NATO leaders began to plan for the possibility of a ground war. On May 18, effectively retracting his earlier remarks, President Clinton claimed that he had "always said that . . . we have not and will not take any option off the table." Benjamin S. Lambeth, *NATO's Air War for Kosovo: A Strategic and Operational Assessment* 44, (RAND Corporation, 2001) (http://www.rand.org/pubs/monograph_reports/MR1365). The prospect of a ground war may (or may not) have motivated Serbia's eventual capitulation. For a critique of the view that the threat of a ground war motivated Serbia's surrender, *see* Andrew L. Stigler, *A Clear Victory for Air Power: NATO's Empty Threat to Invade Kosovo,* 27 Int'l Sec. 124 (2002/3).

7 Lambeth, *supra* note 6, at 25. Throughout the campaign, NATO efforts to cut off supply lines and communications links to Serbian forces into Kosovo were ineffective. *See* Daalder & O'Hanlon, *supra* note 5, at 239–40.

8 Lambeth, *supra* note 6, at 29, 31.

9 *Id.* at 36.

pillars of Milosevic's power—the political machine, the media, the security forces, and the economic system."[10]

NATO leaders convened a summit in Washington, D.C. on April 23–25 to commemorate the Alliance's 50th anniversary. The event proved to be a watershed in the conduct of the war. The very existence of the Alliance was seen to depend on a victory in Kosovo. The war became a war to save not only the Albanian Kosovars but also NATO. NATO's Master Target File grew from 169 targets at the start of the campaign to 976 by early June. "[T]he new goal became punishing Belgrade's political and military elites, weakening Milosevic's domestic power base, and demonstrating . . . that he and his fellow perpetrators of the abuses in Kosovo would find no sanctuary."[11]

The campaign was also expanded in ways that directly affected the Serb civilian population. On May 3, NATO dropped a cluster bomb, CBU-104(V)2/b, on five transformer yards in Serbia's power grid, thus temporarily cutting off electrical power to 70 percent of the country. (This was a "soft" attack insofar as it was intended not to cause damage that would render the grid inoperative for a prolonged period.) The announced intent of the strikes was to shut down the supply of power to Serbian forces in Kosovo and to confuse Serbian air defenses, but "[v]ery likely an unspoken intent was also to tighten the air operation's squeeze on the Serbian political leadership and rank and file. Whatever the case, the attack moved NATO over a new threshold and brought the war, for the first time, directly to the Serbian people."[12] Three weeks later, beginning on May 24, NATO struck Serbia's electric power generating system "with real determination. . . . [I]n perhaps the single most attention-getting strike of the entire air war up to that point, the Yugoslav electrical grid was severely damaged over the course of three consecutive nights. . . . Those attacks, directed against electrical power facilities and related targets in Belgrade, Novi Sad, and Nis, the three largest cities in Serbia, shut off the power to 80 percent of Serbia, leaving millions without electricity or water service."[13]

By this point, the tide had turned against Serbia. On May 27, the ICTY announced indictments of Milosevic and four other senior Serbian leaders on charges of war crimes and crimes against humanity. NATO air strikes continued (including an accidental hit, with civilian casualties, on a train crossing the Varvarin Bridge on May 30), but Serbian will to fight was waning. On

10 *Id.* at 39.

11 *Id.* at 38–39. *See also* Cordesman, *supra* note 2, at 21 ("The Alliance leaders formally decided to further intensify the air campaign by expanding the target set to include military-industrial infrastructure, media responsible for promulgating propaganda, and other strategic targets."). Daalder and O'Hanlon produced a graphic of the average number of daily targets in NATO's campaign for the periods March 24–April 25 and April 26–June 9. The graphic demonstrates sharp increases in targeting lines of communication/transportation, command and control, and Serbian forces, and little increases or even decreases in targeting support/infrastructure, oil production, and Serbian air defenses. *See* Daalder & O'Hanlan, *supra* note 5, at 120.

12 Lambeth, *supra* note 6, at 41.

13 *Id.* at 42. For further background on these attacks, *see* Ward Thomas, The Ethics of Destruction: Norms and Force in International Relations 165–67 (2001).

June 9, Serbia signed an agreement with NATO providing for the withdrawal of Serbian forces from Kosovo. On June 10, that withdrawal began, NATO Secretary General Solana announced the suspension of the bombing campaign, bringing the operation formally to an end on June 20, and the U.N. Security Council adopted SC Resolution 1244.

This apparent politico-military success was not achieved without controversy, however, albeit for entirely predictable reasons. Admittedly, NATO seems to have taken the *jus in bello* very seriously in the pursuit of its humanitarian objectives. NATO's political and military leaders had kept a watchful eye on the legality of their tactical operations in Serbia, perhaps because their militaries had internalized *jus in bello* norms at the institutional and operational levels as well.[14] Yet, NATO leadership sought throughout the campaign to combine two strategic goals that were, to some extent, at odds: fighting a "zero-casualty war" insofar as it concerned its own military personnel,[15] and holding "collateral damage" to Serbian civilians to a minimum. That said, subject to the constraint of holding NATO casualties to the vanishing point, NATO target selection was deeply influenced by the desire to hold civilian casualties down—partly because of genuine humanitarian and legal concerns and because of the belief that a war fought to uphold human rights should not be conducted in a way that caused many civilians to die, yet also partly to prevent public opinion in the allied countries from turning against the war. Thus, according to one commentator,

> the goal of avoiding civilian casualties affected the target selection process, operational details and rules of engagement, and the types of technologies used. Lawyers reviewed each proposed target, with many targets vetted by as many as nine people in different locations before being approved. Potentially sensitive targets, including those in downtown Belgrade and those in which civilian casualties were deemed likely, were reviewed by officials in each of the nineteen NATO capitals, sometimes at very high levels. Indeed, Lt. Gen. Michael Short, commander of NATO's Joint Air Force Component, commented that in the final days of the war, low likelihood of collateral damage "was the litmus [test] that we used to pick a target."[16]

14 *See* USAF Lt. Col. John G. Humphries, *Operations Law and the Rules of Engagement,* 6 Airpower J. 38 (1992) (describing internalization of international legal norms by U.S. military planners and operators especially in post-Vietnam War period). For a description of NATO's target selection process in the Kosovo War, including legal review, *see* Lambeth, *supra* note 6, at 186–89. Target selection and weaponry choices were heavily influenced by political rather than "military" considerations, to the point that some targets (*e.g.*, the Lola Utva aircraft repair factory in Pančevo) seem to have been picked, not so much for their military value, but because they were located away from civilian homes. Even some high-ranking NATO military officers concluded that the Alliance lacked a coherent military strategy. *See id.* at 199–203. Similarly, a military adviser for Human Rights Watch concluded that "Allied Force was neither calibrated nor intelligible. Rather, it was a succession of unfocused and unconvincing air excursions—experiments in communication by detonation." William M. Arkin, *Smart Bombs, Dumb Targeting,* 56 Bull. Atomic Scientists 46, 48 (May/June 2000). Arkin acknowledged, however, that "for all the criticism of targeting, Allied Force was fought with the utmost concern for civilian casualties and damage." *Id.* at 52.

15 *See* A.P.V. Rogers, *Zero-Casualty Warfare,* 837 IRRC 165 (2000) (*available at* http://www.icrc.org/eng/resources/documents/misc/57jqcu.htm).

16 Thomas, *supra* note 13, at 162–63.

Nonetheless, the toll of Serbian civilian deaths (using either NATO's or Human Right Watch's figures) was about 500. (The Serb government put the figure at between 1,200 and 5,700.)[17] Thus, NATO's conduct of hostilities received a significant amount of criticism from a variety of sources holding very different political and ideological perspectives—prominently including Western-based NGOs, such as Amnesty International, Human Rights Watch, and the International Committee of the Red Cross (ICRC). Their criticisms, in particular, eventually prompted the inquiry by the ICTY prosecutor that is the focus of our case study. One particularly well-informed criticism came in a report by Human Rights Watch, entitled *Civilian Deaths in the NATO Air Campaign.* It examined sixty-two of what it believed were ninety separate incidents involving civilian deaths in NATO's bombing campaign. Of these sixty-two, it contended that nine were attacks on non-military targets that it considered illegitimate. Human Rights Watch then called "on NATO governments to establish an independent and impartial commission, competent to receive confidential information, that would investigate violations of international humanitarian law and the extent of these violations, and would consider the need to alter targeting and bombing doctrine to ensure compliance with international humanitarian law."[18] The Human Rights Watch Report, along with criticisms from other sources,[19] led the ICTY prosecutor to appoint the committee that produced the Final Report to the Prosecutor.

2. Establishment of the ICTY—Its Origins, Legality, Organization, and Jurisdiction

a. Origins of the ICTY

On February 22, 1993, the United Nations Security Council, "[e]xpressing once again its grave alarm at continuing reports of widespread violations of international law occurring within the territory of the former Yugoslavia, including reports of mass killings and the continuance of the practice of 'ethnic cleansing,'" and "[d]etermining that this situation constitutes a threat to international peace and security," decided "that an international tribunal shall be established for the prosecution of persons responsible for serious violations of international humanitarian

17 *See* Daalder & O'Hanlon, *supra* note 5, at 240–42 (analysis of incidents of "collateral damage").

18 Cordesman, *supra* note 2, at 112.

19 Anthony Cordesman, a prominent U.S. strategic analyst and the author of an exhaustive review of the Kosovo campaign, wrote of this report: "The Human Rights Watch Report is as thorough, conscientious, and balanced a report as it is possible for a private organization to conduct. There are a number of US government analysts who privately admit that it is almost certainly more accurate in broad terms than NATO or US government reporting. It also tracks in broad terms with the results of two reports by the Organization for Security and Cooperation in Europe (OSCE) on human rights violations in Kosovo. These OSCE reports indicate that the NATO air campaign was considerably more costly than NATO and the US have reported, but that the collateral damage was minimal and unintentional, and that the Serbian violations of human rights were deliberate and massive. Cordesman, *supra* note 2, at 112.

law committed in the territory of the former Yugoslavia since 1991."[20] the ICTY. hout controversy, however. the puirs.ons, uh,pter of this volume. the *jus ad bellum*, in the conThe Council requested the Secretary General to provide it with a report on how to implement its decision. On May 3, 1993, the Secretary General filed the requested report,[21] which set forth the legal basis for the establishment of the proposed Tribunal and provided the articles of a draft "Statute" for it, including provisions relating to its jurisdiction, its organization, investigative and pre-trial proceedings, trial and post-trial proceedings, cooperation and judicial assistance, and other general provisions. On May 25, 1993, the Security Council, acting under its Chapter VII powers, adopted the Statute proposed by the Secretary General,[22] creating an international court, the ICTY, "for the sole purpose of prosecuting persons responsible for serious violations of international humanitarian law committed in the territory of the former Yugoslavia between 1 January 1991 and a date to be determined by the Security Council upon the restoration of peace."[23]

By the time the ICTY was created in 1993, there had been ample precedent for an international criminal tribunal. But the ICTY was, in fact, the first international criminal tribunal in the (near) half century that had elapsed since Nuremberg and Tokyo. The idea appears to have originated with the French,[24] for internal French political reasons,[25] but then received decisive support, with apparently more idealistic motives, from both the outgoing Bush Administration

20 S.C. Res. 808 (1993).

21 *See* S/25704.

22 *See* S.C. Res. 827 (1993).

23 *Id.* at ¶ 2. The ICTY's Statute has been amended repeatedly since 1993. The ICTY website, http://www.icty.org/, includes an excellent collection of the documents relating to the establishment, mission, and work of the Tribunal.

24 In the case of the ICTY, the idea for its establishment seems to have come from a distinguished French jurist, Robert Badinter, and from the French Foreign Minister Roland Dumas, who saw merit in the proposal when Badinter approached him with it. Dumas apparently saw the idea of a tribunal as a means of diverting the criticisms that were beginning to mount against the Western government's inactivity in the face of atrocities in Bosnia. Western public opinion was increasingly aware of the presence of Bosnia Serbian concentration camps in which Bosnian Serbs were being starved or killed, of the bombardment of the Bosnian capital of Sarajevo, and of other atrocities. At the same time, however, Western publics (at least as their political leaders understood them) were unwilling to support military intervention in the former Yugoslavia. Dumas saw the idea of a tribunal for the former Yugoslavia as a political solution to the dilemma posed by French and other Western public opinion. *See* Pierre Hazan, Justice in a Time of War: The True Story Behind the International Criminal Tribunal for the Former Yugoslavia 14–15 (James T. Snyder trans. 2004).

25 Dumas eventually overcame the resistance of French President François Mitterand to the proposal. According to French journalist and author Pierre Hazan, "the future tribunal [was] conceived at the time as a salve for French public opinion and as political insurance against eventual postwar accusations of complicity. Only marginally [was] it envisaged as a dissuasive weapon against the belligerents, without which this idea cannot go beyond the stage of pious vows." Hazan, *supra* note 24, at 16.

and new Clinton administration.[26] Yet, even after the ICTY was established, it remained caught in the dilemmas created by its founders' conflicting purposes.[27]

b. Legality of the ICTY

As noted above, Security Council Resolution 827, which created the ICTY, was an exercise of the Security Council's Chapter VII powers, which authorize the Council to take appropriate action upon determining the existence of "any threat to the peace" (U.N. Charter, Art. 39). One might reasonably have wondered, however, whether the atrocities taking place within Bosnia or, indeed, the whole of the former Yugoslavia, constituted a "threat to the peace" outside that area. More generally, one might wonder if there were any limits to the Council's power to determine whether a "threat to the peace" existed and, if there were such limits, whether the Charter had left it to the Council itself to police those limits, or instead allowed for the possibility of judicial supervision of the Council's determinations. In short, the issue was whether a "threat to the peace" existed as a political question committed to the Council alone or, at least in some cases, whether it was a judicial question.

The issue had arisen in (but was not decided by) *Questions of Interpretation and Application of the 1971 Montreal Convention Arising from the Aerial Incident at Lockerbie (Libya v. United States).*[28] Libya had refused to extradite two of its national suspected of terrorist attacks on a Pan Am flight over Lockerbie, Scotland in December 1988 and a French UTA flight over Niger in September 1989. In Resolution 731(1992), the Council had determined Libya's refusal to extradite the two men as "a threat to international peace and security." But Libya had not threatened or used force against any other state. Was the Council's finding simply a transparent fiction? And if it were, could the ICJ declare it to be so?

---

26 Dumas' proposal gained traction, upsetting other Western diplomats engaged in delicate negotiations with the Serbians and believing themselves close to a peace accord. U.S. Secretary of State Lawrence Eagleberger, in a speech in December 1992, accused Serbian President Slobodan Milosevic and Bosnian Serb leaders Radovan Karadzic and Ratko Mladic of war crimes. Although Eagleberger was about to leave office with the outgoing Bush Administration, his speech had a powerful effect. The first planning for an international tribunal got underway in early 1993. France, Germany, and Italy supported the concept. The United States, under the new Clinton Administration, proposed the creation of a working group at the United Nations to draft a statute for such a tribunal. Despite lingering misgivings, the main Western powers accepted the idea of a tribunal, and the other P5 members of the Security Council, China and Russia, were persuaded to go along. *See* Hazan, *supra* note 24, at 30–37.

27 In the words of one commentator:

> The Americans [saw] the ICTY as both an instrument that [could] permit them to preserve, even reinforce, their moral position in the face of the Bosnian conflict without having to deploy soldiers and one that [gave] them political weight they [could] bring to bear on events. The French want[ed] above all else to allay public rancor, while also hoping that the tribunal [could] have some dissuasive power over the belligerents. The British still fear[ed] that the court [would] threaten the search for a political solution to end the war. The Russians and Chinese [were] wary of the precedent created by a supranational tribunal brought into being and dominated by the West. . . . The Security Council [was] afraid of its own creation.

Hazan, *supra* note 24, at 45.

28 1992 ICJ 114 (Apr. 14). For analyses, *see* Bernhard Graefrath, *Leave to the Court What Belongs to the Court: The Libyan Case,* 4 Eur. J. Int'l L. 184, 200–05 (1993); and Derek Bowett, *The Impact of Security Council Measures on Dispute Settlement Procedures,* 5 Eur. J. Int'l L. 89, 93–96 (1994).

In the 1995 *Tadic* Case,[29] the ICTY's Appeals Chamber (Cassese, P.) examined the merits of the question whether its establishment by the Security Council was legally invalid. First, the Appeal Chamber held that it had (incidental) jurisdiction to examine the claim that it lacked (primary) jurisdiction because its establishment was invalid—the so-called "competence to determine its own competence." Second, it held that it was not precluded from examining that claim by because it posed a "political" question or "non-justiciable" issue. Relying (chiefly) on the practice of the Security Council, the *Tadic* Court held that even if the conflict in the former Yugoslavia was taken to be purely an "internal" one, the Council could determine it to be a threat to international peace and stability. "Indeed, the practice of the Security Council is rich with cases of civil war or internal strife which it classified as a 'threat to the peace' and dealt with under Chapter VII, with the encouragement or even at the behest of the General Assembly, such as the Congo crisis at the beginning of the 1960's and, more recently, Liberia and Somalia. It can thus be said that there is a common understanding, manifested by the 'subsequent practice' of membership of the United Nations at large, that the 'threat to the peace' of Article 39 may include, as one of its species, internal armed conflicts."[30] Similarly, the Appeals Chamber dealt with the objections that the Council had no authority to establish the ICTY because 1) the power to establish international criminal tribunals is not enumerated in the U.N. Charter as among the Council's powers; 2) the Council, as an executive organ, is constitutionally or inherently incapable of creating a judicial organ; and 3) the establishment of the ICTY did not and could not promote international peace, as the ongoing conflicts in the former Yugoslavia attest. The Appeals Chamber rejected all of these contentions.

Despite these lingering questions as to its legitimacy,[31] the ICTY's work from 1993 to the present has generally been well-received.[32]

c. Organization of the ICTY

The ICTY was the first international criminal tribunal with jurisdiction over war crimes and crimes against humanity since the 1945 International Military Tribunal at Nuremberg. It consisted of three organs: the Chambers (including both several Trial Chambers and one Appeals Chamber); the Office of the Prosecutor (OTP); and a Registry. The ICTY was fortunate in one of

29 *Prosecutor v. Tadic,* Decision on the Defense Motion for Interlocutory Appeal on Jurisdiction, Decision of Oct. 2, 1995 (*available at* http://www.icty.org/x/cases/tadic/acdec/en/51002.htm).

30 *Tadic, supra* note 29, at ¶ 30. Would this mean that whatever the circumstances in which an "internal" armed conflict takes place, the Council may determine it to be a threat to international peace and security? If there were a civil war in the remote Pacific island Republic of Vanuatu, and no other nation was threatened with spillover effects from it, could the Council validly find that to be such a threat?

31 *See* Martti Koskeniemi, *The Place of Law in Collective Security,* 17 Mich. J. Int'l L. 455, 483 (1995/6).

32 For an appraisal of the ICTY's effectiveness, *see* Jelena Subotić, Hijacked Justice: Dealing With the Past in the Balkans (2009). For an assessment of the ICTY's contribution to *jus in bello* case law, *see* Michael N. Schmitt, *Military Necessity in International Humanitarian Law: Preserving the Delicate Balance,* 50 Va. J. Int'l L. 795, 817–22 (2010).

its early appointments: the distinguished, energetic, and resourceful Italian legal scholar Antonio Cassese was selected as the Appeals Chambers' first President. "The Office of the Prosecutor has a dual role: investigating violations of international humanitarian law and prosecuting cases of such violations in court."[33] According to Article 16 of the ICTY Statute, the Prosecutor "shall act independently as a separate organ of the International Tribunal."[34] The prosecutor was to be appointed by the Security Council, to serve a four-year term. The prosecutor's staff, forming the Office of the Prosecutor, was to have an investigation unit and a prosecution unit.

The OTP inquiry into NATO's conduct in the Kosovo War gave rise to the question whether the Prosecutor had any discretion whether to investigate or prosecute criminal charges and, if so, what the extent of that discretion was. Article 18(1) spoke to that question by stating that the Prosecutor "shall initiate investigations *ex officio* or on the basis of information obtained from any source . . . [and] shall assess the information obtained and decide whether there is sufficient cause to proceed." That language does not expressly provide for—although it also does not preclude—the kind of "inquiry" or preliminary investigation that is embodied in the Final Report to the Prosecutor. As to prosecution, Article 18(3) stated that "[u]pon a determination that a prima facie case exists, the Prosecutor shall prepare an indictment. . . ."[35] A subsequent decision of the ICTY revealed the Prosecutor had discretion, albeit not unlimited, both to investigate and to prosecute.[36]

d. Jurisdiction of the ITCY

Of particular relevance to the Final Report to the Prosecutor are the provisions of the ICTY Statute addressing the Tribunal's "competence" or jurisdiction. The Secretary General's report noted four "fundamental elements" of the ICTY's competence: "*ratione materiae* (subject-matter jurisdiction), *ratione personae* (personal jurisdiction), *ratione loci* (territorial jurisdiction) and *ratione temporis* (temporal jurisdiction)."[37]

---

33 Sonja Boelart-Suonimen, *The International Criminal Tribunal for the former Yugoslavia and the Kosovo Conflict*, 837 IRRC 217 (2000) (*available at* https://www.icrc.org/eng/resources/documents/misc/57jqd2.htm).

34 *See* Updated Statute of The International Criminal Tribunal for the Former Yugoslavia, Art. 16 (*available at* http://www.icty.org/x/file/Legal%20Library/Statute/statute_sept09_en.pdf).

35 *See id.* at Art. 18.

36 *Delalic, Mucic, and Landzo*, IT-96-21-A, Appeals Chamber, Feb. 20, 2001, at ¶ 602 ("In the present context, indeed in many criminal justice systems, the entity responsible for prosecutions has finite financial and human resources and cannot realistically be expected to prosecute every offender which may fall within the strict terms of its jurisdiction. It must of necessity make decisions as to the nature of the crimes and the offenders to be prosecuted. It is beyond question that the Prosecutor has a broad discretion in relation to the initiation of investigations and in the preparation of indictments. . . . It is also clear that a discretion of this nature is not unlimited. A number of limitations on the discretion entrusted to the Prosecutor are evident in the Tribunal's Statute and Rules of Procedure and Evidence.").

37 S/25704 at ¶ 31.

In terms of *subject matter jurisdiction*, the proposed ICTY Statute conferred on the ICTY the powers to prosecute persons "committing or ordering to be committed grave breaches of the Geneva Conventions of 12 August 1949" (Article 2),[38] and of persons "violating the laws or customs of war" (Article 3). The Secretary General pointed out that international humanitarian law included both conventional and customary law, and that some of the major conventional law had become customary law. Specifically, the Secretary General identified the four 1949 Geneva Conventions, the fourth Hague Convention and annexed Regulations of 1907 on the laws and customs of land war, the 1948 Genocide Convention, and the 1945 Charter of the International Military Tribunal, as "beyond doubt . . . part of international customary law."[39] The 1977 Additional Protocols I and II were not included in this list. (Neither, of course, did the Secretary General's report deny that they, or parts of them, were customary law.)

As to personal jurisdiction, the Secretary General observed that S.C. Res. 808, read together with the resolutions that had preceded it, had intended the proposed Tribunal to exercise jurisdiction over natural persons, thus creating a regime of individual criminal responsibility.[40] Accordingly, Article 6 of the proposed Statute vested personal jurisdiction "over natural persons," and Article 7(1) provided that a "person who planned, instigated, ordered, committed or otherwise aided or abetted in the planning, preparation or execution of a crime referred to in articles 2 to 5 of the present Statute, shall be individually responsible for the crime."

As to territorial and temporal jurisdiction, the Secretary General explained that "the territorial and temporal jurisdiction of the International Tribunal extends to serious violations of international humanitarian law to the extent that they have been 'committed in the territory of the former Yugoslavia since 1991.'"[41] Article 8 of the proposed Statute embodied that understanding.

Considering the ICTY's jurisdictional provisions as a whole, it is clear that the ICTY had personal, territorial, and temporal jurisdiction over the NATO political leaders, military officials, and personnel who planned or executed NATO's aerial campaign in Serbia and Kosovo (both of them parts of the territory of the former Yugoslavia) from late March until mid-June 1999.[42] The question of subject-matter jurisdiction is somewhat more complicated, in part because some of the major NATO states involved in the Kosovo campaign (the United States and France among them) were not parties to Protocol I, and in part because there was doubt about whether and

38 For a superb account of how "grave breaches"(a concept originally relating to the duty of parties to a treaty to implement certain of its provisions into national criminal law) mutated into *international* war crimes, *see* Marko Divac Öberg, *The Absorption of Grave Breaches into War Crimes Law*, 91 IRRC 163 (2009).

39 S/25704 at ¶ 35.

40 *See* S/25704 at ¶ 50.

41 S/25704 at ¶ 62 (quoting S.C. Res. 808 at ¶ 1).

42 *See* Boelart-Suonimen, *supra* note 33 ("[T]here is little doubt that the conflict in Kosovo, which between March and June 1999 involved the FRY, the KLA and NATO countries and was waged mainly in the territory of the FRY, falls within the jurisdiction of the Tribunal.").

how far Protocol I could be said to be established "customary law." [43] Hence, insofar as Article 3 of the ICTY Statute subsumed Protocol I, its application to those non-party nations was open to argument.

The *Tadic* case, which we have already discussed in relation to the legality of the ICTY, is a fundamental decision in the ICTY's jurisprudence also for at least two other reasons. First, it delineated the scope of Article 3 of the ICTY Statute—the substantive criminal provision of greatest relevance to our case study, and in any event, perhaps the most significant substantive provision of the Statute for the ICTY's case law. Second, *Tadic* also laid down several conditions (the "*Tadic* conditions") for criminal conduct to fall within Article 3.

Under *Tadic*, in general, Article 3 subjects persons to criminal liability for violations of the laws and customs of war other than those specified elsewhere in the Statute. As more precisely explicated in *Tadic*, Article 3 "is a general clause covering all violations of humanitarian law not falling under Article 2 or covered by Articles 4 or 5, more specifically: (i) violations of the Hague law on international conflicts; (ii) infringements of provisions of the Geneva Conventions other than those classified as 'grave breaches' by those Conventions; (iii) violations of common Article 3 and other customary rules on internal conflicts; (iv) violations of agreements binding upon the parties to the conflict, considered qua treaty law; i.e., agreements which have not turned into customary international law. . ."[44]

A mere violation of one or more of these rules would not necessarily constitute a crime, however. The *jus in bello* was not originally created as a criminal law regime, and violations of its rules did not, as such, establish individual criminal liability. Hence, before such liability could be found for a violation, further conditions would have to be shown to exist. *Tadic* notes two of these. First, it requires that the violation must be "serious," that is, it must

> constitute a breach of a rule protecting important values, and the breach must involve grave consequences for the victim. Thus, for example, the fact of a combatant simply appropriating a loaf of bread in an occupied village would not amount to a 'serious violation of international humanitarian law' although it may be regarded as falling foul of the basic principle laid down in Article 46, paragraph 1 of the Hague Regulations.[45]

Second, *Tadic* imposes the condition that "the violation of the rule must entail, under customary or conventional law, the individual criminal responsibility of the [defendant]."[46] Since "[i]

---

43 *See, e.g., S. v. Petane*, Cape Provincial Division, Nov. 3, 1987, 1988 (3) So. African L. Repts. (*available at* http://www.icrc.org/ihl-nat.nfs/39a82e2ca42b52974125670050814 4/50c59239).e1b869ed) (Protocol I not deemed customary law).

44 *See supra* note 29, at ¶ 89.

45 *Id.* at ¶ 94.

46 *Id.*

n customary international law, war crimes generally require intentional or reckless conduct,"[47] those forms of *mens rea* will usually also be elements of a criminal violation.

e. The ICTY Prosecutor and NATO

During and after the NATO campaign in Kosovo, the ICTY prosecutor (at the time, Louise Arbour) received many complaints alleging violations of the law and customs of war by NATO forces. In a Press Release of March 31, 1999, Prosecutor Arbour noted that she had "received requests from persons and groups urging me to indict various NATO and other officials for war crimes in relation to the air strikes conducted in Serbia" and commented that "[t]here is no doubt in my mind that the jurisdiction of the Tribunal over Kosovo is well known to all . . . The Tribunal has jurisdiction over [war crimes] by anyone."[48] Shortly afterward, NATO acquiesced in the Prosecutor's jurisdiction. On May 14, 1999, Arbour took the unusual step of establishing an *ad hoc* committee (the Review Committee) to assess the information she had received and to assess whether there was a sufficient basis to proceed further with a full, in-depth investigation of the allegations made about NATO's conduct of hostilities. The Review Committee was an advisory body; the Prosecutor herself retained the ultimate power to decide whether to go forward with an investigation.

The Review Committee completed its work by the end of May 2000, and recommended to the Prosecutor that the OTP conduct no investigation into the NATO bombing campaign. That document, which was subsequently released, is what we here call the Final Report to the Prosecutor. The stated basis for the Review Committee's recommendation was this: "[i]n all cases, either the law is not sufficiently clear or investigations are unlikely to result in the acquisition of sufficient evidence to substantiate charges against high level accused or against lower accused for particularly heinous offenses."[49]

On June 2, 2000, Arbour's successor as Prosecutor, Carla Del Ponte, announced at a meeting of the Security Council both the recommendation of the Review Committee and her decision to adopt that recommendation. Del Ponte said:

47 Öberg, *supra* note 38, at 171; *see, e.g., Prosecutor v Blaskic*, IT-95-14-T, at ¶ 152 (2000) ("[A]ccording to the Trial Chamber, the *mens rea* constituting all the violations of Article 2 of the [ICTY] Statute [containing grave breaches] include both guilty intent and recklessness which may be likened to serious criminal negligence."). *See generally* Knut Dormann, Elements of War Crimes under the Rome Statute of the International Criminal Court: Sources and Commentary 488–93 (2002).

48 Anne-Sophie Massa, *NATO's Intervention in Kosovo and the Decision of the Prosecutor of the International Criminal Tribunal for the Former Yugoslavia Not to Investigate: An Abusive Exercise of Prosecutorial Discretion?*, 24 Berkeley J. Int'l L. 610, 617 (2006).

49 International Criminal Tribunal for the Former Yugoslavia: Final Report to the Prosecutor by the Committee Established to Review the NATO Bombing Campaign Against the Federal Republic of Yugoslavia (June 8, 2000), 39 I.L.M. 1257, at ¶ 90 [hereinafter the Final Report to the Prosecutor or the Final Report] (*available at* http://www.icty.org/sid/10052).

> In 1999, my predecessor, Justice Arbour, established a working group within her office, comprising military lawyers, military analysts and other experts, to examine and assess all complaints and allegations and accompanying material. In addition, the team has assessed all new allegations and materials subsequent to their arrival in my office. Analysis of the material has, quite properly, taken some time, and has involved an examination of all facts and a detailed legal analysis of all aspects of the Tribunal's jurisdiction.
>
> I am now able to announce my conclusion, following full consideration of my team's assessment of all complaints and allegations, that there is no basis for opening an investigation into any of these allegations or into other incidents related to the NATO bombing. Although some mistakes were made by NATO, I am very satisfied that there was no deliberate targeting of civilians or of unlawful military targets by NATO during the bombing campaign.[50]

Subsequently, as she had indicated she would, the Prosecutor made the Final Report publicly available.

Part B now presents the factual and legal background for the aspects of the Final Report that deal with the legality of NATO targeting decisions and practices in two important cases, together requiring application of the *jus in bello* principles of distinction and proportionality, as well the special problem of human shields. With that background, Part C provides you study questions to focus your reading of the Final Report to the Prosecutor, as well as excerpts of the relevant portions of the Report itself. Part D provides extensive and critical legal commentary on the Final Report, and Part E then treats the Final Report as a vehicle for an analysis of the realist and legalist perspectives on the *jus in bello.*

50 Security Council, 4150th mtg., June 2, 2000, S/PV.4150 at 3 (remarks of Prosecutor Del Ponte).

B. THE *JUS IN BELLO* IN THE ATTACKS ON THE GRDELICA GORGE BRIDGE AND ON THE SERBIAN TV AND RADIO STATION (RTS)

We turn now to the sections of the Final Report to the Prosecutor that deal with two incidents involving attacks on what NATO claimed to be valid military objectives. The first of these was an attack on the railway bridge over the Grdelica Gorge on April 12, 1999. The second was the bombardment of the Serbian TV and Radio Station (RTS) in Belgrade on April 23, 1999.

In subpart A below, we focus on the attack on the Grdelica Gorge Bridge. In subpart B, we shall take up the attack on RTS. We identify and provide background discussion of the facts and the basic legal questions, but include a substantial discussion of the threshold legal question of applicable law and raise the increasingly problematic question of the use of so-called "human shields" to complicate the task of compliance with the *jus in bello.*

1. The Attack on the Grdelica Gorge Bridge

The details of NATO's attack on the Grdelica Gorge railway bridge can be found in the selections from the Final Report to the Prosecutor below. Here it is sufficient to say that on April 12, 1999, at about 11:40 A.M., a NATO aircraft (a U.S. F-15E) launched two laser-guided bombs at a designated target, the Grdelica Gorge railway bridge near Leskovac in eastern Serbia. The first bomb was launched by the pilot (or possibly a second crew member, a weapons system officer) just as a five-carriage passenger train began crossing the bridge. After the pilot realized that the first bomb had struck a train rather than the bridge, the pilot circled back and launched a second bomb, perhaps seven to eight seconds later. In the interval between the first and second strike, the train had moved forward along the bridge, so that the second bomb caused additional damage to the train. At least ten people died and fifteen were injured as a result of the attack. Videos of both strikes are available on the internet, and we encourage students to view them.

The most relevant provision of the ICTY Statute appears to be Article 3, which empowers the ICTY to "prosecute persons violating the laws or customs of war."[51] Of those "laws or customs," the most obviously relevant would seem to be Articles 52(2), 51(5)(b), and 57(2) of Additional Protocol I—that is, in essence, the principles of distinction and proportionality, as formulated in Protocol I. Article 52(2)("General Protection of civilian objects") states the principle of distinction as follows:

51 Article 2 of the ICTY Statute, which confers jurisdiction with respect to grave breaches of the 1949 Geneva Conventions, would also apply. All NATO states had ratified those treaties. But their relevance to the incidents here is not apparent. *See generally* W.J. Fenrick, *Attacking the Civilian as a Punishable Offense,* 7 Duke J. Comp. & Int'l L. 539, 559–62 (1997); Massa, *supra* note 48, 619–20.

> 2. Attacks shall be limited strictly to military objectives. In so far as objects are concerned, military objectives are limited to those objects which by their nature, location, purpose or use make an effective contribution to military action and whose total or partial destruction, capture or neutralization, in the circumstances ruling at the time, offers a definite military advantage.

Article 51(5)(b) formulates the principle of proportionality as forbidding:

> An attack which may be expected to cause incidental loss of civilian life, injury to civilians, damage to civilian objects, or a combination thereof, which would be excessive in relation to the concrete and direct military advantage anticipated.

Finally, Article 57(2) ("Precautions in attack") states:

> 2. With respect to attacks, the following precautions shall be taken:
>
> (a) those who plan or decide upon an attack shall:
> (i) do everything feasible to verify that the objectives to be attacked are neither civilians nor civilian objects and are not subject to special protection but are military objectives within the meaning of paragraph 2 of Article 52 and that it is not prohibited by the provisions of this Protocol to attack them;
> (ii) take all feasible precautions in the choice of means and methods of attack with a view to avoiding, and in any event to minimizing, incidental loss or civilian life, injury to civilians and damage to civilian objects;
> (iii) refrain from deciding to launch any attack which may be expected to cause incidental loss of civilian life, injury to civilians, damage to civilian objects, or a combination thereof, which would be excessive in relation to the concrete and direct military advantage anticipated;
>
> (b) an attack shall be cancelled or suspended if it becomes apparent that the objective is not a military one or is subject to special protection or that the attack may be expected to cause incidental loss of civilian life, injury to civilians, damage to civilian objects, or a combination thereof, which would be excessive in relation to the concrete and direct military advantage anticipated . . .
>
> (c) effective advance warning shall be given of attacks which may affect the civilian population, unless circumstances do not permit.

The United States is not a party to Protocol I. Hence, U.S. forces serving with NATO in the Kosovo campaign would be subject to criminal prosecution for their role in this incident only if Articles 52(2), 51(5)(b), and 57(2) were part of the "customs" of war. Accordingly, the first legal question is whether these provisions have attained the status of customary law. We address this threshold question now and return to the application of the Protocol's principles after you have had an opportunity to study the Final Report to the Prosecutor itself.

Some judges and scholars consider Articles 52(2), 51(5)(b), and 57(2) of Additional Protocol I to be customary law. Thus, W.J. Fenrick, former Senior Legal Adviser to the OTP (and reputed draftsman of the Final Report),[52] maintained that "[t]he Protocol I definition of military objective is the definition generally accepted today."[53] Likewise, Michael Bothe found that "there is no doubt" that the principle of distinction, as formulated in Article 52(2), "is a rule of customary international law and its binding force is, thus, not limited to the parties to Protocol I."[54] U.S. Navy Rear Admiral Horace Robertson, Jr. affirmed that "the principle of the military objective . . . essentially as articulated in Protocol Additional I" had met "general acceptance" as "customary international law."[55] Ove Bring thought it was "probably correct" to perceive Article 52(2) as "a codification of traditional customary law applied during World War II and earlier."[56] In a carefully reasoned opinion in 2005, the Eritrea-Ethiopia Claims Commission found that Article 52(2) "is widely accepted as an expression of customary international law."[57] Also in 2005, the ICTY Trial Chambers in the *Strugar* case declared that Article 52 was a "reaffirmation and reformulation of a rule that had previously attained the status of customary international law."[58]

But other scholars and experts have struck a more cautious note. Adam Roberts criticized the Final Report for affirming that Article 52 "is 'generally accepted as part of customary law'" because the Report "nowhere mentions the declarations made in respect of that article by many States, including NATO members."[59] Burrus Carnahan pointed out that "formulation of a gener-

52 Fenrick, whose service with the ICTY began in 1992, had previously been the Director of Law for Operations and Training in the Canadian Department of Defense and was a retired Canadian Armed Forces Frigate Captain. He is considered to have been the primary draftsman of the Final Report. *See* Michael Mandel, *Politics and Human Rights in International Criminal Law: Our Case Against NATO and the Lessons to be Learned From It*, 25 Fordham Int'l L. J. 95, 117 (2001). Captain Fenrick has been widely recognized as a leading scholar of the law of war.

53 W.J. Fenrick, *Targeting and Proportionality during the NATO Bombing Campaign Against Yugoslavia*, 12 Eur. J. Int'l L. 489, 494 (2001). *See also* Massa, *supra* note 48, at 620.

54 Michael Bothe, *Targeting*, in Andru E. Wall, ed., Legal and Ethical Lessons of NATO's Kosovo Campaign 173, 176 (2002).

55 Horace B. Robertson, Jr., *The Principle of Military Objective in the Law of Armed Conflict*, 8 U.S.A.F. Acad. J. Legal Stud. 35, 57 (1997/8).

56 Ove Bring, *International Humanitarian Law After Kosovo: Is Lex Lata Sufficient?*, *in* Andru E. Wall, ed., Legal and Ethical Lessons of NATO's Kosovo Campaign 257, 259 (2002).

57 Eritrea-Ethiopia Claims Commission, *Partial Award, Western Front, Aerial Bombardment and Related Claims, Eritrea's Claims 1, 3, 5, 9–13, 14, 21, 25 and 26*, at ¶1132 (2005), 45 ILM 396, 418 (2006).

58 *Prosecutor v. Strugar*, IT-01-42-T, Trial Chamber II, Judgment, at ¶ 223 (Jan. 31, 2005).

59 Adam Roberts, *The Laws of War After Kosovo*, in Andru E. Wall, ed., Legal and Ethical Lessons of NATO's Kosovo Campaign 401, 422 (2002). For a summary of these reservations and interpretations, *see* Julie Gaudreau, *The Reservations*

ally acceptable definition of a lawful target has been one of the most vexatious problems facing jurists in the law of armed conflict."[60] Then U.S. State Department Deputy Legal Adviser Michael Matheson stated in 1987 that it was "difficult to say exactly which of the rules contained in [Protocol I] currently are part of customary law . . . [[I]t may be possible in many cases to say that a general principle is an accepted part of customary law, but to have considerable disagreement as to the precise statement of that general principle."[61] In identifying "a few examples of the basic principles contained in Protocol I that we believe should be observed and in due course recognized as customary law, even if they have not already achieved that status," Matheson referred to the principle that "while civilian populations inevitably will be affected by lawful military actions, acts of violence will be directed solely against legitimate military objectives. . . ."[62] Matheson was apparently speaking in an official or semi-official capacity. U.S. military documents also deviate to at least some extent from Article 52(2). The 1988 U.S. Naval Handbook adopted an arguably broader definition of "military objectives" than Protocol I's.[63] Likewise, in

---

to the Protocols Additional to the Geneva Conventions for the Protection of War Victims, 849 IRRC 143 (2003).

60 Capt. Burrus M. Carnahan, *Protecting Civilians Under the Draft Geneva Protocol: A Preliminary Inquiry,* 18 A.F.L. Rev. 32, 46 (1976). Carnahan also noted that the definition of military objectives found in Protocol I apparently originated in a 1969 resolution of the Institute of International Law. *See id.* at 47; *see also* Jirí Fuchs, *Shot in the Dark: International Law of Targeting in Theory and State Practice,* 3 Acta Soceitatis Martensis 21, 24–25 (2007/8). Carnahan's evidence refutes Ove Bring's claim that Article 52(2) codifies customary law from World War II and before.

61 Michael J. Matheson, *Customary Law and Additional Protocol I to the Geneva Conventions for Protection of War Victims: Future Directions in Light of the U.S. Decision Not to Ratify,* 81 Proc. Am. Soc. Int'l L. 26, 29 (1987) [hereinafter Matheson, *Customary Law*]. *See also* Michael J. Matheson, *Session One: The United States Position on the Relation of Customary International Law to the 1977 Protocols Additional to the 1949 Geneva Conventions,* 2 Am. U. J. Int'l L. 419, 226–27 (1987).

62 Matheson, *Customary Law, supra* note 61, at 29, 30.

63 *See* Naval Manual (1995), 8.1.1, cited in Fuchs, *supra* note 60, at 33. Under that provision, objects which by their nature, location, purpose, or use would effectively contribute to the enemy's war-fighting or war-sustaining capability would constitute military objectives. This definition of military objective is understood to permit the targeting of the enemy's economic assets if they are sufficiently related to its war effort. For example, the Union Army's destruction of the Confederacy's cotton stores would be considered valid because of cotton's role in sustaining the Confederate war effort. *See* Waxman, *supra* note 3, at 10 & n.19. On the extent to which the ostensible difference between the Naval Manual's definition and that of Article 52(2) might be narrowed, *see* Robertson, *supra* note 55, at 45–46, 50–51 (1997/8); Lieut. David A. Melson, *Targeting War-Sustaining Capability at Sea: Compatibility with Additional Protocol I,* 2009 Army Law. 44 (2009).

We note that the U.S. interpretation has been bolstered by the Eritrea-Ethiopia Claims Commission's 2005 decision in *Partial Award, Western Front, Aerial Bombardment, supra* note 57. The Commission (over a solitary dissent) affirmed that Ethiopia's aerial attack on Eritrea's Hirgigo power plant targeted a lawful military objective under Article 52(2). The Hirgigo plant was still under construction at the time of the strike. Upon completion, it would have replaced a much older plant at Grar, which was supplying power to Massawa, the location of a port and naval base that were indisputably military objectives. In holding the Hirgigo plant to have been a valid objective, the Commission accepted Ethiopia's argument that the plant, thought still not producing power, was nonetheless making an "effective contribution" to Eritrea's campaign, because "a State at war should not be obligated to wait until an object is, in fact, put to use when the purpose of that object is to make an effective contribution to military action once it has been tested, commissioned and put to use." *Id.* at para. 120. Further, the Commission held that the attack on the plant offered Ethiopia a "definite military advantage" in part because of its economic importance to Eritrea. "[T]he fact that the power station was of economic importance to Eritrea is evidence that damage to it, in the circumstance prevailing in late May 2000 when Ethiopia was trying to force Eritrea to agree to end the war, offered a definite advantage. 'The purpose of any military action must always be to influence the political will of the adversary.' . . . The infliction of economic loses from attacks against military objectives is a lawful. . . ." *Id.* at para. 121. The dissent argued that "[t]he infliction of economic loss or the undermining of moral through the destruction of a civilian object, or the probability that the destruction may bring the decision-makers to the negotiation table, do not make the object a military objective." *Id.* at para. 4 (Separate Op. of van Houutte).

its 2003 Military Commission Instructions, the U.S. Defense Department "appear[ed] to have adopted a substantially broader definition of military objective" than Article 52(2).[64] (The 2010 *Manual for Military Commissions: United States* includes a revised definition of "military objective" that is appreciably closer to Article 52(2)).[65] At least from the U.S. perspective at the time of the Final Report, therefore, it seemed doubtful whether Article 52(2) correctly formulated the principle of distinction or stated a recognized rule of customary law.[66]

A similar dispute surrounds Protocol I's formulation of the principle of proportionality (in Articles 51 and 57). In *Public Committee against Torture in Israel*, the Supreme Court of Israel (although without much analysis) appeared to hold that Article 51(5)(b) was customary international law.[67] Likewise, Ove Bring has claimed that the principle of proportionality as expressed in these Protocol I provisions "is arguably a codification of traditional customary law."[68] But W. Hays Parks, then the Special Assistant to the Judge Advocate General of the U.S. Army, emphatically disagreed with Bring's view that Protocol I's formulation of the proportionality principle stated a rule of customary law.[69] In a classic study published in 1990, Parks reported that "[i]n the course of American military review of Protocol I, it was concluded that the concept of proportionality is not a rule of customary law, as it has been represented."[70] Parks also pointed out that "there remains a substantial lack of agreement as to the meaning of the provisions in Protocol I relating to proportionality. This is a rather disconcerting situation given that other lawyers are claiming that the concept of proportionality is customary international law."[71]

---

64 William J. Fenrick, *Riding the Rhino: Attempting to Develop Usable Legal Standards for Combat Activities,* 30 B.C. Int'l & Comp. L. Rev. 111, 121 (2007); *see also* Carolin Wuerzner, *Mission Impossible? Bringing Charges for the Crime of Attacking Civilians or Civilian Objects Before International Criminal Tribunals,* 90 IRRC 907, 915–16 (2008).

65 *See Manual for Military Commissions: United States,* Pt. IV, definition 1(a)(1)(B) (2010 ed.) (*available at* http://www.defense.gov/news/2010_Manual_for_Military_Commissions.pdf).

66 For a defense of Article 52 from the standpoint of a military lawyer, *see* A.P.V. Rogers, *Law on the Battlefield* 70–71, 78–79 (2d ed. 2004).

67 *Public Committee against Torture in Israel v. Gov't of Israel,* HCJ 769/02, at ¶ 43 (Sup. Ct. Israel 2005).

68 Bring, *supra* note 56, at 257, 262.

69 W. Hays Parks, *Commentary, in* Legal and Ethical Lessons of NATO's Kosovo Campaign 281, 291 (Andru E. Wall, ed., 2002).

70 W. Hays Parks, *Air War and the Law of War,* 32 A.F. L. Rev. 1, 173 (1990) [hereinafter Parks, *Air War*].

71 *Id.* at 175. *See also* W. Hays Parks, *The Protection of Civilians from Air Warfare,* 22 Israel Y.B. on Human Rts. 65, 90–97 (1998) [hereinafter Parks, *The Protection of Civilians*] (amassing evidence of state practice to show that civilians have historically been accorded different levels of protection and that states have taken different views as to their obligations to avoid or minimize civilian losses).

2. The Attack on the RTS Station

In studying the Grdelica Gorge Bridge incident, we consider some of the main questions of distinction and proportionality to which NATO's campaign gave rise. Here we shall investigate another important, and related, issue raised by the campaign and, more specifically, by the bombing of RTS: the question of responsibility for collateral damage, including the death of civilians.

The circumstances in which that question arose were as follows. On April 12, 1999, NATO issued a general warning to Western media outlets that the RTS station in Belgrade might be attacked. Western journalists were accordingly warned by their employers to stay away from the building before the attack. It would appear that some Serbian government officials may have learned of an attack indirectly, through Western media sources. NATO did not, however, issue a specific warning of an imminent attack, either to Serbia or to anyone else. It is reported that NATO officials in Brussels had told Amnesty International that a specific warning would have endangered NATO pilots executing an attack. As noted, the attack on RTS occurred at 2:20 A.M. on April 23, 1999, some eleven days after the general warning had been given. Article 57(2)(c) of Protocol I states: "effective advance warning shall be given of attacks which may affect the civilian population, unless circumstances do not permit."

NATO's April 23, 1999 attack on the central studio of RTS, the state-owned broadcasting facility located in the heart of Belgrade, Serbia's capital city, probably caused more controversy than any of its other attacks on Serbian targets.[72] The attack resulted in between ten and seventeen civilian deaths. The attack interrupted RTS broadcasting for only a few hours—an outcome that NATO had apparently foreseen. NATO defended the attack on RTS on the grounds that it was part of a concerted attack aimed at disrupting and degrading Serbia's C3 (Command, Control, and Communications) network. NATO alleged that the RTS facilities in Belgrade were being used as radio relay stations and transmitters to support Serbian military and special police forces, so that they represented a legitimate military objective. In general, "dual use" objects such as a broadcasting station may be considered legitimate military objectives if they are integrated into the enemy's C3 system.[73]

---

72 Six Serbian nationals subsequently brought suit in the European Court of Human Rights on behalf of themselves and their deceased children and a deceased spouse against 17 NATO states that were parties to the European Convention on Human Rights, alleging that the bombardment of the RTS station in Belgrade violated various provisions of that Convention, including the right to life and freedom of expression. The Grand Chamber of the European Court unanimously found the complaint inadmissible on jurisdictional grounds. *See Bankovic et al. v. Belgium et al.*, App. No. 52207/99, Eur. Ct. H.R. (2001), 41 I.L.M. 517. For a critical analysis of the decision, *see* Erik Roxstrom, Mark Gibney & Terje Einarsen, *The NATO Bombing Case* (Bankovic et al. v. Belgium et al.) *and the Limits of Western Human Rights Protection*, 23 Boston U. Int'l L. J. 55 (2005).

73 For example, the *San Remo Manual* holds that enemy merchant ships may be considered legitimate targets for "being incorporated into or assisting the enemy's intelligence gathering system, *e.g.*, engaging in reconnaissance, early warning, surveillance, or command, control and communications missions." San Remo Manual on International Law Applicable to Armed Conflicts at Sea, 12 June 1994, ¶ 60 (*available at* https://www.icrc.org/ihl/INTRO/560?).OpenDocument. There remains a question whether a broadcasting station must be contributing to the enemy's action when attacked. For an

Much of the controversy over the bombing of RTS arose from the fact that NATO may have targeted the station because it was used to broadcast political propaganda in favor of the Serbian government. To quote from the Final Report (which itself quotes official NATO sources):

> [T]he bombing was also justified on the basis of the propaganda purpose to which it was employed:
>
> "[We need to] directly strike at the very central nerve system of Milosovic's regime. This of course are those assets which are used to plan and direct and to create the political environment of [in]tolerance in Yugoslavia in which these brutalities can not only be accepted but even condoned. [. . .] Strikes against TV transmitters and broadcast facilities are part of our campaign to dismantle the FRY propaganda machinery which is a vital part of President Milosevic's control mechanism."
>
> In a similar statement, British Prime Minister Tony Blair was reported as saying in *The Times* that the media "is the apparatus that keeps him [Milosević] in power and we are entirely justified as NATO allies in damaging and taking on those targets" (24 April, 1999). In a statement of 8 April 1999, NATO also indicated that the TV studios would be targeted unless they broadcast 6 hours per day of Western media reports: "If President Milosevic would provide equal time for Western news broadcasts in its programmes without censorship 3 hours a day between noon and 1800 and 3 hours a day between 1800 and midnight, then his TV could be an acceptable instrument of public information."[74]

NATO's critics contended that if NATO had targeted RTS, not because of its role in the C3 system, but to silence its propaganda, it would be questionable whether NATO had truly aimed at a military objective as defined in Article 52(2). Thus, George Aldrich, a U.S. State Department official and later a judge on the U.S-Iran Claims Tribunal, wrote that

> if the television studios . . . were targeted merely because they were spreading propaganda to the civilian population, even including blatant lies about the armed conflict, it would be open to question whether such use could legitimately be considered an 'effective contribution to military action.' . . . [I]t is not a given that every object that may be used to strengthen civilian morale is, by virtue of such use, a legitimate military objective. Certainly, churches, schools, and medical facilities are important to civilian morale but are not, as a consequence, military objectives, and

argument that NATO's justification was too general and failed to show that the attack on RTS was militarily useful in the "circumstances ruling at the time," *see* Bring, *supra* note 56, at 257, 260–61.

74 Final Report to the Prosecutor, *supra* note 49, at ¶ 74.

> I have never seen it suggested that newspapers or civilian radio and television stations become military objectives because they are used to influence the population and maintain its morale.[75]

Further, even if RTS' propaganda had been making an "effective contribution" to Serbia's military action, critics contended, it might well not have been the case that shutting RTS down would have offered NATO a "definite military advantage," as Article 52(2) also requires. Aldrich again said, "The adverse political and psychological effects of an effort to deprive the population of a source of information, along with the probable consequent deaths and injuries among the civilian staff of the studio, might well outweigh any benefits that could result from the destruction of the studio."[76]

Another NATO critic, Paolo Benvenuti, argued that the civilian deaths at the RTS station were not in fact "collateral" to NATO's attack. Benvenuti argued that NATO's bombing of the RTS station was "not an unwanted, collateral effect" of its attack on Serbia's C3 system, but was intentional. From that he deduced that "the civilian casualties as 'collateral damage' appear to be caused willfully."[77] Although we admit to finding Benvenuti's reasoning hard to follow,[78] he may be pointing to the "pretext problem," the problem that "attacks aimed at undermining civilian morale could be justified by the dual-use nature of the targets chosen, even if the intended military impact were in fact secondary or even fictitious."[79]

Two related issues may be identified here. The narrower issue is whether NATO's attack on the RTS satisfied complied with Article 57(2)(c). (That issue is the focus of the Final Report, ¶ 77). The larger issue is whether the military commanders of an attacking state breached the laws and customs of war by causing excessive civilian losses if the defending state deliberately chose

---

75 George H. Aldrich, *Yugoslavia's Television Studios as Military Objectives,* 1 Int'l L. Forum du Droit Internationale 149, 150 (1999). *See also* Andreas Laursen, *NATO, the War Over Kosovo, and the ICTY Investigation,* 17 Am. U. Int'l L. Rev. 765, 783–84 (2002).

76 Aldrich, *supra* note 75, at 150. Aldrich's reference to the possible political and psychological effects of bombing RTS may suggest that his comments would be better framed as part of a proportionality analysis than as part of an Article 52(2) analysis. In any case, Aldrich was surely right in supposing that if political and psychological effects can be considered when evaluating whether a broadcasting facility is making an "effective contribution" to a war effort, similar effects must also be relevant in assessing whether an attack on the facilities obtained an overall "military advantage."

77 Paolo Benvenuti, *The ICTY Prosecutor and the Review of the NATO Bombing Campaign against the Federal Republic of Yugoslavia,* 12 Eur. J. Int'l L. 503, 521 (2001).

78 Benvenuti may have assumed that NATO's attack on the RTS station was impermissible because it was not a military object (although the C3 system was). In that case, NATO would have been targeting a civilian object, in which the presence of civilians was to have been expected—so that their deaths would not have been "incidental." But that seems to assume that NATO could and should have attacked the elements of the C3 system without attacking the facilities where they were located. Alternatively and more plausibly, Benvenuti may have been arguing that NATO was attacking the RTS station both as a military objective (part of the C3 system) and as a civilian objective (a civilian broadcasting station). The reasoning would then be that inasmuch as NATO was attacking a dual-use target as a civilian objective—even if disabling that use was only a secondary purpose of the attack—the civilian casualties that ensued from that attack were not "incidental," but intentional or willful.

79 Ward Thomas, *Victory by Duress: Civilian Infrastructure as a Target in Air Campaigns,* 15 Sec. Stud. 1, 19 (2006); *see also* Waxman, *supra* note 3, at 21.

not to evacuate its civilians from what it knew or should reasonably have foreseen would be the site of an attack. This larger issue is related to (though it is not identical with) what is often called the problem of "human shields."[80] The Final Report briefly noted and commented on the larger issue when it said that

> UK Prime Minister Tony Blair blamed Yugoslav officials for not evacuating the [RTS] building, claiming that "[t]hey could have moved those people out of the building. They knew it was a target and they didn't . . . [I]t was probably for . . . very clear propaganda reasons." . . . [K] nowledge on the part of Yugoslav officials of the impending attack would not divest NATO of its obligation to forewarn civilians under Article 57(2).[81]

Other commentators have offered a defense of the bombing of RTS that is similar to Prime Minister Blair's. For example, Col. Frederick Borch contended that

> even if one assumes for the sake of the argument that the civilian casualties were excessive, the true cause of this collateral damage was not NATO's bombardment. On the contrary, the deaths and injuries resulted from Belgrade's failure to protect its own citizens in light of the warning received some ten days earlier. If the Milosevic government had informed the station's employees that their workplace was a possible target, at least some of these civilians would not have been in the building when it was hit: the missiles would most likely have harmed no one.[82]

Borch based his argument in part on Article 58(c), which requires all parties to the conflict, "to the extent feasible," to "take . . . other necessary precautions to protect the civilian population, individual civilians and civilian objects under their control against the dangers resulting from military operations." But even assuming that the Serbian government had failed to discharge that obligation to the RTS personnel whom NATO killed or injured, the question would remain whether its failure would have exonerated NATO, or at least mitigated any responsibility NATO had for the deaths that resulted from its attack, in view of Article 51(7), which declares that "[a] ny violation of these prohibitions shall not release the Parties to the conflict from their legal obligations with respect to the civilian population and civilians, including the obligation to take the precautionary measures provided for in Article 57."

---

80 *See* Michael N. Schmitt, *Human Shields in International Humanitarian Law,* 47 Colum. J. Transnat'l L. 17 (2009). One reason why the larger issue is not identical with the human shields problem is that the use of civilians as human shields seems to imply a measure of intentionality, either on the part of the state that is using civilians to guard against attacks, or on the part of civilians who volunteer for such a role. But a party to the conflict might leave civilians in harm's way through simple negligence or through reckless indifference.

81 Final Report to the Prosecutor, *supra* note 49, at ¶ 77.

82 Col. Frederick L. Borch, U.S. Army, *Targeting After Kosovo: Has the Law Changed for Strike Planners?,* 56 Naval War Coll. Rev. 64, 73 (2003).

C. STUDY QUESTIONS AND EXCEPTS FROM THE FINAL REPORT TO THE PROSECUTOR

1. Questions Before Reading the Final Report to the Prosecutor, Excerpts on the Grdelica Gorge Bridge Incident

1) Did the attack on the Grdelica Gorge Bridge, "in the circumstances ruling at the time," offer NATO a "definite military advantage"? If so, what was that advantage?

2) Was the bridge making "an effective contribution" to Serbia's "military action"? If so, how?[83]

3) Should the specific incident of the attack on the bridge be assessed for compliance with Protocol I's proportionality requirements? Was it an "attack" for purposes of Article 51(5)(b)? Within the meaning of Article 57(2)(b)?

4) Should that incident instead be integrated into a more complex pattern of attacks on Serbia, and the proportionality requirements applied only to that pattern as a whole? Would that be consistent with the definition of "attack" in Article 49(1)?

5) If the specific incident should be integrated into a more complex pattern of attacks, how would you characterize that pattern? How would you assess whether that pattern of attacks satisfied the proportionality requirements of Protocol I?

6) Should the relevant NATO commanders have restricted air strikes on the Grdelica Gorge Bridge and similar targets to night-time operations? If so, should they be subject to criminal prosecution if they had not?

83 In considering the first and second question, students should take account of the remarks of The Eritrea-Ethiopia Claims Settlement Commission in its 2005 opinion *Partial Award, Western Front, Aerial Bombardment, supra* note 57. First, the Commission was "of the view that the term 'military advantage' can only properly be understood in the context of military operations between the Parties taken as a whole, not simply in the context of a specific attack." *Id.* at ¶ 113. Second, the Commission ruled a power plant that was still under construction and that would have soon replaced a power station that *was* supplying a naval base was making an effective contribution to military action when it was struck. *Id.* at ¶ 121.

7) What obligations did the Serbian government have to protect the civilians who were likely to be using facilities like the Grdelica Gorge Bridge? See Articles 57(4)[84] and 58 (a) and (c).[85] How does Article 51(8) bear on your answer?[86]

8) Is it reasonable to subject individual pilots and unit commanders to the requirement of assessing proportionality during actual combat, even at the risk of personal criminal liability?

9) Did the pilot or crew in this incident demonstrate recklessness in dropping the second bomb? If so, should he or she have been prosecuted?

10) One author (a Colonel in the Spanish Air Force) has suggested that a good functional test of proportionality is to ask whether an aerial attack against a hostile target would be carried out if the target were on the attacker's territory that the enemy was occupying. In the latter case, the "incidental" civilian casualties would be the attacker's own population.[87] Do you agree?

2. Excerpts from the Final Report to the Prosecutor on the Grdelica Gorge Bridge Incident[88]

The Attack on a Civilian Passenger Train at the Grdelica Gorge on 12/4/99

58. On 12 April 1999, a NATO aircraft launched two laser guided bombs at the Leskovac railway bridge over the Grdelica gorge and Juzna Morava river, in eastern Serbia. A 5-carriage passenger train, travelling from Belgrade to Ristovac on the Macedonian border, was crossing the

84 Article 57(4) provides: "In the conduct of military operations at sea or in the air, each Party to the conflict shall, in conformity with its rights and duties under the rules of international law applicable in armed conflict, take all reasonable precautions to avoid losses of civilian lives and damage to civilian objects."

85 Articles 58(a) and (c) provide:

The Parties to the conflict shall, to the maximum extent feasible:

(a) without prejudice to Article 49 of the Fourth Convention, endeavour to remove the civilian population, individual civilians and civilian objects under their control from the vicinity of military objectives; . . .

(c) take the other necessary precautions to protect the civilian population, individual civilians and civilian objects under their control against the dangers resulting from military operations.

86 Article 51(8) provides: "Any violation of these prohibitions shall not release the Parties to the conflict from their legal obligations with respect to the civilian population and civilians, including the obligation to take the precautionary measures provided for in Article 57."

87 *See* Javier Guisández Gómez, *The Law of Air Warfare,* 323 IRRC 347 (1998) (*available at* http://www.icrc.org/eng/resources/documents/misc/57jpcl.htm).

88 Final Report to the Prosecutor, *supra* note 49, at ¶¶ 58 *et seq.*

bridge at the time, and was struck by both missiles. The various reports made of this incident concur that the incident occurred at about 11.40 a.m. At least ten people were killed in this incident and at least 15 individuals were injured. The designated target was the railway bridge, which was claimed to be part of a re-supply route being used for Serb forces in Kosovo. After launching the first bomb, the person controlling the weapon, at the last instant before impact, sighted movement on the bridge. The controller was unable to dump the bomb at that stage and it hit the train, the impact of the bomb cutting the second of the passenger coaches in half. Realising the bridge was still intact, the controller picked a second aim point on the bridge at the opposite end from where the train had come and launched the second bomb. In the meantime the train had slid forward as a result of the original impact and parts of the train were also hit by the second bomb.

59. It does not appear that the train was targeted deliberately. US Deputy Defense Secretary John Hamre stated that "one of our electro-optically guided bombs homed in on a railroad bridge just when a passenger train raced to the aim point. We never wanted to destroy that train or kill its occupants. We did want to destroy the bridge and we regret this accident." The substantive part of the explanation, both for the failure to detect the approach of the passenger train and for firing a second missile once it had been hit by the first, was given by General Wesley Clark, NATO's Supreme Allied Commander for Europe and is here reprinted in full:

> "[T]his was a case where a pilot was assigned to strike a railroad bridge that is part of the integrated communications supply network in Serbia. He launched his missile from his aircraft that was many miles away, he was not able to put his eyes on the bridge, it was a remotely directed attack. And as he stared intently at the desired target point on the bridge, and I talked to the team at Aviano who was directly engaged in this operation, as the pilot stared intently at the desired aim point on the bridge and worked it, and worked it and worked it, and all of a sudden at the very last instant with less than a second to go he caught a flash of movement that came into the screen and it was the train coming in. Unfortunately he couldn't dump the bomb at that point, it was locked, it was going into the target and it was an unfortunate incident which he, and the crew, and all of us very much regret. We certainly don't want to do collateral damage. The mission was to take out the bridge. He realised when it had happened that he had not hit the bridge, but what he had hit was the train. He had another aim point on the bridge, it was a relatively long bridge and he believed he still had to accomplish his mission, the pilot circled back around. He put his aim point on the other end of the bridge from where the train had come, by the time the bomb got close to the bridge it was covered with smoke and clouds and at the last minute again in an uncanny accident, the train had slid forward from the original impact and parts of the train had moved across the bridge, and so that by striking the other end of the

> bridge he actually caused additional damage to the train."(Press Conference, NATO HQ, Brussels, 13 April).

General Clark then showed the cockpit video of the plane which fired on the bridge:

> "The pilot in the aircraft is looking at about a 5-inch screen, he is seeing about this much and in here you can see this is the railroad bridge which is a much better view than he actually had, you can see the tracks running this way. Look very intently at the aim point, concentrate right there and you can see how, if you were focused right on your job as a pilot, suddenly that train appeared. It was really unfortunate. Here, he came back around to try to strike a different point on the bridge because he was trying to do a job to take the bridge down. Look at this aim point – you can see smoke and other obscuration there – he couldn't tell what this was exactly. Focus intently right at the centre of the cross. He is bringing these two crosses together and suddenly he recognises at the very last instant that the train that was struck here has moved on across the bridge and so the engine apparently was struck by the second bomb." (Press Conference, NATO HQ, Brussels, 13 April).

60. Some doubt has since been cast on this version of events by a comprehensive technical report submitted by a German national, Mr Ekkehard Wenz, which queries the actual speed at which the events took place in relation to that suggested by the video footage of the incident released by NATO. The effect of this report is to suggest that the reaction time available to the person controlling the bombs was in fact considerably greater than that alleged by NATO. Mr. Wenz also suggests the aircraft involved was an F15E Strike Eagle with a crew of two and with the weapons being controlled by a Weapons Systems Officer (WSO) not the pilot.

61. The committee has reviewed both the material provided by NATO and the report of Mr. Wenz with considerable care. It is the opinion of the committee that it is irrelevant whether the person controlling the bomb was the pilot or the WSO. Either person would have been travelling in a high speed aircraft and likely performing several tasks simultaneously, including endeavouring to keep the aircraft in the air and safe from surrounding threats in a combat environment. If the committee accepts Mr. Wenz's estimate of the reaction time available, the person controlling the bombs still had a very short period of time, less than 7 or 8 seconds in all probability, to react. Although Mr Wenz is of the view that the WSO intentionally targeted the train, the committee's review of the frames used in the report indicates another interpretation is equally available. The cross hairs remain fixed on the bridge throughout, and it is clear from this footage that the train can be seen moving toward the bridge only as the bomb is in flight: it is only in the course of the bomb's trajectory that the image of the train becomes visible. At a point where the bomb is within a few seconds of impact, a very slight change to the

bomb aiming point can be observed, in that it drops a couple of feet. This sequence regarding the bomb sights indicates that it is unlikely that the WSO was targeting the train, but instead suggests that the target was a point on the span of the bridge before the train appeared.

62. It is the opinion of the committee that the bridge was a legitimate military objective. The passenger train was not deliberately targeted. The person controlling the bombs, pilot or WSO, targeted the bridge and, over a very short period of time, failed to recognize the arrival of the train while the first bomb was in flight. The train was on the bridge when the bridge was targeted a second time and the bridge length has been estimated at 50 meters (Wenz study para 6 g above at p.25). It is the opinion of the committee that the information in relation to the attack with the first bomb does not provide a sufficient basis to initiate an investigation. The committee has divided views concerning the attack with the second bomb in relation to whether there was an element of recklessness in the conduct of the pilot or WSO. Despite this, the committee is in agreement that, based on the criteria for initiating an investigation (see para. 5 above), this incident should not be investigated. In relation to whether there is information warranting consideration of command responsibility, the committee is of the view that there is no information from which to conclude that an investigation is necessary into the criminal responsibility of persons higher in the chain of command. Based on the information available to it, it is the opinion of the committee that the attack on the train at Grdelica Gorge should not be investigated by the OTP.

3. Questions Before Reading Excerpts from the Final Report to the Prosecutor on the Bombing of the RTS Station

1) Was the RTS station in Belgrade a legitimate military objective? What "definite military advantage" in the "circumstances ruling at the time" could NATO reasonably have anticipated? What should, and should not, have counted as a "military" advantage?

2) In evaluating NATO's attack under Protocol I's proportionality requirements, assume that NATO was or should have been aware that its planned attack would have shut the RTS station down for only a few hours. On that assumption, was the attack lawful?

3) Is it correct to "integrate" NATO's attack on the RTS station with its attacks on other Serbian C3 (command, control, and communications) targets in assessing the proportionality of the attack on the station?

4) In assessing the proportionality of NATO's attack, what weight should be given to the Serbian civilian population's dependence on broadcasting for information that would be necessary or useful for many purposes, especially in wartime (for example, the names of persons killed, injured or missing in the war; locations of air raid shelters or warnings of possible attacks; news about the availability of food supplies and places where food might be obtained; news about power outages, weather or traffic; etc.)?

5) Suppose that NATO's true purpose in attacking the RTS station was to damage Serbia's "propaganda machine." Would that fact alone show that the attack failed to observe the distinction and proportionality requirements of Protocol I?

4. Excerpts from the Final Report to the Prosecutor on the Bombing of the RTS Station[89]

71. On 23 April 1999, at 0220, NATO intentionally bombed the central studio of the RTS (state-owned) broadcasting corporation at 1 Aberdareva Street in the centre of Belgrade. The missiles hit the entrance area, which caved in at the place where the Aberdareva Street building was connected to the Takovska Street building. While there is some doubt over exact casualty figures, between 10 and 17 people are estimated to have been killed.

72. The bombing of the TV studio was part of a planned attack aimed at disrupting and degrading the C3 (Command, Control and Communications) network. In co-ordinated attacks, on the same night, radio relay buildings and towers were hit along with electrical power transformer stations. At a press conference on 27 April 1999, NATO officials justified this attack in terms of the dual military and civilian use to which the FRY communication system was routinely put, describing this as a "very hardened and redundant command and control communications system [which ...] uses commercial telephone, [...] military cable, [...] fibre optic cable, [...] high frequency radio communication, [...] microwave communication and everything can be interconnected. There are literally dozens, more than 100 radio relay sites around the country, and [...] everything is wired in through dual use. Most of the commercial system serves the military and the military system can be put to use for the commercial system [...]." Accordingly, NATO stressed the dual-use to which such communications systems were put, describing civilian television as "heavily dependent on the military command and control system and military traffic is also routed through the civilian system" (press conference of 27 April, *ibid*).

89 Final Report to the Prosecutor, *supra* note 49, at ¶¶ 71 *et seq.*

73. At an earlier press conference on 23 April 1999, NATO officials reported that the TV building also housed a large multi-purpose communications satellite antenna dish, and that "radio relay control buildings and towers were targeted in the ongoing campaign to degrade the FRY's command, control and communications network". In a communication of 17 April 1999 to Amnesty International, NATO claimed that the RTS facilities were being used "as radio relay stations and transmitters to support the activities of the FRY military and special police forces, and therefore they represent legitimate military targets" (Amnesty International Report, *NATO/Federal Republic of Yugoslavia: Violations of the Laws of War by NATO during Operation Allied Force,* June 2000, p. 42).

74. Of the electrical power transformer stations targeted, one transformer station supplied power to the air defence co-ordination network while the other supplied power to the northern-sector operations centre. Both these facilities were key control elements in the FRY integrated air-defence system. In this regard, NATO indicated that "we are not targeting the Serb people as we repeatedly have stated nor do we target President Milosevic personally, we are attacking the control system that is used to manipulate the military and security forces."

More controversially, however, the bombing was also justified on the basis of the propaganda purpose to which it was employed:

> "[We need to] directly strike at the very central nerve system of Milosovic's regime. This of course are those assets which are used to plan and direct and to create the political environment of tolerance in Yugoslavia in which these brutalities can not only be accepted but even condoned. [....] Strikes against TV transmitters and broadcast facilities are part of our campaign to dismantle the FRY propaganda machinery which is a vital part of President Milosevic's control mechanism."

In a similar statement, British Prime Minister Tony Blair was reported as saying in *The Times* that the media "is the apparatus that keeps him [Milosević] in power and we are entirely justified as NATO allies in damaging and taking on those targets" (24 April, 1999). In a statement of 8 April 1999, NATO also indicated that the TV studios would be targeted unless they broadcast 6 hours per day of Western media reports: "If President Milosevic would provide equal time for Western news broadcasts in its programmes without censorship 3 hours a day between noon and 1800 and 3 hours a day between 1800 and midnight, then his TV could be an acceptable instrument of public information."

75. NATO intentionally bombed the Radio and TV station and the persons killed or injured were civilians. The questions are: was the station a legitimate military objective and; if it was, were the civilian casualties disproportionate to the military advantage gained by the attack?

For the station to be a military objective within the definition in Article 52 of Protocol I: a) its nature, purpose or use must make an effective contribution to military action and b) its total or partial destruction must offer a definite military advantage in the circumstances ruling at the time. The 1956 ICRC list of military objectives, drafted before the Additional Protocols, included the installations of broadcasting and television stations of fundamental military importance as military objectives (para. 39 above). The list prepared by Major General Rogers included broadcasting and television stations if they meet the military objective criteria (para. 38 above). As indicated in paras. 72 and 73 above, the attack appears to have been justified by NATO as part of a more general attack aimed at disrupting the FRY Command, Control and Communications network, the nerve centre and apparatus that keeps Milosević in power, and also as an attempt to dismantle the FRY propaganda machinery. Insofar as the attack actually was aimed at disrupting the communications network, it was legally acceptable.

76. If, however, the attack was made because equal time was not provided for Western news broadcasts, that is, because the station was part of the propaganda machinery, the legal basis was more debatable. Disrupting government propaganda may help to undermine the morale of the population and the armed forces, but justifying an attack on a civilian facility on such grounds alone may not meet the "effective contribution to military action" and "definite military advantage" criteria required by the Additional Protocols (see paras. 35-36, above). The ICRC Commentary on the Additional Protocols interprets the expression "definite military advantage anticipated" to exclude "an attack which only offers potential or indeterminate advantages" and interprets the expression "concrete and direct" as intended to show that the advantage concerned should be substantial and relatively close rather than hardly perceptible and likely to appear only in the long term (ICRC Commentary on the Additional Protocols of 8 June 1977, para. 2209). While stopping such propaganda may serve to demoralize the Yugoslav population and undermine the government's political support, it is unlikely that either of these purposes would offer the "concrete and direct" military advantage necessary to make them a legitimate military objective. NATO believed that Yugoslav broadcast facilities were "used entirely to incite hatred and propaganda" and alleged that the Yugoslav government had put all private TV and radio stations in Serbia under military control (NATO press conferences of 28 and 30 April1999). However, it was not claimed that they were being used to incite violence akin to *Radio Milles Collines* during the Rwandan genocide, which might have justified their destruction (see para. 47 above). At worst, the Yugoslav government was using the broadcasting networks to issue propaganda supportive of its war effort: a circumstance which does not, in and of itself, amount to a war crime (see in this regard the judgment of the International Military Tribunal in Nuremberg in 1946 in the case of Hans Fritzsche, who served as a senior official in the Propaganda ministry alleged to have incited and encouraged the commission of crimes. The IMT held that although Fritzsche clearly made strong statements of a propagandistic nature,

it was nevertheless not prepared to find that they were intended to incite the commission of atrocities, but rather, were aimed at arousing popular sentiment in support of Hitler and the German war effort (*American Journal of International Law*, vol. 41 (1947) 328)). The committee finds that if the attack on the RTS was justified by reference to its propaganda purpose alone, its legality might well be questioned by some experts in the field of international humanitarian law. It appears, however, that NATO's targeting of the RTS building for propaganda purposes was an incidental (albeit complementary) aim of its primary goal of disabling the Serbian military command and control system and to destroy the nerve system and apparatus that keeps Milosević in power. In a press conference of 9 April 1999, NATO declared that TV transmitters were not targeted directly but that "in Yugoslavia military radio relay stations are often combined with TV transmitters [so] we attack the military target. If there is damage to the TV transmitters, it is a secondary effect but it is not [our] primary intention to do that." A NATO spokesperson, Jamie Shea, also wrote to the Brussels-based International Federation of Journalists on 12 April claiming that Operation Allied Force "target[ed] military targets only and television and radio towers are only struck if they [were] integrated into military facilities ... There is no policy to strike television and radio transmitters as such" (cited in Amnesty International Report, *ibid*, June 2000).

77. Assuming the station was a legitimate objective, the civilian casualties were unfortunately high but do not appear to be clearly disproportionate.

Although NATO alleged that it made "every possible effort to avoid civilian casualties and collateral damage" (Amnesty International Report, *ibid*, June 2000, p. 42), some doubts have been expressed as to the specificity of the warning given to civilians by NATO of its intended strike, and whether the notice would have constituted "effective warning ... of attacks which may affect the civilian population, unless circumstances do not permit" as required by Article 57(2) of Additional Protocol I.

Evidence on this point is somewhat contradictory. On the one hand, NATO officials in Brussels are alleged to have told Amnesty International that they did not give a specific warning as it would have endangered the pilots (Amnesty International Report, *ibid*, June 2000, at p. 47; see also para. 49 above re: proportionality and the extent to which a military commander is obligated to expose his own forces to danger in order to limit civilian casualties or damage). On this view, it is possible that casualties among civilians working at the RTS may have been heightened because of NATO's apparent failure to provide clear advance warning of the attack, as required by Article 57(2).

On the other hand, foreign media representatives were apparently forewarned of the attack (Amnesty International Report, *ibid*). As Western journalists were reportedly warned by their employers to stay away from the television station before the attack, it would also appear that some Yugoslav officials may have expected that the building was about to be struck.

Consequently, UK Prime Minister Tony Blair blamed Yugoslav officials for not evacuating the building, claiming that "[t]hey could have moved those people out of the building. They knew it was a target and they didn't ... [I]t was probably for ... very clear propaganda reasons." (*ibid,* citing *Moral combat – NATO at war,* broadcast on BBC2 on 12 March 2000). Although knowledge on the part of Yugoslav officials of the impending attack would not divest NATO of its obligation to forewarn civilians under Article 57(2), it may nevertheless imply that the Yugoslav authorities may be partially responsible for the civilian casualties resulting from the attack and may suggest that the advance notice given by NATO may have in fact been sufficient under the circumstances.

78. Assuming the RTS building to be a legitimate military target, it appeared that NATO realised that attacking the RTS building would only interrupt broadcasting for a brief period. Indeed, broadcasting allegedly recommenced within hours of the strike, thus raising the issue of the importance of the military advantage gained by the attack *vis-à-vis* the civilian casualties incurred. The FRY command and control network was alleged by NATO to comprise a complex web and that could thus not be disabled in one strike. As noted by General Wesley Clark, NATO "knew when we struck that there would be alternate means of getting the Serb Television. There's no single switch to turn off everything but we thought it was a good move to strike it and the political leadership agreed with us" (*ibid,* citing "Moral combat, NATO at War," broadcast on BBC2 on 12 March 2000). At a press conference on 27 April 1999, another NATO spokesperson similarly described the dual-use Yugoslav command and control network as "incapable of being dealt with in "a single knock-out blow (*ibid*)." The proportionality or otherwise of an attack should not necessarily focus exclusively on a specific incident. (See in this regard para. 52, above, referring to the need for an overall assessment of the totality of civilian victims as against the goals of the military campaign). With regard to these goals, the strategic target of these attacks was the Yugoslav command and control network. The attack on the RTS building must therefore be seen as forming part of an integrated attack against numerous objects, including transmission towers and control buildings of the Yugoslav radio relay network which were "essential to Milosevic's ability to direct and control the repressive activities of his army and special police forces in Kosovo" (NATO press release, 1 May 1999) and which comprised "a key element in the Yugoslav air-defence network" (*ibid,* 1 May1999). Attacks were also aimed at electricity grids that fed the command and control structures of the Yugoslav Army (*ibid,* 3 May 1999). Other strategic targets included additional command and control assets such as the radio and TV relay sites at Novi Pazar, Kosovaka and Krusevac (*ibid*) and command posts (*ibid,* 30 April). Of the electrical power transformer stations targeted, one transformer station supplied power to the air-defence coordination network while the other supplied power to the northern sector operations centre. Both these facilities were key control elements in the FRY integrated air-defence system (*ibid,* 23 April 1999). The radio relay and TV transmitting station

near Novi Sad was also an important link in the air defence command and control communications network. Not only were these targets central to the Federal Republic of Yugoslavia's governing apparatus, but formed, from a military point of view, an integral part of the strategic communications network which enabled both the military and national command authorities to direct the repression and atrocities taking place in Kosovo (*ibid,* 21 April 1999).

79. On the basis of the above analysis and on the information currently available to it, the committee recommends that the OTP not commence an investigation related to the bombing of the Serbian TV and Radio Station.

D. COMMENTARY ON OTP LEGAL ANALYSIS AND THE LEGALIST-REALIST DEBATE

Before offering some thoughts based on the Final Report to the Prosecutor concerning the realist-legalist debate, we first analyze the legal issues addressed by the Report.

1. Analysis of the Final Report to the Prosecutor

Overall, assessments of the Final Report to the Prosecutor have been predominantly critical. It seems fair to say, as one strong critic of the Report does, that "while favorably welcomed by NATO members and some writers, [the Report] generated strong and persistent criticism from the majority of scholars, who questioned the Prosecutor's impartiality and expressed their suspicions that political rather than legal considerations, had influenced her decision."[90] We assume, for purposes of discussion, unless otherwise specified, that Articles 52(2), 51(5)(b), and 57(2) of Additional Protocol I provide the governing law—that is, in essence, that the principles of necessity, distinction, and proportionality, as formulated in Protocol I, are customary law.

2. The Attack on the Grdelica Gorge Bridge

The attack raises at least two important issues. First, was the bridge a military object, in accordance with military necessity and distinction? Second, did it satisfy the proportionality requirement?

a. The Railway Bridge at Grdelica Gorge as a Military Object

Without any analysis, the Final Report to the Prosecutor reached the conclusion that "the bridge was a legitimate military objective."[91] This is strange, if only because Human Rights Watch had explicitly denied that NATO's attacks on Serbia's bridges were directed to lawful military objectives.[92] Furthermore, the issue is less clear than the Report's conclusory judgment would indicate. If nothing else, the definition in Article 52(2) is situation-dependent: rather than listing military objects and objectives, it sets out a flexible test for determining what does,

90 Massa, supra note 48, at 611–12.

91 Final Report to the Prosecutor, *supra* note 49, at ¶ 62.

92 *See* Human Rights Watch, Vol. 12, No. 1, *Civilian Deaths in the NATO Air Campaign* (Feb. 2000), cited in Major Jeanne M. Meyer, *Tearing Down the Façade: A Critical Look at the Current Law on Targeting the Will of the Enemy and Air Force Doctrine*, 51 A.F. L. Rev. 143, 165 & n. 120 (2001).

and what does not, qualify as such.[93] Moreover, bridges are in any case "dual use" objects: they can be used for military or civilian traffic, or both. Finally, there was substantial evidence that NATO was targeting Serbian infrastructure at least partly for the purpose of demoralizing the Serbian population, rather than because of that infrastructure's contribution to Serbia's military efforts.[94] For example, one NATO general had said that "[j]ust focusing on fielded forces is not enough. . . . The people have to get to the point that their lights are turned off, their bridges are blocked so they can't get to work."[95] The OPT might well have assessed NATO's attacks on Serbian transportation infrastructure (and on the Grdelica Gorge Bridge) in light of such purposes, whose validity is very doubtful under Protocol I.

Yoram Dinstein, the eminent Israeli legal scholar of the law of war, is firmly of the view that most bridges qualify as military objects under Article 52 of Protocol I, because of their nature, purpose, use, and location. Dinstein argued that "[w]hen constructed for the engineering needs of major highways and road tracks, [bridges] are surely integrated in the overall network: like the roads and the tracks that they serve, they constitute military objectives by nature."[96] Further, Dinstein argued, most bridges would qualify as military objects because of their purpose, use and above all, location. "Every significant waterway or similar geophysical obstruction to traffic (like a deep ravine) may become a military barrier, and there comes a time when the strategy of either Belligerent Party would dictate that all bridges (including pedestrian overpasses) across the obstacle have to be destroyed or neutralized."[97]

But Michael Bothe argued that when one takes account of the specific characteristics of the humanitarian intervention in Kosovo, the Grdelica Gorge Bridge should not have been liable to attack. First, NATO's campaign was an air war; the political leadership of the NATO countries had all but ruled out the possibility of opening a land campaign. Thus, argued Bothe, there was no "front" to this war, and hence no possibility of interdicting the transportation of troops or supplies over bridges to the "front." While NATO's air strikes on bridges could indeed interfere with the movements of military forces or matériel within Serbia, Serbia's bridges did not seem to be making an "effective contribution" to Serbia's defense against NATO's aerial campaign (the only offensive NATO was mounting); nor did NATO seem to gain any discernible "military

93 *See, e.g.*, Fenrick, *supra* note 53, at 495 ("The Protocol I military objective was, presumably, intended to, at a minimum, shift targeting decision-makers away from a list-oriented approach to military objectives and towards a situation-dependent, criterion-oriented approach.").

94 That evidence included a Report of the Defence Select Committee of the U.K. House of Commons, issued on Oct. 24, 2000. *See* Benvenuti, *supra* note 77, at 508–09 (quoting from and discussing that report).

95 Olivera Medenica, *Protocol I and Operation Allied Force: Did NATO Abide by Principles of Proportionality?*, 23 Loy. L.A. Int'l & Comp. L. Rev. 329, 423 (2001) (citations omitted).

96 Yoram Dinstein, The Conduct of Hostilities under the Law of International Armed Conflict 101 (2d ed. 2010).

97 *Id.* at 101–12. *See also* Carnahan, *supra* note 60, at 48–49 (removal of original phrase "installations and means of transport" from list of presumptively civilian objects during negotiation of Protocol I "implies that means of transportation need not be regarded as objects normally dedicated to civilian purposes").

advantage" in that campaign from attacking them.[98] Second, Bothe argued that, while NATO's air attacks on bridges could indeed have (and probably were intended to have) a damaging impact of Serbian morale, that is not a legitimate "military" advantage under Protocol I: "the advantage of softening the adversary's will to resist is not a 'military' one and, thus, cannot be used as a legitimation for any targeting decision."[99] We set aside, for the moment, Bothe's more fundamental argument questioning whether and how far Protocol I—or at least, Article 52—can apply in a war of humanitarian intervention such as that in Kosovo.[100]

Bothe's argument assumes that bridges and other traffic infrastructure are only valid military targets in a land war with a discernible "front." One might well question that assumption.[101] Ruth Wedgwood has argued that, even if Serbia did not face NATO land forces on any "front," the possibility always remained that NATO would open one, and the attacks on the bridges thus served a traditional military purpose in light of that possibility.

> NATO's destruction of the bridges over the Danube in the Kosovo campaign may be understood as a stratagem to force Milosevic to gamble between theatres for the placement of his armor. (He could head north to meet a possible NATO invasion from Hungary, or south to meet a NATO invasion from Albania while continuing his ethnic cleansing operations. With the severance of bridges across the Danube, he had one vulnerable flank.)[102]

But, even if Wedgwood's analysis is correct, it would not seem to apply to the bridge *at Grdelica Gorge*, which does not span the Danube, but rather the Južna Morava River, which enters the Danube near Smederevo, north of Lapovo.

What military advantages did NATO, in fact, perceive in targeting the Grdelica Gorge Bridge? One answer given by U.S. military sources was that "bridges were often selected for attack for reasons other than their role in transportation (for example, they were conduits for

---

98 *See* Bothe, *supra* note 54, at 179; *see also* Michael Bothe, *The Protection of the Civilian Population and NATO Bombing on Yugoslavia: Comments on a Report to the Prosecutor of the ICTY*, 12 Eur. J. Int'l L. 531, 534 (2001).

99 Bothe, *supra* note 54, at 180.

100 Bothe claimed that discussing NATO's targeting practices and decision-making within the framework of Article 52 "introduces a basic ambiguity, or a fictitious character" into the review. He claimed that, where the goal of the conflict is

> not the military defeat of an adversary, but the protection of the human rights of the population, the traditional notion of military advantage loses much of its significance. In the Kosovo campaign target selection was made on the basis of the fiction that military advantage and military victory in the traditional sense were sought. . . . The only real goal was a change of attitude of the Belgrade government.

Bothe, *supra* note 54, at 181.

In short, this argument suggests that humanitarian interventions are subject to a higher minimum standard for *jus in bello* than other kinds of armed conflicts, forming a kind of *lex specialis*. The logic of his argument, however, may well challenge in general the modern principle that the *jus in bello* is independent of the *jus ad bellum*, an issue we address in our concluding chapter.

101 In addition to the argument considered in the text, to the extent, if any, that NATO was seeking to assist the activities of the Kosovo Liberation Army against Serbian forces, there was a "front" in Kosovo.

102 Ruth Wedgwood, *Propositions on the Law of War after the Kosovo Campaign*, *in* Legal and Ethical Lessons of NATO's Kosovo Campaign 433, 435 (Andru E. Wall, ed., 2002).

communications cables, or because they were symbolic and psychologically lucrative)."[103] There is no evidence in the Final Report, however, that NATO attacked the Grdelica Gorge Bridge because it was a "conduit . . . for communications cables." (Even if that had been the purpose, the question whether the cables were themselves valid military objects would then have arisen.) And if NATO attacked the bridge because it was "psychologically lucrative," there would have been a serious question whether that gain could count as "a definite military advantage" under Article 52(2). Indeed, the Report itself opined that damaging civilian morale "as such" was not a legitimate military objective.[104]

Ultimately, the Report did accept NATO's explanation that the bridge was part of a resupply route for Serbian forces in Kosovo.[105] If NATO reasonably believed that the bridge was part of the Serbian military's resupply route and targeted it for that purpose, the bridge might well have qualified as a military object under Article 52(2).[106] Nonetheless, the plain language of Article 52(2) does suggest one could reasonably question whether even an attack designed to prevent Serbian Army attacks on the Albanian Kosovar population would offer a definite advantage to NATO military operations. If "definite military advantage" is construed, instead, to encompass the larger policy objectives (i.e., the humanitarian purposes) of those military operations, it would open the door to an interpretive approach that could reduce the effect of Article 52(2), without any obvious principle of limitation; it might threaten to expand the meaning of Article 52(2) to permit attacks on a range of targets previously deemed free from attack; and, it might risk re-introducing the Scylla of the broadest conception of military necessity the *jus in bello* has finally rejected. On the other hand, if reasonable limits are imposed to cabin the meaning of "definite military advantage," then the requirements of humanitarian law (as expressed in Protocol I) may form a Charybdis that risks international criminal prosecution and thus conflicts with, deters, and impedes the defense of human rights through humanitarian intervention.[107]

---

103 Meyer, *supra* note 92, at 165.

104 *See* Final Report to the Prosecutor, *supra* note 49, at ¶ 55; *see also* Fenrick, *supra* note 53, at 497 ("Neither the civilian population *nor civilian morale* constitute legitimate military objectives.") (emphasis added).

105 *See* Final Report to the Prosecutor, supra note 49, at ¶ 58 ("The designated target was the railway bridge, which was claimed to be part of a re-supply route being used for Serb forces in Kosovo.").

106 This account seems to have become the official U.S. position. *See* Borch, *supra* note 82, at 69 ("NATO planners had selected the Grdelica bridge for attack because it was part of a resupply route for Serb forces in Kosovo.").

107 Fenrick argued that a facility that is being used as the site of "a serious violation of international humanitarian law" may "lawfully be attacked even if it did not meet the criteria for a military objective." Thus, he suggested, the gas chambers at Auschwitz might lawfully have been attacked "because of some generalized right to prevent the continuing commission of crimes." Fenrick, *supra* note 53, at 496. We have no doubt whatever that the Allies might "lawfully" have attacked Auschwitz. But saying that does not meet the question whether such an attack would have been consistent with Article 52(2) of Protocol I. Further, if an implicit exception is to be made from Article 52(2), the question of its scope needs to be addressed. Should non-military objects be subject to attack if, for example, they are serving as the site for the commission of serious breaches of humanitarian law (as Fenrick indicates)? Must those offenses be criminal (as Fenrick also suggests) and, if so, who makes that determination? What if humanitarian law is not being violated, but human rights law is?

b. NATO's Attack on the Bridge and Protocol I's Proportionality Requirement

Proportionality might well seem to have been the central question for the Final Report to address in connection with the incident at the Grdelica Gorge Bridge. Yet the Report does not even glance at it. (We shall consider shortly below why it does not.) The Report acknowledges that "at least" ten people died and "at least" fifteen were injured in the attacks. To be sure, one cannot judge whether or not the attack was "proportionate" simply by considering, *ex post,* the actual number of civilian casualties and other losses. Rather, one must take an *ex ante* perspective (whether that of a "reasonable military commander," as the Final Report assumes,[108] or that of a "reasonable person," as the ICTY Trial Chambers would later hold in *Galic*).[109] Still, the fact that the civilian losses in this incident were fairly high would seem to have warranted more careful scrutiny than the OTP gave to the proportionality issues.

One crucial issue in determining whether the attack on the Grdelica Gorge Bridge satisfied the proportionality requirements in Protocol I is whether the calculus should focus only on the advantages reasonably anticipated from that attack itself (and, correspondingly, on the incidental losses that might reasonably have been anticipated to result from that attack), or rather on the anticipated advantages and losses that might reasonably be anticipated from a broader pattern of attacks. There is a good deal to be said on all sides of this question.[110] Very closely related to this is the question whether Articles 51 and 57 apply in whole or in part at the level of the individual combatant, given the lower-level combatant's lack of knowledge or authority, or only reach higher-ranking officers in control of the process of target selection.[111] Thus, for some, the issue is related to the question of command responsibility for war crimes at the

108 *See* Final Report to the Prosecutor, *supra* note 49, at ¶ 50.

109 *See* Judgment in the Case the Prosecutor v. Stanislav Galic Stanislav Galic Sentenced to 20 Years' Imprisonment, CVO/ P.I.S/ 807e (December 5, 2003) [hereinafter *Galic*] (*available at* http://www.icty.org/sid/8148).

110 *See* Capt. Burrus M. Carnahan, *The Law of Air Bombardment in its Historical Context,* 17 A.F. L. Rev. 39, 57 (1975).

111 *See, e.g.,* Parks, *Air War, supra* note 70, at 176. As Parks noted,

> In many cases, small unit commanders or individual pilots will not be possessed of sufficient information to weigh a decision regarding proportion. Most small unit commanders have a limited objective that is part of an overall attack, just as individual pilots will be assigned a particular target to attack as part of an overall strike force; their latitude in achieving their objectives is limited at best. Neither may be briefed as to the value of their objective or target within the overall scheme of attack, and the value may fluctuate depending upon the success or failure of the overall attack.

Id.

highest, including the political, level.[112] But, in all cases, consideration of these issues should be informed by a practical understanding of the targeting process in the specific military operations at issue.[113]

In general, three approaches can be identified: (1) the proportionality analysis should generally be applied to some aggregation or integrated pattern of individual-level tactical or operational "attacks," but generally not at the tactical or operational level; (2) the proportionality analysis should generally be applied at the tactical or operational level, if also, in proper cases, to aggregations or patterns of such attacks; and (3) the test's appropriate level of application is a matter of context. These different positions tend not to be sharply distinguishable. In all of them, the primary focus has been on aerial attacks. We consider each in turn.

i. The Broad Theory of Proportionality

First, as Fenrick has noted, "one cannot always assess proportionality on a bullet-by-bullet basis or even on the basis of attacks on individual military objectives."[114] Earlier, Fenrick's careful review of Protocol I's negotiating record had led him to conclude that "'[a]ttack' for the purposes of the proportionality rule would normally envisage military operations directed against several military objectives."[115] Likewise, Dinstein maintained that "a large-scale attack may be

112 Whether or not individual pilots and small unit commanders *should* be held responsible for making proportionality calculations, the drafters of Protocol I seem to have made at least parts of its proportionality rules applicable at the individual level. *See* Massa, *supra* note 48, at 624 (Article 57(1) "applies to all levels of the military structure"); *id.* at 625 (Article 57(2)(b) "not only applies to military planners and commanders but also to the members of the armed forces who carry out the attack"); Jean-François Quéguiner, *Precautions Under the Law Governing the Conduct of Hostilities,* 88 IRRC 793, 803 (2006) (Article 57(2)(b) "must be interpreted as imposing a special and personal obligation on all members of the armed forces to cancel or suspend an attack when they acquire, in the course of an operation, information that was not available at the planning stage."); Carnahan, *supra* note 60, at 60 (arguing that the negotiating record supports view that the duty to call off an attack prescribed by Article 57(2)(b) "would apparently fall on any officer with appropriate authority and not merely on the initiating commander"). On the other hand, Article 57(2)(a) seems to be directed only to higher-ranking officers. *See* Art. 57(2)(a), *supra* text accompany notes 51-52 ("those who plan or decide upon an attack"); *see generally* Lieut. Col. William J. Fenrick, *The Rule of Proportionality and Protocol I in Conventional Warfare,* 98 Mil. L. Rev. 91, 107–08, 111–12 (1982); and Carnahan, *supra* note 110, at 60 (suggesting that this clause "follows the decision in the *High Command Case* in which the United States Military Tribunal at Nuremberg held that German staff officers who aided commanders by drafting and processing illegal orders were themselves guilty of war crimes").

113 Michael Schmitt helpfully distinguished between "planned" and "immediate" aerial targets. The former are known to exist in an operational area and are attacked in accordance with an air tasking order, mission-type order, or fire support plan. They may be either "scheduled" or "on call." The latter are not identified or selected for attack in the normal planning process but are either "unplanned" or "unanticipated" targets. Schmitt further divided the U.S. air targeting process into six phases: 1) combat objectives and guidance (in which the commander sets campaign objectives and issues appropriate guidance); 2) target development (in which the adversary's military, political, and economic systems are studied; the value of potential targets is assessed; and the application of legal requirements considered); 3) weaponeering and 4) force application (in which the weapon to be used is selected and a weapons system is matched to an aim-point); 5) execution planning (which designs the mission that will carry out the strike); and 6) combat assessment (which follows the execution of an attack and determines whether a re-attack or attack on other targets is required). *See* Michael N. Schmitt, *Precision Attack and International Humanitarian Law,* 87 IRRC 445, 450–53 (2005). The actual execution of a strike by an individual pilot or crew thus occurs only after five planning stages have been completed.

114 Fenrick, *supra* note 53, at 499.

115 Fenrick, *supra* note 112, at 111.

looked at as a single 'complex mosaic.' The attacker may argue that an air raid of no perceptible military advantage in itself is justified by misleading the enemy to shift its strategic gaze to the wrong sector of the front."[116] In the particular context of attacks on bridges, Dinstein argued that "[t]here is nothing wrong in a military policy striving to effect a fragmentation of enemy land forces through a destruction of all bridges—however minor in themselves—spanning a wide river."[117] If a city has six bridges that could be used for military transport, and the destruction of any single bridge would cause harm that was excessive in relation to the military advantage that the attacker reaped from destroying it, it might still be lawful and proportionate for the attacker to destroy all six bridges.[118]

A similar position seems to be reflected in some of the understandings that state parties have given to Protocol I. For example, the United Kingdom ratified the Protocol on the understanding of Articles 51 and 57 that "the military advantage anticipated from an attack is intended to refer to the advantage anticipated from the attack considered as a whole and not only from isolated or particular parts of an attack."[119] Nine other states (Australia, Belgium, Canada, France, Germany, Italy, the Netherlands, New Zealand, and Spain) have a similar understanding.[120]

ii. The Narrow Theory of Proportionality

Nonetheless, powerful arguments based on the text, intentions of the parties as revealed by the conduct of their operations, and the purposes of these provisions can be given for a second, much narrower interpretation of an "attack." First, Articles 51 and 57 refer to "attacks," not to "patterns of attacks" or "campaigns." That suggests a narrow meaning for "attack." Further, in calculating proportionality, incidental losses are to be weighed against the "concrete and direct military advantage" anticipated from an attack. Those limitations must be given effect, and they suggest a focus on the specific tactical and operational considerations of a particular attack.[121] Second, the understanding of Articles 51 and 57 held by the U.K. and other NATO states as evidenced in their military operations, as well as evidenced in relevant international jurisprudence, indicates that something well short of a completed campaign,[122] or even of a pattern of attacks, is the proper unit to consider when evaluating proportionality; it could thus include a series of

116 Dinstein, *supra* note 96, at 94–95.

117 *Id.* at 102.

118 *See* Quéguiner, *supra* note 112, at 804.

119 United Kingdom Reservation/Declaration Text (July 2, 2002) (*available at* http://www.icrc.org/IHL.nsf/NORM/0A9E03F0F2EE757CC1256402003FB6D2?).

120 *See* Gaudreau, *supra* note 59.

121 *See* Laursen, *supra* note 75, at 795–96.

122 *See* Fenrick, *supra* note 51, at 548 ("One cannot, for example, assert that it will only be possible to determine whether or not military activity complied with the proportionality principle at the end of the war or a lengthy campaign.").

attacks on various interconnected targets within a city or other delimited zone, or even just a single but large-scale raid on a city, rather than a more extensive and temporally discontinuous series of attacks, such as (in Dinstein's examples) a policy of destroying all the enemy's bridges over a major river or the Normandy invasion. Also, as we have seen, the ICTY Trial Chambers in *Galic* concluded, albeit well after the issuance the Final Report, that the firing of two mortars within a few minutes of each other into the improvised football field at Dobrinja was an "attack" that could be reviewed under the proportionality requirement.[123] Finally, the purposes of Article 57(2) are, arguably, often better served by a narrow interpretation of the term "attack," since information becomes available at an operational level that can falsify proportionality judgments made at a higher and earlier level of decision-making.[124]

iii. The Context-Sensitive Theory of Proportionality

A third possibility is that context should determine how the proportionality requirement is to be applied. Fenrick has outlined such an approach, as follows:

> it is suggested that proportionality can be determined using a variety of scales ranging from the tactical level (military objective by military objective), to a much bigger scale, as long as the more general context is taken into account. For example, if it is essential to block military traffic across a river and the enemy forces may use three bridges to cross the river, it may well be permissible to inflict greater collateral losses for destroying the last bridge because of the resultant greater military advantage. The military objective scale [*i.e.,* what we have been calling the "tactical" or "operational" level] is commonly used in modern state practice, particularly in assessing the legitimacy of aerial attacks. It was also used in the *Galic* Trial Chamber.[125]

Thus, in some circumstances, it should be applied to an entire campaign; in others, to an integrated series of attacks, even if temporally discontinuous; in others, to "attacks" in a narrow, tactical sense.[126]

---

123 *See Galic, supra* note 109.

124 According to one author:

> Article 57(2)(b) is based on the premise that a mistake might have been made [at the planning stage] as to the nature of the target, or that new information could become available and radically change one's assessment of the nature of the target. . . . [I]f, before launching a first salvo against a bridge, a tank driver notices that a crowd of fleeing civilians have taken refuge under the targeted bridge, the driver cannot assume that the planners have correctly considered the principle of proportionality and continue his mission in willful blindness and impunity. He must, at the very least, suspend his attack in order to allow the civilians to evacuate, or to request that his orders be confirmed in the light of these new circumstances.

Quéguiner, *supra* note 112, at 805.

125 William J. Fenrick, *Riding the Rhino: Attempting to Develop Usable Legal Standards for Combat Activities,* 30 B.C. Int'l & Comp. L. Rev. 111, 125 (2007).

126 Of course, this approach does not decide the question of when the broader "context" of an attack should be considered.

The Final Report did not directly address these issues in its review of the incident at the Grdelica Gorge Bridge. The Report's analysis of the strike on the Grdelica Gorge Bridge can be faulted because it neither affirms nor denies that the incident was an "attack" to which proportionality requirements applied. The focus of the Report's analysis is on the question of *mens rea.* It simply does not address whether the strike was an *actus reus* under Article 57(2). If, however, the strike were assessed for proportionality, it is far from clear that it would have satisfied those requirements.

For one thing, the NATO attack occurred shortly before noon, at a time when it was surely reasonably foreseeable that the bridge might be used by civilians, including those aboard passenger trains.[127] There is no evidence in the Report to suggest that an attack during ordinary working hours and in broad daylight was necessary, rather than an attack at night, when the civilian population would have been less likely to be using the bridge. In comparable situations, military commanders have sought to minimize casualties by ordering night strikes: for example, this happened in the Second Gulf War in 2003.[128] Indeed, after a mid-day attack on a bridge in the town of Varvarin on May 30, 1999 in which nine civilians were killed and forty others injured, NATO ordered its air pilots not to attack bridges during daylight hours, on weekends, on market days, or on holidays.[129] While that change in targeting policy cannot, of course, be construed as an admission of fault (for it might be interpreted instead as evidence of a good faith effort to minimize civilian casualties), it does provoke questions about NATO's previous practice.

More importantly, what about the second strike on the bridge? Here, a bomb was launched seven or eight seconds after the pilot (or weapons systems officer) had spotted the crossing train. According to NATO's Supreme Allied Commander for Europe, General Wesley Clark, the pilot's

> mission was to take out the bridge. He realized when it had happened that he had not hit the bridge, but what he had hit was the train. He had another aim point on the bridge, it was a relatively long bridge and he believed he still had to accomplish his mission, the pilot circled back around. He put his aim point on the other end of the bridge from where the train had come, by the time the bomb got close to the bridge it was covered with smoke and clouds and at the last minute again in an uncanny accident, the train had slid forward from the original impact and parts of the train had moved across the bridge, and so by striking the other end of the bridge he actually caused additional damage to the train.[130]

---

127 One might also ask whether it was feasible for NATO commanders to have checked railway schedules or monitored traffic over the bridge to determine when passenger trains were likely to be crossing.

128 *See* Quéguiner, *supra* note 112, at 800.

129 *See* Medenica, *supra* note 95, at 424.

130 Final Report to the Prosecutor, *supra* note 49, at ¶ 59 (quoting the General). The Report does not comment on General Clark's credibility. More skeptical observers have noted that Clark's presentation relied on what NATO later admitted was a highly speeded-up video of the events. This discovery was made by a private German citizen, Ekkehard Wenz, an opponent of the war, whose analysis was reported in a German newspaper. The OPT Report refered to Wenz's work, but

There are questions here both of distinction ("Did the pilot or weapons systems officer target the train, a civilian object, or the bridge, a military object?") and of proportionality ("Should the pilot or crew have cancelled or suspended the attack in accordance with Article 57(2)(b)?"). In either case, for criminal liability to attach, it would be necessary to show, not simply that a (serious) breach of an applicable rule had occurred (the *actus reus* component), but also that the attacker had either intended to breach the rule or had shown reckless disregard of it. (the *mens rea* component).[131] It is therefore insufficient to say that "the crew intended its second bomb to hit a point on the bridge some distance away from the train; that it in fact struck the train was . . . an accident."[132] The question remains whether even if the pilot or crew did not intend to strike the train, the decision to fire the second bomb was reckless in the circumstances.

The Final Report discloses that "[t]he committee ha[d] divided views concerning the attack with the second bomb in relation to whether there was an element of recklessness in the conduct of the pilot or [weapons system officer]."[133] It is not at all difficult to understand why some members of the OTP staff should have suspected that the attacker was "reckless." Indeed, as one sharp critic of the Final Report has argued, the second attack, in light of the uncertain conditions concerning the further risk to civilians created by the first attack, suggests the mission's objectives completed disregarded the risk of civilian casualties.[134]

To be sure, any reasonable finding that the pilot or crew had been reckless would need to take account of the limited time available in which to make a decision whether or not to launch a second bomb; the possibility of genuine uncertainty whether a passenger train had in fact begun to cross the bridge; and the chances that a second strike at the other end of the bridge might not cause further damage to the train or its passengers. Legal second-guessing of split second decisions made in the heat of combat is apt to be both facile and censorious. Hays Parks is right to remind prosecutors and legal scholars (themselves often without any combat experience) of the difficulties of decision-making under what Clausewitz called the "friction of

---

does not use it to undermine Clark's account. *See* Michael Mandel, *Politics and Human Rights in International Criminal Law: Our Case Against NATO and the Lessons to be Learned From It,* 25 Fordham Int'l L. J. 95, 122 (2001).

131 *See, e.g.,* Borch, *supra* note 82, at 70.

132 Borch, *supra* note 82, at 70.

133 Final Report to the Prosecutor, *supra* note 49, at ¶ 62.

134 Tania Voon, *Pointing the Finger: Civilian Casualties of NATO Bombing in the Kosovo Conflict,* 16 Am. U. Int'l L. Rev. 1083, 1102 (2001). Voon wrote that:

> [a]fter the initial launch, the controller was aware of the presence of civilians in the area and, presumably, the direction in which the train was traveling. Therefore, the impossibility of viewing the whole bridge on a tiny screen provides even less justification for launching the second bomb than the first. Moreover, the fact that the bridge was now obscured by smoke does not exonerate the controller for hitting the train a second time. On the contrary, the covering of smoke should have made the controller even more hesitant to continue—he was required [under Article 57(1)] to take "constant care" to spare civilians. As Amnesty International points out, NATO's explanation of the second bombing suggests that the controller understood the mission to be to destroy the bridge, regardless of the cost in civilian casualties.

Id.

war."[135] There is also the question whether, even if the reviewer concluded that the attacker had probably been reckless, the incident was insufficiently serious to warrant prosecution, given the limits of prosecutorial resources. A.P.V. Rogers considers that "the air-crew were concentrating on hitting the bridge but did not reach classroom levels of perfection in the agony of the moment. Errors of judgment such as this are not the stuff of criminal prosecutions."[136]

3. The Attack on the RTS Station

We now consider three legal issues in relation to the NATO attack on the RTS Station: first, was that attack proportionate; second, did NATO comply with any applicable duty of precaution or duty to warn; and, third, was NATO, Serbia, or NATO and Serbia in proportion to their responsibility liable for harm to civilians caused by the attack? We consider these three issues in turn.

a. The Proportionality of the Attack on the RTS Station

As noted earlier, the Final Report did not directly address the proportionality of the attacks on the Grdelica Gorge Bridge. In discussing NATO's bombing of the Serbian TV and Radio Station RTS, however, the Report suggested that the proportionality assessment should consider an integrated series of attacks, rather than an isolated incident. Thus, the Final Report noted that the bombing of RTS "was part of a planned attack aimed at disrupting and degrading the C3 network. In coordinated attacks, on the same night, radio relay buildings and towers were hit along with electrical power transformer stations."[137] But the Report then concluded that "the attack [on RTS] appears to have been justified by NATO as part of a more general attack aimed at disrupting [Serbia's] Command, Control and Communications network, the nerve center and apparatus that keeps Milosevic in power,"[138] and it accepted NATO's rationale that proportionality required "an overall assessment of the totality of civilian victims as against the goals of the military campaign."[139]

---

135 Parks, *Air War, supra* note 70, at 182–85.

136 Rogers, *supra* note 66, at 77.

137 Final Report to the Prosecutor, *supra* note 49, at ¶ 72.

138 *Id.* at ¶ 75.

139 *Id.* at ¶ 78. The Report stated: "The proportionality or otherwise of an attack should not necessarily focus exclusively on a specific incident." Examine in this regard ¶ 52, above, referring to the need for an overall assessment of the totality of civilian victims as against the goals of the military campaign. The Report went on to say, "With regard to these goals, the strategic target of these attacks was the Yugoslav command and control network. The attack on the RTS building must therefore be seen as forming part of an integrated attack against numerous objects, including transmissions towers and control buildings of the Yugoslav radio relay network. . . ." *Id.*

The Report's discussion of the RTS incident thus opens the question whether the proportionality analysis should be applied to: 1) the attack on RTS; 2) the concerted attacks on the date of April 23, 1999 on RTS, the electrical power transformer stations, and any other C3 elements NATO targeted within Belgrade; and 3) NATO's "more general attack" over the course of its air campaign on "numerous objects" throughout Serbia, including transmissions towers and control buildings of the Serbian radio relay system, electricity grids that fed Serbian military C3 structures, and other C3 assets scattered about in various Serbian cities.[140] In light of those remarks, it is even possible to read the Final Report as implying that the bombing of RTS in itself was not an "attack" within the meaning of Article 57(2), and therefore not subject to its proportionality requirements at all.[141] If that were indeed the view that the Report took, it would explain why the Report made no reference to proportionality in reviewing the legality of the strike on the Grdelica Gorge Bridge: that incident in itself was not an "attack," but merely part of a larger and more systemic "attack" against Serbian infrastructure.

Oddly, however, the Final Report does in fact apply proportionality analysis to the RTS incident in itself. It says that "[a]ssuming the station was a legitimate objective, the civilian casualties were unfortunately high but do not appear to be clearly disproportionate."[142] It is hard to see how to square that judgment with the Report's view that the proportionality analysis "should not necessarily focus exclusively on a specific incident."[143] It appears that in making its proportionality assessment, the Report was balancing the civilian losses foreseeably incurred in "a specific incident" against the military advantages anticipated from a more general series of attacks against targets of a specific type (*e.g.*, bridges or C3 assets). But that, of course, cannot be right: a valid proportionality analysis cannot weigh defender's civilian losses from a single incident against attacker's accumulated military gains from an integrated series of incidents. Plainly that would load the dice in favor of the attacker: it would be a rare case in which a specific incident caused disproportionate civilian casualties, unless the incident was part of a larger pattern of disproportionate attacks.[144]

---

140 One analyst of the campaign maintains that most of NATO's planning did not, in fact, "integrate" attacks in ways that served coherent military purposes. He wrote:

> [A]lthough the methodology of effects-based targeting had long since been elevated to a high art, most of the attack planning throughout Allied Force was not driven by desired effects but rather entailed simply parceling out sortie and munitions allocations in boilerplate fashion, without much consideration given to how neutralizing a target might contribute to advancing the operation's objectives. A typical example involved attacking refineries, factories, and bridges in ones and twos over time rather than as interconnected components of a larger entity whose simultaneous destruction might instantly undermine Yugoslavia's capacity to function effectively.

Lambeth, *supra* note 6, at 201.

141 *See* Laursen, *supra* note 75, at 790–92.

142 Final Report to the Prosecutor, *supra* note 49, at ¶ 77.

143 Final Report to the Prosecutor, *supra* note 49, at ¶ 78.

144 *See* Aaron Schwabach, *NATO's War in Kosovo and the Final Report to the Prosecutor of the International Criminal Tribunal for the Former Yugoslavia,* 9 Tul. J. Int'l & Comp. L. 167, 182 (2001) ("Casualty averaging seems to indicate that almost

The Final Report may well be right in thinking that a single, discrete incident is not always the appropriate unit to consider in making an evaluation of proportionality. In the case of the Grdelica Gorge Bridge, it might be appropriate to subsume that "attack" within the larger NATO plan of attack on bridges and other transportation facilities throughout Serbia. But then, in reaching a judgment, the cumulative (anticipated) effect on Serbian civilians and civilian objects from the totality of those attacks should be considered.[145] If on the other hand the strike on the Grdelica Gorge Bridge is considered, in itself, an "attack" subject to proportionality review, the anticipated civilian losses should be weighed against the "direct" and "concrete" military advantages expected from that strike.

b. NATO Compliance With its Article 57(2)(c) Duty of Precaution or Duty to Warn

Article 57(2)(c) states that "effective advance warning shall be given of attacks which may affect the civilian population, unless circumstances do not permit."[146] The obvious purpose of the provision is to enable the government that will be defending against the attack to evacuate its civilians before the attack occurs, or at least to advise those civilians that an attack is expected so that they can remove themselves and their belongings if they wish to do so. The warning can be addressed either to the defending government or to the civilians who will be at risk or to both. To say that the warning must be "effective" is not to say that it must succeed, but that it must be reasonably designed to succeed.[147]

Here it is fair to say that NATO did not give a warning at all—certainly not an "effective" warning. At best, NATO forewarned foreign media journalists (or their employers) to expect an attack on the RTS station. Perhaps NATO expected these journalists to pass the warning on to their Serbian colleagues. Perhaps NATO thought that the absence of foreign journalists at the station would itself warn the Serbs who worked there. In either case, NATO did not warn either the Serbian government or the Serbian civilians who were most at risk from an attack. That conclusion stands even if it turned out that "some Yugoslav officials may have expected that the building was about to be struck."[148]

Even assuming that in warning the foreign journalists to expect an attack on RTS, NATO had also implicitly warned the Serbs, there would still be a question whether that warning was

no single incident involving civilian deaths can ever be disproportionate unless it is part of a larger pattern of incidents involving excessive civilian deaths.").

145 The Final Report seems to agree with this in ¶ 52, when it says that "an *overall* assessment of the totality of civilian victims" is to be measured "against the goals of the military campaign." Final Report to the Prosecutor, *supra* note 49, at ¶ 52 (original emphasis).

146 Protocol Additional to the Geneva Conventions of August 12, 1949, and Relating to the Protection of Victims of International Armed Conflicts (Protocol I) art. 57(2)(c), June 8, 1977, 1125 U.N.T.S. 3. [hereinafter Protocol I]

147 *See generally* Rogers, *supra* note 66, at 87–88, 99–100.

148 Final Report to the Prosecutor, *supra* note 49, at ¶ 77.

reasonable in the circumstances. NATO gave a non-specific warning to foreign media on April 12. The attack occurred on April 23—some eleven days later. The time-lag between the "warning" and the attack was long enough that Serbian civilians who were employed at the RTS station might reasonably have assumed that the danger had passed, or that the "warning" was disinformation intended to keep them from work rather than to prevent them from being hit. On the other hand, the fact that NATO's attack occurred at 2:00 A.M. surely indicates an intent to minimize civilian casualties.

Article 57(2)(c) includes an exceptional clause, however, thus reflecting a balance between humanitarian interests and military necessity. The Final Report referred to evidence that NATO did not warn the Serbs to expect an attack on the RTS station because "it would have endangered the pilots."[149] If that was NATO's motive, then presumably it did not wish to lose the advantage of surprise. While that seems like an acceptable justification, it raises the question whether NATO had not lost (some of) the advantage of surprise by forewarning the foreign journalists.

In any case, the question remains as to the meaning and scope of the exceptional clause. The Final Report does nothing to illuminate what that provision means when it requires an effective warning "unless circumstances do not permit." An answer might be sought by considering two earlier provisions of Hague Law that were apparently models for Article 57(2)(c). The first of these is Article 6 of the 1907 Hague Convention IX Concerning Bombardment by Naval Forces in Time of War, which reads:

> Art. 6. If the military situation permits, the commander of the attacking naval force, before commencing the bombardment, must do his utmost to warn the authorities.[150]

Plainly this provision does not impose an absolute duty on naval commanders to warn land targets of an attack. At most, a commander must "do his utmost" to warn the defending authorities, and even that much effort is required only if "the military situation permits." If Article 57(2)(c) is to be construed along these lines, then NATO would surely be excused from failing to forewarn the Serbs of the attack on the RTS station, if such a warning would have endangered its pilots.

The other precursor provision is Article 26 of the 1907 Hague Convention IV respecting the Laws and Customs of War on Land. That provision reads:

149 Final Report to the Prosecutor, *supra* note 49, at ¶ 77.

150 Convention (IX) concerning Bombardment by Naval Forces in Time of War. The Hague, art. 6, Oct. 18 1907, 36 Stat. 2351 (1907).

> The officer in command of an attacking force must, before commencing a bombardment, except in cases of assault, do all in his power to warn the authorities.[151]

Based on the language and negotiating record of this provision, one might infer that the "assault" exception includes any case in which surprise was an element of the attack.[152] However, subsequent arbitral case law had read the exception both narrowly, so as to exclude surprise attacks from the exception and, broadly, so as to subsume aerial attacks within them.[153] On the assumption that Protocol I was intended to incorporate both Article 26 of the Hague Regulations and Article 6 of Hague Convention IX, then, it is open to debate whether the exception in Article 57(2)(c) covers or does not cover attacks in which surprise is an element. Rogers is surely right, however, in concluding that the exception will "cover the need to protect surprise" and indeed "seems to be of broader application."[154]

c. Liability for Civilian Losses Caused by the Attack on RTS

Assume, for purposes of our analysis, that the RTS station was a legitimate military objective that NATO might have attacked consistently with the principle of distinction, and that the chief legal questions remaining, therefore, concern whether an attack would not satisfy the requirements either of proportionality or of precaution (i.e., the duty to warn) in Articles 51 and 57. However, assume also that Prime Minister Blair was correct in claiming that the Serbian government was aware that NATO would attack the RTS Station and nonetheless did not evacuate the civilians working within it. Who then should be held legally accountable for the civilian deaths that resulted from NATO's attack? Would the answer be different if the question concerned moral rather than legal responsibility?

The most directly relevant Protocol I texts are found in Article 51(7) and (8), which read:

> 7. The presence or movements of the civilian population or individual civilians shall not be used to render certain points or areas immune from military operations, in particular in attempts to shield military objectives from attacks or to shield, favour or impede military operations. The Parties to the conflict shall not direct the movement of the civilian population or individual civilians in order to attempt to shield military objectives from attacks or to shield military operations.

151 Convention (IV) respecting the Laws and Customs of War on Land and its Annex: Regulations concerning the Laws and Customs of War on Land, art. 26, Oct. 18, 1907, 36 Stat. 2227 (1907).

152 *See* Carnahan, *supra* note 60, at 62.

153 *Id.*; Carnahan, *supra* note 110, at 45–46; Howard S. Leroy, *Limitation of Air Warfare*, 12 Air L. Rev. 19, 27 (1941).

154 Rogers, *supra* note 66, at 100. *See also* US Army Maj. John Embry Parkerson, Jr., *United States Compliance with Humanitarian Law Respecting Civilians During Operation Just Cause*, 133 Mil. L. Rev. 31, 50 (1991).

> 8. Any violation of these prohibitions shall not release the Parties to the conflict from their legal obligations with respect to the civilian population and civilians, including the obligation to take the precautionary measures provided for in Article 57.[155]

Notably, Article 51(7) imposes a duty on all "parties to the conflict"—including the party defending against an attack—not to use "the civilian population or individual civilians . . . to shield military objectives from attacks."

Thus, Prime Minister Blair might be understood to have been claiming that the Serbian authorities were using the civilians working at the RTS station in that way. Assuming, again for purposes of analysis, that NATO did breach its duties under the *jus in bello*, and that Blair was right about Serbia's violation of Article 51(7), would that have relieved NATO from any liability for having caused disproportionate or "excessive" civilian casualties in striking that station? Does Article 51(8) imply, instead, that even if Serbia culpably defaulted on its obligations to its own civilians by leaving them in harm's way, nonetheless NATO would still be fully bound by Articles 51 and 57? Would NATO then be responsible for all civilian losses or only for any "excessive" civilian losses caused by its (otherwise lawful) attack?

There would seem to be three possible answers: that NATO was solely liable for any excessive casualties; that Serbia was solely liable; and that liability should be apportioned between NATO and Serbia.[156] Roughly analogizing to the Anglo-American common law of torts, the first answer is consistent with the basic rule of liability of the tortfeasor for all the harm caused by his or her negligence, assuming the lesser negligence of Serbia is regarded as inoperative or that Serbia had the so-called "last clear chance" to avoid the harm; the second to the traditional common law rule of contributory negligence; and the third to the more recent common law doctrine of comparative negligence.[157] The first view seems closest to the language of Article 51(7) and (8); the second is closer to the traditional, pre-Protocol I *jus in bello;* while the third has the support of many legal experts and scholars.[158]

i. NATO's Liability—The Text of Protocol I and Policy-Based Objections

The first view has been defended by Yves Sandoz, a leading legal expert associated with the ICRC. Sandoz wrote:

155 Protocol I, *supra* note 146, at arts. 51(7) & (8).

156 *See* Schmitt, *supra* note 80, at 49–54.

157 *See generally* Epstein & Sharkey, Cases and Materials on Torts 145–370 (10th ed. 2012).

158 There is a related but separate question if human shields take on that role voluntarily, rather than being forced into it unwillingly by the defender. Such persons may reasonably be regarded as combatants rather than civilians. *See* Schmitt, *supra* note 80, at 45–48. We can set that issue aside. Here we are concerned with the cases in which the defender either intentionally, recklessly, or negligently leaves or places civilians under its control in harm's way when the civilians are either unaware of the danger or have been forced into it.

> Protocol [I] is very clear in imposing on a Party to the conflict a requirement not to use civilians to protect its military objectives. Nevertheless, it is also true that it requires as well that the attackers take into account the situation as it is in reality. They can't just ignore the fact that civilians are used as "human shields." But this is common sense. Imagine your own citizens being used; you cannot pretend you just don't care. And it is also true if innocent civilians of one party, particularly children, are used for this purpose. This element has to be taken into account in the balance and the crime of your enemy does not give you the right to ignore the situation created by that crime.[159]

Sandoz' reading of Article 51(7) and (8) seems to be clearly supported by the text.[160] Nonetheless, if that is what Protocol I, in fact, provides, it is subject to strong policy-based objections.

For one thing, liability rules that hold an attacker solely liable for any excessive casualties can be viewed as unfair. By effectively ignoring the defender's responsibility for causing the civilian casualties, the rules treat similarly situated parties differently (assuming again the basic premise of the moral equality on the field of battle of the parties to the dispute, consistent with the independence of the *jus ad bellum* from the *jus in bello*).[161] Even if the attacker is at fault for killing disproportionately many civilians, so too is the defender at fault by intentionally (or negligently) exposing them to that risk.[162] Indeed, without challenging the independence principle, it may even be said on practical grounds that the parties are not truly "similarly situated," such that the defender should be assigned a greater responsibility than the attacker for protecting the civilian population in the area of danger because the defender can exert more control over the location and movement of that population.[163] Moreover, it has been noted that it is "logically proper to place the primary responsibility for the safety of the civilian population on the belligerent that governs the population."[164] A defending party (whether in its own territory or on occupied territory) generally knows the location of its civilians and can warn them of an expected attack, direct them to shelters, assist them in leaving the danger zone, or (with some limits imposed by Article 49 of the Fourth Geneva Convention) evacuate them; the attacker can

159 Yves Sandoz, *Commentary, in* Legal and Ethical Lessons of NATO's Kosovo Campaign 273, 276 (Andru E. Wall, ed., 2002); *see also* Enzo Cannizaro, *Contextualizing Proportionality: Jus ad Bellum and Jus in Bello in the Lebanese war,* 88 IRRC 779, 789–91 (2006).

160 Article 51(8) states that the defender's breach shall not "release" the attacker from its antecedent obligations. One might perhaps construe this language so as to be consistent with the claim that the defender's breach might nonetheless "diminish," "lessen," or "qualify" the attacker's obligations. But as a matter of the intent of the drafters of Protocol I, especially the ICRC, third world states, and neutrals such as Sweden and Switzerland, that seems unlikely. *See* Parks, *Air War, supra* note 70, at 163–64.

161 *See supra* Part I, Chapter 1.

162 In other words, Protocol I ignores or underplays the fact of joint causality in bringing about civilian casualties. *Cf.* Ronald Coase, *The Problem of Social Cost,* 3 J. Law & Econ. 1 (1960).

163 *See* Parks, *Air War, supra* note 70, at 153.

164 Carnahan, *supra* note 110, at 59.

warn of an attack, but can do little else.[165] Indeed, a defender who intentionally places civilians in harm's way seems to be even more clearly accountable for any harms those civilians suffer in an otherwise lawful attack, much as one who seeks the harm caused by the attacker is deemed to have assumed the risk of that harm.[166]

Moreover, Protocol I's liability regime creates incentives for a defender to leave or place civilians in harm's way (even if the defender breaches an Article 51(7) duty by doing so).[167] Thus Protocol I's rules do not serve the fundamental policy of protecting civilians as effectively as they should. Rather than being pro-civilian, the liability rules are pro-defender. Far from being the same, those two policies are in fact at odds.

Furthermore, the liability rules in Protocol I operate in favor of states that (1) are more likely to be defenders than attackers because they are at a disadvantage in terms of military air power, and (2) are willing to accept the loss of their own civilians' lives if that will create an opportunity to exploit those losses for propaganda purposes against their attacker. In other words, Protocol I (deliberately[168]) created an asymmetric advantage for (usually oppressive and undemocratic) combatants such as North Vietnam in the Vietnam War, Serbia in the Kosovo War or Iraq in the two Gulf Wars as against the militarily stronger Western democracies, especially the United States, that were likely to be their attackers. That conscious preference is plainly contrary to the general *jus in bello* policy of not skewing the rules in favor of one type of belligerent against another. Post-1977 practice bears out the claims that Protocol I's liability rules operate both to limit the airpower capabilities of the great powers (and Israel), and to encourage the use of civilians as human shields.[169]

Finally, under Protocol I's definition of an "attack," a defender will often also be an "attacker" in the very incident in which excessive civilian casualties occur. Under Article 49(1), '"Attacks' means acts of violence against the adversary, whether in offence or in defence." Thus consider a case in which A, a party to the conflict, initiates an aerial attack on military objective M on territory being defended by opposing party D. Suppose that D has effective anti-aircraft defenses that it deploys against A's attacking aircraft, which of course are themselves legitimate military

165 In the terms of torts law scholarship, the defender is thus the "cheapest cost avoider." Assigning it the chief responsibility for protecting the safety of the civilian population it controls will hold the combined costs of casualties and precautionary measures to a minimum. *See* Guido Calabresi, The Costs of Accidents (1970).

166 *See* Epstein & Sharkey, *supra* note 157, at 343–47 (discussing so-called "primary" assumption of risk).

167 *See* Parks, *Air War, supra* note 70, at 163.

168 *Id.* at 160–64. Parks' review of the Diplomatic Conference concludes that "Protocol I is a conscious effort by the ICRC, Switzerland, and Sweden—working through the Third World—to shift responsibility for collateral civilian casualties from the defender to the attacker." *Id.* at 164.

169 These claims are documented in Parks' *Air War and the Law of War.* Parks, *Air War, supra* note 70, at 165–68. More recently, similar claims have been made with respect to the war in Afghanistan. *See* Charles J. Dunlap, Jr., *Does Lawfare Need an Apologia?* 43 Case W. Res. J. Int'l L. 121 (2010) (arguing that NATO's 2007 announcement that it would not fire on positions if it knew that civilians were nearby encouraged use of human shields by Taliban and that 2009 imposition of special restrictions on airstrikes led to increased Afghan civilian deaths).

objects. In order to avoid the dangers posed by D's "attacks" on its aircraft, A's targeting is less accurate, resulting in the unintended dropping of bombs on civilians near M. Whose "attack" has caused any excessive civilian casualties—A's attack on M, or D's attack on A's aircraft?[170]

ii. Serbia's Liability under the pre-Protocol I Regime

An alternative view is that the Protocol I liability regime, at least if interpreted as Sandoz does, is badly flawed, and that the general rule should be that the defender is liable for "disproportionate" civilian casualties, at least when the defender culpably (i.e., intentionally or negligently) leaves or places civilians in the way of harm from an expected, and otherwise lawful, attack. Hays Parks contended that this was, in fact, the general pre-Protocol I regime:

> In customary international law the primary responsibility for preventing civilian casualties rests on the defender and the individual civilian, with little or no responsibility imposed upon an attacker. The reason for the existing rule is simple. Under most circumstances, the attacker has no idea where civilians are located and, except for a warning, has no way of controlling the location or movement of individual civilians or the civilian population; the civilian population is in the exclusive control of the defender.
>
> The practice of *all* nations that carried out aerial bombardment operations during World Wars I and II establishes clearly that *no* nation concerned itself with the risk of injury to the civilian population of an enemy nation incidental to the conduct of military operations. Protocol I constitutes an improvement in the law of war in recognizing that an attacker should, in most cases, give consideration to minimization of collateral civilian casualties. The issue is the degree to which an attacker should assume this responsibility. If the new rules of Protocol I are to have any credibility, the predominant responsibility must remain with the defender, who has control over the civilian population.[171]

This approach has some resemblance to the common law rule of contributory negligence, which cuts off any liability of an otherwise negligent tortfeasor, subject to certain exceptions,[172] if the plaintiff's own negligence has contributed causally to the accident that is the subject of the lawsuit.[173] As Parks formulated his view, however, the attacker will and should bear some responsibility for the collateral damages caused by its attacks, at least when it has failed to consider and take reasonable precautions to minimize the resulting civilian casualties.

170 *See* Carnahan, *supra* note 110, at 60.

171 Parks, *Air War, supra* note 70, at 153–54; *see also id.* at 162.

172 *See* Epstein & Sharkey, *supra* note 157, at 325–30 (for example, the "last clear chance" doctrine).

173 *See Butterfield v. Forrester,* 11 East 60, 61, 103 Eng. Rep. 926, 927 (1809) (drunken "riding" from a public house constituted contributory negligence); *Py. Ry. Co. v. Aspell,* 23 Pa. 147 (1854); Epstein & Sharkey, *supra* note 157, at 302–25.

There seems to be little support for the broad view that the defender should be held solely liable for any disproportionate or excessive civilian casualties caused by an attacker.[174] Such a position would, like its polar opposite, treat attackers and defenders asymmetrically, conferring a built-in advantage on attackers. Moreover, it is reasonable to expect attackers to take precautions to minimize civilian casualties when faced with a defender's wrongdoing, even if they should not be required to avoid all such losses by calling off an attack when the defender's wrongdoing has made such losses likely. As before, the policy goal of protecting civilians should underpin the controlling liability regime; and that goal is not well served by absolving an attacker of all responsibility for collateral civilian losses.

iii. Loss-sharing by NATO and Serbia

A third view is that collateral civilian losses should be *discounted* when assessing the proportionality of an attacker's actions if the defender has intentionally (or, arguably, negligently) left or placed them in harm's way. The United Kingdom's 2004 Manual of the Law of Armed Conflict takes such a position:

> Even where human shields are being used, the proportionality rule must be considered. However, if defenders put civilians or civilian objects at risk by placing military objectives in their midst or by placing civilians in or near military objectives, this is a factor to be taken into account in favour of the attackers in considering the legality of attacks on those objectives.[175]

Several distinguished legal scholars have taken similar approaches, including Parks (whose views are discussed above), Dinstein, and Rogers.[176] But the formulations differ, and it is not always clear precisely how the defender's breach of duty affects the attacker.[177] One possibility is that the defender's breach might, at least in some undefined circumstances, altogether relieve the attacker of liability for a disproportionate attack. But what would such circumstances be, and how could the analysis be reconciled with Article 51(8)? Another possibility is that the defender's breach might be factored into the proportionality calculus so as to weight it more heavily on the attacker's favor. To simplify: if a planned attack would be considered "disproportionate" if it were anticipated to cause 100 civilian casualties but not if it were anticipated to cause 75 casualties, and if the defender's breach would account for 30 of the 100 anticipated casualties (leaving the attacker responsible for only 70 casualties), then the attacker could

174 *See* Schmitt, *supra* note 80, at 49.

175 U.K. Manual of the Law of Armed Conflict at ¶ 2.7.2 (2004); *see also id.* at ¶ 5.22.1.

176 For a survey of these opinions, *see* Schmitt, *supra* note 80, at 51–53.

177 Likewise, differences have arisen in formulating the broad idea of "comparative" negligence. *See, e.g., McIntyre v. Balentine,* 833 S.W.2d 52 (Tenn. 1992).

launch the attack without violating the proportionality requirement. Again, if some share of the civilian casualties in a disproportionate attack were attributable to the wrongdoing of the defender, that fact might be held to mitigate any compensatory damages that the attacker was found to owe, and to require that the defender also contribute to the victims' compensation.[178] Yet another possibility would be to consider the attacker's exposure to criminal liability on a charge of a disproportionate attack: the existence of an Article 51(7) breach by the defender might serve to excuse the individual from liability, to mitigate the seriousness of his or her offense, or to justify a reduction in his or her sentence.

Another Approach? None of the three positions reviewed above seems altogether satisfactory. Even the third approach, which attempts to balance humanitarian and military considerations fairly, leaves much that is ambiguous and uncertain. Is another approach available?

We offer the following approach for consideration. Our starting-point is the assumption that attackers will generally care less about the lives and safety of enemy civilians than they will about their own or those of allied parties. (Remember that NATO warned Western journalists, but not Serbian journalists, of its planned attack on RTS.) Thus, one would expect an attacker to show a higher level of care for civilians when attacking a part of its own or a friendly party's territory that is occupied by its enemy than when attacking the enemy's own territory, and historical evidence seems to support this inference.[179] We submit that, to guard against this natural tendency toward bias, which conflicts with the moral equality of the combatants and their populations, an attacker's liability for excessive casualties should be greater in circumstances where it is less likely to demonstrate such heightened care, and it should be less in circumstances where it is more likely to demonstrate such care.

Let us illustrate this by reference to the War in Kosovo. Suppose that Serbia sought to deter a NATO attack on a valid military objective by placing a large number of Kosovar Albanian civilians around it. Serbia, of course, placed little value on the life or safety of its Kosovar Albanian minority. NATO, which was fighting to protect that minority from Serbian persecution, attached considerable value to it. Suppose that NATO, despite knowing or having reason to believe that Kosovar Albanian civilians had been placed near its intended target, went forward with its attack, with the result that many of the civilians were killed. In that case, we submit, Serbia, but not NATO, should be subject to legal and criminal liability for any excessive civilian losses.

A more difficult case is that in which Serbia either intentionally or recklessly left ethnic Serbian civilians, without their knowledge or consent, in a position of danger near an expected NATO target. On the one hand, NATO would be expected to care less about causing Serbian

178 *See* Protocol I, *supra* note 146, at Art. 91 ("A Party to the conflict which violates the provisions of the Conventions or of this Protocol shall, if the case demands, be liable to pay compensation. It shall be responsible for all acts committed by persons forming part of its armed forces.").

179 Thus, Allied Air Forces in the Second World War followed a policy of precision bombing when attacking German targets in German-occupied France, but less discriminate policies when attacking German targets in Germany. *See* John Finnis, Joseph Boyle & Germain Grisez, *Nuclear Deterrence, Morality and Realism* 264 (1987).

civilian casualties than about causing them among the Kosovar Albanian population. On the other hand, Serbia itself would have demonstrated that it attached little value to the lives or safety of some part of its own population for which it might have been expected to have shown more care. In those circumstances, we think that legal or criminal liability should be apportioned between NATO and Serbia. For example, if a NATO planner were found to have acted criminally (because disproportionately) in ordering an attack on the target, Serbia's action should be held to mitigate, or conceivably even excuse, the offense, or to justify a reduction in the sentence.[180] Should not the Serbian officials who were responsible for breaching Serbia's duty to protect its own civilians also be chargeable with criminal liability for any excessive Serbian casualties?

In short, while we do not here challenge the principle of independence between the *jus ad bellum* and the *jus in bello*, a subject we consider in detail in Part IV, we do suggest the legal rules ought to take into account the gravity of the violation of the parties in light of their pre-existing prejudices, creating default rules that realistically take into account their actual conditions and prejudices in the conduct of armed conflict. This lines of analysis direct us now takes us to the tension between realist and legalist interpretations of international law, which we believe is central to any reading of the Final Report's analysis and omissions.

180 We leave for students' consideration what the liability rules should be if Serbia had been simply negligent in exposing the Serbian civilian population to undue risk.

E. THESIS: THE FINAL REPORT TO THE PROSECUTOR AS A TEST CASE FOR LEGALISM AND REALISM

Does the Final Report to the Prosecutor tend to support "legalist" claims about the importance of law in international relations? Does it support "realist" claims that in international relations, the quest for power and security counts for far more? Or does it simply not support either view?

1. The Legalist View

From a "legalist" perspective, the very existence of the Final Report can be seen as a decisive event. The Western powers, acting through the Security Council, had established the first post-Nuremberg international tribunal to prosecute, try, and punish war crimes. However cynical their motives in establishing this tribunal may have been, once it was created, it had a dynamic of its own. Having created a criminal court with broad jurisdiction over the conflicts in the former Yugoslavia, the great powers in NATO could not disavow that institution when it unexpectedly applied the very same rules to NATO that the NATO powers had intended it to apply only to Serbian, Croatian, and other warring forces in the former Yugoslavia.[181] Legalists see a pleasing irony in this. Power wishes to use law for its own purposes. But law has a logic of its own that may come to constrain the very power that created it.[182] When law turns on power in that way, power is helpless to resist it without exposing as a falsehood its claim to be upholding universal legal norms. The Nuremberg and Tokyo courts might have been viewed, fairly or unfairly, as the mere instruments of "victors' justice." But that could not be said of the ICTY, which reviewed the conduct of both the strong and the weak by the same impartial standards.

True, legalists may well complain that Final Report did not lead to the further investigation and prosecution of any NATO defendants, or enable the ICTY to resolve the legal questions that the Report itself admitted were close ones.[183] But the bare fact that NATO was called

181 Hazan, *supra* note 24, at 131–32, 138.

182 *See* Hazan, *supra* note 24, at 199 ("[T]he ICTY demonstrated that a tribunal created as an alibi can progressively escape from its creator to generate new initiatives. . . .").

183 Antonio Cassese, the President of the ICTY from its foundation in 1993 until 1997, was apparently of the opinion that the prosecutor should have brought a case against NATO before the ICTY. *See* Natalino Ronzitti, *Is the Non Liquet of the Final Report by the Committee Established to Review the NATO Bombing Campaign Against the Federal Republic of Yugoslavia Acceptable?*, 840 IRRC 1017 (2000). In a different context, Judge Cassese expressed a strong normative preference for judicial resolution of questions about the legality of military actions. Addressing the Israeli Supreme Court decision in *Public Comm. Against Torture in Israel v. Gov't of Israel, supra* note 67, Cassese wrote:

> In a true democracy, the rule of law and respect for human rights (two pillars of democracy) require that the conduct of the executive be subjected to oversight as much as possible; in many cases it is appropriate for that oversight to be judicial in nature – particularly when fundamental rights are at stake. In addition, such judicial scrutiny is fully consonant with, and indeed implicitly required by, the very purpose and object of international humanitarian law. The more frequently courts of law pronounce upon the permissibility or impermissibility of military actions, the more extensive and forceful are preventive restraints on military behavior; hence the greater the effective protection of basic values that international humanitarian

to account by the ICTY Prosecutor took the authority of law in international relations to an unprecedented level. Moreover, once the ICTY itself had become established, the international community began actively to extend the rule of law to other situations of mass violence and armed conflict.[184] At first, it created special, *ad hoc* tribunals to deal with such situations, like the International Criminal Tribunal for Rwanda. Then, as a culminating achievement, it created the International Criminal Court under the Rome Statute. After being neglected for decades after 1945, the law of war crimes has acquired vitality, influence, and reach that are unparalleled: the entire area of armed conflict is progressively being "legalized."[185] The Final Report, therefore, has its place in an irreversible "march forward for international justice."[186]

Yet, the very achievement to which the legalist narrative points as crowning this development—the creation of the International Criminal Court—can be cited as showing the weakness, if not the potential failure, of the legalist project. The world's leading military power, the United States, has declined, in three successive Administrations, to become a party to the Rome Statute. (Indeed, having signed but not ratified that treaty in the Clinton Administration, the U.S. Congress deliberately unsigned it in the George W. Bush Administration.[187] And in 2005, Congress enacted the American Servicemembers' Protection Act to guard against the possibility that U.S. Armed Forces personnel might be forcibly subjected to trial before the International Criminal Court.[188]) Other major military powers, including China, Russia, India, and Israel, are also non-parties.[189] While the future of the International Criminal Court is of course impossible to predict, it may well turn out to be merely a criminal court for defendants from the underdeveloped world.[190] So it may be that the irony here is deeper than the more naïve legalists understand. The experience of the NATO powers with the ICTY may have alerted the United States and other leading military powers to the dangers of subjecting themselves to criminal liability when engaging in armed conflict. Rather than having come to accept and respect the "rule of

law aims at safeguarding (such as shielding life and limbs of non-combatants from the devastation of war, and introducing a modicum of humanity into the conduct of hostilities).

Antonio Cassese, *On Some Merits of the Israeli Judgment on Targeted Killings*, 6 J. Int'l Crim. J. 339 (2007). In the event, of course, the "executive" arm of the ICTY—the Office of the Prosecutor—had to decide whether to submit a case against NATO to the Court. Had the Court made that decision itself, it would have been in the position of being both accuser and judge.

184 *See* Hazan, *supra* note 24, at 198.

185 For analysis of the meaning of "legalization" and the suggestion that some areas of international affairs are being increasingly "legalized," *see* Kenneth W. Abbott, Robert O. Keohane, Andrew Moravesik, Anne-Marie Slaughter & Duncan Snidal, *The Concept of Legalization*, 54 Int'l Org. 401, 408 (2000).

186 Hazan, *supra* note 24, at 199. For a sophisticated, and not unsympathetic, critique of a naïve legalist narrative, *see* Frédéric Mégret, *The Politics of International Criminal Justice*, 13 Eur. J. Int'l L. 1261, 1281–83 (2002).

187 *See* Hazan, *supra* note 24, at 200–01.

188 22 U.S.C.A. § 7427(a) (2008).

189 *See* The States Parties to the Rome Statute (*available at* http://www.icc-cpi.int/Menus/ASP/states+pasrties/) (listing state parties to Rome Statute as of Oct. 12, 2010).

190 *See* Eric Posner, The Perils of Global Legalism 202 (2009).

law" in armed conflict, they may increasingly understand law as a kind of weapon that can be used to weaken or constrain them. "Lawfare" is viewed with growing suspicion as a kind of "warfare," and the Final Report has undoubtedly contributed to that trend.[191]

2. The Realist View

The French journalist Pierre Hazan, in his valuable book on the ICT, disclosed parts of an internal and confidential ICRC legal memorandum on the Final Report. This confidential document was a scathing review of the work of the ICTY Prosecutor. According to it,

> Neither the ICTY, nor international law in general nor international humanitarian law has come out greater from the report of the commission established by the prosecutor of the ICTY. . . . The clear partiality taken in the establishment of facts, the legal approximations and errors, render the document little credible or indefensible before a lawyer who knows international law well. . . . This document also helps one understand better the frankly negative positions of [Serbia] and of Russia vis-à-vis the ICTY. Such a difference in approach, depending on whether the alleged war crimes are ascribed to [Serbia] or to NATO, is indeed shocking.[192]

The ICRC memorandum all but accused the OTP of raw bias in NATO's favor. "We are struck (and ill at ease) in reading the [OTP] report to note to what degree the commission relies on the public declarations of NATO or of its Member countries to establish the facts that form the foundation of its analysis. . . . We may reasonably ask the question if this *a priori* favoritism to one of the parties of the conflict is compatible with the Prosecutor's avowed impartiality."[193] The ICRC memorandum singles out for particular criticism the Final Report's review of the incident at the Grdelica Gorge Bridge and the bombing of the RTS station in Belgrade. On the former event, the ICRC memorandum found that the rule of proportionality had likely been violated by the NATO pilot's or crew's second strike:

---

191 The term "lawfare" was introduced in a widely influential 2001 article by U.S.A.F. Major General (Ret.) Charles Dunlap, Jr. *See* Charles J. Dunlap, Jr., *Law and Military Interventions: Preserving Humanitarian Values in 21st Century Conflicts* (Carr Center for Human Rights, John F. Kennedy School of Government, Harvard University, Working Paper, 2001) (http://www.ksg.harvard.edu/cchrp/Web20WorkingPapers/Use20of20Force/Dunlap2001.pdf.). That paper, of course, was published not long after the Final Report. Dunlap has noted the "truly remarkable velocity" with which the term has gained use in less than a decade. *See* Dunlap, *supra* note 169, at 1.

192 Hazan, *supra* note 24, at 135. The ICRC memorandum is echoed on this point by the Chief of Prosecutions for the Special Court for Sierra Leone, who was "stunned" by the Final Report's reliance on NATO sources. In his view, "[i]t is doubtful that such a Report will contribute efficiently to enhance the Prosecutor's credibility and to demonstrate her impartiality." Luc Côté, *Reflections on the Exercise of Prosecutorial Discretion in International Criminal Law*, 3 J. Int'l Crim. J. 162, 182 (2005).

193 Hazan, *supra* note 24, at 135–36.

It is doubtful that this rule has been respected in this specific case, and the commission admits elsewhere having doubts on the subject. One can, in consequence, only regret that the prosecutor has refused to pursue its investigation further.[194]

The ICRC memorandum specifically contrasts "the meticulous work the prosecutor must have put into establishing the individual responsibility of [Serbian defendants]" with its unwillingness to assign individual responsibility to NATO pilots and crews.[195] On the bombing of the RTS station, the ICRC memorandum found it "profoundly regrettable" that the Final Report was not clearer on the question whether the station was a military object. "[A] more thorough investigation to establish the facts and, thus, the nature of the military objective or otherwise of the studios would have been useful in order to establish whether a criminal procedure was justified."[196] And it found the Final Report's explanation of NATO's failure to warn the Serbs of the planned attack on RTS as a theory that:

> nears perversity. . . . [OTP regarded] the fact that NATO had warned foreign journalists (but not Yugoslav ones) of the attack and that these foreign journalists were, therefore, not in the studios the night of the attack [as] substitutes for warning the Yugoslav authorities. As they did not react to this subtle warning to evacuate the studios, the Yugoslav authorities are, therefore, at least partially responsible for the fact that the attack caused civilian casualties. Nice logic![197]

The obvious inference, if one accepts these characterizations of the Final Report, is that the prosecutor was under NATO's influence and that the Report was a whitewash. NATO controlled the ICTY's (and thus OTP's) financing. Without funds from the West, the ICTY would have been shut down. NATO forces in Kosovo and elsewhere in the former Yugoslavia executed (or, often, chose not to execute) the prosecutor's arrest warrants, gathered (or declined to gather) evidence for the prosecutor's use, and protected OTP investigators from attack. The NATO powers conceived the very idea of the ICTY and provided it with political support at the United Nations. Although the NATO powers were often unhelpful to the ICTY and frictions between the two institutions had sometimes been acute, the ICTY and the OTP would have been unable to function without NATO's backing, and NATO publicly reminded the prosecutor of this dependence while the Final Report was being drafted.

> NATO spokesman Jamie Shea reprimands the prosecutor by recalling the old saying, "Don't bite the hand that feeds you." Reminding the tribunal that it is a tributary of political, financial, and

194 *Id.* at 136.

195 *Id.* at 136–37.

196 *Id.* at 137.

197 *Id.*

military support of the West, he notes, "The people of NATO are the ones who apprehend the war criminals indicted by the Tribunal." He hammers the point home, saying, "We all want to see war criminals judged and I am certain that, when Prosecutor [Louise] Arbour returns to Kosovo and sees the facts, she will indict the Yugoslav nationals, and no other nationality."[198]

On this realist account (which also voices an angry and disappointed legalism), the Final Report reflects the instrumentalization of law in the service of power. Is this view correct?

3. Neither Legalism nor Realism?

Might it be that, for all its flaws, the Final Report to the Prosecutor reached essentially the right conclusion? Assuming, rightly, that the prosecutor had some discretion under the ICTY Statute whether or not to investigate and prosecute NATO on the charges OTP explored,[199] was it a wise, or at least a defensible, use of that discretion not to prosecute? Consider and evaluate the following arguments:

1) Granted, the Final Report relied very heavily on NATO's own statements in making its findings of fact. But how else could the OTP have gathered evidence for use against NATO if NATO proved unwilling to provide it? The OTP frequently relied on NATO forces for gathering evidence for use against Serbian defendants; but it could hardly have used the defeated Serbian forces to extract evidence against potential NATO defendants. To be sure, Article 18 of the ICTY Statute vests the prosecutor with the "power to question suspects, victims and witnesses," and to "collect evidence," and Article 39 of the ICTY Rules of Procedure provides that the prosecutor may "summon and question suspects." But these provisions are not self-executing. They assume that the prosecutor would be able to compel the production of witnesses and testimony in the event of a government's unwillingness to comply.[200] If NATO proved to be unwilling to respond to the prosecutor's demands, how could the prosecutor have forced it to do so?[201] (Is it obvious that Western public opinion would have taken the prosecutor's side in a showdown, rather than their own governments'?) Moreover, the Final Report also made extensive use of

198 *Id.* at 132.

199 *See* Côté, *supra* note 192, at 165.

200 This basic point is ignored by Ronzitti. *See* Ronzitti, *supra* note 183.

201 NATO gave a merely "general reply" in May 10, 2000 to a questionnaire the OTP submitted to it on February 8, 2000. *See* Benvenuti, *supra* note 77, at 506.

evidence from non-NATO sources, such as Serbia, UNEP, Amnesty International, and Human Rights Watch.

2) Granted also, the Final Report made some debatable judgments of law. But executive agencies (and the OTP was the executive arm of the ICTY) must make judgments of law. They can only execute the law if they have first interpreted it.[202] And in the circumstances of its Report, OTP often had to make those judgments without the benefit of prior judicial interpretation. No doubt OTP's judgments on close questions might reasonably be criticized. But might they not also have been reasonably criticized if they had come out the other way?

3) Judge Antonio Cassese, the former President of the ICTY, acknowledged that "most rules of international humanitarian law on the conduct of hostilities . . . are rather broad and ambiguous; hence they do not offer great certainty to combatants."[203] Given the ambiguity and uncertainty of many of the relevant rules, did the prosecutor have a reasonable chance of obtaining criminal convictions for violations of them? Could NATO defendants not have made persuasive arguments that the relevant rules were so ambiguous, vague, or unsettled that it would be a denial of elementary due process to convict them? Moreover, even if the prosecutor believed that she had a chance of obtaining a conviction (in, say, the Grdelica Gorge Bridge case), was she not also entitled (indeed, should she not have been expected) to make her own independent judgment about the fairness of subjecting defendants to criminal trials on charges of violating laws that, in a Western system, might well be considered void for vagueness?[204]

4) Furthermore, was the prosecutor not justified, when evaluating the prospects for a successful case, in taking account of the jurisdictional problem caused by the fact that neither the United States (which flew 80% of NATO's attack sorties) nor France was a party to Protocol I?

---

202 *Contra* Ronzitti, *supra* note 183 ("[I]t is precisely the task of the Tribunal to interpret and 'clarify' the law.").

203 Cassese, *supra* note 183.

204 Justice Robert Jackson explained the void-for-vagueness doctrine in *Musser v. Utah*, 333 U.S. 95, 99 (1948), as follows:

> Statutes defining crimes may fail of their purpose if they do not provide some reasonable standards of guilt. ... Legislation may run afoul of the Due Process Clause because it fails to give adequate guidance to those who would be law-abiding, to advise defendants of the nature of the offense with which they are charged, or to guide courts in trying those who are accused.

The ICTY prosecutor appears to have the authority not to institute a prosecution based on an independent determination that the charge would not satisfy the standards of due process, which of course implicates basic human rights. *See Prosecutor v. Delalic, Mucic, Delic and Landzo* ("Čelebići Case"), AC, ITCY, at ¶ 604 (Feb. 20, 2001) ("[T]he Tribunal, which encompasses all of its organs, *including the Office of the Prosecutor*, must abide by the recognised principles of human rights." (emphasis added)).

5) OTP concluded that NATO had sought, with overall success, to comply with the applicable rules of war law throughout its campaign. That conclusion seems to have been well-founded. None of the complaints or evidence brought to the OTP's attention suggested that NATO's political and military leadership had been hostile or indifferent to their forces' legal obligations. Even if there were arguable violations (as with the second strike at the Grdelica Gorge Bridge), they seem to have been rare, and to have occurred at a tactical or operational level. Given the limits on OTP's personnel and other resources, and given the gravity of the crimes it was otherwise committed to prosecuting (including those for which Slobodan Milosevic, a sitting head of state, had been indicted), was it not a sensible use of those resources not to prosecute low-level NATO defendants?[205]

6) Was the prosecutor completely barred from considering the political consequences of initiating a prosecution against NATO?[206] She was aware that her work depended critically on NATO's continuing support. Without NATO's assistance, the trial and punishment of some of the most unspeakable crimes committed in the course of the four Yugoslav Wars could well be aborted or end in failure. Even assuming the charges against NATO could be proven, they were minor in comparison with those laid against the major non-NATO defendants. But prosecuting NATO could have undermined the entire enterprise of the ICTY. The quest to end impunity, if carried out too zealously, might defeat itself.

7) Moreover, apart from the severe damage to the ICTY's mission that could well resulted from prosecuting NATO, could the prosecutor reasonably have taken account of the broader consequences for the cause of human rights? The NATO publics had shown themselves restive at the thought of armed intervention in Kosovo, hence, NATO's "zero casualty" policy. But if NATO's intervention on behalf of the Albanian Kosovars resulted in the indictment and conviction of NATO defendants as war criminals, would those publics not be still more reluctant, in the future, to go to the aid of victims of mass human rights abuses? And if the liberal Western democracies did not aid such victims, then who would? Prosecuting NATO might burnish the prosecutor's reputation for impartiality, but at what cost to the innocent victims of future wars?

205 *See* Côté, *supra* note 192, at 175 ("International criminal justice remains largely symbolic and has limited resources that require exemplary selective prosecutions.").

206 For discussion, *see id.* at 169–71.

Chapter 3

The ICTY Office of the Prosecutor's Report on NATO's Aerial Campaign in the War in Kosovo—International Environmental Law and the *Jus in Bello*

In this chapter we again consider the Final Report to the Prosecutor, which examined the possibility that NATO violated the *jus in bello* during its aerial campaign in Serbia to defend Kosovo. But we now move to more recent developments in the law of war concerning obligations relating to the environment. We detail a potentially rich, emerging body of law that relates to the protection of the environment during at least some kinds of armed conflicts between at least some states. The matter is highly disputed. Before turning to that body of law and our case study, however, we provide the international law background in which this new body of law of armed conflict is emerging. In light of the relatively recent vintage of this body of law, our analytical commentary at the end of this chapter will look to rational choice theory and constructivism to account for how this body of law has developed, as well as how it may and should continue to develop.

A new set of international environmental law concepts have emerged in the 20th century. In addition, the specific implications of environmental awareness for the possession and disposition of weapons and their related materials and components has resulted in a body of international treaty law governing the testing and disposition of those materials and components. We take each development in turn.

1. The New International Environmental Law—Liability, Care, Notification, Assistance, Precaution, and Erga Omnes Obligations

Discussion of international environmental liability must begin with the famous *Tail Smelter Case* of 1911, in which an arbitral body awarded the United States injunctive relief and reparations from Canada because of air pollution affecting the State of Washington caused by the emission of sulphur dioxide fumes from a smelter owned by a Canadian corporation in Trail, British Columbia.[1] The Tribunal declared: "no State has the right to use or permit the use of its territory in such a manner as to cause injury by fumes in or to the territory of another or the properties or persons therein, when the cause is of serious consequence and the injury is established by clear and convincing evidence."[2] By 1972, the United Nations Conference on the Environment, meeting at Stockholm, declared unanimously in Principle 21 of its Declaration that all states are responsible for ensuring "that all activities within their jurisdiction and control do not cause damage to the environment of other states or areas beyond the limits of national jurisdiction."[3] That said, the Stockholm Declaration recognized that liability for failure to perform this obligations remained unsettled, declaring in Principle 22: "States shall cooperate to develop further the international law regarding liability and compensation for the victims of pollution and other environmental damage caused by activities within the jurisdiction and control of such States to areas beyond their jurisdiction."[4] In sum, the principle of state responsibility to injured states for trans-border environmental harm was beginning to receive general acceptance.

At roughly the same time, moreover, the International Court of Justice gave indirect impetus to environmental obligations. In the *Barcelona Traction Case*, the Belgian Government espoused the claims of Belgian shareholders in a Spanish corporation for expropriation by the Spanish

---

1 *See Tail Smelter Case (U.S. v. Canada),* 3 U.N. Rep. Int. Arb. Awards 1911, 1905 (1941).

2 *Id.* at 1965.

3 Stockholm Declaration on the Human Environment, adopted by the UN Conference on the Human Environment at Stockholm, June 16, 1972, Section I of Report of the United Nations Conference on the Human Environment, Principle 21, UN Doc. A/CONF.4814 and Corr.1 (1972), *reprinted in* 11 I.L.M. 1416 (1972) [hereinafter "Stockholm Declaration"].

4 *Id.*, Principle 22.

Government. In dictum, distinguishing these indirect claims from the types of claims third parties might bring, the Court said:

> When a State admits into its territory foreign investments or foreign nations, whether natural or juristic persons, it is bound to extend to them the protection of the law and assumes obligations concerning treatment to be afforded them. These obligations, however, are neither absolute nor unqualified. In particular, an essential distinction should be drawn between the obligations of a State towards the international community as a whole, and those vis-à-vis another State in the field of diplomatic protection. By their very nature the former are the concern of all States. In view of the importance of the rights involved, all States can be held to have a legal interest in their protection; they are obligations *erga omnes*.[5]

The Court seemed to limit the obligations *erga omnes*, however, to obligations that "derive, for example, in contemporary international law, from the outlawing of acts of aggression, and of genocide, as also from the principles and rules concerning the basic rights of the human person, including protection from slavery and racial discriminations."[6] Yet, within less than two decades, the *Restatement (Third) of Foreign Relations Law of the United States*, which reflected the consensus of expert international legal opinion in the United States, although not the official government position, was able to conclude that the class of *erga omnes* obligations could now also include environmental harms.[7] Thus, a shift began to emerge, developing a conception of international environmental responsibility that treated environmental harms as potential threats to humanity as whole. This shift may have been attributable to intervening experience in state practice, including declarations flowing out of the Chernobyl incident, and the work of international publicists at the International Law Commission of the United Nations.

On April 26, 1986, at the civilian nuclear power facility at Chernobyl in Ukraine, then a part of the former Soviet Union, an explosion released significant amount of radioactivity. Only days later, when increased levels of radioactivity were detected in Scandinavia and the countries of Eastern Europe, did the Soviets admit that there had been an explosion. Even after it was clear the explosion would have global effects, the Soviets initially failed to supply details, which were to come only much later.[8] Some argued that the Soviet failure to notify and warn their neighbors had violated Article 198 of the Law of the Sea Convention, which provides that a state, damaged or in imminent danger of being damaged by pollution, "shall immediately notify other

---

5 *Case Concerning the Barcelona Traction, Light and Power Company, Limited (Belgium v. Spain)*, Second Phase, 1970 ICJ Rep. 3, ¶ 33.

6 *Id.* at ¶ 34.

7 *See* 2 Restatement (Third) of the Foreign Relations Law of the United States, Section 902 cmt. a (stating that "any state may call on a violating state to terminate a significant injury to the general environment" as an example of "[w]hen a state has violated an obligation owed to the international community as a whole").

8 *See generally* Lori Damrosch et al, International Law Cases and Materials 1519 (4th ed. 2001).

States it deems likely to be affected by such damage, as well as the competent international organizations."[9] Arguably, however, the self-judging "it deems likely"-formula gave the Soviets a plausible legal defense. But the immediate international reaction to the incident eliminated this loophole in short order. At a record-pace, under the auspices of the International Atomic Energy Agency (IAEA), stronger obligations were established for future Chernobyl-like situations. First, the *Convention on Early Notification of a Nuclear Accident* created an absolute obligation to report to neighboring states.[10] Second, the *Convention on Assistance in Case of a Nuclear Accident or Radiological Emergency* created an obligation to "cooperate," provided mechanisms to seek and request assistance, and assured the "best efforts" of the IAEA to facilitate that cooperation, which presumably enabled it to exercise its powers, including the imposition of sanctions, to further that cooperation.[11] In short, in response to the horrors of Chernobyl, the international community carved out an area in which national sovereignty would be subordinated to collective needs.

By 1992, the United Nations Conference on Environment and Development, held in Rio de Janeiro, declared a deeper commitment to international environmental protection.[12] The Rio Declaration renewed and extended the Stockholm Declaration's Principle 22, stating in its Principle 13 that states "shall also cooperate in an expeditious and more determined manner to develop further international law regarding liability and compensation for adverse effects of environmental damage caused by activities within their jurisdiction or control to areas beyond

9 United Nations Convention on the Law of the Sea, Art. 198, opened for signature Dec. 10, 1982, UN Doc. A/CONF.62/122, *reprinted in* 21 I.L.M. 1261, 1309 (1982) [hereinafter "LOS Convention"].

10 *See* Convention on Early Notification of a Nuclear Accident, 25 I.L.M. 1369, 1370 (1986). Article 1(1) provides:

> This Convention shall apply in the event of any accident involving facilities or activities of a State Party or of persons or legal entities under its jurisdiction or control, referred to in paragraph 2 below, from which a release of radioactive material occurs or is likely to occur and which has resulted or may result in an international transboundary release that could be of radiological safety significance for another State.

Article 2(a) then states that

> [i]n the event of an accident specified in article 1 (hereinafter referred to as a "nuclear accident"), the State Party referred to in that article shall ... forthwith notify, directly or through the International Atomic Energy Agency (hereinafter referred to as the "Agency"), those States which are or may be physically affected as specified in article 1 . . . .

As if to confirm the mandatory character of this obligation, Article 3 goes on to provide that, "[w]ith a view to minimizing the radiological consequences, States Parties may notify in the event of nuclear accidents other than those specified in article 1."

11 Convention on Assistance in Case of a Nuclear Accident or Radiological Emergency, 25 I.L.M. 1369, 1377 (1986). Article 1(1) provides:

> "The States Parties shall cooperate between themselves and with the International Atomic Energy Agency (hereinafter referred to as the "Agency") in accordance with the provisions of this Convention to facilitate prompt assistance in the event of a nuclear accident or radiological emergency to minimize its consequences and to protect life, property and the environment from the effects of radioactive releases.

Article 1(3) also provides that:

> The States Parties request the Agency, acting within the framework of its Statute, to use its best endeavours in accordance with the provisions of this Convention to promote, facilitate and support the cooperation between States Parties provided for in this Convention.

12 United Nations Conference on Environment and Development: Rio Declaration on Environment and Development, adopted at Rio de Janeiro, June 14, 1992, 31 I.L.M. 874 (1992).

their jurisdiction."[13] Principle 15 provided, perhaps in light of Chernobyl, that: "In order to protect the environment, the precautionary approach shall be widely applied by States according to their capabilities. Where there are threats of serious or irreversible damage, lack of full scientific certainty shall not be used as a reason for postponing cost-effective measures to prevent environmental degradation."[14] Finally, generalizing the *Convention on Early Notification of a Nuclear Accident*, Principle 18 provided: "States shall immediately notify other States of any natural disasters or other emergencies that are likely to produce sudden harmful effects on the environment of those States. Every effort shall be made by the international community to help States so afflicted."[15] In sum, parallel bodies of hard, treaty law and soft, declaratory UN instruments converged on new international environmental norms that recognized the paramount interests of humanity in the protection of the international environment.

Meanwhile, the International Law Commission of the United Nations (ILC) initiated a project on the codification of the law of state responsibility, which included, inspired by *Barcelona Traction*, an effort to develop the concept of *erga omnes* obligations into more precise rules that might be adopted by states or serve as authority for international adjudication.[16] The ILC project finally came to fruition in 2001, in so-called "Draft Articles on State Responsibility for Internationally Wrongful Acts," also known as the Draft Articles.[17] It should be noted, however, that the UN General Assembly responded equivocally to the ILC project, saying that it merely "[*t*]*akes note* of the articles on responsibility of States for internationally wrongful acts, presented by the International Law Commission, the text of which is annexed to the present resolution, and commends them to the attention of Governments without prejudice to the question of their future adoption or other appropriate action."[18] That said, the Draft Articles reflected forty years of analysis by the world's leading international law scholars and practitioners, who had been elected by the General Assembly and were backed by the ILC's prestige and pedigree.[19] As a consequence, the Draft Articles have served more as a kind of restatement of international law than a model, multilateral treaty. Most critically for our purposes, Draft Article 48 provides:

13 *Id.* at 31 I.L.M. at 878.

14 *Id.* at 31 I.L.M. at 879.

15 *Id.* Principal 24 also called for "further developed" in the law of war. *See infra* note 60.

16 *See* Damrosch, *supra* note 8, at 1513.

17 *See* James Crawford, The International Law Commission's Articles on State Responsibility: Introduction, Text and Commentaries (2002). The official text and commentary appear in the ILC's 2001 report. Draft Articles on Responsibility of States for Internationally Wrongful Acts, in Report of the International Law Commission on the Work of Its Fifty-third Session, UN GAOR, 56th Sess., Supp. No. 10, at 43, UN Doc. A/56/10 (2001).

18 GA Res. 56/83, operative para. 3 (Dec. 12, 2001) (*available at* http://www.un.org/docs) (footnotes omitted) (italics in original).

19 *See generally* B. G. Ramcharan, The International Law Commission: Its Approach to the Codification and Progressive Development of International Law (1977); Ian Sinclair, The International Law Commission (1987); and Arthur Watts, The International Law Commission 1949-1998 (3 vols. 1999).

1. Any State other than an injured State entitled to invoke the responsibility of another State in accordance with paragraph 2, if

   (a) the obligation breached is owed to a group of States including that State, and is established of the protection of a collective interest of that group; or

   (b) the obligation breached is owed to the international community as a whole.

2. Any State entitled to invoke responsibility under paragraph 1 may claim from the responsible State:

   (a) cessation of the internationally wrongful act, and assurance and guarantees of non-repetition ...; and

   (b) performance of the obligation of reparation in accordance with the preceding articles, in the interest of the injured State or of the beneficiaries of the obligation breached.[20]

Draft Article 48 thus confirmed and generalized *Barcelona Traction*'s dictum concerning the possibility of *erga omnes* obligations. What is critical, again for our purposes, is that paragraph 10 of the ILC Commentary on Article 48 states that:

> Whereas the category of collective obligations covered by paragraph 1(a) needs to be further qualified by the insertion of additional criteria, no such qualifications are necessary in the case of paragraph (1)(b). All States are by definition members of the international community as a whole, and the obligations in question are by definition collective obligations protecting interests of the international community as a whole. Of course such obligations may at the same time protect the individual interests of States, as the prohibition against aggression protects the survival of each State and the security of its people. Similarly, individual States may be specially affected by the breach of such an obligations, for example a coastal State specially affected by pollution in breach of an obligation aimed at protection of the marine environment in the collective interest."[21]

The Draft Articles and their commentary, in treating environmental wrongs as potential violations of *erga omnes* obligations, thus confirm in more precise legal terms the decision of

20 Crawford, *supra* note 17, at 276.

21 *Id.* at 278, ¶ 10.

Stockholm and Rio conferences to treat international environmental wrongs as threats to humanity as a whole.

2. Use and Disposition of Environmentally-Sensitive Weapons

Presently we will turn to the special provisions of the *jus in bello* relating to the environment. However, it may be worthwhile to consider how the possession, testing and disposition of environmentally-dangerous materials in the weapons stockpiles of states, especially stockpiles of weapons of mass destruction, have increased military sensitivity to the potential environmental harms that would be caused by the use of such weapons. In fact, important arms control treaties of the last generation may well be viewed, at least in part, as environmental protection treaties.

Nuclear testing throughout the 1950s received ever-increasing international attention. By 1961, a substantial majority of states were prepared to say at the United Nations General Assembly that use of nuclear weapons as a weapon of war violated the Charter of the United Nations. [22] At the same time, these states adopted a resolution calling for the "cessation of all nuclear tests in all environments under control and inspection machinery adequate to ensure compliance with its terms."[23] It was the Cuban Missile Crisis of 1962, however, bringing the world to the brink of nuclear war, that appears to have persuaded the United States, the Soviet Union, and the United Kingdom in 1963 to conclude a so-called Limited (or Partial) Test Ban Treaty open to adherence to all states.[24] Article I provides:

1. Each of the Parties to this Treaty undertakes to prohibit, to prevent, and not to carry out any nuclear weapon test explosion, or any other nuclear explosion, at any place under its jurisdiction or control:

   (a) in the atmosphere; beyond its limits, including outer space; or under water, including territorial waters or high seas; or

   (b) in any other environment if such explosion causes radioactive debris to be present outside the territorial limits of the State under whose jurisdiction or

22 *See* Declaration on the Prohibition of the Use of Nuclear and Thermonuclear Weapons, G.A. Res. 1653 (XVI) (1067th plenary mtg., Nov. 28, 1961) (*available at* http://www.worldlii.org/int/other/UNGARsn/1961/59.pdf).

23 *See* Resolution on the Urgent Need to Ban Nuclear Weapons Tests Under Effective International Control, op. ¶ 2(a), G.A. Res. 1649 (XVI) (1049th plenary mtg., Nov. 8, 1961) (*available at* http://www.worldlii.org/int/other/UNGARsn/1961/59.pdf).

24 *See* Treaty Banning Nuclear Weapon Tests in the Atmosphere, in Outer Space and Under Water, 14 U.S.T. 1313, TIAS 5433, 480 UNTS 43 (entered into force October 10, 1963) (text and ratifications *available at* http://www.state.gov/t/isn/4797.htm).

> control such explosion is conducted. It is understood in this connection that the provisions of this subparagraph are without prejudice to the conclusion of a Treaty resulting in the permanent banning of all nuclear test explosions, including all such explosions underground, the conclusion of which, as the Parties have stated in the Preamble to this Treaty, they seek to achieve.

France and the People's Republic of China did not become parties, however. In fact, continuing French nuclear tests in the Pacific ultimately brought claims by Australia and New Zealand at the ICJ to compel France to cease atmospheric nuclear testing, which were dismissed only when France declared in a binding unilateral treaty instruments that it would discontinue testing.[25] A Comprehensive Test Ban Treaty (CTBT) remains aspirational,[26] as it will enter into force by its terms only when all nuclear-capable states, meaning the states listed in Annex 2 as possessing nuclear reactors, ratify. Although it was signed by President Clinton, the U.S. Senate voted against its ratification, and many other required states are even farther away from ratification.[27] Yet, the development of so-called Nuclear Free Zones in, among other theaters, Latin America and the Pacific, and the resistance of states in those zones to permit even the "innocent passage" of nuclear-powered or nuclear weapons-capable nautical platforms, surface ships and submarines, for fear of, among other things, environmental harm, has severely burdened the operations of the nuclear-weapons capable states.[28]

The Chemical Weapons Convention (CWC),[29] which required destruction of large quantities of noxious materials, also raised awareness of the environmental implications of possession of weapons of mass destruction in another way. For the United States, as one author has observed:

> [T]he CWC [mandates] the peaceful dismantling of massive national arsenals of now obsolete, but still exceptionally lethal chemical weapons (CW) agents, armaments, and facilities—and the destruction must be accomplished relatively promptly, reliably, and under the supervision of international inspectors. In the United States, however, long-standing environmental legislation, starting with the National Environmental Policy Act of 1969 (NEPA) and continuing through

25 *See The Nuclear Test Cases (Australia and New Zealand v. France)*, 1974 ICJ Rep. 253, 457–58.

26 *See* Comprehensive Test Ban Treaty, opened for signature 24 September 1996, 35 I.L.M. 1439 (1996).

27 *See generally* Damrosch, *supra* note 8, at 1085. For a status report, *see* Daryl Kimball, The Status of the Comprehensive Test Ban Treaty: Signatories and Ratifiers, March 2014 (*available at* http://www.armscontrol.org/factsheets/ctbtsig). For the current U.S. Executive Branch position, *see* Comprehensive Nuclear Test-Ban Treaty (*available at* http://www.state.gov/t/avc/c42328.htm).

28 *See* Ronald F. Lehman, II, International Arms Restraint by Treaty, Law and Policy, *in* National Security Law 523, 589–92 (John Norton Moore & Robert F. Turner eds, 2nd ed., 2005). For the right of "innocent passage" of even military ships, *see* LOS Convention, Art. 23, *supra* note 9 (confirming the right to innocent passage for even such vessels, albeit subject to "carrying documents" and observance of agreed "precautionary measures").

29 *See* Convention on the Prohibition of the Development, Production, Stockpiling and Use of Chemical Weapons and on Their Destruction, 32 I.L.M. 800 (1993) (entered into force for U.S. on April 29, 1997).

a sequence of resource-specific antipollution enactments, mandates punctilious adherence to procedural safeguards (such as the preparation of disclosive Environmental Impact Statements) and compliance with stringent national and local substantive standards on emissions, hazardous wastes, community participation, and safety. . . . At present, there is no established technology that can credibly promise to dismantle the United States CW stockpile in a manner that is entirely consistent with both of these sets of legal compulsion.[30]

Indeed, compliance remains incomplete. According to a non-official source, as of February 2014:

The United States and Russia possess the largest remaining chemical stockpiles among Convention members and both states have missed their destruction deadlines. Both countries asked to extend their original 10 year deadline for total destruction because of complications in the process and environmental concerns. The U.S. has destroyed nearly 90 percent of its declared 31,000 ton stockpile and Russia has destroyed 57 percent of its declared 41,000 metric ton stockpile.[31]

Yet, grappling with the burden of destroying so many noxious materials has forced states to internalize the full cost of their possession.[32]

In sum, it is possible that the experience of negotiating and implementing the Partial Test Ban Treaty and the Chemical Weapons Convention—to take only two examples, since one might also consider, among many others, the Ottawa Landmines Convention or the Biological Weapons Convention[33]—may have brought home to many states the environmental implications

30 David A. Koplow, *How Do We Get Rid of These Things?: Dismantling Excess Weapons While Protecting the Environment*, 89 Nw. U. L. Rev. 445, 446 (1995).

31 James Lewis, Fact Sheet: Chemical Weapons and Their Destruction, The Center for Arms Control and Non-Proliferation, Feb. 4, 2014 (*available at* http://armscontrolcenter.org/issues/biochem/fact_sheet_cw/).

32 The disposition of fissionable nuclear materials, such as enriched uranium, as a consequence of arms control treaties fortunately has presented a challenge of lesser magnitude. One creative vehicle for the disposition of nuclear-weapons-grade material turned out to be its conversion into nuclear material for civilian power reactors, based on a proposal by an MIT physicist. *See* John Neff, A *Grand Bargain*, The New York Times (Oct. 24, 1991) (*available at* http://fissilematerials.org/library/A_Grand_Uranium_Bargain.pdf). Under treaty concluded on February 18, 1993, Russia agreed to transfer to the United Sates Department of Energy, on commercial terms to be negotiated later, significant quantities of Russian highly-enriched uranium for conversion into low-enriched uranium to power civilian nuclear power plants. *See* Agreement Between the Government of the Russian Federation and the Government of the United States of America Concerning the Disposition of Highly-Enriched Uranium, 1993 WL 152921 (*also available at* http://www.armscontrol.ru/start/docs/heu93t.htm, and at http://energy.gov/sites/prod/files/pi_iec_local/098b7ef98002cabd.pdf). For a report on the implementation and completion of the project by the U.S. Enrichment Corporation, the now privatized former uranium enrichment services component of the U.S. Department of Energy, *see* Megatons to Megawatts (*available at* http://www.usec.com/russian-contracts/megatons-megawatts).

33 One could also examine the role of the Convention on the Prohibition of the Use, Stockpiling, Production and Transfer of Anti-Personnel Mines and on Their Destruction, concluded Sept. 18, 1997, opened for signature on December 3, 1997, and it entered into force on March 1, 1999 (the Landmine Treaty or Ottawa Conventions) (*available at* http://www.un.org/Depts/mine/UNDocs/ban_trty.htm). One can also examine the Convention on the Prohibition of the Development, Production and Stockpiling of Bacteriological (Biological) and Toxin Weapons and on Their Destruction,

of their possession of such weapons. The cumulative effect of these developments—together with domestic debates ad litigation for domestic environmental harms,[34] as well as for harms committed to U.S. soldiers deployed overseas[35]—may have brought home the potential environmental effects of conventional warfare too, particularly in light of the changing underlying international environmental law culminating in the Rio Declaration and the ILC's Draft Articles on State Responsibility. We turn now to the development of international law relating to the use of weapons themselves, the environment aspects of the *jus in bello*, as background to a discussion of the treatment in the Final Report to the Prosecutor of the environmental effects of the NATO's aerial campaign against Serbia to save Kosovo from a humanitarian disaster.

---

signed April 10, 1972, entered into force March 26, 1975, 26 U.S.T. 583, TIAS 8062, 1015 UNTS 163 (*available at* http://www.state.gov/t/isn/bw/c48738.htm).

34 For a discussion of the extensive litigation in the United States concerning the application of the National Environmental Policy Act, *see supra* notes 29–31 and accompanying text (implementation of the Chemical Weapons Convention); *see also* John C. Gruden, Environmental Law and National Security, *in* Moore & Turner, *supra* note 28, at 1297–1363.

35 *See* Dave Philipps, *U.S. Military Is Scrutinized Over Trash Burning in Afghanistan,* The New York Times (July 22, 2014) (*available at* http://www.nytimes.com/2014/07/23/us/us-military-is-scrutinized-over-trash-burning-in-afghanistan.html?ref=world&_r=0).

In what follows we shall review the early history of the environmental *jus in bello*; describe the tectonic shift in the law during the post-Vietnam era; analyze the critical elements of modern conventional law, the key provisions to Protocol I to the Geneva Conventions, and discuss important interpretive issues; and, finally, we turn to the potential status of the Protocol as evidence of customary international law and its potential application to the NATO aerial campaign against Serbia, in the context of the Final Report to the Prosecutor.

1. The Pre-History of the Environmental *Jus in Bello*

Warfare has nearly always been accompanied by the devastation of the natural environment. Whether in enemy territory or on their home soil,[36] military commanders have regularly practiced scorched earth policies, deforestation, the diversion of waters, crop destruction, and the like as means and methods of warfare.[37] (Thucydides tells us of Athens' repeated use of environmental warfare against Megara and other enemy cities.[38]) Furthermore, even when operational methods have been directed at human rather than natural targets, the incidental effects on the environment may be devastating—as, for example, with the trench warfare of the First World War and the aerial bombardments, including the atomic blasts at Hiroshima and Nagasaki, in

36 Destruction of the environment can of course be done by the defender as well as by the invader. Thus, for example, the Gauls deliberately devastated their own lands and property in order to deny supplies to Caesar's invading Roman army. *See* Archer Jones, The Art of War in the Western World 72–73 (1987). During the Renaissance, Leonardo da Vinci recommended poisoning the fruit trees along an advancing enemy's line of march. *See* Richard M. Price, The Chemical Weapons Taboo 21 (1997). And in October 1914, faced with an advancing German army, the Belgian defenders opened the seagates and allowed water to inundate much of the area between Nieuwpoort and Diksmuide. See Ian F. W. Beckett, The Making of the First World War 25-30 (2012).

Environmental destruction can also be used by invaders to cover retreats. In 1916, the German Army's "Alberich" operation called for a retreat from the front trenches to a better defensive position. The operation wrought extensive devastation to northern France, pursuant to the German Army's objective of leaving the returning Allies to '"find a countryside completely sucked dry.' . . . The operation was minutely planned. Nothing was spared, not the wells, which were made 'unusable,' not even the orchards, which were felled to prevent soldiers from taking shelter under them." Isabel V. Hull, Absolute Destruction: Military Culture and the Practices of War in Imperial Germany 259 (2005).

For other historical examples of wartime harm to the environment, *see, e.g.,* Michael N. Schmitt, *Humanitarian Law and the Environment,* 28 Denv. J. Int'l L. & Pol'y 265, 266–67 (1999/2000); Michael D. Diederich, Jr., *"Law of War" and Ecology–A Proposal for a Workable Approach to Protecting the Environment through the Law of War,* 136 Mil. L. Rev. 137, 143 & n. 36 (1992).

37 To consider the United States' military history alone regarding environmental warfare, *see* Burrus M. Carnahan, Lincoln on Trial: Southern Civilians and the Law of War 77–99 (2010), Lisa M. Brady, *The Wilderness of War,* 10 Envtl. Hist. 421 (2005) (Civil War versus the Confederacy); Lance Janda, *Shutting the Gates of Mercy: The American Origins of Total War, 1860–1880,* 59 J. Mil. Hist. 7 (1995) (the Plains Wars against Native American tribes); and Philippe Sands, *Remarks,* in *The Gulf War: Environment as a Weapon,* 85 Proc. Am. Soc. Int'l L. 214, 215 (1991) (the War in the Philippines); and the Vietnam War (discussed below). The American Civil War is especially notable in this regard. For instance, General William T. Sherman "not only carried on war against the enemy's resources more extensively and systematically than anyone else had done, but he developed a deliberate strategy of terror directed against the enemy people's minds." Russell F. Weigley, The American Way of War: A History of United States Military Strategy and Policy 149 (1973).

38 *See* Thucydides, *History of the Peloponnesian War,* Bks. II, 31 and IV, 45, 53, 56 and 66.

the Second World War. More recently, worldwide attention was focused on Iraq's systematic destruction of virtually all Kuwait's oil installations during the First Gulf War, which set some 500 wells on fire and wasted two to six million barrels of oil per day, and which shrouded much of the Gulf region in a pall of smoke.[39]

Despite their destructiveness, such means and methods of warfare were long considered acceptable.[40] The Roman historian Livy recounts the dream of the Carthaginian general Hannibal in the Second Punic War against Rome, in which he "saw behind him a serpent of immense size, moving along and felling all the bushes and trees in its way: and after it, followed a dark cloud with loud thundering in the air." In his dream, Hannibal asked a messenger from the god Jupiter to explain "what was the nature of this great commotion, or what it portended," and having been told "that it meant the devastation of Italy," was then "ordered to proceed in his course, and not to enquire farther, but let the decrees of the destinies remain in obscurity."[41] On the whole, environmental devastation during war was treated fatalistically, as if it were indeed among the decrees of the destinies. In a later book, Livy recounts the speech of a group of Athenian ambassadors, complaining to an Aetolian assembly of the harms their city had suffered in wartime at the hands of King Philip V of Macedon. The Athenians

> represented, in a deplorable light, the miserable devastation and ruin of their country; adding, that, "they did not complain on account of having, from an enemy, suffered hostile treatment; for there were certain rights of war, according to which, as it was just to act, so it was just to endure. Their crops being burned, their houses demolished, their men and cattle carried off as spoil, were to be considered, rather as misfortunes to the sufferer, than as ill-treatment."[42]

To be sure, there were protests, though these were made more often in the name of humanity or of policy rather than of law. For example, the seventeenth century international lawyer Hugo Grotius devoted a chapter of his great work, *The Rights of War and Peace*, to explaining the need

39 *See* Adam Roberts, *Environmental Destruction in the 1991 Gulf War,* 291 IRRC 538, 541 (1992); *see also* Maj. Gen. Robert E. Linhard (USAF), *Protection of the Environment During Armed Conflict and Other Military Operations,* 69 Int'l L. Stud. 57, 59–60 (Richard J. Grunawalt, John E. King & Ronald S. McClain eds., 1996).

40 There were some limited exceptions to this rule. For example, poisoning wells was prohibited under the rules of ancient Greek warfare. William V. O'Brien & Anthony C. Arend, *Just War Doctrine and the International Law of War,* 1 Military Medical Ethics 221, 223 (2003) (*available at* http://www.Bordeninstitute.army.mil.published___volumes.ethicsVo11.html). And the Jewish rules of warfare forbade the unnecessary destruction, in a discretionary war, of trees in and around a besieged city. See Deut. 20:19; Ariel Ehrlich, Military Law: Morality and War in Judaism (2008) (*available at* http://www.jewishvirtuallibrary.org/iscoursce/ejud___0002___0014_0_ 13895.html).

41 Titus Livius (Livy), *The History of Rome,* Book XXI, sec. 22 (George Baker trans. 1823). Although Hannibal used only the means and methods of warfare available to armies in the ancient world, the scars his campaigns inflicted on the Italian landscape were enduring. The British historian Arnold Toynbee was able to discern those effects when viewing the route of Hannibal's armies from the air. *See* Arnold Toynbee, 1 Hannibal's Legacy: Rome and Her Neighbors after Hannibal (1965).

42 Livy, *History of Rome, supra* note 41, at Book XXXI, sec. 30. The Athenian delegation did complain vociferously, however, about Philip's attacks on the human environment, including temples and gravesites.

for moderation in causing environmental damage during wartime.[43] (Grotius may have had in mind the actual or contemplated destruction of his native Holland's dykes during the Dutch war for independence from Spain in the late sixteenth century.[44]) Although Grotius stated that it was not his "Design to enquire, what it is advantageous to do or not to do, but to reduce the extravagant Licence of War to what natural Equity allows, or what is best among Things lawful,"[45] his recommendations are based more on prudence, morality, or religion than on law.[46] Further, Grotius may have been "well aware that such expressions of concern were exceptional and probably influenced conduct little."[47] Nonetheless, Grotius' admonitions were not without effect on the practice of states.[48]

But another eminent early modern authority on international law, the eighteenth century author Emer de Vattel, was perhaps more representative when he argued that "wasting" a country, and even "ravaging" it, could be lawful:

> Thus, we waste a country, and destroy the provisions and forage, that the enemy may not find a subsistence there: we sink his ships when we cannot take them or bring them off. All this tends to promote the main object of the war: but such measures are only to be pursued with moderation, and according to the exigency of the case. Those who tear up the vines and cut down the fruit-trees, are looked upon as savage barbarians, unless when they do it with a view to punish the enemy for some gross violation of the law of nations. They desolate a country for many years to come, and beyond what their own safety requires. Such a conduct is not dictated by prudence, but by hatred and fury.

---

43 *See* Hugo Grotius, *The Rights of War and Peace,* Bk. III, ch. 12 ("Concerning Moderation in Regard to the Spoiling the Country of Our Enemy, and Such Other Matters") [1625] (Richard Tuck, ed. 2005).

44 The Dutch had themselves broken open their dykes in 1572, in order to blockade a garrison in Middelburg; in 1573, in order to impede a Spanish siege at Alkmaar; and most notably in 1574, in order to let in enough water for a fleet of barges to raise the siege of Leiden. The Spanish military gave serious thought to breaking the dykes themselves in order to flood some of the Dutch provinces. In the end, King Philip II of Spain overruled his military advisers and forbade the operation. The King rested his decision, not on considerations of law or morality, but because the flooding of Holland would damage the prosperity of the neighboring provinces and because it would earn Spain a reputation for cruelty. *See* Matthew C. Waxman, *Strategic Terror: Philip II and Sixteenth-Century Warfare,* 4 War in History 339, 344–47 (1997) (translating Philip II's instructions); and Geoffrey Parker, *Early Modern Europe, in* The Laws of War: Constraints on Warfare in the Western World 40, 46–47 (Michael Howard, George J. Andreopoulos & Mark R. Shulman eds., 1994).

45 Grotius, *Rights of War and Peace, supra* note 43, at sec. viii, ¶ 1.

46 For example, he urged for "our Christian imitation" the practice of "put[ting] not only the Husbandmen [*i.e.,* peasantry] beyond the hazard of War, but also their Cattle with which they plow, and their Seed which they carry to the Field." *Id.* at sec. v, ¶ 4.

47 Christopher D. Stone, *The Environment in Wartime: An Overview, in* The Environmental Consequences of War: Legal, Economic, and Scientific Perspectives 16, 16 (Jay E. Austin & Carl E. Bruch eds., 2000).

48 The French devastation of the Palatinate between 1674 and 1689 was widely criticized by other states as contrary to the law of nations. France defended its actions by arguing that it was necessary for it to create an uninhabitable zone to impede any army seeking to invade it. But the French argument was generally rejected on the grounds that the military advantage was outweighed by the injury inflicted on civilians. *See* Capt. Burrus M. Carnahan, *The Law of Air Bombardment in Historical Context,* 17 A.F.L. Rev. 39, 40 (1975).

> Ravaging and burning. On certain occasions, however, matters are carried still farther: a country is totally ravaged, towns and villages are sacked, and delivered up a prey to fire and sword. Dreadful extremities, even when we are forced into them! Savage and monstrous excesses, when committed without necessity! There are two reasons, however, which may authorise them,—1. the necessity of chastising an unjust and barbarous nation, of checking her brutality, and preserving ourselves from her depredations. Who can doubt that the king of Spain and the powers of Italy have a very good right utterly to destroy those maritime towns of Africa, those nests of pirates, that are continually molesting their commerce and ruining their subjects? But what nation will proceed to such extremities, merely for the sake of punishing the hostile sovereign? It is but indirectly that he will feel the punishment: and how great the cruelty, to ruin an innocent people in order to reach him! The same prince whose firmness and just resentment was commended in the bombardment of Algiers, was, after that of Genoa, accused of pride and inhumanity. 2. We ravage a country and render it un-inhabitable, in order to make it serve us as a barrier, and to cover our frontier against an enemy whose incursions we are unable to check by any other means. A cruel expedient, it is true: but why should we not be allowed to adopt it at the expense of the enemy, since, with the same view, we readily submit to lay waste our own provinces?[49]

And echoes of Vattel's reasoning were heard even in twentieth century warfare. For example, after learning of the destruction that the German Army was leaving behind in its retreat in France, President Woodrow Wilson warned Germany in early 1918 to stop these "acts of inhumanity, spoliation, and desolation," or the Allies would not sign an Armistice.[50] At the ensuing Cabinet meeting in Germany, General Ludendorff defended the Army's actions as "limited to what was militarily necessary."[51] Ludendorff was, however, overruled: the Cabinet's action may have saved Belgium's coal mines (but not those of France) from destruction.[52]

---

49 Emer de Vattel, *The Law of Nations, Or, Principles of the Law of Nature, Applied to the Conduct and Affairs of Nations and Sovereigns, with Three Early Essays on the Origin and Nature of Natural Law and on Luxury (L.F. ed.)* Book III, ch. 9, ¶¶ 166–67 [1797)] (Béla Kapossy & Richard Whitmore eds., 2008).

50 Hull, *supra* note 36, at 260.

51 *Id.*

52 *Id.* Another somewhat earlier example is found in a self-described "Tactical Textbook for Imperial Soldiers" published by the Victorian military officer, Col. C.E. Caldwell, and entitled *Small Wars* (Col. Peter S. Walton (ed.) 1990) (2d ed. 1899)). Col. Caldwell wrote bluntly and did absolutely nothing to hide the racism characteristic of his period and class. In discussing wars of the kind British forces were by then long accustomed to fighting against "primitive" or "savage" peoples, he explained matter-of-factly that

> [t]he destruction of crops and stores of grain of the enemy is another way of carrying on hostilities. This method of warfare is more exasperating to the adversary than carrying off livestock; for while they appreciate the principle that the victor is entitled to the spoils, wanton damage tends to embitter their feeling of enmity. The same applies to the destruction of villages so often resorted to in punitive expeditions, but it hardly does so to the same extent, since the dwellings of those races can be reconstructed easily while their food supplies, if destroyed, cannot be replaced. . . . The most satisfactory way of bringing such foes to reason is by the rifle and sword. . . . Sometimes, however, the circumstances do not admit of it, and then their villages must be demolished and their crops and granaries destroyed; still it is unfortunate when this is the case.

Id. at 40–41.

Thus, scant attention was paid to the legal protection of the environment until the 1970s, even though "the artillery barrages of the First World War and the bombing of the Second World War caused severe environmental damage."[53] One rare exception was the trial in *United States v. List* of the German General Lothar Rendulic before an American War Crimes Tribunal after the Second World War.[54] Among the charges for which Rendulic was indicted was that, while in command of the German Army's retreat from an expected Russian advance in the winter of 1944–45, he had laid waste to the county of Finnmark in the northernmost parts of Norway and the northern half of the county of Tromsö.[55] Although the Soviet Army was not in fact in pursuit of him, the war crimes tribunal evaluated Rendulic's conduct in light of the honest but mistaken belief he had formed at the time that it was.[56] Consequently, he was acquitted of the charge. The legality of his "scorched earth" policy—given his state of knowledge—was not contested.[57]

2. The Developing Environmental *Jus in Bello*

The current legal landscape looks very different.[58] The situation began to change significantly because of widespread revulsion against environmentally-hostile tactics practiced by U.S. forces during the War in Vietnam, including the use of defoliants, Daisy-cutter bombs, and Rome ploughs.[59] This sentiment also dovetailed with the emergence of the environmental movement

53 A.P.V. Rogers, Law on the Battlefield 163 (2d ed. 2004). On the effects of the industrialized warfare, *see* John U. Nef, War and Human Progress: An Essay on the Rise of Industrial Civilization 365–67 (1950).

54 *See The Hostages Trial (U.S. v. List)*, VIII WCR 34, 69. Extensive excerpts from the opinion, together with excerpts from the prosecution's and defense's arguments, may be found in Gary D. Solis, The Law of Armed Conflict: International Humanitarian Law in War 286–90 (2010). For a discussion of the activity of other post-Second World War tribunals in this area of the law, *see* Betsy Baker, *Legal Protections for the Environment in Times of Armed Conflict,* 33 Va. J. Int'l L. 351, 375 (1992/3).

55 The Charter of the International Military Tribunal had defined war crimes to include "plunder of public or private property, wanton destruction of cities, towns or villages, or devastation not justified by military necessity." *See* Baker, *supra* note 54, at 374.

56 *See* Lt. Col. William J. Fenrick, *The Rule of Proportionality in Conventional Warfare,* 98 Mil. L. Rev. 91, 115–16 Bernard L. Brown, *The Proportionality Principle in the Humanitarian Law of Warfare: Recent Efforts at Codification,* 10 Cornell Int'l L.J. 134, 150 (1976/77).

57 *See, e.g.*, Geoffrey Best, *War & Law Since* 1945 328–30 (1994) (criticizing result in Rendulic case).

58 In 2009, the United Nations Environment Program (UNEP) published a useful and comprehensive survey of the current state of the law. *See* UNEP, *Protecting the Environment During Armed Conflict: An Inventory and Analysis of International Law* (Nov. 2009).

59 *See* Schmitt, *supra* note 36, at 267 ("The Vietnam War represented a watershed in the symbiotic relationship between warfare and the global citizenry."); Peter J. Richards & Michael N. Schmitt, *Mars Meets Mother Nature: Protecting the Environment During Armed Conflict,* 38 Stetson L. Rev. 1047, 1053–54 (1999) (noting that while earlier conflicts had caused greater environmental degradation, the War in Vietnam "signaled a paradigmatic shift in environmental valuation and prioritization" in large part because it coincided with the growth of the environmental movement). *See generally* Arthur H. Westing for the Stockholm International Peace Research Institute, *Ecological Consequences of the Second Indochina War* (1976); Jeanne Mager Stellman, Steven D. Stellman, Richard Christian, Tracy Weber & Carrle Tomosallo, *The Extent and Patterns of Usage of Agent Orange and Other Herbicides in Vietnam,* 422 *Nature* 681 (2003).

and the growing worldwide concern for environmental protection that the movement reflected.[60] In the event, two major treaties were concluded in the 1970s that in whole or in part were intended to protect the natural environment during times of armed conflict: the 1976 ENMOD (Environmental Modification) Convention[61] and the 1977 Additional Protocol I to the 1949 Geneva Conventions.[62] In a nutshell, the rules of Protocol I "apply to any attack which has an impact on the environment (the environment as victim)," while the ENMOD Convention "envisages the manipulation of the environment for hostile purposes (the environment as weapon)."[63] To illustrate: Protocol I would apply to such tactics as deforestation for the purpose of denying enemy forces protective cover; the ENMOD Convention would apply to tactics such as seeding the clouds in order to produce flooding.[64] Protocol I includes two clauses, Articles 35(3) and 55, which are of particular interest to the environmental warfare section of Final Report we discuss below. The ENMOD is, both in general and for the War in Kosovo, "probably marginal."[65] We shall return to Protocol I in the next section.

"Rome ploughs" were heavy tractors with large blades that were used to split, cut down, and scrape away trees. Their use cleared roughly two percent of the surface of Vietnam to bare earth and deforested extensive forests near Saigon. In addition to attacking the environment, the United States sought to *manipulate* it for military purposes: it attempted to interdict the flow of supplies along the Ho Chi Minh trial by seeding clouds, in the hope that the ensuing rains would make the trail impassable. *See* Schmitt, *supra* note 36, at 268.

60 This concern found expression at the international level, as, for example, in the U.N. General Assembly's 1982 World Charter for Nature, which affirmed that "Nature shall be secured against degradation caused by warfare or other hostile activities." *See* G.A. Res. 37/7, 3 U.N. GAOR Supp. No. 51, U.N. Doc. A/37/51, ¶ 5 (1982); *see also* Baker, *supra* note 54, at 356. Likewise, Principle 24 of the Rio Declaration on Environment and Development, *supra* note 12, states that "[w]arfare is inherently destructive of sustainable development. States shall therefore respect international law providing protection for the environment in times of armed conflict and cooperate in its further development, as necessary."

61 Convention on the Prohibition of Military and any other Hostile Uses of Environmental Modification Techniques, 16 I.L.M. 88 (1978). For a useful analysis and evaluation of ENMOD, *see* Charles R. Wunsch, *The Environmental Modification Treaty*, 4 ASILS Int'l L. J. 113 (1980).

62 Protocol Additional to the Geneva Conventions of August 12, 1949, and Relating to the Protection of Victims of International Armed Conflicts, done at Geneva, June 8, 1977, entered into force, Dec. 7, 1978, 16 I.L.M. 1391 (1977) [hereinafter Protocol I]. Although the United States has not ratified Protocol I, operational instructions for U.S. military forces, including rules of engagement, nonetheless "spell out the key environmental provisions of that instrument." Arthur H. Westing, *In Furtherance of Environmental Guidelines for Armed Forces during Peace and War*, *in* The Environmental Consequences of War: Legal, Economic, and Scientific Perspectives 171, 176 (Jay E. Austin & Carl E. Bruch eds., 2000).

63 Michael Bothe, *The Protection of the Environment in Times of Armed Conflict*, 34 German Y.B. Int'l L. 54, 57 (1991). *Accord* Josef Goldblat, *The Environmental Warfare Convention: How Meaningful Is It?*, 6 Ambio 216 (1977).

64 *See* Schmitt, *supra* note 36, at 269. This is not, of course, to say that it is always clear which treaty to apply. For example, the Iraqi destruction of Kuwait's oil installations might arguably be covered by both treaties. *See* Roberts, *supra* note 39, at 544.

65 Bothe, *supra* note 63, at 57. On the other hand, consider the possibility that the ENMOD Convention serves the interests of its parties by deterring investment in research and development of novel, highly expensive, if also potentially effective, military technologies. *See* Eric A. Posner, *A Theory of the Laws of War*, John M. Olin Law & Economics Working Paper No. 160 (2d Series) at 8 (laws of war may be designed to limit the efficiency of military technology) (*available at* http://www.law.uchicago.edu/Laeecon/index.html).

Although they are the most prominent treaties for protecting the environment in wartime, ENMOD and Protocol I do not exhaust conventional international *jus in bello* on the subject.[66] Prominent among other environmentally-relevant treaties is the Incendiaries Protocol (Protocol III to the 1980 Convention on Certain Conventional Weapons). [67] The War in Vietnam seems to have provided an impetus for this treaty: United Nations General Assembly Resolutions had condemned the use of incendiary weapons, particularly napalm, and a 1973 Report by the Secretary General invited diplomatic consideration concerning the use of such weapons.[68] Yet that debate continues for the United States, for today the status of the United States as a party is in dispute, as international resistance to U.S. "understandings" of the treaty, providing in effect an escape clause, call into question whether the U.S. instrument of ratification has brought the treaty into force for the United States. [69]

Even if the United States were deemed to be a party, the treaty's impact may be debatable. Admittedly, the Incendiaries Protocol prohibits in Article 2(2) "in all circumstances to make any military objective located within a concentration of civilians the object of attack by air-delivered incendiary weapons."[70] Article 2(3) relates to "other than air-delivered incendiary weapons," and prohibits their use

66 For surveys of potentially relevant treaty provisions, including protections for property afforded by both Hague and Geneva law, *see, e.g.* William H. Boothby, *Weapons and the Law of Armed Conflict* 87–92 (2009); Adam Roberts, *The Law of War and Environmental Damage, in The Environmental Consequences of War: Legal, Economic, and Scientific Perspectives* 47, 50–57 (Jay E. Austin & Carl E. Bruch eds., 2000); John H. McNeill, *Protection of the Environment in time of Armed Conflict: Environmental Protection in Military Practice,* 69 Int'l L. Stud. 536, 539–40 (Richard J. Grunawalt, John E. King & Ronald S.McClain eds., 1996). For example, Article 23(g) of the Annex to the 1907 Hague Convention (No. IV) Respecting the Laws and Customs of War on Land, entered into force Jan. 26, 1910, makes it "especially forbidden" to "destroy or seize the enemy's property, unless such destruction or seizure be imperatively demanded by the necessities of war." Arguably, the destruction of "property" encompasses at least some environmental harms. *But see* Michael Bothe, *Criminal Responsibility for Environmental Damage in Times of Armed Conflict,* 69 Int'l L. Stud. 473, 475–76 (Richard J. Grunawalt, John E. King & Ronald S. McClain eds., 1996) (pointing out that although Iraq's destruction of Kuwait's oil wells was destruction of "property" and, because it had no apparent military necessity, was "wanton," nonetheless the environmental damage consisted chiefly in harms to waters or the air, and "it is at least not a matter of course to conclude that this damage to the environment also constitutes a destruction of property").

67 *See* Protocol on Prohibition or Restrictions on the Use of Incendiary Weapons, (Protocol III), Geneva, 10 October 1980.

68 *See Napalm and Other Incendiary Weapons and All Aspects of Their Possible Use,* U.N.G.A. Res. 3076 (XXVIII) of Dec. 6, 1973.

69 The United States, despite earlier misgivings, recently ratified this Protocol and, in early 2009, deposited its consent to be bound by it, subject to the reservation of its right to use incendiary weapons against military objectives located in concentrations of civilians where it is judged that such use would cause fewer casualties and/or less collateral damage. The United States also attached an "understanding" to its consent. Unusually, some seventeen European states objected in February 2009 to these conditions, thus signaling their refusal to accept the proposed reservation. As of the time of writing, the disagreement remains unresolved. *See* Jeff Abramson for Arms Control Association, U.S. Incendiary-Weapons Policy Rebuffed (*available at* http://www.armscontrol.org/act/2010__04/Incendiary); *see also* Michael N. Schmitt, *Military Necessity and Humanity in International Humanitarian Law: Preserving the Delicate Balance,* 50 Va. J. Int'l L. 795, 815 (2010).

70 For analyses of this Protocol, *see* William H. Boothby, *Weapons and the Law of Armed Conflict* 199–208 (2009); Frits Kalshoven & Liesbeth Zegveld, *Constraints on the Waging of War: An Introduction to International Humanitarian Law* 162–65 (2001); W. Hays Parks, *The Protocol on Incendiary Weapons,* 279 IRRC 535 (1990). For a summary of the negotiations and drafting history, *see* R.R. Baxter, *Conventional Weapons under Legal Prohibitions,* 1 Int'l Sec. 42, 48–49,

to make any military objective within a concentration of civilians the object of attack . . . except when such military objective is clearly separated from the concentration of civilians and all feasible precautions are taken with a view to limiting the incendiary effects to the military objective and to avoiding, and in any event to minimizing, incidental loss of civilian life, injury to civilians and damage to civilian objects.[71]

An "incendiary weapon" is defined in Article 1(1) as "any weapon or munition which is primarily designed to set fire to objects or to cause burn injury to persons through the action of flame, heat, or a combination thereof, produced by a chemical reaction of a substance delivered on the target." Article 1(a) provides that such weapons may take the form of "flamethrowers, fougasses, shells, rockets, grenades, mines, bombs and other containers of incendiary substances." But Article 1(b)(i) and (ii) exclude "munitions which may have incidental incendiary effects, such as illuminants, tracers, smoke or signaling systems" and

munitions designed to combine penetration, blast or fragmentation effects with an additional incidental effects, such as armor-piercing projectiles, explosive bombs and similar combined-effects munitions in which the incendiary effect is not specifically designed to cause burn injury to persons, but to be used against military objectives, such as armored vehicles, aircraft and installations or facilities.

Because incendiary weapons may cause serious harm to the natural environment (among other things, they may give rise to uncontrollable fires over large swathes of territory), the Incendiaries Protocol, by restricting their use, contributes to environmental protection.

Nonetheless, its impact may well be limited. First, it is designed to protect human beings, not the environment in itself. Indeed, it seems to confirm the legality of some direct attacks on the environment: Article 2(4) forbids attacks on forests or "other kinds of plant cover" with incendiary weapons unless they are "used to cover, conceal or camouflage combatants or other military objectives, or are themselves military objectives." Second, it does not prohibit the use of such incendiary weapons as bombs, napalm, or flamethrowers against military targets (indeed, it establishes the legality of such weapons). Third, weapons that produce incidental incendiary

53–55 (1977). For practical guidance on its application, see UK Ministry of Defence, The Manual of the Law of Armed Conflict 110–12 (2004).

71 One writer advances the view that "[i]n practice [Article 2(3)] will mean that, even if civilians are present, incendiary attacks can be made if the civilians have taken shelter in bunkers or are at such a distance from the objective that the effects of the incendiary weapon will not be felt by them." W.J. Fenwick, *The Conventional Weapons Convention: A Modest but Useful Treaty*, 279 IRRC 498, 508 (1990).

effects are excluded.[72] Fourth, the Protocol as a whole applies only to international armed conflict, and thus not to civil war or other internal armed conflicts.[73]

3. The Environmental Protections Afforded by Additional Protocol I

As mentioned above, Additional Protocol I includes two provisions relating expressly to the environment; both provisions were at issue in the Final Report. The first of these is Article 35(3), which appears among the "Basic Rules" governing the "Means and Methods of Warfare." Article 35(3) provides that:

> It is prohibited to employ methods or means of warfare which are intended, or may be expected, to cause widespread, long-term and severe damage to the natural environment.

The second environmental clause in Protocol I is Article 55, entitled "Protection of the natural environment," which reads:

1. Care shall be taken in warfare to protect the natural environment against widespread, long-term and severe damage. This protection includes a prohibition of the use of methods or means of warfare which are intended or may be expected to cause such damage to the natural environment and thereby to prejudice the health or survival of the population.

2. Attacks against the natural environment by way of reprisals are prohibited.[74]

---

72 "The combined incendiary-effect exclusion limits the scope of the definition. A substantial number of modern incendiary weapons are in fact combined-effects munitions and outside the scope of the definition. Older weapons such as those used in World War II and napalm are, however, within the definition." Fenwick, *supra* note 71, at 507.

73 *See* Parks, *supra* note 70, at 550. That is not necessarily to deny that particular provisions of the Protocol might not apply to internal conflicts, however. *See* Denise Plattner, *The 1980 Convention on Conventional Weapons and Applicability of Rules Governing Means of Combat in a Non-International Armed Conflict,* 249 IRRC 551, 563 (1990) (suggesting that Article 2(2) "might also be applicable to all armed conflict").

74 *See* Protocol I, *supra* note 62. Students should note the ambiguity – if also the potential power – of Art. 55(1). Thus, Karen Hulme distinguishes three possible understandings of the opening sentence of that clause: 1) it might simply "encapsulate[] the *raison d'etre* or . . . the 'underling concept' of the provision;" 2) it might "in fact weaken the provision" by allowing some latitude for judgment; or 3) by "recogniz[ing] the value of the environment to humanity" as "so important that that value can limit the actions of parties to armed conflict," it could serve as "a lasting reminder . . . that humankind must continue to protect the environment in armed conflict." Karen Hulme, *Taking care to protect the environment against damage: a meaningless obligation?,* 92 IRRC 675, 677 (2010). The "real issue," as Hulme rightly says, is to decide "the level of protection that can be afforded the environment during armed conflict." *Id.* at 681. Hulme argues that "the provision is [not] without meaning altogether. States parties will, at the very least, need to undertake an assessment of potential environmental impacts of their proposed actions." *Id.* at 680.

In addition to these two specific provisions, Protocol I protects the environment through other, more general clauses. Indeed, it has been said that "[p]robably the most significant environmental protections in Additional Protocol I are located in Articles 52, 51(5)(b), and 57(2)(a)(iii)."[75] The Final Report's discussion of environmental law in fact relies more on these clauses than on Articles 35(3) and 55.

Broadly speaking, these general provisions impose restrictions of necessity, discrimination and proportionality on targeting. Article 52(2) confines permissible targeting "strictly to military objectives," which it limits "to those objects which by their nature, location, purpose or use make an effective contribution to military action and whose total or partial destruction, capture or neutralization, in the circumstances ruling at the time, offers a definite military advantage." Civilian objects encompass "all objects which are not military objectives as defined in paragraph [52(2)]."[76] In other words, the universe of potential targets is divided into two exhaustive and exclusive categories—the military and the civilian—and only the former may permissibly be targeted. It follows that "civilian objects shall not be the object of attack or of reprisals."[77] The term "civilian objects" can "reasonably be interpreted to include all elements of the environment, which, in the relevant times and circumstances, do not constitute a clear, well-defined military objective or advantage."[78] (The International Red Cross has sought to make this explicit in its Article 9 of its *Guidelines for Military Manuals and Instructions on the Protection of the Environment in Times of Armed Conflict* (1996),[79] which states that "[t]he general prohibition on destroying civilian objects, unless such destruction is justified by military necessity, also protects the environment.") If so, both Articles 35(3) and 55 should be understood to afford the environment at least as high a level of protection as that provided by these other requirements of Protocol I.[80] "Thus, Articles 35 and 55 prohibit causing [widespread, long-term and severe] damage to the environment even where the environment constitutes a military objective or where the damage to the environment may be considered as not being excessive in relation to the military advantage anticipated."[81] Under Protocol I, therefore, a military commander 1) may not intentionally target the natural environment unless it is a military objective, 2) even then, may not cause environmental damage that is disproportionate in relation to the military advan-

75 Richards & Schmitt, *supra* note 59, at 1072.

76 *See* Protocol I, Art. 52(1), *supra* note 62.

77 *Id.*

78 Richards & Schmitt, *supra* note 59, at 1072–73; Hulme, *supra* note 74 at 678 ("the general view is that unless the environment (or part of it) fulfills the definition of provided by Article 52(2) of Protocol I it should be considered as *prima facie* civilian").

79 31 IRRC 230 (1996).

80 *See, e.g.*, Baker, *supra* note 54, at 369 ("[A]rticle 35(3) of Protocol I is arguably not subject to the military necessity exception.").

81 Bothe, *supra* note 63, at 56; *see also* Richards & Schmitt, *supra* note 59, at 1062 (quoting U.S. Army's 1998 *Operational Law Handbook*); *see also* Schmitt, *supra* note 36, at 283 (discussing comparable provision in Rome Statute).

tage anticipated from the attack, and 3) even then, may not use means or methods intended or expected to cause widespread, long-term, and severe environmental damage.

There has been some uncertainty over the precise relationship between Articles 35(3) and 55.[82] As the language of these provisions suggests, Article 35(3) appears to be concerned with the protection of the natural environment solely for its own sake,[83] while Article 55(1) prohibits harms to the environment at least in part because of their human consequences ("and thereby to prejudice the health or survival of the population").[84] Thus, Yoram Dinstein has suggested that the reference in Article 55 to human consequences "appears to restrict its range to environmental damage that specifically prejudices human health or survival."[85] If so, Article 35(3) might be characterized as a kind of "Hague" law, while Article 55 might be seen as "Geneva" law.[86] But how should the two interests—human and environmental—be weighed in the event they conflict?

Richards and Schmitt posit a situation in which a commander is considering whether to launch an attack through a village or around it in an unpopulated but environmentally fragile area on the village's outskirts. Assume that the attack through the village is militarily necessary (there is a valid military objective on the other side of the village) and proportionate (the expected harm to the village from the attack would be outweighed by the military advantage secured). Assume also that the attack through the environmentally fragile area would cause widespread, long-term and severe harm to it. Must the commander attack through the village, even though such an attack would result in human casualties, while the attack through the outskirts of the village would not? While observing that an approach in which environmental

---

82 For example, the U.K. *Manual of the Law of Armed Conflict* finds that "[t]he only difference of substance is that while Article 35 relates to all methods of warfare whether on land, sea, or in the air wherever in the world they are utilized, Article 55 only relates to environmental damage on the territory or in the territorial sea of a state party to the conflict." UK Ministry of Defence, *supra* note 70, at 76.

Another analysis states that "Article 55 does more than merely restate Article 35, para. 3. It establishes a general obligation to protect the environment during the conduct of hostilities, but that obligation is directed to the protection of civilians, whereas Article 35, para. 3, aims to protect the environment as such." Antoine Bouvier, *Protection of the Natural Environment in Time of Armed Conflict,* 285 IRRC 567 (1991). But the protection afforded by Article 55 appears to extend, not merely to civilians, but also to military personnel. The article refers to the "population," as distinct from the "civilian population." The omission of the qualifier "civilian" seems to have been intentional. *See* Alexandre Kiss, *Les Protocoles Additionels aux Conventions de Genève de 1977 et la Protection des Biens de l'Environnement, in Studies and Essays in International Humanitarian Law and Red Cross Principles in Honour of Jean Pictet* 181, 190 (Christophe Swarinski ed., 1984).

83 *See* Tara Weinstein, *Prosecuting Attacks that Destroy the Environment: Environmental Crimes or Humanitarian Atrocities?,* 17 Geo. Int'l Env'l L. Rev. 687, 702 (2004/05) ("Article 35 . . . considers protection of the environment beyond humanitarian effects – representing a departure from traditional humanitarian law.").

84 "Article 55 brings back . . . 'other considerations' in the form of humanity, thereby articulating a prescriptive standard measured by impact on human beings. . . . A review of the negotiating record suggests that this ambiguous approach was intended to satisfy two competing camps, those who advocated the 'intrinsic value' approach of Article 35(3), and their opponents who advocated framing restrictions in human terms." Richards & Schmitt, *supra* note 59, at 1063. *See also* Schmitt, *supra* note 36, at 276–77.

85 Yoram Dinstein, *Protection of the Environmental in International Armed Conflict,* 5 Max Planck Y.B. of U.N. Law 523, 531 (Jochin A Frowein & Rudiger Wŭlfrum eds., 2001); *see also* Kiss, *supra* note 82, at 185, 190.

86 Schmitt, *supra* note 36, at 275.

values trump human ones "is inconsistent with the humanitarian concerns underlying the entire body of the law of armed conflict," the authors acknowledge that "consensus even on this most basic level . . . may not necessarily be easy to achieve."[87]

Another significant interpretative problem posed by Articles 35(3) and 55 arises from the reference in both of them to "widespread, long-term and severe damage."[88] The terms are undefined in the Protocol, and "the *travaux préparatoires* for Additional Protocol I provide little guidance on the meaning of the terms aside from reference by some delegates to 'long-term as a period measured in decades.'"[89] Some commentators have suggested that the language should be construed in the same way as similar language in Article I(1) of the ENMOD, which requires state parties not to engage in the military or other hostile use of environmental modification techniques having "widespread, long-lasting or severe effects," and the Final Report has been criticized for failing to do so.[90] Although the ENMOD, like Protocol I, does not include definitions of these terms, the Conference of the U.N. General Assembly's Committee on Disarmament (CCD) provided the following definitions:

> It is the understanding of the Committee that, for purposes of this convention, the terms "widespread," "long-lasting" and "severe" shall be interpreted as follows:
>
> (a) "widespread": encompassing an area on the scale of several hundred square kilometers;
>
> (b) "long-lasting": lasting for a period of months, or approximately a season;
>
> (c) "severe": involving serious or significant disruption or harm to human life, natural and economic resources or other assets.[91]

But reading Protocol I as if it were on all fours with the ENMOD would seem to be mistaken, for at least two reasons. First, the language in Protocol I is conjunctive: it refers to "widespread, long-term *and* severe damage." Thus, all three tests have to be met before a violation can be found. ENMOD's language by contrast is disjunctive: it speaks of "widespread, long-lasting

87 Richards & Schmitt, *supra* note 59, at 1086. *See also* Schmitt, *supra* note 36, at 313–14.

88 *See* Bothe, *supra* note 63, at 56 (finding the interpretative problems "enormous").

89 Richards & Schmitt, *supra* note 59, at 1066.

90 *See, e.g.*, Paolo Benvenuti, *The ICTY Prosecutor and the Review of the NATO Bombing Campaign against the Federal Republic of Yugoslavia*, 12 Eur. J. Int'l L. 503, 509–10 (2001); Thilo Marauhn, *Environmental Damage in Times of Armed Conflict—Not "Really" a Matter of Criminal Responsibility?*, 840 IRRC 1029 (2000).

91 Understanding Relating to Article I, Report of the Conference of the Committee on Disarmament, U.N. GAOR, 31st Sess., Supp. No. 27, at 91–92, U.N. Doc. A/31/27 (1976). On the purpose and effect of this "understanding," *see* Ingrid Detter, The Law of War 270 (2d ed. 2000).

or severe effects." Finding a violation therefore requires that only one of the tests be satisfied. Second, the CCD report on ENMOD, after the language quoted above, went on to say:

> It is further understood that the interpretation set forth above is intended exclusively for this Convention and is not intended to prejudice the interpretation of the same or similar terms if used in connection with any other international agreement.[92]

Thus, it seems to be an error to assume that the terms "widespread," "long-term" or "long-lasting," and "severe" necessarily have the same meaning in both treaties.[93]

What then does Protocol I mean in referring to "widespread, long-term and severe damage"? While there is no general agreement, some commentators have taken the view that "the threshold understanding of what constitutes 'widespread, long-term and severe damage is too high to provide any real protection in conventional warfare . . . Arts. 35(3) and 55 will not impose any significant limitation on combatants waging conventional warfare."[94] In its 2009 study of the environmental law of war, the United Nations Environment Programme (UNEP) reached a similar conclusion:

> The common core of [Arts. 35(3) and 55] is the prohibition of warfare that may cause "widespread, long-term and severe damage to the natural environment." The scope of these provisions initially appears extensive. However, important questions remain with regard to the threshold at which the damaging activity violates international law. Indeed this triple standard is a cumulative requirement, meaning that to qualify as prohibited "damage," the impact must be widespread and long-term and severe. The Protocol fails to define these terms, resulting in a high, uncertain and imprecise threshold.
>
> One commentary on Article 35(3) has accordingly noted that it would "not impose any significant limitation on combatants waging conventional warfare. It seems primarily directed instead to high-level decision-makers and would affect such unconventional means of warfare as the massive use of herbicides and chemical agents which could produce widespread, long-term and severe damage to the natural environment."

---

92 *Id.* Furthermore, the *travaux* for Protocol I also contain evidence (in the form of statements by the Italian and German delegations) that the terms used in that instrument was not necessarily to be construed in the same way as they were construed in other international legal instruments. *See* Kiss, *supra* note 82, at 185 & nn. 20, 21. For further commentary on the differences between the standards of Protocol I and ENMOD, *see* Schmitt, *supra* note 36, at 279–80.

93 *See* Weinstein, *supra* note 83, at 708 ("These definitions, while helpful, are specific to ENMOD only."); *but see* Howard S. Levie, *The 1977 Protocol I and the United States,* 38 St. Louis U.L.J. 469, 478–79 (1993/94).

94 Baker, *supra* note 54, at 368, 370. *See also* Schmitt, *supra* note 36, at 278 ("[T]he required three-part test clearly sets a very high standard of harm before the articles are violated."). Hulme observes that "the real obstacle to lowering the threshold lies with the term 'widespread'. . . . [A]n area the size of the New Forest in the UK (measuring approximately 377 square kilometers), or even a whole country (for example, the Maldives, measuring 300 square kilometers) would need to be damaged." Hulme, *supra* note 74, at 683.

The relevance of these two provisions and the effectiveness of the protection they provider in practice, therefore, seem limited.[95]

Consistent with these pessimistic conclusions, the U.S. Defense Department took the view, in an April 1992 report to Congress on the First Gulf War, that even if Protocol I had applied to that conflict (and neither the United States nor Iraq were parties to it), the environmental devastation caused by Iraq's destruction of Kuwait's oilfields might not have violated Arts. 35(5) and 55:

> Even had Protocol I been in force, there were questions as to whether the Iraqi actions would have violated its environmental provisions. During that treaty's negotiation, there was general agreement that one of its criteria for determining whether a violation had taken place ("long term") was measured in decades. It is not clear whether the damage Iraq caused, while severe in the layman's sense of the term, would meet the technical-legal use of that term in Protocol I.[96]

In short, UNEP and prior U.S. state practice call into question whether Protocol I's environmental provisions would affect future U.S. military operation in any significant way. Indeed, in the context of NATO's aerial campaign in Serbia, Protocol I's applicability to combined NATO operations might also be doubtful, since neither the United States nor France—two of the larger NATO powers at war in Kosovo—was a party to Protocol I.

4. Protocol I, Customary Law, and the Final Report to the Prosecutor

Therefore, it was a matter of some concern to the ICTY Prosecutor whether Arts. 35(3) and 55 of Protocol I had been (or had become) customary law (and not simply treaty law). Article 3 of the ICTY's Statute (the most relevant provision in that instrument for prosecuting alleged environmental war crimes) made the ICTY competent to prosecute "persons violating the laws and customs of war." Were either U.S. or French defendants to be prosecuted for violations of

95 UNEP, *supra* note 58, at 11.

96 Roberts, *supra* note 39, at 545. *See also* Weinstein, *supra* note 83, at 707 ("[M]any have questioned whether Iraq violated existing international law."). However, Saddam Hussein and other Iraqi officials responsible for the policy of destroying the Kuwaiti oil fields might have been criminally liable for wanton destruction of property in violation of Hague and Geneva law, including Article 23(g) of the Hague IV Regulations and Article 147 of the Fourth Geneva Convention. *See* Howard S. Levie, *Comment: Criminal Responsibilities for Environmental Damage,* 69 Int'l L. Stud. 491, 495–96 (Richard J. Grunawalt, John E. King & Ronald S.McClain eds., 1996). *Cf. N.V. de Bataafsche Petroleum Maatschappli & Ors. v. The War Damage Comm'n* (Ct. App. Sing. 1956), *reprinted in* 51 Am. J. Int'l L. 802, 808 (1957) (Japanese Armed Forces' seizure and exploitation of privately owned oil resources in occupied Dutch East Indies constituted a "violation of the laws and customs of war").

Protocol I's environmental clauses, therefore, the Prosecutor would have had to show that those clauses embodied customary law.[97]

To resolve this question, one might look for guidance to the ICJ's *Legality of Nuclear Weapons* opinion, which we shall discuss in detail in the next chapter. It should be noted, as background, that the Court made clear that international environmental law—such as any applicable obligations of prevention, notification, cessation and reparation—do not operate independently of, or in parallel with, the law of armed conflict. Rather, the Court treated humanitarian law principles as the controlling *lex specialis*, albeit one that incorporated environmental considerations, thus stating: "States must take environmental considerations into account when assessing what is necessary and proportionate in the pursuit of legitimate military objectives. Respect for the environment is one of the elements that go to assessing whether an action is in conformity with the principles of necessity and proportionality."[98] Yet, in paragraph 31 of that opinion, the Court also wrote:

> Articles 35, paragraph 3, and 55 of Additional Protocol I provide additional protection for the environment. Taken together, these provisions embody a general obligation to protect the natural environment against widespread, long-term and severe environmental damage; the prohibition of methods and means of warfare which are intended, or may be expected, to cause such damage; and the prohibition of attacks against the natural environment by way of reprisals. . . . These are powerful constraints for all the States having subscribed to these provisions.[99]

Thus, some critics of the Final Report take these statements as an affirmation by the ICJ that Articles 35(3) and 55 in fact reflect customary law.[100]

But the ICJ may merely have been restating what those articles say, rather than affirming them to be customary law. (Not only did the ICJ not explicitly affirm that they were customary rules, but it described them as constraints on the states that "hav[e] subscribed" to them. If the ICJ believed them to be customary law, it would presumably have described them instead as constraints on all states, other perhaps than "persistent objectors.") Furthermore, Judge Fausto Pocar, a former President of the ICTY, has observed that:

97 Article 3 of the ICTY Statute also made the Court competent to prosecute "wanton destruction of cities, towns or villages, or devastation not justified by military necessity." This provision might be understood to include offenses against customary law, even if not embodied in the environmental provisions of Protocol I. *See* Baker, *supra* note 54, 375–76.

98 *Advisory Opinion on the Legality of the Threat or Use of Nuclear Weapons*, 1996 ICJ Rep. 226 (July 8, 1996), at 242, ¶ 30.

99 *Id.* at ¶ 31.

100 *See* Benvenuti, *supra* note 90, at 509 (claiming that the Prosecutor had attributed "the opposite opinion" to the ICJ, and saying that that error was "a symptom of [her] inadequate approach").

> the obligation to protect the natural environment against widespread, long-term and severe damage, which includes the prohibition of the use of methods or means of warfare which are intended or may be expected to cause such damage (Article 35(3)), in particular when the health or survival of the population may be prejudiced (Article 55), finds no clear precedent in existing customary law, as was acknowledged by some States who participated in the drafting of Protocol I. Although subsequent development of a customary principle of respect for the environment in warfare may be in progress, its scope is certainly far from being assessed and recognized.[101]

Meanwhile, the official position of the United States appears to be that it accepts that some provisions of Protocol I were or have become customary law—for example, Articles 35(1) and (2)—but it denies that either Article 35(3) or Article 55 has that status.[102]

In 1999, UNEP commissioned a "Balkans Task Force" (BTF) to produce a report on the environmental consequences of the war in Kosovo. The core conclusions of report, entitled *The Kosovo Conflict: Consequences for the Environment & Human Settlements* (1999) (UNEP Report),[103] are cited in the Final Report and form part of the basis for the Prosecutor's *nolle prosequi* determination. Here we will briefly describe one of the more detailed studies in the UNEP Report, because consideration of the facts of a particular case helps in probing the Prosecutor's judgments.

The BTF identified environmental "hot spots" in four cities where damage was caused by the war and where it found urgent remedial action to be needed in order to avoid risks to health and long-term ecological damage. One of the four cities was Pančevo, a Serbian town of about 80,000 inhabitants on the Danube River, about 20 km northeast of the Serb capital Belgrade. Pančevo was a major industrial complex that included a petrochemical plant, a fertilizer plant and a major oil refinery. The city's industrial area was heavily targeted for NATO airstrikes during the campaign. Altogether NATO made two air strikes on the petrochemical complex and fertilizer plant in April 1999 and seven attacks on the oil refinery between April and June. Air strikes in mid-April had reportedly forced the evacuation of much of the city's population.

The BTF found that the air strikes had caused various hazardous substances to be released into the environment, either through damage to storage facilities or through fires. At the petrochemical plant, 2.100 tons of toxic ethylene diochloride and 8 tons of metallic mercury leaked into the soil, the plant or a nearby canal, and 460 tons of vinyl chloride monomer (VCM) burned (releasing highly dioxins). The air strikes also caused an estimated 80,000 tons of oil and oil

101 The Hon. Fausto Pocar, *To What Extent Is Protocol I Customary International Law?*, (Legal And Ethical Lessons of NATO's Kosovo Campaign), 78 Int'l L. Stud. 337, 348–49 (Andru E. Wall ed., Naval War College 2002). *See also* Christopher Greenwood, *Customary Law Status of the 1977 Geneva Protocols, in* Humanitarian Law of Armed Conflicts: Challenges Ahead, Essays in honour of Frits Kalshoven 93, 104–05 (Astrid J.M. Delissen & Gerard J. Tanja eds., 1991).

102 *See* Thomas Michael McDonnell, *Cluster Bombs Over Kosovo: A Violation of International Law?*, 44 Ariz. L. Rev. 31, 105–06 (2003).

103 The Kosovo Conflict: Consequences for the Environment & Human Settlements (1999) (*available at* http://www.grid.unep.ch/btf/final/).

products to burn at the refinery. At the fertilizer plant, managers released about 250 tons of liquid ammonia into the canal as a preventive measure, out of fear that an air strike on stored ammonia could cause large numbers of human casualties: the release of the ammonia was probably responsible for killing fish in the Danube River.

The BTF could obtain no evidence on pre-war levels of contamination in the area. However, there were indications of substantial pre-war damage. Workers in the industrial complex had suffered from a so-called "Pančevo cancer," which was likely to have resulted from exposure to VCM. The plants were also found to have employed technology from the 1960s and 1970s. Likewise, it appeared from an analysis of sediment core taken from the canal that the oil released as a result of the air strikes had added a layer of acute contamination to an area that had already suffered from chronic petrochemical pollution.

The UNEP Report observed that a NATO representative had been quoted as saying:

> NATO had two types of targets. There were tactical and strategic targets. The oil refinery in Pančevo was considered a strategic target. It was a key installation that provided petrol and other elements to support the Yuigoslav army. By cutting off these supplies we denied crucial material to the Serbian forces fighting in Kosovo. When targeting is done, we take into account all possible collateral damage, be it environmental, human or to the civilian infrastructure. Pančevo was considered to be a very, very important refinery and strategic target, as important as tactical targets inside Kosovo.[104]

Accepting, for purposes of discussion, the foregoing statement of facts, please consider the following questions before you read the excepts from the OPT on damage to the environment as a possible violation by NATO of the *jus in bello* in its aerial campaign against Serbia to prevent, according to NATO, a humanitarian catastrophe, perhaps even genocide, in Kosovo.

We then close with a thesis concerning rational choice and constructivist accounts on the *jus in bello*, especially as applied to environmental harms.

104 UNEP, *supra* note 58, at 33.

1. Questions Before Reading Final Report Excerpts on Damage to the Environment

1) Do you agree that "it would appear extremely difficult to develop a *prima facie* case [against NATO] on the basis of [Arts. 35(3) and 55]"?

2) Is the "*prima facie* case" standard the correct one for the Prosecutor to use in deciding whether to pursue a further investigation?

3) If "long-term" damage needs to be measured in years (or decades) rather than in months, would that not mean, in effect, that many serious violations of Arts. 35(3) and 55 would have to go unprosecuted?

4) If the damage done to the environment by Iraq's destruction of Kuwait's oil fields in the First Gulf War apparently did not cross the threshold of Articles 35(3) and 55, was the Prosecutor not clearly right in holding that the environmental damage caused by NATO's air strikes did not?

5) On the other hand, if the environmental damage Iraq caused did not cross that threshold, what kind of wartime damage to the environment would do so?

6) The Prosecutor notes (¶ 17) that the UNEP Report "suggests that much of the environmental contamination which is discernible cannot unambiguously be attributed to the NATO bombing." Does the incidence of significant pre-war environmental contamination at some of its target sites (such as Pančevo) relieve NATO of all responsibility for causing environmental damage at those sites? Does it mitigate NATO's responsibility? Or does it establish NATO's responsibility, assuming that NATO planners were or should have been aware that by launching their attacks they were aggravating already serious environmental hazards?

7) Was the existence or likelihood of pre-existing contamination at target sites like Pančevo reasonably foreseeable by NATO planners? Should it have become so between over the course of NATO's air strikes on the same industrial area between April and July? If so, how, if at all, should that matter to NATO's criminal liability?

8) Was the Pančevo oil refinery a "military objective" within the meaning of Article 52(2) of Protocol I? Did it make an "effective contribution to military action"? Did its total or partial destruction "in the circumstances ruling at the time" of the air strikes, "offer[] a definite military advantage"?

9) Was the petrochemical plant in Pančevo a "military objective"? What about the fertilizer plant? The Final Report states (at ¶ 22) that the "targeting by NATO of Serbian petrochemical industries may well have served a clear and important military purpose." True?

10) Suppose that NATO had struck the fertilizer plant before its managers had dumped the liquid ammonia in it. Would NATO have been (potentially) liable under Protocol I liable for any resulting environmental damage? Or would the managers have been at least partly liable for not having dumped the ammonia?[105]

11) If you think that NATO would have been relieved of at least some part of its liability by the managers' failure to act, can the Prosecutor be right in implying that NATO was at least partly excused by their decision to take action?

12) The Prosecutor states (¶ 19) "the principle of proportionality is more easily stated than applied in practice." How would you apply it to the air strikes in Pančevo? In determining the balance between military advantages and environmental (or other) harms, would you view the entire course of air strikes on targets in that city's industrial complex, from April through July, as a single whole? Would you aggregate the attacks on each individual target (the oil refinery, the petrochemical plant)? Or would you consider each air strike on each individual target separately from any other strike on that or another target?

13) Are the special difficulties in applying the proportionality principle in the case of damage to the natural environment (as distinct from other civilian objects)?

14) Can military advantage be balanced against environmental harm in any case, or are the two values utterly incommensurable? If they can be balanced, is it possible to do

105 Note that if NATO attack on the fertilizer plant had triggered a massive explosion of the liquid ammonia stored inside it and so resulted in numerous civilian casualties, environmental harm, and other damage, the Serbs might (reasonably) have perceived that attack as a war crime, especially if the requisite *mens rea* was imputed to the attacker. *See* James D. Morrow, *The Laws of War, Common Conjectures, and Legal Systems in International Politics*, 31 J. Leg. Stud. S41, S53 (2002) ("During the Italian campaign of World War II, a German bombardment hit an American supply dump of chemical weapons and released a cloud of poison that drifted toward the German lines. This cloud could easily have been interpreted as an illegal chemical weapons attack by the Germans.").

so only in easy cases? If so, is the proportionality requirement, in this area at least, extremely weak or even useless?

15) Even if environmental harm can generally be balanced against military advantage, was Kosovo a special case of balancing environmental harm to humanity against humanity's interest in preventing another genocide? Would it be possible to construct special sub-rules depending on the type of armed conflict at issue? Would this rupture the distinction between the *jus ad bellum* and the *jus in bello*? (Compare Part III, Chapter 2(D)(3)(c)(iii).)

2. Excerpts from Final Report to the Prosecutor on Damage to the Environment106

14. The NATO bombing campaign did cause some damage to the environment. For instance, attacks on industrial facilities such as chemical plants and oil installations were reported to have caused the release of pollutants, although the exact extent of this is presently unknown. The basic legal provisions applicable to protection of the environment in armed conflict are Article 35(3) of Additional Protocol I, which states that '[i]t is prohibited to employ methods or means of warfare which are intended, or may be expected, to cause widespread, long-term and severe damage to the natural environment' and Article 55 which states:

1. Care shall be taken in warfare to protect the natural environment against widespread, long-term and severe damage. This protection includes a prohibition of the use of methods or means of warfare which are intended or may be expected to cause such damage to the natural environment and thereby to prejudice the health or survival of the population.

2. Attacks against the natural environment by way of reprisals are prohibited.

15. Neither the USA nor France has ratified Additional Protocol I. Article 55 may, nevertheless, reflect current customary law (see however the 1996 Advisory Opinion on the Legality of Nuclear Weapons, where the International Court of Justice appeared to suggest that it does not (ICJ Rep. (1996), 242, para. 31)). In any case, Articles 35(3) and 55 have a very high threshold of application. Their conditions for application are extremely stringent and their scope and contents imprecise. For instance, it is generally assumed that Articles 35(3) and 55 only cover very significant damage. The adjectives 'widespread, long-term, and severe' used in Additional

106 Final Report to the Prosecutor by the Committee Established to Review the NATO Bombing Campaign Against the Federal Republic of Yugoslavia (*available at* http://www.icty.org/x/file/About/OTP/otp_report_nato_bombing_en.pdf).

Protocol I are joined by the word 'and', meaning that it is a triple, cumulative standard that needs to be fulfilled. Consequently, it would appear extremely difficult to develop a prima facie case upon the basis of these provisions, even assuming they were applicable. For instance, it is thought that the notion of 'long-term' damage in Additional Protocol I would need to be measured in years rather than months, and that as such, ordinary battlefield damage of the kind caused to France in World War I would not be covered.

The great difficulty of assessing whether environmental damage exceeded the threshold of Additional Protocol I has also led to criticism by ecologists. This may partly explain the disagreement as to whether any of the damage caused by the oil spills and fires in the 1990/91 Gulf War technically crossed the threshold of Additional Protocol I. It is the committee's view that similar difficulties would exist in applying Additional Protocol I to the present facts, even if reliable environmental assessments were to give rise to legitimate concern concerning the impact of the NATO bombing campaign.

Accordingly, these effects are best considered from the underlying principles of the law of armed conflict such as necessity and proportionality.

16. The conclusions of the Balkan Task Force (BTF) established by UNEP to look into the Kosovo situation are:

> "Our findings indicate that the Kosovo conflict has not caused an environmental catastrophe affecting the Balkans region as a whole. Nevertheless, pollution detected at some sites is serious and poses a threat to human health. BTF was able to identify environmental 'hot spots', namely in Pancevo, Kragujevac, Novi Sad and Bor, where immediate action and also further monitoring and analyses will be necessary. At all of these sites, environmental contamination due to the consequences of the Kosovo conflict was identified. Part of the contamination identified at some sites clearly pre-dates the Kosovo conflict, and there is evidence of long-term deficiencies in the treatment and storage of hazardous waste. The problems identified require immediate attention, irrespective of their cause, if further damage to human health and the environment is to be avoided."

17. The OTP has been hampered in its assessment of the extent of environmental damage in Kosovo by a lack of alternative and corroborated sources regarding the extent of environmental contamination caused by the NATO bombing campaign. Moreover, it is quite possible that, as this campaign occurred only a year ago, the UNEP study may not be a reliable indicator of the long term environmental consequences of the NATO bombing, as accurate assessments regarding the long-term effects of this contamination may not yet be practicable.

It is the opinion of the committee, on the basis of information currently in its possession, that the environmental damage caused during the NATO bombing campaign does not reach the

Additional Protocol I threshold. In addition, the UNEP Report also suggests that much of the environmental contamination which is discernible cannot unambiguously be attributed to the NATO bombing.

18. The alleged environmental effects of the NATO bombing campaign flow in many cases from NATO's striking of legitimate military targets compatible with Article 52 of Additional Protocol I such as stores of fuel, industries of fundamental importance for the conduct of war and for the manufacture of supplies and material of a military character, factories or plant and manufacturing centres of fundamental importance for the conduct of war. Even when targeting admittedly legitimate military objectives, there is a need to avoid excessive long-term damage to the economic infrastructure and natural environment with a consequential adverse effect on the civilian population. Indeed, military objectives should not be targeted if the attack is likely to cause collateral environmental damage which would be excessive in relation to the direct military advantage which the attack is expected to produce (A.P.V. Rogers, "Zero Casualty Warfare," IRRC, March 2000, Vol. 82, pp. 177-8).

19. It is difficult to assess the relative values to be assigned to the military advantage gained and harm to the natural environment, and the application of the principle of proportionality is more easily stated than applied in practice. In applying this principle, it is necessary to assess the importance of the target in relation to the incidental damage expected: if the target is sufficiently important, a greater degree of risk to the environment may be justified.

20. The adverse effect of the coalition air campaign in the Gulf war upon the civilian infrastructure prompted concern on the part of some experts regarding the notion of "military objective." This has prompted some experts to argue that where the presumptive effect of hostilities upon the civilian infrastructure (and consequently the civilian population) is grave, the military advantage conferred by the destruction of the military objective would need to be decisive (see below, paras. 40–41). Similar considerations would, in the committee's view, be warranted where the grave threat to the civilian infrastructure emanated instead from excessive environmental harm resulting from the hostilities. The critical question is what kind of environmental damage can be considered to be excessive. Unfortunately, the customary rule of proportionality does not include any concrete guidelines to this effect.

21. The military worth of the target would need to be considered in relation to the circumstances prevailing at the time. If there is a choice of weapons or methods of attack available, a commander should select those which are most likely to avoid, or at least minimize, incidental damage. In doing so, however, he is entitled to take account of factors such as stocks of different weapons and likely future demands, the timeliness of attack and risks to his own forces (A.P.V.

Rogers, ibid, at p. 178). Operational reality is recognized in the Statute of the International Criminal Court, an authoritative indicator of evolving customary international law on this point, where Article 8(b)(iv) makes the infliction of incidental environmental damage an offence only if the attack is launched intentionally in the knowledge that it will cause widespread, long-term and severe damage to the natural environment which would be clearly excessive in relation to the concrete and direct overall military advantage anticipated. The use of the word 'clearly' ensures that criminal responsibility would be entailed only in cases where the excessiveness of the incidental damage was obvious.

22. Taken together, this suggests that in order to satisfy the requirement of proportionality, attacks against military targets which are known or can reasonably be assumed to cause grave environmental harm may need to confer a very substantial military advantage in order to be considered legitimate. At a minimum, actions resulting in massive environmental destruction, especially where they do not serve a clear and important military purpose, would be questionable. The targeting by NATO of Serbian petro-chemical industries may well have served a clear and important military purpose.

23. The above considerations also suggest that the requisite mens rea on the part of a commander would be actual or constructive knowledge as to the grave environmental effects of a military attack; a standard which would be difficult to establish for the purposes of prosecution and which may provide an insufficient basis to prosecute military commanders inflicting environmental harm in the (mistaken) belief that such conduct was warranted by military necessity. (In the Hostages case before the Nuremberg Military Tribunals, for instance, the German General Rendulic was acquitted of the charge of wanton devastation on the grounds that although Rendulic may have erred in believing that there was military necessity for the widespread environmental destruction entailed by his use of a 'scorched earth' policy in the Norwegian province of Finnmark, he was not guilty of a criminal act (11 Trials of War Criminals, (1950), 1296)). In addition, the notion of 'excessive' environmental destruction is imprecise and the actual environmental impact, both present and long term, of the NATO bombing campaign is at present unknown and difficult to measure.

24. In order to fully evaluate such matters, it would be necessary to know the extent of the knowledge possessed by NATO as to the nature of Serbian military-industrial targets (and thus, the likelihood of environmental damage flowing from their destruction), the extent to which NATO could reasonably have anticipated such environmental damage (for instance, could NATO have reasonably expected that toxic chemicals of the sort allegedly released into the environment by the bombing campaign would be stored alongside that military target?) and whether

NATO could reasonably have resorted to other (and less environmentally damaging) methods for achieving its military objective of disabling the Serbian military-industrial infrastructure.

25. It is therefore the opinion of the committee, based on information currently available to it, that the OTP should not commence an investigation into the collateral environmental damage caused by the NATO bombing campaign.

D. THESIS: RATIONAL CHOICE AND CONSTRUCTIVISM IN ENVIRONMENTAL WAR

We offer a baseline account from rational choice and constructivist perspectives of ordinary principles of military necessity. We then use that baseline analysis to explain an important difference in the *jus in bello* with respect to environmental harm.

1. Rational Choice and Constructivist Accounts of the *Jus in Bello*

While it is both plausible and attractive to see *jus in bello* as the outcome of balancing military necessity against "humanity," any balancing process requires an understanding of the values that are being balanced against each other; and, just as "military necessity" is not self-defining, the principle of humanity can be equally imprecise. We offer a range of competing accounts.

One possibility, according with realist accounts of military necessity, is that when states attempt to frame *jus in bello* rules, they balance their expectations of what their own military needs and interests will be against their interest in protecting their own populations.[107] Schmitt seems to adopt this understanding of the "principle of humanity" when he writes: "Legitimate states are . . . obliged to ensure the well-being of their citizenry, for the provision of 'public goods,' such as physical safety, underpins the social contract between a state and its people. The principle of humanity, which operates to protect the population (whether combatants or noncombatants) and its property, advances this imperative."[108]

Another possibility, drawing perhaps on cosmopolitan or constructivist logic, is that the "principle of humanity," to which military necessity is counterpoised, reflects a concern for humanity as such, rather than simply for each state party's own population. On this approach, the *jus in bello* would reflect a balance between military interests and a concern for humanity

---

107 Consider, for example, the Hague Peace Conference of 1907, which debated whether to extend indefinitely an earlier five-year ban on the discharge of explosives or projectiles from "balloons" (*i.e.*, dirigibles). That five-year moratorium had been adopted in the earlier Hague Peace Conference of 1899 as a compromise measure, reflecting differences between France, Britain, Germany, and the United States (all of which opposed any restrictions), and Russia and smaller powers on the other (which favored an absolute prohibition). As of 1899, Russia's dirigible program had been a failure, French and German programs were nearing success, and Britain considered that the use of dirigibles as a military platform might compensate for the numerical weakness of its land forces. By 1907, the strategic environment had changed. The French and Germans, who had made significant advances with their air arms, again opposed a prohibition; Russia, which had been modernizing its military forces since its crushing defeat in the Russo-Japanese War, switched sides and joined France and Germany; Italy, which was beginning an ambitious airship program, also joined the opposition; Austria-Hungary, which considered that the advent of airpower left it more vulnerable, supported the ban; and Britain, now believing that airpower eroded its military advantages, also switched sides and favored the ban. On this occasion, no compromise could be reached. *See* Ward Thomas, The Ethics of Destruction: Norms and Force in International Relations 99–102 (2001); Donald Cameron Watt, *Restraints on War in the Air Before 1945, in* Restraints on War: Studies in the Limitation of Armed Conflict 57, 59–61 (Michael Howard ed., 1979).

108 Michael N. Schmitt, *Military Necessity in International Humanitarian Law: Preserving the Delicate Balance,* 50 Va. J. Int'l L. 795, 799 (2010).

at large. While not explicitly grounded on constructivist logic, this is probably the more general understanding of a majority of writers on *jus in bello*.[109]

Finally, some have argued that the *jus in bello* rules do not reflect a balancing process at all. Indeed, they question whether concerns for "humanity" as such figure significantly or at all in framing and following *jus in bello* rules. Eric Posner, writing from a rational choice perspective, argues that states usually have important non-humanitarian interests in observing restraints on warfare. For example, destructive methods may leave behind territories and inhabitants that are worth much less to their conqueror. Fewer deaths and less suffering may make peace easier to achieve and, once achieved, to maintain.[110] In general, restraints on war might be due to what Clausewitz called "intelligence," rather than to altruistic concern for the welfare of war's victims. More boldly, Posner suggested that *jus in bello* rules can generally be seen as the outcomes of two common state interests: an interest in having less effective weaponry and tactics; and an interest in having more destructive weaponry and tactics. In a very simplified form, Posner's argument is, essentially, this. States are better off if they can limit the efficiency or effectiveness of weapons. That is so because, as the efficiency of weaponry increases, states will have the incentive to invest greater resources in predation (military technology) rather than in peaceful production. As states invest more in predation, however, they all become worse off together: they find themselves in an arms race situation, akin to that of the prisoner's dilemma. By prohibiting or restricting efficient weaponry, the *jus in bello* makes war and predation more expensive, and hence less inviting than productive uses of capital.[111]

As for destructiveness, the logic works roughly as follows. As weaponry becomes more destructive, wars become more costly: even if victory is achieved by using destructive weapons, the victor gains less because the prize has been devalued. Hence, in general, states should want *jus in bello* rules that promote the destructiveness of weapons (even as they inhibit their

109 *See, e.g., Supreme Court of Israel: Beit Sourik Village Council v. Gov't of Israel*, 43 ILM 1099, 1112 at ¶ 35 (2004); Jean Pictet, The Principles of International Humanitarian Law 27–30 (1966); and Jacques Meurant, *Inter Arma Caritas: Evolution and Nature of International Humanitarian Law*, 24 J. Peace Res. 237, 244–45, 247 (1987).

110 *See* Col. Charles J. Dunlap, Jr., *A Virtuous Warrior in a Savage World*, 8 U.S.A.F. Acad. J. Legal Stud. 71, 88–89 (1997/8) (emphasizing importance of following law of war for maintaining military discipline); *see* also A.P.V. Rogers, *War Crimes Trials Under the Royal Warrant: British Practice 1945–1949*, 39 Int'l & Comp. L. Q. 780, 780–81 (1990) (listing factors that motivate atrocities by soldiers in wartime).

111 Michael Walzer referred to primitive wars fought by bows and arrows, in which it is unlawful for a warrior to feather an arrow. Unfeathered arrows are far less effective than feathered ones, but their use leads to more wounds and deaths. Walzer remarked that this "is a good rule, . . . and we may fairly condemn the warrior who first arms himself with the superior and forbidden weapon." Michael Walzer, Just and Unjust Wars: A Moral Argument With Historical Illustrations 42 (3d ed. 2000). From Posner's perspective, this rule is a case in which the law of warfare (rightly) promotes inefficiency.

A more modern example is that of siege warfare. (Siege warfare continues to be practiced, as in the Bosnian Serb Army's 1992-96 siege of the city of Sarajevo.) Under the traditional rules of war, an enemy commander was permitted to compel civilians attempting to flee a besieged city to return to it. The justification for this harsh rule was that the more of its inhabitants who remained in the city, the sooner would it be starved out. This rationale was invoked successfully by the German General von Leeb when he was charged with war crimes for having threatened to shell Russian civilians seeking to flee Leningrad, which he was besieging in 1941. *See* Walzer at 166. Under Article 54 of Protocol I, however, "[s]tarvation of civilians as a method of warfare is prohibited." Consequently, besieged cities can no longer be taken by starving their civilian population. *But see* Rogers, *supra* note 53, at 102–03. In Posner's terms, the law has been reformulated here to promote inefficiency.

efficiency), because the less rewarding war is, the less of it there will be. Thus, there will be a tendency for *jus in bello* rules to retard military efficiency but to promote destructiveness.[112]

Posner points out, however, that states' willingness to agree on such rules will be affected by factors such as inequalities in their wealth and power. In fact, one might tempted to say that Posner deconstructed the standard account so as to reveal that "humanity" relates to "efficiency" as "military necessity" relates to "destructiveness." Thus, on Posner's theory, we would expect *jus in bello* generally to permit inefficient but destructive tactics or weaponry (explosive shells, incendiaries), to forbid efficient but non-destructive weaponry (poisons,[113] asphyxiating gas, dum-dum bullets), to be contested with respect to efficient and destructive weapons (nuclear-armed missiles, land mines, cluster bombs) and to tolerate or ignore inefficient non-destructive weapons (if only because they are unlikely to be used[114]). Our point is not to defend a rational choice account of the *jus in bello* (like Posner's), but to suggest that there may well be an alternative to the standard accounts that explain *jus in bello* as a balance between military and humanitarian interests.

2. Rational Choice and Constructivist Critiques of Military Necessity in the Context of Environmental Harm

a. Rational Choice

If Posner's account is correct, however, it does explain the different shape of *jus in bello* with respect to environmental harm. We have already noted that, under Protocol I, a military commander 1) may not intentionally target the natural environment unless it is a military objective, 2) even then, may not cause environmental damage that is disproportionate in relation to the military advantage anticipated from the attack, and 3) even then, may not use means or methods intended or expected to cause "widespread, long-term and severe" environmental damage,

112 Posner's theory may be indebted to the views of M.W. Royse, who maintained that "a weapon will be restricted in inverse proportion, more or less, to its effectiveness; that the more efficient a weapon or method of warfare the less likelihood there is of its being restricted in action by the rules of war." M.W. Royse, Aerial Bombardment and the International Regulation of Warfare 131–32 (1928).

113 On the origins of the longstanding prohibition on poison as a means of warfare, *see* Richard M. Price, The Chemical Weapons Taboo 18–30 (1997). In essence, Price argued that poison came to be condemned because it was an (inexpensive) "weapon of the weak" that could be used to great effect, especially in the early modern period, to bring about the death of kings, who were unprotected from it by their control over other instruments of warfare.

114 The "military balloon" or dirigible may have fallen into this category (although in 1899 its use was restricted for a five-year period, *see supra* note 106). At any rate, one delegate to the 1907 Hague Peace Conference, Marius de Robilant, seemed to have thought of the dirigible in this way. He argued against banning it on the grounds that "[i]t will never be as formidable as a war-ship; the projectiles which it can discharge will never be as effective as those discharged with terrifying swiftness from guns of large and small caliber; always subject to the control of its pilot, it will not present for neutrals any of the dangers threatened by anchored or floating contact mines; *there is therefore no reason to be greatly frightened if they cannot be forbidden.*" Thomas, *supra* note 107, at 87 (emphasis added).

although the precise scope of the latter obligation is a matter of debate, as is whether it has been accepted by all states.[115] What is noteworthy, for our purposes, is that Protocol I and, in the view of many, customary international law have imposed an absolute ban on harms that would otherwise be justified by ordinary rules of necessity, distinction, and proportionality. Why should this be so?

Under the rational choice analysis we have presented, rules that maximize military destructiveness can be efficient *ex ante*, because they deter war and induce states to reach settlements that would avoid the destructive outcomes that such wars would impose on both parties. But the rules that encourage destructiveness necessarily contemplate a failure rate in war avoidance; yet, in those cases, ordinary principles of necessity, distinction and proportionality attenuate the level of harm, with respect to the collateral effects on both civilian life and civilian property. Environmental harm, such as contamination to waterways, may have substantial spillover effects for third parties, such as downstream riparians not involved in the combat. In short, the separate requirement that environment harm not be "widespread, long-lasting and severe" serves as a proxy for cumulative destructiveness that exceeds the level the principles of necessity, distinction and proportionality incentivize. If this is so, then the question of interpretation in this requirement, at least under the discretion enabled by treating it as a requirement of customary international law, should further that purpose. In other words, the debate concerning whether the rules is conjunctive or disjunctive—"widespread, long-lasting and severe" or "widespread, long-lasting, or severe"—is best read as an measure of cumulative risk. Thus, states, scholars and judges should interpret the rule as a standard that focus on the whether or not a state has created excessive harm in relation to the destruction that would have been foreseeable *ex ante* through ordinary military operations and ordinary civilian harms.

A number of objections might be raised to this analysis. For example, a state might conclude that the environmental harms it causes will be suffered asymmetrically—meaning that only victims and their neighbors, and few if any of the attacker's allies, would suffer the lion's share of environmental harm. A state might conclude that the probability of it suffering as the victim of an attack, or as the neighbor or ally of the victim of an attack, is also asymmetric—meaning that it might be able to discount or even ignore the destructiveness of environmental harms from its cost-benefit calculus in a particular war (or asymmetric harm in all wars or a sub-class of wars); Indeed it may even ignore environmental effects in its view of the optimal set of rules. Something like this might explain U.S. resistance to Protocol I as a matter of customary international law.

Moreover, for all other states too, if a rational choice theory found it difficult to construct sufficiently precise categories of sub-rules, depending on the nature of the armed conflict or other relevant criteria, to enable states to make efficient choices *ex ante*, a single rule in the form of Protocol I (as adapted by customary international law) might be preferable. Because of

115 *See supra* notes 74–96 and accompanying text.

legal uncertainty, a rational choice theory would not consider the special context of the NATO operation, an attempt to prevent genocide in Kosovo, as bearing on the rule or its application. In short, a rational choice theory might continue to separate the *jus ad bellum* from the *jus in bello*, simply because the alternative would entail too much legal uncertainty.

b. Constructivism

Constructivism yields a much different approach in how, when and by whom environmental warfare concerns ought to be addressed. To begin with, in both ordinary and environmental harms, a constructivist approach should diverge from the rational choice approach in treating humanity's costs as costs that should be internalized by all parties in the development of the *jus in bello.* Perhaps also a focus on principles of humanity might make it more than likely that a constructivist would consider the special circumstances of the NATO aerial campaign against Serbia and, accordingly, weight the risk of a potential genocide as greater than the risk of significant, albeit discrete, environmental harm to Serbia and even to innocent third-party neighbors of Serbia. Accordingly, a constructivist might be inclined to prefer a more fact-specific, contextual, and *ex post* standard rather than a rule that would give states optimal incentives *ex ante.*

Along these lines, a constructivist might view environmental and human rights duties equally as obligations *erga omnes,* arguably giving all states an equal right and interest in their enforcement. Thus, in measuring between incommensurables *ex post* and in a case-specific way, the constructivist might prefer collective decision-making—to ensure that weighing of the relative values between environmental harm and the prevention of gross violations of human rights is not mediated exclusively by states likely to view those values through the lens of their parochial national interests. A constructivist might well conclude that the path to international stability and justice requires assessment of these questions from a cosmopolitan perspective. It would be through this process of collective decision-making that, according to constructivism, global values and global governance could be fashioned. Indeed, from this perspective, it is possible the constructivist approach might well open the door to the conclusion that global cosmopolitanism demands that no individual state or "people" should have the right to exist if, as a consequence, the whole human environment (or a substantial portion of it) were to be destroyed.

We now turn to that question in the context of the ICJ Nuclear Weapons Advisory Opinion.

Chapter 4

Jus in Bello: The Nuclear Weapons Case

A. Introduction: The "Balance of Terror" in the Dock Before the International Court of Justice?

Writing in the early 1930s, the Italian historian Guglielmo Ferrero said: "for the Western world war is no longer an intermittent danger, a threat and a terror from without; it is an obsession which unnerves us from within and feeds on itself, like all fixed ideas."[1] The same could now be said of the Western world in the early twenty-first century. So unlikely does major war seem, at least between Western states, that some analysts have concluded that war as an institution is being abandoned—as the institution of dueling once was.[2] The great wars that ravaged Europe in the twentieth century no longer seem possible on a continent that they utterly transformed, causing its peoples and leaders to re-imagine the very idea of statehood.[3] Visions of war as the cathartic release from the boredom of ordinary life, as the recovery of the deep but half-forgotten ties that unite a people, or as the call to a supreme sacrifice on the sacred altar of the nation—visions that enthralled many in the excited crowds in Berlin, Paris, Vienna, London, and St. Petersburg celebrating the outbreak of the First World War [4]—melted away in the massive, industrialized killing that followed,[5] and died altogether a generation later in the fires of Warsaw, Rotterdam, Hamburg,

1 Guglielmo Ferrero, Peace and War 1 (Bertha Pritchard trans. 1933).

2 *See* John Mueller, Retreat from Doomsday: The Obsolescence of Major War (1989) (noting cultural changes leading to "obsolescence" of major wars); *see also* Carl Kaysen, *Is War Obsolete? A Review Essay,* 14 Int'l Sec. 42 (1990) (providing an economic, political and technological framework for cultural shifts leading to "obsolescence" of war); and Michael Mandelbaum, *Is Major War Obsolete?,* 40 Survival 20 (1998). *But see, e.g.,* Meredith Ruth Sarkees, Frank Whelon Wayman and J. David Singer, *Inter-State, Intra-State and Extra-State Wars,* 47 Int'l Stud. Q. 49 (2003) (suggesting that there may be a "disturbing constancy" in warfare).

3 *See* James J. Sheehan, Where Have All the Soldiers Gone? The Transformation of Modern Europe (2008).

4 On the popular enthusiasm for the war at its outbreak, *see* Hew Strachan, 1 The First World War: To Arms 103–10 (2000). But Alexander Watson describes a more subdued popular reaction to the outbreak of war. *See* Ring of Steel: Germany and Austria-Hungary in World War I at 61-73 (2014).

5 On the effects of the First World War in promoting aversion to war throughout the West, *see* John Mueller, Cataclysm: Reflections on the Recent Transformation of World Politics 133–53 (1995). The scale and horror of the First World War are scarcely imaginable to those now living. Indeed, they were incomprehensible to those who lived through it. Europe had not seen a Continent-wide conflict since the Napoleonic Wars. The overall death toll from the War amounted to between nine and ten million. *See* David Stevenson, Cataclysm: The First World War as Political Tragedy 442 (2004) (estimating a grand total of war dead at 9,450,000). France lost nearly one in every five men mobilized, some 10.5%

and Hiroshima. Political unification, economic interdependence, cultural interpenetration, the integration of military forces, planning, and weaponry brought about through NATO, the rise of mass tourism, the interconnectedness created by the communications media, and (not least) the persisting memory of the last great wars have all combined to free Europe from the unnerving "obsession" of which Ferrero spoke. The "Long Peace" that was maintained for almost half a century during the Cold War has persisted and seemingly grown even more entrenched: the habits of peace beget a longer peace. Wars the European continent has seen since the collapse of Soviet Communism in 1989, though violent and destructive, have been local, confined, and far smaller in scale than the two great wars of an earlier period. Despite terrorist attacks in New York City, Washington D.C., London, and Madrid, Western populations seem to enjoy a security from foreign invasion that has no obvious parallel in their history, at least since the Roman Empire. Even the fear that terrorists may obtain weapons of mass destruction and use them against Western population centers seems, to some observers, to be badly overstated.[6] Although the threat of

---

of the nation's active male population: "[a]bout 1,400,000 French lost their lives; well over 1,000,000 had been gassed, disfigured, mangled, amputated, left permanent invalids." Eugen Weber, The Hollow Years: France in the 1930s 11 (pb. ed. 1996). German, Austro-Hungarian, and British losses, though less, were commensurable. On average, almost 900 Frenchmen and 1,300 Germans died every day between the outbreak of the War in August 1914 and the armistice of November 1918. *See* Stéphane Audoin-Rouzeau & Annette Becker, 14-18: Understanding the Great War 21–22 (Catherine Temerson trans. 2002). In a single day, July 1, 1916, the beginning of the British offensive at the Somme, some 20,000 men in the British and Dominion forces were killed and another 40,000 wounded—deadlier statistics than for any day in the Second World War on any front. *Id.* at 23. French casualties on that day amounted to 7,000 and German casualties are estimated between 9,000 and 12,000. Stevenson at 137. Between February 21 and December 18, 1916, the German Army lost 434,000 men in its single, unsuccessful attempt to destroy the French Army at Verdun, and a further 500,000 men countering the Allied offensive in July, 1916 at the Somme. *See* David Stone, Fighting for the Fatherland: The Story of the German Soldier from 1648 to the Present Day 276 (2006). Likewise, the defense of Verdun cost the French Army 500,000 men, while the Somme offensive produced a total of 600,000 British and French casualties. *Id.* Neither of these two great battles proved to be decisive. Indeed, after the battles, positions at the Front had hardly changed.

Although generally not exposed to the hazards of the Front, civilians as well as combatants suffered fearfully from the War. One of the main causes of such suffering was the (questionably legal) British naval blockade of Germany. One estimate finds that the British blockade was responsible for 726,766 deaths in Germany between 1915 and 1918. *See* Michael Glover, The Velvet Glove 125 (1982); *see also Secretary of State to the Ambassador in Great Britain (Page), December 26, 1914, in* II Department of State: Policy of the United States Toward Maritime Commerce in War 240 (Carlton Savage ed., 1936); John W. Coogan, The End of Neutrality: The United States, Britain, and Maritime Rights, 1899-1915 169–220 (1981) (considering the legality of the British blockade); and Daniel M. Smith, *Robert Lansing and the Formulation of American Neutrality Policies, 1914-1915,* 43 Miss. Valley Hist. Rev. 59 (1956).

Moreover, the nature of the violence to which these forces (largely recruited from the civilian population) were exposed was unprecedented. The War saw the use of new and dreadful weapons of destruction, including the tank, the flamethrower, the mortar, the hand grenade, the submarine, the airplane, and poison gas. The machine gun, a fairly primitive weapon when the War began, became a fearsome defensive weapon, capable of dealing out death and injury on an industrial scale. In time, machine guns came to develop "firepower equivalent to that of a platoon and a half." They were so devastating that "[w]hen French troops were mown down in Lorraine early in the war, the Germans themselves were appalled by the results." Martin Van Creveld, The Changing Face of War: Lessons of Combat from the Marne to Iraq 50 (2006). British Prime Minister Lloyd George attributed almost 80% of the War's casualties to the machine gun. With deadly efficiency and "mechanical casualness," a machine gun could wipe out an entire battalion (600 to 800 men) in 3 minutes. *See* John Ellis, Social History of the Machine Gun 142 (1975). Combat on the Western Front took place mainly over a "terrain swept by bullets, shells and gas." Audoin-Rouzeau & Becker, *supra,* at 27. About 40% of all those mobilized were wounded at least once, and "the gravity and type of wounds inflicted . . . had no precedent. Direct hits from large-calibre shells can literally pulverize the body, leaving no identifiable remains. Very large pieces of shrapnel can actually slice a man in half." *Id.* at 24. And despite medical advances, "[t]he fate of those who were wounded was by and large atrocious." *Id.*

6 *See* John Mueller, Atomic Obsession: Nuclear Alarmism from Hiroshima to Al-Qaeda 161–234 (2009); *see also* Christoph Wirz & Emmanuel Egger, *Use of Nuclear and Radiological Weapons by Terrorists?,* 87 IRRC 497 (2005).

major war has by no means receded entirely—a catastrophic war between India and Pakistan, for instance, seems entirely possible—the Western world seems, to itself, to be a zone of peace.

Even the invention of nuclear weaponry did not shatter the "Long Peace" that the West enjoyed after the end of the Second World War. On the contrary, as we have seen, Kenneth Waltz and others have argued that the threat of nuclear war, coupled with bipolarity, brought about that very peace. Moreover, the possibility of nuclear conflict between the two superpowers arguably contributed to the Cold War peace, and even to the Western victory, in a variety of other ways. For one thing, the leaders of the two superpowers became highly cautious and circumspect in their dealings with each other in periods of tension or crisis. Events that in a pre-nuclear age might have led the powers to war no longer did so.[7] For another thing, reliance on the threat of nuclear retaliation spared the West the need to remain continuously militarized, as it would have had to do if it intended to counter the larger forces of the East solely by means of conventional warfare. As large and costly as Western military establishments became, they arguably would have had to be far larger and costlier if the West had attempted to match or outstrip the East's non-nuclear, conventional forces.[8] The cost-savings made possible by reliance on the threat of "massive retaliation" with nuclear rather than conventional forces were vast. Writing in 1959, John Herz wrote that "policies for effectively combating Communism without banking exclusively on deterrence through the 'big' weapon would seem to call for three types of expenditure, each of which would amount to something like the present, full-size

7 *See* McGeorge Bundy, Danger and Survival: Choices About the Bomb in the First Fifty Years (1988).

8 NATO's early strategic planning reveals how strong the Alliance's desire to control costs was. That concern eventually led to the adoption of the policy of "massive retaliation." As early as 1949, NATO's Defense Committee emphasized that the Allies "should bear in mind that economic recovery and the attainment of economic stability constitute important elements of their security." Gregory W. Pedlow, *DC 6/1 The Strategic Concept for the Defence of the North Atlantic Area, in* NATO Strategic Documents 1949-1969, at 4 (*available at* http://www.nato.int/docu/stratdoc/eng/a491201a.pdf). Yet the Military Committee noted in 1950 that the Allies should not "be misled into planning in the frame of mind prevailing at the end of World War II, which was largely based on the enormous military power available to the Allies at that time." Gregory W. Pedlow, *MC 14 Strategic Guidance for North Atlantic Regional Planning*, in NATO Strategic Documents 1949-1969, at 4 (*available at* http://www.nato.int/docu/stratdoc/eng/a500328c.pdf). Finding that the Alliance would need many years to restore their conventional forces to their World War II levels, while the Soviets had meanwhile maintained or increased their capabilities, the Military Committee said that "special emphasis must be laid on the necessity for developing methods to compensate for [NATO's] numerical inferiority." *Id.* Another early document, DC 13 (1950), called for the Alliance to raise its conventional forces to much higher levels by 1954. *See* Gregory W. Pedlow, *DC 13 North Atlantic Treaty Organization Medium Term Plan, in* NATO Strategy Documents 1949-1969, at 1 (*available at* http://www.nato.int/docu/stratdoc/eng/a500328d.pdf). It envisaged that NATO forces would include 90 divisions, 8,004 combat aircraft, 3,264 naval aircraft and 2,324 warships. *See* Gregory W. Pedlow, *The Evolution of NATO Strategy, 1949-1969*, in NATO Strategy Documents 1949-1969 XIV (*available at* http://www.nato.int/docu/stratdoc/eng/intro.pdf). In 1952 at Lisbon, the North Atlantic Council again set ambitious goals for 1954, including a total of 96 divisions. *Id.* at XVI–XVII. By this point, however, Member States were proving to be unwilling, for both political and financial reasons, to bear the expected costs of creating such large conventional forces. A shift in policy was signaled by the Eisenhower Administration's "New Look," encapsulated in NSC 162/2 of October 30, 1953, which placed much greater weight on the use of nuclear weapons in the Alliance's defense. *See* A Report to the National Security Council, No. 162/2, Oct. 30, 1953 (*available at* https://fas.org/irp/offdocs/nsc-hst/nsc-162-2.pdf). In late 1953, the United States began to deploy nuclear weapons into Europe. Finally, in 1956, NATO formally adopted the doctrine of massive retaliation in MC 14/2. *See* Gregory W. Pedlow, *MC 14/2 Overall Strategic Concept for the Defence of the North Atlantic Treaty Organization Area, in* NATO Strategy Documents 1949-1969 (available at http://www.nato.int/docu/stratdoc/eng.inro.pdf).

American-type budget for defense."[9] Relieved of the need to mobilize vast numbers of their populations and huge quantities of their resources for conventional war, Western governments could allow civil society to flourish, protecting civil liberties from what would truly have been oppressive "garrison states."[10] Furthermore, by economizing on their defense budgets, Western governments were able to direct more of their resources to social welfare programs, thus confirming the idea that the state existed chiefly for the purpose of ensuring the prosperity and well-being of its citizens. Lower defense budgets also underwrote lower taxes and thus expanded the scope for private investment and consumption. The liberty and prosperity enjoyed by Western populations caused admiration and envy among the populations of the East, helping eventually to bring about the fall of Communism and the West's Cold War victory.

Nonetheless, beneath the surface calm, anxiety lingered—and still lingers. Given the choice between a world with or without nuclear weapons, there would surely be few world leaders who would prefer the former. The fear of a nuclear holocaust, even if waning, is still woven into the fabric of everyday life. The "balance of terror" that is said to have kept the Cold War peace was exactly that—a balance of "terror." In his separate "declaration" in the International Court of Justice's (ICJ) 1996 advisory opinion to the General Assembly on *The Legality of the Threat or Use of Nuclear Weapons*,[11] which furnishes the case study for this chapter, the ICJ's then-President, Judge Bedjaoui, captured this fear when he wrote:

> With nuclear weapons, humanity is living on a kind of suspended sentence. For half a century now these terrifying weapons of mass destruction have formed part of the *human condition.* Nuclear weapons have entered into all calculations, all scenarios, all plans. Since Hiroshima, on

9 John H. Herz, International Politics in the Atomic Age 286 (1959). Herz envisaged three categories of expenditure: continuing the current defense effort, which then was devoted mainly to nuclear forces; ramping up conventional and limited nuclear forces; and foreign aid to the developing world "of a dimension hardly conceived of at present." *Id.* at 286–87.

10 President Eisenhower, whose administration initiated the policy of "massive retaliation," saw the dangers of militarization clearly, and worked hard to avoid them. Eisenhower repeatedly emphasized that "we must not destroy what we are attempting to defend"—and what he sought to defend was an open society, protective of the liberties of its people. See John Lewis Gaddis, Strategies of Containment: A Critical Appraisal of American National Security During the Cold War 133 (2005). "Should we have to resort to anything resembling a garrison state," Eisenhower said, "then all that we are striving to defend would be weakened and, if long subjected to this kind of control, could disappear." *Id.* In a memorandum to Secretary of State John Foster Dulles in 1953, Eisenhower expressed the fear that the burden of an arms race would in time "either drive us to war or into some form of dictatorial government." Bundy, *supra* note 7, at 251. The Eisenhower Administration, accordingly, veered away from the strategic planning of the last year of the Truman Administration, finding its projected conventional rearmament to be inordinately expensive—a shift that, as noted above, was reflected in NSC 162/2. *See* Laurence Freedman, The Evolution of Nuclear Strategy 76–78, 81–84 (1981). Under Eisenhower, defense spending fell from 13.8% of the Gross National Product in 1953 to 9.1% in 1960, and while the share of the defense budget that went to the Army dropped significantly, the share of the Air Force rose. See Geir Lundestad, East, West, North South: Major Developments in International Relations Since 1945 127 (Gail A. Kvam trans. 5th ed. 2005). Eisenhower's willingness to rely on a nuclear deterrent made it possible to control defense expenditures even while pursuing the "containment" of the Soviet Union.

11 *The Legality of the Threat or Use of Nuclear Weapons, Advisory Opinion,* 1996 IJC, at 226 (July 8) [hereinafter "LTUNW"] (declaration of President Bedjaoui (translation) (*available at* http://www.icj-cij.org/docket/index.php?p1=3&p2=4&k=e1&p3=4&case=95).

> the morning of 6 August 1945, fear has gradually become man's first nature. His life on earth has taken on the aspect of what the Koran calls "a long nocturnal journey," like a nightmare whose end he can not yet foresee.[12]

The "long nocturnal journey" which the Koran describes,[13] and to which President Bedjaoui alludes, was one that, in traditional Islamic belief, took the Prophet Mohammed to the Further Mosque[14] in the city of Jerusalem, where God granted him a decisive Revelation that Mohammed brought back to mankind on his return.[15] There were those who had hoped that the ICJ's opinion on the legality of nuclear weapons would end humanity's "long nocturnal journey" after Hiroshima with a revelation of a kind—one that, in declaring all threats or uses of nuclear weaponry to be unlawful, would lead the nuclear-armed states to eliminate them and the non-nuclear-armed states to abandon any thought of acquiring them.

By any reckoning, the ICJ's opinion "represents a thought-provoking, if not amazing, moment in the history of international law."[16] Yet the reactions to it, including those of individual judges of the ICJ itself, ranged the spectrum from finding it "appalling"[17] to judging it to be "one of the most important decisions in the history of the Court and of the law of warfare."[18] The critical defect for some (or, in the minds of others, merit) of the opinion was that it appeared not to decide the central question presented to the Court: whether the threat or use of nuclear weapons was categorically forbidden by international law and, if not, in what circumstances such threat or use might be permissible. David Kennedy summed up the situation by asking if the Court was both being

> crafty and craven. [Was] it fudging to find that international law both is and is not complete, covers and does not cover nuclear weapons, which are (generally) illegal, except when they are not? [Was] it equivocating to exhort the nuclear powers to consider their obligations, while remembering their rights, without clarifying what those might be...? And all this seven to seven (or was it ten to four)—deferral, denial, disappointment.[19]

---

12 LTUNW, *supra* note 11, at 46 ¶ 2.

13 The Koran, Ch. 17, sec. 1.1, Al-isrā', "The Night Journey."

14 For the Islamic traditions surrounding Mohammed's night journey and the influence of Mohammed's journey on later Islamic spirituality, *see* Karen Armstrong, Muhammed: A Biography of the Prophet 138–42 (1993). Encyclopedia of Islam and the Muslim World 482 (Richard C. Martin, et al., Macmillan Reference 2003).

15 *Id.*

16 Paul W. Kahn, *Nuclear Weapons and the Rule of Law*, 31 N.Y.U. J. L. & Pol. 349, 360 (1999).

17 Vaughan Lowe, *Shock Verdict: Nuclear War May or May Not be Unlawful*, 55 Cambridge L.J. 415, 415 (1996).

18 Peter Weiss, *Notes on a Misunderstood Decision: The World Court's Near Perfect Advisory Opinion in the Nuclear Weapons Case* (July 22, 1996) (*available at* http://lcnp.org/wcourt/Notesonthedecision.htm).

19 David Kennedy, *The Nuclear Weapons Case, in* International Law, The International Court of Justice and Nuclear Weapons 462, 465–66 (Laurence Boisson de Chazournes & Philippe Sands eds., 1999).

In what follows, we shall first describe the background to the ICJ's opinion, including the nature of the ICJ's advisory function and, in the light of that function, the Court's decision not to consider the parallel request by the World Health Organization (WHO). We shall then pose study questions introducing the readings in this chapter (paras. 78–82, 85–87, 90–92, 94–99, and 104–105), which supply the critical elements of the ICJ's reasoning in its response to the General Assembly's request. In the following commentary, we explain several of the international law doctrines needed for a full understanding of what the Court did (and did not do) and discuss the important objection of critics that the Court failed to decide the question put to it, which constituted (for some) an impermissible gap in the law, a so-called *non liquet.* Assuming this contention has some merit, we conclude with two contrasting "theses" concerning whether a gap really exists and how it might be filled. The first thesis argues that the Court, within a positive law framework, could have reached a conclusion that nuclear weapons are absolutely prohibited, but only through strained reasoning. The second thesis argues that the Court might have more easily reached the conclusion that there is an absolute prohibition, but only within an international law framework that incorporates natural law reasoning. In short, for us, this suggests that, in addition to political considerations, the Court's jurisprudential commitments, particularly its resistance to natural law reasoning, shaped its response to the General Assembly's request for guidance.

B. THE ICJ'S ADVISORY OPINIONS ON THE LEGALITY OF NUCLEAR WEAPONS

The International Court of Justice (the ICJ), located at The Hague in The Netherlands, is the judicial arm of the United Nations, corresponding roughly to the Judicial Branch of the United States federal government.[20] Article 33(1) of the United Nations Charter contemplates the peaceable settlement of international disputes by (among other means) recourse to "judicial settlement." The ICJ was created, in large part, to further that purpose. It was established in 1945 under the Statute of the International Court of Justice,[21] which is annexed to the Charter of the United Nations. The ICJ was the direct successor to the Permanent Court of International Justice (the PCIJ), which was created as part of the Versailles settlement after the First World War. Both courts grew out of the earlier state practice of resolving disputes by international arbitration, which had yielded such successful results as the *Alabama Claims* arbitration of 1872 (resolving a dispute between the United States and Great Britain) and which had led to the proposals for a Permanent Court of Arbitration at the Hague Peace Conferences of 1899 and 1907.[22] The ICJ consists of 15 judges elected by the General Assembly and the Security Council for (renewable) 9-year terms. The judges are by custom selected to represent the main forms of the world's civilizations and legal traditions. In essence, this means that each of the world's principal regions has one or more representatives on the Court.[23]

The ICJ may hear and decide two types of cases—"contentious cases," or legal disputes between states that they submit to the Court for adjudication, and "advisory opinions" on legal questions referred to the Court by any of the five organs of the United Nations and, if authorized, sixteen specialized agencies. [24] The ICJ has jurisdiction to decide a contentious case only if the states concerned have accepted its jurisdiction, which they may do by entering into a special agreement to submit a dispute to the Court, by ratifying a "jurisdictional clause" in a treaty (e.g., Article I of Optional Protocol Concerning the Compulsory Settlement of Disputes to the 1963 Vienna Convention on Consular Relations[25]), or through the reciprocal effect of declarations

---

20 To pursue this rough and possibly misleading analogy, the Security Council corresponds to the Executive Branch, the General Assembly to the Legislative Branch (or, better perhaps, to the House of Representatives), and the United Nations Secretariat to the federal administrative bureaucracy.

21 1945 Statute of the International Court of Justice, 3 Bevans 1179; 59 Stat. 1031; T.S. 993; 39 AJIL Supp. 215 (1945) [hereinafter 1945 Statute of the IJC](*available at* http://www.icj-cij.org/documents/index.php?p1=4&p2=2&p3=0).

22 A valuable history of the origins of the ICJ can be found at the Court's website. History, Int'l Ct. of Just. (*available at* http://www.icj-cij.org/court/index.php?p1=1&p2=1). For a concise survey and appraisal of the Court's work, *see* James Crawford & Tom Grant, *International Court of Justice, in* The Oxford Handbook of the United Nations 193 (Thomas G. Weiss & Sam Daws eds., 2007).

23 *See Members of the Court,* Int'l Ct. of Just (*available at* http://www.icj-cij.org/court/index. php?p1=1&p2=2).

24 *Jurisdiction,* Int'l Ct. of Just. (*available at* http://www.icj-cij.org/jurisdiction/index.php?p1=5).

25 March 19, 1967, 596 U.N.T.S. 261, 21 U.S.T. 77, T.I.A.S. 6820 (*available at* https://treaties.un.org/doc/Treaties/1967/06/19670608%2010-36%20AM/Ch_III_6p.pdf). For discussion of the Optional Protocol's application to the United States, see Medellín v. Texas, 552 U.S. 491, 507–09 (2008).

they have made under the ICJ Statute ("compulsory jurisdiction"). In this Chapter we shall be concerned with the Court's advisory procedure.[26]

In July 1996, the ICJ responded to two requests, both from United Nations bodies, for an advisory opinion on the legality of nuclear weapons. The first request was made in 1993 by the World Health Organization (WHO).[27] The second was made in 1994 by the United Nations General Assembly.[28] The ICJ has authority to provide advisory opinions under Article 65(1) of its Statute, which reads:

> The Court may give an advisory opinion on any legal question at the request of whatever body may be authorized by or in accordance with the Charter of the United Nations to make such a request.[29]

The WHO purported to be authorized to seek an advisory opinion from the Court on the basis of Article 96(2) of the United Nations Charter, which provides that:

> specialized, which may at any time be so authorized by the General Assembly, may also request advisory opinions of the Court on legal questions arising within the scope of their activities.[30]

The General Assembly invoked Article 96(1) of the United Nations Charter as authorization for it to seek an advisory opinion:

> The General Assembly . . . may request the International Court of Justice to give an advisory opinion on any legal question.[31]

In the first of its two opinions, the Court ruled by a vote of eleven to three that it was unable to give the advisory opinion that the WHO had sought. In the second opinion, it ruled that the request for an advisory opinion from the General Assembly was appropriate, and therefore took up the substantive question that the General Assembly had addressed to it.

---

26 Again, readers are referred to the Court's website for a fuller discussion of how the Court works. *See The Court,* Int'l Ct. of Just. (*available at* http://www.icj-cij.org/court/index.php?p1=1&p2=16).

27 *See* World Health Assembly Resolution WHA 46.40, ¶ 1 (May 14, 1993).

28 *See* GA Res. 49/75K (Dec. 15, 1994).

29 1945 Statute of the IJC, supra note 21, at art. 65(1).

30 *See* U.N. Charter art. 96(2). The WHO plainly satisfied the requirement that it be "authorized by the General Assembly." *See* G.A. Res. 124 (II), at 28, U.N. Doc. A/449, at 28 (Nov. 15, 1947); *Legality of the Use By a State of Nuclear Weapons in Armed Conflict, Advisory Opinion,* 1996 I.C.J. 4, at 66, 72 at ¶¶ 11-12 (July 8) [hereinafter "WHO Opinion"].

31 U.N. Charter art. 96(1).

The Court's jurisdictional ruling on the WHO request deserves brief consideration here.[32] The Court found that "three conditions must be satisfied in order to [find] the jurisdiction of the Court when a request for an advisory opinion is submitted to it by a specialized agency."[33] The first condition was that the specialized agency be duly authorized to request advisory opinions from the Court—a requirement plainly met here. The second condition was that the "opinion requested must be on a legal question."[34] Rejecting both the argument that the WHO's question was "essentially political" rather than "legal" and the argument that WHO had been politically motivated in seeking the Court's opinion,[35] the Court ruled that the second test was also satisfied. The third condition prescribed by Article 96(2) was that the question posed by the WHO must arise "within the scope of [its] activities." On that issue, the Court ruled that while the WHO may legitimately examine the effects of nuclear weapons on public health and the means of countering such effects, it was not competent to address the legality or illegality of these (or any other) weapons. Thus, the Court had no need to consider whether, assuming it had jurisdiction to render an advisory opinion on the WHO's question, it should use its discretion to decline the WHO's request.[36]

The Court offered three main arguments for its conclusion. The first, and most formalistic argument, was that the question posed by the WHO "relate[d] . . . not to the effects of the use of nuclear weapons on health, but to the legality of the use of such weapons in view of their health and environmental effects. Whatever those effects may be, the competence of the WHO to deal with them is not dependent on the legality of the acts that cause them."[37] The Court also advanced a second argument based on the "principle of specialty," which governs international organizations like the WHO. International organizations are the creations of states; they are not states themselves. Accordingly, their powers are only those that states confer on them, either expressly or by implication. The Court argued that "to ascribe to the WHO the competence to address the legality of the use of nuclear weapons—even in view of their health and

32 For analysis of and commentary on the WHO Opinion, *see* Dapo Akande, *The Competence of International Organizations and the Advisory Jurisdiction of the International Court of Justice*, 9 Eur. J. Int'l L. 437 (1998); Judith Hippier Bello and Peter H.F. Bekker, *Legality of the Use by a State of Nuclear Weapons in Armed Conflict*, 91 Am. J. Int'l L. 134 (1997); Michael Bothe, *The WHO Request, in* International Law, The International Court of Justice and Nuclear Weapons 103 (Laurence Boisson de Chazournes & Philippe Sands eds., 1999); and Antonio F. Perez, *The Passive Virtues and the World Court: Pro-Dialogic Abstention by the International Court of Justice*, 18 Mich. J. Int'l L. 399 (1997).

33 WHO Opinion, *supra* note 30, at 71, at ¶ 10.

34 *Id.* at 71, at ¶ 10.

35 *Id.* at 72–73, at ¶¶ 15–17. Non-governmental organizations espousing the cause of nuclear disarmament had concededly been very active in persuading the WHO—against the advice of its own legal counsel—to seek an advisory opinion. *See* Nicholas Rostow, *The World Health Organization, the International Court of Justice, and Nuclear Weapons*, 20 Yale J. Int'l L. 151, 155–60 (1995). *But see* Virginia Leary, *The* WHO *Case: Implications for Specialised Agencies, in* International Law, The International Court of Justice and Nuclear Weapons 112, 122–26 (Laurence Boisson de Chazournes & Philippe Sands eds., 1999) (discussing the views of WHO's legal counsel).

36 That the Court has discretion whether or not to furnish an advisory opinion is reflected in the language of Article 65(1), which states that it "may"—not "must"—give such an opinion. *See* LTUNW, *supra* note 11, at ¶ 14.

37 WHO Opinion, *supra* note 30, at 76, at ¶ 24.

environmental effects—would be tantamount to disregarding the principle of specialty; for such competence could not be deemed a necessary implication of the Constitution of [the WHO] in light of the purposes assigned to it by its Member States."[38] Finally, the Court made what might be called a "structural" argument, namely, that the WHO's involvement in the issue relating to use of force would intrude on the organs of the United Nations with competence in that area.[39]

Commentators have differed over the quality and persuasiveness of the *WHO Opinion*'s reasoning. Michael Schmitt concluded that "[t]his was a well-reasoned decision, that preserved the systemic integrity of access to the Court. It was also well-advised from a practical point of view, for the issue on the merits could still be reached through consideration of the General Assembly's much more jurisdictionally sound request."[40] Dapo Akande, on the other hand, criticized the *WHO Opinion* sharply, arguing (among other things) that while

> there may be a certain intuitive feeling that the WHO should not be used to engage in political action and that the prevention of the use of nuclear weapons is political, it must be remembered that the ruling of the Court is not only confined to the use of nuclear weapons but extends to "all hazardous activity." Thus, the WHO is prevented from dealing with the *legality* of any activity that is dangerous to health. Would this have been the holding of the Court if the question had been whether the WHO is competent to propose a convention banning or restricting the use of narcotic substances or tobacco or outlawing the use of asbestos building materials or prohibiting the use of infected blood in transplants?[41]

Michael Bothe was critical of the Court's first two arguments but (without endorsing it) found the third, structural reason to be "a good, sophisticated and systematic legal argument [that is] difficult to reject, at least on an abstract level."[42]

---

38 *Id.* at 79, at ¶ 25.

39 The ICJ opined, as follows:

> The WHO Constitution can only be interpreted. . . by taking due account not only of the general principle of specialty, but also of the logic of the overall system contemplated by the Charter. . . . [WHO's] responsibilities are necessarily restricted to the sphere of public "health" and cannot encroach on the responsibilities of other parts of the United Nations system. And there is no doubt that questions concerning the use of force, the regulation of armaments and disarmament are within the competence of the United Nations and lie outside that of the specialized agencies.

WHO Opinion, *supra* note 30, at 80, at ¶ 26. For the concept of a "structural" argument in American constitutional law, *see* Charles Lund Black & Charles L. Black, Jr., Structure and Relationship in Constitutional Law (2000).

40 Michael Schmitt, *The International Court of Justice and the Use of Nuclear Weapons,* 7 USAFA J. of Legal Stud. 57, at 62 (1997), *reprinted in* 2 *Naval War C. Rev.* 91 (1998). *See also* Michael J. Matheson, *The Opinions of the International Court of Justice on the Threat or Use of Nuclear Weapons,* 91 Am. J. Int'l L. 417, 419 (1997) ("the Court was entirely correct in rejecting the WHO request").

41 Akande, *supra* note 32, at 447.

42 *See* Bothe, *supra* note 32, at 103, 108.

Even before the ICJ ruled on the General Assembly's request, the use or threat of use of nuclear weapons had been the subject of animated discussion by judges,[43] legal scholars,[44] and moralists.[45] Even after the Court's opinion, the flow of commentary has continued unstaunched,[46]

---

43 *See* The Text of the *Shimoda* Case, *supra* Chapter 1.B.

44 Books and articles written by legal scholars before the ICJ's opinion include: Francis A. Boyle, *The Relevance of International Law to the "Paradox" of Nuclear Deterrence,* 6 Nw. U. L. Rev. 1407 (1986); Ian Brownlie, *Some Legal Aspects of the Use of Nuclear Weapons,* 14 Int'l & Comp. L. Q. 437 (1965); Eric Castren, *The Illegality of Nuclear Weapons,* 3 U. Tol. L. Rev. 89 (1971); David Kennedy, *A Critical Approach to the Nuclear Weapons Problem,* 9 Brook. J. Int'l L. 307 (1983); Myres McDougal & Norbert Schlei, *The Hydrogen Bomb Tests in Perspective: Lawful Measures for Security,* 64 Yale L.J. 648 (1955); Elliott Meyrowitz, *The Laws of War and Nuclear Weapons,* 5 Brook. J. Int'l L. 227 (1983) [hereinafter Meyrowitz, *Laws of War*]; Elliott Meyrowitz, *The Opinions of Legal Scholars on the Legal Status of Nuclear Weapons,* 24 Stan. J. Int'l L. 111 (1987) [hereinafter Meyrowitz, *Legal Status of Nuclear Weapons*] (surveying the literature)]; W. Michael Reisman, *Nuclear Weapons in International Law,* 4 N.Y.L. Sch. J. Int'l & Comp. L. 339 (1982); Rostow, *supra* note 35; and Georg Schwarzenberger, The Legality of Nuclear Weapons (1958).

45 Works on the morality of the use or threat of use of atomic or nuclear weapons include: G.E.M. Anscombe, *War and Murder, in* Walter Stein (ed.), Nuclear Weapons: A Catholic Response (1961); John Finnis, Joseph Boyle, Jr. & Germain Grisez, Nuclear Deterrence, Morality and Realism (1987); Gregory S. Kavka, Moral Paradoxes of Nuclear Deterrence (1987); Anthony Kenny, The Logic of Deterrence (1983); Steven Lee, *The Morality of Nuclear Deterrence: Hostage Holding and Consequences,* 95 Ethics 549 (1985); Steven Lee, *Morality, the SDI, and Limited Nuclear War,* 17 Phil. & Pub. Aff. 15 (1988); Steven Lee, *Morality and Nuclear Weapons Policy,* 19 Phil. & Pub. Aff. 93 (1990); Marc Trachtenberg, *Strategists, Philosophers, and the Nuclear Question,* 95 Ethics 728 (1985); and Michael Walzer, Just and Unjust Wars: A Moral Argument with Historical Illustrations ch. 17 (3d ed. 2000).

There is also a growing literature on the subject of the morality of the Allied policy of "saturation" bombing of population centers in Germany and Japan during the Second World War. Works include: Michael Bess, Moral Dimensions of World War II, ch. 10 (2006); John W. Dower, Cultures of War: Pearl Harbor, Hiroshima, 9-11, Iraq chs. 8–9 (2010); Jörg Friedrich, The Fire: The Bombing of Germany, 1940-1945 (Allison Brown trans. 2006); Stephen A. Garrett, Ethics and Airpower in World War II: The British Bombing of German Cities (1993); A.C. Grayling, Among the Dead Cities: The History and Moral Legacy of the QWW II Bombing of Civilians in Germany and Japan (2006); Charles S. Maier, *Targeting the City: Debates and Silences about the Aerial Bombing of World War II,* 859 IRRC 420 (2005); Martin Middlebrook, The Battle of Hamburg: Allied Bomber Forces Against A German City In 1943 (1980); Richard Overy, Why the Allies Won ch. 4 (1993); Ronald Schaffer, Wings of Judgment: American Bombing in World War II (1985); Walzer, Just and Unjust Wars, *supra,* at ch. 16. A classic older study concerning the morality of the Allied policy of saturation bombing is John Cuthbert Ford, S.J., *The Morality of Obliteration Bombing,* 5 Theol. Stud. 261 (1944). For other expressions of contemporary moral reactions to the policy, compare Vera Brittain, *Massacre by Bombing: The Facts Behind The British-American Attack on Germany,* 10 Fellowship 50 (1944) with J. M. Spaight, Bombing Vindicated (1944).

The subject of the morality of the Allied bombing policy has also been dealt with in drama by the German playwright Rolf Hochhuth in his *Soldiers: A Necrology on Geneva* (trans. 1970). Several German novelists have written about the aerial attacks, including Hans Erich Nossack, an eyewitness to the raid on Hamburg. *See* Hans Erich Nossack, The End: Hamburg 1943 (Joel Agee trans. 2004); *see also* W.G. Sebald, On the Natural History of Destruction (Anthea Bell trans. 2003).

46 Books and symposia dealing primarily with the General Assembly Advisory Opinion include: International Law, The International Court of Justice and Nuclear Weapons (Laurence Boisson de Chazournes & Philippe Sands eds., 1999); Ved P. Nanda & David Krieger, Nuclear Weapons and the World Court (1998); and *Symposium: Contemporary Issues in Controlling Weapons of Mass Destruction,* 8 Duke J. Comp. & Int'l L. 1–134 (1997); *see also* William H. Boothby, Weapons and the Law of Armed Conflict ch. 13 (2009).

Articles dedicated primarily to the merits and consequences of the General Assembly Advisory Opinion include: Dapo Akande, *Nuclear Weapons, Unclear Law? Deciphering the Nuclear Weapons Advisory Opinion of the International Court,* 68 Brit. Y.B. Int'l L. 165 (1997); Peter H.F. Bekker, *Advisory Opinions of the World Court on the Legality of Nuclear Weapons,* ASIL Insights (Nov. 1996) (*available at* http://www.asil.org/insight5.cfin);

Roger S. Clark, *The International Court of Justice: Advisory Proceedings for The Legality of the Threat or Use of Nuclear Weapons Question Presented by the General Assembly: The Laws of Armed Conflict and the Use or Threat of Use of Nuclear Weapons,* 7 Crim. L. F. 265 (1996); Yoram Dinstein, *The Laws of Air, Missile and Nuclear Warfare,* 27 Israel Y.B. Hum. Rts. 1, 11–15 (1997); Richard A. Falk, *Nuclear Weapons, International Law and the World Court: A Historic Encounter,* 91 Am. J. Int'l L. 64 (1997); Judith Gardam, *Necessity and Proportionality in Jus Ad Bellum and Jus In Bello, in* International Law, The International Court of Justice and Nuclear Weapons 275 (Laurence Boisson de Chazournes & Philippe Sands eds., 1999); Christopher Greenwood, *The Advisory Opinion on Nuclear Weapons and the Contribution of the International Court to International Humanitarian Law,* 316 IRRC 65 (1997); Christopher Greenwood, *Jus ad Bellum and Jus in Bello in the Nuclear Weapons Advisory Opinion, in* International Law, The International Court of Justice and Nuclear Weapons 247 (Laurence Boisson de Chazournes & Philippe Sands eds.,1999);

including judicial decision-making as well as legal scholarship.[47]

After disposing of the jurisdictional issue of the General Assembly's competence to seek an advisory opinion,[48] and deciding that there was no "compelling reason" not to accede to the General Assembly's request,[49] the Court paused to consider the General Assembly's formulation of the question: "Is the threat or use of nuclear weapons in any circumstances permitted under international law?" Some states had objected to that formulation, understanding it to convey the implication that unless some treaty or rule of customary law specifically authorized the threat or use of nuclear weapons, they would be impermissible. Such a starting-point, those states contended, would be flawed. Those states cited the views of the Permanent Court of International Justice (the PCIJ) in the *S.S. Lotus* Case.[50] Relying on the *Lotus* Case, those states argued that they were "free to threaten or use nuclear weapons unless it can be shown that they are bound not to do so by reference to a prohibition" in either treaty or custom.[51] Other states argued that the *Lotus* case was inapplicable. The Court found no need to decide the issue because all the states appearing before it, nuclear and non-nuclear alike, either accepted, or did not dispute, "that their independence to act was indeed restricted by the principles and rules of international law, more particularly humanitarian law."[52]

Nicholas Grief, *Legality of the Threat or Use of Nuclear Weapons,* 46 Int'l & Comp. L. Q. 681 (1997); Stephen J. Hadley, *Debate: Policy Constraints in Using Nuclear Weapons,* 8 Duke J. Comp. & Int'l L. 23 (1997); Gen. Charles A. Horner, *Debate: Policy Considerations in Using Nuclear Weapons,* 8 Duke J. Comp. & Int'l L. 15 (1997); Kahn, *supra* note 16; David Kennedy, *The Nuclear Weapons Case, in* International Law, The International Court of Justice and Nuclear Weapons 462 (Laurence Boisson de Chazournes & Philippe Sands eds., 1999); Marcelo G. Kohen, *L'avis Consultative de la CIJ sur la Licéité de la Menace ou de l'emploi d'armes Nucléaires et la Function Judiciaire,* 2 Eur. J. Int'l L. 336 (1997); Marcelo Kohen, *The Notion of 'State Survival' in International Law, in* International Law, The International Court of Justice and Nuclear Weapons 293 (Laurence Boisson de Chazournes & Philippe Sands eds., 1999); Martti Koskenniemi, *The Silence of Law/The Voice of Justice, in* International Law, The International Court of Justice and Nuclear Weapons 488 (Laurence Boisson de Chazournes & Philippe Sands eds., 1999); Vaughan Lowe, *Shock Verdict: Nuclear War May or May Not Be Unlawful,* 55 Cambridge J.L. 415 (1996); Matheson, *supra* note 40; T.H. McCormack, *A* Non-liquet *on Nuclear Weapons—The ICJ Avoids the Application of General Principles of International Humanitarian Law,* 316 IRRC 76 (1997) (*available at* https://www.icrc.org/eng/resources/documents/misc/57jnfq.htm); W. Michael Reisman, *The Political Consequences of the General Assembly Advisory Opinion, in* International Law, The International Court of Justice and Nuclear Weapons 488 (Laurence Boisson de Chazournes & Philippe Sands eds., 1999); Schmitt, *supra* note 40, at 57; and Michael N. Schmitt, *Nuclear Weapons and the World Court,* USAFA J. Leg. Stud. (1998) (*available at* https://www.usafa.edu/df/dfl/documents/schmitt.doc).

47 *See Lord Advocate's Reference No. 1 of 2000 by Her Majesty's Advocate in terms of Section 123 of the Criminal Procedure (Scotland) Act 1995, Referring for the Opinion of the High Court Points of law arising in relation to charges upon which, on trial of indictment in the Sheriff's Court at Greenock there were acquitted . . . Angela Zelter [et al.],* Appeal Court, High Court of Justiciary (Scotland), Misc 11/00 (2001) (*available at* http://www.scotcourts.gov.uk/search-judgments/judgment?id=32858aa6-8980-69d2-b500-ff0000d74aa7).

48 LTUNW, *supra* note 11, at ¶¶ 10-13.

49 *Id.* at ¶¶ 14–19.

50 *The Case of the S.S. Lotus (France v. Turkey),* 1927 P.C.I.J. (ser. A) No. 10 (Sept. 7).

51 LTUNW, *supra* note 11, at ¶ 21.

52 Id. at ¶ 22. Some commentators have questioned this ruling. Greenwood, for instance, found it convincing insofar as it is a rejection of the claim that one side or the other had the burden of proof, since he considered such considerations to be out of place in an advisory, rather than contentious, opinion. On the other hand, he noted, "the underlying question of principle—whether the Court should be looking for a permissive rule or a prohibition—cannot be so easily set aside and was discussed at length in several of the Separate and Dissenting Opinions." Christopher Greenwood, *Jus ad Bellum and Jus in Bello in the Nuclear Weapons Advisory Opinion, in* International Law, The International Court of Justice and Nuclear Weapons 247, 250 (Laurence Boisson de Chazournes & Philippe Sands eds., 1999).

Turning to the substantive question, the Court began by seeking to determine, in a very methodical way, what broad categories of international law were or were not applicable. It considered, in turn, human rights law, environmental law, United Nations Charter law, treaty law, customary law, humanitarian law, and the law of neutrality. Some states had argued that human rights law was applicable, including both Article 6(1) of the International Covenant on Civil and Political Rights (ICCPR)[53] and the Genocide Convention.[54] The Court had little difficulty in finding the Genocide Convention inapplicable, on the grounds that it required a specific intent to destroy a racial or other protected group as such. Even though a nuclear attack might cause massive casualties, the Court ruled that the requisite intent would still have to be found before the attack could be considered genocidal.[55] As to the ICCPR, the Court rejected the claim that it did not apply to armed conflict, but found that when so applied, the determination of what constituted an "arbitrary" deprivation of life was to be decided by reference to humanitarian law, the *lex specialis* that "is designed to regulate the conduct of hostilities."[56] Thus, the Court would be required to look outside the ICCPR to determine whether human rights law had been violated; in itself, the ICCPR added nothing of substance to humanitarian law. Some states also contended that the use of nuclear weapons would violate any of a number of international environmental treaties and agreements, such as Additional Protocol I to the Geneva Conventions.[57] The Court rejected these arguments, too, on the ground that "the existing international law relating to the protection and safeguarding of the environment does not specifically prohibit the use of nuclear weapons."[58] Nonetheless, the Court ruled that "States must take environmental considerations into account when assessing what is necessary and proportionate in the pursuit of legitimate military objectives," even when using nuclear weaponry (albeit as part of the *lex specialis* of the

53 International Covenant on Civil and Political Rights, Dec. 16, 1966, 999 U.N.T.S. 171. Article 6(1) provides that "[e]very human being has the inherent right to life. This right shall be protected by law. No one shall be arbitrarily deprived of his life."

54 Convention on the Prevention and Punishment of the Crime of Genocide, Dec. 9, 1948, 78 U.N.T.S. 277.

55 LTUNW, *supra* note 11, at ¶ 26.

56 *Id.* at ¶ 25. Again, commentators offer different appraisals of the Court's reasoning. *Compare* Greenwood, *supra* note 52, at 255 ("The Court's conclusion, though no doubt very unwelcome to some human rights lawyers, is plainly correct.") *and* Matheson, *supra* note 40, at 417 (1997) ("[T]hese conclusions of the Court on the relevance of human rights . . . are correct. They underline the important point that the rules developed for peacetime circumstances cannot be applied in an unqualified manner to the conduct of armed conflict.") *with* Vera Gowlland-Debbas, *The Right to Life and Genocide: The Court and International Public Policy, in* International Law, The International Court of Justice and Nuclear Weapons 315, 326 (Laurence Boisson de Chazournes & Philippe Sands eds., 1999) ("[I]nterpretation of Article 6 in time of armed conflict cannot *exclusively* be made in the light of" humanitarian law). The Court has also been praised by some, and criticized by others, for ruling that the ICCPR applies to international armed conflict. *Compare* Akande, *supra* note 46, at 175 ("[T]he reiteration that the rights under the ICCPR continued to apply in wartime would seem to point to important procedural rights for victims of atrocities committed during armed conflicts.") *with* Robert J. Delahunty & John C. Yoo, *What is the Role of International Human Rights Law in the War on Terror?*, 69 DePaul L. Rev. 803 (2010).

57 Protocol Additional to the Geneva Conventions of 1949 (Protocol I), entered into force Dec. 12, 1978 (not ratified by the United States). Art. 55(1) of Protocol I prohibits "the use of methods or means of warfare which are intended or may be expected to cause [widespread, long-term and severe] damage to the natural environment."

58 LTUNW, *supra* note 11, at ¶ 33.

jus in bello, rather than under international environmental law).[59] In sum, having pared away human rights law and environmental law, the Court then turned to "the most directly relevant applicable law," namely, the law "relating to the use of force enshrined in the United Nations Charter and the law applicable in armed conflict which regulates the conduct of hostilities, together with any specific treaties on nuclear weapons."[60]

With this admittedly brief introduction, we now provide the most relevant portions of the ICJ's General Assembly Advisory Opinion. We first provide questions to help you focus your reading of those excerpts. (In footnotes, we provide detailed commentary on the academic and other responses to the issues raised by the questions we have posed. We urge you to return to the footnotes, after studying the ICJ Opinion and considering our commentary in Part D of this case study.)

59 *Id.* at ¶ 29.

60 *Id.* at ¶ 34.

C. STUDY QUESTIONS AND EXCERPTS FROM THE ICJ'S GENERAL ASSEMBLY ADVISORY OPINION

1. Study Questions Before Reading the ICJ's General Assembly Advisory Opinion

1) Why does the Court, in paragraph 105(2)(D), assert that "[a] threat or use of nuclear weapons should also be compatible with the requirements of the international law applicable in armed conflict"? Why does it not say "must be compatible"?[61]

2) Paragraph 2(E) is divided into two sub-paragraphs. In the first of these by a seven-to-seven vote, the Court states: "the threat or use of nuclear weapons would generally be contrary to the rules of international law applicable to armed conflict, and in particular . . . humanitarian law." What does the Court mean by saying that this is only generally, rather than absolutely, so?[62]

3) Does the Court leave open the possibility of a lawful use of nuclear weapons that was also contrary to humanitarian law? Is that a tenable reading of what the Court did (or may have done)?[63]

---

61 If the Court means to say that the applicability of humanitarian law to nuclear weapons is a *desideratum* but not yet a fact, why has it stated in paras. 85–88 of its opinion that "[i]n the view of the vast majority of States as well as writers there can be no doubt as to the applicability of humanitarian law to nuclear weapons. The Court shares that view." *Id.* at ¶¶ 85–88.

62 Is Judge Higgins right in saying that the Court "leaves open the possibility that a use of nuclear weapons contrary to humanitarian law might nonetheless be lawful"? LTUNW, *supra* note 11, at ¶ 29 (Higgins, J., dissenting); *see also id.* at 426 (Shahabuddeen, J., dissenting) ("The implication of [para. 2(E)] is that, in the view of the Court, it is possible that the use of nuclear weapons could be lawful 'in an extreme circumstance of self-defense, in which the very survival of a State would be at stake,' and hence even if humanitarian law would otherwise be violated."). In framing your answer, consider and contrast the conflicting comments of two dissenting judges:

> Higgins: "What does the term 'generally' mean? Is it a numerical allusion, or is it a reference to different types of nuclear weapons, or is it a suggestion that the rules of humanitarian law cannot be met save for exceptions? If so, . . . what are any exceptions to be read into the term 'generally'? Are they to be linked to an exceptional ability to comply with humanitarian law? Or does the term 'generally', especially in light of paragraph 96, suggest that if a use of nuclear weapons in extreme circumstances of self-defense were lawful, that might *of itself* exceptionally make such a use compatible with the humanitarian law?"

LTUNW, *supra* note 11, at ¶ 25 (Higgins, J., dissenting).

> Weeramantry: "The word 'generally' admits of many meanings, ranging through various gradations, from 'as a general rule; commonly', to 'universally; with respect to all or nearly all.' Even with the latter meaning, the word opens a window of permissibility, however narrow, which does not truly reflect the law."

LTUNW, *supra* note 11, at ¶ 435 (Weeamantry, J., dissenting).

63 Consider the Separate Opinion of Judge Ranjeva, noting especially his understanding of the Martens Clause:

> Paragraph 2E deals with the law of armed conflict and with humanitarian law, the second branch of law applicable to the threat or use of nuclear weapons (see para. 34). The law of armed conflict is a matter of written law, while the so-called Martens principle performs a residual function. "Two consequences flow from this: firstly, this law of armed conflict cannot be interpreted as containing lacunae of the sort likely to warrant reserve or at least doubt; secondly, nuclear weapons cannot

4) Does humanitarian law generally (or always) prohibit the threat of using nuclear weapons? Does other international law applicable to armed conflicts prohibit such threats? In the case of the threatened use of nuclear weapons by the United States against the forces of Saddam Hussein during the First Gulf War, in response to the use of chemical or biological weapons by Iraq.[64] What would be your view of the proposal, entertained by NATO during the Cold War, of using "demonstration" nuclear weapons to deter further advances by Warsaw Pact forces if in a conventional war NATO forces were being overrun?[65]

5) "[A]ssuming that the first sentence [of 2(E)] admits of circumstances where the use of nuclear weapons would be legal, is the circumstance set out in the second sentence the only possible exception to the rule in the first? Do the two sentences contain a rule and an exception, or is the second sentence free standing? Was the Court saying that even where the use of nuclear weapons would be contrary to humanitarian law, it could not rule on its legality where such use is in self-defence where the survival of a State is threatened?"[66]

> be used outside the context of the law of armed conflict. Moreover, *since no State supported the principle of a régime of non-law,* the use of these weapons must be in conformity, from the standpoint of the law, with the rules governing such conflict.

LTUNW, *supra* note 11, at 301 (separate opinion of Judge Ranjeva).

If Judge Ranjeva is right in thinking that the Martens Clause performs the "residual function" of closing any gaps in humanitarian law, and if no state (including the nuclear weapons states) had argued for a carve-out for nuclear weapons from the application of humanitarian law to all forms of weaponry, *see* LTUNW, *supra* note 11, at ¶ 86, does not that law cover the case of the use of nuclear weapons in self-defense, when the survival of a state is at stake? *See* Greenwood, *supra* note 52, 247, 263–64 (examining the contention that, although "the use of nuclear weapons would inevitably violate the *jus in bello*[,] the Court was leaving open the possibility that, in some undefined circumstances, the *jus ad bellum,* in the form of an extreme case of self-defence, would nevertheless justify their use").

64 What do you make of the case described in Judge Schwebel's dissent (LTUNW, *supra* note 11, at 323–29 (Vice-President Schwebel dissenting)) of the (implicit) threat that U.S. Secretary of State James Baker conveyed to Iraqi Foreign Minister Tariq Aziz that the United States would use nuclear weapons against Iraq during the First Gulf War if Iraq struck first against Coalition forces with (illegal) chemical or biological weapons? In fact, although the Iraqis could not have known it, President George H.W. Bush had previously decided not to use nuclear weapons, even in retaliation for Iraqi first use of chemical weapons. (Bear in mind that Iraq had used chemical weaponry in its war against Iran. Citing evidence that Secretary Baker's implicit threat effectively deterred Iraq, Judge Schwebel wrote:

> Thus there is on record remarkable evidence indicating that an aggressor was or may have been deterred from using outlawed weapons of mass destruction against forces and countries arrayed against its aggression at the call of the United Nations by what the aggressor perceived to be a threat to use nuclear weapons against it should it first use weapons of mass destruction against the forces of the coalition. Can it seriously be maintained that Mr. Baker's calculated – and apparently successful – threat was unlawful? Surely the principles of the United Nations Charter were sustained rather than transgressed by the threat.

LTUNW, *supra* note 11, at 327 (Vice-President Schwebel dissenting); *compare* Falk, *supra* note 46, at 69 (discussing Gulf War case).

65 *See* Horner, *supra* note 46, at 16. According to General Horner, the idea was "to detonate a nuclear weapon in an isolated area to prevent casualties with the hope that the Russians would retreat or stop the war." *Id.*

66 Akande, *supra* note 46, at 204. In considering your answer to question 5, consider Judge Fleischhauer's statement, as follows:

> [A]lthough recourse to nuclear weapons is scarcely reconcilable with humanitarian law . . . recourse to such weapons could remain a justified legal option in an extreme situation of individual or collective self-defense in which the threat or

6) What does the Court mean in paragraph 105(2)(E) by an "extreme" situation "in which the very survival of a State would be at stake"? Does "survival" mean physical survival, as in the case of a massive attack with weapons of mass destruction, or does it contemplate some extreme degree of loss of "territorial integrity or political independence" within the meaning of Article 2(4) of the UN Charter?[67]

> use of nuclear weapons is the last resort against an attack with nuclear, chemical or bacteriological weapons or otherwise threatening the very existence of the victimized State.

LTUNW, *supra* note 11, at 308 at ¶ 5 (separate opinion of Judge Fleischhauer). Is Judge Fleischhauer indicating his belief that the only situation in which the use of nuclear weapons might be lawful is that in which a state uses them as "the last resort" in lawful self-defense of its very survival? Is that also a fair reading of the second sub-paragraph in 2(E)?

Like Judge Ranjeva, Judge Schwebel assumed that the requirements of humanitarian law would apply to any use of nuclear weapons in combat. But, he also argued that in some circumstances, not limited to state survival, such use would or could be compatible with those requirements, especially proportionality. He used this illustration:

> For example, the use of a nuclear depth-charge to destroy a nuclear submarine that is about to fire nuclear missiles, or has fired one or more of a number of its nuclear missiles, might well be lawful. By the circumstances of its use, the nuclear depth-charge would not give rise to immediate civilian casualties. It would easily meet the test of proportionality; the damage that the submarine's missiles could inflict on the population and territory of the target State would infinitely outweigh that entailed in the destruction of the submarine and its crew. The submarine's destruction by a nuclear weapon would produce radiation in the sea, but far less than the radiation that firing of its missiles would produce on and over land. Nor is it as certain that the use of a conventional depth-charge would discharge the mission successfully; the far greater force of a nuclear weapon could ensure destruction of the submarine whereas a conventional depth-charge might not.

LTUNW, *supra* note 11, at 319–20 (Vice-President Schwebel dissenting).

Notice that Judge Schwebel's example seems to be intended to show, not that some uses of nuclear weapons might be exceptions to an otherwise universal prohibition on the use of such weapons, but that they might be compliant with the requirements of humanitarian law. Is his example convincing? Assume that the applicable test of "proportionality" is that laid down in Protocol I, Article 57(2)(a)(iii), which requires military commanders to "refrain from deciding to launch any attack which may be expected to cause incidental loss of civilian life, injury to civilians, damage to civilian objects, or a combination thereof, which would be excessive in relation to the concrete and direct military advantage anticipated." *See also* Art. 51(5)(b) (condemning as an unlawfully indiscriminate attack one which "may be expected to cause incidental loss of civilian life, injury to civilians, damage to civilian objects, or a combination thereof, which would be excessive in relation to the concrete and direct military advantage anticipated.").

If you conclude that the use of a nuclear depth-charge in the circumstances postulated by Judge Schwebel would satisfy this test (if only because the collateral damage to civilians has been assumed to be small), do you think that the use of a conventional depth-charge would nonetheless be required in order to comply with Article 57(4), which requires commanders to "take all reasonable precautions to avoid losses of civilian lives and damage to civilian objects"? How would your conclusions be affected if there were a serious risk that the use of any type of depth-charge against a nuclear-armed submarine would be likely to set off a vast underwater nuclear explosion? Assuming that Judge Schwebel's proportionality analysis is correct, does it do anything to sustain the legality of the policy of nuclear deterrence?

67 In his Separate Opinion, Judge Guillaume, in discussing the right of self-defense under Article 51 of the Charter, argued that "no system of law, whatever it may be, could deprive one of its subjects of the right to defend its own existence and safeguard its vital interests. Accordingly, international law cannot deprive a State of the right to resort to nuclear weapons if such action constitutes the ultimate means by which it can guarantee its survival." LTUNW, supra note 11, at Guillaume, at ¶ 8 (separate opinion of Judge Guillaume). Does, or should, an "extreme circumstance of self-defense, in which the very survival of a State would be at stake," include a situation in which a state's "vital interests" are at stake? Is it true that "no system of [international] law could deprive [a state] of the right to defend its own existence," even if that defense necessitated the use of nuclear weapons?

In considering your answer, take account of President Bedjaoui's remarks, which read as if they were a *riposte* to Judge Guillaume's:

> A state's right to survival is also a fundamental law, similar in many respects to a "natural" law. However, self-defense—if exercised in extreme circumstances in which the very survival of a State is in question—cannot produce a situation in which a State would exonerate itself from compliance with "intransgressible" norms of international humanitarian law. In certain circumstances, therefore, a relentless opposition can arise, a head-on collision of fundamental principles, neither one of which can be reduced to the other. The fact remains that the use of nuclear weapons by a State in circumstances in which its survival is at stake risks in its turn endangering the survival of all mankind, precisely because of the inextricable link between terror

7) Assume that paragraph 2(E) embodies a ruling that the use of nuclear weapons might be lawful in a situation in which a state is defending itself against unlawful aggression and has no alternative but a nuclear response if it is to survive. Under that reading of the Court's *dispositif*, would it matter whether this would be the *first use* of nuclear weapons in the conflict? Or might such use be lawful even if the state's survival were threatened by overwhelming conventional forces? Would it matter whether the aggressor was a nuclear-armed state (or allied with one), so that any first-use entailed the risk of nuclear escalation?[68] (Please consider in this connection our discussion of nuclear non-proliferation commitments in Part I Chapters 2B and 2C of this book.)

> and escalation in the use of such weapons. It would thus be quite foolhardy unhesitatingly to set the survival of a State above all other considerations, in particular above the survival of mankind itself.

LTUNW, *supra* note 11, ¶ 22 (declaration of President Bedjaoui (translation)).

See generally Schmitt, *supra* note 40, at 78. Matheson likewise noted that "survival" might refer to the political survival of a state's government, the survival of a state as an independent entity, or the physical destruction of a state's population. *See* Matheson, *supra* note 40, at 430. Some commentators take the position that the Court is referring here to physical survival or to the absorption of the functions of statehood by another state. *See* Peter Weiss, *The World Court Tackles the Fate of the Earth: An Introduction to the ICJ Advisory Opinion on the Legality of the Threat or Use of Nuclear Weapons,* 7 Transnat'l L. & Comp. Probs. 313, 325–29 (1997).

68 Consider, in this connection, two sets of security assurances provides by nuclear weapons states in connection with the NPT. The so-called "positive security assurances" (PSAs) were first enunciated by the Security Council as part of the implicit *quid pro quo* for the conclusion of the NPT, which divided the world into a group of states that could possess nuclear weapons (nuclear-weapons states or NWS) and states that would be barred from possessing nuclear weapons (non-nuclear-weapon states or NNWS). The Security Council "recognize[d] that aggression with nuclear weapons or the threat of such aggression against a non-nuclear-weapon State would create a situation in which the Security Council and above all it nuclear-weapon State permanent members, would have to act immediately in accordance with their obligations under the United Nations Charter," and it "[w]elcome[d] the intention expressed by certain States that they will provide or support immediately assistance, in accordance with the Charter, to any non-nuclear-weapon State Party to the Treaty on the Non-Proliferation of Nuclear Weapons that is a victim of an act or an object of a threat of aggression in which nuclear weapons are used...." S.C. Res. 255, op. ¶ 1 (June 19, 1968).

In addition, so-called "negative security assurances" (NSAs) were unilaterally announced by the United States in 1978. Under those assurances, which were most recently restated in 2010,

> The United States reaffirm[ed] that it [would] not use nuclear weapons against non-nuclear-weapon States Parties to the Treaty on the Non-Proliferation of Nuclear Weapons except in the case of an invasion or any other attack on the United States, its territories, its armed forces or other troops, its allies, or on a State towards which it has a security commitment, carried out or sustained by such a non-nuclear-weapon State in association or alliance with a nuclear-weapon State.

Daryl Kimball, U.S. "Negative Security Assurances" At a Glance, Arms Control Association Factsheet (*available at* https://www.armscontrol.org/factsheets/negsec).

Significantly, after the WHO and General Assembly made their requests but before the ICJ rendered its opinions, these NSAs were reaffirmed in 1995 by the United States, and comparable formulations were submitted by the other members of the Permanent Five of the U.N. Security Council, all of which lawfully possessed nuclear-weapons under the NPT. This appears to have been part of the implicit *quid pro quo* for the permanent extension of the NPT in 1995 at the end of its initial 25-year term. *See* S. C. Res. 984, op. ¶ 1 (April 11, 1995) (incorporating by reference the texts of those NWS assurances). Resolution 984 also updated the "positive security assurances" made in S.C.Res. 255—this time implicitly including France and the People's Republic of China, which in the interim had become NPT NWS Parties. *See id.* S.C. Res. 984, op. ¶ 3.

The NWS have also undertaken separately to provide NSAs by express treaty commitments in protocols to treaties establishing regional "nuclear free zones," such as the U.S. commitment in support of the Western Hemispheric nuclear-free zone established under the Treaty of Tlatelolco. For example, Article 3 of Protocol II to the Treaty of Tlatelolco, to which the United States is a party, provides: "The Governments represented by the undersigned Plenipotentiaries also undertake not to use or threaten to use nuclear weapons against the Contracting Parties of the Treaty for the Prohibition of Nuclear Weapons in Latin America." Additional Protocol II to the Treaty for the Prohibition of Nuclear Weapons in Latin America and the Caribbean (entered into force May 12, 1971) (*available at* http://disarmament.un.org/treaties/t/tlateloco_p2).

8) On the same assumption about the meaning of 2(E), might it be lawful for a state whose own survival was not at risk but that was allied to a state whose survival was at stake because of unlawful aggression to use nuclear weapons to defend its ally?[69]

9) Might the use of tactical nuclear weapons be, in some circumstances, legally permissible?[70] Even taking into account only the principle prohibiting the use of weaponry that causes unnecessary suffering to combatants, is this view consistent with the Court's opinion and *dispositif*?

10) Does the opinion suggest that the legality (or potential legality) of the use of nuclear weapons when state survival was at risk turn on whether the state was or was not acting lawfully under the *jus ad bellum*? Would this be consistent with the traditional law of war?[71] Is the Court in paragraph 2(E) simply confused and

---

69 Notice that Judge Fleischhauer appeared to think that "self-defense," as used in 2(E), included collective self-defense, as it does in Article 51 of the Charter. In view of Article 51's reference to both individual and collective self-defense, that inference seems logical. Yet, as Michael Schmitt pointed out, the Court's opinion refers only to the possible legality of the use of nuclear weapons by a state when "its" survival would be at stake. *See* Schmitt, *supra* note 40, at 66.

Former U.S. Air Force General Charles A. Horner pointed out in 1997 that NATO's "tactical nuclear weapons" strategy meant that "we would use nuclear weapons if the Russian army invaded the Fulda Gap [in Germany], as this event marked the point at which we could no longer defend our position with conventional means." Horner, *supra* note 46, at 16. Assume that if Warsaw Pact conventional forces had succeeded in breaking through NATO's defenses at the Fulda Gap, the "very survival" of the state of West Germany would have been at stake. Although West Germany was a NATO member, it had no nuclear weaponry of its own. Under paragraph 2(E), might West Germany's nuclear-armed NATO allies lawfully have used nuclear weapons in West Germany's (collective) self-defense? What if the Warsaw Pact had previously deployed only conventional means of warfare? What if the Warsaw Pact had used non-nuclear weapons of mass destruction first? *See* LTUNW, *supra* note 11, at 308 at ¶ 5 (separate opinion of Judge Fleischhauer) ("[R]ecourse to such weapons could remain a justified legal option in an extreme situation of individual or collective self-defense in which the threat or use of nuclear weapons is the last resort against an attack with nuclear, chemical or bacteriological weapons or otherwise threatening the very existence of the victimized State."). Might the use of nuclear weaponry by the nuclear members of NATO have been defended legally on the grounds that it was in their "vital interests" to prevent the collapse of the West German state?

70 According to one commentator, "in so far as there may exist smaller weapons of a tactical kind for use of the battlefield and the fallout and long-term effects of which may be controlled, it would appear that there is no doubt as to their legality, provided it could be maintained that the suffering caused to combatants was not disproportionate or unnecessary in view of the military end to be achieved." Leslie C. Green, The Contemporary Law of Armed Conflict 131–32 (2d ed. 2000).

71 The long-prevailing view of the relationship between *jus ad bellum* and *jus in bello* has two aspects: a "symmetry thesis," holding that the content of *jus in bello*, including both obligations and rights, is identical for all combatants in an armed conflict; and an "independence thesis," which holds that the *jus in bello* obligations and rights of the combatants are independent of the justice or legality of the war they are waging under the *jus ad bellum*. *See* David Rodin, *The Liability of Ordinary Soldiers for Crimes of Aggression*, 6 Wash. U. Global Stud. L. Rev. 391, 391 (2007). Consequently, the conduct of states is measured under *jus in bello* in the same way, regardless of whether they are aggressors or victims engaged in lawful self-defense. *See* Walzer, *supra* note 45, at 38–40; Rostow, *supra* note 35, at 173–73 & n.135 (collecting authorities). The *"Hostages" Case (U.S. v. List)* at Nuremberg is directly on point:

> We concur in the views expressed in the following text on the subject: 'Whatever may be the cause of a war that has broken out, and whether or no the cause be a so-called just cause, the same rules of International Law are valid as to what must not be done, and must be done by the belligerents themselves in making war against each other; and as between the belligerents and neutral States. This is so, even if the declaration of war is *ipso facto* a violation of International Law, as when a belligerent declares war upon a neutral State for refusing passage to its troops, or when a State goes to war in patent violation of its obligations under the Covenant of the League or of the General Treaty for the Renunciation of War. To say that, because such a declaration of war is *ipso facto* a violation of International Law, it is 'inoperative in law and without any judicial significance,' is erroneous. The rules of International Law apply to war from whatever cause it originates. Oppenheim's *International Law*, II Lauterpacht, p.174.

conflating the two kinds of law?[72] More charitably, is it saying that the right of lawful self-defense might supersede the *jus in bello*? Or is it implicitly denying that the traditional bifurcation of the two types of war law can stand when nuclear war is in question?[73] But, suppose one interprets the Court to be saying that an aggressor, having committed an act of aggression, has "limited its right to survival which belongs to both *jus ad bellum* and *jus in bello,*" and therefore has no right to use nuclear weapons consistently with *jus in bello,* even if they were needed for its survival.[74] Would it follow that such an aggressor also would have no right to use lawful, conventional weapons if use of those weapons were needed for its survival?

11) Assume that any state using nuclear weapons, in order to be (at least potentially) in compliance with the law, would have to satisfy both the applicable requirements of the *jus ad bellum and* all requirements of the *jus in bello* on each occasion of such use. How would you undertake the proportionality analysis required by the *jus in bello.* How does, or would, the Court?[75] (Please refer back to your study of the law

---

The Hostages Trial: Trial of Wilhelm List and Others, U.S. Military Tribunal, Nuremberg, Case No. 47, 8 United Nations War Crimes Commission, Law Reports of Trials of War Criminals 60 (1949) (*available at* http://lawofwar.org/List%20Case.htm).

In the *General Assembly Advisory Opinion* itself, Judge Koroma noted that the laws of armed conflict "were intended to be applied in all cases . . . without any particular consideration of the status of the parties to the conflict —whether they were victims or aggressors." LTUNW, *supra* note 11, at 302 (Koroma, J., dissenting). Likewise, Judge Shahabuddeen explained:

> A State using force in self-defense is acting legally under the *jus ad bellum.* But, whether a State is acting legally or illegally under the *jus ad bellum,* if it is in fact using force it must always do so in the manner prescribed by the *jus in bello.* It is the *jus in bello* which lays down whether or not a particular means of warfare is permissible.

LTUNW, *supra* note 11, at 418 (Shahabuddeen, J., dissenting).

Since this is so, how could the legality (or potential legality) of the use of nuclear weapons when state survival was at risk turn on whether the state was or was not acting lawfully under the *jus ad bellum*? How could the use of nuclear weaponry be (potentially) lawful if the state that used it were acting in lawful self-defense, but not if it were the aggressor? *See* Rein Müllerson, *On the Relationship Between Jus ad Bellum and Jus in Bello in the General Assembly Advisory Opinion, in* International Law, The International Court of Justice and Nuclear Weapons 267, 267–68 (Laurence Boisson de Chazournes & Philippe Sands eds.,1999).

72 *See* McCormack, *supra* note 46 ("This finding [in 2(E)] . . . represents a staggering confusion between the *jus ad bellum* and the *jus in bello.*").

73 For the argument that the traditional distinction should apply, even in the "extreme circumstances" in which a state's survival is at stake, *see* Jasmine Moussa, *Can Jus ad Bellum Override Jus in Bello? Reaffirming the Separation of the Two Bodies of Law,* 90 IRRC 963, 968–72 (2000). For further discussion of symmetry and independence, *see infra* Part IV.

74 Müllerson, *supra* note 71, at 272.

75 Judge Higgins suggested that a state could satisfy the latter requirements (or more precisely, the *jus in bello* proportionality requirement) only if the state's survival was at stake precisely because the state's continued existence would weigh so heavily in the proportionality calculus. She wrote:

> One is inevitably led to the question of whether, if a target is legitimate and the use of a nuclear weapon is the only way of destroying that target, any need can ever be so necessary as to occasion massive collateral damage upon civilians. . . . It must be that, in order to meet the legal requirement that a military target may not be attacked if collateral civilian casualties would be excessive in relation to the military advantage, the "military advantage" must indeed be one related to the very survival of a State or the avoidance of infliction (whether by nuclear or other weapons of mass destruction) of vast and severe suffering on its own population; and that no other method of eliminating this military target be available.

LTUNW, *supra* note 11, at 365–66 at ¶¶ 20–21 (Higgins, J., dissenting). Is this a satisfactory way of showing that the use of nuclear weapons might be satisfy the proportionality test of the *jus in bello* but only when state survival is at stake?

of war principles in the context of the ICTY's Final Report to the Prosecutor in Part III of Chapter 2.)

12) Is the Court's theory akin to a common law right of private or public necessity? On these alternative characterizations, what would be the remedial consequences for the harm caused to innocent civilians and/or environmental effects?[76] (Again, consider in connection with these questions your study of the ICTY's Final Report to the Prosecutor in Part III, Chapter 3.)

13) Should the ICJ have taken the case? Recall that its advisory decision authority and practice might have enable the Court to decline to answer, as it did in the case of the WHO's request. In practice, was the same result achieved by other means? Was its legitimacy increased or undercut by its performance?[77] Would its legitimacy have been undercut even more had it more fully responded? Indeed, would a response have increased the likelihood of the use of nuclear weapons by supplying criteria for their use, thereby undermining the current so-called nuclear taboo?[78]

---

76 For a discussion of the remedial effects of these common law doctrines, see Richard A. Epstein & Catherine M. Sharkey, Cases and Materials on Torts 44–55 (10th ed. 2012) (writing that private necessity entails a duty to provide compensation, while acting to serve a public necessity does not entail a duty to provide compensation).

77 Michael Schmitt found something to praise in the Court's decision to deal with the "highly politicized, extremely difficult" issue of the legality of nuclear weapons, but also argues that the Court's ultimate inconclusiveness displays the limits of legalism and the power of realism. Schmitt wrote:

> [P]erhaps the Court went as far as it could have gone, given the realities of the global context in which it was operating. Had it gone further, it would have been ignored. Surely, no one would argue that the nuclear States would suddenly have dispensed with their nuclear arsenals if only the International Court of Justice had decried their use as illegal. In light of this reality, if it had gone one step further and declared use illegal in all circumstances, the Court would have been highlighting its own relative impotence. So, for the same institutional reason the Court benefited by taking the case, it needed to avoid deciding it definitively. It could, of course, have held use legal, but the opinion makes clear that as a whole the Court was heavily predisposed towards the opposite conclusion. Thus, [the Court's opinion] was an exercise in jurisprudential realism.

Schmitt, *supra* note 40, at 81. *See also* Kahn, *supra* note 16, 413–14. Kahn wrote:

> There is always a risk of pretension in the legal voice: the pretension that law's empire knows no limits. The nuclear weapons case shows us that there really are limits. The decision ends in an embarrassing silence, broken only by the Court adding its plea to that of millions of others, that the nuclear-weapons states should get on with the business of negotiating an end to the nuclear confrontation. At this level, however, the Court's voice is no louder or more convincing than that of anyone else.

But see Perez, *supra* note 32, at 409 (arguing that the ICJ "discharged both its 'grand' responsibility to articulate [legal] principles and its 'dialogic' function of stimulating constitutional debate at the political level" at the Security Council and General Assembly).

78 Martti Koskenniemi defended the Court's unwillingness to decide, on the basis of a proportionality calculus, whether the use of nuclear weapons might be lawful in some scenarios. He argued:

> Had it done so, it would have instituted a public, technical discourse for the defence of the killing of the innocent. By lifting the matter onto the level of judicial reason, the Court would have broken the taboo against any use of nuclear weapons. It would have opened a professionally honourable and perhaps even a tragically pleasurable way of addressing the unaddressable. The (massive) killing of the innocent would have become another contextual determinant, a banal "factor" in an overall balancing of the utilities, to be compared with the equally banal factors of sovereignty, military objectives, and so on. . . . Unlike taboo, rational argument cannot put nuclear weapons in a class of their own, to be treated outside the normal logic of identity and difference, legal analogy and "distinguishing."

Koskenniemi, *supra* note 46, at 488, 496–97.

In retrospect, did the decision matter?[79] What factors, or theory of international law and politics, can best explain the Court's performance and the current state of affairs evidencing limited, if any, progress toward nuclear disarmament?[80] (Please reconsider your earlier study of rational choice theory and social constructivism.)

2. Readings: General Assembly Advisory Opinion, paras. 78–82, 85–87, 90–92, 94–99, and 104–105

79 Schmitt also argued that in practical terms, the effect of the decision would be "marginal" or "*de minimis.*" In part this is because para. 2(E) can be read (in light of the *Lotus* rule) to be permissive, and in part because states typically characterize their nuclear policies as wholly self-defensive. Schmitt wrote:

> Key to the opinion's *de minimis* practical effect is the Court's non-decision on the issue of self-defense. In that international law is prohibitory in nature, uncertainty must be resolved in favor of allowing a State to perform the act in question; a presumption in favor of the absence of limitations on State action exists. That being the case, nuclear weapons States can treat the Court's quandary over how to resolve the self-defense issue as the functional equivalent of a finding that it could identify no bar to use of their weapons in survival situations. This allows them to maintain their arsenal under the guise of survival based self-defense.

Schmitt, *supra* note 40, at 80.

80 In a powerful and illuminating article, Paul Kahn offered a different account from either Schmitt's or Koskenniemi's of the Court's failure to reach a definitive answer on the legality of using nuclear weapons in state survival situations. In his view, "the legal resources that bear on the problem are in equipoise. To resolve the issue, the Court would have to find a ground of normative priority between two distinct approaches to international law. Neither approach, however, is more important, basic or essential than the other." The first approach he calls "legitimacy," the second, "justification." On "legitimacy," he wrote:

> On this view, the legitimate authority of international law arises out of the consent of the states that bear the legal obligation. Accordingly, to understand the content of the law, we need to trace the character and implications of state consent. . . . Interpretation of law, on this view, must link the content of law to its origin in state consent. Legal claims that extend beyond that consent are illegitimate.

Kahn, *supra* note 16, at 367. On "justification," he wrote:

> The other approach locates the normative claim of international law in the expression of principles of moral behavior among states. To understand the demands that law makes upon the state, we interpret these principles in light of an understanding of justice among states. On this view, we must distinguish the origin of law from the content of law. While much of international law may emerge from the consensual actions of states, the content of that law is not bound by those consensual acts. When we argue about the content of the law, we look to the justifications for legal norms, which means that we look to the moral principles that inform the specific, positive provisions of the law. Judge Ranjeva expresse[d] this perspective when he [wrote]: "The moral requirements are not direct and positive sources of prescriptions or obligations but they do represent a framework for the scrutiny and questioning of the techniques and rules of conventional and consensual engineering."

Id. at 367–68. One could view Kahn's distinctions as mapping onto the distinction we shall later pursue between positivist and rationalist legalism.

In light of these two contrasting visions of international law, Kahn analyzed the crucial holdings of the *General Assembly Advisory Opinion* Court's dilemma as follows:

> The Court's ultimate muteness in this case reflects the central dilemma of contemporary international law. This is the problem of understanding the place of the state in a system that simultaneously recognizes the state as the source of norms and interprets those norms in a transnational, principled fashion. . . . It is not the form of the legal argument, but the double character of the content of the law that causes the dilemma here. This is a substantive conflict about the place of state sovereignty in the international legal order. If all law must be interpreted through the lens of state sovereignty, we get one answer to the nuclear weapons issue: the answer that protects deterrence and stumbles over an ultimate right of self-defense. If all law is interpreted through a transnational moral principle of justice, survival of mankind cannot be a value subordinate to state sovereignty. Contemporary international law is caught between these two quite different value schemes: one reflecting the international order as a system of sovereign nation-states and one reflecting transnational norms independent of those states. The nuclear weapons case brings these two different schemes into conflict, without offering any legal grounds for their reconciliation.

Id. at 337–74.

disabled men or make their death inevitable". The aforementioned Regulations relating to the laws and customs of war on land, annexed to the Hague Convention IV of 1907, prohibit the use of "arms, projectiles, or material calculated to cause unnecessary suffering" (Art. 23).

78. The cardinal principles contained in the texts constituting the fabric of humanitarian law are the following. The first is aimed at the protection of the civilian population and civilian objects and establishes the distinction between combatants and non-combatants; States must never make civilians the object of attack and must consequently never use weapons that are incapable of distinguishing between civilian and military targets. According to the second principle, it is prohibited to cause unnecessary suffering to combatants: it is accordingly prohibited to use weapons causing them such harm or uselessly aggravating their suffering. In application of that second principle, States do not have unlimited freedom of choice of means in the weapons they use.

The Court would likewise refer, in relation to these principles, to the Martens Clause, which was first included in the Hague Convention II with Respect to the Laws and Customs of War on Land of 1899 and which has proved to be an effective means of addressing the rapid evolution of military technology. A modern version of that clause is to be found in Article 1, paragraph 2, of Additional Protocol I of 1977, which reads as follows:

> "In cases not covered by this Protocol or by other international agreements, civilians and combatants remain under the protection and authority of the principles of international law derived from established custom, from the principles of humanity and from the dictates of public conscience."

In conformity with the aforementioned principles, humanitarian law, at a very early stage, prohibited certain types of weapons either because of their indiscriminate effect on combatants and civilians or because of the unnecessary suffering caused to combatants, that is to say, a harm greater than that unavoidable to achieve legitimate military objectives. If an envisaged use of weapons would not meet the requirements of humanitarian law, a threat to engage in such use would also be contrary to that law.

79. It is undoubtedly because a great many rules of humanitarian law applicable in armed conflict are so fundamental to the respect of the human person and "elementary considerations of humanity" as the Court put it in its Judgment of 9 April 1949 in the *Corfu Channel* case (*I.C.J. Reports 1949*, p. 22), that the Hague and Geneva Conventions have enjoyed a broad accession. Further these fundamental rules are to be observed by all States whether or not they have ratified the conventions that contain them, because they constitute intransgressible principles of international customary law.

80. The Nuremberg International Military Tribunal had already found in 1945 that the humanitarian rules included in the Regulations annexed to the Hague Convention IV of 1907 "were recognized by all civilized nations and were regarded as being declaratory of the laws and customs of war" (*Trial of the Major War Criminals, 14 November 1945-1 October 1946*, Nuremberg, 1947, Vol. 1, p. 254).

81. The Report of the Secretary-General pursuant to paragraph 2 of Security Council resolution 808 (1993), with which he introduced the Statute of the International Tribunal for the Prosecution of Persons Responsible for Serious Violations of International Humanitarian Law Committed in the Territory of the Former Yugoslavia since 1991, and which was unanimously approved by the Security Council (resolution 827 (1993)), stated:

> "In the view of the Secretary-General, the application of the principle *nullum crimen sine lege* requires that the international tribunal should apply rules of international humanitarian law which are beyond any doubt part of customary law . . .
>
> The part of conventional international humanitarian law which has beyond doubt become part of international customary law is the law applicable in armed conflict as embodied in: the Geneva Conventions of 12 August 1949 for the Protection of War Victims; the Hague Convention (IV) Respecting the Laws and Customs of War on Land and the Regulations annexed thereto of 18 October 1907; the Convention on the Prevention and Punishment of the Crime of Genocide of 9 December 1948; and the Charter of the International Military Tribunal of 8 August 1945."

82. The extensive codification of humanitarian law and the extent of the accession to the resultant treaties, as well as the fact that the denunciation clauses that existed in the codification instruments have never been used, have provided the international community with a corpus of treaty rules the great majority of which had already become customary and which reflected the most universally recognized humanitarian principles. These rules indicate the normal conduct and behaviour expected of States.

83. It has been maintained in these proceedings that these principles and rules of humanitarian law are part of *jus cogens* as defined in Article 53 of the Vienna Convention on the Law of Treaties of 23 May 1969. The question whether a norm is part of the *jus cogens* relates to the legal character of the norm. The request addressed to the Court by the General Assembly raises the question of the applicability of the principles and rules of humanitarian law in cases of recourse to nuclear weapons and the consequences of that applicability for the legality of recourse to these weapons. But it does not raise the question of the character of the humanitarian law which would apply to the use of nuclear weapons. There is, therefore, no need for the Court to pronounce on this matter.

84. Nor is there any need for the Court to elaborate on the question of the applicability of Additional Protocol I of 1977 to nuclear weapons. It need only observe that while, at the Diplomatic Conference of 1974-1977, there was no substantive debate on the nuclear issue and no specific solution concerning this question was put forward, Additional Protocol I in no way replaced the general customary rules applicable to all means and methods of combat including nuclear weapons. In particular, the Court recalls that all States are bound by those rules in Additional Protocol I which, when adopted, were merely the expression of the pre-existing customary law, such as the Martens Clause, reaffirmed in the first article of Additional Protocol I. The fact that certain types of weapons were not specifically dealt with by the 1974-1977 Conference does not permit the drawing of any legal conclusions relating to the substantive issues which the use of such weapons would raise.

85. Turning now to the applicability of the principles and rules of humanitarian law to a possible threat or use of nuclear weapons, the Court notes that doubts in this respect have sometimes been voiced on the ground that these principles and rules had evolved prior to the invention of nuclear weapons and that the Conferences of Geneva of 1949 and 1974-1977 which respectively adopted the four Geneva Conventions of 1949 and the two Additional Protocols thereto did not deal with nuclear weapons specifically. Such views, however, are only held by a small minority. In the view of the vast majority of States as well as writers there can be no doubt as to the applicability of humanitarian law to nuclear weapons.

86. The Court shares that view. Indeed, nuclear weapons were invented after most of the principles and rules of humanitarian law applicable in armed conflict had already come into existence; the Conferences of 1949 and 1974-1977 left these weapons aside, and there is a qualitative as well as quantitative difference between nuclear weapons and all conventional arms. However, it cannot be concluded from this that the established principles and rules of humanitarian law applicable in armed conflict did not apply to nuclear weapons. Such a conclusion would be incompatible with the intrinsically humanitarian character of the legal principles in question which permeates the entire law of armed conflict and applies to all forms of warfare and to all kinds of weapons, those of the past, those of the present and those of the future. In this respect it seems significant that the thesis that the rules of humanitarian law do not apply to the new weaponry, because of the newness of the latter, has not been advocated in the present proceedings. On the contrary, the newness of nuclear weapons has been expressly rejected as an argument against the application to them of international humanitarian law:

> "In general, international humanitarian law bears on the threat or use of nuclear weapons as it does of other weapons.

International humanitarian law has evolved to meet contemporary circumstances, and is not limited in its application to weaponry of an earlier time. The fundamental principles of this law endure: to mitigate and circumscribe the cruelty of war for humanitarian reasons." (New Zealand, Written Statement, p. 15, paras. 63-64.)

None of the statements made before the Court in any way advocated a freedom to use nuclear weapons without regard to humanitarian constraints. Quite the reverse; it has been explicitly stated,

> "Restrictions set by the rules applicable to armed conflicts in respect of means and methods of warfare definitely also extend to nuclear weapons" (Russian Federation, CR 95/29, p. 52);

> "So far as the customary law of war is concerned, the United Kingdom has always accepted that the use of nuclear weapons is subject to the general principles of the *jus in bello*" (United Kingdom, CR 95/34, p. 45);

and

> "The United States has long shared the view that the law of armed conflict governs the use of nuclear weapons — just as it governs the use of conventional weapons" (United States of America, CR 95/34, p. 85).

87. Finally, the Court points to the Martens Clause, whose continuing existence and applicability is not to be doubted, as an affirmation that the principles and rules of humanitarian law apply to nuclear weapons.

*

88. The Court will now turn to the principle of neutrality which was raised by several States. In the context of the advisory proceedings brought before the Court by the WHO concerning the *Legality of the Use by a State of Nuclear Weapons in Armed Conflict*, the position was put as follows by one State:

> "The principle of neutrality, in its classic sense, was aimed at preventing the incursion of belligerent forces into neutral territory, or attacks on the persons or ships of neutrals. Thus: 'the territory of neutral powers is inviolable' (Article 1 of the Hague Convention (V) Respecting the Rights and Duties of Neutral Powers and Persons in Case of War on Land, concluded on 18 October 1907); 'belligerents are bound to respect the sovereign rights of neutral powers . . .' (Article 1 to the Hague Convention (XIII) Respecting the Rights and Duties of Neutral Powers in Naval War, concluded on 18 October 1907), 'neutral states have equal interest in having their rights respected by belligerents . . .' (Preamble to Convention on Maritime

> Neutrality, concluded on 20 February 1928). It is clear, however, that the principle of neutrality applies with equal force to transborder incursions of armed forces and to the transborder damage caused to a neutral State by the use of a weapon in a belligerent State." (Nauru, Written Statement (I), p. 35, IV E.)

The principle so circumscribed is presented as an established part of the customary international law.

89. The Court finds that as in the case of the principles of humanitarian law applicable in armed conflict, international law leaves no doubt that the principle of neutrality, whatever its content, which is of a fundamental character similar to that of the humanitarian principles and rules, is applicable (subject to the relevant provisions of the United Nations Charter), to all international armed conflict, whatever type of weapons might be used.

*

90. Although the applicability of the principles and rules of humanitarian law and of the principle of neutrality to nuclear weapons is hardly disputed, the conclusions to be drawn from this applicability are, on the other hand, controversial.

91. According to one point of view, the fact that recourse to nuclear weapons is subject to and regulated by the law of armed conflict does not necessarily mean that such recourse is as such prohibited. As one State put it to the Court:

> "Assuming that a State's use of nuclear weapons meets the requirements of self-defence, it must then be considered whether it conforms to the fundamental principles of the law of armed conflict regulating the conduct of hostilities" (United Kingdom, Written Statement, p. 40, para. 3.44);
>
> "the legality of the use of nuclear weapons must therefore be assessed in the light of the applicable principles of international law regarding the use of force and the conduct of hostilities, as is the case with other methods and means of warfare" (*ibid.*, p. 75, para. 4.2 (3));

and

> "The reality . . . is that nuclear weapons might be used in a wide variety of circumstances with very different results in terms of likely civilian casualties. In some cases, such as the use of a low yield nuclear weapon against warships on the High Seas or troops in sparsely populated areas, it is possible to envisage a nuclear attack which caused comparatively few civilian casualties. It is by no means the case that every use of nuclear weapons against a military objective would inevitably cause very great collateral civilian casualties."

(*Ibid.*, p. 53, para. 3.70; see also United States of America, CR 95/34, pp. 89-90.)

92. Another view holds that recourse to nuclear weapons could never be compatible with the principles and rules of humanitarian law and is therefore prohibited. In the event of their use, nuclear weapons would in all circumstances be unable to draw any distinction between the civilian population and combatants, or between civilian objects and military objectives, and their effects, largely uncontrollable, could not be restricted, either in time or in space, to lawful military targets. Such weapons would kill and destroy in a necessarily indiscriminate manner, on account of the blast, heat and radiation occasioned by the nuclear explosion and the effects induced; and the number of casualties which would ensue would be enormous. The use of nuclear weapons would therefore be prohibited in any circumstance, notwithstanding the absence of any explicit conventional prohibition. That view lay at the basis of the assertions by certain States before the Court that nuclear weapons are by their nature illegal under customary international law, by virtue of the fundamental principle of humanity.

93. A similar view has been expressed with respect to the effects of the principle of neutrality. Like the principles and rules of humanitarian law, that principle has therefore been considered by some to rule out the use of a weapon the effects of which simply cannot be contained within the territories of the contending States.

94. The Court would observe that none of the States advocating the legality of the use of nuclear weapons under certain circumstances, including the "clean" use of smaller, low yield, tactical nuclear weapons, has indicated what, supposing such limited use were feasible, would be the precise circumstances justifying such use; nor whether such limited use would not tend to escalate into the all-out use of high yield nuclear weapons. This being so, the Court does not consider that it has a sufficient basis for a determination on the validity of this view.

95. Nor can the Court make a determination on the validity of the view that the recourse to nuclear weapons would be illegal in any circumstance owing to their inherent and total incompatibility with the law applicable in armed conflict. Certainly, as the Court has already indicated, the principles and rules of law applicable in armed conflict — at the heart of which is the overriding consideration of humanity — make the conduct of armed hostilities subject to a number of strict requirements. Thus, methods and means of warfare, which would preclude any distinction between civilian and military targets, or which would result in unnecessary suffering to combatants, are prohibited. In view of the unique characteristics of nuclear weapons, to which the Court has referred above, the use of such weapons in fact seems scarcely reconcilable with respect for such requirements. Nevertheless, the Court considers that it

does not have sufficient elements to enable it to conclude with certainty that the use of nuclear weapons would necessarily be at variance with the principles and rules of law applicable in armed conflict in any circumstance.

96. Furthermore, the Court cannot lose sight of the fundamental right of every State to survival, and thus its right to resort to self-defence, in accordance with Article 51 of the Charter, when its survival is at stake.

Nor can it ignore the practice referred to as "policy of deterrence", to which an appreciable section of the international community adhered for many years. The Court also notes the reservations which certain nuclear-weapon States have appended to the undertakings they have given, notably under the Protocols to the Treaties of Tlatelolco and Rarotonga, and also under the declarations made by them in connection with the extension of the Treaty on the Non-Proliferation of Nuclear Weapons, not to resort to such weapons.

97. Accordingly, in view of the present state of international law viewed as a whole, as examined above by the Court, and of the elements of fact at its disposal, the Court is led to observe that it cannot reach a definitive conclusion as to the legality or illegality of the use of nuclear weapons by a State in an extreme circumstance of self-defence, in which its very survival would be at stake.

* * *

98. Given the eminently difficult issues that arise in applying the law on the use of force and above all the law applicable in armed conflict to nuclear weapons, the Court considers that it now needs to examine one further aspect of the question before it, seen in a broader context.

In the long run, international law, and with it the stability of the international order which it is intended to govern, are bound to suffer from the continuing difference of views with regard to the legal status of weapons as deadly as nuclear weapons. It is consequently important to put an end to this state of affairs: the long-promised complete nuclear disarmament appears to be the most appropriate means of achieving that result.

99. In these circumstances, the Court appreciates the full importance of the recognition by Article VI of the Treaty on the Non-Proliferation of Nuclear Weapons of an obligation to negotiate in good faith a nuclear disarmament. This provision is worded as follows:

> "Each of the Parties to the Treaty undertakes to pursue negotiations in good faith on effective measures relating to cessation of the nuclear arms race at an early date and to nuclear disarmament, and on a treaty on general and complete disarmament under strict and effective international control."

The legal import of that obligation goes beyond that of a mere obligation of conduct; the obligation involved here is an obligation to achieve a precise result — nuclear disarmament in all its aspects — by adopting a particular course of conduct, namely, the pursuit of negotiations on the matter in good faith.

100. This twofold obligation to pursue and to conclude negotiations formally concerns the 182 States parties to the Treaty on the Non-Proliferation of Nuclear Weapons, or, in other words, the vast majority of the international community.

Virtually the whole of this community appears moreover to have been involved when resolutions of the United Nations General Assembly concerning nuclear disarmament have repeatedly been unanimously adopted. Indeed, any realistic search for general and complete disarmament, especially nuclear disarmament, necessitates the co-operation of all States.

101. Even the very first General Assembly resolution, unanimously adopted on 24 January 1946 at the London session, set up a commission whose terms of reference included making specific proposals for, among other things, "the elimination from national armaments of atomic weapons and of all other major weapons adaptable to mass destruction". In a large number of subsequent resolutions, the General Assembly has reaffirmed the need for nuclear disarmament. Thus, in resolution 808 A (IX) of 4 November 1954, which was likewise unanimously adopted, it concluded

> "that a further effort should be made to reach agreement on comprehensive and co-ordinated proposals to be embodied in a draft international disarmament convention providing for: . . . *(b)* The total prohibition of the use and manufacture of nuclear weapons and weapons of mass destruction of every type, together with the conversion of existing stocks of nuclear weapons for peaceful purposes."

The same conviction has been expressed outside the United Nations context in various instruments.

102. The obligation expressed in Article VI of the Treaty on the Non-Proliferation of Nuclear Weapons includes its fulfilment in accordance with the basic principle of good faith. This basic principle is set forth in Article 2, paragraph 2, of the Charter. It was reflected in the Declaration on Friendly Relations between States (resolution 2625 (XXV) of 24 October 1970) and in the Final Act of the Helsinki Conference of 1 August 1975. It is also embodied in Article 26 of the Vienna Convention on the Law of Treaties of 23 May 1969, according to which "[e]very treaty in force is binding upon the parties to it and must be performed by them in good faith".

Nor has the Court omitted to draw attention to it, as follows:

> "One of the basic principles governing the creation and perform-

> ance of legal obligations, whatever their source, is the principle of good faith. Trust and confidence are inherent in international co-operation, in particular in an age when this co-operation in many fields is becoming increasingly essential." (*Nuclear Tests (Australia* v. *France), Judgment, I.C.J. Reports 1974*, p. 268, para. 46.)

103. In its resolution 984 (1995) dated 11 April 1995, the Security Council took care to reaffirm "the need for all States Parties to the Treaty on the Non-Proliferation of Nuclear Weapons to comply fully with all their obligations" and urged

> "all States, as provided for in Article VI of the Treaty on the Non-Proliferation of Nuclear Weapons, to pursue negotiations in good faith on effective measures relating to nuclear disarmament and on a treaty on general and complete disarmament under strict and effective international control which remains a universal goal".

The importance of fulfilling the obligation expressed in Article VI of the Treaty on the Non-Proliferation of Nuclear Weapons was also reaffirmed in the final document of the Review and Extension Conference of the parties to the Treaty on the Non-Proliferation of Nuclear Weapons, held from 17 April to 12 May 1995.

In the view of the Court, it remains without any doubt an objective of vital importance to the whole of the international community today.

* * *

104. At the end of the present Opinion, the Court emphasizes that its reply to the question put to it by the General Assembly rests on the totality of the legal grounds set forth by the Court above (paragraphs 20 to 103), each of which is to be read in the light of the others. Some of these grounds are not such as to form the object of formal conclusions in the final paragraph of the Opinion; they nevertheless retain, in the view of the Court, all their importance.

* * *

105. For these reasons,

THE COURT,

(1) By thirteen votes to one,

Decides to comply with the request for an advisory opinion;

IN FAVOUR: *President* Bedjaoui; *Vice-President* Schwebel; *Judges* Guillaume, Shahabuddeen, Weeramantry, Ranjeva, Herczegh, Shi, Fleischhauer, Koroma, Vereshchetin, Ferrari Bravo, Higgins;

AGAINST: *Judge* Oda;

(2) *Replies* in the following manner to the question put by the General Assembly:

A. Unanimously,

There is in neither customary nor conventional international law any specific authorization of the threat or use of nuclear weapons;

B. By eleven votes to three,

There is in neither customary nor conventional international law any comprehensive and universal prohibition of the threat or use of nuclear weapons as such;

IN FAVOUR: *President* Bedjaoui; *Vice-President* Schwebel; *Judges* Oda, Guillaume, Ranjeva, Herczegh, Shi, Fleischhauer, Vereshchetin, Ferrari Bravo, Higgins;

AGAINST: *Judges* Shahabuddeen, Weeramantry, Koroma;

C. Unanimously,

A threat or use of force by means of nuclear weapons that is contrary to Article 2, paragraph 4, of the United Nations Charter and that fails to meet all the requirements of Article 51, is unlawful;

D. Unanimously,

A threat or use of nuclear weapons should also be compatible with the requirements of the international law applicable in armed conflict, particularly those of the principles and rules of international humanitarian law, as well as with specific obligations under treaties and other undertakings which expressly deal with nuclear weapons;

E. By seven votes to seven, by the President's casting vote,

It follows from the above-mentioned requirements that the threat or use of nuclear weapons would generally be contrary to the rules of international law applicable in armed conflict, and in particular the principles and rules of humanitarian law;

However, in view of the current state of international law, and of the elements of fact at its disposal, the Court cannot conclude definitively whether the threat or use of nuclear weapons would be lawful or unlawful in an extreme circumstance of self-defence, in which the very survival of a State would be at stake;

IN FAVOUR: *President* Bedjaoui; *Judges* Ranjeva, Herczegh, Shi, Fleischhauer, Vereshchetin, Ferrari Bravo;

AGAINST: *Vice-President* Schwebel; *Judges* Oda, Guillaume, Shahabuddeen, Weeramantry, Koroma, Higgins;

F. Unanimously,

There exists an obligation to pursue in good faith and bring to a conclusion negotiations leading to nuclear disarmament in all its aspects under strict and effective international control.

Done in English and in French, the English text being authoritative, at the Peace Palace, The Hague, this eighth day of July, one thousand nine hundred and ninety-six, in two copies, one of which will be placed in the archives of the Court and the other transmitted to the Secretary-General of the United Nations.

(Signed) Mohammed BEDJAOUI,
President.

(Signed) Eduardo VALENCIA-OSPINA,
Registrar.

President BEDJAOUI, Judges HERCZEGH, SHI, VERESHCHETIN and FERRARI BRAVO append declarations to the Advisory Opinion of the Court.

Judges GUILLAUME, RANJEVA AND FLEISCHHAUER append separate opinions to the Advisory Opinion of the Court.

Vice-President SCHWEBEL, Judges ODA, SHAHABUDDEEN, WEERAMANTRY, KOROMA and HIGGINS append dissenting opinions to the Advisory Opinion of the Court.

(Initialled) M.B.
(Initialled) E.V.O.

D. COMMENTARY AND THESES ON THE ICJ ADVISORY OPINION

We now provide commentary on the ICJ's Advisory Opinion. First, we consider the question whether the ICJ's performance constituted an impermissible failure to decide. Then, assuming the Court did, at least in part, fail to decide the question put to it, we turn to two theses we wish to advance concerning the Court's performance. First, we want to make clear, even though the Court's opinion fails to do so explicitly, that the Court could have found a weak positive law basis in treaty law to prohibit absolutely the use of nuclear weapons. Our second thesis, however, is that the Court could have relied on natural law to declare the illegality of a policy of nuclear deterrence, but that would have forced it to reach outside the philosophical premises of most current practitioners of international law.

1. What did the ICJ Actually Decide?: The ICJ's Holdings and Question of a Non-liquet

For purposes of analysis, and as a preface to considering alternative positivist and naturalist legal pathways available to the ICJ, we will present a detailed exegesis of the Court's opinion and its reasoning to prepare the way for an assessment of the criticism that the Court's produced an impermissible and avoidable *non-liquet.*

a. What Did the ICJ Decide and Not Decide?

Having disposed of other bodies of law, it is fair to say that the ICJ rested its analysis on the *jus ad bellum* and the *jus in bello.* With respect to the *jus ad bellum,* discussing the U.N. Charter, the Court focused on two core provisions. One was Article 2(4), which enjoins all Member States to "refrain in their international relations from the threat or use of force against the territorial integrity or political independence of any State;" the other was Article 51, which preserves (but constrains) "the inherent right of individual or collective self-defense if an armed attack occurs against a Member of the United Nations." The Court observed that neither these nor any other Charter provisions "expressly prohibit[], nor permit[], the use of any specific weapon, including nuclear weapons."[81] However, if nuclear weapons were unlawful per se by treaty or customary law, their use would not become lawful "by reason of [their] being used for a legitimate purpose"—such as lawful self-defense— "under the Charter."[82]

Further, any use of weaponry—including nuclear weaponry—that purported to be a legitimate measure of self-defense under Article 51 would be subject "to the conditions of necessity

81 LTUNW, *supra* note 11, at ¶ 39.

82 *Id.*

and proportionality."[83] However, "the proportionality principle may thus not in itself exclude the use of nuclear weapons in self-defense in all circumstances."[84] The Court rebuffed the argument that the risks of escalation inherent in the use of nuclear weapons precluded any such use from satisfying the requirement of proportionality. On the other hand, it refused to accept that "tactical nuclear weapons exist which are sufficiently precise to limit those risks."[85] The Court also turned down the invitation to rule that the policy of nuclear deterrence was per se unlawful (or lawful). Observing that "States sometimes signal that they possess certain weapons to use in self-defense," the Court found that whether such signaled intentions constituted a forbidden "threat" under Article 2(4) of the Charter depended on a variety of factors. More specifically, even though "the policy of deterrence, by which those States possessing or under the umbrella of nuclear weapons seek to discourage military aggression . . . necessitates that the intention to use nuclear weapons be credible," that "threat" cannot in and of itself be said to be contrary to Article 2(4).[86] Whether or not the "threat" posed by a credible deterrence policy intended as a means of defense[87] would be permissible would depend on whether "it would necessarily violate the principles of necessity and proportionality."[88] Later, the Court confirmed that it "does not intend to pronounce here upon the practice known as the 'policy of deterrence.'"[89] This, as former Acting Legal Advisor to the U.S. Department of State Michael Matheson has noted, "is a very significant point."[90] Yet, the Court declined to give definitive answers to three other questions: whether the use of nuclear weapons would be permissible or impermissible: 1) in the context of belligerent reprisals;[91] 2) if authorized by the Security Council under its Chapter VII

83 *Id.* Subsequently, the ICJ has confirmed its view that that "necessity" and "proportionality" are requirements of the *jus ad bellum*. *See, e.g., Armed Activities on the Territory of the Congo (Democratic Republic of the Congo v. Uganda) Congo v. Uganda,* 2005 ICJ Reports 168, 315 at ¶¶ 31-34 (Dec. 19) (separate option of Judge Kooijmans); *id.* at 338 at ¶14 (separate option of Judge Simma) (available at http://www.icj-cij.org/docket/index.php?p1=3&p2=3&code=co&case=116&k=51/) . Schmitt explained the "necessity" test in the context of Article 51 as follows: "Necessity requires a State to resort to force only if there are no reasonable alternatives. While the standard is subjective, it is well accepted." He found the "proportionality" test to be disputed, and noted that the Court did not illuminate it: "The proportionality principle . . . raises the question of what is proportional to what—the armed attack to which it is responding, the danger facing the State, or the amount of force necessary to cause the offending state to desist? . . . [T]he Court elected not to address [this issue]." Schmitt, *supra* note 40, at 66.

84 LTUNW, *supra* note 11, at ¶42.

85 *Id.* at ¶ 43. The Court's reference to "tactical" nuclear weapons is one indication (among several) that it considered itself to be ruling on the legality of the use of *any type* of nuclear weapon, even miniaturized ones. *See also id.* at ¶ 89 (referring to "whatever type of weapons"); and *id.* at ¶ 94 (discussing "low yield, tactical nuclear weapons").

86 *Id.* at ¶ 48.

87 The Court here seems to be considering both individual and collective self-defense. For the background law governing these doctrines, *see* Part II, Chapters 2 and 4, *supra.*

88 *Id.* at ¶ 48.

89 *Id.* at ¶ 67; *see also id.* at ¶ 96.

90 Matheson, *supra* note 40, at 431.

91 LTUNW, *supra* note 11, at ¶ 46.

enforcement powers;[92] or 3) "by a State within its own boundaries"—as, for example, in the case of a civil war.[93]

Having addressed U.N. Charter law, the Court, in the final and most substantive parts of its opinion, then turned to *jus in bello.* Here, it first addressed "whether there are specific rules in international law regulating the legality or illegality of recourse to nuclear weapons *per se*"; second, it examined "the principles and rules of humanitarian law applicable in armed conflict, and the law of neutrality."[94] The Court's examination of the "specific rules of international law is divided into two parts: one discussing conventional or treaty law[95]; the other addressing customary international law.[96] The Court introduced its discussion of both topics by stating that neither body of law contains

> any specific prescription authorizing the threat or use of the nuclear weapon . . . in general or in . . . the exercise of legitimate self-defense. Nor, however, is there any principle or rule of international law which would make the legality of . . . nuclear weapons . . . dependent on specific authorization. State practice shows that the illegality of the use of certain weapons as such does not result from an absence of authorization but, on the contrary, is formulated in terms of prohibition.[97]

The latter sentence may provide the key to the Court's reasoning.[98] On the basis of its review of a range of treaties concerning weaponry, the Court found that states outlaw particular kinds

92 *Id.* at ¶ 49. *See Case Concerning Questions of Interpretation and Application of the 1971 Montreal Convention Arising from the Aerial Incident at Lockerbie (Libya v. U.K.,* Preliminary Objections, Judgment, 1998 ICJ Reports 9, 73–81 (Feb. 27) (Schwebel, J., dissenting); Dapo Akande, *The International Court of Justice and the Security Council: Is There Room for Judicial Control of Decisions of the Political Organs of the United Nations?,* 46 Int'l & Comp. L. Q. 309 (1997); *see also* Perez, *supra* note 32, at 435–36 & n.172 (1997) (noting arguments that the Council had authorized threat or use of nuclear weapons against Iraq in First Gulf War if Coalition had sufficient reason to believe that Iraq had nuclear capability such as to warrant deterrence).

93 LTUNW, *supra* note 11, at ¶ 50. Does the Court's decision, or rather non-decision, here leave open the possibility that China might lawfully use nuclear weapons in an effort to regain control of its "province" of Taiwan, or that nuclear weapons might lawfully be used in a war to reunite the Korean peninsula?

94 *Id.* at ¶ 51.

95 *Id.* at ¶¶ 52–63.

96 *Id.* at ¶¶ 64–73.

97 *Id.* at ¶ 52.

98 As further discussed below, some critics of the opinion have argued that it is unduly "positivistic." Is there some justice in that complaint, at least with regard to this part of the opinion? In presuming that treaties relating to weaponry or other aspects of armed conflict do not apply to nuclear weapons unless they specifically say so, is the Court not implicitly taking the view that states reserve their freedom of action in this area unless they explicitly disavow it? And is not that presumption founded on the view of state sovereignty laid down in the *Lotus* rule? Judge Ranjeva raised a similar point in questioning whether the Court was right to suggest that nuclear weapons posed an exception to the rules of armed conflict. He wrote:

> If such a [exception] must exist, it can be deduced only from the intention of the States authors of and parties to these instruments. The fact that the case of nuclear weapons was deliberately not addressed during the negotiation and conclusion

of weaponry by treaty law when the treaty prohibition is specifically addressed to that kind of weaponry. So, for example, the prohibition on the use of poisonous gas in war was accomplished by the 1925 Geneva Gas Protocol,[99] which specifically banned such weaponry.[100] Further, interpretation of the scope of a treaty prohibition is to be guided by the subsequent practice of the states that are parties to it. So, state practice under the Gas Protocol establishes that it covers "weapons whose prime, or even exclusive, effect is to poison or asphyxiate."[101] Applying this approach, the Court "does not find any specific prohibition of recourse to nuclear weapons in treaties expressly prohibiting the use of certain weapons of mass destruction."[102] Likewise, based on its survey of the treaties that do regulate nuclear weaponry in various ways (e.g., the 1968 Nuclear Non-Proliferation Treaty), the Court found that, although this body of treaty law "could . . . be seen as foreshadowing a future general prohibition by themselves," it nonetheless did not view it "as amounting to a comprehensive and universal conventional prohibition on the use, or threat of use, of those [nuclear] weapons as such."[103]

The question of whether customary law prohibited nuclear weapons as such confronted the Court with two opposing lines of state practice. On the one side, there was the longstanding practice of the nuclear states of engaging in the policy of deterrence. On the other side was "the important series of General Assembly resolutions, beginning with resolution 1653 (XVI) of 24 November 1961, that deal with nuclear weapons and that affirm, with consistent regularity, the illegality of nuclear weapons."[104] The nuclear states argued that the Court should not regard the General Assembly's repeated declarations as constituting international law, even of a customary kind; that the resolutions were also not declaratory of a customary rule of prohibition; that although large majorities of the General Assembly had voted for their adoption, they, the "specially affected" states, had opposed those resolutions;[105] and that the decades-long practice of non-

> of the major conventions on the law of armed conflict has been repeatedly stressed. Accordingly, it is difficult to see how these plenipotentiaries could envisage exceptions of such importance . . . .

LTUNW, *supra* note 11, at 302 (separate opinion of Judge Ranjeva). Which side should bear the burden of determining the scope of the treaties' coverage, and why?

99 Geneva Protocol for the Prohibition on the Use in War of Asphyxiating, Poisonous or Other Gases, and of Bacteriological Methods of Warfare, June 17, 1925, entered into force Feb. 8, 1928, *reprinted in* D. Schindler and J. Toman, The Laws of Armed Conflicts 116 (1988).

100 LTUNW, *supra* note 11, at ¶ 55.

101 *Id.* at ¶ 55.

102 *Id.* at ¶ 57.

103 *Id.* at ¶¶ 62–63.

104 *Id.* at ¶ 68.

105 The practice of states whose interests are "specially affected" may play a particularly important role in determining whether a customary norm has emerged. *See North Sea Continental Shelf Case (Federal Republic of Germany/ Netherlands),*1969 ICJ Rep. 43 (Feb. 20), at ¶ 74. In his dissent, Judge Schwebel gave great weight for this reason to the practice of nuclear deterrence as against

> otherwise adverse international opinion. This is the practice of five of the world's major Powers, of the permanent members of the Security Council, significantly supported for almost 50 years by their allies and other States sheltering under their

use of nuclear weapons did not evidence "an existing or nascent custom," but merely reflected the fact that "circumstances that might justify their use have fortunately not arisen."[106] The states arguing for illegality contended that the General Assembly's resolutions "did no more than apply to nuclear weapons the existing rules of international law applicable in armed conflict; they were no more than the 'envelope' or *instrumentum* containing pre-existing customary rules."[107]

Although the ICJ accepted that "General Assembly resolutions, even if they are not binding, may sometimes have normative value," it nonetheless concluded that the series of resolutions in question had fallen "short of establishing the existence of an *opinio juris* on the illegality of the use of [nuclear] weapons."[108] In its view, the "emergence, as *lex lata,* of a customary rule specifically prohibiting the use of nuclear weapons as such has been hampered by the continuing tensions between the nascent *opinio juris* on the one hand, and the still strong adherence to the practice of deterrence on the other."[109] Thus, the conflict between the two opposing forms of state practice precluded a finding that a prohibitive customary rule had become established.

Having reached the conclusions that neither customary nor conventional international law provides either "any specific authorization" or "any comprehensive and universal prohibition" on the threat or use if nuclear weapons,[110] the Court turned finally to "the question whether recourse to nuclear weapons must be considered as illegal in the light of principles of international humanitarian law."[111] The Court identified two "cardinal principles" of humanitarian law. The first is often called the principle of distinction: "States may never make civilians the object of attack."[112] The principle of distinction entails a corollary in the law of weaponry: the principle of discrimination, or the prohibition on the use of "weapons that are incapable of distinguishing

> nuclear umbrellas. That is to say, it is the practice of States . . . that together represent the bulk of the world's military and economic and financial and technological power and a very large proportion of its population.

LTUNW, *supra* note 11, at 311, 312 (Schwebel, J., dissenting). Judge Shahabuddeen, also dissenting, challenged that reasoning. He said,

> Where what is in issue is the lawfulness of the use of a weapon which could annihilate mankind and so destroy all States, the test of which States are specially affected turns not on the ownership of the weapon, but on the consequences of its use. From this point of view, all States are equally affected . . . .

Id. at 375, 414 (Shahabuddeen, J., dissenting); *see also id.* at 277 (declaration of Judge Shi) ("Policy of deterrence "has no legal significance from the standpoint of the formation of a customary rule prohibiting the use of nuclear weapons as such."); and *id.* at 429, 535–36 (Weeramantry, J., dissenting) ("A balanced view of the matter is that no one group of nations—nuclear or non-nuclear—can say that its interests are specially affected.").

106 *Id.* at ¶ 66.

107 *Id.* at ¶ 69.

108 *Id.* at ¶¶ 70–71.

109 *Id.* at ¶ 73.

110 *Id.* at ¶ 105.

111 *Id.* at ¶ 74. The Court also examined the question presented in light of the law of neutrality. Our readings omit that brief discussion.

112 *Id.* at ¶ 78.

between civilians and military targets."[113] The second principle relates to combatants rather than to civilians: "it is prohibited to cause unnecessary suffering to combatants."[114] This principle too has a corollary in the law of weaponry: "it is accordingly prohibited to use weapons causing [combatants] such [unnecessary] harm or uselessly aggravating their suffering."[115] Despite the fact that these principles had evolved before the invention of nuclear weapons, the Court agreed with "the vast majority of States as well as writers" that these principles applied to nuclear weapons.[116] Nonetheless, the consequences of applying the principles to nuclear weapons remained "controversial."[117] After surveying the arguments on both sides, the Court arrived at an ultimate conclusion that it asserted as not "definitive"—namely, that

> in view of the present state of international law viewed as a whole . . . and of the elements of fact at its disposal, the Court is led to observe that it cannot reach a definitive conclusion as to the legality or illegality of the use of nuclear weapons by a State in an extreme circumstance of self-defense, in which its very survival would be at stake.[118]

It should be noted that the vote on paragraph 105(2)(E), a crucial part of the *dispositif,* split evenly at seven to seven. Normally the ICJ has fifteen judges,[119] with nine constituting a quorum (so ties are normally impossible).[120] Owing to the death of the fifteenth judge, however, the Court had only fourteen members when the opinion was delivered. In that case, the Court's statute provides that the President (or acting President) of the Court "shall have a casting vote."[121] Thus, President Bedjaoui cast a (second) vote in favor.[122]

b. Was the Opinion an Impermissible *Non-liquet*?

We consider, first, whether the Court expressly or by implication produced a *non-liquet*, which in turn depends on the meaning of the term. We next consider whether a *non-liquet* was permissible in the context in which the Court operated.

---

113 *Id.*

114 *Id.*

115 *Id.*

116 *Id.* at ¶¶ 85–86.

117 *Id.* at ¶ 90.

118 *Id.* at ¶ 97.

119 *See* 1945 Statute of the IJC, *supra* note 21, art. 3(1).

120 *Id.* at art. 25(3).

121 *Id.* at art. 55(2).

122 *See* Falk, *supra* note 46, at 64.

We direct the reader's initial attention to two significant parts of the opinion that occurred not long before the Court's conclusion was announced. First, in paragraph 94, the Court considered an argument by the nuclear states that the "'clean' use of smaller, low yield, tactical nuclear weapons" should be held to be lawful. The Court found itself unable to reach that conclusion because those states had not shown "what, supposing such limited use were feasible, would be the precise circumstances justifying such use; nor whether such limited use would not tend to escalate into the all-out use of high yield nuclear weapons."[123] Second, in paragraph 95, the Court observed that "[i]n view of the unique characteristics of nuclear weapons," their use "seems scarcely reconcilable" with the requirements of humanitarian law. In almost the same breath, however, the Court found itself unable to say "with certainty" the use of nuclear weapons would "necessarily" violate humanitarian law "in any circumstance." Further, in paragraph 96, the Court said that it "[could not] lose sight of the fundamental right of every State to survival, and thus its right to resort to self-defense, in accordance with Art. 51 of the Charter, when its survival is at stake." Finally, the coda to the Court's opinion concerned the Non-Proliferation Treaty.[124] The Court called attention to Article VI of that treaty, which imposes on all parties a duty, among things, to "pursue negotiations in good faith . . . on a treaty on general and complete disarmament under strict and effective international control"; and, as though to implore states to make a political decision to prioritize nuclear disarmament, it described fulfillment of that treaty obligation "an objective of vital importance to the whole of the international community today."[125] Thus, in light of the Court's express refusal to opine, and its arguable substitution of political appeal for legal guidance, some of the judges and many, perhaps even most, of the scholarly commentators on the *General Assembly Advisory Opinion* seem to have been persuaded that in a crucial part of its *dispositif*, paragraph 105(2)E, the ICJ arrived at a *non-liquet* ("not clear") judgment—meaning, effectively, that it was unable, or unwilling, to say what the law was.[126]

---

123 LTUNW, *supra* note 11, at ¶ 94. The Scottish Appeal Court in the *Zelter* case, *supra* note 47, takes the ICJ's opinion to be concerned only with "weapons of mass destruction, potentially catastrophic in their destructive potential, with the capacity to cause untold human suffering and the ability to cause damage, including genetic defects and illness, for generations to come." *Id.*at ¶ 71. The Scottish Court therefore seemed to conclude that the ICJ's judgments do not concern "an identifiable and distinct class of small scale or tactical nuclear weapons," so that "[t]he question of whether weapons capable of mass destruction can be used on a small scale, or tactically, or in some other limited way, is another matter ...." *Id.* We are uncertain whether the Scottish Court is saying that the ICJ's advisory opinion does not extend to "small scale or tactical nuclear weapons" or that the advisory opinion does not consider whether large-scale nuclear weapons ("weapons of mass destruction") might be used "tactically," so that their destructive effect are limited.

124 *Id.* at. ¶¶ 98–103.

125 *Id.* at ¶ 103.

126 Judge Simma has subsequently written that the concept of *non liquet* "concerns a judicial institution being unable to pronounce itself on a point of law because it concludes that the law is not clear." *Accordance with International Law of the Unilateral Declaration of Independence in Respect of Kosovo, Advisory Opinion,* 2010 ICJ. Rep., at ¶ 9 (July 22) [hereinafter *Unilateral Declaration of Independence in Kosovo*] (declaration of Judge Simma). He distinguished non liquet, so understood, from the situation in which "the international legal order might be consciously silent or neutral on a specific fact or act." *Id.* The situations Judge Simma contrasts are apparently one in which the law is "not clear" and another in which the law is "consciously silent or neutral." It appears that most of the commentators who understand the LTUNW Court's conclusion in ¶ 105(2)(E) to be *non liquet* take it to be the first rather than the second type of situation.

Yet, it is hard to imagine a more evenly divided, and uncertain, result. Accordingly, commentators have analyzed the split vote in light of the individual opinions of the judges,[127] and have drawn different inferences from their analyses.[128] At the outset, it should be noted that the concept of a *non-liquet* is subject to varying interpretations; there is, indeed, extensive scholarly literature on the subject.[129] At a threshold, it might be questioned whether the concept even applies at all to advisory opinions, in which no precise set of facts and claims exist, rather than a contentious case, which would avoid the question entirely.[130] However, at least one, highly

---

Judge Simma's reference to a court's "being unable to pronounce itself on a point of law" introduces another complication. Did the LTUNW Court conclude that it was institutionally incapable of giving a definitive answer to the General Assembly's question (even if such an answer could, in principle, be given)? In other words, was it suggesting that a judicial resolution of the legal question was not possible (or prudent), although a *political* resolution of the legal question might be? Or was it instead signifying its belief that a "gap" in the law existed, at least at present—so that no institution could give a definitive answer?

127 On the various forms in which the judges of the ICJ may cast their individual opinions ("declarations," "separate opinions, " "dissents"), *see* Farrock Jhabvala, *Declarations by Judges of the International Court of Justice*, 72 Am. J. Int'l L. 830 (1978).

128 Judges Bedjaoui, Ranjeva, Herczegh, Shi, Fleischhauer, Vereshchetin, and Ferrari Bravo voted in favor of para. 105(2) (E); Judges Schwebel, Oda, Guillaume, Shahabudden, Weeramantry, Koroma and Higgins voted against. Each judge also wrote an individual opinion, variously styled "Declaration," "Separate Opinion" or "Dissenting Opinion."

One of the major enigmas in the opinion is how to interpret the split vote. As noted, commentators read the outcome differently in light of their understanding of the individual opinions. According to Michael Matheson,

> the opinions of at least six judges (including at least two of those concurring in the Court's opinion) seem to take the view that there are indeed circumstances in which the use of nuclear weapons would not be unlawful, and the opinions of several others do not give a clear indication of their view on this question. Only three judges clearly expressed the contrary conclusion that all uses of nuclear weapons would be unlawful.

Matheson, *supra* note 40, at 433. Richard Falk analyzed the outcome very differently. He asked:

> Does [the vote] suggest a 50:50 split with respect to legality? Not really. If the decision is read as in important respects constraining the discretion of states to threaten to use or use nuclear weapons, the three dissenting judges who believe that nuclear weapons are categorically illegal can be counted as part of the majority, creating a ten-to-four vote. Furthermore, the arguments of the seven judges who dissented (counting Judge Gilbert Guillaume's "individual opinion" as a dissent) lack any internal coherence, and only Judges Stephen Schwebel, Higgins and Guillaume gave support to the claim of the nuclear weapons states that, although international law applies, it does so only in the context of an actual threat or use of nuclear weapons.

Falk, *supra* note 46, at 67. Dapo Akande's analysis found that "whilst 4 judges explicitly endorsed the legality of some uses of nuclear weapons, 6 judges, in their opinion, supported the view that all uses would be unlawful. If one adds to this the fact that the tenor of Judge Bedjaoui's opinion is generally against legality in any circumstance, the number is 7–4 (with three wavering) against legality in any circumstances." Akande, *supra* note 46, at 168 n. 6. And Michael Schmitt wrote:

> On the legality issue alone (self-defense aside) . . . the 'actual' vote was 10-3-1. . . . [R]educed to common cores of understandings, all judges agreed that it would be quite difficult to employ nuclear weapons in a fashion consistent with international law, seven would preclude use in any but situations of self-defense involving the survival of the State (and maybe not even then), and three would find use unlawful in any circumstances.

Schmitt, *supra* note 40, at 77.

129 Articles and book chapters primarily on this aspect of the LTUNW case include: David Bodansky, *Non Liquet and the Incompleteness of International Law, in* International Law, The International Court of Justice and Nuclear Weapons 153 (Laurence Boisson de Chazournes & Philippe Sands eds., 1999.); Thomas M. Franck, *Fairness and the General Assembly Advisory Opinion, in* International Law, The International Court of Justice and Nuclear Weapons 511 (Laurence Boisson de Chazournes & Philippe Sands eds., 1999); Iain G.M. Scobbie, *The Theorist as Judge: Hersch Lauterpacht's Concept of the International Judicial Function,* 2 Eur. J. Int'l L. 264, 285–91 (1997); Prosper Weil, *"The Court Cannot Definitively . . ." Non Liquet Revisited,* 36 Colum. J. Transnat'l L. 109 (1998).

130 *See* LTUNW, *supra* note 11, at 311, 322–23 (Schwebel, J., dissenting). *See also* Weil, *supra* note 129, at 116–18 (discussed below); *see* Perez, *supra* note 32, at 433–34 (arguing that, because law is meaningful on precise sets of facts, which are not presented in advisory opinions, the *non-liquet* concept is inapposite).

influential member of the Court, Judge Higgins, argued forcefully and unambiguously against the Court's opinion on the ground that it was an impermissible *non-liquet*,[131] even if a majority of its members disagreed.[132]

The issue thus merits substantial attention. Yet, explicating the meaning of *non-liquet* may well require an examination of the underlying theory of international law, rather than merely a technical analysis of the Court's advisory opinion authorities and practice. In perhaps the most important and influential essay on the subject, Prosper Weil distinguished between two views: first, that international law is a "closed" or "logically complete" system; second, that though international law is not "closed" and may therefore contain "gaps," it also "has built-in mechanisms to fill these gaps automatically."[133] The view that law is a "closed" system is associated with legal scholars such as Ronald Dworkin, whose idealized judicial "Hercules" is able to provide a legally correct answer to any question of law presented to him.[134] (Among international lawyers, Hans Kelsen also espoused this view.[135]) On this approach, "[t]he completeness of the system does not only exist *de facto* but *de jure*. Gaps are regarded as logically impossible because of the very structure of the system."[136] The alternative view described by Weil holds it that law (or at least international law), though it may include "gaps," develops at the hands of judges in such a way that any "gaps are doomed to wane."[137] Judges routinely develop law by interpreting existing rules, extrapolating from or distinguishing precedents, concretizing abstract principles, and in other ways. There are also, Weil argued, "two self-curative methods specific to the international legal system"—namely, "recourse to general principles of law and recourse to equity."[138]

Weil traced the view that international law is a perfectly "closed" system back to the doctrine of *The Lotus* case. The "starting point" of the view that the international legal order is closed is

> the sovereignty of states. International law exists only to limit the states' inherent freedom of action. States, thus, are obliged to act only insofar as there exists a prescriptive rule, and they are

131 *See* LTUNW, *supra* note 11, at 591 at ¶ 36 (Higgins, J., dissenting) ("It is also, I think, an important and well-established principle that the concept of *non liquet*—for that is what we have here—is no part of the Court's jurisprudence.").

132 *See* Perez, *supra* note 32, at 433 ("It is not clear, however, that the ICJ's formulation was in fact a *non-liquet*, at least in the sense of a gap in the law leaving the ICJ no choice but to abstain."); and *id.* at 432 ("That the ICJ's non-decision was a *non-liquet* was a distinctly minority view [on the Court].").

133 Weil, *supra* note 129, at 110.

134 *See, e.g.*, Ronald Dworkin, *Hard Cases*, 88 Harv. L. Rev. 1057, 1083 (1975). Presumably, if Judge Simma is right, Dworkin must be wrong, at least as to international law— for on Simma's view, international law may be *consciously silent* on a given question.

135 *See* Hans Kelsen, Principles of International Law 438–39 (1966).

136 Weil, *supra* note 129, at 112.

137 Id. at 110.

138 *Id.* Both general principles of law and equity are recognized as sources of international law in Article 38 of the Statute of the International Court of Justice.

obliged not to act only if there exists a prohibitive rule. Without any prescriptive or prohibitive rule, states may act as they want, unfettered by law.[139]

And that, he said, "is, in a nutshell, the doctrine of the celebrated *Lotus* judgment."[140] Weil argued that in several of its cases, the ICJ appeared to have adopted the view that international law is closed, and accordingly "tipped the balance in favor of the *Lotus* approach."[141] For instance, in the *Nicaragua* Case, the Court had said that "in international law there are no rules, other than rules as may be accepted by the State concerned, by treaty or otherwise, whereby the level of armaments of a sovereign State can be limited."[142] More recently, in its 2010 decision in the *Kosovo Declaration of Independence* case, the ICJ concluded that Kosovo's declaration of independence "did not violate any applicable rule of international law"[143]—leading Judge Simma to lament that the Court had upheld the *Lotus* principle.[144]

Weil disagreed with the view that the international legal order is closed, and accordingly believed there is a place for *non-liquet* in the ICJ's jurisprudence. But, he distinguished between the Court's contentious cases and its advisory opinions. In contentious cases, the states that are parties to an international dispute look to the Court to resolve their disagreement. Having voluntarily consented to the jurisdiction on the Court, the states involved have a right to expect the Court to exercise the authority they have granted to it—in other words, to settle the dispute.[145] Even if the existing law on the point in dispute is unclear, the disputants can be understood to have agreed to confer on the Court "the normative and quasi-legislative power" to develop the law in a fashion that will resolve their dispute.[146] But "[a] quite different situation is presented when the I.C.J. is called up to give an advisory opinion."[147] There the function of the Court is not to resolve a disagreement between states but to offer legal advice to an organ of the United Nations. The Court has no duty to resolve the question presented to it; it may be appropriate for the Court, even as it agrees to provide advice on the question, to respond that in the present

139 *Id.* at 112.

140 *Id.*

141 *Id.* at 113.

142 *Military and Paramilitary Activities in and against Nicaragua (Nicaragua v. United States)*, 1986 ICJ 14, 135 (June 27). *See also* the discussion in LTUNW, *supra* note 11, at 287, 291–92 (separate opinion of Judge Guillaume) (defending the *Lotus* rule and citing *Nicaragua* in its support).

143 *Unilateral Declaration of Independence in Kosovo, supra* note 126, at ¶ 122.

144 *Id.* at ¶ 2 (Declaration of Judge Simma).

145 In this respect, the adjudication of a contentious case between states resembles arbitration practice. *See Island of Palmas Case (United States v. Netherlands.)*, 2 Rpt. Int'l Arbitral Awards 829, 869 (1928). In that celebrated decision, the arbitrator, Max Huber, observed that it was the "evident will" of the disputants to terminate the dispute and avoid *non liquet*. *See also* LTUNW, *supra* note 11, at 575–76 (Koroma, J., dissenting) (citing arbitral practice and arguing that ICJ jurisprudence has followed it).

146 Weil, *supra* note 129, at 115.

147 *Id.* at 116.

stage of international law's development, there is simply no answer, or no complete answer, to that question. The matter is therefore not one of judicial or institutional infirmity; the Court does answer the legal question posed. Rather, the deficiency is in the law, which the Court found, in its present state, to be unsettled or unclear.[148]

Weil believed that, "[r]ight or wrong, *non liquet* was the court's main answer in its [General Assembly Advisory Opinion]."[149] Consequently, he argued that the Court in that case chose not to draw on the *Lotus* principle and did not imply a permissive rule from the absence of a prohibitive one. The Court was, so to say, adopting a three-valued, rather than a two-valued, deontic logic: the use of nuclear weapons, even in legitimate self-defense when the survival of a state was at stake, was neither permitted nor forbidden, but legally neutral.[150] Because no norm —permissive or prohibitive—had emerged from international law's norm-creating process, there was "simply no legal truth."[151] Thus, if it was a *non-liquet*, it was not an impermissible *non-liquet*. In short, the Court was not, as many of its critics contended, acting as a political court. Rather, it was properly exercising its discretion not to legislate based on systemic default rules.

Although some judges noted the issue but failed to express a view,[152] a close reading of several the Court's individual opinions in light of Weil's analysis sheds significant light on the Court's understanding of the task it faced and the conclusions it drew, tending to support Weil's assessment. President Bedjaoui, for one, specifically cautioned against interpreting that ruling "as contemplating the possibility of States using nuclear weapons in exceptional circumstances."[153] Distinguishing and criticizing the rule of the *Lotus* case, he wrote:

> In 1927, the Permanent Court, when considering a much less important question, in fact concluded that behavior not expressly prohibited by international law was authorized by that fact alone. In the present Opinion, on the contrary, the Court does not find the threat or use of nuclear weapons to be either legal or illegal; from the uncertainties surrounding the law and the facts it does not infer any freedom to take a position. Nor does it suggest that such license could in any way whatever be deduced therefrom. Whereas the Permanent Court gave the green light

---

148 One notable commentator takes exactly the opposite view:

> [E]ven though judicial prudence is a political virtue, there seems to be more room for its exercise in contentious cases than in the advisory role of the Court. The Court seems to get things backwards. Parties to a dispute may have a legal right to obtain an adjudicative resolution from the Court, but advisory opinions should be assessed in terms of the possibility of an actual contribution to an international problem or dispute.

Kahn, *supra* note 16, at 365.

149 Weil, *supra* note 129, at 117.

150 For discussion of this possibility, *see* Scobbie, *supra* 129, at 288–89.

151 Weil, *supra* note 129, at 119.

152 Not all of the judges expressed an opinion on this matter. *See, e.g.,* LTUNW, *supra* note 11, at 330, 373–74 (Oda, J., dissenting); *Id.* at 375, 389 (Shahabudeen, J., dissenting) (suggesting uncertainty as to whether the Court reached a *non liquet* conclusion); *see also id.* at 426.

153 *Id.* at 268, 270 at ¶ 10 (declaration of President Bedjaoui).

of authorization, having found in international law no reason for giving the red light of prohibition, the present Court does not feel able to give a signal either way.[154]

Given President Judge Bedjaoui's critical role in tipping the balance of the Court towards equipoise, his refusal to "legislate" to "close the gap" in international law was particularly significant.

Judge Vereshchetin also believed that paragraph 105(2)(E) represented a *non-liquet*, a result he considered permissible in an advisory opinion. He discussed the view that the international legal order was "complete" and that the Court should therefore never reach a *non-liquet*; the view that, even if there were "gaps" in the legal order, the Court should close them; and the view that *non-liquet* was permissible. He observed that this debate predominantly, if not exclusively, related to contentious cases. And he noted that in this case, the Court had been asked for an advisory opinion. Further, it had not been asked to fill any "gaps" in the law. Indeed, several states had specifically asked it not to act legislatively. Finally, he argued that even if the Court had been invited to act legislatively, it should not, in an advisory opinion, have done so:

> Even had the Court been asked to fill the gaps, it would have had to refuse to assume the burden of law-creation, which in general should not be the function of the Court. In advisory procedure, where the Court finds a lacuna in the law or finds the law to be imperfect, it ought merely to state this without trying to fill the lacuna or improve the law by way of judicial legislation. The Court cannot be blamed for indecisiveness or evasiveness where the law, upon which it is called to pronounce, is itself inconclusive. Even less warranted would be any allegation of the Court's indecisiveness or evasiveness in this particular Opinion, which gives an unequivocal, albeit non-exhaustive, answer to the question put to the Court.[155]

Vereshchetin thus argued that states, not the Court, had the obligation to remedy the incompleteness of the law. He said,

> [T]he construction of the solid edifice for the total prohibition on the use of nuclear weapons is not yet complete. This, however, is not because of the lack of building materials, but rather because of the unwillingness and objections of a sizeable number of the builders of this edifice. If this future edifice is to withstand the test of time and the vagaries of the international climate, it is the States themselves—rather than the Court with its limited building resources—that must shoulder the burden of bringing the construction process to completion.[156]

154 *Id.* at 271 at ¶ 14 (declaration of President Bedjaoui) (footnote omitted).

155 *Id.* at 279–80 (declaration of Judge Vereshchetin).

156 *Id.* at 279, 281 (declaration of Judge Vereshchetin).

Justice Guillaume's analysis, albeit in dissent, indirectly supports Judge Vereshchetin's reading of paragraph 105(2)(E). As an outspoken defender of the *Lotus* rule, he consequently was committed to viewing the international legal order as "closed" or "complete." Consistently with those views, he criticized the Court for concluding that in the extreme circumstances envisaged in paragraph 2E, it could not say definitively whether the threat or use of nuclear weapons was lawful or unlawful. "In other words, it concluded that in such circumstances the law provided no guide for States. But if the law is silent in this case, States remain free to act as they intend."[157] Implicitly, like Vereshchetin, he saw the need for states, rather than the Court, to legislate.

Judge Fleischauer's maintained that the international legal order was incomplete because it had not developed any higher-order principle or rule for ranking the competing claims of humanitarian law and the law of self-defense:

> To end the matter with the simple statement that recourse to nuclear weapons would be contrary to . . . humanitarian law, would have meant that . . . humanitarian law, was given precedence over the inherent right of individual or collective self-defense which every State possesses as a matter of sovereign equality and which is expressly preserved in Article 51 of the Charter. . . . [T]he denial of the recourse to the threat or use of nuclear weapons as a legal option in any circumstances could amount to a denial of self-defense itself if such recourse was the last available means by way of which the victimized State could exercise its rights under Article 51 of the Charter. A finding that amounted to such a denial would not, in my view, have been a correct statement of the law: there is no rule in international law according to which one of the conflicting principles would prevail over the other. . . . The principles and rules of humanitarian law and . . . the inherent right of self-defense, which are through the very existence of the nuclear weapon in sharp opposition to each other, are all principles and rules of law. . . . [T]hey are of equal rank and they can be altered by law. They are justiciable. Yet international law has so far not developed . . . a norm on how these principles can be reconciled in the face of the nuclear weapon. . . . [T]here is no rule giving prevalence of one over the other. . . .[158]

In short, Judge Fleischhauer implicitly underscored Weil's three-cornered conception of international law, as well as Judge Vereshchetin's call for legislation by states rather than the ICJ to "alter by law" to fill in the gap left by competing principles.

On the other hand, the views of two (and perhaps three) dissenting judges found the Court's posture indefensible. In her forceful dissent, Judge Higgins, in reference to paragraph 105(2), wrote "[t]hat the formula chosen is a *non liquet* cannot be doubted."[159] But then she added that it was "an important and well-established principle that the concept of *non liquet*—for that is

157 *Id.* at 287, 291 at ¶ 9 (separate opinion of Judge Guillaume).

158 *Id.* at 305, 306 at ¶ 3, 308 at ¶ 4 (separate opinion of Judge Fleischhauer).

159 *Id.* at 583, 590 at ¶ 30 (Higgins, J., dissenting).

what we have here—is no part of the Court's jurisprudence."[160] Elaborating on that claim (and responding, perhaps, to Judges Vereshchetin and Fleischhauer), she argued:

> It is exactly the judicial function to take principles of general application, to elaborate their meaning and to apply them to specific situations. This is precisely the role of the International Court, whether in contentious proceedings or in its advisory function. . . . Even were there . . . an 'antinomy' [in the law] . . . the judge's role is precisely to decide which of two or more competing norms is applicable in the particular circumstances.[161]

Also dissenting, Judge Schwebel similarly interpreted the result in paragraph 105(2)(E) as a *non-liquet.* He called this "an astounding conclusion." He then observed that

> the Court conclude[d] on the supreme issue of the threat or use of force of our age it has no opinion. In "an extreme circumstance of self-defense, in which the very survival of a State would be at stake," the Court [found] that international law and hence the Court have nothing to say. After many months of agonizing appraisal of the law, the Court discover[ed] that there is none.[162]

But Judge Schwebel's primary line of argument was, rather than that the Court should fill in a gap, that there was no gap at all. He contended, instead, that the answer should have been that international law does contemplate circumstances, admittedly extreme circumstances, in which nuclear weapons may be used.[163] Finally, Judge Koroma, albeit with some uncertainty, also interpreted the Court's ruling in 2E as an (impermissible) *non liquet.* But he too rejected the notion that there was a gap, observing:

> [T]he court's findings could be construed as suggesting either that there is a gap, a lacuna, in the existing law or that the Court is unable to reach a definitive conclusion on the matter because that law is imprecise or its content insufficient or that it simply does not exist. It does not appear to me any new principles are needed for a determination of the matter to be made. All that was requested of the Court was to apply the existing law. A finding of *non liquet* is wholly unfounded in the present case.[164]

---

160 *Id.* at 583, 591 at ¶ 36 (Higgins, J., dissenting).

161 *Id.* at 583, 591 at ¶ 32, 592 at ¶ 40 (Higgins, J., dissenting). Note that Judge Higgins' conception of the judicial role assumes that there may be "gaps" in the law, but that if so, the courts have a duty to fill them as cases arise.

162 *Id.* at 311, 322 (Schwebel, J., dissenting).

163 *See supra* notes 64–66 (accompanying study questions 4 and 5).

164 *Id.* at 556, 558 (Koroma, J., dissenting); *see also id.* at 559.

In sum, at least some share of the dissenters' objections was a disagreement with the proposition that there was a gap in international law. Thus, the dissenters, with the possible exception of Judge Higgins, did not directly rebut Weil's claim that international law is an open system subject to closure by the exercise of judicial discretion, and that the ICJ's exercise of its discretion not to legislate in this matter was not improper.

Let us assume, however, that in this crucial part of its judgment, paragraph 105(2)(E), the Court did indeed reach a *non-liquet* conclusion (in the strong the sense of finding a gap in the law it was incapable of resolving, rather in the weak sense of a gap it could resolve but had simply exercised discretion not to resolve). We invite students to reflect on this fundamental question: If the international legal order at this moment gives no answer to the question whether the use of nuclear weapons would be lawful or unlawful in an extreme case of legitimate self-defense when a state's survival is at stake, why should that be so?

Now, we advance two arguments that are related to, but different, from Weil's position: first, under a positive law theory of international law, the Court could have reached a somewhat strained conclusion that that there was absolute prohibition; second, the Court could have reached the same conclusion more directly on natural law grounds.

2. Thesis One: The Court Could Have Based an Absolute Prohibition on the Use of Nuclear Weapons on Treaty Law

In his dissenting opinion, Judge Koroma faulted the Court for its "extreme positivism." In particular, he objected that the Court had engaged in "a futile quest for [a] specific legal prohibition [in conventional or treaty law that] can only be attributable to an extreme form of positivism, which is out of keeping with the international jurisprudence."[165] But is that so? Here we consider two possible "positivist" arguments, both based squarely on treaty law, that could have led the Court to affirm that conventional law—albeit not in express terms—imposed a universal prohibition on the use of nuclear weapons. The first argument is based on the Geneva Gas Protocol of 1925; the second on the NPT.

a. The Geneva Gas Protocol

In his lengthy and powerful dissent, Judge Weeramantry argued that the Geneva Gas Protocol of 1925 would prohibit the use of nuclear weapons in war.[166]

165 *Id.* at 575 (Koroma, J., dissenting).

166 *Id.* at 508-12 (Weeramantry, J, dissenting).

To begin with, the Geneva Gas Protocol was drafted in sweeping terms.[167] It prohibits "the use in war of asphyxiating, poisonous, or other gases, and of all analogous liquids, materials or devices." The treaty does not, however, specify the meaning of "analogous materials or devices." Relying on the "clear" practice of states, the Court found that the parties to the Protocol had not treated it as covering nuclear weapons.[168] Judge Weeramantry argued, however, that the Geneva Gas Protocol's text left ambiguity to be resolved by the subsequent practice of states. He argued that that "poison" is generally defined as a "substance which, of its own force, damages health on contact with or absorption by the body"; that the effects of the radiation caused by a nuclear detonation has the same effects and symptoms as "poison" in that definition; that such "radiation" is also a "substance" or (in the Gas Protocol's terms) a "material," rather than merely a ray or light or other such insubstantial thing; and thus that radiation involves contact of the body with damaging "materials." In any case, he argued, it is also a "device." Thus, he considered it "irrefutable" that "nuclear weapons are covered by the Geneva Gas Protocol.[169]

Weeramantry's reasoning tracked an argument originally advanced in 1958 by a leading British legal scholar, Georg Schwarzenberger, in the following form:

> If it could be established that the use of all nuclear weapons involved necessarily the discharge of gases enumerated in the Protocol, it would settle matters conclusively between the Parties to the Protocol. Even if this were not so, the words "all analogous liquids, materials or devices" are so comprehensively phrased as to include any weapons of an analogous character, irrespective of whether they were known or in use at the time of the signature of the Protocol. If the radiation and fall-out effects of nuclear weapons can be likened to poison, all the more can they be likened to poison gas which is but an even more closely analogous species of the genus "poison." For the same reason, the prohibitions of chemical and bacteriological warfare contained in the Protocol must be taken to be merely declaratory of international customary law and equally binding on all States. It, then, becomes irrelevant whether any particular State is a party to the Geneva Protocol of 1925.[170]

Effectively, then, Judge Weeramantry adopted Schwarzenberger's argument that nuclear radiation is a "material" or "device" that is "analogous" to a "poisonous gas." In response to the United

167 The Protocol grew out of earlier treaties, including the Treaty of Versailles and the (unratified) Treaty on Submarine and Gas Warfare, relating to poisonous gas. *See* R.R. Baxter & Thomas Buergenthal, *Legal Aspects of the Geneva Protocol of 1925,* 64 Am. J. Int'l L. 853, 857–61 (1970).

168 *See* LTUNW, *supra* note 11, at ¶ 55. Although the Court did not cite it, reliance on the subsequent practice of state parties to a treaty may be relevant to its interpretation. *See* Vienna Convention on the Law of Treaties, art. 31(3)(b), 1155 U.N.T.S. 331 (entered into force Jan. 27, 1980) [hereinafter VCLT].

169 *See* LTUNW, *supra* note 11, at 511 (Weeramantry, J, dissenting).

170 Schwarzenberger, *supra* note 44, at 38. *See also* Meyrowitz, *Legal Status of Nuclear Weapons, supra* note 44, at 126–28. Others have advanced similar arguments. *See, e.g.,* Jill M. Sheldon, *Nuclear Weapons and the Laws of War: Does Customary International Law Prohibit the Use of Nuclear Weapons in All Circumstances?,* 20 Fordham Int'l L. J. 181, 244–45 (1996/97).

States' argument that the Gas Protocol was not intended to apply to weapons that merely produced asphyxiating or poisonous byproducts, Weeramantry contended that if radiation is a major byproduct of the use of a nuclear weapon, then no exception from the Gas Protocol can be claimed for it. The known and foreseeable effects of the major byproducts of the nuclear weapon render it illegal under the Protocol, even if it would be compliant with the Protocol in their absence.[171] The broad language of the prohibition, which extends to "all analogous liquids, materials or devices," indicates that the Protocol was intended to apply to kinds of weaponry that were not yet in existence when the Protocol was adopted, including arguably nuclear weapons. Furthermore, to the extent that the dispute over the application of the Protocol turns on whether nuclear radiation is "analogous" to a poisonous or asphyxiating gas, Judge Weeramantry might also have invoked the Martens Clause as a rule of construction that favors disambiguation of a treaty's terms to accord with the Protocol's humanitarian purposes.[172]

Judge Weeramantry's argument is not, of course, free from doubt. One author argued that because radiation is neither a solid, a liquid, or a gas, it cannot be understood to be either a "poisonous gas" in itself nor even an "analogous" liquid, material, or device.[173] He added it has that radioactive fallout is also not within those terms, noting that, although early radioactive fallout results in the exposure of the body to gamma rays or beta burns, the major effects of these types of radiation on the body are dissimilar to those of poison or poison gas.[174] The same author conceded, however, that "nuclear radiation does cause certain internal reactions within the body which are similar to poisoning."[175] It is true, as Paul Kahn wrote, that the effects of nuclear weapons are radically different in scale from the effects of poison gas.[176] Indeed, Kahn contended that "[i]f nuclear weapons are illegal, it cannot be because the world just happened to be lucky enough to have hit upon the right language in a conventional treaty arrangement prior to their invention."[177] But the

171 *See* LTUNW, *supra* note 11.

172 *See* Antonio Cassese, *The Martens Clause: Half a Loaf or Simply Pie in the Sky?*, 11 Eur. J. Int'l L. 187, 212 (2000) (Martens Clause "may serve as fundamental guidance in the interpretation of international customary or treaty rules. In case of doubt, international rules, in particular rules belonging to humanitarian law, must be construed so as to be consonant with general standards of humanity and the demands of public conscience"). For further discussion of the Martens Clause, *see supra* Chapter 1.B.

173 For an opposing view, *see* Capt. Fred Bright, Jr., *Nuclear Weapons as a Lawful Means of Warfare,* 30 Mil. L. Rev. 1, 20 (1965).

174 *Id.*

175 *Id.* at 21.

176 Thus, Kahn is on stronger ground when he argued that

> [t]here is a difference in kind between mustard gas in the trenches of the First World War and mutual assured destruction. Warfare has moved from a limited instrument of state policy to a decision about the meaning and shape of history. . . . The conditions for the continuation of civilization did not just happen to be legally regulated in prior considerations of appropriate conduct on the battlefield. . . . [T]he search for a legal instrument's meaning cannot go forward independently of the context of its application. Principles are not abstractions that rule blindly.

Kahn, *supra* note 16, at 387–88.

177 *Id.* at 387.

framers of the Geneva Gas Protocol designed it to reach forward into the future, banning hitherto-uninvented weaponry that was sufficiently "analogous" to the poison gas used in the First World War. If the language they used covers radioactive weaponry, that would not be a mere fluke.

Judge Weeramantry's argument would not support an absolute ban, moreover. The Geneva Gas Protocol permits two reservations: one that would allow a state party to agree to be bound only in relation to other states that were parties, and the second of which would allow the release of a state party from its obligations if an enemy states used gas warfare against it. For that reason, the Gas Protocol has become known as a "no first use agreement."[178] Because the major nuclear states have made such reservations,[179] even if the Gas Protocol extended to nuclear weapons, it would at best ban only their first use. In sum, the highly technical nature of this positivist argument leaves it open to similarly technical limitations.

b. The Non-Proliferation Treaty

We have thus far neglected what the (unanimous) Court seemed to regard as an important part of the *dispositif*: paragraph 105(2)(F), which states that "[t]here exists an obligation to pursue in good faith and bring to a conclusion negotiations leading to nuclear disarmament in all its aspects under strict and effective international control." In the body of its opinion, the Court rested that statement on Article VI of the Non-Proliferation Treaty (NPT), which it read to create a legal obligation "to achieve a precise result—nuclear disarmament in all its aspects.[180]

Could the Court have based a prohibition on the use of nuclear weapons on the obligations created by the NPT? Timothy McCormack, in making this argument, begins with the premise that the NPT was "an interim agreement between [the nuclear-armed] States on complete nuclear disarmament."[181] But from the fact that the non-nuclear weapon states (NNWS) have accepted the right of the nuclear weapon states (NWS) to possess nuclear weapons on an interim basis, it does not follow that they have also accorded the latter states the right to use them in that period. Rather, the right of the nuclear-armed states to retain possession of their weaponry is merely a realistic concession to the fact that unilateral disarmament would be likely to be neither feasible nor desirable. The structure of the NPT

178 *See, e.g.*, Richard M. Price, The Chemical Weapons Taboo 95 (1977).

179 Edward M. Spiers, A History of Chemical and Biological Weapons 50–51 (2010). Among the parties with reservations are the nuclear-armed states of France, India, Israel, Russia, the United Kingdom, and the United States. The People's Republic of China issued a statement in 1952 in which it said that it considered itself bound on condition of reciprocity by all other parties. *See* Geneva Protocol Reservations, Stockholm International Peace Research Institute (*available at* http://archives.sipri.org/contents/expcon/cbwarfare/cbw__research__dov/cbw__historical).

180 *See* LTUNW, *supra* note 11, at 264 at ¶ 99. (We have analyzed the NPT in detail in Chapter 2.B above. We also have discussed the PSAs and NSAs recognized in Security Council Resolution 984, made in connection with the indefinite extension of the NPT in 1995. *See supra* note 68 (discussing question 7)).

181 *See* McCormack, *supra* note 46.

presupposes that the parties accepted the possession of nuclear weapons by the five nuclear-weapon states as a fact. The compromise reached in the treaty was for the [NNWS] Parties to forego the right to develop, acquire, stockpile, test and use nuclear weapons in exchange for access to nuclear technology for peaceful purposes and for the obligation of the [NWS] to negotiate in good faith for the elimination of their nuclear-weapon stockpiles. . . . [NWS] have not taken this obligation seriously. . . . The preamble and entire text of the NPT show that its purpose is to prevent the horizontal spread of nuclear weapons and to achieve their eventual elimination. Thus, the vast vertical proliferation among the [NWS] is in clear disregard for the objects and purposes of the treaty, as well as for some of its specific obligations.[182]

Accepting McCormack's account of the NPT, the Court could arguably have found that the nuclear-weapon states were in material breach of the obligations that the treaty imposed on them, not only to negotiate in good faith, but also to disarm.[183] The NWS' continued possession of their nuclear arsenals—and, *a fortiori*, any use of them—would therefore also be in breach of the NPT. (Further, even if it could have been argued that the NWS had had insufficient time in 1996 to negotiate complete disarmament, it would be far harder to make that argument today. Indeed, the non-nuclear state of the Marshall Islands has recently petitioned the Court to revisit that issue, claiming that five nuclear weapon state parties to the NPT and four nuclear non-party states are in breach of the NPT or customary law.[184] The Court's finding of a material breach would have authorized the NNWS to claim the right to terminate or suspend the operation of the NPT, surely an unwelcome prospect for the NWS. And even if it had not led the NNWS to terminate or suspend the NPT, a finding by the Court that the treaty had actually been breached might, on its own, have done much more to prompt the NWS to disarm than the Court's mere reminder to those states that they had agreed to do so.

However, this argument, too, is not free from doubt. An alternative view might be that a material breach by the NWS would give only all states unanimously the remedy of termination, or only all "specially affected" states the right to suspend the NPT.[185] But the remedial consequence might

182 *Id.*

183 A "material breach" of a treaty includes "the violation of a provision essential to the accomplishment of the object or purpose of the Treaty." VCLT, *supra* note 168, at art. 60(3)(b).

184 *See* International Court of Justice, *Obligations Concerning Negotiations Relating to Cessation of the Nuclear Arms Race and to Nuclear Disarmament (Marshall Islands v. Pakistan),* Order (July 9, 2015), http://www.icj-cij.org/docket/files/159/18724.pdf.).

185 The VCLT provides that termination of a multilateral convention, such as the NPT, for material breach requires a unanimous determination by the non-breaching parties or, in a special case, that "a party specially affected by the breach to invoke it as a ground for suspending the operation of the treaty in whole or in part in the relations between itself and the defaulting state. . . . " VCLT, supra note 168, at arts. 60(2)(a) and (b). It is at least arguable that unanimous consent to termination would be required for termination of the NPT. Moreover, even if "specially affected" states might escape some NPT obligations, the NNWS could not suspend their non-possession obligation against only a defaulting state, as contemplated by the VCLT, because the non-possession obligation runs to all states and, therefore, if suspended against one would be suspended as against all. For the ICJ's discussion of whether NPT states can fall into the "specially

be, rather than to terminate the right of NWS to possess or use nuclear weapons in self-defense,[186] merely to revive any right to possession or use that NNWS may have surrender through their acceptance of NNWS status as NPT Parties. Also, the Security Council's Resolution 984, welcoming the indefinite extension of the NPT may evidence a common international understanding that the NPT NWS had not yet materially breached their obligations; and the extension itself may operate as a waiver by NPT NNWS parties of their right to asserting a claim of material breach.[187] While the Court was not prepared to go that far, it refused—after discussing the substantial state practice predicated on the NPT relied upon by the NWS to argue for the legality of possession and potential use[188]—to "view these elements as amounting to a comprehensive and universal conventional prohibition on the use, or the threat of use, of [nuclear weapons] as such."[189]

But these objections may only obscure the essential truth of the claim that NWS have not lived up to their side of their Faustian bargain under the NPT, thereby defeating the "object and purpose" of the NPT. Even if the NPT Parties through extending the NPT indefinitely waived their rights to terminate or suspend the NPT, in effect reviving the right of NWS to possess or use in self-defense, the ICJ could reasonably have deemed the right of any state to possess or use nuclear weapons as predicated on a duty owed, independent of the NPT, *erga omnes* to the international community as a whole. States possessing nuclear weapons, including those that are not parties to the NPT or in breach of their NPT obligations as NNWS that possess nuclear weapons capabilities, could have breached this separate this duty. This breach of international obligation could have authorized the ICJ to conclude that the possession, and *a fortiori* use, of nuclear weapons no longer was lawful. Acknowledging that the argument is difficult does not imply that, employing accepted norms of international legal discourse, it was impossible.

3. Thesis Two: The Court Could Have Based an Absolute Prohibition on the Policy of Nuclear Deterrence on Natural Law

Commentators have remarked on the fact that none of the ICJ judges rested his or her analysis squarely on natural law.[190] Nothing in the Court's jurisprudence would seem to have barred

affected" category based on their status as NWS or NNW, for purposes of finding state practice that constitutes evidence of customary international law, *see supra* note 105.

186 The VCLT provides as a default rule that termination does "not affect any right, obligation or legal situation of the parties created through the execution of the treaty prior to its termination." VCLT, *supra* note 168, at art. 70(1)(b). Arguably, the defensive posture of all the NWS is predicated on arrangements and investments undertaken because of the NPT, thereby conferring vested rights to NPT NWS Parties.

187 *See supra* note 68 (discussing question 7).

188 *See* LTUNW, *supra* note 11, at 248–53 ¶¶ 58–63.

189 *See id.* at 253 ¶ 63.

190 Falk, *supra* note 46, at 66. Falk went on to point out, however, that the three dissenters favoring an unconditional ban seem to have blended natural law reasoning into their analyses. *Id.*

natural law reasoning, however. Under Articles 38(c) and (d) of the ICJ's Statute, the Court may apply "the general principles of law recognized by civilized nations" and, subject to some qualifications, "the teachings of the most highly qualified publicists of the various nations."[191] Textually, both clauses seem to allow for the possibility of introducing natural law doctrine into the Court's decision-making.[192] Furthermore, Baron Descamps, the President of the Advisory Committee of Jurists on the Statute of the Permanent Court of International Justice, argued that the reference to "general principles of law" in Article 38 of the PCIJ's Statute, which corresponds to the same reference in the ICJ's Statute, "was necessary to meet the possibility of a *non liquet*."[193] Just as natural law had traditionally functioned to furnish a rule of decision when no positive rule had been declared, so the general principles of law "could provide a reservoir from which apparent gaps in the corpus of international law may be filled."[194] Arguably, therefore, rather than reaching a *non-liquet* in paragraph 105(2)(E), the Court, following its Statute did not have discretion not to decide and should have decided the issue in light of the general principles of law or, what may effectively be the same, natural law.

Recall that the Court did not rule on the legality of the policy of nuclear deterrence.[195] From one point of view, this non-ruling seems prudent: the policy of deterrence had arguably functioned to protect the world from nuclear war during the Cold War; and, even in the Cold War's aftermath, when the Court's was considering its legality, nuclear deterrence might conceivably have served a similar function. From another point of view, however, the Court's decision not to rule on this fundamental issue seems shocking: how could it not evaluate the legality of the strategies of "mass retaliation" or "flexible response" when those strategies, if carried out, might have led to planetary destruction? Here we consider the possibility that, if the Court had been willing to employ natural law reasoning, it would have ruled that the policy of nuclear deterrence, as practiced by the nuclear states, was absolutely prohibited.

---

191 Notice, for example, that Article 38(c) speaks of "general principles," as opposed to specific "rules," or "standards;" that the "principles" are principles "of *law*;" and that the principles are "recognized"—rather than "instituted" or "established;" and that they are recognized by "nations" (which may mean "peoples") rather than "states."

192 *See Case Concerning Pulp Mills on the River Uruguay (Argentina v. Uruguay)*, Judgment of Apr. 20, 2010, 2010 ICJ Rep., at ¶¶ 8–47 (separate opinion of Judge Cançado Trindade) (reviewing authorities, including negotiating history of precursor provision in Statute of the Permanent International Court of Justice referring to "general principles of law," negotiating history of ICJ Statute, and PCIJ and ICJ case law shedding light on meaning of phrase). In the course of his learned and valuable opinion, Judge Cançado Trindade stated that

> Principles of International Law are guiding principles of general content, and, in that, they differ from norms or rules of positive international law, and transcend them. . . . Irrespective of the distinct approaches to them, those principles stand ineluctably at a superior level than the norms or rules of positive international law. Such norms or rules are binding, but it is the principles which guide them. Without those latter, rules or techniques could serve whatever purposes. This would be wholly untenable.

Id. at ¶ 39. *See also Ethiopia v. South Africa, Liberia v. South Africa, Second Phase*, 1966 ICJ Rep. 6, 298 (Tanaka, J., dissenting) ("[I]t is undeniable that in Article 38, paragraph 1(c), some natural law elements are inherent."); and Stephen Hall, *The Persistent Spectre: Natural Law, International Order and the Limits of Legal Positivism*, 12 Eur. J. Int'l L. 269, 292–307 (2001).

193 Hall, supra note 192, at 296.

194 *See id.* at 296–97.

195 *See* LTUNW, *supra* note 11, at 254 at ¶ 67.

Influential thinkers in the natural law tradition, many but not all of them Roman Catholics, have appraised the policy of nuclear deterrence over several decades. The culmination of their work was the important 1987 book, *Nuclear Deterrence, Morality and Realism* (*NDMR*), co-authored by John Finnis, Joseph Boyle, and Germain Grisez.[196] The writers argued forcefully, on the basis of what they called "the common morality," that the policy of nuclear deterrence, as practiced during the (then still ongoing) Cold War, was immoral and ought to be ended, unilaterally if necessary—even if unilateral nuclear disarmament by the Western powers would lead to Soviet domination. By the common morality, the writers meant "the Jewish and Christian morality which, though often violated, provided standards of moral assessment formative of our civilization and still accepted by many."[197] Although not explicitly cast as "natural law" reasoning, *NDMR* can readily be understood in that sense; and we shall read it so. So understood, it lays out a naturalist case for a complete legal prohibition on the policy of nuclear deterrence.

NDMR is a rich, many-layered and complex work, whose many subtle arguments we can hardly hope to summarize or even allude to here. Stripped down to its most basic and essential elements, its argument for a ban on nuclear deterrence is this:

1) The policy of nuclear deterrence, in order to be credible and effective, requires a threat to kill innocents (primarily, the millions of civilians living in the major population centers of the nuclear armed antagonists of the Cold War);

2) That threat necessarily involves an intention to kill those innocents;

3) It is always impermissible to form an intent to do what is known to be impermissible to do;

4) It is known to be impermissible to kill innocents; therefore,

5) It is impermissible to intend to kill innocents; therefore,

6) The policy of nuclear deterrence is impermissible.

Our main focus will be on proposition (3), which has come to be known as the "principle of wrongful intent." However, brief explanations of propositions (1), (2) and (4) are in order.

As to propositions (1) and (2), we note that the *General Assembly Advisory Opinion* seems substantially to accept them. The Court wrote that "[s]ome states put forward the argument that possession of nuclear weapons is itself an unlawful threat to use force. In order to be effective,

196 John Finnis, Joseph Boyle, & Germain Grisez, Nuclear Deterrence, Morality and Realism (1988) [hereinafter "NDMR"].

197 *Id.* at 66.

the policy of deterrence, by which those States possessing or under the umbrella of nuclear weapons seek to discourage military aggression by demonstrating that it will serve no purpose, necessitates the intention to use nuclear weapons be credible."[198] The Court then went on to state that the question whether the policy of deterrence is a "threat" forbidden by Article 2(4) of the U.N. Charter depends on the circumstances.[199] But it seems to assume that the policy requires a "threat," whether lawful or unlawful, and that that threat carries with it an "intention" to use nuclear weapons.

NDMR substantiated proposition (1) by citing statements by Western political and military leaders, over many decades, that the policy of nuclear deterrence depended on a credible threat to destroy the main population centers of the Soviet Union. It also sought to refute the claim that the West could avoid a threat to kill the innocents by adopting a counterforce deterrent strategy rather than a countervalue one. (A "counterforce" strategy involves threats solely against military targets; a "countervalue" strategy involves threats against cities.) In order to be effective, *NDMR* contended, nuclear deterrence requires countervalue threats: if the Soviets could threaten Western cities, but the West could only threaten Soviet military targets, then the Soviets could attack Western cities without fearing that the West would use nuclear weapons at all—for any Western use could trigger a further Soviet strike on Western cities, and the West would never permit that to happen.

Proposition (2) is the subject of a detailed defense in *NDMR*. The writers contended that purported targeting objectives do not define "intent": even if Western nuclear weapons are ostensibly targeted on Soviet military forces or objects in or near Soviet cities, the Western state targeting them in fact intends to kill the cities' populations, because it is *their* destruction, not that of the military objectives, that the West wants the Soviets to fear. Furthermore, *NDRM* argued, the threat cannot realistically be considered a "bluff." As an empirical matter, there is no evidence to think that any U.S. President has ever formed such a secret intention; and even if one had, his successor might not. As a conceptual matter, *NDRM* argued, nuclear deterrence involves the coordination and cooperation of large numbers of people, in the military and government, acting in accordance with institutional rules, practices, and procedures. Deterrence is therefore a "social act," not an individual one. Thus, even if the U.S. President had secretly resolved not to order a strike, the social act of nuclear deterrence would have a retaliatory purpose or intent. (One way to understand this argument is to see it as designed to identify the most relevant moral agent here as a corporate actor—the United States—rather than any individual official. As a corporate actor, the United States as such can be said to have "intentions" and "purposes" of its own.)

Proposition (4) is undoubtedly a part of the "common morality." In *NDMR's* view, common morality draws a distinction between those who may in some circumstances intentionally be

198 LTUNW, *supra* note 11, at 246 at ¶ 48.

199 *Id.* at 247 at ¶ 48.

killed, and those who may never intentionally be killed: the latter are the "innocent." The writers explained:

> In common morality, the only persons who may be intentionally killed are those convicted of certain crimes, and those engaged in a forcible violation of society's just order, whether by an attack from without or by gross criminal conduct within. Nothing can justify intentionally killing other persons who, as the tradition developed, came to be classed together as "innocents." In ordinary language, of course, "innocence" often means absence of moral guilt. But here the word does not have that meaning. It refers to all those whose killing, under common morality, cannot be justified.[200]

In the context of nuclear deterrence policy, the "innocent" can be broadly equated with "civilians" or "non-combatants."

Although each of the propositions reviewed above might be questioned (much of *NDMR* is in fact devoted to defending them), the crux is in proposition (3), the principle of wrongful intent. Intuitively, the principle of wrongful intent seems well-founded. If I know that it would be wrong for me to kill my neighbors, then surely it is also wrong for me to form the intention of killing them. True, criminal law does not punish intent formation as such; it typically requires at least an attempt to carry out the intention, or an overt act in furtherance of a conspiracy to carry it out. Still, even if a wrongful intention lies outside the reach of criminal law in the absence of some observable act, that result may be owed largely to the difficulty of proving a bare intent. Furthermore, until an intention begins to initiate in action, it can be abandoned; and that consideration, too, counsels against punishment for a wrongful intention. Nonetheless, an intention to do what is known to be a wrongful act is itself wrongful: if my fully formed intention to kill my neighbor is frustrated by her sudden heart attack as I am poised to attack, I am still deserving of condemnation. The principle of wrongful intent also applies to conditional intentions (such as are found in nuclear deterrence policy). Suppose I intend to kill my neighbor if he walks on my lawn again. As it happens, he moves away and does not cross my lawn again. I am still bad, even if (perhaps) not as bad as if he had walked over the lawn and I had killed him. Thus, if the principle of wrongful intent is accepted, then there would seem to be a powerful naturalist argument for holding a nuclear deterrence policy like those of the Cold War to be illegal, as contrary to the "general principles of law" mentioned in Article 38(c) of the ICJ Statute.

But does the principle of wrongful intent extend to the special conditions of nuclear deterrence? Moral philosopher Gregory Kavka argued that the principle of wrongful intent, though generally true, does not apply in the special case of what he called "deterrent intentions." Kavka defined "deterrent intentions" as "those conditional intentions whose existence is based on the agent's desire to thereby deter others from actualizing the antecedent condition to the

200 NDMR, *supra* note 195, at 86–87.

intention."[201] Kavka pointed out that such intentions "are rather strange. They are, by nature, self-stultifying: if a deterrent intention fulfills the agent's purpose, it ensures that the intended (and possibly evil) act is not performed, by preventing the circumstances of performance from arising."[202] Moreover, a person who forms a deterrent intent may very strongly desire not to have to carry it out: the desire to form the intention is distinct from the desire to execute it. So, although the person forming a deterrent effect may (conditionally) intend to do what is known to be wrong, that person may have no desire to do (and a strong desire not to do) what is wrong.[203] An example will make this clearer. Kavka's is this:

> if I know I can prevent you from thrashing me only by sincerely threatening to retaliate against your beloved and innocent brother, it may not be wrong for me to do so. Since the intentions behind the threats of those who practice nuclear deterrence are presumably of this sort, these threats are not necessarily wrong.[204]

Three features of this example should be noticed. First, for a deterrent threat of retaliation to be permissible, it must be known to be effective—or at least to be reasonably effective—in preventing the threatened person from doing the harm (here, your thrashing me). Second, the deterrent threat must be the only way of effectively (or reasonably effectively) preventing that harm. Third, the threatened retaliation may then involve inflicting an injury on an innocent person, though it is not clear how much innocent suffering might be defensible under this line of reasoning.

Yet, if these conditions were satisfied, if the intentions involved in nuclear deterrence do fall within that class Kafka describes, and if Kafka is right in constructing an exception to the principle of wrongful intent, then the natural law argument sketched out above could fail.

---

201 Gregory S. Kavka, Moral Paradoxes of Nuclear Deterrence 20 (1987)

202 *Id.*

203 In the Catholic Natural Law tradition, this might be akin to the distinction between "formal" and "material" cooperation with evil. In the case of formal cooperation, which is never permissible, one's subjective intent is to pursue the wrongful aim of another. In the case of material cooperation, which may be justified in certain circumstances, one subjectively does not seek to achieve a wrongful result and acts to cooperate in evil only to avoid a greater evil. *See generally What is the Principle of Cooperation with Evil,* National Catholic Bioethics Center (*available at* http://ncbcenter.org/document.doc?id=139); cf. Catechism of the Catholic Church, 433–35 (U.S. Catholic Conference, 1994) (Eng. Trans.). Rather than using the traditional distinction of Catholic natural law philosophy between "formal" and "material" cooperation, the Catechism focuses instead on "*circumstances,* including consequences," as secondary elements of a moral act, which attenuate moral responsibility, although it insists that "*circumstances* can make neither good nor right an action that is in itself evil." *Id.* at 434, ¶ 1754 (emphasis in the original).

204 *Id.* at 82.

Part IV

Concluding Thoughts: The Relationship Between the *Jus ad Bellum* and the *Jus in Bello*

As we began this book with Thucydides, so now we end it. In his *History of the Peloponnesian War,* Thucydides described an episode that took place in 413 B.C. and that he appeared to think epitomized all the horror and cruelty of that war. A force of 1,300 Thracian archers arrived in Athens too late to join the Athenian contingent that was sailing under Demosthenes to Sicily as reinforcements. Athens was unwilling to pay them, and so sent them home under the command of the Athenian general Diittrephes, with instructions to harass the enemy *en route.* In the course of their return journey, the Thracians landed in Bœotian territory, surprised the virtually defenseless city of Mycalessus, and massacred its inhabitants, young and old, male and female, alike. In particular, they broke into a boys' school and slaughtered every child in it.

Here, in Hobbes' translation, is how Thucydides told the story (*History of the Peloponnesian War,* Book VII, 29-30):

> The Thracians, therefore, that came too late to go with Demosthenes, they presently sent back, as being unwilling to lay out money in such a scarcity: and gave the charge of carrying them back to Diitrephes, with command as he went along those coasts, (for his way was through the Euripus), if occasion served, to do somewhat against the enemy. He accordingly landed them by Tanagra, and hastily fetched in some small booty. Then going over the Euripus from Chalcis in Eubœa, he disbarked again in Bœotia and led his soldiers towards Mycalessus; and lay all night at the temple of Mercury undiscovered, which is distant from Mycalessus about sixteen furlongs. The next day he cometh to the city, being a very great one, and taketh it: for they kept no watch, nor expected that any man would have come in and assaulted them so far from the sea. Their walls also were but weak, in some places fallen down, and in others low–built: and their gates open through security. The Thracians entering into Mycalessus, spoiled both houses and temples, slew the people, without mercy on old or young, but killed all they could light on, both women and children; yea, and the labouring cattle, and whatsoever other living thing they saw. For the nation of the Thracians, where they dare, are extreme bloody, equal to any of the barbarians. Insomuch as there was put in practice at this time, besides other disorder, all forms of slaughter that could be imagined: they likewise fell upon the school–house, which was in the city a great one, and the children newly entered into it; and killed them every one. And the calamity of the

whole city, as it was as great as ever befell any, so also was it more unexpected and more bitter. . . . Thus went the matter at Mycalessus: the loss which it received being, for the quantity of the city, no less to be lamented than any that happened in the whole war.

In Thucydides' narrative of the atrocities at Mycalessus, we already find many of the most important issues that will occupy us here concerning the means and methods of warfare. At least five issues, all of which are relevant to modern *jus in bello,* spring to mind:

1) Did Diitrephes order the massacre? Even if he did not, was he responsible, as the commanding general, for not having restrained it?[1]

2) Is it permissible to attack a city—even an enemy city—if it is (effectively) defenseless?[2]

3) Is the destruction of temples, or places of worship generally, permissible in war?[3]

4) Is the indiscriminate killing of innocent civilians, including those who, because of age, cannot take up arms, permissible?[4]

5) Does the intentional killing of children deserve particular condemnation?[5]

---

1 *See In re* Yamashita, 327 U.S. 1, 15 (1946) ("It is evident that the conduct of military operations by troops whose excesses are unrestrained by the orders or efforts of their commander would almost certainly result in violations which it is the purpose of the law of war to prevent. Its purpose to protect civilian populations and prisoners of war from brutality would largely be defeated if the commander of an invading army could, with impunity, neglect to take reasonable measures for their protection. Hence, the law of war presupposes that its violation is to be avoided through the control of the operations of war by commanders who are to some extent responsible for their subordinates.").

2 *See* Hague Convention (IV) Respecting the Laws and Customs of War on Land and in Its Annex: Regulations Concerning the Laws and Customs of War on Land, Oct. 18, 1907, 36 Stat. 2277, art. 25 [hereinafter Hague Convention No. IV] ("The attack or bombardment, by whatever means, of towns, villages, dwellings or buildings which are undefended is prohibited.").

3 *See supra* note 2, Hague Convention No. IV, art. 27 ("In sieges and bombardments all necessary steps must be taken to spare, as far as possible, buildings dedicated to religion . . . "); Hague Convention for the Protection of Cultural Property in the Event of Armed Conflict, art. 4(1), entered into force Aug. 7, 1956 (*available at* http://www.icomos.org/hague/hague.convention.html). In ancient Greece, the major pan-Hellenic temples at Olympus, Delphi and elsewhere were regarded as sacred and inviolate, and no violence was permitted within their walls. *See* François Bugnion, *The Origins and Development of the Legal Protection of Cultural Property in the Event of Armed Conflict* (2004) (*available at* http://www.icrc.org/web/eng/siteeeng0.nsf/htm/65SHTJ).

4 *See* Declaration Renouncing the Use, in Time of War, of Explosive Projectiles Under 400 Grammes Weight, St. Petersburg, 1868, Preamble (*available at* http://www.icrc.org/ihl.nsf/FULL/130?OpenDocument) ("[T]he only legitimate object which States should endeavour to accomplish during war is to weaken the military forces of the enemy.").

5 *See* Convention on the Rights of the Child, art. 38(4), entered into force Sept. 2, 1990 (*available at* http://www2.ohchr.org/english/law/crc.htm) ("In accordance with their obligations under international humanitarian law to protect the civilian population in armed conflicts, States Parties shall take all feasible measures to ensure protection and care of children who are affected by an armed conflict."); *see also* Denise Plattner, *Protection of Children in International Humanitarian Law,* 240 IRRC 140 (1984).

Thucydides did not directly answer any of these questions.[6] He merely described the events in question, and reported on what the prevailing reaction to them was. Yet his judgment seems unmistakable: these are outrages against morality that no necessities of warfare could justify or excuse.[7]

Thus, consistent with the realist approach we exposed in our initial discussion of Thucydides' presentation of the Athenian Debates concerning whether to use force, he provided no full theory of a law of war, marking out distinct boundaries between the *jus ad bellum* and the *jus in bello*, much less relating the two. We now turn to the question of the relationship between the two bodies of international law concerning the use of force we have treated in Parts II and III of this book, the *jus ad bellum* and the *jus in bello* – a question that lies at the very heart of the law of war. We outline the modern position and its critics, particularly in the context of humanitarian intervention. Next, we consider the debate in the context of the most pressing issue of our time, the problem of terrorism. Finally, we conclude with comments based on the competing methodological approaches we have considered in this volume as possible approaches to address the fissures or lacunae these emerging problems have identified in the law of war.

Other questions might also be posed. Did the women of Mycalessus deserve special protection? *See* Françoise Krill, *The Protection of Women in International Humanitarian Law*, 249 IRRC 337 (1985); *see also* Judith Gardam, *Women and the Law of Armed Conflict: Why the Silence?*, 46 Int'l & Comp. L. Q. 55 (1997) (critique of existing laws of war provisions from feminist viewpoint and argument for a new protocol for women in wartime). What about the Thracians' destruction of the city's working cattle? Could any survivors of the massacre at Mycalessus remain alive for long without livestock for use in raising crops? If the cattle were indispensable to Mycalessus' continued survival, would their slaughter be forbidden? *See* Protocol Additional to the Geneva Conventions Relating to the Protection of Victims of International Armed Conflicts, art. 54(2), June 8, 1977, 1125 U.N.T.S. 3 [hereinafter Protocol I] ("It is prohibited to . . . destroy . . . objects indispensable to the survival of the civilian population, such as . . . livestock."); *see also* Ameur Zemmali, *The Protection of Water in Times of Armed Conflict*, 308 IRRC 550 (1995).

6 Thucydides did refer, however, to these conventions supplying answers to these questions as "the common institutions of Greece." Thucydides, *History of the Peloponnesian War* 3.69.1 (Hobbes translation). For commentary, *see* Trevor J. Quinn, *Thucydides and the Massacre at Mycalessus*, 48 Mnemosyne 571 (1995).

7 Contrast the view of von Clausewitz, who said that "[w]ar is an act of force to compel our enemy to do our will. . . . [A] ttached to force are certain self-imposed, imperceptible limitations hardly worth mentioning, known as international law and custom, but they scarcely weaken it." Carl von Clausewitz, On War 83 (Michael Howard & Peter Paret (trans.) 1976).

First, we trace the origins of the modern position and explicate the legal materials supporting and resisting it. Second, we discuss academic commentary calling the modern position into question.

1. The Modern Position—Origins and Current State Practice

The long-prevailing (and still dominant[8]) view of the relationship between *jus ad bellum* and *jus in bello* has two aspects: the "symmetry" doctrine (also called the principle of belligerent equality), holding that the content of *jus in bello,* including both obligations and rights, is identical for all combatants in an armed conflict; and the "independence" or "separation" doctrine, which holds that the *jus in bello* obligations and rights of the combatants are independent of the justice or legality of the war they are waging under the *jus ad bellum.*[9] Consequently, the conduct of states is measured under *jus in bello* in the same way, regardless of whether they are aggressors or victims engaged in lawful self-defense.[10] It seems generally accepted that these doctrines survive the supposed "outlawry" of war (other than in self-defense or as authorized by the Security Council) under the U.N. Charter.[11] But, as we shall see, the doctrines also have powerful critics.

For post-Westphalian international law, it is possible to trace the explicit separation of *jus in bello* from *jus ad bellum* to four eighteenth century writers: Christian Wolff, Emer de Vattel,

8 *See* Christopher Greenwood, *The Concept of War in Modern Law,* 36 Int'l & Comp. L. Q. 283, 289 (1987) ("[M]ost writers, including those who argue that an aggressor is not permitted to profit from his wrongdoing, accept that humanitarian law must apply to both sides in any conflict.").

9 *See* David Rodin, *The Liability of Ordinary Soldiers for Crimes of Aggression,* 6 Wash. U. Global Stud. L. Rev. 391, 391 (2007); Adam Roberts, *The Equal Application of the Laws of War: a Principle Under Pressure,* 872 IRRC 931, 932 (2008). Roberts' nomenclature is deliberately different from Rodin's.

10 *See* Michael Walzer, Just and Unjust Wars: A Moral Argument with Historical Illustrations 38–40 (3d ed. 1977); Nicholas Rostow, *The World Health Organization, the International Court of Justice, and Nuclear Weapons,* 20 Yale J. Int'l L. 151, 173 & n. 135 (1995) (collecting authorities).

11 In 1999, Secretary General Kofi Annan promulgated *Guidelines for UN Forces Regarding Respect for International Humanitarian Law,* UN Doc. ST/SGB/1999/13 (August 6, 1999). These guidelines make "fundamental principles and rules of international humanitarian law" applicable to "United Nations forces when in situations of armed conflict they are actively engaged therein as combatants, to the extent and for the duration of their engagement. They are accordingly applicable in enforcement actions, or in peacekeeping operations when the use of force is permitted in self-defence." *Id.; see also* United Nations, Dep't of Peacekeeping Operations, *United Nations Peacekeeping Operations: Principles and Guidelines* 15–16 (2008). For a review of the current *jus in bello* rules applicable to U.N. peace enforcement and peace keeping actions, *see* Roberts, *supra* note 9, 952–56.

Earlier writers had noted the existence of disagreements about the applicability of *jus in bello* restrictions to Security Council-authorized peace enforcement operations. Judith G. Gardam, *Legal Restraints on Security Council Military Enforcement Action,* 17 Mich. J. Int'l L. 285, 317–18 (1995/96) ("It is by no means 'uncontested' that the rules of customary international law apply to the forces acting in pursuance of Chapter VII Security Council powers. . . . There is no straightforward resolution to the question of the *ius in bello* and the Security Council."). Some scholars had indicated that they believed that the Council could vary the requirements of humanitarian law with respect to the military actions it had authorized. *See* Theodor Meron, *Prisoners of War, Civilians, and Diplomats in the Gulf Crisis,* 85 Am. J. Int'l L. 104, 108 (1991).

Jean-Jacques Rousseau, and Immanuel Kant.[12] Wolff, an important influence on both Vattel and Kant, argued that war was to be considered as just on both sides of a conflict, so that the *jus in bello* applied to all belligerents in the same way: "What is rightly allowable for one belligerent is also allowable for the other without any consideration of the justice of the war."[13] Vattel followed Wolff in emphasizing (as many later authors in the tradition also did) the moral and epistemological difficulty of determining which of the belligerents was fighting justly and which not. He argued "regular war, as to its effects, is to be accounted just on both sides," and hence that "whatever is permitted to the one in virtue of the state of war, is also permitted to the other."[14] Rousseau took the emerging doctrine to a new level by propounding both the idea of "belligerent equality," at least as to individual combatants, and a form of the doctrine of noncombatant immunity. For Rousseau:

> [w]ar is not . . . a relationship between one man and another, but a relationship between one State and another, in which individuals are enemies only by accident, not as men, nor even as citizens, but as soldiers. . . . Since the aim of war is the destruction of the enemy State, one has the right to kill its defenders as long as they bear arms; but as soon as they lay down their arms and surrender they cease to be enemies or the enemy's instruments, and become simply men once more, and one no longer has a right over their life. It is sometimes possible to kill the State without killing a single one of its members; and war confers no right that is not necessary to its end.[15]

Finally, in his *Philosophy of Law*, Immanuel Kant explicitly distinguished "[t]he Right of going to War" from "Right during War."[16]

The classic modern statement of the still-dominant, dualistic view is found in one of the Nuremberg cases, the U.S. Military Tribunal's Opinion in *The Hostages Trial: (U.S. v. List)*. There the Court, relying the eminent U.K. authority Hersch Lauterpacht, said:

---

12 Indeed, it would be possible to locate the distinction even before the eighteenth century. *See* Joachim von Elbe, *The Evolution of the Concept of Just War in International Law*, 33 Am. J. Int'l L. 665, 676–81 (1939); William G. Grewe, *The Epochs of International Law* 209–14 (Michael Byers trans. 2000). For hints in the Spanish neo-scholastic tradition, *see supra* Part II, Chapter 1.

13 Christian Wolff, *Ius Gentium Methodo Scientifico Pertractatum* (1749), *in* The Classics of International Law, vol. II, 455 (1934).

14 Emer de Vattel, *The Law of Nations; or, Principles of the Law of Nature, Applied to the Conduct and Affairs of Nations and Sovereigns* Book III, ch. 12, §§ 191–92.

15 Jean-Jacques Rousseau, The Social Contract and other Later Political Writings 46–47 (Victor Gourevitch ed. 1997).

16 Immanuel Kant, The Philosophy of Law: An Exposition of the Fundamental Principles of Jurisprudence as the Science of Right ¶ 53 (W. Hastie trans. 1887); *see also* Jasmine Moussa, *Can Jus ad Bellum Override Jus in Bello? Reaffirming the Separation of the Two Bodies of Law*, 872 IRRC 963, 966 (2008). For an attempt to derive substantive rules of *jus ad bellum* and *jus in bello* from Kant's teachings, *see* Brian Orend, *Kant's Just War Theory*, 37 J. Hist. Phil. 323, 339–50 (1999).

We concur in the views expressed in the following text on the subject: "Whatever may be the cause of a war that has broken out, and whether or no the cause be a so-called just cause, the same rules of International Law are valid as to what must not be done, and must be done by the belligerents themselves in making war against each other; and as between the belligerents and neutral States. This is so, even if the declaration of war is *ipso facto* a violation of International Law, as when a belligerent declares war upon a neutral State for refusing passage to its troops, or when a State goes to war in patent violation of its obligations under the Covenant of the League or of the General Treaty for the Renunciation of War. To say that, because such a declaration of war is *ipso facto* a violation of International Law, it is 'inoperative in law and without any judicial significance,' is erroneous. The rules of International Law apply to war from whatever cause it originates."[17]

Even recently, similar views are found, though more guardedly expressed, in the Report of the Office of the Prosecutor commissioned by the International Criminal Tribunal for the Former Yugoslavia to investigate allegations of war crimes by NATO forces during the war in Kosovo (the OTP Report).[18] The relevant parts of the OTP Report read:

32. The precise linkage between *jus ad bellum* and *jus in bello* is not completely resolved. There were suggestions by the prosecution before the International Military Tribunal at Nuremberg and in some other post World War II war crimes cases that all of the killing and destruction caused by German forces were war crimes because the Germans were conducting an aggressive war. The courts were unreceptive to these arguments. Similarly, in the 1950's there was a debate concerning whether UN authorized forces were required to comply with the *jus in bello* as they represented the good side in a battle between good and evil. This debate died out as the participants realized that a certain crude reciprocity was essential if the law was to have any positive impact. An argument that the "bad" side had to comply with the law while the "good" side could violate it at will would be most unlikely to reduce human suffering in conflict.

33. More recently, a refined approach to the linkage issue has been advocated by certain law of war scholars. Using their approach, assuming that the only lawful basis for recourse to force is self defence, each use of force during a conflict must be measured by whether or not it complies

17 *The Hostages Trial: Trial of Wilhelm List and Others*, U.S. Military Tribunal, Nuremberg, Case No. 47, 8 United Nations War Crimes Commission, Law Reports of Trials of War Criminals 60 (1949) (citing and quoting Oppenheim's *International Law*, II, Lauterpacht, 174). Likewise, in the Preamble to Additional Protocol I, the parties "reaffirm. . . that the provisions of the Geneva Conventions . . . and of this Protocol must be fully applied in all circumstances to all persons who are protected by those instruments, without any adverse distinction based on the nature or origin of the armed conflict or on the causes espoused by or attributed to the Parties to the conflict."

18 *See* International Criminal Tribunal for the Former Yugoslavia: Final Report to the Prosecutor by the Committee Established to Review the NATO Bombing Campaign against the Federal Republic of Yugoslavia (June 8, 2000), 39 I.L.M. 1257 (2000) (*available at* http://www.icty.org/sid/10052).

with the *jus in bello* and by whether or not it complies with the necessity and proportionality requirements of self defence. The difficulty with this approach is that it does not adequately address what should be done when it is unclear who is acting in self defence and it does not clarify the obligations of the "bad" side.

34. As a matter of practice, which we consider to be in accord with the most widely accepted and reputable legal opinion, we in the OTP have deliberately refrained from assessing *jus ad bellum* issues in our work and focused exclusively on whether or not individuals have committed serious violations of international humanitarian law as assessed within the confines of the *jus in bello.*

Thus, the OTP reaffirms the modern distinction, even as it faced the question in the most extreme circumstances involving an arguably problematic case under the *jus ad bellum*, collective humanitarian intervention without prior Security Council authorization.

Yet, as the OTP Report states, there has been persistent criticism of the reigning doctrine—even if the criticism continues to represent a minority position. This opposing view was articulated by Sir Hartley Shawcross, the Chief British prosecutor during the Nuremberg Trials before the IMT. He argued: "The killing of combatants is justifiable . . . only where the war itself is legal. But where the war is illegal . . . there is nothing to justify the killing and these murders are not to be distinguished from those of any other lawless robber bands."[19] Interestingly, another Nuremberg prosecutor, Justice Robert Jackson, Chief Prosecutor for the United States, seems to have disagreed. Jackson said: "If certain acts in violation of treaties are crimes, they are crimes whether the United States does them or whether Germany does them, and we are not prepared to lay down a rule of criminal conduct against which we would not be willing to have invoked against us."[20]

The logic of Nuremberg seems to point Shawcross' way, however, not Jackson's. If waging an aggressive war is a crime, how can the soldiers who lend themselves to the pursuit of that crime not be personally implicated in it? True enough, combatants in many wars could plead ignorance of the criminal designs of their political and military leaders. But could that be said of the troops Hitler deployed, for example, against Poland, Holland, Norway, or Greece? Could they have understood their role as anything but that of aggressors? More generally, if individual soldiers can tell the difference between a manifestly illegal order and one that is not, then why assume that they cannot also tell the difference between a manifestly illegal or unjust war and

19 Walzer, *supra* note 10, at 38 (citations omitted).

20 United States v. Noriega, 746 F. Supp. 1506, 1535 (S.D. Fla. 1990) (quoting International Conference on Military Trials, London, 1945, Dept. of State Pub. No. 3080 (1949), 330).

one that is not?[21] Individual combatants might also plead that they were coerced into fighting—an ordinary conscript can do little, if anything, to escape the demands of the modern state at war.[22] But setting aside the question whether individuals have the duty to resist the demands of an aggressor state like Nazi Germany, even at the risk of their own lives, many members of Hitler's armed forces were willing, even enthusiastic, participants in his plans of conquest. Further and more generally, what are we to say of soldiers who are not conscripts, but long-term professionals or volunteers? In any case, would not a decision to hold soldiers criminally liable for refusing to take part in a war of aggression tend to deter aggressive wars by raising the stakes for those who fight for the aggressor?

If Nuremberg posed a problem for the doctrine of the separation of *jus in bello* from *jus ad bellum,* the adoption of the U.N. Charter intensified the difficulty.[23] The Charter was understood to have abolished any putative sovereign "right" to go to war; to be lawful, international wars had either to be authorized by the Security Council or undertaken in self-defense. Scholars in the 1940s and 1950s debated whether the new international legal regime created by the Nuremberg Trials and the Charter entailed these consequences.[24] One of them, Hersch Lauterpacht, explained the difficulty in this way:

> It would seem logical and fully consistent with principle that so far as war has ceased to be a right—or an exercise of power—authorized by international law, an illegal war - that is, a war resorted to contrary to the fundamental obligations accepted by a state and aiming at abolishing

21 *See* Michael L. Gross, Moral Dilemmas of Modern War: Torture, Assassination, and Blackmail in an Age of Asymmetrical Conflict 31 (2010) ("Wars that blatantly violate the territorial integrity of another nation (other than wars of humanitarian intervention) or subjugate a peace-loving people should trigger the same response as a manifestly unlawful order."). One might argue that the point holds particularly true of soldiers fighting for liberal Western societies, where opinions and information about the justice and legality war in which they fight is readily available on the internet and the media and in which the claims made by their government—as in the Second Gulf War—are likely to be vehemently and publicly contested. Conversely, the point seems to be less true of the soldiers of states, for example, North Korea or pre-war Iraq, in which the flow of information and the expression of political opinion are severely restricted.

22 *See* Walzer, supra note 10, 39–40. For criticism of Walzer on these points, *see* Brian Orend, The Morality of War 107–09 (2007).

23 In the ensuing discussion, as previously, we shall continue to refer to the "*jus ad bellum*," even though the normative doctrine of traditional just war theory arguably no longer reflects positive international law (if it ever did), and even though the conception of a "*bellum justum*" has arguably been wholly superseded by the post-Charter conception of a "*bellum legale*." See Josef L. Kunz, Bellum Justum *and* Bellum Legale, 45 Am. J. Int'l L. 528 (1951).

24 Many argued that they did not. *See, e.g.,* Quincy Wright, *The Outlawry of War and the Law of War,* 47 Am. J. Int'l L. 365, 373, 375 (1953). One qualification: Wright also believed that if specifically authorized by the United Nations, states could take some measures going beyond the normal *jus in bello* rights of belligerents in relation to enemies or neutrals. *Id.* at 371. He also affirmed, however, that the United Nations "could not authorize acts which international law regards as war crimes nor could it deprive individuals, even though acting in behalf of an aggressor state, of human rights protected by international law and the law of war." *Id.* at 375. *See also* Richard R. Baxter, *The Role of Law in Modern War,* 47 Proc. Am. Soc. Int'l L. 90, 95–96 (1953) (criticizing proposal that laws of war should not apply to United Nations actions, and noting that U.N. Command in Korean War voluntarily applied humanitarian principles to its operations). For surveys and appraisals of the legal scholarship from the period dealing with this issue, *see* Robert D. Sloane, *The Cost of Conflation: Preserving the Dualism of Jus ad Bellum and Jus in Bello in the Contemporary Law of War,* 34 Yale J. Int'l L.47, 70–72 (2009); *see also* Alexander Orakhelashvili, *Overlap and Convergence: The Interaction Between Jus ad Bellum and Jus in Bello,* 12 J. Conflict & Security L. 157 (2007).

> the institution of war as such—should no longer confer upon the guilty belligerents all the rights to which he was entitled under traditional international law. *Ex injuria jus non oritur* ["No right arises out of a wrong" or, more freely, "No one may profit from his wrongdoing"] is a well-established principle of law.[25]

Even if Lauterpacht's argument had much, in principle, to commend it, courts and commentators (including, later, Lauterpacht himself[26]) have tended to reject its logic.[27]

Thus, one Nuremberg Court, the U.S. Military Tribunal in *The Justice Trial (In re Altstötter et al.)*, addressed the issue in a highly pragmatic way:

> If we should adopt the view that by reason of the fact that the war was a criminal war of aggression every act which would have been legal in an offensive war was illegal in this one, we would be forced to the conclusion that every soldier who marched under orders into occupied territory or who fought in the homeland was a criminal and a murderer. The rules of land warfare upon which the prosecution has relied would not be the measure of conduct and the pronouncement of guilt in any case would become a mere formality.[28]

As a practical matter, there was surely good sense in this decision. If every combatant in Hitler's forces were to have been held criminally liable and punished for participation in an aggressive war, the objectives of achieving a stable, peaceful and democratic post-War Germany would have been undercut, enormous bitterness toward the victorious Allies would have been

25 H. Lauterpacht, *Rules of Warfare in an Unlawful War*, in George A. Lipsky (ed.), Law and Politics in the World Community: Essays on Han's Kelsen's Pure Theory and Related Problems in International Law 89, 91–92 (1953) [hereinafter Lauterpacht, Rules of Warfare].

26 Lauterpacht later answered his own question by arguing, in effect, that without the principle of belligerent equality, war would degenerate into barbarism:

> it is impossible to visualize the conduct of hostilities in which one side would be bound by the rules of warfare without benefiting from them and in which the other side would benefit from rules of warfare without being bound by them. Accordingly, any application to the actual conduct of war of the principle *ex injuria jus non oritur* would transform the contest into a struggle which is subject to no regulation at all. . . . Unless hostilities are to degenerate into a savage contest of physical forces freed from all restraints of compassion, chivalry, and respect for the dignity of man, it is essential that the accepted rules of war in that—humanitarian—sphere should continue to be observed.

Lauterpacht, *Rules of Warfare, supra* note 25, at 92. Elsewhere, Lauterpacht argued that

> [t]he reasons which make it imperative to permit the full application, during the war and as between belligerents, of the rules of war are especially cogent when it is borne in mind that in the present state of international organization there may be no means, so long as the war lasts, by which an authoritative judgment can be arrived at on the question as to which belligerent side is the aggressor.

H. Lauterpacht, *The Limits of the Operation of the Law of War*, 30 Brit. Y.B. Int'l L. 206, 220 (1953). Lauterpacht's later arguments reflect two of the main lines of reasoning for maintaining the distinction between *jus ad bellum* and *jus in bello*: one which relies chiefly on the absence of an authoritative adjudicator of the question of a war's justice or legality; the other pointing to the harmful consequences that arguably would flow from rejecting the dichotomy.

27 *See, e.g.*, Myres S. McDougal, *Law and Minimum World Public Order: Armed Conflict in Larger Context*, 3 U.C.L.A. Pac. Basin L.J. 21, 30 (1984).

28 Marco Sassòli, Antoine A. Bouvier & Anne Quintin, *How Does Law Protect in War?*, Int'l Committee of the Red Cross 665 (*available at* https://www.icrc.org/eng/resources/documents/publication/p0739.htm).

generated at every level of German society, and resources that could have been dedicated to rebuilding an economy that was vital to Europe's recovery would have been consumed in protracted litigation. Pragmatically, if not logically, the decision seems sound.[29]

Indeed, even though the Nuremberg courts did not accept Shawcross' argument, other courts dealing with the legal problems raised by the War found it to be a serious one.[30] In a 1956 case before the Singapore Court of Appeal, addressing the legality of the Japanese Army's seizure of privately owned Dutch oil during the Japanese conquest and occupation in the Second World War of the Dutch East Indies, the Court considered the argument that the seizure was illegal because the war that Japan had waged against the Netherlands was illegal and aggressive:

> Certainly this contention raises grave issues, reaching and extending far beyond the present case, touching indeed the springs of international law. The compelling logic of those who assert that all legal rights should be refused to an aggressor is opposed by persuasive reasoning of those who maintain that such rules of war as are accepted by States should continue to prevail, notwithstanding the illegality of the war. Learned jurists differ profoundly on this matter and municipal courts have yet to give a decisive answer. In this state of uncertainty of the law, it is not, I think, desirable to express views on a matter which is not necessary for the decision in this case, and accordingly I do not pass upon it.[31]

In short, in light of the U.N. Charter, many courts and commentators have begun to find the underlying logic of the distinction problematic, and thus have avoided the question or justified their continued observance of the principle of separation on pragmatic grounds.

Post-U.N. Charter developments in state practice in codifying and developing by treaty the *jus in bello* seem also to have evidenced emerging doctrinal tension and significant uncertainty over the relationship between *jus ad bellum* and *jus in bello.* Protocol I itself provides a good example of this uncertainty. Although its Preamble reaffirms that *jus in bello* rules apply "without any adverse distinction based on the nature or origin of the armed conflict or on the causes espoused by or attributed to the Parties to the conflict," the substantive provisions of the Protocol emphasize that these rules must also regulate "armed conflicts in which peoples are fighting against colonial domination and alien occupation and against racist regimes in the

29 It can also be argued that the Nuremberg Courts' decision to preserve the immunity of combatants for an illegal aggressor in a criminal war facilitated future war. "Without the international law privilege for common soldiers, which shields their violent acts from prosecution even when committed in violation of *jus ad bellum,* individuals would be placed in the position of submitting to conscription at the peril of international legal culpability." Nathaniel Berman, *Privileging Combat? Contemporary Conflict and the Legal Construction of War,* 43 Colum. J. Transnat'l L. 1, 12 (2004). Without preserving the immunity, the democracies would have found it more difficult to recruit and command their troops.

30 For a review of the relevant case law, *see* Orakhelashvili, *supra* note 24.

31 *N.V. de Bataafsche Petroleum Maatschappli & Ors. v. The War Damage Comm'n,* (Ct. App. Sing. 1956), *reprinted in* 51 Am. J. Int'l L. 802, 811–12 (1957). For a contemporaneous comment, *see* "B," *The Case of the Singapore Oil Stocks,* 5 Int'l & Comp. L. Q. 84, 90–92 (1956).

exercise of their right to self-determination."[32] Although the Protocol does not affirmatively privilege the "peoples" that are fighting wars against colonization or apartheid over their state antagonists,[33] it is plainly designed, as both its proponents and critics argued, to tilt the rules of war in a way that served the cause of national liberation forces in the Third World.[34] To that extent, therefore, the Protocol can fairly be said to have woven *jus ad bellum* considerations into *jus in bello* rules.[35]

A similar ambiguity surrounds the Rome Statute of the International Criminal Court (the ICC).[36] Article 8 of that treaty specifies the "war crimes" over which the ICC is to have jurisdiction. These crimes essentially comprise infractions of established *jus in bello* rules.[37] Article 5(1)(d) separately gives the ICC jurisdiction over "[t]he crime of aggression"[38]—which is, effectively, the crime of violating the *jus ad bellum*. But Article 5(2) also specifies that the ICC is to exercise jurisdiction over the crime of aggression only after "a provision is adopted in accordance with [later articles of the Rome Statute] defining the crime and setting out the conditions under which the Court shall exercise jurisdiction with respect to this crime."[39] One might point to the separate treatment of most war crimes and the singular crime of "aggression" as evidence that the international community still upholds the distinction between *jus ad bellum* and *jus in bello*. Further, one could argue that the treaty-makers' inability to define the crime of "aggression" demonstrated that there is no international consensus over what makes a war "unlawful" or "unjust." On the other hand, the 2010 Review Conference of the Rome Statute in Kampala was able to adopt a resolution amending the Rome Statute so as to include the definition of aggression contemplated in Article 5(d).[40] That definition, moreover, is based on the General

32 Protocol, I, *supra* note 5, art. I, sec. 4.

33 *But see* Samuel Estreicher, Privileging Asymmetric Warfare? Defender Duties Under International Humanitarian Law (2010) New York University Public Law and Legal Theory Working Papers, Working Paper 193 at 2 ("Sadly, . . . what the parties achieved can be argued to have privileged certain aspects of guerilla strategy and thus to detract from the overall aim of enhancing the protection of civilians.").

34 *See, e.g.*, Sloane, *supra* note 24, at 65.

35 *See, e.g.*, Jeremy Rabkin, *Proportionality in Perspective: Historical Light on the Law of Armed Conflict*, 16 San Diego Int'l L. J. 263, 327-28 (2015) ("The truth is that AP-I itself implicitly recognizes that different wars authorize different rules, or that different rules may apply to different sides in the same war. . . . [I]t offers another reminder that we cannot, after all, think about *jus in bello* . . . in complete abstraction from *jus ad bellum*"); *see also* Berman, *supra* note 29, at 21. G.I.A.D. Draper, *Wars of National Liberation and War Criminality*, *in* Restraints on War: Studies in the Limitation of Armed Conflict 135, 147, 157 (Michael Howard ed., 1979).

36 *See* Rome Statute of the International Criminal Court, U.N. Doc. A/CONF.183/9 (as corrected by the procés-verbaux of 10 Nov. 1998, 12 July 1999, 30 Nov. 1999, 8 May 2000, 17 Jan. 2001, and 16 Jan. 2002) (entered into force July 1, 2002) (*available at* http://legal.un.org/icc/statute/english/rome_statute(e).pdf) [hereinafter "Rome Statute"].

37 *Id.* at art. 8

38 *Id.* at art. 5(1)(d)

39 *Id.* at art. 5(2).

40 *See* ICC Press Release, *Review Conference of the Rome Statute Concludes in Kampala* (June 12, 2010) (*available at* http://www.icc-cpi.int/NR/exeres/CF95BB41-B15A-45DA-B8CF-33E873E73829.htm).

Assembly's resolution 3314 (XXIX) of December 14, 1974—arguably indicating, again, that there is an international consensus on defining what constitutes an illegal war.

But the definition adopted at Kampala does not permit the ICC to exercise jurisdiction over this crime until 2017, and in other ways reflects political compromises.[41] Moreover, both Obama Administration and some legal scholars have continued to emphasize the inherent indeterminacy of the concept of "aggression."[42] Others argue that the attempt to define the crime of "aggression" violates basic human rights norms of due process and undermines the U.N. Charter framework.[43] And even if the crime of aggression is eventually to be considered, initially, exclusively a "leadership" crime rather than one that ordinary individual combatants commit,[44] that categorization would arguably entrench a potentially ever-widening persisting distinction between the *jus ad bellum* and much or most of the *jus in bello.*

Another example of the tension in current law can be found in "soft law" efforts to codify the *jus in bello*, such as the 1994 *San Remo Manual on International Law Applicable to Armed Conflicts at Sea* ("the Manual").[45] The Manual was drafted over six years and is the work of leading governmental and academic experts on the law of naval warfare. The International Committee of the Red Cross (ICRC) played a major role in the conferences. Although non-binding, the Manual is intended to encapsulate areas of broad agreement as to the current content of the customary law of naval warfare.[46] Article 6 of the Manual appears to be a straightforward statement of the general view of the relationship between *jus in bello* and *jus ad bellum*:

> The rules set out in this document and any other rules of international humanitarian law shall apply equally to all parties to the conflict. The equal application of these rules to all parties to the conflict shall not be affected by the international responsibility that may have been incurred by any of them for the outbreak of the conflict.[47]

---

41 *See The Crime of Aggression*, Coalition of the Int'l Crim. Ct. (*available at* http://www.iccnow.org/?mod=aggression).

42 The Obama Administration has criticized the Kampala definition, in part on grounds of its "uncertainty." *See* Beth Van Schaak, *U.S. Policy on Crime of Aggression Announced* (April 21, 2015) (*available at* http://justsecurity.org/22248/u-s-policy-icc-crime-aggression/). For legal scholars, *see, e.g.*, Andreas Paulus, *Second Thoughts on the Crime of Aggression*, 20 Eur. J. Int'l L. 1117, 1119–24 (2010); *see also* Roberts, *supra* note 9, at 956–57 (explaining the persisting difficulties in agreeing which side is more justified in resorting to force). The extensive historical record demonstrates repeated failure to arrive at a generally accepted, but also reasonably determinate, definition of "aggression." *See* Benjamin B. Ferencz, Defining International Aggression: The Search for World Peace, A Documentary History and Analysis, vol. 1 (1975).

43 *See* Michael J. Glennon, The Fog of War: Pragmatism, Security, and International Law ch. 9 (2010).

44 *See* Antonio Cassese, *On Some Problematical Aspects of the Crime of Aggression*, 20 Leiden J. Int'l L. 841 (2007).

45 San Remo Manual on International Law Applicable to Armed Conflicts at Sea, 12 June 1994 (*available at* https://www.icrc.org/ihl/INTRO/560?OpenDocument) [hereinafter "San Remo Manual"].

46 *See* Louise Doswald-Beck, *San Marino Manual on International Law Applicable to Armed Conflict at Sea*, 309 IRRC (1995) (*available at* http://www.icrc.org/eng/resources/documents/misc/57jmst.htm).

47 San Remo Manual, *supra* note 45, at art. 6.

Thus, consistent with the principle of separation, in stating that a party shall not be denied "equal application" of the *jus in bello* rules that it embodies because of that party's "international responsibility" for a conflict, the Manual denies that a wrongdoer under the *jus ad bellum* ceases to benefit from the principle of belligerent equality under the *jus in bello.*

However, the Manual affirms the principle of belligerent equality only in cases in which one of the belligerents is acting in lawful self-defense under Article 51 of the U.N. Charter. The Manual considers that belligerent equality is at least partly abrogated when the Security Council has determined a belligerent to be to be an aggressor. Under Article 7, such a state forgoes a belligerent's right under the traditional *jus in bello* to equal treatment by neutral states:

> Notwithstanding any rule in this document or elsewhere on the law of neutrality, where the Security Council, acting in accordance with its powers under Chapter VII of the Charter of the United Nations, has identified one or more of the parties to an armed conflict as responsible for resorting to force in violation of international law, neutral States:
>
> (a) are bound not to lend assistance other than humanitarian assistance to that State; and
>
> (b) may lend assistance to any State which has been a victim of a breach of the peace or an act of aggression by that State.[48]

Thus, the Manual, taking into account the new legal situation that might be created by the Security Council's Chapter VII powers to preempt traditional international law, and to the extent determined by the Security Council, does (at least in that special circumstance) seem to be prepared to disregard the principle of separation. The Manual is silent, however, as to the extent to which the Council actually possesses such an international legislative power in respect of the interaction between the *jus ad bellum* and *jus in bello.* For our purposes, the point is that international military law experts have now evidenced some discomfort too with an absolutist approach to the principle of separation.

The recent practice of states through the Security Council's decisions does not, however, definitively establish a practice under which the Council may, as foreseen by the Manual, modify the relationship between the *jus ad bellum* and the *jus in bello.* For example, consider Security Council Resolutions 1483 (2003)[49] and 1511 (2003),[50] which in substance confirmed the status of the Coalition forces that had invaded Iraq as the occupying power. Assuming (as is, of course, very arguable) that the Coalition's invasion of Iraq was illegal, one might be tempted to view

48 *Id.* at art. 7.

49 *See* S.C. Res 1483 (May 22, 2003).

50 *See* S.C. Res. 1511 (October 16, 2003).

the resolutions as nonetheless endorsing its temporary presence there. If so, then the Coalition's violation of *jus ad bellum* would not, in the Council's view, disentitle it from exercising the prerogatives and enjoying the benefits that accrue under the *jus in bello* to an army of occupation. On this view, the Council's practice would provide evidence for the dualist position that the illegality of a war does not alter the position of belligerents under the *jus in bello*. The alternative (and probably better) view, however, is that there is "nothing in these resolutions implying the legality of the presence of the coalition troops or validating the original use of force."[51]

Finally, the infrequent judicial decisions that touch on the question also do not indicate a settled position, or even a marked trend. In the International Court of Justice's *Nuclear Weapons Case*, the Court seemed to many commentators to be conflating *jus ad bellum* and *jus in bello* when it stated, in a split 7 to 7 holding, that which "the threat or use of nuclear weapons would generally be contrary to the rules of [*jus in bello*]," it nonetheless could not "conclude definitively whether the threat or use of nuclear weapons would be lawful or unlawful in an extreme circumstance of self-defence, in which the very survival of a State would be at stake."[52] This may reasonably, but not unquestionably, be understood to imply that the principle of belligerent equality does not always hold. Although states are "generally" not permitted by *jus in bello* to use or threaten to use nuclear weapons, still a state that is the victim of unlawful aggression may use such weapons against the aggressor if its "very survival" is at stake.[53]

Another significant case bearing on our question is the House of Lords March 3, 2006 decision in *R. v. Jones*.[54] The lead opinion for Lord Bingham, after reviewing existing law, held that "the core elements of the crime of aggression have been understood, since at least 1945, with sufficient clarity to permit the lawful trial (and, on conviction, punishment) of those accused of this most serious crime."[55] Yet the Lords also declined to enforce the international prohibition on the crime of aggression in the absence of a decision by Parliament to penalize it by a domestic statute. Furthermore, Lord Bingham opinion suggested that aggression would be "a leadership crime: it cannot be committed by minions and footsoldiers."[56]

---

51 Orakhelashvili, *supra* note 24, at 181. *See also* Robert J. Delahunty, *The Battle of Mars and Venus: Why Do American and European Attitudes to International Law Differ?*, 4 Loy. U. Chi. Int'l L. Rev. 10, 45–47 (2006) (discussing background to, and import of, Resolution 1483).

52 Legality of the Threat or Use of Nuclear Weapons, Advisory Opinion, 1996 ICJ Rep. 226, 266 (July 8) [hereinafter Legality of Nuclear Weapons].

53 *See* Sloane, *supra* note 24, at 91.

54 [2006] UKHL 16, 45 I.L.M. 992 (2006). For commentary, *see* Donald M. Ferencz, *Introductory Note to United Kingdom House of*Lords R. v. Jones, et al., 45 I.L.M. 988 (2006).

55 *Id.* at ¶ 19 (Opinion of Lord Bingham of Cornhill.)

56 *Id.* at ¶ 16.

2. Debating the Modern Position

We now consider the factors giving rise to renewed debate of the modern position. Then, we describe the opposing camps. Finally, we critique each set of views.

a. Factors Giving Rise to Renewed Debate

It may be largely because of the changing nature of war, the debate over the relationship between *jus ad bellum* and *jus in bello*, seemingly concluded by the 1960s,[57] has recently resumed.[58] The renewal of the debate was occasioned, in large part, by the War in Kosovo, which provoked the question whether the standards of conduct in a military "humanitarian intervention" ought to be held higher—or, others argued, lower—for the intervening forces.[59] On the one side, it was argued that since the NATO countries had premised their intervention on a concern for human rights, they had accordingly assumed a heightened obligation to wage the war with respect for civilian life and property, even though that might mean exposing their own combatants to significantly greater risks.[60] As Michael Walzer argued at the time, "*You can't kill unless you are prepared to die.*"[61] Likewise, Paul Kahn maintained that "combatants are allowed to injure each other just as long as they stand in a relationship of mutual risk. The soldier who takes himself out of battle is no longer a legitimate target"—or, by the same reasoning, a legitimate attacker.[62] Moreover, it was argued, a willingness to use tactics that lessened risks to Serbian non-combatants even while raising those for the NATO forces would have been

---

57 *See* Judith Gail Gardam, *Proportionality and Force in International Law,* 87 Am. J. Int'l L. 391, 393 (1993) (stating, from the standpoint of the early 1990s, that "the relationship between the two [bodies of law] has . . . remained largely unexplored").

58 *See* Sloane, *supra* note 24, at 53.

59 For example, the Independent International Commission on Kosovo recommended that

> the ICRC or other appropriate expert body prepare a new legal convention for military operations that are . . . instances of . . . humanitarian intervention. This convention should impose more constraints on the use of force than are embodied in the law of war as now generally interpreted. A less ambitious alternative, recommended by Amnesty International, would be to accept stricter adherence to the existing standards of international law, particularly as already embodied in Protocol I.

The Independent International Commission on Kosovo, The Kosovo Report 66 (2000) (*available at* http://www.reliefweb.int/library/docuyments/thekosovoreport.htm). *See also id.* at 59 ("[T]he Commission believes that a greater obligation is imposed on the intervening side to take care of the civilian population in a humanitarian campaign. . . . The Commission believes that this proposal should be formalized in international law, perhaps in the form of a 'Protocol III' to the Geneva Conventions."); *id.* at 70 ("There must be even stricter adherence to the laws of war and international humanitarian law than in standard military operations. This applies to all aspects of the military operation, including any post cease-fire occupation.").

60 *See* Sloane, *supra* note 24, at 50–51, 94. *See generally* Walzer, *supra* note 10, at 156 ("[I]f saving civilian lives means risking soldier[s'] lives, the risk must be accepted. But there is a limit to the risks that we require. . . . We can only ask soldiers to minimize the dangers they impose."). For a critique of NATO's decision to fly at a minimum altitude of 15,000 feet, *see* Olivera Medenica, *Protocol I and Operation Allied Force: Did NATO Abide by Principles of Proportionality,* 23 Loyola of L.A. Int'l & Comp. L. Rev. 329, 405–09 (2001). For a defense, *see* Michael N. Schmitt, *Military Necessity and Humanity in International Humanitarian Law: Preserving the Delicate Balance,* 50 Va. J. Int'l L. 795, 822–23 (2010).

61 Michael Walzer, Arguing About War 101 (2004) (original emphasis).

62 Paul W. Kahn, *The Paradox of Riskless Warfare,* 22 Phil. & Pub. Pol'y Q. 2, 3 (2002).

a test of the genuineness of NATO's professed humanitarian motives: in other words, *jus ad bellum* was to be measured in part by *jus in bello*.[63] Thus, for example, if military necessity as a constraint would not protect the retreating forces of a clearly defeated enemy who have not laid down its arms, such as Iraqi forces retreating during the First Gulf War, then perhaps *jus ad bello* proportionality principles would argue for a normatively more attractive result in which American forces should have exercised greater restraint.[64]

On the other side, it was argued that precisely because NATO's motive was to uphold and protect human rights, the legal constraints on its conduct of hostilities ought to be relaxed, especially if compliance would have made it harder to achieve the Alliance's main objective.[65] It was also suggested, from the human rights side, that the Serbia's election of the Milosevic government, and especially the indifference of the majority of its population to the atrocities that its government was planning or committing against the Kosovar Albanians, stripped Serbs of the immunity that *jus in bello* ordinarily affords to civilians and made it legitimate for NATO targeting to "undermine [civilians'] morale and disrupt [their] comfort"—that is, deliberately to target civilian population centers and objects.[66] And, from the military side, one commentator argued:

> We need a new paradigm when using force against societies with malevolent propensities. We must hold at risk the very way of life that sustains their depredations, and we must threaten

63 *See, e.g.*, David Luban, *Intervention and Civilization, in* Global Justice and Transitional Politics: Essays on the Moral and Political Challenges of Globalization 79, 82 (Pablo De Greiff & Ciarin Cronin eds., 2002).

64 According to Christopher Greenwood, *jus ad bellum* applies at every stage of an armed conflict. Thus a state, even if acting in lawful self-defense and conformably to the *jus in bello*, "must also show that all its measures involving the use of force, throughout the conflict, are reasonable, proportionate acts of self-defence." Christopher Greenwood, *The Relationship Between Jus ad Bellum and Jus in Bello*, 9 Rev. Int'l Stud. 221, 233 (1983). Greenwood illustrated this by the British Navy's sinking of the Argentine cruiser *General Belgrano* during the 1982 Falklands/Maldives War. In his view, an armed conflict between Britain and Argentina had arisen, and an Argentine warship was unquestionably a lawful military objective for Britain under the *jus in bello*. Nevertheless, the sinking of the *Belgrano* was legally and politically controversial: critics challenged whether it was a necessary and proportionate act of self-defense. Greenwood contended that the controversy demonstrates the continuing applicability of *jus ad bellum* to (at least many forms of) armed conflict. Applying Greenwood's analysis, one might ask whether the Coalition's continuing attacks on the defeated and desperate Iraqi forces in the First Gulf War, even though permissible under *jus in bello*, were unreasonable and unlawful under the *jus ad bellum*.

65 *See* Ruth Wedgwood, *Propositions on the Law of War after the Kosovo Campaign,* 78 Int'l L. Stud. 433 (Andru E. Wall (ed.), Naval War College 2002). Wedgwood wrote that:

> th[e] asserted independence of the two regimes may be no more than a fiction. Defeating Nazism, for example, required measures that are now seen as harsh and even punitive. Even where their legality is conceded under the earlier standards of air war, it is commonly taught in American military curricula that their repetition would now be illegal. It may be that our real judgment of their contemporaneous legality is affected by the radical evil represented by Nazism—an ideology posing an ultimate threat to human welfare. Kosovo, in its smaller venue, may be another illustration of that same quiet linkage. This was not a war to settle a commercial dispute, or remap the location of a boundary valued because of its mineral deposits, but rather a war to prevent ethnic expulsions. As such, its speedy conclusion was necessary. A gradual war of attrition that might defeat Belgrade in slow motion was unacceptable in light of the human survival at stake in the conflict itself. Whether one's framework is utilitarian or pure principle, it is possible to admit that the merits of a war make a difference in our tolerance for methods of warfighting.

Id. at 434–34.

66 Geoffrey Robertson, Crimes Against Humanity: The Struggle for Global Justice 483–84 (3d ed. 2006), *criticized in* Robert J. Delahunty & John C. Yoo, *What is the Role of Human Rights Law in the War on Terror?*, 59 DePaul L. Rev. 803, 848 (2010).

to destroy their world as they know it if they persist. This means the air weapon should be unleashed against entire new categories of property that current conceptions of [*jus in bello*] put off-limits.[67]

In short, what the critics share is a belief that the reasons for the violation of the *jus ad bellum* matter in the application of the *jus in bello.*

Yet, the nature of the intervener may matter as well. The view that humanitarian intervention—which is characteristically, though not always, undertaken by major Western states—should not be governed by the ordinary rules of *jus in bello* may well reflect the way in which democracies, especially the United States, tend to fight contemporary war, especially air war. Some scholars contend that "democracies could be more likely to target noncombatants because the vulnerability of leaders to public opinion makes them wary of incurring heavy costs on the battlefield for fear of losing support at home. This fear could compel democratic elites to target noncombatants to avoid costs or to win the war quickly."[68] Other scholars have argued that U.S. military doctrine has placed increasing, if arguably legally questionable, emphasis on targeting civilian infrastructure, in the hopes of draining off political support for hostile governments.[69] This may well have been true in the Kosovo War.[70]

---

67 Charles J. Dunlap, Jr., *The End of Innocence: Rethinking Noncombatancy in the Post-Kosovo Era,* Strat. Rev. 14 (2000). Col. Dunlap would not, however, target either civilians or civilian objects, and would reserve air campaigns of the sort he describes for conflicts with societies whose "moral compass" was "wildly askew." *Id.*

68 Alexander B. Downes, *Desperate Times, Desperate Measures: The Causes of Civilian Victimization in War,* 30 Int'l Sec. 152, 153–54 (2006); *see also* Dan Reiter & Allan C. Stam, Democracies at War 167–72 (2002); Bruce Bueno de Mesquita & Randolph M. Siverson, *War and the Survival of Political Leaders: A Comparative Analysis of Regime Types and Accountability,* 89 Am. Pol. Sci. Rev. 841 (1989).

69 *See* Ward Thomas, *Victory by Duress: Civilian Infrastructure as a Target in Air Campaigns,* 15 Security Stud. 1 (2006); *see also* Yoram Dinstein, The Conduct of Hostilities under the Law of International Armed Conflict 93 (2d edn. 2010) (arguing that forcing a change in negotiating attitudes "cannot be deemed a proper military advantage"); Ruth Wedgwood, *Proportionality and Necessity in American National Security Decision Making,* 86 Proc. Am. Soc. Int'l L. 58, 61–62 (1992) ("[T]he political desirability of concluding a conflict in the shortest possible time does not excuse us from observance of tactical and strategic proportionality."). The chief doubts about the legality of the asserted practices seem to derive from Additional Protocol I, and particularly from its formulation of the principle of distinction. As we saw in Part III Chapter 1, Protocol I's formulations have themselves been subject to serious criticism.

70 *See* Michael N. Schmitt, *Asymmetrical Warfare and International Humanitarian Law,* 62 A.F. L. Rev. 1, 31 (2008) ("[T]he logic of [effects-based operations], particularly when applied in a coercive campaign, will sometimes lead planners towards targeting non-military objectives."). "Effects-based operations" aim to produce specific effects through target engagement, such as the decapitation of the Iraqi political leadership. *See id.* at 29. The War in Kosovo "serves as a classic 'coercive' campaign, for its intent was never to defeat President Slobodan Milosevic's army. Rather, it was to compel a return to the bargaining table and end systematic and widespread mistreatment of the Kosovar Albanian population." *Id.* at 30.

Did NATO's air campaign bring about Milosevic's capitulation? In particular, did it succeed in causing so much discontent within the civilian population of Serbia that Milosevic surrendered because of fear of internal threats to Milosevic's regime? Some informed analysts conclude that this was at least *part* of the explanation for Serbia's defeat. *See* Daniel L. Byman & Matthew C. Waxman, *Kosovo and the Great Air Power Debate,* 24 Int'l Sec. 5, 19–20 (2000). They also point out, however, that "a recurring historical lesson is that attempts to force an adversary's hand by targeting its populace's will to resist may backfire. Coercion often stiffens an adversary's determination, as the leadership and the country as a whole unite against the coercer." *Id.* at 20 (footnote omitted). *See also* Thomas, *supra* note 69, at 15–19 (questioning whether it "pays to make civilians suffer" from aerial bombardments, both generally and in the case of the Kosovo War).

More fundamentally, the debate over the proper standard for assessing NATO's conduct of hostilities in Kosovo reflected a recurring dilemma within what the historian Michael Howard once called "the liberal conscience."[71] When democratic societies go to war, they often wage it with extraordinary zeal and ferocity, owing in part perhaps to a belief in the justice of the causes for which they fight.[72] On the other hand, the late twentieth-century liberal conscience seems "to have required Western states, if they were to fight, to fight in ever more bloodless and 'humane' ways (at least as far as their own armed forces were concerned)."[73] In the Kosovo War, the dilemma became acute. On the one side, it seemed to be a "good war" fought by Western liberal democracies against a semi-autocratic ruler who was pursuing a policy of ethnic cleansing, if not genocide[74]; on the other hand, that very purpose seemed to require that the war be as sparing as possible of civilian casualties, both Kosovar and Serbian, while the fragility of the political support for the campaign dictated that NATO's own casualties be held to a minimum.

But the identity of the target seems to matter as well. Further impetus for renewed debate comes from the War on Terror. On the one side, Osama bin Laden himself seemed to be saying that the civilians in the Twin Towers were legitimate targets because he was waging a *jihad*—the Koranic equivalent of a just or lawful war—against the United States.[75] Other Islamic radicals have reportedly been elaborating a "*jihad* etiquette"; the Egyptian legal scholar Yusuf al-Qaradawi argues that the killing of Israeli civilians is permissible because they are subject to compulsory military service, and the Saudi cleric Abdullah bin Nasser al-Rashid takes the position that civilians may be targeted for killing in retribution for an enemy attack on Muslim civilians.[76] On the other side, although the United States never argued that the laws of war should be relaxed in its favor, critics of its policies contended (rightly or wrongly) that its view of the legal status of al Qaeda and Taliban captives demonstrated that it was exempting itself from ordinary *jus in bello* rules.[77] In any case, it might be argued that a different legal regime from the

---

71 *See* Michael Howard, War and the Liberal Conscience (1978).

72 *See, e.g.*, John W. Dower, Cultures of War: Pearl Harbor, Hiroshima, 9-11, Iraq (2010). The belief that democracies tend to fight heavily moralized—and therefore, *unlimited*—war has had notable exponents. *See, e.g.*, Walter Lippmann, The Public Philosophy (1955).

73 Nicholas Rengger, *On the Just War Tradition in the Twenty-First Century*, 78 Int'l Aff. 353, 356 (2002).

74 Of course, a good many people doubted whether Kosovo was a "good" war. *See, e.g.*, Christine M. Chinkin, *A "Good" or a "Bad" War?*, 93 Am. J. Int'l L. 841 (1999); Michael Mccgwire, *Why Did We Bomb Belgrade?*, 76 Int'l Aff. 1 (2000). Others defended it. *See, e.g.*, Lawrence Freedman, *Victims and Victors: Reflections on the Kosovo War*, 26 Rev. Int'l Stud. 335, 358 (2000) ("Milosevic needed to be opposed because he represented an ethno-nationalist ideology that had already proved itself as a truly malign influence in European politics."). *See generally* Robert J. Delahunty & Antonio F. Perez, *The Kosovo Crisis: A Dostoievskian Dialogue on International Law, Statecraft, and Soulcraft*, 42 Vand. J. Transnat'l L. 15 (2009).

75 Bin Laden is reported to have said that because they were "supporting US economic power," the individuals at work in the Twin Towers were not true civilians, and hence were legitimate targets. *See* Dino Kritsiotis, *On the Jus ad Bellum and Jus in Bello of Operation Enduring Freedom*, 96 Am. Soc. Int'l L. 35, 39–40 & 26 (2002).

76 *See* Michael Moss & Souad Mekhennet, *The Guidebook for Taking a Life*, The New York Times (June 10, 2007) (*available at* http://www.nytimes.com/2007/06/10/weekinreview/10moss.html?_r=0).

77 For a defense of the United States' legal position on whether al Qaeda and Taliban captives were entitled to prisoner of war status, *see* Robert J. Delahunty, *Is the Geneva POW Convention "Quaint"?*, 33 Wm. Mitchell L. Rev. 1635 (2007). For

jus in bello applicable to inter-state warfare should govern hostilities between the United States and its allies and "transnational" terrorist groups like al Qaeda. Combatants for such groups are unlikely to be induced to lay down arms by the offer of prisoner-of-war treatment, would also be unlikely to reciprocate such treatment with respect to their captives, disregard the basic legal norms governing the conduct of war (including civilian immunity), and belong to organizations that have no discernible political goals which might become the subject of negotiation and compromise that could bring the conflict to an end.[78] Thus, like humanitarian intervention, in the war against terror, the way democracies tend to fight war may drive *jus in bello* doctrine in a particular direction.[79]

b. The Opposing Camps

Recently, the debate has intensified, with leading scholars taking opposing positions on the relationship between *jus ad bellum* and *jus in bello.* On the one side, figures such Antoine Bouvier,[80] Enzo Cannizaro,[81] Yoram Dinstein,[82] Christopher Greenwood,[83] Françoise Hampson,[84]

---

criticism of the Bush Administration's position, *see* Gary D. Solis, The Law of Armed Conflict: International Humanitarian Law in War 214–16 (2010). For a balanced overview of this controversy by a (subsequently appointed) Judge of the International Court of Justice, *see* Christopher Greenwood, *International Law and the "War against Terrorism"*, 78 Int'l Aff. 301, 313–16 (2002). For a review of different approaches to the category of "unlawful" or "unprivileged" combatants, *see* Curtis A. Bradley, *The United States, Israel & Unlawful Combatants*, 12 Green Bag 2d 397 (2009).

78 *See* Gross, *supra* note 21, at 47 ("But the war on terror may be . . . a fight to the death. International terrorists can count none among them who aim solely to destroy military targets. Aggression of the worst sort, unmitigated by any nationalist agenda, belies any claim to just cause, while no prospect of a political settlement or response in kind offers any ground for extending combatant equality. . . . It appears, then, that international terrorists warrant some status that combines criminality with combatancy."). We discuss Gross' view in more detail later, *see infra* notes 145 & 156.

79 *See* James D. Morrow, *When Do States Follow the Laws of War?*, 101 Am. Pol. Sci. Rev. 559, 571 (2007). Morrow stated:

> Although democracies are more likely to live up to their [*jus in bello*] commitments, such commitments also reinforce reciprocal response against enemies who violate the standards of those commitments. Faced with nonstate opponents who do not recognize the laws of war and adopt atrocity as their central strategy, the willingness of the Bush Administration to stretch and perhaps break the standards of humane treatment is not surprising . . . . Arguments in favor of those standards will carry more weight with those responsible for policy when they emphasize self-interest in following those standards over legal obligations to do so. After all, the laws of war exist because national leaders have seen such restrictions on violence during wartime as being in their interest when they can be enforced.

Id.

80 *See* Antoine Bouvier, *Assuming the Relationship Between Jus in Bello and Jus ad Bellum: An "Orthodox" View*, 100 Proc. Am. Soc. Int'l L. 109 (2006).

81 *See* Enzo Cannizaro, *Contextualizing Proportionality: Jus ad Bellum and Jus in Bello in the Lebanese War*, 88 IRRC 779, 787 (2006).

82 *See* Yoram Dinstein, *Comments on War*, 27 Harv. J.L. & Pub. Pol'y 877 (2004),

83 *See* Greenwood, *supra* note 64.

84 Françoise Hampson, *Winning by the Rules: Law and Warfare in the 1980s*, 11 Third World Q. 31, 41–42 (1989) (describing the distinction as "[p]erhaps the greatest achievement of humanitarian law").

Jasmine Moussa,[85] Sir Adam Roberts,[86] Marco Sassòli,[87] and Robert Sloane[88] have defended (with various qualifications) the "orthodox" view of belligerent equality and the independence of the two bodies of law. On the other side (though with strikingly different normative perspectives) are such scholars as Eyal Benvenisti,[89] Nathaniel Berman,[90] Geoffrey Best,[91] William Bradford,[92] Stephen Carter,[93] Charles Dunlap, Jr.,[94] Michael Gross,[95] Thomas Hurka,[96] Frédéric Mégret,[97] Thomas Nagle,[98] Alexander Orakhelashvili,[99] Brian Orend,[100] Carsten Stahn,[101] and Ruth Wedgwood.[102] But the differences, though genuine and substantial, are not as stark as they might at first appear. Thus, although Sloan argued that "the dualistic axiom remains indispensable to the law of war," he insists that "it cannot be applied acontextually—for example, without considering, descriptively, the comparative power of the parties, the technology available to each, and the nature of the conflict."[103] Sloane also, though guardedly, admitted the possibility of an exception from "the dualistic axiom" for certain cases of military humanitarian intervention: "Contrary to the dualistic axiom, it *may* be that in certain cases (in particular, where intervention in arguable

---

85 *See* Jasmine Moussa, *Can Jus ad Bellum override Jus in Bello? Reaffirming the Separation of the Two Bodies of Law,* 872 IRRC 963 (2008).

86 *See* Roberts, *supra* note 9.

87 *See* Marco Sassòli, Ius ad Bellum *and* Ius in Bello—*the Separation Between the Legality of the Use of Force and Humanitarian Rules to be Respected in Warfare: Crucial or Outdated?, in* International Law and Armed Conflict: Exploring the Faultlines —Essays in Honour of Yoram Dinstein 241 (Michael N. Schmitt & Jelena Pejic eds., 2007).

88 *See* Sloane, *supra* note 24.

89 *See* Eyal Benvenisti, *Rethinking the Divide Between Jus Ad Bellum and Jus in Bello in Warfare Against Nonstate Actors,* 34 Yale J. Int'l L. 541 (2009).

90 *See* Berman, *supra* note 29, at 28, 56–57.

91 *See* Geoffrey Best, War & Law Since 1945 235–47 (1994).

92 *See* William Bradford, *Barbarians at the Gates: A Post-September 11th Proposal To Rationalize the Laws of War,* 73 Miss. L.J. 639 (2004).

93 *See* Stephen L. Carter, The Violence of Peace: America's Wars in the Age of Obama 62 (2011) (finding that the distinction rests on "shaky foundations" insofar as it assumes the "invincible ignorance" of individual combatants).

94 Dunlap, Jr., *supra* note 67.

95 *See* Gross, *supra* note 21.

96 *See* Thomas Hurka, *Proportionality in the Morality of War,* 33 Phil. & Pub. Aff. 34, 44–45 (2005).

97 *See* Frédéric Mégret, *Jus in Bello and Jus ad Bellum,* 100 Proc. Am. Soc. Int'l L. 121 (2006).

98 *See* Thomas Nagle, *War and Massacre,* 1 Phil. & Pub. Aff. 123, 123 (1972).

99 *See* Orakhelashvili, *supra* note 24. Orakhelashvili would not, however, go so far as to impose *criminal* liability on individual combatants *merely* because they were fighting for an aggressor.

100 *See* Brian Orend, The Morality of War 107–10 (2006).

101 Carsten Stahn, "*Jus ad bellum,*" "jus in bello" . . . "jus post bellum"?—*Rethinking the Conception of the Law of Armed Force,* 17 Eur. J. Int'l L. 921 (2007).

102 *See* Wedgwood, *supra* note 65, at 434–35.

103 Sloane, *supra* note 24, at 53.

violation of the dualistic axiom is the sole way to stop serious human rights atrocities), the same values that underwrite that axiom should countenance limited exceptions to it."[104] On the other side, though he argued rigorously against dualism on the basis of the principle that an aggressor should not profit from its illegal conduct, Orahelashvili would not go so far as to impose criminal liability on individual combatants *merely* because they were fighting for the aggressor. Moreover, even those who, like Michael Schmitt, accept that the independence of the two bodies of law is "foundational" under existing law, also acknowledge that if one belligerent considers the other to be in serious breach of the *jus ad bellum,* that will likely make a difference to the way in which it regards its enemy's claims under the *jus in bello.*[105]

Before turning to the merits of the dispute, it will be useful to indicate what is not at issue—or at least, what is not truly central to the issue. Three such areas may be identified.[106]

First, both sides seem generally to agree that the requirements of *jus ad bellum* and *jus in bello* are cumulative: both sets of norms apply to international (and perhaps other) armed conflict. In particular, both the requirement of (what we may similarly call "strategic") proportionality that applies through the *jus ad bellum* and the requirement of (say to say, "tactical") proportionality that applies through the *jus in bello* must be satisfied.[107] Support for this proposition comes from the ICJ's *Nuclear Weapons* opinion: the Court says there that "a use of force that is proportionate under the [*jus ad bellum*] law of self-defence, must, in order to be lawful, also meet the requirements of the law applicable in armed conflict which comprise in particular the principles and rules of humanitarian law."[108] Thus, even if a state is waging war lawfully and justly, either as a valid exercise of self-defense or pursuant to the Security Council's authorization, its conduct

---

104 *Id.* at 107 (emphasis in original).

105 Michael N. Schmitt, *Asymmetrical Warfare and International Humanitarian Law,* 62 A.F. L. Rev. 1, 39–40 (2008). The point is noted in other writers as well. *See, e.g.,* Gardam, *supra* note 57, at 412.

106 In addition to the three areas specified in the text, we note that there is some support on both sides for the view that an aggressor is not necessarily entitled to all of the traditional rights of a belligerent under the law of neutrality or the law of military occupation. In those areas, the illegality of an aggressive war might operate to deny an aggressor some or all of the usual benefits that accrue to a belligerent under the *jus in bello. Cf.* Adam Roberts, *Prolonged Military Occupation: The Israeli-Occupied Territories Since 1967,* 84 Am. J. Int'l L. 44 (1990). But we note that there is related case law cutting the other way. *See* Sassòli, *supra* note 87, at 241, 249 (discussing *Partial Award, Central Front, Ethiopia's Claim 2* at ¶ 78, Eritrea-Ethiopia Claims Comm'n (Fed. Rep. of Ethiopia v. State of Eritrea), The Hague, Apr. 28, 2004).

What we are chiefly considering here is whether a belligerent's traditional *jus in bello* rights and obligations on the battlefield or post-capture are altered by the legality or illegality of its decision for war.

107 *See* Greenwood, *supra* note 64, at 230–31. Orakhelashvili, *supra* note 24; Cannizaro, *supra* note 81, at 791–92. For explanations and illustrations of the two types of proportionality, *see, e.g.,* Sloane, *supra* note 24, at 52–53; Moussa, *supra* note 85, at 975–76.

What exactly does it mean to say that the two proportionality tests are "cumulative"? Gardam opined that the *jus ad bellum* proportionality test is not satisfied merely by a review of planning decisions at the onset of a campaign. Rather, in her view, "[e]ach time" targets are selected, "the relationship between the destruction of the target or targets and the scope of [the lawful objective of the war] would . . . require[] assessment." Gardam, *supra* note 57, at 404. Over and above that, a separate review of whether the proportionality requirements of the *jus in bello* (as specified, for example, in Article 51 of Additional Protocol I) would be met. It is doubtful that Gardam's view of existing law is generally accepted.

108 Legality of Nuclear Weapons, *supra* note 52, at ¶ 42.

of hostilities must comport with the requirements of *jus in bello*. (The same is true, of course, of an aggressor.)

Second, non-compliance with the *jus in bello* may create a kind of back-flow that could call into question whether the state in breach is genuinely waging a just or legal war under *jus ad bellum* precepts. This, at least, is true if one assumes that the justice or legality of going to war is not (always) fully and finally determinable in the circumstances prevailing at the outbreak of the conflict, but that any judgment made at that time is revisable in light of later events. Frédéric Mégret, who advances this view, suggested that:

> a state's performance at the level of the *jus in bello* . . . should be taken into account in evaluating the legality of its intervention under the *jus ad bellum*. . . . Rather than what seems the standard practice of a "once and for all" evaluation of the legality of a state's participation to a war, one would be confronted with a more continuous evaluation.[109]

Thus, a state that is waging what seems initially to be a legitimate war of self-defense, but that repeatedly commits atrocities in the conduct of that war may be held, in retrospect, not to have been fighting in accordance with the *jus ad bellum* after all.[110]

Third, in light of the Kampala Conference's amendment to the Rome Statute, there may be an emerging consensus supporting individual criminal liability for political and military leaders for violating the norms of *jus ad bellum*. Although this development stems from Nuremberg, it nonetheless represents a departure from the usual practice of applying *jus ad bellum* only at the level of states and *jus in bello* only at the level of individuals. But this should not yet represent the breakdown of the traditional *jus ad bellum/jus in bello* distinction. This is because it also seems widely agreed that criminalizing aggressive war would not yet by itself entail individual criminal liability under the *jus in bello* for combatants outside those leadership circles solely on the basis of their participation in that war. Thus, if what has been called the problem of

109 Mégret, *supra* note 97, at 122–23. Sloane, on the other side of the debate, seems to accept this. *See* Sloane, *supra* note 24, at 67–67. So, apparently, does Gardam. *See* Gardam, *supra* note 57, at 405 (citing Walzer, *supra* note 10). In a similar vein, Cannizaro noted that third states and international organizations pointed to the high level of collateral damage incurred in Israel's 2006 campaign in Lebanon as proof that Israel had failed to satisfy the *jus ad bellum*'s proportionality requirement. Cannizaro, *supra* note 81, at 792. *But see* Moussa, *supra* note 85, at 977.

110 Relatedly, a change in a belligerent's basic strategic objectives may affect judgments about the belligerent's standing under the *jus ad bellum*. The U.S-led war in Korea was authorized by the Security Council, and therefore must be counted as a "just" or "lawful" war under the relevant Charter standard. Nonetheless, if the decision of the U.N. forces to advance beyond the 38th parallel marked a fundamental change in the strategic aims of the war—from the defense of South Korea to the destruction of the Communist government of the North—the question would arise whether the U.N. forces were continuing to fight a "just" war. Likewise, if the Coalition forces seeking to oust Iraq from Kuwait in the First Gulf War had pressed their campaign to the point of seeking regime change in Iraq, the fact that the Security Council had authorized them to eject the Iraqi forces from Kuwait would not necessarily establish that they were continuing to wage war "justly" and "legally."

the "innocent soldier" can be backed out of the dispute,[111] the area in dispute is significantly narrower.[112]

c. A Critique of the Debate

Why, then, do some legal scholars maintain the traditional independence of *jus in bello* from *jus ad bellum*, while others deny it? Two main arguments can be distilled from the debate. One goes to the question whether and how the illegality of a war can be authoritatively determined, the other to the question of the consequences that would flow from negating the traditional distinction.[113]

Some writers find it more or less unproblematic to determine whether a belligerent is an "aggressor" or not. Although these writers may derive the relevant tests from the U.N. Charter, they do not consider it necessary to await a ruling from the Security Council on whether any particular belligerent is an aggressor. It is possible and even desirable for individual states to apply the Charter rules on their own, without an institutional determination. Thus, Orakhelashvili wrote that "[t]he legal position under *jus ad bellum* is clear enough to help identifying the aggressor even without the institutional determination."[114] But other writers take (as it seems to us) a more prudentially circumspect view. Sloane contended that:

> despite the postwar effort to subject war to law, the *jus ad bellum* remains, as it has been historically, manipulable and highly politicized. In contrast, the *jus in bello* . . . strives to remain agnostic about the architectural goals of war . . . Th[e] model, which denies the dualistic axiom and instead affords the perceived defender more leeway in its application of the *jus in bello* than it does the perceived aggressor . . . is, as experience attests, simply unrealistic.... Absent an authoritative decision on force's legality, which an institutionally paralyzed Security Council [can] seldom provide, each belligerent would inevitably justify force by reference to the Charter, typically as self-defense under Article 51.[115]

As to the consequences that would flow through the negation of the distinction, Moussa provided a succinct and forceful statement of the view that they would be morally and practically intolerable:

111 *See* Roberts, *supra* note 9, at 957–59.

112 *See* Orakhelashvili, *supra* note 24.

113 Both defenses of the traditional distinction were foreshadowed in Lauterpacht. *See supra* notes 25–26.

114 Orakhelashvili, *supra* note 24.

115 Sloane, *supra* note 24, at 69, 71.

> The humanitarian argument in favour of the separation principle is convincing: essentially, victims on both sides of a conflict are equally worthy of protection. Equally cogent are the pragmatic considerations; it could never be hoped that the belligerents would respect humanitarian law if there were not some element of reciprocity in its application. Arguably, linking *jus in bello* to *jus ad bellum* would lead to either of two equally undesirable scenarios. The first is that *jus in bello* would not apply to a war of aggression in its entirety and hence would bind neither of the parties. Needless to say, such an invitation to unrestricted warfare must be rejected on moral and humanitarian grounds. The second scenario is that *jus in bello* restricts only the aggressor and not the party acting in self-defence. Such a proposition is equally problematic, as, without the element of reciprocity, it is inconceivable that either party will respect the principles of international humanitarian law.[116]

But Moussa's contentions are not unanswerable. We consider each argument, the moral argument and the pragmatic argument, in turn.

As to her "humanitarian" or moral argument, is it really true that the "victims" on both sides of a conflict are "equally worthy of protection"? Do we, on reflection, want to say that about either the Serbian civilians who enthusiastically supported Milosevic's program of ethnic cleansing or Hitler's soldiers who invaded Russia in the hope of settling there as colonists?

In Tolstoy's great novel *War and Peace* (1869), shortly before the Battle of Borodino against the invading French Army in 1812, Prince Andrei Bolkonski remarks to his friend Pierre Bezukhov:

> I would not take prisoners. Why take prisoners? It's chivalry! The French have destroyed my home and are on their way to destroy Moscow, they have outraged me and are outraging me at every moment. They are my enemies. In my opinion they are all criminals . . . . They should be executed.[117]

Why, one might ask, is this way of thinking wrong? No doubt the Russian side would be restrained by the knowledge that if it gave no quarter to the French and executed all its French prisoners, the French would retaliate against the Russians. But that answer collapses the "moral" argument into the "pragmatic" one.

Moussa's "pragmatic" argument maintains that, if *jus in bello* were not applicable equally to all parties to a conflict, both sides (or at least the disadvantaged side) would engage in unrestrained and inhumane warfare. But if reciprocity has the effects that she attributes to it, that

116 Moussa, *supra* note 85, at 967.

117 Leo Tolstoy, War and Peace, Book X, ch. XXIV at 1824 (*available at* http://www.planetpdf.com/planetpdf/pdfs/free_ebooks/War_and_Peace_NT.pdf).

would not necessarily follow.[118] On the contrary, if both parties were concerned about the treatment of their soldiers who had fallen into the enemy's hands, both sides could have an incentive to treat their captives humanely, even if neither side had legal obligation to do so. The same would hold true if only one side had a legal obligation toward its captives and the other did not, because the side that was disadvantaged would treat its captives humanely if, but only if, the advantaged side reciprocated that treatment. Moussa's "pragmatic" argument for maintaining the distinction seems instead to undermine it, by making the *jus in bello* seem either redundant or useless. For, where reciprocity is effective, the *jus in bello* is not needed to secure humane treatment; and, where reciprocity is ineffective, the *jus in bello* is likely to be so as well.[119]

Of course, that response is too simple and schematic. Moussa was right to argue that if one belligerent believes that its standing under the *jus ad bellum* justifies it in breaching *jus in bello* rules, then it may set off a downward spiral in which both sides increasingly disregard *jus in bello* restraints. History reveals many examples of this kind of thing. To illustrate the potential dynamic, consider the case of the British blockade of Germany in the early months of the First World War.

On February 4, 1915, the German government proclaimed a "blockade" of British ports in which they threatened to sink every merchant ship believed to be British, with a view to preventing commodities of any kind, including food, from reaching the British Isles. The British government promptly, and correctly, denounced that measure as a violation of the applicable laws of naval warfare. On March 1, 1915, the British government announced a retaliatory "blockade" against Germany, designed to be more protective of neutral shipping and non-combatant crews, but nonetheless intended to prevent any foreign goods from entering Germany and any German goods from going abroad. The British took the position that even if their countermeasure violated the law (which it did), Germany's previous misconduct justified Britain in doing so. The British Tory Party leader Arthur Balfour argued that "[i]f the rules of warfare are to bind one belligerent and leave the other free, they cease to mitigate suffering; they only load the dice in favour of the unscrupulous."[120] Moreover, British Prime Minister Herbert Asquith

118 Gardam appeared to make the same assumption as Moussa, saying that "[a]ny retreat from th[e] position [of independence of *jus in bello* from *jus ad bellum*] will result in the application of *lower* standards by states." Gardam, *supra* note 57, at 394 (emphasis added). But where the conditions for reciprocation exist, the standards as between belligerents are likely to be the same, not necessarily lower, even if *jus in bello* rights and obligations are altered by *jus ad bellum* considerations.

119 Moussa's argument also leaves unexplained why states should be required to comply with the rules of *jus in bello* when their antagonists conspicuously do not. Yet it is clear that "there is an obligation to respect the law that does not depend completely on reciprocity." Roberts, *supra* note 9, at 943. Thus, Article 60(5) of the Vienna Convention on the Law of Treaties specifies that although a party to a multilateral treaty may in some circumstances be entitled to suspend performance because of another party's material breach, this is forbidden with respect to "provisions relating to the protection of the human person contained in treaties of a humanitarian character, in particular provisions prohibiting any form of reprisals against persons protected by such treaties." Vienna Convention on the Law of Treaties, art. 60(5), 1155 U.N.T.S. 331 (entered into force Jan. 27, 1980).

120 James Wilford Garner, International Law and the World War (vol. 2) 322 (1920). Garner's work is the most authoritative contemporaneous treatment of the legal issues arising out of the First World War. For a more recent appraisal, *see* Isabel

argued that Britain's violation of *jus in bello* was warranted because the extent and seriousness of Germany's violations demonstrated that Germany was waging (in *jus ad bellum* terms) an unjust war. "[I]n dealing with an opponent who has openly repudiated all the restraints of law and humanity, we are not going to allow our efforts to be strangled by a net-work of judicial meshes."[121] Later, in response to neutral criticisms, Sir Edward Grey declared that Britain and her allies "were bound 'to take every step in their power' to overcome an enemy which had committed so many shocking violations of the recognized rules and principles of civilized warfare."[122] The episode of the British blockade illustrates exactly what defenders of the independence of *jus in bello* from *jus ad bellum* fear will happen if the distinction is abandoned. Belligerents will claim that because they are fighting a just or legal war (a belief in which they are likely to be fortified by their opponent's *jus in bello* violations), they are therefore free not to allow themselves to be "strangled" by *jus in bello* restraints.

But sometimes, rather than setting off a downward spiral, retaliation may induce the original offender to return to compliance with the applicable rules of war. We offer two illustrations. First, after President Abraham Lincoln's Emancipation Proclamation in the American Civil War, the Union Army began recruiting freed African-Americans into its ranks and even deploying them in combat. Viewing this as a form of slave rebellion, the Confederate Congress threatened to enslave any African-American Union soldiers who fell into Confederate hands. In response, President Lincoln issued General Order 233, which threatened reprisals against Confederate prisoners in Union hands if the Confederates put this plan in effect.[123] Although Lincoln's threat did not altogether deter Confederate forces from killing or enslaving captured African American soldiers,[124] it was generally successful in securing its objectives.[125]

V. Hull, A Scrap of Paper: Breaking and Making International Law During the Great War (2014).

121 *Id.* at 321.

122 *Id.* at 325. On the circumstances of Britain's decision and the U.S. reaction to it, *see* John W. Coogan, The End of Neutrality: The United States, Britain, and Maritime Rights 1899–1915 223–36 (1981).

123 We note that, even if it had been carried out, Lincoln's threat would not have violated the Lieber Code, which provided the *jus in bello* instructions for the Union Army. *See* Article 59 ("All prisoners of war are liable to the infliction of retaliatory measures."). But even under that Code, retaliation was disfavored. Article 27 says that civilized nations acknowledge retaliation as the sternest feature of war," and Article 28 says that "[r]etaliation will therefore never be resorted to as a measure of mere revenge, but only as a means of protective retribution, and moreover cautiously and unavoidably—that is to say, retaliation shall only be resorted to after careful inquiry into the real occurrence and the character of the misdeeds that may demand retribution." Int'l. Comm. of the Red Cross, Instructions for the Government of Armies of the United States in the Field (Lieber Code) (n.p. 1863) (*available at* http://www.icrc.org/ihl.nsf/FULL/110?OpenDocument).

124 *See* Theodore S. Woolsey, *Retaliation and Punishment,* 9 Proc. Am. Soc. Int'l L. 62, 64 (1915).

125 In the "Fort Pillow Massacre" of early 1864, Confederate forces under General N.B. Forrest slaughtered over three-fourths of the black Union soldiers (and about two-fifths of the white Union soldiers) after taking the garrison. Although Lincoln considered retaliation, he ordered none, possibly because he discovered upon careful investigation that Forrest had neither ordered nor authorized the massacre. *See* James Ford Rhodes, History of the United States of America, vol.5, ch. xxix at 510–12 (1920 ed.).

Second, consider a similar example from the First World War.[126] Toward the beginning of the War, the British captured some 39 German officers and men from two submarines that had been attacking British and neutral merchant shipping. Much of the British public believed that such attacks were criminal, and demanded that the men be tried for murder. In the event, the British government (chiefly at the instigation of First Lord of the Admiralty Winston Churchill) decided to keep these men segregated from other prisoners of war, holding them in naval detention barracks (several of them in solitary confinement). Learning of this and fearing that the men would be tried, the German public demanded counter-measures from its own government. The German government decided to confine an equal number of British prisoners of war (most of them from distinguished backgrounds) in separate facilities (in solitary confinement), and awaited details of the treatment accorded to the German mariners. In the event, if the British government had intended further harm to its captives (which, in fact, is doubtful), the German threat of reprisal succeeded in deterring it.[127]

In sum, the most common arguments—both for and against maintaining the independence of *jus in bello* from *jus ad bellum*—appear to be inconclusive. Yet the question (or questions) increasingly demands an answer: if the two bodies of law are in conflict and must be prioritized, then which one should trump?

On one side of the question is whether *jus in bello* requirements can eviscerate *jus ad bellum* rights. Implicitly, this issue arose in the context of whether the use of nuclear weapons in ways that would necessarily violate minimum standards for avoiding environmental harm or the otherwise applicable requirements of necessity, distinction, and proportionality under the *jus in bello* would thereby deprive a state under the *jus ad bellum* of the right to use force.[128] We return to this issue later in this chapter.

On the other side is the question whether *jus ad bellum* rights can diminish, or even eliminate, certain *jus in bello* rights. The difficulties in maintaining the dualist position are particularly acute in two forms of contemporary warfare: 1) armed humanitarian intervention and 2) combat with terrorist organizations such as al Qaeda or, more recently, the Islamic State of Iraq and Syria ("ISIS"). As already noted, both in this chapter and elsewhere, we have already considered obliquely the question of *jus in bello* in humanitarian wars when examining the OTP

---

126 The *jus in bello* prevailing at the time prohibited "ill-treatment of prisoners of war." Sir Thomas Barclay, *Violations of Law of War*, in Law and Usage of War: A Practical Handbook of the Law and Usage of Land and Naval Warfare and Prize at 139 (1914). Under Article 67 of the Lieber Code,

> The law of nations allows every sovereign government to make war upon another sovereign State, and, therefore, admits of no rules or laws different from those of regular warfare, regarding the treatment of prisoners of war, although they may belong to the army of a government which the captor may consider as a wanton and unjust assailant.

Lieber Code, *supra* note 123. For a summary of the post-War case law relating to German mistreatment of British prisoners of war, *see The British Cases*, 16 Am. J. Int'l L. 633 (1922).

127 Garner, *supra* note 120, at 50–51.

128 *See supra* Part III, Chapters 2 (environmental) & 4 (nuclear).

Report on NATO's campaign in Kosovo.[129] And, even before 2001, lawyers counseling U.S. military forces were uncertain what rules would apply in situations such as the 1992 humanitarian intervention in Somalia, the intervention in Haiti on behalf of its ousted (but democratically-elected) President, or the intervention in Iraq to protect the Kurdish population there from Saddam Hussein.[130] But after the attacks on the United States on 9/11, these questions were raised more urgently about U.S. actions in the War on Terror.

Assuming the existence of an armed conflict to which some form of *jus in bello* applied, then, were the United States and its allies bound by the same rules as al Qaeda, or did al Qaeda occupy a different—and lower—legal plane? We now directly consider an argument for linking *jus in bello* to *jus ad bellum* in the contemporary conflicts involving international terrorist organizations like al Qaeda.

129 *See supra* Part III Chapter 2.

130 *See* Major Timothy P. Bulman, *A Dangerous Guessing Game Disguised as Enlightened Policy: United States Law of War Operations During Military Operations Other Than War*, 159 Mil. L. Rev. 152, 167–71 (1999).

As we have already observed,[131] there is considerable controversy over what form of *jus in bello* applies to conflicts such as that between the United States and al Qaeda. Rather than attempting to answer which form of *jus in bello*, if any, is in fact applicable, let us instead ask the prescriptive question: what *jus in bello* rules should apply in such a conflict?[132] First, we consider the question in general terms, focusing on the anomalous situation created by asymmetric warfare between a conventional military power and new kind of enemy represented in al Qaeda. Then we turn to the specific question of the U.S. conflict with al Qaeda.

1. Differentiating in Terms of the Belligerent?

It is plausible to start with the assumption that the rules of *jus in bello* should be neutral as between types of belligerents—that they should not be skewed in favor of one kind of party to a conflict rather than another. If *jus in bello* rules fail to be neutral, the disadvantaged parties will be unlikely to comply with them. And a core objective of the *jus in bello*—to restrain the inhumanity of war—will be defeated by such noncompliance. But *jus in bello* rules may be discriminatory, not only on their face, but also in their effects. Thus, the prevailing rules for maritime war at the outbreak of the First World War permitted belligerents to engage in naval blockades in certain circumstances.[133] On their face, the rules were nondiscriminatory. But in practice, they favored the British blockade of Germany, which chiefly involved the use of surface ships,[134] and disfavored the German blockade of Britain, which relied upon a relatively new weapon, the

131 *See supra* Part III Chapter 1.

132 We shall, of course, be assuming in what follows that an armed conflict did exist, so that *jus in bello* was applicable.

133 As of the beginning of the war, the five generally accepted principles of the law of naval blockade were found in the 1909 Declaration of London. However, the Declaration had not been ratified by any of its signatories, including the world's preeminent naval power, Great Britain. Hence the belligerents did not consider it to be legally binding. Although Germany and Austria-Hungary offered to observe the principles of the Declaration of London if Britain and her Allies reciprocated, their offer was refused. For a statement and explanation of the then-general rules, *see* Michael G. Fraunces, *The International Law of Blockade: New Guiding Principles in Contemporary State Practice*, 101 Yale L. J. 893, 895–98 (1992). For a statement of contemporary customary rules regarding blockades, *see* San Remo Manual, supra note 45, at arts. 93–104.

134 The British blockade was itself legally very questionable. *See Declaration of London*, 9 Am. J. Int'l L. 1 (1915) (exchange of diplomatic correspondence between the United States and the United Kingdom); *see also* Edwin Borchard & William Potter Lage, Neutrality for the United States 198–211 (2d edn. 1940); Garner, *supra* note 120, at 319–22 (1920); E.G. Trimble, *Violations of Maritime Law by the Allied Powers During the World War*, 24 Am. J. Int'l L. 79, 93–99 (1930); and Richard W. Van Alstyne, *The Policy of the United States Regarding the Declaration of London, at the Outbreak of the Great War*, 7 J. Mod. Hist. 434 (1935).

submarine.[135] The law, at least in the Anglo-American view,[136] would not permit Germany to fight the kind of naval war that would have been most effective for it.[137] Not surprisingly, therefore, Germany fell out of compliance with the law.[138] Although German non-compliance did not lead to an immediate change in the law, and the duty of submarines to respect the traditional rules was reaffirmed at Nuremberg,[139] both the Allied and Axis Powers employed similar forms of blockade in the Second World War.[140]

To encourage compliance, therefore, it is necessary for *jus in bello* rules to take account of the realities of armed conflict. They must not be framed so as to deny a certain kind of combatant a genuine opportunity to win. That reasoning underlay the international community's decision in the 1970s to amend the 1949 Geneva Conventions by adopting Protocol I, which was designed to eliminate what was seen as the Conventions' bias in favor of states, especially European colonial powers, and to accommodate the methods of guerrilla fighters in wars of decolonization.[141] Protocol I thus affords to guerrilla fighters combatant status and privileges and protections akin to those that the earlier Conventions had afforded to regular, uniformed combatants in national armies, even though guerrillas often engage in combat without wearing uniforms or other distinctive markings and seek to blend into the surrounding civilian population. As Marco Sassòli explained, the *jus in bello* cannot prohibit every efficient method available to guerrillas to win a war of national liberation.

---

135 Pre-war law had little to say specifically about submarines. The 1913 Oxford Manual of the Laws of Naval War, which purported to be a statement of the customary rules of naval warfare, refers briefly to torpedoes and submarine mines, but otherwise offers nothing explicitly directed to submarine warfare. By contrast, the Manual sets out detailed provisions on the law of seizure and prize procedure. *See* Manual of the Laws of Naval Warfare, Oxford, Aug. 9, 1913 (*available at* http://www.icrc.org/ihl.nsf/FULL/265?OpenDocument).

136 *See* Henry Goudy et al., *Report of the Committee on the Legal Status of Submarines*, 4 Trans. Grotius Soc, xxxi, xxxiv (1918) (acknowledging that although "[t]he law and practice prior to the present war . . . was anything but settled," it was agreed by legal experts in the Allied and neutral countries "that 'unrestricted submarine warfare' as conducted in the present war by the Central Powers [*i.e.*, Germany and her allies] is contrary to the laws and usages of war hitherto accepted by the whole civilised world, even including the latter Powers."). For a post-War American perspective on the legal issues, *see* Garner, *supra* note 120, at 371–80. On the reasons underlying Anglo-American view, *see* Karl Lautenschlager, *The Submarine in Naval Warfare, 1901–2001,* 11 Int'l Sec. 94, 97, 100–02 (1986/87).

137 Among the problems was that submarines, unlike more traditional warships, were unable to carry many persons on board, and thus could rarely rescue the crews of the vessels they had sunk. Furthermore, if they surfaced before firing in order to warn a targeted enemy merchantman, difficulties in maneuvering made them vulnerable to being rammed.

138 Germany's first attempted submarine blockade in 1915 was formally ended six months after it began, largely because of pressure from the neutral United States. The German attempt at a submarine blockade was resumed in February 1917, in the hopes of defeating Britain before the United States could mobilize. *See* Lautenshlager, *supra* note 136, at 111–13; Alexander Watson, Ring of Steel: Germany and Austria-Hungary at War 1914-1918 at 416-24 (2014); Ian F.W. Beckett, The Making of the First World War 25-43 (2012).

139 *See* the Nuremberg judgment against Admiral Dönitz and Raeder, *International Military Tribunal (Nuremberg), Judgment and Sentences,* 41 Am. J. Int'l L. 172, 302–09 (1947) (if a submarine commander is unable to conform to the rules for the sake of his own vessel's safety, he must allow safe passage to the merchant vessel).

140 *See* Fraunces, *supra* note 133, at 901.

141 *See* Berman, *supra* note 29, at 21–23.

> Certainly, it would . . . be preferable for the protection of the civilian population if combatants always clearly distinguished themselves from the civilian population and if military objectives were kept far from concentrations of civilians. However, under such rules, certain belligerents would not have the slightest chance of overcoming the enemy, even though they might be fighting for a cause which is lawful under *[j]us ad bellum*. Inevitably, therefore, [*jus in bello*] had to be adapted to make such fighting, and victory, possible. Thus, Protocol I had to lower the distinction requirement to what is both possible to comply with in a guerrilla war and the minimum necessary to ensure respect for the civilian population.[142]

If the *jus in bello* was modified to meet the exigencies of guerrillas in the wars of decolonization, should it also be modified to meet the circumstances of the War on Terror? It might at first seem logical to do so: al Qaeda's terrorist practices do not seem far removed from those of the guerrilla warriors in the decolonization period. As Nathaniel Berman has correctly pointed out,

> from the perspective of the actual conduct of armed conflicts, rather than their goals, the current wave of terrorism and counter-terrorism does not present wholly novel challenges to the laws of war. Rather, it only presents in purer form the "*in bello*" challenges posed by anti-colonial and anti-occupation struggles—purer because divested of any "*ad bellum*" resemblances to inter-state conflicts.[143]

Should the *jus in bello* therefore be adapted to give al Qaeda a fair chance of victory by enabling it to wage the only kind of war it realistically can?

One could argue that there simply is no way in which that could be done, if only because the concept of "victory" has no meaning for al Qaeda. There is no possibility of reaching a negotiated political settlement with al Qaeda, because it does not have political objectives.[144] Unlike the national liberation movements that aimed at acquiring political authority and establishing a state, al Qaeda presents no intelligible political demands; its terrorism is sacred and apocalyptic, not revolutionary. Likewise, al Qaeda could not possibly satisfy the "proportionality" requirement of *jus ad bellum,* because it has no strategic aims to which its violence might, or might not, be proportionate. There is also no way in which the *jus in bello* could be adjusted to al Qaeda's methods of waging war in order to ensure a minimum of respect for civilians. Unlike national liberation movements, al Qaeda is not interested in reducing the harms that its methods cause

---

142 Sassòli, *supra* note 86, at 252–53.

143 Berman, *supra* note 29, at 23.

144 For discussion of the objectives and motives of radical Islamist movements, *see* Part I Chapter 2.C. *See also* Faisal Devji, Landscapes of the Jihad: Militancy, Morality, Modernity (2005) (arguing that al Qaeda has "ethical" rather than "political" aims); Delahunty, *supra* note 77, at 1637–38. The case of ISIS is different, for that organization undoubtedly has political aims of the highest order. Indeed, its fundamental objective seems to be to overturn the entire post-Westphalian state system. *See* Andrew Phillips, *The Islamic State's challenge to international order,* 68 Australian J. Int'l Aff. 495 (2014).

to civilians; for its signature method consists precisely in committing atrocities against civilians. Finally, there is no possibility that al Qaeda members could be induced to show restraint or even reciprocity in warfare by the offer of humane treatment if they were captured—for, inasmuch as they are willing or even eager to accept martyrdom, neither humane nor inhumane treatment after captivity will influence them.

The argument here is similar to one put forward by the Israeli political scientist Michael Gross. Gross wrote:

> International terrorists can count none among them who aim solely to destroy military targets. Aggression of the worst sort, unmitigated by any nationalist agenda, belies any claim to just cause, while no prospect of a political settlement or response in kind offers any ground for extending combatant equality. The fight will be long, tedious and, most likely, to the death. It appears then, that international terrorists warrant some status that combines criminality with combatancy.[145]

Viewing international terrorists in this light does not imply that, if captured, they may be treated cruelly or inhumanely during either interrogation or detention. At a minimum, the requirements of the Torture Convention, which are also generally accepted as customary law, would apply to their captivity. Those requirements prohibit, not only torture, but also "other cruel, inhuman or degrading treatment or punishment."[146]

A *jus in bello* regime for regulating the conflict with international terrorism that started from the assumptions outlined above would depend on and derive from the *jus ad bellum.* The starting-point for such a regime would be, not so much the justice or legality of the war being waged against international terrorism by the United States and other states, as the complete absence of any justice or legality on the side of al Qaeda and similar organizations. If a specialized *jus in bello* were developed for this specific type of conflict, it would justify denying belligerent equality to al Qaeda on the basis of al Qaeda's position under the *jus ad bellum.*

With these considerations in mind, let us briefly consider the *jus in bello* regime that has been emerging in the United States' War on Terror.

---

145 Gross, *supra* note 21, at 47.

146 The Torture Convention is not limited to situations of armed conflict. Rather, it applies in all circumstances, both of peace and war. Strictly, therefore, the Convention does not fall under the rubric of *jus in bello*, though in application it overlaps with it. For the European Court of Human Rights' application of the Torture Convention to the U.S. Central Intelligence Agency's "rendition" program and the Polish government's role in it, *see Al-Nashiri v. Poland* (E.Ct H.R. 2014) (*available at* http://hudoc.echr.coe.int/sites/eng/pages/search.aspx?i=001-146044#{"itemid":["001-146044"]}).

2. The United States Legal Regime in its Conflict with al Qaeda

During the years since the attacks of 9/11, the United States has gradually fashioned a legal regime with respect to international terrorists that incorporates many of the features described above. In important respects, these emerging rules provide less favorable treatment for al Qaeda operatives than that they would enjoy under the *jus in bello* regulating international armed conflict or wars of national liberation. Although the United States has not explicitly sought to justify these rules in terms of al Qaeda's weak position under the *jus ad bellum,* that argument is available to it. If such an argument were to be advanced, it would affirm a conceptual link between *jus ad bellum* and *jus in bello.*

First, al Qaeda operatives are considered to be "combatants" who may properly be targeted with lethal force. Further, the constitutional restrictions that attach to the use of lethal force by law enforcement officers against dangerous criminal suspects (as in the "fleeing felon" rule[147]) do not govern the use of force against al Qaeda. Second, al Qaeda operatives are held not to be privileged combatants because unlike regular combatants, such as uniformed soldiers in a state's armed forces, they are not considered to have the legal right to use violence against enemy combatants or civilians.[148] Third, because they are understood to be unprivileged combatants, when they kill civilians, as well as regular military personnel, they are subject to prosecution before ordinary U.S. civilian courts under domestic criminal law on a charge of murder.[149] Fourth, under American judicial,[150] legislative,[151] presidential,[152] and administrative[153] decisions, captured al Qaeda combatants are held to enjoy a measure of protection under the *jus in bello*—specifically, the protections afforded by "common" Article 3 of the 1949 Geneva Conventions. As we have already explained, this clause provides that "persons taking no active part in the hostilities," including "those placed hors de combat by . . . detention," shall be "treated humanely," and therefore shall not be subject to "violence to life and person, in particular murder of all

147 *See Tennessee v. Garner,* 471 U.S. 1, 12 (1985). For discussion of the fleeing felon rule and its inapplicability to the U.S. conflict with al Qaeda, *see* Delahunty & Yoo, *supra* note 66, at 823.

148 *See* Solis, *supra* note 77, at 211 ("Being an unlawful combatant/unprivileged belligerent is not a war crime in itself. Rather, the price of being an unlawful combatant is that he forfeits the immunity of a lawful combatant . . . and he may be charged for the [*jus in bello*] violations that he committed.").

149 *See id.*

150 *See Hamdan v. Rumsfeld,* 548 U.S. 557 (2006).

151 The Military Commissions Act, subs. 6(c) of Pub. L. 109-366 and the Detainee Treatment Act of 2005. sec. 1003 of Pub. L. 109-148 and sec. 1403 of Pub. L. 109-163.

152 Executive Order No. 13440 sec. 3 (July 20, 2007), rescinded by Executive Order No. 13491 (Jan. 22, 2009); Executive Order No. 13491 sec. 6 (Jan. 22, 2009).

153 *See* FM 2-22.3 (FM 34-52), *Human Intelligence Collector Operations* vii-viii; ¶ 5.68; ¶¶5.74-75 (Headquarters, Dep't of the Army, Sept. 2006); Department of Defense Directive No. 2310.01E, sec. 4.2 and Enclosure 4 (Sept. 5, 2006); Office of the Secretary of Defense, Memorandum for Secretaries of the Military Departments, July 7, 2006, cited in Delahunty, *supra* note 77, at 1649 n. 47.

kinds, mutilation, cruel treatment and torture" or "outrages upon personal dignity, in particular, humiliating and degrading treatment."[154] Fifth, al Qaeda operatives are also held to be under the legal obligation to comply with the requirements of common Article 3, and they may be criminally prosecuted and tried before military commissions if charged with grave breaches violations of those requirements.[155] In other words, they may be prosecuted as war criminals, not merely as criminals.[156]

In certain ways, the United States' conception of the rules of *jus in bello* that are appropriate for this conflict differs from that of other concerned parties, such as the ICRC —in particular, with respect to targeting and interrogation. In both these instances, the United States could argue that al Qaeda's position under the *jus ad bellum* warrants the imposition of *jus in bello* rules that are less favorable than the rules applicable to other types of conflict. As to targeting, the United States under both the Obama Administration and the second Bush Administration has taken a broader view than the ICRC of the definition of an enemy "combatant." This difference obviously affects the legality of targeting decisions: persons whom the ICRC might consider to be "civilians," and hence impermissible targets, are "combatants" for the United States, and hence lawful objectives.[157]

Second, as to interrogation, the Obama Administration has decided that, as a general matter, the interrogation of captured al Qaeda operatives will be regulated by the rules that apply to the interrogation of any other type of captured combatant, including the regular forces of a state enemy's military. Thus, the rules for interrogation in the United States' conflict with al Qaeda will normally not differ from those followed in any other conflict. However, Executive Order No. 13491, which President Obama issued on January 22, 2009, entitled *Ensuring Lawful Interrogations,* limited interrogation techniques and treatment to those authorized by and listed in Army Field Manual 2 22.3 (2006).[158] But the Administration reserved the possibility of departures from those rules in exceptional cases involving the capture of particular "high value" terrorists.[159] The possibility of such exceptional departures could again be defended as an appro-

154 *See supra* Part III Chapter 1, note 187.

155 *See* Solis, supra note 77, at 211 (unprivileged belligerents may be tried "before either military or domestic courts").

156 *See id.* at 99–101 (discussing emerging practice of "war crimes" prosecutions in non-international armed conflicts). In this respect, current U.S. practice differs from Gross' paradigm. Gross argued that international terrorists should not be considered "war criminals." But if al Qaeda operatives enjoy the protection of common Article 3, it is reasonable to subject them to liability for violating it.

157 For analysis of the differences between the current U.S. position on defining combatancy and that of the ICRC, *see* Robert J. Delahunty, *Obama's War Law,* 11 Engage 80 (2010).

158 *Human Intelligence Collector Operations,* Dep't of the Army (Sept. 6, 2006).). The Field Manual has recently been superseded by the *Department of Defense Law of War Manual* (June 2015) (*available at* http://www.dod.mil/dodgc/images/law_war_manual15.pdf).

159 This was accomplished by Sec. 5 of E.O. 13491, which created a Special Interagency Task Force on Interrogation and Transfer Policies. The Special Task Force was charged, *inter alia,* with studying and evaluating the interrogation practices and techniques in the Army Field Manual would provide "an appropriate means of acquiring intelligence necessary

priate reflection of the *jus ad bellum*, though any "heightened" interrogation methods that might be employed would unquestionably have to comply with the Torture Convention.

To conclude, the lynchpin of the theory is, plainly, its denial that al Qaeda has any intelligible political objectives. This may or may not be true, because al Qaeda at least professes the overall strategic aim of restoring the Islamic caliphate. Perhaps one should give little or no weight to that claim, but the question would need to be considered. More damagingly for the theory, al Qaeda arguably *does* have some discernibly political aims in at least some of the conflicts in which its forces engage with U.S. forces. Al Qaeda operatives joined with Iraqi insurgent groups to oust the United States and its coalition partners from occupied Iraq. And al Qaeda combatants are fighting alongside Taliban rebels to bring down the Karzai government of Afghanistan and force the withdrawal of U.S. and other Allied forces. Moreover, even the 9/11 attacks can be seen as attempts to dislodge U.S. forces from Saudi Arabia.[160] But while these immediate goals are certainly political, it is arguable whether or not they constitute the kind of acquisition of territory or people typically associated with wars of liberation, let alone inter-state wars.

But even assuming that al Qaeda has no discernible political objectives, the theory has limitations. Even if it could serve to justify a special *jus in bello* regime for al Qaeda, the justification would not carry over for the original (or continuing) U.S. conflicts with Taliban. Unlike al Qaeda, Taliban, even after being ousted from power in Afghanistan, can be seen as an embryonic government, akin to the national liberation movements protected under Protocol I. Indeed, at the start of its conflict with the United States, the Taliban was the government of Afghanistan. However, intermediate cases may arise for offshoots of core al Qaeda, which may well be pursuing like the Taliban, the immediate, traditional political objective of state-building as well as core al Qaeda's millenarian objectives. Such mixed-motive cases would be extremely problematic.

In sum, even if the theory has *some* application, its reach would be limited. Thus, the relationship between the *jus ad bellum* and the *jus in bello* remains unsettled in the context. Although many distinguished scholars and military analysts argue powerfully that the traditional independence of the two bodies of law should be maintained, that distinction has come under increasing pressure as a result of the humanitarian interventions of the 1990s and the U.S. counter-terrorism policies of the early 2000s. Although we make no pretense of resolving those debates here, the legal framework that appears to be emerging from the U.S. War on Terror might be defended by an argument that linked *jus ad bellum* and *jus in bello* together. But that theory could not serve as a complete justification for the legal U.S. regime.

---

to protect the Nation" when employed by the CIA or other non-military agencies and, if not, to recommendation "additional or different guidance."

160 See Fawaz A. Gerges, The Far Enemy: Why Jihad Went Global 57 (2005).

In the previous sections, one might say that we have considered the relationship between the *jus ad bellum* and the *jus in bello* in inductive terms—studying particularly difficult borderline cases, such as humanitarian intervention and terrorism, to draw possible inferences of general applicability. We now consider whether alternative theoretical approaches may allow us to deduce general propositions concerning the preferred relationship between the *jus ad bellum* and the *jus in bello.*

One such approach would be to consider the question from the standpoint of the role of force in the development of the international system—more specifically, how the question fits into the larger issue of the kind of international system toward which we are moving. A purposive conception of world order may well relate the *jus ad bellum* and the *jus in bello* in ways that privilege uses of force that further certain preferred outcomes in world order, whereas uses of force that evidence retrograde tendencies or forces should be discouraged with more restrictive rules of law. Alternatively, one could try to focus on the underlying moral basis for decision-makers, adapting traditional Just War Theory (JTW) to modern circumstances.

In general terms, we would describe the first set of approaches as primarily, although not completely, teleological and the second set of approaches as primarily, but not exclusively, deontological. Our discussion will be necessarily incomplete and merely suggestive. Nonetheless, it may serve to prompt further research and reflection.

1. Rational Choice vs. Constructivist Approaches to a New Law of War

The contrasting visions between rational choice theory (to a great extent reflected in neo-realism) and of social constructivism (to a great extent reflected in neo-liberalism) provide a useful framework for analysis of the true relationship between *jus ad bellum* and *jus in bello.*

On one hand, rational choice theory views global order as a question of welfare maximization, one that takes into account global market failures, particularly the production of global public goods. From this standpoint, the use of force should be privileged when it is based on a global public welfare cost-benefit calculation. One recent and important example is legal scholar John Yoo's argument that the United States and its allies ought to be able to launch "wars of global welfare," wars to produce "global public goods."[161] The NATO intervention against Serbia to save Kosovars is, for Yoo, an easy case, irrespective of any international law doubts.[162] Acknowledging that the U.S.-led invasion of Iraq was more complicated, Yoo nonetheless draws on hegemonic stability theory to argue that the rules of international law ought to encourage

161 *See* John Yoo, Point of Attack: Preventive War, International Law and Global Welfare 107–29 (2014).

162 *Id.* at 123.

hegemons such as the United States to intervene in places such as Iraq because otherwise global public goods will not be produced, to the detriment of the world order and the U.S. alike. "A hegemonic power . . . will not provide public goods unless it is able to realize benefits that either approximate or exceed the costs of keeping world order."[163]

Thus, while Yoo continues to observe the distinction between the *jus ad bellum* and the *jus in bello*,"[164] he does argue for revising the *jus in bello* rules of occupation that currently require occupiers to respect the sovereignty of the occupied state. Instead, in war for global welfare, occupiers, such as the United States and its coalition partners in Iraq, should be able to choose *post-bellum* terms of occupation that will further global order.[165] Thus the logic of Yoo's position calls for a substantial re-ordering of the current *jus ad bellum* and a case-by-case revision of the current *jus in bello* to further global welfare-enhancing purposes. In making that argument, he assumes (as rational choice theorists are apt to do) a kind of value-monism. That is to say, he seems to see the apparent plurality of values relevant to the normative evaluation of a choice for war or the ways of conducting it as reducible to the single, calculable medium of "welfare maximization."

At the other end of the spectrum, constructivist thought seems to contemplate a single global order, rather than ad hoc collections of states acting in the service of a single substantive criterion. This conception of international order is not limited to welfare maximization—presumably, in part, because it views any conception of global welfare as a subjectively-created, or discursively and inter-subjectively-created, construct. From this standpoint, Yoo's theory rests on a mistake. Instead, constructivism would treat both *jus ad bellum* and *jus in bello* as socially-constructed concepts of varying value, depending on the degree to which the constructivist project of a world-state has been realized. As the project gradually comes to fruition, *jus ad bellum* and *jus in bello* both begin to disappear, since all world-state law governing the use of force is criminal law. In the interim, those elements of the *jus ad bellum* and the *jus in bello* that are best representations of the state of affairs that would exist in the world-state would be privileged, and the elements that would be reflect international hierarchy (or anarchy) would be given less weight. The *jus ad bellum* that is legitimated by international institutions and collective decision-making would be furthered, and the *jus ad bellum* rules that recognize the status of opponents of the world state would be depreciated.

Along these lines, one neo-liberal, neo-constructivist political scientist Daniel Deudney imagines a world-state based on so-called "republican security theory," under which international anarchy and international hierarchy are replaced with a system of international and domestic checks and balances, a so-called international *negarchy*.[166] Indeed, the "Philadelphia

163 *Id.* at 127.

164 *Id.* at 110–11.

165 *Id.* at 186-88.

166 Daniel H. Deudney, Bounding Power: Republican Security Theory from the Polis to the Global Village 27–60 (2007).

system" of the initial U.S. Constitution the framework for the Constitution would serve as the model for such a system.[167] Thus, for Deudney, it was thus tragic that:

> With the end of the Cold War and the collapse of the Soviet Union, it seemed the moment had finally arrived when the United States had the power and the influence to realize its long deferred agency for the substantial replacement of interstate anarchy. But instead of moving toward the realization, the United States . . . increasingly opposed or rejected major republican security initiatives such as the International Criminal Court, the expansion of international peacekeeping capabilities, and a comprehensive nuclear test ban.[168]

In short, at the end of the Cold War, any opportunity for proto-world state—with a collective criminal-law approach to inter-state violence through a law of crimes, an international police, and the beginning of a ban on private self-defense—passed as quickly as the opportunity presented itself.

But was such a proto-World State ever really at hand or even imaginable in the foreseeable future? As one perceptive commentator, political scientist Randall Schweller, argues, increasing limits on state power are producing, not checks and balances capable of providing moderate amounts of both liberty and order, but rather a state of maximal *entropy*—a disorder so pervasive that the hegemon's capacity and willingness to produce global public goods is irreversibly becoming weaker and weaker as time passes.[169] Schweller's theory is predicated, in part, on the premise that war has become so costly for great powers that the cycle of hegemonic wars has now been brought to an end.[170] He argues that it was precisely through those hegemonic wars that new international orders were created and that those new orders experienced conditions that allowed new hegemons to engage in, among other things, productive institution-building.[171] He noted that global catastrophes may yet occur, such as pandemics, but such events will not leave the world with a new hegemon capable of establishing a new order in the aftermath of the collapse of the old institutional order by constructing new international institutions for the production of global public goods.[172] As hegemony irreversibly weakens, *dissensus* increases.

167 *Id.* at 161–89.

168 *Id.* at 189.

169 *See generally* Randall L. Schweller, Maxwell's Demon and the Golden Apple: Global Discord n the New Millennium (2014).

170 *Id.* at 22–23. Others argue that hegemonic war (or competition with ensuing discontinuous change in international law and institutions) remains possible. *See, e.g.*, Phillip Bobbitt, The Shield of Achilles: War, Peace, and the Course of History (2002) (arguing that the next, post-Cold War struggle in hegemonic competition will come as a struggle between three versions of a so-called "market-state"—a quasi-libertarian U.S. version; a mercantilist Chinese version; and a social democratic European version).

171 *See* Schweller, *supra* note 169, at 50–54.

172 *Id.* at 145–46.

The hegemon becomes less generous or far-sighted in producing global public goods, as its return on investment declines and immediate needs increase; others increasingly find that the benefits of independent action exceed the benefits the hegemon provides. Thus, production of global public goods by even a *posse comitatus* or militia of interested states (a "coalition of the willing") becomes less and less plausible.[173] It would be implausible, *a fortiori*, to look to the creation of the world-state imagined by constructivists that would be charged with responsibility for criminalizing current international and non-international armed conflict, much less to a global civil society enforcing international taboos or capable of creating global public goods through consensus.[174] In short, on this view, hegemonic stability, a republican security regime, and the world-state are all fantasies belied by our probable return to the formlessness of the entropic void.[175]

2. A Return to Just War Theory

Recognizing, without fully endorsing, Schweller's dystopic vision, at a minimum one could question whether a rational, welfare-maximizing approach, executed by the dominant nation-states, whether or not liberal democracies, would be deemed politically illegitimate. If not, it inevitably would face too much resistance to be implemented. Similarly, a neo-constructivist cosmopolitan approach might be a Frankenstein's Monster, imposing a global tyranny rather than checks and balances, blocking plural institutional developments that would serve as laboratories for future growth and progress in the human conditions. In any event, until "the owl of Minerva spreads its wings" and we know which of these futures will unfold,[176] we need to search for an approach that does not depend exclusively on prophecy; and, with this intuition, it seems useful to explore how one continuous ethic of decision-making that is not dependent on any particular global geometry could resolve the increasingly tense relationship between the s *jus ad bellum* and the *jus in bello*. International lawyers are, as Michael Walzer once wrote, moral and political philosophers.[177] To address explicitly the moral dimension of our inquiry, therefore, we turn to a seminal JWT debate in the wake of the U.S. invasion of Iraq between

173 *Id.* at 149–50.

174 *Id.* at 117–18.

175 Genesis, Chapter 1, Verse 2 The Jerusalem Bible (1966).

176 But as Hegel said, the future may only reveal itself when it becomes the present, for the "owl of Minerva spreads its wings only with the falling of the dusk." G.W.F. Hegel, The Philosophy of Right 13 (T. M. Know, trans., Oxford Univ. Press 1967).

177 *See* Walzer, *supra* note 10, at xiii ("Policy-oriented lawyers are in fact moral and political philosophers, and it would be best if they presented themselves that way.").

George Weigel, an American Catholic historian and philosopher, and Dr. Rowan Williams, the Protestant Archbishop of Canterbury.[178]

Briefly stated, Williams argued that JWT mandates a presumption against war, which he formulated as a general presumption against violence. In this formulation, he collapsed the distinction between the *jus in bello* and the *jus ad bellum*, for every act of violence becomes subject to the moral framework he constructs. Any state violence, he argued, is a deviation from Christianity's commitment to human freedom, which in turn is subject to limitation only when required by the common good. Thus: "The point is that coercion is simply not to be justified unless it is answerable to a clear account of the common good. Even the security of a specific state has to be seen in light of this broader framework."[179] Hence, Williams continued, even state violence internationally must also be justified in light of this broader framework. But, recognizing the current defects in the legitimacy of international order, he left open the door to alternative institutional arrangements, "instead of complete reliance on the current Security Council framework,"[180] through which the process of justification will occur. Moreover, he saw instrumental value in a presumption against violence. For it is precisely the need for justification, overcoming a presumption against violence, that Williams holds will help to further the democratic ethic that "the professed wisdom of any leader or any party is challengeable"[181]; facilitate the participation of epistemic communities (such as "lawyers, NGOs, linguists, anthropologies, religious communities, journalists, strategist, military and diplomatic historians"), who may "know things that government sometimes does not"[182]; and serve to "sustain the self-critical habit on a nation and its political classes"[183] facing even existential threats.

While Williams thus opened the door to the possibility that states may relinquish the right to exist, he did not in general argue for an anti-pluralist world-state, a world-state defined in terms of republican security theory's checks and balances (or so-called *negarchy*), or suggest procedures that might risk a world-state characterized by excessive entropy. But he did seem to place process above order in the hierarchy of values. Thus, the presumption against violence that he found in JWT not only ensures the substantive legitimacy of a decision to subordinate individual liberty to the common good but, perhaps more importantly, also enables a process of moral formation for a democratic political community which, in light of the traditional

178 *See* George Weigel, *Moral Clarity in a Time of War, in* First Things (Jan. 2003) (*available at* http://www.firstthings.com/article/2008/01/001-moral-clarity-in-a-time-of-war-30); Archbishop Rowan Williams, *Just War Revisited* (Oct. 14, 2003) (*available at* http://rowanwilliams.archbishopofcanterbury.org/articles.php/1827/just-war-revisited-archbishops-lecture-to-the-royal-institute-for-international-affairs); and George Weigel & Rowan Williams, *War & Statecraft, in* First Things (March 2004) (*available at* http://www.firstthings.com/article/2007/01/war-amp-statecraft-9).

179 Williams, *supra* note 178.

180 *Id.*

181 *Id.*

182 *Id.*

183 *Id.*

JWT theory of "right" or legitimate authority, is the ultimate author of violence. Yet, under this approach, if democratic responsibility is critical to *the jus ad bellum*, then decision-maker and warrior become one and the same, and thus *jus in bello* may well become increasingly more difficult to cabin from the *jus ad bellum*.

Weigel, by contrast, regarded the presumption against war as a late 20th century heresy against traditional JWT—indeed, as a turn to a pacifist ethic that has for long been an undercurrent, and in his view, deviation from the main channel of Christian thought on questions of war and peace. For Weigel, JWT "is theologically and historically embedded within a more comprehensive theory of statecraft, a theory which stresses the prior obligation of public authority to advance and defend the peace of right order (*tranquillitas ordinis*), which is composed of freedom, justice, and security. . . ."[184] This is neither a theory for the production of global public goods through hegemonic stability theory nor a constructivist project for the creation of a world-state nor a republican community of states governed by internal and external checks and balances. Nonetheless, because it is committed to the global common good (albeit in the form of value pluralism, as opposed to the single goal of welfare maximization), as its *telos*, it cannot be constrained by any presumption for or against violence. Because that goal is multi-value and not rigorously defined, moreover, it requires "a context-setting moral judgment about the obligation of pubic authority to pursue the peace of right order."[185]

Weigel argued that the Security Council in current circumstances is wholly disqualified to serve as a public authority capable of making these contextual and multi-value judgments; hence it cannot serve as a "superior authority" contemplated by JWT. Rather, he argued that it is political leaders of states with official responsibility—rather than citizens or, quite pointedly, religious communities—who must discharge the duties of statecraft, "because . . . the ruler is under a prior moral obligation, a responsibility to defend the peace of right order."[186] Thus, Weigel's view reaffirms the classical distinction between the *jus ad bellum* and the *jus in bello*, by separating the author of the decision to exercise *jus ad bellum* rights and duties from the *jus in bello* responsibilities of the agents of the decision-maker. But perhaps more central to his position is that the "presumption against war" is "a functional pacifism whose primary objection to the use of armed forces has to do with who is using, that, the West, understood as an oppressor culture."[187] In short, the exercise of power by the West in pursuit of world order, for Weigel, is not intrinsically oppressive or wrongful.

Plainly, Weigel and Williams do divide on questions of authority—namely, whether only rulers or also the ruled bear moral responsibility for international violence. If so, then their disagreements may simply reflect the difference between, on one hand, a pragmatic realist

---

184 Weigel, *supra* note 178.

185 *Id.*

186 *Id.*

187 *Id.*

appreciation that the monopoly of state power by government makes the effective locus of moral decision-making always a state official and, on the other, a commitment to rule of law and democratic responsibility as a way of fashioning human flourishing. Plainly also they divide on a baseline view whether international order—based on Western, and primarily U.S., power to suppress international terrorism or promote international human rights—is itself a worthy goal. Williams, in contrast to Weigel, would appear to prefer an international order that reflected the broader range of values experienced in the global community, including other faith traditions such as Islam, Hinduism, or Buddhism (or even non-faith moral traditions such as Taoism). Such an order, he seems to think, would ultimately be more responsive to global needs and therefore more stable.

If so, then the core differences between Weigel and Williams could collapse into the difference between hegemonic stability theory from a rational choice perspective and the constructivist project of fashioning a stable cosmopolitan order that transcends a system of sovereign states. Weigel might be assuming that democratic decision-making is not (currently) possible everywhere, but Williams might be assuming that public deliberation and justification are necessary elements of all moral reasoning everywhere. Ironically, then, Weigel's view would appear to privilege Western-style democratic capitalism's pro-democratic intervention in the less than democratic-capitalist parts of the world, even though Weigel's theory is not predicated on direct democracy in an international forum; whereas William's view is structured to reduce Western pro-democratic intervention, albeit on a theory that purports to be grounded in (internationalized) direct democracy. Perhaps then what really divides Weigel and Williams is their relative appreciation for virtual representation or indirect democracy, on one hand, and direct democracy, on the other; or, put more ominously, between a ruler's despotism masquerading under a Divine Right of Kings, on one hand, and, on the other, a majoritarian and imperialist tyranny disguised by direct democracy, not unlike an agitated Athenian *polis*.

Yet, even if all these distinctions have some validity, possibly a deeper explanation of the difference between Weigel and Williams lies elsewhere—in an underlying divide between the Catholic and Protestant streams of Christianity those two thinkers represent; a difference that, in turn, may depend on their underlying views of the intrinsic morality, indeed sinfulness, of killing in war. To explicate that difference requires a reconstruction of medieval JWT.[188]

This reconstruction would begin with an understanding that early Christian thought maintained what was, in effect, a pacifist position, and that it was only establishment of Christian state power, with Constantine and his successors, that made necessary St. Augustine's reformulation of traditional Christian teaching to tolerate Christian participation in publicly-sanctioned

188 A major scholarly effort to reconstruct the standard narrative of the evolution of JWT is found in Philip Wynn, Augustine on War and Military Service (2013). Wynn attempts to demolish the account that locates the "origin" of medieval and later JWT in the writings of St. Augustine. *See also* Robert J. Delahunty, *The Returning Warrior and the Limits of Just War*, 16 Rutgers J. of L. and Religion 219 (2014) (analyzing origins of medieval just war theory in terms of the "Papal revolution" of the twelfth century).

violence. It would then argue that, even after Augustine, much of traditional Christian thought deemed all killing in war to be presumptively sinful and, thus, to require absolution and repentance. Under this view, the critical move in the Roman Church's acceptance of the non-sinfulness of authorized killing in war was the Gregorian Revolution, beginning in the late 11th century, under which Pope Gregory VII began to fashion something approximating a state apparatus under Church authority. Undoubtedly, the establishment of Church autonomy from secular authority within defined spheres played an important role in the emergence of an independent civil society and, as a consequence, the Western concept of rule of law.[189] However, this transformation in the Church's administrative structure included the development of military capacities, which required, as a consequence, a doctrinal shift in the Church's understanding of the intrinsic morality of killing in authorized warfare. With this change, Popes and their allies could more easily induce warriors to participate in so-called just wars, including, for example, both internal crusades within Christendom (to cleanse heresy from the body of the Church) and external crusades against non-Christian (Moslem or pagan) enemies to recover the Christian position in Spain, the Holy Land and elsewhere. In short, these institutional shifts and geopolitical considerations served as an impulse to exculpate Christians under objective moral law from responsibility for what their consciences subjectively might otherwise inform them were intrinsically wrongful acts.[190]

On this view of post-medieval Catholic theology, the obligation of the ruler to pursue the *tanquillitas ordinis*, without a presumption that violence was or was not intrinsically wrongful, served as the mechanism though which Papal and state power could recruit and entice warriors to participate in morally-problematic endeavors. For, after all, if the ruler, such as Shakespeare's Christian King Henry V, bore responsibility to God for the whole wrong to all who suffer, his obedient subjects would be relieved of responsibility for that whole wrong,[191] though not for their responsibility for their own sins committed before the war and implicitly not for those committed during war itself.192 On this line of thought, *jus ad bellum* is necessarily separate

189 *See generally* Francis Fukuyama, The Origins of Political Order: From Prehuman Times to the French Revolution 245–89 (2011).

190 *See generally* Delahunty, *Returning Warrior, supra* note 188.

191 *See* William Shakespeare, Henry V, Act IV, Scene i, ll. 134–46, *in* The Riverside Shakespeare 957 (1974) (according to a solider, Williams: "If the [King's] cause be not good, the King himself hath a heavy reckoning to make, when all those legs and arms and heads chopped off in a battle shall join together at the latter day [Judgment Day], and cry all, 'We died at such a place'—some swearing, some crying for a surgeon, some upon their wives left poor behind them . . . some upon their children rawly left. I am afeard there are few die well that die in a battle for how can they charitably dispose of any thing, when blood is their argument? Now, if these men do not die well, it will be a black matter for the King that led them to it; who to disobey were against all proportions of subjection.").

192 *Id.*, Act IV, Scene I, ll. 155–58, 161–64, and 172–73 (King Henry, having impersonated a Sir Thomas Erpingham on the eve of battle to measure the moral of his soldiers, replies to Williams' claim: "The King is not bound to answer the particular endings of his soldiers, the father of his son, nor the master of his servant; for they purpose not their death when they purpose their services. Besides, there is no King, be his cause never so spotless, if it come to the arbitrement of swords, can try it out with all unspotted soldiers. Some, peradventure, have on them the guilt of premeditated and contriv'd [murder] . . . Now, if these men have defeated the law and outtrun native punishment, though they can outstrip men,

from *jus in bello*, and decisions whether to participate in the use of force to pursue internal order and external justice are not complicated by the ruler's indirect moral responsibility for placing warriors in moral jeopardy, since the soldier can avoid perdition by complying with the law of war. If, on the contrary, moral jeopardy remains for the warrior, regardless of whether *jus ad bellum* criteria are satisfied, then surely the perceived sinfulness of killing in an otherwise lawful and moral war would serve as a practical constraint on the ability of rulers to use force in pursuit of the *tranquillitas ordninis*. On this line of thought, the *jus in bello* cannot be isolated from the *jus ad bellum*. Moral responsibility will always inhere in the direct act of killing, although gradations of sinfulness will depend on the circumstances of the act of killing; and those circumstances will include a warrior's awareness of the degree of justification under *jus ad bellum* criteria, as Shakespeare observed, in the larger play of which the killing she commits is only a scene. In sum, perhaps, when Weigel insisted there is no presumption against war, he may have been influenced by the moral irrelevance, the non-sinfulness, of the act of killing for the warrior who complies with the *jus in bello*. Perhaps, then too, when Williams insisted on a presumption against war, he was influenced by a belief that every act of violence is sinful and entails moral responsibility for the direct instrument of that violence, even if the warrior's superiors have complied with the *jus ad bellum*. Not far from the surface of this debate may be the underlying tension between, on one hand, the Catholic belief in justification through God's mercy, works, and absolution coupled with penance and, on the other hand, the Protestant, particularly Lutheran, belief in light of inescapable human sinfulness in justification by faith and God's mercy alone rather than in the corrupted works of man.

We do not believe, however, that one needs to reach these foundational questions to construct a normatively attractive theory linking the *jus in bello* with the *jus ad bellum*. Both *jus ad bellum* and *jus in bello* are indispensable. The question is how to combine them. A moral equilibrium cannot simply dispense, as pre-World War I international law largely did, with the *jus ad bellum*. We are long past the days in which war can be considered as a type of duel, governed by a detailed protocol but requiring no more justification than a perceived "slight." But neither should *jus in bello* be pressed to the point of superseding or radically destabilizing the underlying purposes of the *jus ad bellum*—that is, of securing the rights of communities to survive and flourish in an international environment that remains post-Westphalian and so reflects moral pluralism. The justice of a war can be a thumb – if a light one – on the scales that weigh

they have no wings to fly from God. . . . Every subject's duty is the King's, but every subject's soul is his own."). While here Shakespeare's Henry speaks only to the consequences of death not in a state of grace occasioned by the death in war, his general thesis of the moral responsibility of each soldier for his own conduct provides the basis for a separate *jus in bello*. For an interpretation of the incident, *see* Robert J. Delahunty, *The Conscience of a King: Law, Religion, and War in Shakespeare's King Henry V*, 53 J. Cath. Leg. Stud. 129, 173-6 (2015).

a rightful belligerent's conduct under the *jus in bello.* Democratic statesmen of the stature of Lincoln, Churchill and Franklin Roosevelt have thought so; and they were right.[193]

Taking into account constructivist insights in the emerging process of globalization and the insights of rational-choice theory in effective international institutional design, a presumption against action to support world order cannot be adopted uncritically. To that extent, Weigel seems correct: protecting the global *tranquillas ordinis* may well require violence wielded by a Great Power, even unilaterally. Yet, as we have observed in our study of Thucydides' account of the Peloponnesian War and of our discussion of the nuclear bombing of Hiroshima and Nagasaki, even if a war begins initially in compliance with the *jus ad bellum,* the circumstances of war progressively dehumanize all the participants and inevitably escalate violence in ways that do serious damage to pre-war understandings of acceptable conduct under the *jus in bello.* Even the side whose initiation of war is "right" under the standards of JWT must continuously reflect on that fact, on peril of corrupting or destroying the "justice" of the cause for which it fights.

In this process of sustained and critical reflection, legalism plays a vital, but not an exclusive, role. Strict compliance with *jus in bello* rules may shelter atrocious conduct (like the needless destruction of a shattered and defeated Iraqi Army); on the other hand, it may also cause irreparable damage to the very interests in restraint, moderation and humanity that it seeks to protect. In the aftermath of a major war's horrifying violence, the legalist response through formal rule construction is almost inevitable, but it is also ultimately reactive and unstable as memory fades and the conditions giving rise to particular rules disappear. As Jeremy Rabkin has recently reminded us, rules in themselves are indispensable and yet insufficient. "The appeal of a rule is that it obviates many disputes about the application of a general aim or standard in concrete circumstances. The reason we do not have rules for everything is that we often cannot reduce complex considerations to a single fixed rule. . . . Humanity often has a greater stake in who prevails in war than in how they came to prevail."[194]

Our tentative suggestion, therefore, is that, while Weigel was correct that the *jus ad bellum* begins without presumptions, Williams was also correct that self-doubt and self-criticism are essential features of any morally-attractive decision-making process in relation to war. On our view, the *jus ad bellum* decision must remain under continuous review and self-criticism, which in turn must affect judgments of necessity, distinction, and proportionality in the *jus in bello.* As time passes, and as the morally-significant errors and unanticipated harms latent in every decision become more transparent, we believe the *jus in bello* must be refined to accommodate the

193 This is not, of course, to say that these great leaders fought their wars without observing any limits whatever. Quite the opposite is true. But the restraints that they respected were not always legal ones. Thus, it has been said of Winston Churchill: "Political realist and tough fighter that he was, he was prepared to go far in pursuit of victory in war . . . but there was a limit beyond which even he would not go. This limit was not one prescribed by international law; it was a principle from the codes of the knight and the gentleman." Geoffrey Best, Churchill at War 269 (2005).

194 Rabkin, *Proportionality in perspective, supra,* note 35, at 340.

increased moral responsibility decision-makers bear for the unintended consequences of their decisions—a duty, so to speak, to review, reflect, and revise. Indeed, moral responsibility in such cases calls not only for additional restraint by the "ruler" but also for conscientious debate and criticism by the ruled and, at the extreme, conscientious objection by warriors. In this sense, we would collapse the *jus ad bellum* and *jus in bello* into a continuous ethic of moral decision-making – if you will, a kind of self-correcting feedback loop.

If continuing compliance with the deontic criteria (i.e., legitimate authority, just cause and right intention) and the prudential criteria (i.e., probability of success, a balance of advantages or proportionality of ends, and last resort) of the *jus ad bellum* become suspect over time, application of the *jus in bello* ought to evidence enhanced requirements of necessity, distinction and proportionality. At the outermost, perhaps a state that deeply violates *jus ad bellum* and *jus in bello* criteria may have forfeited the right to survive at all cost, while a fundamentally virtuous state may be able to impose greater costs on others, including even the destruction of another state, to ensure its own continuation. Weigel, thus, was right that there may be a duty to act, for those who have the power and the virtue to act; but Williams might also be right that the duty to act can never be an excuse for the moral responsibility to review, reflect, and revise. Justice among nations seems to require nothing less.

Index

www.ingramcontent.com/pod-product-compliance
Lightning Source LLC
LaVergne TN
LVHW081958200926
848481LV00010B/2765